Early Childhood Development

A MULTICULTURAL PERSPECTIVE

Fifth Edition

Jeffrey Trawick-Smith

EASTERN CONNECTICUT STATE UNIVERSITY

Merrill
Upper Saddle River, New Jersey
Columbus, Ohio

Library of Congress Cataloging in Publication Data

Trawick-Smith, Jeffrey W.
  Early childhood development : a multicultural perspective/Jeffrey Trawick-Smith. — 5th ed.
    p. cm.
  Includes bibliographical references and index.
  ISBN 0-13-501646-0
  1. Child development.   2. Early childhood education.   3. Multicultural education.   4. Cognition in children.   5. Observation (Educational method)   6. Children with disabilities—Education.   I. Title.
  LB1115.T73 2010
  372.21—dc22

2008038453

Vice President and Editor in Chief:
  Jeffery W. Johnston
Publisher: Kevin M. Davis
Development Editor: Christina Robb
Editorial Assistant: Lauren Carlson
Senior Managing Editor: Pamela D. Bennett
Senior Project Manager: Mary M. Irvin
Senior Art Director: Diane C. Lorenzo

Project Coordination: Elm Street Publishing Services
Cover Design: Kellyn Donnelly
Cover Image: SuperStock
Photo Coordinator: Shea Davis
Operations Specialist: Laura Messerly
Vice President Director of Sales and Marketing: Quinn Perkson
Marketing Coordinator: Brian Mounts

This book was set in Goudy by Integra Software Services Pvt. Ltd. It was printed and bound by Edwards Brothers. The cover was printed by Phoenix Color Corp.

Photo Credits: Scott Cunningham/Merrill, pp. 3, 279, 355, 368; Barbara Schwartz/Merrill, pp. 4, 16, 35, 42, 160, 171, 182, 373, 448; Anne Vega/Merrill, pp. 11, 27, 110, 132, 138, 149, 189, 203, 206, 267, 304, 318, 405, 418, 427, 470; Corbis Digital Stock, p. 15; Bill Anderson/Photo Researchers, Inc., p. 49; Laima Druskis/PH College, p. 65; Knut Mueller/Das Fotoarchiv./Peter Arnold, Inc., p. 76; Blend Images/Alamy, p. 82; Index Open, pp. 87, 169; Laura Dwight/Creative Eye/Mira.com, p. 92; Susan Leavines/Photo Researchers, Inc., p. 100; Frank Siteman, p. 105; Elizabeth Crews Photography, p. 107; Susan Woog Wagner/PH College, p. 127; Amy Etra/PhotoEdit Inc., p. 156; Krista Greco/Merrill, pp. 197, 295; Pearson Learning Photo Studio, pp. 227, 342; Dan Floss/Merrill, pp. 231, 308; Julie Peters/Merrill, p. 240; Nancy Sheehan Photography, p. 255; Robert Harbison, p. 329; Susan Ragan/AP Wide World Photos, p. 334; Hope Madden/Merrill, p. 393; Bill Bachmann/The Image Works, p. 436; Purestock, p. 463; Myrleen Ferguson Cate/PhotoEdit Inc., p. 481.

Pearson® is a registered trademark of Pearson plc
Merrill® is a registered trademark of Pearson Education, Inc.

Pearson Education Ltd., London
Pearson Education Singapore Pte. Ltd.
Pearson Education Canada, Ltd.
Pearson Education—Japan
Pearson Education Australia, Limited

Pearson Education North Asia, Ltd., Hong Kong
Pearson Educación de Mexico, S.A. de C.V.
Pearson Education Malaysia Pte. Ltd.
Pearson Education Upper Saddle River, New Jersey

Merrill
is an imprint of

www.pearsonhighered.com

10 9 8 7 6 5 4 3 2 1
ISBN 13: 978-0-13-501646-6
ISBN 10:   0-13-501646-0

To my parents, who taught compassion, understanding, and tolerance by living example.

This edition is dedicated to the memory of Phyllis Waite: community activist, strong and loving mother and grandmother, and committed leader of the Mashantucket Pequot Tribal Nation.

Preface

Early Childhood Development: A Multicultural Perspective, Fifth Edition, is a book about the development of all children in the world. It examines the physical, social, emotional, linguistic, and intellectual characteristics of children of diverse cultural backgrounds within and outside the United States. It discusses typical as well as atypical development; children with challenging conditions are profiled.

The book can be used as the primary text for child development or early child development courses in community colleges or four-year programs in education or psychology. It can also be used as a supplementary text in graduate-level, life-span human development courses where a goal is to promote cultural understanding and sensitivity. Some of my colleagues have used it as a supplement in courses in multicultural education or the antibias curriculum. The book is intended to assist future teachers, child care providers, and family service and mental health professionals in understanding and celebrating the rich diversity of development among children in all neighborhoods in the United States and around the globe.

TEXT ORGANIZATION AND FEATURES

An initial examination of the contents will show that the book resembles other texts in child development. It includes current and important issues and topics. The book is organized in a conventional ages-and-stages format. A closer look, however, reveals several unique features. First, each topic is examined from a multicultural perspective. Sections on language development, for example, include descriptions of second-language learning and the linguistic development of non-English speakers. Chapters on intellectual development highlight cultural diversity in cognitive styles. Attachment patterns and peer relations among children of diverse backgrounds are explored. Cultural variations in motor play and development are examined.

A second unique feature is that topics in atypical development and special education are smoothly integrated into the core development chapters. For example, autism and serious emotional disturbance are fully examined in sections on social development, and mental retardation and learning disabilities are extensively described in chapters dealing with cognition. One purpose of the text is to assist professionals working with children and families in understanding and appreciating the characteristics of children with challenging conditions who will be increasingly integrated within regular classrooms.

A final important feature of the book is its real-life, practical orientation. It is intended as a hands-on guide, with suggestions for professional practice presented in each chapter. A special **Assessing Young Children** feature helps professionals interpret the behaviors of children in classrooms and use this information to plan programs, guide classroom interactions, and enrich development. Each chapter ends with a **Research into Practice** section that outlines practical classroom and parenting applications. A **Child Guidance** feature in each chapter highlights a proven research-based technique for enhancing children's social, emotional, cognitive, or language growth. The chapters include numerous stories drawn from diverse cultures within and outside the United States, which bring theory and research to life.

WHY STUDY CHILD DEVELOPMENT FROM A MULTICULTURAL PERSPECTIVE?

Why is a multicultural focus in child development so important? During the 21st century, traditionally underrepresented groups—often called minorities—will constitute a new majority within the United States. Children from families of historically underrepresented groups make up a growing percentage of the preschool and school-age population. Early childhood classrooms are becoming increasingly diverse, and teachers and other professionals must be prepared to meet the unique needs of young children of varying backgrounds. Even teachers of monocultural classrooms must assist their students in understanding and appreciating other cultures. A primary goal in early childhood education today is to provide the skills, understanding, and sensitivity that children need in a pluralistic society. This textbook is designed to assist professionals in meeting that goal by providing a culturally sensitive account of developmental processes.

NEW FEATURES IN THE FIFTH EDITION

This fifth edition includes many new topics and issues. One new emphasis is on **societal trends** that influence young children's development. Sections on the effects of **electronic media** on children's development have been added. Research is presented on how television, DVDs, and computers can influence language and intellectual and social behavior. The growing problem of **childhood obesity** is more fully addressed throughout the book. New evidence is included on the factors that lead young children to become overweight—even those factors that occur before birth! Strategies to prevent obesity in the home and classroom are discussed.

The effect of the current **standards movement** in early childhood education on children's development is explored in this edition. Political and social pressures for accountability and assessment, and their influence on behavior and learning, are examined.

This new edition examines the useful applications of the **information processing theory**. This is a theory that focuses on how young children attend to, remember, and retrieve information they gather in their lives. New strategies, based on this theory, are suggested for promoting positive relationships with peers and prosocial skills and for reducing aggression. Finally, Chapter 18, "Parents, Families, and Children: A Multicultural Perspective," has been revised to describe the diversity of families in American society and their many strengths and challenges. A special emphasis is placed on **family stressors** and how children are able to cope with these. The various **risk factors** that families face and the **protective factors** that help children to survive are examined. **Cultural and socioeconomic influences** on family life are more fully explored.

In addition to these new sections, the book contains discussions of more than 800 new research studies and articles on early childhood development that have been published since the last edition. These include recent and remarkable investigations on how the brain works as a child is acquiring new words, becoming attached to parents, listening to music, or interacting with peers. Studies that use new computer technology to explore the precise ways that children solve problems or learn grammatical rules are presented. Most important, much new research is cited that supports the basic premise of this book: that culture and families influence the ways young children develop.

SUPPLEMENTARY MATERIALS

The following supplements to the textbook are available for download on www.pearsonhighered.com. Simply click on "Educators"; enter the author, title, or ISBN; and select this textbook. Click on the "Resources" tab to view and download the supplements detailed below.

Online Instructor's Manual with Test Bank

An online instructor's manual (0-13-501651-7) includes a discussion of critical topics for each chapter and a set of cooperative learning activities that instructors can use in their classes. Two or more of these activities are provided for each chapter in the book. These creative, field-tested activities may be copied for classroom use. The instructor's manual also contains a test bank with three different types of items: recall, analysis and application, and essay questions.

Online Test Gen

The computerized test bank software, Test Gen (0-13-501649-5), allows instructors to create and customize exams. Test Gen is available in both Macintosh and PC/Windows versions.

Online PowerPoint Slides

The PowerPoint slides (0-13-501689-4) highlight key concepts and summarize text content. These guides are designed to provide structure to instructor presentations and give students an organized perspective on each chapter's content.

Downloadable Course Cartridges

Available for both BlackBoard (0-13-501648-7) and WebCT (0-13-501647-9), the online course cartridges contain the Test Bank content in a format to use with either online learning application.

ACKNOWLEDGMENTS

Writing a book of this kind is a challenge. Such an undertaking is not possible without support and encouragement from many individuals. I would like to thank my family—Nancy, Benjamin, and Joseph—for their patience during my work on this project. They helped me to know when it was time to step away from the computer, put down the manuscript, and take a moment to enjoy fully what is most important in life: their love.

I want to thank Elsa Nuñez, the president of Eastern Connecticut State University—a visionary, a leader, and a warm, encouraging colleague—who has recognized, supported, and inspired my scholarship. I also wish to thank my university colleagues, particularly Leah Barbuto, Theresa Bouley, Diane Ceretto, Julia DeLapp, Patty Gardner, Ann Gruenberg, Jamie Klein, Sudha Swaminathan, and June Wright, who kept me thinking and laughing during the project.

I would like to give a special thanks to Patty Martinez-Meritt from the University of Alaska, who has, with her students, provided so many wonderful ideas and suggestions for the book over the years. I want to thank Rachel Levin for her thorough search for new studies on young children's development.

I would like to acknowledge those individuals who provided the stories, quotes, and cultural descriptions that enrich this book. In particular, I would like to thank Deb Adams, Ingrid Eschholz, Tuala Fitzgerald, Ivy Goduka, Jill Huels, Diana Kimiatek, Hari Koirala, Lirio Martinez, Elsy Negron, Randy Rush, Wilson Soto, and Asomgyee Pamoga. Other people provided technical expertise in the writing of some sections. I want to thank David Trawick for his comments and suggestions on chapters addressing genetics and medical issues. Jeff Danforth provided helpful insights regarding children with ADHD, not to mention a very fine blues tape. June Wright provided materials and ideas on multiple intelligences and brain research, and Ann Gruenberg shared perspectives on atypical development.

I wish to thank Christina Robb and Kevin Davis at Pearson/Merrill for keen professional insights, kindness, and tireless patience. They understand well the emotional needs of an author who is writing a complex textbook. The entire editing, production, and marketing staff of Pearson/Merrill was remarkably helpful and supportive.

The suggestions and comments of the following reviewers of the earlier editions were invaluable: Mae P. Arntzen, Mott Community College; Toni Campbell, San Jose State University; Linda A. Carson, Des Moines Area Community College; Susan Bertram Eisner, Hood College; Kathleen E. Fite, Southwest Texas State University; Rey A. Gomez, Arizona State University; Craig H. Hart, Brigham Young University; Alice S. Honig, Syracuse University; Ivy N. Goduka, Central Michigan University; James E. Johnson, Northeastern State University; Sim Lesser, Miami Dade Community College, Kendall; Jeanne B. Morris, Illinois State University; Cathy Nathan, Texas Tech University; Sherrill Richarz, Washington State University; Barbara J. Rodrigues, University of Central Florida; Bobbie H. Rowland, University of North Carolina, Charlotte; Michelle L. Rupiper, University of Nebraska, Lincoln; and Nancy E. Sayre, Clarion University. I'd like to acknowledge as well the reviewers who made suggestions for improving the previous edition: Christine Chaillé, Portland State University; Colleen Finegan, Wright State University; Laura Gruntmeir, Redlands Community College; Cathy Nathan, Texas Tech University; and Michelle L. Rupiper, University of Nebraska, Lincoln. I'd like to thank the reviewers of the fifth edition for their suggestions for improvement: Yash Bhagwanji, Florida Atlantic University; Herman Knopf, University of South Carolina, Columbia; Andrea McCourt, Texas Tech University; Robin Ocheltree, Arizona State University; and Kresha Warnock, Ball State University.

Finally, I would like to thank the children and families whose behaviors and learning serve as the basis for many stories in the book: Benjamin, Joseph, Matthew, Meggie, Sam, Alex, Brenna, and Haley; the children and families of the Child and Family Development Resource Center of Eastern Connecticut State University, the Hartford Public Schools, the Windham Public Schools, the Temple Early Childhood Education Center, the former John Marshall Elementary School in Louisville, Kentucky; the Christian Center Child Care Center in Bloomington, Indiana; the University of Minnesota Child Care Center in Minneapolis, Minnesota; the Oak Grove Montessori School in Mansfield, Connecticut; and the preschool and kindergarten of the Universidad de Puerto Rico, Colegio Universitario Tecnologico de Bayamon, Bayamon, Puerto Rico.

Jeffrey Trawick-Smith

Brief Contents

Contents

Special Features

CHAPTER 1

Studying Early Childhood Development in a Diverse World

GUIDING QUESTIONS

1. What is early childhood development?
2. How can a knowledge of early childhood development guide interactions with children?
3. How can this knowledge guide curriculum planning?
4. How can an understanding of early childhood development guide the observation of children and the identification of special needs?
5. How can a knowledge of early childhood development promote an understanding and appreciation of diversity?
6. How can this knowledge guide advocacy and the shaping of public policy?
7. Why should professionals study child development from a multicultural perspective?

The purpose of this book is to assist present and future teachers of young children in using knowledge of child development within child care, preschool, kindergarten, and primary-grade classrooms. It is a practical guide to what young children are like and how this knowledge can be used to enhance your professional practice. My focus in this book is on diversity and development, with a major thesis being that individual children learn and behave in different ways. Children of diverse cultural and socioeconomic backgrounds and those with challenging conditions and special needs vary in their language, social style, self-perceptions, and physical competence because of unique life experiences. I will describe and celebrate this diversity. A significant message I want to convey is that there is not just one way to grow up.

Understanding development and its cultural variations is essential for effective teaching, as the following story reveals:

Three 4-year-olds—Sarah, Peter, and Alonzo—are working with clay at the art table in a child care center. Their teacher, Ms. Sekar, has placed individual balls of clay on small wooden boards so that each child can select one to work with. Knowing that children at this age have a difficult time sharing, she reasons that dividing the clay into individual portions will avert conflict. She quickly discovers, however, that her careful planning has just the opposite effect.

Peter looks over with an expression of concern at Sarah's clay. "She's got more than me!" he complains to Ms. Sekar.

"Oh, no, Peter, she doesn't," she assures him. "I put just the same amount of clay in all the balls. You have just as much as she does."

Peter is not satisfied. "No! Hers is fatter!"

Ms. Sekar notices that Sarah's clay ball is pushed flatter, giving it a wide appearance. "Oh! Hers is fatter, you're right. But yours is ..."—she searches for the right word here—"...taller." She sees immediately that this argument has gone over Peter's head.

As Peter continues to protest, Alonzo discovers that he needs more clay for a sculpture he is working on. Smiling, he casually leans over and pinches off a large chunk from Peter's ball. Alonzo's actions are more than Peter can bear. "No!" he screams, beginning to cry and trying to grab back some of his clay from Alonzo. Alonzo gives a look of total surprise at Peter's outburst.

After comforting Peter, Ms. Sekar engages all three children in an elaborate negotiation: "Peter seems to be upset because he doesn't have as much clay as everyone else. What can we do about this?"

"Give me back my clay," Peter offers, still angry.

"We could put all the clay together," Alonzo suggests. Sarah agrees.

"We could try that," Ms. Sekar responds with enthusiasm. "We could make a huge ball. Then you could tear off the clay you need. What do you think?"

"What if I can't have enough?" asks Peter tearfully.

"There is so much clay," the teacher answers. "I think you'll have plenty to use. Should we try it?"

Peter finally agrees. They combine their clay into one large chunk and place it in the center of the table. As the children work, they help themselves to more clay as they need it. This seems to make everyone happy. Ms. Sekar is pleased at how cooperative these young children are in sharing from this "community" lump of clay.

This child care provider has resolved a classroom conflict by applying principles of child development. Because she has read about young children's thinking and social behavior, she is aware that 4-year-olds can be egocentric—that is, so self-oriented that they are unable to fully understand others' perspectives. Because she anticipates difficulties over sharing, she attempts to avoid conflicts by dividing the clay into individual balls. She quickly realizes, however, that she has created more problems than she has prevented.

She knows, again from child development research, that children's thinking is based on the appearance of things: what you see is what you get. From Peter's perspective, the ball that looks fatter must contain more clay. The caregiver immediately recognizes the futility of trying to convince him that the balls are of equal size.

In resolving the conflict between Alonzo and Peter, the teacher has relied on her knowledge of cultural diversity in child development. She knows that, in Alonzo's family, collective behavior rather than individual ownership is emphasized. Because joint ownership is the norm in Alonzo's culture, his act of taking clay is simply an innocent effort to share materials.

By involving the children in the resolution of this conflict, she has relied on new research showing that very young children can be quite cooperative and can resolve their own conflicts with adult assistance. Her final solution reflects her knowledge of the intellectual and social abilities and limitations of this age group.

This example shows that child development research and theory can be extremely useful in the classroom when applied in concert with careful observation and the wisdom of experience.

WHAT IS EARLY CHILDHOOD DEVELOPMENT?

Anyone who spends time with children knows that they change in many ways as they grow older. What may not be as obvious is that these changes are qualitative as well as quantitative. Children do not simply acquire more knowledge, social ability, or physical proficiency with age; their thinking and behavior become qualitatively different over time.

One way to understand qualitative change in development is to reflect on your own life experience. Think back to what you were like 10 years ago. Are you the same person? How have you changed? It is likely that you are quantitatively different; you have more knowledge, a broader repertoire of social skills, or even—like me—a few new gray hairs. But you are also likely to be qualitatively different. Your interests have probably changed. You probably solve problems differently or use new methods to learn. You may have a clearer picture of your

Teachers can apply knowledge of child development to curriculum planning and classroom interaction.

career goals. Children also become very different human beings with each developmental period, as the following vignette illustrates:

> Three-year-old Daisuke shows great anxiety every time the heater blower turns on in his child care center. His caregiver intervenes to help assuage his fears.

DAISUKE:	I don't like that thing!
CAREGIVER:	Yes. That heater is old and loud. It's just a heater, though. Let me show you. (Leads the child over to the heating unit) See? It's just a machine.
DAISUKE:	Just an old machine.
CAREGIVER:	That's right. Can you see down inside here? See the parts of the machine in there? That's what makes the noise.
DAISUKE:	Yeah. The machine goes r-r-r-r. (Makes a blower noise)
CAREGIVER:	Right. So when it comes on, you won't be afraid, right?
DAISUKE:	Yeah.

> Minutes later, the blower turns on again. Daisuke clings to the caregiver in terror.
> Approximately a year later, the caregiver has another conversation about the blower with this same child.

DAISUKE:	Remember that heater? (Points to the heating unit)
CAREGIVER:	Sure. You didn't like the noise it made.
DAISUKE:	I was afraid of it when I was little. I thought it was a...monster. (Laughs)
CAREGIVER:	I remember that.
DAISUKE:	It's just the machine inside that makes that awful racket!

Why is this child, at age 4, no longer afraid of the heater? It isn't just because he has more knowledge of how it works. Indeed, he had learned a good deal about the heater from his caregiver when he was only 3. He could even verbalize that it was "just an old machine" that made a frightening noise. Yet his fear persisted. At age 4, he is able to think in a completely different way. His intellectual abilities have changed qualitatively as well as quantitatively. He is no longer completely fooled by how things look or sound (i.e., if the blower sounds like a monster, it must be a monster). He can now use a new kind of reasoning to overcome the misleading appearance of things (i.e., the blower may sound like a monster, but it is really a machine making noise).

In all areas of development, children gradually transform into unique individuals. At each stage, they pose new and fascinating challenges for parents and professionals. What we expect of them, how we interact with them, what we plan for them to do, and how we meet their social and emotional needs and those of their families are all influenced by a knowledge of these qualitative changes in development.

In this book, **development** is defined as the process by which humans change both qualitatively and quantitatively as they grow older. It is not just adding more knowledge or ability with time; it is the process of transforming, of becoming completely new. **Early childhood development** is defined as the development of children from conception and birth through age 8.

WHY STUDY EARLY CHILDHOOD DEVELOPMENT?

This book is intended to be a practical guide for teachers and other professionals working with young children and their families. It addresses developmental problems and issues in the classroom. It can be used to guide professional practice in at least five ways, as summarized in Table 1-1.

development: The process by which humans change both qualitatively and quantitatively as they grow older.

early childhood development: The development of children from conception and birth through age 8.

TABLE 1-1
Five Ways This Book Can Guide Professional Practice

The Book Can Guide	Example
Interactions with children	A teacher reads in Chapter 12 that the preschool years are a period of magical thinking and irrational fears. So, when a 4-year-old shows anxiety about going onto the playground, she understands the source of the problem and designs a sympathetic, cognitive-based strategy to alleviate the child's fear.
Curriculum planning	A teacher is designing a science activity to teach about seeds in a primary-grade classroom. He reads in Chapter 14 that most children of this age enjoy playing games with rules, so he develops a science board game. He also reads that there are cultural differences in regard to competition, so he designs the game so that all children win and competition is minimized.
Observation and identification of children with special needs	Based on information in Chapter 9, an infant caregiver accurately identifies a 7-month-old who has not become securely attached to her parents. Guided by research, she implements a warmth and responsiveness strategy to help the child bond to others.
Understanding and appreciation of diversity	A primary-grade teacher plans to have children read independent research reports to the whole class. However, he reads in Chapter 16 that children of some culture groups express themselves using a storytelling style. So, he gives students an option of telling the group about their projects.
Advocacy and the shaping of public policy	A kindergarten teacher is concerned about the problem of bullying on the playground and in the school bus. Citing research from Chapter 13 showing that this negative social behavior forms very early in life, she advocates for a preschool to grade 12 antibullying program at a local school board meeting.

A Guide to Interactions with Children

We know that young children think and act differently from adults. They use a different form of language, interact with other people in distinct ways, and apply unique meanings to social events. The things that make them worry, cry, or laugh are unique and sometimes unpredictable. Their interests and motivations are peculiar to their developmental level. They have a great need to scream and run and play, to throw things, and to joke and giggle with peers. Without a deep understanding of what young children are like, adults will have difficulty communicating with and comforting them, challenging their thinking, and helping them solve problems with peers. The following story shows how a thorough and sympathetic understanding of childhood can enhance professional practice:

Janny and Molly are playing together in the block area of a kindergarten classroom. Janny has just knocked down Molly's block structure, causing great upset. The teacher quickly moves over to the area as a loud conflict ensues.

MOLLY: (Crying) Janny, you kicked my building. I'm going to kick yours! (Angrily kicks at Janny's blocks!)

JANNY: No! (Begins to cry and pushes Molly)

TEACHER:	(Moving between the two children) Oh! You are both so angry. What's up here?
MOLLY:	She knocked down my building. (Screaming at Janny) I hate you!
JANNY:	(Crying, speaking to the teacher) She pushed me!
MOLLY:	You knocked over my building, Janny!
TEACHER:	(To Molly) I know you must be so upset. You worked very hard on that building.
MOLLY:	And Janny knocked it down.
TEACHER:	Yes. But she wasn't trying to, were you Janny?
JANNY:	No. And she just pushed me.
TEACHER:	(To Janny) Well, she was very angry. (To Molly) I don't think Janny meant to knock down your building. Sometimes these accidents happen. What can we do here?
MOLLY:	Well . . . Janny has to build it.
TEACHER:	(To Janny) Can you help Molly rebuild her building?
JANNY:	Okay. And maybe we could make a queen's castle.
MOLLY:	(In an enthused tone) All right.

In responding to this conflict, the teacher has applied an understanding of the unique ways children interpret and solve social problems. She knows that young children sometimes assign hostile intent when accidents occur. Molly truly believes that Janny intended to destroy her block structure. Instead of reprimanding Molly for pushing, then, the teacher acknowledges how angry and upset she must be. She also points out to Molly that the toppling of the blocks was accidental. She knows that helping a child read social situations more accurately will promote positive social development.

This caregiver also applies knowledge of how very young children resolve conflicts. She keeps Janny involved in the discussion, aware that children are often able to settle their own disputes with adult assistance. She also knows that anger toward peers rarely lasts long at this age. Indeed, within a short period of time, the two children have worked out a reconciliation. Had the teacher quickly separated these angry children, a wonderful opportunity for learning conflict resolution skills would have been missed.

A Guide to Curriculum Planning

The ideas presented in this book can also guide curriculum planning. A full understanding of the thinking and behavior of young children is critical in developing activities and materials that are appropriate for this age group. Overlooking developmental characteristics can lead to an inappropriate curriculum, or what Elkind (2007) calls "miseducation" and Sutton-Smith (1999) refers to as "cognitive child labor." Classrooms that present young children with taxing, passive, and overly abstract academic activities still exist. Such classrooms do not reflect a knowledge of child development.

The following vignette illustrates how a teacher's understanding of typical and atypical child development enhances curriculum:

A preschool teacher sets out trays of cornmeal for children to play with. They can draw in the cornmeal, wipe away their marks, and draw again. A child who is experiencing delayed development of large motor skills is attempting to join another child in this activity. As he tries to draw, he knocks the tray to the floor, and the cornmeal spills out. His peer expresses concern.

RUBEY:	Look! He spilled it all out!
TAYLOR:	(Looks down, says nothing)
TEACHER:	Oops! That tray slides off the table so easily.

RUBEY: He knocked it!
TEACHER: It was an accident. I have that problem sometimes. I've knocked things
           off a slippery table. What can we do to attach the tray so it doesn't slide?
TAYLOR: Glue it, I think.
TEACHER: Well, then the tray would stay stuck forever. How about if I clamp it?
           (She retrieves a metal clamp from the woodworking area, clamps the tray
           to the table, and adds more cornmeal) There. Try that.

The two children draw in the cornmeal for many minutes without further spills.

Here the teacher has provided an appropriate learning material that reflects an understanding of young children's development. The activity is concrete and open ended and, therefore, meets the learning needs of children of this age. The activity also reflects an understanding that end products are not as important to young children as the process of creating. A positive feature of the cornmeal activity is that children can create and re-create many times without concern about finished products.

Based on observations and an understanding of the development of children with special needs, the teacher has quickly assessed that Taylor's motor limitations make this activity inaccessible to him. Her knowledge of motor development has sensitized her to developmental delays and has guided her adaptation of materials to meet his special needs.

A Guide to Observing Children and Identifying Special Needs

Observation is the cornerstone of effective teaching. Teachers and child care providers usually base intervention and curriculum planning decisions on the careful observation of children's developmental needs. This book assists professionals in observing children. It suggests key areas of development to study and describes the diverse behaviors and characteristics that can be expected at various developmental levels. In addition, it guides teachers in identifying children with special needs. Certain behaviors suggest developmental delay or at-risk status. An infant who displays very little motor activity, a preschooler who is limited in language, or an elementary school child who is rejected by peers may require special intervention. Focused observation not only can identify these potential problems but also can suggest causes and remediation.

In the following example, a caregiver uses child development research to identify a child with special needs:

A 5-month-old has just been enrolled in a child care center. Her caregiver spends much time observing her during her first few days. He notices that the infant is less alert and responsive to adult contact than the other babies. He has read that this is an age when most infants show great interest in other people. He expects to see much smiling, cooing, and other social behaviors.

He knows that social interaction varies across cultures. For example, in some families, babies are held or spoken to less often. However, babies of all cultures have some mechanism for making contact with other people, and this infant does not respond at all to his efforts to interact.

The caregiver discusses his concerns with the infant's parents. Together they seek assistance from a medical/social service team in the community. An assessment reveals that the infant has a hearing impairment. With this information, the caregiver can adapt interactions to meet the child's special needs. He focuses more on physical and visual stimulation, using touch more than language to make contact.

A Guide to Understanding and Appreciating Diversity

This book can also help teachers recognize and appreciate the wide variety of behaviors and characteristics that are typical among a given group of children. A fundamental message of the book is that no two children are alike. Behaviors and characteristics vary because of temperament, culture, gender, socioeconomic status, and a host of other factors. Children are not deficient or at risk because they develop in unique directions. They may display alternative ways of interacting with the world because of their life experience.

Knowledge of child development ultimately helps teachers be sensitive to typical variations in child behavior, as the following story reveals:

A 5-year-old Japanese American child, Misaka, has just been pushed off a tire swing on the playground at school. After discussing the event with the aggressor, the teacher attempts to comfort the victim.

Teacher: Are you all right, Misaka?
MISAKA: (Smiles broadly, says nothing)
TEACHER: It looks like you're okay. Did you get hurt?
MISAKA: (Continues to smile, still does not speak)
Teacher: Something doesn't seem quite right here. Why don't we sit together for
               a few minutes and relax. (Pulls the child onto her lap)

After several minutes of sitting together, Misaka begins to speak to the teacher.

Misaka: (Tears forming in his eyes) He pushed me off.
TEACHER: Yes. I'll bet that hurt.
MISAKA: (In an angry tone) I don't like him!
TEACHER: You really sound angry. Let's talk about this a little.

The teacher and Misaka quietly discuss the incident until playground time is over.

Initially, this teacher misreads Misaka's smile as a sign that he is happy and unaffected by the aggression. She then remembers that smiling can mean different things in different cultures. In some Japanese American families, a smile is used to conceal embarrassment, sorrow, or anger. The teacher wisely stays with and nurtures the child until he is ready to express his feelings.

A Guide to Advocacy and the Shaping of Public Policy

Many teachers and caregivers see their professional roles as extending beyond the four walls of their classrooms (NAEYC, 2004; Robinson & Stark, 2002). They recognize that they must bring about change in the community and the larger society in order to improve the lives of children and families. Often, they become advocates who lobby policymakers, write letters to the editors of their local newspapers, participate in political action groups, or campaign for candidates who support programs for children. This book serves as a guide for such advocacy. Research and theories cited in these chapters show that working to improve community services and to influence public policy will have a direct impact on children's development (Bronfenbrenner, 2006; J. L. Robinson, 2000; Roosa, 2000). Each chapter presents ideas for advocacy and the shaping of public policy to benefit children and families.

In the following vignette, a teacher uses his knowledge of children's physical development and health to support important legislation:

A second-grade teacher is concerned about one of his students, Giovanny, who has been suffering persistent illnesses, including an ear infection that comes and goes. The teacher is aware that illness is a leading cause of children missing school and, thus, falling behind in their learning. He knows that this is a particular problem for children who live in poverty, like Giovanny. If Giovanny remains unhealthy, his learning and development will be seriously impaired.

The teacher talks with Giovanny's mother, a single parent, about the problem and is startled by her response.

Mother: I just try to keep Giovanny in bed so he can get better. That's all I can do when he gets sick.
TEACHER: He really needs to see a doctor.
MOTHER: Can't afford a doctor for every little thing.
TEACHER: But this is pretty serious. These ear infections, especially.
MOTHER: I don't have any insurance. And the state says I make too much money to get any help from them.
TEACHER: Isn't there a special state program?
Mother: Yeah, there was, but they took that away.

The teacher is surprised. Surely Giovanny's mother doesn't make so much from her low-paying job that her family can't receive free medical services. On investigating, he learns Giovanny's mother is correct. The new governor in the state, in an effort to address a budget deficit, has pushed for an end to the "Healthy Kids" program that provides health insurance for children of the working poor.

The teacher organizes a campaign among colleagues and parents in the school to reinstate this program. They call legislators, attend a public hearing, and write letters to the local newspaper. One of their most powerful arguments is that illness can undermine goals for education in the state—goals that the governor champions. Absences will affect achievement test scores and threaten state and federal mandates for school improvement, they point out. With the help of similar groups throughout the state, they eventually succeed. The legislature overwhelmingly votes to reinstate the program, with the governor's support.

This teacher is inspired to take action by his knowledge that illness is a serious threat to learning and development. He uses research on poor health, absence, and school success to convince the legislators that providing health insurance for all children will help meet a politically popular goal.

WHY STUDY EARLY CHILDHOOD DEVELOPMENT FROM A MULTICULTURAL PERSPECTIVE?

During this new century, children of traditionally underrepresented groups—often called minorities—will constitute a new majority within the United States. Currently, African Americans, Latinos, Asian Americans, and Native Americans constitute one-third of the U.S. population. It is projected that, within 50 years, they will account for more than half (U.S. Bureau of the Census, 2007)! Because families of these ethnic backgrounds are generally younger than those of other cultural groups, their children will represent a growing percentage of the preschool and school-age population. As families become more diverse, child and family professionals must be prepared to meet their unique needs.

Children of different cultures vary in the ways they communicate and interact with adults and peers (Klein & Chen, 2001), in how they play and learn (Farver, Xu, Eppe, & Lonigan, 2006; Johnson, Christie, & Wardle, 2005; Rakoczy, 2005), and in how they view teachers and school (Okagaki & Frensch, 1998). Parental socialization practices and beliefs vary markedly across cultures (Deater-Deckard, 2005; Zhang & Fuligni, 2006). Professionals must come to understand, appreciate, and show sensitivity to these differences as they interact with children and families. They must devise ways to provide their students with knowledge of people of other cultures and with positive and significant cross-cultural experiences.

Unfortunately, children of color are often underrepresented or misrepresented in child development research (McLoyd, 2006; M. B. Spencer, 2006). Many studies are conducted with only white, middle-class children (Trawick-Smith, 1993). Some textbooks and articles on children and families have been found to reflect a Euro-American bias in which the behaviors and development of white, middle-class children are considered typical and those of other cultures are viewed as "abnormal, incompetent, and change worthy" (McLoyd, 1990b, p. 263). Children from non-European cultures or from low socioeconomic backgrounds have been considered "culturally deprived" (Bereiter & Engelmann, 1966) because they speak, learn, or interact with peers in ways that are different from those of white, middle-class children. This belief has led some teachers and child care providers to confuse cultural differences with developmental deficits.

A major purpose of this book is to help professionals appreciate that many developmental variations are, in fact, differences that can be explained by life experience. These differences are quite often adaptive. Unique behavior, language, and learning patterns of children of a particular cultural group are acquired for a reason (McLoyd, 2006; Trawick-Smith & Lisi, 1994; Quintana et al., 2006). They help the child get along in his or her family and community and are valued, expected, and encouraged by parents, other adults, and peers. Behaviors that vary from those of children in mainstream society may be very typical within the child's own cultural milieu.

In this book, great care has been taken to differentiate between developmental deficits—real, special needs that can and should be addressed through intervention—and cultural differences—variations in development that are part of the rich cultural history of children

Knowledge of child development can help teachers to understand and appreciate diversity.

and families. The following definitions of key phrases used in this book will help clarify distinctions among different sources of diversity:

unique/diverse needs: The distinct needs of each individual child that are not related to background or disability.

special needs: The needs of children that result from developmental delays or disabilities.

cultural/ethnic diversity: Variations in development and behavior that are due to a child's cultural background.

socioeconomic status (SES): A measure of a family's overall economic and social status, determined by level of education, income, place of residence, and occupation of primary wage earners.

children of color/children of historically underrepresented groups: Children of non-European, non-Caucasian ethnic background. These phrases replace the traditional word *minority*.

- *Unique diverse needs.* These phrases refer to the social, emotional, and learning needs of all individuals regardless of gender, ethnicity, or intellectual ability. Each individual within a classroom will have unique ways of learning or interacting with others, and in no group of students will all individuals be alike.
- *Special needs.* This refers to the needs of children with social, emotional, intellectual, or physical delays or disabilities. The term *special* is borrowed from the field of special education. This terminology should not be confused with *cultural needs*. You should not assume that children of some ethnic groups necessarily have special needs.
- *Cultural/ethnic diversity.* These phrases refer to variations in needs or play and the learning styles of children of various cultural groups. For example, children of different cultures have different styles of communicating. *Diversity* must not be confused with *deficit*. Differences across cultures are just that—differences to be celebrated, not deficits to be remediated.
- *Socioeconomic status (SES).* This is a measure of a family's overall economic and social status, determined by level of education, income, place of residence, and the occupation of primary wage earners. Children's development will vary because of socioeconomic status. Children of poverty, for example, will have unique needs, as will those from extremely wealthy families. *Socioeconomic status* must not be confused with *cultural or ethnic diversity*. Children of color, for example, are not necessarily of low socioeconomic status. These phrases also must not be associated with *special needs*; children of poverty do not automatically have developmental delays.
- *Children of color/children of historically underrepresented groups.* These phrases will be used in this book to replace the traditional word *minority* to describe children of non-European, non-Caucasian ethnic background. Although cumbersome, they are more accurate because persons of color could soon represent a majority of the population in some sections of the United States. In addition, these terms are viewed as more positive. All too often, *minority* is construed as a negative term.

SUMMARY

Development is a process by which humans change qualitatively and quantitatively over time. A knowledge of this process helps professionals interact with young children in effective ways, plan curriculum, observe and identify students with special needs, understand and appreciate cultural diversity, and participate in advocacy and the shaping of public policy. Studying child development from a multicultural perspective is important because the United States is becoming more diverse and there are cultural variations in the ways children think, learn, play, interact, and communicate.

RESEARCH INTO PRACTICE

CRITICAL CONCEPT 1

Development is defined as the process by which humans change as they grow older. This change is not just quantitative in nature; humans do not just acquire more knowledge and ability but change qualitatively as well. At each stage, humans think, behave, and perceive the world very differently.

Application #1 Assess qualitative changes in your students over time, not just quantitative increases in knowledge as measured by achievement or IQ tests. Observe how children solve math problems or think through scientific experiments, for example. You will learn more about development than if you only check to see if children get the right answer.

Application #2 Provide classroom experiences that help children think, interact with peers, and feel good about themselves. Activities that merely focus on learning facts may not promote qualitative aspects of development.

CRITICAL CONCEPT 2

A wealth of research exists on what children are like and how they develop in the early years. This research can guide professional practice.

Application #1   Child development research can guide you in interacting with children in ways that promote positive behavior and learning.

Application #2 Child development research can assist you in creating a developmentally appropriate curriculum—one that excites, engages, and challenges your students.

Application #3   Child development research can help you observe typical and atypical development and identify children who have special needs—developmental delays or disabilities that may require special intervention.

Application #4   Child development research can help you understand and appreciate cultural and developmental diversity and distinguish cultural differences from developmental deficits.

Application #5   Child development research can guide you in advocacy activities and the shaping of public policy. You can use research findings to sway public opinion and persuade legislators to enact legislation that supports children and families.

CRITICAL CONCEPT 3

Since the American population is becoming more diverse, it is important for professionals to study child development from a multicultural perspective. Children of different cultures vary in the ways they communicate and interact with adults and peers, in how they play and learn, and in how they view teachers and school. Parenting practices and beliefs vary across cultures as well.

Application #1   Adapt your interactions and the activities you plan for children to meet unique cultural needs. Based on research on developmental diversity, you can create culturally sensitive classrooms by modifying learning experiences, classroom management strategies, communication styles, methods of assessment, and modes of interacting with parents and families.

Application #2   Be cautious in assessing the needs of young children, carefully differentiating between cultural differences and true developmental deficits. Understand and celebrate cultural differences; avoid trying to change these. You should only address true developmental deficits through intervention or referral to specialists.

Application #3   Monitor your own attitudes and beliefs to guard against false assumptions about children. Young children of color do not always live in poverty. Children in poverty do not always have special needs. Such sweeping conclusions can lead to ineffective and insensitive caregiving and teaching.

CHAPTER 2

Historical Perspectives and Research in Early Childhood Development

GUIDING QUESTIONS

1. How have Western perspectives on childhood changed from the 1500s to the present?
2. How have non-Western perspectives on childhood differed from those in Europe and America?
3. How have research methods changed throughout the history of child study?
4. What are correlational and experimental studies of children, and do they differ?
5. How are qualitative/ethnographic methods of studying children different from quantitative methods?
6. What are the major types of action research in the classroom?
7. In what situations would professionals use quantitative observations in the classroom? Qualitative observations?
8. What are the key steps in writing anecdotal records?
9. What kinds of information are commonly included in a case study?

This chapter examines the roots of child study. It explores historical views of childhood as well as past and present research methods. Not only are these topics of scientific and historical interest, but they are of practical importance as well. Ideas about child rearing and development from long ago are still reflected in many current caregiving and teaching practices. Research findings can also directly influence adult–child interactions in the home and classroom. The following story shows how historical views and early research affect a novice teacher's classroom practice.

A student teacher, Stephen, has planned a small-group activity for a preschool class. However, as he begins, he encounters an unanticipated difficulty. One of the children will not stay seated in the circle he has created. She continues to jump up, talk in a loud voice, and stand in front of other children so that they cannot see.

"Susan, you need to sit down," he says. She sits quietly for a moment or two, but as he continues, she jumps up again.

Look!" she cries out. "There are monkeys up in the tree! My other teacher read this!"

"Susan, if you can't sit quietly, I'll have to move you away from the group," warns Stephen sternly. He has read about the time-out strategy in an introductory psychology

text. When he was young, his own teachers used this technique to deal with misbehavior. When the child interrupts again, Stephen takes quick action: "I'm sorry, Susan. You'll need to sit on a chair at the back of the room. I warned you." With this, he tries to lead the child to the chair, but she resists vigorously.

"No!" she screams. "I won't!" Other children begin to laugh, and the student teacher senses that he is losing control. Recognizing that he is in trouble, he looks to his supervising teacher, Ms. Laiti, who has just entered the classroom. This experienced teacher comes to the rescue. "Susan, why don't you sit on my lap while we hear the rest of the story?" This seems to satisfy the child. Stephen struggles to regain his composure and continues with his activity.

Stephen, an inexperienced student teacher, has responded to a classroom dilemma in an ineffective way. Warnings and time-outs—the only strategies he can think to try in this situation—are not useful in dealing with this particular child. These techniques have been found not to work well for some students, especially if they are not implemented thoughtfully (Larzelere, 2006; Larzelere & Kuhn, 2006; H. M. Walker, 1995). Ms. Laiti, who is more experienced, handles the problem more smoothly. She bases her actions on what she knows about this child and about the characteristics of 4-year-olds generally.

Why did Stephen act as he did? Novice teachers often rely on the thinking and practices of their own teachers or parents. Some of the strategies he tries—giving a warning and then issuing a time-out, for example—were prominent practices two decades ago when he was growing up. There could be something of the old view, "Children should be seen and not heard," reflected in his response to this child. His insistence that students sit quietly, listen, and display absolute deference during his story reading may also reveal an attitude—prevalent in years past—that children are simply little grown-ups who can learn and behave as adults if properly trained. In studying the history of childhood, Stephen might be surprised to discover the roots of the beliefs and dispositions that led him to react as he did.

There is usually a lag between the emergence of new ideas about child development and their implementation in professional practice. It takes a long time for new research findings and innovative theories to find their way into the classroom because research is often reported in scholarly journals or in papers that are presented only to other researchers. It is critical for teachers of young children to stay up to date, but to do so takes time and an ability to decipher "researchese."

This chapter has several purposes. The first is to present a brief history of thinking and research in child development. The reader will see how perspectives on childhood have changed over time and will come to see that some lingering classroom practices are really grounded in the thinking of the past. A knowledge of the historical roots of child study helps teachers and caregivers reflect on their own classroom practice and identify strategies that reflect dated notions of childhood.

A second purpose of this chapter is to familiarize readers with research methodology so that scientific journals will not appear as imposing. The intent is not to turn readers into researchers but to assist them in reading and interpreting studies that have practical classroom implications. The focus will be on critical analysis of research because all studies on human subjects are necessarily flawed. In particular, this chapter will raise a concern about whether current and past research have adequately reflected the cultural diversity within our society.

HISTORICAL PERSPECTIVES ON CHILDHOOD

Western Perspectives

Until the Middle Ages, there was no concept of childhood in the minds of many adults in Western society. Children were considered to be infants until they were 6 or 7 years of age—nonpersons who were sometimes uncared for and unwanted (Aries, 1973; Corsaro, 2005; King, 2007). They died in great numbers during this time, many at birth. Infanticide was not uncommon through the 17th century; healthy and unhealthy infants were drowned or abandoned. Clearly, many adults living in Europe during this time placed little value on the early years of child development.

Once children reached the age of 7, they were often viewed as little adults. This perspective is reflected in the paintings of earlier centuries. Children are often shown with mature adult faces, sitting calmly and piously alongside adult family members (Bjorklund & Bjorklund, 1992; deMause, 1995; King, 2007). With this perception came

Some current classroom practices are rooted in outmoded historical beliefs about how children should learn and behave.

the expectation that children would behave like grown-ups. This attitude lingers among some adults to this day.

It is important to note that many Western parents did love and care for their children during these early centuries. Hanawalt (2002) argues that the grim picture of childhood in medieval times has been overdrawn by some historians and that many parents struggled and sacrificed for the survival of their sons and daughters in the face of great adversity.

During the Renaissance in Western society, children came to be viewed, for the first time, as distinctly different human beings. Parents became preoccupied, however, with rooting out "inherent evil" (King, 2007; Pollock, 1987). Children were believed to have been born "bad," and it was the role of adults to train them in the teachings of the church and to "beat the devil out of them" when they strayed. This belief that children are innately immoral persisted through the 18th century. Harsh training and a focus on "breaking the will" of children can be seen even today among some misguided parents and teachers (deMause, 1995).

In Europe and the United States, the 19th and 20th centuries were periods of relative enlightenment in regard to the treatment of children. A new emphasis was placed on socialization. "The raising of a child became less a process of conquering... than of training" (deMause, 1974, p. 52). When the Industrial Revolution brought about the need for a large labor force, concern about the welfare of children whose parents were at work began to be expressed. Public schools and eventually child care programs were established to socialize children in every aspect of development. Improvements in health care led to a drastic reduction in childhood mortality. The late 20th century, generally, brought a growing concern for children's physical, emotional, social, and intellectual needs.

Western perspectives on childhood throughout history are presented in Figure 2-1, which shows that caring and concern for children have been relatively recent historical phenomena in Europe and America.

These historical trends have led historian deMause (1995) to predict a period of "helping" in Western society in which adults will at last come to recognize children's needs and will nurture and guide early development. Unfortunately, research on those in poverty and on traditionally underrepresented ethnic groups in Europe and America suggests that not all children have enjoyed these advances in care and understanding (Canino & Spurlock, 2000; Children's Defense Fund, 2007; Huston, McLoyd, & Garcia Coll, 1994). Until the mid-20th century, for example, children in poverty were sometimes economically exploited by employers and even by their own parents. Some were forced to work long hours under horrendous conditions in factories and on farms (Kessen, 1965). To this day, children of color, in particular, live in poverty in disproportionately high numbers (Children's Defense Fund, 2007).

Zigler and Finn-Stevenson (2007) have suggested that the 1970s ushered in a shift away from concern about children and families. They cite an increase in reports of child abuse and neglect cases since that time, accompanied by a decrease in family services to address these problems. They point to complex family stressors that may put children's development in new jeopardy: divorce, substance abuse, domestic violence, and parental depression. A new concern is children's exposure to violence; a growing number of children witness violent acts in their homes and neighborhoods (Canino & Spurlock, 2000; Garbarino & Kostelny, 1996; Harpaz-Rotem et al., 2007). Children in poverty are significantly more likely to experience the violent death of a family member or friend (Children's Defense Fund, 2007). It must be concluded that not all children in modern Western society are receiving the care and support they deserve. The needs of families and young children are still not being fully met in contemporary America, and it is important for teachers of young children to serve as advocates. (See the Advocacy and Public Policy box in this chapter for an example.)

Another recent trend in American society that has affected views on childhood is the **standards movement.** Because child and family services are expensive, a growing number of legislators and community leaders have called for clear standards and greater accountability

standards movement: A recent trend by legislators, policy makers, parents, and educators to set clear standards for educational achievement in early childhood programs and to establish vigorous systems of assessment and accountability.

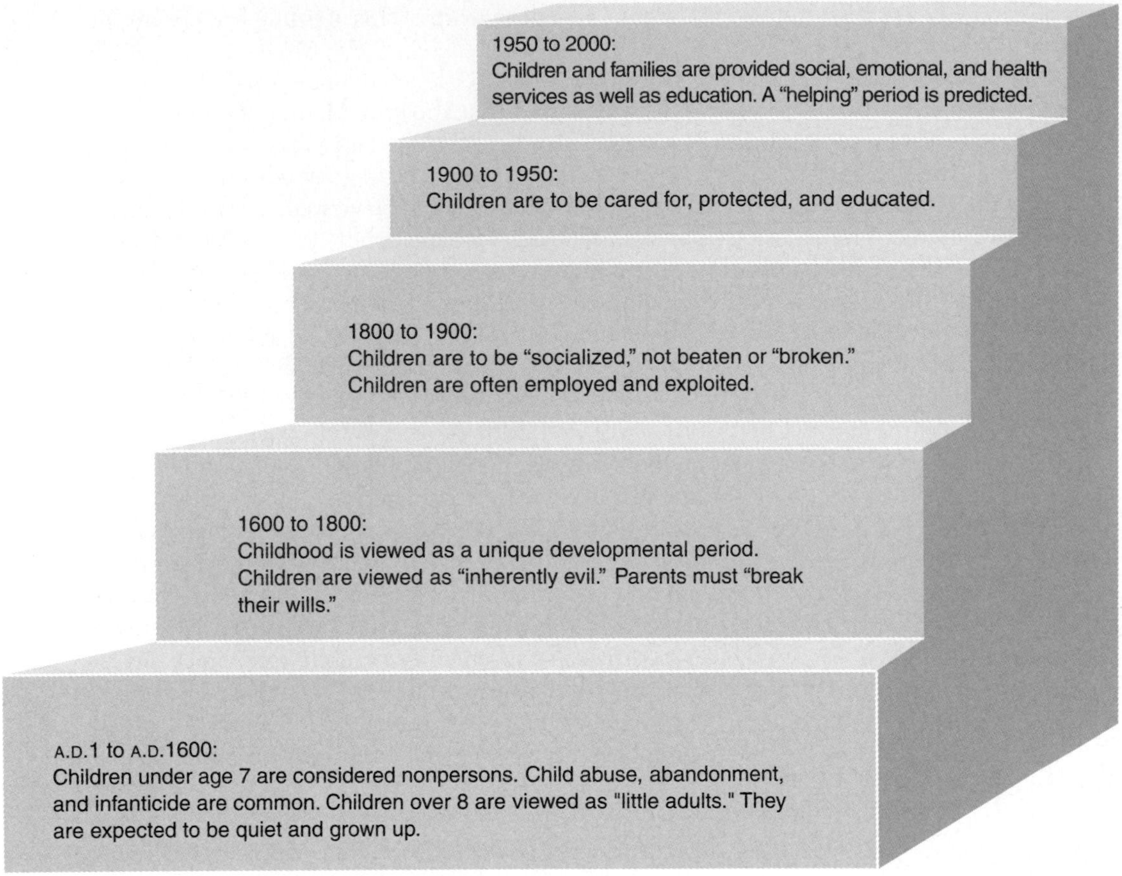

1950 to 2000:
Children and families are provided social, emotional, and health services as well as education. A "helping" period is predicted.

1900 to 1950:
Children are to be cared for, protected, and educated.

1800 to 1900:
Children are to be "socialized," not beaten or "broken." Children are often employed and exploited.

1600 to 1800:
Childhood is viewed as a unique developmental period. Children are viewed as "inherently evil." Parents must "break their wills."

A.D.1 to A.D.1600:
Children under age 7 are considered nonpersons. Child abuse, abandonment, and infanticide are common. Children over 8 are viewed as "little adults." They are expected to be quiet and grown up.

FIGURE 2-1   A history of perspectives on and treatment of children in the Western world is presented. The figure shows that care of and concern for children is a relatively recent historical occurrence in the United States and Europe.
SOURCE: DEMAUSE, 1995; POLLOCK, 1987.

in government-funded programs. There has been a push to improve measures of educational success, even at the youngest age levels. Examples of this trend are the federal No Child Left Behind Act of 2002 and the Head Start Child Outcomes Framework (U.S. Department of Health and Human Services, 2008). These initiatives mandate higher educational standards and increased assessment of learning. The standards movement has been viewed as a mixed blessing for children in America (Scott-Little, Kagan, & Frelow, 2003). On the one hand, it has led to higher expectations and a greater appreciation of what children are able to learn. Curricula in schools have become more challenging, for example. The movement has led to a belief that all children—even those in poverty—can excel if we hold high (and measurable) expectations for them.

The movement has created hardship for some children as well (Frost, Wortham, & Reifel, 2008). New academic pressure has taken a toll on some children. School phobia, academic failure, grade retention, and even expulsion have been observed at a very early age (Perry, Dunne, McFadden, & Campbell, 2007). Curricula in some schools have become narrowly focused only on "testable" skills and knowledge. Opportunities for play, even recess, have been reduced (Pellegrini, 2005). It is important for teachers of young children to seek a balance in their classrooms between academic experiences that meet standards and those that allow children to play, socialize, and make choices in their learning.

ADVOCACY AND PUBLIC POLICY

Raising Awareness of the Problems Faced by America's Children

As discussed in this chapter, historians report that we have entered a "period of helping" in which adults in our society recognize and fully meet the needs of children (deMause, 1995). Many Americans—including community leaders—believe that children are faring quite well in our country. However, research does not support such a positive view (Children's Defense Fund, 2007). Professionals can play an important role in raising public awareness of the many ongoing problems faced by young children in our country: poor health care, malnutrition, low academic achievement, and even abuse and neglect. A message to be conveyed to the public is that we have a long way to go in fully meeting the needs of America's children.

A common approach to raising awareness is to cite statistics in letters to the editor of local newspapers or presentations at public hearings. Numbers and tables can lack emotional impact, however, and may not convince community leaders of the severity of these problems. A more powerful advocacy method is to invite policymakers to visit children and families in their homes, neighborhoods, and schools to witness firsthand some of the challenges they face. Such is the approach of the Child Watch Visitation Program of the Children's Defense Fund. This program "adds the faces and stories of real children to the statistics and reports... and moves executives, clergy, legislators, and other community leaders out of their offices, corporate boardrooms, and legislative chambers, and into the world of the real children and families whose lives they affect every day with their decisions" (Children's Defense Fund, 2007, p. 1).

In one community, program participants invited legislators and business executives to visit local soup kitchens, Head Start centers, and public assistance agencies to observe poverty close up. In another, Child Watch invited community leaders to hear the testimonials of parents living in poverty who discussed the importance of food and nutrition programs. In a particularly innovative strategy, Child Watch members in a third community invited civic leaders to a lunch with families receiving public assistance. Each leader was given an envelope of pretend money with which to buy a meal. Some received adequate funds, some only half of what was needed to eat, and many only empty envelopes. This was a powerful simulation of the day-to-day struggles of those without enough money to feed their families.

Professionals can plan such face-to-face encounters between policymakers and families in their local communities or become involved in the national Child Watch program (childrensdefense.org).

Non-Western Perspectives

Historical information on attitudes and care of non-Western children is scarce. Historical work most often cited in child development texts focuses on European and, later, American perspectives (Aries, 1962; deMause, 1974). Following are some of the viewpoints and approaches of African, Native American, Asian, and Puerto Rican societies toward children over the centuries.

African History.   The views of some non-Western societies can be traced through descriptions of family life centuries ago. Accounts of the strong kinship and tribal bonds of early African families, for example, suggest that adults showed a high degree of concern and caring toward children, as they did toward members of their families and communities (Hale & Franklin, 2001; Hale-Benson, 1986; Nsamenang, 1995, 2004). Mother–child relationships were especially strong in early Africa. Nobles (1985) has suggested that this special bond preceded the slavery era and that the strong role of the mother is still an important element in African American family life.

Native American History. Early descriptions of Native American families also portray close familial and tribal ties (Adair & Braund, 2005; Joe & Malach, 1998). Although great diversity exists among tribes, a theme woven through the ancient stories, family histories, art, and music of most Native American cultures is the interdependence among and respect for all living things. Children were a significant part of the natural order and, therefore, were highly cherished and protected. Communities and families adopted a clear division of labor and a sense of social responsibility. Child rearing was a collective endeavor performed by mothers and fathers, older tribal members, and older and even same-age children. Children were socialized from the earliest days to become part of a group yet were afforded much opportunity for individual expression through art and music. Individual differences were accepted as part of the natural scheme. The high value placed on both social relationships and individual expression is fundamental to Native American life to this day (Blanchard, 1983; Spring, 1998; Swanton, 2006).

Ancient stories portray the very humane treatment of Native American children in centuries past. Training "occurred in close contact with many people who praised, advised, guided, urged, warned, and scolded, but, most importantly, respected children" (Blanchard, 1983, p. 118). Although infant mortality may have been viewed as necessary for population control in early centuries, the birth of a healthy child was cause for tribal celebration.

Chinese and Japanese History. Early attitudes toward children in China and Japan were influenced by the writings of Confucius (551–479 B.C.). Confucianism's focus on interpersonal harmony led to the belief in both societies that children are inherently good—a perspective that did not emerge in Europe until many centuries later. A respect for children can be found in descriptions of early Chinese and Japanese life. The education of children was a concern even in ancient times (Ho, 1994; Lee & Mock, 2005; Shibusawa, 2005). Between the 16th and 19th centuries, Japanese and Chinese children were encouraged to learn through observation and imitation; question asking was valued. In the 18th century, Kibara (1710) wrote that children should be guided in self-directed learning. He recommended only moderate amounts of punishment or reinforcement.

In China, as early as the 13th century, infancy was recognized as a unique period in development. According to Chinese philosopher Wang Zhong-Yang, the first 60 days of life were a "sensitive period." The emergence of smiling and walking represented milestones in human growth. It was proposed that the strength of parent–child bonds could lead to a successful transition from infancy to childhood.

Slavery and Colonialism. The experience of childhood in some non-Western cultures from the 18th to 20th centuries was strongly influenced by slavery and colonialism. Ogbu (1992) has argued that the experience of oppression added a new dimension to the lives of nondominant cultural groups generally and children in particular. As families were enslaved or tribes and communities conquered, new parental values and child-rearing practices emerged by necessity.

Ethnic studies scholars have identified several ways that the lives of children and families have been affected by oppression (Garcia Coll & Pachter, 2002; McLoyd, Aikens, & Burton, 2006). These are presented in Table 2-1. As shown in the table, families of subjugated cultures became more **collective** in their thinking and action. Family and nonfamily members banded together, often pooling resources and sharing caregiving tasks.

Puerto Rican families of the late 19th century, for example, are described as close-knit and mutually supportive. Strong kinship bonds were considered an important adaptation to the conditions of social and economic injustice of the time (Halgunseth, 2004; Sanchez-Ayendez, 1988). These bonds have historically extended beyond family lines. Early practices such as *compadrazgo* (coparenting by relatives and nonrelatives) and *hijos de crianza* (informal

collective families: Families that are more likely to collaborate in daily life, pooling resources, sharing household tasks and child-rearing responsibilities, making group decisions, and banding together in the face of adversity.

TABLE 2-1
The Influences of Oppression on the Lives of Children and Families

Characteristics of Historically Oppressed Families	Example
Collectivism	Persons of historically oppressed groups have more often lived in extended families, which include parents, grandparents, and even aunts and uncles.
	Family members have often pooled resources and sacrificed individual goals for the good of the family. Collective child care has been common.
	Neighbors and friends who are like family " have banded together in the face of adversity.
	Children have been taught "enmeshment"— a strong attachment to family and culture.
Firm and directive parenting	Parents of historically underrepresented groups have often directly regulated children's behavior in an effort to protect them from the dangers of racism and physical violence.
	Children have been encouraged to be obedient and not "talk back" to those in authority—particularly slaveholders or powerful members of the dominant culture.
Valuing or devaluing Western education	Some children of historically oppressed groups have been urged to "exceed white children" in their achievement in Western schools.
	Some children of historically oppressed groups have been taught to reject the learning and values of Western schools.

adoption of children by nonfamily members) reflect a commitment to shared child rearing among all community members. Close friendships among individuals living in proximity to one another were common. The phrase *como de la familia* (like one of the family) is used to this day to refer to these special mutually supportive nonfamily relationships.

Similar kinship and "para-kinship" relationships have been described in early African American culture as well (Hale, 1994; Hale & Franklin, 2001). The experience of slavery led to powerful family bonds. It was through the family that "the slave received affection, companionship, love, and empathy . . . and some semblance of self-esteem" (Staples, 1988, p. 305). Nonfamily adults also played a role in child rearing, particularly when families were separated by the sale of parents or by a slaveholder's death. To this day, "a strong desire exists among Black people to be related to each other" (Hale-Benson, 1986, p. 16).

As shown in Table 2.1, child-rearing techniques also changed as a result of oppression (Garcia Coll, 1990; Garica Coll & Pachter, 2002). Parents often adopted **firm and directive socialization practices** to protect their children from dangers inherent in slavery or colonization. African slave parents, for example, took on the vital responsibility of restricting children's actions to avoid their harsh punishment by slaveholders. They encouraged self-sufficiency at an early age; children needed to get along on their own, especially in cases where parents were sold or the family was split up in other ways. Survival demanded that children become mature

firm and directive socialization practices: Techniques of child guidance, more common in families of traditionally oppressed cultures, in which behavior is closely monitored and regulated in order to keep children safe from danger.

before their time. They were urged to work hard, complete required tasks, and never complain (Johnson & Staples, 2004). Slave parents did not hesitate to use the "switch" when children became dangerously insolent (Hale, 1994; Hale & Franklin, 2001).

Among the Plains Indians during western expansion, parents taught young children— even infants—not to cry. This was an adaptive practice designed to keep children from giving away their location to the enemy. Keeping children under control was, again, a necessity for survival among Native American cultures (John, 1988; Tafoya & Vecchio, 2005).

Firm and directive parenting, which may be observed to this day among some families of traditionally oppressed peoples (Brooks-Gunn & Markem, 2005; Hale, 1994; Hale & Franklin, 2001; Hale-Benson, 1986), has historical roots. It is important to point out that such child-rearing styles are not wrong or deficient; such directive interactions have allowed children to survive over the centuries. In neighborhoods where violence and drug use are common, it is still imperative for parents to closely scrutinize and direct children's activities. Doing so leads to positive child development among some groups (Baumrind, 1994; Garcia Coll et al., 1998).

Beliefs about children's education and success in the dominant culture were also affected by colonization and slavery, as shown in Table 2-1. In some cultures, oppression led to **valuing Western education** and academic achievement within the dominant society. In others, there occurred **a devaluing of Western education,** in which families rejected mainstream paths to success. Both attitudes may be viewed as adaptive; both represented the best thinking by parents in how to help their children develop in positive directions. Hale-Benson (1986) has noted a strong achievement orientation among African American families. Since the time of emancipation, parents have encouraged their children to be ambitious and hardworking and to "exceed white children's behavior and performance" (p. 48). This has not meant that parents wish children to abandon their African heritage. Many families focus on striving for success in the dominant culture while maintaining pride in one's African traditions.

In contrast, for centuries some Native American families have encouraged children to actively reject the values and practices of the dominant culture (Canino & Spurlock, 2000; Whitesell, Mitchell, Kaufman, & Spice, 2006; Wise & Miller, 1983). Some parents have emphasized schooling less and have focused instead on teaching competencies that are more highly valued in Native American tradition. In such families, children may come to judge their self-worth not on success as defined in Western terms but on achievements related to their own culture. Lefley (1976) found that children of Seminole and Miccosukee tribes in Florida had significantly higher self-esteem when they had not been acculturated into the dominant society. Generally, traditional modes of interaction have enhanced positive development in some groups.

In summary, children of the world have diverse histories that explain variations in development and parenting. Understanding and appreciating children's unique historical roots is important for teachers of young children in interpreting classroom behavior and family relationships today.

valuing/devaluing Western education: Responses of cultural groups to the mainstream educational system. In some cultures, education is viewed as a way to better oneself; in others, children are encouraged to reject mainstream educational institutions.

RESEARCH ON YOUNG CHILDREN

Much of the information in this book has been drawn from research on young children's development. Because research on humans is necessarily flawed, findings merely provide good guesses about the relationships between children's behavior, learning, or other characteristics and their experience and genetic makeup. As a result, professionals working with young children should be guided by research findings but not enslaved by them. They must be able to weigh the results of a particular work and judge its relevance to classroom practice based on the methods used or the sample selected.

A History of Child Study

For centuries, scientists and philosophers have been interested in children's development. The aim of early work in child study was to describe normal development and determine its causes. What was considered normal, however, was often what society at the time defined as acceptable thought or behavior. John Locke (1632–1704) and Jean-Jacques Rousseau (1712–1778), who were among the first Western writers to recognize the importance of environment in children's development, wrote about the origins of "goodness" and "sinfulness" in childhood. Goodness, from their perspective, was adherence to the teachings of the church and the mores of industrialized society. Any deviation from the mainstream thought or behavior of this historical period likely would have been viewed as aberrant.

Pioneers in the field of child study conducted descriptive observations of children in an effort to plot the course of normal development. Johann Heinrich Pestalozzi (1746–1827) and Charles Darwin (1809–1882) published biographies of their own children in an attempt to capture milestones of human growth. Obviously, the study samples of these scientists were limited. What they were, in fact, observing were the behaviors of children from privileged European families at that time. Diary studies often reflected the biases of a particular era. Diarists often emphasized or exaggerated information that supported current norms, systematically omitting information that might be deemed "shameful" by the community (Pollock, 1987).

G. Stanley Hall (1844–1924), an eminent psychologist at the turn of the 20th century, was the first to test child development theories using larger and more representative samples of children. Hall invented a now common research tool, the questionnaire, to gather data. Later researchers extended Hall's scientific methodology in the study of children, selecting even larger samples and using more formal, controlled, and objective observation techniques (Gesell & Ilg, 1949; Shirley, 1933). The results of these studies were often reported in **normative charts,** which presented milestones in physical, mental, or social development for each age level of childhood. A sample normative chart for motor development is presented in Table 2-2.

A problem with these studies was that they usually included only white, middle-class children. For example, Shirley's (1933) study of motor milestones in infancy—sometimes cited in child development textbooks today—was conducted with babies of white families in Minnesota. Would these same findings have been obtained if the study had included children from other cultural groups within the United States or in the world as a whole?

normative charts: Graphic representations of the stages or milestones children pass through as they develop.

Recent research on young children has become exceedingly sophisticated. Much of the information shared in this book has been derived from these more modern studies.

Age	Motor Development Milestone
1 month	Raises chin up off the ground
2 months	Raises chest up off the ground
4 months	Sits with adult support
7 months	Sits alone
9 months	Stands holding onto adults or furniture
10 months	Creeps
14 months	Stands alone
15 months	Walks alone

TABLE 2-2
Example of a Normative Chart for Motor Development in Infancy

SOURCE: Gesell & Ilg, 1949; Shirley, 1933.

Several types of research designs are commonly employed to investigate specific aspects of young children's development, including correlational, experimental, qualitative, and ethnographic studies. Each will be discussed in the following sections.

Correlational Studies

In a **correlational study,** two or more behaviors or developmental characteristics are observed for a particular group of children, and an effort is made to determine whether relationships exist among them. Is the babbling of infants related to the amount of time parents spend talking with them? Is achievement in first-grade reading related to self-esteem? These kinds of questions are asked and answered in correlational studies. In each case, groups of children are observed, tested, or otherwise assessed, first on one factor and then on another. The scientist then determines whether relationships exist between the two factors.

I conducted a correlational study in which I examined relationships between children's overall social competence and their ability to persuade their peers (Trawick-Smith, 1992). First, teachers rated a group of preschool children on social ability. Later, the subjects were observed playing with peers. A coding system was used to determine whether these children were effective in persuading playmates to do things. A relationship was found between overall social competence and persuasiveness. Children who were rated as competent could more effectively get peers to perform tedious tasks for them (e.g., "Will you pick up my blocks for me?"), to accept new play themes (e.g., "Do you want to play circus?"), or to give over desired objects (e.g., "Can I have one of your long blocks?").

Some correlational studies are **cross-sectional,** in which factors of interest are examined by observing a group of children of many different ages only once or a small number of times. An example is a study by McClelland, Acock, & Morrison (2006) on the relationship between early learning–related skills (such as independence, self-regulation, and cooperation) and reading and math achievement across the elementary years. Rather than follow a single set of children from kindergarten to sixth grade—a time-consuming and costly approach—the researchers studied children of varying ages (from 5 to 11 years) during one time period. They discovered that there was a relationship between these learning skills and math and reading achievement at all age levels. However, the association was the strongest for children between the ages of 5 to 7 years. The researchers conclude that learning skills have the strongest relationship to reading and math ability from kindergarten to second grade.

In **longitudinal** correlational research, a group of children is followed over a period of time to observe changes in their behavior and development at various age levels. One such study focused on solitary/withdrawn behavior of young children and its relationship to acceptance by peers and self-esteem over time (Nelson, Rubin, & Fox, 2005). In this study, a single group of children were identified and measured at 4 years of age and again at 7 years. Researchers found that solitary and withdrawn behavior was related to poor acceptance by peers at both age levels. Only at age 7, however, were these solitary/withdrawn behaviors found to be related to low self-esteem. They speculate that, as withdrawn children get older, their solitary behavior and related rejection by peers in the preschool years leads them to perceive themselves more negatively at age 7.

A caution must be issued about correlational studies: just because two characteristics or behaviors are found to be related does not mean that one causes the other. If the amount of parent language is related to infant babbling, can we assume that the former caused the latter? Or could infants' babbling have, instead, caused parents to speak to them more often? It seems plausible that highly vocal babies would elicit increased response from adults. Teachers must be careful in interpreting and applying correlational research. Although scientists often conclude that one factor causes another, many alternative explanations are possible.

correlational study: A type of research in which two traits are measured and their relationship is examined.

cross-sectional study: Research in which a trait is studied by examining children of many different ages at one time, and developmental trends are determined by comparing one age group to another.

longitudinal study: Research in which a group of children is studied over a long period of time to observe changes in behavior and development at various ages.

Experimental Studies

In an **experimental study,** the researcher intervenes in some way in children's lives and observes what happens. Will teaching parents to respond to babies when they cry lead to healthy emotional development? Will reading books to preschoolers promote their language and literacy? These are the sorts of questions an experimental study attempts to answer. In each case, the researcher causes something to occur in the lives of children and then measures the outcome. Often the goal of such investigations is to determine whether an intervention causes a positive change in children's learning or behavior.

Experimental studies can be quite short in duration. Several researchers, for example, designed a six-week experiment to test strategies for improving young children's attitudes toward those of different cultures (Cameron, Rutland, Brown, and Douch, 2006). They assigned children from ages 5 to 10 years to one of four groups. One group was read stories about Euro-American children and those of historically underrepresented backgrounds interacting together in positive ways. After each story, children were guided in talking about the traits of individual characters, without any mention of culture. A second group was read the same stories but then was asked to discuss the cultures of the characters and to name the ways those of each cultural group were alike. In a third group, the same stories were read and children were asked to identify commonalities of the characters but also to discuss their cultural differences. A control group of children who did not receive any special treatment was also studied. Researchers found that all the children who had heard and discussed the stories held more positive views toward those of different cultures than the control group. Among the experimental groups, those who had discussed *both* similarities and cultural differences of the characters in the story held the most positive attitudes. The authors conclude that a strategy of both celebrating differences and noting similarities across cultures may be the most powerful method for reducing children's prejudices.

Experimental studies can also be longitudinal. In a classic study of impoverished children in Colombia, researchers provided a group of families with food supplements for children and parents, beginning at midpregnancy (Super, Herrera, & Mora, 1990). Another group was provided with both food supplements and twice-weekly visits from a parent educator to promote cognitive development. A third group, which did not have access to these services, was used as a control. All children were followed until age 6. Those who received food supplements fared better on physical and intellectual growth measures than those who did not receive the supplements. The group that received both food supplements and home visits was even better off in these areas. The researchers concluded that nutritional and educational intervention can, over time, reduce the physical and intellectual risks of impoverished environments.

The results of experimental studies often lead researchers to conclude that one factor has caused another to occur. If the children who were provided with nutritional and educational services were better off than those who did not receive these services, it is likely that the intervention caused positive outcomes. This interpretation of findings is illustrated in view (a) of Figure 2-2.

Caution must still be used in interpreting the results of experiments, however. Other interpretations are possible, as depicted in views (b), (c), (d), and (e). Child and family characteristics, positive parent interactions, or even biased research may explain positive outcomes rather than the services themselves.

Multicultural Critique of Traditional Research

Multicultural scholars (Quintana et al., 2006; Banks, 2003; McLoyd, 2006; Ogbu, 1992) have raised concerns about traditional research methods, particularly in the study of children of diverse cultural backgrounds. They argue that some researchers have systematically excluded subjects from traditionally underrepresented groups. Further, when children of nondominant cultural groups are included in studies, they are regularly compared with their

experimental study:
Research in which a treatment, such as an educational intervention, is administered to subjects. An experimental group receives the treatment, a control group does not, and the researcher compares the outcomes of the two groups.

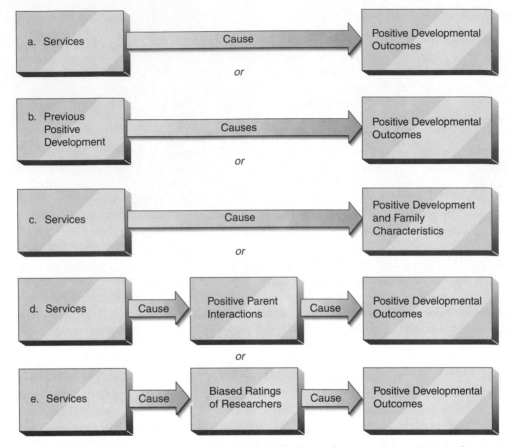

FIGURE 2-2   There are many ways to interpret the findings of an experimental study. Several alternative explanations are possible for the outcomes of a nutritional services study, for example: (a) The services themselves caused positive development. (b) The children selected for the study were more advanced in their development before the study even began. (c) Families who volunteered their children for the study were more concerned and caring. These positive family characteristics enhanced development. (d) The nutritional services caused parents to change in some way—to become more positive or nurturing with their children, for example. These changes resulted in positive outcomes. (e) Researchers who were studying the effects of nutritional services subconsciously rated children higher in development if they received these services.

white, middle-class peers on measures or behaviors that reflect the dominant culture's values. Children who speak Spanish as their primary language, for example, have been compared with their Anglo peers on measures of standard English competence. In such comparisons, children of traditionally underrepresented groups are often portrayed as less competent.

Professionals must use care not to assume that conclusions and recommendations of researchers always apply to all individuals or ethnic groups. Some scholars have advocated qualitative and ethnographic studies that are more sensitive to and appreciative of cultural differences (Heath, 2003; Ogbu, 1992).

Qualitative/Ethnographic Studies

Correlational or experimental studies make extensive use of **quantitative methods** in which children are observed and their behaviors are tallied or rated numerically. These numbers are then entered into sophisticated computer programs, and in-depth statistical analyses are

quantitative methods: Research methods in which children are observed and their behaviors counted or rated numerically. The numbers that are obtained are then entered into computer programs and analyzed statistically.

In an ethnographic study, the researcher attempts to write a "thick" description of all that children say and do.

performed. An alternative methodology gaining support among researchers in the field is **qualitative research.** This method involves open-ended observations of children, usually in natural settings. The purpose is to provide a "thick description" (Denzin & Lincoln, 2001) of children's development that captures all aspects of their lives: classroom environment, friendships, parents and family life, and community.

The results of qualitative studies are usually presented as rich and detailed narratives that illustrate children's development. A qualitative study of how preschool children learn to read, for example, could include in-depth descriptions of how individual subjects used books over a long period of time. The researcher reviews and interprets these descriptions. Qualitative researchers do not often draw sweeping, universal conclusions about all children in the country (or the world) from their findings. Instead, their purpose is to describe individual behavior or development within a particular environmental context. This methodology, then, moves away from an effort to identify what is normal for all children.

In one descriptive study of play behavior, 12 preschool children were observed interacting during make-believe in a natural classroom setting (Trawick-Smith, 1998a). The purpose was to ascertain what children do during metaplay—that is, when they temporarily stop their make-believe, step out of their pretend roles, and argue or negotiate about what will happen next. In the study, detailed descriptions of children's metaplay negotiations were given. The following is one excerpt:

ROSITA: (Holding up a wooden dowel) This will be my magic witch wand.
AIDA: That stick?
ROSITA: It's a witch wand to . . . um . . . cast the spell, all right?
AIDA: What's it do?
ROSITA: Let's say if the princess goes like this (makes noises, waves the dowel), then it makes things into gold, all right, Aida?

Researchers examined the transcriptions for patterns or trends in behavior and identified several distinct metaplay negotiations.

qualitative research: Research that involves writing a rich description of behaviors and development rather than counting or quantifying observations.

Another type of qualitative research is **ethnography.** This method uses the traditional procedures of the anthropologist to study children's development within cultural context. Researchers who follow this methodology spend a great deal of time as participants in the culture of subjects being studied. (Ethnographic researchers might even live in the same community as subjects.) In so doing, they come to more fully understand and appreciate the culture within which children grow and develop.

Some newer studies have been done within the culture of the preschool or child care classroom. Here the researcher spends a long period of time with students, teachers, parents, and administrators, coming to know the environment as a participant observer. The researcher takes field notes of experiences and observations and gathers other kinds of information about subjects.

For example, one researcher visited a preschool classroom taught by a male teacher in week-long, 3 hour classroom visits over the course of a year (Sumsion, 2005). She was interested in determining whether interactions with this teacher would reduce gender stereotypes. As she visited, she would observe children's play, gather drawing samples, and conduct informal interviews. Using information gathered from these visits, she concluded that simply having a male teacher did not reduce children's stereotyped thinking. She concluded that teachers, whether male or female, should more actively engage children in discussions about gender in order to reduce gender biases.

Ethnographic investigations capture the rich complexity of culture and context. Good ethnographers fully understand and appreciate the diverse histories, life experiences, world-views, competencies, and socialization practices of cultural groups, and they describe these in their reports. Ethnographic research probably provides the fullest picture of child development from a multicultural perspective.

Action Research in the Classroom

Teachers and caregivers of young children can conduct child development research themselves. Whenever they observe children in the classroom in a thoughtful and organized way, they are engaged in **action research**—informal research used to answer pressing questions related to classroom life. Some action research methods resemble those used in correlational or experimental studies, while others are equivalent to methods used in qualitative and ethnographic research.

Quantitative Classroom Observation. Sometimes teachers want to gain a quick understanding of children's growth and development in particular areas. In these cases, quantitative observation methods may be useful. One of the most common is the **developmental checklist** of milestones or behavioral characteristics of interest to a teacher. Children are observed and rated on each item on the checklist according to a predetermined coding system. Sample items from a checklist that assesses preschoolers' social development are presented in Table 2-3.

Teachers using this checklist would determine whether children could perform each of these social tasks independently, with adult assistance, or with direct adult guidance. Results would indicate which students needed support in social interactions and the areas in which they required assistance. Data from a developmental checklist can also provide parents with an overview of development.

Other quantitative research methods can be adapted for use in the classroom. For example, a child care provider may want to determine how frequently a particular child engages in literacy activities during the day, or a kindergarten teacher may wish to record the number of contacts students make with peers. In these instances, a coding system (similar to those used by researchers) can be developed to tally how often these behaviors are performed.

ethnography: A type of research in which investigators spend significant time working or living with a group—a classroom, a family, or a community—and write qualitative descriptions of their observations.

action research: Informal research conducted by teachers and caregivers to answer pressing questions related to teaching, learning, and children's development.

developmental checklist: A classroom observation system in which a teacher or caregiver rates children's attainment of certain developmental milestones, such as resolving conflicts or playing cooperatively with peers.

Social Skill	Teacher Rating
Interacts with peers	I
Uses language with peers to express needs or ideas	I
Plays cooperatively with peers	AA
Shares toys and materials	AA
Enters peer groups effectively	DG
Elicits and maintains the attention of peers	AA
Resolves conflicts with peers	DG

Coding System:

I = Can perform the skill independently

AA = Can perform the skill with some adult assistance

DG = Needs direct guidance from adults in performing the skill

TABLE 2-3
Checklist Assessing Social Development of Preschoolers

Several types of coding system procedures are used. In **event sampling,** teachers make a check or notation on a coding sheet every time a particular behavior is observed. For example, a teacher who is interested in how frequently children exhibit aggressive behavior will carefully watch for aggressive interchanges and make a tally or check mark whenever these occur. Over time, data may be collected concerning which children are most aggressive or how prevalent aggression is within the whole classroom.

In **time sampling,** teachers observe children at regular intervals and record interactions that occur within that time frame. For example, a teacher might make a brief observation of a child's interactions every 10 minutes during a free-play period in the classroom and note whether the child is playing alone or with other children. Throughout the morning, the teacher would continue gathering data on the child's social contact at 10-minute intervals, placing a check mark under "playing alone" or "playing with peers" on a coding sheet. Over time, the teacher would get a picture of how frequently children interact with others. More elaborate time-sampling systems can be developed. Table 2-4 presents a coding sheet that allows the teacher to code, at once, the level of social involvement and the type of play a child is exhibiting. At some regular interval—say, every 5 minutes—a teacher using this

event sampling: A method of observing children in which a teacher or researcher records the number of times a particular behavior or event occurs.

time sampling: A research method in which a teacher or researcher observes children at regular time intervals and records interactions that occur during that period.

| Level of Social Participation | TYPE OF PLAY | | | |
	Functional Play	Construction Play	Dramatic Play	Games
Solitary play	///	/////		
Parallel play		//	//	
Associative play		////	/	
Cooperative play		////		///

"/" indicates an observation of that play category during a 5-minute period.

TABLE 2-4
Sample Coding Sheet for Observing Social Participation and Type of Play

SOURCE: Parten, 1932; Piaget, 1962; Rubin, Maioni, & Hornung, 1976.

system would make a check mark corresponding to the type of play (e.g., construction play) and the level of social participation (e.g., cooperative play) the child exhibited.

Teachers can design their own observation systems to study behaviors of interest or concern. Great care must be taken, however, to clearly and objectively define behaviors to be studied. In a coding system for aggression, for example, should name-calling be considered an aggressive act? Should a check mark be made when a child physically resists a peer's attempt to snatch a toy? These issues must be resolved before observation begins. In designing observation systems, teachers must also be cautious not to select behaviors that are valued only by the dominant culture. For example, a social interaction rating scheme would be considered culturally biased if it included the item "establishes eye contact with peers and adults." Although looking directly at a speaker is a part of typical communication within Euro-American society, eye contact is viewed as a sign of disrespect in other cultures (Sanchez-Burks & Lee, 2005).

Qualitative Classroom Observation. Qualitative methods of classroom observation may be most useful to teachers because they are relatively easy to administer and because they provide rich descriptive information about children that can be shared with parents and other professionals. In addition, they avoid the cultural bias that can exist in coding systems. Consider the following comparison of qualitative versus quantitative observations of aggression:

OBSERVATION #1 (QUANTITATIVE):

A teacher uses a coding sheet to tally the frequency of aggressive acts by a particular child. A total of five tally marks are made on the sheet during a single morning of observation.

OBSERVATION #2 (QUALITATIVE):

A teacher writes the following descriptions of classroom events that took place during a morning observation:

> Nader builds with blocks, stacking them higher and higher until the structure teeters. Laticia enters the play area and comments to Nader, "I can do a taller one! That's not a very good one." Nader does not look up and continues to build. "That's a stupid one!" Laticia says in a loud voice.
>
> Laticia moves to Nader's building and kicks it, toppling the blocks. Nader screams in anger and pushes Laticia backward before I can move over to intervene. Laticia falls and is crying loudly as I enter the area.

In a previous quantitative observation, it was found that Nader frequently engages in aggression. However, that finding does not give a full picture of the circumstances surrounding these aggressive acts. Nor does it provide information to assist in solving this classroom problem. In the qualitative description, events leading up to aggression can be studied. Nader has been provoked; many observations of this kind may suggest that he is actively rejected by peers and may be the target of negative social behaviors. In the description, Nader's reaction to the provocation is revealed. Actually, he displays quite remarkable restraint when the first taunts are made. It is only after a severe offense has taken place that he strikes out. From this information, intervention strategies can be designed to address Nader's peer rejection or to help him learn nonviolent ways to react to his classmates' negative behaviors. Such qualitative descriptions may also help the teacher in promoting Laticia's social development.

There are many types of qualitative observation methods. Two that are commonly adopted for use in classrooms are **anecdotal records** and **case studies.**

anecdotal records: A qualitative research method—often used in the classroom—in which children's behavior is observed and recorded in a rich narrative.

case studies: A qualitative research method—often used in the classroom—that involves gathering in-depth information on an individual child or family and writing an extensive narrative profiling development.

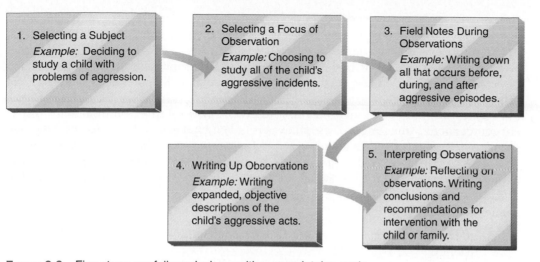

FIGURE 2-3   Five steps are followed when writing anecdotal records.

Anecdotal Records.   The anecdotal record is the qualitative observation method most often used by teachers. In this method, notes are taken about classroom observations and then rewritten later in a fuller, more descriptive way. An example of the steps that are followed in writing anecdotal records is presented in Figure 2-3.

1. *Selecting a child or children to be observed.* Sometimes an individual student is the focus of the study. At other times, whole-classroom observations are conducted. Observations in a particular play area or center are also common.

2. *Selecting the focus of the observation.* Teachers often focus their observations on a particular behavior or area of development. In most instances, the observation is structured to gather information to solve a particular classroom problem. However, sometimes teachers watch classroom interactions generally and record whatever seems noteworthy. This can lead to important unanticipated discoveries about classroom life.

3. *Taking notes during observations.* The teacher takes brief notes during the observation, jotting down key events and behaviors and the names of the children involved. An effort is made to record dialogue. Even writing short phrases can remind the observer later of conversations that took place. The observer carefully records the setting and time of day for all entries. Taking notes while teaching is a difficult task. Experienced teachers often carry a small notepad and make brief observations and notations when a break in classroom activity occurs.

4. *Writing up observations.* When time allows, teachers write up their anecdotal records in a more descriptive form. It is important to reconstruct observations as soon as possible after they take place. Although these descriptions are rich and detailed, they are accurate and objective, describing behavior rather than interpreting it (e.g., instead of writing, "Sonia was angry this morning," a teacher would write, "Sonia had a frown on her face and spoke to everyone in a loud voice").

5. *Interpreting anecdotal records.* After several records are written, teachers begin to reread and interpret them. They may look for patterns of behavior across observations or search for solutions to problems revealed in these narrative descriptions. They may share excerpts from these records at parent conferences or with teams of intervention professionals.

Case Studies. On occasion, a teacher wishes to do a more comprehensive study of a particular child. Classroom observations may not provide all the needed information. A child intervention team—composed of teachers, social workers, school psychologists, or other professionals working together to address the needs of an individual child—may require in-depth information on the child's family and community life as well as school-related behaviors. In such instances, a case study may be written.

A case study is an accumulation and interpretation of information from many different sources across time. A good case study certainly includes anecdotal records; however, other sources of information are also used. Summaries of interviews with parents or descriptions of visits to a child's home may be incorporated. Data on the community or the child's neighborhood can be added. The following information is commonly included in a case study:

1. Anecdotal descriptions of classroom behavior
2. Information on peer relations, classroom friendships, and interactions with teachers
3. Descriptions of previous school experience (i.e., records from other child care providers, attendance records, developmental checklists from earlier years)
4. Physical descriptions/health and medical information
5. Interests and activity patterns in school (i.e., data on what the child does frequently during free play and which materials he or she uses, results of interviews with the child about his or her interests)
6. Informal observations of competence (i.e., language samples, collections of drawings, photographs of block structures)
7. Formal assessments of the competence (i.e., results of developmental screenings, clinical interviews)
8. Descriptions of the child's family life and culture (i.e., summaries of parent interviews, descriptions of home visits, socioeconomic information)
9. Descriptions of the child's neighborhood
10. Descriptions of what the child does outside of school (titles of favorite books, diaries of television viewing, checklists of nonschool activities)

After this information has been assembled, a descriptive narrative is written to summarize and interpret the findings. Conclusions and recommendations are often included. The case study may be shared with other professionals or parents, adhering to rules of confidentiality. It may be included as part of the teacher's ongoing classroom record of the child's development.

SUMMARY

Views of childhood have changed over the centuries in both Western and non-Western cultures. Some of the Western perspectives of long ago—that children should be "seen and not heard" and that they should learn and behave just like adults—persist to this day, even among some teachers. Historical views of childhood within non-Western cultures also endure. Parents of cultural groups that have been oppressed, for example, may believe that children need firm, directive parenting as a way of protecting them from adversity. The methods for studying child development have also changed over the years. Early researchers attempted to describe normal child development based on the mores and religious beliefs of the day. Modern researchers use sophisticated quantitative and qualitative methods. In quantitative studies, children's behaviors or traits are rated or tallied numerically. Resulting numbers are analyzed statistically. In qualitative studies, researchers describe the behaviors of children in rich, open-ended ways. Qualitative methods, including anecdotal records and case studies, are most useful for teachers because they yield in-depth profiles of children that can be used in teaching and can be shared with parents.

RESEARCH INTO PRACTICE

CRITICAL CONCEPT 1

Western perspectives on childhood have changed throughout history. Historical accounts in Western society portray children as being treated poorly in early centuries but cared for more compassionately in modern society.

Application #1   Become a historian in your own field by studying how viewpoints on learning and development have evolved over time. In so doing, you can borrow from the rich traditions of great thinkers and early practitioners and can discover and better understand the historical roots of many current classroom beliefs and practices.

Application #2   Reflect on the historical origins of your own perspectives and classroom methods. Identify any strategies you use that are based on outdated beliefs about children. Traditional practices such as the "sit still and listen" approach, for example, are based on old views of childhood and should be modified or abandoned in favor of newer strategies.

CRITICAL CONCEPT 2

In spite of improvement in the treatment of children in Western societies in recent times, services and educational opportunities are still not available to all children. Some children are in great need, even in modern America.

Application #1   Assist families in accessing social, nutritional, and health care services in a time of scarce community resources. Without support in these areas, children cannot learn and develop in classrooms.

Application #2   Becomes an advocate for policies and programs that provide children and their families with adequate services. Political action is an important role of modern early childhood educators.

CRITICAL CONCEPT 3

Non-Western perspectives on childhood are unique because of history. Many of the beliefs about children and socialization practices of families in non-Western cultures are related to the experiences of slavery and oppression.

Application   Accept and appreciate cultural differences in parenting that stem from historical experiences of oppression. More directive and protective parenting and an emphasis on obedience are examples of logical adaptations in parenting that result from cultural adversity.

CRITICAL CONCEPT 4

Many of the ideas in this book are derived from research on young children. Although research studies yield important information, flaws and biases are common.

Application #1   Familiarize yourself with research methods so that you can critically evaluate new information on child development.

Application #2   Because of common flaws in research methods, be cautious in interpreting findings. Study findings must be viewed not as truths but as "good guesses" about what children are like.

CRITICAL CONCEPT 5

Qualitative and ethnographic studies are gaining favor among child development researchers. In these studies, children's behavior and development are richly described rather than simply counted or scored. Such research is viewed as less culturally biased and more useful for practicing classroom professionals.

Application #1   Use anecdotal records as a means of describing and assessing children's learning, behavior, and overall development.

Application #2   Write case studies of individual families and children, particularly those with special needs, when a more in-depth examination of development is needed.

CHAPTER 3

Theories of Child Development

GUIDING QUESTIONS

1. What is a theory, and how can it be useful in working with young children and their families?
2. What are the key tenets of maturationist theory, and what are their implications for working with young children?
3. What are the major criticisms of maturationist theory from a multicultural perspective?
4. What are the key principles of behaviorist theory, and how are they applied in the classroom?
5. What are the key professional and multicultural criticisms of behaviorist theory?
6. What are the fundamental tenets of psychoanalytic theory, and how can these be useful in working with young children?
7. What are the major professional, multicultural, and feminist criticisms of psychoanalytic theory?
8. What are the key principles of the cognitive-developmental theory, and what are their implications for teaching?
9. What are the major criticisms of cognitive-developmental theory raised by researchers and multicultural scholars?
10. What are the main ideas underlying sociocultural theory, and how do they guide classroom practice?
11. What are researchers' and multicultural scholars' criticisms of sociocultural theory?
12. What are the primary beliefs of information processing theorists, and how can these be applied in the classroom?
13. What concerns have been raised about the information processing theory, and how adequate is it in explaining learning in different cultures?
14. What are the major tenets of the ecological systems theory, and how do these influence advocacy and public policy?
15. In what ways does the ecological systems theory more fully address cultural diversity and development than other theories?

Researchers and educators hold several distinct sets of beliefs, or theories, about how children grow and develop. One theory holds that children simply mature as they grow older. Another is that the environment shapes what children become. In some theories, genetics and environment are believed to interact to influence learning and behavior. In this chapter, we will review seven theories of child development. The major tenets of each theory will be demonstrated by applying them to the following real-life classroom dilemma:

Four-year-old Adam moves into the block area of his Head Start classroom, where two other children have built a make-believe car out of large blocks. As he enters, one of the two children announces loudly, "Adam can't play!" Adam ignores this statement and sits down on the pretend car beside his two peers. He snatches a plastic firefighter's hat from the head of the child who has just called out. The child protests loudly,

"No, Adam! Give it back!" Adam pushes him off the car with great force. His victim begins to cry and call for a teacher's assistance.

The teacher, Ms. Rodriguez, moves into the area quickly. She is very familiar with the problem she now faces; Adam has been hitting, kicking, and pushing other children since he began the Head Start program 3 months ago. Adam's aggression seems to have increased lately. Talks with Adam's mother have not helped. She is very concerned about his classroom behavior but is having great difficulty coping with the problem. As an unemployed single parent, she is struggling to make ends meet. She has suffered from depression and is receiving mental health services. She is 20 years old and has three other children.

Ms. Rodriguez now stands before Adam and the child he has just assaulted. She must make an on-the-spot decision about how to respond. What specific steps should she take? What should she say to Adam? To his victim? What long-term strategies should she adopt to help Adam learn less aggressive ways of interacting with peers?

How this teacher responds will depend, in part, on what she believes about why Adam behaves as he does. If she believes that he has learned aggressive behaviors from watching violent models in the neighborhood or on television, she will select one kind of intervention. If she believes that he has severe underlying emotional challenges that must be addressed, she will attempt a different strategy. If she believes that he lacks knowledge about how to interact positively with others, she will consider a third approach. Perhaps she perceives that some combination of these conditions is at the root of Adam's difficulties, in which case she will decide on yet another intervention. In other words, the teacher's decision about how to deal with Adam's aggression will depend on her theory about his development.

A **theory** is a system of beliefs about something. A child development theory is an integrated collection of beliefs about why children behave, think, and feel as they do. A theory might include beliefs about the nature of learning and development, the role of heredity and environment, and how adults, other children, schools, and communities contribute to the development process. Adam's teacher will base her decisions about Adam on a complex system of beliefs pertaining to these issues.

theory: A system of beliefs about something. A child development theory is a collection of beliefs about why children behave, think, and feel as they do.

35

TABLE 3-1
Theories of Child Development

Theory	Prominent Theorists	Assumptions About Child Development
Maturationist theory	Gesell	Human traits are determined primarily by genetics. Children simply mature with age; environment plays a minor role.
Behaviorist theory	Skinner, Watson, Bandura	Human traits are acquired through experiences within the environment. Adults can purposefully shape desired learning and behavior through positive reinforcement.
Psychoanalytic theory	Freud, Erikson	Emotional development stems from an ability to resolve key conflicts between desires and impulses and pressures from the outside world. Adults can promote children's emotional health by providing appropriate opportunities for the gratification of drives.
Cognitive-developmental theory	Piaget	Intellectual development is internal and personal. Knowledge is constructed actively by learners, who struggle to make sense out of experience. Learners assimilate new ideas into what they already know but also adjust previous thinking to accommodate new information.
Sociocultural theory	Vygotsky	Adults and peers can "scaffold" children's learning by asking questions or challenging thinking. Through social interaction and verbalization, children construct knowledge of the world.
Information processing theory	Siegler, Dodge	Knowledge is acquired by applying specific thinking processes in order to pay attention to, store, remember, retrieve, and modify information over time. Children learn in social situations by noticing social cues, storing these in memory, and retrieving and applying them in subsequent interactions with others.
Ecological systems theory	Bronfenbrenner	Development is influenced by the personal, social, and political systems within which children live. Interactions among the family, school, community, social and political system, and the individual child will determine developmental outcomes.

Several prominent, contrasting theories about child development are presented in Table 3-1. Each is based on research and a set of assumptions about the nature of human experience. No single, universally accepted theory exists. Researchers and practicing teachers may hold one perspective or another, or they may hold an eclectic view that attempts to blend the beliefs of several distinct viewpoints. Some theories are interrelated and complementary; others offer conflicting perspectives on childhood.

Theories about children are extremely practical. It is a myth that a theory is abstract and esoteric and holds little value in the real world. A theory can guide professional practice by ensuring that there is an underlying purpose for classroom routines and that the process of educating young children is carried out consistently. It can help a teacher solve a problem like Adam's. Very specific and useful strategies can be derived from each major theoretical perspective.

MATURATIONIST THEORY

The **maturationist theory,** one of the oldest theories of development, holds that children learn and behave as they do because they have inborn predispositions to do so. From this perspective, most of what we become as humans is genetically predetermined. Some children are talented in the arts, for example, because of inherited, genetically derived traits. Some are aggressive because of inborn temperament. From this view, all children, regardless of background or culture, acquire the same basic abilities and knowledge—how to walk, talk, and read, for example—at about the same age and in a relatively fixed order because these skills emerge in a way that is predetermined at birth.

This theoretical perspective assigns relatively little importance to the child's environment (Gesell, 1933). For example, to the maturationist, parenting and teaching are far less important than genetics. Social class and culture are not particularly emphasized. In its purest form, this theory suggests that children simply mature as they get older; they will turn out as they will, with little influence from the outside world.

A metaphor used by maturationists is that of a growing plant. Children's development is seen to be like the blossoming of a flower or the growth of a seed. Given the basic nutrients of life—loving care, safety, and a healthy diet—children will grow and flourish in a predetermined way just as a plant does. Major environmental obstacles may slow the path of growth, like a plant not receiving enough sun or water, but once essential needs are restored, the child will continue to flourish.

Early maturationists (Gesell, 1933; G. S. Hall, 1893) sought to describe how social, physical, intellectual, and personality characteristics unfold as children mature. The focus was on providing a profile of *normal* maturation. Gesell conducted controlled observations of thousands of children in order to identify **developmental milestones**—that is, specific characteristics that could be expected to emerge in children at various age levels (Gesell & Ilg, 1949). His work was made available to parents who used his developmental time schedules to assess their own children's growth. So, his research served to relieve anxiety in some parents and intensify it in others.

According to Gesell and his colleagues, major developmental and behavioral problems stem from an environment that restricts maturation (Ilg & Ames, 1965). Children who are placed in rigidly academic classrooms or are expected to perform difficult tasks before they are ready also are likely to exhibit problematic behaviors.

Modern maturationists have focused more directly on how genetics contributes to development (Plomin, 1995; Scarr, 1993). Although the research methods of these scientists vary, their assumptions about child development are generally the same: genetics and maturation have a more powerful effect on behavior and learning than the environment. These authors provide evidence that at least some developmental characteristics, particularly physical ones, emerge in a fixed order at about the same age. A classic study by W. Dennis and M. G. Dennis (1940) of Hopi Indian children learning to walk is a good example. These researchers found that infants who were strapped to cradle boards—rigid boards that held children upright and greatly restricted their movement—learned to walk at the same time as infants whose parents had given up this old custom.

Gesell himself conducted an experiment in which one infant twin was taught to climb up and down stairs and the other twin was not. The trained infant showed advanced

maturationist theory: A theory that holds that most of what humans become is predetermined by genetics and that traits inherited from ancestors simply unfold as children mature.

developmental milestones: Specific characteristics that are expected to emerge in children at various age levels.

stair-climbing ability for only a short time; the untrained twin quickly caught up when given experience with stairs (Gesell & Thompson, 1929).

Other studies of twins also lend credence to a maturationist view. Identical twins raised apart have been found to show surprisingly similar characteristics in many different areas of development, including activity level, sociability, attention span, impulsivity, introversion/ extroversion, and propensity to mental health problems such as schizophrenia (Goldsmith et al., 2007; Plomin, 2008). Other research has shown that personality traits such as boldness or timidity can be identified in infancy and that these persist into adulthood (Kagan, 1994; Moffitt et al., 2007). One well-known longitudinal study showed that infant personality types—"easy," "difficult," and "slow to warm up"—could still be observed in adult subjects (A. Thomas & Chess, 1977). Of special interest to parents and teachers are studies showing that the characteristics of a **difficult temperament** in infancy—harsh and negative reactions to new or frustrating situations, irregular patterns of sleeping or eating, and numerous adjustment problems—continue in later childhood and adolescence (Pesonen et al., 2003). From a maturationist perspective, these traits are genetically determined and will unfold regardless of environmental intervention.

Working with Adam

How would maturationists explain Adam's aggressive behaviors? What strategies would they recommend to address the problem? This theoretical perspective suggests two overall causes of Adam's difficulty. First, Adam could be acting the way he is simply because he is immature. From this perspective, positive social behaviors unfold over time with maturation, so less mature children are not able to interact effectively with peers. It is possible that Adam is not developmentally ready for participation in such a large Head Start group. One very controversial strategy that is often suggested by maturationists is to postpone Adam's enrollment in a preschool setting until he is more mature. In a year's time, he may gain social abilities that will allow him to function more positively. This strategy often has been called *buy a year*.

Another maturationist explanation for Adam's behavior is that he may have been born with a difficult temperament. If Adam's challenging interactions are displayed across all play settings or times of day and if he seems truly unable to gain control of these negative behaviors, he may have inherited a personality that is difficult. How can teachers and caregivers respond if Adam's problems are purely genetic? It is recommended that classroom and home environments be restructured to accommodate these personality traits. Because children like Adam may have difficulty with transitions and new situations, these should be carefully planned and minimized. Establishing a regular, predictable routine; maintaining constancy in the physical play space; and making other efforts to create a sameness in Adam's experiences will be helpful from this viewpoint. Because children with difficult temperaments often react severely to being held or restrained, great effort should be made to avoid these behaviors in interactions.

Adults should also practice tolerance and acceptance from a maturationist view. Teachers might ignore the little things in Adam's classroom behavior and tolerate minor oppositional behaviors without reaction. Challenging interactions are viewed simply as part of Adam's personality. The following vignette shows the maturationist theory in practice:

> Adam has just entered the art area where a group of children are cutting with scissors. All the available scissors are being used. He tries to snatch a pair away from Samantha, a child who is working there. A teacher witnesses the incident from a distance.

ADAM:	(Pulling on the scissors) Give me these!
SAMANTHA:	(Clinging to the scissors) Adam! No! (Looks to the teacher for help)
TEACHER:	(In a calm voice) Adam, Samantha is using those scissors.
ADAM:	(Still pulling on the scissors, says to Samantha in a threatening voice) You better give me those!

difficult temperament: A disposition that is characterized by harsh and negative reactions to new or frustrating situations, irregular patterns of sleeping or eating, and numerous adjustment problems.

TEACHER: (Retrieves another pair of scissors from a cupboard) Here's another pair. Why don't you use these? I'll sit with you, and you can tell me about what you're working on. (Gently guides Adam to his own seat and sits next to him)

In this interchange, the teacher shows understanding and tolerance for Adam's severe outburst. Rather than using harsh or punitive methods, he has calmly resolved the dilemma by redirecting Adam's activity. With maturation, Adam may eventually be able to regulate his own social behaviors.

Critique and Multicultural Analysis

Many studies do not support a pure maturationist perspective. Even Gesell (1933) found that environment plays an important role. Research on twins has shown that a significant portion of behavior and development can be explained by life experience. For example, follow-up studies on temperament show that personality can change over time as a result of environmental factors (Kagan et al., 1994). Research on IQ shows that there exists a **heritability ratio** —a mathematical estimate of the role of genetics in determining intelligence. By most researchers' estimates, more than half of "innate" intelligence can be explained by environment (Davis, Arden, & Plomin, 2008).

In addition to the challenges to maturationism presented by research, a growing number of professionals are raising concerns about the educational and political implications of such a theory (Boykin, 1994; Derman-Sparks, Phillips, & Hilliard, 1997). Concern has been expressed that a maturationist perspective could lead some parents and professionals to give up on children like Adam, reasoning that if challenges are predetermined, it is fruitless to intervene. If problems are to be solved by pure maturation, then a wait-and-see approach would be taken for even the most severe problems of child development. Some have suggested that the "buy a year" strategy might better be phrased "lose a year" since opportunities to address the child's difficulties would be lost (Shepard, 1994; Stipek & Byler, 2001). Detractors of maturationist theory contend that, although its messages of tolerance and acceptance of differences are valuable, care should be taken not to assign too great a role to genetics. Doing so could lead to a pattern of inaction in the home and classroom when children are in need of support.

The staunchest opponents of maturationism argue that it leads to cultural bias (Dei, Mazzuca, McIssa, & Ogbu, 1997; Padilla et al., 1991). These authors point with alarm to the early work of Arthur Jensen, a prominent educational psychologist who created a furor with an article titled "How Much Can We Boost IQ and Scholastic Achievement?" In the article, Jensen (1969) implies that African American children have lower IQs than Euro-American children because of genetically derived intellectual deficiencies. He proposes that educational programs for these lower-IQ students be focused on simplistic thinking processes and that they be guided toward professions that do not require abstract reasoning or problem solving. The dangers of a maturationist theory are obvious from Jensen's work: the argument of genetic determinism can be used, as it has been for centuries, to advance a belief that some races are inferior.

Ogbu (1994) argues that racial differences in children's behavior and learning are just that—differences, not genetic deficits. These differences stem from the unique experiences, histories, and worldviews of particular cultures. Cultural variations—diverse languages and dialects, learning styles, or patterns of interaction, for example—are derived from social experience. Such variations should be understood and appreciated, not remediated.

True deficits in competence do exist among individuals of all cultures. These also can be traced to life experiences, such as oppression, poverty, poor health care, or inadequate schools. These factors can be successfully ameliorated through intervention. From Ogbu's perspective, environment, including culture, is the most critical element in child development.

heritability ratio: A mathematical estimate of the relative role of genetics in determining intelligence.

BEHAVIORIST THEORY

The **behaviorist theory** offers a very different perspective on child development. Behaviorists contend that most of what children are and will become is derived from experience. At birth, from this view, a child's mind is a "blank slate" or an "empty vessel" to be gradually filled by the environment. Development in all areas—from personality type to ability to read to career preference—is a result of environmental influence.

Behaviorist theory assigns great importance to the role of adults and holds that parents and teachers must purposefully shape children's learning. Although most behaviorists believe that children are born with certain rudimentary facilities—for example, a fundamental ability to learn and a nervous system that allows perceptual and motor growth—they argue that maturation and genetics are relatively unimportant in human development. One of the first behaviorists in America, John B. Watson, summarized this theoretical perspective in its purest form when he described the newborn baby as merely "a lively bit of squirming flesh, capable of making few simple responses" (1929, p. 47).

A critical tenet of behaviorist theory—and one from which the theory's name originated—is that all learning is really just observable behavior. From this perspective, even such complex tasks as reading, talking, or solving a calculus problem are behaviors that can be observed and measured. Reading, for example, may be viewed as the behavior of saying aloud or to oneself the sounds and words represented on a printed page. From a behaviorist view, advancement in any area of learning is simply a change in behavior. Becoming a more competent reader, for example, is the process of being able to say new sounds, bigger words, or longer sentences as they appear on the page. The job of the teacher or parent is to present new skills in small and logically sequenced units and then to shape children's acquisition of these in special ways.

Classical and Operant Conditioning

behaviorist theory: A theory that holds that most of what humans become is shaped by the environment.

classical conditioning: A strategy for shaping behavior in which a neutral stimulus is paired with a pleasurable one. Eventually, the subject responds in the same way to the neutral stimulus as to the pleasurable one, even when the pleasurable stimulus is no longer present.

operant conditioning: A form of training in which a desired behavior is immediately rewarded. When this occurs, that behavior is performed more frequently.

Watson was the first to apply one form of behaviorism, **classical conditioning,** to children's learning. In classical conditioning, adults shape children's behavior by pairing a neutral event (e.g., riding in a car on a long trip) with something that is naturally either pleasurable or unpleasurable (e.g., eating cookies). Over time, children begin to respond to the neutral stimulus in the same way they would the pleasurable one even when the pleasurable stimulus is not present (e.g., a child would feel content and happy riding in a car even when not provided with cookies).

Watson's now famous experiment with an 11-month-old child, Albert, further illustrates this method. At the beginning of the experiment, Albert had shown no fear of rats. During the conditioning period, he was presented with a rat and, at the same moment, a startling noise. This created great upset. (This experiment was conducted before the American Psychological Association had written modern rules of research ethics.) Over time, Albert became afraid of rats because he learned to associate their presence with the loud noise. Even when the noise was no longer made, he cried when rats (and later other furry objects) were presented to him. He had learned a conditioned response, albeit a useless and perhaps troublesome one: to cry in the presence of rats and similar stimuli. This proved, according to Watson, that through environmental conditioning a child could be shaped, behavior by behavior, to become almost any type of person (Watson, 1929).

A more modern application of behaviorism has been provided by B. F. Skinner (1948), who developed a system of **operant conditioning** based on the work of Watson and others. In operant conditioning, children's desirable behaviors are rewarded systematically by adults. When this occurs, they are more likely to perform those behaviors. Children who are rewarded for using the toilet independently, for example, will do so more often. If parents wish their children to sit quietly at the dinner table, they should reward them for this behavior after it occurs.

A principle of operant conditioning is that the behavior of children and adolescents can be shaped only gradually. When a toddler is just starting to use the toilet, for example, rewards should be given for small steps—say, just trying to get to the bathroom on time. Breaking down learning into manageable units and rewarding small steps forward are key features of operant conditioning.

Skinner (1948) wrote at length about the kinds of responses adults should give for positive behavior. Reinforcers such as verbal praise and tangible rewards (i.e., snacks, toys, stickers, special privileges) should be given only after positive behaviors have been performed. Punishment should not be used; undesirable behavior should simply be ignored. A good deal of patience is required, then, in carrying out Skinnerian parenting or teaching!

Social Learning Theory

If reinforcement should not be provided until after desirable behaviors are performed, how do teachers or parents induce children to act in positive ways to begin with? An adult could wait a long time for a child to share a toy, speak a new word, or say "thank you" to a parent by mere accident. Albert Bandura (1991) formulated a theory to take this problem into account—**social learning theory.** Following his theory, desirable behaviors are modeled by adults. Children imitate these. If they are rewarded for doing so, they will perform these behaviors more frequently.

Bandura's theory is based on the assumption that humans acquire new behaviors merely by observing others perform them. For example, children will learn to share by watching others do so. They will learn how books work by observing parents or teachers reading them. Bandura's work lends support to the adage "Children are more likely to do what we do than what we tell them to do."

Bandura (1965) argues that children and adolescents are most apt to learn behaviors they observe if they see these being reinforced. In his classic social learning study, he found that children were more likely to behave aggressively if they watched a model punch a doll and then receive rewards for this. Much positive social behavior, Bandura contends, is learned by witnessing others perform positive acts and then seeing them praised or rewarded. A practical application of Bandura's work is that a teacher or parent can help one child interact positively by openly praising another who is behaving appropriately.

Working with Adam

From the perspective of Skinner or Bandura, Adam's problems are behavioral, as are all aspects of child development. So, strategies need to be implemented to change Adam's social interactions in the classroom to induce him to perform kind or cooperative behaviors. A systematic reward system should be established in which Adam's positive social behaviors—no matter how fleeting—are reinforced with stickers, special privileges, or snacks. Later, the teacher might move to social reinforcers, such as praise. Such strategies have often been called "catching children being good" since prosocial behaviors in a child like Adam may be very infrequent. While implementing these strategies, misbehavior should be ignored. This will ensure that Adam is not inadvertently rewarded for his aggression by adult attention. If Adam's behavior becomes too disruptive or dangerous, a time-out might be given in which Adam would be asked to sit away from the group. Skinner argues that a time-out is not a punishment. (However, many practicing teachers who have witnessed children's negative emotional responses to this practice disagree.)

social learning theory: A theory that holds that humans learn new behaviors by imitating the people around them. When they are rewarded for this imitation, they will perform these behaviors more frequently.

Behaviorists believe that adults should praise desirable behavior while ignoring disruptive or antisocial behavior.

Behaviorists would also suggest that positive models of prosocial behavior be provided. Teachers or parents might go out of their way to model kindness and cooperation themselves and to avoid harsh responses such as shouting or physical punishment. In addition, adults could purposefully praise the positive interactions of Adam's peers in his presence. This would show that such behaviors are rewarded. The following vignette illustrates behaviorist theory in practice:

Two children are playing cooperatively in the sandbox on the playground. Adam moves in, shouting and snatching sand toys away from them. His peers initially ignore him and keep playing. A teacher quickly intervenes.

TEACHER: (Speaking to the two children who are playing cooperatively) Samantha and Stuart, I like how nicely you are playing together. You are sharing your toys and being kind to each other.

SAMANTHA: (In a proud tone) Yeah. We're nice friends.

TEACHER: Yes. (Presenting several new digging toys) Would you like to play with these?

ADAM: (Shouting at his peers) You can't play with those. You get out of here!

TEACHER: (Ignores Adam's outburst and continues to talk to the two other children) Maybe I'll play with you. (Sits down and begins to work in the sand with the two children)

ADAM: (Throws a handful of sand out of the sandbox and screams) I'm going to get all this sand out of here! (Now throws a bucket out of the sandbox)

TEACHER: (Ignores Adam, speaks to the two others) What are you working on here, a castle?

STUART: Yeah. It's a castle for . . . pirates, I think.

ADAM: (Watches a moment, then speaks in a quieter tone) I'll help pile the sand. (Scoops sand into a bucket and offers it to his peers) Here. You put this on.

TEACHER: Adam, great! You're helping us out. (Hands a digging toy to him) Would you like to use this to help us with our castle?

In this situation, a teacher has ignored Adam's misbehavior and, in his presence, rewarded two children who are cooperating. She patiently ignores Adam's undesirable behaviors. Adam finally displays positive social interaction. The teacher then quickly praises and rewards these prosocial acts.

Critique and Multicultural Analysis

Behaviorism has come under criticism in recent years (Crain, 2005; Overton & Ennis, 2006). A major concern has been that modeling and reinforcement do not fully explain learning. The case of language development illustrates this clearly. The behaviorist view is that language learning is shaped through reinforcement—that is, when very young children imitate adult utterances, they are praised or rewarded (Skinner, 1957). Research suggests that this is simply not how language is acquired (Hollich, Hirsh-Pasek, & Golinkoff, 2000; K. Nelson, 1998). Children invent their own unique utterances when they learn to talk. For example, children might first use the correct form of "took" and then, out of the clear blue, use their own version: "taked" or even "takeded." Is it likely that this new, incorrect form was imitated from an adult model? Would adults systematically praise this misstatement? Another example is the child's invention of new words. Could the child who refers to a bald adult as having a "barefoot head" possibly have heard this from an adult model?

In fact, classic parenting studies show that adults do not praise the correctness of children's language (R. E. Owens, 1994). For example, if a child were to declare "I pushed Sarah," it is unlikely that an adult would respond with, "I like the way you used the past tense form correctly." Instead, adults usually reply to the content of children's utterances.

Children and adolescents demonstrate countless novel behaviors and learning in other areas that cannot be explained by an imitation and reinforcement theory. Why do very young children believe that a cow is a "doggie"? Why will they argue that 10 cookies spread out in a long line are more than 10 cookies that are bunched together on a plate? Can these ideas possibly be observed in or reinforced by adults? How can a group of 9-year-old friends invent a secret language, complete with its own words, sounds, and special symbols, that they write on their notebooks at school? Could they have imitated this language from others? Would a teacher have somehow reinforced this in the classroom? (Likely, just the opposite is true.) Most researchers now believe that learning is more complex than merely copying the behavior of others (R. M. Thomas, 2004). Development is internal and personal; more often, it involves the mental action of children rather than any external behavior by adults.

Multicultural critiques of behaviorism abound. Serious questions have been raised about the practice of excessively praising or rewarding children's behavior (Corpus & Lepper, 2007; Hitz & Driscoll, 1988; Kohn, 2001), particularly in children of historically underrepresented groups (Garcia Coll, Meyer, & Brillon, 1995; Maynard, 2002). Some families or cultural groups virtually never use positive reinforcement, yet their children grow and learn. Stars, stickers, and verbal praise do not appear, then, to be a necessary ingredient for positive development. Children whose family experiences do not include constant praise may be overwhelmed, in fact, by teachers who rely on tangible rewards or lavish accolades. In some Asian and Native American families, for example, where modesty is valued, praise can even create discomfort and embarrassment (Klein & Chen, 2001). Research suggests that for children of all cultures, praise can actually inhibit learning, creativity, and even self-esteem (Hitz & Driscoll, 1988; Kohn, 2001).

A number of other questions about behaviorism have been raised by multicultural scholars: *Which* behaviors should be reinforced (Boykin, 1994)? Who should decide this? On whose values, histories, and worldviews should these decisions be based? Can and should all children's behavior be shaped to conform to standards of mainstream America? Boykin and

Toms (1985) have argued that tenets of behaviorism have been used "to promote Anglo-Saxon ideals" (p. 35). Problems arise, they suggest, when adults reward behaviors that are not valued by a child's cultural group. Worse yet, some behaviors that are reinforced in school may be in conflict with the values of one's own family.

For example, in one commonly used primary school curriculum, children are rewarded for establishing eye contact and taking turns talking in a group. These are not behaviors that are valued or appreciated in all cultures. In some Mexican American, African American, and Korean families, eye contact is a sign of disrespect, and quietness is highly valued (Chan, 1998). In some Latino families, talking all at once in a group—thus helping one another get a right answer in class—is a sign of being considerate (Rothstein, Trumbull, Daley, & Isaacs, 2001). Yet just the opposite is what is reinforced in American schools. Behaviorism, then, can lead to "mixed socialization messages" (Boykin & Toms, 1985, p. 36) that create conflict and confusion for children of historically underrepresented groups.

Educational programs designed around behaviorist principles do not always have a good track record in meeting socialization or learning goals, particularly for children of low socioeconomic status or those from traditionally underrepresented groups. A number of longitudinal studies have found, for example, that African American children—particularly boys—fare less well in behaviorist classrooms (Burts, Schmidt, Durham, Charlesworth, & Hart, 2007; Hart, Burts, & Charlesworth, 1997; Marcon, 2002; Schweinhart & Weikart, 2006).

PSYCHOANALYTIC THEORY

psychoanalytic theory: A theory that holds that emotional development is influenced by tensions between internal desires and impulses and the demands of the outside world. The resolution of these tensions is needed to become a healthy adult.

id: Freud's term for the part of the mind that contains instinctual urges and strives for immediate gratification but is kept in check by the ego and the superego.

ego: Freud's term for the part of the mind that is rational and regulates and redirects the instinctual impulses of the id.

superego: Freud's term for the part of the mind that comprises the conscience, including the values and mores of one's culture.

The **psychoanalytic theory** varies from other child development perspectives in that it focuses exclusively on the formation of personality. Psychoanalysts contend that children's emotional health stems from an ability to resolve key conflicts between their internal desires and impulses and pressures from the outside world. For example, infants feel an urgent need for pleasurable oral stimulation and experience great tension until this desire is satisfied. However, in the real world, babies cannot nurse all the time, so they must control their urges to some degree until an appropriate opportunity presents itself. In adolescence, strong sexual urges arise. Emotionally healthy youth are able to regulate these feelings and to find socially approved outlets for sexual tension. Those who cannot do this may be at risk; they may engage in early and unsafe sexual activity, for example.

From a psychoanalytic perspective, a healthy child is one who learns to walk a fine line between immediate need fulfillment and the control of urges. Parents and teachers play a critical role in the process. They must provide just the right amount of freedom and nurturance. If they allow too little or too much gratification, according to the psychoanalytic theory, the child or adolescent may fail to mature emotionally.

The best-known psychoanalytic theorist was Sigmund Freud (1938), a physician who formulated a perspective of personality development based on his observations of neurotic adult patients. He postulated that instinctual urges—such as the need for oral pleasure—are located in the **id**, a significant part of the mind. According to Freud, the id creates a constant pressure to satisfy basic drives, many of which derive from sexual feelings. If the id were the only aspect of personality, humans would seek to gratify their needs without delay. However, the **ego** emerges in early infancy to keep the id in check. The ego, another fundamental component of the mind according to Freud, is more rational and regulates and redirects the instinctual impulses of the id so that need fulfillment is sought only at appropriate times. At the end of early childhood, the **superego** appears within the personality. This component of the mind comprises the conscience; all the values and mores of one's culture are included.

This is how these three systems of the mind interact, according to Freud: A 5-year-old has an urge to obtain a toy that another child is using. The id drives her to snatch the toy and run off. The ego redirects her, however, to delay this behavior because the moment is not right; the child using the toy is older (and bigger) and might resist. In addition, a teacher hovers nearby. At the same time, the superego informs the child of important societal rules. The superego reminds her that being a "good girl" means sharing and taking turns, so the child refrains from taking any action at all.

Erikson's Ages of Emotional Development

Erik Erikson (1963, 1982), another psychoanalyst, elaborated on and extended Freud's theory. He proposed eight *ages* through which humans must pass from birth to adulthood if they are to feel competent and self-fulfilled. They are presented in Table 3-2.

Like Freud, Erikson proposed that healthy personality growth is characterized by a resolution of inner conflicts. Each stage of emotional development, from Erikson's view, involves a struggle between two opposing emotional states—one positive, the other negative (see Table 3-2). These polar states push and pull at the individual, creating tension and posing unique interpersonal problems. For Erikson, the individual's primary psychological work at a particular stage is to resolve this emotional conflict in a positive direction. The role of teachers and parents in this process is to help children pursue the positive emotional states that are critical to each stage of development.

As shown in Table 3-2, the first four of Erikson's stages involve emotional conflicts that confront children. The earliest conflict—between trust and mistrust—occurs in infancy. Emotionally healthy babies, according to Erikson, acquire **trust**—a sense that they have nurturing, responsive caregivers who meet their basic needs. They come to view the world as safe and predictable. They enter into trusting relationships, first with primary caregivers and later with other human beings. *Security* is another word that describes this emotional state. Although humans will always experience feelings of mistrust about their relationships or the security of the world, from Erikson's view, the emotionally healthy baby is essentially trusting of the world and the people in it. Children who are abused or neglected, whose caregivers do not respond to their needs, or who for other reasons come to doubt the trustworthiness of the world will not resolve this emotional conflict in a positive way. They may be impaired from entering into relationships with others and may be unable to advance to later stages of emotional development.

The second of Erikson's conflicts—between autonomy and shame and doubt—occurs during the toddler years. Once children trust adults and know that their basic needs will be met, they are willing to venture out away from the safety of parents and family. They now wish to become individuals apart from those with whom they have bonded. In striving for individuality, children often assert themselves, rebel against rules, and assume a negative affect when confronted with adult control. Erikson argues that the emotionally healthy toddler gradually acquires a sense of **autonomy**—a feeling of individuality and uniqueness apart from his or her parents. Children who are overly restricted or harshly punished for attempts at becoming individuals will come to doubt their individuality and suffer shame. Gradually, such children can become timid, lack confidence in their abilities, and assume identities as mere extensions of their parents.

Erikson contends that children who develop a strong sense of autonomy as toddlers will acquire a sense of **initiative** in their preschool years. This emotional state includes a desire to take action and assert oneself. Children with initiative wish to create, to invent, to pretend, to take risks, and to engage in lively and imaginative activities with peers. If adults encourage these efforts, a sense of initiative will flourish. However, when adults criticize children or in other ways lead them to believe their efforts are wrong, feelings of guilt arise. Moderate feelings of guilt can play a positive role in development, of course. They can lead children to assume responsibility for their own behaviors, for example. Overwhelming guilt, however, inhibits emotional growth.

trust: Erikson's term for an emotional state, often acquired in infancy, in which children feel secure and know that basic needs will be met by caregivers. Such experiences as child abuse or neglect will lead infants to an opposite state—*mistrust* of the world and the people in it.

autonomy: Erikson's term for an emotional state, often acquired in toddlerhood, in which children strive to be independent and separate from parents. Children who are overly restricted will feel *shame and doubt.*

initiative: Erikson's term for an emotional state, often acquired in the preschool years, in which children assert themselves, make creative attempts, take risks, and reach out to peers. Children whose initiatives are thwarted will experience an opposite emotional state: *guilt.*

TABLE 3-2
Erikson's Eight
Ages of Emotional
Development

Stage	Approximate Age	Description
Trust vs. mistrust	Birth to 18 months	Children must come to trust that basic needs will be met by caregivers and that the world is a predictable and safe place. Otherwise, they will develop feelings of mistrust in others and the world.
Autonomy vs. shame/doubt	18 months to 3.5 years	Children must acquire a sense of independence from parents and a belief that they can do things on their own. If children are overly restricted when asserting their independence, they will develop feelings of shame and doubts about their individuality.
Initiative vs. guilt	3.5 to 6 years	Children must feel free to act, to create, to express themselves creatively, and to take risks. Children who are inhibited in these pursuits can become overwhelmed with guilt.
Industry vs. inferiority	6 to 12 years	Children must come to feel competent in skills valued by society. They need to feel successful in relation to peers and in the eyes of significant adults. If they experience failure too often, they will come to feel inferior.
Identity vs. role confusion	Adolescence	Adolescents must develop a clear sense of self. They must acquire their own unique roles, values, and place in society. If they are unable to piece together these elements into a coherent view of self, role confusion results.
Intimacy vs. isolation	Young adulthood	Young adults must be willing to risk offering themselves to others. An inability to give to another can lead to feelings of isolation.
Generativity vs. stagnation	Mature adult	Adults must gain a sense that they have contributed to the world in some lasting fashion. Through child rearing, civic deeds, or paid work, they must come to feel they have in some way given to others. Those who do not achieve this sense may suffer stagnation—a sense that there is no direction or purpose to one's life.
Integrity vs. despair	Older adult	Older adults must come to feel great satisfaction with the events and accomplishments of their lives. They must look back on their experiences with pride and acceptance. Those who cannot feel this satisfaction as life draws to an end suffer great despair.

SOURCE: From *Childhood and Society* by Erik H. Erikson. Copyright 1950 © 1963 by W. W. Norton & Company, Inc.

industry: Erikson's term for an emotional state, often acquired in the elementary years, in which children feel competent because of successes in and out of school. Repeated failure will result in an opposite emotional state: *inferiority*.

Preschool children are content to make many creative attempts regardless of the outcome. However, during the early elementary years, from Erikson's viewpoint, children wish to master real skills—the skills of older children and adults. They want to read and write like grown-ups, to excel at sports and other games, and to be strong and smart. Erikson maintains that children who have genuine successes in childhood and whose accomplishments are accepted and appreciated by adults and peers will develop a sense of **industry**—a feeling of competence. Conversely, those who consistently experience failure and lack of acceptance will develop a sense of inferiority.

Working with Adam

Psychoanalysts would view Adam's difficulties as primarily emotional. They would search for solutions to his problems by exploring his early life and, in particular, his mother's socialization practices. (Recall that his mother is very young, has four children, and suffers from depression.) Was Adam's mother warm and nurturing? Did she promote trust? Did she allow him to become autonomous and to take initiative? Or did she inhibit his efforts at self-expression? Answers to these questions would guide decisions about intervention.

Children who are aggressive, like Adam, very often have not formed secure attachments to parents or other adults (S. Calkins, 2004; Mitchell-Copeland, Denham, & DeMulder, 1997). They may, in Erikson's words, "mistrust" their environment and the people in it. A first step in working with Adam, then, might be to create for him a safe, predictable classroom environment and a strong bond with a teacher. An orderly classroom with stable enrollment and staffing and a consistent routine could help establish trust. A certain teacher might be assigned to spend time with Adam, giving warmth and nurturance and responding with enthusiasm to his accomplishments. Over time, Adam might come to trust this teacher. This attachment could facilitate positive relationships with other teachers and peers. Because bonds take time, this adult might continue to work with Adam for an extended period. The staff might rethink the practice of graduating children to a new classroom and teacher each year, for example.

Because a lack of trust is at the root of Adam's difficulty, from a psychoanalytic standpoint, great care would be taken to avoid harsh, punitive discipline, which is so common in the lives of aggressive children. Punishments for aggression (even Skinner's time-out) would, at best, control short-term behavior; at worst, they would engender further hostility and mistrust in Adam.

Once Adam has become attached to one or a small number of adults, he could be encouraged to be autonomous in his play and learning. He should be allowed to make choices, express himself, take risks, and explore his environment with minimal restriction. This is not to say that he should be allowed to do whatever he wishes. Psychoanalysts believe that adults must provide limits; need gratification must be controlled and redirected, or children become too egocentric and demanding.

Later, if Adam shows a healthy sense of autonomy, he could be encouraged to take initiative. From a psychoanalytic viewpoint, play and art activities that allow interpersonal expression would be most important during this period. These experiences would allow Adam to make creative attempts and to become bold and confident. They would also provide him with an opportunity to *work through* troublesome life experiences.

In the primary grades, Adam would need to experience success. According to Erikson, it is real achievement that nurtures a child's sense of industry. If Adam were to fail constantly in school or with friends and family, he would develop a sense of inferiority.

Critique and Multicultural Analysis

A number of concerns have been raised about the psychoanalytic theory and its usefulness in teaching and parenting. The most commonly cited weakness is that it does not explain development of the whole child but only a narrow range of emotional states (R. M. Thomas, 2004). How can a psychoanalytic perspective inform the teaching of reading or mathematics in the classroom? What implications does it hold for enhancing motor development? The theory does not seem to appreciate the interrelatedness of intellectual, physical, social, and emotional growth.

Another common criticism has been that the entire theory is based on personal observations of a small sampling of individuals. Freud, for example, drew his conclusions from case studies of 19th-century Viennese adult psychiatric patients, most of whom were white, upper-middle-class women. There have been recent charges that some of his case studies were of composites rather than real people! Although Erikson observed children in a variety of cultures, his work is also based on the subjective interpretation of a small number of cases (R. M. Thomas, 2004).

Multicultural and feminist scholars have elaborated on these limitations. Boykin and Toms (1985) have argued that some psychoanalytic stages of personality development, such as autonomy, reflect Anglo-Saxon ideals that are not appreciated in all cultures. Some ethnic groups value collective thought and action, so they emphasize behaviors such as relying on other people, checking with others before taking action, and sharing possessions. In some Japanese American families, for example, a sense of belonging and collectivism—not individual autonomy—are goals in child rearing. Similar values of collectivism have been reported in African American, Puerto Rican, and Native American cultures (DeGenova, 1997; Shulruf, Hattie, & Dixon, 2007).

Gilligan (Gilligan, 1993a; Gilligan, Brown, & Rogers, 1990) further suggests that psychoanalytic theories tend to view the development of male children as normal or ideal and thus portray unique features of female development as deficient. For example, from Gilligan's view, separating from parents and becoming an autonomous person are uniquely important to the personality formation of boys, while attachment and intimacy are the norm for girls. Yet psychoanalytic theorists interpret separation as healthy and intimacy as a sign of overdependence.

Taken together, these criticisms suggest that not all children can be expected to develop through stages of emotional growth as Erikson and Freud have described them. Some children will form stronger bonds with family and community than will others. Some will display less autonomy and initiative, others more.

COGNITIVE-DEVELOPMENTAL THEORY

The **cognitive-developmental theory** holds that mental growth is the most important element in children's development. Cognitive developmentalists argue that almost all aspects of human life—even making friends, feeling happy or depressed, or enjoying a sunny day—are directly influenced by thinking and language. Making friends, for example, is determined in part by one's knowledge of peers and how they behave. Feeling sad often stems from one's mental interpretation of events of personal predicaments.

Intellectual functioning is extremely complex and internal from a cognitive-developmental perspective. A skill such as reading or performing a new math operation is not learned merely by a change in behavior, as behaviorists might contend. Nor do these skills simply unfold, as maturationists might argue. Learning such skills involves intricate and internal mental actions; the learning occurs through elaborate processes inside the learner's mind, not outside it.

One of the most influential of the cognitive developmentalists, Jean Piaget (1896–1980), integrated elements of psychology, biology, philosophy, and logic into a comprehensive explanation of how knowledge is acquired. A fundamental principle of his theory is that knowledge is constructed through the action of the learner (Piaget, 1971). (Students of Piaget have often used a carpentry metaphor to describe this action; his theory is often referred to as "constructivism" [R. A. DeVries, Zan, Hildebrandt, Edmiason, & Sales, 2001].) The action to which Piaget refers might be physical. For example, a baby comes to know about a rattle by banging it and listening to the noise it makes. Learning also involves mental action: the learner must do something mentally with new information to really learn it.

Piaget's idea that learning involves action is illustrated by the following example. A toddler who lives in the city takes a ride in the country with her father. She sees a cow and calls out "doggie!" The father responds, "That's a cow." They pass another cow, and another, and eventually the child calls it by its correct name. What has happened here

cognitive-developmental theory: A theory of human development holding that knowledge is actively constructed by the child and that active problem solving, social interaction, and language are necessary for learning.

Jean Piaget is the most noted cognitive-developmental theorist.

appears simple but is actually quite complex. When the child came across this strange new animal, she had to fit it into something she already knew about; that is, she had to make sense of her experience based on previous understandings. She knew about dogs, so she decided that this must be an example of a dog. She had fit this large animal with horns into her mental category *dog*. Piaget (1971) calls this step in the learning process **assimilation.** The child has assimilated this new phenomenon into something she already knows about.

However, the child would still not have learned much had assimilation been the only step. Another mental action was necessary. As the child looked at the cow, noticed its size and horns, and heard it say "moo," she became puzzled. Puzzlement is critical for learning, according to Piaget. "This is a little different from a dog," she may have thought. So, she had to adjust her previous conception of animals a bit. Piaget calls this process of modifying previous understandings **accommodation.** The child may have created two categories of animals, perhaps "doggies" and "great big doggies with horns." (A child in one research study actually invented the name "biggiedoggie" for cows.) Conveniently, this child's father provided a label for this new category: "cow."

Both assimilation and accommodation are needed for learning. If accommodation did not occur, learners would never modify their thinking about things; in the example, the child would go on calling cows "dogs." If assimilation did not occur, there would be no previous understanding to rely on; the child in the example would be so confused about the appearance of the cow and what it might be that she would be unable to make any sense of it whatsoever. The ideal learning arrangement, according to Piaget, is one in which the child is confronted with a conflict or dilemma that is personally meaningful but causes puzzlement and requires a modification of previous thinking. Learning experiences should have elements of both familiarity and novelty.

Through assimilation and accommodation, Piaget argues, humans advance through stages of intellectual—or **cognitive development.** These stages are presented in Table 3-3.

assimilation: Piaget's term for a learning process in which humans integrate new ideas or information into what they already know about.

accommodation: Piaget's term for a learning process in which humans modify what they already know to make room for new ideas or information.

cognitive development: Mental development, including problem solving and the acquisition of knowledge.

Stage	Age	Description
Sensorimotor	0 to 18 months	Infants rely solely on action and the senses to *know* things. Intelligence is an ability to get what one needs through movement and perception.
Preoperational	18 months to 6 or 7 years	Preschool children can use symbols and internal thought to solve problems. Their thinking is still tied to concrete objects and to the here and now. They are fooled by the appearance of things.
Concrete operational	8 years to 12 years	Elementary school children are more abstract in their thinking. They can use early logic to solve some problems and are less fooled by perception. They still require the support of concrete objects to learn.
Formal operational	12 years to adulthood	Adolescents and adults can think abstractly and hypothetically. They can contemplate the long ago and far away. Their thinking is free from the immediate physical context.

SOURCE: Piaget, 1952, 1954, 1959, 1965.

sensorimotor stage:
Piaget's stage of cognitive development that encompasses infancy, in which thinking is limited to using physical action and the senses to know about things.

preoperational stage:
Piaget's stage of cognitive development that encompasses early childhood, in which children use internal thought, including symbols, but still rely on perception and physical cues in the environment for learning.

concrete operational stage: Piaget's stage of cognitive development that encompasses the elementary years, in which thinking becomes more internal and abstract but in which children still need the support of concrete objects in order to learn.

Each stage of life is marked by qualitatively different kinds of thinking, according to Piaget. Babies are in the **sensorimotor stage;** they rely purely on action and the senses to know things. Knowledge, to a baby, is getting the things he or she needs through movement and perception. Preschoolers are in the **preoperational stage;** they are able to use internal thought, including symbols, but still rely on perception and physical cues in the immediate environment for learning. Children in the primary grade years are in Piaget's **concrete operational stage;** their thinking and learning have become more internal and abstract. Still, elementary school students need the support of concrete objects in order to learn. Second-grade children will better learn about place value in math, for example, if they are able to discover it by acting on concrete materials. It is not until children reach the **formal operational stage,** according to Piaget, that they can engage in purely abstract thought that is not tied to the physical world. This may not occur until adolescence or early adulthood.

Working with Adam

Cognitive developmentalists would believe that Adam's difficulties with peers stem from a lack of **social cognition**—that is, an inability to understand social situations or the outcomes of social behaviors. They would cite research showing that highly aggressive children who often inaccurately interpret their peers' actions and motives (Crick & Ladd, 1993; Dodge et al., 2003) are usually not aware of alternative strategies for solving social problems (Nelson & Crick, 1999; Trawick-Smith, 1990). From the cognitive-developmental perspective, Adam may lack important social knowledge. An intervention should be aimed at teaching him how to interpret social situations.

One strategy would be to have Adam view videotapes or observe real-life interactions of peers playing in a variety of social situations. Teachers would then ask questions to guide his interpretation: What happened when Lawanda pushed Miko? How did Cheryl get Ahman to play with her? How did Hannah feel when Nemah yelled at her? In each case, the teacher would be trying to help Adam learn about social behaviors and situations. Teachers could also intervene in Adam's own conflicts to achieve this same goal. Interventions such as asking "What happened when you pushed Seth?" would guide Adam in interpreting the less-than-positive outcomes of aggressive behavior.

Teachers could also assist Adam in generating alternative solutions to social problems. When angry conflicts come up, for example, the teacher could ask the child to consider nonaggressive strategies: "What else can you do, besides hitting, if you're angry?" or "Can you think of a better way to get the blocks than just grabbing them?"

Besides these focused interventions, cognitive developmentalists would propose creating a classroom environment for Adam that facilitates general cognitive development (R. A. DeVries et al., 2001; Schweinhart & Weikart, 2006). A program that encourages children to play, solve problems, and make sense of novel objects and situations would enhance general intellectual ability and, in turn, social cognition.

Critique and Multicultural Analysis

Because Piaget relied on observations of a small number of typically developing children to formulate his theories, some have asked whether he has described accurately the understandings and behaviors of all children at each stage of development. Research indicates, for example, that children may be more intellectually competent than Piaget has suggested (Flavell, 1996). In addition, some have argued that his observations reflect the development only of children of his particular culture (Braga, 2007). For example, a series of classic studies of Mexican children who had extensive experience with pottery making at an early age showed an understanding of quantity at a much younger age than Piaget's theory would have predicted (Price-Williams, Gordon, & Ramirez, 1969). Other of Piaget's ideas—his emphasis on autonomy in thinking and learning, for example, or the value he placed on games in childhood—have been criticized as Western and male oriented (Ardila & Keating, 2007; Gilligan, 1993a; Harrison, Wilson, Pine, Chan, & Buriel, 1990). These elements of his theory, it is argued, reflect the competitive, individualistic society in which he lived and worked.

In spite of these criticisms, many multicultural scholars view cognitive-developmental perspectives as quite sensitive to cultural and gender diversity (Ogbu, 1992; R. M. Thomas, 2004). Miller-Jones (1988) advocates a cognitive-developmental theory, for example, because it focuses on developmental processes—such as assimilation and accommodation. It does not emphasize the acquisition of specific knowledge or skills, which can vary in importance across cultures. She argues that not all children will learn to tie shoes or use a spoon at a particular age, as Gesell would suggest. Nor will all acquire certain, specific academic or social skills that are shaped by dominant culture, as Skinner would propose. But all children of the world will learn—through assimilation and accommodation—the skills, knowledge, beliefs, and values important to their own family and culture.

SOCIOCULTURAL THEORY

The **sociocultural theory** is also concerned with intellectual development. Theorists of this group, however, believe that thinking and learning are not as internal and individual as Piaget proposed but rather are highly influenced by language, social interaction, and culture. The most prominent sociocultural theorist is Lev Vygotsky (1896–1934), whose work is currently receiving much attention in the field of education. Vygotsky's personal history is quite fascinating. A prolific writer from the former Soviet Union, his most significant work

formal operational stage: Piaget's most advanced stage of cognitive development that encompasses adolescence and adulthood, in which thinking is purely abstract and not tied to the immediate, physical world.

social cognition: The ability to understand social situations, including skill at recognizing the outcomes of one's own behaviors and the actions and motives of others.

sociocultural theory: A theory that holds that thinking and learning are highly influenced by social interaction, language, and culture.

was written during a 10-year period. He died of tuberculosis at age 38. His work was suppressed by the Soviet government for a long time and was not translated into English until the early 1960s. Yet his impact on recent thinking in child development has been profound.

Vygotsky's views are similar to Piaget's in a number of areas. He argues that children construct knowledge through action. When children solve problems with concrete objects, they acquire new concepts (Vygotsky, 1962). He also describes stages of intellectual development, as Piaget has done, but his theory differs from Piaget's in one fundamental way: he assigns greater importance to external influences—language, social interaction, and the larger society.

Vygotsky's theory is illustrated in Figure 3-1. He proposed that children engage in two distinct and independent mental activities in the earliest months of life—nonverbal thought and nonconceptual speech. In **nonverbal thought,** children observe objects or events or perform actions without using language. An example would be an infant pounding a rattle and attending to its sound. In **nonconceptual speech,** a child utters words or phrases without thinking fully about what they mean. Examples are playful babbling or the rote recitation of a song.

nonverbal thought: An early form of mental activity in which children observe objects or events or perform actions without using language.

nonconceptual speech: An early form of language in which children utter words or phrases without thinking fully about what they mean.

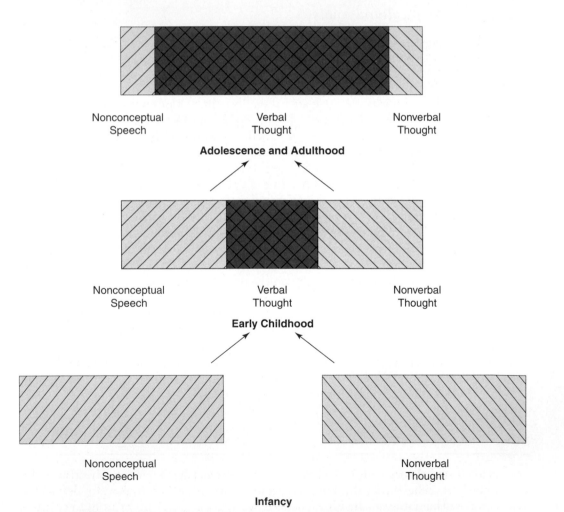

FIGURE 3-1   According to Vygotsky, speech and thought are separate processes in the early years. As children get older, they integrate the two into verbal thought. By adolescence, most mental activity involves verbal thought.

To Vygotsky, language and thinking are, at first, separate processes. Intellectual development involves connecting language and thinking. A toddler gradually associates the sound of a rattle, for example, with verbal labels—*rattle, noise,* or *loud.* Only when language and thought are related in this way can children think in more complex ways.

During the preschool and primary years, according to Vygotsky, children engage in much **verbal thought,** in which language and thinking are integrated and mutually supportive. Verbal thought allows the acquisition of complex concepts. An understanding of size, for example, is enhanced when children can use words like *small* or *smallest* and *big* or *biggest.* **Self-directed speech** is a behavior that shows that young children are using language to guide learning. In self-directed speech, children talk to themselves, naming objects or narrating their actions—particularly as they solve problems. When playing a number game, for example, a kindergartner might be overheard counting out loud. Vygotsky notes that the more difficult a problem is, the more frequent a young child's self-directed speech is. Until 7 or 8 years of age, there is still much isolated nonverbal thought and nonconceptual speech. Young children continue to engage in rote verbalizations or perform actions without using language.

In adolescence and adulthood most thinking is accompanied by language, as shown in Figure 3-1. When solving problems or learning new concepts, adults essentially speak to themselves. Of course, much of this language is internal, but adults sometimes engage in out-loud self-directed speech when a learning task is difficult. It may be that readers of this book are muttering these passages aloud as they struggle to understand Vygotsky's theory!

According to Vygotsky, then, language is not merely a mode of expression—a reflection of what children already know, as Piaget described it—but also a fundamental tool for constructing knowledge. Needless to say, a quiet classroom where children just sit and listen is not optimal for learning from this view. When teachers use language and encourage children to do the same, they are enhancing thought as well as speech.

Vygotsky's theory contains practical ideas for promoting intellectual development. He proposes that teachers and parents **scaffold** children's learning—that is, use language and other social interactions to guide thinking. Here is how scaffolding works: When children are faced with problems they can solve on their own, adults should not interfere. Independent thinking is an ultimate goal of teaching or parenting from Vygotsky's view. However, if tasks are so challenging to a child that they are insurmountable, adults should offer direct solutions. There are times, however, when problems or tasks are only slightly above a child's ability level. Here adults can ask questions or give hints that allow the child to solve problems independently. When adults indirectly guide children's own thinking and learning in this way, intellectual growth occurs. Parents and teachers should watch, then, for moments when indirect guidance can be given. Such periods are in what Vygotsky calls the **zone of proximal development.** This zone is represented in Figure 3-2.

An example of learning to read illustrates Vygotsky's ideas of scaffolding and the zone of proximal development: A 6-year-old is reading a picture book and becomes stuck on a word. If she is completely stumped, her parent should assist her very directly. He might read the text for her or even guide her to an easier book. If, however, the child quickly figures out the word and continues with the story, the parent should not interfere at all. Independent reading is the ultimate goal. But what if the child is close to figuring out the word on her own? This would be a situation within the zone of proximal development and a moment when an adult might be most effective in promoting literacy. The parent might give a hint or ask an interesting question to guide the child in solving her own problem. "Look at the picture," the parent might suggest. "What is the wolf doing? Does that help you figure out the word?" Or the parent might offer the sound of the word's first letter: "P-p-p. What word in your story would start with that sound?" To Vygotsky, such interactions are most powerful in promoting learning.

verbal thought: A kind of thought in which language and thinking are integrated and mutually supportive. In verbal thought, children use language—such as verbal labels and self-directed speech—to guide learning.

self-directed speech: A verbal behavior in which children talk to themselves, naming objects or narrating their actions—particularly as they solve problems.

scaffold: To use language and social interaction to guide children's thinking. When scaffolding, adults offer direct solutions to problems, indirectly guide them with hints or questions, or allow them to think completely independently, depending on what they need to learn.

zone of proximal development: A situation in which a problem or task is only slightly above a child's ability level. In this zone, adults can ask questions or give hints that allow the child to solve the problem independently.

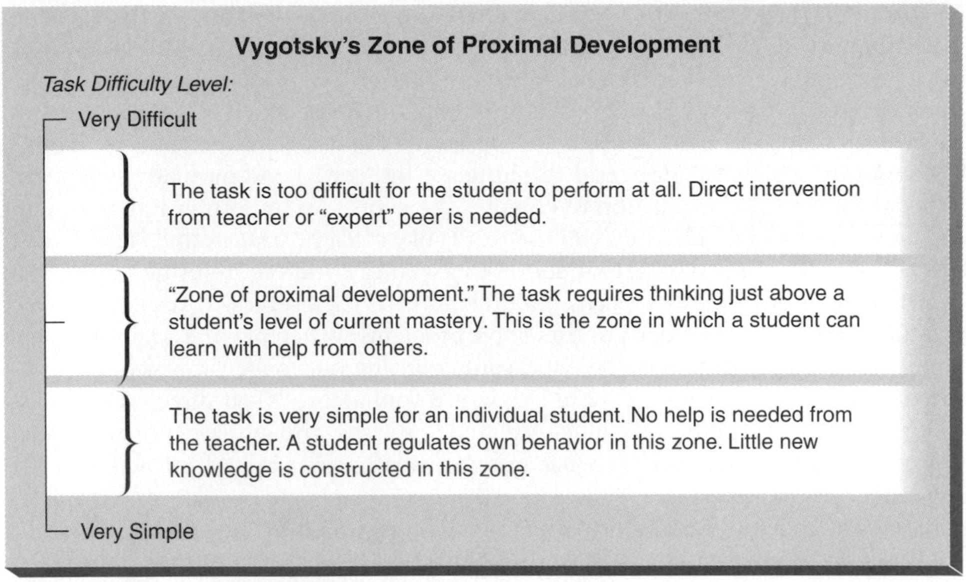

Vygotsky's Zone of Proximal Development

Task Difficulty Level:

— Very Difficult

The task is too difficult for the student to perform at all. Direct intervention from teacher or "expert" peer is needed.

"Zone of proximal development." The task requires thinking just above a student's level of current mastery. This is the zone in which a student can learn with help from others.

The task is very simple for an individual student. No help is needed from the teacher. A student regulates own behavior in this zone. Little new knowledge is constructed in this zone.

— Very Simple

FIGURE 3-2   The zone of proximal development is a period during problem solving when a task is just beyond a child's level of mastery. This is a time when an indirect prompt or question can help children solve the problem independently.

SOURCE: Vygotsky, 1978.

Working with Adam

Vygotsky's ideas for helping Adam would be similar to Piaget's. He would propose intellectual interventions—strategies to help Adam think about social problems and solve them independently. Following Vygotsky's framework, scaffolding would be the primary tool to accomplish this. Teachers might watch for an opportunity when a question or suggestion would help Adam resolve a conflict with a peer on his own: "You both want the same riding toy? What would be a good way for you both to use it?" Of course, if such prompts did not help Adam, a more directive intervention could be tried: "One thing you could do is take turns." However, if Adam was able to solve the difficulty on his own, a watch-and-wait strategy could be chosen with no intervention. From Vygotsky's view, Adam's teachers should decide in each circumstance how much assistance to give him.

Similarly, Adam's interpretation of social problems could be scaffolded. If Adam pushed another child, a prompt might help him discover, on his own, the negative outcome of this act: "What happened when you pushed Jamal? How did it make him feel?" Once again, if indirect prompts did not work, a more directive intervention could be used: "I think Jamal got hurt. See how he's crying?" The hope is that Adam would eventually be able to interpret social events independently.

Vygotsky would also recommend that language be used to guide Adam in thinking about and solving social problems. Teachers might offer phrases to help him remember appropriate social responses. After an aggressive interchange, for example, a teacher might say, "If you're mad, you should say, 'I don't like that!'" Words might also be offered to help Adam understand his own feelings or those of his classmates: "He's very sad that you pushed him" or "I can see you're very angry." Encouraging Adam to talk through conflicts out loud would help him think in more complex ways about social relationships.

Critique and Multicultural Analysis

Because of Vygotsky's untimely death, his work is considered to be incomplete and sketchy (R. M. Thomas, 2004). Much of his writing has only recently been available to Western scholars, so it is relatively new to mainstream psychology. A small but growing cadre of modern researchers are now extending and testing his theory (Berk & Winsler, 1995; Reunamo & Nurmilaakso, 2007; Rogoff, 1997, 2001, 2003). Although some have criticized his ideas as merely reflecting the Marxist–Leninist thinking of his time and culture (Bruner, 1984), much research supports his perspective (Rogoff, 2003). Vygotsky's theory has been viewed as particularly practical, with direct applications to teaching (Bodrova & Leong, 1996, 2003a; Trawick-Smith, 2008) and parenting (Freund, 1989). This is likely due to a tradition among Soviet psychologists to seek solutions to community problems or to improve the well-being of disadvantaged groups within society (R. M. Thomas, 1999).

The sociocultural theory receives high marks from multicultural scholars because it views development as social and collective rather than purely individual (Rogoff, 1997, 2001, 2003). Vygotsky's concepts of collaborative learning and joint problem solving relate well to the collective orientation of many non-Western families. His beliefs about testing and assessment, for example, are viewed as particularly sensitive to other cultures. He argues that scores on individually administered tests are not good measures of competence for most children. What a child is able to do with help from others is what is most indicative of intelligence. Thus, banding together with others to solve problems— as is common in many non-Western families—is more significant than individual achievement.

Vygotsky's theory is one of the few that appreciates the influence of culture on development. From his view, teachers and parents impart to children not only specific social skills and academic knowledge but also the values and customs of the larger society. Further, individual learners can have an impact on culture. The zone of proximal development is said to be a "transaction" in which children and adults influence one another's thinking (Rogoff, 1997).

INFORMATION PROCESSING THEORY

The **information processing theory** is another theory concerned primarily with intellectual development and learning. Information processing theorists believe, as Piaget and Vygotsky did, that humans learn by actively constructing meaning from the world around them. When confronted with a new or puzzling phenomenon, they use previous knowledge and thinking skills to make sense out of it. One way that information processing theory differs from the ideas of Piaget and Vygotsky is in the importance it places on specific thinking processes, such as paying attention and remembering (Siegler, 2000, 2007). Also, many information processing theorists reject Piaget's fixed stages of cognitive development, believing instead that thinking changes gradually and smoothly over time as the mind becomes more efficient (Klahr & MacWhinney, 1997). Children's growing awareness of and ability to control their own thinking also accounts for changes in their cognitive competence, from this view (Siegler, 2007b).

Information processing theorists often use the computer as a metaphor for what humans do when they are thinking. A young child who sees or hears something new—say, a word to describe an unfamiliar fruit at the family dinner table—retrieves this information, stores it, remembers it, and modifies it over time, similar to the way a computer operates. Like a hard drive, the child's memory is limited and can become overloaded if too many mental actions are required at one time. If three or four new foods appear on the table at once, for example, the child may not be able to learn and remember the names of all of them. With age, the

information processing theory: A theory of development that emphasizes how children learn in specific situations, relying on memory, attention, and other learning processes. This theory compares the learning process with the way a computer stores, modifies, and retrieves information

child's mind works more efficiently and can store greater amounts of information, as if its owner has acquired an upgrade and additional memory.

Information processing researchers study two specific thinking processes that contribute to learning—**attention** and **memory.** In order for children to learn, from this view, they must pay careful attention to the things that are most important in a learning task. In a math lesson, for example, children must focus their attention on a particular aspect of the shapes being categorized—the number of sides they have. They must ignore other, irrelevant stimuli—the size of the shapes, the color of the marker the teacher is using to explain the problem, even the joke a nearby peer is whispering to a friend. Very young preschoolers tend to focus on many different aspects of a situation, almost at random. They give less thought to what is most important to look at or listen to. Older preschoolers, 4- and 5-year-olds ,are better able to focus on those things that are critical for solving a problem or pleasing adults (Jones, Rothbart, & Posner, 2003; Miller & Seir, 1995). At this age their control over attention still comes and goes. One minute they might focus on an important aspect of a preschool activity but the next be distracted by something occurring in another part of the room. Only in later childhood are their attention abilities finely honed.

Learning also requires that children store new information in memory, according to the information processing theory. Remembering things well requires that children actively select what is important to remember and use specific strategies to store this information (Cowan, 2007). For example, elementary school children can repeat over and over to themselves information to be remembered, a learning strategy called *rehearsal.* They can also use a technique called *organization*, in which they arrange like ideas in groups within their memory storage and label them verbally. For example, a child trying to remember the names of types of transportation might store these in groups, under the labels, "things that go through the air," "things that go in the water," and "things that go along the ground." Preschoolers lack the ability to use these strategies effectively. Also, they are less clear on what "remember" means. They have been found to define "know" or "remember" as "getting the right answer," for example (Lockl & Schneider, 2006; Miscione, Marvin, O'Brien, & Green, 1978). Still, preschoolers are aware of and have some control over knowing and remembering processes. They understand that "know," "remember," and "pay attention" involve doing something special in the mind. When a parent says "Now remember," or a teacher says "Try to learn this," children give special attention to the information that follows. They are more likely to retain it than if they were not given these cues (J. Flavell, Green, & E. R. Flavell, 1995; Peskin & Astington, 2004).

Over the last few decades, a group of researchers—calling themselves **social information processing theorists**—have begun applying tenets of the original information processing theory to the study of social behaviors and social problems of young children (Dodge & Rabiner, 2004; Lemerise, Gregory, & Fredstrom, 2005; Rah & Parke, 2008). They have argued that thinking processes, such as attention and memory, influence social interactions of children in the same way they guide other kinds of learning. In any social situation, they argue, children follow a series of mental steps to understand the behaviors of others and to decide how to respond. First, they pay attention to, encode, and interpret **social cues** in the situation—actions, facial expressions, tone of voice, spoken words—that help them figure out what is occurring and why. If a child has knocked over another child's block structure, for example, the victim might study the perpetrator's face for signs of intentionality, such as smiling or laughter. The child might observe whether the action appeared to be an accidental bump into the structure or a purposeful kick. Note that the ability to perform this step requires the child to pay attention to aspects of the situation that really matter, just as in other learning settings.

Next, the child must relate these cues to previous social experiences that have been stored in long-term memory. The child might reflect on prior interactions with this particular peer or on whether peers who knock over blocks are usually trying to be mean. Based on stored information as well as social cues, the child clarifies the situation and sets goals for the interchange. The child might decide to simply build another building and ignore the

attention: A mental strategy in which learners consciously control what they focus on, so they concentrate on only one or several of the most relevant phenomena at a time.

memory: Events or experiences that are stored in the mind and can later be retrieved.

social information processing theory: An information processing theory that explains how children attend to, interpret, store in memory, and later retrieve the social cues they observe in interactions with others.

social cues: Actions, facial, expressions, tone of voice, spoken words, and other social signals performed by peers that help young children interpret social situations.

peer's behavior. Or, the child might choose to communicate anger or even retaliate. Because this step is guided by memories of previous experience, the information the child has selected to store away is very important. It determines whether the child will rely on accurate and useful information from the past or that which is less helpful. As in all types of learning, memory is critical, from an information processing perspective.

In yet another step in responding to a social situation, the child now weighs the various options for responding to the situation. Should the child kick the perpetrator's block structure down? Should there be angry words? Should the action be ignored? This includes more interpretation, based on stored memories. The child considers what the consequences may be for each action. What have peers or teachers done in the past in reaction to this sort of retaliation? Will they get angry? On the other hand, will the peer keep knocking over the blocks, if the child does nothing? Finally, the child decides on and performs a response. Although the steps are many and seemingly complex, social information processing theorists argue this mental process can take place in a matter of seconds.

During and after the social situation, the child stores the entire experience in memory to be referred to later. Thus, each interchange adds to the child's stored information about the social world. Children who engage in this mental processing are often, though not always, able to resolve social problems positively. However, children who store inaccurate information or lack an ability to follow these steps at all do not have positive relationships with peers. Children who are extremely angry or hostile, for example, will react with little thought, often assuming peers have sinister motives and striking out aggressively (del Castro, Slot, Bosch, Koops, & Veerman, 2003).

Working with Adam

Information processing theorists would recommend strategies for working with Adam that are similar to those Piaget and Vygotsky would suggest. They would propose that teachers help Adam to better *process* social situations as they occur. However, these theorists would be more specific about the steps they would suggest teachers follow. When Adam appears angry and about to become aggressive, for example, they would encourage teachers to prompt him to pay careful attention to relevant social cues from peers—their frowns, tears, complaints, or the way they move away from him or leave the play area. ("Look at how children walk away when you yell at them. They don't want to play with you anymore.") If peers bump or crowd Adam, a teacher might point out cues that help him see they were not trying to be mean. ("Look at their faces. See how they're smiling? They want to play with you, not bother you.") Teachers can also help Adam to retrieve and reflect on previous experiences during social interactions. They might ask, "How can you tell when someone does something that's an accident? What do they usually say?" or "Does Jasmine usually try to be mean to you, or is she usually very friendly?" Finally, teachers can help Adam consider alternative social behaviors, based on previous experiences. A teacher might say, "What's something you can do if you don't want children to play with you?" or "What would be something else you could do, besides pushing, if you want someone to leave you alone?" Helping Adam to monitor the outcomes of his selected response would help him to refine his stored social understanding: "What did she do when you said, 'You're too close to my building'? She moved back a little, didn't she, and said, 'sorry.'" Social information processing theories would argue that as Adam acquires new learning processes, his social interactions will become more positive (Dodge & Rabiner, 2004).

Critique and Multicultural Analysis

Some scholars believe that the information processing theory focuses too narrowly on specific learning situations and the ways individuals think about and learn from these (Keating, 1996; Tooby & Cosmides, 1992). The theory ignores, these scholars contend, some of the broad, cognitive processes—assimilation and accommodation or logical reasoning—that Piaget described (Turiel, 2002). Also, some believe the theory is not detailed enough in describing the nature of stored memories. How is social information, which is so helpful to children according to the social information processing theory, organized in the mind? How does a child retrieve and apply this information to a particular social interaction? Such questions have not been fully answered.

Does information processing theory accurately describe the learning of children of all cultures? Some have raised concerns that research supporting this theory has too often been conducted with Euro-American children and that cultural influences have not been adequately studied (Rogoff, 2003). Others point to studies that show that specific learning processes, such as memory or paying attention, can vary depending on cultural traditions, practices, and language (H. Hernandez, 2001). In one study, for example, children from Mexico were found to be able to attend to more sights, sounds, and verbal instructions at one time than Euro-American or Mexican American children (Cerrea-Chavez, Rogoff, & Arauz, 2005). The researchers conclude that children in Mexico are encouraged to pay attention to and learn from the multifaceted activities of their active families, whereas children in American schools are taught to focus on just one thing at a time (e.g., "Look right at me" or "Listen to what I'm saying"). In another study, children from China were found to have a larger memory storage than American children—but only for memory of numbers (Geary, Bow-Thomas, Liu, & Siegler, 1996). Researchers suggest that this is due to language differences. Number words in China are shorter in length and can be spoken more quickly than English number words. What appears to be advanced memory storage, then, may simply be an ability of Chinese children to remember words that are shorter than those learned by American peers.

In spite of these concerns and minor cultural variations, many researchers believe information processing theory is compatible with cognitive-developmental and sociocultural theories, reviewed above (Arsenio & Lemerise, 2004). They see the theory as particularly useful in explaining how children learn in specific social situations.

ECOLOGICAL SYSTEMS THEORY

ecological systems theory: A theory of development that emphasizes the influence of the many institutions and settings—the community, the school, the political system—within which children live. This theory holds that individual development does not occur in a psychological vacuum but is affected by larger society.

ecology: The many different settings or institutions that affect human development.

microsystem: The layer of environmental influences on development that includes all institutions and experiences within the child's immediate environment. The family, the school, and peers are examples.

The **ecological systems theory** focuses most directly on child and adolescent development within the larger world. Unlike the perspectives previously reviewed, this theory emphasizes the influence of the many institutions and settings—the community, the school, the political system—within which children live. Urie Bronfenbrenner (1995), the leading proponent of this theory, has been critical of psychologists and educators who focus only on individual growth and behavior without regard for the social, political, or economic conditions in which children grow up. He maintains that the family, local social service agencies, schools, state and federal governments, the media, and the current political thinking of the time all must be considered in a comprehensive explanation of human development.

Bronfenbrenner uses the word **ecology** to refer to the settings and institutions that influence the growing human being. He suggests that there are multiple ecologies—that is, many different settings—that affect development. Further, he proposes that these ecologies lie in distinct layers or ecological systems around the developing human. Figure 3-3 illustrates graphically how these ecological systems interact with one another and the individual child.

As shown in the figure, the first layer, the **microsystem,** most directly affects development. The microsystem comprises all institutions, experiences, and influences within the child's immediate environment. These include the family, pediatric services, some social services, the school, teachers or child care providers, and peers. The child both influences and is influenced by these persons and institutions. For example, a child's social behavior is enhanced by certain teacher interventions, and the teacher interventions are affected by the child's behavior.

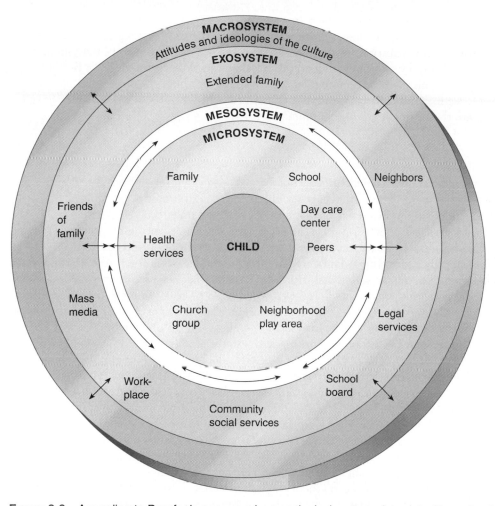

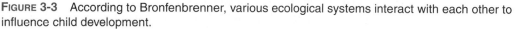

FIGURE 3-3 According to Bronfenbrenner, various ecological systems interact with each other to influence child development.

SOURCE: Kopp, C. B., & Krakow, J. B. Child Development in Social Context. Copyright 1982 by Addison Wesley Publishing Co., Inc. Reprinted by permission.

Institutions within the microsystem influence one another; for example, parents are affected by schools and schools by parents. A teacher may provide information to a pediatrician about a medical problem; the pediatrician may, in turn, make recommendations for in-class adaptations to address the problem. Bronfenbrenner has argued that these interconnections make up the second ecological layer—the **mesosystem.** When strong, supportive linkages exist among persons or organizations in the microsystem, according to ecological systems theory, positive child and adolescent development is enhanced.

Additional ecological systems affect children indirectly. As shown in the figure, the **exosystem** is composed of institutions or persons that do not actually touch children's lives but that indirectly affect their experiences. For example, the legal services system, a friend of the family, or the public assistance office may not directly promote social or intellectual growth of children. However, they may enhance the mental or physical health of the family, provide resources needed for adequate nutrition or shelter, or improve the effectiveness of parents. These positive influences will, in turn, promote healthy child development.

mesosystem: The layer of environmental influences on development that is composed of the interconnections among the persons or organizations within the microsystem. Parent–teacher communication and collaborations between child care centers and public schools are examples.

exosystem: The layer of environmental influences on development that is composed of institutions or persons that do not actually touch children's lives but that indirectly affect their experiences. The legal services system or the public assistance office are examples.

The final ecological system shown in Figure 3-3 is the **macrosystem,** which contains the overarching values, ideologies, laws, worldviews, and customs of a particular culture or society. Although institutions of the macrosystem seem far removed from individual child development, they are extremely influential. An example of this is provided by Berk (2006), who reports that child abuse is more prevalent in societies where the use of physical punishment or force in child rearing is accepted. In cultures where values of respect and caring for children are the norm, abuse is less common.

Working with Adam

In previous sections, we have identified a number of classroom interventions based on theories of child development. These strategies would be viewed as too narrow by ecological systems theorists. Addressing individual behavior, feelings, or social understandings merely within the school setting would affect only one small element within Adam's microsystem. From an ecological systems perspective, a much broader social intervention would be needed.

A first step in addressing Adam's challenging behaviors would be to create supportive linkages among the microsystem institutions in his life. Teachers, social service professionals, medical personnel, and Adam's mother would need to collaborate in finding solutions to his difficulties. For example, the teacher might arrange for a planning meeting with Adam's mother and other significant family members, social and mental health service providers, and other professionals working with Adam and his family. A collaborative intervention—to be implemented in the home, the classroom, the community center, or home-visiting program—might be devised. For example, the psychoanalytic approach of promoting attachment could be implemented collaboratively across settings in Adam's microsystem. Individuals in each setting would provide predictable, nurturing, and responsive environments that enhance emotional bonds. Regular meetings could then be held between the parent and teacher to discuss problems and successes in implementation.

The teacher might visit Adam's home, and his mother might be invited into the classroom. Parent education programs might be planned. The purpose of these initiatives would be to increase interconnections between school and family—that is, to strengthen the mesosystem. Following ecological systems theory, the teacher might adopt strategies to address other ecological systems. Assistance might be given to Adam's mother to obtain mental health services or to access resources to feed and clothe her family. The teacher might even assist in crisis management, helping the mother obtain legal services or career counseling when needed. Although such support activities are viewed by some as exceeding the limits of a teacher's role, they are absolutely crucial exosystem interventions from an ecological systems perspective. Without them, no amount of in-class intervention will have a lasting impact.

Finally, the teacher might even launch a campaign to alter problematic elements in Adam's macrosystem. Political action against elected officials who threaten to cut child and family services might be undertaken. Lobbying activities to promote the regulation of television violence might be initiated. Advocacy would be a regular professional responsibility of teachers from this perspective. These efforts would be based on a fundamental principle of ecological systems theory: child development problems are best addressed within a compassionate and caring society that values and protects its children.

macrosystem: The layer of environmental influences on development that contains the overarching values, ideologies, laws, worldviews, and customs of a particular culture or society. A society's respect and caring for children is an example.

Critique and Multicultural Analysis

Few research studies have examined child development from the perspective of ecological systems theory. Such work is exceedingly time consuming and challenging (M. B. Spencer, 1985). Identifying all the macrosystem, exosystem, mesosystem, and microsystem variables that affect children's social or intellectual development would be a formidable, if not impossible, undertaking. Studies have been conducted to determine some of the microsystem and exosystem causes of childhood problems. Certain **risk factors**—conditions that may lead to poor development—have been identified. These include poverty, lack of social services, violence in the community, poor housing, family disharmony, and child abuse (Deng & Roosa, 2007; Werner & Smith, 1992). Conversely, **protective factors**—conditions that may insulate children from the negative effects of poverty or community violence—have been studied (Garbarino, Dubrow, Kostelny, & Pardo, 1992; J. L. Robinson, 2000). Among these are a positive home environment, attachment to parents, adequate housing and safe neighborhoods, and a positive preschool experience. Very few theorists of any field would deny the importance of these factors in shaping children's development.

The ecological systems theory has been viewed as culturally sensitive. It not only accepts cultural differences but also fully integrates these differences into an explanation of human development. Customs, language, worldviews, and histories of particular ethnic groups—all part of the macro-, exo-, and microsystems—are viewed as fundamental aspects of the developmental process. For example, the learning and behavior of African American children should not be studied in isolation from the social and political world. The historical roots of slavery, experiences of oppression, conditions in the immediate neighborhood, and economic hardship would be considered integral aspects of the developmental process (M. B. Spencer, 1999).

Because ecological systems theory focuses on the social, political, and economic contexts in which development occurs, it is believed to be most useful in identifying social issues concerning children in poverty or those of historically underrepresented groups. Unlike perspectives that focus on individual development, ecological systems theory informs policymaking and advocacy activities. (See the Advocacy and Public Policy box in this chapter for an example.) In fact, Bronfenbrenner's model has been a favorite among child development advocates and activists (Garbarino & Kostelny, 1992; M. B. Spencer, 1999; Zigler, 1998).

risk factors: Conditions in a child's life that can lead to poor development, including poverty, community violence, and child abuse.

protective factors: Conditions that might insulate children from the negative effects of risk factors. Attachment to parents and positive preschool experiences are examples.

ADVOCACY AND PUBLIC POLICY

Reducing the Stigma of Parental Depression

Research has demonstrated that children of parents who are depressed are at risk of behavioral and emotional problems (Dawson et al., 2003; Lundy et al., 1999). Parental depression is the most powerful predictor of childhood depression (Verdeli, 2004). One reason for this is that depression affects the quality of parent–child interactions. Unfortunately, many parents who are depressed will not seek treatment because of the societal stigma associated with this disorder (Glass, 2003). Depression has been viewed by many as a human weakness; those with this disorder have often experienced discrimination.

Following Bronfenbrenner's ecological systems theory, presented in this chapter, teachers and caregivers can address this problem at various levels. At the microsystem level, for example, they can offer special support in the classroom to a child whose parents are depressed. They can assist a parent in obtaining mental health services from a community agency—an exosystem strategy. These efforts will greatly assist individual children and families.

Professionals can also take action to reduce the effects of parental depression on all children in the community through a macrosystem intervention. They can serve as advocates for families by working toward reducing the stigma of depression in society as a whole. They might organize schoolwide programs in which mental health professionals are invited to present information on depression to parents and other members of the community. They might write school newsletters or letters to the editor of the local newspaper that dispel prevalent myths about depression. The National Institutes of Mental Health (NIMH, 2004) suggest that the following key points be emphasized: (a) depression is a

(continued)

very common illness, afflicting more than 18 million Americans; (b) for the majority of sufferers, the disorder can be effectively treated; (c) depression does not stem from "personal weakness," sufferers cannot simply "pull themselves together" and recover, and treatment is critical; and (d) women, particularly mothers, are prone to this disorder.

Professionals can become involved in addressing the stigma of depression and other mental health disorders at a national level. They might join the campaign of Mental Health America (http://www.nmha.org) to pass state and federal legislation requiring full med-

ical insurance coverage for the treatment of mental illnesses. They might help organize local chapters of the National Depression and Bipolar Support Alliance (http://www.dbsalliance.org) or the Partnership Network of the National Institutes of Mental Health (http://www.nimh.nih.gov/health/outreach), organizations committed to educating the public on the nature and treatment of depression and other mental illnesses. Through such advocacy, professionals can help parents who suffer depression surmount the societal obstacles to treatment and, in turn, help their children enjoy an emotionally healthy childhood.

Summary

A child development theory is a system of beliefs about how children grow, learn, think, and behave. There are several prominent theories of child development; each can be applied to solving social problems or promoting learning in a classroom. From a maturationist perspective, teachers and caregivers should adapt environments to the inborn, genetically determined needs and characteristics of children. In contrast, behaviorists would urge that desirable behaviors be shaped through the direct use of rewards and modeling. Cognitive-developmental theorists would suggest that most classroom problems can be solved by supporting intellectual development. From this view, children would be guided in actively and personally constructing knowledge about the world. From a sociocultural perspective, this construction of

knowledge can be greatly enhanced when adults use rich language and provide for peer interactions. Information processing theorists also believe social interactions can support learning—particularly if children are guided in learning processes, such as attending and remembering, and in accurately interpreting social cues. Ecological systems theorists would contend that positive development is ensured only when all influences on children—direct and indirect—are addressed. Teachers should work with families and social service agencies and should even try to change society as a whole. Some theories—sociocultural and ecological theories, for example—are preferred by multicultural scholars because they acknowledge the powerful effects of families and culture on children's development.

Research into Practice

Critical Concept 1

A theory of child development is a belief system about how and why children grow, learn, and behave as they do. Theories are very practical; they can guide adults in making decisions about teaching and caring for children.

Application   Clarify your own theories about children and how they develop. A clearly articulated theory leads to thoughtful and consistent parenting and teaching.

Critical Concept 2

Seven predominant theories of child development can be identified in the literature. All hold some value in resolving classroom dilemmas. Each provides useful guidance to parents and teachers.

Application   Become familiar with alternative theories of child development. Borrow critical concepts and strategies from each theory in your professional practice.

Critical Concept 3

The maturationist theory holds that most of what children become is inherited; behaviors and abilities simply unfold as children mature.

Application #1   Recognize that some characteristics of children are genetically determined at birth. Appreciate and accept diverse interpersonal styles or temperaments that are part of children's biological heritage.

Application #2   Adapt classrooms to meet the unique inborn traits of individual children rather than expect children to adapt to classrooms.

CRITICAL CONCEPT 4

Behaviorist theory holds that the child is a blank slate at birth and is simply filled in over time by experience. From this perspective, adults can use rewards, praise, modeling, and other tools to shape children's development in any desired direction.

Application #1   Use positive feedback and other rewards to influence children's behavior.

Application #2   Behave as you wish children to behave, thereby modeling desirable behavior. Children are more likely to do what adults do than what adults tell them to do.

CRITICAL CONCEPT 5

The psychoanalytic theory is concerned mainly with personality formation. Psychoanalysts characterize psychological growth as a process of resolving emotional conflicts between instinctual desires and the demands of the real world.

Application #1   Be nurturing and responsive to the needs of infants and toddlers so that children of this age will acquire feelings of trust.

Application #2   Encourage autonomy—an emotional state in which children strive to be independent and separate from parents. Allowing exploration and self-expression and avoiding punishment or overrestriction are ways to do this.

Application #3   Promote a sense of initiative by encouraging children to assert themselves, make creative attempts, take risks, and reach out to peers.

Application #4   Promote a sense of industry—a feeling of being competent—by providing many experiences with success both in and out of school.

CRITICAL CONCEPT 6

Cognitive-developmental and sociocultural theorists view mental growth and language as most critical; they view development as the active, internal construction of knowledge. These theories are often viewed as more culturally sensitive than other perspectives on child development.

Application #1   Provide interesting experiences, ask questions, and pose challenges that lead young children to actively solve problems and construct their own understandings of the world.

Application #2   Scaffold children's learning by asking questions, prompting, or giving hints when a child is within the zone of proximal development—that is, when the solution to a problem is just beyond the child's level of ability.

CRITICAL CONCEPT 7

The information processing theory describes how children use memory, attention, and other specific learning processes to learn in new situations. Social information processing theorists show how the theory is useful in helping children process and resolve social problems, using previously stored experiences to guide them.

Application #1   Help children to become aware of and use attention and memory to solve problems by pointing out the things that are most important for them to attend to or remember.

Application #2   Guide children in social situations by helping them pay attention to social cues—smiling, crying, shouting—of peers and to reflect on past experiences in resolving conflicts.

CRITICAL CONCEPT 8

Ecological systems theories hold that developmental processes do not occur in a psychological vacuum but rather that individual child development is influenced by factors in the immediate environment as well as society and culture as a whole. Ecological systems theories are thought to be most useful in defining social issues and guiding social policy decisions.

Application #1   Realize that classroom intervention alone will not ensure positive child development. Family, community, and societal factors must also be optimal for children to learn and be healthy.

Application #2   Help parents and families access community resources. They should become knowledgeable about and establish relationships with local service agencies and should ensure that parents have access to these agencies.

Application #3   Expand your role as a professional to include advocacy. Lobby your local, state, and federal legislators; organize community or parent advocacy groups; and in other ways work to ensure a child-caring community and society.

CHAPTER 4

Genetics, Prenatal Development, and Birth

GUIDING QUESTIONS

1. What are the biological steps by which genetic information from the mother and father are joined to create a unique human being?
2. How are genetics and culture interrelated?
3. What are the major stages of prenatal development, and how are these affected by such environmental influences as drugs, poor health and nutrition, and teen parenthood?
4. What are the complex physical reactions in a mother that lead to childbirth?
5. How are Western and non-Western childbirth practices alike and different?

In this chapter, genetics, prenatal development, and childbirth are examined. A full understanding of these topics requires knowledge of the unique histories, worldviews, and family practices of diverse cultural groups, as the following story reveals:

Mr. Salazar, the director of a social services program, has just learned that a young Native American mother he is working with, Rose, has become pregnant. Because Rose's first child has had a variety of developmental and health problems, he tries to invite her to a free health clinic offered by his program. He has difficulty contacting her, though. When he calls her home, Rose's grandmother—who speaks mainly Chippewa—answers the phone. She has difficulty understanding him. Although he leaves messages, Rose does not return his calls.

Mr. Salazar decides to go to Rose's home to tell her about the health clinic. When he finds no one there, he sits on the front porch of the family apartment, waiting. One hour passes, then another, but his resolve grows. He will continue to wait because he believes the well-being of a new and developing human being is at stake. If he can arrange for prenatal health care and nutritional services, this new child will get off to a much better start than Rose's first child did.

When Rose finally arrives, Mr. Salazar tries to explain his visit: "I want to invite you to a clinic so that your new baby will be healthy." Rose looks down and does not answer. "Good health and nutrition are very important for a developing fetus," he persists. The mother still does not reply but quietly excuses herself and walks into her apartment, closing the door behind her. He stands a moment on the front steps, puzzled over what has just transpired.

Later, Mr. Salazar complains to a friend, a Midewiwin who is a social service worker: "I can't believe she cares so little about her unborn fetus. Will this new child stand a chance if Rose doesn't get decent prenatal care?"

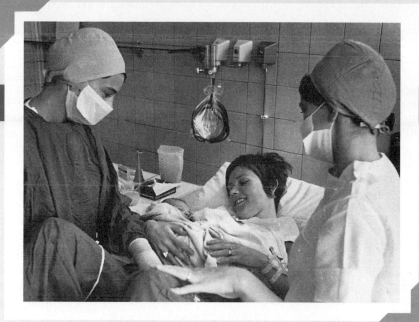

His friend laughs. "Oh, she cares a great deal for her children, I'm sure. You have a lot to learn about our culture. It's just very difficult for her to come to your clinic; there are barriers that you don't know about."

"Barriers? The clinic is free!" Mr. Salazar responds. "Why can't she come just this one day, for her child?"

"You don't understand. There are cultural barriers," his friend explains. "This is one reason for the high mortality rate of Native American newborns in our country." He goes on to describe the traditions and values of many Native American families. He explains that they often have a great need for privacy; many Native Americans, particularly women, have a tradition of personal modesty. The crowded, public setting of a health clinic and the intrusive examinations that are likely to be given may be too intimidating. Even Mr. Salazar's unexpected visit to her apartment must have caused great consternation.

He goes on to explain that Native Americans have a rich history of health care and medical treatment that is overlooked and often denigrated by Western doctors. The herbal remedies and tribal ceremonies used by Native Americans to prevent illness reflect a worldview in which humans must be in harmony with nature. Medical care is an extended-family matter; all close relatives are often involved in treatment. Western medical experts have not recognized the value of these practices until recently, the director's friend asserts. Doctors are finally appreciating that Native American and Western techniques can be integrated to effectively address health issues.

Mr. Salazar, with the help of his friend, eventually arranges for Rose's family—including her grandmother—to receive medical and prenatal care at a small nearby clinic where staff are sensitive to cultural traditions. Several months later, the director is pleased to learn that Rose has given birth to a healthy baby.

This story illustrates how culture can influence development in the very earliest stages of life—even before birth. Such seemingly physiological processes as fetal health and birth weight can be affected by cultural beliefs and practices.

GENETICS: THE BIOLOGICAL STEPS TO BECOMING A UNIQUE HUMAN BEING

ovum: The egg, contributed by the mother, that will grow into a developing human if fertilized by a sperm cell.

genes: Segments of DNA molecules, passed along from parents to offspring, that determine the characteristics of a developing human.

DNA (deoxyribonucleic acid): Long, double-stranded molecules that make up chromosomes. Genetic information is carried in DNA within cells.

chromosomes: Chemical structures contained in the nucleus of all human cells that carry all the genetic information necessary for the development of a unique individual.

meiosis: A special cell division process that leads to the formation of a father's sperm cell and a mother's ovum.

zygote: A fertilized egg, resulting from the union of sperm and ovum at conception, that contains a full complement of 46 chromosomes.

mitosis: The process of cell division and duplication in which each new cell receives an exact copy of the original cell's chromosomes.

dominant gene: A gene for one trait that overpowers a gene for an alternate trait.

recessive gene: A gene for one trait that is overpowered by a dominant gene for an alternate trait. A recessive gene expresses itself only when paired with another recessive gene.

What children become as they grow up is determined, in part, by what they have inherited biologically. There is much debate about how much influence genetics has on development, but most researchers agree that genetics and experience interact to affect how children turn out (Scarr, 1993; Segal, McGuire, Havlena, Gill, & Hershberger, 2007).

Genes and Chromosomes

The process of child development begins at conception, although parental lifestyles even before conception may influence children's growth. Following sexual intercourse, millions of sperm cells from the father travel up the fallopian tubes in the mother's body toward the egg, or **ovum.** Only one cell can successfully penetrate the ovum. Once this penetration occurs, the egg becomes immediately resistant to other sperm cells. A remarkable chemical reaction then takes place: the nuclei of these two tiny cells combine and share information that will determine the traits of a new and unique person.

Information about the characteristics of parents and their ancestors is carried in the sperm and egg in **genes;** these comprise molecules of deoxyribonucleic acid, or **DNA.** Genes are ordered along larger bodies called **chromosomes,** which are contained in the nucleus of all human cells. Chromosomes carry all the genetic information necessary for the development of a unique individual; they help determine such diverse traits as eye color, temperament (Chess & Thomas, 1987; Kagan et al., 1994; Rothbart, 2007), and even—some have claimed—political orientation (Eaves, Eysenck, & Martin, 1989).

Typical cells in the body contain 46 chromosomes. Sperm and egg cells are unique, however, in that each contains only 23 chromosomes. They were formed within the father's testes and the mother's ovaries by a special cell division process called **meiosis.** When the sperm and egg combine during conception, so do the chromosomes in their nuclei. The result is a fertilized egg, or **zygote,** with a full complement of 46 chromosomes that determine what the developing person will inherit from both parents.

The zygote begins to divide and duplicate almost immediately after conception through a process called **mitosis.** At the same time, it begins a journey of several days down the mother's fallopian tube. It eventually becomes embedded in the soft tissue of the mother's uterus. Here it continues to divide and grow at a remarkable rate into what will eventually become a new person.

When the egg and sperm join, the mother's and father's genes combine to determine the characteristics of this unique person. But what happens when the mother's genetic information leads to a particular trait and the father's leads to just the opposite? In most cases, the gene for one of these traits will be **dominant**—that is, it will win this genetic tug-of-war and express its characteristics in the developing human. If the mother contributed a dominant gene for tallness, for example, the child would become tall. The gene for shortness—the **recessive gene**—would not express itself. A recessive gene expresses itself only when it is paired with another recessive gene.

In actuality, genetics is not quite so simple. Most traits involve a combination of several genes, and sometimes traits are blended. The environment also plays a role in whether genetic information inherited by the child will actually be expressed. A good example is the inheritance of general intelligence. One's IQ is determined, in part, by genetics; however, most geneticists believe that there is no such thing as a "smart" gene. What a person inherits from parents at conception is a "heritability range"—that is, a range of potential intellectual abilities (Scarr, 1993). For example, a child might inherit the potential to be of moderate to high intelligence but achieve only moderate intelligence because of a limited environment. Another child might inherit a potential for only low to moderate ability but achieve the same moderate level of ability because of a more supportive environment. In each case, the level of intellectual capacity depends on both genetics and life's opportunities.

Of all the human traits determined at conception, perhaps none is as significant as gender. All human cells contain a special pair of chromosomes: an XX pair in females and an XY pair in males. This single pair of chromosomes—one contributed by the mother, the other by the father during conception—determines the gender of the developing person. The mother's egg can contribute only an X chromosome, while the father's sperm cell can contribute either an X or a Y. If a sperm cell containing an X chromosome penetrates an egg (which always has an X), a female is conceived. If an egg is fertilized by a sperm cell with a Y chromosome, a male is conceived. It is the genetic contribution of the father, then, that determines gender.

Twins can result from one of two genetic processes. Sometimes, at the time of conception, two separate eggs are released from the mother's ovaries and are fertilized by two different sperm cells. The result is that two genetically distinct siblings are born at the same time. These "fraternal" twins (not exclusively fraternal, of course, because they could be sisters or a brother and sister) are no more alike than other siblings. They have developed from separate zygotes containing different genetic information. *Identical* twins occur in the rare instance when a fertilized egg divides immediately after conception into two separate zygotes. Both zygotes travel down the fallopian tube into the uterus and grow separately into genetically identical persons. Identical twins are necessarily of the same gender since they have developed from the same sperm cell and egg. Twins occur in about 2% of births, and about two-thirds of these are fraternal.

Hereditary Diseases

Some problems in development before birth can be attributed to genes and chromosomes. Sometimes these can lead to physical malformations, mental retardation, or poor health. One condition caused by chromosomal abnormalities is **Down syndrome.** Individuals with this condition have received three number 21 chromosomes instead of the typical pair. Moderate to severe mental retardation, problems with the heart and other organs, and unique physical features such as reduced stature and somewhat flattened facial features are common characteristics of a child with Down syndrome. The condition occurs in 1 out of 500 to 1 out of 700 births; the possibility increases with the age of the mother (Ataullah & Freeman-Wang, 2005; Neuhäuser & Krackow, 2007). Down syndrome is the most common genetic cause of mental retardation. The second most common cause is **fragile X syndrome,** which results from a brittle or separated X chromosome. It is believed that this condition contributes to some cases of infantile autism, a serious emotional and behavioral disorder that will be examined in a later chapter (Hessl et al., 2002).

In **Rh disease,** another genetically related problem, the infant inherits blood from the father that is incompatible with that of the mother. If the fetus inherits Rh-positive blood from the father and the mother is Rh negative, the mother's body will produce antibodies that can become toxic. The result can be fetal anemia, jaundice, mental retardation, and death. A family's firstborn child is not at great risk since not enough time has elapsed for antibodies to form before the child is born. Subsequent children are most affected. Fortunately, through careful screening of the mother's blood before birth, the problem can be avoided. A special serum can be administered to destroy Rh-positive blood cells as they enter the mother's body during her first delivery. This inhibits the formation of antibodies that can affect the development of subsequent children. Prenatal health screening is critical, then, to avoid the damaging effects of this condition.

Down syndrome: A genetic condition, caused by an extra chromosome, that can lead to mental retardation, heart problems, motor delays, and unique physical features such as reduced stature.

fragile X syndrome: A genetic condition, caused by a brittle or separated X chromosome, that can lead to mental retardation and infantile autism.

Rh disease: A genetic condition, caused by inheriting blood from the father that is incompatible with that of the mother, that can lead to anemia, jaundice, mental retardation, and death.

Some genetically derived problems afflict only males or females; these derive from abnormalities of the X and Y chromosomes that determine gender. Diseases that affect only males include **hemophilia,** a condition that limits blood clotting and leads to internal bleeding, and **Klinefelter's syndrome,** which can result in sterility, physical malformation, and mental health problems. Only females are afflicted with Turner's syndrome, a condition that leads to physical malformation and sterility.

Genetics from a Multicultural Perspective

How are genetics and culture interrelated? Are some cultural variations in child development inherited biologically? Can culture actually influence how some genes are expressed in the developing person? These questions are debated by geneticists and multicultural scholars. Sandra Scarr (1993) has summarized the relationships among genetics, culture, and individual variation in this way: "Becoming human is one matter. Becoming French, Mongolian, or African-American is another. Becoming George Sand, Genghis Khan, or Martin Luther King, Jr. is still another" (p. 1333). Her point is that there are at least three significant sources of variation in human development: the biological evolution of the species, the cultural heritage, and the genetic makeup of the individual human being. All these factors interact with and support one another. Scarr rejects the notion that one factor is predominant: "For too long, psychologists have argued nature *versus* nurture, biology *versus* culture, as though one cause excluded the other" (p. 1335). A full understanding of human genetics requires an understanding of the complex ways that all three factors interact.

Becoming Human

Genetics regulates most directly the process of becoming human. All children inherit certain *species-specific* characteristics—for example, language, smiling, general intelligence, and emotionality—that can be observed across all cultures and in all individuals. All cultural groups provide opportunities for children to acquire such traits. However, these opportunities tend to differ from one culture to another. For example, all societies have some mechanism for teaching language, but their teaching methods differ. That so many fundamental characteristics can be observed across cultures suggests that human beings are really more alike than they are different, regardless of where they grow up or what their individual circumstances may be.

Becoming an Individual

There are, of course, individual differences in development. To use Scarr's example, Martin Luther King, Jr. and Genghis Khan were clearly unique human beings! These individual variations may be determined partly biologically from Scarr's view. One child may suffer from a hereditary disease that will contribute to lifelong atypical development or poor health. Another may inherit genetic information that will partially explain a pleasant temperament or difficulty learning math. Experience plays a key role, however, in determining how these inherited traits will actually be expressed as the human develops. According to Scarr (1993), environments provide a "range of opportunities" for development (p. 1336). A child with Down syndrome may become more or less intellectually competent, depending on environment. A child born with a predisposition to be of pleasant temperament may be less positive if the environment does not nurture this inborn trait.

Scarr (1993) has argued not only that environment can shape the way children turn out but also that children can "create their own environments" (p. 2). Using the previous example, a child who has inherited, biologically, a pleasant temperament may elicit positive

hemophilia: A genetically derived condition that limits blood clotting and can lead to internal bleeding.

Klinefelter's syndrome: A genetically derived condition that can result in sterility, physical malformation, and mental health problems.

behaviors from parents or peers. When adults respond to a pleasant manner with support and nurturance, the child may become even more positive in interactions. Thus, it is the child's temperamental disposition that may lead to a nurturing environment, not the other way around!

Becoming an Individual Within a Cultural Group

How does culture influence development? How do African Americans become African American and Mongolians become Mongolian? Within a particular cultural group, there is vast individual variation in development that stems from the genetic and environmental influences that were discussed previously. Japanese American children, for example, vary greatly in social competence, temperament, and learning style (Ishii-Kuntz, 1997b; Yuko, Masaharu, & Masako, 2007). Given such variety within cultures, can one conclude that there are no cultural differences? Are all individuals so different that it is pointless to think about cultural diversity in development? Derman-Sparks et al., (1997) have described a "denial of differences" view in which the rich cultural diversity within our society is not appreciated. Differences among cultural groups do exist, of course. Some of these differences are genetically derived, and others are rooted in the unique experiences of groups throughout history.

Cultural Differences Related to History and Experience. Most cultural differences have evolved, from Scarr's (1993) perspective, as groups have adapted to the unique challenges of their surroundings. Cultures have defined what is important for children to know, believe, and be able to do based on what is needed for survival of the group. Although genetics has provided the raw materials to develop these abilities, it is cultural experience that defines the specific behaviors and knowledge that children acquire.

Ogbu (1992) gives an example of how challenges from the outside world have led some cultures to adopt distinct child-rearing practices. Some African American parents have adopted a directive parenting style that has evolved to keep children from harm in an inhospitable, biased society (Baumrind, 1994; Brody & Flor, 1998; Rudy & Grusec, 2006). This parenting style has been found to lead to positive development for African American children, even though it may be viewed as authoritarian by those in the dominant culture. In some Native American families, maintaining cultural values is critical. Sometimes traditional public schooling is seen as a threat to this. As a result, success in school is not always highly valued by parents, which may explain the high dropout rate in some Native American communities (Kawamoto & Cheshire, 1997; Slonim, 1991; Sutton & Broken Nose, 2005). An important point to remember is that such cultural differences are logical, purposeful, and directly related to experience. They are not genetically derived deficits, as some writers have asserted (Herrnstein & Murray, 1994).

Cultural Differences Related to Genetics. Some cultural variations can be related directly to genetics. For example, differences have been found across ethnic groups in the motoric activity of infants (Nugent, Lester, & Brazelton, 1989; Paludi, 2002; van Haastert, de Vries, Helders, & Jongmans, 2006). Stature and weight vary across cultures; children of Asian ancestry have shorter stature, broader hips, and shorter arms and legs, and those of African descent are relatively taller and have longer limbs.

Certain hereditary diseases are more prevalent within particular ethnic groups (Milunsky, 1992; Pearce, Foliaki, Sporle, & Cunningham, 2004). African American children are more likely to suffer from **sickle-cell anemia,** a disorder that causes severe pain, heart and kidney problems, and early death. In some African communities, 30% of newborns carry the gene that causes this disorder. Asians are more likely to inherit **thalassemia,** a red blood cell disorder that causes damage to vital organs. Children of European or Pueblo Indian ancestry are

sickle-cell anemia: A genetically derived condition, more common in African Americans, that causes severe pain, heart and kidney problems, and early death.

thalassemia: A genetically derived blood disorder, more common in Asians, that causes damage to vital organs.

more often afflicted with **cystic fibrosis,** an enzyme disorder that causes mucus to form in the lungs and intestinal track. **Tay–Sachs disease,** an enzyme-related condition that causes the brain and nervous system to deteriorate, more often strikes Jews of eastern European descent.

Although these diseases are purely genetic in origin, anxieties about children's afflictions and parents' responses when they occur have become a part of cultural heritage. The story of Randy illustrates this point:

> Randy is a 36-year-old African American professor at a small eastern university. He has just been released from the hospital, where he fought a life-threatening bout with pneumonia. This is not the first time he has had to cope with serious illness; his crises are numerous and come on quickly and without warning. "Another battle is won for now," he comments to well-wishers at a faculty meeting.
>
> One day, at age 13, after choir practice at church, Randy sat down in a pew next to his grandmother, resting his head against her shoulder. She had always been there for him, he was thinking; at that moment, his stomach began to hurt. His abdominal pains grew over the next few days, and his mother's usual remedies didn't seem to be working. Randy was eventually admitted to the hospital. He remembers his mother crying and recalls being confused at her sadness. This was just a stomachache, after all; surely he would get better. Only later would he learn that he'd been diagnosed with a genetic disease, sickle-cell anemia, which meant he had little chance to live a full life. "It is pretty hard to deal with at age 13," Randy recalls. "I was young and looking forward to life. And now I was being told that I would die."
>
> The stomach crisis finally passed, but in no time another challenge arose. Randy developed sores around his ankles that grew and became more and more painful. These were leg ulcers, he was told, the first of many he would suffer. They would last 30 to 60 days. He remembers having trouble walking to school because of the pain. Some days he could not put on his shoes.
>
> But Randy survived. He finished high school and went off to college. Here, stress, financial worries, and poor diet led to numerous visits to the campus infirmary. He joined ROTC, hoping to become an officer in the Air Force. He suffered a devastating blow when he underwent a routine physical examination and was told the Air Force would not commission him because of his disease. Yet Randy persevered. He became a certified teacher, earned a master's degree, and then completed a doctoral program at a prestigious university. He had certainly beaten the odds.
>
> When asked why he has survived so long, Randy answers without hesitation, "Religion. My family has always been deeply religious. I have a strong mother, a strong father. They were strong believers, and I was brought up in the church." Randy believes it is not a coincidence that his ailment first began in church with his grandmother nearby. That early experience represents, for him, how religion and a supportive extended family have gotten him through.
>
> Randy is clearly aware of what the future might hold. He could die suddenly of a stroke or organ failure. "Sometimes I ask, 'Why me? What would life be like if I did not have the disease?' But then I ask, 'Would I value life as much if I didn't have it?'"

Randy's observations mirror the view of many scholars that the strength of black families and their religious orientation have allowed survival of the culture in adversity (Hale 1994; McAdoo, 2007; Nobles, 2007).

Cultural Differences Versus Genetic Deficits. We can conclude that cultural differences in child development—which surely do exist—stem mostly from the unique experiences and histories of various ethnic groups. For centuries, however, biology has been used to perpetuate

cystic fibrosis: A genetically derived enzyme disorder, more common in Pueblo Indians and Europeans, that causes mucus to form in the lungs and intestinal track.

Tay–Sachs disease: A genetically derived enzyme, more common in Jews of eastern European descent, that causes deterioration of the brain and nervous system.

racism. For example, a genetic argument has been used to espouse the intellectual superiority of one culture over another. Although few modern-day social scientists assert that some cultures are inferior, work suggesting this continues to be published. One such book, *The Bell Curve*, by Richard Herrnstein and Charles Murray (1994), received much attention in the popular press. Its authors note that a disparity exists between the IQs of certain ethnic groups and white Americans. They hint that the IQ advantage for whites is explained, in large measure, by genetics. Many criticisms have been raised about this work. Some have challenged the statistics reported. Others have raised questions about whether measures of IQ favor persons of white, middle-class background. Still others point out that individuals from underrepresented groups lack the resources and opportunities enjoyed by the dominant culture. The IQ disparity, they argue, is really a disparity of access (Klebanov & Brooks-Gunn, 2008; Timberlake, 2007).

Unfortunately, such books tend to revive archaic beliefs about "cultural deficits." They suggest that individuals within a particular cultural group are deprived because their values, socialization practices, or competencies do not match those of the dominant culture. Such perspectives are extremely dangerous from a public policy and education standpoint. It will be argued throughout this book that cultural differences are just that: differences. They may be explained by experience or genetics or an interaction of these, but they are always to be appreciated as part of the rich diversity that makes up our world.

PRENATAL DEVELOPMENT

Once the sperm and egg have joined, the zygote (or fertilized egg) travels down the fallopian tube, becomes embedded in the uterine wall, and begins to grow rapidly. Three distinct stages of **prenatal development** can be identified. These are described in Table 4-1.

prenatal development: The development of the human organism after conception and before birth.

Stage	Age	Significant Developments
Period of the ovum	Conception to 2 weeks	Cell differentiation occurs. Embryoplast cells form; these will become the developing person. Trophoblast cells are differentiated; these will develop into the placenta and other important external tissues. Miscarriage is most common during this period.
Period of the embryo	2 to 8 weeks after conception	The heart, brain, lungs, digestive system, kidneys, and liver all are formed. The heart begins to beat. Facial features—eyes, nose, ears, mouth, tongue, tooth buds, and upper and lower jaws—develop. The placenta, umbilical cord, and amnion form. The length of the embryo is about 1.5 inches.
Period of the fetus	8 weeks to birth	Further development and growth of organs and limbs occurs. Brain growth is especially rapid. The fetus begins to open and close eyes and even suck a thumb. This is often considered a period of less risk. However, poor maternal health and nutrition still put the fetus at risk.

TABLE 4-1
Stages of Prenatal Development

The **period of the ovum,** which lasts about 2 weeks after conception, involves the rapid growth of a shapeless mass of cells. However, cell differentiation has already begun during this period. As described in the table, specialized cells are created that will grow into all the important tissues and organs of the developing human. The period of the ovum is one of risk for development; miscarriages—that is, spontaneous abortions—occur most often during this early stage.

The second period of prenatal development, the **period of the embryo,** begins about 2 weeks after conception and extends to approximately the eighth week. Amazingly, almost all major organs and structures of the human body are formed during this stage, and many begin to function. Also during this period, important organs begin to form outside the embryo. These include the **placenta,** a soft mass that allows the flow of nutrients from the mother to the embryo, and the **umbilical cord,** the lifeline that transports these nutrients. An important, protective fluid-filled sac, the **amnion,** has now formed around the developing organism. The rapid growth of the embryo makes this a period of some developmental risk. Environmental influences such as maternal drug use or illness can have a devastating effect during this stage. Maternal nutrition is critical for the embryo's development.

The final prenatal stage, the **period of the fetus,** is marked by continued development of the organs and by rapid growth. Because many of the organs have already formed, the fetal stage is often considered a less critical period. However, important development occurs at each prenatal stage. For example, brain growth is extremely rapid in the final 3 months of prenatal development (and for many months after birth!) Maternal nutrition is extremely important, then, during this time. Most doctors urge a healthy maternal lifestyle during all 9 months of pregnancy to ensure positive fetal development.

The three stages of prenatal development and the significant physical growth that occurs in each are presented in Figure 4-1, which also shows periods of risk in the formation of various organs and systems.

Environmental Influences on Prenatal Development

Environmental agents can negatively influence prenatal development. These include poor nutrition, drugs, and maternal illness during pregnancy. Because of some of these factors, children of color have a rockier road to travel from conception to birth. On almost any measure of fetal development or neonatal health, Caucasians fare better than African Americans, Puerto Ricans, Native Americans, Mexican Americans, and Asian Americans. For some traditionally underrepresented groups, the infant mortality rate is almost twice as high as that for whites (Children's Defense Fund, 2007; Grantham-McGregor, Powell, Walker, Chang, & Fletcher, 1994).

Why are such problems more common among certain ethnic groups? One explanation is poverty. Poverty rates are higher for almost all underrepresented populations (Garcia Coll, 1990; Shi et al., 2004; U.S. Bureau of the Census, 2000). Poverty is among the most debilitating of conditions in prenatal development (Shonkoff & Phillips, 2007).

Drugs. Substance abuse by a pregnant mother can have catastrophic effects on the developing fetus. Heroin use, for example, has been associated with premature birth, physical malformations, respiratory difficulties, lower birth weight, and greater risk of death at birth (Steinhausen, Blattmann, Pfund, 2007; D. Young, 2007). Further, newborns of heroin-addicted mothers become addicted because they have ingested the drug through the placenta since conception. These babies begin their lives suffering withdrawal symptoms. Long-lasting negative effects may result from early exposure to heroin, although the lasting impact of in utero exposure to drugs is still debated (Steinhausen, Blattmann, & Pfund, 2007).

Cocaine use has caused growing concern in recent years. An inexpensive form of this drug, crack, is so accessible that its abuse has become the fastest-growing drug problem in

period of the ovum: The first period of prenatal development, during the first 2 weeks after conception, when the developing human is a rapidly growing shapeless mass of specialized cells.

period of the embryo: The second period of prenatal development, from 2 to 8 weeks after conception, when all major organs and structures of the body are formed.

placenta: A soft mass that allows the flow of nutrients from the mother to the embryo during prenatal development.

umbilical cord: A cord that transports nutrients from the mother to the fetus during prenatal development.

amnion: A protective, fluid-filled sac that forms around the embryo during prenatal development.

period of the fetus: The third period of prenatal development, from 8 weeks after conception to birth, when there is rapid growth and continued development of organs.

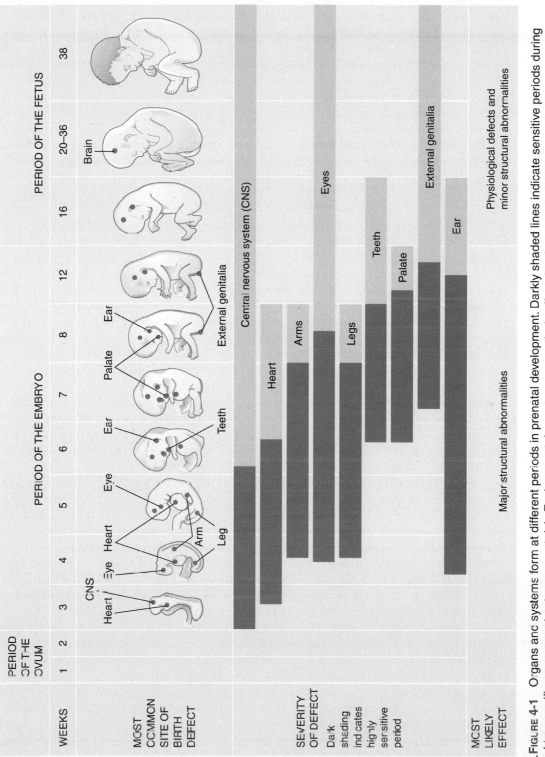

.FIGURE 4-1 Organs and systems form at different periods in prenatal development. Darkly shaded lines indicate sensitive periods during which specific organs or structures are at risk. Environmental agents can negatively affect development during these periods.

SOURCE: Moore, K. L. *Before We Are Born,* 4/e. Copyright © 1993, with permission from Elsevier.

our country. Crack-addicted mothers have a greater chance of miscarriage or premature delivery. Their newborns are more likely to suffer brain damage, low birth weight, and other physical malformations (Covington, Nordstrom-Klee, Ager, Sokol, & Delaney-Black, 2002; Steinhausen et al., 2007). These "crack babies" must suffer withdrawal periods that are significantly longer than those for children born to heroin-using mothers (Anderson & Choonara, 2006; Wallis, 1986).

Mothers who use illegal drugs are more likely to smoke and use alcohol as well, compounding the risk (Friedman & Polifka, 1996). Maternal smoking has been linked to miscarriage, premature delivery, and low birth weight (Edwards & King, 2007; Floyd, Rimer, Giovino, Mullen, & Sullivan, 1993). Even smoking by fathers has been associated with genetic abnormalities and low birth weight, perhaps because mothers living with smoking spouses inhale secondhand smoke (Hofhuis, de Jongste, & Merkus, 2003; Friedman & Polifka, 1996). Evidence suggests that effects of smoking may be long term. Children of smoking mothers have been found to be less responsive, fussier, and more sluggish during infancy and to perform poorly on attention and picture-recognition tasks in the preschool years (Chavkin, 1995; Diaz, 1997). They also have been found to be less competent readers and to have social adjustment problems in later childhood (Fergusson, Horwood, & Lynskey, 1993). In 70% of cases of **sudden infant death syndrome (SIDS)**—a condition that causes healthy babies to suddenly die in their sleep—mothers smoked during pregnancy and after (Hunt & Hauck, 2006; Gordon et al., 2002).

Alcohol use during pregnancy has also been related to physiological difficulties in newborns. Mothers who drink heavily during pregnancy may give birth to babies with **fetal alcohol syndrome,** a condition that can lead to nervous system impairment, mental retardation, hyperactivity, and deficiencies in weight, height, and brain size. Adolescents who were fetally exposed to alcohol are more likely to exhibit learning and adjustment problems (Colburn, 1996). Even one drink a day may have negative effects on fetal development (Mariscal et al., 2006). Most doctors recommend that pregnant women abstain from alcohol completely.

Commonly used over-the-counter or prescription drugs may also threaten prenatal development. Such diverse medications as aspirin, tetracycline, and Valium have been found to lead to complications and health problems. So many drugs are used by some mothers during pregnancy that when fetal problems arise, it is difficult to pinpoint which drug is the cause (Friedman & Polifka, 1996; Robins & Mills, 1993).

Sometimes the effects of drugs are not clearly known for many years. For example, in the case of diethylstilbestrol (DES), a drug prescribed between 1945 and 1970 to prevent miscarriage, no discernible consequences were observed immediately after birth. It was only when the female offspring of mothers who took the drug reached adolescence that its effects became known. The daughters were found to have a higher rate of vaginal cancer and to be more likely to have miscarriages when they became pregnant (Friedman & Polifka, 1996; Rosenblith, 1992). Male offspring of DES users are more likely to have genital abnormalities; whether they have a greater cancer risk is still being debated (Wilcox, Baird, & Weinberg, 1995).

Mothers in poverty are more likely to abuse illegal drugs, probably because of the stress associated with being poor. These mothers obviously have fewer resources and are more likely to be unemployed. They are also more likely to become victims of violence and to live with other persons who abuse drugs. Not surprisingly, poor mothers suffer a higher rate of depression and psychiatric disorders (Petterson & Albers, 2001; Robins & Mills, 1993). Drug abuse may reflect a struggle to find some comfort in a difficult life. Unfortunately, it can have disastrous effects on a developing fetus.

Poor mothers of all cultures abuse drugs. However, mothers of historically underrepresented groups are more likely to use highly addictive drugs, heroin and cocaine in particular. Data have

sudden infant death syndrome (SIDS): A leading cause of death among infants in which a baby stops breathing without cause, usually at night.

fetal alcohol syndrome: A condition caused by a mother's heavy drinking during pregnancy that can lead to nervous system impairment, mental retardation, hyperactivity, and deficiencies in weight, height, and brain size.

also suggested that drug use in large cities is more prevalent among young mothers of color (Anthony & Petronis, 1989). Hence, newborns of poor mothers or those of underrepresented groups are somewhat more likely to suffer the negative effects of in utero drug exposure. These statistics demonstrate a need for enhanced education and prenatal health care, particularly among younger women of these populations. The statistics also suggest that programs to end poverty and support low-income mothers can contribute to positive child development.

A word of caution must be issued about ethnicity, class, and drug use. Just because some forms of substance abuse are more prevalent among those in poverty or those of underrepresented groups does not mean that all, or even many, individuals in these populations use drugs. Among all women of childbearing age, for example, only 5% use cocaine; when women under age 22 are excluded, the rate drops to 3% (Chavkin, 1995; Robins & Mills, 1993). So drug use cannot be considered common in any class or culture.

Nutrition and Health. Poor nutrition and maternal illness can influence fetal development. Because the developing fetus receives nutrients from the mother through the placenta, a malnourished mother is likely to give birth to a malnourished baby. It is a myth that a fetus can miraculously extract needed nutrients from the mother even when she is not eating well. Babies of malnourished mothers are often born prematurely or die soon after birth; those who survive are likely to suffer from low birth weight (Filippi et al., 2006) or cognitive delays later in life (Shenkin, Starr, & Pattie, 2001). This may be due in part to the fact that malnutrition during important periods of fetal brain growth can impede nervous system development. Autopsies have revealed that the brains of stillborn babies of malnourished mothers were smaller and composed of fewer brain cells than those of well-nourished mothers (Goldenberg, 1995).

A growing concern regarding poor maternal diet during pregnancy is that it contributes to childhood obesity (Breier, Vickers, Ikenasio, Chan, & Wong, 2001). **Obesity,** a health problem to be addressed in later chapters, is a condition in which one's body fat exceeds normal levels. This can lead to high blood pressure, heart disease, diabetes and other serious health problems in later life (Reilly et al., 2003). How can a pregnant mother's poor diet lead her child to become obese? If a fetus does not receive adequate nutrients during gestation, physiological changes may occur that cause the body to store fat (McNeely, Fujimoto, Leonetti, Tsai, & Boyko, 2007). Even though the child may be born underweight, a predisposition to fat storage remains throughout life (McNeely et al., 2007; Taylor & Poston, 2007). From this early fetal experience of poor nutrition, the child's body has been programmed to eat as if it were still deficient of nutrients.

Maternal illnesses also can have a serious effect on prenatal development. Rubella—a relatively mild disease for the mother—can cause a range of disorders in the developing fetus, including congenital heart disease, central nervous system disorder, or death (Kleigman, Behrman, Jenson, & Stanton, 2007). Although the damaging effects of rubella have been nearly eradicated in the United States, due to immunization, they persist in underdeveloped countries with poor health care (Robertson, Featherstone, Gacic-Dobo, & Hersh, 2008). The human immunodeficiency virus (HIV), which causes the fatal disease AIDS, can be transmitted from an infected mother to her fetus (Turchi, Duarte, & Martelli, 2008). The virus can even be passed from mother to child through breast milk (Coovadia et al., 2007).

In the United States, newborns of traditionally underrepresented groups may be less healthy than those of Euro-American ancestry. As stated previously, they are more often of low birth weight and are more frequently born prematurely (Kistka et al., 2007; U.S. Department of Health and Human Services, 2008). African American newborns show a greater incidence of general nutritional deficiency; anemia among poor African American and Latino babies is as high as 20% to 40%. Southeast Asian babies also are more often impaired by iron deficiency (Nutritional Status of Minority Children, 2004).

obesity: A condition in which one's body fat exceeds normal levels and can lead to health problems in later life.

Poverty and cultural barriers to health care may lead to poor prenatal development.

These cultural gaps in health status are due primarily to poor prenatal care for some groups (Children's Defense Fund, 2007; Garcia Coll, 1990). A major barrier to adequate health care for many mothers is economic; good nutrition and regular medical visits can be expensive. A number of government programs have been established to address this problem. An example is the WIC program (Special Supplemental Food Program for Women, Infants, and Children), which is designed to provide low-income pregnant mothers with high-protein and iron-fortified foods, nutritional education, counseling, and regular medical evaluation. Research over several decades has shown that the program has had positive effects on families who participate (Buescher & Horton, 2001; Ponza, 2004). Children whose mothers received this prenatal support were found to have advanced cognitive abilities at age 5 (Hicks, Langham, & Takenaka, 1982; Settings, 2006). They were also less likely to be victims of abuse and neglect (Lee & Mackey-Bilaver, 2007).

These findings suggest that such comprehensive social programs are a powerful way to bolster the health status of our nation's children. Unfortunately, the actual cash value of many government programs for children and families has declined in recent decades (Children's Defense Fund, 2007; Ewen & Matthews, 2007). Advocates of young children must regularly remind policymakers that investments now in prenatal health care will lead to long-term savings as children continue to grow and develop in healthy ways throughout their lives. (See the Advocacy and Public Policy box in this chapter for an example of such advocacy.)

There are noneconomic cultural barriers to prenatal care as well. Spanish-speaking pregnant mothers have been found to be reluctant to go to clinics or other medical care facilities where only English is spoken (Clark & Redman, 2007; Torres, 2005). Cultural beliefs and practices create obstacles to health care and social services. John Red Horse (1983) tells a story that illustrates this point:

Margaret was a single, Native American mother with a newborn baby. When she was hospitalized for an extended period with a heart problem, her child was placed in a foster home, and a caseworker was assigned to monitor family needs. Margaret came to be friends with the foster parent over time; in her culture, friendships are like family relationships.

ADVOCACY AND PUBLIC POLICY

Providing Prenatal Care for Immigrant Mothers

As described in this chapter, prenatal care is widely acknowledged as one of the most powerful and cost effective ways to ensure that infants are born healthy and continue to thrive into childhood (Children's Defense Fund, 2007). A variety of state and federal programs are designed to provide such care to all pregnant mothers. More than 80% of mothers in the United States begin to receive prenatal care within the first 3 months of pregnancy.

There is one group living in the United States that may not receive adequate prenatal care: immigrant mothers. These include pregnant women who have entered the country legally or without appropriate documentation. Some citizens and policymakers believe that providing prenatal services to immigrant mothers will strain already tight local and state budgets and will encourage illegal immigration. Recent federal legislation has allowed and even encouraged state and local governments to deny prenatal care to some immigrant mothers and allows states to choose to deny such mothers nutritional benefits from the WIC program, described in this chapter.

It is important to note that this legislation limits publicly funded care for children who, once born, will immediately become U.S. citizens (National Council of State Legislatures, 2004). The net effect of such legislation is relatively straightforward: it denies some children living within the American borders a healthy beginning to life. Although immigration issues are complex and emotionally charged, many teachers and caregivers believe it is important to advocate for prenatal care for all children regardless of their mothers' backgrounds.

Professionals can educate the public about the disastrous effects of poor prenatal care—premature birth, low birth weight, poor brain growth, and a higher rate of infant mortality (Goldenberg, 1995)—through letters to the editor and presentations at public forums. They can lobby state and local policymakers to expand levels of funding for the prenatal care of immigrant mothers—those who are both documented and unauthorized. They might join the national campaign of Children's Health Matters (http://www.childrenshealthmatters.org) to support and extend the federal Immigrant Children's Health Improvement Act, which ensures health coverage for immigrant children and pregnant women. Such advocacy will help ensure that all children born in America begin life well nourished and healthy.

There came a time when Margaret's health had deteriorated and she became preoccupied with her own medical problems. During this period she did not ask to see her baby. Neither the caseworker nor the foster parent took the initiative to arrange for a visit; however, both became angry that Margaret did not demand one. They wondered why she did not wish to see her own child. When Margaret was eventually released from the hospital, she received a hostile greeting from the foster parent and discovered that the caseworker had initiated court action to terminate her parental rights.

Both the caseworker and the foster parent had completely misunderstood Margaret's behavior because they did not understand her culture. In some Native American families, child care is a collective family and community affair. Since the foster mother was like a relative, Margaret had no concern about leaving her child in her care for a long period. She knew her baby would be well taken care of. Margaret, in fact, had wanted very much to see her child; however, demanding to do so was not part of her cultural communication style.

It was only after many interviews that Margaret's motives were finally understood in cultural context and her family life restored.

This story raises an important issue: What would happen if Margaret became pregnant again? This would certainly be a high-risk pregnancy; her health status and low income would suggest a need for rigorous health and nutritional intervention. But after the experience described here, would Margaret be willing to visit a clinic or hospital for prenatal care? Her introduction to Western health care and social service systems nearly led to a disastrous outcome for her family. Lack of cultural sensitivity and understanding by some medical and social service professionals can be a very real barrier to prenatal care (Park, Vincent, & Hastings-Tolsma, 2005).

Teen Pregnancy

It has long been argued that teenage mothers have an increased rate of complications in pregnancy and childbirth because their young bodies are not yet ready to provide for optimal fetal development. One theory is that a young girl's body, which is undergoing a growth spurt itself, will compete with the developing fetus for nutrients. Indeed, babies of teenage mothers may be at risk; they suffer a higher incidence of infant mortality and a greater likelihood of mental deficiencies after birth. It is now believed, however, that these risks are not associated solely with the age of the mother. Teenage mothers are more likely to live in poverty and so have poor medical care and fewer nutritional resources. These factors likely account for many of the problems of fetal development among teenage mothers. When adequate prenatal care is provided, teenage mothers are more similar to older mothers in the outcomes of their pregnancies (Chandra, Schiavello, Ravi, & Weinstein, 2002; Fraser, Brockert, & Ward, 1995).

Teenage pregnancies occur in all cultures and socioeconomic groups (Hyde & Delameter, 1999). However, the newborns of low-income teenage mothers from historically underrepresented populations may be most at risk (Gold, Kennedy, Connell, & Kawachi, 2002). Because poor health care and nutrition are a major threat to fetal development in teenage pregnancy, the economic and cultural barriers to medical and nutritional services for some cultural groups create special problems for poor young mothers and their fetuses.

There has been a decline in the rate of teen pregnancy and related high-risk births in the United States over the last decade. This has been attributed to greater education about human sexuality, birth control, pregnancy, health care, and nutrition (Santelli, Lindberg, Finer, & Singh, 2007). School and community education programs are most effective if provided well before young women are at risk of becoming pregnant. (Potential young fathers also need these programs!) Some experts have advocated extensive health programs in late elementary or early middle school (Rodriguez & Moore, 1995). In addition, culturally sensitive health clinics within middle and high schools and community centers may help break down barriers to prenatal care for teenagers who do become pregnant.

Although teenage pregnancies more often result in medical complications for poor and underrepresented cultural groups, there may be greater support within families for young mothers of these populations. Several generations often live together in families of traditionally oppressed peoples (Costanzo & Hoy, 2007). For example, three to four times as many African American children as Anglo children have grandparents living in their homes (U.S. Bureau of the Census, 2004). Grandparents of historically underrepresented groups have been found to be more involved than their white counterparts in the lives of their grandchildren (Cherlin & Furstenberg, 1986; Simmons & Dye, 2003). Grandmothers in some cultures provide special support in prenatal, perinatal (during birth), and postnatal care (J. L. Pearson, Hunter, Ensminger, & Kellam, 1990). They may guide young mothers in eating well and preparing for childbirth. Teenage mothers and their newborns suffer fewer problems of development when they live with their parents before, during, and after birth (Kalmuss, Namerow, & Cushman, 1991; Pearson et al., 1990). Grandmothers not only contribute support during pregnancy and birthing for their teenage daughters but also play a critical parenting and parent educator role within extended families.

CHILDBIRTH

After 9 months of prenatal development, a series of complex physical reactions takes place, and the birth process begins. Muscular contractions in the mother's body work to thin and open the cervix—the lower part of the uterus—so that the baby can be pushed into the birth canal. Eventually, the baby is expelled through the vagina; soon after, the placenta is expelled as well. There are three distinct stages in the childbirth process, called **labor:** dilation, expulsion of the fetus, and expulsion of the placenta.

The longest stage of labor is *dilation*, in which continuous contractions prepare the cervix for delivery. The contractions begin at regular intervals, perhaps 15 to 20 minutes apart, and become more frequent and intense. The increasing intensity of contractions can cause significant discomfort to the mother. As the cervix dilates, the amnion—the fluid-filled sac surrounding the fetus—ruptures, letting out the fluid. When this occurs, it is said that the mother's *water has broken*.

Contractions continue for an average of 12 to 14 hours for first births and 4 to 6 hours for subsequent deliveries. Near the end of this stage, mothers experience a particularly intense period of labor called *transition*, during which the cervix is stretched around the baby's head.

Expulsion of the fetus is a much shorter stage of labor, usually less than an hour for first births and half an hour for subsequent deliveries. During this stage, the mother experiences the infamous *urge to push*, an involuntary and unrelenting need to push the baby out with abdominal muscles. The mother's pushing, coupled with continued contractions, moves the baby down the birth canal and out of the vagina into the world.

The moment they are born, babies exhale and often begin to cry. Once they are breathing, their dependence on nutrients through the placenta has ended. The umbilical cord is cut and clamped, and they begin their lives independent from the mother's body.

The arrival of a new baby distracts most parents from the shortest and final stage of labor: *expulsion of the placenta*. During the 5- to 10-minute wait for the placenta to detach from the uterine wall and be expelled, new parents are usually holding and caressing their baby. (Perhaps they are also engaging in friendly disputes about family resemblances and name choices!) The entire birthing process is illustrated in Figure 4-2.

Western Childbirth Procedures

Modern technology has given rise to a set of standard medical procedures used frequently in hospital births in Western societies. These include the fetal monitor, which measures fetal heart rate and detects distress, and anesthesia, medication to ease the mother's discomfort. During many Western births, an episiotomy is performed just before the expulsion of the fetus. This involves making a small incision in the vagina to avoid tearing during delivery. *Forceps* are sometimes used to assist in difficult labors during the expulsion of the fetus; these are large metal tongs that are fitted around the newborn's head to gently ease the baby from the birth canal. A *vacuum extractor*—a device that pulls the baby from the birth canal by applying a suction to the scalp—is being employed more frequently, as it is believed to be safer for the newborn. In some instances, a *cesarean section* is performed, in which the newborn is surgically removed from the uterus through the abdomen. The usual reason for a cesarean is fetal distress, although some physicians routinely perform these for mothers who have previously given birth in this manner.

Concern has been raised about whether some of these procedures are needed. There is some evidence that anesthesia or forcep deliveries can lead to complications after birth (Brockington, 1996; Lurie, Glezerman, & Sadan, 2005). The use of a fetal monitor may result in more cesareans, as medical personnel may misread typical fluctuations in heart rate as signs of distress (Quilligan, 1995). This is a problem because a cesarean is major

labor: The process of giving birth, which occurs in three stages: dilation, birth of the baby, and expulsion of the placenta.

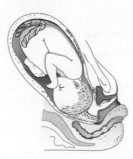

a. Lightening

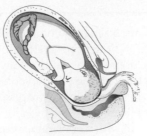

b. Contractions and breaking of the bag of waters

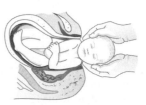

c. Dilation of the cervix

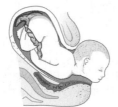

d. Visible head. Beginning of birth.

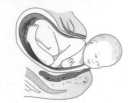

e. Delivering the head

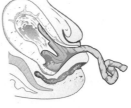

f. Delivering the shoulders

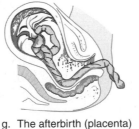

g. The afterbirth (placenta)

h. Expelling afterbirth

FIGURE 4-2   Labor and delivery advance in steps. Labor involves processes shown in views a, b, and c. The stages of birth are shown in views d through f.

SOURCE: Schiamberg, L. B. (1988). *Child and Adolescent Development*. Upper Saddle River, NJ: Macmillian. Reprinted by permission.

abdominal surgery that carries risks and may greatly impede the mother's recovery and ability to parent during the period directly following birth. These concerns have led some parents to demand more natural approaches to childbirth.

The **natural childbirth** movement has flourished in the United States during the past few decades. More and more parents are asking that birthing be comfortable, family oriented, and nonmedical. A number of specific "innovations" have found their way into American hospitals, many of which have actually been practiced in many cultures for centuries. Western hospitals are now providing *birthing rooms*—cozy, homelike spaces where mothers and family members can feel more at ease during the birth process. Most have adopted policies that allow—and often encourage—fathers to observe and participate in labor and delivery (Wilcock, Kobayashi, & Murray, 1997). A major goal of natural childbirth is to avoid the use of drugs during labor. These home-like birthing practices have been found to reduce the number of medical interventions and to increase the satisfaction of parents with the birthing process (Hodnett, Downe, Edwards, & Walsh, 2008).

natural childbirth: The process of giving birth in a comfortable, family-oriented, and nonmedical way while avoiding the use of drugs.

Two physicians whose writings have directly influenced natural childbirth practices in this country are Ferdinand Lamaze and Frederick Leboyer. Lamaze (1958) first introduced the notion that mothers be prepared for birth through education and exercise. He suggested a series of breathing techniques to use during labor that would relax and focus the mother, oxygenate the baby, and reduce discomfort without the use of drugs. He also was one of the earliest Western writers to advocate that fathers or other companions play a key role in the birth process. Leboyer (1975) was most concerned about treatment of the newborn immediately after birth. He noted that delivery rooms were traditionally loud and bright and proposed dimming lights, reducing sound, and providing newborns with warm baths and much skin-to-skin contact with parents.

Many of these ideas resemble childbirth beliefs and traditions of non-Western cultures or those of earlier eras. Some of these recent natural childbirth trends, however, are still quite Western in flavor. Anthropologist Brigitt Jordan (1993) has noted that in the United States, male doctors usually make key decisions in the process, even in natural deliveries, whereas "giving birth in most societies is women's business" (p. 3). (It is interesting that two male physicians are the pioneers in modern birthing practice in Western society!) The vast majority of natural births still take place in hospitals in the United States and in many European countries; this is not the case in most other societies (Declercq, Sakala, Corry, & Applebaum, 2007).

Childbirth Across Cultures

Every culture has specific beliefs and practices regarding bringing new babies into the world. Although an astounding variety of childbirth methods exist, all cultures provide a common set of processes and supports that are needed to ensure a healthy and joyous delivery (Jordan, 1993).

Childbirth Support. In all cultures, some person (or persons) is responsible for educating the new mother and supporting her through the birth process. The background and training of support persons vary, depending on how a particular culture defines the birth event (Jordan, 1993). For example, in the United States, childbirth is most often considered a medical process, so physicians or medically trained practitioners support the mother. In other cultures, nonmedical personnel are primary supports. These may include nonspecialists such as family members, neighbors, or friends. The United States is one of the few countries in the world where nonfamily, nonmedical support persons have not been regularly included in the birth process (Declercq et al., 2007). However, this trend is changing.

In many cultures, births are attended by **midwives,** childbirth specialists (usually women) who, by virtue of their own experience and perhaps some medical training, have been assigned this role in the community. In the Yucatán, midwives are responsible for assisting with almost all births. Midwives are well respected in Yucatán towns, as Jordan (1993) describes: "There is no particular deference in her interactions with medical doctors. She acknowledges their expertise in certain areas...but she is also aware of her own special expertise" (p. 14). Other support persons are always present during delivery in the Yucatán: the mother and father, family members, neighbors, and friends of the woman giving birth. These individuals come and go during labor, taking turns providing support.

In South Africa, midwives and doctors are often joined in births at home or the hospital by additional trained *childbirth companions*. These professionals are assigned solely to meet the mother's emotional needs. They offer praise, comfort, support, and advocacy during labor and delivery and remain constantly with the mother, when medical staff are required to leave. Mothers who are supported by these companions report more positive birthing experiences and less harsh treatment by doctors or midwives (Brown, Hofmeyr, Nikodem, Smith, & Garner, 2007).

A growing number of American births include a midwife, although attending physicians generally maintain direct control over the process (Kennedy, Shannon, Chuahorm, & Kravetz, 2004). In some subcultures of the United States, childbirth support comes

midwives: Childbirth specialists generally not relatives or doctors—who provide emotional and physical support to mothers during labor and delivery.

In all cultures, there is a person who is responsible for educating a new mother and supporting her through the birth process.

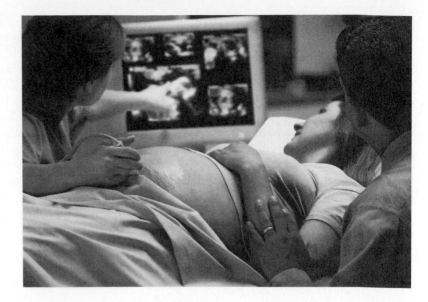

exclusively from family or community members because of a lack of resources. Onnie Lee Logan (1991), a "granny midwife" in Mobile, Alabama, until 1984, delivered countless babies in her low-income African American community without any medical support because none was available: "Let me tell you about white doctors at this time. I don't think they paid too much attention to black families then, because the spirit of white people didn't go out for the black people. They didn't care" (p. 56). In this case, a non-medical childbirth support system emerged in the community as a result of poverty and prejudice. It appears to have been an effective system; since granny midwifery was outlawed in Alabama in 1984, maternal and infant death rates have climbed in the state (Logan, 1991). One reason could be that mothers in rural towns are now required to drive hours to reach hospitals for obstetric care.

Childbirth Education and Preparation. All societies have some provision for preparing mothers for childbirth, although the length and nature of this preparation vary. In the United States, preparation for childbirth is formal and extensive. Not only do obstetricians and hospitals provide education, but many families participate in Lamaze classes or other programs of childbirth preparation. In these classes, mothers are taught about nutrition and the physical stages of labor. They practice breathing exercises that will assist with the discomfort of contractions. Education is critical, according to Lamaze (1958), because knowledge of the process reduces fear and helps the mother relax during labor. Fathers or other birthing coaches are sometimes trained in childbirth classes as well. Such childbirth classes are attended primarily by middle-class parents. Twenty percent of pregnant mothers in the United States—primarily those in poverty—receive no childbirth preparation (or prenatal care) at all (Klerman, 2000; Park et al., 2005; Wilcock et al., 1997).

In the Yucatán, childbirth preparation is brief and informal. It usually takes place during labor (Jordan, 1993). This may be partly because of a belief that childbirth is necessarily frightening and painful. Extensive preparation aimed at convincing mothers otherwise would be pointless. In fact, women come to believe, through stories passed down for generations, that pain is an expected and normal part of bringing children into the world—the experience that sets women apart from men. Fathers are encouraged to attend the delivery, primarily to appreciate the suffering required to bring a child into the world.

The Yucatán midwife may make several prelabor visits to the pregnant mother to ascertain the due date and give a *sobada*—a soothing abdominal massage. However, most instructions about birthing are given during childbirth itself. Lessons are provided by all in attendance: midwife, family, friends, or neighbors; no one person is solely responsible for informing parents about what is occurring.

When Onnie Lee Logan (1991) practiced midwifery in Mobile, virtually no formal childbirth preparation was available for poor African American families. Granny midwives, when available, provided informal childbirth preparation methods: "In those days I had to go out and have a meetin' with 'em befo' I delivered their baby. When they engage you that they wanted you to deliver their baby, you in turns would have to make from two to three trips to visit that mother to outline things, to see how the situation was goin' on, and to he'p her make preparations" (p. 92). Midwives' preparations went far beyond birthing education, however: "When they go on a delivery, they didn't just go on a delivery. They do the cookin' and washin'. It wasn't so much the midwifin'. They was there to he'p with everything they could" (p. 52).

Childbirth Procedures. Delivery practices also vary by culture. In a typical American birth, parents are provided with a pleasant, homelike birthing room in a hospital where they stay throughout labor and delivery (Wilcock et al., 1997). This is in contrast to earlier practice, when mothers were moved from a labor room into a sterile, bright delivery room to give birth. Today, the typical American mother strives to take as few medications as possible during labor, although some do request anesthesia if contractions become too painful. Others receive Pitocin, a drug to stimulate labor, if the cervix is not dilating quickly. American hospitals place a great value on speed of delivery. Doctors often administer Pitocin after what would be judged a very short period of time in some cultures (Jordan, 1993).

During labor, the mother is accompanied by a *coach*. This is usually the father, although sometimes it is a childbirth educator or friend. Hospitals usually limit the number of persons in attendance. The coach guides the mother in breathing exercises during contractions and serves as an advocate. During the birth itself, mothers are often asked to assume the flat-on-the-back *lithotomy* position. The United States is the only country in the world where mothers historically have been asked to lie down to give birth (Roberts & Hanson, 2007). Many hospitals now use birthing chairs or allow the mother to squat (Wilcock et al., 1997).

During birth, an *episiotomy* is likely to be performed, and forceps or a vacuum extractor may be used. These practices may be other signs of time urgency on the part of American medical personnel (Jordan, 1993). In many cultures, such procedures are virtually never performed. Delivery takes longer in those communities, but healthy babies are born.

After birth, American parents are allowed a bonding period with the newborn that lasts from 20 minutes to an hour. The baby is then taken to the hospital nursery, examined, and washed. A number of medical procedures are followed. Many American hospitals now allow rooming-in, in which the mother (and usually the father) may keep the baby with her or him in the hospital room. When parents sleep, the newborn is usually returned to the nursery.

In the Yucatán, mothers give birth in their own homes surrounded by neighbors and family and a community midwife. A blanket screen is provided for privacy, but this does not isolate the mother completely from the ongoing activities of the household. The mother is in control of decision making during labor and delivery; attendants are there only to support her. Medications are not administered to control pain, nor are breathing or relaxation techniques used. Mothers are taught to accept that childbirth is painful and are expected to express their discomfort in an outpouring of emotion.

At the time of delivery, the Yucatán mother lies semi-upright in a hammock. In most societies, mothers are upright in delivery; this position is reportedly more comfortable, and the baby is expelled more easily (Jordan, 1993). During delivery, one of the support persons is positioned at the mother's head so she can wrap her arms around this person for comfort and support. Other attendants gather around her. The midwife assists in the delivery, easing the baby out after the head has appeared. No modern tools or technology are used. Occasionally, the midwife will bring medical instruments, such as a thermometer, a suction for mucus, or surgical scissors, to cut the umbilical. The midwife never performs episiotomies or forcep deliveries.

After birth, the Yucatán midwife does not treat the newborn in a particularly delicate way. The baby is passed from person to person, and the grandmother often holds and caresses the baby while the midwife sponges the mother. The baby stays with the family from this time on. Any formal medical evaluations are conducted within the family's home by a visiting physician or nurse (Jordan, 1993).

Onnie Lee Logan's (1991) midwife experiences were similar. With no medical instruments, medications, or medical personnel in attendance, childbirth among the poor in Mobile was natural by necessity. Birthing often took place in homes with no running water or heat. Usually, the mother and her own mother attended. The father was only occasionally involved. During labor, the granny midwife's role was one of giving emotional support: "I'll tell you one thing that's very impo'tant that I do that the doctors don't do and the nurses doesn't do because they doesn't take time to do it. And that is I'm with my patients at all times with a smile and keepin' her feelin' good with kind words" (p. 32).

The childbirth techniques Logan describes, which were passed down from her mother, are only now finding their way into modern obstetric practice in hospitals: "During labor I keep them on their feet where in the hospital they buckle them down. I'd let my mother stay on her feet until she'd have to lay down" (Logan, 1991, p. 141). About episiotomies, Logan writes, "I do all my work keepin' 'em from having lacerations and havin' to have stitches. That doctor would've took her in there and give her a long laceration to get the baby" (p. 142). Logan's strategy was to apply hot compresses, a technique that "I didn't get in class at the bo'd of health neither. It was given to me by God...and they dilate so good without me doin' any lacerations at all" (p. 142).

Logan writes about the advantages of an upright birthing position and hints at why the flat-on-the-back method is so popular among obstetricians: "There are so many women that want to have babies in that sittin' position. It's not unusual. It feels good. The mother gets mo' relief. Now it might not be mo' relief for you but it will be for her" (1991, p. 151). After birth, Logan's babies would stay with their parents at home. However, the poor conditions of the family residence were often cause for concern. She would clean the house and stoke the woodstove and even tear sheets to use as baby blankets if the family had none.

Sometimes Logan found herself playing unusual roles to support the newborn and the family. On one cold morning after a birth, representatives of a stove company arrived to repossess a woodstove—the family's only source of heat. Thankfully, she was there to intervene: "I said, 'You move that stove outa here I'm gonna have you arrested....This lil infant just been born.... I'm gonna have you arrested for takin' all the heat from these po' people that they got" (1991, p. 107). The men agreed to leave the stove and return when the weather was warmer.

SUMMARY

Following a complex set of biological processes, children inherit genes from their parents that contain information about all kinds of human characteristics. Physical, social, and even emotional traits can be passed along through these genes; however, genetics alone does not explain how children turn out. Individual experience, culture, health, and nutrition play a role. Environmental hazards or genetic disorders can impede positive development.

The childbirth process itself can influence what children will be like. A healthy birthing experience can lead to positive outcomes; complications at birth can threaten children's well-being. Birthing practices vary across cultures. However, in almost all societies, childbirth is a joyful experience in which the mother receives preparation and education prior to delivery and much support during childbirth.

RESEARCH INTO PRACTICE

CRITICAL CONCEPT 1

Child development begins long before birth. Genetic information is passed on from ancestors through a miraculous series of chemical processes.

Application: Accept and appreciate some differences in temperament, physical growth, sociability, and intellectual competence as part of individual children's biological inheritance.

CRITICAL CONCEPT 2

Genetics alone does not explain how children will turn out; the environment and culture play important roles.

Application   Recognize variations in development that are due to unique cultural experiences. Such traits as social competence, temperament, learning style, and even performance in school may be the result of cultural beliefs and histories. Accept and celebrate these variations in the classroom.

CRITICAL CONCEPT 3

Hereditary diseases can threaten healthy development. Some genetic disorders, such as sickle-cell anemia and Tay-Sachs disease, are more prevalent in certain cultural groups.

Application #1   Recommend prenatal genetic tests, such as amniocentesis or chorionic villus biopsy (to be described in the next chapter) for parents in high-risk cultural groups. Findings of these tests can determine the presence of disorders.

Application #2   Recommend genetic counseling for parents of high-risk families. In such counseling, professionals help parents determine the odds of transmitting genetic diseases to their offspring. Such counseling can also prepare parents whose developing fetus has been diagnosed with genetic disorders.

CRITICAL CONCEPT 4

Prenatal development occurs in three distinct stages—the periods of the ovum, embryo, and fetus. Environmental conditions, such as drug use, poor maternal health and nutrition, and teen pregnancy, can negatively influence development in each of these stages.

Application #1   Urge mothers to abstain from alcohol, tobacco, and other drugs during pregnancy. Even common over-the-counter or prescription drugs should not be used without guidance from a physician.

Application #2   Encourage mothers to eat healthy foods during pregnancy. The developing fetus acquires nutrients directly from the mother's diet. A poorly nourished mother will give birth to a poorly nourished baby.

Application #3   Advocate for greater public funding for prenatal care for all mothers—even those of unauthorized immigrant status.

Application #4   Assist low-income and teenage mothers in accessing adequate health care and nutritional services during pregnancy. They should maintain relationships with the local WIC office and other social service agencies that provide prenatal care and support.

CRITICAL CONCEPT 5

For certain cultural groups, prenatal development and childbirth are influenced by barriers to medical care.

Application #1   Advocate for adequate and culturally sensitive health care and nutritional services for pregnant mothers.

Application #2   Help medical personnel to be sensitive to alternative medical beliefs and practices among cultural groups, including diverse childbirth preparation and practices.

Application #3   Help medical personnel to be sensitive to the anxieties and unique emotional needs of pregnant mothers of diverse cultural backgrounds.

Application #4   Encourage medical institutions to provide personnel who can speak the native languages of families in the community.

Application #5   Encourage professionals and family members to accompany pregnant women on health care visits or during delivery.

CRITICAL CONCEPT 6

The childbirth process itself can influence growth of the newborn. Birthing practices vary across cultures. However, in almost all societies, childbirth is a joyful experience in which the mother receives preparation and education prior to delivery and much support during childbirth.

Application #1   Help parents and families to become knowledgeable about the birthing process. Childbirth preparation classes or other childbirth education activities are important. Most societies have some form of birthing preparation.

Application #2   Help families to arrange for support during labor and delivery to assist the mother physically and emotionally. In most societies, a spouse, parent, friend, or village midwife attends the birth of a child.

Application #3   Help families who wish to give birth without the use of drugs to learn and use Lamaze techniques or other relaxation and natural pain reduction methods. These will reduce the need for medication during labor and delivery.

CHAPTER 5

The Newborn

GUIDING QUESTIONS

1. What are the physical characteristics of newborns, and what are their patterns of growth during the first few weeks of life?
2. What are the characteristics and cultural variations of newborn psychological states?
3. Why is sleeping important for a newborn, and what causes variations in sleeping patterns?
4. What are the developmental benefits of alert and waking states, and how do these vary across cultures?
5. Why is newborn crying critical for development, and how should caregivers and parents respond to it?
6. What are the benefits of breastfeeding to babies in both industrialized and underdeveloped countries?
7. What are reflexes, and how are they important for infant development, parent–child relationships, and health care?
8. What is habituation, and how can it be useful in studying newborns' knowledge and abilities?
9. How are special needs identified in newborns, and what are some of their causes?
10. How do prematurity and low birth weight affect newborn development across cultures and socioeconomic levels?
11. What is sudden infant death syndrome, and what steps can be taken to protect newborns from this condition?

This chapter examines the characteristics and development of newborn babies. During the first few weeks after birth—sometimes called the **neonatal period**—infants have a unique look, sound, and feel. They are more helpless, fragile, and dependent than they will ever be again. Their needs for nurturance and sustenance seem endless. Some new parents are not fully prepared for life with a neonate, as the following story illustrates:

Yolanda, a 16-year-old, is about to become a new mother. Throughout her pregnancy and during a rough labor and delivery, all she can think about is how wonderful her life will be as a parent. Her son will be the smartest, happiest baby, she asserts. He will love her and care for her as he gets older; she is his mother! Her friends will come by to admire him as he smiles and coos. She and her son will play games and spend all waking hours outside of school together.

When Yolanda is discharged from the hospital, she goes to her parents' home, where she and her son will live until she finishes high school. On the first day out of the hospital, her son just sleeps. She is disappointed that he is not awake and playful. She wants him to get to know her; she wants to tickle, rock, and hold him. These are the things that mothers and babies should do together, she thinks. However, he just sleeps. "Don't worry, girl. You'll have plenty of time to be together," her mother says with a knowing look.

neonatal period: A developmental period during the first few weeks after birth when babies have a unique appearance and are more helpless, fragile, and dependent than they will ever be again.

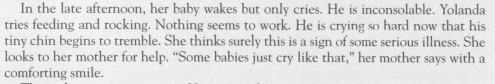

In the late afternoon, her baby wakes but only cries. He is inconsolable. Yolanda tries feeding and rocking. Nothing seems to work. He is crying so hard now that his tiny chin begins to tremble. She thinks surely this is a sign of some serious illness. She looks to her mother for help. "Some babies just cry like that," her mother says with a comforting smile.

The nighttime is even worse. Her son awakens many times. By morning, Yolanda is tired, worried, and disbelieving that this is now her life. The romantic images of motherhood have vanished. Then her son gazes into her eyes as she feeds him. Holding her warm little son somehow makes up for all the hours of anxiety and fatigue.

This young mother has learned that newborns have unique needs and dispositions. Their repertoire of play activities is limited; they mostly sleep, cry, and eat. As this mother found out, life with a newborn is a challenging yet emotionally satisfying experience.

PHYSICAL CHARACTERISTICS OF NEWBORNS

Newborn babies are quite striking in appearance. They are remarkably small. Great poets and essayists have for centuries attempted to capture in rhyme and verse the absolute tininess of newborns—their minuscule fingers and toes and their delicate, wee bodies. The sheer smallness of a newborn can be quite startling to unprepared parents. Some perfectly healthy babies can weigh as little as 5 pounds, so small they can be held in one hand!

Many newborns have puffy facial features right after birth; their eyes may look particularly swollen. One parent who is fond of sports analogies suggested that his newborn baby looked like a prizefighter who had just gone 12 rounds. This puffiness is due to fluids accumulating in the head when the baby assumed a head-down position before and during delivery. The puffiness fades in the first few days after birth.

Contributing to the newborn's interesting appearance is a condition called *molding*, in which the head is squeezed and sometimes misshaped during the trip through the mother's relatively small birth canal. Some babies' heads are so distorted in the process that parents become alarmed. However, their heads resume a typical rounded shape within the first few days after birth. How can this squeezing occur without causing damage to the newborn? Before and after birth, babies' bones consist mainly of cartilage and so are very soft. A newborn's head also has an open space between the bone tissue called the *fontanelle*. This allows the baby's head to safely compress during birth. Babies whose heads are even an inch or two larger than the mother's pelvis can be born without complication.

At birth, newborns are often covered with a white, waxy substance called vernix caseosa. This is secreted from glands around hair follicles and forms a protective coating and lubricant that smooths the baby's passage down the birth canal.

The body of the newborn is oddly proportioned. The relative size of neonatal body parts reveals growth patterns that will guide development throughout early childhood. One of these growth patterns is the **cephalocaudal growth gradient,** which refers to the tendency of human development to proceed from the top down. Infants' and children's heads and brains grow more rapidly than their legs and feet. Nowhere is this more obvious than in the newborn. At birth, babies' heads are disproportionately huge. Because of this, when parents hold newborns, they must give careful support to the head, which wobbles on less-than-well-developed neck muscles. The top-heaviness of newborns as compared with older children and adults is illustrated in Figure 5-1.

Another growth pattern that is obvious in the newborn is the **proximodistal growth gradient,** which refers to a growth trend that proceeds from the center of the body out. Infants' and children's trunks develop more rapidly than their appendages; large movements precede the refined use of fingers or toes. Newborns' potbellied appearance is due to this proximodistal pattern. Their trunks and internal organs grow most rapidly, while their legs, arms, hands, and feet remain relatively small and less developed.

The way newborns look may play a critical role in their development. Their tiny, disproportionate features suggest helplessness and vulnerability, which could prompt human parents to nurture and protect them. Lorenz (1971) has proposed that "babyish features"

cephalocaudal growth gradient: The tendency for human development to proceed from the top down so that infants' and children's heads and brains grow more rapidly than their legs and feet.

proximodistal growth gradient: The tendency for human development to proceed from the center of the body out so that infants' and children's trunks develop more rapidly than their appendages and large movements precede the refined use of fingers or toes.

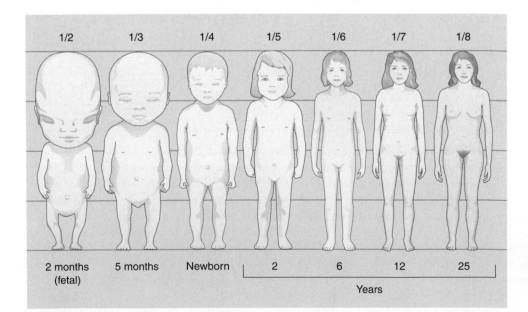

FIGURE 5-1 The cephalocaudal growth gradient—the tendency to develop from the top down—is obvious in the body proportions of newborns, children, and adults.
SOURCE: Schiamberg, L. B. (1988). *Child and Adolescent Development.* Upper Saddle River, NJ. Macmillan. Reprinted by permission.

trigger a "nurturing impulse" in both human and nonhuman adults. His theory is stated most pragmatically by an exhausted father who had been up all night with his crying newborn: "She was asleep, then she was awake. Asleep, awake. If she hadn't been quite so cute, I never would have put myself through this ordeal."

NEWBORN PSYCHOLOGICAL STATES

Newborns engage in a relatively limited number of activities during their first days of life; they watch the world go by, cry on occasion, and sleep a great deal. These various experiences have been categorized into what child specialists call **psychological states** (Ingersoll & Thoman, 1999; Peirano, Algarín, & Uauy, 2003), which are listed in Table 5-1.

Each is described in relation to how aroused and alert the infant is. As can be seen in the table, three of these are sleeping states. How much time newborns spend in specific states and how rapidly, predictably, and good-naturedly they shift from one state to another will vary from one infant to another. Significant differences in infant state patterns exist across cultures.

Sleeping

Newborns spend a significant portion of their lives sleeping. Excited first-time parents or grandparents, eager to get to know a little newcomer, will express disappointment at how few waking hours there are to talk or play. In the first weeks of life, a baby may sleep between 16 and 20 hours in each 24-hour period (Ingersoll & Thoman, 1999; Peirano et al., 2003). Unfortunately for tired parents, these hours of sleep are not continuous; in fact, new babies

psychological states: Distinct categories of newborn experience or activity, such as sleeping or crying, that vary according to how aroused or alert the infant is.

TABLE 5-1
Newborn Psychological States

State	Characteristics
Sleep	Newborns' eyes are closed. They are not aroused or stimulated by moderate noise or other sensations. Newborns are in a sleep state for the vast majority of a 24-hour period.
Regular sleep	Newborns exhibit no movements; their eyes are still. Breathing is regular, slow, and quiet.
REM sleep	Newborns twitch, whimper, and grimace. Their eyes can be seen moving beneath closed lids. The brain is particularly active during this state.
Drowsiness	Newborns are in a state between sleep and wakefulness. They are still and quiet; their eyes open and close. They can be roused into full wakefulness by stimulation. Newborns are often in this state before sleep.
Alert	Newborns are quiet and attentive to stimuli. They intensely study persons and objects around them. It is believed that in this state newborns come to learn about their world.
Awake and active	Newborns are highly active. They flail their limbs and turn their heads in gross, global movements. It is believed that in this state newborns acquire motor abilities.
Crying	Newborns emit loud, distressing sounds. They flail limbs; their faces are often contorted. Different cries have been identified—those that communicate hunger, pain, and anger.

usually take brief naps of about 4 hours, followed by periods of wakefulness. Needless to say, full nights of sleep are a thing of the past for parents of newborns.

Sleep may be one way that infants take breaks from the barrage of overwhelming stimuli in their new worlds. In several studies, researchers found that infant stress is reduced during sleep (Larson, White, Cochran, Donzella, & Gunnar, 1998; Watamura, Donzella, Kertes, & Gunnar, 2004). Babies in this research were found to have less cortisol—a chemical produced under stressful conditions—in their saliva following nap times. (Interestingly, this lower level of cortisol was also found in babies after long car rides even if they did not sleep during the trip.) Environmental conditions that prohibit sleep, such as loud noise or a lack of adequate space or time for naps in child care, may put young babies at risk.

As infants get older, they tend to sleep for longer continuous periods and remain awake for more extended intervals as well. By 6 or 7 months, many babies begin sleeping for a full night. Not all infants are aware that this is how they are to behave, however; my son, for example, did not quite master the art of sleeping through the night until age 5! In fact, an *average* infant may not truly exist with regard to sleep patterns. Tremendous individual variation in sleeping routines exists within all cultures (Sadeh, Raviv, & Gruber, 2000). Some children sleep for long periods right after birth; some sleep infrequently, even into childhood.

What causes sleep pattern variation? Babies may be born with biological clocks that regulate cycles of eating and sleeping. Evidence of this comes from studies showing that day–night rhythms can be identified in early infancy and remain constant through the first year of life (Ingersoll & Thoman, 1999; Peirano et al., 2003). These variations have also been found to be related to such diverse factors as birth weight, the frequency and kind of parent–child interactions, and even the age of the mother.

Another source of variation in newborn sleep patterns is culture. Parents of diverse ethnic backgrounds adopt very different practices in regard to sleeping arrangements. In many families in Africa, India, Okinawa, the Philippines, and Mexico, for example, babies sleep with a mother or grandmother for more than a year after birth (Whiting & Edwards, 1988). Mayan infants often sleep with their mothers into the second year of life (Morelli, Rogoff, Oppenheim, & Goldsmith, 2002). This is true of several underrepresented ethnic groups within the United States as well (Bornstein, 1995; Germo, Chang, Keller, & Goldberg, 2007). Some Appalachian children sleep with their parents until age 2, for example (Stein, 2001), and Korean American children sometimes sleep with their mothers until age 5 (Owens, 2004; Yang, & Hahn, 2002). Although these sleeping practices are sometimes misunderstood by people of Euro-American cultures, they are quite typical of other cultural groups around the world. Sleeping situations may have an impact on infant sleep–wake patterns. Infants who sleep next to their mothers, for example, may have their needs for comfort or hunger met immediately without significant arousal from sleep (Morelli et al., 2002). Those who sleep in another room or whose parents hold back from responding to nighttime crying may be more likely to be aroused from sleep.

As shown in Table 5-1, infants experience several different sleep states. Perhaps the most fascinating and puzzling of these is irregular sleep, during which **rapid eye movement (REM)** occurs. REM sleep is one of life's great mysteries. In this sleep state, the brain is especially active; adults often dream during REM. Infants in REM sleep twitch, whimper, and grimace, while in regular sleep they are passive and motionless. Even more mysterious is the fact that babies are in REM sleep for much longer periods than adults; more than 30% of a newborn's life is spent in this sleep state (Peirano et al., 2003; Whitney & Thoman, 1994).

Why do babies spend so much time in REM sleep? The *autostimulation theory* holds that REM sleep exercises the nervous system. Newborns need stimulation but spend very little time awake; therefore, their brains provide much-needed internal stimulation while they are in REM sleep. Research supports this theory. When babies spend more time awake, their REM sleep periods have been found to be reduced (Boismier, 2004).

rapid eye movement (REM) sleep: An important sleep state in which infants spend more time than adults and where the brain is especially active. This state may provide needed exercise for the newborn's nervous system.

Alert and Waking Activity States

Most child psychologists agree that **alert and waking states** are most critical for infant development. It is during these periods that babies explore their world and exercise their senses and motor abilities. One argument for soothing crying babies very quickly is that in calmer waking states they are able to learn more about their new world and the people in it (Colombo, 1993; Dearing, McCartney, Marshall, & Warner, 2001). To spend useful time in alert and waking states, then, babies must be able to soothe themselves or be soothed by parents when they are upset. Infants who are in a crying state for inordinate amounts of time or who are easily drawn from quiet, alert activity to extreme upset may not benefit from the same level of cognitive and social stimulation.

The length of time babies spend in waking and alert states and their ability to return to these states quickly after upset vary across cultures (Tronick, 2007). Biological factors as well as differences in parenting practices may account for these variations. Chinese American, Japanese American, Puerto Rican, and Navajo infants have been found to spend particularly long periods of time in quiet, alert states (Bornstein, 2002; Chisholm, 1989; Garcia Coll, Meyer, & Brillon, 1995). Infants of these ethnic groups have also been found to be more easily soothed or better able to console themselves when upset, and they are less easily perturbed when alert and active.

In one study, babies of diverse backgrounds were presented with a variety of objects, pictures, and sounds. Puerto Rican babies were more alert when these stimuli were presented. They could more easily follow the direction of both moving objects and sounds. In contrast to other subjects in the study, Puerto Rican babies virtually never cried even when stimulation was increased (Garcia Coll, Surrey, & Weingarten, 1998). In other research, Caucasian newborns have been found to be more easily perturbed and excitable, Chinese babies to be less so, and African American babies to spend more time than babies of other cultural groups in motor activities during waking states (Garcia Coll et al., 1998; Kagan et al., 1994; Tronik, 2007).

What is the importance of these cultural comparisons? Differences in infant state may explain why parents of different cultures interact with their babies in different ways. Navajo children are quiet and alert much of the time, and their parents are passive and less verbal in their interactions with them (Chisholm, 1989; Garcia Coll et al., 1998). Euro-American babies may become upset more easily during waking periods; mothers of these cultural groups are found to respond more quickly and often to crying and fussiness (Richman, Miller, & Levine, 1992; Wade, Black, & Ward-Smith, 2005). African American babies are more motorically active during waking hours, and their mothers spend much time in physical play with them (Garcia Coll et al., 1998; Hale, 1994). Adults must strive for a good fit between these unique state patterns and their interactions with babies.

Crying

Crying is the universal way that babies communicate their needs. Adults of both genders, of all ages, and of all cultural groups—whether or not they have children of their own—become troubled or agitated by infant crying (LaGasse, Neal, & Lester, 2005; Wood, & Gustafson, 2001; Zeskind, Klein, & Marshall, 1992). Even newborn babies become upset at the cries of other infants (Dondi, Simion, & Caltran, 1999). It may be that concern about crying is a part of human biological heritage.

Several decades ago, it was believed that parents could accurately determine what their baby was communicating through crying. Unique cries to communicate hunger, anger, pain, and a need for attention were identified by parents and researchers (Wolff, 1969). However, parents may have been relying more on context than the features of crying to determine

alert and waking states:
States in which newborns are attentive and can explore their world and exercise their senses and motor abilities.

Crying is a universal way that newborns communicate needs. How parents respond to crying varies across cultures.

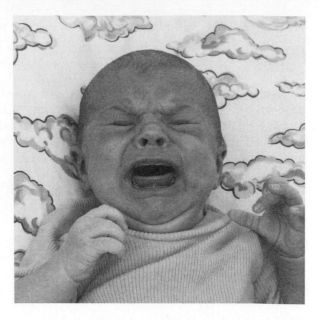

what babies need. When an infant hasn't eaten in a long while and cries, a parent is likely to accurately guess that hunger is the problem. In one study, when parents were played a tape recording of various infant cries, they were far less able to identify which needs were being communicated (Gustafson, Wood, & Green, 2000). What parents can do very well is distinguish their own infant's cries from those of other infants (Holden, 1988). They can also very accurately distinguish urgent cries, which are loud and long, from less urgent ones (Bellieni, Sisto, Cordelli, Buonocore, 2004; Gustafson et al, 2000; Zeskind et al., 1992).

How do parents respond to infant cries? Parents in all cultures take action in some way when their babies are upset. The outdated belief that responding too often to babies' cries will spoil them has been refuted by research. In a classic study by Bell and Ainsworth (1972), children were actually found to cry less in the second 6 months of life if their mothers responded consistently during the first 6 months. These authors suggest there may be a later payoff for early responsive parenting.

Perhaps the most fascinating finding of this research was that infants of responsive mothers were more advanced in communication abilities at age 1. This finding supports the notion that crying is communication; if mothers respond to cries, their babies may more often experience the power of vocalization. This research has led some professionals to urge parents to always respond to babies' cries quickly. However, this formula for infant care may be too simple. Bell and Ainsworth (1972) reported great variation within their responsive parent group in regard to how quickly and by what method mothers soothed their babies. Some mothers were immediate in picking babies up or feeding them; others waited a few minutes to respond. Their babies all cried less and communicated more effectively at age 1.

In a follow-up study, van Ijzendoorn and Hubbard (2000) found that mothers who responded to some kinds of cries but not others (such as fussy cries) had babies who were equally well adjusted and communicative later in life. Further, responding was found to take many forms among the parents studied. They discovered that some important reactions to crying that had not previously been studied (e.g., talking to a baby from across the room) were useful parent responses. Varied and highly social responses to crying—such as engaging in lively play, asking siblings or other family members to intervene, and just being close to the baby—are common in many Italian families, for example (Axia & Weisner, 2002). These strategies work as well at soothing an infant as feeding or snuggling.

Cross-cultural studies have suggested that patterns of responsiveness and crying vary significantly across families and ethnic groups. In some societies, for example, quick responding does not always lead to less crying, as Bell and Ainsworth (1972) have proposed. In research on Bedouin tribespeople in Israel, babies whose parents responded immediately to even minor whimpers or fussiness were found to cry a great deal during the first year of life (Landau, 1982). Constant crying and quick responses to it were viewed as part of cultural tradition within this society. This study raises questions about whether "responding quickly" to newborn cries means the same thing in all cultures. It also suggests that excessive crying may not be viewed as an altogether bad thing within some societies. In other research, some Asian, South American, and Native American mothers were found to swaddle and carry their babies nearly all the time—even when working!—so that crying rarely occurred at all (Tronick, 2007).

Infant crying can serve as a tool for diagnosis of newborn health. Babies' cries have certain common acoustical properties—that is, typical crying has a certain pitch, volume, and duration. Variations in these properties may indicate problems. For example, unusually high-pitched crying and cries that are short in duration have been associated with Down syndrome, encephalitis, undernutrition, and various forms of brain damage (Huntington, Hans, & Zeskind, 1990; Lester, 1987).

Breastfeeding

When babies are not sleeping, crying, or gazing out at the world, they are eating. Newborns eat frequently, consuming small snacks as often as every 2 hours. Before pasteurization of cow's milk, babies in all societies of the world were breastfed. Mothers of wealthy families who chose not to breastfeed their infants hired wet nurses to do so (Zigler & Finn-Stevenson, 2007). Only in recent times has bottle feeding become an option.

Most newborn babies in the world still breastfeed (World Health Organization, 2008). Breastfeeding is most prevalent in less developed countries. In Papua New Guinea, for example, breast milk substitutes are only available by prescription. In Iran, breastfeeding is considered one of the "rights" of infancy (Zareai, O'Brien, & Fallon, 2007). It is also true that children from non-Western countries are likely to be breastfed for longer periods before weaning (Levine, 1996). Babies in rural Africa are usually not weaned until after age 2.

In industrialized societies, mothers began using bottle-fed formula around the turn of the century. By 1966, only 18% of American mothers were breastfeeding; bottle feeding was viewed as a sign of modernization (Guthrie, 1986). There has since been a revival of breastfeeding in the United States, with well over half the mothers in recent years choosing to breastfeed their newborns (National Center for Health Statistics, 2007). Breastfeeding in America varies by culture and socioeconomic status. Middle-class Euro-American mothers are most likely to breastfeed; poor mothers of African American or Latino backgrounds are less likely (Beasley & Amir, 2007).

A wealth of research evidence suggests that breastfeeding can be beneficial to newborns' health (Pan American Health Organization, 2002). Mother's milk and, particularly, colostrum—a clear yellow fluid that is produced before breast milk during the first days after birth—are believed to retard the growth of certain bacteria and to serve as an important immunological agent for babies. Infants who are breastfed have a lower incidence of respiratory infections (Galton Bacharch, 2003), asthma (Oddy, Peat, & deKlerk, 2002), tooth decay (Valatis, Hersch, & Passarelli, 2003), and even leukemia (Shu, Linet, & Steinbuck, 1999). Breastfed babies are less likely to be obese later in childhood (Armstrong & Reilly, 2002). Breastfeeding has been found to significantly reduce the risk of infant mortality because of these many health benefits (Arifeen et al., 2001).

The duration of breastfeeding has been linked to many positive intellectual outcomes for children as well. Those who have breastfed for 6 months or longer score higher on measures of intellectual, verbal, and motor ability in infancy (Dewey, Cohen, & Brown, 2001), childhood (Harwood, Darlow, & Mogridge, 2001), and adulthood (Mortonson, Achaelso, Sanders, & Reinisch, 2001). Breastfeeding benefits mothers as well. Those who breastfeed their infants have a lower risk of breast cancer (Ursin et al., 2007). Mothers are believed to become attached to their babies through breastfeeding interactions (Ford & Labbock, 1993; R. Lawrence, 1991); higher-quality infant–mother relationships have been found among those who breastfeed (Else-Quest & Hyde, 2003). Many pediatricians now recommend breastfeeding, even if only for the first few months after birth.

Concerns have been raised in recent decades about increases in the use of formula feeding in underdeveloped countries. Formula companies, facing shrinking Western markets, had begun to market their products in impoverished countries, touting bottle feeding as a modern alternative to breastfeeding. This tactic has had serious consequences. Not only is formula feeding costly to mothers with scarce resources, but it brings a risk of infection due to the use of contaminated water and lack of proper sterilization (Dorosko & Rollins, 2004). Under pressure from child advocates, some companies have changed these marketing practices. However, bottle feeding has continued at a high rate in some of these impoverished communities (Marino, 2007). (See the Advocacy and Public Policy box in this chapter on promoting breastfeeding in impoverished countries.)

Reflexes

Babies engage in unique movements during the first few months of life. They often exhibit global wiggles, in which their whole body quivers even when only one part is stimulated. For example, tickling a newborn's big toe may cause the whole body to move. This suggests that a newborn's movements are not differentiated; the infant cannot purposefully move just one body part or another. Some believe that swaddling—wrapping the baby's entire body snugly in a blanket—is comforting because it stills these active, uncontrollable, whole-body movements.

Newborns engage in a variety of **reflexes**—involuntary movements that are built into a baby's nervous system. A list of common reflexes, including descriptions and the course of their development, is provided in Table 5-2. These reflexes are part of human biological heritage; they are identical in newborns of all cultures.

As shown in the table, some reflexes simply disappear with development. For example, the moro reflex—a movement in which the arms are thrown outward and then pulled in to the body when there is a loud noise or sudden loss of support—diminishes between 4 and 6 months. Other reflexes may develop into purposeful actions as babies gain control over their bodies. For example, the rooting reflex, in which a baby involuntarily turns the head toward the source of a tickle on the cheek, and the sucking reflex, a rhythmic sucking that occurs when the mouth is stimulated, develop into complex voluntary acts necessary for eating. Babies learn quickly to voluntarily turn the head and accurately seek and find a nipple. They learn to suck more efficiently and to coordinate sucking with swallowing. Some reflexes, then, are absolutely crucial for survival.

In addition to their survival functions, some reflexes can be an important diagnostic tool for pediatricians. Absent reflexes or those that persist when they should normally disappear are associated with a variety of problems, including brain damage. Premature infants have weaker reflexes at birth and are slower to lose them in later infancy (Beckwith & Rodning, 1991). Children living in poverty often have weaker reflexes because of poor health status and low birth weight (Garcia Coll et al., 1998).

reflexes: Involuntary movements, such as sucking, rooting, and grasping, that are built into a baby's nervous system. These are present at birth and disappear at about 6 months of age.

TABLE 5-2
**Newborn Reflexes
and Their
Developmental
Course**

Reflex	Description	Developmental Course
Grasping	Newborn grasps tightly any object—such as a parent's finger—that is placed in the palm.	The reflex becomes less strong at about 4 months when the baby gains voluntary control over grasping. Grasp movements develop into fine motor abilities in later life.
Moro	The arms are outstretched and then pulled into the body in response to a loud noise or sudden loss of support.	The reflex disappears by 5 months.
Rooting	When a finger or nipple is rubbed against the cheek, the head is turned in that direction. The newborn opens the mouth and often sucks.	The reflex becomes less strong at 3 months when the baby gains voluntary control over head turning and searching for nourishment.
Sucking	The newborn sucks when an object comes in contact with the mouth. Sometimes the reflex is exercised in sleep, even without external stimulus.	The reflex becomes less strong at 3 months; the baby gains voluntary control over sucking. Sucking movements become refined; babies learn to adapt their mouths to various-size nipples and eventually to a cup.
Walking	The newborn takes steps when placed on a surface or against a step.	The reflex disappears at about 3 months. It is debated whether the reflex comprises important early practice for later walking.

Reflexes may also serve as the basis for important early parent–infant play, as the following vignette reveals:

A father from the Yucatán has spent little time with his newborn. His wife, her mother, and a midwife have chased him from the room again and again. "The baby's going to sleep," they scold. "Don't bother her." At last the mother and others have stepped over to the cooking area, and he has a moment alone with the baby. He reaches down tentatively and anxiously strokes his tiny daughter's hand. She grasps on tightly to his finger with surprising quickness and strength. This sudden connection to his daughter is startling and wonderful. As he begins to gently move his hand back and forth, the baby clings on. A huge grin crosses his face. "Little girl! Little girl!" he coos and laughs. This game continues for several minutes. At last his mother-in-law returns. "No!" she says. "Go away! You'll bother her!"

Here the grasp reflex has allowed an uncertain parent to have a unique play interaction with his daughter. Since newborns have a limited range of social behaviors, reflexes provide parents with an early and enjoyable, though perhaps primitive, interpersonal contact.

Exploration and Habituation

The word *exploration* often suggests the active and thoughtful study of the world. An explorer is a person who physically travels to new frontiers or into outer space. A scientist is said to explore complex phenomena using sophisticated knowledge and technology. Can newborns, who are unable to purposefully move and who have limited power to interpret

ADVOCACY AND PUBLIC POLICY

Promoting Breastfeeding in Impoverished Countries

As described in this chapter, breastfeeding has many health advantages for all babies and their mothers. This is particularly true in impoverished countries, where poor nutrition and unsanitary conditions are common. When mothers use commercial formula that is mixed with contaminated water, babies will suffer infections that cause diarrhea—the leading cause of death among children worldwide. In addition, formula is expensive—sometimes costing half the entire income of a family in an underdeveloped country. Mothers may overdilute infant formula to make it go further, causing malnutrition. Over 1.5 million infant lives could be saved by increasing the rate of breastfeeding around the world (UNICEF, 2004a).

Why would mothers choose commercial formula over breast milk, which is free and more healthy? Some baby food companies continue to market their products in impoverished communities (IBFAN, 2004). They offer free samples to health centers or directly to mothers. They actively promote their products to health care workers and agencies, sometimes disguising their marketing strategies as "humanitarian aid" to poor countries. The International Code of Marketing of Breastmilk Substitutes (ICMBS)

was adopted by the World Health Organization to discourage these practices, yet violations of this code are frequent.

Professionals can become advocates for breastfeeding within their local communities, educating the families they work with and other parents about the benefits of breast milk. They can urge elected officials to endorse the joint position of the World Health Organization and UNICEF, which states that all governments should (a) support exclusive breastfeeding of infants for at least 6 months and (b) guarantee mothers the right to breastfeed at home, in the community, and at the workplace. Professionals can contact baby formula companies within their communities or states and request their adherence to the ICMBS. (A list of companies that do not comply with this code are provided on the Website of the International Baby Food Action Network at http://www.ibfan.org.) They can help organize activities during World Breastfeeding Week, an annual event sponsored by the World Alliance for Breastfeeding Action (http://www.waba.org.my). Such advocacy will improve the health not only of children in this country but also of those living in poverty around the world.

the world, engage in exploration? Infant research suggests that they can. When a young baby gazes out at a parent or at a mobile dangling over the crib, she is exploring the world. When another listens intently to the sounds of the family dog barking, he also is exploring the world. Not only do newborns perceive sights and sounds, but they can recognize and distinguish among them as well. They have preferences for what they listen to and see. They get bored staring at objects or listening to sounds that are very familiar.

We know that babies are able to explore because of a phenomenon called **habituation** (Bornstein, 1998; Leventhal, Martin, Seals, Tapia, & Rehm, 2007). When newborn babies study an object or a sound for a period of time, they appear to become familiar with it. The stimulus becomes less interesting and exciting to them; they may choose to look away at something else, or they may show less excitement in their body movements. When this occurs, babies are said to have habituated to a particular stimulus. The occurrence of habituation means that very young infants can *know* about something; they become so familiar with its properties that they become uninterested. This explains why an infant's new toy may be exciting for a short period but then loses its appeal. It may also explain why a new noise, such as a dog's bark, at first may be upsetting to newborns but later goes almost unnoticed. Babies who habituate quickly to new stimuli in the first 6 months of life have been found to be intellectually advanced later in childhood (Kavšek, 2004; Rose & Feldman, 1996). This is probably because habituation is a sign that infants are learning about things in their world.

habituation: A psychological process in which infants become so familiar with objects or events that they show disinterest in them. Psychologists have taken advantage of habituation to study what babies know and are able to do.

Psychologists have taken advantage of habituation to study what babies know and are able to do. For example, much of what we know about newborn perception is based on a research technique that relies on habituation. Here's how it works: Let's say a group of researchers is eager to learn whether babies can distinguish their mother's voice from other adult voices. First, they provide newborns with a special nipple that records the frequency of their sucking. They discover that newborns suck especially rapidly when they are exposed to new sounds. Next, they play a tape of an unfamiliar female voice for each of their subjects. They find that babies initially suck wildly in response to this new stimulus. Over time, however, the infants become familiar with the voice; it no longer excites or captivates them, so their sucking slows down. In the middle of the experiment, the voice of each infant's own mother is suddenly played on the tape. The babies' sucking, which had significantly slowed, now increases sharply. In fact, they suck more rapidly in response to their mother's voice than to the stranger's. What can the researchers conclude? That babies must have been able to tell the difference between these voices, that they must know the unique features of their mothers' speech. This habituation research method has also been used to determine babies' abilities to see, touch, smell, taste, and feel motion.

Newborns of some cultural groups habituate faster to new sights and sounds. In several studies, for example, Chinese American, Japanese American, and Navajo infants were found to habituate more quickly than Euro-American babies (Freedman, 1979; Loo, Ohgi, Zhu, Howard, & Chen, 2005). In another investigation, African American and Euro-American babies were found to habituate more rapidly than Puerto Rican babies (Garcia Coll et al., 1998). Puerto Rican infants in this study remained alert and active for longer periods of time when presented with both visual and auditory stimulation.

How can this information be useful? It shows that some infants can be expected to adjust more quickly to new experiences and events than other infants. Some newborns show sustained interest in, but also become upset at, new sights and sounds. In these cases, caregivers and parents should introduce new toys or play environments more slowly. Other newborns may become accustomed to stimuli more quickly, in which case they may enjoy a more frequent change in environment. Given cultural variations in the rate at which babies adapt, caregivers or family service providers working in multicultural settings should be particularly sensitive to the habituation patterns of newborns when suggesting changes in the play environment of a home or center.

NEWBORNS WITH SPECIAL NEEDS

Thus far, we have discussed typically developing newborns. Vast variations exist, however, in neonatal behavior and development. Some newborns have special needs caused by unfavorable conditions before, during, or after birth; by genetics; or by environmental influences. Many challenging conditions are a function of socioeconomic status and culture.

Genetic Disorders

Some children have genetic disorders that inhibit development. Sometimes these can be detected before birth through **amniocentesis**—a procedure by which genetic information is obtained from a small sampling of amniotic fluid as early as the 12th week of pregnancy. In a newer procedure, **chorionic villus biopsy,** tissue is drawn from the outer membrane of the amniotic sac; this procedure allows detection of genetic disorders as early as the 9th week of pregnancy. Conditions that are commonly detected before or right after birth include Down syndrome, Tay-Sachs disease, and cystic fibrosis (described in Chapter 4).

Some disorders escape detection during pregnancy. In these cases, a neonatal assessment by a pediatrician will often indicate problems. Perhaps the most comprehensive and widely used test

amniocentesis: A procedure to detect genetic disorders before birth by obtaining a small sampling of amniotic fluid as early as the 12th week of pregnancy.

chorionic villus biopsy: A procedure in which genetic disorders are detected by sampling fetal tissue from the outer membrane of the amniotic sac as early as the 9th week of pregnancy.

of newborn functioning is the **Neonatal Behavioral Assessment Scale (NBAS),** developed by Brazelton and Nugent (1995). In this assessment, the pediatrician observes or tests the newborn baby's repertoire of behaviors, including reflexes, states, responses to stimuli, and soothability. When NBAS scores are combined with other medical information, many neurological impairments can be detected within the first few weeks after birth (Ohgi et al., 2003).

Environmental Risk Factors

Developmental problems at birth are sometimes the result of **teratogens**—harmful agents in the environment. An example of a teratogen is the drug thalidomide, which was found to cause physical deformities in newborns. New teratogens continue to be identified as risk factors. For example, fathers' and mothers' exposure to Agent Orange during the Vietnam War and to chemical weapons during the Gulf War may threaten healthy fetal development.

Newborns of mothers who smoke, drink, or abuse drugs during pregnancy may show signs of developmental problems at birth, including birth defects and brain damage. For example, newborns who suffer from **fetal alcohol syndrome** (described in Chapter 4) have been found to be more irritable and less easily soothed almost immediately after birth (Elliott, Payne, Morris, Haan, & Bower, 2007). Even one drink a day by the pregnant mother can lead to delays in motor functioning (Mariscal et al., 2006). Newborns whose mothers smoked during pregnancy have been found to be less responsive to stimuli and to cry more intensely during neonatal assessments (Edwards & King, 2007; J. M. Friedman & Polifka, 1996). Even nonsmoking mothers who are exposed to secondhand smoke will give birth to lower-birth-weight babies (Hofhuis, de Jongste, & Merkus, 2003).

Poor Health Status and Prematurity

The infant mortality rate in the United States is alarmingly high. Although the incidence of neonatal deaths has declined in recent years, almost all industrialized nations have lower infant death rates than the United States (Chung & Muntaner, 2006; Hoyert, Mathews, Menacker, Strobino, & Guyer, 2006). What is more disturbing is the disproportionately high percentage of neonatal deaths among babies of historically underrepresented cultural groups in this country. The infant mortality rate for Euro-Americans was recently reported to be 5.8 deaths per 1,000 births. For the same year, African American infant deaths were more than twice as high, at 14.6 per 1,000 (Children's Defense Fund, 2007). Similar trends are found among Native American, Latino, and some Asian groups (Hoyert et al., 2006; U.S. Department of Health and Human Services, 2008). It is important to note that infant mortality rates are high for these underrepresented groups at all socioeconomic levels (Jackson, 2006). Apparently, poverty alone does not explain cultural differences in infant mortality.

Neonatal Behavioral Assessment Scale (NBAS): A rating system that assesses newborn functioning by measuring reflexes, states, responses to stimuli, and soothability.

teratogens: Environmental agents, such as drugs, radiation, or illness, that threaten the development of the fetus.

fetal alcohol syndrome: A condition caused by a mother's heavy drinking during pregnancy that can lead to nervous system impairment; mental retardation; hyperactivity; and deficiencies in weight, and height.

Illness. Some infants suffer from serious illness because of poor health status or genetics. Severe health problems are more common among babies from families of low socioeconomic status. Historically underrepresented ethnic groups are also more likely to be afflicted (Children's Defense Fund, 2007). A high incidence of bacterial meningitis, for example, has been found among Navajo and White Mountain Apache Indian babies (Santosham et al., 2007). Cystic fibrosis is more common in Pueblo Indians and sickle-cell anemia among African Americans.

Impoverished babies, particularly those of African American and Latino cultural groups, also suffer more frequently from milder, common illnesses. Although these affect development less severely, chronic poor health in infancy may have a long-lasting impact on intellectual and social development (Meeks, Gardner, Lozoff, Wasserman, & Pollitt, 2007). The incidence of mild illness among children of color or those in poverty has probably been underestimated. Families with limited resources cannot afford medical visits for less serious health problems, and many have no health insurance (Children's Defense Fund, 2007).

Anemia. Why do some newborns fail to survive? Why are others chronically ill? One reason is poor nutrition. Iron-deficiency anemia is especially prevalent among newborns in the United States (Children's Defense Fund, 2007; Yip, 1990). Chronic anemia has been associated with infant death, poor health, and a broad range of developmental problems in later life (Meeks et al., 2007). Anemia is especially prevalent among infants of African American and Latino families in America; a rate as high as 25% has been found for these groups.

Prematurity and Low Birth Weight. Premature birth and low birth weight contribute to infant mortality and poor developmental outcomes for those who survive. **Premature births** are those that occur at least 3 weeks before the end of the full 38- to 42-week gestational period. Babies who are less than 5.5 pounds (2,500 grams) at birth usually are considered premature also. Premature babies are extremely vulnerable, and their mortality rate is quite high (Shi et al., 2004). Because their biological systems are not fully developed, they often suffer breathing difficulties, problems with temperature regulation, and jaundice. Premature infants behave differently; they are often less alert and responsive and are more difficult to feed. They can also be less predictable in sleep patterns and hypersensitive to stimuli. For these reasons, parents' reactions to them may be less positive. Parents have been found to touch, hold, or talk less frequently to premature babies than to full-term infants (Coppola, Cassibba, & Costantini, 2007).

Although some premature babies have developmental problems later in life, many fare extremely well, gaining weight quickly and showing no signs of difficulty in later childhood (Benasich & Brooks-Gunn, 1996). Positive parenting and other forms of early intervention may make a difference in these outcomes. Premature babies who are held, touched, and talked to frequently gain weight more quickly and are more developmentally advanced than those who do not receive this special intervention (Coppola, et al., 2007; McCarton et al., 1997).

Rates of prematurity and low birth weight vary across cultural and socioeconomic groups in the United States, as shown in Figure 5-2.

premature births: Births in which children are born at least 3 weeks before the end of the 38- to 42-week gestation period or weigh less than 5.5 pounds at the time of delivery. Premature babies have a high mortality rate and may suffer developmental difficulties into childhood.

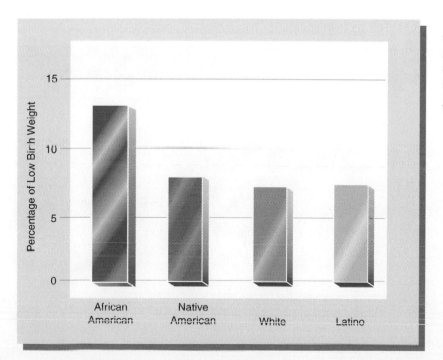

FIGURE 5-2 Percentage of low-birth-weight babies is twice as high in African American families as in Euro-American and other cultural groups.

SOURCE: Adapted from Children's Defense Fund. (2004) *The State of America's Children.* Washington, DC: Author.

African Americans have an exceedingly high incidence of low birth weight (13%). Other groups are also at greater risk (Mathews & MacDorman, 2007). Puerto Rican babies are more likely to be born prematurely (9%). Rates of prematurity are particularly high for babies born to teenage mothers of historically underrepresented groups (Chandra et al., 2002). Euro-American, Cuban American, Mexican American, and Asian American babies have significantly lower rates of low birth weight (about 5.5%). These trends may be explained in part by socioeconomic status; high-risk groups tend to live in poverty at higher rates (Valero de Bernabé, Soriano, & Albaladejo, (2004); Beckwith, & Rodning, (1991). However, culture may also play a role. Linguistic and cultural barriers may keep mothers of some groups from accessing health care or nutritional services (Children's Defense Fund, 2007).

In addition to increasing the likelihood of prematurity and low birth weight, poverty contributes to developmental risks for such infants after birth. In fact, socioeconomic status is the best predictor of how premature babies will turn out; the lower the families' income and education, the more likely babies are to fare poorly (Valero de Bernabé et al., 2004).

Sudden Infant Death Syndrome. Sudden infant death syndrome (SIDS), defined in Chapter 4, strikes fear in the hearts of parents around the world. One out of 360 infants dies of this mysterious condition, which is the leading cause of death for infants before age 1 (Hamilton, et al. 2007). Families of all countries and ethnic groups can be affected. What is frightening about SIDS is that babies simply stop breathing and die silently for no apparent reason, usually at night. The causes of SIDS are unknown. Some pediatricians suspect that SIDS is a generic label used to describe a range of life-threatening conditions. Babies born to mothers who are heavy smokers or who abuse cocaine and heroin are more likely to die from SIDS (Hunt & Hauck, 2006; Gordon et al., 2002). Siblings of babies who have died of the condition are also at greater risk (Hunt & Hauck, 2006).

Other research has focused on the position in which babies sleep. SIDS is more common among those who sleep on their stomachs (Hunt & Hauk, 2006). When infants are routinely put down to sleep on their sides or backs, the risk of SIDS is reduced by 50% (Johannemann, Conkright, & Warner, 2007). Parent educators and family service providers can make two

Low birth weight and premature birth contribute to infant mortality and puts infants who survive at risk.

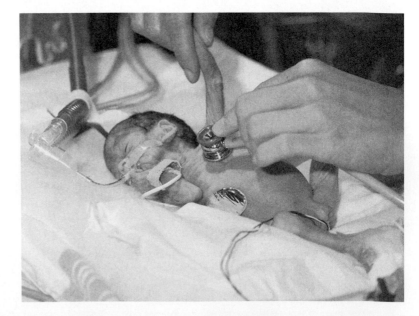

CHILD GUIDANCE: *Joining the Dance of the Newborn*

Parents of newborns often ask: How should I interact with my baby? Should I provide lots of stimulation? Should I ignore fussy crying? Should I hold and carry my baby often? Should I get up in the middle of the night for feedings? Some medical and family service professionals have designed parent education programs to answer these questions. These programs offer direct guidance to parents based on available research: Talk, play, and cuddle with your baby often. Respond quickly to crying.

An alternative view on caring for newborns is that there is no one correct way to parent. Babies have different temperaments and distinct reactions to the world, as do adults. The job of parents, from this view, is to get "into synchrony" with their newborns, to join them in an elaborate dance, following *their* lead (Tronick, Thomas, & Daltabuit, 1994).

Parents can achieve this synchrony by carefully observing their infants' life patterns, beginning immediately after birth. What are their sleeping–waking cycles? When are their babies most often in an alert state and ready to play? At what times of day do they most often become upset? Which events upset them? What responses soothe them most? Recording these observations over several weeks will reveal individual patterns.

At the same time, parents can reflect on their own routines and needs. What interactions do I find most enjoyable when my baby is in an alert state? Do I like to read, sing, or play with her? What soothing techniques seem most natural to me? Does it feel right to snuggle, to feed, or to use a quiet voice from a distance? What are my own sleep needs (so that I am able to be an alert and responsive parent)? How can I adjust these aspects of my life to meet my baby's needs while still leading a happy and fulfilled life?

The dance can now begin. At a certain time of day, a newborn becomes alert and fascinated with the world around her. A parent recognizes this state and chooses to interact with her, wiggling a mobile and moving a rattle across her field of vision. The child shows signs of being overwhelmed, however—turning away and beginning to fuss. The parent, picking up on these signals, adjusts her interactions, quietly singing to her baby instead. This is an interaction that both parent and child enjoy. Later in the afternoon, the baby begins to cry and is inconsolable. The parent has learned from observations that this is a typical, daily pattern. He responds in a way that he has learned will soothe her—snuggling with her, then placing her in a front carrier so that he can go on with life routines. Late that night, after all have gone to bed, the baby cries again. This is a fussy cry, however, different from the afternoon upset. The parent—in need of sleep—waits to respond, knowing that this is usually a short-lived episode and that the baby will soon return to sleep.

Just as dance partners don't plan all their steps before the music begins, parents can't plot out how they will respond to crying or to an alert state. They allow themselves to be guided by the baby's signals as well as their own desires and needs. This approach is useful not only for infants. Adults living or working with children of any age might strive to achieve this synchrony.

quite simple recommendations that will save infant lives: Don't put babies down to sleep on their stomachs, and don't ever smoke around them!

Although babies of all cultural and socioeconomic groups can be stricken by SIDS, those in poverty and of African American and Native American backgrounds are at greatest risk (Alexander, Wingate, & Boulet, 2007; Lahr, Rosenberg, & Lapidus, 2007). Babies of some countries are more likely to be afflicted—those in Australia and New Zealand, for example. In other countries, such as Japan and Sweden, the incidence is quite low.

SUMMARY

Newborns—babies from birth to 3 or 4 weeks—have a unique, even startling, appearance. Their faces are sometimes puffy and their heads distorted from the trip through the birth canal. They are top-heavy, with disproportionately large heads.

Newborns spend much of their time in a variety of psychological states, including sleeping, crying, and exploring their world in an alert and awake state. During awake states, they eat, perform simple reflexes, and study objects and people. When they become familiar with things they have studied, they lose interest. This phenomenon, called habituation, allows researchers to study what babies know and are able to do.

Some newborns develop poorly because of a variety of unfavorable circumstances. There are genetic causes of developmental disorders. Environmental hazards, such as drug and alcohol use during pregnancy, inhibit healthy growth as well. Illness, anemia, prematurity, and sudden infant death syndrome, which threaten newborn development, are more common among children of color and those living in poverty.

RESEARCH INTO PRACTICE

CRITICAL CONCEPT 1

Newborns have a unique appearance, with tiny features, disproportionately large heads, and a look of vulnerability. Right after birth, they may have puffy features and misshaped heads.

Application   Help expecting parents prepare themselves for the distinct—even startling—appearance of their newborns. Encourage them to read, view videotapes, and participate in childbirth classes. Once their child is born, encourage parents to give in to desires to nurture and protect their newborn. These are natural responses due, in part, to their child's look of helplessness and vulnerability.

CRITICAL CONCEPT 2

Newborns spend their time in a narrow range of psychological states. They sleep for many hours. When awake, they cry and eat. Two particularly important states are the alert and waking periods, during which newborns visually explore the world and the people in it.

Application #1   Help parents identify and understand the importance of each newborn psychological state. Babies should be afforded opportunities to spend meaningful time in each state; for example, a soothing, quiet space for uninterrupted sleep and a visually stimulating environment for alert looking should be provided. Parents should respond appropriately to infants' cries for food and nurturance.

Application #2   Encourage parents to learn to read newborn states and adjust interactions accordingly. Babies learn most during the active and waking states; these are important times for moderate stimulation. The drowsy state, in contrast, is a time when babies should not be disturbed.

CRITICAL CONCEPT 3

Breastfeeding is found to have significant developmental and health benefits for both infants and their mothers. Children who breastfeed have a lower incidence of serious illness, tooth decay, and childhood obesity. Mothers who breastfeed show a higher quality relationship with their infants and are less likely to be afflicted with breast cancer.

Application #1   Encourage mothers to breastfeed their infants, even if only for a few months following birth. A longer duration of breastfeeding will lead to even more positive outcomes for children.

Application #2   Encourage new mothers to breastfeed by providing reading materials and Website addresses describing the many health benefits and by introducing them to support organizations, such as the La Leche League (http://www.lalecheleague.org).

CRITICAL CONCEPT 4

During waking states, newborns habituate to familiar sights and sounds; that is, once they come to know something, they grow uninterested in it. They become excited when new objects appear and new events occur.

Application #1   Observe habituation processes in newborns as a way of assessing perceptual and intellectual development. For example, when a baby studies a new mobile and then shows disinterest in it over time, it can be concluded that the child has perceived and learned about the mobile and is now ready for new stimulation. Share ideas on habituation with parents, so they can also note progress in intellectual development.

Application #2   Provide a moderate amount of stimulation for newborns and encourage parents to do so. If the environment does not include interesting events or objects, babies will have nothing to study and habituate to. If too much stimulation is provided, babies may not be able to study and become familiar with any one object or person. They may become overwhelmed by the bombardment of perceptual stimuli.

CRITICAL CONCEPT 5

The time newborns spend in various states and how quickly they habituate to new stimuli vary from one ethnic group to another. This may be due partly to genetics. However, parents of diverse backgrounds respond in unique ways to newborn states. For example, some parents respond quickly with warmth and feeding when babies cry; others are slower to respond or use distracting techniques. These differences in interactions may explain some of the diversity in infant states and behavior.

Application #1   Understand and be sensitive to cultural differences in newborn states and habituation. Care should be taken not to misconstrue neonatal differences as deficits.

Application #2   Adjust interactions to the unique state patterns of individual babies. Babies who are easily upset and cry more often should be soothed and nurtured more. Those who are often awake and active should receive more social stimulation. Babies who habituate more slowly should not be overwhelmed with too many novel objects or people. Slow-habituating babies may warm up slowly to new people, new room arrangements, and new experiences.

CRITICAL CONCEPT 6

Some newborns may be at risk of poor development. Infants of low birth weight can suffer poor developmental outcomes, particularly within families living in poverty. Genetic disorders and illness may also threaten healthy development in the earliest days of life. Sudden infant death syndrome is a life-threatening condition that afflicts a small percentage of infants each year. Some problems stem from barriers to health care for families of historically underrepresented groups.

Application #1   Provide special support for babies in high-risk categories and their families. Low-birth-weight infants, for example, would benefit from greater social and intellectual stimulation in child care. Provide parent education programs to help families of high-risk babies provide positive interaction in the home.

Application #2   Serve as an advocate for families of children in high-risk categories. Helping parents gain access to nutritional and health care services is an important role of the infant care provider in modern life. Actually accompanying family members to a clinic or a public assistance office may be necessary to overcome cultural and linguistic barriers to family services.

Application #3   Guide parents in taking steps to reduce the risk of sudden infant death syndrome. Recommend that babies be put to sleep on their backs or sides—never on their stomachs. Encourage them to never smoke around newborns.

ASSESSING YOUNG CHILDREN: Development of the Newborn

Areas of Development	What to Watch for	Indicators of Atypical Development	Applications
Psychological States	Regular sleeping and alert periods, which increase in duration during the first half year. Crying to communicate needs.	Inconsolable crying of long duration. Infrequent alertness. Peculiar-sounding cries.	Respond to various psychological states based on knowledge of babies' life patterns. Provide stimulation—physical touch or play—at a level that babies desire, during alert states. Soothe babies using a method that matches their individual preferences—snuggling, feeding, or singing.
Reflexes	Strong grasping, rooting, sucking, and other reflexes.	Certain reflexes are not present in the early days of life. Reflexes do not disappear during the first year.	Observe/test infant reflexes to verify healthy development—reflexes appear and disappear at expected age—and identify special needs. Use reflexes as a means of social contact. Guide infants in grasping a finger or wiggling in response to physical touch.
Physical Growth	Birth weight of 5 or more pounds. Rapid growth, particularly of the head and trunk. General good health.	Low birth weight. Poor pediatric evaluation on NBAS. Failure to grow rapidly in the first year. Frequent illness and poor nutritional status.	Provide for good nutrition and health care. Watch for alert states, when perceptual stimulation (e.g., rattles, mobiles, music) and physical play are most effective.

Interpreting Assessment Data: Variations in these areas of development may be a result of individual or cultural factors. Infants may sleep longer at night because they sleep with their parents during the first year. Babies who cry more often may have a less positive inborn temperament. Unpredictable variations in psychological states or peculiar-sounding crying may indicate a challenging condition, however. Low birth weight and poor nutrition could be the result of poverty or poor prenatal care. Further professional evaluation is needed when such indicators are present. Nutritional and educational intervention may be recommended.

CHAPTER 6

Infant Physical Growth and Brain Development

GUIDING QUESTIONS

1. What are the major trends in physical growth during infancy?
2. What motor abilities are acquired during this developmental period, and how do these vary across cultures?
3. What new motor and self-help skills are acquired in toddlerhood, and how do they differ from one culture to another?
4. What are the major advancements in infant perceptual development related to vision, hearing, taste, smell, and touch?
5. What are the characteristics of infant brain growth, and why is the infant brain considered to be *super-dense*?
6. What classroom adaptations can be made to meet the needs of infants with perceptual and motor challenges?

Infancy is the period from birth to age 2. In this chapter, trends in infant physical and motor growth are explored, and the remarkable growth of the infant brain is examined. Cultural differences in child-rearing practices or beliefs that lead to variations in these areas are considered, as are atypical patterns of development. Interventions to support children with challenging physical conditions also are presented.

The following story shows why information on infant physical growth is essential for both new parents and professionals who work with them:

"Why isn't Ding Fang walking yet?" a parent suddenly asks Ms. McBride, a child care provider, when he brings his infant daughter into her center early one morning. Ms. McBride is taken aback; this baby is only 13 months old, can already stand alone, and shows no signs of motor delay. She is surprised that the father would have this concern, but she understands that he—like so many other first-time parents—is anxious about his child's development. Because few infants have arrived yet and Ms. McBride has two assistants, she is able to leave the play area for a few minutes. She invites the father into her office, where she shows him developmental charts of typical infant motor development.

"If you look here," she says, "you can see that Ding Fang is right on track in terms of her motor abilities. She can stand up already; you can see from the chart that many babies her age are not able to do this yet."

The father explains, "I see other babies about Ding Fang's age in our apartment complex who are walking already. Some have been walking for quite a while. I wondered if something was wrong. Ding Fang seems very quiet—relaxed, you know? She doesn't try to get up and run like the other children."

Ms. McBride responds in a reassuring tone, "Babies are all different. Some walk early, some a bit later. Some are more active than others. Some babies are very bold, very eager to get up and be on their own—and run away from their parents," she adds with a laugh. "Other babies seem to be in no rush to move on their own. All of these patterns are typical. Ding Fang is just following her own path to being a grown-up child. She will walk very soon, I know."

The caregiver in this story has demonstrated sensitivity to a parent's need for reassurance about his child's development. She knows that parents compare their babies' growth patterns with those of other babies. When an infant who lives next door is showing advanced motor development, parents make comparisons—and worry.

In supporting this father, the caregiver has relied on knowledge of infant motor development. She is aware of the normative data—information about how babies develop on the average. She also knows that there is typical variation in infant motor growth and that physical development and activity level vary across families and cultures. Because of temperament or family life experience, children of some ethnic groups are more bold and active, while others are less so. Recognizing that Ding Fang's quieter, less active style may be part of her cultural heritage, she conveys to the child's father that diverse patterns of motor activity are common.

PHYSICAL GROWTH AND MOTOR DEVELOPMENT

A grandfather who sees his 4-month-old grandaughter for the first time in a month exclaims, "She's a completely different person!" He has this impression because infants grow so rapidly and acquire so many new motor abilities between birth and age 2 that they seem to become new people with each passing week.

Trends in Physical Growth

By the second year, many children are four times as heavy and more than a foot longer than they were at birth. Babies' bodies change structurally as well. Although they remain top-heavy, their legs and trunk grow rapidly and begin to catch up with the rest of the body during the second year. A layer of subcutaneous fat, commonly called *baby fat*, gives the young baby a plump appearance. This layer of fat cushions and provides a source of nutrition to the very young infant. By age 2, toddlers have lost some of this subcutaneous fat and, with it, their roundish appearance.

During infancy, muscle and bone tissue grow rapidly, explaining the remarkable increase in strength, coordination, and stamina that occurs during this period. A brain growth spurt also takes place, causing babies to gain physical competence by leaps and bounds. These rapid changes invariably cause unexpected mishaps: a 6-month-old may suddenly roll off a changing table, or a 9-month-old may stand for the first time and, without warning, pull a plate off the table. Before parents can adjust to one new stage of motor development, babies may have acquired even more sophisticated modes of locomotion that pose additional challenges. Keeping up with infant motor development requires vigilance and great energy!

Descriptions of "typical" physical growth are often based on observations of white, middle-class infants from the United States (Garcia Coll et al., 1998). However, there is much variation across cultures in babies' sizes and the pace of their physical growth. For example, Southeast Asian infants and toddlers tend to be shorter than Euro-American babies (Herman-Giddens et al., 1997). Many African and African American infants are advanced in motor development and physical growth (Paludi, 2002). Some children living in poverty are smaller because of malnutrition (Children's Defense Fund, 2007). Even within cultures, tremendous variation in size and motor ability exists among typically developing children.

Motor Abilities

Motor abilities emerge in a relatively predictable order in infancy. Babies creep before they walk. When they begin to walk, they hold on to a hand or a piece of furniture until they can manage alone. They swipe at objects before they can accurately reach out and grab them. They can seize stationary objects before they can grab moving ones. They grasp objects by trapping them between their fingers and palm before using the thumb and index finger in a more sophisticated **pincer grasp.** The order in which these abilities are acquired is the same among most children around the world (de Onis, 2006).

Early child development researchers have studied the emergence of these infant motor behaviors and have created developmental profiles—sometimes called **normative charts**—that show the average age at which certain behaviors first appear (Gesell, 1933; Shirley, 1933). These charts are still used by pediatricians and parents to judge developmental advancement. A chart depicting general motor milestones in infancy is shown in Table 6-1; the progression of infants' grasping abilities is shown in Table 6-2.

Caution must be used in interpreting these developmental profiles, however. Although the sequence of motor development is relatively fixed, not all children acquire motor abilities at the same pace. Individual differences in creeping, for example, can vary by 7 or 8 months for typically developing children. The age at which babies walk also varies significantly among individuals (Ivanenko, Dominici, & Lacquaniti, 2007). Developmental charts can cause undue anxiety among parents if misinterpreted. Some parents may even attempt direct training of motor skills, causing frustration for both themselves and their children.

Motor development profiles are often created from observations of white, middle-class children. Children of other cultural groups may acquire physical abilities at a much different pace than is indicated on these charts. African and African American babies, for example, have been observed to be advanced in motor competence (Paludi, 2002; Rosser & Rudolph, 1989). Children of some Asian cultures are slower to acquire certain motor skills (Mayson, Harris, & Bachman, 2007).

pincer grasp: An advanced form of grasping, acquired at around age 1, in which the thumb and forefinger are used to hold small objects.

normative charts: Graphic representations of the stages or milestones children pass through as they develop.

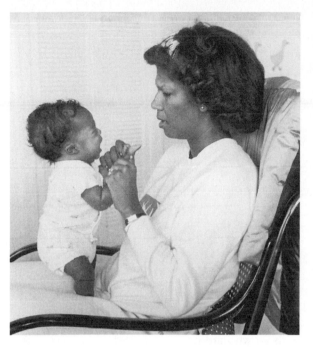

There is cultural variation in infant motor development. African and African American babies tend to be advanced in physical abilities.

How can cultural and individual differences in motor development be explained? Some believe that these differences are the result of biological inheritance (Freedman, 1974). There is research to support this claim. Recall W. Dennis and M. G. Dennis's (1940) study of Hopi Indian infants, in which those who had been tightly swaddled and strapped to a cradle board walked at about the same age as those who were not confined in this way. Remember also the study by Gesell and Thompson (1929). A child who was trained to climb

TABLE 6-1
**Motor Milestones
in Infancy**

Milestone	Average Age
Raises head; can lift chin up from floor or bed	1 month
Raises chest up off the floor or bed	2 months
Sits up with adult support	2.5 months
Bats at objects; cannot accurately grasp them	3 months
Reaches for and grasps objects	6 months
Sits alone steadily	6.5 months
Stands with adult support	8 months
Stands up holding onto furniture	9 months
Creeps	10 months
Walks when led by an adult	11 months
Stands alone	11 months
Walks alone	12 months
Climbs stairs	13 months
Walks down stairs with both feet on each step	26 months

SOURCE: Bailey, 1969; Shirley, 1933.

TABLE 6-2
Development of Grasping in Infancy

Grasping Ability	Average Age
Swipes at objects; makes no contact	16 weeks
Swipes at objects; makes contact; does not grasp	20 weeks
Makes primitive grasping movement with fingers; object still not accurately held	20 weeks
Squeezes and holds object between fingers and palm; thumb is not used	24 weeks
Squeezes object between fingers and thumb	28 weeks
Picks up objects between thumb and index finger (pincer grasp)	52 weeks

stairs displayed better stair-climbing ability than her twin sister, but her sibling quickly caught up. These researchers concluded that babies will ultimately follow their own unique maturation patterns regardless of environmental influences.

Others argue that environment and culture explain this diversity in motor functioning. Chisholm (1989), for example, offers an explanation for why infants who are strapped to cradle boards during the day are as advanced as those who are not so confined. He observed that Navajo infants were more active and interacted very frequently with parents when off the board. He proposes that these babies received adequate practice in motor activities during evening periods. Garcia Coll and colleagues (1998) have provided evidence that African American babies are advanced in motor skills because of the way they are handled by parents and other family members. They cite research indicating that interactions between African American parents and babies are more active, less likely to involve quiet toys, and more likely to involve physical touch. This research suggests that the babies of middle-class African American parents who have adopted more Westernized parenting styles are less motorically advanced.

In some cultures, a goal of parent–infant interaction is promoting motor competence. Ugandan parents and West Indian parents from Jamaica engage in training activities to promote sitting alone or moving independently (Hopkins & Westra, 1990; J. E. Kilbride & P. L. Kilbride, 1975). In contrast, parents from Japan and southern Mexico report discouraging rapid motor development (Greenfield, 1995; Mayson et al., 2007).

Cultural variations in development may, then, be the result of a unique blend of parenting values and practices, family life, and genetic contributions from ancestors.

Toddler Motor Development and Self-Help Skills

During the last half year of infancy—from approximately 18 months to 2 years—children enter a new period of development called *toddlerhood*. Changes in intellectual, language, and motor growth mark this as an especially challenging and fascinating period. Toddlers, for the first time, move primarily in an upright position. This ability opens new worlds for them. High surfaces are now accessible; they can reach for and pull down family heirlooms or favorite furnishings. Childproofing homes and teaching babies not to touch become critical parenting issues. Toddlers can walk and even run—and this includes running away. They hold powerful aspirations to be on their own and to explore without adult intrusion. Parents must be extremely vigilant with children at this age.

Toddlers are much stronger than younger infants. For example, many toddlers do not wish to be confined for the endless period—in child time—that it takes to change a soiled diaper. They will wiggle and struggle, jump up half clothed, and make a break for the door.

Toddlers cut most of their teeth between 18 months and 2 years. This allows them to eat meats and other foods that were difficult before. It also allows them to bite—including, unfortunately, siblings and peers. Teething also creates the challenge of dental care. Pediadontists ask parents to rub or brush babies' teeth, procedures that require risky sojourns into the mouths of babies just learning the power of their jaws.

In toddlerhood, fine motor abilities that require the coordination of fingers and thumb are acquired. Once they master the pincer grasp, toddlers can engage in fine motor play: they can make simple puzzles, work with modeling clay, or tear paper. They can also open cabinets, take the tops off household cleaners, or pick up (and usually place in their mouths) small objects, such as pennies or an older sibling's marbles. Childproofing is especially important in toddlerhood, as choking is a major concern at this age.

Childproofing from a Multicultural Perspective. Childproofing takes many forms and is influenced by cultural values and practices. In some families, home environments are fully redesigned during toddlerhood so that babies can touch anything they wish. The goal is to encourage autonomy and reduce reprimands and restrictions. In other families, toddlers are required to learn rules for what may be touched or played with. Infractions are met with hand slapping or firm reprimands. It may be that this early form of discipline has a goal of "toughening" children or protecting them from dangers in their neighborhoods (Hale, 1994; Ipsa & Halgunseth, 2004).

A classic study by Levine (1996) shows the diversity of childproofing strategies used in the world. He observed that in a village in western Kenya, babies were reared outdoors for the most part. The risks to these toddlers were great, including the danger of burns from cooking fires and falls off cliffs or into rivers, lakes, and dye pits. In this case, the challenge was not childproofing the home but childproofing the whole world! The solution? Parents of this village carried their toddlers on their backs from the time they could walk until they were old enough to understand rules and the dangers around them. This represents an interesting reversal of the common trend of carrying babies only until they can walk on their own. In this Kenyan village, carrying became necessary only when babies learned to move around.

As children become more advanced motorically, they are expected to perform certain self-help tasks. Which tasks are to be learned and how quickly children are expected to learn them are defined by particular cultures. In some cultural groups, early independence and self-care are highly valued (Hale, 1994; Ipsa & Halgunseth, 2004); in others, children are expected to rely heavily on parents until quite late in childhood (Powell, Yamamoto, Wyatt, & Arroyo, 1997; Yu & Kim, 1983) and are even given lessons in how to "graciously receive help" (Gonzalez-Mena, 2008, p. 21).

Eating. Eating with a toddler is a fascinating experience that varies across cultures. As a father, I've made many enlightening observations of toddlers' eating habits: the creative mixing of foods, experiments with the aerodynamics of breakfast cereals, and tests to determine how persistent parents will be in retrieving dropped spoons. In one fascinating observation, my oldest son was seen holding his spoon in a particularly mature manner with his left hand while shoveling food into his mouth with his right.

In some families, toddlers are expected to sit for meals and eat with a spoon or another eating implement as early as age 2. Such behaviors as throwing food or using one's hands to eat are discouraged. In white, working-class families in America and Europe, self-control and neatness are often expected at an early age (L. W. Hoffman, 1991; Morton, 2007; Wang, Wiley, & Zhou, 2007). In other cultures, rules at mealtime are not so rigid, nor are they imposed so early. In Nyansongo, Kenya, toddlers eat off the plates of others, including their younger siblings (Whiting & Edwards, 1988). Variation in how toddlers

Toddlers move quickly and hold powerful aspirations to be on their own and explore without adult intrusion.

eat is a function of the foods eaten in a particular culture and the implements used. It is easy to see how much less challenging it would be to learn to use a spoon than to use chopsticks, for example.

The following story, told to me by an American researcher working in an East African village, illustrates how eating expectations vary drastically from one culture to another:

A researcher sits on the ground to eat an evening meal with a large family. There are no eating implements; food is eaten with the fingers. The researcher studies a toddler who has invented a novel system of raising his bowl to his lips and pouring rice into his mouth as if drinking from a cup. Much rice spills onto the ground; at most half of the food actually reaches his mouth. The father takes the child's hand and shows him how to pick up food with his fingers. The researcher and father speak in the family's language:

RESEARCHER: So, you teach your child to use fingers to eat?
FATHER: He wastes too much food when he eats like this (demonstrates the child's original eating method). He eats like an animal and wastes food.
RESEARCHER: (Laughs) So, you tell your child, "Be sure to eat with your fingers."
FATHER: (Looks puzzled, doesn't understand the joke)
RESEARCHER: (Laughing still) Well, see, in my family my mother was always telling me, "Don't eat with your fingers. Use a spoon or fork." I just think it's funny that you tell your child just the opposite.
FATHER: How do you feel your food that you eat? Part of enjoying a meal is feeling the foods, running your fingers over vegetables or the grains of rice. (He demonstrates) It is a pleasure to eat in this way.

It is important for parents and professionals working with children and families to consider cultural variations when pursuing goals of teaching table manners or proper eating habits. American eating styles are not necessarily valued in all cultures.

Toileting. Toddlerhood is often a time when American parents decide to train their children to use the toilet independently. Brazelton (1962) has suggested that children at this age are both psychologically and physiologically ready to learn this new skill. Many parents, however, view toilet training as a trying experience. Often they feel a sense of urgency about their child's accomplishing bladder and bowel control. Anxieties are exacerbated by the fact that many child care centers will not admit children who do not use the toilet independently. From a friend, I heard the following story that highlights the frustrations of toilet training:

> Two-year-old Nathan's parents decided to encourage independent toileting by giving him a small plastic dinosaur every time he successfully used the toilet. This seemed to work for a while, but Nathan began to have an increasing number of accidents. During one such event, Nathan's mother asked him what the problem was: "You've been going in the toilet, and I give you a dinosaur each time. But now you're going in your pants again." The toddler responded with a sly smile, "I want two dinosaurs, Mommy."
>
> His mother reflected: Nathan may not use the toilet, but he has certainly learned how to negotiate!

In the United States, parents take many different approaches to toilet training. White, middle-class parents often adhere to a "child-oriented approach" suggested by traditional baby experts (Brazelton, 1962; Spock & Rothenberg, 1985). In this method, parents wait until they are absolutely certain the child is ready, then use gentle reminders, modeling, and positive guidance to help children achieve independent toileting (Blum, Traubman, & Nemeth, 2004). Some middle-class American parents have adopted behaviorist strategies in which rewards and praise are used to shape independent toileting behaviors (Azrin & Foxx, 1974; Pupillo, 2007).

It is important to note that these strategies are used primarily in white, middle-class families in America. African and African American parents and grandparents more often use reprimands and punishments for bowel or bladder accidents. They also are more likely to expect independent toileting at an early age (Hale, 1994; Sun & Rugolotto, 2004). These practices reflect cultural values of early self-sufficiency and autonomy. In Korean American and Japanese American families, parents are more likely to be casual in their approaches to toileting and tolerant of later mastery (Powell et al., 1997; Yamamoto & Kubota, 1983; Yu & Kim, 1983). One early study of Japanese Americans found that the longer a family had lived in the United States, the more urgency parents felt about toilet training (De Vos, 1954). Middle-class American beliefs about the need for early training appear to become integrated over time into traditional Japanese American family life.

In other parts of the world, parents report that toileting of toddlers is not a problem or even a goal of socialization. After extensive observations in many non-Western countries, Whiting and Edwards (1988) reported that toileting was seldom mentioned by parents in discussions of child-rearing issues. He found that in some warm climates, babies often run unclothed for most of the day and urinate or defecate where they wish. The extent of parents' efforts in these communities may be to gently lead them farther away from important living areas, such as places of food preparation.

In a classic study of toileting practices in East Africa, M. W. DeVries and M. R. DeVries (1977) describe a process in which babies at 3 weeks old are taken to a special place outdoors to urinate. This occurs day and night. At the phenomenally early age of 5 months, many babies of this community begin to communicate a need for elimination with noises or body movements.

Despite the varieties of routines for toilet training in the world, all typically developing children acquire the procedures unique to their culture and often at about the same age. Regardless of whether harsh reprimands, rewards, or modeling are used or even when no conscious effort to train is made at all, most children achieve bladder and bowel control by age 3. Parents' selection of toileting techniques, then, may be more a function of family and cultural beliefs than of any real advantage one strategy has over another.

PERCEPTUAL DEVELOPMENT

Long ago it was believed that babies were born into a confusing world of fuzzy shapes and strange, garbled sounds. Most parents and even researchers thought that only older infants could see faces, recognize voices, or distinguish among tastes and smells. New techniques for studying infant perception have shown, however, that babies have quite remarkable perceptual abilities right after birth.

Vision

Newborns see objects quite well that are between 7 and 15 inches away (Ricci et al., 2008). Interestingly (and perhaps not coincidentally), this is approximately the distance a parent's face is from an infant who is being held. Babies' visual ability increases over the first few months of life; it is estimated that by age 1, they see as well as they ever will (Haith, 1990; Turati & Simion, 2002).

One way we know that young babies can see clearly is that they like to look at some patterns or objects for longer periods of time than they do others (Frick, Colombo, & Saxon, 1999; Slaughter, Heron, & Sim, 2004). Infant visual preferences are illustrated in Figure 6-1.

It has been discovered that newborns prefer patterns over solid shapes (Fantz, 1963; Rose, Feldman, & Jankowski, 2004), moderately complex patterns over either simple or complex ones, curved lines over straight ones, and large squares over small ones (Colombo, Frick,

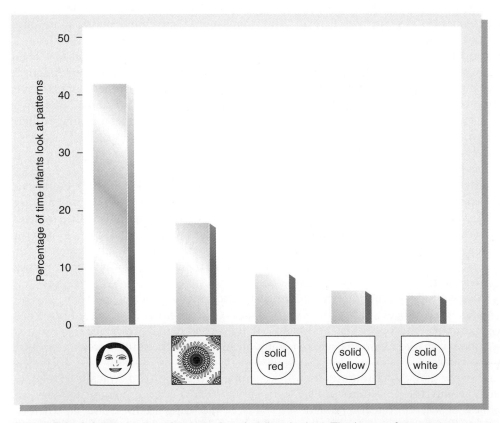

FIGURE 6-1 Infants show preferences for what they look at. The human face appears most interesting to them.

SOURCE: Fantz, R. L., The origin of form perception. *Scientific American*, 204.

Ryther, & Gifford, 1996). By 4 months, babies can also distinguish among colors and prefer blue and red to yellow—the same color preferences as adults (Bornstein, 1992; Franklin, Pilling, & Davies, 2005).

One thing that newborn babies may prefer to look at are human faces (de Haan, Johnson, Maurer, & Perrett, 2007; Rose, Futterweit, & Jankowski, 1999). Remarkably, by 3 months, babies show a preference for looking at faces of their own race (Kelly et al., 2005). In one study, newborns looked longer at drawings of faces with features displayed in typical order than at face-like drawings in which features were randomly arranged (Fantz, 1963). Later studies have not replicated these findings, however (Bhatt, Bertin, Hayden, & Reed, 2005; Small, 1990). It may be that very young infants do not recognize faces per se but look at them intently because they are such interesting visual patterns. A 6-week-old baby's smile at the appearance of his mother's face, for example, may merely be a response to a high-contrast image. Parents aren't aware of this, however; they report that the infant's gaze is a sign that "my baby knows me." Thus, newborns' innate visual interests, present at birth, may promote parent bonding.

Babies have been found to differ in their looking behaviors (Rose et al., 2004). Younger babies are "long lookers"—that is, they study a new object once but for a long period of time. As babies grow older, they often become "short lookers," studying new objects briefly but again and again. They quickly move their gaze from one feature of an object to another or from object to object. Interestingly, babies who perform short looking early in infancy are found to be better able to process information and, thus, to learn (Rose et al., 2004). Babies who continue a long-looking pattern of visual behavior are less competent in processing information.

Tracking and scanning are two special abilities that assist babies in viewing the world. **Tracking** is the ability to visually follow a moving object with one's eyes. Newborn babies make attempts to move their heads and readjust their eyes to keep interesting objects in their field of vision (Gamé, Carchon, & Vital-Durand, 2004). Their efforts are jerky, inefficient, and poorly controlled, however. They must turn the entire head and then refocus every few inches as an object moves in front of them. They follow objects moving only side to side in their field of vision. They rarely look up and down. Tracking rapidly becomes smoother and more accurate during the first 6 months of life.

Tracking ability varies by culture. Puerto Rican babies, for example, have been found to track objects more efficiently than babies of other cultural groups (Garcia Coll et al., 1998). This might be due to biological inheritance. Unique cultural experience might also play a role since tracking ability can be influenced by practice (Slaughter et al., 2004). For example, babies may learn to track more efficiently in larger extended families—common in Puerto Rico—where there is much movement and many interesting persons to observe. This theory is supported by the finding that, early in life, babies are more likely to track human faces than other objects (Gamé et al., 2004).

Scanning is a visual ability to look over all the features of an object and get a complete picture of what it is like. When adults examine an unfamiliar painting or an artifact in a museum, they quickly scan its visual details and get a sense of it as a whole. Newborns cannot do this. Instead, they tend to look at only one feature of a stimulus—at just one corner of a triangle or one car of a teddy bear, for example. Within 3 months after birth, babies become much more competent in scanning an entire object (Bronson, 1994). They quickly look at one feature and then another until they have processed the whole object. It is easy to see how a short looker—a baby who quickly shifts gaze from one feature of an object to another, as described previously—will be better able to scan a full object. Long-looking babies may continue to study just one feature for long periods (Rose et al., 2004).

Another visual ability of infants is depth perception. In a classic study, Gibson and Walk (1960) discovered that babies as young as 6 months would not crawl out over a **visual cliff** even when they were encouraged to do so by their mothers. (The cliff, of course, was a

tracking: The ability to visually follow a moving object with one's eyes. Tracking becomes smoother and more accurate during the first 6 months of life.

scanning: The visual ability to look over all the features of an object and to get a complete picture of what it is like. Babies become competent in scanning an entire object by 3 months of age.

visual cliff: A research apparatus designed to show that babies have depth perception. Babies are encouraged to crawl out over a clear plastic surface that appears to be a deep drop off; if they do not, depth perception can be inferred.

perfectly safe surface covered with clear plastic that only gave the appearance of being a deep abyss.) Babies' refusal to venture out over the cliff provided clear evidence that they could perceive depth at this young age. In more recent studies, 10- and 12-month-olds were found to have quite sophisticated distance perception—a form of depth perception (Kavšek, 2007; McKenzie, Skouteris, Day, Hartman, & Yonas, 1993). In this research, babies were found more often to reach for objects that were close to them but less often for those that were far away. Even newborns—only days old—have been found to widen their eyes, pull back their heads, and hold up their hands when they view objects moving toward them (Bower, 1975).

Experience in crawling has been found to contribute to an ability to visualize depth and distance (Witherington, Campos, Anderson, Lejeune, & Seah, 2005). A baby who has an opportunity to crawl in an unrestricted environment may have many practical experiences with height—a tumble off a sofa or an inability to reach a cookie on a kitchen counter, for example. A baby who is more often confined in a playpen or crib may not come to visualize or understand concepts of *far away* or *a long way down* as quickly.

Hearing

Babies can hear quite well, perhaps even before birth. In one study, fetuses as early as 26 weeks after conception were found to respond to sounds with accelerated heart rates and increased movement (Lee, Brown, Hains, & Kisilevsky, 2007). Newborns can distinguish among sounds of different kinds—high and low pitches or loud and soft noises (Leibold & Werner, 2007). Certain sounds, such as lullabies, singing, or heartbeats, tend to soothe them. Others, such as sudden, high-pitched noises, agitate them (Cathey, 2006; Sansavini, Bertoncini, & Giovanelli, 1997).

Newborns tend to cry at the sound of other infants' crying (Dondi et al., 1999; Sagi & Hoffman, 1976). An implication of this finding is that humans may be born with an innate propensity to distinguish and become upset over human cries. Parents may more readily respond to the cries of their own babies because they are naturally predisposed to be disturbed by this sound.

Babies are more attentive to certain sounds. They prefer singing and women's voices (Vouloumanos & Werker, 2007), and they are especially attentive to the voices of their own mothers (Purhonen, Kilpeläinen-Lees, Valkonen-Korhonen, Karhu, & Lehtonen, 2004). They can discriminate among individual consonant sounds, even those of other languages (Werker & Tees, 2002; Werker & Yeung, 2005)! Babies as young as 2 days old can distinguish adult-to-child speech (which is characterized by especially exaggerated, higher-pitched intonation) from adult-to-adult speech (Cooper & Aslin, 1990; Kitamura et al., 2001). Five-month-olds are able to discriminate between intonations indicating approval (i.e., "Very good!") and disapproval (i.e., "No!") even when uttered in different languages (Fernald, 1993; Werker et al., 2006).

Abilities to locate the direction of sounds, search for and track their sources, and selectively listen to one sound over another are acquired as early as 5 months (Lewkowicz, 1996; Pickens, 1994). Cultural differences in these abilities have been observed. For example, Puerto Rican infants have been found to track sounds more accurately than Caucasian or African American infants (Garcia Coll et al., 1998). Again, such differences may be due partly to genetics and partly to unique family or community experiences.

How can researchers possibly determine what newborn babies can hear or not hear? They use the habituation technique, described in the previous chapter. They monitor sucking or heart rate as babies listen to sounds—say, a voice saying a *b* sound in English. Eventually, babies grow uninterested, and their heart rate and sucking slow.

At this point, the voice changes to a *d* sound, and these biological functions all increase again. What does this indicate? The baby can hear the difference and shows renewed interest.

Taste and Smell

Taste and smell develop early among the senses. The ability to discriminate among smells and tastes may be acquired well before birth (Hummel, Roudnitzky, Kempter, & Laing, 2007). Newborns can distinguish among five tastes: sour, bitter, salty, sweet, and neutral (Rosenstein & Oster, 1988; B. A. Smith & Blass, 1996). They have clear taste preferences, sucking on a sweet solution more continuously and slowly, as an adult might savor a gourmet meal (Blass & Ciaramitaro, 1994). Readers who have a sweet tooth may find it interesting to know that their cravings may be part of biological inheritance, present at birth. In contrast, newborns do not appear to like salty solutions: they suck these in short bursts and for only brief periods. The craving for salty snacks prevalent in some American cultures, then, may be an acquired taste.

Newborns can distinguish between pleasant and unpleasant smells (Case, Repacholi, & Stevenson, 2006). They also can detect where an odor is coming from. When an unpleasant smell comes from one direction, they rapidly turn their heads the opposite way (Rosenstein & Oster, 1988).

Taste and smell are critical for neonatal survival. Infant preferences for certain sweetish, nonsalty solutions will facilitate early nursing. A series of studies has suggested that odor guides newborn feeding as well. Babies only a few days old prefer the odor of their own nursing mothers' breast pads to the smells of those of unfamiliar lactating women (Doucet, Soussignan, Sagot, & Schaal, 2007; Porter & Winberg, 1999). These authors conclude that odor may attract babies and direct their search for the nipple. These odor preferences do not exist among bottle-fed babies, suggesting that such preferences arise from early experience with maternal smells. Another study has found that female babies are more likely to show these preferences than are males, suggesting a genetic cause (Makin & Porter, 1989). Again, a complex interaction of heredity and experience may be at work in infants' acquisition of perceptual abilities.

Touch

The sense of touch develops before birth and plays a critical function in human development throughout life. Parental touch has a positive effect on infant emotions and health. Babies are soothed by being stroked or patted. Parental touching has been found to elicit smiles, gazes, and increased attention from very young babies (Ferber, Feldman, & Makhoul, 2007; Stack & Muir, 1992). A routine of warm touching can lead to positive developmental outcomes for at-risk babies (Ferber et al., 2005; Scafidi et al., 1986). Touch may be a primary way that parents communicate with their babies or initiate play (A. S. Carter, Mayes, & Pajer, 1990). It also serves as a medium for learning about things. For example, 8-month-olds have been found to recognize and remember the shapes and textures of objects (Catherwood, 1993; Streri & Féron, 2005). Even newborns can distinguish among tactile stimuli and discriminate between touches to one part of the body or another (Kisilevsky, Fearon, & Muir, 1998). Touch is often used in conjunction with other senses to interpret the world (Sann & Streri, 2007). For example, looking and touching may be used together to recognize a toy.

Sadly, babies can also feel pain—from an injection or a circumcision without anesthesia (Bartocci, Bergqvist, Lagercrantz, & Anand, 2006). A current debate among pediatricians is whether babies should receive anesthesia for minor medical procedures and, if so, how much may be safely administered.

BRAIN GROWTH

neurons: Cells in the brain that transmit and retrieve messages to and from all organs and muscles.

dendrites: Elongated tissues on a neuron that receive messages from the axons of other nerve cells.

axon: A long thread of tissue that extends out from the cell body of a neuron and sends messages to the dentrites of other nerve cells.

neurotransmitters: Chemicals secreted from neurons that are responsible for transmitting messages from one cell to another in the nervous system.

synapse: A juncture between the axon of one neuron and the dendrites of another through which neural messages are transmitted.

All areas of development are regulated by one marvelous organ—the brain. One of the most significant physical changes in infancy is brain growth. A baby's brain develops at an astonishing rate; by age 3, it is as complex as it will ever be (Franceschini et al., 2007)!

How the Brain Works

The brain is composed of billions of nerve cells, called **neurons,** that are designed to send and retrieve information across organs or muscles. A neuron is illustrated in Figure 6-2.

Each neuron is made up of a cell body that is surrounded by **dendrites,** elongated tissues that receive messages. A very long thread of tissue, the **axon,** extends out from the cell body toward other nerve cells. The purpose of the axon is to send messages. If an infant decides to reach out and grasp a favorite toy, a signal is sent from one neuron to another—from the axon of one cell to the dendrite of the next. In this way, the message is passed along to the muscles and perceptual organs that are needed for this movement.

The message in one cell is transmitted to another via chemical secretions called **neurotransmitters.** These travel out of the axon of one cell and pass into the dendrites of the next through a juncture called a **synapse.** The number of synapses in the brain increases rapidly during infancy and accounts for the remarkable intellectual growth during this period. **Myelin** also helps neural messages travel efficiently from one cell to another. This is a fatty sheath that surrounds the axon and ensures that signals travel efficiently, quickly, and accurately.

The brain is organized into regions. Each of these is responsible for specific functions. *Sensory* regions send and receive information regarding the sense organs. *Motor* regions regulate movement. *Association* regions are responsible for complex thought processes. The **frontal cortex** is an important area of the brain that develops rapidly beginning at about

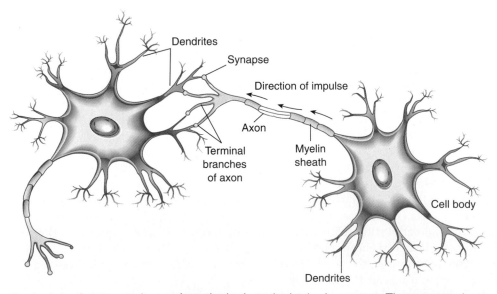

FIGURE 6-2 A message is sent from the brain to the body via neurons. The message is passed across cells through neurotransmitters that travel from the axon of one cell to a dendrite of another. This occurs at a juncture called a synapse. Myelin, an insulating sheath around the axon, ensures that the message travels accurately from cell to cell.

8 months. This area is associated with the ability to express and regulate emotions. (Note that 8 months is about the age at which most babies become securely attached to their parents.)

The brain is also organized into right and left hemispheres. In right-handed individuals, the left hemisphere governs analytical thinking and language, and the right hemisphere governs spatial and auditory perception. The left hemisphere controls the right visual field, and the right hemisphere controls the left visual field. This specialization of left and right sides of the brain has been referred to as **brain lateralization.**

The Super-Dense Infant Brain

The number of neurons and the connections among them—the synapses—increase at a startling rate in the early years. By age 2, the number of synapses reaches an adult level. By age 3, a child's brain has 1,000 trillion synapses—twice that of any reader of this textbook (Paterson, Heim, Friedman, Choudhury, & Benasich, 2006)! Infants' brains have been referred to, then, as **super-dense.** They contain more complex neural connections and have a higher metabolic rate (i.e., they use more energy) than at any other period of life (Chugani, 1997).

Babies acquire more synapses than they will need. So, after age 3, some of these connections are eliminated. In the elementary years, as many synapses are lost as are added. By adolescence, the loss of synapses far outpaces their acquisition. Typical, 18-year-olds have lost roughly half their infant synapses. After infancy, then, brain growth is a pruning process in which brain connections that are not used or needed disappear (M. H. Johnson, 1997, 2000). Figure 6-3 shows this trend.

Which synapses are kept, and which are discarded? Scientists believe this is a "use it or lose it" process (Franceschini et al., 2007). Synapses that have not been used often enough disappear, while those that have been reinforced through experience become permanent. For example, if babies exercise synapses in the cerebral cortex that are responsible for thinking and language, these will be maintained. Babies will, thus, become more competent in these areas. Children who do not use these synapses, however, may be hampered in language or thinking.

This pruning and reinforcing of synapses explains, in part, why there are cultural variations in skills and thinking (R. Shore, 1997). Children growing up in hunter-gatherer societies might, at an early age, acquire neural connections needed for efficient hunting. For

myelin: A fatty sheath that surrounds the axon and ensures that signals travel efficiently, quickly, and accurately.

frontal cortex: A region of the brain that develops rapidly at 8 months of age and is associated with the ability to express and regulate emotions.

brain lateralization: The organization of the brain into right and left hemispheres, with each hemisphere performing unique and specialized functions.

super-dense infant brain: The brain of the infant, which grows more rapidly and has more connections (synapses) among nerve cells than an adult brain.

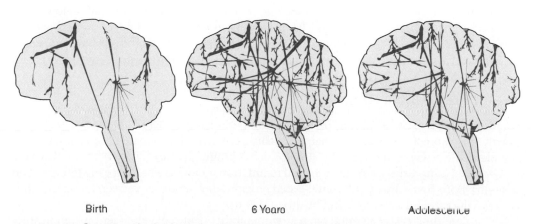

Birth   6 Years   Adolescence

FIGURE 6-3 Synapses in the brain increase rapidly in the early years. The number of synapses actually decreases in adolescence and adulthood as neural connections are pruned.

SOURCE: From Chugani, "Neuroimaging of developmental nonlinearity and developmental pathologies," in R. W. Thatcher, et al., eds. Developmental Neuroimaging: Mapping the development of brain and behavior. Copyright © 1997 Academic Press. Reprinted by permission of Elsevier.

such children, synapses that promote perception and motor coordination might be used and maintained. Growing up in crowded, urban apartment buildings, Shore suggests, might reinforce synapses that allow children to filter out certain kinds of stimuli. Brain growth is an interaction, then, between biology and cultural experience.

Promoting Infant Brain Growth

How can parents and caregivers nurture the brain growth of babies they care for? One obvious way is through early stimulation. Providing perceptual, motor, and language experiences for babies will enhance the formation of dendrites and increase the number of synapses (Chugani, 1997). Of course, overstimulation—a constant bombardment of sights and sounds—would work against healthy brain growth. Such experiences might cause stress, leading to interference in neural development (Gunnar, 1996).

The most powerful influence on infant brain growth, however, is attachment—the process by which infants bond emotionally with significant adults in their lives. When babies receive warm, responsive care from parents and other caregivers, they come to know and trust these adults. The resulting bond literally protects the human brain from stress or trauma (Gunnar, 1996; Watamura et al., 2004). Here's how it works: When babies experience stressful events, levels of a hormone called **cortisol** are elevated in the body. Cortisol threatens brain development by reducing the number of synapses and leaving neurons vulnerable to damage. Babies who suffer great trauma—as in the case of child abuse or neglect, for example—are at risk of poor brain growth because of these high cortisol levels. In particular, areas of the brain that regulate emotions are affected (Perry, 1996). Infants under great stress are more likely to suffer anxiety, impulsivity, hyperactivity, and poor control of their emotions later in life.

Babies who are securely attached to caregivers, however, are less likely to produce cortisol under stressful conditions (Hertsgaard, Gunnar, Erickson, & Nachmias, 1995; Mörelius, Nelson, & Gustafsson, 2007). When they do, the levels of this hormone are far lower than in children who are not securely attached. Thus, a warm bond with parents and other caregivers—so important for security and happiness—also has a positive impact on physical brain development.

The process may be more complex, however, than simply asking all parents and child care providers to stroke, rock, or snuggle with babies more often. The findings of one study suggest that it is the long-term, emotional bond of babies to their parents that reduces cortisol and nurtures the brain, not any specific parenting behavior (M. Lewis & Ramsey, 1999). In this research, mothers' soothing behaviors during an inoculation visit to a doctor's office did not result in lower cortisol levels. The authors conclude that what may be most important in protecting the brain is a baby's overall view that her or his parents are dependable and caring. Soothing behaviors are only one of several interactions, over the course of infancy, that will lead to this protective attachment.

Prime Time for Brain Growth

Because the brain grows so rapidly in infancy, this period is considered a *prime time* for neural growth. R. Shore (1997) argues that a primary responsibility of parents and infant care providers is "the day-to-day care of young children's brains" (p. 26). Even infants with severe brain-related disabilities—autism or mental retardation—can benefit from early intervention programs. Both home-based and center-based programs for infants have been found to significantly reduce cognitive, social, and health problems.

This prime time is also a period of great vulnerability. Brain development is significantly impaired by *in utero* exposure to drugs, child abuse, maternal depression, and other factors (Cirulli, Berry, & Alleva, 2003; Swain, Lorberbaum, Kose, & Strathearn, 2007). Even in these cases, however, early intervention can offset such negative influences if provided in the first 3 years of life (Ramey & Landesman-Ramey, 1996).

cortisol: A hormone that increases in the body with stress and threatens infant brain development by reducing the number of synapses and leaving neurons vulnerable to damage.

CLASSROOM ADAPTATIONS: INFANTS WITH PERCEPTUAL-MOTOR CHALLENGES

Genetic disorders and complications before or during birth can adversely affect infant motor development and perception. Some disabilities are detected early in infancy or even before birth. However, their full impact on babies' abilities to move around and explore objects and people may not be fully realized until the middle of the first year. A baby with a particular challenge may interact quite typically in the early weeks of life. Only later, when smiling, grasping objects, and sitting up are expected, do the adverse effects of the disability become obvious.

Caregivers can adapt infant care environments to address specific special needs (Hooper & Umansky, 2008). Through the design of classroom space, selection of play objects, and purposeful interactions with babies, caregivers have been found to promote positive development among infants with a variety of disabilities.

Visual Impairment

One out of 3,000 babies is born with a **visual impairment;** the most common cause is *retinopathy of prematurity*, a condition related to low birth weight (McLean, Bailey, & Wolery, 2003). Visual impairments are difficult to detect, yet it is extremely important to diagnose them early. Eighty percent of infant learning involves vision; early detection allows parents and professionals to develop special interventions for those who can't see well (Olusanya, 2005). What can parents, child care providers, and pediatricians look for in identifying visual problems in the first year of life? McLean et al. (2003) suggest the following indicators:

1. A lack of visual curiosity
2. Closing one eye when viewing objects
3. Widely roving eye movements
4. Side-to-side movement of the head, without fixing the eyes in a steady gaze
5. Excessive blinking or rubbing of the eyes
6. Sensitivity to sunlight.[*]

Professionals working with babies and their families might watch for these signs. The American Academy of Pediatrics now recommends an immediate screening by a medical team for babies whose parents report a concern of any kind. Babies with visual impairment but with no other disabilities will develop early motor skills at a typical pace (Fazzi et al., 2002). However, at a point when most infants begin to reach for and grasp objects, visually impaired babies will not. At an age when most typically developing babies are beginning to crawl or walk, those who cannot see well remain relatively stationary (Ashkenazy, Cohen, Ophir-Cohen, & Tirosh, 2005). Several theories have been offered to explain such motor delays (Fraiberg, 1977). In typical homes or child care centers, babies' movements are often guided and motivated by vision. Visually impaired babies move less because they are not visually inspired to get somewhere. They don't reach as often because they are not motivated to obtain an object they cannot see.

While visual impairment inhibits motor development, motor delays can, in turn, impair visual abilities. Physically challenging conditions have been found to contribute to poor visual discrimination skills (Hooper & Umansky, 2008). One theory to explain this finding is that motor play is necessary for training the visual and auditory systems. Children

visual Impairment: A condition characterized by blindness or severely limited vision that can impair motor, cognitive, and other areas of development.

---

[*]From Mary Mclean, Mark Wolery & Donald B. Bailey Jr., *Assessing Infants and Preschoolers with Special Needs*, 3/e. Published by Allyn and Bacon/Merrill Education, Boston, MA. Copyright © 2004 by Pearson Education. Adapted by permission of the publisher.

who cannot crawl, climb, or jump lack important perceptual experiences. A harmful, circular relationship may, then, emerge: Children may not play because they cannot see well. Their lack of play experiences leads to further impairments in their vision.

How can caregivers adapt classrooms to support the development of infants with visual impairment? The following strategies are recommended by early intervention specialists (Howard, Williams, Port, & Lepper, 2004; Hooper & Umansky, 2008):

1. *An enlarged motor play space with safe challenges.* Caregivers can provide a safe, open motor area where children with visual impairment can move and explore without constant adult guidance. (Overdependence on adults has been found to impede the development of infants with this disability.) Obstacles, such as large pillows or soft ramps for children to crawl over or around, can be included. Not only will such spaces promote physical development, but they will encourage infants to use their *residual vision*—the limited vision they do have.

2. *Auditory toys.* One caregiver working with an infant with a visual impairment said that she "made everything in her classroom jingle." What she meant by this was that almost every toy in her center made noise. Objects that produce sound—squeaking toys and musical instruments, for example—can be purchased. A jingle bell can be attached to objects that do not make sound—stuffed animals, beanbags, or plastic baby books—to help infants with visual impairment find and play with them.

3. *Identification patches.* Highly tactile objects—toys that are rough, smooth, soft, warm, or cold—have been found to encourage exploration and play among infants with visual impairment. An identifying patch can be added to objects that are not highly textured so that babies can identify them without seeing well. A special toy, for example, or the chair a toddler sits in at snack time can be marked by gluing on a piece of Velcro. The child can feel for this to identify these objects.

Hearing Impairment

One out of every 750 healthy infants is born with a **hearing impairment** (McLean et al., 2003). This condition is far more prevalent among premature babies (17%) and those who require neonatal intensive care (up to 78%). As with visual impairments, auditory problems are very difficult to detect—particularly moderate hearing losses. Nearly 20% of auditory impairments are not detected until the age of 18 months or later (Holstrum et al., 2008). McLean and her colleagues (2003) offer the following as key indicators of hearing loss:

1. Decreased or abnormal quality of vocalization
2. Failure to respond to sudden, loud sounds
3. Failure to respond to or locate the direction of a parent's voice
4. A sudden smile or look of surprise when an adult who has been speaking to the infant picks the child up
5. Favoring one ear over the other by turning the head in just one direction to listen or by holding an auditory toy just to one ear
6. Difficulty in discriminating among early words
7. Tugging or pulling at the ears
8. Discharges from the ear canal.[*]

hearing impairment: A condition caused by a variety of factors that is characterized by deafness or severely limited auditory perception and can lead to language, motor, and other developmental delays.

Professionals should watch for these indicators in the infants they work with and encourage parents to do so. In addition, they should advocate for legislation requiring all hospitals

---

[*]From Mary Mclean, Mark Wolery & Donald B. Bailey Jr., *Assessing Infants and Preschoolers with Special Needs*, 3/e. Published by Allyn and Bacon/Merrill Education, Boston, MA. Copyright © 2004 by Pearson Education. Adapted by permission of the publisher.

ADVOCACY AND PUBLIC POLICY

Supporting Hearing Screening for Infants

As discussed in this chapter, hearing impairments can have a profound effect on children's development. On each day, 33 babies are born with a hearing loss in America, making this one of the most common birth defects (American Speech–Language–Hearing Association, 2008). Intervention for children with hearing impairments can be highly effective when implemented early in life. Unfortunately, nearly 20% of hearing impairments are not detected until the age of 18 months or later. One way to ensure that all children with this condition are identified is to provide a screening procedure at the time of birth. The ideal place for this to occur is in hospitals and clinics where babies are delivered. Currently, 85% of newborns are now screened. This means that a portion of infants, in a country with the most advanced health care in the world, still do not receive these early screening services. More worrisome is the fact that only half of those infants who are screened and found to have a hearing loss receive intervention services before age 6 months. Professionals can advocate for state and federal legislation mandating and funding hearing screening and intervention for every newborn in America.

Professionals can contact legislators in states that currently do not have laws mandating newborn hearing screening in hospitals and birthing centers. (A list of states that do not have such laws is provided on the American Speech–Language–Hearing Association Website at http://www.asha.org.) Professionals should urge legislators to sponsor bills with the following provisions: (a) mandatory screening at all hospitals and maternity centers for all newborns, prior to discharge, using auditory brain stem response, otoacoustic emissions, or other means approved by health professionals; (b) a formal procedure for informing parents of results of the screening and making recommendations for follow-up testing and treatment prior to the newborn's discharge; and (c) mandatory reimbursement for screening by all health insurers, hospitals, medical service corporations, and health maintenance organizations.

Professionals might also contact federal congressional leaders to ask their support for increased funding for the Early Hearing Detection and Intervention (EHDI) program, which provides federal funds for states to carry out these screening procedures and to conduct research on the effectiveness of these programs. In recent budget-tightening years, continued appropriations for this program have been threatened. Through such advocacy efforts, all children with hearing impairments may one day be identified and receive intervention within days after birth.

and maternity centers to screen newborns for hearing loss prior to discharge. (See the Advocacy and Public Policy box in this chapter.)

Hearing impairment influences many areas of development. As with visual disabilities, this challenging condition can inhibit motor competence. Babies with poor or no hearing may acquire motor skills much like unimpaired infants for a number of months. When they have acquired motor abilities that allow them to respond to auditory stimuli, however, their challenging condition becomes more obvious (Holstrum et al., 2008). They may not crawl, reach, or bounce in response to music, voices, or other sounds.

The vast majority of studies on hearing disability in infancy focus on delays in language development. Hearing-impaired babies show significant problems in learning to talk (Castrogiovanni, 2008). Concerns that hearing-impaired babies will fail to form positive relationships with parents have also been raised (Moeller, 2007). However, research suggests that when parents are physically warm and responsive in their interactions, their hearing-impaired babies become as securely attached as those who hear well.

Adaptations can be made in infant care centers to meet the needs of children with hearing impairment. The following are recommended strategies (Hooper & Umansky, 2008; Holstrum, Gaffney, Gravel, & Oyler, 2008; Howard et al., 2004):

1. **Rich visual and tactile cues.** Caregivers can provide toys that are visually rich and tactile so that children with hearing impairment can explore using a variety of senses. Any classroom activities or objects that require auditory discrimination can be accompanied by visual cues. For example, a caregiver recently helped a toddler with hearing loss participate in a group song by providing him with a drum to beat. She modeled the rhythm—the places in the song when the drum was to be struck—by using her own drum. The child watched her and pounded along to the music, enjoying a rich rhythmic experience even though he could not hear the music clearly.

2. **Using total communication.** Caregivers can use **total communication**—a system in which manual signals, along with spoken words, are used to communicate with infants and toddlers with hearing impairment. This can include formal sign languages, such as American sign language, but also informal gestures and facial expressions (e.g., waving goodbye, making exaggerated faces of delight). Early intervention specialists suggest that these should be accompanied by verbalizations. This allows children to develop their *residual hearing*—the hearing ability they do have—and to acquire an ability to read lips.

3. **Assistive devices for hearing loss.** A range of assistive devices are now used with infants and toddlers that help them hear more clearly. These range from traditional hearing aids to directional microphones and *completely in the ear canal* (CIC) devices. These must be carefully matched to the infant's age, cognitive ability, and degree of hearing loss.

4. **Acoustical adaptations to the classroom.** Classrooms can be adapted to reduce background noise that impedes an infant's ability to discern voices and other important sounds. Placing acoustical tiles on ceilings and even walls and placing rugs or full carpeting on the floor can help children with hearing impairment focus on relevant auditory cues.

Other Conditions That Affect Perception and Motor Ability

Many other disorders can hamper perceptual and motor development. Down syndrome can produce motor delays that are observable in infancy. Physical malformations resulting from the disorder can also affect perception. Eye cataracts, for example, are prevalent in babies with Down syndrome. Cerebral palsy, a condition caused by brain damage from oxygen deprivation or trauma before or during birth, often leads to blindness, deafness, or permanent impairment of motor abilities.

Early intervention can significantly affect the degree to which disabilities interfere with perceptual and motor development. In several studies, children with Down syndrome and other challenging conditions were provided with intensive services, including home-based intervention, parent support, and social services (Dunst, 2007; Shonkoff, Hauser-Cram, Krauss, & Upshur, 1992). Infants achieved an 8-month gain in motor development, with some advancing by as much as 12 months. These outcomes are remarkable given the perceptual and motor delays these babies exhibited before the study. The researchers concluded that a multidisciplinary, family-based intervention can significantly enhance motor skill among babies with disabilities.

INFANT OBESITY

As discussed in Chapter 4, **childhood obesity** is a growing health problem in the United States. It has been linked to a variety of health risks in adulthood, including heart disease and diabetes (Reilly et al., 2003). Obesity is determined by calculating the **body mass index (BMI),** a formula in which one's weight is compared with one's height (BMI = weight in lbs./height in inches^2 × 703). A score of 30 or higher is considered an indicator of obesity. For children, the identification of obesity is a little more complicated because the amount of fat and muscle change with age. A child's BMI is usually compared with a profile of BMIs for other children her age and gender in order to determine obesity.

total communication: A system of communication in which manual signals, such as sign language, informal gestures, and facial expressions, are used along with verbalizations to communicate with children with hearing impairment.

childhood obesity: A condition in which one's body fat exceeds normal levels and can lead to health problems in later life.

body mass index: A measure of health status, computed by considering weight in relation to height (the formula for calculating BMI is weight/height^2).

Should we begin worrying about obesity in infancy? A traditional view has been that plump babies are healthy ones, that "baby fat" is a characteristic of a thriving, well-fed child. In fact, infant obesity predicts a number of health problems, not the least of which is later childhood and adult obesity.

A number of factors contribute to this health risk. There is a strong link between poverty and infant obesity (Olson & Strawderman, 2008). This may be due to material malnutrition during pregancy (McNeely et al., 2007). If a fetus does not receive adequate nutrients in gestation, changes may occur in the body that prompt fat to be stored. It is as if infants, born hungry, increase their fat storage in preparation for future food shortages. This predisposition to fat storage can remain throughout life (Taylor & Poston, 2007). Infants of some ethnic groups are more likely to be obese (Q. Zhang & Wang, 2004). Mexican American infants, for example, are more frequently overweight (Buekens, Notzon, Kotelchuck, & Wilcox, 2000). This may be due to genetics, the higher incidence of poverty, or infant feeding practices within this cultural group. (Buekens et al., 2000). A growing rate of infant obesity in India has been associated with undernourishment (and a resulting predisposition to fat storage) during fetal development (Yajnik, 2007).

One way to lower the risk of infant obesity is through breastfeeding. Countless studies have shown that children who are breastfed are less likely to be overweight in infancy, later childhood, and adulthood (Davis, Weigensberg, Shaibi, & Crespo, 2007; Harder, Bergmann, Kallischnigg, & Plagemann, 2005). Delaying the introduction of solid foods until at least 17 weeks has also been found to reduce obesity risk (Sellwood, 2008). Mothers who smoked during pregancy have been found more likely to have obese infants and children, even after social factors such as poverty and lifestyle were controlled (Oken, Levitan, & Gillman, 2008). A way to protect an infant from problems of obesity, then, is for the mother to maintain her own good nutrition and health during pregnancy.

CHILD GUIDANCE: *A Cognitive Approach to Teaching Self-Help Skills*

Caregivers and parents use a variety of techniques to help toddlers learn self-help skills, for example, how to dress themselves, eat with a utensil, or use the toilet independently. Behaviorist strategies, such as giving rewards or praise, are commonly used. An alternative to these methods is a cognitive approach in which adults help toddlers to *understand* the purposes and consequences of caring for themselves in daily life. Among the strategies used in this approach are verbalizing and explaining, pointing out consequences, questioning, redirecting, and choice giving. Each of these will be illustrated using a toileting example:

Verbalizing and explaining. A caregiver begins by verbalizing the importance of using the toilet independently. The explanation must be simple and concrete: "When children get older, they can use the toilet all by themselves" or "If you go to the bathroom right in the toilet, your pants stay nice and dry."

Pointing out consequences. When a child has an accident, the caregiver calmly (and without judgment) points out the consequences of this in a concrete way: "Oops. You didn't make it to the toilet. Your pants are all wet. Feel. See how wet they are?" When a child uses the bathroom independently, the caregiver comments on the outcome of this as well: "Ooh, feel! You went right in the toilet, and your pants are dry. We don't need to change them."

Questioning. When accidents or successes occur, the caregiver asks simple questions about this: "You went right in the toilet. How do your pants feel now?" or "Oops. You didn't use the toilet. So what do we need to do now?" After the child answers, the caregiver responds: "Right, your pants are all dry, aren't they?" or "Yep, we need to change your pants because they're wet."

Redirecting. At the first sign of bladder or bowel urgency, the caregiver guides the child to the bathroom, using language: "Hey, why don't you come use the bathroom so your pants stay nice and dry? Then you can come back and play."

Choice giving. The caregiver gradually gives over more and more responsibility to the child by giving choices: "I can help you to use the toilet, or you can do it all by yourself. You decide."

The purpose of these strategies is to help children understand why using the toilet is important. From a cognitive perspective, understanding leads to greater personal commitment to learning these skills. Of course, these techniques can be applied to teaching toddlers other skills, such as dressing, eating, and picking up toys.

SUMMARY

Infancy, a period from birth to age 2, is marked by rapid physical growth. Babies change in appearance and acquire many new motor abilities. These abilities vary among babies of different cultural backgrounds. Parents of some cultures are more active and physical in their parenting; parents of other cultures are less so. As a result, infants in these families vary in their physical competence. As children enter toddlerhood, they acquire self-help skills, such as using the toilet and eating with a utensil. Which skills they learn and at what age will be determined by family and cultural values and practices. Infants also acquire new perceptual abilities. They can see, hear, touch, smell, and taste very well by the end of this developmental period. Their brains also grow rapidly. In fact, their brains become more dense and complex than at any other point in development. Perceptual and motor impairments can inhibit development. The negative effects of visual, hearing, motor, and other disabilities can be offset, to some degree, by early intervention and classroom adaptations.

RESEARCH INTO PRACTICE

CRITICAL CONCEPT 1

Physical growth is rapid in infancy. Babies acquire many new motor abilities and self-help skills during this developmental period. They also acquire new perceptual abilities; they can see, hear, touch, taste, and smell as well as adults by age 6 months. Physical growth and perceptual and motor development progress in a relatively fixed order. For example, babies swipe at objects before they can grasp them; they hold objects between their fingers and palm before they can use their pincer grasp.

Application #1 Become familiar with the order in which physical traits and perceptual and motor abilities are acquired. Using this information, you can assess progress in physical growth and identify babies with physical challenges.

Application #2 Create infant play environments that promote large motor development. In child care, equipment should be provided to meet the needs of a variety of levels of competence. Mats or carpeting allow younger infants to wiggle, scoot, roll, and crawl. Cushioned stairs and platforms, ramps, and low climbing equipment are useful for older babies and toddlers.

Application #3 Promote perceptual development by providing interesting and safe toys for babies to look at, listen to, touch, and even smell and taste. Toys that stimulate several different senses, such as objects that are visually interesting and also make noise, are particularly useful in infant perceptual and motor development.

CRITICAL CONCEPT 2

There is great individual variation in the age at which perceptual and motor abilities are acquired. Culture may be one factor that influences the pace of motor development. The games parents play with their babies, their carrying practices, and the kinds of toys available can affect physical competence. How quickly toddlers learn self-help skills such as toileting also can be influenced by cultural beliefs and practices.

Application #1 Caregivers should be aware of cultural differences in motor and perceptual development. Care should be taken not to misconstrue such physical differences as deficits.

Application #2 Create a multicultural motor curriculum for babies by interviewing parents about what games are played in the home. The traditional chants, songs, finger plays, and games of diverse cultural groups can be introduced to babies of all cultures in infant care.

Application #3 Discuss family expectations for children's learning of self-help skills such as toileting and eating. Consensus should be reached on goals for independence that reflect cultural beliefs and traditions but do not cause stress in children.

CRITICAL CONCEPT 3

The brain grows and develops at a remarkable rate in infancy. A typical 3-year-old has twice the number of synapses—connections among brain cells—as an adult. After age 3, children lose synapses they do not use. Stimulation and warm, responsive caregiving are needed to ensure that important brain cell connections are created and maintained.

Application #1 Provide intellectual and language stimulation—talking, singing, reading to, and playing with infants. Care should be taken not to overstimulate babies, however, since overstimulation can lead to stress and impede neural development.

Application #2 Provide nurturing and responsive care to facilitate attachment. Using warm, physical touch and responding quickly to needs, adults can create positive emotional bonds with babies. These bonds not only enhance feelings of security but also will protect infants' brains from damaging environmental influences.

CRITICAL CONCEPT 4

Perceptual and motor development are affected by challenging conditions. Genetic disorders or environmental trauma before or during birth can significantly impair physical growth. Adaptations in child care programs and intervention programs that provide services to babies and their families can offset the negative effects of these disorders.

Application #1   Work in your community to establish home-based and center-based early intervention programs that provide services to infants with special needs and their families.

Application #2   Adapt play environments and toys to meet the needs of babies with challenging conditions. Infants with visual impairments, for example, can be provided with toys that are rich to the touch or create interesting sounds.

Application #3   Provide emotional support to families of infants with special needs. Caregivers can encourage parents to express frustrations and anxieties. Parent support groups can be organized in infant care centers or community agencies.

ASSESSING YOUNG CHILDREN: Infant Physical and Motor Development

Areas of Development	What to Watch For	Indicators of Atypical Development	Applications
Large motor abilities	Large muscle skills: grasping, creeping, and standing in the first year; walking, running, jumping, and climbing in the second.	Typical motor development only until a time when grasping, sitting up, or walking are expected; then, significant delays.	Provide a large, safe motor area where children are able to move around and explore with minimal adult restriction. Include challenging obstacles— large pillows; soft, vinyl ramps; and low, carpeted steps and platforms—to encourage large motor problem solving.
Perceptual and fine motor abilities	Increasing ability to hear, see, touch, taste, and smell stimuli during the first months of life. Increasing skill in coordinating senses and fine motor actions (e.g., looking at and picking up a small object).	Failing to respond to visual or auditory stimuli. An inability to coordinate perceptions (e.g., failure to turn one's head in the direction of a sound).	Create multisensory play environments. Provide toys of varying textures and colors and ones that produce sound. A soft environment can be achieved by including carpeting, pillows, and stuffed animals.
Self-help or family life skills	An ability to eat with a spoon and sit at a table during meals by age 2. An ability to take off or put on some items of clothing by this age. An ability to use the toilet independently by age 3.	An inability to perform such simple self-help functions as feeding oneself or using the toilet by age 3.	Interview families about cultural goals for learning self-help skills. Encourage these skills through a positive, gentle, cognitive approach that helps toddlers learn the purposes for and consequences of developing these abilities.

Interpreting Assessment Data: Variations in these areas of development may be due to differences in cultural practices or family life experience. Infants whose parents play with them actively will show more advanced motor abilities. Children of some cultural groups will not acquire specific self-help skills because these are not stressed within their families. An inability to attend to stimuli or to perform simple motor activities may be the result of challenging conditions, such as visual or auditory impairment. Significant delays may also be common for children with cerebral palsy or Down syndrome. Early intervention in infant care centers or homes can enhance the perceptual development of infants with these special needs.

CHAPTER 7

Cognitive Development in Infancy

GUIDING QUESTIONS

1. What are Piaget's six substages of infant cognitive development, and how do babies think and solve problems during each of these periods?
2. How accurately does Piaget's theory of infant development describe children from diverse cultures?
3. What are the characteristics of infant memory, and how does this cognitive ability change during the first 2 years of life?
4. What are the two styles of memory during infancy, and how do these influence development?
5. What types of play are observed in infancy, and how do these develop in the first 2 years of life?
6. What are the variations in infant cognitive development caused by culture and poverty?
7. What are some causes of cognitive disabilities in infancy, and what types of interventions or classroom adaptations address these?

This chapter describes the intellectual development of children between birth and age 2. The ways that infant thinking and learning differ from that of older children or adults will be explored. The following story illustrates why intellectual development—sometimes called **cognitive development**—of babies is fascinating and important. The problem solving of the two infants in the story shows the remarkable cognitive changes that children go through as they develop during this 2-year period.

A Bedouin Arab mother works busily in the kitchen, one of only two "rooms" in the tent where her family lives in the Negev Desert in Israel. Her two infants are nearby. She continually shooes her oldest, a 16-month-old, away from the cooking fires. Her 4-month-old lies next to her on a pile of blankets. When this youngest infant begins to fuss, the mother hangs a piece of rope over a pole so that it dangles just inches from her baby's face. (There are virtually no toys in this home; anything that is available—pieces of cloth, wood, furniture, and even animals that wander through the tent—becomes a plaything for the children.)

The strategy works. The 4-month-old wiggles with excitement. As he does, he accidentally bats the rope with his hand and makes it swing. This causes much smiling and additional wiggling; once again, his hand sends the rope swinging. All this activity captures the attention of the 16-month-old, who stops playing and studies carefully this interesting toy. After a moment, she toddles over to her brother, draws back an arm, takes aim, and smacks the rope. This sends it swinging violently, so much so that it comes loose and falls on her brother. "Uh-uh," she says looking anxiously toward her

cognitive development:
Mental development, including problem solving and the acquisition of knowledge.

mother. The 4-month-old is smiling, however, and wiggling more actively than ever. He appears to believe that his wiggles and this interesting new result—the rope falling right onto his stomach—were somehow related.

The mother scolds her oldest, replaces the rope toy, and resumes her work.

The Arab mother in this story has demonstrated the seemingly universal understanding that dangling an interesting object is an excellent way to divert infant upset. More important, the story illustrates the differences in cognition between babies of different ages. The 4-month-old performs only random actions that create accidental results. From his playful activities, it is obvious that he does not understand the clear connection between flailing arms and the swinging rope. He simply acts, and when something interesting occurs, he keeps performing this action.

In contrast, the 16-month-old is very purposeful and reflective in her behavior. She studies the rope, moves closer to it, carefully measures the length and speed of her swing, and accurately sends the rope swaying. She plans to swat the toy and then carries out her plan in an impressive manner—too impressive, perhaps. She quickly realizes that her action has caused a problem, one that could lead to a scolding from her mother. She uses vocalizations and sophisticated facial expressions to communicate her anxiety. The story shows the phenomenal difference in thinking between two infants who are just a year apart in age!

PIAGET'S VIEW OF INFANT INTELLIGENCE

The most well-known description of infant cognitive development is provided by Jean Piaget (1952). He refers to the developmental period between birth and age 2 as the **sensorimotor stage.** In Piaget's view, thinking at this age involves getting things done physically by using the senses. There is no infant thought without action, he argues. Babies' thinking is very different, then, from the internal, reflective thought processes of adults. Whereas adults contemplate, analyze, infer, or imagine, babies just act.

To clarify, imagine that a highly desirable object is out of your reach, say, on a high shelf. How would you go about getting it? You would probably hesitate a moment and think

sensorimotor stage: Piaget's stage of cognitive development that encompasses infancy, in which thinking is limited to using physical action and the senses to know about things.

through the problem, picturing alternative strategies in your mind. If a chair was nearby, you might envision dragging it close to the shelf to stand on. In no time at all, you would have formulated a plan, carried it out, and retrieved the object. According to Piaget's theory, young babies would follow a very different process in retrieving a toy that is out of reach. With little hesitation, they would swat at the object. Or they might cry for an adult to get it for them. They would do these things without a clear understanding of what the results might be. Before a certain age, babies would not engage in careful reflection or thoughtful planning; they would simply take action.

Over the course of 2 years, babies' thinking gradually becomes more reflective. When faced with this same problem, 2-year-olds would contemplate more thoroughly the steps they might take to get the toy. They might try several different techniques, perhaps even inventing novel approaches. They might try to climb the bookshelf like a ladder, for example. (Such creative problem solving poses many challenges for parents.) To Piaget, it is this shift from simple action to more internal thinking that marks infant cognitive development.

Piaget's Substages

Piaget plotted intellectual advancement from pure sensorimotor action to internalized thinking. He described six substages through which infants develop on their way to becoming more sophisticated thinkers. These substages are presented in Table 7-1.

TABLE 7-1
Piaget's Substages of Infant Cognitive Development

Substage	Age	Description
Reflexes	0 to 1 month	Infants perform simple, involuntary reflexes.
Primary circular reactions	1 to 4 months	Infants engage in circular actions with their bodies. A movement or vocalization is made; this creates an interesting sensation and is repeated. There is yet no understanding of cause and effect.
Secondary circular reactions	4 to 8 months	Infants engage in circular reactions that involve other objects. They may shake a rattle, note an interesting result, and shake it again. There is still no understanding of cause and effect.
Coordination of secondary circular reactions	8 to 12 months	Infants can perform a series of actions that have been performed in previous substages. They may shake, then bang, then chew a rattle. They understand that certain actions cause certain consequences. So, they engage in goal directed behavior—they set out to cause something to happen.
Tertiary, circular reactions	12 to 18 months	Infants can perform novel, never-before-tried actions to solve problems; for example, they may use trial and error to obtain an interesting object placed high on a kitchen counter.
Mental combinations	18 to 24 months	Infants can solve some problems using mental images. They can think through their actions without actually performing them. They can study and later imitate the behaviors of others.

SOURCE: Piaget, 1952.

Substage 1. In the first substage, from birth to 1 month, babies have a very limited repertoire; they do little more than wiggle reflexively, according to Piaget. Significant development occurs during this short period, however. Reflexes are refined and organized. For example, newborns must adapt and gain control over their sucking reflex in order to retrieve nutrients from the nipple of a bottle or their mother.

Substage 2. During the second substage, between 1 and 4 months, babies begin to engage in **primary circular reactions.** These are actions involving babies' own bodies that are performed by accident but then repeated because they produce interesting sensations. For example, a baby may flail arms and legs, notice the fascinating feel of this, and continue to perform these actions. A less positive example of a primary circular reaction was performed by my son when he was only 2 months old: By chance, he had reflexively grasped hold of a clump of his own hair and pulled. The initial sensation was interesting enough, and the pulling continued. In no time, however, this action began to hurt. I eventually had to rescue him, interrupting the circular reaction by helping him loosen his grasp on his hair.

These are called *circular reactions* because the infant as yet has no clear understanding, from Piaget's perspective, of what causes what. The wiggles and the sensation simply go together. A circular reaction is illustrated in Figure 7-1.

Substage 3. In substage 3 of infant cognitive development, between 4 and 8 months, babies engage in **secondary circular reactions.** These are repetitive actions that involve other objects: toys, clothing, and even parents. For example, a baby might grasp a rattle, wiggle it by accident, notice the interesting noise it makes, and keep wiggling. As another example, I attached a mobile to the sleeve of my 6-month-old son's shirt with string. He swung his arms wildly as he watched the butterflies on the mobile fly about. This went on and on, and over time the butterflies fell off one by one. The toy manufacturer clearly had not built a toy sturdy enough to survive the rigors of secondary circular reactions!

I have found that banging things is a prevalent secondary circular reaction among infants at this age. In fact, I've named this "the period of incessant pounding" since my own children seemed to take such pleasure in loud, headache-producing bangs that tended to go on and on. It is hard to say how long a baby might persist in creating this repetitive racket. Few parents

primary circular reactions: Actions involving babies' own bodies, usually emerging at 1 month of age, that are performed by accident but then repeated because they produce interesting sensations.

secondary circular reactions: Repetitive actions in infancy, usually emerging between 4 and 8 months, that are performed on toys or other objects.

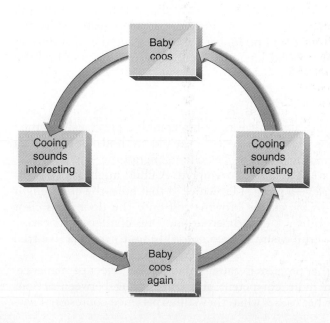

FIGURE 7-1 A primary circular reaction in early infancy. Cooing causes interesting sounds; these sounds cause continued cooing. The reaction goes round and round, with no understanding of beginning or end.

have the stamina to find out. They often create distractions or redirect babies to quieter toys. A consolation for a parent enduring many minutes of spoon banging is that this is an important intellectual activity.

Substage 4. Between 8 and 12 months, significant advancements occur. A new kind of action emerges at this substage: the coordination of secondary circular reactions. Babies combine several behaviors they have practiced in earlier stages. They may reach out, grasp a rattle, shake it, and then bang it against a table. More important, babies of this period are, for the first time, able to understand that certain actions cause certain consequences. For example, they can tell the difference between the act of banging a rattle and the noise that results from this action.

Piaget invented a research method for studying this new causal thinking. He presented babies with an interesting toy that was placed out of their reach on a blanket. The blanket was within their grasp, and they were shown how to pull it toward themselves to get the toy. After infants had retrieved the objects several times by pulling the blanket, the toy was again placed out of reach. This time, however, it was placed next to the blanket, not on it. The infants were then allowed to solve the problem on their own. Before 8 months, babies were confused by the task. They would pull on the blanket again and again even though the toy was not sitting on it. They were not able to think carefully about cause and effect. Their blanket pulling was, likely, a secondary circular reaction.

After 8 months, however, babies were quite shrewd in solving the problem, showing they understood cause and effect more clearly. They could recognize that pulling the blanket worked only when the toy was sitting on top of it. When the toy was not on the blanket, they would abandon blanket pulling and try completely different strategies. They might attempt to reach for the toy directly, for example, or look to their parents for help.

Another kind of thinking that emerges in substage 4 is **object permanence**—an understanding that objects exist even if they cannot be seen or heard. Piaget has proposed that very young babies are unable to think about things they cannot perceive. When a favorite toy is hidden away in a toy box, for example, it simply does not exist in the mind of a 4-month-old. By 8 months, however, babies begin to contemplate objects that are not present. They may look around for misplaced toys or missing family members.

Piaget developed a research method to study the development of this kind of thinking as well. He showed babies of different ages a toy; just as they reached for it, he hid it behind a screen. Infants in substages 1, 2, or 3 no longer reached or searched for the object after it was hidden. When they could no longer see it, they acted as if it did not exist. In contrast, babies in substage 4 and later substages did search for and find the missing object.

Substage 5. Substage 5, from 12 to 18 months, is characterized by increasingly novel actions. According to Piaget, infants at this age not only combine previously learned strategies but also try new ones to achieve their goals. If the old methods for getting an object that is out of reach—say, standing on tiptoes, reaching, or grasping—do not work, a brand-new, never-before-tried action might be attempted. A child might pull a chair over to the kitchen counter to retrieve a plate of brownies. If that fails, the child might try using a tool—perhaps a toy—to knock the brownies off onto the floor. It is clear that toddlerhood is a time of significant experimentation. One challenge in caring for children of this age is their powerful desire to accomplish things through active trial and error.

Children of substage 5 make further progress in causal thinking and object permanence. Although they become more and more competent at distinguishing between actions and consequences or determining what causes what, they still experience confusion. Flaws

object permanence: An understanding, usually emerging between 8 and 12 months of age, that objects still exist even if they cannot be seen.

in causal thinking are common at this age and can create challenges for parents, as the following story reveals:

> A father from a small village in Guatemala is puzzled over the fact that every time he wears an old straw hat, his 15-month-old daughter shows great upset. What is particularly odd is that he has worn the hat often from the time his daughter was born, but never, until now, has she shown this strong reaction. He tries to think of every possible reason for the problem. Does the hat look like something frightening? Does it represent a bad experience for her? It is only as he is preparing for a trip to visit relatives in another village that he discovers the source of the difficulty. He realizes that he wears the hat when he travels. His last two trips, he recalls, were to take his daughter to a clinic in nearby Guatemala City—once for immunization injections and a second time for treatment of an illness. It is clear that his daughter is associating his hat with frightening and, in one case, painful visits to the nurse.

Other examples abound of how early causal thinking creates challenges. In American homes, some toddlers cry at signs of their parents' departure, such as when a sitter arrives or a mother puts on her coat. Others may climb into a high chair in the middle of the afternoon because they see parents working in the kitchen and assume it is dinnertime.

Substage 6. Substage 6, from 18 to 24 months, is characterized by **internalized thought.** The older toddler can, for the first time, solve problems by thinking them through using reflection and mental images. At this substage, a child studies a problem before acting and engages in less physical trial and error. For example, one child simply studied an adult unclasping a childproof safety lock on a kitchen cabinet and then later unclasped it on the first try to obtain a yummy snack of dog biscuits. So, this substage can also be a challenging period because of toddlers' intellectual as well as physical development!

By substage 6, babies can find objects that were hidden hours or even days earlier. I learned this when one of my sons, as a toddler, hid his own shoes in a grocery bag in the kitchen one evening. The next day, his mother and I panicked as we tried to find the shoes while dressing him for child care. The shoes were nowhere to be found. He smiled as he watched us search frantically. When this grew tiresome, he toddled into the kitchen, pulled the shoes from their hiding place, and offered helpfully, "Here y'go, Daddy."

Although many advancements take place by substage 6, there are still many limitations in thinking. One characteristic that persists into toddlerhood is **egocentrism.** This is a type of thinking in which children are unable to understand that there are other viewpoints in the world besides their own. People at every age show some egocentrism, but infants are especially egocentric. Some child specialists have even suggested that babies view the entire world as being simply a part of themselves.

One difficulty that arises because of egocentrism is a tendency for toddlers to erroneously believe that their own actions have caused completely unrelated consequences. A child who has just been scolded for running toward a busy road, then later stumbles and skins a knee, may believe the naughty act caused the fall. The following is another example:

> A 23-month-old has been diagnosed with an ear infection and is required to take a nasty-tasting antibiotic. Her father has a difficult time getting her to swallow the medicine. The child turns her head, spits, and cries. Eventually, she gives in and swallows. When every drop is gone, her father soothingly says, "There ya' go."
>
> After a number of days of this routine, the toddler begins to say, "de go," "de go," every time she sees her father approach with the full medicine spoon. These verbalizations become more urgent as he places the spoon near her mouth. He eventually realizes that his daughter is saying, "There ya' go." She has associated this phrase with the end of an unpleasant experience and believes that saying these words will *cause* the medicine giving to stop.

internalized thought: A kind of thinking, emerging between 18 and 24 months of age, in which problems are solved by thinking them through, using reflection and mental images.

egocentrism: A type of thinking, common in infancy and early childhood, in which children are unable to understand that there are other viewpoints in the world besides their own.

Between 18 and 24 months, infants begin to solve complex problems, often studying objects or people first, before acting.

Her behavior can be explained by flaws in her causal thinking; she misinterprets which event is the cause and which is the effect. Egocentrism also plays a role. She believes her words have such power that they can stop an unpleasant occurrence. It is important for parents and professionals who work with infants and families to understand such limitations in toddlers' thinking. Adults need to be very explicit in discussing causes and effects. Simply saying "No!" when a child touches something dangerous, for example, may not clarify which action caused the reprimand. If the child happened to be rubbing an eye at about the same time, the unintended message would be that if you rub your eye, you will get a scolding. "You can't touch that burner, because it's hot" would be a much more effective way to help a toddler learn.

A Multicultural Critique of Piaget's Theory

Piaget's descriptions of infant development have been found to be quite accurate. Researchers have tested his theories for decades and have found that babies appear to acquire cognitive abilities in the order that Piaget described (Bjorklund, 1997; Flavell, P. H. Miller, & S. A. Miller, 1993). The primary challenge to Piaget's work has come from those who note that infants have greater cognitive competence than he suggested (Bremner, 2002; Gelman & Williams, 1997; Kirkham, Slemmer, & Johnson, 2002; Luo, 2007). For example, studies have shown that object permanence may be present quite early in life (Luo, Baillargeon, Brueckner, & Munakata, 2003). Babies appear to understand the existence of some objects earlier than others. They show upset at the disappearance of a parent, for example, before they are able to search for missing toys in Piaget's task.

One reason for Piaget's underestimation of babies' cognitive abilities may be the lack of sophisticated research technology available when he was formulating his theory. His observations were done with smaller numbers of subjects in naturalistic settings without the complex laboratory equipment available today. In addition, his studies were limited to children of European background.

In spite of Piaget's misjudgment about the pace at which babies develop cognitive competence, his work continues to be viewed as the definitive account of infant cognition.

The most important part of his theory—his descriptions of how and in what order cognitive skills emerge—has held up extremely well over time.

Multicultural scholars (Christopher & Bickhard, 2007; Hale, 1994; Ogbu, 1992) have argued that Piaget's view of cognitive development is more sensitive to cultural diversity than other theories of human development. They point out that Piaget's framework focuses on universal thought processes, such as causal thinking and object permanence, rather than emphasizing the content of knowledge, which is shaped by culture. From a Piagetian perspective, exactly what babies know or are able to do—whether they can recognize a grandmother, turn the pages of a book, or speak the word "doggie," for example—is not as important as general mental functioning. The ability to recognize a particular object is not as critical as being able to retrieve, explore, search for, or solve problems with it within the environment. This culture-neutral element of Piaget's work has led Hale-Benson (1986) to conclude that "major aspects of his theory can be applied to all human societies and groups, and differences in performance can be accounted for without imputing inferiority or deficiency" (p. 24).

Research has, for the most part, found that Piaget's descriptions of infant cognitive development are accurate for babies of any cultural group. For example, in an early study, middle-class Euro-American babies were compared with those from two small villages in Guatemala in their performance on such Piagetian tasks as object permanence (Kagan, 1977). "Remarkable concordance" (p. 278) was discovered among these infants in the sequence with which they acquired cognitive skills. Small differences in the ages at which certain skills emerged were found. Babies from the isolated and impoverished villages were slightly delayed in learning some skills. Nonetheless, the similarities between the two groups of babies were marked. Findings of many later studies further support Piaget's idea that cognitive development proceeds, for all babies, in predictable steps (D. H. Feldman, 2004).

OTHER COGNITIVE ABILITIES IN INFANCY

Besides the cognitive abilities that Piaget identified, several other aspects of infant mental functioning have been explored by researchers: memory, attention, and pretend play.

Memory

Babies can remember persons, actions, and objects at a very early age. In a classic memory study, 8-week-olds were found to remember a learned behavior for up to 2 weeks (Rovee-Collier, Griesler, & Earley, 1985). In this investigation, a ribbon was attached from a mobile to the legs of infant subjects. At first, these young babies did not seem aware that they could make the mobile move by kicking; they were taught to do so by researchers. Two weeks later, babies were again attached to the mobile. Without hesitation, they began to kick their legs, suggesting they had remembered the situation and the actions from previous experience. At periods beyond 2 weeks, however, babies no longer kicked when the ribbon was attached.

Follow-up studies found that babies did not remember how to kick unless the entire setting was exactly the same as it was when the first experience occurred (Hartshorn & Rovee-Collier, 2003; Rovee-Collier, 1997). For example, if babies were trained to kick a mobile in one setting—say, in their crib at home—and were later placed in a different crib or provided with a different kind of mobile, they were not able to reenact the original behavior. This suggests that young babies may not remember specific events. Instead, they may recollect whole situations, or "spatiotemporal maps," as these authors call them.

A baby's thinking might go like this: "I recognize this place, the softness of the pad I'm laying on, this person standing nearby, the set of butterflies dangling over me, this funny ribbon attached to my leg. The whole scene is familiar. So I remember that kicking and butterfly wiggling go together." If anything is out of place, though, if things look or feel different, the whole experience vanishes from the baby's memory.

In many studies, babies have been found to acquire impressive visual memory skills by the age of 6 or 7 months (Rose, Feldman, & Jankowski, 2001, 2004). **Visual memory** is an ability to recognize objects that were seen at an earlier time. In these investigations, babies were shown various stimuli—abstract patterns, faces, or three-dimensional objects—until they became fully familiar with them. Later the babies were shown each picture or object again, along with a new, dissimilar one. The babies were observed to stare longest at the new, never-before-seen object. It was concluded in these studies that they remembered the original stimulus—so well, in fact, that it was no longer that interesting to them. A new object or picture held their attention far longer.

By age 13 months, children have been found to recall complex actions after significant delays. In several studies, children of this age could reproduce a series of actions (e.g., making a track and rolling a toy car down it) even a week after they had observed these actions performed by an adult (Bauer & Hertsgaard, 1993; Brugger, Lariviere, Mumme, & Bushnell, 2007; Wenner & Bauer, 2000). A significant finding of this study was that adult verbal cues (e.g., "Remember when we made the car go down the track?") increased the accuracy of infant memory. An implication is that parents and caregivers can use language such as "Don't touch!" or "That's very hot!" to help even preverbal 1-year-olds learn and remember important behaviors.

How long do these memories last? Will babies recollect experiences in later childhood? Astounding results of one study (Perris, Myers, & Clifton, 1990) show that 2½-year-olds could reenact a task they had performed just once at age 6 months! So, early experiences appear to stay in children's memories for a long time. These findings reaffirm the importance of providing positive home and classroom environments for babies. The experiences parents or caregivers provide at this age will have a lasting influence.

Infant memory appears to be related to later cognitive abilities (Rose et al., 2004). Babies' visual memory has been found to be associated with language and reading ability, quantitative competence, and general intelligence at age 6 (Colombo, 1993; Rovee-Collier, Hayne, & Colombo, 2002). In a summary of 23 studies of infant memory, McCall and Carringer (1993) concluded that infants' ability to remember is associated with IQ scores at age 8. In fact, these authors suggest that infant memory tasks are a better way to predict later cognitive functioning than traditional infant intelligence tests.

Attention

An ability that is related to memory is *attention*. Babies who can attend to objects and study their features in an efficient way may remember them for longer periods (Rose et al., 2004). Some babies have been found to attend more intensely to new objects and to familiarize themselves with these very quickly. These babies tend to be intellectually advanced later in life (Colombo, 1993; McCall & Carringer, 1993). The style of attending may also affect infant learning. As reported in Chapter 6, some babies attend by taking brief looks—referred to as **short looking**—at many different aspects of an object— that is, by looking at one feature, then another. Babies who are **long looking** study objects by looking at only one feature for a long period of time. Babies who are short looking have been found to process information more quickly than long-looking ones (Rose et al., 2004). It is believed that the brief looks allow infants to gain a better understanding of the whole object, not just one part. For example, a child looking only at the ear of a stuffed bear may not become familiar with the whole toy; a child who studies the ear, then a leg, and then the eyes will.

visual memory: An ability, acquired by 6 or 7 months of age, in which an infant recognizes objects that were seen at an earlier time.

short looking: A style of attending in which infants take brief looks at many different aspects of an object, looking at one feature, then another. This style allows them to process information more quickly.

long looking: A style of attending in which infants study objects by looking at only one feature for a long period of time. This style causes them to process information more slowly.

Researchers have found that babies who are long looking can be encouraged to take more frequent looks (Jankowski, Rose, & Feldman, 2001). In this fascinating study, a group of babies were presented with an interesting pattern; however, different features of the pattern were spotlighted with a red beam every few seconds. A child might fix on one corner of a pattern, but then a light would illuminate a different corner, drawing the baby's attention to that. In essence, long-looking babies were induced to be short-looking ones. Results indicate that this strategy helped babies process whole stimuli more efficiently.

What are the implications of this research for parenting or caregiving? As adults play with babies, they might draw their attention to specific aspects of a toy, a book, or even themselves. "Look at this butterfly on your shirt" and "Look at my mouth. See how I'm smiling at you?" are examples.

Infant Play and Cognitive Development

Play is a common activity in infancy. One sophisticated form of playing—pretend play—is particularly useful in enhancing intellectual abilities before age 3. The following story provides an excellent illustration of pretend play in the early years:

> Alonzo, an 18-month-old, is playing in a barren courtyard outside his apartment in a housing project in an urban neighborhood. His mother sits on the front steps, keeping a watchful eye on her son. She is saddened that he doesn't have a pleasant space to play in or toys to use. The playground in the project is in disrepair and unsafe.
>
> She notices that Alonzo has created a play environment for himself. He has found the only object in the area, half of a clay brick, and is pushing it along the cracked sidewalk leading up to their front door. He displays an impressive repertoire of car noises: engine roars, fire sirens, and an occasional tire squeal. His mother smiles. She is fascinated and amazed by his ingenuity.

People from all socioeconomic backgrounds and cultures engage in play from the time they are very young. Play has been defined as any behavior that is nonliteral, intrinsically motivated, self-chosen, and pleasurable (J. E. Johnson et al., 2005). Thus, play can include dress-up, playing checkers, rolling down a hill on the playground, or swinging on a swing. These activities make childhood fun, but they are also critical for cognitive development.

Motor Play. One early form of play is the spontaneous, repetitive, physical activity of early infancy called **motor play.** An infant's circular reactions (described earlier in this chapter) are usually quite playful (Garner, 2006). Rhythmically banging a rattle, for example, is enjoyable and intrinsically rewarding, so it can be considered playing. Cooing and babbling are really spontaneous play with sounds. Several examples of infant motor play are presented in Table 7-2.

Some early motor play is social; babies play with other people even in the earliest months of life. In many cultures, parents are the first playmates; they initiate or respond to playful infant behaviors. When they do this, they are not only making warm contact with their children but also promoting intellectual growth (Frost et al., 2008). For example, when an African American father plays a traditional game of faces by letting his baby touch his face and then putting his own hands on hers, he is promoting early causal thinking. The baby learns that her action—touching—causes the father to respond in kind (Hale-Benson, 1986).

When a mother in a Euro-American family plays peekaboo, she is teaching her infant a lesson in object permanence. If the mother's face disappears, does it still exist? The solution to the riddle is sudden and thrilling as the mother's face reappears, accompanied by the high-pitched vocalization, "Peeeeek-a-booooo." When a mother in India plays the traditional Bengali game Kan Dol Dol, in which she and her baby hold one another's ears and

motor play: Spontaneous, repetitive, physical activity, common in infancy, that is nonliteral, intrinsically motivated, self-chosen, and pleasurable.

TABLE 7-2
Examples of Infant Motor Play

Type of Play	Examples
Primary circular reactions	An infant accidentally makes a "raspberry" noise with tongue and lips. This creates an interesting sound. He playfully repeats this vocalization again and again.
	A father tickles his infant daughter. She shrieks with delight. He tickles her again. She responds with another giggle. They continue with the game in an endless chain of tickles and shrieks.
Secondary circular reactions	The sleeve of an infant's shirt is attached by a thread to a mobile dangling over his crib. He wiggles accidentally and causes the butterflies on the mobile to flutter about. He shows a brief expression of surprise, then wiggles again.
	An infant playfully pounds a toy plastic hammer on the tray of her high chair. She pounds for a minute or more, then stops, smiles, and looks at her father. Then she pounds again. The game continues until her father distracts her with a quieter toy.
Imitation games	An Indian mother and her infant son play a traditional Bengali game, *Kan Dol Dol.* The mother gently holds the baby's ears and begins to sing. The baby reaches out and grabs his mother's ears; he vocalizes in unison with her song.
	A father claps his hands in a playful gesture. His baby smiles, wiggles, and imitates the gesture.
Simple pretense	A baby lays her head on a pillow and closes her eyes pretending to sleep. "Night, night," her father says. A smile crosses her face. She opens her eyes and laughs.
	A baby pretends to drink from an empty cup. Then she holds the cup to her mother's mouth; the mother makes noises to indicate she is drinking. The baby places the cup to her own mouth again and imitates her mother's sounds.

sing, she is facilitating imitation. In the game, the baby emulates the mother's actions and intonations (Roopnarine, Hossain, Gill, & Brophy, 1994).

In some cultures, young babies have nonparent playmates as well. Older siblings are sometimes primary playmates (Punch, 2007; Youngblade & Dunn, 1995). In one small Italian village, infants were observed playing with extended family members and even neighbors as often as with parents (New, 1994). Cousins and neighbor children were particularly frequent playmates; they would engage babies in games of practice walking or *batti, batti, le, manini,* a version of patty-cake. These experiences with other children are important, and not just socially. All the noisemaking and pounding, laughter and surprise, wiggling and bouncing that characterize early social motor play provide unique opportunities for babies to construct their understanding of the world.

Pretend Play. **Pretend play** is a very useful form of play that emerges in later infancy. In this activity, babies transform themselves into make-believe people, animals, or objects. They may pretend to be a parent feeding a baby or a doctor giving immunizations. They often change real objects into imaginary ones. They might use an old gourd, for example, as if it were a real cup filled with juice or hold a toy telephone as if it were a real one. Often, infants carry out increasingly complex make-believe enactments in such play. For example, a child

pretend play: A form of play in which children transform themselves into make-believe characters, change real objects into imaginary ones, and carry out complex make-believe enactments.

who is pretending to be the village metalsmith will pound a rock as if it were real metal and create noises that simulate the sounds of a hot tool being plunged into cold water.

Vygotsky (1976) argued that this kind of play is practice at symbolizing. Symbolizing is a mental activity in which an abstract symbol is used to stand for an idea or an object that is not present. The words on this page are symbols, as are spoken words. When a child pretends to drink juice from a gourd, the gourd is a symbol that represents a real cup that is not present. So, early pretend play is important practice at using *symbolic thought* (Frost et al., 2008).

Pretend play emerges as early as age 1 and becomes more complex and frequent through toddlerhood (Lillard, 2007; Trawick-Smith, 1991). The earliest form of infant pretend play—called **simple pretense**—involves the make-believe use of familiar objects to enact customary routines (Bosco, Friedman, & Leslie, 2006). A 14-month-old might take a cup and pretend to drink; another might lie on a pillow and pretend to sleep. In the second year, babies begin to use two or more objects in these simple pretend enactments (McCune, 1995). A pillow and a blanket might be used to pretend to sleep, or a toy pitcher might be used to pour pretend liquid into a toy cup. In simple pretense, children usually play themselves as they perform these actions. It is easy to see that these activities involve early symbolic thought: objects are being used to play out events that are not really occurring. The objects and actions are symbols, not unlike words and text.

Parents and caregivers can promote simple pretense at age 1 by providing familiar, realistic props—toy cups, telephones, pillows, and blankets, for example. They might also model or prompt the make-believe use of these items. For example, a parent might drink from a toy cup and say to the baby, "Would you like some juice?" Such adult interventions have been found to promote more complex levels of pretend play (Tamis-LeMonda & Bornstein, 1991). Parents and caregivers can also arrange for babies to interact with playmates of the same age. Even very young infants have been found to engage in more simple pretense when playing with peers than when playing alone (Lyytinen, 1995).

During the second year, play takes a significant leap forward. For the first time, children use objects in their play to represent things that are completely different. A wooden rod might be used as a spoon or a cylinder-shaped block as a cup. This sort of play involves sophisticated symbolizing. For example, it is intellectually challenging for Alonzo, the 18-month-old in the story at the beginning of this section, to imagine that a brick is a car because these two things are so totally different. As children demonstrate this more symbolic form of make-believe, their parents and caregivers can provide more challenging play props. Nondescript items, such as blocks or cardboard boxes that represent nothing in particular, might be offered with suggestions for how these might be incorporated into pretend play (e.g., "This block can be your telephone").

The use of pretend objects in play may vary by culture. In more *object-oriented* cultures, babies are more often guided in these object transformations by parents. Bornstein, Haynes, Pascual, Painter, and Galperin (2002) found that U.S. mothers would often prompt their 20-month-olds to use toys in imaginary play actions. For example, a parent might say, "Here's your telephone. Can you dial your grandma? You dial like this, see? And then you talk in here." In contrast, these researchers found that Argentinian mothers were more *people oriented* in their play interactions. Toys and other objects were used mainly as a means for stimulating parent-child language. A parent might say, "I'm going to call you on the telephone now. Hello, Roberto? Hello? How are you today?"

Variations in Infant Cognitive Development

Cognitive development varies among individual infants. There are many sources of this variation: Some children may simply have unique developmental time clocks that cause them to follow their own idiosyncratic paths toward healthy, typical childhood. Others have

simple pretense: The make-believe use of familiar objects to enact customary routines, such as using a toy cup to pretend to drink.

During later infancy, some children
begin to play with peers.

family or community experiences that lead to unique patterns of intellectual growth. Some
suffer debilitating conditions, such as illness, genetic disorder, or poverty, that influence
their cognitive development.

Culture and Infant Cognition

Cultural experience can influence cognition in infancy. The pace at which babies acquire
cognitive skills sometimes varies across cultures. In a classic study in Botswana, for example,
!Kung babies were found to be significantly advanced in their performance on various cognitive tasks as compared with Euro-American babies (Konner, 2007). Although infants of
both cultures were found to acquire cognitive skills in the same order, !Kung babies were
several months ahead of their American peers in the acquisition of these skills.

How can these cultural differences be explained? It may be that some cultural traditions
or socialization practices lead to advancement in certain intellectual abilities. For example,
in the Botswana study, the advanced mental abilities of !Kung infants were attributed to
the high frequency of social and cognitive stimulation in !Kung family life. A typical day for
a !Kung baby includes a phenomenal degree of parent–infant play. Toys are provided, and
mobiles and other objects are hung from cribs. !Kung mothers wear elaborate ornamental
necklaces that babies play with as they sit in their mothers' laps. !Kung babies also spend an
extensive period of time each day in a vertical posture, which may facilitate alertness and
sensorimotor exercise.

Such parenting practices are culturally derived, a part of !Kung tradition. These interactions are encouraged and expected in that part of the world, and community life is structured
to allow parents to care for babies in this way.

A word of caution is in order: These same child care practices might be impossible to carry
out within another culture. In fact, these practices may not even be desirable for babies from
other ethnic backgrounds. The point of cross-cultural research is not to identify successful
practices from one culture to transfer them to another but rather to gain an understanding
and appreciation of rich cultural variation in cognition among babies.

Researchers may find cultural differences in infant cognition for other reasons. In his
classic cultural critique of research on intelligence, Nyiti (1982) proposes that problems in

the way cognition is tested cause babies of one culture to be found less competent than those of another. He points out that researchers are often of different ethnic backgrounds than babies of the particular cultural group being studied. Babies may have difficulty relating to and understanding these culturally different adults. For example, when Euro-American researchers use English to ask bilingual Puerto Rican toddlers to play with certain objects, they may confuse, distract, or otherwise inhibit them from showing what they can really do.

Nyiti (1982) also suggests that findings of cultural differences may be explained by poor estimates of age in some communities. Within many cultures, birth dates and precise ages are not considered important. Parents simply do not think about infant development in terms of months beyond birth. So, they tend to make inaccurate guesses about the ages of their children and inadvertently provide researchers with flawed data.

Finally, some cultural differences in infant cognition may result from babies' unfamiliarity with the toys or objects used in studies. Native American babies may not be drawn to or interested in looking at the same objects as Euro-American babies. For example, if a toy holds no personal or cultural meaning to an 8-month-old Navajo infant, the infant may not eagerly search for it in an object permanence task. Babies from Kenya, Zambia, and Guatamala, who rarely played with objects or toys in their homes, were found to show little interest in looking at or pursuing objects of any kind (Super, 1990).

Although real cultural differences do exist, they may be highly distorted when research techniques are not culturally sensitive. Care must be taken not to interpret diversity in infants' pace of intellectual development as an indicator of cultural deficiency.

Poverty

Poverty is one of the most debilitating conditions for children (R. H. Bradley & Corwyn, 2003; Luthar, Cicchetti, & Becker, 2000; Werner, 1995). Infants from impoverished homes are more likely to suffer delays in cognitive development and language. The longer babies live in poverty, the more severe these delays. Being poor in infancy can have lasting effects. Research shows that children living in poverty as infants are less competent in school-related cognitive tasks later in life (Chilton, Chyatte, & Breaux, 2007; Grantham-McGregor et al., 2007a). However, being from a low-income family does not automatically mean that a baby will have cognitive deficiencies. Some infants who live in poverty develop quite typically. A range of family and neighborhood factors determines the developmental impact that poverty will have (Caughy, Campo, & Muntaner, 2003). These are presented in Figure 7-2.

Babies of low-income families who live in safer and less crowded homes are more likely to acquire typical cognitive and language competence (R. H. Bradley & Corwyn, 2002). However, babies who do not receive adequate nutrition or who are not well cared for—sadly, two common consequences of impoverished family life—may show intellectual delays.

Nutritional Deficiency. Poor nutrition is common among low-income families. Iron-deficiency anemia and protein deficiency are especially prevalent among poor African American and Latino babies and among those from economically underdeveloped countries. Babies suffering these conditions perform poorly on measures of infant cognitive development (Walker et al., 2007). One explanation for the devastating effects of malnutrition is that during the crucial period when babies are experiencing rapid brain growth, a lack of nutrients can seriously inhibit neurological development.

Parenting. Parents in poverty are often under a great deal of stress, which can negatively influence parent–child relationships. Parents who are suffering either chronic poverty or sudden economic decline become increasingly punitive and coercive and less supportive and warm over time in interactions with their children (R. H. Bradley & Corwyn, 2003; Raver,

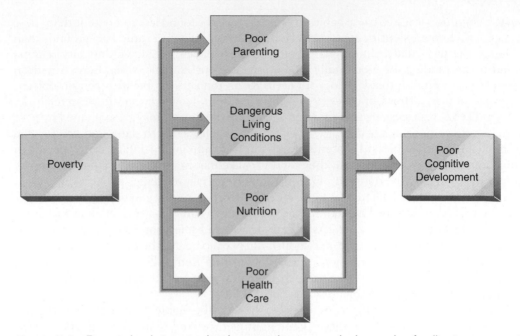

FIGURE 7-2   Poverty leads to poor developmental outcomes by increasing family stressors and creating unhealthy home and community environments.

Gershoff, & Aber, 2007; McLoyd, 1990a). This has a particularly devastating effect on infants. Babies in poverty who receive less responsive, accepting, stimulating, or organized care have been found to display poor cognitive functioning. Babies whose parents are more positive survive experiences of poverty with little cognitive delay. In low-income Haitian American families, for example, warm and positive parenting was found to significantly enhance the intellectual abilities of high-risk 1-year-olds (Widmayer et al., 1990).

CHALLENGING CONDITIONS AND INFANT COGNITION

Other sources of variation in infant cognitive development include illness, injury, genetic disorder, and other challenging conditions. For example, children with **Down syndrome** are often significantly delayed in mental development. Cognitive difficulties of infants with Down syndrome are less apparent in the early months of life. By the second year, however, these babies show significant delays in the acquisition of cognitive, language, and play skills (Cicchetti & Beeghly, 1990; Hooper & Edmondson, 2008). The degree to which the disorder affects cognitive growth in infancy is related, once again, to parenting. Babies who receive significant social, intellectual, and motor stimulation from parents or other adults will show substantially more advanced cognitive development than babies who do not receive this care (Iarocci, Virji-Babul, & Reebye, 2006; Kaplan, 1996).

Challenging conditions are also caused by problems during birth. Sometimes babies have trouble getting enough oxygen during the birth process. Blood vessels may break in a baby's head during a difficult labor, restricting oxygen flow. A baby may become tangled in the umbilical cord. In some cases, babies have trouble breathing right after birth and require neonatal oxygen intervention in which an oxygen face mask or even a ventilator must be provided. These experiences may affect brain development and thereby cause cognitive delays in infancy. For example, babies who suffered oxygen deprivation or hemorrhaging at

Down syndrome: A genetic condition, caused by an extra chromosome, that can lead to mental retardation, heart problems, and unique physical features such as reduced stature.

birth have been found to perform less well on learning tasks at 13 months of age (Mercuri, & Barnett, 2003; Millar, Weir, & Supramaniam, 1992).

Low birth weight can also affect cognitive development in infancy (Cooke & Foulder-Hughes, 2003). Since babies born in poor families and those from historically underrepresented cultural groups are more likely to be afflicted by this condition, it is difficult to distinguish its effects from those of poverty or racial barriers to health care. It is now believed, however, that low birth weight in itself can create cognitive difficulties that are noticeable in the first 2 years (Cooke & Foulder-Hughes, 2003; Bhutta et al., 2002).

Such factors as health care, a nurturing family, and social services influence the outcomes for low-birth-weight babies. A stimulating home environment and responsive parents, for example, have been found to promote positive development among low-birth-weight infants (Brooks-Gunn, Klebanov, Liaw, & Spiker, 1993; Hogan & Park, 2003). Medical and social support before, during, and after pregnancy have also been linked to positive outcomes (Paneth, 1995). These factors have even greater impact if they are continued throughout childhood (Malik & Spiker, 2004; McCarton et al., 1997).

Families, Culture, and Infants with Special Needs

Families of infants with special needs can suffer great stress (Carpenter, 2007; Palfrey et al., 2005). The identification of cognitive delays, neurological impairment, or Down syndrome in infancy can create feelings of guilt, frustration, or anxiety among parents (Seligman & Darling, 2007; Umansky, 2008b). Mothers of infants with special needs have been found to suffer especially high levels of stress. Stress reactions are greatest if a child's condition is severe or if the causes of the impairment cannot be clearly identified (Wallander & Noojin, 1995).

One study found that fathers of exceptional infants also experience anxiety. They worry about different things than mothers do, however (Shonkoff et al., 1992). Mothers more often suffer global stressors such as depression, anxiety about day-to-day parenting, or feelings of incompetence. Fathers are more narrowly concerned about poor attachment. They are most likely to worry that they will not come to love or bond with their child because of challenging conditions.

A number of factors have been found to reduce stress in families of infants with special needs. Extensive child and family services, including early educational intervention, home visitation by professionals, and parent support groups, can reduce parent anxiety (Palfry et al., 2005). Informal social support from relatives and friends is also related to family adjustment. Parents who are aided by grandparents or caring neighbors will cope more successfully (P. Beckman, 1991).

Cultural traditions and values may help some families cope with the stresses of raising an infant with special needs. Parents who belong to historically underrepresented groups more often live in extended families. African American, Puerto Rican, Asian American, and Native American households, for example, are likely to be multigenerational. Friends and neighbors commonly assist in child rearing and family problem solving within these cultural groups. Informal social support networks—groups of relatives and friends who support one another emotionally and financially—are formed as an adaptive strategy for surviving the challenges of poverty or racial bias (Caughy et al., 2003; Harrison et al., 1990). Such support networks have been found to significantly reduce stress among parents of infants with special needs (P. Beckman, 1991). A neighbor might provide a regular respite for a weary single mother. An experienced grandmother might assist a young father in learning to meet an infant's unique needs. Such informal social support might be as psychologically helpful to some families as formal intervention.

In cultures that accept and appreciate diversity of development, the anxiety associated with special needs might be lessened. For example, in some Native American families, less importance is placed on the timing of children's development (Blanchard, 1983; Seligman & Darling, 2007). Parents of such families may believe that babies will walk and talk when they will. Individuality, including developmental exceptionality, is tolerated and even celebrated (Frankland, Turnbull, Wehmeyer, 2004; John, 1988; Kawamoto & Cheshire, 1997). Such acceptance reflects historical perspectives on the natural order of things. All that exists is good and right, according to ancient Native American beliefs (Kawamoto & Cheshire, 1997). There are really no abnormalities from this view. Differences are to be appreciated because they are part of nature.

Parents in some societies have little concern about developmental delay in infancy because issues of basic survival are so overriding. In his classic research in West Africa, for example, Levine (1996) reports that mothers in communities facing starvation and high infant mortality had very little interest in their infants' cognitive development. Neurological impairments or mental retardation would likely go unnoticed in such communities. Keeping one's baby alive might be the only measure of positive developmental outcome in such families. Impairments that would draw great attention in one society, then, would receive scant notice in another.

Early Intervention

The negative influence of some of the factors described in previous sections may be reduced through early intervention. Babies who are at risk of intellectual delay may be provided with nutritional, educational, or family services that can greatly offset the damaging effects of poverty, malnutrition, poor health, or genetic disorder.

Nutritional Intervention. A number of studies have shown that the negative effects of debilitating conditions can be significantly reduced by providing nutritional guidance and resources to mothers during pregnancy and food supplements to their infants after they are born (Engle et al., 2007; Grantham-McGregor et al., 2007a). In a series of studies, Guatemalan mothers and children living in poverty were provided nutritional supplements (Khandke, Pollitt, & Gorman, 1999; Pollitt, Gorman, Engle, Martorell, & Rivera, 1993). The children showed advanced cognitive abilities throughout infancy. An important finding of these studies was that the cognitive advantages lasted for a long period of time. Even in adolescence, those who had received nutritional services were found to have advanced intellectual abilities! In studies in the United States and Europe, prenatal nutrition and health care were found to reduce preterm deliveries and low birth weight as well as the cognitive difficulties associated with these conditions (Valero de Bernabé, Soriano, & Albaledejo, 2004; G. R. Alexander, Weiss, & Hulsey, 1991).

Unfortunately, there has been less interest in the United States in recent years in implementing health-and nutrition-related interventions. Instead, greater emphasis has been placed on intellectual and social interventions in the home or classroom. The power of early nutrition has been often overlooked, yet it may be the most effective intervention for supporting the development of babies in poverty. Professionals working with infants and families should address nutritional needs as the very first step in any intervention plan. They should also become advocates for publicly funded nutrition programs—both within the United States and around the world—to promote the health and cognitive development of all infants.

Family and Parent Interventions. As described in a previous section, poor parenting and a less supportive home environment are among the negative effects of poverty. Effective parent behaviors—such as verbalizing, responding, and providing nurturance—are associated with positive infant cognitive development, particularly among babies with special needs. Family and parent interventions to enhance these parent behaviors are a powerful method, then, of providing early support for babies' development.

Home-based programs have been designed to assist parents, grandparents, siblings, and other caregivers in learning to perform nurturing and cognitively stimulating interactions. These programs can have a profound influence on babies. For example, such interventions have been found to significantly enhance the intellectual abilities of babies with Down syndrome and those in poverty (C. T. Ramey & S. L. Ramey, 1998; Reynolds, 2004). These strategies have also been discovered to enhance the emotional well-being of parents (Warfield, Hauser-Cram, Krause, Shonkoff, & Upshur, 2000). The more intensive and comprehensive the services, the greater their impact appeared to be on parent attitudes and mental health.

These studies illustrate how important parent support and education are in child development. Professionals can make a difference by assisting families in providing nurturing environments for their babies; however, parent programs must be culturally sensitive to be effective. Parent education programs, for example, must reflect the many culture-specific ways that parents show warmth, provide stimulation, and respond to babies' needs. They should not be aimed at merely teaching parents to engage in white, middle-class caregiving. Home-based interventions must also be delivered in a sensitive, respectful manner. Home visitors should strive to understand and encourage the wide range of effective approaches to caregiving found across cultural groups (Bennett et al., 2008; Engle et al., 2007; McCurdy, Gannon, & Daro, 2003).

Educational Interventions. Infant education programs have been found to be especially effective for at-risk children. In such home- or center-based programs, professionals provide direct intellectual or social stimulation. In one program, a home visitor might play causality or object permanence games with babies right in the family home. In another, a caregiver might stimulate the language of toddlers in a child care center. These programs have been found to produce long-term positive results for children with Down syndrome or other genetically derived challenging conditions (Bricker & Cripe, 1992). Furthermore, children in severe poverty have been found to make significant intellectual gains when such programs are combined with health care and nutritional supplements (Grantham-McGregor et al., 2007a).

The positive effects of early intervention are greater if they are begun in early infancy and continued into the school-age years (McCarton et al., 1997; C. T. Ramey & S. L. Ramey, 1998). For professionals working with children and families, then, a guiding principle should be to intervene early and maintain services in the child's and family's lives for as long as possible.

Services for infants and toddlers with special needs are now mandated and funded through the federal Individuals with Disabilities Education Act (IDEA). One part of this legislation provides for the identification of children with disabilities from birth to age 3 and for appropriate interventions to address their developmental needs. Professionals who work with young children should become advocates for IDEA. (See the Advocacy and Public Policy box in this chapter.)

Well-designed child care alone can lead to gains in infant cognition. In one study, in fact, poor children who began a center-based program before their first birthday performed better on later school-related cognitive tasks than children who had entered centers later in life (Caughy, DiPietro, & Strobino, 1994). A key to ensuring this positive effect of child care is *quality*. Many infant and toddler programs in the United States have been found to be of low quality (Burchinal & Cryer, 2003). In programs where child care providers created a stimulating, language-rich environment and interacted with infants in positive ways, babies' intellectual abilities were greatly enhanced (Burchinal & Cryer, 2003; National Institute of Child Health and Human Development, 2000).

High-quality child care is expensive (Phillips et al., 2000b). It requires a low adult-to-child ratio and extensive caregiver training and education. Public funds are not adequate to ensure that all American families have access to high-quality infant care. Professionals should advocate for better federal and state support of child care—particularly infant and toddler care. (See the Advocacy and Public Policy box in Chapter 5.)

To summarize the preceding sections, a source of variation in infant cognitive development is the availability of nutritional, family, and educational services. Do infants and their families

Supporting Birth to Age 3 Intervention Programs

This chapter highlights the importance of early identification and intervention for infants with special needs. Infant intervention programs have been found to have significant and long-lasting effects on cognitive development (C. T. Ramey & S. L. Ramey, 1998). Intervention services to infants with special needs and their families have been mandated nationally by Part C of the Individuals with Disabilities Education Act (IDEA), which was enacted in its current form by the U.S. Congress in 1997 (U.S. Department of Education, 2004). This part of the bill funds and mandates collaborative efforts among public and private organizations (including schools and child care centers) in all states to identify, evaluate, and provide appropriate services to infants and toddlers who have at least one formally diagnosed developmental delay. It includes a requirement for periodic follow-ups on children who are referred for services to determine their current developmental status.

Under this legislation, more than 200,000 infants and toddlers are currently receiving services; 41% of these children live in poverty (Children's Defense Fund, 2007). Most families receiving services under Part C participate in more than one intervention program, including family services, speech and language therapy, occupational and physical therapy, and special education. The majority of infants and toddlers served have been given positive progress ratings by their providers (U.S. Department of Education, 2004).

The contributions of IDEA Part C to the welfare of America's children are obvious. Still, many believe improvements can be made. Only half the infants and toddlers eligible for services under the act currently receive them (Zero to Three, 2004). There is evidence that the quality of services and the professional training of personnel funded through this legislation is inconsistent across states (National Association for the Education of Young Children, 2004). For these reasons, a number of organizations call on professionals to advocate for greater funding and new language to mandate increased quality when the bill is reauthorized on each fiscal year. The National Association for the Education of Young Children (http://www.naeyc.org), the Council for Exceptional Children (http://www.cec.sped.org), and Zero to Three (http://www.zerotothree.org) all propose an increase in funding of at least 30%. Professionals can join the efforts of these groups to ensure that infants with special needs will be identified and served early in life.

have access to such services in the United States? Research indicates that infants of middle- or upper-middle-class backgrounds do (Phillips et al., 2000). Children of these socioeconomic levels were more likely to receive nutritional and health services and to be enrolled in high-quality educational programs. Infants living in poverty often did not have these resources and services.

CLASSROOM ADAPTATIONS: INFANTS WITH COGNITIVE DISABILITIES

As described in this chapter, educational programs can enhance the development of infants and toddlers with cognitive disabilities. What specific practices in infant care centers lead to these benefits? Many babies with cognitive challenges are delayed in their overall development—that is, they move, think, and solve problems like children who are many months younger than they are. Therefore, an important classroom adaptation is to include activities designed for children who are still in the very earliest stages of the sensorimotor period. The following examples are offered by specialists (Howard et al., 2004; McCormick, 2003; Umansky, 2008a):

1. *Large motor activities.* Many children with cognitive delays exhibit poor motor development. Caregivers can plan activities that encourage the use and coordination of large muscles and that promote balance, locomotion, and variability of movement. They might provide floor-time activities, in which babies are encouraged to roll, sit

up, and crawl on soft mats or pillows. They might initiate retrieving games in which infants are guided in obtaining out-of-reach objects by stretching, rotating their bodies, rolling, scooting, or creeping. Older children might be guided in basic walking or crawling by designing play spaces with soft, carpeted steps or foam inclines.

2. **Multisensory activities.** Some infants with cognitive disabilities have difficulty processing sensory stimuli. Caregivers can design sensory-rich play spaces to address this deficit. To encourage the coordination of the several senses, **multisensory materials** can be included—brightly colored mobiles, for example, that also play music or textured blocks that are of many different colors for stacking. A soft stuffed animal that squeaks or jingles could be offered.

3. **Object permanence activities.** Understanding the existence of objects that are out of sight can be challenging for infants and toddlers with special needs. Caregivers and parents can introduce **object permanence activities**—games that help children learn that things still exist even if they can no longer be seen. For younger infants, simple games like peekaboo (in which one's face vanishes, then reappears) can be useful. For older infants and toddlers, hiding games can be planned. An object might be hidden under one of several screens and then babies are encouraged to search for it. For toddlers, a beanbag could be hidden in different places in the room. An important part of this game would be to hide the object in a different location each time. Thus, children come to understand that the object exists apart from its hiding place.

4. **Causality materials.** As discussed in an earlier section, causality is a difficult concept that may not be readily acquired by children with special needs. **Causality materials**— toys or objects that cause things to happen—might be included in the classroom: a squeeze toy, a pull toy that makes a noise when dragged across the room, or a rattle that makes an interesting noise when shaken or pounded. A mobile might be attached to the sleeve of a very young infant. Each reflexive wiggle would cause the mobile to move.

Note that such activities are useful for all infants. Caregivers would adapt these to be more basic and simple and would give more direct guidance for those with cognitive delays.

multisensory materials: Play materials for infants that encourage the coordination of two or more senses. A brightly colored mobile that also plays music is an example.

object permanence activities: Play activities for infants, such as hiding games, that help children understand that objects exist even if they are out of sight.

causality materials: Play materials for infants, such as pull or squeeze toys, that cause things to happen and help children understand cause and effect.

CHILD GUIDANCE: *Facilitating Toddler Make-Believe*

Toys that encourage make-believe are not always included in programs for toddlers. Yet children as young as age 1 have been found to engage in simple pretense, in which they carry out basic make-believe actions with realistic props. A toddler might pretend to eat from a bowl and drink from a cup. Another might hug and rock a doll, then cover it with a blanket. Caregivers can guide children in playing this way, using a five-step play intervention strategy:

1. Caregivers begin by creating a center in the classroom that includes only a small number of very familiar housekeeping props—eating utensils, toy telephones, and blankets and pillows for pretending to sleep. (Unfamiliar, theme-related props—farmers' tools or menus from a restaurant, for example, which are common in preschool classrooms—are not appropriate for this age group.)

2. Caregivers then model or prompt simple pretense. They might announce, "I'm so sleepy. I'm going to

bed now," and then lay down, cover themselves, and close their eyes. Or they might prompt a child to do the pretending by saying, "Here, would you like some juice?" then handing over a cup.

3. As children become more competent in their play, the caregiver adds more props. These are still familiar objects related to family life.

4. Once children are performing many simple actions— called *self-as-agent enactments*—the caregiver includes dolls in the center for the first time and initiates parenting play. As children pretend to dress, bathe, or rock the dolls, the caregiver prompts them now and then to pretend that the *doll* is doing the eating, drinking, crying, or talking. This is called *other-as-agent play*. "I think the baby is upset. What is she saying to us?" a caregiver might ask. Or the caregiver might say, "Let's say the baby is drinking the juice now because she's really thirsty," to prompt this kind of pretense.

(continued)

5. After children have performed these simple enactments for several months, the caregiver includes a small number of nonrealistic objects for the first time. Blocks, rubber shapes, soft rods, and cardboard pizza rounds are examples. The caregiver now shows how these objects can be used to stand for things that are completely different. A caregiver might pretend to drink from a cylinder-shaped block, then offer it to a child and say, "Do you want to drink some juice?" The teacher might hand a rod to a child and suggest, "Here's a spoon to stir the soup." These enactments will lay the groundwork for more elaborate and social forms of symbolic play in the preschool years, to be described in Chapter 12.

SUMMARY

Babies think in very different ways than do older children or adults. Piaget called the period from birth to age 2 the sensorimotor stage because infants solve problems mainly through action and simple perception. He identified substages that children pass through, from the purely reflexive activities of the newborn to the more internal and symbolic thinking of the toddler. During this period, children come to understand that objects exist even when they cannot be seen. They gain a simple understanding of cause and effect and an ability to remember things and to engage in pretend play. Other cognitive abilities are also acquired during infancy: memory, attention, and play. Cognitive development varies from culture to culture and can be adversely affected by poverty and disabilities. A variety of interventions have been found effective in enhancing the cognitive development of infants with special needs.

RESEARCH INTO PRACTICE

CRITICAL CONCEPT 1

Infants make impressive strides in cognitive development. According to Piaget, they pass through six substages of intellectual growth and acquire the abilities to find objects and cause events to occur. They can remember things, attend to specific features of objects and people, and engage in simple pretend play.

Application #1 Use knowledge of Piaget's substages of infant development to assess children's developmental progress and to plan appropriate play activities.

Application #2 Initiate object permanence activities, such as hiding games, peekaboo, and drop the spoon, to promote children's understanding that things exist even when they cannot be seen.

Application #3 Provide causality materials that help babies understand cause and effect. Toys involving an action that produces an interesting result are ideal. Other examples are squeeze toys that make interesting noises or pull toys that make popping sounds when dragged along the floor.

CRITICAL CONCEPT 2

Infants acquire other cognitive abilities, such as memory, attention, and play. These become increasingly sophisticated during the first 2 years of life.

Application #1 Play memory games with older infants. Verbal labeling games, such as pointing to objects and asking, "What's that?" and hiding games, such as "Where's the ball?" are examples. Using verbal cues, such as "Remember what the dog's name is?" will facilitate memory.

Application #2 Enhance attention by pointing out the details of objects as babies handle them. Statements such as "Look at the doll's feet" or "You've got buttons on your shirt" are examples. These strategies help children become short looking, a style that promotes learning.

Application #3 Introduce motor activities that are social, involve turn taking, and are related to the infant's culture. Peekaboo; *batti, batti, le, manini*; and *Kan Dol Dol* are examples.

Application #4 Provide props and initiate activities that promote pretend play. A pretend play space can be provided in which children can be encouraged to play out simple make-believe enactments with realistic props. Drinking and eating, pounding with a plastic hammer, and talking on a toy telephone are examples.

CRITICAL CONCEPT 3

Children of different cultures may show different cognitive abilities or may acquire these abilities at different rates. For example, in societies in which babies are stimulated by adult contact throughout the day, advanced infant cognition may be observed. Generally, variations in infant development reflect the rich cultural, developmental, and socioeconomic diversity of our country and our world.

Application #1   Understand and appreciate variations in cognitive development in infancy. Care should be taken not to confuse cultural differences with deficits.

Application #2   Interview parents to learn about the games and activities that are used to promote cognitive development at home. This information can be used to infuse rich cultural play traditions in infant care.

CRITICAL CONCEPT 4

Poverty, malnutrition, and genetic disorders can interrupt cognitive development in infancy. Early intervention can offset some of these negative influences.

Application #1   Identify challenging conditions in the babies you work with. This requires that you understand the behaviors and intellectual characteristics that indicate atypical development. Identifying special needs and accessing services to address those needs are among the most important responsibilities of infant care providers.

Application #2   Be aware of the devastating effects of poverty and poor health care on infant development. Become an advocate for early education and for nutritional, health, and family support services.

ASSESSING YOUNG CHILDREN: Infant Cognitive Development

Areas of Development	What to Watch For	Indicators of Atypical Development	Applications
General Cognitive Abilities	Increasingly complex circular reactions: first repetitive actions with one's own body, later actions performed on other objects. An ability, by 8 months, to search for objects when they are not in view. By this same age, making frequent attempts to cause events to occur through physical action. An ability, by 18 months, to study and think about problems internally before trying to solve them.	Failure to progress beyond primary circular reactions (e.g., simple actions with one's own body). An inability, at 8 months, to retrieve toys, signal for help from an adult, or solve other problems that require causal thinking. A tendency to solve all problems by physical trial and error after 18 months.	Provide play environments with many objects. Include toys that allow babies to cause things to happen—rattles, pull toys, mobiles, or squeeze toys. Play hiding games and provide toys in which objects disappear (e.g., placing shapes in a sorter box) that require babies to think about things that are not visible.
Specific Intellectual Skills	An ability, by 6 months, to remember familiar persons or objects for short periods. An ability to perform simple make-believe enactments with one's own body by age 1 year (e.g., pretending to sleep). Skill in pretending with other people or dolls by 18 months.	Showing poor memory of familiar persons or objects. Continuing to engage in simple, repetitive motor play without make-believe beyond 18 months.	Alternate available toys so that some are put away for a week or more, then reintroduced. Guide infants in recognizing things they have not seen in a while—"Look! Remember we used to squeeze the toy like this?" Provide realistic play props and guide older infants in using these to perform simple pretense—"Can you drink juice from the cup?"

Interpreting Assessment Data: Variations in these areas may be due to culture and family life experience. Cognitive abilities such as object permanence or remembering specific objects will vary depending on the availability of toys within the home. The types of play children engage in—make-believe, active motor play, or quieter pursuits—will be determined by culture and family preference. Children who cannot solve problems of cause and effect or who *never* engage in make-believe may be at risk, however. Illness, injury, or genetic disorders may be a cause; further evaluation is needed. Nutritional, family, and educational intervention can often offset the negative effects of these conditions.

CHAPTER 8

Infant Language and Literacy

GUIDING QUESTIONS

1. What is the difference between receptive and productive communication in infancy?
2. In what ways do babies communicate before they can talk?
3. What are overgeneralization and overrestriction in infants' first words?
4. How do children in bilingual families acquire and use early words from two completely different languages?
5. What are the features of two-word utterances in toddlerhood, and why are these called telegraphic speech?
6. What are the unique characteristics of the two-word utterances of toddlers in bilingual families?
7. What aspects of literacy can be learned before age 2, and what can adults do to enhance this learning?
8. What are some causes of language delays in infancy, and how can adults adapt interactions and play environments to address these?

This chapter will examine infant language and literacy development. Babies use language at a surprisingly early age. They can understand words and phrases before adults are even aware that they can. They display an impressive repertoire of verbalizations to convey needs or express ideas. Sometimes these language behaviors are not easy for some adults to recognize and interpret, as the following story reveals:

> A mother has brought her 10-month-old son to a parent conference in her older daughter's elementary school. As the teacher and mother chat, the young toddler plays with toys in the classroom. Suddenly the child blurts out, "Huh-duh, huh-duh!" and points to the door. The teacher is puzzled. What could the child be trying to communicate? She is even more surprised by the mother's response: "No, sweetie. You can't go out now. We'll go in a few minutes." The baby doesn't seem satisfied. "Huh-duh," he says in an angry tone. "No. You can't go right now," the mother responds gently. The baby finally goes back to playing, and the mother and teacher resume their discussion. Later, the teacher comments on the mother's remarkable ability to understand her baby's messages. The mother explains, "I've just gotten to know his little language. I'm pretty good at figuring out what he's trying to say."

Is the baby in this story really using language as his mother thinks? Are such garbled utterances really words? What is real language, and when does it first emerge in human development? How is language development affected by the type of language spoken or the number of different languages to which one is exposed? These questions, which language specialists—known as **psycholinguists**—ask as they watch linguistic abilities unfold in the early years, will be addressed in this chapter.

psycholinguists:
Researchers and other specialists who study children's language abilities.

RECEPTIVE COMMUNICATION

Language understanding is often called **receptive communication** by psycholinguists. Babies understand words long before they can actually speak them (Bruce & Hansson, 2008). An implication of this is that adults should speak to their babies even before their babies have begun to talk. At what age children will first benefit from this adult conversation is not known. Even in the first year of life, babies can show us they understand words. When asked, "Where's Mommy?" a baby may point or smile (Bernardis, Bello, Pettenati, Stefanini, & Gentilucci, 2008; Goldin-Meadow, 2000). Babies may be able to comprehend even earlier in life but lack the motor skills to show what they know. To be safe, it is advisable to speak to babies at birth, if not before. Some mothers make it a practice to have long conversations with their fetuses while pregnant! Even if babies don't clearly interpret adult messages in their early months, such conversations are good practice for parents.

Speech Perception

Babies are born with **speech perception**—an ability to perceive and process language differently from other sounds. For example, in brain-wave studies, newborns display more activity in the left side of their brains when they hear language and more activity in the right side when they hear music (Callan et al., 2006). Because language is believed to originate in the left hemisphere of the brain, hearing speech may exercise the early linguistic functions of the nervous system.

Psycholinguists have found that babies are quite competent in perceiving speech sounds (Vouloumanos & Werker, 2007). Within the first few months of life, they can distinguish among some consonant and vowel sounds (Werker & Tees, 2002; Werker & Yeung, 2005), intonations, pitch (Kitamura et al., 2001; Katz, Cohn, & Moore, 1996), and loudness (Cathey, 2006; Fernald, 1993). In a controversial study, W. S. Condon and Sander (1974) reported that babies wiggle in concert with the rhythms of human voices. All this research suggests that infants are wired for language learning at birth.

receptive communication: The ability to understand language. Receptive communication usually precedes the ability to actually speak language.

speech perception: An ability, present at birth, to perceive and process language differently from other sounds.

149

In fact, babies may be better able to distinguish among speech sounds of different languages than adults are (Werker & Tees, 2002; Werker & Yeung, 2005). A classic study by Trehub, Schneider, Thorpe, and Judge (1991) demonstrates this. These researchers found that English-speaking babies were able to distinguish between two Czech sounds even though their parents could not. In a similar investigation, Eimas and Tartter (1979) discovered that Japanese babies had little trouble discriminating between the English sounds for the letters "l" and "r" even though Japanese adults in the study were unable to do this. Children of both bilingual and monolingual homes appear to be equally competent in differentiating speech sounds of different languages, even languages that sound very similar (Bosch & Sebastian-Galles, 1997). These findings suggest that babies may be born with a capacity to learn any language, but their speech perception narrows over time to include only the speech sounds of their own culture's language.

Understanding Words

Sometime in the second half of the first year, infants begin to understand words. From here on, babies' word learning advances at such a remarkable pace that one researcher has referred to them as "vacuum cleaners for words" (Hollich et al., 2000, p. 1). In nearly magical fashion, they sweep up and store the words of family members and caregivers! One reason for this rapid word learning is the rapid development and organization of the brain. Brain studies show that 13-month-old infants use both hemispheres of the brain as they process words they don't understand (Mills, Plunkett, Prat, & Schafer, 2005). By 20 months, only the left hemisphere—that responsible for language learning—is used for both known and unknown words. This suggests that left hemisphere language regions that are responsible for language have become specialized.

The first words babies can understand are usually labels for objects (e.g., ball, door, mommy). There are a variety of theories about why this is so. Parents may use object words more in their talk to babies (Waxman & Braun, 2005). In fact, it has been proposed that adults use so many labels for things that babies come to believe that all words are names of objects (Markman, 1992). Other theories of word acquisition are more complex. Hollich and colleagues (2000) believe that a cluster of factors, including object naming by adults, social interactions, and a baby's ability to study and understand objects, all contribute, in concert, to word learning.

First words are influenced by culture: Spanish babies learn Spanish words, English babies English words, and so on. More than this, however, different types of words are emphasized in different cultures. For example, in a culture in which compliance and directive parenting are the norm, the word *no* is learned earlier (Shatz, Grimm, Wilcox, & Niemeier-Wind, 1989). Babies in Italy understand quite early in life the names of different kinds of pasta (Tomasello & Mervis, 1994).

PRODUCTIVE COMMUNICATION

productive communication: Behavior in which babies convey messages to others, including actual speaking but also gestures, noises, and crying.

Productive communication is behavior in which babies convey messages to others. Early words are often considered the first instances of productive communication. However, there is evidence that gestures, noises, and even crying constitute the earliest forms of personal expression (Southgate, van Maanen, & Csibra, 2007; Goldin-Meadow, 2000). The baby in the story at the beginning of this chapter was expressing an idea with his "huh-duh" comment. Psychologists consider communication to be any symbolic expression that holds meaning. So, the infant's garbled babble might rightfully be considered true productive communication.

Crying

Crying is one of the earliest forms of infant productive communication. Through cries, babies convey upset and can show the intensity of their disturbance by varying the pitch and duration of their cries and the number of pauses between bursts of crying (Cecchini, Lai, & Langher, 2007; Zeskind et al., 1992). Debate continues about whether very young infants can communicate specific needs, such as hunger, pain, anger, or fear, by altering the acoustical properties of their cries. Many parents swear that this is so. Early studies showed that parents and trained professionals could differentiate among various kinds of cries. More recent investigations have found that even experienced parents are not accurate in reading the precise meaning of their own babies' cries (Gustafson et al., 2000). In these studies, infant crying was tape-recorded and played back for parents out of context. Without the aid of context—a knowledge that it was almost feeding time, that the baby had not been changed in a while, or that the baby had an ear infection, for example—parents had a very hard time interpreting their babies' cries.

Crying varies significantly among individuals. Temperament and family circumstances may influence the amount of crying. Babies of different ethnic groups show different crying patterns. Among many Euro-American babies, for example, crying is a preferred method of communication, while Navajo, Chinese American, and Japanese American babies cry less often (Chisholm, 1989; Freedman, 1979; Kagan et al., 1994).

If crying is communication, is it somehow linked to later language development? A classic study by Bell and Ainsworth (1972) indicated that babies whose parents responded quickly to their cries were less likely to cry in the second year of life and were more advanced in communicative competence. It may be that responding to crying shows the power of vocalization and that babies with responsive parents graduate more quickly from this early form of communication to actual language.

Parents of different cultures will, of course, respond in different ways to infant crying. Some offer a pacifier, others play or talk, and others snuggle and nurse (Tronick et al., 1994). There is no one correct way to respond to crying. All these methods may enhance infants' communicative competence.

Noises and Gestures

As babies get older, they make noises and gestures to communicate. By age 1, infants of most cultures understand when others point to things, and they, too, will point to refer to objects (Southgate et al., 2007; Goldin-Meadow, 2000). At about the same time, culturally defined gestures emerge: a Japanese baby might demonstrate early bowing (Ogura, Yamasjota, Murase, & Dale, 1993), a Euro-American baby might wave "bye-bye" or clap in excitement, and a Mexican infant might make the movements of *tortillitas*, a version of patty-cake (Jackson-Maldonado, Thal, Bates, Marchman, & Gutierrez-Clellan, 1993).

Noises are also used to communicate ideas. A child may make a "r-r-r" noise to refer to a car, a moaning sound for cows, or a "sh-sh-sh" sound to show running water (Reich, 1986). A frightening and dismaying example is offered by a father living in an urban housing project in America. He says that his 1-year-old daughter says "puh-puh-puh" to indicate gunshots in the neighborhood.

Babbling

Babbling is repetitive vocalization that babies perform during much of the first year of life. Stages of babbling are presented in Table 8-1. Most psycholinguists do not think that

babbling: A repetitive vocalization by babies that is believed to be playing with noise rather than true communication.

**TABLE 8-1
Stages of Babbling**

Stage	Description
Pretend crying stage	Infants produce fussy, cry-like sounds that are not true cries.
Vowel cooing stage	Infants produce long strings of open vowel sounds (e.g., "oooooooh," "aaaaaah").
Consonant cooing stage	Infants produce strings of consonant-like sounds (e.g., "raspberry" noises with lips and tongue or drawn-out "k" and "g" noises emitted from the back of the throat).
Lallation stage	Long consonant–vowel–consonant strings (e.g., "mamamamama," "babababa").
Shortened lallation stage	Shorter consonant–vowel–consonant utterances (e.g., "mama," "lala").
Expressive jargon stage	Long, complex babbles that sound identical in intonation to adult speech.

babbling is true communication but rather that the infant is playing with noise. Much early babbling involves a primary circular reaction, as described in the previous chapter: the baby accidentally makes a noise, which creates an interesting sensation, which causes the baby to repeat the vocalization.

Early coos contain only open vowel sounds. By 4 or 5 months, more consonants are added. During this stage, babbling becomes more elaborate and more highly influenced by the speech of others. Babies' babbles begin to include certain pauses, stresses, and other acoustical features that closely resemble those of adult speech (Davis, MacNeilage, Matyear, & Powell, 2000). At this young age, babies are beginning to match their vocalizations to those of others. One reason for this may be mothers' feedback when babies babble. One study found that when babies babble in vowel sounds resembling adult language, mothers were more likely to respond with verbalizations, as opposed to gestures or smiles (Gros-Louis, West, Goldstein, & King, 2006). Mothers may be subconsciously teaching their children the exact sounds of their home language.

Near the end of the first year, long strings of vowel-consonant-vowel patterns are uttered (Stoel-Gammon & Vogel Sosa, 2007). By 10 or 11 months, babies' babbling is an **expressive jargon** that is so similar to adult speech in complexity and intonation that it sounds as if the baby were speaking in full, albeit incomprehensible, sentences.

Early babbling includes a wide variety of speech sounds, many of which are not used in the baby's native language. Babies begin to babble at about the same age, using the same broad repertoire of noises regardless of the specific language or languages spoken in the home (Oller, Eilers, Urbano, & Cobo-Lewis, 1997; Nathan, Ertmer, & Stark, 2006). During the second half of the first year, however, babbling appears to be somewhat influenced by the family's native language. Babies of diverse cultural and linguistic groups babble in noticeably different ways. In one study, even untrained listeners could guess the home languages of babies from distinct linguistic backgrounds (Blake & Boysson-Bardies, 1992). Family dialect, however, does not appear to influence babbling; African American and Euro-American babies use roughly the same English sounds and intonations in their babbling.

By the second half of the first year, babies growing up in bilingual homes may show distinct patterns in their babbling, depending on the extent of their exposure to two different languages (Genessee & Nicoladis, 2007). Those more fully exposed to two separate language systems often demonstrate a broader repertoire of babbling sounds. Research has not yet

expressive jargon: A type of babbling that is so similar to adult speech in complexity and intonation that it sounds as if the baby were speaking in full sentences.

been conducted to determine if this bilingual babbling contributes to later language competence. At the very least, it may be concluded that bilingual babblers are practicing a wider range of speech sounds than monolingual babblers.

If babbling is not a form of true communication—that is, if it is not used to express needs or ideas—then is it useful for later language learning? One function it does have is to induce "conversations" with parents. When a baby engages in expressive jargon, for example, a parent is likely to respond verbally. Often complex interchanges, involving turn taking and lively intonation, follow (Pine, Lieven, & Rowland, 1997). Babbling is a playful behavior that allows babies to make verbal contact with others.

Some argue that babbling can be analyzed to identify potential language problems later in life. One study found that babies who were slower in beginning to babble had smaller vocabularies at age 3 (Oller, Eilers, Neal, & Schwartz, 1999). Paul (1999) argues, however, that there is much typical variation in the onset of babbling because of culture, home environment, and temperament. She warns against using early babbling to falsely label babies as *at risk*. Some babies simply watch and listen for longer periods, she argues, before trying to vocalize themselves.

First Words

Between 8 months and 18 months, babies speak their first words. It is very difficult to tell exactly when this occurs because a baby's early words are often unintelligible and their meanings unclear to adults. Eventually, new words can be understood. It is important to know, however, that babies' meanings for the words they speak may be very different from adults' meanings for those same words (Lu, 2000). Just because a baby can utter a word does not mean that he or she understands its full meaning. The following story illustrates this:

> A father is playing with his 1-year-old daughter in the backyard of their apartment building. "Pelota!" ("Ball!"), he calls out as he throws her a large rubber ball. To his astonishment, she tries to throw the ball back. It flies into the air, almost behind her. "Pelota!" she calls as she does this. The father becomes truly excited—his daughter has not spoken this word before.
>
> Later, in the apartment, the father tries to show his wife and her mother that their toddler has learned a new word. He hands the ball to her, but she will not name it. He rolls it to her and says, "Pelota." No success. The wife and grandmother laugh, thinking that surely parental pride has gotten the best of him.
>
> As his wife leaves for work, he tries again to show her that her daughter has learned a new word. He rolls the ball to her across the lawn. She smiles, picks it up, but says nothing. With a laugh, the mother leaves. The moment she is gone, the daughter flings the ball back toward her father. "Pelota!" she calls out.

The father has just received a practical lesson in language development. He finally understands why his 1-year-old daughter would not speak this new word in the apartment. To her, *pelota* does not simply mean "*ball*" but "*throw the ball high up in the air in the back yard*." Only later, through much experience with balls of various kinds and in many different contexts, will the baby gradually come to understand the full, adult meaning of the word.

Two kinds of errors are typical when toddlers begin to use words. The first is **overgeneralization,** in which babies overgeneralize a new word so that it refers to many more things than it should. For example, a baby will use the word *car* to mean cars, trucks, tractors, and even strollers. Another will use the word *papa* to refer to any adult male: the mailman, a tribal elder, a doctor at the clinic. As children hear a word and use it in many contexts, they

overgeneralization: A language characteristic of toddlers and young children in which a word is used to describe more objects, events, or ideas than it should. For example, a child uses the word *car* to stand for cars, trucks, vans, and buses.

gradually construct a more accurate meaning and reduce the various generalizations of the word.

A second common error is **overrestriction.** Toddlers will often use a word to refer to a narrower range of things than an adult would. The previous story is an example: the child uses *pelota* only if she is throwing the ball in the back yard. Egocentrism at this age contributes to overrestriction. The word *shoes* may be restricted to the meaning *my own shoes*, and the word *cup* might mean only *my own red cup*. In these cases, babies need to broaden the meaning of words. Through experience with language, they gradually construct a fuller definition.

Which words do babies speak first? Two types of words that are likely to emerge early are names of things, such as *ball*, *dog*, and *daddy*, and social expressions, such as *bye-bye*, *no*, and *want* (L. R. Gleitman & H. Gleitman, 1992; Sebastián-Gallés, 2007). Children who first acquire mainly the names of things are known as **referential.** Those who initially learn more social expressions are called **expressive.** Many factors determine which category of language learning style a child will fall into. Temperament may lead some children to be more wary of people and less likely to use social words. Children who are exposed to few toys and objects but to many people in their homes or neighborhoods may learn social words initially.

Culture may influence whether children will be referential or expressive. Euro-American babies, for example, speak more nouns as first words—that is, they are referential (Fernald & Morikawa, 1993; Lu, 2000). Euro-American mothers often emphasize object labeling and direct language teaching in their interactions with their babies. These mothers are regularly observed playing a labeling game in which they quiz their children on the names of things: "What's this? It's a book. Can you say 'book'?"

In contrast, Japanese American babies tend to use more social expressions, and their mothers focus more on social behaviors in their interchanges with babies. These mothers have been observed using toys or other play objects primarily to engage their babies in social interaction. This trend reflects *omoiyari*, a traditional concept that emphasizes harmony in human interactions (Gopnik & Choi, 1995; Kita & Ide, 2007). These differences reflect culturally derived parenting practices and socialization beliefs that result in Japanese American infants learning more verbs and social words but fewer nouns than Euro-American babies.

The structure of language itself may also influence first word use. English has been referred to as "noun dominant," so English-speaking children may be referential more often (Gopnik & Choi, 1995). In languages such as Japanese and Korean, nouns are less frequent and are often deleted. So, expressive language styles may emerge more often among children speaking these languages.

Culture, of course, determines precisely which words will be uttered first. In studies of word acquisition, toddlers were found frequently to include names of animals and sounds, childhood games, and food and drink among their first 50 words (Childers & Tomasello, 2006; Tomasello and Mervis, 1994). It is easy to see that words in these different categories would vary significantly across cultures and across ethnic groups within the United States. Families eat different foods, have different pets or other experiences with animals, and have their own traditional childhood activities. These unique experiences determine early words.

Early Words in Bilingual Families. At least half of all children in the world are bilingual or multilingual, including a growing number of children in the United States (U.S. Bureau of the Census, 2004). How does the experience of bilingualism influence word learning? The steps in bilingual word acquisition are depicted in Figure 8-1.

In the earliest stages of word learning—before 18 months of age—babies acquire new words from both languages as if they were all part of a single vocabulary—sometimes called a

overrestriction: A language characteristic of toddlers and young children in which a word is used to describe fewer objects, events, or ideas than it should. For example, a child uses the word *shoes* to mean only his or her own shoes.

referential language learning style: A style of language learning in which a young child acquires the names of objects earliest in development.

expressive language learning style: A style of language learning in which a young child acquires social words, such as *bye-bye* and *no*, earliest in development.

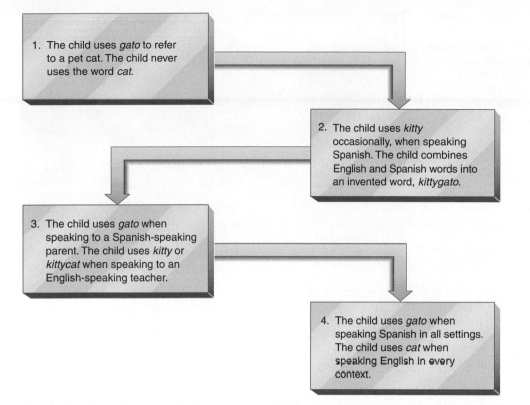

FIGURE 8-1 Learning a word in two languages follows a series of steps. Shown here are the steps a preschooler follows in learning the English word *cat* and the Spanish word *gato*.

mental dictionary. For example, a child from a farming family that speaks both English and German might use the German word for horse (*pferd*) and the English word for pig. In an English/Spanish-speaking family, a child might refer to some foods in English (e.g., apple) and others in Spanish (e.g., *platano* for banana).

The proportion of words in this early dictionary that are of one language or another is determined by how much exposure a child has to each language (Genesee & Nicoladis, 2007). A child who grows up in a bilingual, English/Spanish family, where Spanish is spoken 80% of the time, will have a vocabulary that contains more Spanish words than English. A child from a Vietnamese American family, whose parents rarely speak English to her, will have a mental dictionary with more Vietnamese words in it.

It is rare for toddlers to use words from both languages to describe the same concept or object. Very young children almost always opt to name something consistently in one language or the other (Singleton, 2007). By 18 months of age, infants begin to use some *mixed speech*; a baby might learn the names of a few especially important items in *both* languages. This is more common in homes where one parent speaks one language and the other a different language. In this case, a toddler might say "ball" to one adult and "pelota" to another (Deuchar & Quay, 1999; Quay, 2004). This ability to figure out which adult speaks which language and to adapt speech accordingly is really quite remarkable at such a young age!

In some instances, toddlers combine the words of two languages into a single utterance (e.g., *kittygato* for cat). Whether babies will use one language more than another, use some words of both languages to express ideas, or engage in mixed speech will be determined by

mental dictionary: A child's total vocabulary, including words in all the languages being learned.

Toddlers from bilingual families learn the names for some objects in one language and the names for other objects in the second language.

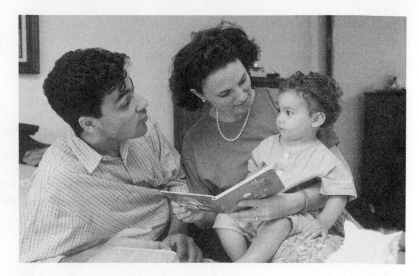

the nature of the bilingual environment in which they grow up (Deuchar & Quay, 1999; Quay, 2004). There are infinite varieties of bilingual family settings:

- A baby lives with a Spanish-speaking grandmother and an English-speaking mother.
- A baby grows up in a home where only Cherokee is spoken. At age 1, she attends a child care center where only English is spoken.
- A baby grows up with parents and older siblings who speak an African American dialect at home and in the neighborhood but standard Euro-American English in more formal settings.
- A baby grows up in a home where parents speak Spanish as their native language but wish to speak only English around their children to help them assimilate into American life.

Diversity in language environments explains the rich variation in communication style and competence during the early years.

A question frequently asked by parents is whether babies living in bilingual environments will suffer delays in vocabulary growth. It would seem that bilingual babies might experience complex and perhaps confusing verbal environments. In a bilingual home, for example, every object would have at least two words to describe it. This concern has arisen from early studies that only looked at bilingual children's ability to learn English. Not surprisingly, babies who grow up in homes where both Spanish and English are spoken have been found to have smaller usable English vocabularies (Uccelli & Páez, 2007).

It is easy to see why such studies do not reflect the best ways to look at bilingual vocabulary development. Bilingual babies learn some of their words in one language and others in another language. Measuring vocabulary by looking only at words of one of the languages does not provide a complete picture. When the vocabularies for all languages spoken in the home are added together, virtually no difference is found between monolingual and bilingual children in the number of words learned in the early years (Bialystok, McBride-Chang, & Luk, 2005). In fact, children of bilingual homes might be somewhat advanced in both verbal and nonverbal intelligence (Padilla et al., 1991).

Two-Word Utterances

Between 18 months and 2 years, babies begin putting words together. Although their first sentences are only two words long, they can express amazing numbers of ideas or relationships between objects and actions (Gerkin, 2007; Lu, 2000). The following English toddler utterances, for example, are likely to get immediate attention from adults:

"All broke."
"Kitty bye-bye."
"Book flush."
"Me bite."
"Oh-oh paint."
"All wet."

Using just two words, toddlers comment about objects or events, announce actions, and even confess to all manner of misadventures. To express ideas with two words is a significant intellectual achievement. For the first time, toddlers must contend with word order, or what psycholinguists refer to as **syntax.** To appreciate the complexity of combining words, consider the sentence "Car go," which a baby uses to mean "The car went down the street." In this utterance, the baby has provided a stripped-down version of an adult sentence. This is the simplest utterance possible that will still have meaning. All but the most important words necessary to convey the message are left out. Some psycholinguists have referred to this as **telegraphic speech** because of this economy of expression. Babies speak as though they were paying for every word!

In a two-word utterance, babies must make challenging decisions about word order. In "Car go," the baby places the agent, "car," before the action, "go," thus following the basic rules of sentence construction in English. Even very young toddlers make few word-order errors (e.g., "Go car"). Most psycholinguists believe that babies apply simple rules of their native language to construct their early sentences. Of course, they don't consciously think about rules as they speak. Children, generally, have a **tacit knowledge of language;** it is an "I can do it, but I can't tell you how I do it" form of thinking.

Two-Word Utterances in Bilingual Families. Bilingual babies progress to two-word utterances at about the same age as monolingual babies. For those learning two or more languages, however, putting words together poses special challenges, especially if the languages are very different. Every language has a unique word order. Verbs appear at the ends of sentences in some languages and in the middle in others. Adjectives follow nouns in some languages and precede them in others. So, babies growing up in bilingual families have two sets of rules to learn and apply as they create simple sentences.

How do toddlers put two-word utterances together when faced with contrasting rules about word order? They work out quite ingenious solutions to the problem. Some babies simply select one of the languages they hear around them and apply only its rules. A baby who speaks both Spanish and English, for example, may rely just on the rules of Spanish word order even when speaking English. For example, in Spanish adjectives often follow nouns, as in *el gato blanco*. So, a toddler might apply this rule to English utterances as well and say "the cat white" instead of "the white cat." Other babies have been found to actually invent their own unique word-ordering system that is a combination of the languages spoken in the home (Genesee & Nicoladis, 2007).

Bilingual babies also face challenges in picking just the right words to create simple sentences. One problem is that words work differently in different languages. In Chinese, for example, many words can act as both a noun and a verb. This is less frequent in English (the word *plan* is one example) (Aaronson & Ferres, 1987). So, a child who speaks both Chinese and English is more likely to create a simple English sentence such as "I noising" to mean "I am making noise."

syntax: The part of language that involves creating sentences, including word order, sentence length and complexity, and the use of clauses and word endings.

telegraphic speech: Early utterances of young children, such as "Throw ball," that contain only the words necessary to convey the message. Less important words, such as articles, are omitted.

tacit knowledge of language: A subconscious ability to apply rules of language without thinking about them.

THE MEDIA

Do Television and Computers Teach Babies to Talk?

By 3 months, 40% of American infants view television, DVDs, or videos for at least an hour each day (Zimmerman, Christakis, & Meltzoff, 2007). By age 2, 90% of children are exposed to these media. For parents with stressful lives, this high rate of viewing may be because they use television or DVDs as "electronic babysitters." In other cases, babies are incidentally exposed to television because their older siblings or parents are constantly watching. However, a growing number of parents expose their infants to electronic media because they believe this is educational. They are swayed by claims from software and broadcasting companies that babies can actually acquire language, as well as new knowledge, by watching specially designed DVDs or television programs. A growing number of research studies have found this is not the case.

Until recently the research on the effects of media on babies has been inconclusive. Babies have been found to acquire vocabulary by regularly watching certain television shows but to suffer vocabulary delays when watching others (Linebarger, 2005). Amount of viewing has been linked to irregular sleep schedules and sleep disorders (D. A. Thompson & Christakis, 2005). On the other hand, research has shown that infants can learn social behaviors and emotions when watching television (Mumme & Fernald, 2003). Findings of a new study on more than 7,000 infants may have settled the matter and have certainly surprised and alarmed parents and educators (Zimmerman et al., 2007). These investigators discovered that for each hour per day of daily television or DVD viewing, infants learned six to eight fewer words than those not exposed to these media. The authors conclude that, not only is television not a good way to promote infant language, but it may actually be harmful. They speculate that this is due to the reduction in face-to-face communication between children and parents that occurs during viewing.

This study, along with several smaller ones with similar results, have led the American Academy of Pediatrics to recommend that children under the age of 2 not be exposed to any sort of visual electronic media. Professionals should help parents plan alternative social and language-rich activities to engage in during family times.

Because of the complexity of two-word sentence construction, babies from bilingual homes often engage in language switching, in which words from two languages are blended in a single utterance. For example, a baby who speaks both Swedish and English may say "Titta, bunny" for "Look, bunny" or "Horsie sova" for "Horsie sleep." In some cases, babies will take words with the same meaning from each language and combine them into a two-word utterance, such as when a baby who speaks both German and English says "bitte please." It has been well documented that parents and other adults grow anxious hearing these early language mixtures. Many believe these constructions to be confusing and damaging to language learning. A temptation is to correct toddlers, but this tactic is counterproductive. In their preschool years, bilingual children will be able to separate effectively the two or more languages they hear (Quay, 2004; Lanvers, 2001).

TODDLER LITERACY

Babies in some cultures are exposed to written as well as oral language. In American families, adults and toddlers of all cultural groups spend time together reading stories or browsing other written materials. When parents read with babies, they promote early literacy skills, such as how to handle books or turn pages. Such experiences show that reading is interesting and worthwhile. In shared reading activities, babies learn that stories are read with a certain pacing and intonation. Schickedanz (1999) has observed that even fairly young babies who have been read to often will babble in a unique way, called book babble, during a reading session.

When reading to their toddlers, parents have been found to scaffold early literacy learning. **Scaffolding,** an idea drawn from Vygotsky's (1978) work, is the process by which adults give support or guidance for some parts of a task or activity and then gradually give over regulation of the experience to children. In so doing, adults help children become more and more independent in their thinking and actions. Parents have many ways of scaffolding children's learning during a reading session. One parent might first turn pages of a book and then ask the child to do so. Another might point to pictures and ask the child to name them and then later encourage the child to do so independently. A third parent might ask children to guess what happens next. For example, a father might ask, "What do you think she saw?" and the child might respond, "Bunny!"

The following vignette illustrates adult scaffolding of a child's early literacy:

A grandmother and a 2-year-old sit in the kitchen of their apartment looking at a department store catalog. The child sits in the grandmother's lap holding the reading material in front of him.

GRANDMOTHER:	(Pointing to a picture on a page) What's this, Terry?
CHILD:	Man.
GRANDMOTHER:	That's a man isn't it?
CHILD:	A man.
GRANDMOTHER:	But what about over here? (Points to another part of the page)
CHILD:	Man…mans.
GRANDMOTHER:	Yeah. That's two men, right, Terry? Two men.
CHILD:	Two
GRANDMOTHER:	That's right. (Turns page and waits without speaking)
CHILD:	Wa dis?
GRANDMOTHER:	What is that?
CHILD:	Shush caysh.
GRANDMOTHER:	(Laughs) Yeah. Suitcase. (Waits again)
CHILD:	(Turns page on his own) Wa dat?

The reading continues with the toddler now turning the pages, asking and then answering his own questions about the pictures.

This grandmother is scaffolding her grandchild's reading experience. At first she directly manages the page turning and question asking, but soon she gives over regulation of the activity to the child. Initially she pauses to allow him to ask the questions and, next, allows him to turn the pages himself. This vignette illustrates another important point: not all infants have their earliest print experiences with storybooks (Pellegrini, Perlmutter, Galda, & Brody, 1990). Magazines, signs, and the text on cereal boxes may be more prevalent in some families or cultural groups. Parents should be encouraged to make use of any materials in the home to enhance infant literacy.

Some child and family services programs, such as Head Start, Even Start, and the Family Resource Center, now include literacy interventions for infants and toddlers (Gilliam & Zigler, 2000). (See the Advocacy and Public Policy box in this chapter for ideas on how professionals can initiate such community-based infant literacy programs.) Only a few studies have been conducted to examine the effects of these strategies. In one investigation, a training program was designed to teach child care providers to engage in literacy activities—such as shared book reading—with at-risk infants and toddlers (M. B. Armstrong, 1998). The intervention was found to increase caregivers' skills and to promote children's literacy understandings at age 2. In two similar studies, caregiver

scaffolding: A process by which adults give support or guidance for some parts of a task or activity and then gradually give over regulation of the experience to children, allowing them to become more independent in their thinking and actions.

When adults read to toddlers, they often "scaffold" early literacy learning.

ADVOCACY AND PUBLIC POLICY

Organizing a "Born to Read" Program

As discussed in this chapter, children as young as age 1 enjoy and benefit from reading books. Infants can learn to handle books and turn their pages. They understand how stories sound and even babble in unique, story-like utterances when read to (Schickedanz, 1999). Most literacy programs for young children and their families, however, focus on older children—preschoolers or those in the elementary grades. A new program called "Born to Read," developed by the Association for Library Service to Children, is an exception. In this program, local libraries collaborate with other community organizations to conduct outreach activities that promote infant and toddler literacy. (Such outreach is critical since families with babies—particularly those with low literacy levels—rarely visit the library.) A library might partner with local social services agencies, the school district, and child care and Head Start centers to identify families with infants who could benefit from a literacy program. Because a focus is on teen parents and their infants, a Born to Read partnership often includes an adolescent parent program.

Identified families are provided with packets of books that are appropriate for infants. Bibliographies of additional children's books, tips on reading strategies, and follow-up games and activities are presented in newsletters, in brochures, or through direct contact. In one innovative approach, a library held a baby shower for expecting teen mothers that included infant books as shower gifts. According to one librarian, participating in the program in Florida, these strategies "strengthen the library's relationships with so many community agencies, give the library a whole new visibility, and spin off into other areas of community involvement."

The Association for Library Service to Children invites professionals to set up Born to Read programs within their own communities. Involvement of teachers and caregivers is especially encouraged since these professionals are specialists in early literacy. Guidelines for starting a Born to Read program, including information on possible funding sources, can be obtained on the organization's Website (http://www.ala.org/alsc). Becoming involved in such an initiative will help provide children with a solid, early foundation in literacy development.

CLASSROOM ADAPTATIONS: INFANTS WITH LANGUAGE DELAYS

Some children have language delays. Typically developing 1-year-olds babble in highly expressive jargon, acquire first words, then create two-word utterances. Babies with challenging conditions often do not exhibit this same behavior (Buschmann et al., 2008). The absence of these language features usually prompts parents or caregivers to suspect that the child has a challenging condition. Several conditions that affect language development are presented in Table 8-2.

Condition	Effects on Infant Language
Hearing impairment	Babbling is typical until age 6 months, but vocalizations begin to decrease in the second 6 months of life. More complex babbling and expressive jargon do not appear.
Down syndrome	Babbling and early words are delayed. Babies respond less often to others' language, make fewer requests, and initiate conversations infrequently.
General language delay	Babbles or words resemble the vocalizations of much younger, typically developing children. Language may or may not catch up with that of nondelayed peers over time.

TABLE 8-2
Some Challenging Conditions That Affect Infant Language

training was found to have a positive impact not just on infants but on the home literacy environment as well (Barratt-Pugh, Rohl, Oakley, & Elderfield, 2005; Hardman & Jones, 1999). After the training, more books for babies were found in both the child centers and the homes of participants. More frequent adult–infant reading interactions were observed in both home and center settings. These studies suggest that it is never too early to read to children.

Hearing Impairment and Infant Language

Some language delays in toddlerhood have clearly specified causes. Hearing impairment is an example. **Hearing impairment,** which is caused by a variety of environmental and genetic factors, is characterized by complete deafness or severely limited auditory perception. This condition can lead to language, motor, and other developmental delays. In the early months of life, babies with hearing impairments vocalize in much the same way that hearing babies do. In fact, their babbles are so typical that many parents do not even suspect problems at this age (Holstrum, Gaffney, Gravel, Oyler, & Ross, 2008; Yoshinaga-Itano & Appuzo, 1998). By 6 months, however, the vocalizations of these infants decrease significantly. They often do not progress to complex babbles and expressive jargon as typically developing babies do (Goldin-Meadow, Mylander, & Butcher, 1995; Scheiner, Hammerschmidt, Jürgens, & Zwirner, 2004).

From this point on in development, hearing impairment can severely disrupt all aspects of language development. Early detection and intervention can significantly reduce these negative effects, however. Two studies demonstrate this clearly. In one, babies with hearing impairments that were identified before 6 months were compared with those whose hearing losses were not discovered until after 18 months

hearing impairment: A condition caused by a variety of factors that is characterized by deafness or severely limited auditory perception and can lead to language, motor, and other developmental delays.

(Yoshinaga-Itano & Appuzo, 1998). The former group, whose disabilities were detected early, scored far higher on measures of receptive and expressive language and cognitive abilities later in childhood. In a similar investigation, children whose hearing impairments were identified prior to age 4 months or after age 2 years were compared (Wake, Poulakis, Hughes, Carey-Sargeant, & Rickards, 2005). Once again, those whose impairments were discovered early fared far better later in life. They scored higher not only on measures of language development but on assessments of social development as well. A crucial role of professionals who work with families and children is to assist in the early identification of hearing loss. They should also advocate for legislation mandating early hearing screening in hospitals and doctors' offices (see the Advocacy and Public Policy box in Chapter 6).

Several fascinating studies suggest that some babies with hearing impairments do, in fact, continue to progress in communicative ability, using a different kind of system to communicate. Those who are exposed to American Sign Language early in life, for example (see Figure 8-2), learn this communication system in precisely the way that hearing babies learn oral language (Goldin-Meadow et al., 1995).

In several studies, young babies with hearing impairments whose families used sign language at home were found to babble with their hands in a playful, repetitive manner, just as hearing babies might repeat consonants in babbling (Petitto, Holowka, Sergio, Levy, & Ostry, 2004; Petitto & Marentette, 1991). For example, one infant used the sign for "ba" repeatedly, much like a speaking baby's typical consonant–vowel voice play "ba, ba, ba."

Babies with hearing loss who have not been exposed to sign language sometimes invent their own system of gestures to communicate (Goldin-Meadow et al., 1995). Once again, this system develops following a pattern that is similar to typical language development. At about the age when first words emerge, babies who cannot hear will begin to use single gestures to stand for objects or actions. For example, a baby might use a twisting motion to express a desire for a certain container to be opened. At the age when typically developing toddlers are using two words, babies with hearing impairments will combine two gestures to express elaborate ideas. It is evident that they have the same strong need to communicate and will construct a way to do this in the absence of hearing and speech abilities.

How can child care providers adapt their interactions with infants who have hearing impairments to promote communication? Crais and Roberts (2003) recommend the following:

1. *Be responsive.* Caregivers should respond quickly and with interest to all initiatives of infants with hearing impairments—whether they are gestures, facial expressions, attempts at verbal communication, or even noises. These interactions show the power of language and encourage children to continue communicating.

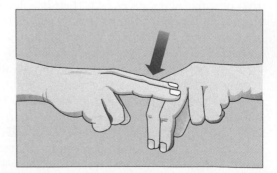

FIGURE 8-2 Infants who are exposed to American Sign Language have been found to babble with hand signs.

2. **Use language.** Caregivers should use language with infants who have hearing impairments even if very little of their speech can be heard. This will allow children to develop their residual hearing—the hearing ability they do have. It will also encourage them to study facial expressions related to language and eventually to read lips.

3. **Use total communication.** While communicating with infants, caregivers should use exaggerated gestures, facial expressions, and physical touch as well as language. This will help infants learn to derive messages using several different senses.

4. **Practice turn taking.** Even with nonverbal infants and toddlers, turn-taking *conversations* can be initiated. A caregiver can model a gesture (e.g., pointing to an object and naming it), then pause to give the child a turn to copy this behavior. A caregiver might engage the child in bye-bye play, making a gesture and verbalizing, then allowing the child to do so. Handing-back-and-forth and trading games can be introduced. The caregiver can hand a toy to the child and say, "Here." Then the caregiver can give a gesture to request the object back and say, "Thank you!" when the child complies.

Down Syndrome and Infant Language

Another clearly identified source of language delay is Down syndrome. Babies with this condition show significant disruption in language development within the second half of their first year. In addition to experiencing oral language delay, babies with Down syndrome show difficulty in general communication with parents (Moore, Oates, Hobson, & Goodwin, 2008). They may pay less attention and give fewer verbal responses when parents speak to them. In addition, they make fewer requests and initiate fewer conversations.

Language delays of infants with Down syndrome vary in degree, depending on the severity of the condition. Some babies with the condition are only slightly delayed in communication; others are significantly so. Early intervention can reduce the negative impact of Down syndrome on language. In several studies, for example, a language enrichment intervention that was taught to mothers of babies with Down syndrome led to increases in word acquisition (Girolametto, Sussman, & Weitzman, 2007; Girolametto, Weitzman, & Clemments-Baartman, 1998).

General Language Delay

Some language problems have no apparent cause. Some toddlers have been found to acquire many or most aspects of language more slowly even when they suffer no obvious perceptual or cognitive problems. These children have limited vocabularies or do not begin to use words until very late. Some have trouble understanding words spoken to them. Although a variety of terms have been used to describe this phenomenon, the phrase **general language delay** is probably most common. Language delays are believed to be just that: general delays in all or most aspects of communicative development.

Some researchers find that the language of children with delays is identical to that of younger, typically developing children (Ratner, 2008). The term *delay* causes some confusion, however. It implies that such children will simply catch up with their peers in language competence over time. This is not always the case. Children with general language delays in toddlerhood or in the preschool years are more likely to have language and academic problems and to be identified as having learning disabilities later in life (Buschmann et al., 2008).

general language delay: A condition in which a child's language development lags behind that of other children of the same age, with no apparent perceptual or cognitive cause.

Toddlers with language delays are usually defined by what they are not rather than by what they are (S. R. Easterbrooks, 2008). They are *not* mentally retarded. They do *not* have genetic disorders. It is likely, then, that this category of disorder represents a whole range of different and perhaps unrelated conditions that have diverse causes. Early researchers believed that minimal brain dysfunction—minor and undetectable damage to the brain—is responsible for much language delay (Tallal, 1987). Newer studies are now suggesting a genetic link (Oliver & Plomin, 2007). Other causes have also been suggested, such as poverty, family stress, nonresponsive parenting, and poor health (Carson, Perry, & Diefenderfer, 1999; Prathanee, Thinkhamrop, & Dechongkit, 2007). There is no one profile of a child with language delay, then, and no single intervention that is successful in all cases.

Researchers have proposed a number of classroom strategies for enhancing the language development of infants with Down syndrome or those with general language delays (Crais and Roberts, 2003; S. R. Easterbrooks, 2008):

1. *Naming objects, actions, and events.* Children with disabilities often have limited vocabularies. A powerful vocabulary-building strategy is to name all objects, actions, or events during the day. During motor play, a caregiver might say, "You're *jumping.* Jump, jump, jumping!" A caregiver might label a toy a toddler is using: "You have a doll. It's a doll."

2. *Responding with expansion and expatiation.* When children with disabilities speak, an adult can guide them toward more complex syntax in a way that does not interrupt the conversation. In one technique, **expansion,** the teacher simply restates the one- or two-word utterance of a child in a more elaborate form. If a child says, "Ball," a caregiver might restate, "It's a big, red ball!" In **expatiation,** the caregiver restates the utterance but then adds more language, furthering the conversation (e.g., "Yes, it's a ball. Are you throwing the ball to Jeremy?"). Whether to use expansion or expatiation will depend on the age and competence level of the child.

3. *Engaging in naturalistic conversation.* Although some researchers have found direct teaching of vocabulary to be useful for toddlers (Owens, 1996), most psycholinguists recommend that naturalistic conversations be used for enhancing language. These are authentic, unobtrusive, and engaging conversations with children during play or classroom routines. A caregiver might comment on what a toddler is doing at the water play table: "Look at that! You're just pouring and pouring the water." When toddlers talk in these contexts (e.g., "More"), the caregiver can respond enthusiastically using expatiation (e.g., "Oh, you're finished with your raisins! I'll give you some more."). These conversations can be initiated even with very young babies (e.g., "Look at you shaking that rattle. It goes jingle, jingle, jingle.").

expansion: A language teaching technique in which an adult restates a one- or two-word utterance of a child in a more elaborate form.

expatiation: A language teaching technique in which an adult restates a one- or two-word utterance of a child but then adds more language, furthering the conversation.

language differences: Variations in language due to cultural or linguistic background, not to be confused with deficits in language caused by challenging conditions.

Unfortunately, some children have been identified as having language delays merely because they are from families of different cultures or because they speak different dialects or languages. Child and family professionals should take great care not to assume that **language differences** are deficits. Family service providers or child care teachers should not, for example, expect infants from bilingual homes to speak English as quickly as native English speakers. Differences in communicative styles must also be appreciated (Zamborlin, 2007). For example, quietness may be a sign not of delay but rather of a culturally derived communicative style (Klein & Chen, 2001). A quiet style might also be a common response to the overwhelming experience of learning a new, second language.

CHILD GUIDANCE: *The Naming Game*

As infants acquire language, they become eager to learn the names of objects and persons around them. "Wha dat?" ("What's that?") is a very common question as early as age 1. Caregivers can take advantage of this fascination with words by initiating a naming game to promote vocabulary growth. The game can be played in distinct phases, beginning in the first half year of life and continuing through toddlerhood.

In phase 1, an adult simply names objects that a baby sees or holds, using an exaggerated intonation (e.g., "That's a ball" or "Look, you have a bear. It's a bear."). This phase can be initiated long before a baby can even speak words. In phase 2, which begins after a child is speaking one-word utterances, the adult introduces the "What's that?" question. As the child sees or handles objects, the adult says, "Look! What's that?" then pauses to allow the baby to answer. Initially, the baby may have little to say. So, after a brief wait, the adult answers the question: "That's a book." Over time, the child will begin naming objects, particularly those that are very familiar (e.g., "Book!"). The adult now restates the word with much enthusiasm: "Right! That's a book!"

Phase 3 begins when babies start asking for the names of things on their own. At this point, the adult gives over much of the regulation of the game, including the question asking, to the child. For example, a child, holding out a jonquil she has just snatched from a vase on the dining room table, asks, "Dat?" The adult names the object for the baby with enthusiasm (e.g., "Oh, that's a flower") while at the same time quickly rescuing the flower and returning it to its vase. Over time, these questions increase in frequency, and the game can become quite exhausting for adults. Children, in contrast, can play forever, without tiring. Answering each and every question is important for language learning, however. (It is a myth that children ask these questions merely for attention or to torment their weary parents.)

SUMMARY

Babies acquire receptive communication—the ability to perceive and understand speech—before they can actually talk. Productive communication—the ability to communicate to others through words, crying, noises, and even nonvocal means, such as gestures—often emerges before age 1. Children's early language is quite different from that of adults. The words they use hold unique meanings. The word *ball* could stand, too broadly, for all round objects or, too narrowly, for just one specific red ball in a child's room. Early sentences often do not include articles or even subjects or verbs. Children growing up in bilingual homes have the special challenge of sorting out the rules of two different languages spoken around them. They initially learn words from both languages as if they were part of one big vocabulary. They confuse the grammatical rules of one language with the other.

Babies not only acquire oral language but can also begin to enjoy and understand books. A variety of challenging conditions can lead to language delays. Child care providers can adapt their interactions to promote language development in infants with hearing impairments, Down syndrome, or general language delay.

RESEARCH INTO PRACTICE

CRITICAL CONCEPT 1

Infants begin to understand language long before they can talk. At birth, they can distinguish speech from other kinds of sounds and recognize the voices of significant adults. In the second half of the first year, they are able to understand words and phrases.

Application #1 Talk to babies, and encourage parents to do so, starting at birth, even though babies are not yet talking themselves. Rich conversation directed toward infants will stimulate language centers in the brain and promote later communicative competence.

Application #2 Because it is not known precisely when infants understand words, be careful about what you say around them. Toddlers who are not yet speaking may still comprehend a sensitive or confidential topic discussed by adults in their presence.

CRITICAL CONCEPT 2

Early in life, babies communicate through crying, making noises, smiling, gesturing, and pointing.

Application Watch for and respond to infants' nonverbal communication. Responding quickly to signals such as crying and smiling will show babies the pleasure and the power of vocalization and will encourage them to refine their communicative abilities.

CRITICAL CONCEPT 3

Near age 1, babies can speak words. Vocabulary grows exceedingly quickly during the first 2 years of life. The first words babies learn are often names of things they can act on, such as *ball,* or words that have social meaning, such as *bye-bye.*

Application #1   Provide a language-rich environment for babies since language grows so quickly during the first 2 years of life.

Application #2   Name objects that children look at and play with. After children learn the names of things, point to objects and ask, "What's that?"

Application #3   Use social words with infants, such as *bye-bye, night-night,* and *hi.* Encourage babies to use these words, as in "Say 'bye-bye' to grandma."

CRITICAL CONCEPT 4

Bilingual children learn words in two different languages and combine these into one large mental dictionary. Sometimes they become confused about which language to speak at which time, and sometimes they combine words from the two languages into a single utterance.

Application #1   Appreciate the challenge of learning more than one language and be patient with children who show confusion in word learning.

Application #2   Labels for objects and social words should be spoken in both languages to infants who are bilingual. Learn enough words in a baby's native language to be able to name important objects or events in their lives, such as *lunch, naptime, bathroom,* and *goodbye.*

Application #3   In assessing language development, consider the size of children's full mental dictionary, not just their English vocabulary. Asking bilingual children to name objects or pictures in both their native language and the language being learned will give a true picture of semantic development.

CRITICAL CONCEPT 5

Two-word utterances are constructed in toddlerhood. At this point, children must learn early rules of word order. They can accurately place the agent before the action, as in "Daddy throw" rather than "throw Daddy." Infants who are bilingual have a harder time learning word-order rules since they often must acquire two very different sets of language rules.

Application #1   Talk with toddlers using simple sentences that clearly identify the agent, action, and object. Overlay these statements across children's activities, as in "You're throwing the bean bag" and "Jamal took your block."

Application #2   Understand how challenging it is to learn the syntax of two different languages. Be patient when children use the word-order rules of one language when speaking in another. Such errors are a fundamental part of bilingual development.

CRITICAL CONCEPT 6

Toddlers who are read to will acquire early literacy abilities and dispositions. They learn to handle books or turn pages and discover that reading is interesting and worthwhile. They come to understand that stories are read with a certain pacing and intonation.

Application #1   Read to babies very early in life. Books published specifically for infants that are chew resistant and waterproof and include bright colors, textures, and even sounds are ideal.

Application #2   Scaffold children's literacy learning as you read to them. In scaffolding, read the story but at the same time give over some of the responsibility for reading to the child. For example, encourage a toddler to turn pages, name the illustrations, or guess what a particular animal or character in the story might say next (e.g., "woof-woof" or "baa").

CRITICAL CONCEPT 7

Challenging conditions can cause language delays that may be identified in infancy. Hearing impairment, Down syndrome, and general language delay are examples.

Application #1   Provide conversation-rich play environments that allow children with special needs to acquire language in naturalistic settings.

Application #2   Adapt your interactions with children who have special needs to enhance language. Respond to children quickly, using rich language and whole communication in which gestures, facial expressions, and physical touch are also used. Expand children's one-word utterances, rephrasing them in longer, more complex sentences. You can name objects, persons, and actions in children's lives.

Application #3   Teach children to engage in turn-taking conversations with objects. Handing objects back and forth or trading objects are examples. These strategies teach children with special needs the social rules of communication.

ASSESSING YOUNG CHILDREN: Infant Language and Literacy Development

Areas of Development	What to Watch For	Indicators of Atypical Development	Applications
Oral language abilities	Uses crying, gestures, and babbling to communicate needs or make contact with others. Babbles speech sounds that are found in the child's family's language. Understands some words by 1 year. Utters single words by this age. Speaks two-word utterances between 18 months and 2 years.	Failure to cry or in other ways communicate needs. An inability to understand or respond to language by age 1 year. Failure to use one-word utterances by 18 months. Use of only one-word utterances beyond 2 years.	Provide language-rich play experiences. Talk to babies even before they are able to speak. Name objects, persons, or actions, using an enthused intonation. Use total communication, in which gestures, facial expressions, and physical touch are used, as well as oral language.
Literacy skills	Responds to children's literature or other adult reading material with smiles, coos, or animated babbling by age 2. By this same age, shows an understanding of how books work (e.g., how pages turn).	An inability to attend or respond positively to shared reading experiences with an adult.	Read to babies regularly. Scaffold their use of books. Encourage them to turn pages and point to and name illustrations.

Interpreting Assessment Data: Variations in language and literacy are due to the specific languages spoken in the home and cultural differences in reading preferences. Children will babble different sounds and will utter one or two words less early in life if they are trying to learn two languages simultaneously. They may be more attentive to magazines or mail-order catalogs than to children's books if these are more common in their home. Significant delays in understanding and production of simple one- or two-word utterances, however, may indicate challenging conditions, such as hearing impairment or general language delay. Further evaluation and early language intervention may be needed.

CHAPTER 9

Infant Social and Emotional Development

1. What are trust and mistrust, and how do these form in infancy?
2. What are separation anxiety and stranger anxiety, and how do they vary across families and cultures?
3. What are the major types of secure and insecure attachment that can form in infancy, and how do these affect later development?
4. What are some causes of cultural variation in infant attachment?
5. How is infant attachment affected by special needs, family stress, early intervention, and child care?
6. What is autonomy, and how does it vary across cultures?
7. What are the major temperaments that have been identified in infancy, and how do these vary across cultures?
8. What are some key emotions that infants can express, and how do interactions with adults and cultural beliefs influence their acquisition?
9. How does egocentrism affect infant relationships?
10. What are the effects of special needs on infant attachment and social relationships?
11. What adaptations can be made for infants with special needs that promote healthy social and emotional development?

This chapter examines infants' social and emotional development. Infants form strong bonds with caregivers very early in life. They come to know, become attached to, and show a desire to be with a small and very select group of people in their lives. The wonderful emotional bonds formed with infants are among the greatest rewards of parenting or caregiving. But these strong bonds also pose challenges, as the following story reveals:

A mother and father are saying goodbye to their 18-month-old on her first day in child care. The mother squeezes the little girl tightly and for a long time; she seems reluctant to let go. Next, the father gives a hug. The toddler smiles and appears to be enjoying this affection. They stand together for many minutes, and the parents appear to grow increasingly anxious.

"We need to go now, sweetie," the father finally says. The toddler still smiles. "We'll be back, though, okay?" he reassures her as the two start to move toward the door. Their daughter toddles after them, giggling as if they are playing a game. "Bye-bye, Sarah," the mother says in a shaky voice. The toddler's smile quickly disappears. "Bye-bye?" This phrase holds a great deal of meaning.

"No!" the child screams, at last understanding what is happening. "No go, Mommy!" She is crying now. The mother and father cease their retreat. The mother approaches the upset child and gives her another hug. "We'll be back," she soothes. This has no effect. The child's screams intensify.

A caregiver moves in quickly, carrying a picture book. She hugs the little girl and tries to distract her. "Would you like to come over and read with me?" The toddler calms a bit, but as her parents move closer to the door, she begins to wail again. As the parents walk out, her upset is most intense. All day long at work, the parents are haunted by the sounds of their child's screams. They will replay this nightmarish experience in their heads for years to come.

The toddler, however, stops crying within a few minutes after their departure. She now sits in the caregiver's lap, happily turning the pages of a storybook.

This vignette shows the strength of early attachments. It also illustrates that bonds are bidirectional. Parents are as fearful about separating from their infants as their infants are about being separated from their parents.

Babies can form such close relationships with many different people—parents, grandparents, siblings, child care providers, and neighbors (Ahnert, Pinquart, & Lamb, 2006; Cugmas, 2007; Waters & Cummings, 2000). Whom babies become attached to is not as important as that they have at least one person in their lives whom they care about and who cares about them deeply. These relationships in infancy are crucial for later healthy development. Forming bonds with others in the early years has been found to protect children emotionally from the negative effects of poverty, domestic and community violence, parental substance abuse, and other stressors that threaten mental health (Hamilton, 2000; Weinfield, Whaley, & Egeland, 2004).

TRUST AND ATTACHMENT

The work of Erik Erikson (1963), which was discussed in Chapter 3, is very useful in examining infant social and emotional development. According to Erikson, a critical emotional struggle in infancy is between *trust* and *mistrust*. Emotionally healthy babies come to understand that they have nurturing, responsive caregivers who meet their basic needs. They come to view the world as safe and predictable. They enter into trusting relationships with caregivers and, later, with other human beings. *Security* is another word to describe this emotional state.

A degree of mistrust is also healthy and important for survival. For example, it causes an infant to be hesitant about crawling away from a parent to explore a dangerous set of cellar stairs. Humans will always experience some feelings of mistrust in which doubts about their relationships or the security of the world emerge. However, the emotionally healthy baby is, for the most part, trusting of the world and the people in it.

Babies who are abused or neglected, who do not have caregivers who respond to their needs, or who for other reasons have come to doubt the trustworthiness of the world will not resolve this emotional conflict in a positive way. They may be impaired from entering into relationships with others and may be wary of new situations or people. They may be unable to advance to later stages of psychosocial development, so they are more likely to suffer mental health problems later in life.

Attachment Formation

A critical part of achieving trust, from Erikson's view, is the ability of babies to come to know and bond with caregivers. Forming an emotional bond with others in infancy is called **attachment.** In his classic work on infants, John Bowlby (1969) described attachment as a bidirectional process in which babies and parents (or other caregivers) make contact with one another in ways that lead to emotional bonds. Babies perform social behaviors—smiling, making eye contact, and cooing—that capture adults' attention and elicit strong feelings of caring and concern. Caregivers respond to these behaviors with warmth and social contact. Thus, babies and significant adults become attached to one another.

A traditional view has been that infants form attachments only with their mothers. Extensive cross-cultural research has shown, however, that this is not the case. Babies most often form attachments to multiple caregivers. It is estimated that only 10% of infants are still attached to only one adult at 18 months of age (Lewis, Feiring, & Rosenthal, 2000). Babies form attachments to fathers that are as strong and secure as those formed with mothers (Grossmann et al., 2002; van Ijzendoorn & DeWolf, 1997). In most two-parent families, babies become attached to both father and mother at approximately the same time (Lamb, 2005). In cultures in which grandparents, aunts and uncles, or other relatives live in the home, attachment to nonparent caregivers is common. In these cases, babies form attachments to these adults at the same time that they bond with the mother. In many cultural groups, older siblings have caretaking responsibilities, so bonding with siblings is common (Dunn, 1992; Earl, 2006; Teti & Ablard, 1989).

Bowlby (1969) identified stages that infants go through in the formation of bonds with caregivers. In the early months, babies show great interest in all people. They smile and babble at others and grasp onto their fingers or hair. This is an important stage. Babies who do not show interest in those around them may be at risk for later emotional difficulties. Bowlby observed that babies between 4 and 6 months of age begin to prefer interacting with certain familiar people. They smile and coo more intensely at caregivers and show puzzlement or wariness around strangers. By 6 months of age, they show an intense desire to be with just these familiar caregivers and show concern when they are not present.

Separation Anxiety and Stranger Anxiety

Between 6 and 8 months of age, babies show **stranger anxiety,** a fear of unfamiliar persons that often results in great upset (Murray, Cooper, Creswell, Schofield, & Sack, 2007;

attachment: The bidirectional process by which infants and other people—particularly parents—form emotional bonds with one another.

stranger anxiety: A fear of strangers who are not primary caregivers that often appears between 6 and 8 months of age.

Infants and toddlers become attached to adults who are warm and responsive.

R. A. Thompson, 1997). The following story highlights the problems that occur during this period:

A woman from Puerto Rico is saddened when her son, his wife, and her beloved 4-month-old grandson leave the island to live in New York City. She has become very close to her grandchild. He always smiles so brightly when she enters the room, and he seems to enjoy being held and carried by her. When she hugs and kisses him good-bye at the airport, he responds by flashing a big smile and pulling her hair.

Two short months later, the family decides that the grandmother should come live with them on the mainland. She is thrilled, in part because she will be with her grandchild again. During the long flight, she thinks about nothing but him. She anticipates his smiling face at their reunion. On arriving, she excitedly rushes into the airport waiting area, where she spots her daughter-in-law cradling her cherished infant grandson. She scoops up the tiny baby in her arms, hugs him, and then holds him away from her so she can see his beautiful face. She is confronted with a look of terror. The baby bursts into trembling sobs, bends away from her, and reaches toward his mother. The grandmother is crushed. What could have occurred to sour their wonderful relationship after only 2 months?

After 6 months of age, babies begin to show **separation anxiety,** a fear of being separated from caregivers (Eisen & Schaefer, 2005; Vondra & Barnett, 1999). They show upset when their parents leave them. Sometimes only a brief departure to another room will trigger distress. Separation anxiety is very familiar to professionals who work with infants and their families. A parent educator may have trouble arranging a meeting of a parent support group because half the participants' babies show great upset at being left with a sitter. A child care provider may find the first days of a school year challenging if many new babies (and parents) are anxious about separating.

separation anxiety: A fear of being separated from primary caregivers or left alone that often appears between 6 and 8 months.

Stranger anxiety and separation anxiety vary from infant to infant and situation to situation. A baby who is with a parent or caregiver—preferably sitting securely on a familiar lap—is less likely to become upset over the appearance of strangers. In the previous story, the grandmother would have done well to allow her grandson's parents to hold him while they became reacquainted. Early experiences with being away from caregivers and meeting strangers will reduce both types of anxiety (R. A. Thompson & Limber, 1990).

Some babies are cared for by extended family members and neighbors from the time they are born. This type of collective child rearing is an adaptive strategy among parents of historically underrepresented groups (Paludi, 2002). Babies in such families tend to show less upset at the appearance of strangers and at the departure of parents.

Other cultural practices and beliefs influence stranger anxiety and separation anxiety. Babies in rural Uganda were found to display greater upset at separation from parents than those in the United States (Ainsworth, 1977). This difference was explained by variations in departure patterns of parents in these cultures. In rural Uganda, parents rarely leave their babies, but when they do, they are gone for long periods. For example, a mother might stay with her baby every waking moment until it is time to harvest garden vegetables. When this time comes, however, an extensive separation is necessary. African babies in this study had had little practice at separating. In addition, they had come to understand that a parent's departure meant a long separation, so their separation anxiety was great. Figure 9-1 shows similarities and differences in separation anxiety patterns across cultures.

Cultural beliefs about infant care may affect separation anxiety and stranger anxiety in infants. Fathers and mothers of some ethnic groups believe that babies should never be cared for by nonparent providers. When these parents are forced to separate from their children because of work obligations, they tend to suffer severe anxiety. They may have strong negative feelings about leaving their babies in child care (Klein & Chen, 2001; Peleg, Halaby, & Whaby, 2006). Some Korean American parents, for example, report a reluctance to have their children cared for in centers, by babysitters, or even by relatives (Seo, 2006).

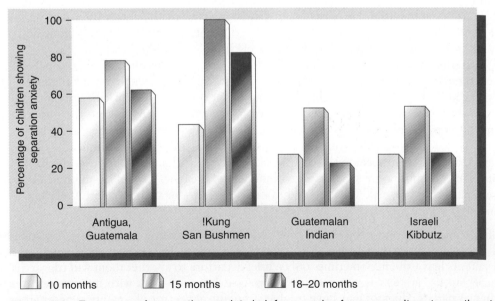

FIGURE 9-1 Frequency of separation anxiety in infancy varies from one culture to another. In all cultural groups, such anxiety becomes most intense in children at 13 to 15 months of age.

Data from Kagan, J., Kearsley, R. B., & Zelazo, P. R. (1978). *Infancy: Its Place in Human Development.* Cambridge, MA: Harvard University Press.

How do negative parental attitudes and feelings affect infant anxiety? Parents may inadvertently communicate their worries to children at the time of departure. Mothers or fathers leaving their children in infant care, for example, can express upset through language or facial expression. Such behaviors may increase infant distress (Hock, McBride, & Gnezda, 1989; Hsu, 2004).

Several well-known studies have addressed practical solutions to the problems of separation anxiety and stranger anxiety. Research by Weinraub and Lewis (1977) and Lollis (1990) found that 2-year-olds showed less upset at parents' departure in child care when the separation was explained to them clearly ahead of time. Separation was also found to be smoother if the departing parent suggested activities for the child to engage in during separation. An important practical finding of these studies was that toddlers cried more on separation if the parent sat and actually played with them for a time before leaving them. The most effective strategy for parents, then, may be to point out play activities to their children but not to play along with them.

Types of Attachment

Mary Ainsworth, Everett Waters, and other colleagues have engaged in extensive research to refine understandings of infant attachment (Waters & Cummings, 2000). They devised a research method for examining the quality of attachment called the **strange situation procedure.** In this procedure, babies are placed in a playroom. First, the baby plays with toys in the presence of the mother. Next, the mother leaves, and an unfamiliar person enters. The mother returns briefly, then leaves again, and the baby plays alone. Many babies in this situation cry when their mothers depart, but this reaction is not the important point of the procedure. What is significant, according to these attachment researchers, is what babies do when the mother returns. Some babies greet their mothers joyously; others do not. It is the nature of the reunion, from this perspective, that reveals the quality of the mother–child bond.

Using this technique, researchers have discovered that several types of attachment exist. These are summarized in Table 9-1. Babies can be categorized as having a **secure attachment** or insecure attachment. Roughly 70% of babies in the United States form secure attachments (Bakermans-Kranenburg & van Ijzendoorn, 2006). A baby who is securely attached will play happily with toys during the mother's presence in a strange situation. On her departure, the baby may cry, but the reunion will be a happy one. The baby may hug or cling to the mother for a time but will quickly stop crying.

strange situation procedure: A research method used to assess the quality of attachment of babies to their caregivers. The procedure involves observing the responses of a child to a number of conditions, including the departure of a parent and the arrival of a stranger.

secure attachment: A category of attachment in which an infant has securely bonded with a parent or significant other. In the strange situation procedure, infants who are securely attached will show some distress on separation from caregivers but quickly re-establish warm interactions when reunited.

TABLE 9-1
Types of Attachment

Attachment Type	Description
Secure	Plays happily within a strange play setting if a parent is present. May cry when the parent leaves the room but will greet the parent joyously at their reunion.
Insecure/avoidant	May or may not cry at a parent's departure from a strange play area. Ignores and even moves away from the parent when he or she returns.
Insecure/ambivalent	May show great upset when a parent leaves a strange play area. Continues to be inconsolable when the parent returns. Will alternate between desperate clinging and angry rejection during the reunion.

Babies who are insecurely attached behave differently in a strange situation. Ainsworth, Blehar, Waters, & Wall (1978) identified two distinct behavioral patterns among insecure babies. Babies who have an **insecure/avoidant attachment** may or may not show upset when their mothers leave. However, they will completely ignore them when they return. Such a baby may actively move away from the mother or ignore her efforts to make contact when she comes back into the play area.

Babies who have **insecure/ambivalent attachment** alternate between extreme upset and angry rejection when the mother returns to the playroom. Such a baby may first cling to the mother during their reunion and then push her away. Insecure/ambivalent babies are often inconsolable on the parent's return. A third, less common type of insecure attachment is now being studied: **disorganized attachment** (Bakermans-Kranenburg & van Ijzendoorn, 2006; Vondra & Barnett, 1999). Babies of this type show confusion when their mothers return to the play area. They may, at first, behave as an ambivalent child might—clinging, then pushing away. Abruptly, they might show signs of avoidant attachment, actually ignoring their mothers. Sometimes they "fall into a depressed huddle or jerk back with a fearful expression" (Vondra & Barnett, 1999, p. 33) as if so disoriented by the situation that they are unable to act at all.

Once babies can be identified as securely or insecurely attached, do they remain that way throughout life? Research suggests that these attachment patterns can be quite stable through adulthood (Fraley, 2003; Waters & Cummings, 2000). Many babies who are insecurely attached become insecure adults. Most babies who are securely attached may stay that way through adolescence even if they suffer negative life events (Hamilton, 2000). However, there are individuals who become more securely attached to parents or other caregivers as their lives change. If a family service provider works with parents on becoming more responsive and nurturing, their children may become more securely attached. If a family is able to move out of poverty, parents may become more attentive, also enhancing secure attachment. Some young children become attached to preschool teachers and caregivers. So, attachment classification is relatively fixed over the course of life but is "open to revision" (Waters & Cummings, 2000, p. 684).

Attachment, as determined by the strange situation paradigm, appears to affect development in later childhood and adolescence. Infants who are securely attached tend to be more friendly and competent and to have more positive views of themselves in later childhood (Allen et al., 2007). In contrast, babies who are insecure/avoidant tend to become more aggressive, more impulsive, and less cooperative (Calkins, 2004). Babies who are categorized as disorganized in their attachment are also more likely to be aggressive and hostile in later years. As high as 40% of babies in this classification have been found to have neurological impairments (Vondra & Barnett, 1999).

Babies who are insecure/ambivalent tend to become timid, dependent, and whiny in later childhood (Shulman, Elicker, & Sroufe, 1994). They are also more inhibited in their exploration and play with peers (Bohlin, Hagekull, & Andersson, 2005). In the elementary years and in adolescence, they are more likely to be identified as having social and emotional problems (M. Lewis et al., 2000).

Cultural Variations in Infant Attachment

Babies of many cultural groups around the world fall into secure or insecure categories of attachment at approximately the same rates as American infants: 70% are securely attached, 20% to 25% are insecure/avoidant, and 5% to 10% are insecure/ambivalent (Bakermans-Kranenburg & van Ijzendoorn, 2006). Several studies raise questions, however, about whether babies' behavior in Ainsworth's strange situation paradigm is a universal indicator of attachment. In studies of Japanese babies, more than 40% showed insecure/ambivalent

insecure/avoidant attachment: A category of attachment in which an infant has not securely bonded with a parent or significant other. In the strange situation procedure, babies who have an insecure/avoidant attachment may or may not show upset when their mothers leave but will completely ignore them when they return.

insecure/ambivalent attachment: A category of attachment in which an infant has not securely bonded with a parent or significant other. In the strange situation procedure, babies who have an insecure/ambivalent attachment will alternate between desperate clinging and angry rejection when reunited with a parent.

disorganized attachment: A category of attachment in which an infant has not securely bonded with a parent or significant other. In the strange situation procedure, babies who have disorganized attachment appear disoriented on their reunion with caregivers and may cling to, push away from, or even ignore them.

attachment, compared with 5% to 10% in other cultural groups (Rothbaum, Weisz, Pott, Miyake, & Morelli, 2000; S. Chen, 1996; Takhashi, 1990). The Japanese babies in these studies were so upset at the mother's departure that they could not be consoled during the reunion phase of the procedure. Similar findings were obtained in a study of Chinese American infants in a child care setting (Kagan, Kearsley, & Zelazo, 1978). When placed in several strange situations, Chinese babies showed less secure attachment, staying closer to their mothers and playing less. Studies of infants in northern Germany indicate a higher rate of insecure relationships, particularly insecure/avoidant attachments (K. Grossman, K. E. Grossmann, Spangler, Seuss, & Unzner, 1985; Rothbaum, Weisz, Pott, Miyake, & Morelli, 2001). In the United States, African American babies have been found to be less securely attached than their Euro-American peers (Bakermans-Kranenburg & van Ijzendoorn, 2006). Is it plausible that so many babies in these cultural groups are at risk of poor attachment to parents?

Several explanations have been offered for these cultural differences. Japanese American and Chinese American babies spend far less time away from their mothers than do babies of other cultures. Their upset at separation from their parents may be so severe that reunion behaviors are negatively affected (S. Chen, 1996; Rothbaum et al., 2000; Tan, 2004). Some attachment researchers now believe that, for some cultures, this research method is simply not valid (Waters & Cummings, 2000). In fact, nonstop crying for long periods after separation may be an expected and culturally correct response for babies in societies where infant–mother bonds are sacred. Anything but great anxiety on the part of the baby—or the mother—during and after time apart could be interpreted as a sign of a less strong relationship.

The high rates of insecure/avoidant attachment in German communities could be the result of cultural values and socialization practices as well (Grossman et al., 1985). Northern German mothers are found to engage in independence training in which children are encouraged to separate from their families at a young age. Closeness and dependence are discouraged. It is understandable, then, that babies of these cultural groups would be more likely to ignore mothers on reunion in the strange situation procedure.

Caution must be used, then, in relying on separation and reunion behaviors to measure attachment. More culturally sensitive methods of observing infant–caregiver bonds may be needed (Rothbaum & Morelli, 2005; Waters & Cummings, 2000).

Parenting Behaviors, Attachment, and Culture

Parenting behaviors influence attachment formation. The two examples that follow show contrasting styles in parent interactions. Which style is more likely to support strong emotional bonds?

EXAMPLE 1

As a woman in a small village in India works in the garden outside her home, her 4-month-old granddaughter sleeps in a basket nearby. The baby awakes and begins to cry. The grandmother scoops the baby up, hugs and comforts her, and then straps the baby to a sling across her abdomen. She then returns to her gardening, stooping over the vegetables and pulling weeds in a rhythmic motion. The baby falls asleep, cradled securely against her grandmother, gently rocking with her movements.

EXAMPLE 2

A mother in a city in Kenya has just acquired a crib for her 5-month-old son. Enthused about what she perceives to be a modern European child care method, she places her sleeping baby in the crib in his room and leaves to run errands. After a time, the infant awakes and cries in hunger and anxiety. No one is in the home to comfort him. Even when the mother returns home, she does not respond to her baby's cries. She wishes to train her baby to stay in the crib while she does her work.

Two dimensions of parenting, illustrated in the first example, have been found to lead to secure attachment in babies: responsiveness and warm physical contact (De Wolf & Ijzendoorn, 1997; Posada et al., 1999; Raval et al., 2001). Responsiveness involves carefully interpreting babies' signals—the cries, whimpers, eye contact, noises, or other behaviors that express their needs—and responding in appropriate ways. Quickly picking up and rocking a baby who is crying for contact is an example of responsiveness. Reacting slowly and then giving a baby a bottle when that is not what is desired would be a less responsive interaction. The grandmother in Example 1 is a responsive caregiver. She accurately reads her granddaughter's crying as a desire to be held, and then she reacts quickly.

Warm, physical contact is a separate dimension of parenting. Nurturing parents spend lots of time in physical contact with their babies, holding them, bouncing them, playing with them, or simply gazing into their eyes. The grandmother in example 1 manages to provide warm, physical contact while continuing with her work. When she straps her granddaughter close to her body, the baby immediately falls back to sleep.

Do warmth and responsiveness lead to attachment in all cultures? Some cross-cultural research suggests that these basic attachment processes are universal. However, variations exist in the exact ways that parents respond or provide nurturance. In Ainsworth's (1977) classic study in Uganda, nursing a baby during upset was found to be an important behavior for promoting attachment. African mothers who nursed in response to infant crying were more likely to have securely attached babies. In the United States, however, where nursing was less common at the time, it was less important to the attachment process. In fact, babies in U.S. homes frequently became attached to parents or other adults who were not responsible for feeding them. Other methods of warm contact, such as snuggling or rocking, were discovered to be more likely to promote bonds.

Ainsworth concluded that responsiveness and warmth are important caregiving behaviors in all cultures, but how these are expressed varies greatly. Each family, she argues, has a unique **cluster of attachment behaviors** that are necessary for strong emotional bonds. The behaviors of one culture may be irrelevant in another, so there may be no one best way to create positive relationships with babies.

Looking through the lens of one's own cultural values and customs, it is easy to form an opinion that the attachment practices of another culture are deficient. Levine (1996) provides an example of this in his observations of impoverished families in Africa. Babies in the communities he visited were held and fed with very little affection. He notes that most Westerners would consider this a negative pattern of interaction. After all, in European and Euro-American families, warmth and responsiveness include smiling, stroking, and hugging. The absence of these nurturing behaviors might be construed as a sign of poor relationships. A careful and unbiased look at these interactions suggests just the opposite, however. Levine describes how babies' cries for food or contact received immediate response in these communities. Children rarely had to wait to have their needs met. They became attached to adults as securely as in any other community. The lack of affect in parenting is part of the tradition in this cultural group, Levine explains. It represents a kind of emotional distancing from children that is common in communities where infant mortality rates are very high.

Professionals working with infants and families must remember that the attachment behaviors valued in their own cultures may be different from those of families they work with. Great care must be taken not to misinterpret cultural expressions of warmth or responsiveness. A parent may respond to a baby's signals with rough-and-tumble play or humor.

cluster of attachment behaviors: The unique set of parenting behaviors of a particular family or culture that lead to the secure attachment of infants.

Warm contact may include being carried in a backpack or being bounced on a knee. Some attachment behaviors may be delivered without a great deal of affection or enthusiasm, but they are effective parenting interactions nonetheless.

Attachment and Infants with Special Needs

A common assumption is that infants with special needs will have difficulty forming secure bonds with their caregivers. The following story illustrates this belief:

> A single mother has been attending a support class for parents of infants with Down syndrome. The focus of this class is on initiating play and responding to infant cries. She grows more and more irritated as she listens to her instructor talk about risk factors and concerns about attachment. "You'll need to make a special effort to form an attachment with your baby," he tells the class. "Children with Down syndrome may not become attached to you easily. And some of you may have trouble forming bonds to your baby. Has anyone felt that this has been a problem?"
>
> The mother can stay quiet no longer. "No. I never feel that way. Are you saying we won't love our babies as much? That they won't love us? I can't believe that. I'm offended, in fact."
>
> The instructor is startled, but he tries to maintain composure. "I'm not saying you won't love your baby. I'm saying that sometimes parents and children have a harder time connecting with one another, so it makes sense to try extra hard to create bonds. That's the nature of this condition."
>
> The mother is not satisfied. "I don't buy it. Not at all. I know my baby, and he knows me. Down syndrome or no, he and I already have this attachment you're so worried about. Quite honestly, I think you underestimate the love we have inside of us."
>
> The instructor nods humbly and moves on to another topic. At the end of the session, he thinks about the experience. Perhaps he has underestimated what parents know and feel about their own babies. He pledges that in the future he will not jump to conclusions so quickly about parents' relationships with their children.

It is not surprising that this parent educator worries that infants with challenging conditions will not become securely attached to caregivers. Infants with various cognitive and social disorders can create stress for parents. Parents' responsiveness or warmth might be negatively affected. Infants with certain challenges might have poor relationships with parents because they have impaired communication systems. Babies with hearing impairments, for example, might have poor verbal interactions with parents, and this could disrupt attachment.

For the most part, however, research suggests that strong parent–infant bonds form in the most trying of circumstances. Children with profound disabilities will still become attached to caregivers. In a study of 53 infants with Down syndrome, for example, only 13% showed clear signs of insecure attachment (Vondra & Barnett, 1999). This is a lower rate than might be found in a sample of typically developing babies. Infants with hearing impairments have been found to form secure attachments to parents in exactly the same way that babies with normal hearing do (Lederberg & Mobley, 1990). It appears that verbal communication is not absolutely necessary for positive relationships with caregivers. Physical touch, facial expressions, and motor play interactions may serve just as well. The only developmental disability that reliably predicts insecure attachment is autism and, even then, only if the condition is severe (Naber et al., 2007).

Very similar findings are reported in studies of low-birth-weight babies and of babies who experienced complications during birth (M. A. Easterbrooks, 1989; Pederson & Moran, 1995). In spite of the stresses and challenges associated with these conditions, both mothers and fathers were found to form healthy, positive attachments to their babies and vice versa.

There are several conditions that are more likely to threaten attachment formation. Some researchers report an interruption of attachment behaviors in interactions between parents and infants with facial deformities (Weiss, Wilson, Hertenstein, & Campos, 2000; Langlois, Ritter, Casey, & Sawin, 1995). Although parents of babies with cleft palates or more severely disfiguring syndromes report that their interactions are positive, they tend to hold their babies less often, interact with them less frequently, and provide less warmth. Such interactions could affect attachment. The results of several studies, however, challenge this assertion (Murray et al., 2008; Speltz, Endriga, Fisher, & Mason, 1997). A majority of babies with cleft lips or palates, in these investigations, were found to be securely attached.

Cross-cultural studies have shown that severe infant malnutrition negatively affects attachment (Valenzuela, 1990; Walker et al., 2007). Malnourished babies may be more irritable and may recover less quickly from upset than well-nourished children. It could also be that their parents have emotional difficulties that affect their parenting.

In studies of responses to atypical crying, parents and nonparent adults were found to rate cries of brain-damaged infants as sounding less pleasant and in some cases ignored them (Frodi & Senchak, 1990; Zeifman, 2004). If these findings can be generalized to other types of impairments, the atypical crying of infants with special needs might fail to elicit the warm parental responses that Ainsworth believes are so important.

In a major summary of many different studies of attachment and infant problems, van Ijzendoorn, Goldberg, Kroonenberg, and Frenkel (1992) conclude that most children with challenging conditions—from Down syndrome to low birth weight—form secure attachments at the same rate as typically developing infants. However, these authors did find significant attachment problems when the parents themselves faced challenging conditions. Problems such as substance abuse or psychiatric disorder among caregivers are linked to insecure attachment among all babies, not just those with special needs. So, the mental health and coping abilities of *adults* may be far more critical in the process of attachment than the childhood disorders themselves.

Attachment and Family Stress

What adult problems contribute most to poor attachment? Parental depression is a major risk factor (Mcquaid, Bigelow, McLaughlin, & MacLean, 2008; Wiedman & Garfield, 2007). A depressed parent may find it difficult to respond quickly and with warmth to infant initiatives. Highly depressed or anxious mothers with typically developing babies have been found more likely to experience attachment difficulties than emotionally healthy mothers of infants with special needs (Lyons-Ruth, Connell, Grunebaum, & Botein, 2006).

Another threat to secure attachment is poverty (Raikes & Thompson, 2005). In fact, babies who become securely attached in early infancy may become less securely attached in later years if their families fall on hard times. The experience of poverty has been found to cause infant illness and fatigue. It may result in disruptive family events, such as repeated moves to new housing or sudden changes in caregiving arrangements. Poverty increases parent stress, which can lead to depression, anger, and a lack of sensitivity to babies' needs. All these features of poverty can disrupt a strong infant–parent bond.

Attachment Interventions

Social and mental health services can significantly improve these parent–child relationships. Lyons-Ruth and colleagues (1990) provided emotional support to depressed mothers through a professional home visitor and direct training in child care techniques. They were also invited to a weekly parent support group. These investigators found that infants of participating mothers were more securely attached and performed higher on measures of cognitive development. In two other studies, low-income mothers were taught to read the signals of their babies and to respond to these in positive ways (van den Boom, 1995; Wendland-Carro, Piccinini, & Millar, 1999). Following both interventions, mothers were found to respond more quickly and warmly to their infants—that is, to perform more often those critical attachment behaviors that Bowlby (1969) described.

A problem with the idea of attachment interventions is that different cultures have different ways of interacting and bonding with infants. A responding behavior in one culture may not be effective in another. In such cases, efforts to teach specific parenting behaviors may be fruitless. These concerns have been borne out in research. In a program designed to teach attachment-related interactions to high-risk mothers, a curriculum of games and activities was implemented during home visits and classes at a child development center (Spiker, Ferguson, & Brooks-Gunn, 1993). The effects of the intervention were minimal though positive. However, white parents showed more positive outcomes than African American parents. It was concluded that the procedures and parenting techniques being taught were geared primarily to the dominant Euro-American culture.

In contrast, a number of very effective attachment interventions are more culture neutral. One unique intervention involved simply giving U.S. mothers front carriers that resembled the homemade slings used in African villages. When mothers used these, they were in close, continual physical contact with their babies (Anisfeld, Casper, Nozyce, & Cunningham, 1990). Parents were not taught to interact with their children in any special way; they simply were given the carriers when their babies were 3 months old. At 13 months, babies of all cultural groups—white, African American, and Latino—were more securely attached to their mothers than those whose mothers did not receive the carriers. An important finding was that precise parenting interactions did not seem to make a difference. Breastfeeding, for example, did not lead to more positive attachment. Close body contact led to positive findings regardless of how mothers interacted with their babies as they carried them. Similar findings are reported by Gribble (2007) who notes more positive developmental outcomes for at-risk children of diverse backgrounds whose parents were given close-to-the-body slings to carry them.

In another culture-neutral intervention (Lieberman, Weston, & Pawl, 1991), Mexican American and Central American mothers with insecurely attached babies were provided informal, open-ended support sessions designed to "respond to the affective experiences of mother and child" (p. 202). No direct teaching was involved, although professionals made suggestions or provided developmental information when it was helpful. At the end of the program, babies were more securely attached, and mothers displayed more frequent interactions and greater empathy.

Taken together, these studies highlight the importance of culturally sensitive intervention. Parent education or support efforts will be ineffective if parents are advised to perform behaviors that are inconsistent with the values or socialization practices of their cultural group.

Infant Care and Attachment

In the United States, as a growing percentage of mothers enter the workforce, more and more infants are being cared for outside the home. Concerns are being raised about the effects of infant care on the attachment process. Will babies who spend long hours in child care become insecurely attached? How can parents be responsive and warm, provide regular physical contact, and in other ways foster strong emotional bonds when they are away from their babies all day? Some research has assuaged parents' fears. In a review of many studies on infant care, Phillips, McCartney, Scarr, and Howes (2000a) conclude that babies in child care centers were found to be as securely attached as those who were cared for by parents at home.

Other research, however, has rekindled fears about infant care. A team of researchers with the National Institute for Child Health and Human Development (NICHD), who are conducting a large longitudinal study on child development, report that children who have attended child care beginning in infancy are more likely to be insecurely attached and to exhibit problem behaviors, assertiveness, and aggression later in school (National Institute of Child Health and Human Development Early Child Care Research Network, 2008). (This and other studies also indicate that these same children may enjoy cognitive and school achievement benefits in later life [Vandell, 2007]).

Caution must be used in interpreting any of these findings. Research on infant care, as with all studies on human beings, has flaws. For example, Thompson (1988) argues that the strange situation method for studying insecure attachment—which many of these studies used—is not always a good measure of how well babies have bonded to their parents. In a society in which infants now separate and reunite on a daily basis, he argues, reactions to the strange situation procedure may mean something very different than when Ainsworth was first conducting her studies. The following vignette illustrates this possibility. Is the baby in this story insecure/avoidant in his attachment to his mother, or is some new process at work that reflects modern life in child care?

> When a mother says goodbye to her toddler in a child care center, he becomes more upset than usual. He did not sleep well the night before, and she had to get him up early because she has a morning meeting. He was cranky in the car all the way to the center, and when she leaves him, he cries and becomes angry. She feels extremely guilty at work for many hours afterward.
>
> During her lunch hour, she decides to visit the center to see how her son is getting along. Perhaps a little bonding time might make him feel more loved and make her feel less guilty. When she enters the center, her son is absorbed in play at the water table. He and another child are laughing and splashing. When her son sees her, his smile disappears. "No! No!" he calls out, assuming that she is picking him up for the day. He completely rebuffs her overtures. She backs away and watches.
>
> Her son's caregiver offers comforting words. "He's having a lot of fun there. I don't think he wants to go home just yet." She returns to work relieved that her son is in good hands and enjoying the day.

Most caregivers and parents who have babies in child care centers have observed similar interactions. In the early morning, children might prefer to stay at home, but by the end of the day they don't want to leave the center. The behaviors of the child in the story are apt to give the misimpression that he is insecurely attached. However, the true feelings underlying these interactions indicate otherwise. The child's behaviors may simply show that he has adapted to a life filled with separations and reunions, alternate caregivers and new situations, and early mornings and late nights. A new way of observing attachment may be needed, one that is sensitive to the modern, complex lives of working parents and their children.

Most researchers studying the effects of child care are no longer comparing children in care versus those at home. Why? As one child specialist states, "You'd have a hard time even finding a sample of children who are *not* cared for outside the home!" Working parents and child care are aspects of modern life that are here to stay in the United States. The question now being asked is this: What are the effects of high- versus low-quality child care on babies? Studies are beginning to show that babies in high-quality infant care are generally securely attached to parents and their child care providers (Fuller, Holloway, & Liang, 1996; Love et al., 2003; NICHD Early Child Care Research Network, 2005). Those in poor-quality programs—of which, sadly, there are many—may be at risk. One way professionals can support healthy attachment is by helping parents select high-quality caregiving arrangements for their babies. In addition, they can advocate for an increase in federal funds to support high-quality infant care throughout the country. (See the Advocacy and Public Policy box in this chapter.)

ADVOCACY AND PUBLIC POLICY

Increasing Funding for High-Quality Infant Care

This chapter presents research on the effects of infant care on attachment and overall emotional development. Findings suggest that care outside the home prior to age 1 does not disrupt the attachment process or lead to negative social outcomes as long as that care is of high quality. What constitutes high-quality infant care? First, caregivers of high-quality programs are responsive, warm, and knowledgeable about child development; they have completed extensive training or college course work in early childhood education (Whitebrook, Phillips, & Howes, 1993). High-quality infant care programs also have an optimal adult-to-child ratio, adequate play space and materials, and a small group size. Sadly, many infant care programs in the country have been rated quite poorly in these areas (Cost, Quality, and Child Outcomes Study Team, 1995).

Professionals can promote high-quality infant care in a variety of ways. Those who work directly with babies can provide nurturing and responsive care and create play environments that are spacious, well equipped, and safe. They can advocate for a high adult-to-child ratio and small group sizes in the programs where they work. They can pursue training and educational opportunities to enhance their own professional development.

High-quality infant care is expensive. Professionals must also advocate for increased federal and state funding to ensure that all babies are cared for in high-quality centers and homes. They can lobby their state legislatures to increase local funding for child care. They can contact their U.S. senators and representatives to urge greater allocations for the Child Care and Development Block Grant—a federal program that provides for child care subsidies for families living in poverty. They can also ask Congress to increase amounts in their education, labor, health, and human services appropriations for professional development for child care providers and for improvements in infant care quality—two areas where funding has been frozen at the same level for a number of years.

What is the best approach for contacting legislators? The National Association for the Education of Young Children provides an "action center" on its Website (http://www.naeyc.org) that makes the advocacy process easy. The center includes mailing and e-mail addresses of legislators in all states, sample letters that advocate for specific legislation (including increased funds for child care), and state-by-state and federal updates on the status of key pieces of legislation. Periodically checking the Website and writing letters to policymakers will help promote high-quality infant care and, in turn, the positive social and emotional growth of American babies.

AUTONOMY

Marked changes in social behavior occur during the second year of life. Consider the following examples:

- A baby who has enjoyed playing quietly outside her urban apartment building suddenly shows great interest in a busy parking lot nearby. The more her mother scolds her for going close to this dangerous area, the more interested she seems. Before long, on every trip outdoors, she makes at least one run for the parking lot.
- A baby of pleasant temperament suddenly begins to say "no" to almost anything. He screams "no" when it is bedtime, dinnertime, or even time to go out to play. At one point his mother offers ice cream. "No!" he shouts as he simultaneously reaches for the bowl and spoons ice cream into his mouth.
- A father always dresses his daughter for child care. One morning, the toddler insists on dressing herself. She struggles with the task, trying to put her shoes on before she has put on her pants. "No! I do it," she protests when her father tries to help. Because of this, the father is more than an hour late for work.

What has occurred to bring about such changes? When toddlers become more intellectually competent, they tend to be more curious and eager to explore—even dangerous parking lots. When they discover that "no" is a powerful social word that has great impact on family members, they want to use it. When they acquire new motor abilities, they want to exercise them.

Significant social and emotional changes lead babies to behave in new and challenging ways in the second year of life. Erikson's work, described in Chapter 3, is helpful in understanding these changes. Erikson argues that once children are trustful of adults and know that their basic needs will be met, they are willing to venture away from the safety of parents and family. Often they use their parents as a "secure base" from which to explore (Waters & Cummings, 2000). Like a mountain climber who can revisit his base camp in bad weather, toddlers will venture out from their parents but return quickly if they need reassurance. One day, my 15-month-old son raced away from me at an airport but got only several feet away from me before he ran into a strange man who did not look particularly friendly. Panic spread across his face, and he toddled quickly back to me. After a few reassuring minutes on my lap, he was off again!

Toddlers now wish to become individuals apart from the adults with whom they have bonded. With this striving for individuality, they often assert themselves, rebel against rules, and assume a negative affect when confronted with adult control. According to Erikson (1963, 1982), these challenging though necessary behaviors are explained by the next emotional conflict humans encounter: *autonomy* versus *shame and doubt*.

The emotionally healthy toddler, according to Erikson, gradually acquires a sense of *autonomy*—a feeling of individuality and uniqueness apart from parents. Children who are overly restricted in their attempts to become individuals (e.g., incessant hand slapping when they try to explore forbidden objects around the home) will come to doubt their individuality. They will eventually suffer shame for their efforts. Such children can become timid and lack confidence in their abilities. They may assume identities as mere extensions of their parents.

How do children become autonomous? Erikson has proposed that creating environments in which children can become independent in thought and action will contribute to a sense of autonomy. Parents should encourage children to assert themselves. They should hold back from harshly reprimanding their children's initiatives, according to Erikson.

In some families, toddlers are discouraged from separating from their parents; instead, dependence and "enmeshment" are encouraged.

Cultural Variations in Autonomy

During a recent meeting of a parent support group, a mother spoke at length about the frustrations of living with a toddler. She described negative and defiant behaviors that she attributed to "the terrible twos." Another mother remarked that she had experienced none of these challenging interactions. Her son was pleasant, quiet, and compliant; there were no strains whatsoever on family relationships. Yet another mother commented that her son had shown early defiant behaviors but that she had acted swiftly to counteract them. Through firm discipline, she explained, she had kept her toddler from developing negative attitudes and conduct. From discussions such as these, it is easy to see why autonomy is expressed differently by different toddlers.

Cultural beliefs, methods of discipline, or infant personality may explain why each family faces unique experiences in toddlerhood. Behaviors during this period are so diverse across cultures and sexes, in fact, that some have concluded that Erikson's descriptions of autonomy are inaccurate (Edwards, Knoche, Aukrust, Kumru, & Kim, 2006; Gilligan, 1993a; Klein & Chen, 2001).

In many cultures, toddlers are discouraged from separating from parents. In these families, children are carried and breastfed and sleep with adults throughout infancy and even into older childhood (Garcia Coll et al., 1995; Harkness & Super, 1996). Toddlers of these cultural groups may not display the extreme separation behaviors that Erikson described (Edwards et al., 2006; Tobin, Wu, & Davidson, 1989). In other cultures, self-sufficiency is encouraged very early in life (Hale, 1994). Children of these groups may demonstrate expressions of independence that are stronger than even Erikson would have predicted (Keller, Demuth, & Yovsi, 2008; Slonim, 1991).

Other cultural beliefs and practices may affect the degree to which children seek autonomy. Native American parents have been found to emphasize restraint and control in toddlerhood, not independence and self-expression. From birth, bonds with family are emphasized, and individualism is scorned (Garcia Coll et al., 1995; Kawamoto & Cheshire, 1997). Likewise, in many Japanese American and Chinese American families, dependence is prolonged; children never completely separate from families and parents (Chan, 1998; Ishii-Kuntz, 1997a; Rothbaum et al., 2000). In one interesting study (Wang, Wiley, & Zhou, 2008), Chinese American families were found to offer praise at dinnertime only for child behaviors that reflected "interdependence"—that is, asking for help, relying on family members in feeding, or listening to others. In contrast, Euro-American parents primarily praised behaviors that showed independence, such as eating on one's own.

Puerto Rican mothers have been found to value physical closeness, respect for and obedience to adults, tranquil behavior, and good manners in toddlerhood (Dixon, Graber, & Brooks-Gunn, 2008; Harwood, Miller, & Irizarry, 1995). Although many mothers of this group report a need to instill some degree of autonomy to ensure survival, they do so reluctantly. One Puerto Rican mother justifies giving some amount of independence in this way: "Maybe the moment will come when they won't need me because I will be too old, and then I will be sure that they are going to be able to face their problems" (Harwood et al., 1995, p. 115). It is clear that this parent is concerned with autonomy only because a separation might be necessary someday, not because it is a positive step toward emotional well-being, as Erikson proposed.

Gender may influence whether toddlers are encouraged to be autonomous. Some have speculated that, in Western society, independence is a characteristic of males, not females (Gilligan, 1993a). One study found that Latino and African American parents often place greater demands for obedience and respect for authority on girls (Dixon et al., 2008). In contrast, Whiting and Edwards (1988) report that in a number of non-Western cultures, independence increases with age only in girls. It is likely that boys and girls of all cultures eventually come to recognize themselves as unique individuals. However, it cannot be assumed that all toddlers will assert their individuality in flamboyant ways, strike out on their own, or shun their parents in the process. So, professionals should not attempt (or urge parents to attempt) to shape all children to conform to Erikson's ideal.

TEMPERAMENT

Parents often report that infants exhibit unique personality types, even in the earliest days of life. A mother might exclaim, "He just smiles and coos all the time. He's just a good baby. He always has been!" A father might say, "She's so different from my first child. Right from the day she was born, I could tell she'd be a feisty one." Sometimes these unique personality types are surprising and puzzling to parents, as the following story reveals:

> A child psychologist has been working with babies and their families for many years. He has also studied child development extensively through formal course work and independent reading. He believes he is well prepared to meet the emotional needs of his own daughter when she is born.
>
> Knowing the research by Mary Ainsworth, he and his wife try hard to be responsive to their daughter's crying. Even when she cries in the middle of the night, they take turns getting up to comfort and feed her. Though they find this to be exhausting, they believe it's what their daughter needs for healthy emotional growth. This is what the research suggests. They keep waiting for the payoff that Ainsworth describes in her work: that babies whose parents are responsive will cry less in later infancy.
>
> But this predicted reduction in crying never occurs. His daughter shows negative reactions to her world as intensely at age 2 as she did at birth. "Oh well," the father finally concludes, after 2 years of life with this sensitive and strong-willed little child. "I guess this is simply the way she is."

A scientific term for "the way she is" is **temperament**—a basic disposition that can be observed throughout a person's development. Babies are often born with temperaments that can influence their social relationships and emotional health for years to come. A number of these temperament types have been identified by infant researchers. They are summarized in Table 9-2.

Alexander Thomas and Stella Chess (1977) were among the first to conduct studies of infant temperament. In a famous longitudinal investigation, they found that babies could be categorized into three personality types that could be identified at birth: easy, difficult, and slow to warm up. Babies with an **easy temperament** have sunny dispositions, are friendly around strangers, and are easily consoled. Parents of newborns with easy dispositions tend to believe parenting is "a piece of cake," "a breeze." They may not understand why other parents suffer such stress raising their newborns.

Babies in the **difficult temperament** category cry easily, show less positive affect, and react negatively to new circumstances and unfamiliar people. They may show powerful outbursts of upset, which can include inconsolable crying, spitting food, and pulling hair. Parents of difficult babies often ask themselves, "What am I doing wrong?" The caregiver in the story, for example, has learned that no amount of good parenting will change some aspects of a baby's fundamental disposition. Babies with a **slow-to-warm-up temperament** are very wary of strangers and reluctant to separate from parents. They may show less overt emotion, positive or negative.

Among the babies that Thomas and Chess studied, 35% could not be classified. Some babies, then, will have clearly identifiable and persistent personality traits, and others will not.

temperament: A basic disposition that can be observed throughout a person's development. Babies are born with temperaments that can influence their social relationships and emotional health.

easy temperament: A disposition in which infants have sunny dispositions, are friendly around strangers, and are easily consoled.

difficult temperament: A disposition in which an infant cries easily, shows less positive affect, and reacts negatively to new circumstances and unfamiliar people.

slow-to-warm-up temperament: A disposition in which an infant is wary of strangers, is reluctant to separate from parents, and shows less overt emotion, positive or negative.

Temperament	Characteristics
Active	Shows a need for constant motion. Wiggles and bangs objects. Constantly seeks interaction and stimulation.
Bold	Takes initiative in interactions with parents and, later, peers. Is relatively fearless in exploration and play.
Difficult	Erupts in powerful outbursts of upset. Shows negative reactions to new situations or people. Cries often and is not easily consoled.
Easy	Shows a sunny disposition and frequent smiling. Adjusts smoothly and happily to new situations or caregivers.
Fearful	Becomes more easily afraid of new or puzzling situations. Will show greater wariness or upset when confronted with the "visual cliff" experiment, for example.
Shy	Shows a reticence to interact with others. Is quieter and less vocal around strangers.
Slow-to-warm-up	Exhibits wariness of new situations or people. Is less positive in affect and more likely to cling to caregivers.
Timid	Takes less initiative. Is wary of strangers. Shows caution in exploration and play.

TABLE 9-2
Infant Temperaments

SOURCE: Chess & Thomas, 1990; Kagan, 1994; Snidman, Kagan, Riordan, & Shannon, 1995.

In addition, it is important to note that, within each category, babies have various degrees of a particular personality trait. Among difficult babies, for example, some are extremely negative, others less so.

An amazing finding of Chess and Thomas's (1990) research is that subjects still showed roughly the same personality types in adolescence! It is easy to imagine how children of various personality types might behave as they get older. Readers have likely met easy adults who have friendly, easygoing personalities; difficult adults who respond less positively and get upset easily at change or new circumstances; and slow-to-warm-up individuals who are shy, timid, and reserved. Other researchers have also found that inborn infant temperament types persist into later childhood and adolescence (Kagan, 1994; Rothbart, 2007; Rothbart & Bates, 2006; Snidman et al., 1995). A high rate of mental health disorders and conduct problems in school have been found among those born with difficult temperaments (Caspi, Henry, McGee, Moffitt, & Silva, 1995; Henry, Caspi, Moffitt, & Silva, 1996; Newman, Caspi, Moffitt, & Silva, 1997; Sanson, Hemphill, & Smart, 2004). Those with shy or slow-to-warm-up temperaments are more likely to be inhibited and avoid social interactions (Henderson, Marshall, Fox, & Rubin, 2004). This suggests that personality type can predispose children to risks.

Temperament and Attachment

Does temperament affect the quality of parents' or caregivers' relationships with babies? The infant in the following vignette has a difficult temperament that has caused stress and sleeplessness for his parents. Will his negative interactions, over time, interfere with family bonds?

Two young parents are trying to wash clothes at the laundromat, but their 10-month-old seems determined to keep them from doing their work. He cries out in high-pitched, ear-splitting screams. Other people at the laundromat give disapproving looks and move away. The father rocks and bounces his son, then gives him a pacifier, but the baby spits it out and resumes his angry wail. Now the mother takes a turn. She rattles her keys in front of his face. This tactic works for half a minute. The baby studies and grasps the keys, then loses interest and throws them forcefully to the floor. After much effort, the parents give up trying to console their angry baby. They throw their half-clean wash into a basket and head for home.

Surely these interactions will take a toll on infant–parent relationships. How can these parents provide the warmth and responsiveness necessary to promote attachment? How can this baby, in a perpetual state of upset, bond with them? Amazingly, attachment does occur! In study after study, babies of all temperaments—including personalities as difficult as that illustrated in the story—are found to become securely attached to their parents at exactly the same rate (Mangelsdorf, Shapiro, & Marzolf, 1995; van den Boom, 1995). It makes no difference whether babies are grouchy and unsmiling, timid and quiet, passive and unplayful; parents find ways to create positive interactions and foster warm bonds. This fact speaks to the powerful, loving urge of parents and babies to form relationships with one another.

Temperament and Culture

Within all cultures, some babies are difficult and others easy; some are shy and others bold. There are, however, some personality trends that can be observed within specific cultural groups. These are likely the result of biological heritage. For example, very early in life, babies of Chinese American and Japanese American families have been found to be less irritable and excitable and more easily calmed, or, in a word, easy (Camras, Oster, Compos, & Bakeman, 2003; Freedman, 1979; Kagan et al., 1994). Italian infants are found to exhibit these same temperamental traits (Axia & Weisner, 2006). These charactersitics persist at least through infancy. Although very early experience could explain some of these personality differences, researchers conclude that genetics is most influential (Garcia Coll, 1990).

In other studies, Navajo babies also were found to cry infrequently and to be more easily consoled and less perturbable (Chisholm, 1989; Freedman, 1974). It is interesting to note that parents in these cultural groups also tend to be quieter and less excitable (Fajardo & Freedman, 1981; Joe & Malach, 1998). Do these parents and children have similar traits because of genetics? Or do parents adapt their interactions to meet the temperamental needs of their babies? It is difficult to answer these questions. However, it is clear that a "goodness of fit" in personality traits exists among family members in Navajo culture. The quiet, easy temperaments of infants and the less excitable personalities of parents are a good match.

In a cross-cultural comparison, Puerto Rican babies were found to be less upset and to cry less often in new situations than Caucasian and African American babies (Garcia Coll, Sepkoski, & Lester, 1981). African American newborns were more active. Garcia Coll et al. (1995) interpret these differences as evidence of biological contributions to personality. They suggest, however, that maternal health and nutrition during pregnancy and, later, parent interactions contribute as well. For example, if a baby has a difficult temperament, suffers poor intrauterine development, and has a parent who responds more negatively, an extremely challenging personality type may emerge. If any one of these variables is changed, however—say a baby enjoys healthy prenatal development or has parents who respond more positively—a less difficult temperament pattern may result.

A difficult temperament is viewed in most cultures as a risk factor. In a classic study in Africa, however, difficult temperament was actually found to promote survival and healthy development. M. V. DeVries and Sameroff (1984) found that Masai Kenyan babies with difficult temperaments were more likely to thrive during a 10-year drought because their fussiness and crying ensured that they would be adequately fed by their mothers. These findings demonstrate that certain personality types may be more highly valued in one culture than in another (Harwood et al., 1995). Would Masai mothers even use the somewhat pejorative term *difficult* to describe this powerful temperament that ensures survival?

EARLY EMOTIONS

Early infant emotions both shape and are shaped by relationships with others. Babies express contentment when they are nurtured; they show distress when an unfamiliar adult picks them up. An intriguing question is whether infants feel the same way about things as adults do. To examine this issue, researchers have conducted studies in which they have observed and rated infant expressions. Babies have been found to make certain facial contortions when angry and others when surprised. Contentment is easy to spot: babies smile and even laugh. Figure 9-2 illustrates several of these infant expressions. Researchers study these expressions and their development and speculate on what babies feel. They also plot the ages at which particular emotions emerge in human development.

Parents appear to play a critical role in teaching babies emotions. They demonstrate various emotional states through exaggerated facial expressions or intonation. Babies can discriminate among these different expressions only days after birth (Izard, 2002; Izard & Harris, 1995). In a study in which parents were instructed to interact with their babies "still-faced"—showing no emotion—their 6-month-olds wiggled, changed their own facial expressions, and eventually turned away or even cried (Moore, Cohn, & Campbell, 2002). This shows how important emotional expressions are in communication with infants.

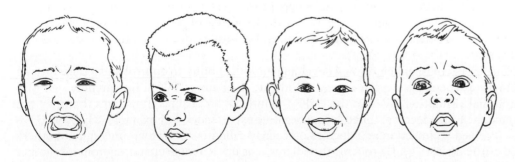

FIGURE 9-2   Distinct infant facial expressions have been identified and studied in order to learn about the development of early emotions.

SOURCE: From Krantz, M., *Child Development, 1/e.* © 1994 Wadsworth, a part of Cengage Learning, Inc. Reproduced by permission. www.cengage.com/permissions.

By 10 months of age, babies can distinguish among facial expressions that look similar but represent very different emotions (Ludeman, 1991). For example, they show different reactions to happy and sad faces even when these look very much the same. Ten-week-olds were found to look longer at faces that showed more intense anger than those showing moderate anger and at faces that displayed fear (Creswell et al., 2008).

Visual cues may not be the only way babies notice emotions in parents. In one study, touch, in the absence of facial expression, was effective in communicating feelings of excitement or comfort to 3- to 6-month-olds (Muir, 2002). In other studies, vocalization was found to play a role in imparting feelings (Baldwin & Moses, 1996; Mumme, Fernald, & Herrera, 1996; Vaish & Striano, 2004). For example, when mothers read stories to babies using various emotional intonations (e.g., happy, sad, angry), babies as young as 5 months were found to differentiate among these vocalizations.

Babies rely on adult expressions to guide their own feelings. For example, babies who see mothers displaying positive facial features show less distress in the presence of a stranger (Stenberg, 2003) and are more likely to explore an unusual object (Svejda & Campos, 1982). In one study, babies were persuaded to cross a visual cliff if their mothers showed an encouraging expression (Striano & Rochat, 2000). In a process called **social referencing,** babies refer to adult emotional reactions to determine how they should feel.

Another way that adults transmit feelings is through their responses to infant emotional expressions. Adults are quite accurate in interpreting infant expressions of happiness, sadness, surprise, interest, fear, contempt, anger, and disgust (Izard & Harris, 1995). So, they may be sensitive to infant emotions, allowing them to respond appropriately. Interestingly, abusive parents were found to misread their infants' emotional states (Kropp & Haynes, 1987). They could not pick up on their children's distress signals, for example. This might explain, in part, their devastating reactions to their children and the poor developmental outcomes that result. Interestingly, parents who were themselves abused are the least accurate in identifying the emotions of their children (Leerkes & Siepak, 2006).

The emotions that children learn and express may be influenced by attachment (Kochanska, 2001). Babies who are insecurely attached express the emotions of fear, distress, and anger earlier and most often. Securely attached babies, in contrast, express more joy. As securely attached babies develop during the first 2 years, their expression of anger declines even further. It may be that the comfort of a warm bond with a parent leads children to acquire the more positive emotions more readily. Another possibility is that babies who exhibit positive affect elicit more nuturing responses from their parents, which, in turn, leads to secure attachment. One recent study supports this explanation (Donovan, Leavitt, Taylor, & Broder, 2006). These authors report that the frequency of positive emotional expressions by infants at age 6 months predicted warmth and sensitivity in their mothers in their second year of life.

One aspect of infant emotional development is the ability to control and reduce intense feelings, particularly negative ones (Rothbart & Bates, 2006). Researchers call this **emotional regulation.** Even in the earliest months of life, babies show signs that they can reduce their own levels of upset during negative experiences. For example, a baby who has just received an injection at a doctor's office may calm herself by focusing on her mother's face or the doctor's gentle touch. A toddler who is upset about separating from his mother on his first day in child care may focus intently on a book that a caregiver is reading to him. It is believed that many babies reduce negative feelings in this way—by attending intensely to things unrelated to the source of their bad feelings. Adults seem instinctively to know this is so. How often have you seen a parent try to calm a baby by pulling out a set of car keys to look at and play with?

social referencing: The process by which infants refer to adults' emotional reactions—their voices and facial expressions—to determine how they should feel about persons, objects, or situations.

emotional regulation: The ability of infants to control and reduce intense feelings by attending intensely to things—a parent's face or a set of keys—that are unrelated to the source of those feelings.

Adults teach children emotions through the use of exaggerated facial expressions.

In one study, babies who were able to control their emotions by focusing their attention in this way were found to be more competent socially in the preschool years (Belsky, Friedman, & Hsieh, 2001). Interestingly, even babies who had highly negative emotions were found to be more socially competent in later life if they could focus their attention well. The investigators conclude that this ability to attend reduces negative emotions and protects children from becoming overwhelmed by negative events in their lives.

Emotions and Culture

Does culture influence the expression of early feelings? Cross-cultural research suggests that basic human emotions are universal (Ekman, 1994; Elfenbein & Ambady, 2002). Such feelings as fear, happiness, and anger are part of human interactions within all cultural groups and are expressed through similar facial expressions. What may vary by culture, however, are the times and places when certain emotions may be expressed. In which situations are smiling or laughter appropriate? When may anger be openly communicated? Rules about the expression of emotions vary by culture and are learned even by very young children.

Children of Japanese and Chinese families are often taught—through direct guidance or example—to avoid outward expressions of anger (Slonim, 1991). African and African American children, in contrast, are encouraged to express feelings openly. Euro-American children display a moderate amount of emotional expression. Children living in Nepal are taught differently about expressing emotions, depending on whether they live in Tamang or Brahman villages (Cole, Tamang, & Shrestha, 2006). Tamangs, who live in small settlements in the foothills of the Himalayas, discourage expressions of anger in their children, but encourage open discussion about feelings of shame. In contrast, Brahman families, who live at lower elevations in the middle belt of Nepal and follow Hindu traditions, allow expressions of anger and discussion about angry feelings, but discourage expressions of shame. So, even within a single, small country, major cultural differences exist in how children are taught to express feelings.

Hale-Benson (1986) warns that professionals working with children and families must take into account the feelings and orientations of the cultural groups they work with and not insist that children or their parents express emotions in an open way (e.g., "If you're angry, talk about it. Tell me how you feel!"). Such outward expressions may not be culturally appropriate. Nor should family service providers or teachers deny children these expressions when they are culturally meaningful (e.g., "Calm down, Jamal. You're getting too excited and loud.")

INFANT RELATIONSHIPS AND EGOCENTRISM

An infant trait that influences social relationships is *egocentrism*, described in Chapter 7. Recall that this is a kind of thinking in which young children have difficulty understanding the perspectives of other people. Infants and toddlers have trouble, for example, recognizing others' needs or feelings, as the following examples illustrate:

- A pregnant mother, suffering from morning sickness, slumps in the bathroom with terrible nausea. Her toddler son pulls on her shirt from behind, begging to have his favorite book read "right now."
- A toddler becomes enraged when another child comes to the child care center with shoes identical to her own. "Mine!" she screams. Even though she has her own shoes on, she insists that her peers' shoes are hers as well.

It is clear from these examples that babies often think their needs are most important and that everything in the world belongs to them. It is easy to see how this kind of thinking influences social interactions. Such displays of egocentrism have led some to label this period of development the *terrible twos*.

Research shows that while toddlers are egocentric, they can also be very kind and sociable. They share objects with their parents and other toddlers without being asked, give spontaneous hugs, and interact quite well with peers—smiling, laughing, and offering toys as they play (Zahn-Waxler, Radke-Yarrow, Wagner, & Chapman, 1992; Volbrecht, Lemery-Chalfant, Aksan, Zahn-Waxler, & Goldsmith, 2007). How can these behaviors be reconciled with the view that these babies are unable to understand the perspectives of others? It may be that there is an ongoing struggle in the second year of life between the needs of self and the desire to be with others. The following story illustrates this idea:

A toddler and her father walk along a city sidewalk in Manhattan. The father holds on tight to his daughter's hand. In her other hand she holds a bagel, which she chews vigorously as they walk. After a number of blocks, the bagel is quite wet from the toddler's saliva. She accidentally drops it onto the dirty sidewalk. "Oh-oh," she says, scooping the bagel back up.

"Dirty," the father says. "You can't eat that. Don't eat that dirty bagel."

"No eat," the toddler responds, shaking her head but clinging to the bagel. She looks over at a man sitting on a bench, a complete stranger. She pulls free from her father and toddles over to him. "Here. You have this," she says, offering her filthy, saliva-soaked bagel to the stranger. Her father grabs hold of her hand again, offers a brief apology to the man, and guides his daughter away.

Here, the elements of egocentrism and kindness are blended. It is a relatively egocentric idea that someone else would wish to eat a spoiled food item that the child has been eating. (The thinking goes: if I eat it, someone else will want to.) However, there is kindness and unselfishness in the act of offering it to someone else. No one asked the child to do this. Such acts of spontaneous kindness are common at this age.

guided peer watching: A classroom strategy in which caregivers direct children's attention to the play of their peers (e.g., "Let's watch what Charlene is doing").

Children of all cultures show evidence of early empathy. However, they may express their concern for others in different ways. In one study, children from Germany and Israel, two Western cultures, engaged in active helping behaviors when they believed an adult experimenter was in trouble (Trommsdorff, Friedlmeier, & Mayer, 2007). In contrast, children from Indonesia and Malaysia reacted with personal distress but less prosocial action. Both of these responses show early empathy but reflect the unique social styles of individual cultural groups.

CLASSROOM ADAPTATIONS: THE SOCIAL AND EMOTIONAL DEVELOPMENT OF INFANTS WITH SPECIAL NEEDS

As described previously, infants with special needs can become securely attached to their parents and other caregivers (Vondra & Barnett, 1999). Those who form these bonds often acquire a sense of autonomy, described by Erikson, and display a full complement of mainly positive emotions that allow them to enter into positive relationships with others. However, some babies with special needs are at risk of poor social and emotional development (Odom, 2002; Meadan & Monda-Amaya, 2008). An infant with a hearing impairment may not be as responsive to adults or peers; strong bonds with these individuals may not form (Holstrum et al., 2008). A child who has been abused may not easily acquire feelings of security or contentment (Gushurst, 2003).

Infant care providers can adapt their classroom interactions to support babies who are at risk. The following are strategies that have been found to promote healthy social and emotional development among infants with a variety of challenging conditions (Terpstra & Tamura, 2008; Umansky, 2008b):

1. **Nurturing, responsive care.** To address issues of mistrust or poor attachment, caregivers can provide high levels of physical warmth to babies with special needs. Holding, snuggling, bouncing, and other types of physical contact and play are important for all babies but particularly for those with challenging conditions. Caregivers should also respond quickly to crying or expressions of need. Immediate responses to infants with special needs will promote a sense of security.

2. **Quiet, safe, consistent environments.** Providing a play environment that is comfortable, soothing, and predictable is especially critical for babies with special needs. Classrooms that are free of sudden, loud noise and other harsh stimuli are important. Very predictable environments can help such infants develop a sense of trust. A single caregiver who interacts in consistent ways can be assigned to each baby who is at risk. (High rates of staff turnover—a problem in infant care—can threaten this sense of consistency.) For toddlers with special needs, predictable routines are comforting. Caregivers can ensure that play, snack, nap, and going-home times occur in a relatively fixed order and follow a familiar routine.

3. **Positive interactions with peers.** As babies with special needs get older, they may need support in interacting with peers in positive ways. Caregivers can be active in facilitating social play. They might begin by engaging toddlers in **guided peer watching**—a strategy in which they direct children's attention to the play of others ("Why don't you sit here with me and we'll watch what Jeremy is doing. Look! See? He's putting the baby to bed"). Once babies show an interest in other children, they can be encouraged to play close to their peers (e.g., "Come sit near Celeste and play with your train"). Simple sharing and turn-taking activities, conversations, and social routines with peers can be prompted. A caregiver might say, "Can you give Nikko one of your animals? Great! That's so nice. See how he's smiling?" A child might be encouraged to wave and say "bye-bye" to each peer as she is leaving the center for the day. Nurturing behaviors toward peers can be

CHILD GUIDANCE: *Setting Limits for Toddlers*

As discussed in this chapter, Erikson (1982) proposed that toddlers need to acquire a sense of autonomy in order to grow emotionally. However, this does not mean that children of this age should be allowed to do whatever they wish. Limits or rules are needed to keep children safe. This is especially true in some neighborhoods where there is more traffic, greater risk of violence, or other threats. In some cultures, certain rules, even at this age, are a very important part of family tradition. Respecting and obeying elders, for example, may be more critical in a Native American family than in a Euro-American family. Toddlers, themselves, feel safer knowing that there are limits. Two-year-olds are more likely to explore new environments, for example, if they trust that a parent or caregiver will stop them from doing anything harmful.

How do adults establish limits for such young children in a way that adheres to cultural beliefs yet does not inhibit autonomy? First, parents and caregivers should reflect on which limits they believe are most important. Effort should be made to identify only a small number of rules that really matter. It is important for adults of any culture to provide a minimal set of limits—simple boundaries for behavior—within which there are many opportunities to move around, explore, play, and express oneself.

As adults think about these *rules that matter*, they should consider culture, family beliefs and traditions, and environmental factors. What are the specific behaviors that are valued by the family and that are really needed to keep children safe? A parent might decide that, at a neighborhood park, her child's activities should be limited to a small, safe play area around a playscape. She decides that leaving this space will not be allowed. Within this area, however, her child is able to play, climb, and express himself without restriction. A caregiver at a child care center might have a different set of limits. Because the playground is completely safe and fenced, she does not establish rules about where children can play. They may move freely, wherever they wish, without constraint.

A parent of a culture that values respect for elders may believe that a politeness rule is one that really matters. The father may set limits on the ways that his toddler talks to adults in the family. Loud expressions of anger or negativism are not allowed. Still, the child has opportunities to assert herself—even in negative ways—in other settings: while playing with peers or siblings or when engaging in pretend play with dolls. A caregiver at a university lab school that serves middle-class, Euro-American children might have a very different set of limits regarding interactions with adults. He may tolerate a great deal of negativism ("No!") and informal interaction with caregivers (e.g., addressing them by first name). He sets rules regarding other behaviors that are more important for this particular group of children.

A parent from a culture that values self-control at an early age may set a limit that certain objects in the home cannot be touched. Another parent or caregiver might childproof the environment instead so that the toddler can touch and play with any object in the home.

What happens when toddlers break a rule? Once again, families of different cultures will use different strategies. Some adults will ignore most misbehavior, refusing to respond to children who have broken rules. Others will use a firm reprimand. Still others will impose a brief time-out in the child's bedroom or on a chair in the child care center. Some adults will redirect children, simply guiding them to more appropriate actions: "You can't play in the bathroom. Come out with me and play at the water table." Regardless of how an adult responds, the consequence of breaking a rule should not be too harsh. Fear of severe reprisal will inhibit autonomy and threaten attachment.

In summary, there is no one correct set of limits that adults should impose on toddlers. A wide variety of culture-specific responses to misbehavior are appropriate. The guiding principles are (a) avoid establishing too many rules or rules that are not really important and (b) do not enforce these too harshly.

prompted (e.g., "He's upset. Can you give him a nice pat? Just pat his arm to make him feel better").

4. ***Modeling positive affect and social interactions.*** Social behaviors and emotional states are often acquired by watching adults, but infants with special needs may not emulate adult models as readily. Caregivers can display positive affect and social behavior in more exaggerated ways when interacting with babies who have challenging conditions. A caregiver might use exaggerated facial expressions of delight, surprise, and puzzlement, accompanied by matching language. Smiling, touching, hugging, and offering verbal expressions of concern when upset occurs can be modeled in a highly obvious manner. In the presence of infants with special needs, caregivers might demonstrate sharing, turn taking, pretend play, and other social behaviors they would like children to acquire.

SUMMARY

Emotionally healthy infants acquire a sense of trust by becoming attached to one or several caregivers. These bonds lead to positive social and emotional development in later years. Infants who are insecurely attached to parents may be at risk. Some may become highly aggressive; others may become withdrawn and anxious. Children of some cultural groups are more likely to be categorized as insecurely attached. However, they may simply have been taught to be more or less dependent by their families, and this can affect assessments of their attachment. Other factors, such as temperament, challenging conditions, early intervention, and child care, can influence attachment. Children who become securely attached gradually acquire a sense of autonomy—a feeling of individuality and power. How autonomy is defined and encouraged varies across cultures, however. In some families, autonomous behaviors are discouraged; children are expected to remain dependent on family members into adulthood.

Infants often display unique temperaments—dispositions that remain constant throughout development. Several specific temperaments have been studied, such as easy, difficult, and slow-to-warm-up. Each affects infant behavior and relationships. Infants learn a range of basic emotions by studying the behaviors of adults. When they observe caregivers' facial expressions or verbalizations of excitement, happiness, or concern, they share these emotions. These emotional and social responses of babies are affected by egocentrism—an inability to fully understand the viewpoints of others.

Children with special needs may require extra adult support in achieving these social and emotional milestones. Caregivers can adapt interactions with infants with challenging conditions to promote healthy social and emotional growth.

RESEARCH INTO PRACTICE

CRITICAL CONCEPT 1

Infants of all cultures develop a sense of trust and form attachments to significant adults in their lives—parents, caregivers, relatives, neighbors, and peers. Children who are abused or neglected or who have not formed secure attachments to others acquire a sense of mistrust and may suffer poor mental health.

Application #1 Be nurturing in your interactions with infants. Behaviors such as warm physical touch, smiling, and being close help babies become attached to adults.

Application #2 Respond to infants' cries or bids for attention. Babies become attached to adults who respond to their initiatives predictably and in interesting ways.

Application #3 Be culturally sensitive in showing warmth and responsiveness. In some cultures, warm physical touch is not the norm. Parents respond in different ways to crying. Find a good match between your interactions and the cultural experiences of infants.

CRITICAL CONCEPT 2

In the second year, children who have become securely attached to others will begin to strive for a sense of autonomy. They will wish to become individuals separate from their parents. Whether children will become fully independent, however, depends on culture. In some families, dependence is highly valued and individualism discouraged.

Application #1 Understand and appreciate some toddlers' need to become independent. Tolerating assertive and sometimes negative behaviors and allowing a degree of freedom and choice are critical for many children at this age.

Application #2 Understand why some parents encourage dependence in their children. Historical experiences, immediate dangers in the neighborhood, or a need for families to band together in the face of adversity may lead parents to discourage independence in their toddlers. Don't adopt complete autonomy as a goal for all children in your care.

CRITICAL CONCEPT 3

Infants' social relationships are also influenced by inborn temperament. Some babies have inherited difficult dispositions, others easy ones. Bold and timid and slow-to-warm-up babies can also be differentiated. Some variations in temperament are due to cultural traditions and differences in parenting styles.

Application #1 Be aware of the role of biology in determining the basic dispositions of some infants. Guilt ridden parents must be helped to understand that a negative or wary temperament may be due not to poor parenting but to inborn characteristics.

Application #2 Accept and appreciate the inborn traits of babies. For example, working with or raising difficult children may require a great deal of patience and tolerance.

CRITICAL CONCEPT 4

Babies acquire a range of emotions and facial and vocal expressions to represent them. Interactions with family members will assist babies in emotional development.

For example, a parent's own expressions of sadness or surprise will help infants differentiate these feelings.

Application #1 Use facial expressions and gestures to transmit emotions to babies. Engage in up-close, face-to-face interactions in which you show surprise, happiness, or puzzlement.

Application #2 Use facial expressions to show caution or fear when infants are in jeopardy. Displaying an obvious look of concern when a toddler wanders toward a busy road or climbs too high on a climber will transmit the message that there is danger.

CRITICAL CONCEPT 5

Egocentrism—an inability to understand others' perspectives—is a cognitive characteristic that influences social relationships in infancy. Babies tend to believe that the whole world centers on them. Egocentrism does not seem to inhibit kindness and sharing among toddlers, however. Infant social relations are marked by fascinating blends of self-centeredness and empathy.

Application #1 Understand that egocentrism is a cognitive trait, not a personality flaw. Be tolerant of egocentric behavior and don't always insist on cooperative interactions.

Application #2 Children's egocentrism should not prevent you from trying to instill altruism. Model or prompt kindness and sharing. Even highly egocentric infants will perform these behaviors if encouraged.

CRITICAL CONCEPT 6

Infants with special needs often form attachments to caregivers and acquire early social abilities. However, parents and caregivers may need to adapt their interactions with some babies in order to promote healthy social and emotional growth.

Application #1 Provide warm, responsive caregiving—reacting quickly to upset and initiating much snuggling, holding, bouncing, or other physical play. Design an especially safe, soothing, and predictable environment for babies with special needs.

Application #2 Facilitate high-quality interactions among babies with special needs and their typically developing peers. Encouraging children to watch, talk to, and physically nurture their peers will promote positive social development.

Application #3 Use highly obvious facial expressions, verbalizations, and prosocial behaviors when interacting with infants with special needs. Modeling positive affect, sharing, warm touching, and rich language will help babies with challenging conditions acquire positive emotions and social skills.

ASSESSING YOUNG CHILDREN: Infant Social and Emotional Development

Areas of Development	What to Watch For	Indicators of Atypical Development	Applications
Emotional health	By age 6 months, shows a strong attachment to parents or caregivers through smiling, clinging, and in other ways showing a desire to be near these persons. Shows temporary upset during separation from parents or other caregivers. By age 18 months, exhibits some willingness to separate from parents and other caregivers. Demonstrates an ability to work and play alone some of the time.	Shows a lack of interest in or caring for other human beings by age 6 months. Expresses an inordinate amount of upset or anger when separated from parents or family. Completely ignores parents when reunited with them after child care. Remains clingy and dependent on parents after 18 months.	Respond quickly and with warmth to infant crying and other means of communication. Plan for a baby to visit a new child care center and to spend significant time with caregivers prior to enrollment. Create a play space that allows choice, independence, and exploration.

| Relationships with others | Shows an interest in other children and nonfamily adults. Shows early empathy and kindness toward peers. | Shows no interest in peers or adults. Does not respond to and even becomes troubled by social contact from others. | Display positive emotions, through the use of exaggerated facial expressions, intonation, and touch. Model caring and kindness, displaying nurturing behaviors and expressions of concern when infants become upset. Facilitate peer interactions, prompting infants to touch, talk to, and watch other children. |
| Specific social skills | Makes contact with others through verbalization, playful behavior, smiling, gesturing, or sharing objects. | Performs few social behaviors. Verbalizes little and makes no contact with others. | Model specific prosocial behaviors for toddlers: sharing, smiling, and warm touch. Demonstrate simple play skills—such as simple pretense—and invite children to play near one another. |

Interpreting Assessment Data: Variations in social behavior may be due to cultural and family practices. Babies of some cultures will be more wary or less social because of unique styles of parenting and family interaction. Children whose family values dependence and discourages autonomy may show greater upset during separation from parents. These children may be less independent in toddlerhood. If babies avoid *all* contact with adults and peers, however, or show poor attachment to parents, further evaluation is recommended. Family stressors such as poverty and substance abuse can interfere with positive family relationships. Mental health services for the whole family may be helpful.

CHAPTER 10

Preschool Physical and Motor Development

GUIDING QUESTIONS

1. What are the major trends in physical growth during the preschool years?
2. What gross motor abilities are acquired between ages 2 and 5, and how do these vary across cultures?
3. What are some examples of motor play in the early years within both Western and non-Western cultures?
4. What are the major trends in fine motor development in the early years, and how are these influenced by perceptual skills?
5. How do traditional views of artistic development differ from the perspectives of teachers and parents in Reggio Emilia, Italy?
6. How do boys and girls differ in their motor development during the preschool years?
7. What personal and family life skills are acquired in early childhood, and how are these influenced by cultural traditions?
8. How can professionals and parents adapt interactions and classroom environments to support the motor development of children with physically challenging conditions?

The preschool years—from age 2 to age 5—are marked by significant physical growth and development. This chapter profiles the extraordinary motor advancements that occur during this period. Preschoolers are more coordinated, show surprising strength and speed, and display tireless energy. However, great diversity in these physical changes exists among individuals. The following vignette shows how variations in motor activity and physical play preferences can be seen within a single group of children.

A university child care center in a large Midwestern city serves a culturally diverse group of children. A caregiver, Ms. Shapiro, is challenged to create activities that meet the diverse needs and interests of all the children in her care. She creates a new science center that includes objects from nature that she believes relate to the lives of the children and their families. This center contains items not only from the woods but also from urban environments, such as wasp nests and bird feathers. She asks families to help her collect things for the center; they contribute items that hold cultural meaning. One family offers different types of beans and grains, and another brings in a sampling of vegetables from the family garden.

Ms. Shapiro plans for children to sit in the center and feel, weigh, and examine the items under a magnifying glass. However, what they actually do with the items is quite different. Two children do spend time quietly examining objects. Two others, though, seem far more enamored with the new screen divider that the caregiver

has put up to separate the science center from the rest of the classroom. These children begin a spontaneous, raucous game of peekaboo, taking turns ducking down behind the divider and then popping back up with shrieks of laughter. Soon the game evolves into chasing; the two children pursue one another round and round this interesting screen. Another child takes items off a table and tosses them into the air. She studies these objects as they fall to the floor and break apart. Other children soon join her.

As the students continue with these activities, working together to ensure the demise of her carefully planned center, Ms. Shapiro ponders what has gone wrong.

The caregiver in this vignette has been very careful to provide materials relating to the children's interests. She has demonstrated sensitivity to the unique community and cultural experiences of the families she serves. The problem is that she has failed to recognize another important area of diversity in children's development: *movement*. Individual children move through the world differently. Some are very active, while others prefer quiet solitude and reflection. Some children explore objects by acting on them; they must throw, swing, bang, or bend them to fully understand their properties.

Movement styles and preferences, activity levels, and motor abilities vary across cultures (Hale, 1994; Heo, Squires, & Yovanoff, 2008; Poolton, Masters, & Maxwell, 2007). In some cultural groups, quietness and stillness are valued. In others, animated interaction is the norm. Physical activity also differs by age; younger children have a harder time sitting still for long periods. Perhaps there is a poor match between the activities this caregiver has planned and the motor needs of this particular group. The caregiver in this story might have included in her new center some choices involving greater movement. An object drop area, a pendulum swinging game, or nutcrackers to break open designated materials have been recommended as appropriate science experiences for more active young learners (Trawick-Smith, 1994).

An important message of this story is that culturally sensitive programs for young children must include more than a multicultural curriculum. Simply providing materials or topics that reflect diverse backgrounds is not enough. In preschools, playgroups, or home-based interventions, adequate space must be provided and activities planned to meet cultural, developmental, and motor activity needs. Professionals must engage children in appropriate levels and types of physical activity. Among some groups of children, an active environment not only feels more comfortable but also leads to greater learning (Hale, 1994).

PHYSICAL GROWTH

Some patterns of physical and motor development are universal. Children of all cultures grow physically in certain similar ways during the preschool years. First and foremost, all children of this age do grow; however, growth rate slows during this developmental time period in contrast to the astounding pace of physical development during infancy. The preschool years are a time of slow but steady increase in height, weight, and muscle tone. A look at a 3-year-old and a 5-year-old will reveal the significant physical development that occurs in early childhood.

Preschoolers' bodies now grow faster than their heads. The huge-headed appearance of infancy and toddlerhood gradually disappears as torsos grow longer and stomach muscles stronger. These changes give preschoolers a flatter stomach; the endearing potbelly of infancy gradually fades. A pronounced physical change that occurs during the preschool years is arm and leg growth, although preschoolers remain short-legged in contrast to adults.

These growth patterns lead to a shift in the **center of gravity,** the point at which body weight is evenly distributed. Babies' centers of gravity are high in the body, somewhere in the area of the chest. This makes them very top-heavy and more awkward on their feet, unable to make sudden movements without toppling over (Haywood & Getchell, 2005). A preschooler's center of gravity is nearer the belly button. This lower weight distribution allows children of this age to perform actions that were impossible only a year or two before. Physical changes in the preschool years are also evident in weight increases: a typical preschooler weighs 31% more at the end of this period than at its beginning. (It is interesting to note, however, that in infancy weight increases 300%!)

Preschoolers' height and weight vary significantly, even within single cultural groups. A study of children in the United States, for example, showed that height among 4- and 5-year-olds ranged from less than 90 centimeters to more than 115 centimeters (Haywood & Getchell, 2005). The weight of these same children was even more variable, with a range of 30 to 50 pounds. All children studied were developing in healthy, typical ways. A child's simply being small in the preschool years is not a cause for concern.

Cultural variations in the size of preschool children have been found to exist. Children of Asian ancestry, for example, tend to weigh less and be of shorter stature than those from other groups (Haywood & Getchell, 2005). Genetically derived body structure accounts for most of this variation, but environment may be a factor. For example, the short stature of Southeast Asian children living in poverty has been linked to iron deficiency (Nutritional Status of Minority Children, 2004). In contrast, African and African American preschoolers tend to be taller and heavier. Differences in home and family environments have been cited as one reason for higher weights among these cultural groups. For example, more active play in the early years has been linked to greater muscle tone among African and African American children (Garcia Coll, 1990; Kelly, Sacker, Schoon, & Nazroo, 2006). Higher weight and height among children of African descent is also the result of an inborn body type.

Euro-American and European preschoolers fall somewhere between Asian and African cultural groups in stature. This has led some researchers to refer to such children's height and weight as *typical*, African children's as *precocious*, and Asian American children's as

center of gravity: The point in the body at which body weight is evenly distributed. Center of gravity is lower in the preschool years, allowing children to perform actions that were impossible in infancy.

delayed. These are value-laden words that suggest physical anomalies. In truth, what is typical growth in one culture is very different from that in another. No one cultural growth pattern is the norm.

GROSS MOTOR DEVELOPMENT

Children of all cultures acquire **gross motor abilities**—skills that require the use of large muscles in the legs or arms as well as general strength and stamina. Examples of such skills include running, jumping, throwing, climbing, and kicking. A number of gross motor abilities that are acquired in the preschool years are presented in Table 10-1.

Advancement in these areas often appears to be so rapid that adults come to believe these abilities are acquired overnight. One parent describes the high-speed, death-defying tricycle-riding prowess of a 5-year-old who only several days before was unable to get the trike to move at all. Another parent reports that his 4-year-old, who just weeks before was unable to swing herself, had suddenly begun to perform sophisticated aerial acrobatics on the swing set. How did these abilities emerge so quickly?

Actually, motor development is characterized by a gradual refinement in abilities (Gallahue & Ozmun, 2006; Haywood & Getchell, 2005). Steps toward mastery of a particular skill are many, although each step is not always easily observed. Although a child might demonstrate sudden accuracy in throwing, for example, this skill actually was acquired in small steps. The process began in infancy, with primitive swiping and grasping. In toddlerhood, the child may have begun throwing underhanded. In the early preschool years, the child may have begun to throw overhanded but with awkward body

gross motor abilities: Skills, such as running, jumping, throwing, climbing, and kicking, that require the use of large muscles in the legs or arms as well as general strength and stamina.

TABLE 10-1

Gross Motor Abilities Acquired in the Preschool Years

By the end of the preschool years, children usually can . . .
walk up and down stairs, alternating feet.
walk in straight and circular lines.
balance while walking on tires or balance beams.
climb ladders and climbers, alternating feet.
run with both feet leaving the ground.
stop, start, and change directions quickly when running.
leap off a hill or climber and land squarely on both feet.
jump over blocks, tires, or other obstacles, leading with one foot.
hop on one foot for 10 or more repetitions.
gallop, using one lead foot.
ride tricycles or other riding toys, using the pedals.
stop and start riding toys and steer around barriers.
throw balls and other objects using the whole body and stepping forward with the leg that is opposite the throwing arm.
catch objects using only the hand and arms and bending the elbows to absorb the impact of a throw.
kick objects using a bent knee and a back and forward swing.
swing on a swing independently.

movements (i.e., stepping forward with the same foot as the throwing arm). From the earliest days of life, the child may have practiced the timing of the release of objects. In infancy, the child had to overcome reflexive grasping. In toddlerhood, the child had to learn to let go of an object at just the right time when throwing (Angell & Mason, 2008; Cratty, 1986). It was only after many of these small, unnoticed advancements that the child's throwing competence suddenly would become apparent to adults.

Locomotion abilities—skills involving movement from one place to another, such as walking, skipping, and running—progress in the same way. Although parents or teachers may have suddenly noticed that preschoolers are difficult to keep up with, the speed, balance, and coordination at this age took a long time to develop. In toddlerhood and the early preschool years, their steps were unsure. They stumbled often and tipped over when changing directions or stopping suddenly. They rarely moved directly in a straight line. They did not engage in true running; both their feet did not leave the ground at the same time when they loped along (Adolph, Vereijken, & Shrout, 2003; Cratty, 1986). Gradually, they became more competent in their locomotion. By age 3 they could walk in a straighter line and at 4 in a circular path.

They became better at climbing up- and downstairs. At about age 4, they could alternate steps for the first time when stair-climbing. At this age they could also leap, gallop, and hop. Their running at last became controlled and coordinated. So, by the late preschool years, most children would be off and running, with their parents chasing behind and wondering, "When did they learn to move so quickly?"

There are two distinct kinds of movement abilities: movement consistency and movement constancy (Sugden & Keogh, 1990). **Movement consistency** refers to competence in the performance of basic movement skills such as running or catching. **Movement constancy** refers to an ability to adapt these movements to meet varying environmental challenges (e.g., being able to catch balls of different sizes or being able to run uphill and down as well as on flat surfaces). Both are critical for play and everyday life in all cultures. A child in Chicago learns not only to run, for example, but also to run up and down ramps, over tires, and along balance beams on the playground. A child in rural Guatemala must not only run but also change directions and stop and start quickly when herding farm animals.

Not only must children learn to coordinate the movements of their own bodies, they must often adapt these in relation to what other children are doing (Sugden & Keogh, 1990). In a game of tag, for example, children must do more than simply run. They need to start and stop, shift direction, or speed up in relation to the actions of peers who are pursuing them. Reaction time is also important in many childhood games. Traditional American pastimes such as musical chairs, red light/green light, and slapjack require quick motoric reactions to stimuli.

Cultural Variations in Motor Skills

Because physical growth is most often governed by genetics and maturation, preschoolers across cultures are more alike than they are different in motor development (Haywood & Getchell, 2005). Some cultural variations do exist, however, in the pace with which skills emerge. Children from tribes in Central and South America appear to acquire specific motor skills earlier than Euro-American preschoolers. Similar advanced development was discovered among Asian children (Lester & Brazelton, 1982; Mayson, Harris, & Bachman, 2007). African and African American preschoolers were also found to acquire certain large motor abilities earlier than their Euro-American peers (Harkness & Super, 1996; Kelly et al., 2006). Again, both genetics and experience explain these differences. Garcia Coll, Surrey, and Weingarten (1998) speculate that the way children

locomotion abilities: Skills involving movement from one place to another, such as walking, skipping, and running.

movement consistency: Competence in the performance of basic movement skills, such as running or catching.

movement constancy: An ability to adapt basic movement skills to meet varying environmental challenges. Being able to catch balls of different sizes or to run uphill and down as well as on flat surfaces are examples.

are held and played with by parents and other family members contributes to differences in motor development. Diet and nutrition can also produce variations.

Cultural Variations in Activity Level

Anyone who has spent time with young children is aware of individual differences in their activity levels. Some preschoolers are quiet, while others are extremely active. Activity level generally increases during the first 2 years of life and then, for most children, decreases significantly through age 5 (Eaton & Yu, 1989; Wood, Saudino, Rogers, Asherson, & Kuntsi, 2007). Not all children become less active in the preschool years, however (Haywood & Getchell, 2005). A good deal of evidence suggests that needs and preferences for movement are biologically inherited. For example, studies have shown that identical twins have very similar activity levels, whereas fraternal twins do not (Wood et al., 2007). Boys have been found to be consistently more active than girls, suggesting that high activity level is a sex-linked genetic trait (Denny, 2004; Eaton & Yu, 1989; Pate, Pfeiffer, Trost, Ziegler, & Dowda, 2004).

Children's need for movement varies by culture. This is partly the result of unique biological inheritance (Chess & A. Thomas, 1990; Sallis, Prochaska, & Taylor, 2000). It is also affected by differences in home and family environments (Garcia Coll et al., 1998). A study of Puerto Rican and Euro-American mothers, for example, has shown how values can influence children's activity levels (Harwood et al., 1995). Puerto Rican mothers were more likely than Euro-American mothers to rate active play as undesirable. In contrast, Mexican American and African American parents report that action and rhythmicity are a central part of child rearing and family communication (Hale, 1994; Klein & Chen, 2001; Pate et al., 2004; Sanchez, 1997). Because of differences in parental beliefs and interactions, children of these cultural groups are likely to develop very distinct movement patterns.

The activity levels of individuals of one culture are sometimes misunderstood by those of another. A case in point is the response of some Euro-American teachers, psychologists, or social workers to the active styles of African American preschoolers (Hale & Franklin, 2001). Some adults have been found not only to misinterpret the active play of children of this cultural group but also to try to quiet or slow it down (Hale & Franklin, 2001; Morgan, 1976). For example, a parent educator recently conducted a workshop titled "Quiet Time: Establishing a Calm Routine in Child-Rearing." How might a parent who greatly values active play respond to such a session?

MOTOR PLAY AND CULTURE

Preschoolers of different cultures use motor abilities in different ways as they play. Some may use kicking skills to play a game with a ball, while others may use these to kick rock into the cooking fire. Some may refine kicking to enact pretend martial arts battles, while others might skillfully kick a can along the sidewalk all the way back home from the grocery. This section will provide examples of preschool motor play across cultures.

Running and Walking

In all cultures, running and walking are observed in children's free play. American preschools or child care centers afford many opportunities for varied walking experiences, including tiptoeing quietly to the bathroom, climbing up and down steps, and keeping up with older children on a field trip. All these activities require adaptation in walking behaviors.

It is impossible to keep children from running. Whenever children are given opportunities to move around freely at home or in preschool, much running will occur. Open-ended chasing is a common running game played on American playgrounds. Distinct from organized games of tag with clearly defined rules, chasing involves wild, chaotic running around as one or several children chase after others. Sometimes the chasers and chasees reverse roles without warning. The following is an example of a typical chasing game:

Three children are playing a make-believe game in which one is a giant who chases and captures people.

JENNA: (In a gruff, make-believe voice) Oh, I'm tired, all right? I'm a tired giant. I am going to sleep now. But no one better throw leaves on me during my nap.
EDGAR: (Laughs. Takes a handful of leaves that have fallen on the playground and throws them on the sleeping "giant.")
JENNA: (Doesn't stir; continues to snore loudly)
ROSITA: (With eager anticipation in her voice) Oh, oh. Throw some more leaves on.
EDGAR: (Giggling) I'll do it. (Throws more leaves)

Suddenly Jenna rises up and emits a roar. She darts after one of her classmates, then quickly shifts direction and chases another. At first, the children being chased run quickly; then they slow down, eager to be captured. Jenna grabs hold of Edgar and pulls him back to the leaf pile.

JENNA: (To the captured child) Now you stay there while I take my nap. And I hope no one else throws leaves on me.

The game continues for many minutes. Slight variations occur: children come to the rescue of peers who are captured, the giant keeps sleeping for many seconds while the children throw leaves, or the giant runs in slow motion during the chase.

In this game, children acquire running consistency—that is, basic running skill. However, they also show running constancy as they vary their running movements to meet all kinds of circumstances and to respond to the actions of peers. For example, they must anticipate the direction and speed with which the giant pursues them and vary their own speed accordingly. They run over or under obstacles and up and down a hill on the playground.

Running games are common in other cultures. In Taiwan and mainland China, children at a very young age fly kites (Bai, 2005; H. L. W. Pan, 1994). One child or an adult might pull the string while other children run alongside. Children might gather and run around underneath the flying kite. Although this game is very different from American chase, it also develops children's running abilities. Children must run hard and adapt their running to the conditions of the field and quickly change direction as the wind blows the kite.

In Polynesia, children play a game along the boat ramps near their homes. As the waves rise and break, children run away from them so they do not get wet (Martini, 1994). Teasing is another childhood favorite in this culture. In this game, a group of children tease a younger or same-age peer or sibling and then run away with whoops and laughter. Many Euro-American adults do not consider this to be the most positive form of social play, but it certainly causes children to exercise their running abilities. Polynesian preschoolers also engage in active make-believe that includes imaginary hunting expeditions. They charge after and pretend to kill valley goats, pigs, or dogs.

Preschoolers of all cultures acquire the same motor abilities but use them very differently in their play.

Kepelle village children in Sierra Leone also engage in hunting play, called *Sua-Kpe-pele*, in which chasing of animals is common (Bloch & Adler, 1994). Each type of play poses challenges that require running adaptation, such as changing directions to outrun a wave or pursue a goat.

Climbing and Jumping Down

Climbing competence requires large motor development as well as a positive disposition toward taking risks. For example, when climbing a net ladder, children must not only have strength and coordination but also overcome the anxiety of being up so high. Adults often reassure children who are fearful (e.g., "I'm right here if you need help" or "The ladder is very safe. You won't get hurt climbing up there."). When adults acknowledge children's risk taking (e.g., "Oh, my! Look how high up you are! You're way over my head! How did you climb so far up?"), they instill confidence and a desire for more adventurous play (Gallahue & Ozmun, 2006).

Once children have climbed up on something, they generally jump down. Jumping is a complex action that develops gradually in stages (Haywood & Getchell, 2005). Young preschoolers step off from surfaces rather than jump down from them. As they get older, they begin to actually leap, landing first on one foot and then the other. In these early jumps, children awkwardly throw their arms back and fail to lean forward for balance. The consequence is often a lopsided landing. Children in the early preschool years usually leap from the lower platforms of a climber or bottom rungs of a ladder until their jumping abilities improve. Girls and boys differ in their jumping skill: girls are more precise in their jumps, while boys can leap higher (Cratty, 1986; Pate et al., 2004).

Games involving climbing up and jumping down are common in any culture. Middle-class American children often have access to innovative playground equipment. A growing number of playgrounds at preschools and child care centers—and even the back yards of private homes—include elaborate playscapes that allow safe climbing and jumping. Such sophisticated equipment is not a part of child play experiences in all cultures.

In Puerto Rico, preschoolers might climb on low walls or leap from banks into shallow streams under the watchful eye of a parent or older sibling (Soto & Negron, 1994). Wall and fence climbing are common in urban neighborhoods as well, as the following vignette illustrates:

> Two 4-year-old cousins play together in an urban park. The play area is a grass surface with several broken swings and half-buried concrete sewer pipes. The children are drawn to the periphery of the area, where a 3-foot-high brick wall surrounds the park. They climb up and walk along the wall. Soon they begin a game in which they leap from the wall to the ground. "Look at me, Mama!" one child announces from atop the wall, then he screams and leaps. He lands on both feet but then drops to the ground and rolls over dramatically.
>
> "Be careful now, Jamal," his mother warns. "You're way high up. Don't want skinned knees, now." She says this with a smile, knowing the wall is low enough and the ground is soft enough that there is no real danger.
>
> "Yeah. I can get up high too," says Latonia, trying to best her cousin. She climbs to the top of the wall. "Look at me, Auntie Sarah, I'm jumping!" she screams out in mock horror, sailing through the air and landing on both feet in the grass. The game continues for more than an hour.

Catching and Throwing

Balls predominate in children's play in Western societies (Kaplan-Sanoff, Brewster, Stillwell, & Bergen, 1988). Children acquire throwing and catching abilities gradually. Not until the elementary years will they display highly coordinated ball-handling skills (Haywood & Getchell, 2005). In the early preschool years, children begin to throw overhanded. Their first attempts lack any control, however. Where a thrown object will land is difficult to predict at this age; sometimes it will actually fly backward behind a child. During the course of the preschool years, children's arms become more fluid and less rigid when they throw, and they are better able to time the release of objects. Eventually they begin to use their whole bodies, not just their arms. Near the end of the preschool years, some children learn to step forward with the foot opposite the throwing arm and to shift their weight to get behind a throw. At this point, throws become longer and more accurate.

Catching ability also progresses during the preschool years (Haywood & Getchell, 2005). Initially, children are rigid, passive targets. They simply put out both arms and wait for the object to strike them. If a thrown object happens to come directly between their arms, they may trap it against their chest to make the catch. More often than not, however, the object goes wide, and they make no effort to move their arms or adapt their movements to catch it. Sometimes a ball or beanbag will bounce off their outstretched arms or chests. Their reaction time is simply not quick enough to grab an object as it strikes them. Older preschoolers begin to catch more effectively. They move their arms more quickly and bend them to absorb the impact of the object as they catch it. They become very competent at catching large objects (e.g., a beach ball) by age 5 but still struggle with small balls or other catching toys.

Children will practice throwing without great coaxing from adults. Spontaneous throwing games predominate during free play. Any kind of material might become an object to be thrown. Without warning, very young children are apt to invent indoor throwing games with inappropriate objects that threaten life and limb! In American preschools and child care centers, beanbags or balls of different sizes are provided to stimulate throwing and catching behaviors. In other cultures, balls may not be available, but throwing still predominates in children's play. Turkish children invent their own aiming and tossing games spontaneously, using non-ball objects—sticks, marbles, nuts, stones, or bones (Baran & Erdoğan, 2007). In Polynesia, children throw rocks (Martini, 1994). Preschoolers of this culture can be observed standing for long periods on a bridge tossing large and small stones into the water below. They also throw rocks at cans or toss sticks for a dog to retrieve. A favorite game, even at this young age, is dashing glass soft-drink containers against rocks or throwing them into the water. In another popular game, young children in Polynesia throw lemons at one another. Although these activities may seem unusual and perhaps inappropriate to adults of Western cultures, they are marvelously inventive and reflect the unique play environments of children.

Balancing

When preschoolers grow taller, their center of gravity becomes lower, and their balance improves (Haywood & Getchell, 2005). Balance is required for many games. Children often engage in play in which they deliberately cause themselves to become off balance (Aldis, 1975). Examples include spinning around and around and then trying to walk or sliding down a particularly slippery slide and then trying to regain balance at the bottom. Low balance beams and other equipment are useful for balance play. Playground equipment in parks or preschools in America is often designed to encourage balancing games, as the following story illustrates:

> Two children stand and bounce on one of several old tires that lie horizontally on a playground. One child begins to walk around the tire rim. When she comes to the point where her peer is standing, she stops and says, "Hazel, move!"
>
> "Oh, that's easy," her friend responds and begins to walk around the tire in the same direction. They circle round and round together many times.
>
> "And let's say if you fall off," the first child announces, "you get eaten by…um…sharks, all right? Oh, and let's say we switch directions now, okay?" The two children stop and turn; as they do, they wobble a bit but do not touch the ground. "Those sharks coulda got us!" the first child laughs.

Balancing activities are not limited to games on play equipment. In many cultures, playgrounds are not available, so balancing activities must be improvised from available household or outdoor materials:

> A 5-year-old girl in a village in Senegal invites a slightly younger sibling to play a make-believe balancing game. She fills two large cans with water and balances one of them on her head, demonstrating how it is to be carried. "Don't spill a single bit or the food will be wasted," she instructs in an adult tone. The younger girl places the second can on her head. As the older child begins to walk a winding path, holding herself erect and supporting the can on her head with one hand, her sister follows after. With one careful step after another, they make their way through the village in single file.

This is a typical form of "work-play" among girls of Senegal, performed as preparation for adult responsibilities (Bloch & Adler, 1994).

Rough-and-Tumble Play

Children of all cultures engage in wild, silly roughhousing that looks, from outward appearances, like fighting or aggressive behavior. This form of play is forbidden in many

American schools and households out of concern that it might lead to real fighting. A growing body of research suggests that such **rough-and-tumble play,** which includes wrestling, play fighting, rolling around, or chasing peers—all accompanied by screams, laughter, and noise making—is useful for motor development and social learning (Colwell & Lindsey, 2005; DeWolf, 2001). Such play likely relieves tension, exercises many different muscles simultaneously, leads to close physical contact with peers, and is generally great fun. Rough-and-tumble play with nurturing adults may contribute to greater competence in peer interactions (MacDonald & Parke, 1986; Tamis-LeMonda, 2004). Contrary to what would be expected, this form of play does not lead to aggression, nor does it result in unruly or uncontrollable behavior (Pellegrini & Perlmutter, 1988).

Rough-and-tumble play may be the ideal context for acquiring motor abilities in early childhood. Children who are less active might be enticed into activity by such open-ended, humor-filled interchanges. Children who do not care for organized games might be attracted to the competition-free, highly symbolic features of rough-and-tumble play. Wrestling, running, and shouting on the playground are appropriate and powerful ways to practice motor skills. Very few activities that an adult could invent would lead to the same levels of exercise.

Do children of all cultures engage in rough-and-tumble play? Research on Polynesian children shows that pretend fighting is prevalent in the early years. Groups of multiple ages have been observed waging "war" with one another by wrestling, punching, calling names, and throwing rocks, lemons, or pretend spears (Martini, 1994). Japanese children play a traditional game that resembles sumo wrestling. However, such rough, active play has declined in the past few decades within Japanese society as television and video games have become popular pastimes (Takeuchi, 1994). Whiting and Edwards (1988) observed rough-and-tumble play in six very distinct cultures. In some of these societies, parents were observed teaching young children how to distinguish between rough play and true aggression. At an early age, then, some preschoolers may be tutored in how to modulate their brute force, to hold back from hurting others, or to show clear signs of playfulness, such as smiling or laughing.

Although there may be elements of rough-and-tumble play in all cultures, preschoolers of some families will be rougher and more active than others (Brown & Freeman, 2004). African American children have been found to enjoy very active, physical play

rough-and-tumble play: A form of motor play—including wrestling, play fighting, rolling around, and chasing peers—that relieves tension and contributes to social competence but does not lead to aggression.

Children of all cultures engage in rough-and-tumble play.

(Hale-Benson, 1986). Euro-American children have been found to be moderately rough, and Korean American preschoolers have been found to engage in far less rough-and-tumble play (Farver, Kim, & Lee, 1995).

FINE MOTOR DEVELOPMENT

The ability to coordinate smaller muscles in the arms, hands, and fingers is referred to as **fine motor development.** Remarkable advances in the development of fine motor skills occur during the preschool years. At this age children begin to use these smaller muscles to perform a variety of self-help skills, as the following story illustrates:

> A 4-year-old arrives at a Midwestern child care center in winter. He is wearing a new snowmobile suit, a miniature version of the full-body outfit that an ice fisherman or snowmobile rider might wear in subzero temperatures. His suit is covered with elaborate zippers, buttons, snaps, clasps, and Velcro attachments. One caregiver chuckles at its similarity to a costume from a science fiction movie.
>
> The child is enormously proud of his new suit and rushes around the center showing friends and teachers. "It's like my Dad's, you know. It's a real one. It's for snowmobiles. It's got all this neat stuff. See?" The children are duly impressed. The teachers, who are a bit more practical, are imagining the time it will take to dress this little boy for outdoor play.
>
> Now comes the challenging task of taking the outfit off. It's nice and warm in the center; if the child leaves on his wonderful suit, he will perish from the heat. His teacher reminds him of this and offers help. "Why don't you let me give you a hand. Can I get some of these zippers started for you?"
>
> No!" the child responds vigorously, "I can do all this." It is clear that part of the thrill of wearing the new suit is demonstrating how all the various snaps and zippers work. He sits on the floor beside his cubby and sets to work getting out of the outfit. A small group of admirers, including both teachers and peers, gathers around to watch. He struggles with some parts of the suit but perseveres. It takes him a full 20 minutes to remove it. Everyone applauds when he finishes. He smiles and holds up the suit one last time for all to see before hanging it on a hook.
>
> At this moment, the director pokes her head into the classroom. "Just wanted to remind you that today is our monthly fire drill. We'll be going outside in a few minutes. Be sure to bundle everyone up. It's cold out there."

Although children may struggle a bit with self-help skills such as buttoning, zipping, or eating with utensils, these are mastered, for the most part, by age 4 or 5 (Hurley, 2000). Some children, like the preschooler in the story, show surprising command over small muscles. They are able to tie their shoes or remove elaborate clothing independently. A great deal of variation in fine motor competence will exist, however, among children in a typical child care or preschool setting.

Fine motor abilities are supported by advancements in perception. Preschoolers can see, hear, touch, taste, and smell as well as adults can (Hurley, 2000). Further, they are much better at interpreting what they perceive than they were during infancy. For example, 4-year-olds have been found to be quite sophisticated in noticing details in pictures and making accurate interpretations about what they see (Jones, Swift, & Johnson, 1988). They begin to coordinate these newly acquired perceptual abilities with body movements. A 4-year-old can now skillfully use vision to guide hands in

fine motor development:
The ability to coordinate smaller muscles in the arms, hands, and fingers that allows a child to perform such tasks as tying, buckling, zipping, making puzzles, molding clay, cutting with scissors, and drawing.

TABLE 10-2
**Fine Motor Abilities
Acquired in the
Preschool Years**

By the end of the preschool years, children usually can . . .
eat with a fork and spoon.
spread food with a knife.
put on clothing and shoes independently.
button large buttons on clothing.
zip and unzip clothing.
finger paint.
sculpt with clay.
cut with scissors.
manipulate with accuracy the small pieces of a puzzle or pegboard.
grasp a writing implement or paintbrush using the thumb and fingers.
create representational drawings, including human heads and facial features.
write some primitive, conventional letters or one's name.
coordinate hand and arm movements with vision, hearing, touch, and other senses.

drawing. A 5-year-old can turn the pages of a small book while looking at pictures and print. This ability to integrate movements and perception has been called **perceptual/motor coordination.** Examples of specific fine motor abilities that develop in the early years are presented in Table 10-2.

As with gross motor development, adults are surprised by what they perceive as sudden spurts in their children's fine motor control. A Head Start teacher tells of a child who seemed to struggle with fine motor tasks, then announced one day that she could now tie her own shoes. The teacher watched in amazement as the child successfully demonstrated her newfound skill. A parent describes how a young preschooler suddenly began to draw people—primitive heads with long legs below them. Until this moment, the child had only scribbled. Although adults might marvel at how quickly children gain control over small muscles, this is actually a gradual and complex process.

ARTISTIC DEVELOPMENT

perceptual/motor coordination: The ability to integrate movements and perception. Using vision to guide one's hands in drawing or turning the pages of a book are examples.

scribbling stage: The earliest stage of drawing, when children make marks on paper that gradually become more controlled and contain more circular strokes and discrete shapes. Children in this stage eventually tell stories about their scribbles.

Children of all cultures engage in quiet games that involve the use of small muscles. The types of games vary according to the available toys and cultural traditions. Making puzzles, molding clay, cutting and stacking objects, and building with blocks are common fine motor activities in some cultures. Drawing and other forms of artistic expression are perhaps the most universal form of fine motor play.

Drawing Development: A Traditional View

Children's drawing illustrates fine motor development as well as intellectual growth in the preschool years. Traditional theorists have described stages of drawing through which children progress, beginning with the scribbling stage and advancing to more representational drawing levels (Di Leo, 1982; Lowenfeld, 1947). Descriptions of these stages are presented in Table 10-3.

In toddlerhood and the early preschool years, children often scribble. During the **scribbling stage,** their marks on paper gradually become more controlled, often containing more circular strokes and discrete shapes. Children achieve even greater control when they

Stage	Approximate Age	Description
Scribbling stage	15 months to 3 or 4 years	Large zigzagging lines give way to more controlled and circular markings later in this stage. Eventually, discrete shapes appear. Children begin to name their scribbles as they approach the next stage.
Preschematic stage	3 or 4 years to 6 or 7 years	Early representations are drawn. For the first time, adults can recognize what children have created. Names of drawings stay the same over time. Early drawings are composed of heads with basic features. Over time, arms, hands, legs, and detailed facial features emerge.
Schematic stage	6 or 7 years to 9 or 10 years	Whole scenes that include houses, trees, a sun, and people are created. Figures "float in space" and are out of proportion early in this stage. Later, figures may be anchored to a ground line with a shading of blue at the top of the page representing the sky.

TABLE 10-3
Stages of Drawing in Early Childhood

SOURCE: Adapted from Di Leo, 1982; Lowenfeld, 1947; and Seefeldt, 1987.

learn to hold the drawing implement in their fingers instead of gripping it in their fist and to place their arms down on the table as they draw. Eventually, children name their scribbles or tell stories about them. Even in the early preschool years, then, children exhibit an awareness that art can be used to symbolically represent ideas. The first stories children tell about their artwork are often invented after the drawing is complete. The story of a particular drawing is not fixed in the child's mind and will change over time in the retelling, as the following vignette reveals:

A 3-year-old is using markers to create an elaborate scribble drawing. Her father watches this for a while, then says, "Tell me about what you're drawing."

"Oh" The child thinks a moment. "It's a big bear, I think."

"A bear!" the father enthuses. "Like in the book we just read."

"Yeah, see, he's got sharp teeth, and he roars." The child laughs, then continues with her work.

The father and his daughter eat lunch together. After this, the father asks if she will tell him more about her drawing.

"Okay," the child retrieves her artwork. "She's having lunch," she says, pointing at her scribbles.

"The bear?" the father asks.

"No, not a bear! It's Mom."

"Oh. It's not a picture of a bear?"

The child makes a face of annoyance. "No. I said it's Mommy."

This 3-year-old has made a scribble drawing, then created a story about it based on an event that just occurred (e.g., her father reading a book about a bear). After she has lunch, she changes the story to represent this new experience—a story about eating. In less than a year, this child will begin drawing pictures with a concept already in mind. She will set out to represent an idea in a more planned way. By age 4, the story she tells about her drawing will stay the same even when she is asked about this work weeks or months later.

Children must advance through the scribbling stage before they are able to produce more representational drawings. Even after they have moved on to more elaborate drawing, older preschool children will revisit scribbling for enjoyment or comfort.

In the later preschool years, children enter the **preschematic stage,** in which they begin to create simple representations of the people and things that are important to them. Heads predominate in their drawings during this period. As children progress, they draw stick arms and legs that at first protrude from the heads of their figures and later are attached to bodies drawn below the heads. Other representational figures—trees, houses, animals, clouds, and the sun—emerge in children's drawings as they develop into the early primary grades, although these are often drawn out of proportion or may be shown floating through space. In the elementary years, children enter the **schematic stage,** in which elaborate scenes are created that reflect a greater degree of correspondence to the real world. At this stage, the figures often are anchored to a ground line, and a patch of blue sky may be added above. Samples of children's drawing representing several of these stages of development are presented in Figure 10-1.

preschematic stage: A stage of drawing, during the late preschool years, when children begin to create simple representations of the people and things that are important to them. Heads predominate first in this stage; children then progress to adding stick arms, legs, and bodies.

schematic stage: A stage of drawing, emerging during the elementary years, in which elaborate, whole scenes of people, houses, trees, and the sun are created. In this stage, figures often are anchored to a ground line, and a patch of blue sky is added above.

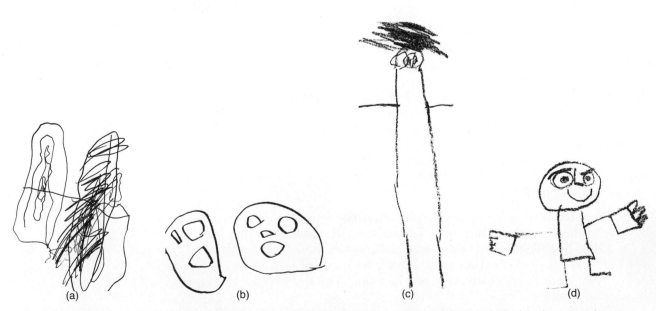

(a)   (b)   (c)   (d)

FIGURE 10-1   Drawing ability develops rapidly during the preschool years. Children first scribble (a), then draw heads (b). Arms, legs, and other body details emerge soon thereafter (c). Some children draw full figures by the end of the preschool period (d).

An interesting feature of children's drawing is repetitive practice. Once children begin making small, circular scribbles, they draw these over and over again on paper. Once they begin to draw heads, they fill pages with them. Preschool teachers begin to worry about the supplies budget as children go through reams of paper, drawing identical heads on each sheet. This repetitive practice may be an effort to gain mastery over newly acquired abilities.

Representing life on paper requires more than skill at controlling a marker or crayon or being able to see the object one is drawing. Drawing also has a cognitive component. Piaget has argued that children are more likely to draw what they know than what they see (Piaget & Inhelder, 1963). For example, children draw transparent houses with visible people. Such a drawing represents not what they actually see when they look at a house but what they know occurs inside: family members sleeping, eating, and playing. Drawing development involves, then, a complex coordination of perceptual, motor, and cognitive skills.

Is drawing a good indicator of fine motor skill in all cultures? In societies where drawing, writing, and other forms of graphic representation are essential, drawing may be an excellent, natural context for observing development (Gandini, 1997a; Golomb, 2007). It is important to note that not all cultural groups use Western writing implements such as pencils, markers, or crayons. For example, to assess drawing development among Yup'ik Eskimo children in southwestern Alaska, one might observe *storyknifing,* an activity in which children draw symbols in mud as they tell traditional stories (deMarrais, Nelson, & Baker, 1994). Even preschoolers (called *tag-alongs* by older Yup'ik children) learn to knife stories along the riverbank.

Some cultures do not value or emphasize drawing or writing at all. In several studies, British and Zambian children were asked to copy two-dimensional figures (Kathuria & Serpell, 1999; Serpell, 1979). British children were more competent in reproducing the figures with pencil and paper. This result could lead to the erroneous conclusion that Zambian children are delayed in motor or cognitive abilities. In fact, Zambian children were advanced in their ability to accurately form these shapes with strips of wire. Simple sculpturing with wire is more prevalent within this culture than Western forms of drawing.

Drawing Development: The Reggio Emilia Perspective

An excellent example of how culture influences artistic development can be found in **Reggio Emilia,** a region in Italy. Over the past several decades, researchers and educators from all over the world have flocked to schools in this area to study the remarkable artistic achievements of very young children who live there (Copple, 2003; Gandini, 1997b; Salmon, 2008). Preschoolers as young as age 3 have been observed creating highly representational works of art. An example of the extraordinary drawing of children in Reggio Emilia is shown in Figure 10-2. From a traditional view, such complex drawings should not emerge until children were well into the elementary years.

Why are children in this part of the world so advanced? Within their culture, the arts are highly valued. Parents and teachers in Reggio Emilia believe that artistic expression is more than just a way of expressing feelings. Drawing, painting, sculpting, and singing are fundamental ways in which children reflect on their learning (Gandini, 1997a). In contrast to many American schools, artistic efforts take center stage in Reggio Emilia classrooms. They may be more highly valued even than traditional mathematics or reading.

Reggio Emilia: A region in Italy in which artistic expression is highly valued, and where young children are found to create highly representational works of art.

"Harvesting Grapes"

FIGURE 10-2   Children in Reggio Emilia, Italy, create highly realistic artwork at an early age. Such complex drawings are not made by American children until the later elementary years.

SOURCE: Edwards, C. et al. 1994, *The Hundred Languages of Children.* Copyright © 1994. Reproduced with permission of Greenwood Publishing Groups, Inc. Westport, CT.

These cultural values lead to specific classroom practices that enhance children's artistic expression. The following are characteristics of Reggio Emilia classrooms for children through age 6 (Gandini, 1997a). Readers might reflect on how these could be implemented in American schools.

1. ***Art is used as a representation of learning.***   The arts are more than simple outlets for personal, creative expression in Reggio Emilia classrooms. Art media are used to help children represent and reflect on their discoveries. If children conduct pouring experiments with water, they then draw, paint, or sculpt what they have discovered. After a field trip to a museum, children use art materials to represent their observations. Art is integrated into meaningful, interdisciplinary projects; it is not considered a separate part of the curriculum.

2. ***Art and all other learning experiences are collaborative.***   Although there are opportunities for children to work alone with art media, most artistic representations are completed in groups. Further, parents are often involved in their children's artistic efforts. They are encouraged to study, reflect on, and even contribute to their sons' or daughters' representations. Teachers are considered "partners" (Gandini, 1997a, p. 19). During representational activities, they ask questions, make suggestions, and guide children's work. This is in marked contrast to the

traditional hands-off approach to art—common in American schools—in which children are simply left alone to create.

3. **Time and space are devoted to artistic representation.** Large spaces are provided in Reggio Emilia classrooms for artistic expression. A special art studio—called an *atelier*—is often provided for use by both children and teachers. There are no time constraints on children's representational activities, so a project may go on for days or even weeks. Children are encouraged to revise earlier drafts of drawings or paintings. In contrast, American schools do not provide such time and space. Children might spend 15 minutes at a small art table, for example, and then place their completed drawings in their cubbies to take home.

4. **A teacher who is trained in the visual arts is available in each school.** Schools in Reggio Emilia have an *atelierista*—a resident artist who guides children in their representations. This teacher works closely with other teachers in the school to integrate the arts into all learning experiences. This is quite a different role from that of the American art teacher who pulls children out of classes to conduct brief lessons in arts and crafts.

5. **Learning experiences are displayed in the classroom using documentation panels.** The works of children, along with writing and photographs, are displayed on beautiful panels throughout the classroom. These are more than decorations. They show children's development and learning. For example, several drafts of a child's self-portrait may be presented—each showing a new, more sophisticated understanding of self. These panels allow teachers and parents to assess children's development. They also allow children to review and reflect on learning and artistic representation.

These unique classroom features represent the value this community places on the arts. Children's advanced artistic development in Reggio Emilia may be more a result of unique cultural traditions and worldviews than of specific teaching practices. Still, many American teachers are implementing Reggio Emilia techniques, with great success, in their own classrooms (Williams & Kantor, 1997).

GENDER AND MOTOR DEVELOPMENT

Researchers have observed gender differences in motor development during the preschool years. Boys have been found to lose baby fat and acquire muscle tone more quickly than girls. They tend to be larger and stronger throughout the early years. Girls are more competent at fine motor activities. This may be because some areas of the brain—those responsible for perceptual-motor abilities—are more fully developed in females during this period (Tanner, 1990). Boys are generally found to be more active; they engage in more rough-and-tumble play than girls (Clark & Paechter, 2007; P. K. Smith, 1997). Boys tend to take more risks and to be more adventuresome in play (Hagan & Kuebli, 2007; Pellegrini & Smith, 1999).

Research on gender and motor development has been conducted mainly with white, middle-class children. For this reason, findings of gender differences are not surprising; this cultural group tends to socialize boys and girls to behave very differently motorically (Hagan & Kuebli, 2007; Jacklin, 1989). In middle-class America, boys are given more practice and encouragement in acquiring large motor skills, and adults hold stereotyped expectations of children's motor abilities (Leaper & Friedman, 2007; Leve & Fagot, 1997). Parents buy different kinds of toys for boys and girls, and these toys accentuate different motor skills (Bussey & Bandura, 1992; Kacergis & Adams, 1979).

It is possible that gender differences are not so great outside Euro-American culture. For example, in studies of children of color in six different societies, including the United States, Whiting and Edwards (1988) found fewer differences in activity level or rough-and-tumble play between boys and girls. It must also be pointed out that even in societies in which boys show greater motor competence, individual differences are great. Many individual boys are less competent than many individual girls. Data on *average* children will not give a full picture of differences among preschoolers.

PERSONAL AND FAMILY LIFE SKILLS

Advances in motor development allow preschoolers to take better care of themselves and to take on simple household responsibilities. In middle-class homes in America, young children perform such self-help tasks as dressing themselves, picking up their toys, bathing, brushing their teeth, and eating with utensils. As early as age 3, many children can accomplish self-help skills, though some require help from adults. For example, assistance is needed in tying shoes, buttoning small buttons, or coordinating a fork and table knife to cut food. Children master most of these self-help skills by age 5.

In many families in the United States, preschoolers are assigned chores related to family life, such as straightening their rooms or helping to wash dishes. Some assist in the preparation of family meals. As they develop their motor abilities, they are able to take on more complex tasks, such as drying dishes with a towel or zipping up a coat, with less adult assistance.

Family chore assignments are more extensive in some cultures than in others. Young children from nonindustrialized countries are often more involved in household work than those in European and American families. Preschoolers in communities in India, Okinawa, the Philippines, Mexico, and Kenya, for example, were observed to perform a range of jobs that most American children would never be assigned (Whiting & Whiting, 1975). Such chores included collecting firewood, fetching water, herding and tending livestock, grinding grain, and harvesting vegetables. Children were also found to perform universal household tasks, such as preparing food, at an earlier age than would be expected in American families. A 2-year-old in India, for example, was observed cutting vegetables with a knife alongside an older sibling (Whiting & Edwards, 1988).

Child care is a family chore that is commonly assigned early in life in some cultures. Very young children have been observed carrying, feeding, or in other ways tending to the needs of their infant siblings (Whiting & Edwards, 1988). A woman from Lebanon recollects the child care duties that were assigned to her when she was only 3 years old, growing up in a small village outside of Beirut:

> I was asked to sit on my bed with my baby brother—only a year younger than me—while my mother went out. "Don't let him go to the bathroom on the bed," my mother would warn. "Make sure he goes right in the pot." So, I would sit for hours watching and playing with him. I would guide him to the pot by the bed when he would need to go. I would play I was a mother and that my brother was my very own baby. This game would continue until my mother returned home.

Child care tasks are regularly assigned to preschoolers in nonindustrialized communities. In the United States, young children of historically underrepresented groups are also more likely to be given caregiving responsibilities (Klein & Chen, 2001; Willis, 1998). In almost all cultures, young girls are more often assigned child care duties (Morelli, 1986; Whiting & Edwards, 1988).

It is easy to see how motor abilities are exercised as young children care for their siblings: they must chase after, hold, carry, and sometimes confine their younger brothers or sisters. The following vignette illustrates the large motor abilities required in infant care:

A 5-year-old girl in a small village in Kenya is up early. She has been assigned the task of child care provider for her infant brother. Her mother and father have already gone to work in the garden, and she is left in full charge of her young sibling. When he awakes and cries, she picks him up and holds him close. As he calms down, she holds on with one arm and reaches with the other for a bottle to feed him. She must grip him tightly as she does this; he is 8 months old and very big for his age.

   After feeding him, she places him into a sling. Her brother wiggles and kicks—he does not seem eager to be confined. She then straps the sling to her back. She stands up, maintaining her balance, then walks off to play with friends in another part of the village.

This young girl exercises the same large muscles a child of another culture might use when climbing on a playscape. She uses large upper-body muscles, and she walks and balances. Her play activities, such as a game of tag, will be particularly challenging with her sibling strapped to her body!

CLASSROOM ADAPTATIONS: PRESCHOOLERS WITH PHYSICALLY CHALLENGING CONDITIONS

Some children have challenging conditions that affect their motor development, including neurological and perceptual disorders, attention-deficit/hyperactivity disorder, and malnutrition. Caregivers and preschool teachers can make adaptations in the classroom to address these challenges.

Neurological and Perceptual Disorders

Cerebral palsy, a disorder that can be caused by oxygen deprivation before or during birth, affects motor coordination and muscle strength. Young children with cerebral palsy vary greatly in the extent of their impairment; some are quite competent in motor skills and can acquire typical play and self-help abilities. Only the most challenging motor abilities may be difficult for them (Umansky & Hooper, 2008). Others have severe multiple handicaps, including visual and hearing impairments (Beckung, Hagberg, Uldall, Cans, 2007; Himmelmann, Beckung, Hagberg, & Uvebrant, 2006). These children may require significant support in play or daily life needs. They may need assistance even to maintain an upright sitting position. Their fine motor activities and eye–hand coordination are often limited.

Down syndrome, described in Chapter 4, is another challenging condition that can cause delays in gross motor abilities. Children with this disorder may have low muscle tone, leading to poor balance (Carmeli, Kessel, Bar-Chad, & Merrick, 2004). They may sit and walk with legs spread far apart for increased stability. They may avoid rotating the trunk or swinging their arms when walking, as typically developing children do. Because of their relatively short fingers, poorly developed bones in their wrists, and general cognitive delay, they also are limited in fine motor activities. In some cases, simply grasping small objects will be a challenge.

Some preschoolers show general motor delays that have no specified causes. In some instances, this is accompanied by delays in language or cognition. This condition may be due to minimal brain damage, perhaps occurring in fetal development or during the birth process, that is imperceptible to physicians in neonatal tests.

cerebral palsy: A disorder that can be caused by illness, injury, or oxygen deprivation before or during birth and that impairs motor coordination, muscle strength, and sometimes hearing and vision.

Down syndrome: A genetic condition, caused by an extra chromosome, that can lead to mental retardation, heart problems, motor delays, and unique physical features such as reduced stature.

Visual impairment and **hearing impairment** often affect motor ability. It is clear that many of the motor play games described previously, such as climbing, jumping, and balancing, will be more challenging for children who cannot see or hear well (Houwen, Visscher, Lemmink, & Hartman, 2008). However, motor play differences between perceptually impaired preschoolers and their peers are minimized when play environments are adapted to accommodate visual or hearing challenges.

Teachers, caregivers, and parents can adapt play equipment, provide sensory-rich materials, and guide children with special needs in their motor activities. When these accommodations are made, differences between the play of children with disabilities and those without are greatly reduced (Prendeville, Prelock, & Unwin, 2006; Ward, Saunders, & Pate, 2006). The following story illustrates how slight adaptations in materials in a preschool program can enhance play experiences for a child with visual impairments:

Cedric, a child who has a visual impairment, tries to join peers who are creating a large mural with markers in the art center. He knocks over a can holding the markers as he reaches for one. Grasping the marker in his fist, he now begins to make marks on the mural.

TADESSE:	(In an angry tone) No, Cedric! You're making a mess. That's just scribbling.
MICHAEL:	(Speaking at the same time as Tadesse) You can't help. You're messing it up. (Now complaining to the teacher, who is approaching) Cedric's messing up our mural!
CEDRIC:	(Says nothing; looks confused)
TEACHER:	(To the other children) Cedric has trouble drawing because he can't see well. (To Cedric) Is it hard for you to see the paper and markers, Cedric?
CEDRIC:	(Nods. Still does not speak.)
TEACHER:	You know, we have templates that help you draw shapes. (Offers metal templates. Takes Cedric's fingers and helps him locate and feel the templates.) See? You can trace inside these and make shapes.
MICHAEL:	Yeah. Like triangles. Can I try one?
TEACHER:	Sure. Shapes would look nice on the mural. (To Cedric) Cedric, let me help you get started.

The teacher takes Cedric's hands and shows him how to trace with markers inside a template. All three children begin to work together using this new medium.

Here the teacher has quickly assessed that a perceptual limitation has made an activity inaccessible. By adapting the materials, she has remedied the situation.

Adults can monitor activities throughout a classroom or home environment and make adaptations to meet special needs. Patz and Dennis (2008) recommend six such adaptations to promote the gross and fine motor development of preschoolers with a variety of challenging conditions:

1. *Positioning children so that they can play and learn.* Some children with motor challenges lack **postural tone**—sufficient muscle strength and control to be able to sit upright or maintain other postures that allow learning and play. Caregivers can provide equipment that helps preschoolers sit upright at a table. Highly resourceful caregivers and teachers (those with carpentry skills) can add the following to a chair to provide special support: an insert in the back to provide extra cushioning, a seat belt, and a footrest. A cutout in the table will allow children to reach desired objects more easily. Figure 10-3 illustrates these adaptations. Special adaptive equipment—adjustable chairs and tables, for example—may be purchased to accomplish these same purposes. Placing toys and learning materials on comfortable carpeting

visual impairment: A condition characterized by blindness or severely limited vision that can impair motor, cognitive, and other areas of development.

hearing impairment: A condition caused by a variety of factors that is characterized by deafness or severely limited auditory perception and can lead to language, motor, and other developmental delays.

postural tone: Sufficient muscle strength and control to be able to sit upright or maintain other postures that allow learning and play. Some children with motor challenges lack posture tone and require support.

FIGURE 10-3 Chair supports, footrests, and cutout tables can help children with physically challenging conditions to learn and play.

SOURCE: Umansky, Warren & Stephen R. Hooper, *Young Children with Special Needs, 3/e.* © 1998. Reprinted by permission of Pearson Education Inc., Upper Saddle River, NJ. Illustration courtesy of Jean Patz.

on the floor and encouraging children to assume a side-lying position will allow greater freedom of movement, control, and involvement in play for some children.

2. **Providing powered wheelchairs.** Children with severe motor impairments may benefit from powered wheelchairs. Recommended for those with cognitive abilities above a 2-year-old level, these motorized chairs have been found to increase communication, play with peers and objects, independence, and motivation to move around the classroom. Wheelchair controls can be activated using different parts of the body. A joystick may be operated with the hand or another extremity. Some chairs may be controlled by moving the head, chin, or tongue. A blowing control system also is available.

3. **Adapting equipment to allow full participation.** Children with motor challenges should be able to join in all activities in all parts of the classroom or playground. Ramps, low steps, and other means of access, along with teacher assistance, are needed to ensure that all children can play on indoor lofts, outdoor climbers, and other equipment.

4. **Providing larger materials.** Children who have perceptual and fine motor difficulties will benefit from larger toys and learning materials. Puzzles with very large pieces and gripping knobs can be provided. Other examples include extra large blocks, pegs and pegboards, paint brushes, and pretend play props. All these items can now be ordered from most early childhood materials catalogs.

5. **Adapting fine motor activities.** Fine motor activities can be adapted for children with physically challenging conditions. Pencils, pens, and drawing implements can be made easier to use by attaching special round, rubber grips to them. These can be ordered from materials catalogs. The same purpose can be achieved by pushing a pen or paintbrush through a large rubber ball. Adhesive strips can be wrapped around such implements to provide a better grip. Nonslip mats can be placed on tables so that children can work with materials with fewer spills. Special scissors can be purchased with a single, large loop that is squeezed so that cutting is easier. Four-loop scissors can also be provided; children place fingers in the inner loops and teachers in the outer ones to guide them. Fine motor materials can be positioned at a level that is comfortable for children with special needs. Children with

some motor challenges may find, for example, that materials positioned at the midline are easier to manipulate. Tables can be adjusted accordingly.

6. *Including materials that exercise small muscles.* A number of common classroom activities are ideal for children with motor challenges. Clay and other molding materials are easy for all children to use and will exercise small muscles. Squeeze toys enhance strength of grip. Dressing boards with snaps and zippers, pop beads, and other manipulatives are useful for promoting coordination.

Attention-Deficit/Hyperactivity Disorder

A motor-related condition that is occasionally identified during the preschool years is **attention-deficit/hyperactivity disorder (ADHD).** Children with this disorder are extremely active and impulsive and are more easily distracted (Loe & Feldman, 2007; Umansky & Hooper, 2008). Debate about what causes this disorder is ongoing; most researchers believe that physiological features in the brain are the source of the problem (Mulder et al., 2008; Rommelse et al., 2008). The behaviors of children with ADHD are more problematic during their school years when long periods of sitting and paying attention are expected (Graham, 2008; Wicks-Nelson & Israel, 2002). However, even children in Head Start, child care, or kindergarten are sometimes identified with ADHD.

A variety of strategies have been proposed for addressing the problem, including family interventions to promote warm, supportive, patient, but firm parenting (Bjornstad, 2007; Kern & DuPaul, 2008; Sroufe, 1997). In some cases, medications such as Ritalin have been prescribed. Although controversial, drugs have been found to increase the attention and reduce the disruptive behaviors of some children with ADHD (Kollins, & Greenhill 2006; Poncin, Sukhodolsky, McGuire, & Scahi, 2007). There have been problems associated with using medications (Wilens et al., 2008), as the following story reveals:

A young single mother living in poverty has just given birth to her third child. She suffers from depression and is receiving counseling and parent support services from a community social service agency. Her oldest son, Bobby, has just been enrolled in kindergarten in the elementary school near her home. On the first day of school, Bobby's mother warns the teacher, "Watch out for Bobby. He's a real terror!" She describes the damage Bobby has done to her apartment and the difficulty she has had controlling him. She speaks loudly and within hearing range of Bobby, who stands, staring blankly. As his mother leaves, she explains that Bobby has been prescribed Ritalin, a drug used to control hyperactivity. "That keeps him from being so off-the-wall," she explains. Bobby takes in the whole conversation.

Over the next few days, the head teacher consults with Bobby's family services team. She learns that Bobby has been identified as suffering from ADHD and has been prescribed Ritalin by a physician. She is quite shocked since she has observed that Bobby is lethargic and sluggish—far from hyperactive. The teacher convinces social service providers, the physician, and Bobby's mother to try a few months without medication. Bobby's behavior changes markedly. He is alert, focused, and involved in classroom activities. He is also remarkably active, yet his behavior is manageable. After several days, the teacher recommends that Bobby no longer be medicated.

Much later, the school psychologist comes to suspect that Bobby has been overmedicated by his mother. In fact, Ritalin was prescribed initially because his mother complained to a physician about Bobby's behavior at home.

This story illustrates the complexity of addressing the special needs of preschoolers. Parenting and home environment, family mental health problems, and poverty interact to

attention deficit/hyperactivity disorder (ADHD): A disorder that is characterized by high activity level, impulsiveness, and an inability to pay attention and that often leads to poor peer relations and school performance.

compound Bobby's emotional and educational difficulties. Although prescribing Ritalin can be effective in controlling the challenging behaviors of some children with ADHD (Poncin et al., 2007), there are no simple solutions. Often elaborate family intervention is also necessary. One concern raised about ADHD is that it is an overdiagnosed condition. Any typically active preschooler may be labeled hyperactive by an uninformed parent or professional. Great care must be taken in the preschool years not to confuse high activity level with ADHD.

Some researchers argue that children of historically underrepresented groups are at risk of being mislabeled (Lynn, 2002; Mandell, Davis, Bevans, & Guevara, 2008; Klein & Chen, 2001). For example, the preference of African American children for highly active play may be misinterpreted as an early sign of ADHD (Hale & Franklin, 2001; Neal, McCray, Webb-Johnson, & Bridgest, 2003). What some professionals have called "hyperactivity," "overstimulation," or "uncontrollable behavior" among African American children, Boykin and colleagues (2005) refer to as "verve." A typical high activity level and authentic ADHD are very different things.

What classroom interactions will support the learning and development of children with ADHD? The following strategies have been recommended by specialists (Howard et al., 2004; Kern & DuPaul, 2008):

1. Provide long periods of time and as much space as possible for children with ADHD to engage in active motor play.
2. Keep very brief those periods that require sitting still and waiting or engaging in unpleasant tasks.
3. Provide constant warmth and support; show children with ADHD that they are accepted and loved.
4. Provide a predictable classroom schedule and avoid sudden, unexpected changes in routine.
5. Ignore minor misbehavior or negativism.
6. Enforce rules that really matter by applying brief consequences for misbehavior.
7. Avoid punishment and eliminate anger and verbal aggression in all classroom interactions.

Malnutrition

Malnutrition can have a devastating effect on motor development in the preschool years. Protein energy malnutrition affects approximately half the world's children (Black, 2008). Limited growth and poor skeletal formation have been found in those suffering from this condition. Malnourished young children have been found to be apathetic, listless, and inactive (Lozoff et al., 2007). Problems of malnutrition are not limited to nonindustrialized countries. The number of families in the United States who do not have enough to eat has risen sharply in recent years (Children's Defense Fund, 2007). Nearly 20% of those now living without adequate food are children. Although American children are not as likely to experience severe malnutrition, they suffer delays in growth and limited perceptual and motor development.

The negative effects of malnutrition can be offset by dietary supplements and medical intervention. These are especially effective when provided early in life and when they are coupled with other kinds of support, such as educational programs or family services (Grantham-McGregor et al., 2007a). Sadly, children who are extremely malnourished in the early years may never reach their full developmental potential.

Professionals can join national and international groups in a campaign against childhood hunger in the United States and the world. (See the Advocacy and Public Policy box in this chapter for ideas on how to become involved.)

ADVOCACY AND PUBLIC POLICY

Ending Childhood Hunger

This chapter presents data showing that hunger persists as a problem for families in the United States. Thirty-five million people—including almost 13 million children—live in households that experience hunger or the risk of hunger (U.S. Department of Agriculture, 2004). This represents more than 1 in 10 households in the United States—an increase of 1.3 million families in 1 year. Members of some of these households—including more than 3 million children—frequently skip meals or eat too little, sometimes going without food for a whole day. Members of other families at risk of hunger—including 10 million children—have low-quality diets or resort to seeking emergency food because they cannot always afford to buy it. Preschool children who experience hunger have high levels of chronic illness, anxiety, depression, and behavior problems. They cannot learn, arriving in their Head Start or child care programs each morning feeling irritable, ill, and unable to concentrate. Hunger leads to poor-quality social interactions among young children. It is extraordinary that these problems exist given America's great resources!

In spite of the growing problems of hunger in the United States, some policymakers have proposed cuts to major federal food programs that provide nutritional supplements to families in poverty. For example, some congressional leaders have proposed cuts in the Special Supplemental Nutrition Program for Women, Infants, and Children (WIC), which provides food for 7 million people who live in families with children under 5 (Children's Defense Fund, 2007). Professionals can advocate for a continuation and expansion of food assistance programs to families and children by joining the campaigns of several active nonprofit organizations. They might participate in the activities of the Food Research Action Center (http://www.frac.org), an advocacy organization dedicated to fighting hunger in America. The center organizes citizens' groups in local communities to plan educational programs and political action to protect and expand national anti-hunger programs, particularly the School Breakfast, Summer Food Service, and WIC programs.

Professionals might join in the efforts of Results (http://www.results.org), another anti-hunger organization that focuses on lobbying, letter writing, direct contact with lawmakers, and other political activities. The group's Website provides regular "action alerts" on key pieces of pending legislation related to hunger and child poverty. It also posts information on how to contact legislators and presents the positions on hunger-related issues of candidates running for public office. Professionals might join Bread for the World (http://www.bread.org), a faith-based organization that advocates for an end to hunger worldwide. This group organizes letter writing, fund-raising, and community educational programs on college campuses and in churches to support U.S. legislation that relates to world hunger. In a campaign under way at this writing, for example, the group is organizing a letter-writing strategy to support a bill in the U.S. Senate to increase funds for WIC. Such initiatives help ensure that children arrive in their preschools and child care centers free of hunger and ready to learn.

Obesity

As described in earlier chapters, a growing nutrition-related problem in early childhood is obesity. The number of preschool children in the United States who are considered obese has doubled in the last three decades (National Center for Health Statistics, 2007). Even children who are not obese in the early years may adopt lifestyles that will lead them to become so in the future. A growing percentage of young children have diets high in fat and calories. As early as middle childhood, those eating such diets are more likely to suffer conditions traditionally viewed as adult problems: high cholesterol, respiratory difficulties, sleep apnea, hip injuries, risk of diabetes, and a variety of psychological difficulties (Deitel, 2006; Dubois, 2008). Preschoolers are also less active than there were in previous decades—particularly at home. Part of this descrease in activity is due to a steady increase in television viewing for this age group (Proctor et al., 2003). Children who are less active in play are at risk of becoming obese in later childhood (Rey-López, Vicente-Rodríguez, Biosca, & Moreno, 2007).

There is a higher incidence of obesity among children living in poverty (Kumanyika, 2007). This may be due to lower levels of parental education that are associated with poor feeding practices. In addition, low SES families often live in neighborhoods where fresh, healthy foods are not available and fast food restaurants are prevalent. High-calorie, high-fat processed foods are often more affordable than healthy alternatives. Finally, children in poverty sometimes live in high-crime neighborhoods, so outdoor play activity is restricted. Children of some ethnic groups are more likely to become obese (Crawford, Story, Wang, Ritchie, & Sabry, 2001). For example, rates of obesity are higher for Mexican American preschoolers, especially for girls (Cossrow & Falkner, 2004; Zive, Frankspohrer, Sallis, & Mckenzie, 2003). This is likely due to high calorie cultural food preferences, low activity level among female children, and the high rate of poverty of this cultural group.

A number of programs have been developed to prevent childhood obesity. The outcomes of these have been mixed. Some programs that combine dietary changes and increased activity level have led to modest reductions in young children's body mass index (Summerbell, et al., 2008). Even if some of these efforts did not lead to major reduction in obesity, all of these programs resulted in greater exercise and an improvement in diet in young children. In a review of 13 obesity prevention programs, two other promising approaches were found: 1) reducing children's exposure to television and television advertising of unhealthy foods and 2) providing school-based programs that promote a wide variety of physical activities for children (Haby et al., 2006). It appears that a multifaceted strategey for preventing early childhood obesity is needed. Professionals can play a role by supporting parents in adopting healthy feeding practices, advocating for a reduction in television viewing, and, most important, providing varied and engaging physical play activities in school.

Early Intervention

Generally, the motor development of young children with special needs is greatly enhanced by early intervention programs that provide classroom or home-based education and parent support (C.T. Ramey & S.L. Ramey, 1998). Early identification of special needs is critical. Some studies suggest that if intervention programs are begun in infancy, children will show fewer delays in later years (McCormick, et al., 2006). However, a summary of a large number of studies has shown that even when interventions are not begun until the preschool years, some children show remarkable improvement in motor and cognitive abilities (Shonkoff et al. 1992). It is never too late for intervention, then.

Do typical American preschool programs or home environments offer adequate opportunities to exercise motor abilities? A study by Poest, Williams, Witt, and Atwood (1992) suggests that they do not. In this investigation, preschoolers were not found to engage in adequate physical activity at school or at home regardless of the season. Even in summer, physical activities were limited for many children. One interesting finding of the study was that preschool teachers with more extensive training in early childhood education provided more physical activity for their students. Trained teachers' knowledge of the importance of motor development in the early years may explain this finding. Another study found that young children engage in more physical activity in programs that are rated as "high quality" and those with more teachers with college degrees (Dowda, Pate, Trost, Almeida, & Sirard, 2004). These studies suggest that parent education programs be planned that focus on the importance of adequate motor play at home.

CHILD GUIDANCE: *Talking with Children About Their Art*

It has long been recommended that adults talk with children about their drawings and other artwork. Not only is this a way to promote artistic development, but it facilitates the expression of ideas and feelings as well (Di Leo, 1982). Schirrmacher (2008) cautions, however, that some adult initiatives actually inhibit artistic expression. A *corrective* strategy, in which the adult critiques the child's work in order to promote drawing ability, can be particularly harmful (e.g., "Are squirrels really red? No. They're brown. Can you draw a brown squirrel?"). Positive evaluations of children's work may also inhibit drawing development. When a preschool teacher says, "Look at Julio's beautiful painting!" she may unintentionally giving a message to other children that their work is not as worthy. She may even implicitly be communicating to Julio that it is only the sort of product he has just created that will win adult praise.

Asking children what they are creating may also discourage artistic efforts. Questions such as "What is that?" or "Is that a car?" imply that the adult cannot recognize what is being represented. Further, such queries suggest that children always must be drawing *something*. How might children answer these questions, Schirrmacher asks, if they are merely experimenting with media and not attempting to represent something specific?

How do adults interact with children to promote artistic development? Schirrmacher recommends that they quietly position themselves near children who are engaged in art. Saying nothing at all at first but merely smiling or studying children's work in a reflective way will show interest and enthusiasm but not impose on children as they create. In addition, this moment of quiet observation will allow the adult to come to understand what children are doing so that an eventual conversation, if there is to be one, will be more meaningful. Schirrmacher suggests that children be allowed to talk first; if they say nothing, this may not be an appropriate moment to initiate a conversation.

When children initiate a discussion, adults can respond with comments or questions regarding the media (e.g., "I see you've used some of this rough material in your collage"), the theme of the work (e.g., "Where are the firefighters going in their truck?"), or the overall composition (e.g., "I see you've made an interesting border around the baby. Tell me about that"). Sometimes it is appropriate to ask questions that elicit a discussion of feelings ("So the little boy is about to get a shot? How does he feel about that?"). What is to be avoided, according to Schirrmacher, is any evaluation—positive or negative.

SUMMARY

The preschool years are a time of slow but steady growth. Children gradually get taller and heavier. Their bodies grow more rapidly than their heads, so they lose the top-heavy appearance of infancy. Preschoolers acquire gross motor abilities, like running, climbing, and hopping. Children all over the world learn these skills and apply them to games that are unique to their own culture. In Taiwan, children may chase kites; in Polynesia, waves; and in the United States, their peers in a game of tag. Preschoolers also acquire fine motor skills, enabling them to make puzzles, use scissors, or zip up their own coats. Fine motor growth leads to advancement in drawing ability. Cultural differences exist in artistic skill. Children of Reggio Emilia, Italy, can produce very sophisticated drawings because of cultural and family influences. Motor development is affected by a variety of factors, including gender. American boys tend to be advanced in motor skills; however, this trend is not as pronounced in some other cultures. Challenging conditions can affect motor development. Caregivers and preschool teachers can adapt their interactions and classroom environments to support motor growth of children with special needs.

RESEARCH INTO PRACTICE

CRITICAL CONCEPT 1

Significant changes in physical growth and motor development occur in the preschool years. Children get taller, stronger, and more coordinated. They acquire gross motor skills (abilities to use the large muscles) and fine motor skills (small-muscle abilities) in a predictable sequence.

Application #1 Provide opportunities for preschoolers to exercise large muscles every day. Create areas in classrooms to ensure active play even in inclement weather. These might include low climbers, tossing games, a balance beam, and any other equipment that will fit well in a classroom.

Application #2 Engage preschool children in games that involve running and walking, such as open-ended chasing on the playground, tag, follow-the-leader, and giant steps.

Application #3 Provide climbing equipment on preschool and child care playgrounds. Safe playscapes with platforms children can jump off of will promote important motor skills.

Application #4 Give preschool children toys for catching and throwing, such as soft, large balls, beanbags, and other objects, both in the classroom and on the playground.

Application #5 Make balancing materials available for preschool-age children. Low balance beams, tires, and taped lines on the sidewalk or classroom floor are examples.

Application #6 Appreciate the importance of rough-and-tumble play. Identify safe areas for rough play, such as soft mats and grassy hills. Institute rules for rough-and-tumble play, such as taking your shoes off when wrestling on the mat. Carefully monitor activities to ensure that rough play does not lead to injury.

Application #7 Offer preschoolers a range of small motor experiences in the classroom. Fine motor development is promoted by art activities such as drawing, painting, sculpting, cutting, and making collages and materials such as blocks, puzzles, books, stringing beads, and felt boards.

CRITICAL CONCEPT 2

Children's motor development varies across cultures. Children in some cultural groups acquire certain abilities quickly, others more slowly. How newly learned motor behaviors are used also differs significantly across cultures. Motor play reflects differences in family life and historical tradition; some children play tag, others fly kites, and still others chase sheep or chickens. All these activities promote the same basic motor abilities.

Application #1 Understand and appreciate cultural differences in motor development. Recognize that some children will be more rough or active and that others will be quieter or less motorically advanced. Take care not to construe these differences as deficits.

Application #2 Create a multicultural motor curriculum in the classroom by interviewing families about motor activities and games played in the home. This information can be used to integrate traditional games of diverse cultural groups into classroom play activities. Children will gain motor skills as well as cultural understanding when playing such games.

CRITICAL CONCEPT 3

Emerging fine motor abilities lead to the development of preschool children's art. Their drawings evolve from simple scribbles to representational people and full scenes. Research on early childhood programs in Reggio Emilia, Italy, suggests that children can express themselves artistically at a very early age. Children from this community have been found to use art media in very sophisticated ways to represent what they have learned. This is due to the special value placed on art in this culture and the unique teaching methods used.

Application #1 Integrate the arts—including drawing, painting, and sculpture—into all learning activities and projects.

Application #2 Give more time for the completion of art projects. Encourage children to work on some representational activities for days or even weeks. Encourage them to make many drafts of a single artwork.

Application #3 Provide collaborative artistic experiences. Encourage children to engage in collective representations with peers, parents, and teachers.

Application #4 Display panels on classroom walls, documenting children's artistic representations. Encourage children and parents to study these panels to assess development and learning.

CRITICAL CONCEPT 4

Girls and boys show different patterns of physical growth and motor activity. Some of these differences are related to genetics, others to experience.

Application #1 Understand and appreciate gender diversity in motor play. Do not misconstrue differences in activity level, accuracy or strength in movement, and play preference as deficits that need to be remediated.

Application #2 Afford girls and boys the same motor play opportunities. Encourage all children to be active in the classroom and on the playground. Be careful not to unintentionally promote stereotypic play.

CRITICAL CONCEPT 5

Advancements in motor development allow preschoolers to perform self-help skills and family chores. The kinds of family tasks young children will be assigned vary by culture. Children of European or American families are often given simple tasks, such as straightening their own rooms or helping to wash dishes. In nonindustrialized countries, they may be asked to garden, herd livestock, and care for younger siblings.

Application #1 Plan classroom activities around caring for oneself and helping family members with chores. Encourage children to reflect on ways they assist their family and friends. Such activities will inspire a desire to contribute to family life and the classroom community.

Application #2 Plan daily chores to be assigned to all children in the classroom. Caring for plants and animals, cleaning up after snack, putting away blocks, or helping a friend with a puzzle will give children a sense of responsibility and belonging.

CRITICAL CONCEPT 6

Some preschoolers have challenging conditions, such as neurological disorders or attention-deficit/hyperactivity disorder, that can impair motor activities. Malnutrition can have a devastating effect on development, resulting in physical delays. Poor motor development can be remediated by nutritional and health services and early intervention.

Application #1   Be aware of the characteristics of children who have physically challenging conditions and who suffer from malnutrition. Early identification of exceptionalities is one of the most important responsibilities of professionals working with young children.

Application #2   Support the motor play of children with special needs. Adapt classrooms, equipment, and materials so that all children have access to games and activities. Guide children with physical challenges in exercising small and large muscles.

CRITICAL CONCEPT 7

Early childhood education programs hold promise for ameliorating poor motor development. However, teachers and caregivers need to do more to enhance the quality and frequency of physical activity in school.

Application #1   Ensure that preschoolers get exercise every day. It is an incorrect assumption that children will get all the exercise they need after school at home or at child care.

Application #2   Redesign organized games so that all children are moving all the time while playing them. Games in which less competent children are quickly eliminated and have to sit out (e.g., musical chairs) or in which only one child at a time gets to run or play (e.g., duck, duck, goose) can be modified so that all players are exercising at once.

ASSESSING YOUNG CHILDREN: Preschool Physical and Motor Development

Areas of Development	What to Watch For	Indicators of Atypical Development	Applications
Large motor abilities	Large motor skills, such as walking, running, climbing, throwing and catching, and balancing, by age 4. An ability to start and stop movements quickly and to coordinate actions with those of others. Play abilities such as riding tricycles or kicking balls.	Lack of coordination, balance, and muscle strength. Poor eye–hand coordination. Highly active, impulsive, uncontrollable play behaviors.	Provide long periods of active motor play, indoors and out, that promote specific motor abilities. Plan activities that include sudden starts and stops and involve chasing peers. Use equipment—including climbers—that are accessible to all children, even those with physically challenging conditions. Research and initiate motor games that reflect the cultural groups represented in the classroom.
Perceptual and fine motor abilities	An increasing ability to perform small-muscle tasks, such as molding clay, making puzzles, and cutting with scissors. An ability, by age 6, to draw recognizable figures—heads and stick bodies, for example.	An inability to handle scissors, puzzle pieces, or drawing implements by age 4. Remaining in the scribble stage of drawing and representing no heads or other recognizable shapes by age 6.	Provide a variety of small motor activities, including puzzles, scissors, table blocks, and dressing boards. Include materials that can be used by children with a wide range of skills, including modeling clay and large crayons. Adapt materials and adjust tables and chairs so that children with fine motor delays can more easily play and learn.

Areas of Development	What to Watch For	Indicators of Atypical Development	Applications
Self-help or family life skills	An ability to perform most self-help tasks: feeding, bathing, toileting, and dressing oneself by age 4. An ability and interest in household chores, such as simple cleaning, caring for one's own toys, and attending to the needs of younger siblings.	Poor self-help skills; dependence on others for dressing or toileting beyond age 4. An inability to perform simple household tasks.	Encourage children to participate in daily classroom care, including cleaning, straightening shelves, caring for plants and pets, and preparing snacks. Encourage independence in self-help tasks, such as toileting and dressing for outdoor play. Interview families about their expectations for children's participation in family life tasks.

Interpreting Assessment Data: Culture and individual variations in development will affect these motor abilities. Children will acquire the motor skills emphasized in their particular community and culture. Those who grow up in cultures where there are no games may not acquire throwing, catching, or kicking skills. In families where artistic expression is highly valued, drawing abilities may develop more quickly. In communities where children must contribute to household work for the survival of the family, life skills will emerge at an early age. Significant delays in *all* large and small motor skills may indicate challenging conditions, however. Children who are exceptionally impulsive and active might be referred for evaluation. A motor-based, stress-free preschool program can benefit children with these challenges. Nutritional intervention with families can also address some motor problems at this age.

CHAPTER 11

Cognitive Development in the Preschool Years

GUIDING QUESTIONS

1. What are the major advancements in cognitive development in the preschool years, according to Piaget?
2. What is perception-based thinking, and what challenges can it pose for children and families?
3. What is unidimensional thought, and how can it affect learning and adult-child interactions?
4. What is irreversibility, and how does it affect problem solving?
5. What is transductive reasoning, and how does it influence children's interpretations of events?
6. What is egocentrism, and what are its implications for parents and teachers of preschoolers?
7. What is symbolic thought, and what are some important abilities it allows?
8. What are three experiments that Piaget invented to study young children's cognition, and what does each show about their thinking?
9. What are the major criticisms of Piaget's theory of preschool cognition?
10. How does Vygotsky's view of preschoolers' thinking differ from Piaget's?
11. Why are language and social interaction more important for learning in children of historically underrepresented groups?
12. What are three theories of the mind that most preschoolers acquire, and why are these important in development?
13. How are theories of the mind affected by challenging conditions, culture, and play?
14. What are the characteristics of young children with mental retardation, and how can caregivers and teachers adapt interactions and classroom environments to meet their needs?

Between the ages of 2 and 5 years, children become quite sophisticated in their thinking. Gone are the primitive circular reactions and the trial-and-error problem solving of infancy. Preschool-age children think problems through before acting. They engage in a new form of reasoning that is both impressive and fascinating. This chapter examines these cognitive advancements in the preschool years.

So remarkable are young children's intellectual abilities that adults sometimes forget that preschoolers are still in the early stages of cognitive development. Parents and professionals continually need to remind themselves that preschoolers think in a way that is qualitatively different from adult thinking. The following vignette shows both the new sophistication of young children's thought processes and the cognitive limitations of this age level:

Three 4-year-olds have just completed a traditional card game, Concentration, in their preschool classroom. "I won!" one young player announces. A teacher approaches and asks, "How do you know?" "Easy. I got the most cards," the child answers proudly.

The teacher continues to question the winner. "Great. How did you figure that out?" "Well, because!" exclaims the child, placing his pile of cards next to each of his

playmates' piles in comparison. "See? I've got more!" "So, you have more because your pile is taller?" the teacher asks. "Yep. Got more cards," he answers confidently.

"Wait a minute!" another child protests. "Let me look at something." He spreads his cards end to end on the floor in a line. This line contains so many cards that it extends from the math area out into the center of the classroom. He makes similar lines next to his own with his playmates' cards.

The teacher, observing this, says, "Now, this is interesting. What are you doing?" "Checking to see if Seth won," this second child responds. "Look. See? His line is longer. You did win, you creepo," he says with a laugh.

The teacher asks, "Does everyone agree? Did Seth win?" There are no more challenges or disputes, so the teacher asks no more questions.

"Let's play again," another child offers. They continue playing and determining the winner of each round in this unique way for the rest of the morning.

It is easy to see from this story how far these preschoolers have advanced intellectually since infancy. They invent a very reasonable method of solving the problem of who won the card game. Coming up with two different ways to determine the winner took complex thought. Even so, these children did not solve the problem as an adult would; they did not think to count the cards. They solved the problem by relying on perception: if a pile of cards *looks like* more, it must *be* more. So, preschoolers' thinking is more internal and sophisticated than in earlier years but is still very much tied to concrete objects in the real, observable world.

COGNITIVE DEVELOPMENT IN THE PRESCHOOL YEARS: PIAGET'S THEORY

To Piaget, the preschool years are a period of transition in cognitive development (1952). Young children gradually leave behind the very early thought processes of infancy, which were tied to the concrete world. They can now think beyond objects or people that are immediately before them and are able to reflect on things they cannot see, hear, touch, or act on. They can imagine objects or people that are not present, contemplate future events, and recall past ones.

However, preschoolers do not use logic as adults do, according to Piaget. Their reasoning is hampered by several mental limitations. They still rely too heavily on their senses in their thinking and are easily distracted by the appearance of things. What they see, hear, or touch can actually hinder their problem solving. The following story illustrates this:

A father is driving his 4-year-old son to child care. He introduces a game to make the long drive fun.

FATHER: Let's play "I'm thinking of something." I'll go first…let me see…ah. I've got one. I'm thinking of something green.

CHILD: Christmas trees?

FATHER: Nope. Great guess, though.

CHILD: (Begins to look around the car) Oh, I know. (Digs through his lunch bag) This apple in my lunch?

FATHER: Please don't take your lunch out, David. I'm afraid you'll lose your apple. You won't have it for lunch, then.

CHILD: (Appears to ignore his father's comment) Well?

FATHER: (Becomes distracted by his driving; appears to forget about the game) Um…oh! No. Not the apple.

CHILD: Give me a hint.

FATHER: It's got wheels …

CHILD: (With great excitement) The car! It's green!

FATHER: (Also enthused) Got it! Okay, now it's your turn.

CHILD: (Begins to look obviously around the car) Oh, I know!

FATHER: Got one?

CHILD: (Stares intently at the steering wheel) You'll never get this one. I'm thinking of something black.

The father begins to guess, intentionally not naming the steering wheel although the child looks right at it. As they pull into the parking lot of the child care center, the father gives up. With much laughter, the child reveals that he was thinking of the steering wheel. His father feigns absolute surprise.

In this story, a 4-year-old has displayed quite sophisticated thinking. In his "Christmas trees" guess, he shows he can contemplate things that are not present and events that have occurred in the past. However, in making the apple his second guess, he shows that his thinking is still quite reliant on what he can see and touch. He looks around the car and into the lunch bag in his hands in search of possible solutions. When it is his turn, he chooses something for his father to guess by scanning his immediate physical environment only. His thinking in this case seems limited to what he can see around him.

Because preschoolers' thinking is still based so much on perception and action, Piaget argued that learning at this age requires an environment that is rich in sensory experience and provides much activity with objects. Through active manipulation of play materials, preschoolers gradually construct an understanding of the world. Passive models of learning in which children are instructed directly by adults are useless at this age from Piaget's perspective.

Characteristics of Preoperational Thought

Piaget (1952) provides excellent descriptions of preschoolers' thinking, or what he calls **preoperational thought.** He identifies several fundamental ways that children of this age think differently from adults. These differences are summarized in Table 11-1.

preoperational thought: A kind of thinking used by most young children in which there is still great reliance on perception and physical cues in the environment to learn and solve problems.

TABLE 11-1

Characteristics of Preoperational Thought in the Preschool Years

Characteristic	Example
Perception-based thinking	A child sees two bowls that each hold exactly 10 mango kernels. In one bowl the kernels are spread out. The child reports that that bowl holds more.
Unidimensional thinking	A father who is building a wall asks his daughter to find him a large, square stone. The child goes off and returns with a small square one. "Too little," the father responds. "I need a *large* square." The child goes off again, this time returning with a huge round stone.
Irreversibility	A young preschooler gets her hands on her older brother's science project for school. She completely disassembles it. Her angry father discovers her handiwork and insists she put all the pieces back together. However, she hasn't a clue how to reverse her efforts and place items back the way they were.
Transductive reasoning	A child pushes his younger brother to get a straw doll. As he plays with the doll, he begins to sniffle. All at once, his angry mother is on him. She snatches the doll away and gives it back to the younger sibling. The child believes he has been punished for sniffling.
Egocentrism	A child who is wearing a new pair of moccasins comes across another child who is wearing an identical pair. He becomes terribly upset. "Those are mine," he wails, even though he can see his own moccasins on his own feet.

Perception-Based Thinking. Young children engage in **perception-based thinking,** in which they are fooled by what things look or sound like and cannot use logic to overcome mistaken perceptions. The following vignette illustrates this early form of thought:

> A 4-year-old child lies in bed on a hot night, unable to sleep. His two brothers are sound asleep next to him. He begins to feel alone and afraid. He wiggles and kicks, hoping to rouse one of his older siblings, but they sleep on.
>
> He suddenly spots the curtains blowing in the window. He is certain that he sees a puma climbing in to eat him, so he cries out. Not only do his brothers wake up, but his mother and grandmother do as well. They rush into his room to determine the problem. "It's a puma!" he cries.
>
> "No. You're frightened by the curtains, silly boy," his grandmother says, turning on the light. "See? Just curtains." The preschooler smiles sheepishly. "Just curtains. Yeah. It's the curtains."
>
> The mother sits on his bed, stroking his head. "Go to sleep," she softly urges. His grandmother turns the lights off, then on, then off again to show him that things look different in the dark.

perception-based thinking: A characteristic of preoperational thought in the preschool years in which children are fooled by what things look or sound like and cannot use logic to overcome mistaken perceptions.

Finally, the child and his brothers fall asleep, and the adults leave the room. A short time later, the preschooler wakes again. "Puma! Puma!" he calls out, and the family comes to the rescue once more. The grandmother and mother give up on explanations and simply close the window.

Why does the child's fear continue? He seems to know that what he sees is a curtain blowing in the window. When the light is on, he can laugh and say, "Just curtains." When the light is off, however, his fear returns. Piaget would suggest that this is due to perception-based thinking. If the curtain appears to be a mountain lion, then it must be a mountain lion. To a preschooler, "what you see is what you get."

Unidimensional Thought. Preschoolers tend to focus on only one characteristic of an object or one feature of a problem at a time. They are said to *center* on a single phenomenon and have difficulty coordinating more than one idea or activity. This is called **unidimensional thought.** What would occur if a child care provider were to say to a classroom of 4-year-olds, "I want you to put your paintings in your cubbies, wash your hands, and get ready for lunch, just as soon as we are finished with our story"? It's unlikely the caregiver would even finish this sentence before children started racing to their cubbies. They would center on the caregiver's first instruction and miss the rest of the message.

Following are two other examples that illustrate this kind of thinking:

EXAMPLE 1

A kindergarten teacher is reading a book about a circus to a group of children. When she turns a page, the children see an illustration of a clown that looks vaguely like a local television character.

HANNA:	Oh, look! Chuckles! It's Chuckles the Clown.
TEACHER:	(Smiles and nods) It looks like Chuckles, doesn't it? (Tries to resume reading)
ALONZO:	Know what? I saw the real Chuckles at the mall.
RHONA:	Chuckles is really a man.
ALONZO:	Yeah, but he's a clown too.
TEACHER:	Okay. Well, let's see what happens next at the circus. (Quickly turns the page and attempts to move on with the story)
ALL CHILDREN:	(In unison) Chuckles!
TEACHER:	(Looks at the book and sees that the same clown is depicted on this page as well. Tries to engage the children in the story.) Let me ask you this: Will the clowns from Clown Town ever find the rest of the circus?
MALCOLM:	Chuckles can do magic. He did tricks at my brother's school ....

The teacher finally gives up reading the book and encourages the children to discuss Chuckles the Clown.

EXAMPLE 2

A teacher asks children in her Head Start class to clean up at the end of the morning. She watches in amazement as two children straighten up the block area. They work for many minutes, placing blocks together that are alike. However, they have come up with a very different categorization scheme than an adult would select. When they have finished, she notices that one shelf contains only triangular blocks and is nearly empty. The other shelf is overflowing with the rest of the blocks. She comments on this to the children:

unidimensional thought: A characteristic of preoperational thought in the preschool years in which children focus on only one characteristic of an object or one feature of a problem at a time and have difficulty coordinating more than one idea or activity.

TEACHER: (Pointing to the shelf with the triangular blocks) So why did you only put a few blocks here?

LEVI: See, this is where we put all the triangles. That's how we did it. Triangles right in here. (Pats the shelf proudly)

TEACHER: (Looking at a second shelf) Oh, this is so full of blocks. They're just falling out. Should we put some of these on the emptier shelf? We could put all the small blocks over there, maybe. (Begins to demonstrate, moving blocks from the full shelf to the nearly empty one)

GABRIEL: No! This is for the blocks that aren't triangles. See? Only the triangles go over there.

YANNIS: (Speaking at the same time as Gabriel) That's how we did it. Triangles (points to the nearly empty shelf) and blocks (points to the full shelf).

The teacher does not intervene further. During the next free-play session, other children decide to reshelve the blocks. This time they use a different categorization scheme so that the blocks are more evenly distributed across shelves.

In both examples, the children have centered on one idea or feature of a phenomenon. In example 1, children are so centered on ideas about a local television character that they have trouble focusing on a story. In example 2, children are centered on just one feature of blocks: "triangleness." Their categorizing is based simply on whether a block is a triangle. They have much difficulty thinking about other dimensions of blocks at the same time.

Irreversibility. Piaget (1952) noted that children have difficulty reversing the direction of their thinking. This is called **irreversibility.** A simple test shows this: Take a group of preschoolers for a walk on the playground. Along the way, stop at eight different spots. At the end of the walk, ask the children, "Can you take me back exactly the way we came?" They will have a very difficult time reversing their steps. They might revisit the various stopping points out of order. Or they might simply walk back to the starting point without stopping at all. The problem is that they cannot reverse their thinking. Here is another example:

irreversibility: A characteristic of preoperational thought in the preschool years in which children are unable to reverse the direction of thinking or action.

Preschool children have trouble reversing operations. When taking a walk, they cannot easily retrace their steps back to the starting point.

Two siblings—a 4-year-old and a 5-year-old—sit at the dinner table, watching as their aunt pours a ladleful of beans onto their plates. Each receives one large ladleful; the aunt is careful to be equitable. But an argument erupts nonetheless. The children's plates are of different sizes, causing the amounts of beans to look different. The 4-year-old insists that she has fewer beans. "See? He has more!" she cries.

The exasperated aunt tries to reason with her. "Let me show you something. I'm going to put your beans *back* into the ladle." She scoops the child's beans back into the ladle and says, "See? It's one ladleful, right?" The aunt returns the child's beans to her plate. "Now I'm putting Reuben's beans back in the ladle. Watch." The aunt performs this operation slowly so that the child can see. "Look. He has one ladleful, too. He has one ladleful, and you have one ladleful. You see?" She returns Reuben's beans to his plate.

All is quiet for a moment, and the aunt believes her explanation has been effective. After a few minutes, however, the 4-year-old protests again. "No! Look! He has more!"

It is easy to see how perception-based reasoning plays a role in this controversy. But irreversibility in thinking is also a source of difficulty. Why can't this upset preschooler understand her aunt's logical explanation that each has received the exact same amount? One problem is that she cannot reverse the process of ladling in her mind even when her aunt demonstrates. She cannot mentally transport her beans, then her brother's, back into the ladle to compare their amounts.

Transductive Reasoning. According to Piaget (1952), preschool-age children are much better able to sort out cause and effect than are infants. However, they are still limited in their causal thinking. They tend to put one immediate event into relationship with another immediate event and assume—sometimes erroneously—that one causes the other. For example, if a child is running around his apartment at the same moment that a plant near a window blows over in the wind, the child may associate the two events and assume that his running caused the plant to fall. Piaget called this faulty causal thinking **transductive reasoning.**

Transductive reasoning can cause stress and guilt in young children. For example, if a child is misbehaving just as police arrive at the apartment door to arrest a relative, she could assume that she caused the arrest and feel guilty (Garbarino et al., 1992). Or if a child is scolded for being too active and loud and then moments later is told that his parents are separating, he is likely to feel guilt at causing the separation (Bagshaw, 2007; Hetherington, Bridges, & Insabella, 1998). Adults must be very careful, then, to clarify for preschoolers the nature of relationships between negative life events.

transductive reasoning: A characteristic of preoperational thought in the preschool years in which children put one immediate event into relationship with another immediate event and assume—sometimes erroneously—that one causes the other.

egocentrism: A type of thinking, common in infancy and early childhood, in which children are unable to understand that there are other viewpoints in the world besides their own.

Egocentrism. Piaget believed that preschool-age children still exhibit **egocentrism**—a difficulty understanding others' perspectives, as described in Chapter 7. Piaget devised an experiment to show this (Piaget & Inhelder, 1963). Children were asked to sit at a table and look at a model of three mountains arranged in a particular design. A doll was positioned across from each child. The child was asked to "draw a picture that shows what the doll sees." Piaget found that children under 6 years of age would usually draw the scene not from the doll's perspective but from their own. Not until the elementary years would they understand that the doll's perspective is different from their own and represent this in their drawings.

Of course, egocentrism can have its challenges. A child may have difficulty understanding that others have needs and desires, as the following story illustrates:

A 5-year-old Indian child in a barrio in Mexico busies himself all morning breaking rocks apart in the courtyard of his family's home. He is so fully engrossed that he does not notice all the activity around him. This is the day that everyone takes their produce to the market to sell. His grandparents, parents, older siblings, an aunt, and several close friends who live in the same complex have just finished packing vegetables to carry to town and are now ready to go.

The child's mother calls to him, asking him to follow along. The preschooler refuses. "No! I have to finish my rocks," he insists. Ignoring the fact that his entire family is packed and waiting, he picks up another rock and begins to pound on it. His mother grasps him by an arm and tries gently to pull him away from his work. He resists. "One more," he compromises. So, while the entire family waits, he pounds the rock for several more minutes until it breaks apart. Satisfied, he joins his family on their trip to the market.

Symbolic Thought. One of the most significant advancements in the preschool years, according to Piaget, is the acquisition of **symbolic thought.** This is a form of thinking in which symbols are used to stand for things that are not present. Language is a good example of symbolic thought. When speaking, children use words as symbols to stand for things. Symbolic thought also occurs in play. A toy telephone is used to make a pretend call, or an empty cup is used to drink pretend milk. Simple words are spoken to represent actions, persons, or objects. In the later preschool years, children begin to use even more abstract symbols, or what Piaget called *signs*. Sophisticated sentences are constructed to stand for whole ideas. Drawing and scribbling are used to "write" stories. Young children engage in complex make-believe in which they use gestures, objects, or their own bodies to stand for things that are completely different.

Piagetian Tasks

Piaget invented fascinating experiments to show some of these unique aspects of young children's thinking. In these experiments, children were asked to perform problem-solving tasks that highlight specific cognitive processes. Some of these tasks and the children's responses to them are described in Table 11-2.

symbolic thought: A form of thinking in which symbols are used to stand for things that are not present. Language, reading, writing, and pretend play all require symbolic thought.

TABLE 11-2
Piagetian Tasks That Show Preoperational Thought

Task	Description and a Preoperational Child's Performance
Conservation of number	A child is shown two sets of objects that are equivalent but are arranged in different patterns. The child will report that one set has more than the other.
Conservation of continuous quantity	A child is shown two differently shaped containers that hold equal amounts of water. The child will report that one container holds more than the other.
Categorization	A child is presented with objects that have multiple attributes; they vary by size, color, and shape. The child is asked to put "the things that are alike together." The child will use only one attribute—say, color—to categorize. For example, all yellow, green, or blue shapes will be placed together regardless of shape or size.

Conservation. Piaget proposed that preschoolers lack **conservation,** an understanding that properties and amounts stay the same even when physical appearances are changed. Adults have acquired conservation. They know, for example, that if orange juice is poured from a small cup into a large cup, the amount remains constant. Young children do not understand this; their lack of conservation can lead to faulty problem solving.

Piaget devised an experiment to show that young children lack **conservation of number.** The steps of the experiment are shown in Figure 11-1. Sitting with individual children, Piaget would spread out two sets of eight objects—say, red and black checkers—on a table. The checkers would be lined up in one-to-one correspondence: each black checker was lined up with a red one (see step a). Piaget would ask the child, "Are there more red checkers, are there more black checkers, or are there the same amount of black and red?" Preschool-age children would invariably announce that the sets were equivalent.

Next, Piaget would reconfigure one line of checkers (see step b). He might bunch the black ones together or spread them out farther than the red ones. The important thing was to make the two sets of checkers *look* different. Preschoolers were then asked, "Are the sets of checkers still the same, or are there more black ones or red ones?" Children would now argue that the spread-out set (or possibly even the bunched-up one) had more. Piaget would challenge children's thinking at this point, asking, "You said before that there were as many red as black checkers. Are you saying now that there are more red ones?" or "Another child told me she thought there were still as many black as red ones. What do you think?" Piaget would even ask children to count the checkers. No matter how many hints were given, however, children under age 5 or 6 would hold to their belief that one set or the other had more.

Why? It is because of all the limitations in thinking just described. Children are fooled by perception. If one set *looks* like more, it must *be* more. No amount of logic will dissuade a young child from believing this. In addition, children of this age center on only one

conservation: An understanding that properties and amounts stay the same even when their physical appearances are changed.

conservation of number: A type of conservation in which children understand that amounts of objects stay the same even if they have been rearranged.

Step a:

Step b:

OR

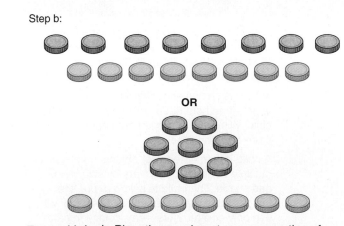

FIGURE 11-1   In Piaget's experiment on conservation of number, children are shown an arrangement of checkers, as shown in step a. Then the checkers are rearranged in different ways, as shown in step b. After the arrangement, preschoolers often report that one group of checkers now has more than the other.

dimension of the problem. They might focus on the length of the line and say, "This one has more because it's longer." Or they might center on thickness of the collection of checkers and claim, "This one has more because it's thicker." They cannot consider both length and thickness at the same time.

Children also struggle with this experiment because they lack reversibility. They cannot mentally rearrange the checkers back into a line after they have observed them being pushed together. Elementary-age children can do this and often will respond to this task by saying, "This is the same because if you spread the checkers back out again, they would be just the same as the other set."

Piaget designed a similar task to show how children lack **conservation of continuous quantity.** This experiment is illustrated in Figure 11-2. In this experiment, Piaget had children watch as he poured the same amount of water into two identical containers (see step a). Next, he would pour the water from one container into a much wider one (step b). The child would watch as this was done. Now the water levels would be very different, as depicted in step c. When preschool children were then asked which container had more, they might say the narrow container had more because the water was "higher" or that the wide container had more because the water was "fatter." Only after age 6 or 7 did children respond that the quantity of water was the same in both containers. Even with repeated hints ("I didn't take any water out; I just poured it into another container"), younger children were fooled.

Again, this task shows perception-based thinking. To the child, one container *looks* like it has more water, so it *must* have more. Unidimensional thinking is evident as well. Children center on the height or wideness of the water but cannot think about both concepts at the same time. Finally, the task demonstrates irreversibility in children's thinking. They cannot mentally reverse the operation. That is, they cannot imagine the water in the new container being poured back into the original one.

conservation of continuous quantity: A type of conservation in which children understand that amounts of liquid or other substances stay the same even when they are put in different-size containers.

Categorization. In a very different experiment, Piaget demonstrated unidimensional thinking by asking children to categorize objects. In this **categorization** task, children were presented with items of different colors and shapes and asked to "put the things that are alike together." Preschoolers would often sort by color (e.g., putting all yellow objects together and all blue objects together), by shape (e.g., putting all triangles together and all squares together), or by size (e.g., putting all large objects together and all small objects together). Rarely did they rely on two or more dimensions at the same time (e.g., putting all large yellow triangles in one pile and all small blue triangles in another and so on). A typical categorization scheme used by preschoolers is presented in Figure 11-3.

categorization: A mental activity in which children put objects that are alike together. Early categorization is based on one characteristic (e.g., size, color, or shape), later categorization on two or more traits (e.g., placing shapes of the same color together).

FIGURE 11-2   In Piaget's experiment on conservation of continuous quantity, children are shown two same-size containers with equivalent amounts of liquid, as shown in step a. Then the contents of one container is poured into a shorter, wider container, as illustrated in step b. In step c, the child is asked, "Which container holds more?" Preschoolers regularly state that one of the containers now holds more liquid than the other.

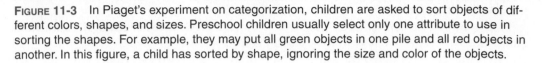

FIGURE 11-3   In Piaget's experiment on categorization, children are asked to sort objects of different colors, shapes, and sizes. Preschool children usually select only one attribute to use in sorting the shapes. For example, they may put all green objects in one pile and all red objects in another. In this figure, a child has sorted by shape, ignoring the size and color of the objects.

Piaget noticed that young children would sometimes shift from relying on one property to relying on another when categorizing. A child might, for example, start out by putting one blue triangle down, then a red one, and then a green one, relying first on shape. But since the last item was green, the child might shift suddenly to the property of color and put down a green square, a green circle, and a green rectangle. Next, the child might switch to rectangles in categorizing. In the end, a child might place all shapes into a single category! Only in the elementary years did Piaget find that children were able to use multiple properties to categorize. After age 6 or 7, children would put blue triangles in one pile, green triangles in a separate pile, and so on. This experiment shows how young children center on one property or another—but not more than one—in problem solving.

CRITICISMS OF PIAGETIAN THEORY

Piaget studied children of Western backgrounds without the benefit of the sophisticated laboratory techniques available today. In spite of this, recent studies have shown that his general descriptions of young children's thinking are quite accurate. Some research findings, however, indicate that he may have underestimated preschoolers' intellectual abilities (Bjorklund, 2005). There are several major reasons for Piaget's misjudgment about preschoolers' cognitive abilities: (a) cultural variations, (b) faulty research methods, and (c) the role of language and social interaction in learning.

Cultural Variations

Children of all cultures show fundamental characteristics of preoperational thought. However, minor variations exist in the performance of specific Piagetian tasks from one cultural group to the next. In a classic study of cognitive development in Mexico, researchers discovered that children of families who make pottery acquired conservation skills much earlier in development than Piaget would have predicted (Price-Williams et al., 1969). How can this be explained? Pottery making would seem to require many judgments about quantity: How much clay should be used to make an urn or bowl of a certain size? How much water should be added to obtain the correct consistency? As children in this community assist their parents in making pots, they have unique experiences with quantity that their European peers do not have.

Children of many Asian cultures have also been found to acquire Piagetian competencies, like conservation, earlier than Euro-American children (Mishra, 2001). One explanation for these differences is that parents in some families value more highly the skills of estimating quantity and emphasize these skills subconsciously in everyday life (Ogbu, 1994). They might guide children's attention to amounts in all family activities by asking questions (e.g., "Can you get enough water to fill the urn?"). In European families, these abilities are not as essential for a successful adult life.

Children of some cultural groups are found to acquire Piagetian cognitive skills more slowly than children in Euro-American cultures: those of Senegal, Algeria, Nepal, most African countries, as well as Native Americans (Mishra, 2001). Does this mean that children of these societies are intellectually inferior? Certainly not. As in the pottery-making example, these findings may simply reflect differences in the particular skills that are valued or emphasized. Abilities needed to succeed in Piagetian tasks may not be as important in some families. For example, quantifying objects may be a less significant aspect of daily life in a community in which sharing and collective ownership are the norm (Klein & Chen, 2001). When everything is shared, there is little need for making judgments about amounts.

Nyiti (1982) has suggested that deficits found in young children of some cultures may be due to cultural bias in research. When Western, English-speaking researchers present Piagetian tasks to children of very different cultures, they may not get a full picture of cognitive competence. Cultural or linguistic barriers may impede performance. Nyiti found, for example, that Micmac Indian children of Nova Scotia showed far lower levels of functioning if they were tested in English instead of their native language.

Finally, it must be acknowledged that some delays in the acquisition of cognitive abilities in certain communities are just that: true delays. Malnutrition, poor health care and education, and violence—which, sadly, afflict nonindustrialized countries most often—may result in poor cognitive development among some children in the world (Farver, Natera, & Frosch, 2002).

Flaws in Research

Research flaws of other kinds also have been cited to explain Piaget's underestimation of preschoolers' abilities. Some researchers have changed Piaget's experiments slightly or designed new ones, using more sophisticated technology. Resulting findings indicate that children may be more competent than Piaget has proposed. For example, several researchers altered Piaget's "three mountains" experiment (discussed earlier) and found that even 2 year-olds could represent what a doll is looking at if provided with appropriate means for reporting this (Borke, 1975; Moll & Tomasello, 2006). Unlike Piaget, these investigators did not ask children to draw the doll's view of the mountains—a very difficult task at this age. Instead, they placed the three mountains on a turntable and asked children to *show* what the doll was looking at by turning it. Even very young preschoolers could turn the turntable one way and say, "I'm looking at this," and then turn it the other way and say, "The doll is looking at this." So, children may be less egocentric than Piaget's original experiments indicate.

Several researchers invented new methods for studying children's unidimensional thinking (N. H. Anderson & Cuneo, 1978; Cuneo, 1980; Yuzawa, Bart, & Yuzawa, 2002). In these studies, preschoolers were shown rectangular cookies that varied in height and width. They were asked which cookies would make them most happy. The overall mass of the cookie was the characteristic that influenced children's answers. Thick, narrower cookies or thin, wide ones were equally likely to be chosen, whereas cookies that were both narrow *and* thin were not selected. So children seemed to be able to take into account both thickness *and* width in solving this problem. Why do children show unidimensional thinking on Piaget's tasks but not on this one? The task may be more interesting when cookies are used instead of checkers. Motivation may be higher when more meaningful (and tasty!) objects are used.

Researchers have shown that when Piaget's conservation tasks are altered, results are quite different. In one now-famous study, the conservation of number task was conducted again in a unique way. Instead of a researcher, a "naughty teddy bear" (a puppet) spread out one row of the checkers (Dockrell, Campbell, & Neilson, 1980). Amazingly, more 4-year-olds could solve the problem under this condition than in Piaget's original experiment. How can the addition of a make-believe animal cause such an improvement in children's thinking? The researchers concluded that the playful atmosphere of the test allowed children to focus on the problem itself rather than on what the adult experimenter was doing and saying. In the original experiment, children may have been distracted by the fact that a very serious grown-up had altered one set of checkers. They may have come to believe that one set of checkers had more than the other because an adult had done something to it. The manner, language, and appearance of adult experimenters might influence children's performance on one-on-one tests.

VYGOTSKY'S PERSPECTIVE ON COGNITIVE DEVELOPMENT

One concern raised about Piaget's theory is that it does not fully recognize the contributions of language and social interaction to development. Many of Piaget's observations were of individual children, and his tasks were designed to be completed by one child at a time. Piaget did not emphasize the role of adults in his work. In his descriptions of his own children at play, references to parents were so rare that some readers have humorously asked, "Where was Mrs. Piaget?"

Vygotsky (1978) has argued that children's thinking is highly influenced by interactions and conversation with other people. If we want to know how children think and learn, he proposes, we need to observe them in natural interchanges with others. The following vignette illustrates how real-life interactions influence children's problem solving:

A kindergarten teacher has placed objects from nature, boxes, markers, and labels on a large table in the science center of his classroom. Children are invited to make a museum here by putting things that are alike together and labeling them "just like in a real museum." Two children are hard at work, creating categories and making labels.

ELORA: I think we should put these nests (holds up a bird's nest) and the bee things (points to a wasp's nest) together, all right, Sean?

SEAN: No, 'cause the bee nests are too small. Small ones go here (points to a pile of small objects of different kinds that he has assembled).

ELORA: (In an annoyed tone) That's not how you do it, Sean. You don't put little things all together at museums. You put nests together and rocks together, like this. (Demonstrates these ideas by moving objects from Sean's pile)

SEAN: (In an angry voice) No! You're messing it up. You're making a mess with my museum!

TEACHER: (Moving over to the science center) What's up here? You both sound angry.

SEAN: (Loudly) Elora moved all my stuff. I made a pile, and she says I can't. See? She moved my things all around.

ELORA: But he's not making a museum. He's just getting the little stuff and putting it here.

TEACHER: So, he's making a pile of little objects. And you want to make different kinds of piles. Is that right? So, what can we do about that?

SEAN: (In a calmer tone) Make Elora put my pile back.

ELORA: We could make a nest pile with big things and a nest pile with little things. All right, Sean? See? (Begins to move objects around the table again)

SEAN: (Shows interest but says nothing)

TEACHER: (To Sean) See what she's doing? She's putting all the nests together, but then you can put the small nests in one place and the bigger nests in a different place.

ELORA: (Already categorizing objects) See, Sean? This is a pile for little nests. And
           you can make a pile for little rocks and…little stuff. (Laughs)
SEAN: Okay, but I do all the little stuff. (Joins Elora in categorizing)

The children in this story are categorizing. Initially, Sean uses a simple feature, size, to create a pile. Elora has a different scheme in mind. The resulting dispute, including intervention by an adult, leads to a very complex, multidimensional categorization strategy. The children sort objects first by their origin in nature and then by size. What led to this advanced mode of thinking? Sean's thought processes were challenged by Elora and by the kindergarten teacher. Would Sean have developed such a sophisticated museum had he not been working with a peer?

Vygotsky (1978) has argued that young children cannot show their highest levels of thinking when they are alone. He suggests that when children get support from a more competent peer or an adult, they are far better at solving problems. When Elora says, "You put nests together and rocks together," she provides a structure for Sean's categorization. At the same time, she encourages his independent problem solving. In other words, she *scaffolds* his problem solving without performing the task for him.

Parents and teachers are also found to naturally scaffold children's learning (Bjorkland & Reubens, 1997; Freund, 1989; Trawick-Smith, 2008). They ask questions or give hints while giving children as much responsibility as possible. The teacher's statements in the story demonstrate scaffolding: "So, he's making a pile of little objects. And you want to make different kinds of piles. Is that right? So, what can we do about that?" Again, a supportive structure is provided for problem solving; the actual solution, however, is left up to the children.

Vygotsky proposed that language plays a particularly critical role in learning. He noted that preschooler's **self-directed speech**—the inner-directed language described in Chapter 3— helps children guide their own attention and to organize ideas internally. When they talk to themselves, children think at higher levels (Fernyhough & Fradley, 2004). Where does private speech come from? To Vygotsky, it originates from verbal instructions and other messages from adults and peers. When a parent says to a child in a mosque, "Sit still and pray," the child may be heard repeating this phrase quietly to guide self-control. When a Head Start teacher says, "Use words when you're angry, don't hit," children may be heard uttering this statement to direct social problem solving. Contrary to Piaget's position, Vygotsky believed that such direct verbal instructions from adults contribute significantly to cognitive development.

To Vygotsky, then, preschoolers would solve problems more competently than Piaget proposed if they were able to talk and socialize. How would Piaget's preschool subjects have performed on his tasks if they had been encouraged to work on them with peers or if an adult had been scaffolding their activities?

Culture and Social and Language Interactions

For preschoolers of some cultures, social and language interaction is especially critical for learning. Children of Euro-American cultures have been described as **field-independent learners** (Guisande, Tinajero, & Almeida, 2007; Rodriquez, 1983); that is, they have a unique cognitive style that allows them to solve problems without much outside assistance. They can focus on the specific steps of a task without being distracted by the full external environment, or the field. They are better able to work alone.

Children in other cultures tend to be **field-sensitive learners.** This means that they rely on the entire environment and everything and everyone in it to solve problems. Mexican American, Puerto Rican, and African American children tend to display this cognitive style. When field-sensitive children perform a Piagetian task, they will not just look at the checkers or the container of water. They will attend to everything around them: the whole room, the noises and voices coming from outside, and even the expressions of the experimenter. Such a

self-directed speech: A verbal behavior in which children talk to themselves, naming objects or narrating their actions— particularly as they solve problems.

field-independent learners: Learners with a cognitive style that allows them to solve problems without much outside assistance and to focus on the specific steps of a task without being distracted by the full external environment, or "the field."

field-sensitive learners: Learners with a cognitive style that leads them to rely on the entire environment and everything and everyone in it to solve problems.

Children of some cultures are very reliant on social interaction and conversation with others in solving problems.

child might search the adult's face, for example, for clues in solving a problem. The most important characteristic of field-sensitive children is a need for social interaction and language in order to learn. This need arises from unique cultural experiences. In particular, the collective behavior and action of family members within some cultures tends to nurture a field-sensitive cognitive style (Klein & Chen, 2001). It is clear that field-sensitive children, more than others, require the kind of social scaffolding that Vygotsky describes.

Unfortunately, the vast majority of preschool and elementary school teachers in the United States are from field-independent cultures. They tend to develop learning activities that are geared to their own cognitive style, such as puzzles to be completed by just one child or easels with space for just one painter at a time. Field-sensitive preschoolers perform less well on some of these tasks (Guisande et al., 2007). Later in life, in a typical test-and-drill elementary school, they are at a special disadvantage (Rodriquez, 1983). An implication of this research is that school and home environments should be structured to allow extensive social interaction and conversation. Cooperative projects and play activities can be designed to meet the needs of preschoolers with diverse cognitive styles.

NEW PERSPECTIVES ON PRESCHOOL COGNITION

Newer theories of young children's cognitive development have been formulated. Siegler (2000, 2004, 2007a, 2007b) argues that Piaget provided an excellent framework for understanding children's *thinking* but offered little detail on how thinking processes are actually acquired over time. "We know little about how children get from here to there," Siegler writes (2000, p. 26). He suggests that memory, attention, and other learning strategies be examined more closely to gain a full understanding of the steps children follow to acquire the cognitive abilities they have. The following story illustrates his idea:

A school psychologist is implementing a new strategy with a kindergarten child, Marnie, in an effort to reduce her aggressive behavior toward her peers. He uses videotaped examples of aggression to help her better understand the consequences of this behavior and to learn alternatives for solving social problems. He invites Marnie's parents to join in the discussion.

PSYCHOLOGIST: Marnie, I want to show you a videotape of children playing. (Starts the tape; points to the screen) See what that little boy is doing?

MARNIE: (Says nothing)

FATHER:	See, Marnie? The little boy's being mean.
MARNIE:	Yeah.
FSYCHOLOGIST:	What happens when the little boy pushes the little girl?
MARNIE:	He grabs the block.
PSYCHOLOGIST:	Right. He got that block he wanted, but what else? What did the other children do when he pushed her?
MARNIE:	I don't know.
MOTHER:	Did you see that part, Marnie? What did the children do?
MARNIE:	I don't know.
PSYCHOLOGIST:	I'm going to show you that part again, all right? Watch carefully. Look at what the other children do. (Rewinds and replays the tape)
MARNIE:	Oh, they're walking away.
PSYCHOLOGIST:	Right. They're angry, aren't they? See their faces? They don't like being pushed. So, see how they move away from the little boy? They don't want to play with him now.
MARNIE:	Yeah. (Points to the screen) That guy's mad.
PSYCHOLOGIST:	He is mad. He's walking away. So, what should the little boy do if he wants a block. What can he do so his friends won't walk away from him?
MARNIE:	I don't know.
MOTHER:	Could he use words instead of pushing?
PSYCHOLOGIST:	That's a good idea. What could he say, Marnie, to get that block?
MARNIE:	"I want a block."
PSYCHOLOGIST:	That might work.
FATHER:	Maybe, "Can I please have that block?" How about that?
MARNIE:	Okay. "I want the block, please."
PSYCHOLOGIST:	What else could the boy do to get the block so that his friends won't be angry?

The session goes on for many minutes. The adults continue guiding the child in thinking about the pushing incident on the videotape.

Piaget would believe that this child gains a new understanding of aggressive behavior through *assimilation* and *accommodation* (described in Chapter 3). In this session, she relies first on her previous concept of pushing: that it's something you can do to get what you want (in this case, a block). This is assimilation. As the adults talk with her, she changes her view a little. This is accommodation. She comes to understand that pushing leads peers to walk away and become angry—something she hasn't thought about before. She also learns that there are other ways to get what you want besides brute force (e.g., asking with words).

Siegler (2007b) would argue that Piaget's explanation is accurate but that the explanation doesn't tell the whole story. There are many questions about *how* the child has learned these ideas that Piaget does not answer with his theory. For example, why does the girl not initially notice children's reactions to pushing on the tape? What causes her to finally focus on this part of the event? Why does she not at first see the anger on children's faces but later say, "That guy's mad"? Siegler would suggest that the girl has applied specific learning strategies that help her better understand this social event. These learning strategies are a fundamental part of cognitive development.

For example, the girl begins to *attend* more carefully to certain features of the pushing incident with help from adults (e.g., "Watch carefully"). She identifies the internal mental states of children on the tape with prompting from the psychologist (e.g., "They're angry, aren't they? See their faces?"). What's missing from Piaget's view, according to Siegler, is a detailed explanation of children's internal learning processes and adults' roles in supporting these.

Attention

One cognitive process that helps the child in this story to learn is **attention**—an ability to focus for an extended period on the important features of a situation or problem. As children get older, they are able to better control what they pay attention to. Very young preschoolers tend to focus on many different aspects of a situation, almost at random. They give little careful thought to what is most important to look at or listen to. Generally, 4- and 5-year-olds are better able to focus on the things that are critical for solving a problem or pleasing peers or adults (P. H. Miller & Seir, 1995). At this age, their control over attention comes and goes. One minute they might focus on an important aspect of a preschool activity but the next be distracted by something occurring in another part of the room.

What helps young children learn to attend to things that matter? Adults often guide their attention. "I want you to pay attention" and "Look carefully at this" are phrases used commonly by parents and teachers. Research suggests that such statements lead to greater control over attention (Flavell, Miller, & Miller, 1993). Marnie, in the previous story, is greatly assisted in paying attention to the consequences of pushing and the angry feelings of peers by adult guidance. Over time she will be able to focus better on these things on her own.

One other thing that will help Marnie control her attention and learning is a theory of the mind, to be considered next.

Theories of the Mind

A fascinating cognitive advancement in the preschool years is a **theory of the mind** (Flavell, 2004). At a surprisingly young age, children begin to understand—or form a theory about—what the mind is, how it works, and how it might be controlled. These understandings help children learn and think at ever-higher levels (Carlson, Mandell, & Williams, 2004). A theory of the mind sounds extremely sophisticated—far too complex, it would seem, for preschool-age children to understand. Yet there is evidence that children as young as age 2 do form such a theory (Carlson et al., 2004). Signs of this can be observed within simple play activities, as the following story reveals:

> A 4-year-old child plays with her 18-month-old brother in her family's small house in rural Kenya. She is playing a chasing game: she taunts her sibling, then runs away from him. He toddles after her, shrieking with delight. At one point she climbs into an enormous basket, and her brother loses sight of her for a moment. "He doesn't know I'm in here," she whispers to her mother, who is working in the kitchen. "He thinks I ran out the door." Sure enough, her brother toddles out the front door looking for her. His mother brings him back in.
>
> The chasing game continues and becomes more wild. Because the house is so small, the noise and activity begin to annoy the mother, who is busy preparing food. At one point the toddler bumps a table, tipping a bowl and sending berries rolling onto the floor. This is all the mother can tolerate. "No more running!" she scolds. "Stop it now!" Her daughter appeals: "He didn't mean to knock over the berries. It was an accident." The mother is not moved by the argument, however, so the girl and her brother find a quieter game to play.

Where is evidence of a theory of the mind in this story? The young girl's language gives one clue. She uses words such as *know, think,* and *mean to*—terms that describe internal mental states. More important, she shows an understanding of the inner workings of the mind that are represented by these words. She demonstrates a grasp of inner motives with the statement "He didn't *mean* to knock over the berries." The utterance "He doesn't *know* I'm in here" displays an awareness that the mind can understand or know about something. The most significant revelation in the story is that this preschooler can comprehend not only her own thinking processes but also

attention: The ability to focus for an extended period on the important features of a situation or problem.

theory of the mind: A belief about what the mind is, how it works, and how it might be controlled that helps children learn and think at ever-higher levels.

those of another person. She can guess—and quite accurately—what her brother knows, thinks, or intends. It is truly amazing that such a young child can contemplate the mind—a highly abstract concept that has puzzled adult philosophers and scientists throughout history!

Why is a theory of the mind important? It is one thing to just think; doing so enables us to learn, solve problems, or make decisions. It is quite another to think about *how* we think. In doing so, we attend to our inner mental processes. For example, we can reflect on the steps our minds go through in learning something, or we can contemplate the source of our feelings or attitudes. When we are aware of our own thought processes, we are able to control or modify them. When we can contemplate the feelings or thinking of others, we can interact with them more effectively.

Psychologists speak of *theories* (plural) of the mind because many believe that children construct understandings of the mind in separate pieces. It is only in adulthood that a coherent, integrated theory of how the mind works is formulated. At least three distinct types of theories of the mind have been found to emerge in early childhood, each of which plays a function in children's cognitive and social development. These are presented in Table 11-3.

Theories About Internal Emotional States. Theories about internal emotional states are particularly useful in social interactions. Five-year-old Marnie, in the story at the beginning of this section, would benefit greatly from a better understanding of the feelings of others. Children who can read emotions are better able to decide how to interact with adults and peers. They can make judgments about when a peer is grumpy and should be left alone or when another is happy and in the mood to play. In some cases, a child's very survival can depend on the theory of the mind, as the following sad story illustrates:

A 4-year-old is playing in her apartment when her father bursts into the room. She has not seen him in a long time because he and her mother separated after a long period of fighting. She wants very much to talk and play with him and to get a hug, but she can tell by the way he has entered that he is angry and drunk. The child knows that, when he gets this way, he can be mean and even physically abusive. So she says

Theory	Description
Internal emotional states	Preschool children can accurately interpret their own emotions and those of others. Further, they know that emotions come from within and may be hidden from other people.
Motives and intentions	Preschool children can interpret others' motives as long as they are obvious. They can also accurately identify the intentions behind actions. Statements such as "He was trying to be mean" and "He didn't mean to; it was an accident" show these theories of the mind.
Knowing and remembering	Preschool children have a general understanding of internal thought processes. They know that "know," "remember," "guess," "forget," and "pay attention" are things that occur in the mind, though they have trouble differentiating among these concepts.

TABLE 11-3
Theories of the Mind That Emerge in the Preschool Years

nothing to her father but backs quietly out of the room. As she exits, her mother enters from the kitchen, yelling at her father. She escapes to the front porch, where she sits with her hands over her ears to muffle the sounds of their argument.

Theories of Motives and Intentions. Another theory of the mind relates to motives. Preschool children are able to interpret, to some degree, their own motives as well as others' (Leslie, Knobe, & Cohen, 2006). Children as young as age 3 have an understanding of what motives are and can distinguish between positive and negative motives. They might report that a peer knocked down a block structure because she was "being mean" or that another shared a snack because he was "being nice." They can analyze their own motives for behavior as "bad" or "good." By the end of the preschool years, they can even identify whether behaviors are intentional or unintentional. By the time children reach age 4 or 5, teachers can help them reflect on social problems by noting that "He didn't mean to" or "It was just an accident."

Interestingly, children who have problems with aggression tend to be less able to accurately describe the intentions of their peers. They more often interpret benign behaviors or accidental mishaps as intentional and malicious (Lemerise & Arsenio, 2000). It is easy to see how this limitation in thinking would affect Marnie's problems with aggression in the previous story. She may be aggressive because she believes, falsely of course, that so many things her peers do are intended to harm her.

Theories of Knowing and Remembering. Preschoolers reveal theories of knowing and remembering when they play. When children announce, "We're the police, remember?" or "I know who you're pretending to be," they are showing a knowledge of these thinking processes. Children as young as 5 have been found to indicate what others know when they participate in classic theories of mind experiment (Call & Tomasello, 1999). Here's how the experiment works: Pairs of children are shown where a toy is hidden within a room. One of the children is asked to leave. The second child watches the researcher hide the toy in a different place. The researcher then asks this second child, "When your friend comes back, where will she look for the toy?" Children who do not understand what a peer *knows* will point to the new hiding place because they can't differentiate between their own thinking and that of others. Children who understand about others' knowing will point to the original hiding place and say, "She'll look here, because that's where it was before she left." By age 5 years, most children accurately perform this task.

Of course, the exact meanings of some of these concepts may not be fully acquired until later childhood (Lovett & Pillow, 1991). Young children have been found to define *know* or *remember* as "getting the right answer," for example. Still, preschoolers are aware of and have some control over knowing and remembering processes. They understand that *know, remember,* and *pay attention* involve doing something special in the mind. When a parent says "Now remember" or a teacher says "Try to learn this," children give special attention to the information that follows. They are more likely to retain it than if they were not given these cues (Flavell, 2004).

Variations in Theories of the Mind

Children begin to formulate theories of the mind at about the same age and in similar ways across many cultures and ability levels.

Challenging Conditions. Even challenging conditions may not impede theories of the mind from being formed. In one study, 4-year-olds with Down syndrome were found to be as capable as typically developing preschoolers at solving tasks that require guessing what others are thinking (Baron-Cohen & Ring, 1994). In other investigations, children with moderate language delays were discovered to perform well on tasks where they were to anticipate others' thoughts (Hughes et al., 2005; Farrant, Fletcher, & Maybery, 2006).

Of course, the more severe these conditions, the more difficult it is for children to form theories of the mind. Children with severe language disabilities, for example, were found to be unable to understand verbal instructions on theories-of-the-mind tasks or to use words like "knowing" or "remembering" (Jenkins & Astington, 1996). For the most part, however, research suggests that most young children—even those with some cognitive impairment— form beliefs about what their parents, peers, and teachers are thinking and feeling.

Autism may be one significant exception. Autism is a condition characterized by a lack of awareness of others, a preference for objects to people, and an intense desire for sameness. Other symptoms include language delays, self-destructive behavior, and repetitive, ritualistic body movements (Honey, Leekam, Turner, & McConachie, 2006). Making sense of multiple stimuli is a problem for autistic children. They have trouble piecing together information from many different sources to gain an understanding of the whole. For example, they tend to have difficulty interpreting the many visual and auditory cues (e.g., words, intonations, and facial expressions) of a person talking. So, the full message is often missed.

Preschoolers with autism often perform poorly on tasks related to theories of the mind. They have difficulty interpreting others' motives, beliefs, and thoughts (Peterson, Wellman, & Liu, 2005; Shaked, Gamliel, & Yirmiya, 2006). In fact, some researchers hypothesize that autistic children's poor social and emotional functioning may be attributed, in large degree, to a failure to form accurate theories of the mind. If autistic children are not aware of the internal feelings of others, they may become less interested in or committed to relationships. They may be less likely also to understand the emotional impact of their social behaviors. If they are not aware of the mental processes involved in paying attention, they may be less likely to guide their minds to focus on important social and learning cues.

Culture and Theories of the Mind. Long ago, a prevalent theory in anthropology was that sophisticated understandings of mental states existed only in modern, Western societies where there was a high level of formal education. Early writers noted that in some cultures dreams are considered predictions about the future and memories thought to be imposed by outside, spiritual forces (Lienhardt, 1961). How could people with such beliefs possibly form accurate theories about mental states?

A fascinating study was conducted in one such culture—a Baka village in the rain forests of Cameroon (Avis & Harris, 1991). People of this village hold spiritual beliefs that would appear to contradict an accurate theory of the mind. They believe, for example, that dreams predict the future. Would preschoolers in this community come to understand internal mental states as Western children do? In the study, 3- and 4-year-olds were presented with theories-of-the-mind tasks in a culturally sensitive way. Two Baka experimenters played a hiding game with subjects, using the foods and implements of the culture. First, children were asked to sit with the two experimenters around a cooking fire. One experimenter, Mopfana, would begin to cook mango kernels but then get up and leave for a moment. The other experimenter, Mobissa, who by virtue of age was of higher status, would then ask the children to play a trick and hide the kernels. (Note the importance of culturally sensitive research methods.) Once the kernels were hidden, Mobissa would ask the children several questions: "When Mopfana comes back, where will he look for the kernels? Before Mopfana opens the lid to the bowl where the kernels are, will his heart feel good or bad? After he lifts the lid, will his heart feel good or bad?" By age 4, the Baka children were very good at accurately predicting thoughts and feelings. The authors conclude that spiritual beliefs in no way limited children's understandings of intentions, thinking processes, and emotional states. Other studies from other parts of the world also report that, in spite of diverse worldviews, many children acquire theories of the mind at about the same time in development (Flavell, 2004).

autism: A condition characterized by a lack of awareness of others, a preference for objects to people, and an intense desire for sameness. Autism can include language delays, self-destructive behavior, repetitive and ritualistic body movements, and difficulty interpreting multiple stimuli.

There may be exceptions, however. In a study in Peru, Junin Quechua children were found to perform less well on theories-of-the-mind tasks through middle childhood (Vinden, 1996). Does this represent a cognitive deficiency? This researcher argues that this finding merely reflects cultural traditions and communication styles. Adults of this community were found to use very few words of emotion, knowledge, or belief. Even in traditional family stories, few references were found to internal mental states. Theories of the mind may emerge earliest, then, in those cultures where the internal workings of the mind are most frequently contemplated and discussed.

ACADEMIC SKILLS AND THE STANDARDS MOVEMENT

As discussed in previous sections, preschool children's new intellectual abilities allow them to perform at higher levels in traditional academic areas. In preschool and child care classrooms, teachers provide developmentally appropriate learning experiences that promote scientific inquiry, mathematical problem solving, reading and writing, artistic representation, and even historical thinking (Bredekamp & Copple, 1997). Research has shown that acquiring academic abilities in preschool can lead to higher achievement in elementary school (McClelland, Acock, & Morrison, 2006). This has led policymakers, community leaders, parents, and educators in the United States to call for greater accountability and assessment in programs for preschool children—particularly those that receive public funding. The thinking goes: if we are paying for programs to assure that children are ready to learn in school, we want concrete evidence that this is being accomplished. What has resulted has been called the **standards movement.** This is a national initiative to identify the specific skills children need to succeed in school and to promote and assess these in a systematic way.

Standards for what children should learn in the preschool years have been written in most states and communities of the country (Neuman & Roskos, 2005). These include clear statements of the specific competencies or behaviors to be acquired and assessments of these. In Connecticut, as an example, the *Preschool Assessment Framework* (State of Connecticut, 2005) includes specific performance standards, such as "orders and compares objects" or "engages in scientific inquiry." Preschool teachers write anecdotal records about students' performance on each of these, then determine children's overall level of competence on each using a rubric. A particular skill for a child is determined to be either "emerging" or "mastered." Nationally, the Head Start program has established the *Child Outcomes Framework* (U.S. Department of Health and Human Services, 2008), which includes indicators of early learning to be promoted and assessed in all Head Start classrooms. Examples include "demonstrates increasing interest and awareness of numbers and counting as a means for solving problems" and "begins to describe and discuss predictions, explanations, and generalizations based on past experiences." Teachers determine children's progress in meeting these indicators through observations during home visits, analysis of children's work and play samples, parent reports, and direct assessment instruments.

The standards movement is controversial (C. Brown, 2007). Many believe that the new emphasis on standards and assessment has improved preschool effectiveness by inspiring teachers to focus more on academic areas of learning. On the other hand, concerns have been raised that this movement has caused teachers to focus exlusively on assessment and testing outcomes and not enough on social development, children's interests, and culturally meaningful areas of learning not addressed in the standards. One study found that teachers of children in poverty, in particular, are overly concerned with literacy and mathematics performance to the exclusion of social skills or children's interests (Lee & Ginsburg, 2007). In addition, the standards movement has led to greater stress among teachers, who are increasingly held accountable for assuring their students are learning (Lambert & McCarthy, 2006). This has even caused some to leave the profession.

standards movement: A national initiative to identify the specific skills children need to succeed in school and to promote and assess these in a systematic way.

Neuman and Roskos (2005) suggest that a resolution to the debate about preschool standards is to assure that performance indicators and assessments are appropriate for young children and include broad areas of development, such as social interaction, creativity, and motor skills. A good example of this is Connecticut's *Preschool Assessment Framework*, which includes measures of children's performance in all domains and equally emphasizes peer interactions, play abilities, artistic representation, and motor development, along with cognitive areas of growth. Further, this framework provides guidance for teachers on developmentally appropriate activities to promote attainment of indicators through playful, social, and culturally meaningful experiences. The standards movement has affected children of all ages and will be revisited in later chapters.

In the previous sections, various aspects of young children's thinking and learning are described. As demonstrated in many of the vignettes, these cognitive abilities can be enhanced by thoughtful curriculum planning and intervention by teachers. It is important for professionals to advocate for high-quality preschool and child care programs for all children. (See the Advocacy and Public Policy box in this chapter for examples of how professionals can support one highly effective early education program—Head Start.)

ADVOCACY AND PUBLIC POLICY

Supporting Head Start

Head Start is the most comprehensive and well-known child development program in America. Funded by the federal government and administered through the Department of Health and Human Services, the program has provided educational, medical, mental health, nutritional, and parent services to young children and families who live in poverty since it was first funded in 1964. Today, the program serves nearly 1 million children from birth to age 5 and their families in a variety of settings, including preschool and infant classrooms and home-based sites. Nearly 75% of children served are of historically underrepresented groups; more than 12% have disabilities.

Research conducted over the past several decades has shown that Head Start can have an impact on young children's learning and school performance as well as on social development and physical and mental health (Barnett, 1995; Heckman, Hsee, & Rubinstein, 2000; Karoly, 1998). One long-term study found that children who attended Head Start had lower rates of grade retention, special education, and delinquency as well as higher reading scores through adolescence (Reynolds & Temple, 1998). In another investigation, Head Start children were found to have a

24% lower high school dropout rate than those who did not attend the program. Garces, Thomas, and Curry (2000) report higher incomes and a greater probability of completing high school and attending college for Euro-Americans who attended Head Start when they were young. These authors found that African Americans who had participated in Head Start were less likely to be charged or convicted of a crime.

Head Start continues to be a popular program; its funding has been reauthorized by Congress each year since its inception. However, funding is not adequate to meet the needs of children living in poverty in the country. Current resources allow Head Start to reach only three out of five eligible preschoolers and only 3% of eligible infants and toddlers (U.S. Bureau of the Census, 2001). Studies of other programs that serve children in poverty suggest that educational interventions that received greater funding achieved even more impressive outcomes than has Head Start (Ramey, Campbell, & Blair, 1998).

Professionals can join the National Association for the Education of Young Children (http://www.nacyc.org), the Children's Defense Fund (http://www.childrensdefense.org), and other organizations in advocating for an expansion

(continued)

of Head Start funding. They can write letters or in other ways contact U.S. senators, representatives, and the president to urge the following: (a) that Head Start funding be expanded so that existing services can be extended to the many children who do not currently receive them, (b) that additional funds be devoted to increasing the educational level and training of Head Start teachers, and (c) that greater funding be made available to improve the quality of educational and other programs of Head Start. Such efforts will help reduce the harmful impact of poverty on young children in America.

CLASSROOM ADAPTATIONS: PRESCHOOLERS WITH MENTAL RETARDATION

A variety of challenging conditions can affect cognitive development. Preschoolers with **mental retardation,** for example, will not solve problems or learn concepts as typically developing children do. Mental retardation is defined as a condition leading to general intellectual impairment and to difficulty in adapting well to life events and circumstances (Umansky & Hooper, 2008). It may have clearly identified organic causes (e.g., Down syndrome or other genetic disorders discussed in earlier chapters) or be of unknown origin. Children with mental retardation progress through the same stages of cognitive development but much more slowly than others. Further, they may never reach the highest levels of cognitive development in adulthood. Figure 11-4 illustrates these variations in the development of categorization. Retardation has been found to affect symbolic functioning. Delays in language, literacy, and play behavior are common (Laws & Gunn, 2004; Stefanini, Caselli, & Volterra, 2007).

Piaget's descriptions of sensorimotor and preoperational stages of development may still be quite useful in observing the play and learning of young children with mental retardation (McLean et al., 2003). Because skills will be acquired in a sequence—if not at a pace—that is similar to typical development, Piaget's framework can reliably guide teaching and parenting of children with this condition. For example, 4- or 5-year-olds with mental retardation may have the characteristics typical of Piaget's late sensorimotor period. Their thinking and problem solving may be tied exclusively to perception and physical action. It is possible that they have not fully acquired the symbolic thought and prelogical problem solving of their typically developing peers. For these reasons, the following adaptations are recommended:

1. *Sensory environments.* An environment can be created that is especially rich in texture and in visual and auditory stimulation. Toys that make noise (e.g., beanbags that jingle), that are brightly colored, or that are particularly interesting to the touch (e.g., stuffed animals or texture blocks) will capture and maintain a child's interest and promote exploration, manipulation, and play. Moderately intense sensory stimulation is important in active preschool programs where there are many other stimuli vying for the attention of a child with special needs (Umansky, 2008a).

2. *Novel materials.* Children with cognitive challenges may lose interest quickly in familiar toys and learning materials (Umansky, 2008a). Caregivers and teachers can regularly add novel objects to revive interest and promote exploration. Placing new scoops at the sand play table or a new tape of animal sounds in the listening center will refocus children with special needs on learning and play tasks.

3. *Graded challenges.* Preschoolers with cognitive disabilities may use materials that are less challenging or uninteresting to their typically developing peers. Yet it is important for children of all abilities to play together. In each learning center or on each table, a variety of activities can be provided—some less challenging, some more

mental retardation: A condition that may or may not have a clearly identified cause and is characterized by general intellectual impairment and difficulty in adapting well to life events and circumstances.

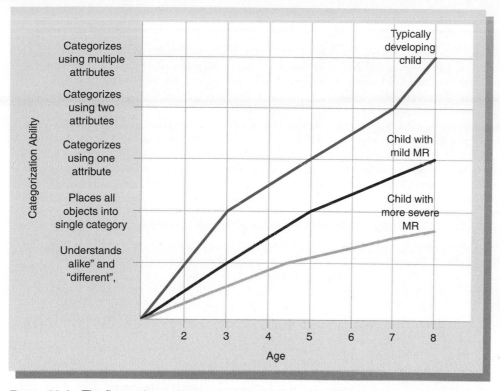

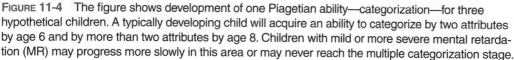

FIGURE 11-4   The figure shows development of one Piagetian ability—categorization—for three hypothetical children. A typically developing child will acquire an ability to categorize by two attributes by age 6 and by more than two attributes by age 8. Children with mild or more severe mental retardation (MR) may progress more slowly in this area or may never reach the multiple categorization stage.

so. Thus, each space in a classroom will have **graded challenges**—materials representing varying degrees of difficulty—that will allow children of all abilities to find something meaningful to do there. A set of simple pouring and splashing toys can be provided along with a more complex floating and sinking experiment at the water table. Simple squeeze toys or stacking rings—designed for infants—can be placed next to more sophisticated math activities in another part of the classroom. Children of diverse abilities can use these materials side by side.

4. *Props for simple pretense.* As described in Chapter 7, toddlers perform a kind of play, called **simple pretense,** in which they carry out simple make-believe acts with real objects. A child might pretend to drink from a toy cup, for example. Some preschoolers with mental retardation will play at this less complex level as well. Although their typically developing peers may be using more sophisticated props— literacy materials, nonrealistic objects, and theme-related props, to be described in the next chapter—children with mental retardation may require far simpler toys. Replicas of familiar household items—dishes, a toy telephone, a plastic steering wheel, and dolls—can be provided to allow children with special needs to play next to their peers in the housekeeping corner.

Children with mental retardation may need more direct guidance in exploring, playing, and interacting with peers (Umansky & Hooper, 2008). Caregivers can adapt materials, on the spot, to make them easier to use. They can more vigorously facilitate interactions with peers. Children with mental retardation may need more assistance with basic self-help tasks.

graded challenges: The provision of play and learning materials in a classroom that represent varying degrees of difficulty so that children of all abilities can find something meaningful to do.

simple pretense: The make-believe use of familiar objects to enact customary routines, such as using a toy cup to pretend to drink.

hands-on/minds-on experience: A learning experiences that allows children not only to handle objects but also to think deeply about these objects—to order, categorize, describe, compare, or artistically represent them.

CHILD GUIDANCE: *Creating Hands-on/Minds-on Experiences*

Most early childhood professionals are aware of Piaget's emphasis on the importance of concrete objects in young children's learning. A phrase that is regularly used to refer to a Piaget-inspired classroom activity is *hands-on*. "Water play is useful for young children because it's 'hands-on,'" a kindergarten teacher explains to parents. A child care provider states at a faculty meeting, "My students engage only in 'hands-on' learning, in which they can manipulate concrete objects." A careful study of Piaget's work, however, suggests that he might not fully agree with these statements. It is true that he believed learning in the preschool years requires concrete experience. Manipulating objects was certainly critical to his theory. However, he did not believe that simply handling objects was enough to ensure preschool cognitive development. Young children need to *think* about the objects they are handling, he argued. Learning, from his view, involves mental as well as physical action.

A new phrase that more accurately captures Piaget's view of cognitive development is *hands-on/minds-on* learning. How does a **hands-on/minds-on experience** differ from a traditional hands-on activity? The following examples illustrate this:

Hands-on Water Play

A child care provider places interesting scoops, cups, tubes, and egg beaters in the water play table and encourages children to pour and splash. A large number of children choose this activity at free play and spend long periods of time there. The caregiver is pleased with the experience because it is very appropriate and engaging.

Hands-on/Minds-on Water Play

Children are playing at the water play table. As their activity wanes a bit, the caregiver moves over and presents a box of interesting objects. "Would you like to play a game? I want you to guess which of these objects will float and which ones will sink. You need to guess first! Put the ones you think will float here (points to a tray) and the ones you think will sink here (points to another tray). Then we'll check to see whether you guessed right."

Children sort the objects into two groups, discussing and arguing as they do. Eventually they agree on which items they think will sink and which will float, and they test their hypotheses.

A Hands-on Light Experience

At the science table, a kindergarten teacher provides many different objects to touch and to look at through a magnifying glass. He also provides two flashlights so that children can experiment with light. Two children choose to play with these. They cause the beams to travel over the ceiling and have races and play tag with their projected circles of light.

Hands-on/Minds-on Light Experience

Two children at a science center explore flashlights. A teacher observes and, after allowing a period of play, moves over with a collection of items—pieces of cloth of different textures, paper and cardboard of various thickness and colors, foil, thin and thick sponges, and other flat materials. "I wonder if light will shine through these things," he says. The children are immediately intrigued. They choose a piece of corduroy cloth to test. As they begin, the teacher asks, "Do you think light will shine through that?" The children make guesses. "Why do you think that?" the teacher asks. The children answer, then test their hypotheses. They continue with the experiment until they have tried out all the items.

All four of these activities are appropriate for young children and are certainly enjoyable. Students benefit from each of these experiences, including positive social interaction. Piaget would argue, however, that the hands-on/minds-on activities would lead to the greatest cognitive advancement. Children need to reflect on the properties of objects, sort them, make guesses about them, and test their guesses. In other words, they need to think deeply about the things they handle. How did these professionals create hands-on/minds-on experiences? First, they planned challenging problems for children to solve. Second, they challenged the children's thinking with good questions.

Summary

Preschool children enter what Piaget called the preoperational stage of development. A cognitive characteristic of this stage is perception-based thinking, in which children rely heavily on their senses rather than logic to interpret the world and solve problems. Another characteristic is unidimensional thinking—the tendency to center on just one aspect of a problem at a time. Children may focus on the height of an object or its width, but they can't consider both simultaneously. In the preschool years, children display irreversibility, an inability to reverse operations in their minds. They engage in transductive reasoning, in which they assume—

sometimes erroneously—that if two events occur together, one must have caused the other. Young children have acquired symbolic thought—an ability to use symbols in make-believe, drawing, and even early writing. Piaget invented a number of experiments to show these aspects of young children's thinking. The most well known of these are his conservation tasks.

Vygotsky's view of cognitive development places greater emphasis on language and social interaction. He argued that a critical aspect of learning is scaffolding, in which adults or other children guide thinking. New research focuses on specific processes by which children learn. Memory, attention, and theories of the mind—understandings of how the mind works—have all been found to contribute to cognitive development. Young children with mental retardation will be delayed in their cognitive development. Teachers and caregivers can provide materials to support their learning.

RESEARCH INTO PRACTICE

CRITICAL CONCEPT 1

Young children make rapid intellectual advancements during the preschool years. They now engage in what Piaget has called preoperational thought, a new form of thinking that allows them to solve problems using some internal reflection. They can now think about objects or people that are not present and can reflect on things they cannot see, hear, touch, or act on. They can imagine objects or people and represent them in make-believe and can contemplate future events and recall past ones.

Application #1 Provide preschoolers with problem-solving activities in classrooms. Puzzles, simple scientific experiments, quantifying and counting games, blocks, and cooking activities are examples of learning experiences that enhance cognitive development.

Application #2 Create elaborate dramatic play centers in classrooms. These should include realistic and nonrealistic props that allow children to play out real experiences in their lives. Typical home-related play materials such as dolls, toy dishes, and plastic tools are important. Provide props that relate to special events or topics in the curriculum. A toy store, post office, or hospital will allow children to expand their make-believe themes.

Application #3 Ask distancing questions—questions that encourage children to think about persons, objects, or events that are not immediately present. Examples are "What did you do yesterday?", "How is a cow different from a person? From a dog?", and "What are you going to do after child care today?" Concrete experiences that help children think about the long ago or far away are useful. For example, showing children tools used long ago and tools used in other cultures helps them begin to think in historic and global perspectives.

CRITICAL CONCEPT 2

Piaget has proposed that preschoolers are still limited cognitively. They think in qualitatively different ways than adults. Their thinking is still perception based, meaning that they rely heavily on the feel, touch, smell, taste, sound, and appearance of things in solving problems.

Application #1 All learning experiences for preschoolers should involve using the senses. Children must touch, examine, and experiment with concrete objects in order to learn.

Application #2 Highly abstract learning experiences, such as rote-memory math or reading exercises or "sit still and listen" instruction, should be avoided in the preschool years. Children cannot learn if they cannot handle and explore real objects.

CRITICAL CONCEPT 3

Piaget has described preschoolers' thinking as marked by fascinating errors in logic. Their reasoning tends to be unidimensional; they often center on just one object or aspect of a problem at a time. They have trouble reversing activities or operations mentally. Their causal thinking, while more sophisticated than in infancy, is still faulty. They engage in transductive reasoning, in which two unrelated events are placed into a causal relationship. Finally, they are still quite egocentric; they have trouble understanding the perspectives of others.

Application #1 Understand and appreciate that misconceptions and unreasonable fears are common in the preschool years and stem from cognitive limitations. Accept errors and misinterpretations of the world as necessary and positive steps toward more advanced reasoning.

Application #2 Take great care in explaining phenomena to children. Engage them in discussions concerning which things are alive and which are not. Provide experiences in which children contemplate things made by humans and things that result from natural causes. Plan opportunities for children to observe natural phenomena.

Application #3 Pose simple problems to help preschoolers think about more than one object, event, or person at a time. Categorization activities are an example. Encourage children to put things that are alike together at the museum table in the classroom. Invite them to categorize blocks with different shapes in the math center. As children work, ask questions or make comments that induce children to think about more than one attribute at a time: "You put all the triangles here? Can you make two piles of triangles, so that the triangles that are alike are together?"

Application #4 Provide activities that prompt children to reverse their activities. Take a small group for a walk on the playground, for example, and then ask, "Can you walk back the same way we came?" Invite children to take their block structures down one block at a time, essentially reversing the building steps. Ask them to tell stories or rhymes backward.

Application #5 Provide with activities that allow them to act on objects and observe results. Activities such as blowing balls through a maze, rolling toy cars down a ramp, swinging a pendulum to knock over bowling pins, and pouring water into different kinds of tubes allow children to experience cause and effect. As children play in these ways, ask causal questions: "What happened when you ———— ?", "What would happen if you ———— ?" or "What can you do to make ———— happen?"

Application #6   Plan classroom experiences in which preschoolers take the perspectives of others. Guessing games that require children to give clues to help other players guess an object or person promote perspective taking. There is no more helpful perspective-taking activity than dramatic play, in which children must assume the roles of others.

CRITICAL CONCEPT 4

Piaget's research methods have come under criticism. Children have been found to be more competent than his early work has suggested. Piaget's ideas were based on observations of children of European background; children of other cultures have been found to differ in cognitive development.

Application #1   Understand and appreciate diversity in preschoolers' cognitive development. Children of some backgrounds acquire concepts earlier than others, and some depend on social interaction and language to solve problems. Care must be taken not to interpret cultural differences in cognition as deficits.

Application #2   Plan a curriculum that matches the cognitive styles of children enrolled in the classroom. In particular, give children of collective cultures, who tend to rely heavily on other people for thinking and learning, opportunities for cooperative and socially active problem solving.

CRITICAL CONCEPT 5

Vygotsky placed greater emphasis than Piaget on the role of social interaction in thinking and problem solving. He found that interchanges with peers as well as adults enhance cognitive development. Vygotsky also viewed language as critically important for learning. As adults and peers talk to children, they aid in the construction of key concepts. Even self-directed speech—the language children use when they talk to themselves as they work and play—is useful in guiding learning.

Application #1   Actively scaffold children's learning, using verbal cues, hints, and questions to encourage independent problem solving.

Application #2   Arrange for learning interactions with peers so that more competent children are able to support those who are struggling. Implement learning centers, cooperative learning groups (small groups who solve problems together), and assigned pair activities—even with very young preschoolers.

Application #3   Allow and even encourage children to talk out loud as they solve problems. Statements such as "Say it to yourself" or "You can talk to yourself while you're figuring it out" will promote the use of self-directed speech.

CRITICAL CONCEPT 6

Other researchers are emphasizing specific learning processes in cognitive development, such as attention and theories of the mind. Young children are beginning to learn how to control their own attention to focus on important aspects of a learning task. They acquire an early understanding of what the mind is and how it works. They develop theories about emotions, motives and intentions, and knowing and remembering. These early theories are formulated by children of all cultures and even by some children with challenging conditions.

Application #1   Guide children's attention to important aspects of a task or learning activity. Pointing to relevant phenomena or making statements such as "Look at this" will help children control their attention.

Application #2   Help children to formulate theories of the mind related to emotional states by conducting class discussions of feelings—sadness, anger, surprise, or joy—and pointing out these emotions in everyday life. Interventions in real social problems are particularly helpful, such as "How did you feel when Jonah said you couldn't play?" or "How do you think Emur felt when you pushed her?"

Application #3   Intervene in classroom conflicts to help children identify motives and intentions: "He didn't mean to knock over your blocks. It was an accident" or "He was just trying to be funny; he wasn't trying to make you mad."

Application #4   Use "mind words" regularly in the classroom to prompt children's thinking about thinking (e.g., "Guess what I'm *thinking*?" or "Who *knows* the answer?")

Application #5   Provide activities that encourage children to remember objects or events. One example is a game in which children are asked to recall objects that are displayed and then hidden. As the game is played, ask questions that help children focus on how the mind works: "How many do you think you will remember?", "What is something you could do to help you remember?", and "If it's too noisy, is it easier or harder to remember?"

Application #6   Provide a dramatic play center, described previously, so that children can play out make-believe feelings and other mental states (e.g., "Let's say you're sad, okay?" or "The king doesn't know we're in the castle, all right?").

CRITICAL CONCEPT 7

Preschoolers with mental retardation may think and solve problems at a level similar to that of children several years younger. Some children with this disability will still be in a sensorimotor period of cognitive development.

Application #1   Provide simpler materials—basic pounding, noisemaking, or causality activities—that are designed for much younger children. These items can be placed next to more complex activities so that children of all abilities can play together.

Application #2 Place simple play props—dolls, dishes, and toy telephones—near more complex thematic play materials that are typically found in preschool classrooms. In this way, children with mental retardation can engage in simple pretending in close proximity to typically developing peers.

Application #3 Provide moderately stimulating toys—those that are colorful, make noise, and are textured—to capture and hold the interest of children with mental retardation. Offer novel objects when this interest in more familiar materials wanes.

ASSESSING YOUNG CHILDREN: Cognitive Development in the Preschool Years

Areas of Development	What to Watch For	Indicators of Atypical Development	Applications
General cognitive abilities	An ability to solve problems using more internal thought. Using private speech—talking to oneself—to guide learning. An ability to solve more complex problems with support from peers or adults. An ability to use symbolic thinking in pretend play, artwork, or storytelling.	Inability to solve problems—such as puzzles or matching games—using concrete objects. Difficulty distinguishing between actions and their outcomes. Delays in symbolic abilities, such as language, drawing, or make-believe.	Plan challenging activities that include problem solving with concrete objects. Provide cooperative learning experiences that encourage children to talk with and help one another on learning tasks. Use language to guide children's problem solving and encourage them to talk with each other and to themselves when learning. Provide symbolic activities—dramatic play, blocks, art, and early writing experiences.
Specific intellectual skills	An ability to solve simple number problems, with occasional errors by age 5. By this same age, an ability to identify objects that are "alike" and "different" and to put similar objects into a single category. An ability to distinguish among simple internal states and mental processes, such as knowing and remembering and feeling happy or sad.	Signs of confusion or frustration when asked to perform number, categorization, or matching tasks. Difficulty in interpreting others' beliefs, feelings, motives, and thoughts.	Provide activities that enhance specific cognitive skills, such as categorizing, ordering, reversing operations, or making judgments about quantity. Talk with children about internal mental states, such as knowing, remembering, or paying attention, and guide them in using these in their learning (e.g., "Here's something you should remember").

Interpreting Assessment Data: Cognitive development varies across families and cultures. Problem-solving abilities with concrete objects, for example, will depend on whether toys and other objects are available in the home. Family life will influence the understanding of quantity. Children in pottery-making families, for example, may be advanced in their ability to judge amounts. *Significant* delays in general problem solving may indicate challenging conditions, however, such as mental retardation and general language delay. A lack of pretend play or an inability to interpret the feelings or intentions of peers may suggest other developmental problems, including autism. Children showing these deficits should be recommended for further evaluation. A preschool program that includes concrete problem-solving activities and pretend play may enhance their cognitive development.

CHAPTER 12

Symbolic Thought: Play, Language, and Literacy in the Preschool Years

GUIDING QUESTIONS

1. What is symbolic thought, and how does it influence children's play and learning activities during the preschool years?
2. What is sociodramatic play, and how is it related to intelligence, creativity, and language?
3. What are the major steps and guidelines for sociodramatic play intervention in the classroom?
4. How is sociodramatic play influenced by class and culture?
5. How do challenging conditions limit sociodramatic play, and how can classroom environments and interactions be adapted to address these limitations?
6. What is phonology, and what are the typical patterns of phonological development in monolingual and bilingual children?
7. What is semantics, and how do children acquire the meanings of words across cultures?
8. What is syntax, and what are the major trends in syntactic development in monolingual and bilingual young children?
9. What is pragmatics, and how do the social rules of language differ between Euro-American and non-Western cultures?
10. What reading and writing abilities do young children acquire, and how do these vary across cultures?
11. What classroom adaptations will support the language and literacy development of children with special needs?

Preschool-age children are highly imaginative. They tell elaborate stories, interpret and reinvent their lives in their drawing and writing, and create fanciful worlds through make-believe. They are able to do all these things because they possess **symbolic thought,** described in Chapter 11. Symbolic thought is the ability to use symbols—whether words, scribbles, toys, or inventive make-believe actions—to represent ideas. The following vignette illustrates the many symbolic abilities of preschoolers:

Two 4-year-olds are playing in a pretend post office in the dramatic play area of their Head Start center. They write on stationery and envelopes and then place their completed letters in a make-believe mailbox provided by the teacher.

OLIA: (In a pretend, adult-like voice) Well, I need to write to my daughter now. She has moved away, and I need to write her. Come on, Marcie. Let's write to our daughters, okay?

MARCIE: How old are they?

OLIA: Let's say they're . . . um . . . teenagers.

symbolic thought: A form of thinking in which symbols are used to stand for things that are not present. Language, reading, writing, and pretend play all require symbolic thought.

MARCIE: Okay. 'Cause teenagers can read 'em. We can write...they can read 'em. Tell 'em to come home, all right? Come home right now. (Makes scribbles on the stationery, as if writing this message in a letter)

OLIA: And write them not to have a baby. (Scribbles intently on her letter)

MARCIE: (Laughs and continues to write) No. The daughters don't have babies.

OLIA: They can have a baby. My sister has a baby. Now look. (Holds up her letter) It says, "Don't have a baby, 'cause that's not...something...." I can't remember what this part says.

MARCIE: Well, I'm going to tell 'em to come home right now.

The two children write and discuss their letters. Finally, they place them in envelopes that they address with scribbles, then mail them at the post office.

OLIA: Let's say I'm the daughter now, and I get your letter, okay? (Takes an envelope from the mailbox and assumes a different make-believe voice) Oh. A letter! What does this say?

MARCIE: (Takes the letter from the other child and runs her fingers along the scribbles) "Dear Daughter. Please come home now. Aren't you scared by yourself? Love, Mommy."

This play episode is filled with examples of symbolic thought. The two children use vocal intonations, gestures, and announcements of make-believe to transform themselves into other characters and the real world into a pretend situation. They use scribbles on paper to stand for ideas that fascinate and perhaps worry them. A play mailbox is transformed into a real one. In these interactions, the children talk, write, read, and pretend. This chapter examines the importance of these activities in young children's development.

SOCIODRAMATIC PLAY

With advances in cognition, preschoolers' play becomes more complex. The simple pretenses of toddlerhood—repetitive, make-believe acts with objects (e.g., pretending to drink from a cup)—have given way to much more complex enactments. These involve other children and

255

include more intricate themes and story lines. Such pretend play, called **sociodramatic play**, predominates children's leisure activities during the preschool years. The following is an example of this play form:

> A 5-year-old girl hums to herself as she builds a platform out of large hollow blocks. She suddenly notices a classmate standing nearby and invites her to play: "Lauren, let's go! The car's ready. You ride in my car too, okay?"
>
> The younger girl, clearly eager to join the play, moves over to the block structure and asks, "Is this a car or a truck? I think it's a truck."
>
> "No, a car." her older playmate responds. "Now I'll be the mother. Hurry, we'll be late! It will never do to be late!" She says this in a particularly serious, adult-like tone. "It's a truck," the younger girl persists.
>
> At this point the older child puts her hands on her hips and exhales, seemingly exasperated. "Now honey, you get in here!" she commands, using her adult voice again. "Okay," her playmate responds, "but it's a truck."
>
> "Yeah, but let's say it's, like, a car-truck, all right?" the older child offers as a compromise. This seems to satisfy her playmate, who now sits down on the blocks.
>
> "Now I'm the mommy, and you're the baby," the older girl directs. Predictably, the younger child responds, "No! I'm not the baby! Let's say we're both mothers, and this will be our baby." At this point she retrieves a doll from the nearby dramatic play area. "This is our baby, Rachel." She speaks now to the doll in a gentle, parental tone: "Rachel, you need to lie down and be good in our truck, 'cause we can't drive when you make all that noise."
>
> The discussion now turns to their destination. "We're going to New York City, okay, sweetie?" the older girl says in her grown-up voice. "Oh, no," counters her playmate. "It's so crowded there today! Let's go to McDonald's instead."
>
> The older child responds, "Well, we'll go to McDonald's first and get our food. Then we better go to New York to the show."

This story shows how sociodramatic play and cognitive development are related. The two girls engage in much high-level thinking as they plan and later embark on a make-believe trip. They must use much language to negotiate the pretend elements of their play. They announce verbally what various play objects represent ("The car's ready") and what will happen next on their make-believe journey ("We're going to New York City"). They also use language to define make-believe roles ("I'm the mommy, and you're the baby"). Without language, children would have a very hard time agreeing on meanings for the many symbols and pretend situations that make up this form of play (Lyons-Ruth, 2006; Rakoczy, 2005).

In sociodramatic play, children try out adult-like phrases and intonations as they enact their make-believe roles. Much representational thought is required, as objects are used to stand for things that are not actually present (such as using blocks to represent a car). Overall, the sociodramatic play setting is a safe and noncritical arena for exercising mental skills. Research has demonstrated that this form of playing contributes to children's development in many ways (Frost et al., 2008; J. E. Johnson, Christie, & Wardle, 2006).

Sociodramatic Play and Cognition

sociodramatic play: A type of pretend play that includes other children and involves complex enactments and intricate themes and story lines.

A circular relationship exists between play and each of three fundamental areas of development: intelligence, creativity, and language. These three intellectual areas contribute to play ability, and play, in turn, contributes to development in these areas. These complex relationships are illustrated in Figure 12-1.

Children who are intellectually competent tend to be expert players. Their cognitive abilities lead to more complex play themes and more symbolic pretend enactments. Such

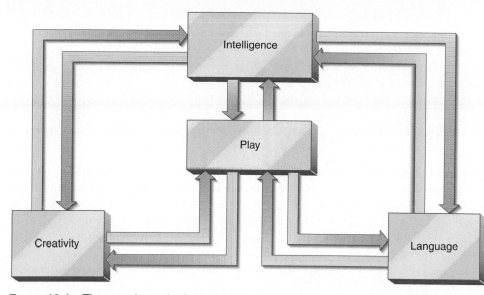

FIGURE 12-1   The complex web of relationships between play and cognition is illustrated. Arrows indicate the direction of effects. Play influences intelligence, for example, and intelligence influences play. More intricate relationships can be seen: play enhances language, language increases intelligence, and the intellectual growth that occurs results in even greater play skills.

children use more language and interact more fully with peers (Dunn, Cutting, & Fisher, 2003; C. Shore, 2006). Conversely, the act of playing enhances intellectual growth (Bergen, 2002, 2006). Those who play often become intellectually competent. A number of classic studies have found that children who frequently engage in sociodramatic play or are encouraged to do so by adults score higher on IQ tests and perform more competently on Piagetian tasks (Christie, 1983; Fisher, 1992; Rubin, Fein, & Vandenberg, 1983). Others have found relationships between sociodramatic play and problem solving (Pepler & Ross, 1981; Wyver & Spence, 1999) and creativity (Dansky, 1980; Russ & Kaugars, 2001).

Strong connections have been discovered between sociodramatic play and language or language-related abilities such as reading (Christie, 1998; Ilene & Davidson, 1998; Lederer, 2002; Trawick-Smith, 2001). Vygotsky (1978) has explained these language–play connections by noting that both involve symbolic thought. He has proposed that sociodramatic play is an important step between the concrete thought processes of early childhood and the more abstract thinking of adulthood. This kind of play allows children to practice using symbols. For example, when children pretend that a wooden rod is a broom or make noises to represent a tornado, symbols are being used: the rod stands for the broom, and the noises stand for the wind, much like words stand for ideas. By age 5, these symbols become very abstract, as the following vignette reveals:

Three 5-year-olds are pretending to be firefighters in a street near their home in Mexico City. They run from one side of the street to the other, making loud siren noises.

OMAR: The fire's burning up. But pretend the fire guys can't get through 'cause of the earthquake.

CARLOS: (Talking at the same time as Omar) Yeah. The earthquake is shaking the place.

LOURDES: No. Let's say we have to put out the fire now. The earthquake stopped, all right? Spray on the fire! (Makes more siren noises)

OMAR: Where is the burning building?

CARLOS: (Looks down the street and points to the wall of a large apartment building) There. It's burning there.

OMAR: It's pretty bad. It's all burned up, I think.

LOURDES: It's burning up. We need to stop it.

CARLOS: We need our hoses. (Looking puzzled, turns to his peers) But we don't have hoses.

OMAR: Like this. (Makes a gesture to show he is holding a fire hose and makes noises that sound like spraying water)

In this play episode, objects and gestures are used to represent things that are completely different. A wall of an apartment complex becomes a burning building. A movement of the hands becomes a fire hose squirting water. A siren noise represents an entire fire truck. These transformations of reality require significant "symbolic leaps" between the real world and an imagined one (B. P. Garner, 2006; Lloyd & Howe, 2003).

Components of Sociodramatic Play

Sara Smilansky, a pioneer in play research, conducted in-depth observations of children's play in Israel and the United States. She identified several critical components of sociodramatic play that can be observed in most children between 2 and 5 years of age: role-playing, make-believe, social interaction, verbalization, and persistence. These are described in Table 12-1.

Smilansky has proposed that, when children display deficits in any of these areas, adults should target these for intervention. She has shown that, through informal play interactions, adults can enhance children's performance of these specific play skills (Smilansky, 1990; Smilansky & Shefatya, 1990).

Sociodramatic Play Intervention

Smilansky (Smilansky, 1990; Smilansky & Shefatya, 1990) suggested four specific steps for intervening in children's sociodramatic play in the classroom. These strategies were designed to enhance the play components shown in Table 12-1 and, in turn, to promote related cognitive and language development. In the first step, children are provided with rich experiences (e.g., field trips and stories) on which they may later base play in the sociodramatic play center. This is an important step, Smilansky (1968) argues, because sociodramatic play involves the reenactment of previously acquired experiences. Children who lack rich experience may not be able to pretend at all (Smilansky & Shefatya, 1990). In the second step, a special play area, equipped with props related to these field trips or experiences, is created within the sociodramatic play center of the classroom. After a trip to the grocery, for example, a make-believe store with empty cans and boxes, plastic produce, and a cash register might be provided.

A third step in the program involves observation of children's play and the identification of individuals who show play deficits. Some children do not interact with peers, for example; others rarely assume the roles of make-believe characters. Some are unable to transform real objects or events into pretend ones. Others quickly switch from one role to another without developing elaborate themes or enactments. Such children are targeted for intervention.

In the final step, teachers and caregivers play along with children to address these observed play deficits, following specific guidelines: They observe first before entering a play setting so that they fully understand children's play in progress. They intervene in sociodramatic play only if it is determined that children need support. Adults can enter play from *inside* the role-playing theme by taking a role themselves. For example, a teacher might enter children's restaurant play by pretending to be a customer who is ordering

Quality Element	Description
Role-playing	Children assume a make-believe role of another person, animal, or object and perform appropriate actions through gestures and verbalizations.
	Example: A child pretends to be a firefighter putting out a pretend fire.
Make-believe (actions)	Children announce make-believe actions and perform these with gestures.
	Example: A child says, "I'm squirting out the fire" and makes a gesture and noises to show this.
Make-believe (objects)	Children use real objects to represent make-believe ones.
	Example: A child uses a wooden rod as if it were a fire hose.
Make-believe (situations)	Children announce make-believe situations.
	Example: A child shouts, "The house is burning, and there are people trapped inside!"
Social interaction	Children coordinate make-believe roles and actions with peers.
	Example: A child helps another pull the fire hose up to the burning house.
Verbalization	Children interact with one another verbally, both inside the make-believe play and outside of it.
	Example: A child states, "Help! The fire's got me!" from inside a make-believe situation.
	Example: The child says, "Let's say you're another fireman, all right?" from outside a make-believe situation.
Persistence	Children maintain their play themes for more than 5 minutes.
	Example: A child engages in firefighter play for 20 minutes without significant interruption.

TABLE 12-1
Sara Smilansky's Sociodramatic Play Quality Elements

SOURCE: Smilansky, 1968; Smilansky & Shefatya, 1990.

lunch. At other times the adult might intervene from *outside* the role-playing, merely asking interesting questions or offering new props. A caregiver might ask a group of children who are pretending to work at a gas station, "What will you use for a hose to pump the gas?" Smilansky warns that adults must not force themselves on children as they play and should honor their students' wishes to be left alone.

In Smilansky's approach, all interventions are aimed at preserving and enhancing the ongoing sociodramatic play theme. Interactions that significantly interfere with activities in progress are inappropriate. One important guideline in Smilansky's strategy is that teachers should intervene for only a short time to enhance one or two play skills; after this, they should withdraw. The goal is to enrich self-directed play, not to provide continuous adult-guided make-believe.

Several researchers have provided additional guidelines for intervening in young children's sociodramatic play based on Vygotsky's work (Bodrova & Leong, 2003a; Trawick-Smith, 2008). These authors suggest that caregivers and teachers *scaffold* children's play by carefully tailoring their interventions to the level of support that children need. As they observe children in play, adults might determine that interactions are rich and meaningful and require no intervention whatsoever. In such cases, a hands-off response is recommended. However, teachers might discover that children in play are confronted with insurmountable challenges—both intellectual and social. For example, a child might not understand what "cooking spaghetti" means and so is unable to help peers cook a pretend meal. An adult would need to intervene directly, by saying, "Why don't I help you. We'll cook the spaghetti in a pan. Can you get one and put some water in it?" Another child might be unable to dress a doll because of motor challenges. Again, direct adult assistance would be needed. Two children might lapse into a screaming match over who gets to be "the mother" in a family play theme and there can be no positive resolution without adult assistance. In these cases, the teacher intervenes in a relatively straightforward manner, perhaps even directly offering a solution.

Often, children are faced with play problems that they can solve on their own with only a little assistance from an adult. This is a situation within what Vygotsky called the *zone of proximal development* (see Chapter 3), in which the most learning and development can occur. When such situations arise in a classroom, teachers and caregivers can offer gentle guidance—interesting questions, hints, or encouragements—that assist children in solving play problems independently. A teacher might ask, "You don't have anything to put out the fire? What would be something we could use as a pretend fire hose?" In this case, the teacher is not solving a problem for children but rather guiding them in solving it on their own. Such support, these authors argue, is most helpful in promoting play development.

Sociodramatic Play, Class, and Culture

Smilansky and other play researchers have reported that children of low socioeconomic status or those from nontechnological societies play less often and less well. In many play studies, children of color in the United States have been found to have specific play deficits (Mendez, Fantuzzo & Cicchetti, 2004). McLoyd (1986) has argued that findings of play deficits among some groups may be the result of culturally insensitive research methods. She points out that toys used in play studies often hold little cultural meaning for some children. When research is conducted within classrooms, some children may be inhibited from showing their true play abilities. In a study I conducted, for example, children from Puerto Rico were found to engage in their most elaborate play outdoors on the playground (Trawick-Smith, 1998c). Others have discovered that naturalistic neighborhood play may be a better context for assessing play skills (Malone, Stoneman, & Langone, 1994; Nwokah & Ikekeonwu, 1998; Roemmich, Epstein, Raja, & Yin, 2007).

In a study where deficits were found among African American kindergartners, subjects were asked to play a "mommy and daddy" role-playing game. In a critique of this investigation, Hughes (1998) notes that 83% of the children in this study lived in single-parent homes. Hale & Franklin, (2001) suggests that the broad range of play activities—particularly active motor play, which is common among African American children—cannot be fully captured by narrow tests of sociodramatic play.

Korean American children have also been found to perform less pretend play (Chen & French, 2008; Farver, Kim, & Lee-Shin, 2000). In fact, it has been observed that they display discomfort when they find themselves in open-ended, "let's pretend" situations (Klein & Chen, 2001). However, children of this cultural group engage in more exploration and show greater cooperation and less aggression than their Euro-American peers. Argentinian children have been found to perform higher rates of pretend play and more "social-oriented" play than Euro-American preschoolers (Bornstein, Selmi, Haynes, Painter, & Marx, 1999; Cote & Bornstein, 2005). Taken together, these studies raise questions about whether there is a single "best way" to play in early childhood. Their findings suggest that caregivers, teachers, and researchers should broaden their definitions of play to appreciate a wider range of in- and out-of-classroom play activities.

Play-Work. Children of low socioeconomic status are more likely to be assigned household tasks at an earlier age than middle-class children (Fasulo, Loyd, & Padiglione, 2007; B. B. Whiting & Edwards, 1988). Obviously, family chores will limit the amount of play time in children's lives. Does this mean that children of poor families do not enjoy the same play opportunities as their middle-class peers? Research suggests that children cleverly integrate work and play during the day into what has been called **play-work.** Descriptions abound of children from many different cultures playing while they do chores. Often, they carry out their household tasks in a make-believe adult manner. West African boys carry sticks as pretend spears while they tend livestock. Their fathers provide them with small tools—replicas of real adult implements—to use in the garden (Edwards, 2000; Bloch & Adler, 1994). Girls are observed pretending to carry water in miniature pots as they follow along behind their mothers, who carry real water vessels.

Children who are assigned child care responsibilities also play as they work (Edwards, 2000; B. B. Whiting & Edwards, 1988). The following story shows how a young child plays a sophisticated make-believe role while contributing in important ways to family life:

> A 5-year-old plays on the living room floor with a neighborhood peer and her 17-month-old sister while her mother works in another part of the apartment. The girl feeds her younger sibling a dry breakfast cereal, one flake at a time, while crooning, "Here ya' go, honey. That's a good girl to eat it all up." Her friend makes a play suggestion: "Let's say these are carrots and vegetables and we try to get our baby to eat them."
>
> "All right," says the 5-year-old. She commands her sister, "Eat those vegetables so you can grow up right, baby." The toddler enjoys the game and gobbles up the cereal. Then the older sister suggests to her friend, "But now let's say it's time for bed, all right?" She scoops her sister up into her arms and carries her to the couch. The baby begins to protest loudly. Her mother calls in from another room. "Samantha, you watch the baby, now."
>
> The child and her friend soothe the crying toddler. They make a pretend bed out of a comforter on the couch and lay the toddler on it. "Night, night," they say in unison as the younger child feigns sleep.

Here a child plays an important caregiving role while carrying on an elaborate make-believe theme with a friend. Would the child show the same level of play ability in an artificial research room or classroom setting?

Nontoy Play. Play studies often involve presenting realistic toys—small replicas of adult-size implements—for children to play with. Such toys are commonly found in Euro-American households in the United States. However, not all children play with realistic toys. Hale-Benson (1986) describes African American children's play as less object oriented and more people centered. She suggests that African American homes are not as likely to contain intricate toys. Instead, play more commonly involves physical interaction with peers, siblings, and parents. She contends that this feature of family life has led some Euro-American educators to erroneously conclude that African American home environments are deficient. Her belief is that toys would only interfere with the play styles of such families. This orientation toward people reflects an African heritage, she contends. She notes that "African children don't play with dolls, they play with their mother's babies" (p. 70).

Commercially made toys are not available in many other cultures. In East India, children play with discarded paper, wood, and clay (Roopnarine, Johnson, & Hooper, 1994). Parents sometimes fashion toys out of available objects, such as rattles made from gourds and stones, play tortoises made from coconut shells, and paper snakes. In sharp contrast, the most popular toys of children in some Japanese families are computer and video games. These are found in more than one-fifth of all households in Japan. Such play is alarming to educators

play-work: A type of play in which children integrate play activities with family chores.

who value traditional sociodramatic play activities. However, research suggests that when Japanese children use certain kinds of computer games, they engage in many of the same play processes as children who use traditional toys (Takeuchi, 1994). Studies have shown that when children play with certain kinds of software and receive adult support, they pretend, socialize, and verbalize with computers at the same rates as when they engage in traditional sociodramatic play (Barbuto, Swaminathan, Trawick-Smith, & Wright, 2003; Trawick-Smith, 1998; Wright and Samaras, 1986)!

An implication of cross-cultural play research for professionals is that home and classroom environments should be planned with great sensitivity to cultural differences. Children of different cultural backgrounds use different kinds of toys, choose different types of play themes, and sometimes integrate work and play. Parent educators should not automatically select a large number of toys to bring into a home until they have made a careful assessment of cultural play preferences. They might guide parents in basic parenting strategies, such as responding and using language, but not always encourage them to pretend with their children. Traditional housekeeping centers with realistic props may not be sufficient to meet all children's play needs in preschool or child care. Simply filling up classrooms with realistic toys to compensate for perceived deficits in children's home environments is ill advised (Hale-Benson, 1986).

CLASSROOM ADAPTATIONS: FACILITATING THE PLAY OF CHILDREN WITH SPECIAL NEEDS

Children with special needs engage in play. Their activities are similar to those of typically developing children, but certain play limitations may be evident. Sometimes children with special needs require extra adult support or modifications in the classroom or home environment in order to play. Without assistance, their activities may be less symbolic or less verbal.

Play and Visual Impairments

Preschoolers with **visual impairment,** discussed in Chapter 6, begin to engage in sociodramatic play at about the same time as typically developing peers. However, they perform fewer make-believe enactments and are less imaginative in their themes. Their play tends to be more solitary and repetitive, and they often seek out adults to play with instead of peers (Bishop, Hobson, & Lee, 2005; Lewis, Norgate, Collis, & Reynolds, 2000). Why does a visual impairment limit play in these ways? One theory is that children who cannot see or who see poorly are challenged in their ability to distinguish fantasy from reality in play. The following play situation illustrates the problem:

> A child who has a visual impairment is playing with peers in the dramatic play area of a child care center. One of her playmates announces, "The phone is ringing," and holds up a toy telephone. His smiles and body language indicate that this is a pretend enactment.
>
> Other children, without visual impairments, immediately understand that he is playing because they can interpret these visual cues. The visually impaired child, however, appears confused. She relies only on his tone of voice to interpret his statement and is not sure whether he is pretending or has actually heard a phone ringing.

Play is sometimes stimulated by novel play objects. Interesting toys or raw materials suggest particular play ideas (Trawick-Smith, 1990). A child with a visual impairment would not be excited by these.

visual impairment: A condition characterized by blindness or severely limited vision that can impair motor, cognitive, and other areas of development.

What can caregivers and teachers do in the classroom to facilitate the play of children with visual impairments? The following suggestions are recommended by specialists (Algozzine & Ysseldyke, 2006; D'Allura, 2002; Rettig, 1994):

1. Give regular tactile tours of the classroom, guiding children with visual impairments in identifying play props or finding the sociodramatic play center by touch.

2. Help children with visual impairments to "rehearse" play with new toys in the classroom. For example, after providing a new toy telephone in the dramatic play area, a teacher can guide a child in identifying the receiver and touch buttons and then help her practice making pretend phone calls. Once the child learns to find and use this prop, the teacher can encourage independent phone play with peers.

3. Assist children with visual impairment in interpreting the make-believe of their peers by using other senses. A caregiver might say, "She's pretending to be a fire-fighter. Can you hear her making those siren noises?" or "Listen! He's pretending to call you; do you hear him? Are you going to answer? You could say, 'Hello.'"

Play and Hearing Impairments

Children with **hearing impairment,** discussed in Chapter 6, are also less likely to engage in make-believe. They symbolize less with objects and participate less often in joint make-believe with peers (Bornstein et al., 1999; K. Johnson, Des Jardin, Barker, Quittner, & Winter, 2008; Keating & Mirus, 2003; Spencer & Meadow-Orlans, 1996; Vig, 2007). A problem for children with hearing impairments is an inability to engage in the sophisticated communication necessary to carry out elaborate pretend play themes (Trawick-Smith, 1994). Preschoolers regularly use language to announce make-believe (e.g., "This is a broom, all right?" or "Let's say we go to the circus, but nobody's there"). Often other playmates disagree with these play suggestions and offer alternatives (e.g., "No. That's not a broom, it's a gun!" or "No, the clowns are there now, all right?"). Thus, preschool play involves elaborate verbal negotiations among players, and children with hearing impairments have trouble participating in such discussions. Not only are they less able to understand their peers' comments, they are also likely to have communicative challenges that make self-expression difficult.

Caregivers and teachers can facilitate the play of children with hearing impairments. The following are recommended strategies (Noll, 2007):

1. Assist children with hearing impairments in communicating their play ideas clearly. A caregiver or teacher might, through exaggerated intonation or sign language, say, "Tell Jeremy what you're doing. Say, 'I'm baking a cake. Want some?'" If communication is very limited, the teacher can encourage the child to *show* what she is playing: "Let's hold up your cake so he can see what you're doing."

2. Interpret for peers the play ideas of children with hearing impairments. A teacher or caregiver might say to several non–hearing impaired children, "She's saying to you that she wants to be the mail carrier. See? She's delivering your mail."

3. Interpret for children with hearing impairments the play suggestions of peers. Through exaggerated voice or sign language, a teacher or caregiver might say to a child with a hearing impairment, "He's telling you a storm is coming. He wants you to hide with him in the box."[*]

hearing impairment:
A condition caused by a variety of factors that is characterized by deafness or severely limited auditory perception and can lead to language, motor, and other developmental delays.

These interventions have been found to be more successful in integrated classrooms or playgroups where hearing and hearing-impaired children play together. In one study, less

[*]From Noll, D. L. (2007). *Activities for social skills development in deaf children preparing to enter the main-stream.* St. Louis: Washington University School of Medicine. Copyright © 2007 Dorie L. Noll. Used with permission.

sophisticated play was observed in self-contained classrooms containing only children with this challenging condition (Esposito & Koorland, 1989).

Play and Cognitive Disabilities

In spite of intellectual challenges, children with **mental retardation** have been observed performing imaginative make-believe roles with peers (Hestenes & Carroll, 2000; Messier, Ferland, & Majnemer, 2008). However, their play abilities—as is true of other areas of their development—may be somewhat delayed. The sociodramatic play of children with mental retardation is very similar to that of typically developing children who are several years younger. For example, they engage in less cooperative play and more often play alone (Hestenes & Carroll, 2000). Their behaviors may be less symbolic and more ritualistic. The following story contrasts the play of a 5-year-old who has mental retardation with that of a typically developing peer:

Thomas, who has mental retardation, joins Keisha, a typically developing child, in a play activity at a community center after-school program.

THOMAS: (Moves over to a pretend kitchen, picks up a kettle, and bangs it on a toy stove) The pot is banging. (Laughs)

KEISHA: (Takes the toy kettle away from Thomas and speaks in an adult tone) No. Don't bang in our house. Too noisy for your father to sleep. Get me some cups to pour the coffee.

THOMAS: (Grabs another pot and a spoon and bangs them together, laughing) I can bang these. (Repeatedly takes the top off the pot and puts it back on again)

KEISHA: No. You need to set the table 'cause you're the youngest boy. You're the brother.

THOMAS: (Says nothing, sits down at the table where dishes have been placed, and begins to drink from a toy cup)

KEISHA: Good coffee. Now I'm going to put out the dessert. But you better not eat any 'til after the lunch, all right? (Begins to bring various additional plates and pots from the toy stove over to the table) Mmm . . . smell the spaghetti sauce. (Holds a pot under Thomas's nose)

THOMAS: (Takes a plastic fork and pretends to eat) Mmm . . . spaghetti.

KEISHA: Didn't I tell you no dessert? (Exhales in pretend exasperation) Well, eat the pie then. It's the lemon kind with sprinkles.

THOMAS: (Pretends to eat with a plastic fork)

The children in this episode are of two different levels of play development. Thomas's activities resemble those of toddlers. He engages in much **functional play:** repetitive action, such as banging dishes or removing and replacing the top to a pot. He uses less language. His pretend enactments are confined to simple eating or drinking actions with toy dishes. He does not fully join in Keisha's elaborate play themes, which are typical for children of this age. The story illustrates how children with cognitive challenges and those who are developing typically can enter into meaningful joint play interactions in spite of play differences.

Interactions like those described in the previous episode do not always occur without adult support. Teachers and caregivers sometimes need to facilitate play between children with cognitive delays and their peers. Several specific recommendations are offered by specialists (Guralnick, 2005; Umansky, 2008a):

1. Help children with cognitive delays learn how to join their peers in play. Teachers and caregivers can model or prompt effective **play entry strategies**—techniques for joining groups of children already playing. Guiding children in using more verbal initiatives and discouraging them from disrupting play themes that are in progress will help them to be more often invited to play. A teacher might say, "Don't grab the

mental retardation: A condition that may or may not have a clearly identified cause and is characterized by general intellectual impairment and difficulty in adapting well to life events and circumstances.

functional play: A type of play, commonly performed by infants and young children with special needs, that involves repetitive motor action, such as banging objects or repeating body movements again and again.

play entry strategies: Techniques that young children use to join groups of peers who are already playing.

blocks. They don't like that. Why don't you say, 'I'm going to make a farm.' Then you can build with the blocks too. I'll help you."

2. Suggest roles in make-believe that children with cognitive challenges are able to play. If typically developing children are pretending to cook a meal for a party, a caregiver might invite a child with special needs to play a simpler role within this theme: "Ima, we need someone to stir this soup. Here's a spoon. Can you stir it for us?"

3. Interpret make-believe for children with cognitive delays. If peers are playing an elaborate pirate theme, a teacher might help a child with special needs understand what they are doing: "They're pretending that the chairs are a ship. The rug is the water. See how they're rocking back and forth? Would you like to ride in the ship too?"

Play and Autism

Unlike the challenges previously described, **autism,** which is defined in Chapter 11, appears to limit sociodramatic play (Honey et al., 2006). Most children with autism engage in very little make-believe. They are more likely to use toys or objects in repetitive motor actions (e.g., banging a pan) and less likely to symbolize with them (Ingersoll & Schreibman, 2006; Rogers, Hepburn, Stackhouse, & Wehner, 2003). Their unique play preferences exacerbate their already fragile relationships with peers.

Why don't children with autism play? Hughes (1998) identifies several distinct perspectives on the question. One view is that children with autism lack a *theory of the mind* (described in the previous chapter). Imagine how an inability to think about the thought processes of others would impede make-believe. To pretend, a child needs to ask, "How would the character I am playing think, feel, and behave?" Further, a child would need to regularly assign beliefs, feelings, and thought processes to other children to sustain elaborate play themes (e.g., "Let's say you don't know I'm hiding in the box, okay?").

Another perspective is that children with autism can't play because they lack **intersubjectivity**—the ability to share a common understanding about something with another person (Kasari, Sigman, Yirmiya, & Mundy, 1993). Typically developing children often achieve intersubjectivity in their play. With peers they settle on a common play theme (e.g., "Let's say the fire is burning up our apartment"). They come to joint understandings about what objects represent (e.g., "This block is our fire hose, all right?"). Because children with autism have trouble coming to these understandings with others, they have difficulty playing. To other children, a rubber shape becomes a cup through discussion and negotiation. To a child with autism, it remains a rubber shape.

From these perspectives, children with autism don't play simply because they can't. Another view is that children with autism—at least those with less severe forms—can play but choose not to. In one study, children with this condition were found to engage in as much pretend play as typically developing children and those with mental retardation when they were encouraged to do so by adults (Boucher, 1996). This has important implications for caregivers, teachers, and parents. Children with autism, who may not be naturally drawn to play activities, may need much support to initiate and sustain their play. Several classroom strategies are recommended to provide this support (S. R. Easterbrooks, 2008; Filipek, Steinberg-Epstein, & Book, 2006; Pollard, 1998):

1. Vigorously intervene in the play of children with autism and encourage and directly teach them to engage in simple pretend actions. A caregiver might say, "Ellie, I'm drinking juice from the cup. See? Why don't you have a drink from it? We can pour some more from the pitcher if you want."

2. Encourage functional play activities—repetitive motor actions—within sociodramatic play settings. For a child with autism who is playing near peers in a pretend

autism: A condition characterized by a lack of awareness of others, a preference for objects to people, and an intense desire for sameness. Autism can include language delays, self-destructive behavior, repetitive and ritualistic body movements, and difficulty interpreting multiple stimuli.

intersubjectivity: The ability to share a common understanding about something with another person.

kitchen, a caregiver might suggest, "Sal, why don't you put the top on the teapot. You can put it on, take it off, and put it on" (demonstrates). The child would be encouraged to continue engaging in this action as children around him carry out more elaborate cooking play. Such functional play is a kind of activity that children with this condition often prefer.

3. Prompt other children in the classroom to engage those with autism in play and to show them how to pretend. A teacher might say to a typically developing child, "Why don't you invite Edwin to your house and show him how you put the baby to bed?"

THE MEDIA

Can Technology Help Children with Autism Learn to Play?

Computers and video technology can promote, but also threaten, healthy development. As discussed in Chapter 8, frequent exposure to computers and television in infancy may delay language and cognitive abilities (Zimmerman et al., 2007). The viewing of electronic media has also been linked to young children's inactivity and obesity (Vandewater, Shim, & Caplovitz, 2003). On the other hand, developmentally appropriate computer software and video material have been found to promote learning, creativity, and social interaction in preschool-aged children (Barbuto et al., 2003; Fish et al., 2008; O'Hara, 2008).

A new and fascinating use of technology is now being studied. Computer programs and video materials have been designed to help children with autism learn to play. In one investigation, children with autism used a virtual reality computer program to create imaginary situations and stories—activities that they had great difficulty with in real-life play settings (Herrera et al., 2008). After a period of this imaginative activity on the computer, their play with peers was found to include more pretend enactments. In another study, specially designed computer software allowed young children with autism to interact in simulated play situations with make-believe peers (Hetzroni & Tannous, 2004). After this intervention, subjects were able to transfer the play skills they had learned to classroom settings.

Video has also been used with success in facilitating the play of children with autism. In one study, young children with this challenging condition viewed video recordings of typically developing children using toys in imaginary ways (Hine & Wolery, 2006). After this intervention, they demonstrated more interest in novel toys and greater competence in toy play. In another investigation, a child with autism acquired new abilities in pretend play by watching his brother demonstrate these abilities on video (Reagon, Higbee, & Endicott, 2006). In a similar study, children with autism who watched peers playing on video were able to emulate the social, communication, and play behaviors they viewed (Newman, Swaminathan, & Trawick-Smith, 2008). Interestingly, those who watched peers interact were more likely to demonstrate target behaviors than those who watched themselves peform these behaviors on video.

Why do computer play and video viewing—relatively passive and often solitary activities—promote social play skills in children with autism? Several explanations have been offered (Bernard-Opitz, Sriram, & Nakhoda-Sapuan, 2001): Children with autism become overwhelmed by the activity level and complexity of real-life play situations. Initially, they may require a more structured environment in order to learn social abilities. Simulated social situations on computers and video may allow them to isolate specific social behaviors or solutions to social problems in a controlled way. Also, most children with autism are relatively skilled at attending and responding to visual cues, such as pictures and animation. They may be better able to maintain their focus on social events when they are presented on a computer screen. This research may cause even the staunchest opponents of electronic media to reconsider the use of technology in the classroom. For certain children, using appropriate programs and creative teaching methods, computers and video can support development (Barbuto et al., 2003).

FIRST- AND SECOND-LANGUAGE ACQUISITION

Children's language grows in four fundamental ways during the preschool years:

1. They learn almost all speech sounds. Their language becomes clearer, and pronunciation, fluency, and intonation all improve. These areas of language development are often referred to as **phonology.**
2. Preschoolers use many words and come to understand word meanings more fully. These aspects of language are sometimes called **semantics.**
3. Preschoolers' sentences grow in length and complexity. They begin to use clauses and complex word endings to extend and enhance their self-expression. Such language features are referred to as **syntax.**
4. Finally, preschoolers become quite adept at using language to influence other people and to accomplish things, socially. This social communication is often called **pragmatics.**

These developments vary depending on whether children are learning one, two, or more languages. Most children in the world are bilingual.

Phonology

Children acquire speech sounds gradually in the early years (Menn & Stoel-Gammon, 2008). Some preschoolers are hard to understand because they have not mastered key sounds, as the following story illustrates:

> A teacher, Ms. Sorenson, is listening attentively to Martin, a 3-year-old, tell her about a movie he went to see with his family. Martin's retelling is difficult to understand. In his excitement, he uses many misstarts or stutters (i.e., "and then… and then…and then, know what happened?"). He has trouble pronouncing certain sounds. At an important point in the story, Ms. Sorenson is having special difficulty understanding him:

phonology: The part of language involving speech sounds, including pronunciation, fluency, and intonation.

semantics: The part of language that has to do with using words and learning word meanings.

syntax: The part of language that involves creating sentences, including word order, sentence length and complexity, and the use of clauses and word endings.

pragmatics: The part of language that involves using words, sentences, and speech sounds to influence people and to accomplish things socially.

Children who are acquiring a second language often substitute the speech sounds of their native language for those of the language they are learning.

MARTIN: (Says something incomprehensible in a passionate tone)

MS. SORENSON: I'm sorry, I didn't quite understand you. Could you tell me again?

MARTIN: (Repeats the same garbled message)

MS. SORENSON: I'm sorry. I just didn't catch it. Say it one more time, sweetie.

MARTIN: (Shows frustration, repeats his utterance)

MS. SORENSON: Oh! I see! How interesting! (She shows enthusiasm even though she
                 still has not understood a word)

Such interchanges are common in the early preschool years. Children have not yet acquired all the sounds of language. Their intonation and fluency are less sophisticated than those of adults. Phonology develops gradually in early childhood, and preschoolers can be expected to struggle with speech sounds throughout much of this period. Harsh correction or insistence that children start over again will not be useful and may even inhibit language learning.

It is understandable that children learn speech sounds slowly; each sound requires a complex manipulation of various parts of the body responsible for speech, called **articulators.** These are illustrated in Figure 12-2.

Articulators include the front and back of the tongue, the teeth, the lips, the roof of the mouth, the vocal cords, and even the lungs. All these must be used in harmony to make a single sound. I invite you to engage in an experiment in order to appreciate the complexity of phonology. Paying great attention to all the parts of your body that are in motion, speak the following letters: *s, v, t, p, o, h, g.* Which different body parts were used? How did the sounds differ from one another in terms of the articulators that were needed? Did you notice that the *v* sound requires use of the vocal cords, whereas the *t* sound does not? Did you discover that, in making the *p* sound, air is obstructed fully and then allowed to burst out of the mouth, but when making the *s* sound, the air seeps out slowly?

articulators: Parts of the body that are responsible for speech production, including the front and back of the tongue, the teeth, the lips, the roof of the mouth, the vocal cords, and the lungs.

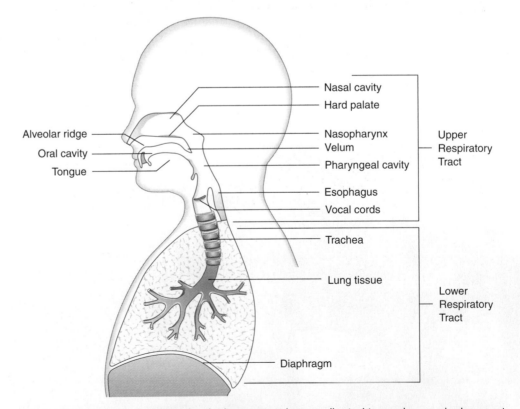

FIGURE 12-2   A large number of articulators must be coordinated to produce a single sound.

Not only must children manipulate numerous articulators to speak a sound, they must connect a string of these together rapidly in order to form words and communicate ideas. It is now believed that children learn a complex set of rules to accomplish this (Beckman & Edwards, 2000). For example, there may be a mental rule that guides children in using a specific cluster of body parts (tongue, teeth, vocal cords, and so on) to make a particular sound. The rule for a *v* sound might be, "Put your upper teeth to your lower lip, let the air seep out, and use the vocal cords to add a nice hum." Of course, children are not really aware of this rule; they can't tell you about it. This is an example of the *tacit knowledge of language*, which was described in Chapter 8.

A different phonological rule might lead children to use a plural *s* that is *voiced* (more like a *z* sound using the vocal cords) when it is added to a word that ends in a vowel. An example in English is *pies*. (If you place your hands on your throat when you say "pies," you can feel your vocal cords at work.) The rule would guide children in using a voiceless *s* (a hiss without vocal cords) when adding it to a word ending in a consonant. *Bats* is an example. (Try the throat test again. The *s* in this word does not lead to a vibration.)

Yet another phonological rule might prompt children to use a sound only with certain other sounds that are compatible within their language. (In English, for example, the sounds *d* and *p* just don't work well together. A rule guides children in not using this combination.)

How do children learn these rules? One theory is that they hear acceptable sounds and sound patterns over and over in the words used most frequently in their language (Beckman & Edwards, 2000; Kong, Beckman, & Edwards, 2007). The first hundred or so words that most children learn, according to this view, will contain almost all the key sounds of their language, many instances of the plural *s* rule, many examples of sounds that are compatible, and so on. As they hear and learn words, then, they also learn rules for how to make the sounds used to pronounce them. Does all this sound complicated? Consider this: Children acquire most of these phonological rules by age 5!

Typical and Atypical Phonology. Speech problems worry parents greatly. A student of mine, who is the father of a toddler, recently informed me, "I'll give my daughter until about age 2 to say these sounds correctly. If she doesn't by then, we'll need to do something." He didn't clarify what that something would be. Direct training? Harsh correction? I did my best to convince him not to worry, that it takes children awhile to learn these complex phonological rules.

When a child cannot pronounce an *l* or *r* sound by age 5 or stumbles over words in stutter-like misstarts, anxiety arises. However, the vast majority of these preschool speech errors are typical. Researchers have identified the approximate ages at which various sounds are first spoken accurately. This information often is presented in developmental charts that caregivers, teachers, or parents use to assess phonological development. A sample phonological chart is presented in Table 12-2.

Age of Acquisition	Girls	Boys
3 years	p, b, m, w, d, n, k, g, h, ng	p, b, m, h, w, d, n, k, t, g
4 years	l	ng
5 years	j, y	y
6 years	sh, ch, r, zh, f, wh	zh, wh, j
7 years	s, z, th, v	f, l, r, ch, sh, s, z, th, v
7 to 9 years	bl, br, dr, fl, dl, kr, pl, skw, sl, str, tr, pr, other blends	bl, br, dr, fl, dl, kr, pl, skw, sl, str, tr, pr, other blends

TABLE 12-2
Typical Order of Acquisition of Specific Speech Sounds for Boys and Girls

As shown in the chart, some sounds emerge early in development; these sounds may be easier for children to pronounce (Menn & Stoel-Gammon, 2008). Others, such as certain consonant sounds and blends, are extremely difficult. These sounds might not be mastered until age 7 or 8.

Sometimes children have phonological challenges that can be identified and addressed in early childhood. There are a number of indicators of serious speech delay. Children who, at an older age, cannot pronounce many early acquired speech sounds may be at risk. For example, if a 5-year-old cannot articulate the sounds *d*, *b*, or *g*—shown in Table 12-2 to be acquired by age 3—a formal speech evaluation may be recommended.

Children who are not stimulable in these early speech sounds may be most in need of intervention. Children are said to be **stimulable** for a particular sound if they can accurately imitate it when it is presented to them by an adult. It is common for children to mispronounce a sound in natural speech but to accurately imitate the sound during a stimulability test. Children who cannot accurately produce early sounds under these controlled circumstances are more likely to require some intervention.

Children who make **unpredictable substitutions** for speech sounds they cannot pronounce are likely to be recommended for formal evaluation. Typically developing young children make regular, logical substitutions when trying to speak sounds they cannot articulate. Some of these regular substitutions include *w* used instead of *r*, as in *wabbit* for *rabbit*, and *d* substituted for *th*, as in *dat* for *that*. These substitutions somehow sound right. They are close enough to the correct sounds that listeners can understand what is being said.

Some children do not make these regular substitutions, however. They may use many different sounds in place of one they cannot pronounce. For example, the child pronounces *rabbit* as *abbit* one time and then as *dabbit* the next. These substitutions may not sound anything like the correct pronunciations, so communication is impeded. Children who make irregular substitutions are at greater risk of later speech delays (Menn & Stoel-Gammon, 2008).

Children who show single-sound stuttering, accompanied by tension or facial grimaces, may also be at risk of later phonological difficulties. Most preschoolers are disfluent; they stumble over words and restart sentences (e.g., "the ball . . . the ball . . . the ball . . ."). Asking children to slow down or start over is not recommended since such disfluencies are typical and will disappear with age.

Occasionally, preschoolers will show **single-sound disfluency** (e.g., "b-b-b-b-ball"), displaying great strain on their faces as they struggle to speak. (In fact, speech and language pathologists sometimes refer to these grimaces as **struggle behaviors.**) In such cases, further evaluation may be recommended. True disfluency is not learned from other children or caused by certain parenting behaviors but has several more basic suspected causes (Furnham & Davis, 2008). A predisposition to stuttering may be genetic (Castrogiovanni, 2008). Abnormal brain activity that occurs during a stuttering event suggests a neurological cause (Packman, Code, & Onslow, 2007). Children with disfluency are also more likely to have other language and intellectual delays (Pamplona, Ysunza, & Gonzalez, 2008). Finally, social and emotional difficulties, such as social anxiety or low self-esteem, may interfere with motor actions required for speech (Furnham & Davis, 2008). Needless to say, a problem stemming from so many sources is challenging to treat. As children get older, stuttering has been found to interfere with social relationships (Adler & King, 1994).

Preschoolers are most likely to be recommended for evaluation and speech therapy when teachers, caregivers, parents, and peers cannot understand them. The bottom line in deciding whether a speech challenge should be addressed is the degree to which a child can communicate. If a child is communicating well, intervention is often postponed (Ratner, 2008).

stimulable: A condition in which a child can accurately imitate a particular sound when it is presented to them by an adult even if they do not pronounce it correctly in everyday speech.

unpredictable substitutions: An indicator of possible speech and language delays in which a child uses many different sounds—not just one predictable one—in place of a sound he or she cannot pronounce.

single-sound disfluency: The most worrisome form of stuttering in which a single sound is repeated (e.g., "b-b-b-b-ball"), often accompanied by tension or facial grimaces, as children struggle to speak.

struggle behaviors: Facial grimaces, contortions of the mouth, and other signs of difficulty in producing speech sounds that are indicators of a more serious form of disfluency.

Phonology in Second-Language Acquisition. When children learn two or more languages, they must acquire several completely different sound systems (Abrahamsson, 2001; Birdsong, 2004; Gonzalez, 1998). Needless to say, it is challenging to coordinate the phonological rules of distinct languages. Children often use the sounds of one language—usually the one that is used in the home—to speak a second. For example, in Spanish, *v* sounds are pronounced as *b*, so Spanish-speaking preschoolers may say "bisit" instead of "visit" when speaking English.

Examples also can be found in the language of young children who speak **African American Vernacular English** (AAVE) (Goldfield & Snow, 2001; Sligh & Conners, 2003), a form of English spoken by African Americans in many communities in the United States. It is a rule-governed language that is as complex and expressive as standard English. African American Vernacular English has its own unique phonology, syntax, and semantics. For example, the standard English sound *th* is pronounced *d*, as in "dis" instead of "this." The standard English suffix-*ing* is pronounced *in* in AAVE, to make "singin" instead of "singing."

It is important to remember that these are language differences, not deficits. The unique phonological features of children's language are to be understood and appreciated. They represent the creative efforts of children to acquire more than one language.

Semantics

Preschoolers' semantics—their knowledge of word meanings—develops quickly. Studies of word acquisition show that children advance from a usable vocabulary of 200 words at age 2 to 10,000 words at age 6 (McMurray, 2007; Marchman & Fernald, 2008). Children know even more words than they speak, so their actual word learning is even more impressive than these data indicate! Word acquisition is particularly rapid among children whose parents frequently respond to their language, play with them often, and accept their unique behaviors (Roberts, Burchinal, & Durham, 1999).

Children can learn a word very quickly, sometimes after only a couple brief exposures to it (Trehub & Shenfield, 2007; Woodward & Markem, 1998). In one study (Klibanoff & Waxman, 2000), for example, preschoolers were presented with a puppet, called Gogi. They were told that the puppet did not speak English yet and that he referred to toy horses as *blickish*. Subjects were then asked, "Can you give Gogi something else that's blickish?" Children would select like objects—different toy horses—to give to the puppet. Very quickly, they incorporated this new, nonsense adjective into their vocabulary.

How can this rapid word learning be explained? First, early specialization of certain language regions of the brain allows greater capacity to learn new words (Mills, Plunkett, Prat, & Schafer, 2005). Also, increases in general cognitive development may promote the acquisition of word meanings. One theory holds that children older than 2 years begin to actively construct categories in their minds for what particular words represent and what they do not represent (D. G. Hall & Graham, 1999; Li, Zhao, & MacWhinney, 2007). When they are first confronted with the word *fuzzy*, used by a parent to describe a stuffed animal, for example, they may associate it with just that single toy. In fact, in the early preschool years, they may be quite reluctant to use the word for anything else. Their thinking is that each word represents one thing, and things can't have more than one name. Over time, they begin to broaden the mental category for fuzzy. They may hear a parent comment on "fuzzy slippers" and a "fuzzy blanket" and begin to add to their original definition. Word learning is an active process, then, in which young children construct meanings based on their experience.

African American Vernacular English: A form of English spoken by African Americans in many communities in the United States that is as complex and expressive as standard English and includes its own unique phonology, syntax, and semantics.

Some believe that social cues are provided by parents, caregivers, and peers that help children construct meanings of new words (Akthar, Carpenter, & Tomasello, 1996; Yu, Ballard, & Aslin, 2005). The following story illustrates this:

A father is reading a book to his 4-year-old daughter.

FATHER: (Reading) The wind was blowing across the desert.
NORA: Yeah, and see the animals are scared. See the rabbits? (Points to the illustration) And the fox is scared.
FATHER: Right. (Turns the page, which shows many other desert animals) You know what I see? A scorpion. He's hiding from the storm, too.
NORA: Scorpion. This one? (Points to the illustration)
FATHER: Right.
NORA: Scorpion. And there's a fox, still. And birds.
FATHER: Right.
NORA: (Points to the scorpion) And… what is it?
FATHER: Scorpion. Can you say it?
NORA: Scorpion.
FATHER: (Turns the page; points to a bird) Is this a scorpion?
NORA: No! (Laughs.)
FATHER: (Points to a mouse) Oh, this is a scorpion.
NORA: (Laughs) That's a mouse! This is a scorpion. See? He has this… tail.

What has this father done to help his daughter learn a new word? He provides a label, *scorpion,* for something the child is not familiar with, then asks questions, poses gentle challenges, and even employs humor to help the child learn what the word means. Such adult interactions promote semantic development.

Young children have been found to construct the meanings of some words very gradually (Tomasello, 2000); some are more challenging than others to learn. For example, opposites, kinship terms, and relational words are quite difficult. Ask a young female preschooler with many siblings, "How many sisters are in your family?" Likely, she will count only her sisters but not include herself in the tally. *Sister* to her may mean "*my* female siblings." Ask another preschooler about things that happened yesterday, today, and tomorrow. Likely, he will confuse these words (e.g., "Tomorrow I went to my grandma's house"). Note that these children understand much of what these words mean but need to refine their understandings slightly. A child may know that *tomorrow* is a word to indicate "one day away from now" but still needs to add "in the future" to its definition.

Overgeneralization errors, described in Chapter 8, are common in early childhood. These are errors in which a child uses a word to stand for far more things than an adult would. For example, the word *bike* might be used to name all riding toys—tricycles, plastic big wheels, two-wheelers, and even wagons or scooters. Later, children actively and gradually refine the meaning of the word.

Children overgeneralize other types of words besides nouns. A 3-year-old, dressing to go outside, might announce to her child care class, "I'm putting my coat off." Is the child completely confused about the meaning of *off?* Not at all. She knows it is a spatial term that refers to the relationship of the coat to her body. Her definition of the word might be simply "where the coat is right now." In other words, she has overgeneralized the word *off* to mean both "on" and "off." Gradually she will sort out the subtle differences between the two words.

Children sometimes overgeneralize verbs and use them in ways not generally acceptable in adult language (Brooks, Tomasello, & Dodson, 1999). For example, children often use

overgeneralization: A language characteristic of toddlers and young children in which a word is used to describe more objects, events, or ideas than it should. For example, a child uses the word *car* to stand for cars, trucks, vans, and buses.

intransitive verbs unconventionally: "You cried her" or "I disappeared it." Sometimes, they use other parts of speech, such as nouns, as verbs: "I'm noising."

Other times, preschoolers will commit **overrestriction** errors (Pan & Gleason, 2008), as discussed in Chapter 8. One child was observed using the word *vehicle* only to refer to cars and trucks that he saw from his second-floor apartment as they moved down the street. He did not use the word to refer to parked cars or even moving cars if he was watching them from the sidewalk. Only when he was in his apartment, looking down, and only when a car or truck was driving by would he say "vehicle."

All these examples show the active, creative process children go through in constructing rules of language.

Semantics and Children with Special Needs.   Occasionally, children will show serious difficulties in learning words. Sometimes these challenges are identified early by teachers and parents. Often they are linked to other challenging conditions. Children with mental retardation have been found to understand and produce words at a level comparable to that of much younger children (Umansky & Hooper, 2008). Children with general language delays often have difficulty retrieving words in speech and are slow to learn the full meanings of new words (Ratner, 2008).

Children show difficulty retrieving words in a variety of ways. They may stutter or pause for long periods while trying to recall simple names or descriptions. They may use the word *thing* with great regularity to name objects. One child who had difficulty with names of things was reported to refer to a spoon as "what you eat breakfast with" and a zipper as "what's on my brother's pants" (Ratner, 2008). In these cases, further evaluation may be necessary.

Semantics and Second-Language Acquisition.   Children who grow up in bilingual or multilingual homes must learn more than one vocabulary. In the early preschool years, children do not easily distinguish between languages (August, Carlo, Dressler, & Snow, 2005; Goldfield & Snow, 2001). Often they treat all words they have learned in both languages as part of the same mental dictionary. Evidence of this may be found in young bilingual preschoolers' common practice of inserting words of one language into sentences spoken in another. For example, a 5-year-old who speaks both Swedish and English says "en block" for "the block" or "Ar det ducks?" for "Is that ducks?" These utterances show that children are not clearly discerning which words go with which language.

Another sign that younger bilingual preschoolers generate one big mental dictionary is that they use words of either one language or another but rarely both to name certain items or activities (Lanvers, 2001). For example, children who speak both Spanish and English may use *gato* for *cat* since they have a cat in their Spanish-dominant home but use *mouse* rather than *raton* to refer to a pet in their English-dominant classroom.

When assessing very young bilingual children's semantic development, it is very important to test competence in both languages. When making a tally of the number of words a child uses, words from both languages must be counted. Tests in which children name pictures or objects are valid only if children are allowed to respond in either language. Otherwise, the assessment will not provide a full picture of a child's vocabulary (Uccelli & Páez, 2007).

One of the most important advancements in preschool bilingual development is discovering the distinction between words of different languages (Ellis, 2000; Hernandez, Li, & MacWhinney, 2005; Goldfield & Snow, 2001). By age 5, children recognize that the words used in one language are somehow different from those in another. They rely on concrete cues in the environment to assist them in making these early distinctions. They notice, for example, that peers or nonfamily adults may not understand certain words they speak. They

overrestriction: A language characteristic of toddlers and young children in which a word is used to describe fewer objects, events, or ideas than it should. For example, a child uses the word *shoes* to mean only his or her own shoes.

may observe that certain words are spoken in the home but never in child care or kindergarten. In fact, they may experience a "language shock" in which they speak in the "wrong language at the wrong time" at school and are derided or ignored. Over time, they may begin to speak the words of just the dominant language in school and words of their family's language only at home.

It is not until the later preschool years—when children begin to understand their bilingualism—that they show a desire to learn words for new objects or ideas in both languages (Gonzalez, 1998; Whyatt, 2008). At this point, interesting inquiries arise in the home or classroom:

> Molly, a 5-year-old English-speaking child, is taking a walk with her bilingual classmate and teacher. A large bird flutters up.
>
> MOLLY: What's that?
> TEACHER: (Laughs) You know what that is, I think.
> MOLLY: (Shakes her head "no")
> TEACHER: That's a bird. You know birds, right?
> MOLLY: (Shows an annoyed expression) No, silly. I know birds. What is it in Wilson's language? (Wilson is a Spanish-speaking peer in her class)

Older bilingual preschoolers also begin to test out the impact of different words for the same object. They may say a word in one language and, if the response is not adequate, say the word in the second language. One child was found to ask for treats or toys in one language and, when his parents did not comply, to make the request again in the second.

The kinds of words spoken in a particular language are determined by culture. Values, customs, and even climate determine which words are important in a particular cultural group. For example, the Inuit and Yupik languages, spoken by indigenous people of Alaska, Canada, and Greenland, have 15 different words to represent the various states of snow (Gray, 2008). Since English is a noun-dominant language, it contains many labels for things (Bassano, Eme, & Champaud, 2005; Tardiff, Gelman, & Xu, 1999). Some speculate that this is because English-speaking societies are object oriented (Gopnik, Choi, & Baumberger, 1996). In contrast, Korean and Chinese languages have fewer nouns, and these societies are believed to be more people oriented.

Children of one culture who are trying to learn the words of another are faced with many challenges. Some words in the second language may have no equivalent in their own. Words that hold important cultural meaning for children may not even exist in another language. The following story shows how even the differences in the semantics of two distinct forms of English can create challenges:

> A readiness test is being administered to a group of African American kindergarten children living in an urban southern neighborhood. The teacher has come to the language section of the test that requires him to read words and ask the children to put an X on corresponding pictures in a test booklet.
>
> The teacher comes to the word *toboggan*, for which children are expected to place a mark on a sled shown in the picture. An uproar occurs, however. A young spokesman for the group complains, "There ain't no toboggan here!" Almost all the other children agree. The testing session collapses into chaos.
>
> It turns out that in this school and neighborhood, a toboggan is a ski cap worn by older males. It is an important part of self-expression on the street. Using toboggan to mean a sled makes no sense to these kindergartners.

Syntax

Syntax refers to the rules that govern the formation of sentences. Children's sentences grow longer during the preschool years. There are several reasons for this. Unlike toddlers, who speak in short, telegraphic utterances, preschoolers use full sentences. The child who said "Move chair" at age 2 now says "I moved the chair" at age 5. All the parts of speech are now present: the agent ("I"), the action ("moved"), and the object ("chair"). In addition, new features emerge. The child begins to use **morphemes**—small words or parts of words that hold meaning. Morphemes include endings such as the past tense *-ed* or the plural *-s* and articles such as *a* and *the*. Most of the important English morphemes are learned by age 4 and are acquired in a surprisingly fixed order (Tager-Flusberg, 2008). A few of these morphemes and the ages at which they are typically acquired are listed in Table 12-3.

Another reason preschoolers' utterances become longer is that they acquire rules for creating negatives, questions, and compound sentences (Tager-Flusberg, 2008). The following examples show these advances. Notice ways in which the 5-year-old's utterances are more complex than those of the 2-year-old:

2-year-old: No bite.
5-year-old: Don't bite me.
2-year-old: Mommy go?
5-year-old: Where did Mommy go?
2-year-old: Ball gone. Flush it down.
5-year-old: The ball is gone because I flushed it, and it went down the toilet.

Most psycholinguists believe that, by age 5, children have learned almost all the rules of adult syntax.

Typical and Atypical Syntactic Development. In some cases, preschool children do not construct sentences in the ways just described. Morphemes might be acquired more slowly, and clauses, negatives, and questions may not be used. These difficulties are more frequent in children with mental retardation, general language delays, and hearing impairment (S. R. Easterbrooks, 2008). Challenging conditions lead not only to delays

morphemes: Small words or parts of words that hold meaning, such as the past tense *-ed* ending, the plural *-s*, and articles such as *a* and *the*.

TABLE 12-3
Some Grammatical Morphemes and Typical Age of Their Acquisition

Morpheme	Example	Age
ing	"See Daddy throw*ing*."	22 to 34 months
in	"Doggie *in* box."	22 to 34 months
on	"Baby *on* chair."	22 to 34 months
Plural *–s*	"My book*s*."	22 to 34 months
Past irregular	"Mommy *went*."	24 to 38 months
's	"Baby*'s* cup."	24 to 36 months
a, the	"Throw *the* ball."	26 to 42 months
Past regular: *-ed*	"Mommy *goed*."	26 to 42 months
Third-person regular: *-s*	"The doggie walk*s* fast."	26 to 42 months
Contractions: *'s, 'm, 're, 've, 'd*	"I*'ve* played that already."	28 to 48 months

in syntax but also to faulty sentence structures. The following utterances of children who are deaf, for example, show that syntactic development is not just slowed but disrupted by hearing impairment (McGuckian & Henry, 2007; Moeller, 2007).

> Who TV watched?
> Tom has pushing the wagon.
> John goes to fishing.

Special intervention is likely to be recommended for children who use such atypical sentences.

Syntax and Second-Language Acquisition. Different languages have different structures. One of the most challenging tasks of second-language acquisition is to understand the syntactic differences between two language systems (Ellis, 1999). Some languages are extremely dissimilar in syntax. For example, the Japanese and Korean languages contain no articles, so children speaking these languages have special difficulty learning English, with its preponderance of *the*'s and *a*'s. In Spanish, adjectives follow nouns, so Spanish-speaking children are likely to struggle with English phrases such as *the green crayon*. *Crayon green* would make more sense to them.

When children are confronted with two or more distinct syntactic structures, they seek creative solutions to the problem. A common strategy is to learn and use the syntax of just one language—usually the one spoken most often in the home—and apply this structure to any language they speak. For example, children who speak both Spanish and English regularly use Spanish sentence structure when they talk in English (Lipski, 2007). Since all nouns are preceded by articles in Spanish, they may use these unnecessarily when forming English sentences: "I am going to the school" instead of "I am going to school." Because *no* is the only word used in Spanish to express negation, sentences such as "He no see nothing" are common.

African American Vernacular English (AAVE) also has a different syntax than standard English (e.g., "My sister, she pretty," "He be runnin' home from school," or "He don't like nobody"). Each of these utterances conforms to language rules that children acquire as they interact with family members and peers. These sentences are syntactically correct for these children. Children who speak AAVE can, of course, learn standard English syntax. A goal in many preschools and kindergartens is to help children learn standard English as a second language. Most psycholinguists recommend an "additive" rather than "subtractive" approach to language education, in which children add new syntactic rules without giving up their own culture's dialect (Soto, 2007; Winsler, Diaz, Espinosa, & Rodriguez, 1999).

Pragmatics

Children learn language so that they can communicate needs, feelings, and intentions and thus become active members of a family, peer group, and society. Language is learned by young children not as a set of abstract rules but as a social and communicative tool to enhance their effectiveness in groups. The most significant language advancement in the preschool years is the ability to use words and sentences to influence other people. Using language socially is called pragmatics.

Young children gradually discover the power of language. They come to realize that, by phrasing requests just so, they can persuade parents to delay a bedtime or give a treat. They learn that, with just the right intonation and sentence structure, they can persuade peers to give them toys or grant them entry into playgroups. The following vignette (Trawick-Smith,

1992) shows how a slight change in phrasing and intonation accomplishes a play goal for one preschool child:

> A child is engaged in a make-believe conversation on a toy telephone in the dramatic play center of her kindergarten. Another child tries to get the phone away from her.
>
> AIDA: (In an alarmed tone) Cheryl, give me the phone! I have to call the police!
> CHERYL: (Gripping the phone defensively and speaking in an annoyed tone) No, Aida! I'm using it!
> AIDA: (In an angry voice, tugging on the phone) Come on, Cheryl!
> CHERYL: (Pulling the phone away) No!
> AIDA: (Pauses a moment, alters her entire demeanor, and speaks in a gentle tone) Cheryl, let's say this is our phone, okay?
> CHERYL: (Looks confused and says nothing)
> AIDA: All right? This is our phone, okay?
> CHERYL: (In a tentative voice) Okay.
> AIDA: (Pauses again) And Cheryl, let's say we call the police now on our phone, okay?
> CHERYL: Okay. (Hands the phone to Aida)

Aida has clearly learned the power of language. She uses subtle alterations in intonation and sentence structure to get what she wants from a peer. Note how she changes her request from "*I* have to call the police" to "let's say *we* call the police." In addition, notice that she uses an "okay?" at the end of her statements. These rephrasings soften her requests and eventually win her the toy she desires.

Each culture has rules for the social uses of language, many of which are acquired during the preschool years. Several that are found in Euro-American cultures are presented in Table 12-4. In the following sections, some of these rules are described.

Rule	Description
Politeness	The speaker listens, responds to questions, and does not make unfriendly demands when talking. *Example:* When speaking to a teacher, a child might request, "Can I have more paint?" rather than demand, "Give me more paint."
Speaking so the listener understands	The speaker adjusts language to the point of view of the listener. The details of the message are clearly spelled out. *Example:* "The bus driver came to my house" instead of "He came over."
Turn taking	The speaker takes a turn talking, then allows the listener to respond. *Example:* "Do you know what?" is followed by a pause for a response.
Talkativeness	The speaker must use just the right amount of language and avoid uncomfortable silences.
Position/body language	The speaker smiles, establishes eye contact, and maintains a comfortable physical distance from the listener.

TABLE 12-4
Some Social Rules of Language in Euro-American Cultures

Politeness. A range of politeness rules exists in many Euro-American families (Haugh, 2007a; Ladegaard, 2004), including the following:

- Be friendly
- Don't impose
- Give listeners a turn
- Request, don't demand
- Answer questions when asked

Children in the preschool years not only learn these rules but also apply them most often when conversing with adults or older peers who have higher social status. They are less likely to be polite when speaking with same-age peers and rarely follow the rules of politeness with younger children. Preschoolers are already tailoring their pragmatic strategies to the social status of listeners.

Speaking So the Listener Understands. Another social rule is that speech must be adapted to match the abilities, interests, and needs of the listener. In the very early years, children often talk *at* one another, not caring whether their messages are getting through. Piaget (1954) referred to such conversations as **collective monologues.** The following collective monologue between two preschool-age siblings was overheard by a social worker visiting their home:

JACOB: (Drawing with crayons) I'm making a huge red plane.
HOUDA: (Also drawing, interrupts Jacob) The house is burning up, and the people have to get out.
JACOB: Wanna see it? (Shows drawing to Houda)
HOUDA: Get out now everyone!
JACOB: (Talks at the same time as Houda) It flies really fast. (Makes an airplane noise)
HOUDA: The little girl can't get out, so the firemen have to help her.

In this interaction, no effort is made to adapt language to the viewpoint of the listener. Neither child, in fact, pays much attention to or tries to capture the interest of the other during the conversation. As they get older, preschoolers acquire more **socialized speech** in which they begin to adjust their language to the listener's perspective and level of cognitive ability (H. Smith, 2007; Bryant, 2008). They may use simplified language and give more detail when talking to younger children than when talking to older peers or adults.

However, even older preschoolers have much to learn about listeners' perspectives. In one fascinating study, children were videotaped talking to relatives on the telephone and in person (Warren & Tate, 1992). On the phone, they were found to use gestures and refer to things that only they could see (e.g., "Look at this, Grandma" or "Know how old I am? This many"). These behaviors indicate that they were still unable to completely adapt their communications to the perspectives of their listeners.

collective monologues: Conversations in which children talk *at* one another, not caring whether their messages are getting through to their listeners.

socialized speech: Verbalizations in which children adjust their language to the listener's perspective and level of cognitive ability, including the use of simplified language when talking to younger children and more complex language when talking to older peers or adults.

Turn Taking. Turn taking is another basic rule of social language observed in many Euro-American families. In a typical conversation, one speaker talks, then another. In the collective monologue presented earlier, turn-taking rules are not in evidence. A number of naturalistic studies of children's play show, however, that turn taking can occur in some conversations in the early years. In a classic study, Garvey (1993) found that preschoolers at play engaged in joint conversations 66% of the time. These subjects also responded appropriately to 59% of their peers' comments. Among 5-year-olds, long turn-taking chains were discovered: one child would speak, another would answer, the original speaker would respond to that comment, and so on. Such research suggests, then, that children make huge strides in the early years in learning the turn-taking rule—especially when they are playing.

Pragmatics and Children with Special Needs. Children who have language and cognitive delays can still be quite effective in their social communication. For example, research has

Hearing-impaired children who learn a manual sign language can interact more effectively in classrooms. Few teachers, however, have learned such a language.

shown that children with mental retardation—even those who show significant delays in language itself—can still communicate very well with peers and adults (Abbeduto & Murphy, 2004). A 5-year-old who is delayed in vocabulary or syntax might still effectively communicate needs, express play ideas, and share humor. Such children often learn turn taking, politeness, and listener-perspective rules at the same age as typically developing children (Ratner, 2008). However, some children with special needs have trouble learning these social rules of language.

Hearing Impairment and Pragmatics. Hearing-impaired children are at risk of poor pragmatics development. Obvious problems include inattention and an inability to respond to others' initiatives (Castrogiovanni, 2008; Shames & Wig, 1986). A peer's invitation to play might go unnoticed, or a caregiver's or parent's question may be unheard. Research suggests that some hearing-impaired children who learn a manual sign language, such as American Sign Language (ASL), have richer social interactions with others than those who have not learned such a communication system (Marschark et al., 2007; P. E. Spencer, 1996). Interactions using ASL may have many of the same social features as oral language, such as turn taking and politeness.

The caveat, of course, is that children with hearing impairments who use ASL must communicate with adults and peers who also use ASL. Although a growing number of families have learned ASL, few teachers and students in preschools and child care centers have (Quigley & Paul, 1987; Singleton & Newport, 2004). Teachers and caregivers might consider learning and using the communicative systems of the children in their classes. Hearing children will benefit from inclusion of this "second language," and children with hearing impairments will have a better chance of forming positive peer relations.

Autism and Pragmatics. Autism also seriously threatens the development of pragmatics. Young children with autistic characteristics are often unresponsive and avoid eye contact with others. They sometimes engage in **echolalia,** in which they repeat, in a meaningless way, the words, syllables, or sounds spoken by others as if echoing them. In almost half of all identified cases, autistic children do not speak at all (Umansky & Hooper, 2008). A number of interventions have shown limited success. Using gestures, modeling, imitation, and

echolalia: A language behavior, common in children with autism, in which a child repeats, in a meaningless way, the words, syllables, or sounds spoken by others as if echoing them.

other non-verbal behaviors to communicate with children with autism have been found somewhat effective (Luyster, Kadlec, Carter, & Tager-Flusberg, 2008). A variety of alternative communication systems have been found to promote communication—a simple sign language, for example (Myers & Johnson, 2007). In one investigation, the effects of a **picture exchange communication system (PECS)** on children with autism was studied (Ganz, Simpson, & Corbin-Newsome, 2008). A PECS is a system in which children are encouraged to make requests by handing pictures of objects they want to adults or peers. Eventually, children learn to put pictures together to create "sentences" and to make more elaborate requests. Childen in this study learned to use this system to better communicate with others, although this did not increase their use of words to express ideas.

Pragmatics and Culture. Most research on pragmatics has been conducted with monolingual Euro-American children. Therefore, the rules of language that have been discussed so far are common in Euro-American families but not necessarily in other cultural groups. Each culture has its own set of rules about how to communicate with others. Professionals who work with children and families need to recognize and appreciate diversity in pragmatics.

Turn Taking and Collective Conversation. Many Euro-American families engage in very orderly conversations that involve turn taking: one speaker takes a turn, then another, and so on (Klein & Chen, 2001). Some child development researchers have come to view this style of communication as the norm. In fact, children who are unable to wait for their turn to speak are sometimes considered deficient in their ability to communicate, self-centered, or lacking impulse control.

Studies of cross-cultural communication patterns reveal that in some families it is the norm to have **collective conversations,** in which all persons speak at once. In many African American, Puerto Rican, and Jewish families, for example, much discourse involves spontaneous and simultaneous talk (Farber, Mindel, & Lazerwitz, 1988; Hale-Benson, 1986; Klein & Chen, 2001; Slonim, 1991). Waiting for a turn, in fact, might result in exclusion altogether from the discussion. It is no wonder that some children have trouble adapting to the typical hand-raising or turn-taking routines of American classrooms.

Amount of Language Used. Some cultures are less verbal than others. In fact, in some families it is a social rule of communication that children use few words or remain silent, particularly in the presence of higher-status group members. Mexican American and Asian families are more likely to emphasize physical cues and touch in communication (Chan, 1998; Mejía-Arauz, Rogoff, Dexter, & Najafi, 2007). Western Apache families also have been found to be quieter (Joe & Malach, 1998; Klein & Chen, 2001). Many Euro-Americans, in contrast, are quite talkative. Professionals must take care not to assume that the style of the dominant culture is the norm or the only correct way for all children and their parents to communicate.

The Meaning of Silence. Silence in conversation means different things in different cultures, as the following vignette illustrates:

Two children—Maura, a Euro-American, and Ding Fang, a Chinese American—have just gotten into a disagreement over a toy in the block area. A teacher, Ms. Miller, intervenes:

MS. MILLER: What's going on over here? It seems like you two are having an argument.
DING FANG: (Looks down, says nothing)
MAURA: (In an angry tone) She took my car. (Now shouting at her peer) I was playing with that, you know!

picture exchange communication system (PECS): A system in which children are encouraged to make requests by handing pictures of objects they want to adults or peers.

collective conversation: A style of communication, common in many cultures, in which speakers all talk at once, with little turn taking.

DING FANG:	(Says nothing, does not establish eye contact)
MS. MILLER:	Is that right, Ding Fang? Did you take Maura's car?
DING FANG:	(Remains silent)
MS. MILLER:	Ding Fang? Can you tell me what happened?
DING FANG:	(Still silent)
MS. MILLER:	Well, you don't seem to want to talk about it right now.
DING FANG:	(Remains silent; looks as if she might cry)
MS. MILLER:	(Recognizes that Ding Fang is upset) You know, maybe this isn't such a good time to talk about it. Why don't we just go look at a book for a while. Would you like to do that?

Initially, Ms. Miller misreads the meaning of silence. She assumes that Ding Fang is either unwilling to cooperate in solving the conflict or does not care how the matter is settled. Quickly, however, she recognizes that Ding Fang's silence means something very different. In Chinese American culture, silence is often used to avoid threatening situations or severe conflict. It is likely that this child is, in fact, very troubled about the incident but is communicating upset in a manner unique to her culture. Thankfully, this responsive teacher quickly caught the message.

Silence has unique meaning in other cultures as well (Albert & Ha, 2004; P. Menyuk & D. Menyuk, 2004). Brazilians and Peruvians, for example, often use silence as a means of greeting guests. Such a welcome might be construed as impolite within Euro-American cultures. Arabs use silence to achieve privacy. For example, an Arab preschooler might simply stop talking as a way of saying "I need to be alone now." Some Euro-Americans, in contrast, are uncomfortable with silence and feel they need to fill in the gaps in conversation.

Body Language and Facial Expression. Body language and facial expression are other important components of communication. Misreading the gestures, expressions, or postures of people from other cultures can lead to irritation and discomfort (Dresser, 2005; Lynch, 1998; Wang & Li, 2007). Avoiding eye contact is a good example. In some cultures, looking a speaker straight in the eye shows interest and attention. In other cultures, eye contact with people in positions of authority is interpreted as a sign of disrespect. In some African American, Puerto Rican, or Mexican American families, for example, children do not look adults directly in the eye, particularly when they are being reprimanded (Wang & Li, 2007). This is in sharp contrast to some Euro-American families who view eye contact as evidence that one is listening. More than one Euro-American teacher has been heard getting a child's attention with the imperative, "Look right at me so I can tell that you're paying attention." In some cultures, a "peripheral gaze" is common during conversation. In others, interaction is simply not possible without direct and continuous eye contact (Irujo, 2004; Wang & Li, 2007).

Smiling is another method of physical communication that varies in social meaning across cultures. Although smiling appears to be a universal expression of positive affect, in some cultures it can mean other things as well (Dresser, 2005; Wang & Li, 2007). In the following story, a family service worker discovers one meaning of a smile for a Japanese American family:

A family service worker, Ms. Amato, makes monthly visits to the home of a Japanese American family who has just moved to the United States. She finds that the family is quite self-sufficient and manages to obtain needed resources from other family members and friends in the community. During her visits, she mainly discusses the adjustment of the children—two young boys—to their new preschool. On this visit, the mother raises a concern.

MOTHER: I don't think the teachers understand my children. They don't know what my children are saying. (Smiles broadly)

MS. AMATO: (Smiles back) Right, that can be a problem. Maybe you should talk with them.

MOTHER: (Still smiling) I don't think they like me coming to visit.

MS. AMATO: (Chuckles) Right, I know all about this. Some teachers are just like that, I guess. They aren't as eager to have parents come into the class-room. You seem to be handling this pretty well, though. Are you going to talk to them?

MOTHER: (Smiles, says nothing)

MS. AMATO: Maybe you should make an appointment to have a chat. You'll work it out.

MOTHER: (Smiles, but tears are forming in her eyes)

MS. AMATO: Oh. You seem upset. This is a bigger problem for you than I thought, isn't it? You're really worried.

MOTHER: (Smiles, wipes away tears, nods)

MS. AMATO: Okay, let's talk this through. Maybe I can help you.

Ms. Amato initially misinterprets this mother's upset for two reasons. First, she reads the mother's smile as a sign that she is handling things well and is not too concerned about the problem with her children's preschool. Second, because the family has managed so well in this country, Ms. Amato assumes she will address this problem on her own, without needing help. Quickly, however, she discovers that her interpretation is incorrect. She has learned through this experience that some Japanese American families use a smile to conceal worry, embarrassment, sorrow, or anger (Dresser, 2005; Wang & Li, 2007). In addition, she has come to know that even the most competent families need support from professionals now and then.

Cultures also have different rules about the amount of touching that is comfortable or appropriate in communication. In Euro-American and British families, touching is less frequent than in many other cultures. Japanese Americans are even less likely to touch one another, particularly when interacting with members of the opposite sex (Axtell, 1991; Dresser, 2005; Wang & Li, 2007). In contrast, Puerto Ricans and African Americans are generally more likely to touch one another in their interactions (Hale-Benson, 1986; Slonim, 1991).

Another component of body language is the use of personal space—the distance one speaker stands from another while conversing. Euro-Americans tend to keep a greater distance between themselves and others during interactions, especially when speaking to people with whom they are not well acquainted. African Americans and Puerto Ricans are more likely to stand close to conversation partners (Wang & Li, 2007). In these groups, the standard conversing distance is the distance for intimate conversation among Euro-Americans. Such differences in the use of personal space have led some Euro-Americans to describe those of other cultures as "too close, too pushy" (Irujo, 2004, p. 144).

Bilingual Preschools

Throughout this section, it has been suggested that professionals show acceptance of children's and families' home languages and diverse communication styles. The reader may have come to ask these questions: If children aren't encouraged to learn the language of mainstream culture, won't they be at a disadvantage in life? Is there a way to promote the learning of standard English while at the same time respecting and enhancing a child's preferred home language, dialect, or unique communication pattern? Providing bilingual education may be the best way to address these issues. In-depth discussions of bilingual programs for older children are presented in later chapters. A new study suggests that such programs might be offered even earlier in life—during the preschool years (Barnett, Yarosz, Thomas, Jung, & Blanco, 2007).

In this investigation, a group of Spanish-speaking 3- and 4-year-olds were randomly assigned to either an existing monolingual English immersion classroom or a two-way immersion classroom, in which English and Spanish instruction were alternated each week. Children in both groups showed gains in language, literacy, and math. There were no significant differences between the groups in English language measures. However, both the native Spanish speakers and the native English speakers demonstrated significant growth on language measures in Spanish. The authors interpret these findings to suggest that a bilingual program can enhance second language acquisition, while at the same time promoting English language at the same level as in a typical English-only preschool.

LITERACY DEVELOPMENT

Some preschoolers read and write very early. They do not do so in the same way as adults, however. In fact, it is sometimes quite difficult to recognize young children's literacy in the home or classroom. A careful observation of preschoolers at play will reveal that a portion of young children are quite active in writing stories, signs, or labels. Some demonstrate an inventive form of reading. The following story shows how these competencies can, at times, surprise and challenge adults:

CHILD: (Holding up a piece of paper with horizontal lines of scribbles written on it) Look! Read this!

TEACHER: Oh! Interesting! You've done some writing. Why don't you read it to me!

CHILD: You read it!

TEACHER: Well … I'd like you to read it to me.

CHILD: (In an annoyed tone) No! You read it!

TEACHER: Since this is your own story, in your own writing, I'd like you to be the one to read it.

CHILD: (Exhaling in exasperation) All right! It says right here, "No other people allowed in the blocks."

Many very young children truly believe that they can read and write and expect adults to be able to interpret what they have written (Boets et al., 2008; Strickland & Schickedanz, 2004). Do these literacy behaviors represent true reading and writing? Research evidence suggests that these primitive scribbles and make-believe reading acts are directly related to later literacy competence (Neuman, 2006; Neuman & Roskos, 1997; Sulzby, 1995; Wu, 2007).

Writing

Children's earliest writing looks like scribbling. Samples of this early written work (created by my son when he was 4 years old) are presented in Figure 12-3. Although primitive, these marks on paper stand for ideas or even whole stories (Aram & Biron, 2007; Short, Harste, Burke, & Short, 1996; Sulzby, 1995). For example, writing sample (a) in the figure is a story about a giant who eats up little boys. Over a 2-month period, the young author read and reread the story. In each rereading, the story became more elaborate but had the same basic plotline.

Figure 12-3 Children's early writing includes scribbles to represent whole stories. By the end of the preschool years, children are using conventional letters with sounds that match some of the words in their stories.

Evidence suggests that these representations are very different from drawing (Boets et al., 2008; Strickland & Schickedanz, 2004; Short et al., 1996). In writing sample (b), one can easily distinguish between the drawing—an airplane—and the accompanying text—the scribble lines—below it. During the preschool years, some children's writing comes to look more and more like adult print (Sulzby, 1995). For example, writing sample (c) looks very much like adult cursive. Writing sample (d) demonstrates that children gradually begin to incorporate letters into their early writings. It is not uncommon for early letters to be inserted without regard to the sounds they represent in conventional writing. Children often include letters from their own names to express messages or stories (Clay, 2001; Ferreiro & Teberosky, 1982).

By the end of the preschool years, some children begin to use letters that are associated with sounds in the message or story they are writing (Clay, 2001; Sulzby, 1995). Often these letters stand for whole words or syllables. The letter *B* might be used to represent the word *baby,* for example. In writing sample (e) in Figure 12–3, the young author has used letters that match sounds in a sign he made for his room: No people allowed. Such early writing represents one of the primary ways children acquire adult literacy in later years (Ehri & Roberts, 2006).

Reading

Some children also begin to read very early, as the following story shows:

> A mother and her 4-year-old wait in line at a bank. As the child scans the large room filled with customers and bank employees, he spies a sign announcing the latest interest rates. He walks to the sign, runs his finger along the print, and reads loudly so that everyone in the bank can hear, "No one is allowed to rob this bank!"

Is this real reading? Research has shown that this behavior is associated with later reading competence (Ehri & Roberts, 2006; Schickedanz, 1999). Children who are read to and are encouraged to interpret print on signs, cereal boxes, or magazines gradually make attempts to construct meaning from print. Preschoolers' abilities to decode printed messages improve gradually until more conventional reading emerges in the early elementary years.

Description	Example
The child believes that words of a story come from the pictures.	A child shouts, "Read!" even on a page in a book that has only illustrations and no print.
The child notices print and understands that the story comes from the text.	A child says, "This letter's in my name!" or jokingly hides the print so the adult can't read.
The child learns the text of the story by heart.	A child sits and "rereads" a memorized story using the exact language and intonation of an adult reader.
The child begins to "map" the story across the print.	A child tries to find the place in the text where the memorized story is written. The child makes matches—sometimes in error—between syllables and words of the story and segments of print.

TABLE 12-5

Stages of Early Shared Book Reading

SOURCE: Schickendanz, 1982, 1999.

Schickedanz (1999) has plotted the development of book reading among children. Her proposed stages are presented in Table 12-5. In the first stage, children do not recognize that the words of a book come from print. Young preschoolers focus on the pictures and may even think that the words originate from these. This poses interesting problems for adults who read to them. In some books, pages occasionally have pictures but no text. When an adult does not read these pages, a child is likely to grow suspicious and protest, "Read it! Come on!" The child assumes that if there are pictures, there must be a story, so the adult must have some other reason for not reading.

In the next stage, children come to understand that the story comes from print (Schickedanz, 1999). They may point to the text or, in an effort at humor, hide the words with their hands so the adult cannot see them. At this stage they may recognize familiar letters: "That letter's in my name!"

An important next step involves memorizing verbatim the story line of favorite books (Schickedanz, 1999). At this point, children will sit and read aloud independently with such accuracy and adult intonation that unknowing teachers or parents will think they are reading conventionally. Such **by-heart reading** allows children to explore their favorite books independently and establish personal relationships with them. Once a particular book is memorized, some children will attempt to match the story line to the printed words. They will run their fingers across the text while retelling the memorized story. If the story and text don't match, they will struggle to solve the problem.

Schickedanz (1999) offers an example of a child reading *Frosty the Snowman* but erroneously mapping each verbal syllable to a single letter in the title: The child points to the F and says "Fro," then points to the r and says "sty," and so on. A problem arises when there is a letter y left over at the end of this. The child exclaims, "This book's not working right!" (p. 72).

In the final stage of Schickedanz's (1999) profile of early readers, children accurately map the story over the print. Some children will begin to read conventionally at this point, she contends, with very little direct reading instruction.

Phonemic Awareness

When young children engage in the kinds of literacy activities described above, they often acquire fundamental language competencies that have been linked to later reading ability.

by-heart reading: A reading behavior in which children recite verbatim the text of a story they have memorized with such accuracy and adult intonation that unknowing teachers or parents will think they are reading conventionally.

Phonemic awareness, one of these competencies, is the ability to hear individual sounds in spoken words and the understanding that speech is made up of sequences of these sounds. For example, a child who has acquired phonemic awareness can accurately answer the questions, "What is the first sound in the word *mop*? What is the last sound?" Phonemic awareness is an auditory ability and does not refer directly to reading printed words. However, it allows children to eventually match the sounds they can hear to the letters that represent them and to "sound out" words they are reading. Research suggests that phonemic awareness in the early years predicts later reading achievement (Castles & Coltheart, 2004).

Some children have special challenges in acquiring phonemic awareness. Those from families of low socioeconomic status perform less well on this skill (McDowell, Lonigan, & Goldstein, 2007). Children who speak a different language may have more difficulty identifying and understanding individual speech sounds in English (Mathes, Pollard-Durodola, & Cardenas-Hagan, 2007). Research suggests, however, that children who achieve phonemic awareness in their native language are able to transfer this skill to the second language they are learning (Quiroga, Lemos-Britton, Mostafapour, Abbott, & Berninger, 2002; Cardenas-Hagan, Carlson, Pollard-Durodola, 2007). Children who do not acquire phonemic awareness through natural reading and writing experiences in the preschool years will benefit from classroom strategies that teach this ability (McIntosh, Crosbie, Holm, Dodd, & S. Thomas, 2007).

Promoting Early Literacy

The literacy abilities described previously seem simply to emerge in young children without much adult involvement. Studies have indicated, however, that adults play a crucial role in facilitating the ability to read and write (Schickedanz, 1999). The following are adult strategies that have been found effective in promoting early reading and writing in homes and classrooms (Neuman, Copple, & Bredekamp, 1999):

1. ***Reading to young children daily.*** The most powerful strategy for enhancing literacy is reading to children regularly (Fletcher & Reese, 2005; Zeece, 2007). Although any kind of experience with books will be useful, certain adult reading behaviors are particularly effective in promoting children's understanding of print. Adults should select high-quality picture books with predictable phrases and plotlines. When they read to children, they should sometimes allow them to handle the book, turn pages, and see print close-up. Having children sit in their laps while reading facilitates this. In classrooms, using **big books** —enlarged versions of children's classics—will allow children to see print as well as illustrations as they are being read to. As adults read, they should discuss the story and ask interesting questions, including prediction questions, such as, "What do you think will happen next?"

2. ***Creating print-rich environments that provide opportunities for early reading and writing.*** Adults can infuse literacy into young children's home and classroom environments. Highly visible and meaningful labels, signs, posters, bulletin boards, name tags, and other examples of print can be included (Christie, 2008; Justice & Vukelich, 2007). Books can be provided in all areas of a classroom, not just the library center (e.g., books about buildings can be placed in the block center). Opportunities to write—sign-in sheets, class journals, waiting lists for favorite toys (e.g., "Sign Up to Use the Water Table"), and blank books—can be included. Adults should draw children's attention to environmental print (e.g., "What do you think this sign says?" or "Look, the sign says the block area is closed"). They can also prompt or model writing as children work and play in the classroom (e.g., "Let's write down what we saw in our science journal").

phonemic awareness: The ability to hear individual sounds in spoken words and the understanding that speech is made up of sequences of these sounds.

big books: Enlarged versions of classic children's books that allow children to see the print and illustrations well.

3. *Planning games and group activities that teach phonemic awareness and alphabet knowledge.* Two skills are highly related to later reading ability: phonemic awareness—the understanding that language is made up of smaller units (words, syllables, and sounds)—and **alphabet knowledge**—the understanding that letters have different shapes and that each is related to a particular sound. Phonemic awareness can be promoted through activities that help children attend carefully to the sounds of language (Gillon, 2004). Reading nursery rhymes and poetry, playing sound games, and singing songs are examples. Alphabet knowledge can be taught by reading (and making) alphabet books, providing alphabet puzzles, and playing letter and sound matching games (Justice, Sofka, & McGinty, 2007).

4. *Engaging children in story writing and invented spelling.* Providing young children with writing materials, such as blank books, clipboards, and photocopies of children's classics with the text removed, will inspire independent story writing. As children write, they should be encouraged to use **invented spelling**—their own, unconventional system of spelling out words based on their understanding of letters and their associated sounds. One child might simply use scribbles to represent a story, another merely the letters in her name. An older preschooler might spell the word *mirror:* "mrr." In any case, adults should encourage children to "write it on your own." Such efforts at figuring out how words are written and spelled lead to greater competence in phonemic awareness, alphabet knowledge, and general reading competence (Sulzby, 1995).

5. *Designing literacy play activities.* Parents and teachers can create special sociodramatic play centers that include literacy props—stationery and envelopes for writing pretend letters, for example. These props may be related to specific play themes. If the sociodramatic play area is organized as a restaurant, for example, menus, order pads, and signs to write the specials of the day are provided. Adults can model how print is used by playing along with children in such centers (Christie, 2008; Roskos & Neuman, 1998). A child who does not play with literacy props in a pretend restaurant center may be prompted to do so through a teacher demonstration: "I think I'll look at the menu and see what I can order." These literacy play centers and interventions have been found to enhance children's understandings of print (Neuman & Roskos, 1997). (See the Child Guidance box in this chapter on promoting literacy play.)

Professionals can help organize literacy programs in their own communities that integrate the previous strategies. They can advocate for greater state and federal funding for such programs. (See the Advocacy and Public Policy box in this chapter for information on one major federal initiative, Early Reading First, that provides grants to support early literacy projects.)

Cultural Variations in Emergent Literacy

Much of the research done on early literacy has been conducted with white, middle-class children (Schickedanz, 1999). However, not all preschoolers arrive in child care or Head Start with the same knowledge of print. Reading and writing mean different things in different cultures, so children of some cultural groups cannot be expected to conform to profiles drawn from studies of middle-class Euro-Americans.

In a few cultures, children never learn to read and write (UNICEF, 2004b). In most families, children do acquire literacy, but reading and writing may be more or less emphasized depending on values and traditions. In traditional African American families, storytelling is emphasized; parents more often tell stories than read them to their children (Flood, Heath, & Lapp, 1997; Hale, & Franklin, 2001). Children's ability to tell meaningful and

alphabet knowledge: The understanding that letters have different shapes and that each is related to a particular sound.

invented spelling: An early form of writing in which children use their own, unconventional system of spelling out words, based on their understanding of letters and their associated sounds.

ADVOCACY AND PUBLIC POLICY

Strengthening the Early Reading First Program

As discussed in this chapter, early literacy experiences can lay the foundation for learning to read and write in school. A new federal program, Early Reading First, has been implemented to prepare young children to enter kindergarten with the necessary language, cognition, and early reading skills to prevent reading difficulties and ensure school success. Signed into law in 2002 as part of the No Child Left Behind Act, the program assists existing early childhood programs—preschools, child care centers, and Head Start facilities—in providing high-quality literacy experiences for young children. Special emphasis is placed on programs in communities where there is a high rate of poverty.

Among the activities that can be funded by grants from Early Reading First are (a) professional development programs that train teachers and caregivers to promote oral language development and literacy in their classrooms; (b) the implementation of new curricula to enhance vocabulary, knowledge of letters and letter sounds, phonemic awareness, and the understanding of the purposes and conventions of print; (c) the purchase of literacy materials that enhance these learnings; and (d) the administration of assessments to identify children at risk of poor literacy development. Information on how to apply for local Early Reading First grants can be obtained at the U.S. Department of Education Website (http://www.ed.gov/programs/earlyreading).

Many professionals believe this program has a positive impact on young children's learning but needs to be strengthened. The International Reading Association (IRA; http://www.reading.org) notes two major weaknesses of the Early Reading First legislation as it has recently been signed into law (IRA, 2004): (a) there is simply not enough money allocated to serve the 2.4 million children in need, and (b) the grants are restricted to projects that employ so-called evidence-based strategies. Some believe this phrase has come to mean that a program must focus exclusively on direct instruction of isolated skills, such as phonics, in order to be funded. The IRA urges professionals to communicate with and educate policymakers about the importance of promoting *multiple methods* of reading instruction in early childhood programs, including instruction embedded in the reading of high-quality children's literature.

Professionals can collaborate with other local agencies to apply for Early Reading First grants. They can urge their U.S. senators and representatives to extend and increase funding for the program along with its companion program for older children, Reading First. They can ask that language be added to the next Early Reading First bill that encourages a wider range of creative approaches to teaching literacy. Through such efforts, the program may reach a larger number of children in need and in more powerful ways.

---

entertaining stories may be more highly valued than reading competence within these families. In some Native American communities, other forms of expression are emphasized. Ceremonies, art, dance, and story-like lessons that preserve the history and values of the culture are the primary modes of communication.

In some societies, writing is common, but the writing implements used are very different from those found in traditional American classrooms. Yup'ik Eskimo children practice *storyknifing*, in which a storyteller relates traditional tales or oral family histories while carving symbols or pictures in the mud with a knife. Preschool-age children watch, listen, and learn the symbol systems their older peers and siblings use. These early observations of storyknifing are believed to support later formal literacy in school (deMarrais, 1998; deMarrais et al., 1994; Demmert, 2001).

What children read varies across cultures. Some spend more time looking at magazines, catalogs, or other factual, nonnarrative texts. Parents interact with their preschoolers in educational ways as they read these materials, much as Euro-American parents do when reading traditional picture books (Pellegrini et al., 1990).

There are three interrelated implications of cross-cultural literacy research for professionals who work with preschoolers and their families:

- Children and families will hold unique and varied attitudes, values, and experiences concerning literacy.
- Opportunities should be provided in the home and school for children to express ideas or tell stories using nonprint media that are valued within their own cultures.
- All types of reading material—including nonliterature text found in letters, fliers, magazines, and mail-order catalogs—must be included in a culturally sensitive literacy program.

CLASSROOM ADAPTATIONS: ADDRESSING LANGUAGE AND LITERACY DELAYS

Most preschools and child care centers are served by a **speech and language pathologist**—a specially trained professional who works with children with language difficulties. Speech and language pathologists conduct regular speech, language, and hearing screenings and assist in more informal assessments in the classroom. When serious language difficulties are identified, they provide interventions to address them. Sometimes they conduct one-on-one sessions outside the center or preschool. More and more speech and language pathologists are delivering services to children right in the classroom. They also rely heavily on caregivers and teachers to help carry out speech and language interventions. The classroom strategies that are recommended most often for supporting children with language and literacy delays are providing a language-rich, conversational environment; planning many opportunities for social interaction and play; and integrating literacy experiences in all areas of the curriculum. Beyond this, teachers and caregivers can help with specific language and literacy problems based on the specific objectives of the speech and language pathologist:

1. *Phonology.* Caregivers and teachers can plan activities that address the specific speech sounds with which a particular child needs help. They can select nursery rhymes, finger plays, poetry, and songs that include specific targeted sounds (e.g., the classic "Riddly, riddly, ree" rhyme if a child is struggling with the *r* sound). Role-playing and puppetry activities in which children are prompted to make specific sounds (e.g., "The snakes all go, 's-s-s'") can be introduced.

2. *Semantics.* Teachers and caregivers can name objects, events, and actions for children who are struggling to learn words. Following a strategy recommended for toddlers, objects in the classroom can be named as children handle them. Verbs, adjectives, and adverbs should also be spoken in enthusiastic ways (e.g., "You're doing that math game so *quickly*. Is that *difficult* for you?") This strategy is most powerful if teachers overlay these words across children's authentic play activities—that is, if a noun or verb is spoken at the moment a child is using a particular object or performing a specific action.

3. *Syntax.* Caregivers and teachers can purposefully use or encourage children to use specific morphemes (the grammatical endings presented in Table 12–3) that they are having difficulty with. A caregiver might enthuse, "You're runn*ing* and runn*ing*, aren't you?" or "How many balls are there? Two balls! Right!" They can also expand a child's shorter or less mature sentences into longer, fuller ones. If a child says, "No want juice," an adult can respond, "Oh, you don't want any more juice?"

4. *Pragmatics.* Providing play and other social experiences will help children with special needs acquire pragmatics. Teachers and caregivers can also plan games and small-group discussions to teach specific social rules of language with which a child might be having

speech and language pathologist: A specially trained professional who works with children with language difficulties. Speech and language pathologists conduct regular speech, language, and hearing screenings and provide home and classroom interventions when serious language difficulties are identified.

CHILD GUIDANCE: *Promoting Literacy Play*

Young children often include literacy activities in their play. A child playing school might pretend to read a book to her "pupils"—a collection of dolls. In a make-believe store, a child might write out a grocery list. Several studies have shown that when adults provide literacy props—implements that encourage make-believe reading and writing—children acquire an understanding of print (Neuman & Roskos, 1997; Roskos & Neuman, 1998). Based on this research, many teachers and caregivers implement a literacy play strategy in their classrooms. Here's how it works: First, they create a special sociodramatic play center that includes many of these props—pens and markers, pads of paper, stationery and envelopes, books, and signs. Often these props are related to special play themes that have been planned. For example, a sociodramatic play area organized as a grocery store might have shopping lists, coupons, sale advertisements, checkbook stubs, and product labels.

Merely offering these props for children to play with may not be sufficient to encourage literacy play, however. Adult intervention is sometimes required. Research has shown that when adults model pretend uses of print, children engage in more frequent literacy activity and acquire important reading and writing skills (Morrow & Rand, 1991; Vukelich, 1991).

A second step in this approach, then, is for adults to enter the play area and demonstrate the use of literacy props. A teacher might facilitate play at a make-believe restaurant, for example, by sitting at a table and saying aloud, "Let's see. I think I'll read the menu and decide what I'm going to order for dinner." A caregiver in a pretend post office might announce, "I think I'll write the address on this envelope so I can mail a letter to my mother."

Teachers and caregivers cannot remain in the sociodramatic play center for long periods. They need to attend to other parts of the classroom and should allow children to play independently. Over time, children who are advanced in literacy may begin to take over this modeling role (Stone & Christie, 1996). Just like adults, they show less experienced peers how to read and write as they play. A highly competent child might show a set of labels and a marker to a peer and say, "See, we have to write the price on all the groceries, like they do at Stop and Shop. See? I'm writing 10 dollars for the carrot."

Although this strategy is most often implemented within the sociodramatic play center, it may be applied in any area of the classroom. Print materials can be placed in the block, art, or science centers, or even outdoors on the playground.

difficulty. Collective tales (in which children take turns telling a portion of the story), the classic game "telephone," and greeting songs ("Where Is Mandy?") are examples of activities that promote the turn-taking rule.

5. *Literacy.* For children who are not showing interest or competence in literacy, books and writing experiences can be included throughout the classroom. For example, journals and pens can be included in the block area if a child with literacy delays often plays there.

lap reading: A classroom strategy in which adults sit with one or several children in their laps and read favorite books, encouraging them to turn pages, point to illustrations, and ask questions.

Lap reading sessions can be implemented with individual children with special needs. In these sessions, adults sit with single children in their laps and read and reread favorite books. Children are encouraged to turn pages, point to illustrations, and ask questions.

SUMMARY

Preschool children acquire symbolic thought—an ability to use symbols such as play props, drawings, or written words—to represent ideas. This type of thinking allows children to engage in sociodramatic play in which they perform make-believe roles and use objects or actions to stand for things that aren't really present. A child uses a block as a telephone, for example, and makes a pretend call. This type of play is related to a variety of cognitive abilities, including general intelligence and creativity. Sociodramatic play varies across cultures. Children who spend more time working in the household or who do not have many toys will play in a different (not deficient) way.

Symbolic thought also leads to advancements in four areas of language: phonology (speech sounds), semantics (word meanings),

syntax (grammar), and pragmatics (social rules of language). Children learning two or more languages at the same time will learn these aspects of language in a different way. They may use a different dialect or insert the words of one language into sentences spoken in another. Children of different cultures may adhere to different social rules of language. Taking turns talking, for example, is important in some cultures but not others. Preschoolers read and write, although not in the way that adults do. Scribble writing and by-heart reading are examples. Adults can plan activities in the home and classroom to enhance these areas of development. Children with special needs may receive services from speech and language pathologists to address language and literacy disorders.

RESEARCH INTO PRACTICE

CRITICAL CONCEPT 1

A major advancement in the preschool years is the acquisition of symbolic thought—a type of thinking in which symbols or internal images are used to represent objects, persons, and events that are not present. Examples of symbolic thought are pretend play, drawing, writing, and speaking.

Application #1 Create classrooms that are rich with symbols. Children should hear much language from both peers and adults and should see print throughout the environment. They should be exposed to the expressive media—art, music, storytelling, literature, and drama—of their own cultures.

Application #2 Provide many opportunities for children to express themselves symbolically. Art, drawing, and writing experiences and musical and dramatic activities will enhance their symbolic thinking.

CRITICAL CONCEPT 2

Symbolic thought is prevalent in the play of young children. When preschoolers engage in sociodramatic play—the imaginative enactment of make-believe roles—much symbolizing can be observed. Children use objects to stand for things that are completely different, and they transform themselves into pretend characters.

Application #1 Create sociodramatic play centers in the classroom to encourage children to pretend. Such centers should include realistic play props related to home themes or topics in the curriculum. For example, if children are studying transportation, a make-believe boat or airport can be created to encourage curriculum-relevant play.

Application #2 The sociodramatic play area should also contain nonrealistic raw materials, such as wooden rods, boxes, and rubber forms. These materials allow children to use objects to stand for things that are completely different. Such transformations require *symbolic leaps*. Transforming a rod into a broom, for example, requires more complex symbolization than using a toy broom as a real one.

Application #3 Intervene in children's play to promote greater symbolization. Encouraging children to take on diverse and highly imaginative roles, to transform objects, and to invent make-believe situations will enhance symbolic thought.

CRITICAL CONCEPT 3

Play differs across cultures. Traditional measures of sociodramatic play may not fully capture the symbolic quality of childhood activities in all families. An example found in many cultural groups is play-work, in which children perform household chores but do so in make-believe ways.

Application #1 Understand and appreciate cultural diversity in play. Be cautious not to infer play deficits when some children do not appear to engage in make-believe. Careful observation may reveal pretend elements in children's work, storytelling, singing, or other nonplay activities.

Application #2 Create culturally sensitive dramatic play centers. Dolls representing diverse races should be provided. Thematic centers that reflect distinct cultural experiences might be developed. As examples, a teacher in California designed a Chinese grocery store in her dramatic play area, a caregiver on a reservation created an apartment with food boxes and toy foods reflecting Navajo cuisine, and a teacher in Chicago developed two separate apartments in the dramatic play area to replicate a multifamily dwelling. Centers such as these allow children to play out themes related to their own families and communities.

CRITICAL CONCEPT 4

Language advances rapidly during the preschool years. Four interrelated areas of language increase in complexity: phonology, or speech sounds; semantics, or word meanings; syntax, or sentence construction; and pragmatics, or social uses of language.

Application #1 Provide language-rich environments for young children. Preschool and kindergarten classrooms should be filled with conversation both among children and with adults. Authentic dialogue, in which children can express ideas of interest to them, will enhance language learning more than artificial language lessons that hold little meaning to children.

Application #2 Evaluate children's language across all four areas of development. Understand and appreciate typical communication errors that are common and necessary in language development. Note difficulties that require special services. Children with extensive articulation errors or disfluency, those who have difficulty learning or retrieving words, and those who do not speak in full sentences may require intervention. Most important, children who cannot communicate effectively with peers or adults may need special support.

CRITICAL CONCEPT 5

Bilingual children follow a distinct path in learning language. They acquire unique phonology, semantics, and syntax that include elements of both languages they are learning. These unique language features are logical and rule governed. Children of diverse cultural backgrounds vary in pragmatics; social rules of communication differ from one family or community to another.

Application #1 Understand and appreciate the unique language patterns of bilingual children. Recognize the distinct forms of English that are spoken by children whose preferred languages are, for example, Spanish, African American Vernacular English, or Japanese. Take care not to interpret diverse language patterns as deficits.

Application #2 Bilingual preschool and kindergarten programs are ideal for language development of all children. Two-way programs, in which both the language of the dominant culture and a second language are used in the classroom, will enhance the communicative competence of all students.

Application #3   Make an effort to become conversant in the primary languages of all children in your classroom. Using key phrases in a child's native language shows respect and eases the overwhelming experience of second-language learning.

CRITICAL CONCEPT 6

Many children begin to read and write in the preschool years. However, their efforts are not always recognized by adults. They write by scribbling and read by pretend book looking. However, these early literacy experiences are the foundation of later reading and writing in school. Literacy experiences vary from one culture or family to another. Not all children come to school with a conventional knowledge of print. However, children of all cultures arrive with skill in personal expression; some families emphasize oral expression, others artistic expression.

Application #1   Develop a writing center in your classroom. Equip the center with such materials as blank books, journals, clipboards, pens and markers, movable alphabets, and a computer. Urge children to write in any way they wish; accept and encourage scribble writing and invented spelling.

Application #2   Read to children daily. Honor requests to read favorite picture books again and again so that children will come to know them by heart. Make books available for children to look at and read on their own throughout the day. Encourage them to retell or reread their favorite books.

Application #3   Adapt literacy experiences to meet the needs of children of diverse cultures. Encourage bilingual children to write in their preferred language, and provide books in their native language. Match reading materials to the family life experiences of all children; include nonbook reading materials, such as magazines, catalogs, and signs. Incorporate opportunities for all types of personal expression, including storytelling, drama, and music.

CRITICAL CONCEPT 7

Some children are delayed in their acquisition of phonology, semantics, syntax, or pragmatics. Some may have special difficulty understanding how print and books work. These language and literacy challenges may be severe enough to require further evaluation and special intervention from a speech and language pathologist—a professional trained to work with children on such disorders.

Application #1   Assess the language of students in informal play settings. Audiotape each child in your class in an informal conversation. Later, analyze the tape in relation to the key areas of language described in this chapter. Refer children that show significant deficits in one or several areas to the speech and language pathologist for further evaluation.

Application #2   Plan activities that follow through on the interventions of the speech and language pathologist. Provide group experiences and play materials that address specific speech sounds, endings, grammatical structures, or word meanings that are being addressed in therapy sessions.

Application #3   Offer lap reading sessions to children who show little interest in or knowledge of print. In these sessions, have individual children sit in your lap; read and reread their favorite books. Encourage children to turn the pages, point to illustrations and print, and talk about the story. Provide literacy play props in the sociodramatic play center. Show children with literacy delays how to use these props in make-believe reading and writing.

ASSESSING YOUNG CHILDREN: Preschool Language and Literacy Development

Areas of Development	What to Watch For	Indicators of Atypical Development	Applications
Oral language abilities	Accurately utters speech sounds that are typically acquired by the child's age. Articulates clearly enough to be understood by peers. Uses a varied vocabulary to communicate. Speaks in sentences of four or five words by age 5. Uses morphemes, such as *ing* or plural *s* by age 4. Uses language in socially appropriate ways.	Poor articulation of speech sounds and an inability to imitate these when presented by an adult. Limited vocabulary. Use of the word *thing* to stand for words the child cannot remember. Absence of morphemes or incorrect uses of these (e.g., "Me go …"). Prevalence of short one- or two-word utterances at age 4. Socially inappropriate language (e.g., talking too much).	Create an environment that includes much play and social interaction. Engage children in natural conversation using strategies that promote specific aspects of language: (a) naming objects and actions (semantics); (b) speaking clear, fluent language in an enthused tone (phonology); and (c) expanding shorter, simpler sentences into fuller ones, using many morphemes (syntax).

| Literacy skills | Early scribble writing by age 4. Writing part of one's name or other letter writing by age 5. By this same age, an ability to point out print and knowledge that it can stand for ideas. Having favorite books and learning to "read" some of these by heart. By age 5, trying to map memorized stories over the text of favorite books. | An inability to handle or look at books (e.g., inability to turn pages or hold the book upright). A lack of attention and positive response in shared reading with an adult. By age 5, an inability to distinguish print from pictures. | Provide writing materials and books in all areas of the classroom. Model the use of these materials in play. Engage in lap reading sessions with each child each week in which the child sits in an adult's lap and listens to and reads favorite books. |

Interpreting Assessment Data: Variations in language and literacy are due to the specific languages spoken in the home and cultural differences in reading preferences. Children will differ in the speech sounds they utter and sentences they speak if they are trying to learn two languages simultaneously. They may learn words and morphemes more slowly if English is not the preferred language of their family. They may be less attentive to children's books and may write less if these are not a regular part of their family life. However, if children cannot communicate verbally with peers or teachers, referral to a speech and language pathologist is recommended. In-class interventions to enhance phonology, grammar, or vocabulary may ameliorate speech deficits. Reading to children in the home or classroom may also address language and literacy problems.

CHAPTER 13

Social and Emotional Development of Preschoolers

GUIDING QUESTIONS

1. What is initiative, and how is it related to self-concept and culture in the preschool years?
2. What is social competence, and what are the characteristics of children of popular, rejected, and neglected peer status?
3. How do friendships influence the social development of preschoolers?
4. What are the five stages of social participation in the preschool years?
5. What are the major theories for how positive and negative social behaviors are acquired?
6. How are altruism and empathy learned?
7. How is aggression learned, and what types of aggression may be observed in the preschool years?
8. How are preschool social competence, social behaviors, and peer relationships influenced by culture?
9. In what ways do poverty, relationships with siblings, child care, and gender affect social development?
10. What classroom adaptations will help children with special needs form positive relationships with peers and acquire social skills?

This chapter explores the social and emotional growth of children between the ages of 2 and 5. During the preschool years, many children become quite self-assured, independent, and social. They acquire the desire and ability to interact with adults and other children. They can persuade peers, gain admission into games or play activities already in progress, and resolve conflicts. Children with social skills are often better liked and have more friends. Such positive peer relationships have been found to predict long-range positive social development and mental health. In fact, having friends and being liked by other children in preschool may be more powerful predictors of later adult happiness than grades in school or scores on achievement tests (Berndt, 2007; Ladd, 2007; Ladd & Burgess, 1999).

Even very young preschoolers display savvy techniques for influencing peers, as the following vignette shows:

Jason, a 2-year-old, watches as Brendan, also 2, plays with a toy car in a family child care home. He says nothing but displays an expression of great interest. He seems to say with his eyes, "I want to play with that car. Now, how am I going to get it?" He decides on a very sophisticated approach to obtain the desired toy.

He looks around the room and spies a smaller, less intricate toy vehicle. He picks this up and offers it to Brendan: "Here. You have this. You have it." As he says this, he holds the toy out toward his peer. Brendan hesitates, then drops the coveted car and

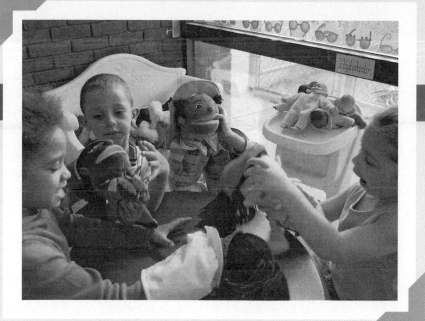

accepts Jason's gift. In an instant, Jason seizes the desired toy and pretends to drive it along the floor.

Jason's behaviors demonstrate tremendous social ability and knowledge. Earlier in life he might have resorted to primitive object-attainment strategies common in toddlerhood, such as snatching the toy and running off or screaming, "Give me it! Mine!" Now he tries a less physical, more social approach. He speculates on what might motivate Brendan to give up the toy—another car. Then, with artfully crafted behaviors and language, he offers it to his peer. The roots of negotiation and compromise can be observed in this simple behavior.

As children get older, their efforts to persuade peers become more sophisticated and highly linguistic. The following story illustrates a 4-year-old's effort to obtain a needed toy:

Lauren is building with blocks. She discovers that she needs a long block, but Hanna is using all these. She asks in a friendly voice, "Hanna, can I have one of the long blocks?" Hanna doesn't even bother to look up from her work. "No," she says in an annoyed tone. Lauren pauses, appearing to be studying the situation and thinking through the possible solutions to the problem.

"If you give me a long block, you can be in my club," Lauren says at last. Suddenly, Hanna is quite interested; she looks up from her block building and asks, "What?"

"Give me the long blocks, and you can be in my club," Lauren repeats. Hanna smiles. "Okay. You can have them all," she says, pushing her entire pile of blocks over to Lauren.

Realizing that her strategy has paid off, Lauren decides to use it again and again. By the end of the morning, every child in the class is vying for membership in her club!

Lauren has developed a clever—if somewhat manipulative—strategy for getting what she needs. She uses both language and knowledge of peer motivations. For example, she shows that she understands the growing need among her age-mates for peer acceptance and group membership.

This chapter describes these and other social behaviors that emerge during the preschool years. It highlights the emotional characteristics of the preschooler and shows how these enhance—or detract from—human relationships.

EMOTIONAL GROWTH IN THE PRESCHOOL YEARS

Early childhood is a crucial period for the formation of positive feelings toward oneself, others, and the larger world. Children who are nurtured, encouraged, and accepted by adults and peers will be emotionally well adjusted. Children who are abused, neglected, or rejected can suffer social and mental health difficulties. Emotional states in early childhood have a powerful impact on social relationships. Children who are emotionally healthy are better able to enter into positive relationships with both peers and adults (Fabes, Leonard, Kupanoff, & Martin, 2001; McElwain, Halberstadt, & Volling, 2007).

Initiative versus Guilt

The work of Erik Erikson (1963, 1982) has long guided teachers, mental health professionals, and parents in understanding the emotional development of young children. Erikson believed that humans must develop through eight *ages* of emotional growth if they are to feel competent and self-fulfilled in their lives (see discussion in Chapter 3). Each age is characterized by an emotional struggle between two polar internal states, one negative and one positive. During the preschool years, this struggle is between initiative and guilt. Emotionally healthy preschoolers will want to take action and assert themselves, according to Erikson. They will wish to create, invent, pretend, take risks, and engage in lively and imaginative activities with peers. Erikson (1963) called this urge to make creative efforts **initiative.** When adults encourage such divergent activities and avoid criticism or excessive restriction, a child's sense of initiative will grow. When children are led to believe their efforts are wrong, they develop a sense of guilt.

This struggle between initiative and guilt explains why many preschool and kindergarten children are so energetic in pursuit of imaginative play activities. It also explains why some children come to view themselves as bad or naughty. Although feelings of guilt have a positive role in development because they lead children to assume responsibility for their own behaviors, Erikson argues that overwhelming guilt inhibits emotional growth. Children who are punished or criticized for their efforts will gradually stop trying and will construct understandings of themselves as bad people. Erikson suggests that adults can promote a sense of initiative by creating noncritical environments in which children are allowed to take risks. Encouragement of creative processes with less emphasis on finished products also will facilitate initiative.

initiative: Erikson's term for an emotional state, often acquired in the preschool years, in which children assert themselves, make creative attempts, take risks, and reach out to peers. Children whose initiatives are thwarted will experience an opposite emotional state: *guilt*.

Social Initiative

One way initiative manifests itself in the developing child is through energetic interactions with peers. Many preschoolers show **social initiative**—an interest in reaching out to others, making social contacts, and trying out social behaviors. The healthy preschool child, from Erikson's perspective, displays an eagerness to engage others. A child who is burdened by guilt is more hesitant in social interactions and is more likely to be rejected by peers.

social initiative: A desire, common in the preschool years, to reach out to others, make social contacts, and try out new social behaviors.

Research suggests that social initiative is critical for positive peer relations. Children who take initiative in play are better able to sustain peer interactions (Ladd, 2005; Ladd & Coleman, 1997; Miller & Coll, 2007) and can more readily enter playgroups (Ramsey, 1989a, 1989b). Such children are also better liked by peers and form friendships more easily (Berndt, 2007). Erikson's interpretation of these findings would be that initiative is necessary for the formation of human relationships. At any age, making friends or becoming intimate necessitates some self-assurance and risk taking.

Initiative and Self-Concept

Self-concept is defined as an individual's theory of self (Butler & Gasson, 2005; Harter, 1990, 2003). One's self-concept includes all self-perceptions of one's own competence and characteristics, including ethnic and gender identity. Because it is a theory, it is continually modified and changed with experience. As children grow older, self-concept is refined and clarified. A person with a positive self-concept is said to be happy with or feel good about his or her self-perceptions. When children proudly announce, "Look at how high up I can climb!" or "I have a lot of friends in preschool!" they are displaying healthy views of self. Obviously, a positive self-concept is critical for happiness and fulfillment throughout life.

According to Erikson, positive self-concept is related to feelings of initiative during the preschool years. A child who makes creative efforts in play or work or who actively engages peers will feel successful. It is the process of doing or creating that is crucial; actual skills or accomplishments are less important to young children from Erikson's viewpoint. Most children with a healthy sense of initiative will feel good about themselves. Only children whose activities are discouraged or harshly criticized by adults will suffer poor self-concept.

Erikson's views are supported by research. Preschoolers do tend to refer to concrete activities and actions—that is, initiatives—in assessing their own competence. Statements such as "I can swing pretty high" and "I can wash my own hair" reflect children's pride in their efforts (Herbert & Stipek, 2005; Stipek & Green, 2001; Tracy & Robins, 2007). Generally, preschool children do have positive self-concepts, as Erikson's theory would suggest. They tend to believe, for example, that they can do almost anything. In one study, even when 4-year-olds had just failed several times to complete a difficult task, they reported that they would be successful on their next try (Stipek & Green, 2001). Preschool children have been described as "exceedingly optimistic in self-ratings of their abilities and expectations for success" (Curry & Johnson, 1990, p. 69).

Erikson's explanation of these early, positive self-perceptions would be that children of this age are focusing on attempts or initiatives—that is, on the processes of playing or working—rather than on the outcomes or end products of their efforts. Preschoolers tend to base views of self on whether they try hard, have friends, and are viewed as "good" children (Herbert & Stipek, 2005). If preschoolers make an effort, get positive responses from peers and adults, and don't break rules, they tend to believe they have been successful. How sad it is that these positive self-concepts often disappear at about school age!

Social initiative appears to make a unique contribution to positive self-concept. Children who take initiative in interactions with peers and are less dependent on adults have been found to be more self-assured and confident in their abilities (Hartup, 1996). To Erikson, such findings show that self-concept and feelings of initiative are inextricably interrelated.

Initiative and Culture

Erikson observed initiative in preschoolers around the world. Findings of several recent cross-cultural studies, however, suggest that initiative may not be universally valued. Parents in China, for example, have been found to actively socialize children to become cautious, inhibited, and self-restrained—characteristics that are contrary to Erikson's conceptions of initiative (Chan, 1998; X. Chen, Rubin, & Sun, 1992; Rubin & Coplan, 2007). In fact, Chinese children who are shy or reticent are called *guai*, a Mandarin word meaning well behaved or good. Parents' efforts to teach reticence appear to be effective: Chinese children have been found to be more reserved and cautious than those from U.S. cultures (X. Chen, Cen, Li, & He, 2005). In fact, Chinese children who are shy tend to be preferred as playmates by peers of their own cultural group (Rubin & Mills, 1988). This finding is in sharp contrast to theory and research on shyness in American children.

self-concept: A person's overall view of self, which includes perceptions about traits, abilities, gender, and ethnic affiliation. As children acquire a self-concept, they strive to answer the question, "Who am I?"

Studies of Mexican American families also reveal that initiative is not a universally valued trait. In several studies, Mexican American parents have been found to emphasize **affiliative obedience,** defined as a high level of obedience to elders or respected authorities and a low level of self-assertion (Baer & Schmitz, 2007; Sanchez, 1997; Zuniga, 1998). Some Mexican American children have been observed to be collective and dependent on family members in solving problems and to take less individual initiative in resolving conflicts with peers (Diaz-Guerrero, 1987; Knight, Cota, & Bernal, 2002). Within this cultural group, such behaviors are important adaptations to conditions of hardship and oppression. They lead to mutual interdependence, or **enmeshment,** of family members, which is crucial for survival.

Diaz-Guerrero (1987) raises questions about whether initiative, self-assurance, and guilt are fundamental personality traits at all or simply patterns of behavior that can vary among individuals depending on the situation. Is it possible, he asks, that children can display initiative in one setting and be hesitant and shy in another? He has observed that Mexican American children show creative and self-assertive attempts in certain situations, such as when playing with peers in the absence of respected adults. They show more restrained, obedient interactions in other situations, such as during a family meal. He suggests that Mexican American children living in the United States might be most healthy if they were able to switch between initiative and restrained obedience according to the context.

Professionals working with children and families must be cautious, then, not to expect all preschoolers to display the high levels of initiative that Erikson described. Children of some cultural groups may have a sense of initiative but choose not to express it fully in some settings, such as at school. Many family service providers have observed children who are reserved and timid in a classroom engaging in active, noisy social play at home or in the neighborhood.

SOCIAL COMPETENCE

The term **social competence** refers to two interrelated aspects of human development: being liked by others and having skills to interact effectively in social settings. Positive peer relationships and social skills in children during their early years are good predictors of overall happiness and mental health in later life (Hartup & Laursen, 1993; Ladd, 2005). Children who are disliked by peers, deficient in social abilities, or aggressive and impulsive in their interactions during their preschool years are more likely to become psychologically troubled adults (Asher & Coie, 1990; Dodge et al., 2003; Polman, de Castro, & Koops, 2007).

Teachers, caregivers, and parents can help children acquire social skills and make friends. In fact, these may be the most important goals of early childhood programs. It is important to keep in mind, however, that social competence is defined differently in different cultures. The social behaviors that predict peer acceptance in one culture may not in another. An active, rough play style, for example, may lead to popularity or rejection, depending on the cultural experiences of playmates. Trying to teach all children precisely the same set of social skills, then, would be a misapplication of the social competence research.

Peer Status: Children Who Are Popular, Rejected, and Neglected

Some preschoolers have a very hard time interacting with peers, while others are quite competent at making friends and winning acceptance and respect from their playmates. Researchers regularly use the **sociometric interview** to assess overall social competence of preschoolers in classrooms. In this technique, children of a particular class are interviewed individually about which peers they like to play with and which they do not. Some children are named often as preferred playmates. Researchers call these children *popular.*

affiliative obedience: A high level of obedience to elders or respected authorities and a low level of self-assertion that is emphasized more in some cultures than in others.

enmeshment: A goal of socialization in some cultures in which children become attached to, cooperate with, and rely on others, particularly their family members.

social competence: The degree to which a person is liked by others and has learned skills to interact effectively in social settings.

sociometric interview: A technique to assess the overall social competence of children in classrooms in which individuals are interviewed about which peers they like to play with and which they do not.

Others are regularly named by their peers as undesirable playmates and are considered to be *rejected*. Children in a third group—those who are *neglected*—are never named by peers at all (Dodge & Price, 1994; Jiang & Cillessen, 2005). **Sociometric status** refers to the category a particular child occupies in a group. What are the children of each category like? What behaviors do they display in a classroom?

Children Who Are Popular.   Children who are of **popular sociometric status** are well liked by peers and have many friends. These children are named often by peers as desired playmates in sociometric interviews. Characteristics of children who are popular—drawn from research—are presented in Table 13-1.

The table shows why children who are popular are so well liked. First, they are very active socially (Trawick-Smith, 1992). They often initiate contact with peers and are energetic in directing play activities. Overall, they are leaders who make many play suggestions and structure the activity of others. In the following scenario, Sheila's behaviors illustrate this active social style:

SHEILA: Now, Lauren, it's time to bathe our babies, okay? Can you come over here and help us? Let's bathe 'em 'cause they're very filthy. So let's really scrub 'em. And I'll be the mamma, you be the older sister, okay? Now you come over now, all right?

LAUREN: All right. (Moves over to Sheila)

SHEILA: Let's say we set up for the party, okay? Some guests are coming at five o'clock. (Now addresses Susan) And let's say you come help too, Susan.

SUSAN: (Says nothing, joins Sheila and Lauren)

SHEILA: Now we need to set the table. You have to put the forks just the right way. Here, I'll show you. (Demonstrates how to set the table) Now you do it, okay, Susan? Oh. There's the phone. (To Lauren) Will you answer that, honey?

sociometric status: A child's relative status in a group of peers—popular, rejected, or neglected—based on a sociometric interview.

popular sociometric status: The peer group status of children who are well liked, have many friends, and are named often as desired playmates in sociometric interviews.

Characteristic	Description
Socially active	Takes initiative in play and makes many social contacts
Highly directive	Takes leadership in play and directs the activities of peers
Linguistically effective	Uses language often and competently to persuade peers or capture and maintain their attention
Positive in affect	Engages in friendly, supportive interactions and avoids bossing, bullying, and whining
Diplomatic	Accepts the suggestions of peers a moderate amount of the time or rejects others' ideas by offering alternatives
Skilled in conflict resolution	Resolves conflicts in nonaggressive ways that are satisfying to all involved
Skilled in playgroup entry	Enters playgroups effectively, using interesting and unobtrusive initiatives
Competent in interpreting social situations	Accurately reads social situations and the characteristics of playmates and selects appropriate behaviors for resolving conflicts

TABLE 13-1
Characteristics of Popular Children

Sheila is exceedingly active in directing peers. Her playmates seem very pleased to be able to play with her and do as she directs—although they have trouble getting a word in edgewise!

Children who are popular are usually those who can use language effectively in social situations (Hart, Olsen, Robinson, & Mandleco, 1997). In the following vignette, Jeremy demonstrates such verbal skill in persuading a peer to help him build with blocks:

JEREMY: (Addresses nearby child in a friendly tone) Help me build my boat, Alonzo.
ALONZO: (Says nothing and does not look up from his own blocks)
JEREMY: (In an angry tone) Alonzo! Help me build it!
ALONZO: (Also angry) No!
JEREMY: (In a friendly tone again) Alonzo, let's say this is our boat. (Points to his block structure) Let's say we build it, all right?
ALONZO: Okay. But I'll do the long blocks. (Helps Jeremy stack blocks)

In this example, Jeremy uses subtle changes in phrasing and intonation to persuade a peer to do what he wants. When his angry demand does not work, he tries a request for joint action: "Let's say we build it, all right?" This tactic leads to success. The child appears to be experimenting with language, trying out options until arriving on phrasing that works. Such verbal skill is common among well-liked children.

Children who are popular are friendly and positive in their interactions with peers. They are less aggressive or bossy and often give positive feedback, attention, and affection to their playmates (Crick, Ostrov, & Werner, 2006). Overall, they are very pleasant children to play with. Such children can be assertive—they are not led around by peers. A moderate amount of the time, they reject the play suggestions or initiatives of their playmates (Trawick-Smith, 1992). When they do reject others' ideas, however, they do so in a tactful manner. Often they give a reason for rejecting another's idea and may offer an alternative course of action. This diplomatic style is profiled in the following example:

JOSEPH: (Placing plastic farm animals in a block structure) I'm building a farm here. Let's say this is a farm.
CEDRIC: (Building with blocks) No, this is a museum where paintings are. See, Joseph?
JOSEPH: No! It's a farm!
CEDRIC: No, 'cause there's not enough room for a whole farm. Let's say it's a museum where farm animals can go. They can go to the museum, okay? See? (Begins placing farm animals in his structure)
JOSEPH: Okay. (Joins Cedric's play theme) But those animals might make a mess at the museum!

Here, Cedric has rejected Joseph's suggestion but has given a reason for rejecting it and offered an alternative play theme. His rebuff of Joseph's idea was not harsh or hostile and did not result in a disruption of the play.

Children who are popular are quite competent at resolving conflicts, and they often do so in friendly, nonaggressive ways (Hartup & Laursen, 1993; Trawick-Smith, 1988). They are more likely to compromise when disputes arise, as the next vignette illustrates:

Two 5-year-olds in Kenya are tending cows in a field near their home. One child invents a game to play.

ADISSU: (Grabs a handful of dirt from the ground and throws it at Nicodemu, laughing) Ha! I'll get you all dirty!
NICODEMU: No! I don't want this game.
ADISSU: (Throws another handful) You try to make me dirty, too. You throw at me.
NICODEMU: (In an angry tone) Stop it! It's getting in my eyes.

ADISSU: (Stops and reflects) Well, we can throw at the cows. See? (Tosses a handful of dirt on the grazing farm animals)

NICODEMU: They might run.

ADISSU: No. See? (In a loud, animated voice) Getting the cows! (Throws dirt)

NICODEMU: (Smiles, begins to throw dirt on the animals as well)

Here, Adissu works out a compromise in a dispute over what to play. He adapts his original play suggestion so that the game is acceptable to his peer. He does so without bullying or aggression. Such give-and-take is quite common among popular children.

To be effective with peers, young children must learn how to enter a playgroup (Brotman, Gouley, & Chesir-Teran, 2005; Putallaz & Wasserman, 1989). Children who are popular are quite savvy at gaining entrance into play in progress. They have acquired social skills that win their acceptance in groups (Harrist & Bradley, 2006; Ramsey, 1989a, 1989b). They do not just ask to play—a strategy that rarely has been found to be successful. Instead, they may simply start playing along with peers, making interesting but unobtrusive contributions to the play theme. They often address one of the children by name. These strategies have been found to be very successful among preschool-age children (Ramsey, 1989b).

One last characteristic of children who are popular is that they can accurately *read* social situations (Dodge & Price, 1994; Lemerise et al., 2005). They seem to be aware of the needs, motives, and behaviors of their peers and of the effects of their own behaviors. They are better able to identify the outcomes of particular social initiatives, for example. They know that pushing or hitting can lead to retaliation and that some children will do what you ask if you are friendly (Trawick-Smith, 1992). They can more accurately name the intentions of peers (Dodge & Price, 1994). This ability to monitor one's social behaviors and those of others may explain why popular children are able to select strategies that are most successful: they have come to learn which strategies work well with peers and which do not.

Children Who Are Rejected.   Children of **rejected sociometric status** are actively avoided by peers. These children are named often by peers as undesirable playmates in sociometric interviews. Characteristics of children who are rejected—drawn from research—are presented in Table 13-2.

As shown in the table, children who are rejected are sometimes disliked because they display antisocial behaviors that are extremely obvious and disruptive (Yoon, Hughes, Cavell, & Thompson, 2000). They are often quite aggressive. **Aggression** is defined as any action that has the intent of harming another either physically or psychologically. This might include hitting, biting, pushing, kicking, or name-calling and other verbal abuse.

rejected sociometric status: The peer group status of children who are actively avoided by peers and who are named often as undesirable playmates in sociometric interviews.

aggression: Any action that has the intent of harming another either physically or psychologically, such as hitting, biting, pushing, kicking, or name-calling and other verbal abuse.

Characteristic	Description
Negative	Displays a negative, obviously unpleasant affect
Whiny	Complains, whimpers, or tattles with regularity
Unpredictably aggressive	Hits, pushes, bites, or verbally assaults peers, often without reason or provocation
Unskilled at interpreting social situations	Misreads social situations and erroneously assigns hostile intent to benign acts of peers
Antisocial and isolated from peers	Avoids others and chooses to play alone

TABLE 13-2
Characteristics of Rejected Children

Interestingly, not all children who are aggressive are disliked. It may be that subtle differences in aggression determine a particular child's peer group status in the classroom (Crick et al., 2006; Dodge & Price, 1994). For example, children who only display **reactive aggression**—aggression in which they resist or strike out in response to peer mistreatment—are not as likely to be rejected. In contrast, children who frequently engage in **hostile aggression**—anger-fueled aggression that is unpredictable, illogical, and unprovoked—are more likely to be disliked by peers. Indirect, verbal aggressive behaviors, such as tattling or name-calling, appear to be especially deplored by children (Putallaz et al., 2007).

It is easy to see why peers stay away from classmates who are unpredictably aggressive. Such children may respond impulsively and unpredictably to the slightest frustration or disagreement with uncontrollable violence. The uncertainty and potential risks of playing with such children tend to offset the benefits of befriending them. The following story illustrates the aggressive and unpredictable behaviors of one rejected child:

> Three children are looking at books in the library corner. Each is absorbed in reading; all is quite peaceful for a while. Without warning, Philip kicks one of the other children who has moved too close. He then grabs the child's book.
>
> PHILIP: (Pulling the book from Albert's hands) Give me this.
> ALBERT: No. Give it back, Philip!
> PHILIP: (Moves toward Albert in a threatening way and uses an angry tone) You better not touch me.
> ALBERT: (Covers his head, expecting to be struck)
> PHILIP: (Pushes Albert) This is my book. (Now turns to Rubin, who has been watching, and snatches his book as well) You give these to me.
>
> Both Albert and Rubin quickly retreat from the library corner to find a teacher. Philip sits down by himself and continues to read.

In this story, Philip becomes suddenly aggressive for no obvious reason. He bullies both of the other boys even though such aggression will drive them from the play area. He seems content to be on his own after they have left.

A characteristic of children who are rejected is an inability to read social situations and to understand the feelings of their peers (Dodge & Price, 1994; Lemerise et al., 2005). For example, rejected children often erroneously interpret the actions of peers as intentional and hostile (Crick et al., 2006; Yoon et al., 2000), as the following vignette demonstrates:

> Sergio has accidentally bumped into Tamara's blocks, toppling a portion of the structure. Tamara immediately attacks, striking her peer several times before a teacher can intervene.
>
> TEACHER: (Alarmed) What's happening here?
> TAMARA: He kicked over my blocks.
> SERGIO: (In tears) I didn't mean to.
> TAMARA: He tried to kick 'em. If he kicks 'em again … (turns to Sergio) I'll hit you again!
> SERGIO: (Sobs loudly) But it wasn't on purpose!
> TAMARA: (Kicking out at Sergio) You better get away from me. Stay outa' my blocks!

Here, Tamara has reacted angrily and has assumed that the other child's action was deliberate. This tendency to assign negative intentions may explain why children who are rejected so frequently strike out, seemingly without provocation.

Some children who are rejected are also isolates. They may choose to play alone and push or hit when others move near them (Ladd, 2006; Rubin & Coplan, 2007). Such children may be most at risk because they not only are difficult to play with but also show no desire to be

reactive aggression:
Aggression in which children resist or strike out in response to peer mistreatment.

hostile aggression:
Anger-fueled aggression that is unpredictable, illogical, and unprovoked.

TABLE 13-3
**Characteristics of
Neglected Children**

Characteristic	Description
Isolated from peers	Plays alone and often retreats when peers approach
Shy	Exhibits reticence and anxiety in social situations
Unskilled at entering playgroups	Lacks the ability to enter playgroups in progress or to join peers in play
Unskilled in capturing peer attention	Lacks the ability to capture and maintain a peer's attention
Unskilled in play leadership	Lacks the social skills or initiative to guide peers' play and make play suggestions

with peers at all. Many children who are rejected suffer low self-esteem, although some hold exceptionally unrealistic, positive views of self (Boivin & Hymel, 1997; Nelson, Rubin, & Fox, 2005). Some children who are rejected, for example, report that they are very well liked by peers when in fact they are not. This is another sign of their inability to accurately interpret social circumstances.

How do children first come to be rejected? They may begin life with a negative inborn temperament (Corapci, 2008; Eley, Lichtenstein, & Stevenson, 1999). They are more likely to have parents who are punitive and authoritarian (Hurt, Hoza, & Pelham, 2007; Nix et al., 1999; Sandstrom, 2007). When they come in contact with peers, a vicious circle emerges: Children who are rejected push, hit, or display negative affect, and their peers move away from them or refuse to play. This rejection may anger them or threaten their positive feelings of self. They respond with even more aggression; their acting-out behavior escalates. Such children are at special risk and are in most need of adult intervention to enhance social relationships (Kupersmidt, Coie, & Dodge, 1990).

Children Who Are Neglected. Children of **neglected sociometric status** are largely ignored by their peers and sometimes even by their caregivers or teachers. These children are rarely mentioned at all in sociometric interviews, as if they did not exist. Characteristics of children who are neglected—drawn from research—are presented in Table 13-3.

As shown in the table, their predominant characteristic is **isolate behavior**—a pattern of interaction in which they rarely initiate contact with others and often retreat when initiatives are directed toward them. Some children who are neglected prefer to be alone (Rubin & Coplan, 2007). Many (though not all) neglected children are shy (Nelson, Rubin, & Fox, 2005; Miller & Coll, 2007).

Observations of the interactions of children who are neglected reveal that they are often quite inept in social settings. They lack the social skills needed to enter a playgroup or to capture the attention of peers. They have difficulty persuading others. Often they respond inappropriately to others' initiatives, as the following vignette shows:

Twana is swinging by herself on an urban playground. Several older children wander over to the swing. They are loud and active.

ROSE: (Laughing, speaking to her peers) Hey, let's swing. (To Twana) We're gonna swing with you, little girl. All right?

TWANA: (Slows her swinging, looks down, says nothing)

CELESTE: (Speaking to Twana) Little girl, what's your name? You got a name?

TWANA: (Looks down, does not respond)

neglected sociometric status: The peer group status of children who are ignored by their peers and who are rarely mentioned at all in sociometric interviews.

isolate behavior: A pattern of interaction in which children rarely initiate contact with others, retreat when initiatives are directed toward them, and often prefer to be alone.

Neglected children are often withdrawn and socially anxious.

CELESTE: (Persisting) Can you swing as high as this? Try it. Try this. (Demonstrates)

TWANA: (Gets off the swing and walks to her mother)

ROSE: (Laughs and says to her peers) Don't think she likes us.

MOTHER: Twana, those girls want to play. You go play with them. You can swing with them.

TWANA: (Shakes her head and hides her face under her mother's coat)

In spite of repeated initiatives by the other children, Twana does not respond. She does not appear interested in social interaction and leaves the area in response to their friendly advances. It is easy to see why peers give up trying to befriend such children and eventually come to ignore them.

Some studies have found that children who are neglected can acquire social skills and may suffer little emotional harm from their "invisible" status among peers (Harrist, Zaia, Bates, Dodge, & Pettit, 1997). They have been found to make friends and interact to some degree with other children. Some show social abilities but only in certain settings or with particular peers. A child who is neglected at school may be very well liked in the neighborhood or among siblings. Observations across situations and areas are necessary, then, in assessing peer neglect (Broberg, Lamb, & Hwang, 1990). It is those children who *never* interact with others and are thus unable to make any friends at all who are at risk, particularly as they get older (Nelson et al., 2005). If a child never initiates contact with peers, adult assistance may be needed.

Children who are neglected may have been born with a **slow-to-warm-up temperament,** described in Chapter 3, which is characterized by quietness and wariness. Caution and timidity in entering into new relationships may be a fundamental aspect of such children's personalities (Kagan, Reznick, & Snidman, 1988; Prior, Smart, Sanson, & Oberklaid, 2000). A circular relationship between temperament and peer interaction emerges: Children who are neglected may be so quiet and cautious that they are ignored. Because they are not invited to participate in play activities, they miss opportunities to refine social skills and gain confidence in peer relations. They grow comfortable playing in isolation. As they further isolate themselves, they are noticed less and less.

slow-to-warm-up temperament: A disposition that is characterized by quietness, wariness, and timidity in entering into new relationships.

Friendships

Most preschool children have at least one reciprocated friendship with a peer (Gifford-Smith & Brownell, 2003; Ladd, Kochenderfer, & Coleman, 1997; E. Lindsey, 2002; B. Vaughn et al., 2001). Those who maintain long-term friendships tend to be more competent socially.

A single friendship can insulate a child from some of the negative effects of being rejected or neglected by peers (Hartup & Moore, 1990). Having a friend may be reaffirming: it shows children that they can be liked, even if only by one other child. In one study, it was discovered that the number of friends children had in kindergarten was related to how well they adjusted to a new school setting (Ladd, Kochenderfer, & Coleman, 1996).

Friendships are very useful for social skills intervention in preschool. Studies have shown that friendships provide unique social opportunities for children. Conflicts among friends are less heated and more likely to end in compromise (Hughes & Dunn, 2007; Hartup, Laursen, Stewart, & Eastenson, 1988). Play between friends is often more positive and advanced (McElwain, Halberstadt, & Volling, 2007; Vaughn et al., 2001). A child is more likely to be accepted into a playgroup when one of the players is a friend (Ramsey, 1989a). Playing with friends enables less effective children to try out new social skills and enjoy greater success (Sebanc, 2003). So, an especially opportune time for teachers to facilitate social skills is when children are playing with their friends.

In some cases, preschool friendships are temporary, lasting only for the duration of a particular play activity or perhaps extending for a day or two. Other friendships are long lasting (Cairns, Leung, Buchannan, & Cairns, 1995). Some years ago, when I was conducting a study of social competence, I accidentally created a friendship between two 4-year-olds—one a rejected child—by frequently bringing them together in a laboratory play setting. Soon teachers reported that the two children were inseparable in the classroom. Years later, I ran into the mother of one of the children, who reported that they were still close friends in middle school!

Social Participation

Most preschool children—regardless of their status in a classroom—play with peers. However, the level of their **social participation**—the degree of their involvement with peers during play—varies considerably. In her classic research, Mildred Parten (1932) discovered stages of social participation that most young children pass through during the preschool years. These are presented in Table 13-4.

In the first of Parten's stages, **unoccupied behavior,** children show little interest in what is going on around them. They do not interact with toys, materials, or peers. Parten proposes that this type of play is most prevalent in toddlerhood but declines as the social world of the young child broadens after age 3. Parten's second stage, **onlooker behavior,** is distinguished by an interest in what others are doing. Children at this stage often watch their peers play.

social participation: The degree of children's involvement with peers during play, ranging from unoccupied and onlooking behavior to cooperative play.

unoccupied behavior: A level of social participation in which children show little interest in what is going on around them and do not interact with toys, materials, or peers.

onlooker behavior: A level of social participation in which a child shows interest in what peers are doing and watches their play but does not interact with them.

TABLE 13-4
Parten's Stages of Social Participation

Stage	Description
Unoccupied behavior	Shows little interest in toys, persons, and activities occurring in the vicinity
Onlooker behavior	Shows an interest in peers and watches their activities intently; engages in no social contact
Parallel play	Engages in activities side by side with peers but rarely converses or interacts
Associative play	Pursues own individual play themes but interacts often; talks to peers and shares materials
Cooperative play	Adopts a single, coordinated play theme with peers; plans, negotiates, and differentiates roles in pursuit of a shared goal

SOURCE: Parten, 1932.

Although onlooking is not social behavior per se, it is considered an important social advancement. When children begin to show interest in others, they are taking a step toward more involved social participation.

Children show they are interested in peers' activities by increasingly watching or hovering around them, according to Parten. Shortly after this interest emerges, they begin to engage in **parallel play,** the next level of social participation. In parallel play, children pursue activities side by side with others. They rarely interact in these endeavors, however, and often do not even speak to one another. Nevertheless, they show enjoyment of the close proximity to their peers. The following vignette illustrates parallel play and a child care provider's role in encouraging it:

Two 3-year-olds are playing in the sandbox on the playground. Another child stands for a long time watching them. A caregiver moves into the area and approaches the onlooking child.

CAREGIVER: Why don't you make a sand pie, too, Markku? Come with me, I'll help you. (Takes the child's hand and walks to the sandbox)

MARKKU: (Says nothing but walks with the caregiver)

CAREGIVER: (In an enthused tone) Now I'm going to make a huge pie. (Begins to make a mound of sand)

MARKKU: (Says nothing but begins to make his own sand mound, occasionally stopping to watch the caregiver and other children as they work)

The caregiver continues to converse with Markku and work with the sand. After several minutes, she withdraws from the sandbox. Markku continues to play with the sand and to watch his playmates. No interaction among the children occurs.

The child care provider in this vignette is facilitating parallel play. Her intervention leads the onlooking child to a more social level of activity than before: Markku now plays right next to the other children and watches and even copies their actions.

Once children are regularly playing parallel to others, a new form of play can be expected to emerge, according to Parten. At this stage, children begin to engage in **associative play,** in which they pursue their own individual play themes yet interact often. In such activity, children might talk to one another about what they are doing or even share materials, as in the following vignette:

Two 4-year-olds play on the ground near their homes in a village in East India. Meena makes noises and speaks to herself in a pretend voice as she moves a clay elephant along the ground. Sarala is playing with a paper snake. She makes impressive hissing noises and drags the toy along the ground. At first, the two children do not speak to one another.

MEENA: (Speaking suddenly) This elephant is so hot in the sun. See? (Points to her clay elephant, then makes a motion showing her elephant is drinking water) See? He's drinking from the river.

SARALA: Yes. My snake is thirsty too. But snakes can't go to the river. (Continues to make her snake slither along)

MEENA: (Places the toy under a structure of sticks) And this is the elephant's house. See? He's going in, but he's not supposed to be in there. (Laughs)

SARALA: (Looks up from her paper snake) Let me see.

MEENA: Here. (Points to the toy under the sticks)

SARALA: Well, my snake needs a house. And she can go inside. Give me those sticks. (Points)

MEENA: (Hands over some sticks, then begins to play with her elephant again)

parallel play: A level of social participation in which children pursue activities side by side with peers but rarely interact or speak to them.

associative play: A level of social participation in which children pursue their own individual play themes yet interact often with peers, talking about what they are doing and sharing materials.

SARALA: (After fashioning a house from sticks, speaks to herself) Now the snake is
            sleeping. But he wakes up when someone walks by and he bites! (Makes a
            hissing sound)

In the associative play depicted in this vignette, the children play with their own toys but occasionally converse with each other, discussing their individual activities. They share materials and exchange ideas. Their play is not as yet fully coordinated, however. They have not adopted a single, cooperative theme. They remain very absorbed in their own personal play pursuits.

The last of Parten's stages, **cooperative play,** often emerges in the later preschool years. This form of play represents the most complex form of social participation. Children now adopt a single, coordinated play theme and plan, negotiate, and differentiate roles in pursuit of their shared goal. In the following story, associative play is transformed into cooperative play by two older preschoolers:

Two 4-year-olds are playing with dolls in the dramatic play area of their Head Start classroom. As they each dress and care for their "baby," they speak to one another about their activities.

MIA: (Dressing a doll) I'm getting ready to go shopping. I need to bundle her up
            'cause it's cold.
JENNIFER: My baby won't stop crying. (Speaking to her doll) What is it? Are you sick
            or something?

The two children continue to play out their own themes for several more minutes.

JENNIFER: She's getting real sick, I think. She could spit up or something.
MIA: Maybe she's got to go to the doctor.
JENNIFER: Yeah. She might need some medicine.
MIA: I'm going to the store, all right? And let's say this is our car, okay? (Points
            to two chairs)
JENNIFER: (In mock urgency) But I need to get to the doctor or the hospital.
MIA: Okay. Let's say you come over and ride with me, all right, Jennifer? And we
            take your baby to the hospital and then get the groceries.
JENNIFER: Okay. Where do I get in?

As the two children drive to town with their dolls, they discuss the illness and what the doctor will do.

In this interchange, Mia and Jennifer gradually merge their individual but similar play themes into a single, coordinated one. They begin to jointly plan their play and to coordinate their make-believe events, actions, and characters. Their activity moves, then, from associative to cooperative play.

According to Parten, many children begin to engage in frequent cooperative play with peers by age 5. This is not to say that they completely abandon earlier play forms. Even very social children occasionally revisit the onlooker or parallel play stage. Often children begin their play at an onlooker or parallel level, then move into cooperative play as their activities proceed (Robinson, Anderson, Porter, Hart, & Wouden-Miller, 2003). However, Parten proposes that the ratio of cooperative play to less social play forms increases in typically developing children.

Positive and Negative Social Behaviors

As previously discussed, social behaviors will determine whether children are accepted or rejected by peers, whether they make friends, and how fully they participate in play activities.

cooperative play: A level of social participation in which children adopt a single, coordinated play theme and plan, negotiate, and differentiate roles in pursuit of a shared goal.

Generally, children who display kindness and caring will make more friends and will be well liked; those who are antisocial in their interactions will not.

Altruism and Empathy. Many preschool children show kindness toward other persons in their interactions. Acts such as sharing a toy, helping with a puzzle, and comforting a crying peer are called **altruistic behaviors.** A traditional view has been that very young children are too egocentric to perform these acts (Piaget, 1952). Research suggests, however, that young children can be very altruistic (Trommsdorff, Friedlmeier, & Mayer, 2007). Preschoolers have been observed showing concerned facial expressions and offering help or consolation when a peer begins to cry. Children as young as age 2 have been found to spontaneously share toys and give affection and help without any prompting from adults.

What can parents, caregivers, or teachers do to promote altruism among young children? Each theory of child development (see Chapter 3) holds its own answer to this question. Maturationists would suggest that humans are born with a sense of **empathy,** an ability to feel vicariously others' emotions or physical pain. From this perspective, when children see peers fall and cry, they can almost feel the hurt and sadness themselves. Support for this perspective comes from studies of newborns who have been found to show great upset when they hear others crying (M. L. Hoffman, 1988; A. D. Murray, 1985). A remarkable finding of these studies was that the more a cry resembled the subject's own crying, the more upset that subject became. For example, the infants would show greater disturbance when listening to cries of a baby their own age than to those of an older child or adult. It is as if these infants could more fully empathize with those who were most similar to them!

Maturationists would suggest that empathy is mainly an inborn trait. All children need for empathy to emerge, from this view, are social experiences in which positive emotions can grow and flourish. As children observe peers' expressions of happiness, sadness, or anger, they come to feel these emotions themselves. They naturally respond in helpful and kind ways when others are upset (Warneken & Tomasello, 2006).

Psychoanalysts would propose that early attachment to parents and other caregivers leads to altruism and empathy. If adults are nurturing in their interactions and convey caring and concern, children will integrate these emotional responses into their own personalities. Research supports this theory. Children who are securely attached tend to perceive their peers in more positive ways and to have more friends than those who are not securely attached (Rah & Parke, 2008). What children need to acquire empathy, from this view, are

altruistic behaviors: Acts of kindness toward other persons, such as sharing a toy, helping with a puzzle, and comforting a crying peer.

empathy: An inborn ability to feel vicariously others' emotions or physical pain.

Preschool children often share, help others, and show kindness with no prompting from adults.

adults—parents and caregivers—who are nurturing and responsive. Parent educators and family service providers might encourage parents to perform attachment behaviors—warm touching, smiles, and enthusiastic responding. Caregivers and preschool teachers might also engage in warm, responsive interactions.

Behaviorist and learning theorists would suggest that these prosocial behaviors are rewarded and modeled by adults. Evidence supporting this view comes from studies showing the power of adult modeling. Research has demonstrated, for example, that when adults display sharing and cooperation in classrooms, their students are more likely to demonstrate these behaviors (Spinrad & Stifter, 2006; Zahn-Waxler et al., 1992). The effects of prosocial modeling have been found to be most powerful when combined with other social skills interventions, such as giving rewards for or pointing out and commenting on kind behaviors (Gibbs, Potter, & Goldstein, 1995). A message from this theoretical perspective is to be kind in interactions with children. Children are more likely to do what adults *do* than what adults *tell* them to do.

From a cognitive-developmental perspective, children construct understandings of altruism and empathy. As their social experience increases, they come to understand that certain social behaviors lead to desirable responses by others. They discover that kind acts, such as helpfulness and cooperation, bring about caring and acceptance by peers and adults. Programs have been developed to help children make these connections (Ladd, 2007). In these programs, adults use a variety of methods to help children notice the outcomes of specific social behaviors and learn to use a variety of prosocial strategies for resolving conflicts. Such programs have been found to promote prosocial behavior.

Ecological systems theorists would argue that altruism and empathy can be fully understood only by studying the family, the community, and society as a whole. Microsystem influences are believed to be at work: children in high-quality child care or Head Start centers that provide warm, responsive care will display more prosocial behavior (Burchinal & Cryer, 2003). Exosystem factors may also play a role: families who receive adequate social and mental health services may suffer less stress and therefore exhibit more positive behaviors in the home. Macrosystem influences are also important: children in societies that value kindness and cooperation are more likely to acquire these prosocial behaviors (Gamble & Modry-Mandell, 2008; Konner, 1993; B. B. Whiting & Edwards, 1988).

Aggression. Negative social behaviors can also be observed among some preschool children. Engaging in these behaviors can lead to peer rejection, a lack of friends, and low levels of social participation.

The most worrisome of these is aggression—defined previously as any physical or verbal behavior that is intended to harm or threaten another. It is important for teachers and parents to distinguish between aggression and a number of common, nonaggressive behaviors:

1. *Rough-and-tumble play.* Rough play, such as wrestling, play fighting, and friendly jostling, is usually not considered aggression. In fact, **rough-and-tumble play** may lead to social competence (DeWolf, 2001; Pellis & Pellis, 2007).
2. *Teasing play.* Taunting or arguing that is nonliteral and nonhostile is also not usually viewed as aggression. **Teasing play** is very common in the interactions of children of historically underrepresented groups (Campos, Keltner, Beck, Gonzaga, & John, 2007; Costibile et al., 1991; Endo, 2007; B. B. Whiting & Edwards, 1988).
3. *Assertiveness.* **Assertiveness,** or sticking up for oneself during disputes, is not usually considered aggression. For example, a child who resists having a toy snatched away by tugging it back and shouting "No!" is displaying assertiveness, not aggression.

rough-and-tumble play: A form of motor play—including wrestling, play fighting, rolling around, and chasing peers—that relieves tension and contributes to social competence but does not lead to aggression.

teasing play: A form of play, common in some cultures, in which children taunt one another or argue in a nonliteral and nonhostile way. Teasing play is not usually considered aggression.

assertiveness: Sticking up for oneself during disputes, such as tugging back a toy that has been snatched away. Assertiveness is not usually considered aggression.

4. *Conflicts and arguments.* A distinction is generally made between aggression and **conflicts and arguments**— disagreements that can be settled verbally (Thornberg, 2006). Conflicts, no matter how loud, do not necessarily involve aggression. The following vignette depicts a nonaggressive conflict:

Two 5-year-olds, Marcus and Jamal, are climbing into a cardboard box and rolling down a hill in their neighborhood. An argument erupts.

MARCUS: Let's say this is our cave and we have to hide in it. Hunters are coming, all right? And so we have to hide.

JAMAL: No! Let's just play. (Climbs into the box and rolls down the hill alone)

MARCUS: (In a loud, angry tone) Jamal! No! Don't roll down! This is the cave, all right?

JAMAL: (Ignores Marcus and drags the box back up to the top of the hill)

MARCUS: (In an angry tone) No, Jamal! This has to be the cave!

JAMAL: We could say it's a cave that can roll down, all right Marcus? (Laughs) It could be a cave that rolls down.

MARCUS: (Laughs) That's funny. It'll be like … a rolling cave. Come on. (Climbs into the box with Jamal and continues to play)

In this play episode, one child becomes angry and shouts at the other. However, no physical or verbal aggression is evident. Marcus and Jamal resolve their conflict independently and in a positive way. Contrast this outcome to that of the next example:

Rachel is building in the block area of her kindergarten. A classmate enters and roughly snatches several of the blocks away.

RACHEL: No! I'm using these. Give them back, Zein.

ZEIN: I need these! I'm building a whole castle.

RACHEL: No! (Snatches one block back)

ZEIN: I hate you. And you're not coming to my birthday party.

RACHEL: (Pushes Zein hard and walks out of the block area)

In this case, aggressive behavior is displayed by both children. Rachel's pushing and Zein's snatching and hateful words would all be viewed as aggressive acts. The important criteria for judging aggressive behavior is whether an action has the effect of hurting another person psychologically or physically.

Professionals who work with young children and their families must be cautious in making judgments about aggressive behavior. True aggression requires immediate adult intervention. However, conflicts or displays of assertiveness may not require adult support. In fact, adult interference could deprive children of opportunities to solve social problems independently.

Adults must also be careful not to misjudge typical play activities of children from diverse cultural backgrounds as aggression. Euro-American teachers have been found to treat culture-specific activities such as teasing or rough-and-tumble play as aggression and to prohibit these within classrooms (Hale-Benson, 1986; Klein & Chen, 2001). Such misinterpretations of play styles can result in barriers to social development for some children.

Researchers find it useful to break down aggression into specific categories, as listed in Table 13-5.

Each kind of aggression has a unique impact on others. As shown in the table, some researchers distinguish between **verbal aggression** and **physical aggression.** The former involves taunts, teasing, threats, or cruel statements intended to harm others psychologically, while physical aggression includes biting, hitting, pushing, or kicking (Bonica, Arnold, Fisher, Zeljo, & Yershova, 2003; Crick et al., 2006; Polman et al., 2007).

conflicts and arguments: Disagreements among children that can be settled verbally and do not involve aggression.

verbal aggression: Nonphysical assaults, such as taunts, teasing, threats, or cruel statements, that are intended to harm others psychologically.

physical aggression: Assaults, including biting, hitting, pushing, or kicking, that are intended to cause physical harm.

Aggression Type	Description
Verbal aggression	Teasing, name-calling, or other verbal taunts intended to harm others psychologically
Physical aggression	Hitting, pushing, biting, or other physical assaults intended to harm others physically
Reactive	Aggression that is provoked by peers; a reaction to peers' taunts or physical assaults
Proactive	Aggression that is unprovoked and often unexpected by peers
Instrumental	Proactive aggression that has a clear goal or purpose, such as obtaining a toy or driving an undesired playmate from a play area
Bullying	Proactive aggression that has no clear goal and is often displaced and hostile in intent

TABLE 13-5
Types of Aggression

SOURCE: Coie, Dodge, Terry, & Wright, 1991; Crick & Dodge, 1996.

Both types of aggression lead to rejection by peers; a hurtful taunt is as distasteful to young children as a punch or kick (Dodge & Coie, 1987)!

Aggressive episodes have been further categorized as either reactive or proactive. Reactive aggression, discussed previously, involves physical or verbal assaults that are provoked. For example, a child who hits back after being hit is said to be performing reactive aggression. **Proactive aggression** involves unprovoked physical or verbal assaults. Children who are reactive—that is, who strike out only when provoked—tend to be less at risk of being rejected (Coie et al., 1991; Dodge & Coie, 1987; Polman et al., 2007). It may be that these children are more predictable in their aggressive behavior. They make fine playmates as long as they are not angered or disturbed.

Proactive aggression may be further classified as instrumental aggression or bullying (Crick & Dodge, 1996; Knoff, 2007). **Instrumental aggression** involves acts that have a goal: to get a toy or to chase undesired classmates from a play area, for example. **Bullying,** in contrast, is aggression without a clear purpose. Often bullying is hostile aggression, as discussed earlier—that is, it stems from rage or upset. It is easy to see why proactive, bullying aggression leads to peer rejection more than any other type. Children who exhibit this behavior tend to be very hostile and unpredictable. Playing with such peers is risky. Sadly, children who are highly aggressive as preschoolers are very likely to become aggressive as older children and adolescents (Campbell, Spieker, Burchinal, & Poe, 2006; Crick & Dodge, 1996).

There is great concern that children who are aggressive will be rejected by peers. It is important to note that their victims may also be at risk. Research suggests that some children are more likely to be victimized than others (Garner & Lemerise, 2007; B. Kochenderfer-Ladd & Wardrop, 2001; Unnever, 2005). This **victim status** may remain stable over time; that is, a 4-year-old who is regularly victimized by peers may still be a victim of aggression years later in middle school. Both boys and girls—particularly those who are withdrawn, anxious, or depressed—may become frequent victims. These children are more likely to report being lonely and unsatisfied with social relationships. They more often avoid going to school later in life. So, the needs of both aggressive children and their victims must be addressed.

How do children learn aggressive behaviors? Again, each theory of child development offers a unique explanation. Maturationists would suggest that some children are born with an aggressive temperament. Such children may have simply inherited a negative or difficult

proactive aggression: Unprovoked physical or verbal assaults. Children who perform proactive aggression tend to be at risk of being rejected.

instrumental aggression: Verbal or physical assault that has a logical goal: to get a toy or to chase undesired classmates from a play area, for example.

bullying: Aggression that is without a clear purpose, often stemming from rage or upset and leading to peer rejection.

victim status: The group status of children who are more likely to be victimized by peers. This status may remain stable over time and can lead to victimization throughout childhood.

disposition that inevitably leads to problematic peer relations. This view is supported by studies finding that twins are very similar to one another in their tendency to be aggressive (Dionne, Tremblay, Boivin, Laplante, Perusse 2003; Eley et al., 1999; van Lier et al., 2007). Interestingly, genetics was found to be the greatest determinant of aggression among girls. Boys' aggression was more highly influenced by environmental factors.

Psychoanalytic theorists would also view aggression as part of a child's biological inheritance (Freud, 1930). However, they would propose that the environment—in particular, the child's interpersonal interactions with parents—determines how aggressive drives are expressed. It is the job of adults to redirect aggressive urges toward positive outlets. From this view, active running and jumping or expressive art activities are strategies that may help children "get out" their aggressive urges.

Behaviorists would argue that aggressive behavior is shaped and rewarded by the environment (Bandura, 1962, 1967). This can occur in several ways. First, children observe and emulate aggressive models. For example, those who watch violent television programs may become more aggressive themselves (D. R. Anderson, Huston, Schmitt, Linebarger, & Wright, 2001; Paik & Comstock, 1994). Children who are physically punished or abused by parents may strike out more often at peers (Grogan-Kaylor, 2005). Second, aggression is rewarded since children who push and hit peers often get what they want. For example, a child who gets a desired toy by pushing a peer receives a *payoff* for his or her aggression.

Cognitive-developmental and social information processing theorists would argue that there is an intellectual component to aggression. Children who are aggressive may be the way they are because they do not *understand* social situations. They may misinterpret the intentions or actions of peers and may be unaware of the consequences of their social initiatives. Such children may not view hitting or pushing as inappropriate because they cannot see clearly the pain and upset it causes. Further, they may not recognize that aggressive acts lead to peer rejection. This cognitive-developmental explanation has been supported by much research. Young children who are aggressive have been found to be less able to accurately read social cues (Dodge & Price, 1994) or to make decisions about which behaviors to perform in which situations (Trawick-Smith, 1992). Further, they are more likely to assign hostile intent to the benign acts of peers (Reid, Salmon, & Lovibond, 2006). For example, when a playmate knocks down their blocks, they are more likely to report that it was done "on purpose" or "to be mean." They are more likely to describe friendly facial expressions as "angry faces" (Hall, 2006).

Ecological systems theorists would propose a broader view of aggression. Harsh parental discipline or television watching would not fully explain the problem from their perspective. Regarding television, they might ask, Why do children in our society watch so much television to begin with? What stresses or lack of child care resources lead parents to use TV as the one-eyed babysitter? Why is children's programming so violent? What marketing trends or profit motivations lead television companies to broadcast damaging programs? What political ideologies dissuade legislators from regulating television programming more fully? A good deal of society-wide soul searching should be done, according to ecological systems theorists, not just finger-pointing at parents who let their children watch too much TV.

Each theoretical perspective is useful in solving problems of aggression. Teachers and parents can model nonaggressive social problem solving and reward children for doing so. They can further reduce exposure to aggressive models by limiting television viewing. They can encourage children to express anger or upset through positive outlets, such as art or music. They can guide children in reflecting on the outcomes of aggressive acts (e.g., "Look what happened when you hit him. See how he's crying?"). Finally, professionals and parents can take political action to change elements within society—such as violent television—that contribute to the problem.

THE MEDIA

Does Television Cause Aggression in Young Children?

As discussed in this chapter, some believe that watching television contributes to problems of aggression in young children. A brief look at prime-time programming reveals a nightly menu of police dramas and action shows in which violence is depicted in ever more graphic ways. Problems among characters are not always solved with words (as every preschool teacher urges students to do) but often with fists and weapons. In the National Television Violence Study—a longitudinal study of media and violence—an assessment was conducted of 3,000 programs per year over a 3-year period, across 26 channels (Wilson, 2008). More than 60% of these programs contained some form of physical aggression. A new concern is early exposure to video game violence. Although preschool-age children play fewer violent video games than older children, they are exposed to these through the play of their older siblings and even parents (Anderson, Gentile, & Buckley, 2007).

If children are exposed frequently to such images, surely they will imitate these aggressive behaviors in the classroom and neighborhood. An extensive review of 50 years of research on the effects of television and aggression confirms this worry (J. Murray, 2008). As just one example of the many thousands of studies conducted over the past few decades, Boyatzis and colleagues (1995) found that after just one viewing of a violent cartoon, children—particularly boys— were more likely to display aggression toward peers. Not only are these findings an indictment of television as a negative influence on child development, but they dispel a common myth: that cartoon violence is less harmful because it does not appear to be real. Violent video games tend to have the same effect on young children (Anderson et al., 2007). The greater exposure to these, the higher the rate of aggressive behavior, especially for boys. Younger children appear to be most vulnerable to social learning from these media (Wilson, 2008).

If television and other video media are so powerful in influencing children's behavior, can they also be used to promote prosocial behavior? There is research to suggest that children who watch programs in which characters are kind and cooperative perform these behaviors more frequently in real life (Singer & Singer, 1998). The problem is that families do not watch very many television shows featuring such positive role models (Wilson, 2008). They prefer popular programs in which depictions of aggression are common and violent characters are rewarded for their aggressive actions. The solution to the problem may be thoughtful guidance from parents on what young children watch. Teachers and caregivers can support parents by providing suggestions for programs that promote positive social behaviors and by encouraging parents to view these with their children. Professionals should also suggest that parents turn their televisions and computers off, now and then, to enjoy positive, real-life interactions with their children

CULTURE AND SOCIAL COMPETENCE

Culture influences children's social interactions, communication patterns, and play interests. Interactions of children of a particular cultural group may be misinterpreted by those who do not understand that culture's unique traditions or interpersonal characteristics. Ogbu (1992) has argued that teachers and family service providers must be cautious not to view social differences as deficits. Variations in social behavior, he proposes, are as much a part of a child's cultural heritage as a family's religious beliefs or holiday celebrations.

Culture and Prosocial Behaviors

Prosocial behaviors, such as altruism and empathy, vary significantly across cultural groups. In a study of six different cultures, B. B. Whiting and J. W. M. Whiting (1975) found great variation in helpfulness and cooperation, for example. Young children in American society scored lowest on measures of these behaviors. The children who scored highest were those of non-Western communities who lived in large families and had parents with extremely challenging workloads. These children were assigned many household tasks, and their work was often critical to the family's survival. Such family circumstances lead children to acquire a "helpful way of life" that will be evident even when adults are not present.

Children in American families are not assigned crucial household work as often. This may be due to a belief that children should enjoy early childhood without the burden of chores. In addition, most American families have more resources than the impoverished non-Western families that Whiting and Whiting studied, so children's work may not be as critical to survival. Helpfulness might not emerge quite as early, then, in the social repertoire of some American preschoolers (Yablo & Field, 2007). This does not represent a deficit; it simply means that within some American families, culture has dictated that helpfulness will evolve more gradually in human interactions.

Hale-Benson (1986) has observed more cooperative behavior among African and African American children and more competition among children of Euro-American backgrounds. She cites a study showing that children from rural Kenya were more cooperative in playing a board game, for example, than less "traditional" urban African children and those from the United States (Munroe & Munroe, 1977). She proposes that cooperation comes more naturally to children who grow up in cultures where collective thought and action are valued. In many Euro-American families, she contends, individual initiative and competition are the norm.

Play

There are cultural differences in play activities as well. Chinese American children initiate play less often and integrate fewer commercial play props and other objects within their play interactions (Chen et al., 2005; Haight & Black, 2002). In contrast, Irish American children often direct the play of peers and regularly choose to play with commercially marketed toys. African or African American children engage in more frequent cooperative play (Hale-Benson, 1986). Children from Euro-American cultures might pursue individual play interests more often. Individual ownership may be more important to families of Euro-American cultures. These children might desire more personal space and individual possession of toys and learning materials. Some African American children may view play items as community property to be spontaneously borrowed and shared.

The following story shows how conflicts arise when these social styles clash:

Sonia approaches Robert, who is painting by himself at an easel in a preschool program.

SONIA: (Smiles and stands very close to Robert) You painting a picture, Robert? That's a sun, right? (Points at the painting) What's this? This a boy or something? Is it a boy or a girl?

ROBERT: (Studies his painting intensely but does not look at Sonia and does not respond)

SONIA: I could paint that boy ... paint him, like, a big brother. All right, Robert? (Grasps a paint brush from the easel)

ROBERT: No! I'm painting, Sonia. Leave me alone!

SONIA: (Begins to paint on Robert's painting) I'll make a boy....

ROBERT: (Screaming loudly) No! (Shouts across the room to the teacher) Teacher! Sonia's ruining my painting!

In this story, a misunderstanding has occurred between two children with different social orientations. Robert believes that the easel, brushes, and painting are his alone. He wishes to produce his very own work of art. Sonia sees the easel as community property. In her family, everyone shares toys and works on tasks together. She cannot understand why her peer would not want company in creating a picture.

Access to Peers

Throughout the preceding sections, we have assumed that preschoolers have access to peers they can play with. Studies in countries around the world, however, suggest that this availability of peers varies greatly (Haight & Black, 2002; Lancy, 1996). In a study of families of 11 different communities, B. B. Whiting and Edwards (1988) conclude that many children of the world stay close to home and play mainly with parents or siblings. They do not, then, form the same kinds of peer relationships as American preschoolers. In fact, some children in non-Western families in this study were found to spend less than half the time that American children do playing with peers. The percentage of time boys and girls from around the world play with peers is presented in Figure 13-1.

Whiting and Edwards also report that work assignments for preschoolers can reduce play time with peers. They observed that, in cultures in which the work burden for parents is great, children spend an inordinate amount of time helping out with household chores. Caring for younger siblings, tending livestock, or completing other family tasks may constitute a larger part of a young child's day in such families. Even though these children often

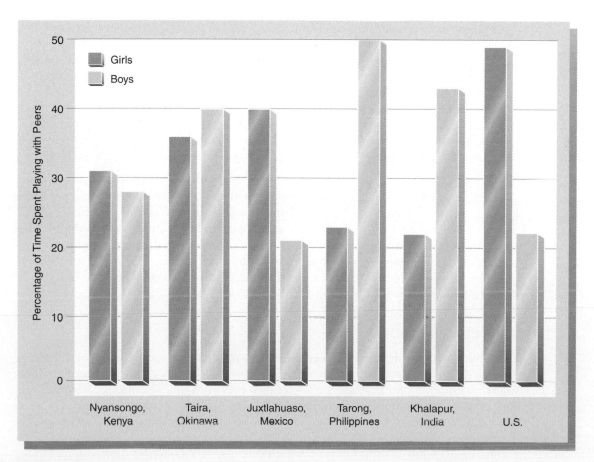

FIGURE 13-1

integrate play and work and include peers in their work tasks (Bloch & Adler, 1994), free play time with same-age playmates is often limited.

Without daily peer interactions, social development would take a very different course than that described by Western researchers. Children whose social access is limited might be less outgoing or more hesitant when they do interact with peers. Social skills might not be acquired as early since opportunities to develop them are lacking. Assessment of social abilities, then, must take into account previous social experiences, which are influenced by cultural values and community circumstances.

Friendliness and Shyness

Friendliness is another dimension of social behavior that varies significantly by culture. Erikson (1963) has described emotionally healthy preschoolers as outgoing and energetic. Parten (1932) has proposed that preschoolers interact with peers more frequently with age. Social initiative has been identified as an important prerequisite to making friends and being accepted by peers. Yet, in some cultures, shyness is more typical. Among Chinese parents, in fact, raising quiet, cautious children is an important goal of child rearing (Chen et al., 2005). This may stem from Confucian philosophy, which holds that self-restraint and hesitancy are signs of maturity and accomplishment. Extreme shyness, which is sometimes considered deviant in Western cultures, is very much accepted and appreciated in China. The following story illustrates this point:

> One of my colleagues arrived in the United States several years ago from China to attend graduate school. While pursuing her studies in psychology, she received much positive response from professors and fellow students for her academic competence. She then accepted a position to teach in an American university. Colleagues made friendly comments about her shyness and recommended that she become more outgoing. It was only then that she was confronted with the idea that she was shy. Until that point, she had not thought about herself in this way.
>
> "I never knew I was shy," she confided. "When I was in China, I never heard of the concept. It was not a characteristic anyone talked about. In China, I was just a person. In America, I am a shy person. It is very strange to suddenly become a new kind of human being."

Research on white, middle-class children suggests that shyness leads to being neglected or, in some cases, rejected by peers. In China, just the opposite is true: X. Chen and colleagues (1992) report that shy children are more likely to be accepted by peers than louder, more active children. Shyness clearly is interpreted differently in different cultures. This research should give pause to professionals who try to increase the sociability of all children. Some children have been socialized to be shy, and efforts to change them are likely to be confusing and futile.

Rough Play and Teasing

Some children appear to be more rough and active in their interactions with peers. In some cases, such children's play initiatives are misinterpreted. Ramsey (2004) reports that Euro-American children and teachers are sometimes overwhelmed and disturbed by the very rough play of children from other cultures. Hale-Benson (1986) proposes that the active and physical play of African American children is often misconstrued as aggressive or hyperactive.

Play arguing and teasing have been found to be very common interactions among young children of some African American, Polynesian, Native American, and Italian families (Campos et al., 2007; Endo, 2007; Bloch & Adler, 1994; Martini, 1994; New, 1994). Such play may involve exchanging silly insults or ribbing younger peers or siblings. Such behaviors, though delivered in jest, can sound antisocial to people from cultures in which such games are not played. Hale-Benson (1986) suggests, however, that these teasing interactions enhance specific areas of social, emotional, and intellectual development. First, they provide an early experience in controlling emotions. The successful player must endure teasing without growing angry or overreacting. Second, teasing behavior involves creativity, verbal competence, and quick thinking. Teachers and caregivers have the difficult task of distinguishing between truly hurtful comments, which comprise verbal aggression, and playful barbs and insults, which may be part of cultural interaction.

Social Interaction and Second-Language Acquisition

One factor that can influence social interactions in preschool peer groups is language diversity. Children who do not speak the language of the majority of classmates in a preschool or peers in a neighborhood may be limited in their social interactions. In an ethnographic study of peer relationships, Meyer, Klein, and Genishi (1994) described the experiences of four Korean-speaking 3-year-olds who were new to an English-dominant preschool. The researchers observed that the four children first interacted only with each other. They formed friendships with one another almost immediately and were inseparable during free play. They would sit together at group time, speaking to one another in Korean. During their interchanges, they were found to acquire critical play, social, and linguistic competencies. Gradually they began to apply these abilities to interactions with their English-speaking peers.

This study suggests that second-language learners might acquire social skills best by first using their native language to interact with peers who are culturally and linguistically similar to themselves. Had the children of the study been required to speak English or to play with English-speaking children, the authors concluded, they might not have acquired important language and social abilities. It was only after they had refined their social and language competencies that they were able to enter into relationships with children of different backgrounds.

Peer Acceptance and Culture

Because children's social behaviors are often different across cultures, it is reasonable to assume that ethnicity might be a cause for peer rejection. It seems likely that a child in preschool or child care who plays and communicates in very distinct ways would be actively avoided by peers. Research findings on peer acceptance and culture provide a cloudy picture, however. Some studies indicate that young children do show same-race preferences in the selection of friends and playmates (Jackson, Barth, Powell, & Lochman, 2006). These biases appear to become stronger in the elementary years. Interestingly, same-race preferences were found to be most prevalent among Euro-American children and less so among African Americans (D. J. Fox & Jordan, 1973).

Other research, however, suggests that preschool children may be more accepting of cultural differences and more regularly enter into cross-cultural friendships than previously cited research would suggest. This is particularly true if children have positive social experiences with peers of other cultures (McGlothlin & Killen, 2005). In a large study of young Euro-American, Latino, African American, and Asian American children, Howes and Wu (1990) report that peer acceptance was not usually related to ethnicity. Children were liked or not based on other interpersonal attributes. Many cross-ethnic relationships, spanning all cultural groups, were observed in this investigation.

Why is there a discrepancy in findings among studies? Ramsey (1995) suggests that school environments might make the difference. Classroom interventions that enhance children's understanding of others' perspectives and behaviors promote cross-cultural peer relationships. For example, a regular **class meeting** in which children talk openly about cultural and racial differences, share concerns and problems with peers, and resolve conflicts can reduce bias. In classrooms where there is less active effort to promote cultural acceptance, cross-ethnic relationships are less likely to form.

OTHER SOURCES OF VARIATION IN SOCIAL COMPETENCE

Children's relationships with peers are influenced by many other factors. Family stressors, child care, gender, and disability can affect the acquisition of social skills and the formation of friendships.

Poverty and Family Stressors

class meeting: A class-room strategy in which children are encouraged to talk openly about cultural and racial differences, share concerns and problems with peers, and resolve conflicts.

Children in poverty are more likely to suffer emotional challenges and, as a result, to be less successful in their relationships with peers (Brophy-Herb, Lee, Nievar, & Stollak, 2006; McLoyd, 1998). While conditions such as poor nutrition and health care may play a role in this problem, most researchers believe that it is poverty's devastating effect on parenting that explains most poor social outcomes. Parents under the stress of poverty may be less effective, more punitive, and less warm with children (Gutman, McLoyd, & Tokoyawa, 2005; McLoyd, 1998). They may direct more anger toward their children than do parents who do not suffer economic hardship. These parenting characteristics have a negative impact on social development. Young children whose parents interact with them angrily or negatively are less effective with peers and less competent in understanding emotions and social situations (Davenport, Hegland, & Melby, 2007; Nix et al., 1999).

Are preschoolers of historically underrepresented groups more likely to be rejected by their Euro-American peers? The research evidence is mixed.

The negative effects of poverty may be seen most clearly in the case of dysfunctional families. Children growing up with such problems as domestic violence, abuse, or parental mental health disorders—all more common among poor families—are at special risk in their social development (McLoyd, 1998). Children whose mothers are depressed, for example, have been found to be more disruptive and less popular among peers (Aikens, Coleman, & Barbarin, 2008). Social problems among these children are less severe, however, when a mentally healthy adult lives in the home. For example, a child who lives with a depressed mother but also with a healthy father or grandmother might have a greater chance of forming positive peer relations (Silverstein & Ruiz, 2006).

Child abuse has a devastating effect on children's social development. Children who are abused have been found to have particularly poor relationships with peers (Teisl & Cicchetti, 2008). Such children are liked less by playmates and have few friends. This may be due, in part, to their own resistance to peer contact. In one study, it was found that children who are abused were approached as often as nonabused children by peers but were far more likely to reject invitations to play (Haskett & Kistner, 1991). Generally, the social profile of preschoolers who are abused matches that of other children who are rejected: they are often negative, unpredictable, and aggressive.

Professionals must address problems of child abuse and neglect in a number of ways. They must learn the key physical and behavioral indicators of maltreatment and must be aware of and fulfill their ethical and legal responsibilities to report any concerns to the local child protection services agency within their community. They must work closely with other professionals and organizations to provide prescribed services to children who are victims of child abuse and neglect. They can help organize community partnerships—broad-based collaborations among schools, social services agencies, faith-based programs, businesses, and families—to protect children. (See the Advocacy and Public Policy box in this chapter for a full discussion.)

Siblings

Siblings can contribute to positive social development; however, most research focuses on problems in sibling relationships. Sibling rivalry, the trauma of a birth of a brother or sister, and aggression are emphasized in studies and in the popular literature. Ironically, another problem related to siblings that receives much attention is *not* having them; over the years, negative stereotypes have emerged about only children. Many popular parenting books paint a no-win situation: siblings cause conflict and family disharmony, yet children's development is negatively affected without them.

Although problems with siblings certainly exist, the impact of siblings on social development may be more positive than negative. Consider the case of sibling rivalry. It is true that conflicts exist, particularly between same-sex siblings of similar age (Martin & Ross, 2005), but this conflict may not be all bad. Older children may gain confidence and leadership ability by directing their younger siblings. Younger children may acquire skills at resisting bullying. Children appear to feel more comfortable in their conflicts with brothers or sisters. Sibling interactions may be ideal contexts for learning to speak one's mind, argue, and resolve disputes.

Children have been found to learn to resolve disagreements with siblings when parents intervene in certain ways to guide them. One study found that a "child-centered" intervention, in which parents would engage arguing siblings in discussion, led to more positive interactions and less conflict over time (Kramer, Perozynksi, & Chung, 1999). Interestingly, this *hands-on* approach had the greatest impact when children were fairly young—in the preschool or early elementary years. Parental intervention was found to be less effective when children reached middle childhood, suggesting that there may be an age—8 or 9 years—at which parents should withdraw a bit and allow children to practice conflict resolution on their own.

Research suggests that sibling relationships are often cooperative and nurturing (Richmond, Stocker, & Rienks, 2005). Children learn many social skills, then, from brothers or sisters. Sibling influence is especially important in the many communities of the world in which a sibling is the caretaker or primary playmate (Haight & Black, 2002; B. B. Whiting & Edwards, 1988).

Parenting guides and the popular literature usually portray the birth of a brother or sister as a traumatic event in the life of a child, but studies have shown that children learn valuable lessons as they adjust to the arrival of a new sibling (Dunn, 2005). A new baby may assist the older child in the process of separating from parents and becoming independent. Children learn to share the affections of their parents. They often acquire nurturing behaviors as they interact with a newborn, particularly in cultures where children are assigned child care responsibilities at a young age (B. B. Whiting & Edwards, 1988).

Does this mean that children who do not have siblings are handicapped in some way? Research dispels the myth that only children are doomed to become self-centered or socially inept. In fact, some studies suggest that only children are advanced in intellectual development, language, and creativity (Mõttus, Indus, & Allik, 2008). A number of fascinating studies on only children have been recently conducted in China, where there are now incentives for families to have only one son or daughter. Chinese only children have been found to have greater cognitive skills, to perform better in school, and to suffer less anxiety and depression than those with siblings (Chen et al., 2005). It appears that siblings are useful but not necessary for social development. No research evidence suggests that only children have delayed social abilities or problematic peer relations.

ADVOCACY AND PUBLIC POLICY

Creating Community Partnerships to Protect Children from Abuse and Neglect

This chapter reviews the harmful effects of abuse and neglect on young children's social and emotional development. An estimated 5 million children are reported annually to public agencies for alleged maltreatment (Stoltzfus, 2002). Nearly 2 million of these reports are investigated by child protection agencies, resulting in nearly 1 million substantiated cases of child maltreatment, usually neglect. While the numbers of children found to be maltreated have declined in the past decade, there continues to be an unacceptably high number of children who are abused and neglected in America. Nearly 8% of these children are abused again within a 6-month period. (In some states this percentage is more than 13%!)

Traditional methods of reporting, investigation by child protection agencies, removal from the home, and foster care have not fully solved the problem. A new approach that requires involvement of every professional (and all citizens) has been proposed by the Center for Community Partnerships in Child Welfare (CCPCW). This community partnership model is based on the simple premise that child abuse and neglect are *everyone's* concern. Broad collaborations among all individuals and agencies must be formed to prevent these problems and to address children's needs when they occur.

In a community partnership approach, teams of professionals, including those from the child protection services agency, are formed to review and make fundamental changes to existing approaches to child protection. A goal of these teams is to make services more collaborative and family centered. One community team might implement a strategy in which professionals, parents, relatives, pastors, and even neighbors come together to develop an action plan for a family where a child is at risk of abuse and neglect. Another team might modify the policies and procedures of the child protection agency so that its employees spend more time in schools and neighborhood organizations getting to better know the community. Yet another team might create neighborhood networks—made up of extended family members, faith-based organizations, businesses, schools, neighborhood associations, and organizations like Boys and Girls Clubs—to help individual families to keep their children safe. A team might create a local governing board for the partnership that includes community residents as well as representatives of various agencies. Professionals working with young children can play a critical role in such initiatives.

The CCPCW has helped organize such partnerships in 50 communities around the country. Community groups can visit the center to receive guidance in forming partnership teams; center personnel will visit local communities to provide this assistance. The center publishes guides for creating partnerships and a monthly journal. More information on the center can be obtained from its Website (http://www.cssp.org/center).

Child Care

If availability of peers influences social development, it stands to reason that young children in child care will show advanced social competence. Many preschoolers in the United States spend more than half of their waking time interacting with other children in centers or family child care homes (Children's Defense Fund, 2007). The relationship between child care and social development is not as clear, however. A large, longitudinal study on child care outcomes, conducted by the National Institute of Child Health and Human Development (NICHD), has yielded mixed results (NICHD Early Child Care Research Network, 2008; Belsky et al., 2007; Burchinal & Cryer, 2003). Children who received high quality care in smaller group settings were found to display more prosocial behavior (as well as advanced cognitive abilities). They also were rated as more aggressive by their teachers, suggesting that they were more outgoing, both positively and negatively. Children cared for in low-quality settings were more likely to engage in negative peer interactions.

One of the most important conclusions of the NICHD researchers was that the impact of child care depends on its quality. **Child care quality** has been defined as the degree to which both structural and dynamic features of care meet the social, emotional, and intellectual needs of young children. *Structural features* include physical and social characteristics of the center or home—staff-to-child ratio, available play space and toys, and group size. *Dynamic features* consist of caregiver behaviors—warmth or responsiveness—that promote children's development. Both of these dimensions are important for assuring that children acquire positive social skills. Unfortunately, research suggests that many children in the United States—particularly those living in poverty—receive care that is rated low on both structural and dynamic dimensions (Fuller, Kagan, Caspary & Gauthier, 2002). Although child care holds promise as a way to resolve serious problems of poor social development, it may also create risks. A national policy is needed in the United States to fund high-quality child care programs in all communities.

Gender and Social Development

Boys and girls can be very different in their social interactions and play. Most parents eventually learn this through experiences like the following:

A single mother has committed herself to raising her daughter free of sex-stereotyped behaviors and self-perceptions. She carefully selects gender-neutral toys for her child. She encourages her daughter to be active and bold—to make independent decisions.

child care quality: The degree to which a child care center includes adequate structural features, such as staff-to-child ratio, available play space and toys, and group size, and dynamic features, such as caregiver warmth and responsiveness.

She carefully screens the television shows her daughter watches to be certain she is not exposed to stereotyped role models.

The mother enrolls her daughter in a child care center. After about a month, she visits the center to observe the classroom and her daughter in action. She is somewhat troubled by what she sees. Her daughter plays only with girls during her visit, and their play involves pretending to cook meals, caring for babies, and dressing up in feminine hats and jewelry. At one point, an active 4-year-old boy approaches her daughter's playgroup with a toy dinosaur. "Dinosaurs are attacking," he calls out. He is quickly rebuffed by the little girls. "We don't need that!" the woman's daughter says, seizing the dinosaur and tossing it to the ground. The boy retreats, and the girls resume their play. The mother shakes her head and wonders what went wrong.

Children of all socioeconomic groups and cultures show gender differences in play. Most children prefer to play with sex-stereotyped toys; boys play with trucks, and girls play with dolls (Freeman, 2007; Hill & Flom, 2007). As early as 2 years of age, they prefer to play with same-sex peers (Hay, Payne, & Chadwick, 2004). Play styles of boys and girls differ markedly. Boys are usually more active and rough in their play, and girls are quieter and more elaborate (Ostrov & Keating, 2004; Gmitrova, Podhajecká, & Gmitrov, 2007). Girls tend to be more wary and timid in their play and more emotionally expressive than boys. Boys are less compliant and more demanding when interacting with adults.

These patterns of social interaction and play—often called **sex-typed or gender-stereotyped behaviors**—are found in all cultures and societies of the world (Turner & Gervai, 1995; B. B. Whiting & Edwards, 1988).

How can these gender differences be explained? How is it that the child in the story, who was raised in a nonstereotyped home environment, displays such sex-typed behavior? There are several prominent perspectives regarding gender identity and sex-role stereotyping. The first perspective is that children acquire sex-typed behaviors because of modeling and reinforcement in the environment (Bandura, 1967). The world is filled with models of stereotyped behavior. Parents may subconsciously act in stereotypical ways, and television regularly depicts men and women in sex-typed roles and interactions (Larson, 2001). As more and more children are cared for in child care in America, peers become important models. Even very young preschoolers have been found to learn gender-typical social skills and play styles from playmates in the classroom (Maccoby, 1999).

This stereotyped behavior is often rewarded in the environment. Parents may reinforce girls to be timid and compliant and boys to be bold and independent. They may do so subconsciously. In one study, for example, parents were found to verbally encourage their children to play with both male and female toys, but their body language gave them away. They moved closer to and became more involved in their children's play when stereotypical toys were selected (Caldera, Huston, & O'Brien, 1989). This may explain why, even in homes where feminist perspectives are taught, children still hold stereotyped views of gender roles (Huston & Alvarez, 1990).

A second perspective of gender differences is that early sex stereotyping stems from cognitive limitations. During the preschool years, children tend to believe that being a boy or girl is determined by clothing, hair, or other physical characteristics (Martin & Ruble, 2004). If you wear a dress, you are a girl, or if you have short hair, you are a boy, the thinking goes. Once children come to view themselves as male or female, according to this perspective, they actively strive to understand their gender role more fully. They observe the behaviors of models around them and develop a theory of what it is to be a boy or girl. Once a gender theory emerges, they strive to conform to it in their behavior and thinking.

sex-typed or gender-stereotyped behaviors: Behaviors in which boys and girls exhibit rigid gender expectations of their culture, including toy and playmate preferences and degree of activity, roughness in play, and compliance with adult requests.

Young children's gender theories are quite rigid and inflexible. Boys may play only with trucks and may become louder and more active than girls. Girls may prefer dolls and conform to a quieter and more passive play style. One reason for such rigid thinking is that society makes stereotyped gender roles so easy to observe and comprehend. Children see that men on TV are more aggressive or have certain kinds of jobs. They see that women play passive, dependent, and nurturing roles. Children tend to pay more attention to the behaviors and traits of TV characters of their own gender (Calvert, Strong, Jacobs, & Conger, 2007; Luecke-Aleska, Anderson, Collins, & Schmitt, 1995). They more readily integrated these characteristics into their theory of boyness or girlness.

If this second perspective is correct, then children should become less stereotyped in their interactions as they develop intellectually. Research shows that this is the case: older and cognitively advanced children have been found to show less rigidly stereotyped beliefs and behaviors than younger or less intellectually competent children (Martin & Ruble, 2004).

How do these two perspectives assist professionals and parents in reducing negative gender stereotypes? Based on the first view, adults carefully avoid modeling or reinforcing stereotypical behaviors. At the same time—relying on the second perspective—they might provide experiences that help children to construct a nonstereotyped theory of gender. Photographs that depict men and women engaged in nonstereotypical work might be presented and discussed. Children's books that show characters engaged in nonstereotyped play activities might be provided. A focus should be on helping children analyze what it means to be a boy or girl.

CLASSROOM ADAPTATIONS: SOCIAL COMPETENCE AND SPECIAL NEEDS

A number of research studies suggest that children with special needs are more likely to be rejected by peers. In fact, some researchers believe that peer rejection and its causes— in particular, hostile, aggressive behavior—are themselves a disability. For example, the condition **serious emotional disturbance (SED),** to be examined in-depth in Chapter 17, is defined in part as an inability to function effectively in social contexts (Umansky & Hooper, 2008).

Much research has focused on specific challenging conditions and their effects on social development. Studies suggest that children with hearing and visual impairments are viewed by peers as less friendly or unable or unwilling to play (Most, 2007; Walker & Berthelsen, 2007). Of course, it is the children's impairments that limit their responsiveness to others' initiatives.

By age 5, children are likely to report negative attitudes toward children with physical disabilities (Frostad & Pijl, 2007; Sirvis & Caldwell, 1995). Perhaps these negative opinions cause children with physical challenges to be excluded from play and, thus, to be less socially competent. Children with mental retardation or learning disabilities also have been found to be deficient in social skills and more often rejected by classmates (Gadeyne, Ghesquière, & Onghena, 2004). Children with autism rarely engage in social play; they often show little interest in peers and tend to be rejected as playmates (Chamberlain, Kasari, & Rothcram-Fuller, 2007; Welteroth, 1999).

Taken together, these studies paint a bleak prognosis for the social development of children with special needs. Are children with challenging conditions destined to be rejected by peers? Will efforts to facilitate social relationships be futile? Actually, the picture is much more complex—and more positive—than early studies would suggest. Peer rejection varies as a function of the particular exceptionality and its extremity.

serious emotional disturbance (SED): A broad term used to describe children who exhibit negative emotional reactions that go beyond typical misbehavior or upset. Children with SED may exhibit externalizing problems, such as aggression, or internalizing problems, such as withdrawn behavior and anxiety.

Handicaps that can actually be observed and understood by young children are less likely to lead to peer rejection (Umansky & Hooper, 2008). Children in wheelchairs, for example, have visible handicaps that are easily explained by parents or teachers, so they are more readily accepted than children who have less obvious impairments. Disorders such as autism are much harder for preschoolers to understand. Children with autism are different in their communication and behavior, which contributes to their rejection by peers. The lack of concrete cues to explain their condition makes it difficult for adults to facilitate their acceptance by peers.

Children with special needs may not experience peer rejection (Frostad & Pijl, 2007). In some cases, they may have a neutral social status—they are neither the most popular nor the most actively rejected (Dudley-Marling & Edmiason, 1985). A significant number of children with special needs may actually be rated as popular by peers, if they are in high-quality, inclusive classrooms (Frederickson, Simmonds, Evans, & Soulsby, 2007). So, although challenging conditions can impede social relationships in the preschool years, such is not always the case.

How can teachers and caregivers adapt classroom activities and interactions to help children with special needs learn social skills and be accepted by their peers? A number of strategies have been suggested (Howard et al., 2004; Umansky, 2008b):

1. *Interventions to increase social participation.* Adults can intervene in play to encourage children with special needs to interact more fully with peers. For some children, a major goal may be to promote parallel play or simple peer watching (e.g., "Why don't we sit together and make a puzzle next to Louisa and Stanley?"). For others, collaborative play might be encouraged (e.g., "We're making dinner. Could you help Jennie stir the pot?").

2. *Classroom adaptations to increase social participation.* Adults can create an environment that is fully accessible to all children. A ramp on a climber will allow children with physically challenging conditions to participate more fully in play. Wide spaces in the dramatic play center will enable children in wheelchairs to join peers in make-believe.

3. *Play materials that increase social participation.* Open-ended play materials allow children of all ability levels to work together. For example, all children can play with modeling clay. A child with Down syndrome might create a simpler sculpture than a typically developing child. A child with autism may prefer pounding and rolling the clay. All are able to participate at some level. For less open-ended materials, adults can create **graded challenges**—that is, choices of activities that vary by difficulty level (see Chapter 11 for a full discussion). A variety of puzzles—some more challenging than others—can be provided, for example, so that all children can work together at the puzzle table.

4. *Interventions that teach specific social skills and language.* Once children with special needs are interacting with peers, adults can help them learn specific social and language skills. Among the abilities that are considered essential for positive peer relationships are getting a peer's attention (e.g., "Tap her on the shoulder and say her name"), joining a play group (e.g., "Why don't we go order lunch at their pretend restaurant?"), and using language to express feelings or resolve conflicts (e.g., "Don't hit. When you're mad, say, 'I don't like that!'").

5. *Guiding children in understanding one another's behaviors.* Some children with special needs have trouble understanding social situations or the behavior of their peers. Adults can intervene to guide them in interpreting peer interactions (e.g., "He didn't mean to knock over your blocks. It was just an accident"). It is equally important to help typically developing children in a classroom understand the behaviors of those with special needs (e.g., "He isn't trying to bother you. He wants to play with you, but he can't use words to tell you that").

graded challenges: The provision of play and learning materials in a classroom that represent varying degrees of difficulty so that children of all abilities can find something meaningful to do.

closed-field play: Play in which just two children are invited to play together without involvement of other children.

open-field play: Play in which two children are encouraged to spend time together but with other children present as well.

CHILD GUIDANCE: *Facilitating Friendships*

As described in this chapter, friendships are important for preschoolers' social development. Not all children have friends, however. Can teachers and caregivers nurture friendships in the classroom? A child development student and I recently worked with a group of Head Start and child care teachers in facilitating friendships among 4-year-olds. The project was very successful; many children in participating classrooms formed reciprocal friendships with peers. These are the steps we asked teachers to follow:

1. *Watching for authentic friendships.* Teachers watched for potential friendships during free play in the classroom. Each child was carefully observed; the names of peers who showed an interest or made frequent contact with a particular child were recorded. A special focus of these observations was on children who were quieter, more aggressive, or had special needs—those who might be having difficulty in making friends. An important part of this step was to identify authentic friendships—not pairs that teachers simply thought would work well together. The point was to find pairs of children that genuinely liked each other.

2. *Planning closed-field friendship interactions.* Once potential friendship pairs were identified, teachers planned **closed-field play** interactions to nurture relationships. These were situations in which just the two children in a pair were invited to play together

without involvement of others. A pair might be invited to join a teacher in another room for a book sharing experience. They might be asked to help get snacks ready. During outdoor time, a pair might be invited back into the classroom to play together, undisturbed, in the dramatic play area. The purpose was to help the two get to know one another in a quieter, less active environment.

3. *Planning open-field friendship interactions.* After pairs of children came to know one another well, **open-field play** interactions were provided. During free play, teachers would guide pairs of children toward an area of the classroom—say, the dramatic play center—to play together. In this step, other children in the class were present as well. The teacher would facilitate the pair's interactions with one another and with other peers.

4. *Planning interactions outside the classroom.* For pairs of children who began to show interest in one another, outside-of-class experiences were planned. Some teachers contacted the families of participating children and encouraged them to arrange home get-togethers for these friendship pairs. One teacher invited friendship pairs—one couple at a time—to her house for dinner! These outside experiences were found to strengthen the in-class relationships that were forming.

SUMMARY

The social worlds of children broaden in the preschool years. Preschoolers often acquire a sense of initiative that leads to energetic and creative play, exploration, and self-expression. They also may acquire social initiative—a desire to make contact with peers and new adults in their lives. Some children come to be popular—well liked by their peers. Others are neglected or rejected by other children. Many children form close friendships with peers, leading to the acquisition of new social abilities. Most children develop through stages of social participation—from unoccupied or onlooker behavior at age 2 to cooperative play in the later preschool years. Some acquire positive social abilities and characteristics—including altruism and empathy.

Others display antisocial behaviors, such as aggression. There are a variety of explanations for why children acquire these social traits. Children may be more or less mature, model the behaviors of those around them, or have cognitive abilities or limitations that affect their understanding of social situations.

Social behavior and peer acceptance are affected by culture. Those of diverse cultural backgrounds will have different social and play styles. Some children will be rejected because peers of another cultural group misinterpret their interactions. Poverty, family characteristics, siblings, child care, and gender also influence social development. Classroom adaptations are needed to support the social behaviors and peer acceptance of children with special needs.

RESEARCH INTO PRACTICE

CRITICAL CONCEPT 1

Once preschool children have become attached to caregivers and are autonomous in their actions and thinking, they often begin to show initiative. Initiative is an emotional state that leads children to make creative attempts, take risks, and

reach out to peers. Erikson has warned that if children are harshly restricted in their initiatives, they will suffer guilt.

Application #1   Create play environments in which children feel safe taking risks, trying out new behaviors, and making creative attempts. Give them opportunities to engage peers in active play. Take care not to stifle initiative. Too many rules or criticism of creative efforts can lead children to suffer guilt.

Application #2 Provide experiences and activities in school that are largely process oriented; that is, experimentation and self-expression should be emphasized, without regard to end products. Blocks, sculpting and drawing materials, dramatic play, and large motor free play are examples of open-ended activities that inspire initiative. In contrast, teacher-directed art projects that require children to produce the same finished product will restrict initiative.

Application #3 Avoid evaluating or comparing children's completed works. Even praise can threaten initiative by giving implicit messages about the efforts of other children. For example, praising one child's painting suggests that there is only one correct way to paint.

CRITICAL CONCEPT 2

Cross-cultural studies have found variation in the degree to which children acquire initiative. Some families discourage individual creative effort and emphasize collective thought and action. Children of these families may be less eager to take risks and to express themselves individually in the child care center or classroom.

Application #1 Understand and appreciate cultural differences in initiative. Take care not to insist that all children take risks or make creative attempts. Caution, ambivalence about individual expression, and a desire to check with others before acting may be part of some children's cultural heritage.

Application #2 Plan classroom experiences that focus on group efforts rather than individual initiative to meet the needs of children of diverse cultural backgrounds. Activities such as collaborative mural painting, joint block building, and cooperative scientific experiments may better match the play styles of children of collective cultures.

CRITICAL CONCEPT 3

Peer acceptance and the formation of friendships are extremely important in the early years. Young children who are not well liked or who are ineffective with peers are at risk. Children who are actively rejected by peers because of aggressive or annoying behavior and those who are neglected because they are shy or nonsocial may need special support in forming peer relationships.

Application #1 Intervene in children's play to teach social skills that will lead to peer acceptance. Model or prompt strategies for joining a play group or getting a peer's attention. Guide children in resolving disagreements in positive, nonaggressive ways. These interventions are especially important for children who are actively rejected or ignored by peers.

Application #2 Facilitate friendships between pairs of children who are having difficulty forming positive peer relationships. Identify potential friendships by observing the play of rejected and neglected children and noting potential classroom friends. Invite identified pairs of children to help prepare snacks or to work on special activities away from the rest of the group. During these experiences, facilitate positive interactions. Ultimately, lasting friendships may form. Encourage parents to assist in the process by inviting potential friends to their homes after school.

CRITICAL CONCEPT 4

Specific prosocial behaviors contribute to successful relationships with peers. These include altruism and empathy. Aggression, in contrast, leads to poor peer relations.

Application #1 Apply cognitive-developmental and information processing strategies in classrooms and centers to teach kindness and reduce aggression. Through intervention, guide children in interpreting the social world. In particular, ask children to reflect on the outcomes of both positive and negative social behaviors. During aggressive conflicts, encourage children to think about and discuss the effects of hitting or pushing and the alternatives for solving social problems.

Application #2 Apply behaviorist and social cognitive learning strategies to promote positive social behavior. Praise children for positive interactions. Model prosocial behaviors. Reduce exposure to negative social models by restricting television viewing at home and by eliminating aggressive behaviors by adults in the classroom. You should refrain, yourself, from angry scolding, for example. Plan parent education programs that promote nonphysical, nonaggressive disciplinary methods.

Application #3 Use psychoanalytic strategies to promote positive social development and reduce aggression. Be warm, positive, and responsive with children who have problems with aggression. Encourage parents to interact in these ways as well. The purpose of these strategies is to facilitate trust and attachment. Such interactions may lead to positive relationships with adults and children. Once bonds with adults have formed, children may begin to successfully enter into relationships with peers as well.

CRITICAL CONCEPT 5

Social interaction and peer acceptance are influenced by cultural background, family stressors, sibling relationships, child care arrangements, and gender. Disabilities such as serious emotional disturbance, perceptual impairments, and physically challenging conditions can limit peer relationships. Children whose patterns of social interaction are considered *different* are sometimes at risk of peer rejection or neglect.

Application #1 Take an active role in promoting positive relationships and interactions among children of diverse cultural and family backgrounds and between boys and girls. Assist children in understanding one another's play preferences and social styles through class discussions or direct intervention (e.g., "He likes to play like that. If it's too rough, just say, 'I don't want to play that way,'" or "She doesn't like to talk when she's in a big group. Maybe you should invite her to look at a book with you in the quiet corner"). Develop an antibiased curriculum in which developmental, cultural, and gender differences are openly discussed and celebrated. Make efforts to ensure diversity in playgroups and to reduce rejection on the basis of race, gender, or disability.

Application #2 Actively facilitate play and social interaction between children with special needs and their typically developing peers. Facilitate conversations between children with language delays and their peers, assist hearing impaired children in understanding their peers' communication, or demonstrate positive ways that children with autism can get their classmates' attention.

ASSESSING YOUNG CHILDREN: Preschool Social and Emotional Development

Areas of Development	What to Watch For	Indicators of Atypical Development	Applications
Emotional health	Shows initiative in projects and play activities. Enters readily into play with peers. Shows a positive view of oneself with statements such as "Look how high I can swing" or "I have lots of friends."	Holds back or hesitates in classroom activities or interactions with peers. Expresses feelings of guilt (e.g., "I am a bad boy") or self-doubt ("I can't do it").	Provide process-oriented experiences, such as art, sociodramatic play, and open-ended motor activity. Encourage creative expression, risk taking, and informal interactions with peers. Avoid evaluation or comparison of children's work and an emphasis on final products.
Relationships with others	Is liked by at least some other children in the classroom or neighborhood. Forms one or more special friendships. Enters into positive relationships with teachers and other adults.	Shows no interest in interacting with peers. Is actively avoided by peers or ignored completely. Forms no close friendships in school or at home.	Interact with warmth and responsiveness so that children become attached to you. Promote positive relationships among children through play intervention. Establish as a goal that each child will form at least one meaningful friendship.
Specific social skills	Shows specific social skills, such as getting a peer's attention, entering a playgroup, or resolving conflicts. Uses language in peer interactions. Shows kindness.	Displays hostile, aggressive behaviors and an inability to solve problems with peers in positive ways. Performs behaviors that peers consider bizarre or disruptive. Shows extreme withdrawal; always chooses to play alone.	Intervene in real-life classroom interactions to teach important social skills. In these situations, model strategies for getting a peer's attention, entering a play group, or resolving a conflict.

Interpreting Assessment Data: Variations in social and emotional development may be due to culture. Some children are less likely to take initiative because dependence and family enmeshment are valued over independence. Children may be quiet and more reluctant to play with peers because their families are less verbal and more cautious and reflective. Some rough play—more common in some cultures than others—may be misinterpreted as aggression by teachers or peers. True rejection by peers or an inability or unwillingness to engage in *any* social interaction is cause for concern, however. Children who are highly aggressive or hostile are at special risk. Such children should be referred for special services as early as such problems are evident. Social intervention strategies such as teaching prosocial skills, social language, and conflict resolution abilities or nurturing classroom friendships may ameliorate these social problems. The earlier social interventions are provided, the more likely they are to be effective.

CHAPTER 14

Physical Growth and Motor Development in the Primary Years

GUIDING QUESTIONS

1. How do physical appearance and stature change during the primary years, and how do such changes vary across cultures?
2. How do poverty, health problems, and violence threaten the physical development of primary-grade children?
3. What motor abilities are acquired in the primary years, and how are these related to brain growth?
4. How do the motor play activities of primary-age children vary across cultures?
5. What are some threats to children's motor play in modern society?
6. What classroom adaptations can be implemented to meet the needs of children with physically challenging conditions and attention-deficit/hyperactivity disorder (ADHD)?

This chapter examines physical growth and motor development during the primary years—ages 6 to 8. Children of most cultures begin formal schooling during this developmental period. The emphasis of schools in almost all societies is on promoting academic learning. Even in nonindustrialized communities, classroom teachers spend the majority of the day providing instruction in traditional subjects, especially language and reading (B. B. Whiting & Edwards, 1988). What appears to be less important to parents, teachers, and even child development researchers is physical growth and motor development during the primary years. Many school districts in America have reduced the number of days children spend in physical education each week, and some are eliminating outdoor play altogether (Clements, 2007; Harkin, 2007).

Trends toward de-emphasizing physical growth and activity have serious implications, as the following story reveals:

A first-grade teacher, Ms. Schreiber, is reading a story to her students during group time. She is having a difficult time holding their attention. This is the first day that a new recess policy has been in effect. Outdoor playtime has been significantly reduced and pushed back until later in the school day. The rationale for the new policy is that recess is a waste of instructional time. The superintendent of this school system believes that increasing instructional time is the best way to improve scores on achievement tests.

And so, Ms. Schreiber struggles along, reading in an animated voice and reminding students to listen. The children wiggle and talk until finally she realizes the futility of continuing with the story. She gathers the children together and takes them outdoors.

The children run and scream for a short while, then Ms. Schreiber leads them back inside. When she resumes the story, her students are very attentive. Just a few minutes of physical activity has made all the difference!

When she relates this experience to the principal of her school, he is not impressed. In fact, he reprimands her for having violated the new policy.

The teacher in this story has learned that cognitive and motor development are interrelated. Children who are healthy, physically fit, and relaxed will perform well in school. Those who have health problems or are in need of physical exercise will perform poorly. Children who do not engage in regular, active play may become inattentive and possibly disruptive.

PHYSICAL APPEARANCE AND STATURE

The rate of physical growth slows considerably in the primary years (Haywood & Getchell, 2005). Children of this age will usually gain only about 2 inches in height and 4 pounds in weight each year. Initially, boys tend to be taller and heavier than girls, but girls generally catch up to them near the end of this developmental period. As legs and torsos become gradually longer and faces thinner, many school-age children begin to take on a slimmed-down appearance that contrasts with the roundish body shape of earlier periods.

A trademark of primary years is the toothless grin. Children at this age lose their baby teeth one after the other. Tooth loss is a significant event of this developmental period and dominates peer conversations.

Cultural Variations in Physical Growth

Much variation in growth exists among typically developing children. Furthermore, height and weight vary across cultural groups (Story et al., 2000). Southeast Asian children continue to be shorter, on the average, than Euro-American children, while African and African American children tend to be longer limbed and heavier. Individual growth trends can differ markedly within each cultural group, however, with some children shooting up quickly during this period, others growing more slowly.

Cultural differences in stature among primary-age children are often due to genetics. However, environment plays a role. Children of some cultural groups who live in poverty are smaller in stature because of poor nutrition and health care (Nutritional Status of Minority Children, 2004). For example, Southeast Asian children of poor families tend to be significantly shorter and lighter. Their small stature is believed to result from a combination of genetics and iron deficiency, which is prevalent among low-income families of this cultural group (Nguyen et al., 2004; S. Walker et al., 2007).

In a study of black South African children, place of residence was found to influence stature in the primary years (Goduka, Poole, & Aotaki-Phenice, 1992). Children living in their homelands were found to be taller and heavier than those whose families had been relocated to resettlement communities during apartheid and those who were living on white-owned farms. These researchers concluded that a complex cluster of community, home, and family factors contributes to general physical development.

Research in China has shown that, in some communities, only children are taller and heavier than those with siblings (Falbo & Poston, 1993). This finding contrasts sharply with research done in the United States reporting no physical differences between only children and others (Brown & Pollitt, 1996). Why the discrepancy? One explanation is that families with only one child receive special support from the government in China as part of a national policy to reduce the population. Since 1979, Chinese parents having only one child have been awarded certificates entitling them to special nutritional or health care benefits. In this case, then, government policy has affected the physical growth of young children.

Other research shows that children in many nonindustrialized countries are taller and heavier if their mothers have obtained a higher level of education (Tucker & Young, 1989). It is clear from these studies that children's stature in the primary years is affected by a complex set of factors that goes beyond health and nutritional influences.

POVERTY AND HEALTH STATUS OF PRIMARY-AGE CHILDREN

Great concern has been expressed around the world about the nutrition and health care of very young children in poverty. Poor prenatal and infant health status, in particular, has been found to predict serious developmental problems later in life (Pollitt, 1994). Are poor health and nutrition as damaging during middle childhood? There appears to be a widespread assumption that older children are somehow less vulnerable to these problems. Research suggests that adequate nutrition is crucial to healthy development in the primary years. Elementary school children who do not have an adequate diet or sufficient medical care have been found to suffer serious developmental problems (Grantham-McGregor, Walker, & Chang, 2007b). They are not protected simply because they have enjoyed good health or nutrition during earlier years. Continuous support is needed—throughout all of childhood—to ensure healthy growth and development.

Illness

Primary-grade children living in poverty are more likely to suffer a number of serious health problems. They are more often afflicted by infectious diseases (Silver & Stein, 2001); more regularly diagnosed with chronic conditions, such as asthma (Almqvist, Pershagen, & Wickman, 2005); and more frequently found to have dental problems (Liu, Probst, Martin, Wang, & Salinas, 2007). Children in poverty miss many more days of school because of physical ailments (Li & Leader, 2007). Such medical problems are also more common among children of parents who are above the poverty line but have low-wage jobs. This is due, in part, to a lack of medical insurance among these families. There are millions of uninsured children in the United States (Children's Defense Fund, 2007). Such children are four times as likely to have necessary medical procedures delayed and five times as likely to use the hospital emergency room as their only source of medical care.

These trends are most pronounced for poor children from historically underrepresented groups. Children of African American, Mexican American, and Native American backgrounds may be at special health risk during the primary years (Miernyk et al., 2000; Olvera-Ezzell, Power, Cousins, Guerra, & Trujillo, 1994; Perrin, Bloom, Gortmaker, 2007). One reason for this is the existence of cultural barriers to family services, as the following story illustrates:

> Marcus lives with his young, single mother in a small apartment in a large urban neighborhood. He has a respiratory ailment and spends much time lying in bed. Marcus has missed many days of school already this year. His mother has no health insurance and is frightened to go to a community clinic near her home.
>
> One morning she finds Marcus coughing and wheezing so violently that she becomes afraid. Seeing no other option, she decides to go to Marcus's school, hoping his teacher or a school nurse can help. She asks a neighbor to stay with Marcus and runs to the school, which is several blocks from her home. She enters Marcus's classroom and rushes to the teacher in a panic.
>
> TEACHER: Hello! I'm glad you stopped in. We really need to talk.
> MOTHER: (Breathless) Can you . . . can you . . . (Struggles with her words)
> TEACHER: (In a concerned tone) Did Marcus not come in with you today? Is he out of school again?
> MOTHER: He's sick . . .
> TEACHER: We need to talk about all of these absences. He's not learning anything in school because he's gone so much. Is he really sick all the time, or does he just like staying at home? It really would be good if you'd see to it that he gets here . . .
> MOTHER: (Begins to cry)
> TEACHER: Oh . . . You seem really upset. Let's sit here a moment. Tell me what's wrong.
>
> The mother finally gets out her story. The teacher arranges for the school nurse to help get Marcus to the clinic. He is diagnosed with asthma. With treatment, he is able to attend school more regularly.

Marcus's family has limited access to health services. His young mother is intimidated by the medical clinic, perhaps because of the complex bureaucracy or the disapproving looks from the staff because of her young age. Even when Marcus is very ill, she is afraid to go. At first, Marcus's teacher misses the mother's pleas for help and begins to deliver a lecture on the importance of attendance. Fortunately, she notices Marcus's mother's upset and helps her get medical care for her son.

Nutrition

Children's health is related to good nutrition. Elementary children who eat well will suffer fewer serious illnesses (U.S. Department of Health and Human Services, 2008). In many parts of the world, children do not have enough to eat. Protein deficiency, anemia, and general starvation are still common in some nonindustrialized countries (Black, 2008). These conditions disrupt healthy development. Children's mental as well as physical and motor competence are impaired by an inadequate diet during middle childhood.

Poor nutrition is common among primary-grade children in the United States as well. Studies of eating habits in the elementary years show that many American children have diets high in saturated fats, salt, and sugar. More than one-third of the calories consumed by typical elementary school children come from nutritionally poor foods (Frary, Johnson, & Wang, 2004). Not surprisingly, problems of inadequate diet are more common among families living in poverty (Olvera-Ezzell et al., 1994).

Obesity

As discussed in previous chapters, a growing concern in the United States is childhood obesity. **Obesity** is defined as a serious medical condition in which a child has a body mass index that lies above the 95th percentile for his or her particular age group. **Body mass index (BMI)** is a formula that determines the ratio of weight in relation to height (see Chapter 6). In recent years, obesity in childhood has increased. In a study of 34 industrialized countries, the United States was found to have the highest rate of school-aged children who are overweight or obese (25% and 7%, respectively). Causes of this epidemic are many—as presented in Chapter 10, the leading culprits are lower activity, increased television viewing, and poor food choices (Frary et al., 2004).

Children of certain historically underrepresented groups are at special risk for obesity. Mexican American children, for example, are more likely to be obese in the elementary years than their Euro-American, African American, and Asian American peers (Flegal, Ogden, & Carroll, 2004; Olvera-Ezzell, Power, & Cousins, 1990). This trend is most pronounced for Mexican American children living in poverty. Contributing to obesity among Mexican American elementary school children are factors associated with being poor: inadequate diet and lack of health insurance and health care. Mothers who believe that they are not in control of their own circumstances are also more likely to have obese children.

Obesity is beginning to affect children in other parts of the world as well. In China, boys who live in urban areas have BMIs that have begun to resemble those of American children (Iwata, Hara, Okada, Harada, & Li, 2003). Obesity is also becoming more prevalent in Eastern Europe and the Middle East (Kelishadi, 2007).

A variety of interventions have been developed to address the problem of childhood obesity. These include reducing high-fat and high-calorie foods in children's diets, discouraging television viewing, and increasing activity levels, both in- and outside of school (Summerbell, et al., 2008). Cultural variations in the causes and nature of obesity, however, require that unique strategies be used in each family. In one program, for example, Mexican American parents were taught to socialize their children to eat healthy foods that were common and meaningful within their culture and to use techniques to discourage overeating that matched the natural parenting styles of this group (Olvera-Ezzell et al., 1990). Parents were encouraged to tailor their interactions to the particular mealtime situation. For example, when coaxing children to try new foods, they were permissive in their responses: "You don't have to eat that, but it's really good!" When they wanted their children to eat healthy foods they were already familiar with, they were more directive: "You need to eat all those vegetables so you will grow." To discourage overeating, they were diplomatic in their mealtime interchanges: "Do you really think you should eat a big second helping of potatoes?" These strategies reflect the unique socialization beliefs and practices of this cultural group.

obesity: A serious medical condition in which a child has a body mass index (BMI) that lies above the 95th percentile for his or her particular age group.

body mass index (BMI): A measure of health status, computed by considering weight in relation to height (the formula for calculating BMI is weight/height^2 × 703).

Injury

Injury is the leading cause of death among primary-grade children (Centers for Disease Control and Prevention, 2008). Each year, 22,000 children die, and 30,000 are permanently disabled because of unintentional injuries. Further, 600,000 children are hospitalized annually with injuries, and many more visit emergency rooms. In the United States, children in poverty—particularly

THE MEDIA

Does Television Contribute to Childhood Obesisty?

Childhood obesity is increasing worldwide. What has changed in the lives of children to explain this health problem? Certainly, children are eating more empty calories and getting less exercise, as emphasized in this chapter. But there may be an underlying culprit that affects both of these factors: the media. Children are watching more television and sitting at the computer for more hours than at any point in history (Ackad, 2007). The increase in these sedentary activities has been linked directly to problems of obesity (Anderson & Butcher, 2006). In one study, the highest rate of obesity among primary-age children was found for those who watched 4 or more hours of television a day (Crespo et al., 2001). Girls and children of historically underrepresented groups were found to watch more television and to be less active. Research suggests that television viewing in childhood has long-term health consequences, such as high blood pressure and high cholesterol in adulthood (Hancox, Milne, & Poulton, 2004).

The most obvious explanation for the link between media use and obesity is that, when children are sitting in front of a television or computer screen, they are not engaged in active play. This reduction in physical activity alone explains much of the problem. One study (Klesges, 1993) suggests that children burn fewer calories watching television than doing nothing at all. In this study, children's metabolic rates slowed to levels lower than those typically found when children are asleep. Metabolic rates slowed significantly more during TV viewing in obese children.

As children watch television, they are also exposed to commercials that promote foods high in sugars and fats (Halford et al., 2004). The number of advertisements for unhealthy foods has increased in recent years (Caroli, Argentieri, Cardone, & Masi, 2004). This not only teaches children poor eating habits but may prompt them to eat more as they're watching.

One solution is to encourage parents regularly to turn off the television and computer and encourage and participate in active play with their children. Reducing television watching and computer use has been found to be one of the most effective components in obesity prevention programs aimed at children (Haby et al., 2006).

those who live in dangerous urban neighborhoods—suffer more injuries (Gilbride, Wild, Wilson, Svenson, & Spady, 2006). Injuries are also more prevalent among children of some historically underrepresented groups. Mexican American children, for example, are more likely to be injured on the playground or in the street (Mull, Agran, Winn, & Anderson, 2001). Temperament may play a role in childhood injuries. Children who are more extroverted, active, and less inhibited suffer more injuries than less outgoing and more cautious children (Morrongiello & Sedore, 2005; Spinks, Nagle, Macpherson, Bain, & McClure, 2008).

Vigilant parents and teachers can safeguard children. Poor supervision has been identified as a major cause of preventable accidents involving children (Schwebel & Gaines, 2007). Risk of injury is highest in single-parent homes, those in which parents are very young, and those in which drugs or alcohol are abused.

How much supervision is required to keep children safe from injury? In one study, this question was asked of mothers, child protection service workers, and health care providers (Peterson, Ewigman, & Kivlahan, 1993). The consensus among these groups was that preschool-age children should receive constant supervision—that is, they should never be out of the sight of an adult. Primary-age children should receive near-constant supervision; they should never play for more than 5 minutes without an adult checking on them. However, study participants agreed that when children were playing in high-risk areas, where busy roads or urban hazards are a threat, even primary-age children should receive constant supervision.

Children who live in violent neighbor-hoods live in constant fear.

Taken together, research on injury paints a troubling picture of the risks to children living in poverty. While parents and child safety experts recommend constant adult vigilance when children play in high-risk neighborhoods, problems associated with poverty—substance abuse and single or teenage parenthood—can result in inadequate supervision.

Violence

During the time it takes you to read this chapter, one child will die from gunfire in this country. This death rate is equivalent to the loss of an entire classroom of children every 2 days (Children's Defense Fund, 2007). The number of reported violent crimes in the United States has actually gone down in recent years. Assaults committed by people younger than 19, for example, has declined by 19% since 1994. Fewer children than a decade ago have been witnesses to or victims of violence. Still, the problem of violence in the lives of children persists. In the words of the Children's Defense Fund (2007), "One child homicide is one too many" (p. 71).

American children younger than 15 years of age are still 12 times more likely to be killed by gunfire than children in 25 other industrialized nations *combined* (Children's Defense Fund, 2007). Elementary school children and adolescents are twice as likely as adults to be victims of violent crime. By age 5, a majority of children now living in low-income neighborhoods in the United States have encountered a shooting. By adolescence, two-thirds have witnessed a homicide. Children of historically underrepresented groups are more likely to be victimized; homicide is the leading cause of death among African Americans younger than age 24 (Reiss & Roth, 1993). Figure 14-1 shows the alarming homicide rates for several cultural groups in the United States. In no other country in the world is violent criminal behavior more prevalent (van Dijk, Mayhew, & Killias, 1990).

Approximately 3 million American children are reported annually to protective service agencies as suspected victims of child abuse. One-third of them were confirmed as victims of abuse (Children's Defense Fund, 2007). Reported cases of child abuse have not declined in spite of recent general drops in crime and improvements in the economy. What is disturbing about these figures is that they represent only a portion of the children who are abused in this country. It is estimated that more than half of violent crimes against children go unreported and unaddressed (Finkelhor, 2004).

Living in violent communities—"urban war zones" as they have sometimes been called—presents emotional as well as physical risks (Garbarino et al., 1992). Preschool children

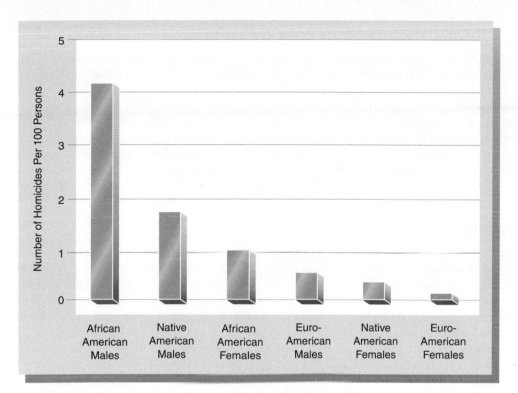

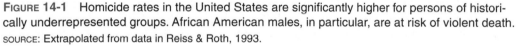

FIGURE 14-1   Homicide rates in the United States are significantly higher for persons of historically underrepresented groups. African American males, in particular, are at risk of violent death.
SOURCE: Extrapolated from data in Reiss & Roth, 1993.

exposed to chronic community violence show passive responses: clinging, fearfulness, bedwetting, and quiet, withdrawn behavior. However, with age, reactions become more overt and problematic in school. Primary-grade children from violent communities exhibit more aggression and conduct problems, poor concentration, forgetfulness, and learning difficulties. Regular experiences with violence at this age may lead to serious psychological disorders. Children may undergo major personality changes. Regression—the resumption of bedwetting or thumb sucking—is common. Children who live in danger often develop feelings of rage and despair. Many experience "psychic numbing," which causes them to stop caring or feeling (Garbarino et al., 1992, p. 57).

All children who live with violence live in fear. Garbarino and his colleagues (1992) tell the story of one young child who lives in terror in a dangerous neighborhood. When asked why he kept an empty deodorant bottle beside his bed, he ran his finger along the label and read, "Guaranteed 100% safe." The intensity of this fear reaction varies according to cultural and family experience. In one study, African American children—particularly girls—were found to worry more about physical harm than their Euro-American peers (W. K. Silverman, La Greca, & Wasserstein, 1995). Such findings are not surprising given the high rate of physical assault and homicide in low-income, predominantly African American neighborhoods.

Children's fear of violence is not limited to urban American neighborhoods. Violence causes psychological harm all over the world. In Mozambique, which has been at war off and on throughout its existence, children are regularly kidnapped, tortured, and killed. A growing number of children are orphans whose parents have been killed in the war. In an interview with 35 Mozambiquan children, 24 reported witnessing at least one violent death (Garbarino et al., 1992).

In Cambodia under Pol Pot's Khmer Rouge regime, the horrors of which were documented in the film *The Killing Fields*, children suffered horrible atrocities. Not only were children, their families, and parents killed in great numbers, but children were sometimes recruited as executioners or enforcers who were forced to kill others in support of the genocidal restructuring of Khmer society.

Some children are able to cope in spite of such atrocities. These children are called **resilient** because they manage to develop in positive directions under terrible circumstances. Many, however, do not survive intact. Although their physical wounds may heal, their psychological scars remain for life. Children of these communities are often numb and unresponsive—out of touch with the world and the people around them (Garbarino et al., 1992). In every community of the world, fear and injury caused by violence have a devastating effect on development.

Homelessness

More than 1 million children will be homeless in the United States at some point during this year (Children's Defense Fund, 2007). Only two decades ago, the homeless population was composed almost entirely of single men who suffered from mental illness (Zigler & Finn-Stevenson, 2007). Today, children account for the fastest-growing segment of the homeless population. In some communities, more than half of all homeless persons are children (Proffitt, 2008).

Living in a car, an abandoned building, or a shelter can have an injurious effect on psychological and physical growth (Buckner, 2008; Gewirtz, Hart-Shegos, Medhanie, 2008). Homeless children are more likely to be depressed and anxious, and they often display conduct problems and aggression. They may also suffer from malnutrition; their health status is generally far poorer than that of children living in poverty who have consistent—if not adequate—housing. They are more often afflicted by chronic illness and are less likely to be adequately immunized against childhood diseases.

It would have been preposterous even 30 years ago to think that homeless children would be living on the streets of America. You may be asking, as you read this section, How could such a problem exist in such an affluent society?

MOTOR DEVELOPMENT IN THE PRIMARY YEARS

In the primary years, children gain greater control over their bodies. The basic large motor skills acquired in the preschool years—running, climbing, jumping, catching, throwing, kicking, and balancing—become refined and coordinated (Haywood & Getchell, 2005). Primary-grade children can now combine running, stopping, starting, and kicking abilities to play soccer. They can coordinate movements and balance to ride a two-wheel bicycle. They use their full bodies in throwing, shifting body weight to one foot in preparation for a throw, and then transferring weight to the other foot as the throw is made. Using this ability, they can excel in catching and throwing games. Specific large motor skills acquired during the primary years and approximate ages at which they appear are presented in Table 14-1.

On the average, boys outperform girls on some large motor skills during the primary years (Cratty, 1986; Tanner, 1990). This may be due to boys' greater weight, height, limb length, and muscle tone at this point in development. In addition, boys are more likely than girls to be encouraged to excel in physical activities. It is important to note, however, that gender differences in motor competence are not great at this age level and that, as individuals, many girls are more competent than many boys. Both boys and girls acquire large motor skills at the same rapid rate throughout the primary years.

resilient: A descriptor for children who are able to cope and develop in positive directions in spite of terrible circumstances in their lives.

TABLE 14-1
**Motor Development
Milestones in the
Primary Years**

Primary children can . . .	by around age . . .
catch a small ball using hands only	6 years
skip using alternate foot	6 years
kick with a mature follow-through of the foot	6 years
hop alternating from one foot to another	6 years
hop accurately into small spaces or squares (as in hopscotch)	6.5 years
swing a bat and strike a ball, rotating the trunk and shifting body weight forward	6.5 years
throw a ball accurately, shifting weight properly and stepping with the foot opposite the throwing arm	6.5 years
balance on one foot without vision	7 years
walk along a narrow balance beam	7 years
perform jumping jacks	7 years
throw a ball or other object 40 to 70 feet	8 years
run between 14 and 18 feet per second	8 years

SOURCE: Cratty, 1986; Haywood & Getchell, 2005.

Children also show more refined abilities in the use of small muscles in the primary years. They can manipulate markers, crayons, and pencils with greater control and can cut accurately with scissors. They are now able to button, zip, snap, and tie independently, which allows them to accomplish their own dressing and undressing. They can coordinate the use of vision, hands, and fingers, which enables them to draw more representational pictures, write legibly, and handle and read books. These advances in motor ability are partly due to increases in muscle tone, strength, and coordination but also to brain growth.

The Body–Brain Connection

Early researchers, such as Arnold Gesell, recognized a connection between the brain and motor ability. However, they viewed motor development as an *outcome* of brain maturation—a physical sign that synapses and nerve cells were forming. A new theory about the body–brain connection has now been proposed. The **dynamic systems theory** (Lockman & Thelen, 1993; Thelen & Smith, 1994; Warren, 2006) is based on research suggesting that motor action, cognitive development, and behavior are all part of a single, dynamic system in the brain. From this perspective, all these components influence one another. Movement can foster brain growth, cognitive development, and learning, not just the other way around. This theory holds that physical play and exercise are critical, in part, because they promote learning and academic success.

Here is an example of how this dynamic system works (Warren, 2006): A child climbs on a climber on the playground. As she does this, she activates and coordinates certain neurons—brain cells—that are needed for this action. If she climbs often, these cells will become organized into a **neural cluster**—a collection of connected brain cells that handle climbing. As the child plays, she combines her climbing with other skills—swinging, jumping, and screaming out to her friends. Each of these actions leads eventually to the formation of new neural clusters. Over time, these clusters connect with one another and become an even larger network of cells, called a **neural map.** A neural map is a complex web of cells that connects a whole region of the brain. From this view, the practice and refinement of specific motor abilities leads to brain organization.

dynamic systems theory: A theory that holds that motor action, cognitive development, and behavior are all part of a single, dynamic system in the brain. From this perspective, motor development and brain growth are interrelated.

neural cluster: A collection of connected brain cells that handle certain movements, such as climbing.

neural map: A complex network of neural clusters that connects a whole region of the brain. The formation of neural maps leads to brain organization.

According to dynamic systems theory, once the brain is well organized in this way, it is better able to learn all sorts of things (Warren, 2006). Imagine that a child is crawling through a maze his teacher has created on the playground. As he does this, he creates neural clusters, which help him understand space and movement. These same clusters of brain cells may later help him with other spatial tasks in the classroom, like interpreting a map or recognizing or writing letters and words. When the brain becomes organized in motor play, it enhances not only movement but also thinking and learning of all kinds.

If, indeed, brain organization and learning are promoted by movement, it behooves adults to offer active play experiences throughout a child's day (Lockman & Thelen, 1993). Denying elementary children—or, for that matter, adolescents or adults—opportunities to move deprives them of key elements in the body-brain system. Children need to jump, run, swing, throw, and balance to become intellectually competent.

MOTOR PLAY AND CULTURE

The ways children use emerging motor skills in play vary considerably from one culture to another. In some cultures, children play sports at a young age. In others, less competitive play pursuits are common. In spite of cultural variations, certain advancements in motor play during the primary years appear to be universal. Common features of children's motor play in all cultures are presented in Table 14-2.

Generally, the somewhat wild and chaotic play actions of preschoolers give way to more organized and rule-governed activities in the primary years (Hughes, 1999; Kyratzis, 2004; B. B. Whiting & Edwards, 1988). Even the roughest and loudest games can involve teams, role assignments, rules, turn taking, or other evidence of organization.

Children in this developmental period often wish to acquire real skills and become grown up. Their play becomes more and more realistic, then, and skill centered (Hughes, 1999). The spontaneous make-believe enactments of the preschool years evolve into serious dramatic productions. Wild chasing games develop into more adult-like sporting events that allow children to show off their motor abilities. The emphasis is on practicing real adult competencies.

Several types of motor play are common across cultures in this developmental period. These are presented in Table 14-3. Some of these play activities are more advanced versions of activities observed in the preschool years. Others are unique to this developmental period.

TABLE 14-2
Elements of Primary Motor Play Found in Most Cultures of the World

Element	Example
Organization and role assignments	In a neighborhood game of war, there are teams, leaders, soldiers, and medics.
Turn taking	In a game of climbing up and jumping off a wall, children announce, one at a time, the kind of jump they will complete and then perform it with peers watching.
Realism	In a game of soccer, children adhere to real adult rules, practice grown-up competencies, and emulate the behavior and language of sports heroes.

SOURCE: Based on Hughes, F. P. (1998). *Children, Play, and Development, 3rd edition.* Boston: Allyn & Bacon.

Type of Play	Example
Functional	Children in Polynesia leap off the bank of a stream, competing to see who can land the farthest out in the water.
Rough-and-tumble	Children in Kenya chase one another and throw dirt and sticks on one another as they tend livestock.
Pretend	Two children in Mexico pretend to be grown-up parents as they care for an infant brother in the neighborhood.
Games with rules	A large group of children gather in a village in Nepal for a game of marbles.
Teasing	Children in northern Italy snatch a toy from a younger sister and hide it, taunting, "I wonder where that doll went?"
Rituals	A group of children gather in a park in Chicago and perform jump-rope chants and rhymes passed down from older siblings.

TABLE 14-3
Types of Motor Play Common Across Cultures

Functional Play

When primary-grade children are released onto the playground after a long morning in the classroom, they can often be observed running, jumping, screaming, and chasing. Many researchers call such open-ended, repetitive motor activity **functional play,** described in Chapter 12 (Frost et al., 2008). One first-grade teacher has a more down-to-earth name for it: "getting the wiggles out." Functional play appears in infancy and is very common in the preschool years. It is frequently observed in the activities of children in societies around the world (Hughes, 1999; Martini, 1994).

How does this type of play change in the primary grades? Such activity is still loud and wild at this age, but it becomes more organized and skill oriented. This more organized pattern is illustrated in the following examples, drawn from observations of different cultural groups and communities:

EXAMPLE 1

Two 7-year-old Polynesian children are running under a bridge, emitting high-pitched screams so they can hear their echoes. One child now stops the other.

CHILD A: Wait. Let's try it with just me going under.
CHILD B: No. We need to run together.
CHILD A: I'll go under first and then you.
CHILD B: Yes, okay.

Child A runs through screaming; child B follows soon after. They giggle at the change in the echoes created by this new approach. They decide to experiment further, first by running faster as they scream, then slower. Then they try whispering as they pass under the bridge and laugh when they find that no echo is created. (Adapted from Martini, 1994)

EXAMPLE 2

Three 6-year-old African American children play in an alley in their urban neighborhood in Chicago. They have pulled an old mattress from a Dumpster and are using it as a trampoline.

functional play: A type of play, commonly performed by infants and young children with special needs, that involves repetitive motor action, such as banging objects or repeating body movements again and again.

MARCUS: (Jumping on the mattress) Look! I'll do this trick. Like in the circus. (Jumps and lands on his stomach)

ALPHONSE: (Laughing) No. That's not how you do it. My turn!

MICHAEL: Is not! I'm next. I can jump higher. (Climbs onto the mattress as Marcus rolls off and begins to jump) Look at this! See how high? (Adapted from Garbarino et al., 1992)

EXAMPLE 3

Two brothers from a small village in Senegal tend cows in a field. One of the children begins to run around, making noises and ducking behind cows to hide from his brother.

BOITSHWARO: Can't catch me!

YAPOYO: I can! (Begins to run after Boitshwaro)

BOITSHWARO: (Circles round and round the herd, then laughs at his brother) You are too slow!

The cows begin to run. The game ends quickly as the boys herd them back into a group.

Each of these games is very different, but all reflect common advancements in functional play. Rules about taking turns are evident in the first two examples. In the second and third examples, children try to display adult-like motor skills: "I'll do this trick. Like in the circus" and "You are too slow!" In spite of the diversity in these activities, all of them show children incorporating similar organization and skill orientation into their actions.

Children in all cultures engage in functional play. However, the frequency of this activity varies significantly from one community to the next. In one study, children in Taiwan were found to engage in almost twice as much functional play as Euro-American children in the United States (H. L. W. Pan, 1994). In another study, African American children of low socioeconomic status were found to engage in this type of active play very frequently. In a study I conducted, Puerto Rican children living on the island engaged in more functional play than either Euro-American or Puerto Rican children living on the mainland (Trawick-Smith, 2000).

Traditionally, functional play has been considered less sophisticated, socially and cognitively, than make-believe or games with rules. High levels of this type of play have often been interpreted as evidence that some children have play deficits (Smilansky, 1968). For example, the fact that African American children living in poverty engage in more functional play has caused some researchers to label them as *deficient*. A look at the previous examples shows, however, that functional play in the primary grades can be socially and cognitively challenging. Such play episodes involve rules, social negotiations, and turn taking, just as in a game of kickball.

Elements of make-believe can also be found in functional play (McLoyd, 1986; Trawick-Smith, 1998c). For example, the children in the second example, who are using a mattress as a trampoline, may be pretending to be acrobats. The children in my Puerto Rican study pretended to be monsters—each with a special name and role in the "monster family"—as they screamed and chased on the playground (Trawick-Smith, 2000).

Rough-and-Tumble Play

rough-and-tumble play: A form of motor play—including wrestling, play fighting, rolling around, and chasing peers—that relieves tension and contributes to social competence but does not lead to aggression.

Rough-and-tumble play is a cousin of functional play. As discussed in earlier chapters, this type of play involves rough but nonaggressive activity, such as wrestling, play fighting, and friendly jostling. There is evidence that this form of play enhances both physical and social development (DeWolf, 2001; Pellegrini, 1995a; Pellis & Pellis, 2007). How does rough-and-tumble play change in the primary years? As with other play forms, it becomes organized and rule governed. Parents and teachers who are familiar with this type of play may be doubtful. It takes careful observation to see the structure in such wild interactions.

B. B. Whiting and Edwards (1988) observed explicitly stated rules within the rough-and-tumble play of children of many different cultures. In a community in the United States, children's play fighting is regulated by boxing rules: gloves were required, time-outs would stop the fighting, and an "I'm sorry" was necessary when a peer got hurt. In Okinawa, primary children's wrestling bouts are very organized, with turn taking, rules, and regulations about not hurting. In Polynesia, children organize their play fighting into "war games," called *keu tou'a*, that include rules, assignments of leader and follower roles, and teams (Martini, 1994). In East India, children shout, wrestle, and squirt water on each other during the *Holi* holiday. In this society, the *Holi* holiday is one of the few times of the year when children engage in open-ended, wild activity. Even so, this play is generally more cooperative and less rough than in Western cultures.

The amount of rough-and-tumble play varies from one culture to another. B. B. Whiting and Edwards (1988) found that childhood roughhousing was particularly common among boys in Okinawa, the Philippines, and Mexico. Ramsey (2004) has observed that children of some historically underrepresented cultural groups in America have a rougher play style that is sometimes less familiar to Euro-American children and adults. Often this activity is misinterpreted as aggression or preaggression. "It's only a matter of time," one teacher commented as she watched two children wrestle on the playground, "before these two will be fighting."

In fact, rough-and-tumble play rarely leads to actual aggression. Primary children appear to clearly understand the differences between play jostling or wrestling and real fighting (DeWolf, 2001; Pellegrini, 1995a). This is true for children around the world. B. B. Whiting and Edwards (1988) drew this conclusion from their observations of rough play in many different cultures: "It might seem ... that ... children are constantly beating one another, but in fact there are surprisingly few incidents of assaulting interactions. ... There is much evidence of children's genuine concern about hurting others" (p. 254).

Pretend Play

One trend in children's play in the primary years is that **pretend play,** defined in Chapter 7, declines as organized games increase (Hughes, 1999). In East India, for example, children at this age are more likely to start a game of marbles or tag than to enact the make-believe game "police and thief" that was a favorite in preschool. In America, second-graders will more often organize a kickball or soccer game during recess than initiate a pretend superhero game.

Why does make-believe disappear? Where does it go? In one study, primary-grade children were found to engage in much make-believe when they were given explicit permission to do so (Trawick-Smith, 1993). It is possible that pretend play disappears because it is not sanctioned beyond the preschool years in most societies. Subtle messages from parents and teachers may let children know that this form of play is immature or otherwise inappropriate. In America, a child might be scolded for using math blocks as rocket ships. In Kenya, a child might be told to stop playing and watch the livestock more closely.

What happens to make-believe? Does it simply vanish after early childhood? Many believe that play goes "underground," that it becomes fantasy or secret play (Trawick-Smith, 1998b). An American primary-grade child might daydream or draw fantastic characters on his notebook in school. An African child might secretly pretend to be a mother while caring for her infant brother. Traditional dramatic play equipment, dolls, and toys may be removed too early from homes and classrooms. With encouragement, older children will pretend in ways that are developmentally useful.

pretend play: A form of play in which children transform themselves into make-believe characters, change real objects into imaginary ones, and carry out complex make-believe enactments.

Given the opportunity, what kinds of pretend play will primary-grade children engage in? As with other forms of play, make-believe becomes exceedingly structured with age (Trawick-Smith, 1993). Children's pretending becomes more elaborate than the spontaneous, free-flowing make-believe of the preschool years, taking on many of the characteristics of adult-level theater. Children spend an inordinate amount of time planning their play, developing complex play settings and assigning roles. Sometimes one or another player becomes the director, guiding play organization and coaching others' performances (e.g., "Okay, him and me are cops, right? And let's say we chase you in our police car and catch you and lock you up in jail, okay?"). Children often enact real-life settings or re-create the scripts of favorite books, television shows, and movies (Hughes, 1999).

Games with Rules

Games with rules—activities that include rules, strategy, and competition—are believed to predominate children's play activities in the primary years (Cherney & London, 2006; Hughes, 1999). Children often spontaneously organize their own ball games, races, or besting contests (e.g., "Let's see who can swing the highest without holding on"). Organized sports are common among primary-grade children in America. It is important to note, however, that the frequency and nature of childhood games vary significantly from one culture to another.

In some cultural groups, games simply are not played. In a study of one small village in Kenya, for example, games were virtually never observed (B. B. Whiting & Edwards, 1988). In another investigation of a small community in Mexico, games were rarely recorded in neighborhood play. Only in school did children of this village participate in organized games. One explanation is that games are not particularly valued within these cultures. Another is that team sports and elaborate games are made impossible by a shortage of players in a village or neighborhood (B. B. Whiting & Edwards, 1988).

Where children do play games, major differences can be found in their content or level of competition. Of course, which games are played will be determined by culture. In America, children play football, T-ball, or soccer. In East India, children play *Kaalla Gjja*, a kind of follow-the-leader game in which all players must imitate precisely the leader's

games with rules: A predominant form of play during the primary years that includes rules, strategy, and competition.

Children in many cultures play games with rules and competition.

elaborate actions (Roopnarine et al., 1994). In Polynesia, children organize themselves into games of *Keu tou'a*, in which one team of children chases another (Martini, 1994). Within some cultural groups, quiet games are the norm: computer and video games in Japan and spinning tops and shooting marbles in Mexico (B. B. Whiting & Edwards, 1988). There are, in fact, as many different varieties of childhood games as there are diverse cultures. Passed down from peers, older siblings, and parents and teachers, games reflect the histories, values, and competencies of the particular society.

One way that games differ is in the amount of competition involved. Among Euro-American and European children, a high degree of competition is common. This likely reflects the attitudes and valued competencies of these cultural groups. Ideals of rugged individualism and corporate competition within these societies may underlie the emergence of competitive games in childhood. Sutton-Smith and Roberts (1970) believe that games serve to socialize children to capitalist values of goal directedness and individual achievement: "In games, children learn all those necessary arts of trickery, deception, harassment, divination, and foul play that their teachers won't teach them" (p. 65). Elkind (2007) warns that intense competition may create undue stress in children, causing their interest in sports and games to decline over time.

In many cultures, intense competition is not a problem because children's games are exceedingly cooperative. Games among children in East India and Polynesia have been described as remarkably noncompetitive (Martini, 1994; Roopnarine et al., 1994). In a study in Oyugis, a small community in western Kenya, children were found to virtually never argue over the rules of games (B. B. Whiting & Edwards, 1988). This may be because competition and individual achievement are less emphasized in these cultures than in others, such as the United States, where very many arguments erupt about rules and winning.

Teasing Play

Teasing play becomes an important play form in many societies as children enter the primary years. Described in Chapter 13, this form of play involves taunting peers or arguing in a playful and nonhostile way. Some adults view this as negative or antisocial behavior. It is unlikely that teachers will rush to encourage teasing games in school! Yet many researchers believe that teasing play in childhood is a highly organized social activity that promotes motor and cognitive development (Campos et al., 2007; Endo, 2007). Hale-Benson (1986) describes a teasing game as a formal rite among older African American children. Called *playing the dozens*, it involves verbal duels between two opponents who trade insults about family members. The contest occurs in the presence of a crowd of peers who encourage and judge the insults with loud reactions.

To play well, a child needs to think quickly and to express taunts and slurs with emotional expression and humor. Most important, children playing the game need to control their emotions; they must not get angry at their opponent's insults. Such control of emotion may be very critical for children living in urban neighborhoods, where rage and hostility are at the heart of many violent acts. Children who learn emotional control through such play may be less likely to become violent when they are older.

Teasing play in Polynesia also reflects a high degree of organization (Martini, 1994). In this culture, teasing is a method of maintaining order and structure in a peer group. A child will tease others as a method of challenging their status and establishing his or her own dominance. Teasing, taunts, and scolding are a form of *status leveling* in which individual children are relegated to lower-status positions in the group. Through the teasing process, clearly identified leaders emerge. Why is leadership so important in Polynesian peer groups? Children in this culture have little contact with parents during the day. They do not request help from adults to resolve conflicts or when a minor injury occurs. They rely on their peers.

teasing play: A form of play, common in some cultures, in which children taunt one another or argue in a nonliteral and non-hostile way. Teasing play is not usually considered aggression.

A peer structure with specific leaders in charge may provide security and comfort to these young children. Thus, teasing is a vital part of peer group organization.

Rituals

Rituals—playful, predictable, often rhythmic routines—are common in the primary years (Hughes, 1999). The following are familiar examples:

- A child on a climber calls down to his peers in a familiar rhythmic chant: "Nya nya nya-nya nya, you can't catch me!" His peers give chase.
- As two children walk along a sidewalk, one announces, "Step on a crack, break your momma's back!" The two children slow their pace and look down, carefully placing each step.

What is fascinating is that many of these rituals have been part of child culture for generations. They are somehow transmitted to children through the ages, although few parents remember directly teaching them to their children.

Much can be learned about a child's culture by observing rituals (Hughes, 1999). A chant such as "one potato, two potato" to determine who goes first or who obtains a certain object may reflect a Euro-American emphasis on turn taking, competition, and rules. Group chants and jump-rope rhymes, common in the play of African American children, might reflect a more collective culture (Hale-Benson, 1986), as might the collaborative hopping chants of children in East India (Roopnarine et al., 1994).

Why do children perform these repetitive rituals? Perhaps they reflect children's need for order and routine at this age. Rituals may serve the function of socializing children into childhood culture (Hughes, 1999). Learning such chants, sayings, and ritual actions may be a way of establishing membership in a peer group. Children who know the rituals are in; those who don't are left out. In essence, the rituals create a special way of interacting or speaking that is exclusively for children.

MODERN THREATS TO MOTOR PLAY

There are threats to motor play in modern life. Technology and even school reform have reduced children's playtime.

Television

As discussed in previous sections, children who watch many hours of television engage in less active play. A study in Japan, for example, showed that outdoor motor playtime dropped by half during the period that television became popular (Takeuchi, 1994). In the United States, television watching has been linked to obesity in childhood and adolescence (Anderson & Butcher, 2006). Great variation in television watching is found across individual families. Of course, in some societies, television is not available. In those where it is available, viewing is common and increasing in all families (Gable, Chang, & Krull, 2007). However, families of low socioeconomic status tend to watch more hours of television than middle class-families (Grund et al., 2001). Children of historically underrepresented groups have also been found to spend more time in front of television than their Euro-American peers (Flores, Tomany-Korman, & Olson, 2005). In contrast, children who spend time in after-school care and summer school programs and those who have older siblings to play with have been found to be less likely to watch television and more likely to engage in active play (Cooper, Charlton, Valentine, & Muhlenbruck, 2000).

rituals: Playful, predictable, often rhythmic routines that children perform and pass on to their siblings and peers in the primary years.

School Policy

Changes in school policy in some communities have threatened opportunities for motor play. One trend observed in schools across the country is the reduction or elimination of recess. Several studies suggest that eliminating active play reduces children's attention in school and their potential for learning (Frost et al., 2008; Pellegrini, 1995b). These concerns are voiced by a first-grade teacher whose school district has just changed the recess policy:

> Our school board has been making a big deal out of increasing our "instructional time." They've added minutes to our school day and days to our school year. Several weeks ago, I received notification that outdoor time would no longer be considered instructional time. The memo read, "Since recess time cannot be counted in the determination of instructional minutes, outdoor free time must be reduced or eliminated or the school day lengthened."
>
> I argued to my principal, "What do they mean, recess isn't instructional time? In my view, there's no greater learning period in the day. Aren't board members concerned about social interaction? Aren't they concerned about health? Don't they understand the connections between the body and the mind? Better they give up math time than recess!" My principal smiled and nodded. He has yet to take action, however, on my concerns.

Perhaps physical education (PE) classes provide adequate exercise to justify reducing recess. A national survey indicates that many schools do not offer PE on a daily basis (Ross & Pate, 1987). More troubling is the finding of one study that a typical 30-minute PE class includes only about 2 minutes of exercise (G. S. Parcel et al., 1987). In the classes that were studied, much of the time was spent waiting for a turn or watching others play after being eliminated from a game.

Pangrazi (2006) argues that an effective PE lesson is one where *all* children move throughout the *entire* class period. A way to accomplish this, he proposes, is to make classes more like the spontaneous free play experiences that occur during recess. Open-ended running, chasing, and roughhousing games should be planned. Chuoke and Eyman (1997) suggest that motor skills and a sense of fair play are best taught within the context of recess, not PE. They urge greater adult involvement in the spontaneous play activities of children on the playground.

School research suggests that motor development is not a priority among many educators. Troubling trends in poor health and learning may be predicted in communities in which the importance of physical play is not appreciated. The good news is that children in some communities find time to play after school. Figure 14-2 shows the percentage of children who play more than an hour a day after school in various countries in the world.

Professionals should become advocates for school recess both within their own schools and communities and in the country as a whole. (See the Advocacy and Public Policy box in this chapter for a description of a national movement to protect children's right to outdoor play.)

CLASSROOM ADAPTATIONS: PHYSICALLY CHALLENGING CONDITIONS

A number of physically challenging conditions affect motor development and physical health in the primary years. Some of these are presented in Table 14-4. Classroom adaptations are often required to promote the learning and social interactions of children with these special needs.

Cerebral Palsy

Children with **cerebral palsy** constitute the largest percentage of primary-grade students with physical challenges who require special services (Koman, Smith, & Shilt, 2005). As described in Chapter 10, this condition results from damage to the brain, often from oxygen deprivation during the birth process or trauma in early childhood. Because those areas of the

cerebral palsy: A disorder that can be caused by illness, injury, or oxygen deprivation before or during birth and that impairs motor coordination, muscle strength, and sometimes hearing and vision.

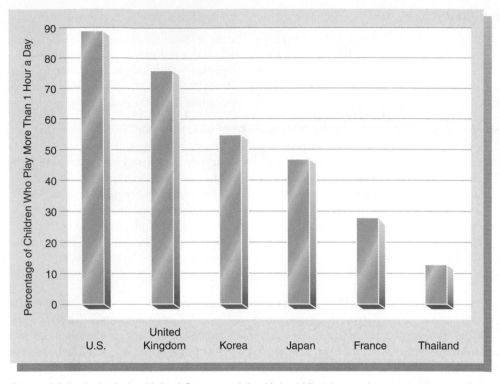

FIGURE 14-2   In both the United States and the United Kingdom, a large percentage of children engage in active play when not in school. In other countries, chores and television may reduce playtime.

SOURCE: Extrapolated from data in Takeuchi, 1994.

TABLE 14-4
Challenging Conditions That Affect Motor Development and Physical Health in the Primary Grades

Condition	Description
Cerebral palsy	Increasing limitations in movement and coordination and declining strength in muscles occur. Braces or a wheelchair may be required to move around.
Duchenne muscular dystrophy	A steady weakening of skeletal muscles and difficulty climbing stairs and running are common. Eventually, lower extremities may weaken to a point where a wheelchair is needed.
Spina bifida	Sensory impairments or walking difficulty are common. More severe cases can result in paraplegia. Serious health problems, including urinary tract disorders and retention of fluid in the brain, are possible.
Attention-deficit/hyperactivity disorder	Extreme activity level and difficulty controlling attention and impulses are common. The disorder is often diagnosed during the elementary grades, as children move from active, play-based settings to quieter, sit-still-and-listen programs in the primary years.

brain responsible for motor coordination are most affected, impairment of fine and large motor abilities often results. Sometimes these motor challenges are accompanied by perceptual and intellectual disabilities (Umansky & Hooper, 2008).

How cerebral palsy manifests itself in the primary years is determined by the type and severity of the disorder. Some children with cerebral palsy show increasing limitations in movement and coordination or declining strength in muscles. Some display jerky, irregular motions and poor balance. Others suffer only fine motor impairments. Many need braces or a wheelchair to move around. Independent forms of movement are possible, however (Umansky & Hooper, 2008). Some children with cerebral palsy are able to roll, others to creep—although they may do so by pulling themselves along with their arms, their legs extended straight out in back. A more advanced form of creeping, sometimes called *bunny hopping,* is sometimes observed. In this method, children, on hands and knees, plant their arms out in front of themselves, then quickly pull their legs forward in a hop. These types of movement are useful for physical development and give children a sense of independence. Special educators recommend that children with cerebral palsy not always be confined to a wheelchair.

Because of motor and speech problems, many children with cerebral palsy have difficulty with academic tasks. Often, limited hand use or speech functions, not cognitive delays, explain academic challenges for children with cerebral palsy in the primary years.

ADVOCACY AND PUBLIC POLICY

Protecting a Child's Right to Play

This chapter reviews the developmental benefits of active motor play for primary-age children. One threat to motor play in America are new policies in some school districts restricting or limiting recess time. An estimated 40% of all elementary schools have either eliminated or are in the process of eliminating recess (American Association for the Child's Right to Play, 2004). Such trends can have negative effects on young children's health, brain growth, and ability to pay attention. One article of the UN's Convention on the Rights of the Child calls for a child's right to "engage in play and recreational activities appropriate to the age of the child" (United Nations, 2004, p. 4).

What can professionals do about the problem? First, they can become advocates within their own schools and communities to restore and/or extend recess time for children. They can educate parents and administrators about the importance of recess through workshops, newsletters, letters to the editor, and appearances on local television and radio. They can organize parent advocacy groups or enlist the local PTA to work toward adequate outdoor playtime. These advocacy efforts should focus not only on providing recess but also ensuring that this play time is of high quality. Recess should be supervised by trained and responsive professionals. Adequate space and equipment must be available so that children can pursue meaningful play activities. Space and equipment must be accessible to all children, including those with physically challenging conditions.

Professionals can become involved in the recess movement on a national level by joining in the campaigns of several play advocacy organizations. The American Association for the Child's Right to Play (http://www.ipausa.org) is the U.S. chapter of an international organization that advocates for quality play for children. The group organizes educational events, such as conferences and workshops; publishes a magazine and newsletter; and helps organize *play days*— events in parks and community centers that bring together parents and children to play together. Another organization, Playing for Keeps (http://www.playingforkeeps.org), coordinates a range of initiatives to educate parents, educators, and toy manufacturers about the benefits of play. They post educational resources on play and plan an annual international conference.

Through local advocacy and involvement in these national organizations, professionals can help ensure an adequate and high-quality recess time in every elementary school.

Duchenne Muscular Dystrophy

Duchenne muscular dystrophy is a hereditary disorder—sometimes difficult to diagnose—that affects motor functioning (McLean, Bailey, & Wolery, 2003). The condition is characterized by a steady weakening of skeletal muscles. Children in the primary years initially may be able to walk and move around the classroom, but climbing stairs, walking on a field trip, and playing a running game may be challenging. Eventually, the child's lower extremities may weaken to a point where a wheelchair is needed.

In the early 1980s, the life expectancy of a child with Duchenne muscular dystrophy was the early teens because of a gradual weakening of the heart muscle or respiratory infection. More recent research has shown that many afflicted with this disease live into young adulthood (Blair & Watson, 2006).

Spina Bifida

Spina bifida is a congenital condition in which the spinal cord and nerve roots are damaged (Umansky & Hooper, 2008). Milder forms may involve slight sensory impairments and walking difficulty. More severe cases can result in paraplegia (paralysis of both legs), severe sensory impairment, and incontinence (inability to control the bladder). Serious health problems, including urinary tract disorders and retention of fluid in the brain, are common. Because of this, support for children with spinal bifida in school often requires the involvement of medical, educational, and social services personnel.

Meeting Special Motor Needs in School

Many elementary schools have adapted classroom space and the curriculum to accommodate children with physical challenges. A child can be given a marker or pen pushed through a rubber ball to assist in drawing or writing. Instead of a traditional desk, an adapted seating device can be provided so that a child can lean or even lie while doing schoolwork. A child can be given a special oversize spoon or a dripless cup to assist in independent eating (Sirvis & Caldwell, 1995). Technology is sometimes used to support learning and social interaction (Goldstein, Cohn, & Coster, 2004). Computers and communication boards—special keyboards or picture displays that children use to express ideas manually—help those with motor delays to communicate.

Duchenne muscular dystrophy: A hereditary disorder affecting motor functioning that is characterized by a steady weakening of skeletal muscles, possibly leading to deterioration of the heart muscle and the need for a wheelchair.

spina bifida: A congenital condition in which the spinal cord and nerve roots are damaged, leading to problems ranging from slight sensory impairments and walking difficulty to paraplegia, severe sensory impairment, incontinence, and retention of fluid in the brain.

The classroom environment, as a whole, can be adapted to assist primary-age children with physically challenging conditions. Worktables and learning centers can be rearranged so that there are adequate pathways for wheelchairs. Carpeted floor space can be created in all learning areas to allow children to work on the floor. Curriculum activities themselves can be altered. Children with physically challenging conditions can be provided larger, easier-to-manipulate materials and can be given more time to complete tasks.

Less attention has been given to adapting outdoor play spaces for primary-grade children with physically challenging conditions. Without such adaptations, children with physical impairments may be unable to engage in motor play and games on the playground. Being denied such opportunities hampers their physical health and social relationships. New play equipment has been designed to meet the needs of children with physical challenges. Accessible playscapes with ramps, support bars, and other devices are becoming more common on school playgrounds. Providing motorized wheelchairs for children with serious motor delays has been found to increase social participation, independent mobility, and play with objects both indoors and on the playground (Patz & Dennis, 2008).

Teachers and parents are acquiring new skills to assist children in play and motor activity. They can guide them in using equipment, facilitate interaction between children with special needs and peers, and ensure safety. These interventions are necessary so that all children will have opportunities to exercise muscles in play.

Attention-Deficit/Hyperactivity Disorder

Children with **attention-deficit/hyperactivity disorder (ADHD)** (described in Chapter 10) are extremely active and have difficulty controlling their movements, attention, and impulses (Rommelse et al., 2007). Although ADHD can be diagnosed in the preschool years, it is most likely to become a concern for parents and teachers in school during the primary grades. This is because children move from home settings or active, play-based classrooms in child care or Head Start to quieter sit-still-and-listen programs in the primary years. Children with ADHD are quickly noticed by teachers; these children have difficulty sitting for long periods, attending to learning tasks, and following rules for quietness and impulse control (Barkley, 1990; Tillery & Smoski, 1994).

What causes ADHD? The most prevalent theory is that it results from neurological impairment. Studies of brain functioning confirm this (Mulder et al., 2008; Rommelse et al., 2008). When adults with ADHD are given a PET scan—a medical procedure that measures activity level in the brain—they are found to have significantly slower brain activity than non-ADHD adults. Ironically, hyperactivity might be caused by a sluggish brain! This explains why Ritalin, which is a stimulant, improves the behavior of some children with ADHD. The stimulant speeds up brain processes and may help children become more alert, attentive, and interested.

ADHD and Culture.   One theory about ADHD is that it is an artifact of culture (Bogdan & Knoll, 1995; Konner, 1993). From this viewpoint, in societies that value sitting still and being quiet, ADHD is a disability. In communities in which quietness is not an important competency—those in which children do not attend school, for example—ADHD is rarely identified. In fact, in some societies, highly active, impulsive behavior is believed to be advantageous to survival!

Multicultural scholars have raised concern that some children of color may be identified as hyperactive, because of their naturally higher activity levels (Mandell, Davis, Bevans & Guevara, 2008). They suggest that at least a portion of these children do not suffer a *real* disability but simply do not conform to norms of quietness in American schools. For example, African American children are more likely to be identified with ADHD (Skounti, Philalithis, & Galanakis, 2007). Hale-Benson (1986) argues that this is due to the high activity level and physical style of play among African American children, which makes them vulnerable to being misdiagnosed.

There are great differences in the prevalence of ADHD across many other ethnic groups and countries (Dwivedi & Banhatti, 2005), suggesting that there is a complex interaction of biological, cultural, and family factors that leads to ADHD identification. A good example is the case of hyperactivity among Japanese American children. Some researchers have noted that hyperactivity is less often identified in children of this cultural group (Skounti et al., 2007). Why? Certainly the disability exists among children of all backgrounds. However, it may not be as easily *identified* among children of this culture. Japanese American children with ADHD live in families with quieter styles of interaction. Their behavior may be less active than that of children with ADHD in other cultures. Their activity level—though high by standards of their own culture—may be considered "within the range of normalcy" by the dominant society. Further, Japanese American parents are more likely to

attention-deficit/hyperactivity disorder (ADHD): A disorder that is characterized by high activity level, impulsiveness, and an inability to pay attention and that often leads to poor peer relations and school performance.

ignore hyperactive behaviors or minimize their significance (Sata, 1983). They disclose problems to teachers or physicians less often, and the condition goes unidentified. It is possible that ADHD is as prevalent in their culture as in others but that cultural factors diminish the frequency of identification.

Meeting the Needs of Children with ADHD in School. A variety of classroom adaptations are recommended for meeting the needs of primary-grade children with ADHD (Lewis & Doorlag, 2005; Umansky & Hooper, 2008):

sociomoral reasoning: An ability to make judgments about right and wrong that may be acquired through the playing of group games.

1. Create learning centers and other work spaces that are cozy, soft, and somewhat (but not fully) partitioned to increase comfort and reduce distraction. A math center, for example, might include carpeting and pillows on the floor and be separated from the rest of the classroom by shelves on two sides.
2. Place quieter, less active centers or worktables far away from more active and louder areas of the classroom to increase attention.

CHILD GUIDANCE: *Facilitating Competitive Games*

Some primary-age children have difficulty with competition in games. They may be unable to cope with losing or may even be poor winners (e.g., "Ha! Ha! I beat you!"). Teachers and caregivers find it challenging to resolve conflicts and assuage hurt feelings that can result from intense competition. More than one professional has decided to do away with games altogether on the playground or in the classroom. "There is already too much competition in our society," one preschool teacher recently pronounced. "Children need to learn to cooperate." She introduced cooperative games that had no winners or losers and eliminated competitive games from her curriculum.

Kamii and DeVries (1980) argue, however, that games with rules and competition are, in fact, very cooperative. These authors propose that playing such games leads to advancement in **sociomoral reasoning**—an ability to make judgments about right and wrong. Here is how they believe this occurs: In a game, each child has an individual goal—to win. However, children enjoy playing games with others and have a desire for game playing to continue. In order to keep playing, children must come to an agreement with other players about rules. They can't simply pursue their personal need to win by breaking these rules, or the game will fall apart and peers will refuse to play. As a game proceeds, a tension mounts between this personal need to win and the need to adhere to social rules so that play continues. Thus, games are a lesson in wanting to win but having to regulate this need—to control personal desires—in order to adhere to the agreements established by a group. Games with competition provide practice at suspending one's own wishes to follow social rules.

For children to benefit from games, Kamii and DeVries suggest that game playing must be relaxed and enjoyable. Teachers can facilitate play to achieve this; the following are suggested strategies (Kamii & DeVries, 1980; Trawick-Smith, 2001):

- Instill a sense of fun and humor in games and communicate that winning is not terribly important.
- Avoid behaviors that fan the fires of competition, such as cheering wildly for winners or giving prizes.
- Adapt rules of a game so that no player is eliminated. For example, in shadow tag (in which a child who is *it* tags others by stepping into their shadows), those who are tagged should not be required to sit out. They might, instead, join *it* in chasing others around the playground.
- Give children the option of playing games with or without winners. For example, one group of children—perhaps because of cultural background or temperament—may not wish to play competitively. In a bowling game, they might be encouraged to just knock over pins without keeping score. Another group, eager to compete, can be guided in doing so.
- Discuss rules with children *prior to the beginning of a game* and facilitate negotiations about whether any rules should be altered. A child might suggest a change in the rules of a board game, for example: "Let's say when you land on this space, you don't have to go all the way back to start. You just go back two spaces."
- Facilitate disagreements as they arise, encouraging children to review and adhere to the rules they have all agreed on.
- Point out the negative effects of breaking rules or teasing (e.g., "See what happened when you didn't play fair? Angelica and Charles don't want to play anymore" or "Did you see how he walked away when you called him the loser? He doesn't want to play another game now").

3. Prepare children with ADHD for upcoming transition times (e.g., cleanup time, getting ready for lunch, or going to recess) far in advance. Children with this condition usually have difficulty coping with change or the interruption of activities.
4. Maintain a predictable routine and avoid sudden changes in schedule.
5. Allow children with ADHD to choose the position in which they wish to learn—lying down, sitting, standing, and even moving around.
6. Encourage children with ADHD to take special breaks from long periods of sitting or working. During a particularly long group time or cooperative learning project, for example, a child might be encouraged to stretch, walk around the classroom, or rest in the book area.
7. Give children with ADHD more time to complete tasks by breaking down projects or assignments into smaller steps or extending their time to work on these. For example, a child might be given extra time to finish writing in her journal as her classmates move on to other activities.
8. Give children with ADHD written or pictorial agendas—lists of activities or projects they wish to accomplish during the day. Encourage them to check off completed items and to share their accomplishments with adults and peers.
9. Provide long periods of time for active motor play.
10. Provide much warmth and attention; show children with ADHD that they are loved.

SUMMARY

The rate of physical growth slows in the primary years. How quickly children develop physically varies across cultural groups. Children of some backgrounds shoot up in height and weight during this period; those of other cultures may not. Such factors as poverty, poor health, injury, community violence, and homelessness can impede physical well-being. Primary-age children acquire many new motor skills. Exercising these motor abilities may enhance brain growth and organization. The specific motor play activities children engage in vary from one culture to another. Children of some backgrounds engage in rough play. Some are more competitive, others less so. Children of some communities play games that are rarely observed in America. Motor development is threatened by aspects of modern life, including television and the reduction of outdoor play time in school. Children with physically challenging conditions may need special support from teachers in school. Teachers can adapt classroom space and the curriculum to assist children with such conditions as cerebral palsy, muscular dystrophy, spina bifida, and attention-deficit/hyperactivity disorder.

RESEARCH INTO PRACTICE

CRITICAL CONCEPT 1

Although children grow at a slower rate in the primary years than they did in earlier periods of development, they still show significant physical development and acquire important motor skills during this time. Physical appearance and stature vary across cultures. Children of some backgrounds shoot up in height and weight during this period; those of other cultures may not.

Application #1   Attend to the physical as well as intellectual development of your students. Because the primary years are still a period of rapid growth, regular assessment by teachers of height, weight, muscle tone and coordination, and overall health status are critical. Children who do not show typical growth patterns must be referred to health professionals.

Application #2   Be aware of cultural variations in stature and physical appearance. Differentiate between cultural differences and deficits in physical growth. Recognize and appreciate cultural differences; address deficits through referral and intervention.

CRITICAL CONCEPT 2

Poor health status and poverty can inhibit growth. Illness, poor nutrition, injury, violence, and homelessness are all more prevalent among children who live in poverty. These factors can have a devastating effect on physical development.

Application #1   Help families access housing, health, and nutritional services for children. If health and safety needs are not met, children cannot learn in school. Writing to local, state, and federal legislators to advocate for family and child services—and encouraging parents to do the same—is part of a teacher's professional role in modern society.

Application #2 Advocate for safe and affordable before- and after-school care for children who live in dangerous neighborhoods. Care that is well supervised and promotes positive physical and social development is needed.

Application #3 Implement comprehensive health education programs in primary-grade classrooms that include topics of safety and nutrition. Include parents, family members, and community health professionals in planning such programs. Offer culturally sensitive activities and projects, such as lessons on nutrition that reflect the unique diets and nutritional socialization practices of families served.

CRITICAL CONCEPT 3

Children acquire new motor skills in the primary years. There are important connections between motor development, brain growth, and learning. Children who exercise during school may achieve greater brain organization and may be better able to attend to learning tasks. Unfortunately, motor play has declined over time in modern society. School reform efforts have reduced and in some cases eliminated outdoor playtime.

Application #1 Become advocates for outdoor play and motor activity during the primary years. Defend the importance of physical play in the face of a movement in American education to reduce or eliminate recess.

Application #2 Incorporate a quiet–active–quiet pattern of interaction into the schedule of your classroom. Follow periods of sitting and listening with more active experiences. Even brief stretching and exercise sessions or short outdoor minibreaks during the school day may enhance learning and brain growth.

Application #3 Integrate large motor and fine motor development activities into the curriculum. Relate dance, sculpture, woodworking, and other activities to topics studied in social studies and science. Aiming games, such as beanbag tossing or bowling, can teach academic skills while enhancing eye–hand coordination.

Application #4 Collaborate closely with health and physical education teachers to design developmentally appropriate motor play opportunities that relate to the curriculum. In physical education classes, introduce games that relate to social studies, mathematics, and science topics.

CRITICAL CONCEPT 4

Primary-grade children use motor skills in their play activities. The kinds of games children choose vary from one culture to another. Some children play highly competitive games with rules; others engage in cooperative pursuits. Rituals and rough-and-tumble play are common in many cultural groups. Children in some communities engage in functional play more often, in which they run, climb, and jump to test their muscles. Teasing may even be considered a form of motor play in some peer groups.

Application #1 Understand and appreciate diversity in motor play. Some children will be less active, less coordinated, or less competitive than others. Adapt motor play activities to ensure that all children can participate and acquire motor abilities at their individual levels of development.

Application #2 Provide a variety of play experiences that are relevant to all cultures represented in the classroom. Be cautious not to misinterpret rough-and-tumble play or teasing as inappropriate. Adapt games with rules to address cultural preferences for more or less competition.

Application #3 Interview parents to get ideas for designing a multicultural motor play curriculum. This curriculum may include traditional games and rituals of cultural groups represented in the school or community. Including jump-rope chants, sayings, songs, and jokes from children's families and communities will promote cultural understanding and sensitivity.

CRITICAL CONCEPT 5

Children with physically challenging conditions, such as cerebral palsy, muscular dystrophy, and spina bifida, may be unable to enjoy motor play with peers because of limited access to play equipment and other barriers. Another challenging condition, attention-deficit/hyperactivity disorder (ADHD), may also limit interactions and play both in and out of school. Children with this condition are extremely active and have difficulty attending to school tasks. They are more likely to be excluded from play by peers.

Application #1 Adapt indoor and outdoor play spaces to provide access for children with special needs. Special ramps, railings, and climbing apparatus are needed to ensure that children with physically challenging conditions can join the play of peers.

Application #2 Adapt classroom activities to allow children with ADHD to learn and interact positively with peers. Eliminate extended periods of sitting and tolerate a degree of movement about the classroom to help children with this condition be successful in school.

Application #3 Intervene in children's motor play to promote positive peer relations among children with physically challenging conditions and their typically developing peers. Suggest activities that all can play. For example, upper-body, nonrunning games, such as beanbag catching or button-button, can be initiated for children in wheelchairs. As children play, facilitate conversations and social contact.

ASSESSING YOUNG CHILDREN: Primary-Age Physical and Motor Development

Areas of Development	What to Watch For	Indicators of Atypical Development	Applications
Large motor abilities	Large motor skills, such as catching with hands only, throwing, balancing on one foot or a balance beam, and kicking with a mature follow-through, by age 8. Game playing with rules and other highly coordinated motor activities by age 8.	Lack of coordination, balance, and muscle strength. Highly active, impulsive, uncontrollable behavior. Inactivity and obesity. Frequent illness and absence from school.	Provide adequate outdoor playtime—including recess and adult-guided physical education. Incorporate movement activities in the classroom during group times or transition periods. Introduce games with rules, and facilitate these to reduce the intensity of competition.
Perceptual and fine motor abilities	An ability to coordinate small muscles to perform school-related tasks, such as reading and writing. Schematic drawings and sculpting that show greater realism and detail.	An inability to handle school-related implements, such as pencils, books, or scissors. Difficulty in holding or manipulating game-playing materials, such as cards or dice.	Provide fine motor activities, such as writing, handling books, building with blocks, and making puzzles. Include art materials throughout the classroom and encourage artistic expression across the curriculum.
Self-help or family life skills	An ability to dress and undress independently and to feed oneself using a fork, knife, and spoon by age 6. Simple cleaning skills and an ability to help with household chores by age 8. Willingness to care for one's classroom and personal cubby or desk.	Poor self-help skills. Dependence on others for dressing, toileting, and caring for one's personal space in the classroom or home.	Encourage independence in dressing, eating, and other self-help tasks. Foster a sense of responsibility for cleaning and decorating the classroom and caring for plants and animals. Provide a personal space for each child to organize and maintain.

Interpreting Assessment Data: Culture affects motor development in the primary years. Some children may be less active or physically able and others more so, depending on motor activities in the family. Racial differences in stature and muscle tone exist. Serious motor delays and poor health may indicate serious problems related to poverty and family stress. Poor nutrition, illness, and injury can impede motor growth. Challenging conditions, such as cerebral palsy, muscular dystrophy, and spina bifida, greatly affect motor abilities. These conditions require special services in school. Children who are highly active and inattentive may have attention-deficit/hyperactivity disorder. Regardless of cause, motor disabilities can be ameliorated through large- and small-muscle play in the classroom and on the playground. Such play is disappearing in some modern elementary schools. Primary teachers should advocate for physical education, recess, and physical therapy services in schools.

CHAPTER 15

Cognition and Schooling

GUIDING QUESTIONS

1. How are school experiences similar and different across cultures?
2. What are intelligence tests, and what are some concerns about them related to multiple intelligences and cultural bias?
3. What are some major features of learning and thinking in Piaget's concrete operational stage of cognitive development?
4. How can Piaget's theory be applied to teaching traditional school subjects, such as social studies, mathematics, and science?
5. What are some criticisms of Piaget's theory related to underestimates of competence and cultural differences in cognitive abilities?
6. How does Vygotsky's view of development in the primary grades differ from Piaget's theory?
7. What are the major types of memory, and how do they differ from one another?
8. What is metacognition, and how does it help children use learning strategies, such as rehearsal, labeling and organization, and paying attention?
9. How does culture affect memory?
10. What are some cultural factors that influence school success?
11. What classroom adaptations can be made to meet the needs of children with cognitive disabilities and those who are gifted and talented?

This chapter examines the intellectual development of primary-grade children. A major focus will be on how primary cognition influences and is influenced by formal schooling. In almost all cultures in which schools exist, formal education begins sometime between age 5 and 8. Why? In some societies, it is a long-standing tradition that children go to school at a certain chronological age. In the United States, for example, age 5 or 6 is considered *school age*, the time when classroom instruction should begin. In many cultural groups, however, chronological age is unimportant. Children are considered ready to learn at whatever point in time they show significant intellectual change. In Taira, Okinawa, parents refer to this as a point when children show they "know what they are doing" or "have sense" (B. B. Whiting & Edwards, 1988). This usually occurs at about age 6 or 7. In one community in Mexico, children are thought to develop "reason" and become "teachable" at about this age (Romney & Romney, 1963).

Of course, psychologists have a more formal explanation for what happens during this period of development. Primary-age children are entering a new stage of cognitive growth known as the concrete operational period. At this stage, children show new intellectual abilities and a growing capacity to use language. They can contemplate more than one idea or element of a problem at a time and begin to construct understandings of numbers, historical time, and map space. It is no coincidence, then, that the period between 6 and 7 years of age is almost universally considered a time to begin formal schooling. Tradition, folk wisdom, and psychology all point to this as a period of significant psychological growth.

Nevertheless, children's cognitive growth in the primary years does not mean they think and learn like adults do (Mueller, 1999; Shayer & Adhami, 2004). Professionals who work with children and their families must understand both the emerging competencies and the cognitive limitations of this period. Expecting too much of children in school can lead to what David Elkind (1987) calls "miseducation." The following story illustrates the problem:

A first-grade teacher, Ms. Baker, has arrived at a dreaded point in her school's mathematics curriculum. She has reached a section in the first-grade math text where she is to teach about clocks and time. She has been through this before. Her students rarely understand the concepts and become confused and frustrated. This year is no exception.

MS. BAKER: (Holding up a model clock) Now, this is 3 o'clock. Can you make your clocks say 3 o'clock? (Watches as children struggle with this problem, moves around helping them) Now. Show me how the clock looks at 3:15. The children look confused.

CELESTE: What? There's no 15.

SONIA: No, it's 15 o'clock, so you don't need a 15.

TAYLOR: Not 15 o'clock, silly. No such thing as that! (Laughs)

MS. BAKER: No. See, 15 is the number of minutes past 3 o'clock.

TAYLOR: Like this. (Begins to count the numerals on the clock face) One, two, three...

SITA: I can't do it!

MS. BAKER: I know. Let's put our clocks down for a while. Time for a story.

This teacher recognizes that an understanding of clock time is beyond the abilities of her students. In fact, she is aware of research that shows children may not fully understand some clock concepts until fifth or sixth grade (Dilworth, Greenberg, & Kusché, 2004; Friedman & Laycock, 1989). She knows enough not to push children to absorb this lesson. She considers this yet another example of how textbook authors and school district curriculum committees sometimes overestimate what children know and are able to do.

SCHOOLING ACROSS CULTURES

Schooling varies from one society to another. In a study of many different cultures around the world, B. B. Whiting and Edwards (1988) found that in some communities education is universal: all children attend school. The United States, the Philippines, and Okinawa are examples. In Kokwet, Kisa, and Kariobangi, Kenya, fewer than half of all children are in school, whereas in Ngeca, Kenya, more than 90% attend. In Nyansongo, Kenya, only boys go to school. Schooling is not, then, a universal part of childhood.

School experiences differ markedly for children who do attend. In Okinawa and the Philippines, school is very informal. Transitions to school are smooth in these communities. Most children are already familiar with classrooms and teachers when they arrive on their first day because most have been enrolled in nursery schools since they were young. The relaxed, informal atmosphere of primary classrooms resembles their earlier educational experiences. Sometimes teachers in these communities are neighbors or friends of the family. Children have often visited the primary school, having accompanied older siblings on some days as a child care arrangement.

In other societies, adjustment to school is more difficult. For example, a study in a community in Juxtlahuaca, Mexico, found that Mixtec children enter a school in a part of town they have never been to and are given instruction in a language different from their own (B. B. Whiting & Edwards, 1988). Teachers and other students treat them poorly, and discrimination is frequent and obvious. Some of these children rebel with bravado or attention-getting behaviors; others become quiet and subservient.

In several small villages in Kenya, teachers—all male—are strict and emotionally distant from their students (B. B. Whiting & Edwards, 1988). Parents in these communities expect schools to require absolute obedience. Interestingly, the parents themselves do not require such compliance from children at home. These parents may have come to view school as the place where conformity and control are first learned.

In some communities, schools emphasize competition and individual achievement, while in others, competitiveness is rare (Feldman, 1998; Slavin, 1997). In Tarong in the Philippines, school achievement is viewed as collective and collaborative, and the only competition is among hamlets, not among individual children. In U.S. schools, in contrast, individual achievement is emphasized. This causes a hardship for some American children of more collective cultural groups—Native American, Southeast Asian, Mexican American, and Pacific Islander children, for example (Landrine, 1995).

In schools of all societies, children are evaluated in some way, and their achievements and behaviors are labeled "right" or "wrong," "good" or "bad" (B. B. Whiting & Edwards, 1988). This means that, in all communities where there are schools, some children are successful, and others are not. Most cultures must deal with a problem called *school failure*. Professionals can advocate for improvements in education to address school failure.

INTELLIGENCE TESTS

intelligence test: A test composed of a series of questions that measure verbal and quantitative reasoning and abstract thinking and is designed to measure innate mental capabilities.

How well children do in school is, in part, a function of their overall intelligence. Important advancements in thinking are necessary for children to learn to read, perform arithmetic computations, and understand history. The nature of intelligence has been a subject of much debate among psychologists.

One approach to assessing children's intellectual ability is to give an **intelligence test** that measures their innate mental capabilities. Two of the most commonly used tests are the Stanford-Binet Intelligence Scale and the Wechsler Intelligence Scales. These are composed of a series of questions that measure verbal and quantitative reasoning and abstract thinking. Intelligence tests are **standardized,** meaning they are administered to large samples of children. Standardization allows test developers to determine how well a typical 7-year-old or 16-year-old performs on test items. In grading these tests, an individual child's scores are compared with the scores of other children of the same age. A 6-year-old who can successfully complete test items that the majority of 6-year-olds cannot is considered mentally advanced. Another 6-year-old who failed to answer test items that most 5-year-olds were able to answer is considered delayed.

Scores on an intelligence test are usually expressed as an **intelligence quotient (IQ).** An individual's IQ is computed by dividing the person's mental age by his or her chronological age. Mental age is determined by performance on the test: a child who performs as most 7-year-olds do has a mental age of 7. Chronological age is actual age in years. If a 6-year-old child is determined to have a mental age of 7 on an intelligence test, the child's IQ would be computed this way: 7 (mental age) divided by 6 (chronological age) equals 1.17. For statistical reasons, the score is multiplied by 100, giving an IQ of 117 for this child. Children who score exactly their chronological age have an IQ of 100, and those who score higher or lower than this are considered advanced or delayed, respectively. An IQ of 70 or lower might indicate mental retardation; an IQ of 130 or higher could signify giftedness.

Uses of IQ Tests in School

IQ tests are sometimes given to school-age children as part of an assessment to diagnose learning problems or to identify special needs. In the past, a single IQ test might be used to identify mental retardation. Children scoring poorly would be placed in special education classrooms. Likewise, gifted children were often identified using a single IQ test. Fortunately, using a single test score to make such important decisions about children's lives is rare today. Teachers, school psychologists, and parents generally obtain information from a variety of sources, including IQ scores, observations, samples of schoolwork, and interviews, when assessing children's intellectual potential.

IQ is highly related to school success (Laidra, Pullmann, & Allik, 2007). Proponents of IQ testing would argue that this is because such tests measure innate intellectual potential. From this view, children who score high on IQ tests have biologically determined abilities that allow them to succeed in school.

Analysis and Multicultural Critique of IQ Testing

IQ testing and the idea of innate intelligence have been challenged over the years (Nell, 2007). Some researchers have argued that there are many different kinds of intelligence that are not measured by traditional IQ tests. Others propose that IQ tests are culturally biased.

Multiple Intelligences. Many believe that there is not a single, general intelligence but **multiple intelligences.** Robert Sternberg (2000, 2003, 2005), for example, has proposed that there are three different kinds of intellectual functioning that vary among individuals. The first is **componential intelligence,** which is related to basic processes of thinking, attending, and remembering. The second is **contextual intelligence,** which is responsible for adapting thinking processes to changes in the environment. This kind of intelligence is necessary for real-life problem solving. A child just entering the fifth grade must not only rely on basic thinking processes to learn but must also accommodate to the demands of a new, more academic classroom. A child of abusive parents who is placed in a foster home

standardized tests: Tests that are administered to large samples of children, allowing developers to determine how well a typical child performs on test items. In grading these tests, an individual child's scores are compared with those of other children of the same age.

intelligence quotient (IQ): A formula for expressing an individual's intelligence as a single score, computed by dividing one's mental age—determined by performance on a test—by his or her chronological age, the person's actual age in years. For statistical reasons, the score is then multiplied by 100.

multiple intelligences: A phrase used to indicate that there are many different kinds of intellectual competence in humans, not just a single, general intelligence.

componential intelligence: A type of intelligence related to basic processes of thinking, attending, and remembering.

contextual intelligence: A type of intelligence—necessary for real-life problem solving—that involves adapting thinking to changes in the environment.

must accommodate thinking and learning to this new home environment. Contextual intelligence is necessary in each case.

Sternberg believes that a third type of intelligence, **experiential intelligence,** allows humans to use previous experience in learning. For example, children who have been read to by parents will rely on these early experiences later in learning to read in school. The ability to use personal life history in this way is an example of experiential intelligence. From Sternberg's view, a test that fails to measure all three types of intelligence will not give a full picture of mental competence.

Howard Gardner (1998, 2000, 2006) has categorized intelligences even more fully. He argues that at least eight distinct intellectual competencies can be identified: linguistic, logical-mathematical, spatial, bodily-kinesthetic, musical, interpersonal (social understanding), interpersonal (self-understanding), and naturalistic. (Gardner has considered a ninth possible intelligence—existential intelligence—but does not believe there is yet enough evidence to distinguish it from other forms.) His multiple intelligences are described in Table 15-1.

Each form of intelligence is independent, from Gardner's view, and is related to functioning in a particular area of the brain. An important element of Gardner's theory is that different cultures appreciate and enhance different intelligences. In Euro-American cultures, for example, linguistic and logical-mathematical competencies are highly valued, especially in school. Children who are capable in these areas are defined as *intelligent* by mainstream American society. Because traditional IQ tests measure primarily linguistic and logical-mathematical abilities, they are considered important measures of intellectual competence in the United States.

In other cultures, very different intelligences may be emphasized. Hale-Benson (1986) suggests that African American children are often competent in kinesthetic intelligence—that is, in body control and movement. In addition, they excel in social understanding, reflecting the "people orientation" and "physicality" of their particular cultural group. In Puerto Rico, many parents and teachers report special competence in musical intelligence among young children (Trawick-Smith, 1998c). Native American children and adults show a keen interest in and sensitivity to nature, suggesting an advanced naturalistic intelligence (Joe & Malach, 1998). A study of children in India found gender differences in which intelligences are strongest (Kaur & Chhikara, 2008). Boys were found to be advanced in bodily-kinesthetic intelligences. Girls showed greater competence in musical intelligence. From Gardner's (1998, 2000) view, these abilities are every bit as important as linguistic or logical-mathematical skills. However, because they are not measured by IQ tests and other traditional assessments of intelligence, such intelligences may not be fully recognized and appreciated in Euro-American schools.

IQ Tests and Cultural Bias. Other concerns have been raised about IQ tests and cultural diversity (Kaur & Chhikara, 2008). In the United States during the 1960s and 1970s, a growing body of research showed that IQ tests favored middle-class Euro-American children. One reason for this was that concepts and language learned in white, middle-class homes were emphasized in these tests. Another was that IQ tests were being standardized using samples of middle-class Euro-American children—that is, they were developed by being given to many children of this dominant cultural group. Norms for performance were then based on white, middle-class scores.

Many studies have verified that IQ tests have favored white, middle-class cultural groups. In a classic investigation, Mercer (1972) showed that African American and Mexican American children who had performed poorly on traditional IQ tests scored much higher on a culture-free test of intellectual adaptability. In a study on transracial adoption (Scarr,

experiential intelligence:
A type of intelligence that allows humans to use previous experience in learning.

TABLE 15-1
**Gardner's Multiple
Intelligences**

Intelligence	Description
Linguistic intelligence	The ability to use written and oral language. This intelligence is used in storytelling, journalism, and fiction writing.
Logical-mathematical	The ability to reason well, use logic, and understand and solve intelligence problems with numbers. This intelligence is used in such fields as computer programming or chemistry.
Spatial intelligence	The ability to perceive visual-spatial phenomena and to graphically represent and orient oneself to these. This intelligence is used in such fields as architecture or interior design.
Bodily-kinesthetic	An ability to use one's entire body to express ideas or to produce things. This intelligence is used in athletics, dance, sculpture, and mechanics.
Musical intelligence	The ability to perceive, create, and perform music. This intelligence is used by musical performers, composers, and music critics.
Interpersonal intelligence	An ability to identify and accurately interpret the behaviors, motives, feelings, and intentions of other people. This intelligence is used by community leaders, counselors, and social service workers.
Intrapersonal intelligence	A knowledge of one's own competencies, motivations, self-perceptions, emotions, temperaments, and desires. This intelligence is used to assess strengths and limitations and to make personal life decisions.
Naturalistic intelligence	An ability to notice similarities or differences and changes in one's surroundings, to categorize or catalog things, and to sense patterns in and make connections to elements in nature. This intelligence is used to explore other species, the environment, and the earth.
Existential (not fully accepted by Gardner)	An ability to ask and ponder fundamental questions about existence. Often called spiritual intelligence, this intelligence is used to write or talk about broad philosophical issues or overarching themes (as opposed to specific knowledge or skills).

SOURCE: Gardner, 1998, 2000, 2006.

Weinberg, & Waldman, 1993), IQ scores of African American children who were adopted in infancy by middle-class Euro-American parents were found to be as much as 20 points higher than those of children living in their own, nonadoptive African American families. Other studies have shown that African American children and those of other historically underrepresented groups perform less well on IQ tests due to "stereotype threat"—an intense anxiety that their performance will verify society's stereotypes toward them (Suzuki & Aronson, 2005). The thinking goes: "If I do poorly, everyone will know that African Americans aren't smart." So strong is this worry, that children may, in fact, do less well. Research also shows that children of some cultural groups perform poorly on IQ measures because test items require their knowledge of the dominant culture (Suzuki & Aronson, 2005).

Since the 1970s, IQ tests have been standardized with more representative samples of children. New tests have been developed with culture-free content. The Kaufman Assessment Battery for Children (K-ABC), for example, has been standardized using a highly representative sample that includes all cultural groups as well as gifted, emotionally disturbed, and learning-disabled children (Kaufman & Kaufman, 1983). Separate norms are established for African American and Euro-American children, so scores are based on what is expected for same-age children of their own cultural group. Test items are often nonverbal and are claimed to be culture free. Verbal items and responses to them may be presented in almost any language. (An illustration of verbal and nonverbal test items is presented in Figure 15-1.) Administrators of the K-ABC may give prompts or guidance when children miss an item. This addresses a problem of field sensitivity, which we will consider next.

Test Setting, Field Sensitivity, and Culture. Even if the content of IQ tests is culture free, children of some cultures may perform poorly if the test setting favors children of certain groups (Steele, 1997). In a review of many studies, Vijver and Tanzer (2004) conclude that when children of color are administered IQ tests in comfortable settings, such as their homes, they score higher than when tested in a less familiar environment by adult strangers.

field-sensitive learners: Learners with a cognitive style that leads them to rely on the entire environment and everything and everyone in it to solve problems.

Another test-taking disadvantage that children of some groups may have is field sensitivity. As discussed Chapter 11, children of historically underrepresented cultures are more likely to be **field-sensitive learners** (Greydanus, 2004; Timm, Chiang, & Finn, 1999). They

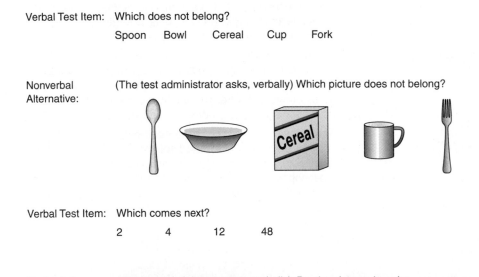

FIGURE 15-1   Verbal and nonverbal test items that resemble those on IQ tests are shown. Modern test developers have tried to use more nonverbal items to reduce racial and linguistic bias.

tend to rely on the entire physical and social environment when solving problems. They more often seek help from others in learning. How does a field-sensitive style affect IQ test performance? Such tests are often delivered individually in stimulus-free rooms, so field-sensitive children cannot rely on peers, teachers, or environmental cues during testing. Research shows that some field-sensitive children will study in vain the expressions of the examiner, ask questions, or scan the room while taking tests (Figueroa, 1980). **Field-independent learners,** who are disproportionately Euro-American, are often task oriented and tend to focus less on other people and more on test problems.

The following vignette illustrates how the content of tests, unfamiliarity with testing situations, and learning style can influence IQ test performance of children from historically underrepresented groups:

> An African American girl from rural Mississippi sits in a quiet conference room with an unfamiliar adult. The man is white and speaks in a different kind of accent than she is used to. He asks her to perform tasks as part of an IQ test. The test items make little sense to her. She is puzzled and anxious during the entire experience. There is no one else in the room to get help from. When she asks the adult for assistance, he smiles, shakes his head, and says, "I want you to do this on your own."
>
> At one point, the test administrator shows her a drawing of a late-model car with a wheel missing and asks her to complete the drawing. The child is distracted, however, by the car itself: it is much bigger and newer than any she has seen in her small, rural town. "What kinda car's that?" she asks. The administrator does not answer her question but repeats the instructions: "Can you finish drawing the car?"
>
> She becomes more confused and anxious. She looks toward the door, hoping her teacher or some children will come in soon. When no one enters, she takes a stab at solving the problem. As she begins to draw, she looks up at the test administrator and studies his face. She wonders, Does his smile mean I'm doing it right?

The child in this story is likely to perform less well on this test because of cultural differences in experience and style. She is uneasy about the strange testing room and the unfamiliar examiner. She is confused by the test's content; the items do not relate to her own life. She appears to be field sensitive in that she focuses on everything around her rather than just on the test. Finally, she yearns for help from others since getting assistance from peers and adults is part of her cognitive style.

PIAGET'S THEORY OF COGNITIVE DEVELOPMENT

A very different view of cognitive development is offered by Piaget (1952), who was not as concerned with the outcomes of intellectual development—as measured by scores on IQ tests—as with the nature of learning and how knowledge is organized within the mind. He sought to describe the specific mental steps children go through to learn and to become competent adults. Because his work focuses on how children construct knowledge, it is considered a more practical theory for teachers and parents (R. A. DeVries et al., 2001).

Assimilation and Accommodation

As described in Chapter 3, Piaget believed that learning and cognitive advancement at any age is the result of **assimilation** and **accommodation.** The following story illustrates these two mental processes in a second-grade class:

field-independent learners: Learners with a cognitive style that allows them to solve problems without much outside assistance and to focus on the specific steps of a task without being distracted by the full external environment, or "the field."

assimilation: Piaget's term for a learning process in which humans integrate new ideas or information into what they already know about.

accommodation: Piaget's term for a learning process in which humans modify what they already know to make room for new ideas or information.

Antonio, a 7-year-old, is observing fish swim in an aquarium in the science center of his classroom. He begins to wonder how fish can breathe underwater. His teacher, Ms. Tashita, moves to his side.

MS. TASHITA: You seem to be very interested in the fish.

ANTONIO: Yeah. But…(Stares at the fish intently and looks puzzled)

MS. TASHITA: What is it? Do you have a question?

ANTONIO: Yeah. How do they breathe in there? (Taps on the side of the aquarium)

MS. TASHITA: Well. How do you breathe?

ANTONIO: (Breathes in and out several times in an exaggerated way) Like this. See? I use my mouth…and…what are they called?

MS. TASHITA: Lungs?

ANTONIO: Yep. And the air goes in, and I can breathe. But the fish don't have any air in there. Only water.

MS. TASHITA: Well, let me explain. Do you know that there is something special in the air that you need to breathe?

ANTONIO: Yeah. Oxygen, I heard about that. Plants need it, and people too.

MS. TASHITA: And fish. They need oxygen.

ANTONIO: But they just breathe the water in. Doesn't the water just get in their lungs? Like this. (Pretends to breathe in water, makes gurgling noises, and laughs)

MS. TASHITA: (Laughs) Well, there is oxygen in water. And the fish have something special that helps them take the oxygen out of the water. Not lungs, like people. Fish have gills.

ANTONIO: Oh! So it's like we take the oxygen out of the air, and fish take it out of water. Like that?

MS. TASHITA: Exactly! You can see the gills near their heads. See? Watch. (Continues to help the child see the gills for several minutes)

The child in this story is engaged in both assimilation and accommodation in coming to an understanding about how fish obtain oxygen. He assimilates information; that is, he integrates this new knowledge into his previous understandings about breathing and oxygen. However, if he only relied on previous knowledge—that is, only assimilated—he would conclude that fish have lungs and breathe water. With questions and prompts from the teacher and through further observation, he changes his previous understandings a little. He adjusts his ideas about water by adding a new feature: it contains oxygen. He adapts his view of how plants and animals obtain oxygen: gills are another way to get oxygen. This is accommodation.

An important aspect of these processes, from Piaget's view, is that the *child* does the assimilating and accommodating, not the teacher. Learning is internal and personal. The child must play an active role in constructing knowledge; the teacher serves only as a *facilitator*.

The Concrete Operational Stage

concrete operational stage: Piaget's stage of cognitive development that encompasses the elementary years, in which thinking becomes more internal and abstract but in which children still need the support of concrete objects in order to learn.

Piaget proposed that children, sometime between the ages of 5 and 7, move into a new, distinct stage of intellectual development: the **concrete operational stage,** defined in Chapter 3. During this period of development, which extends to age 12 or beyond, they gain freedom from some of the cognitive limitations of previous developmental periods, but they still display some cognitive characteristics of preschool-age children.

Many 7-year-olds can successfully complete the conservation tasks, which were discussed in Chapter 11. When shown two identical containers holding the same amounts of water and then watching the water from one container being poured into a container of a different shape, children of this age will report that the amount of water stays the same. Why are children now able to successfully complete such tasks when only 1 or 2 years before they could not? Piaget explains that they have acquired several important cognitive processes that lead to improvement in problem solving and learning. These processes are listed in Table 15-2 and described next.

Decentration. Preschoolers tend to focus on only one aspect of a problem at a time, but children in the concrete operational stage are able to coordinate two ideas at once. This ability is called **decentration** since a child no longer *centers* on just one phenomenon. In the conservation task just described, they can see that the water is *higher* in one container but *wider* in the other. A common response of children at this age would be, "They both have the same amount still because this container is tall, but that one is real fat." They no longer fixate on just one aspect of the problem. They can coordinate ideas of tallness and wideness at the same time.

Decentration allows children in the primary years to learn new school-related concepts. In literacy, for example, children come to see that several dimensions of writing must be considered all at once if others are to read what is written. They learn that they must reproduce the correct shapes of letters but also turn them in the appropriate direction in space (e.g., *b* as opposed to *d*). At the same time, they must attend to the sounds letters represent in conventional writing and, while contemplating all of these things, think about the idea or story they are relating.

Reversibility. Children in the concrete operational stage acquire **reversibility**—an ability to mentally or physically reverse the steps of a process to go back to a starting point. How does this kind of thinking help with school learning? Reversibility is required in many subject areas. Mathematics is a good example:

> A third-grade teacher, Ms. Nagy, sets up a math game in her classroom that requires children to add up points and keep score. As a group of children play, one child accidentally adds too many points to her score sheet and writes down a new, incorrect total: 56. Her peers protest immediately.

decentration: An ability to coordinate two ideas at once and to no longer center on just one phenomenon.

reversibility: An ability to mentally or physically reverse the steps of a process to go back to a starting point.

TABLE 15-2
Intellectual Advancements in the Primary Years

Cognitive Process	Description
Decentration	Children no longer center just on self or on just one aspect or dimension of a problem but can consider multiple factors simultaneously. For example, they can think about a container as both tall *and* thin and another as short *and* wide.
Reversibility	Children can mentally reverse the steps of a process. For example, they can put a toy back together the way it was before or retrace their steps on a walk.
Causality	Children can understand that actions or events cause things to happen. For example, they can see that throwing a ball harder results in its flying farther or that pushing a peer on the playground causes upset and anger.

SOURCE: Piaget, 1952.

ARI:	No, Hanna! Not 56! You don't add 15 points! That's wrong!
TINA:	(Speaking at the same time) You have to take those off!
HANNA:	(Looking confused) What?
TINA:	You can't have 15 points.
HANNA:	(Still confused) How do I take them off?
MS. NAGY:	(Just entering the math center) Sounds like you have a problem with your score.
ARI:	Yeah, 'cause Hanna added too many points. Like 15 points. Now we don't know what to do. And I was winning!
MS. NAGY:	Okay. If Hanna added 15 points to her score and she shouldn't have, what should she do?
ARI:	(Angrily) Tell Hanna she can't play anymore. I was winning!
MS. NAGY:	Oh, I think you should all keep playing. What's something else you could do?
HANNA:	I know! Add 15 to everybody else. Fifteen points to you and you. (She points to one peer, then the other)
TINA:	No, wait. This is how you do it. You take away the 15 points from Hanna. See? 55, 54…(Now she counts silently to herself) back to 41. See? That was your score before, 41. (Scribbles out Hanna's total and corrects it)

How did the children in this classroom think through this problem? They relied on reversibility: they discovered that you can reverse addition by subtracting the same amount. Reversibility problems abound in mathematics and many other school subjects.

Causality. In the preschool years, children tend to believe that if two events occur simultaneously, one must cause the other. If a child knocks over a vase and then hears that her father has a fever, she might believe her mistake caused her father's illness. In the primary years, children begin to understand cause and effect more accurately. They can often see connections between actions—both their own and others'—and consequences. This is called causal thinking or **causality.**

Causality is useful for many learning activities in school. In science experiments, for example, children may be asked to speculate on why ice cubes melt more or less slowly in water of different temperatures or why the plant that gets no light looks different from the one that does.

Piaget notes that children of this age are still struggling to sort out causes and effects. They ask *why* quite regularly in an effort to understand causal relationships: "Why are the leaves falling?" "Why is Janelle upset?" Even at this age, great care must be taken so children do not misinterpret events. The following story shows how a counselor helps a child understand cause and effect clearly:

An 8-year-old, Tamika, is meeting with a counselor, Mr. Blouin, at a community health center. She has been struggling with the divorce of her parents; Mr. Blouin is guiding her in interpreting this troubling event.

causality: An understanding of cause and effect, including an ability to see connections between actions—both one's own and others'—and consequences.

MR. BLOUIN:	Tell me how you're feeling about things today, Tamika.
TAMIKA:	(Forcing a smile) Pretty happy.
MR. BLOUIN:	Happy? Good. Tell me why you're so happy.
TAMIKA:	'Cause I know what to do now.
MR. BLOUIN:	Oh?
TAMIKA:	Yeah, I need to be good in school, that's all. I need to be a nice girl.

MR. BLOUIN:	You are a nice girl in school.
TAMIKA:	But I'm going to be real nice and then Papa will come back, maybe.
MR. BLOUIN:	You think if you change the way you are, your parents will get back together?
TAMIKA:	Yeah, 'cause I was pretty bad, and so Papa went away.
MR. BLOUIN:	Your father didn't leave because you were bad. It wasn't your fault, Tamika.
TAMIKA:	(Begins to cry) Why did he leave us? Why is he so mad?
MR. BLOUIN:	He's not mad at you. He loves you. He knows you're a nice girl at home and at school. He didn't leave because of you. Your mother and father just don't get along anymore, remember? They don't get along, so that's why they're getting a divorce. It's not your fault.

The child in this story is able think about cause and effect but still shows confusion about causal relationships. The counselor tries to clarify the reasons for this family problem and to assure the child that she has not caused it. As shown in the story, faulty causal thinking can lead to feelings of guilt for children in the primary years.

Piaget's Theory and Traditional School Subjects

The advancements in cognition described by Piaget allow concrete operational children to gain greater understanding of traditional subjects in school, such as social studies, mathematics, and science.

The Social Studies. In the social studies, an increased knowledge of time, space, and causality allows the study of history, geography, and economics. Piaget (1971) has shown that children only gradually construct an understanding of time in the early years. Preschoolers can make gross estimates of time; they understand that a day is the length of time that the sun shines, and they can learn the temporal order of key events (e.g., "My grandmother is picking me up after our nap"). In the concrete operational stage, children begin to accurately reflect on the past. They can understand that time is continuous from past to present to future (Seefeldt, 1998) and can distinguish the long ago from the present. However, they are still challenged by time intervals among events of the past. The following interview with a 6-year-old shows that distinctions between long ago and long, long ago are difficult even for school-age children:

RESEARCHER:	Tell me what it was like long ago.
CHILD:	Long ago? Like when children went to schools that had dirt floors?
RESEARCHER:	Sure. Tell me about back then.
CHILD:	Well. There was no electricity. And all the people would ride horses.
RESEARCHER:	Tell me more.
CHILD:	Well, I think back then people wore rags. And they would talk like apes.
RESEARCHER:	Ah. That *is* long ago.
CHILD:	And you know what? There were no electric guitars. (Feigns playing a guitar while making loud guitar noises)

The child in this interview clearly has an understanding of historical time. However, he has difficulty judging the intervals between one historical period and another. Talking like apes, wearing rags, riding horses, and going to a school with a dirt floor are all viewed as having occurred in about the same period.

One thing that helps children acquire this understanding of time is having a parent or teacher who "reminisces" about past events (Fivush, Haden, & Reese, 2006). Teachers should plan conversations in school in which they share stories from their own lives, growing up, as a way of promoting historical thinking. New understandings about time create an emerging interest in the long ago among school-age children (Seefeldt, 1998). Abstract history lessons that require the memorization of dates or complex historical interpretations are still beyond the grasp of children of this age. However, concrete experiences with history, such as school visits by grandparents to talk about the past or children's books that depict periods of long ago, may be very useful for the development of historical understanding.

Piaget (Piaget & Inhelder, 1963) described the gradual acquisition of spatial concepts in early childhood. He found that during the late preschool and early primary years, children think about space in terms of their own movements or actions through it (Hazen, 1982). Their thinking goes, "I know about this space because I walk this way to get to the park" or "I know about this space because I can crawl under it." This conception has been referred to as **action space** (Piaget, Inhelder, & Szeminska, 1960). As children move more fully into the concrete operational stage, they begin to think of space as a whole: directions, locations, and distances are linked together in the child's mind to create a total picture of a familiar area. This type of thinking is called **map space.**

Piaget illustrated these ideas by asking children of varying ages to create "maps" of their school and its surroundings out of sand (Piaget et al., 1960). Preoperational children constructed models that highlighted how they move through, in, and out of the school. Such representations reflect action space from Piaget's view. Concrete operational children added more detail to their maps, including key landmarks. They presented more accurate representations of the area as a whole. These constructions show that children have begun to acquire a conception of map space. Other research verifies that children in the primary grades can create and interpret maps, particularly of familiar areas (Liben & Downs, 2003; Uttal, 2005). Figure 15-2 shows young children's maps of their homes.

Although children in the concrete operational stage can think about map space, they may not be ready for abstract geometry lessons (Seefeldt, 1998). However, concrete experiences with map space, such as drawing maps of the school, creating models of their community with blocks, solving problems with globes, playing map games, and studying maps on the Internet, will be very helpful to them.

Primary-age children begin to understand basic concepts in economics, as well. Several studies have shown that 6-, 7-, and 8-year-olds understand basic ideas of supply and demand, whereas 5-year-olds do not (Leiser & Halachmi, 2006; D. R. Thompson & Siegler, 2000). Advancements in children's causal thinking may explain these findings. Consider the cause-and-effect thinking, for example, needed to solve the following problem, which was posed to children in one of these studies:

> Usually Kathy sold about 10 cups of lemonade each morning, but one morning she sold about 50 cups. Would that make Kathy charge more, or the same, or less money than usual for each cup of lemonade on that day? (Thompson & Siegler, 2000, p. 675)

Only school-age children could recognize that demand would *cause* prices to go up. These findings suggest that economics—rarely studied before high school in the United States—can be included at an appropriate level in the early elementary school curriculum.

Mathematics. As described in earlier sections, reversibility and decentration help children learn mathematics. Several other abilities also enhance learning in this area. Piaget noted that children in the concrete operational stage acquire an understanding of numbers.

action space: An early type of spatial thinking in which young children think about space only in terms of their own movements or actions through it.

map space: A type of spatial thinking in which young children can think about space as a whole and can link directions, locations, and distances together in their minds. This type of thinking allows children to interpret and construct maps.

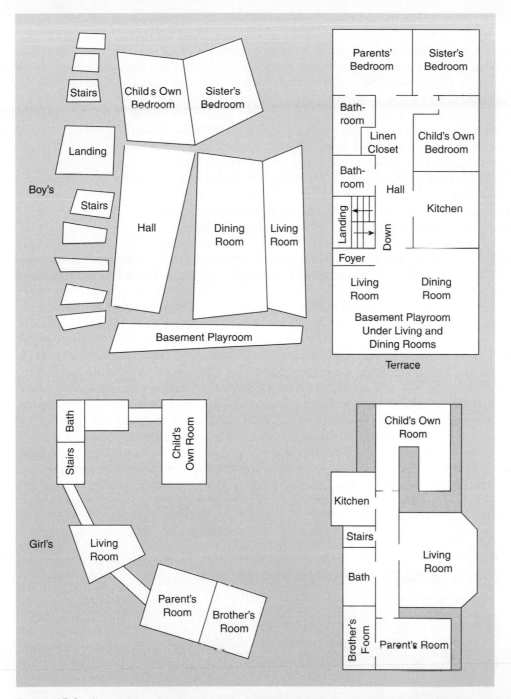

FIGURE 15-2   Two children's maps of their own homes (left) are compared with the actual layouts (right). Although primitive, the children's maps reveal early understanding of map spaces. SOURCE: Stone, L. J., & Church, J. (1984). *Childhood and adolescence,* 5th ed. (p. 401). New York: Random House. Reprinted by permission.

He devised an experiment to show this, which was examined in Chapter 11. Children are shown two rows of checkers of equal numbers. When one row is spread out or pushed together, the child is asked if the amounts are still the same. Recall that preschoolers regularly answer that the spread-out row now has more. They are fooled by perception. Even when asked to count, children of this age cling to their erroneous beliefs.

Piaget found that children in the concrete operational stage are able to use reason to overcome misleading perceptions. When confronted with this same task, they are now likely to count the checkers or simply state, "Both rows have the same because you didn't take any away." Such solutions indicate that children understand numbers. When is a complete understanding of numbers acquired? Possibly not until age 7 or 8. Even children who can count may not use counting as a tool to solve real problems until third grade (Feigenson, Dehaene, & Spelke, 2004; Kamii, 1982). For example, a 6-year-old who has been counting for years may still determine who won a card game by placing the cards in piles and deciding which looks highest. Only later in the elementary years do children exclusively use counting and number concepts to solve problems.

It is important to note that even adults solve some math problems by relying on perception rather than counting. When working with large numbers of objects—say, determining the amount of pasta needed to feed a large family—adults often make estimates. So, it is important for children in the primary grades to practice using different methods of quantifying—counting small numbers of objects but also visually estimating larger ones.

Another mathematics-related competence described by Piaget is **seriation,** the ability to order objects by size or some other dimension. In a classic experiment to test for this skill, Piaget presented children with eight sticks of varying lengths and asked, "Can you make a row of sticks so that you place the shortest one here (points), then the next tallest, then the next tallest, until you put the very tallest one at the other end?" Very young preschoolers struggle with this task and make many errors. Some simply create interesting designs with the sticks! In contrast, 4- or 5-year-olds complete the task with much physical trial and error. They might select two sticks at a time, compare the lengths, then place them in the row. Such a process leads to errors, which the child may or may not notice at the end of the task. By age 7 or 8, children exhibit thoughtfulness and careful planning in solving this problem. They scan the entire collection of sticks and select the shortest. Then they search the pile again for the next tallest. Much of their work on the task is internal, with less physical trial and error. When they can complete the task with few or no mistakes, they are said to have fully acquired seriation.

seriation: The ability to order objects by size or some other dimension. Ordering sticks by length is an example.

New cognitive abilities in the primary years allow children to solve more complex mathematical problems. Concrete objects are still needed, however, for children to learn math concepts.

How is this ability related to mathematics learning? Seriation is the foundation for important later math skills, such as *transitive reasoning*. (Remember high school algebra? If A is greater than B and B greater than C, then A must be greater than C.) But seriation is necessary even in the elementary math curriculum. The following ordering activity from a first-grade curriculum guide is an example:

> Ask children to stand in a line. Introduce the concepts "taller," "tallest," "shorter," and "shortest." Then ask children to rearrange themselves in the line so that "the tallest child is on this side of the room and the shortest is on the other side." As children complete the task, ask questions that guide their problem solving: "How can you figure out where you belong in the line?" or "Are you sure you're in the right spot? How can you check?"

Seriation activities, such as ordering a collection of shells by size or weight, will provide important, early practice at this kind of thinking. As children get older, activities involving numerals are appropriate. A third-grade teacher created a game in which various numeric statements ("3+4," "2×7," "6," and so on) were presented on colorful cards. Children were asked to order these cards based on the amounts they represented.

Science. Cognitive advancements in the preoperational stage contribute to an understanding of scientific concepts. Piaget (1930) noted that preoperational children lack a full understanding of natural causes. They tend to believe that occurrences in nature are the result of human or human-like agents. When a cloud floats by, for example, they believe it must have been moved by someone or must be alive. A child might claim, "The sun comes out because it wakes up" or "Mommy makes night time so people can sleep" (Gelman & Gottfried, 1996; Gottfried & Gelman, 2004). As children enter the concrete operational stage, however, they begin to overcome this limitation in thinking. They are able to think logically about what causes rain or how and why seeds travel from one place to another. The scientific curriculum can be broadened to topics that were incomprehensible to children only a few years before.

A second advancement in scientific thinking, according to Piaget, is **multiple classification**—the ability to categorize objects using more than one attribute. Children in the preoperational stage center on only one dimension when they are asked to group objects. For example, they might rely only on color, putting all the red shapes in one pile and all the blue ones in another. In contrast, concrete operational children can think about two attributes at once. They can classify by both shape and color, placing all *red* triangles in one pile and all *blue* triangles in another. This multiple classification helps children mentally organize scientific information.

When encouraged to make a museum in the classroom with objects from nature, for example, second-graders create displays of *things from the beach* and *things from the woods*. Further, within these categories, they might create separate displays of *living things* (e.g., seaweed, berries, and seeds) and *nonliving things* (e.g., stones, old cans, and bottle tops). So, they can simultaneously think about where objects come from and whether they were ever alive.

With their newfound categorization abilities, concrete operational children can now begin to understand the scientific classification of plants and animals. For example, third-graders will no longer categorize animal pictures as either fish or animals, as they might in preschool. Instead, they will place pictures of fish and birds in separate piles *under* the category *animals*. This ability to categorize phenomena in a hierarchical structure contributes to later understanding of the standard scientific classifications, such as genus and species.

School and Concrete Learning. The remarkable changes in children's thinking in primary years have led some teachers to plan very abstract, academic learning activities for

multiple classification: The ability to categorize objects using more than one attribute.

this age-group. Even public policymakers, not understanding the nature of school-age thinking, are now calling for rigorous drill and testing programs. Piaget would have disapproved. He called this developmental period the *concrete* operational stage for an important reason. Children of this age still need the support of concrete objects in order to learn. Attempts to teach classification or number in an abstract way without real objects would be futile. To teach about weather or animal classification without concrete observations or experiments would likewise be inappropriate. Attempts to move children too quickly into abstract thought have been found to lead to a great deal of stress (Hart et al., 1998).

ANALYSIS AND MULTICULTURAL CRITIQUE OF PIAGET'S THEORY

Concerns have been raised about Piaget's theory of concrete operational thought. He has been criticized for overestimating the age at which concrete operational thinking first appears. In addition, some believe he does not adequately emphasize the role of culture and social interaction in intellectual development.

Underestimates of Competence

A number of studies have found that children can acquire concrete operational thinking at an earlier age than Piaget proposed. When tasks are altered so less complex language and more familiar objects are used, even preschoolers have been found to perform concrete operations. For example, some researchers report that, with training, 4- and 5-year-olds can successfully perform conservation, seriation, or number tasks (Benigno & Ellis, 2004; Blevins-Knabe, 1987; Gelman & Williams, 1997).

Several studies have shown that preschoolers can understand natural causes better than Piaget proposed. In one study, children were asked about phenomena that were very familiar to them—flowers and dogs, for example. The questions posed to them were simpler than in Piaget's experiments (e.g., "Do you think people make dogs?" instead of "Where do dogs come from?"). Children as young as age 3 reported that plants or animals came from nature and were not created by humans (Gelman & Kremer, 1991). In other investigations, researchers have found that 3- and 4-year-olds can perform multiple classification if tasks are presented in a simple way or if the children are encouraged to think about several different traits of the objects they are categorizing (Ross, Gelman, & Rosengren, 2005; Siegel, McCabe, Brand, & Mathews, 1978).

Researchers have also shown that primary children can think at higher levels than Piaget suggested. In several studies, children were found to engage in **propositional logic,** an advanced kind of thinking that Piaget believed only adolescents or adults could use (Brainerd, 1996; Kodroff & Roberge, 1975). Propositional logic involves the interpretation of if/then statements. When these were presented to children in a simple way and included interesting and familiar objects, even 7- and 8-year-olds could understand and explain them. For example, school-age children were asked the following: "If a dog gets wet, it shakes its fur. If a dog shakes its fur, the apartment will get messy. So, if a dog gets wet, then what will happen?" Contrary to what Piaget would have expected, even young school-age children could draw the correct conclusion.

propositional logic: A kind of reasoning that involves the interpretation of if/then statements, such as "If this occurs, then what happens?"

Culture and Cognitive Abilities

There is great individual variation in children's cognitive competence in the primary years. Some children are more advanced than Piaget would have predicted, and others develop more slowly. Flavell et al., (1993) suggest that cognitive ability varies more during the primary years than in any other period. One factor that contributes to this variation is culture.

Cultural Differences in Conservation.   In a classic study conducted in West Africa, primary-grade children were found to be unable to perform conservation tasks (Greenfield, 1966). Remarkably, even older children and adolescents in this investigation had not acquired an ability to conserve. In marked contrast, children living in pottery-making families in Mexico were able to conserve surprisingly early in childhood (Price-Williams et al., 1969). Chinese 6-year-olds were also found to master complex conservation tasks at an earlier age than American children (Zhou, Peverly, Boehm, & Chongde, 2000). Why the discrepancy in these research findings?

Children of different communities and cultures have different motivations and opportunities to learn skills (Greenfield, Keller, Fuligni, & Maynard, 2003). In highly cooperative African communities, personal ownership is de-emphasized, and possessions are more likely to be shared. Because children are accustomed to sharing, disputes over toys or food are less likely. Having the most may not be highly valued in such a family or village, and children who are not accustomed to disagreements over objects and amounts may think about quantity less often. Conservation may be a less important competence in such societies and thus may emerge later in development (Hale-Benson, 1986; B. B. Whiting & Edwards, 1988).

In contrast, Mexican children from pottery-making families think about quantity every day. In helping family members make pots, children must make many judgments about amount. How much clay is needed to make an urn of a certain size? What amount of water is needed to wet a lump of clay to the correct consistency? Children regularly see quantity transformed during the pottery-making process and may puzzle over why there appears to be more clay in a finished pot than in an unformed lump. Judgments about quantity and transformations of mass are all important to family livelihood in this society, so these competencies may arise earlier in life.

In Israel, first- and second-grade children are provided conservation-related activities in school (Cahan, et al., 2008). Not surprisingly, they perform conservations tasks at an earlier age than children of other cultural groups. However, they exhibit the same level of competence as other groups on other cognitive tasks, such as classification. This shows how cultural experience plays a part in children's mastery of specific cognitive skills.

Cultural Differences in Map Reading.   In some cultures, primary-grade children do not acquire an understanding of map space as Piaget described. In a study in one African community (Dart & Pradhan, 1967), even older children and adolescents were unable to understand maps! This is in sharp contrast to some Euro-American communities, where children have been found to accurately interpret maps in the preschool years (Hazen, 1982; Milson, 2007). How can these differences be explained? In some cultures, maps are prevalent and important. Families may travel long distances along roads and highways, and children may watch their parents or grandparents study maps of subway systems, interstate highways, or shopping mall floor plans. Their families may even organize treasure hunts using simple maps during holidays or birthdays. The following is an example of this early map experience:

> During a long drive to Disney World, a 4-year-old announces that she is in need of a restroom. "Can you hold it awhile?" her mother implores, having stopped for gas only several minutes before.
>
> "No!" the child responds with convincing urgency.

"Why don't you look at the map?" the mother suggests, handing a road map to the child, hoping to distract her from her problem. "We're right about here." She points. "I want you to watch and tell me when we get to this little blue square. See? That's how bathrooms are marked on the map. When we get to that square, we will be at the bathroom."

The child studies the map very seriously and runs her finger along the line that marks the highway as she has seen her mother do. In moments, she announces, "I think we're here now. Stop, Mom. We're here now."

"No, honey," her mother answers, "not yet. We have to go along that highway a little more. See?" She points again. "We haven't reached that little square yet."

"But it's just right here!" the child complains, pointing to the rest area symbol on the map. "It's just a little way."

Her mother responds, "Well, on the map it looks like a little way. But a little way on a map is a pretty long way on the real highway." The child reflects on this for several minutes. The rest area finally comes into view. Now the child is even more puzzled.

"No, Mom. This isn't the bathroom. It's not blue. The bathrooms are blue, see?" She shows her mother the blue rest area symbol on the map.

Motivation to study maps may never be greater than in such a situation! It is not surprising that children with such family life experiences will construct map space at an early age. However, in some cultures map reading is not important. If motorized transportation is not used, young children may not travel far from their dwellings, much less away from their villages (B. B. Whiting & Edwards, 1988). In some societies, longer trips take place overland, through forests or deserts, rather than on roads, and precise paths of travel may not be as important as general direction. Even a sense of place or home is not critical in every culture. Some nomadic groups, for example, may not have a geographic home. Where they are and where they go is determined by climate or sources of food. In these instances, map reading is simply not relevant, and opportunities to construct map space are minimal.

Cultural Differences in Math.   Kamii (1985, 1989) has shown that American children have difficulty learning about place value. For example, a first-grade child will often think that the 1 in the number 16 is just a 1, not a 10. So, children of this age struggle when performing multidigit addition or subtraction problems. Other studies have shown that primary children in Korea, Japan, and China surpass American children in their understanding of number (Cai & Nie, 2007; Fuson & Kwon, 1992; Naito & Miura, 2003; Stevenson, Chen, & Lee, 1993).

Why the discrepancy? One theory is that language differences lead to advantages for some cultural groups. The Korean language, for example, has number words that clearly identify place value. Korean number words progress in this way: nine, ten, ten one, ten two, ten three, and so on. The number 2222 is said as "two thousand two hundred two ten two." Because numbers are spoken in this way, it is easier for children to construct an understanding of place value (Fuson & Kwon, 1992). Family attitudes and expectations may also lead to differences in number understanding. In both Korean and Chinese families, parents are found to be more concerned and more demanding about children's performance in math (Ng, Pomerantz, & Lam, 2007; Wang, 2004).

Cultural experiences, values, and even language explain differences in cognition in the primary years. It is important to point out that cultures are not inferior simply because they value certain cognitive abilities less or provide fewer experiences to obtain them. The intellectual competence of school-age children must be judged in relation to the abilities or knowledge needed to function in their own cultural group.

VYGOTSKY'S VIEW OF LANGUAGE AND SOCIAL INTERACTION

A criticism of Piaget's work has been that it does not place enough emphasis on language and social interaction, processes that Vygotsky (1962) has argued play a crucial role in school learning. Language, according to Vygotsky, helps direct children's attention and organize their understandings. Both self-directed speech and the language of others are useful. Primary children often use **self-directed speech,** defined in Chapter 3, to guide their own thought processes and to work through the steps of a complex problem. Such verbalizations are now internalized: children speak to themselves silently as they think and learn. An important advancement during this period is that children can consciously manipulate this language in their minds. They can say to themselves during school, "Now listen to this, it's really important" or "If you put these two triangles together, you make a rectangle." These are instances of what Vygotsky called **verbal thought.**

The language of others also aids learning. Teachers and peers ask questions or give verbal hints within the **zone of proximal development.** Recall from Chapter 3 that this zone is a point at which a problem or task is just beyond a child's current level of mastery. Challenges *not* in this zone are those that are either completely insurmountable or very easy to overcome. A science experiment, for example, may be so difficult that a teacher actually completes most of it for a child or simply ends the activity altogether. In contrast, an experiment may be so simple that a child can perform it easily without any help. A science experience that is moderately challenging and can be completed with indirect assistance, however, is considered to be in the zone of proximal development. Here a teacher can pose an interesting question, point out something that the child has missed, or give a hint to guide the child in independent discovery.

According to Vygotsky, peers can also assist children who are within the zone of proximal development. In the following vignette, an older peer provides guidance, including much language, to help a younger child solve a problem:

> A 6-year-old is gradually constructing an understanding of numbers, although she still struggles with problems of quantity. So, when she attempts to solve quantification tasks, she is often in the zone of proximal development.
>
> After playing a card game with a 9-year-old peer in an after-school program, she becomes puzzled about who won. Her playmate shows her how to determine the winner:

self-directed speech: A verbal behavior in which children talk to themselves, naming objects or narrating their actions—particularly as they solve problems.

verbal thought: A kind of thought in which language and thinking are integrated and mutually supportive. In verbal thought, children use language—such as verbal labels and self-directed speech—to guide learning.

zone of proximal development: A situation in which a problem or task is only slightly above a child's ability level. In this zone, adults can ask questions or give hints that allow the child to solve the problem independently.

Children learn the most when they receive assistance from others within the "zone of proximal development"—a point at which the solution of a problem is just beyond the child's current level of mastery.

"You have to line up the cards and count. See?" The child places the cards in one-to-one correspondence along the table and demonstrates counting.

Later, the 6-year-old is confronted with another problem of quantity. She is arguing with another peer about who got the most raisins for a snack. She solves this problem by relying on the words and thinking of the previous peer: "You have to line them up and count." She repeats this instruction, more to herself than to the other child. When they line up the raisins and count them, they find that both have the same number.

As discussed in earlier chapters, children of some cultural groups may require greater social interaction than others in learning. Those from collective, field-sensitive cultures may be most reliant on external clues, including social input from other people, in learning. Mexican American and African American children, for example, have been found to learn more in school when completing group projects and cooperative learning assignments (Landrine, 1995; Rodriquez, 1983; Slavin, 1997).

MEMORY, METACOGNITION, AND SCHOOLING

School success requires not just acquiring knowledge but also retaining it for significant periods of time. Children must remember ideas or concepts and build on them during later school experiences. *Memory* is critical for long-term success in school. Several types of memory have been identified. These lie along a continuum from very fleeting recollection to long-term retention. These memory types are described in Table 15-3.

TABLE 15-3
Types of Memory

Type	Description	Example
Sensory memory	Sensations or perceptions are acquired through the senses and stored briefly at a subconscious level.	A child breathes in the rich smells at a farm and stores a recollection of these in the brain for a few minutes.
Short-term memory	Perceptions or information are attended to carefully, then organized and stored in the brain. For a short time, these may be consciously retrieved and pondered.	A child pays special attention to the smells on the farm and consciously stores these in the brain, along with other ideas about the farm experience. Later in the day, the child comments on these to a teacher. A month later, however, the child has no recollection of farm smells.
Long-term memory	Perceptions or information are organized and integrated into semipermanent recollections that may be retrieved over a long period of time. Information that holds personal meaning and is related to previous ideas or understandings is most likely to be stored in long-term memory.	A child thinks about and talks with parents and other family members about the rich smells of the farm. The child organizes and integrates ideas about these smells into previous, permanent understandings of smells in different contexts.

Types of Memory

Sensory memory refers to brief recollections of experiences involving the senses. If children from an urban neighborhood visit a farm in the country, the rich smell of fertilizer may register briefly and subconsciously in their minds. They may subconsciously hear the steady hum of milking machines in the barn. Such sensory memories disappear in a matter of seconds unless coded or processed in the mind.

If children attend carefully to these sights and sounds, however, they may enter these sensations into **short-term memory.** In this type of memory, experiences are stored in the brain for a short period of time. Children organize, make sense of, or in other ways process new information in short-term memory. They can consciously retrieve and reflect on the information at some other time. On return to school after the trip to the farm, for example, children can reflect and comment on their observations. Short-term memory vanishes, however, in a relatively short time (Alvarez & Cavanagh, 2004; Baddeley, 2001).

The most important type of memory is **long-term memory,** in which certain images, facts, or concepts are drawn from short-term memory and are permanently stored. Over time, this information is organized and refined. Some have equated long-term memory with knowledge itself. Children are able to construct larger, more complex long-term memories as they get older (Gathercole, Pickering, Ambridge, & Wearing, 2004).

Why is some information stored in long-term memory and some is not? Many believe that children store things in long-term memory that hold personal meaning and interest—things they are curious about or that captivate them. Furthermore, they are more likely to retain information that they can integrate into their previous knowledge. As a result, totally meaningless facts may not be retained because children cannot fit them into what they already know. For example, a child who has no basic concept of time will not retain facts about how clocks work. Information must be both interesting and relevant if children are to retain it.

Metacognition and Memory

As discussed in Chapter 11, young children gradually acquire **theories of the mind;** that is, they come to understand internal emotional states, motives, and thinking processes. By the early elementary years, children know what learning and remembering are and can guide and control these in the mind (Lovett & Pillow, 1991; C. S. Rosen, Schwebel, & Singer, 1997). Their ability to think about and regulate internal cognitive processes is called **metacognition.** In the primary years, metacognition enhances the ability to remember information. Children can now consciously guide their own memory processes, using strategies of rehearsal, labeling and organization, and paying attention.

Rehearsal. Children discover during the primary years that they can remember information for longer periods through **rehearsal.** Rehearsal is the repeating of material verbally or the practicing of actions over and over so they are retained. Several studies have shown that children as young as 6 years old repeat facts or skills again and again that they wish to learn (Flavell, Beach, & Chinsky, 1966; Loomes, Rasmussen, Pei, Manji, & Andrew, (2008); Whitebread et al., 2005). Whereas kindergartners and preschoolers might learn the names of plants in a terrarium by listening and remembering in a haphazard way, first-graders will rehearse these names, saying them aloud or to themselves again and again (Oyen & Bebko, 1996).

Labeling and Organization. Another way to remember new information is by **labeling and organizing** it in some way in the mind as it is being learned. A group of preschoolers might do this when learning about animals in science. As they notice similarities and differences among animals, they might mentally create the categories *birds, fish,* and *other animals.* As children reach the primary years, they become more sophisticated at placing

sensory memory: A kind of memory that involves brief recollections of experiences involving the senses. A sensory memory disappears unless it is processed fully in the mind.

short-term memory: A type of memory in which experiences are stored in the brain for a short period of time. One can organize, make sense of, reflect on, or in other ways process information in short-term memory.

long-term memory: A type of memory in which certain images, facts, or concepts are drawn from short-term memory and are permanently stored. Some equate long-term memory with knowledge itself.

theory of the mind: A belief about what the mind is, how it works, and how it might be controlled that helps children learn and think at ever-higher levels.

metacognition: The ability to think about and regulate internal cognitive processes, such as learning and remembering.

rehearsal: A learning strategy in which learners repeat material verbally or practice actions over and over so they are retained.

labeling and organizing: A learning strategy in which learners place objects, events, or ideas they wish to remember into mental categories and then name them.

objects, events, or ideas into mental classifications to remember them (Plumert, 1994; Shin, Bjorklund, & Beck, 2007). They can also create labels for these classifications (Heyman & Gelman, 1999; Samuelson & Smith, 2000). For example, in a history activity, they might distinguish events of long ago from those of modern times by creating mental labels (e.g., "things that happened when my parents were young," "things that happened after I was born," and so on).

In one study, children as young as age 5 understood that categorizing and labeling objects would help them remember. By age 6, children could even describe how these labeling strategies worked. As one child put it, "I say the names of the different things in my mind. The words make pictures in my brain" (Fabricius & Cavalier, 1989, p. 303).

Paying Attention. With age, children become better at **paying attention** to certain important stimuli in the environment. This ability significantly enhances their ability to remember. Whereas preschoolers attend to almost anything that catches their eye, school-age children are better able to focus on one or several relevant phenomena (Bjorklund, 2004). This ability is crucial in school. Children who can comprehend teacher imperatives such as "Pay attention to what I'm about to say" or "Now follow along with me" will be more successful students.

In a fascinating series of studies, 7- to 10-year-olds were found to pay greater attention to adults whom they perceived to be more powerful and important (Blugental, Lyon, Lin, McGrath, & Bimbela, 1999). Children this age were also discovered to be more attentive if a teacher showed clear emotions (e.g., smiles and sincere expressions) and used a smooth, fluent voice pattern. These findings suggest that children use their knowledge of the relative importance of adults in their lives and the meanings of teacher facial expressions and intonations to decide which things are critical to pay attention to. (By the way, these findings may explain why substitute teachers and student teachers face so many challenges in the classroom. Children in the primary years may perceive them to be less powerful and may read doubt and anxiety in their expressions and voice.)

Metacognition in School. Teachers, counselors, and school psychologists can help children acquire metacognitive abilities by making informal suggestions for how to remember things (Sánchez-Alonso & Vovides, 2007). For example, they can suggest rehearsal strategies with statements like "If you say the names of these plants over and over, you'll never forget them." In one study, children whose teachers frequently made these metacognitive suggestions were found to be more competent in remembering facts (Moely et al., 1992). They were also found to use metacognitive strategies more frequently and effectively on their own. Children who were low or average achievers appeared to benefit most from these suggestions. This research indicates that teachers must not only impart information and skills but also help children learn how thinking and remembering work.

Memory and Culture

What children remember varies from one culture to another (Fivush & Nelson, 2004). For example, Alaskan native children are more likely to remember labels for various categories of snow than the names of plants and animals that are not indigenous to their homeland. Native American children may more easily remember the governance structure of their tribe than the branches of the government of the United States. Memory problems in early childhood may result, in part, from a curriculum that is not wholly relevant to children of diverse backgrounds (H. Hernandez, 2001).

paying attention: A learning strategy in which learners consciously control attention and focus on only one or several relevant phenomena at a time.

Culture affects not only *what* is remembered but also *how* it is remembered, as the following story illustrates:

> A third-grade teacher tries to help a young African American child learn addition and subtraction facts. No amount of drilling seems to help. The teacher begins to worry that the child lacks the capacity to remember.
>
> One day the teacher provides jump ropes for his students at recess. The child he has been concerned about quickly organizes a jump-rope game. As she jumps, the child chants a complex rhyme that takes many minutes to recite. The teacher is amazed at the child's ability to remember such long and complex verses (not to mention her agility with the jump rope). He begins to reassess his theory about the child's poor memory capacity. In fact, he later reexamines his whole approach to teaching mathematics in the classroom: is there a way to incorporate such rhythmic games into his math lessons?

Why can the child in this story remember verses but not math facts? African American children have been found to display a "performer style"—a mode of thinking and learning that includes movement, dance, and music (Hale & Franklin, 2001; Irvine & York, 1995). Such an orientation comes from a high degree of exposure to creative arts in the community. The child in the story relies on movement and rhyme to recall a jump-rope chant. These memory strategies are no less effective than rehearsal, organization, or attention-directing approaches. The teacher in the story wisely considers including these in his teaching.

Research on memory in non-Western cultures confirms that some children and adults remember things in very different ways (Sternberg, 2005). In several studies, people of non-Western communities performed poorly on memory tasks in which objects or words were presented in a nonmeaningful manner (Cole & Scribner, 1977; Paris & Lindauer, 1982). For example, subjects presented with a list of unrelated, isolated words would later remember very few of the items. Further, instruction in memory strategies such as rehearsal and categorization did not improve these subjects' performance. However, they could remember very well objects or events that were incorporated into songs, chants, stories, dances, wood carvings, drawings, and other forms of cultural expression. Names of nearby villages, for example, could be recalled when they were presented in a story.

Euro-American children have been found to be very competent in remembering lists of unrelated words, pictures, or objects, as they have been taught to do in schools in the United States (Rogoff, 1990, 2001). However, they struggle with visual and spatial tasks, such as finding hidden objects, and do not retain information that is shared in a story or song. Mayan children from Guatamala, aboriginal children from Australia, and children from Africa were found to be far better at these latter memory tasks (Dube, 1982; Kearins, 1981; Rogoff, 1986, 2001).

Children of various cultures may even rely on different senses to remember. In one study, African American children were found to retain information longer when it was received auditorily (Kirk, 1972). In contrast, Mexican American and Native American children were found to have better visual memory. Members of these cultural groups might remember information longer when it is presented in a visual way through drawings, photographs, or other graphics.

Memory in some cultures may be more collective than individual (Hirst & Manier, 2008). Families in Western African, for example, have been found to rely on other family and community members, particularly elders, to remember things. The thinking goes: "If I must recall something, I can always ask my grandfather or my mother or my neighbor to tell me the important things to know." This leads to a shared memory within a community that can be passed down from one generation to another. It is in sharp contrast to a Western style of remembering things on one's own, using the memory strategies described above.

CULTURE AND SCHOOL SUCCESS

Cognitive development is not the only factor in school success. A wealth of research over several decades has documented that children of some cultural groups in America fare less well in school than others (Cooper & Jordan, 2004; Okagaki & Frensch, 1998; Todd & Wolpin, 2007). Children of many historically underrepresented groups are more likely to perform poorly, with African American, Mexican American, Puerto Rican, and Native American children particularly at risk of school failure. This risk increases during the school years. In second grade, 15% of Latino and African American children perform below grade level; by sixth grade, 40% of Latino and 50% of African American children are below grade level (Fuligni, 1997). Euro-American children are less likely to fail (Mattison & Aber, 2007; Todd & Wolpin, 2007), and children of some Asian American cultures are most likely to succeed (Okagaki & Frensch, 1998).

Why do these cultural variations exist? Poverty is the main explanation. Cultures with high rates of school failure tend to be those with the highest poverty levels. There are other reasons, however, for cultural differences in school success. When children of the same socioeconomic groups are compared, those of historically underrepresented groups are still found to do less well in school (Kao & Thompson, 2004).

Clashes in Cognitive Style

As discussed earlier, children of different cultures have different cognitive styles—for example, some are field sensitive or more social in their learning, others less so (Greydanus, 2004; Timm et al., 1999). These individual variations derive from the rich traditions of families and cultural groups. They also place some children at risk of prejudice and disadvantage in school. Research suggests that African American children have active, expressive styles of learning that clash with the behaviors required for success in dominant-culture classrooms (Hale & Franklin, 2001; McNeil, Capage, & Bennett, 2003; Yamazaki, 2005).

Similar findings are reported for Mexican American (Irizarry, 2007; Rodriquez, 1983) and Native American (Wise & Miller, 1983) children. Students of these cultures prefer movement, singing, and conversation in learning, whereas traditional American schools expect quiet sitting, listening, and studying. Children of some Asian American cultures, however, show learning styles that are very similar to those of their Euro-American peers (Rennie & Mason, 2007; Slaughter-Defoe, Nakagawa, Takanishi, & Johnson, 1990). Japanese American children, for example, have been found to demonstrate quiet, studious modes of learning that closely resemble those of white, middle-class children (Yamazaki, 2005). Unfortunately, school success may depend, in part, on whether a child's cultural style matches that of the dominant culture.

What can schools do about this? It would seem that the best approach would be to match instruction to the learning style of each cultural group represented in a classroom. African American children should be taught in active, expressive, artistic ways; Asian American children using quieter strategies. Irvine and York (1995) point out that this is nearly impossible and has not been supported by research. What if a teacher has a classroom of students representing four or five different cultures (not uncommon in some parts of the United States)? Would each group be segregated for separate instruction?

Gender or individual differences might lead some children to learn in ways that are quite distinct from others in their cultural group. A Native American child might be quite individual in his cognitive style despite his culture's collective orientation. An Asian child might be very active and expressive even though most peers of her cultural background have a quieter style. There is a danger, Irvine and York (1995) warn, in assuming that everyone of a particular culture will benefit from a certain kind of instruction. Finally, these authors believe that, too often, attempts to match instruction to specific learning styles leads to oversimplification of the curriculum and lowered learning expectations for some cultural groups.

H. Hernandez (2001) proposes a different strategy—**instructional pluralism.** In this approach, a single unit of instruction includes many different learning options. In a lesson on rain forests, for example, a teacher might begin with some direct instruction, a media presentation, and a song, all of which focus on the rain forests in Brazil. After these experiences, children would engage in an active, collective brainstorming session on solutions to the problem of the vanishing Brazilian rain forests. The teacher would then quiet the group with a guided imagery activity in which each child, with eyes closed, would take a silent, mental journey to a rain forest. Follow-up questions would be asked—both right-answer and open-ended ones; children would be encouraged to help each other answer. As a closure activity, children would get to choose either an individual or a group project that might include creative writing, drawing, drama, or even the recitation of facts. Hernandez argues that such lessons address a range of learning needs at one time and help children of one style try learning in another style.

Poor Schools and Teaching

One explanation for poor academic performance by some children is that their schools are ineffective. Comer and his colleagues (2004) have noted that schools serving historically underrepresented groups are often "hierarchical, authoritarian...rigid, and unable to respond" (p. 126) to the needs of diverse groups of children. Teachers and administrators, he contends, unwittingly foster a climate of distrust and alienation (Comer, Joyner, and Ben-Avie, 2004).

Teachers may treat children of color differently from students of the dominant culture. Several classic studies were conducted to examine this problem. In one, significant differences were found between teachers' interactions with Mexican American and Euro-American children (Jackson & Cosca, 1974). These teachers directed 35% more praise statements and 21% more questions toward Euro-American students. They also accepted Euro-American children's ideas 40% more often. These figures may not give a full picture of bias, however. This study was conducted in schools identified as "best" within their districts, and teachers were informed ahead of time that they would be observed for possible bias in their responses to children!

In several similar studies, teachers have been found to interact more frequently with Euro-American children, especially boys (H. Hernandez, 2001; Sadker, Sadker, & Klein, 1991). In one of the most frequently cited studies, conducted in the southwestern United States (Wahab, 1974), children were found to receive teacher attention in a very fixed order: Teachers spoke most often to Euro-American boys; Euro-American girls received the second-highest number of interactions, Mexican American boys were third, and Mexican American girls received the least attention in these classrooms. Such trends may exist even when teachers are of historically underrepresented groups. Several studies have found that African American and Euro-American teachers were equally likely to have poor relationships with, or negative attitudes toward, African American children (Kesner, 2000; V. Washington, 1980, 1982). Regardless of race, teachers in this study directed more negative classroom behavior toward children of this cultural group. Findings of one investigation are more positive and hopeful: Blake and Cutler (2004) found that, in schools where teachers discuss and adopt a uniform philosophy related to celebrating diversity, these negative teacher-child interactions did not exist. These studies should cause even the most experienced professionals to carefully monitor their interactions for bias and inequitable distribution of attention and discuss their attitudes with colleagues.

instructional pluralism: A teaching strategy in which a single unit of instruction includes many different learning options—direct instruction, media presentations, singing, collective brainstorming, guided imagery, creative writing, drawing, drama, or even the recitation of facts.

Family Attitudes Toward School

One widely held belief is that children of historically underrepresented groups perform poorly in school because their families do not value education. Research has shown, however, that parents of all cultural groups value schooling and encourage their children to perform well (Kao & Thompson, 2004; Okagaki & Frensch, 1998). In fact, research suggests that African American and Latino families value success in school more highly than Euro-American families (Fuligni, Witkow, & Garcia, 2005; Stevenson, Chen, & Uttal, 1990). Both Latino and African American parents in this investigation reported more positive attitudes toward homework, grades on achievement tests, and a longer school day. Interest in school was high even among families living in poverty.

Families of some cultural groups may hold less positive attitudes toward Western schooling. Some Native American parents, for example, have been found to view traditional American schools as oppressive or as threatening to cultural traditions and values (Kawamoto & Cheshire, 1997; Wise & Miller, 1983). In addition, some Native American parents hold a strong belief that children should be accepted as they are; they may not support rigorous intervention efforts that they perceive as altering the course of nature (Joe & Malach, 1998; Klein & Chen, 2001). A child with special needs, for example, may not be a cause of great concern to a Native American family; children are as the gods intended them to be. Even these parents value their children's education, however, but they may be more supportive of family and community education activities or of tribal schools.

SCHOOLING AND THE STANDARDS MOVEMENT

Chapter 11 reviews the effects of the **standards movement** on preschool-aged children in the United States. This is a movement to identify the specific skills young children need to succeed in school and to promote and assess these in a systematic way. In the primary grades, teachers are now expected to focus on specific academic skills—particularly in reading, writing, and mathematics—and to rigorously assess these. A driving force behind much of this reform has been the No Child Left Behind Act (NCLB), which was enacted in 2002. This bill mandates that all states set clear standards for achievement of all children and report progress annually to the federal government. Schools that fail to meet annual progress requirements for 5 years are required to make dramatic changes to curriculum and staffing. Parents whose children attend a failing school may send them to another school (see the Advocacy and Public Policy box for more detail).

What has been the effect of this act on children, teachers, and families? The U.S. Department of Education reports some progress in children's learning (U.S. Department of Education, 2007). Reading scores for fourth-graders have risen since the enactment of NCLB. Math scores for both fourth- and eighth-graders have also improved. African American and Latino students, who have historically lagged far behind their Euro-American peers, have made some gains on test scores. Major concerns have been raised, however, about the overall outcomes of this legislation. Some argue that the focus on test scores has narrowed the curriculum so that it addresses only "testable" subjects—primarily reading and math (Hammond, 2005). Science, social studies, the arts, movement, and other areas of learning have been slighted. Others cite the stress NCLB has created for teachers, administrators, children, and parents (Kinsler, 2006; Yeh, 2006). The unrealistic expectations for improvement of test scores have been criticized (Armor, 2006; Wiley, Mathis, & Garcia, 2005). In 2005, for example, between 80% and 96% of all schools in the upper Midwestern states failed to meet required annual progress!

standards movement: A national initiative to identify the specific skills children need to succeed in school and to promote and assess these in a systematic way.

One concern about the standards movement, and NCLB specifically, is its failure to significantly close the achievement gap between Euro-American children and children of color (Fusarelli, 2005). Some researchers have provided evidence that this legislation has actually widened ethnic and socioeconomic differences in school success and has increased segregation in schools (Hammond, 2005; Lewin, 2005). In spite of these and other concerns, most educators and policymakers support some type of continued program to promote academic achievement and assessment. See the Advocacy and Public Policy box in this chapter for ideas on strengthening and modifying the NCLB Act.

ADVOCACY AND PUBLIC POLICY

Strengthening the No Child Left Behind Act

The No Child Left Behind Act (NCLB) is a sweeping educational reform package that was signed into law in 2002. The bill includes four major provisions that have significantly altered education in America: (a) NCLB mandates a system of accountability in which all states and school districts must test children's academic progress and report results in an annual report card to the federal government, to the community, and to parents. Schools that do not show progress on test scores must provide supplemental services, such as free tutoring or after-school assistance, and take other corrective steps. If they still do not make adequate yearly progress after 5 years, they will be required to make "dramatic changes" to the way the school is run—including hiring new teachers. (b) The bill authorizes states and school districts to use up to half the money from some federal grants—which had been previously earmarked for specific purposes—in alternative ways they feel more effectively enhance learning. For example, a school district could use funds for the Safe and Drug-Free Schools program to hire new teachers. (c) NCLB provides that education funds will be directed toward programs that have been shown to be effective through rigorous research. (d) The bill allows parents of children in schools that do not meet state standards for at least 2 years to transfer their children to a better-performing public school within their district. The school district must provide transportation for this purpose. Schools that fail to meet standards for 3 years must provide supplemental services, such as tutoring, after-school programs, and summer school.

NCLB is very controversial. Some believe the act has led to immediate and significant improvement in teaching and learning. Others are skeptical. Most teachers see NCLB as having both strengths and weaknesses (National Education Association, 2004). They believe that the law can have a positive impact if improved. A number of national legislators share their view. At this writing, at least 10 bills are being sponsored by senators and representatives to modify NCLB.

What is the role of professionals in improving NCLB? They should become knowledgeable about key issues regarding the bill. They might study the recommendations of several key groups calling for reform. The National Education Association (NEA; http://www.nea.org), the largest teacher organization in the country, advocates repairing NCLB in several fundamental ways: (a) They argue that the act's mandates should be fully funded. They note that funds are currently not adequate to meet all the requirements of the bill. School districts, particularly those serving low-income families, are struggling financially. The NEA proposes that any sanctions against schools for poor progress should be made only when a school has been given adequate resources to succeed and still fails. (b) The NEA believes the NCLB currently uses a "test-and-punish methodology." They feel that the language of the bill should be made less punitive toward teachers and schools. An underlying assumption of the legislation should be that educators want to do their jobs well but often need assistance to do better. Threatening educators with harsh consequences for poor test score performance will lead to a deterioration of

(continued)

education, not its improvement. They predict that, as written, the bill will cause good teachers to leave high-risk schools and will cause schools to focus too narrowly on test scores rather than broader educational goals. (c) The NEA argues that there should be less reliance on "one size fits all" tests that focus only on reading and math to determine progress. They believe that multiple methods of assessment should be encouraged and funded by the bill so that a more accurate picture of school progress is obtained. Similarly, they propose that multiple forms of evidence about schools and school districts be gathered and used to support improvements. (d) The NEA suggests that the criteria in NCLB for measuring "adequate yearly progress" are unrealistic. Large numbers of schools and school districts are certain to fail, they predict, even those that are high achieving or steadily improving. Reasonable goals for improvement should replace the bill's existing requirements.

Another professional organization, FairTest (http://www.fairtest.org), organizes advocacy around one element of NCLB: its heavy reliance on testing. Through publications and lobbying, this group urges that the bill be modified so that sweeping decisions about schools and teachers are no longer based on single, narrowly focused academic tests. The group argues that children spend too much school time taking or preparing to take tests. FairTest invites parents and professionals to sign a petition, which is posted on its Website, urging for a modification to NCLB.

Professionals can study the issues surrounding NCLB, formulate positions on modifying and/or strengthening the bill, and share their views publicly in letters to the editor or to their legislators. Through advocacy, this monumental education reform act can be made more effective in meeting young children's educational needs.

CLASSROOM ADAPTATIONS: PRIMARY-GRADE CHILDREN WITH COGNITIVE DISABILITIES

Since 1975, with the enactment of Public Law 94–142, the Education for All Handicapped Children Act, students with special needs have been integrated into regular classrooms in the public schools. The trend in recent years has been toward even more inclusive classrooms. Even children with severe disabilities are often placed in regular classroom settings (Simpson, deBoer-Ott, Smith-Myles, 2003; Turnbull & Turnbull, 2001). Primary-grade teachers may work with children with physical challenges, such as sensory or orthopedic impairments, and with children having social and emotional disturbances and autism. It is likely that teachers will have students who face various cognitive challenges.

Approximately 1% of elementary students have mental retardation (Umansky, 2008a). Speech and language disorders affect approximately 1% to 2% of school-age children; however, in most cases the speech or language challenge is related to another, primary disorder. Children with mental retardation and autism, for example, often receive services from speech and language pathologists (Rice & Schuele, 1995).

learning disabilities (LD): Cognitive disabilities characterized by impairment in some specific aspect of learning, such as writing, speaking, or mathematics, and sometimes including perceptual and attention deficits.

Learning Disabilities

The most common yet least understood cognitive disorders among school-age children are **learning disabilities (LD).** Approximately 3% to 4% of children have this condition, although the exact number is difficult to determine because of disagreement about how the disorder is to be defined and identified. One of the most challenging tasks of teachers and psychologists is to accurately identify children with LD.

Learning disabilities are generally described as impairments in some specific aspect or aspects of learning, such as writing, speaking, or mathematics. A general cognitive delay is not a characteristic, however. In fact, children with LD may be extremely competent in some areas of learning but have difficulty in other areas. For example, a child with LD may be poor in math yet competent in reading.

The prevalent theory is that learning disabilities are caused by neurological impairments (Sousa, 2007). However, persuasive arguments have been offered that environmental factors play a role (Harlaar, Spinath, Dale, & Plomin, 2005; Margai & Henry, 2003). Although researchers have yet to agree on the cause of LD, most concur that certain characteristics are common among children with the disorder. Several of these characteristics are described in Table 15-4.

Academic Difficulties. Children with LD usually have difficulties in one or more academic areas. A child may show poor reading comprehension or see letters reversed or transposed in written text (sometimes referred to as *dyslexia*). Another child may show mathematics achievement well below his or her grade level. Sometimes a child is delayed in one or several areas and at grade level or even above in others.

Perceptual-Motor Difficulties. Children with learning disabilities sometimes have perceptual challenges. They may have difficulty accurately interpreting auditory or visual stimuli (Wright, Bowen, & Zecker, 2000). They may not accurately hear the instructions for a science activity, or they may misinterpret a graph in a math lesson. They may become puzzled about direction, confusing left and right, for example, or may show no regular use of either the left or the right hand. Children with LD are sometimes awkward and show poor motor coordination. Their lack of physical competence may cause them to avoid outdoor motor play with peers. These motor difficulties affect school achievement as well. In the words of Umansky and Hooper (2008), "To pay attention to what others say, as well as to one's own thoughts, one's body must cooperate. The bodies of children with learning disabilities do not cooperate with them" (p. 224).

Characteristic	Description
Poor academic achievement	Children with LD often have difficulty in one or several subject areas. Their performance is often uneven; for example, they may excel in math but struggle with writing.
Perceptual-motor difficulties	Children with LD often have trouble interpreting sensory stimuli and distinguishing left from right. They may exhibit a lack of motor coordination.
Speech and language delays	Children with LD often show delays in language, including slow speech and poor word retrieval.
Faulty memory and logic	Children with LD often have trouble remembering or thinking through problems in school.
Hyperactivity/attention deficits	Some children with LD show extreme degrees of activity in school. They may have great difficulty attending to classroom tasks.

TABLE 15-4
Some Common Characteristics of Children with Learning Disabilities

Language and Speech Delays. Some children with LD have language or speech delays. One child might speak very slowly, another in long, loquacious, rambling sentences. Yet another child with LD might show difficulty in retrieving words. For example, in trying to name a ball, such a child might say, "The...the...you know...that...what's it called?...the...thing."

Faulty Memory or Thinking. Children with LD sometimes have trouble remembering or paying attention in class, organizing their work, or following tasks or instructions in order. Sometimes teachers misinterpret these difficulties and claim the child "just doesn't listen" or "never follows directions." On occasion, children with LD become distracted by one small part of a whole and are therefore unable to see the entire field or the big picture. For example, a child looking at a topographical globe of the world might center on the bumps on a particular mountain range and attend to nothing else.

Some children with LD have difficulty with change and become upset or angry if routines are disrupted. A child might become surprisingly upset, for example, when discovering one morning that his cubby or desk has been moved to another location.

Hyperactivity/Attention Deficits. Children with LD are sometimes extremely active and have much difficulty paying attention. Some children are so active that they disrupt the activities of other students in the class. They may have trouble sitting for even brief periods and may be unable to attend to even the simplest of instructions.

Some experts believe that LD and **attention-deficit/hyperactivity disorder (ADHD),** described in Chapter 14, are essentially the same disability because the two conditions so regularly accompany one another. However, research has shown that ADHD can exist with or without LD (Hesslinger, Thiel, van Elst, Hennig, & Ebert, 2002). Some children display a full range of LD characteristics; others only show ADHD-related behaviors.

Some characteristics of ADHD are common among younger children. Preschoolers often are wiggly and inattentive, show difficulty following directions, and use less mature syntax and grammar. How does one determine whether a school-age child is simply exhibiting immature behavior or displaying symptoms of a real disorder? Furthermore, some LD characteristics may be indicators of other disorders, such as underachievement, emotional disturbance, and even mental retardation (S. M. Robinson & Deshler, 1995). Whether a child has LD or some other disorder or is simply immature must be determined by careful observation and assessment.

If a child's challenges are many and severe, a condition such as mental retardation might be suspected. If they are less severe and more specific, LD is a possibility. If the challenges do not greatly affect school success or social relationships, immaturity could be the cause.

Children Who Are Gifted and Talented

Children are said to be **gifted and talented** if they display a superior intellect and/or talents that are advanced for their chronological age. They often are extremely competent in language and may grasp complex ideas quickly. They may not benefit from tedious, step-by-step lessons that laboriously break learning down into chunks of information and may not require drill-and-practice strategies to master concepts. This means that much of a typical school day is unproductive for children who are gifted and talented (McCoach & Siegel, 2003; L. K. Silverman, 1995).

attention-deficit/hyperactivity disorder (ADHD): A disorder that is characterized by high activity level, impulsiveness, and an inability to pay attention and that often leads to poor peer relations and school performance.

gifted and talented: A term used to describe children who display a superior intellect and/or talents that are advanced for their chronological age and who are often extremely competent in language and able to grasp complex ideas quickly.

One trait of children who are gifted and talented is a unique learning style. The following story illustrates the idiosyncratic pattern of development for one young child:

A 5-year-old growing up in southern India has not spoken. He appears alert and interested in the world around him and shows affection toward his family members, but he does not speak. Not one word. Of course, his parents grow worried.

They take him to a clinic where he is examined by a physician. Nothing appears to be wrong physically. His parents try various techniques to encourage him to talk. They offer rewards and demand that he speak before they will meet his needs. They try speaking in just their native language. (Theirs is a bilingual home, and they hope that simplifying the linguistic environment will help.) None of these strategies work.

Then, one day, the child begins to speak: not just one or two words but in long, sophisticated sentences. To the surprise and delight of his parents, he speaks eloquently and fluently in both his native language and English. By the end of his sixth year, he can read and write in both languages.

Children who are gifted and talented face many challenges. They are very much in need of special support in school. They do not always get along well with peers; often they seek the companionship of older children or adults (Gross, 2003). Children who are gifted and talented tend to be highly sensitive and somewhat introverted (L. K. Silverman, 1995). They are not always good students; in fact, underachievement is common.

A number of approaches to meeting the needs of children who are gifted and talented have been proposed. Acceleration of the content and pacing of the curriculum is one promising method. Early entrance into kindergarten and skipping grades are extreme examples. This strategy appears to work well, especially for girls (Neihart, 2007). Because children who are gifted and talented seek the company of older peers, skipping even two or more grade levels has been found to be effective.

Developing special gifted classes before, during, or after school is another strategy. Unfortunately, such programs are often limited (many take place only twice per week) or are eliminated altogether during periods of tight budget constraints. Providing enrichment in the regular classroom is the most prevalent (and least costly!) approach. In this method, teachers provide special experiences to challenge the thinking of children who are gifted and talented in the regular classroom. A problem with this approach is that some teachers confuse enrichment with "MOTS," meaning "more of the same" (L. K. Silverman, 1995, p. 400). Children who are gifted and talented are simply asked to do *more* worksheets or *more* math problems. Such strategies represent a misunderstanding of the needs of these children.

A growing number of children are now identified as both gifted and learning disabled. One out of six children who are gifted may have learning disabilities (Little, 2005). They may show specific reading, math, or perceptual challenges. Eliminating rote memory tasks and timed tests—standard fare in most classrooms—and integrating computer technology into the curriculum are strategies that are believed to support the academic achievement of children who are both gifted and learning disabled (L. K. Silverman, 1995).

Concerns have arisen about the identification of children who are gifted and talented because gifted classrooms are often composed of middle-class Euro-American students and not representative of the cultural composition of the community (L. K. Silverman, 1995). Children of color who are recruited into gifted and talented programs are less likely to remain in these classrooms over time (Moore, Ford, & Milner, 2005). They may not fit in as well with peers of predominantly middle-class backgrounds and do not always conform to the behavioral and learning expectations of teachers.

One reason children of color are underrepresented in gifted programs is because they do not always perform well on traditional assessments of giftedness. For example, an African American child may not perform efficiently on memory or vocabulary tasks because the content of the tasks is not relevant to her life. A Latino child may not score well on an IQ test because he comes from a field-sensitive culture. Teachers and school psychologists should consider using alternate means to determine giftedness among children of diverse cultural backgrounds. Children who show a high degree of competence in movement and the performing arts on the playground or in the neighborhood could be gifted. A child who displays exceptional story- or joke-telling ability may be gifted as well. L. K. Silverman (1995) proposes that children of diverse cultural backgrounds be assessed in the community, not in school. Observations of interactions at church, in the community center, or around the home or apartment may be more useful in identifying children who are gifted and talented from historically underrepresented groups. New, non-verbal, culturally sensitive methods of assessment have been found to more accurately identify African American and Latino gifted children (Naglieri & Ford, 2003).

Meeting Diverse Cognitive Needs in One Classroom

In a single primary classroom, a teacher might work with children who have severe cognitive impairments and those with highly advanced abilities. How can the needs of students with mental retardation and learning disabilities and those with advanced cognitive abilities be met in one class of 20 children? Several strategies are suggested in the literature (Howard et al., 2004, Ormrod, 2007; Umansky & Hooper, 2008):

1. *Graded challenges.* In Chapter 13, **graded challenges** were recommended as a way to encourage greater social interaction. These may also be used to meet diverse cognitive needs. Recall that graded challenges are activity choices—built into any project or instructional material—that are of different difficulty levels. In a math center, for example, activities that are of varying degrees of difficulty are provided. Some involve simple counting, others require addition and subtraction, and still others entail higher level math operations. Children are drawn (or guided) to activities that match their cognitive abilities. Graded challenges work best in classrooms with learning centers and group projects. Whole-group teaching is exceedingly difficult in classrooms of diverse learners!

2. *Cooperative learning and partnering.* In **cooperative learning and partnering,** teachers can plan projects in which children work in pairs or groups. At least some of the time, children should be assigned to these groups by the teacher so that more competent students are matched with those who have cognitive disabilities. More advanced children can then guide those needing assistance. Care should be taken to assign group members who are socially compatible. A very prosocial, gifted, and talented student would make an excellent partner for a child with Down syndrome.

3. *Visual and auditory cues.* Many activities in the primary years require an ability to read. A project based on a children's book or a cooking activity with a written recipe are examples. Children with cognitive impairments will have difficulty with these activities. Teachers can include visual or auditory cues for these children: a recorded

graded challenges: The provision of play and learning materials in a classroom that represent varying degrees of difficulty so that children of all abilities can find something meaningful to do.

cooperative learning and partnering: Classroom strategies in which children work in pairs or groups so that more competent students may be matched with those who have cognitive disabilities.

version of the book or pictures on the recipe—cups and teaspoons and ingredient labels—to guide them in their cooking. More competent partners can be asked to read the text to less able readers as well.

4. *Activities addressing multiple intelligences.* Cognitive disabilities may affect some areas of learning but not others. A child may struggle with reading but be a very competent musician. Even gifted and talented children may not be competent in some areas. They may excel in verbal abilities but have great difficulty with math. Teachers can plan activities that address all areas of learning so that each child has an opportunity to show his or her unique abilities. Gardner's (2006) multiple intelligences, presented in Table 15-1, serve as a handy guide. Teachers might try to plan at least several activities per week that address each of these intelligences.

5. *Flexible scheduling.* Children of diverse abilities take more or less time in learning concepts. Some will finish activities quickly and be ready to move on but will have to wait while other children catch up. Other children will take a long time to finish and may never complete projects or assignments. Teachers can address this pacing problem by adopting **flexible scheduling**—a strategy in which some children are allowed to take as long as they need on a learning task, and others are able to move ahead to more advanced activities if they finish early. Teachers can simply extend a learning period, for example, so that children can complete a science experiment they are working on. They can plan a variety of higher-level activities to keep on hand for children who finish early.

6. *Questions of different cognitive levels.* Questions are powerful teaching tools for primary-grade teachers. Higher level, open-ended questions stimulate advanced thinking (e.g., "Why did the oil and water separate do you think?"). These **questions of different cognitive levels** are ideal for many children—particularly those who are gifted. The more thought-provoking the question, the better! For children with cognitive disabilities, however, such questions are very challenging. Less complex questions would be more appropriate (e.g., "Where is the oil? Can you point to it?"). In planning, a teacher can write out questions that are of many different difficulty levels. These can be asked within the same activity. High level questions can be alternated with lower level ones. Care can be taken to let less able children answer the easier questions; more challenging ones can be directed to cognitively more advanced students.

flexible scheduling: A classroom strategy in which some children are allowed to take as long as they need on a learning task, and others are able to move ahead to more advanced activities if they finish early.

questions of different cognitive levels: Questions that teachers ask that are of many different difficulty levels so that challenging, open-ended questions are alternated with lower level, simple-answer questions.

CHILD GUIDANCE: *Helping Children Invent Their Own Solutions to Problems*

Based on Piaget's work, many primary-grade teachers encourage children to find answers to problems on their own. In a math activity, for example, a teacher might say, "I want you to count how many marbles you have, then divide them into three equal groups." During a science lesson, a teacher might state, "I have trays for all the different animal classifications—mammals, reptiles, and so on. I want you to put these pictures of animals into their correct trays." Such activities allow children to think, interact with peers, and learn important concepts. But do they go far enough?

Constance Kamii (1989) argues that in at least some activities, teachers should not only challenge children to find an answer but also encourage them to invent their own way to solve the problem. How can this be done? A teacher can simply alter the instructions or pose questions in a slightly different way. A teacher might say, "I want you to divide up your marbles so that each of you has the same amount." Here, children are not told to count. That gives away the solution. They are encouraged to solve the problem any way they wish. They may choose to simply guess, use a one-to-one correspondence strategy, or count. They may argue about the best way to divide the marbles. In the end, their solution will be more meaningful and will lead to more complex thinking and social interaction.

(continued)

In a science activity, the teacher might simply instruct children to "put the animals that are alike together." After they have done this, the teacher might ask them, "Why did you group the animals like you did?" In this case, children are able to come up with their own solutions—that is, their own categories—rather than ones the teacher suggests.

To challenge thinking even further, the teacher can ask, at the end of such activities, "Can you think of *another* way to divide the marbles?" or "Can you use *another* way to group the animals?" The emphasis here is on Piaget's cognitive processes—categorizing, for example—not just getting a right answer.

SUMMARY

The primary years, from ages 6 to 8, are marked by rapid cognitive growth. Most children of this age enter the concrete operational stage of development, in which they are able to solve more complex problems and acquire new abilities in language and literacy. For this reason, most children around the world begin formal schooling during this developmental period. There are a variety of perspectives on the intellectual development of primary-grade children. Some believe that innate abilities may be measured by IQ tests. Others, such as Howard Gardner, propose that there are multiple intelligences, including musical, spatial, and even interpersonal, that are not always appreciated in school. Piaget viewed intelligence as the acquisition of specific thinking processes. For children in his concrete operational stage of cognitive development, these processes include reversibility and causality. His work has influenced the primary-grade curriculum development in all subject areas.

Piaget's view of cognitive development has been criticized as underestimating primary-age children's thinking and for failing to appreciate cultural differences in learning. Vygotsky's theory emphasizes the role of culture and language more fully. He argued that verbalizations—both the child's and those of others—are now internalized and help guide learning.

Metacognition—the ability to think about and regulate learning processes—contributes to cognitive development in the primary years. Children are now able to consciously control their learning processes and can use such strategies as rehearsal, labeling and organization, and paying attention.

School success is influenced by factors other than cognitive development; cultural elements play an important role. Clashes in cognitive style, the poor quality of urban schools, and family attitudes toward education all affect learning outcomes. Cognitive disabilities and giftedness also influence school performance. Children with special needs can be successful in school if teachers adapt classroom activities, groups, and schedules.

RESEARCH INTO PRACTICE

CRITICAL CONCEPT 1

Children's success in school is related, in part, to general intelligence. One measure of intelligence is the intelligence quotient (IQ), which is determined by a score on a standardized test. Concerns have been raised about IQ as an adequate measure of intellectual functioning, however. Some researchers have found that IQ tests measure only one narrow type of intelligence and fail to appreciate others. Others have argued that IQ tests favor children of Euro-American backgrounds. IQ test bias has been a persistent concern in American education.

Application #1 Use extreme caution in interpreting IQ scores, particularly those for children from historically underrepresented groups. Be aware that IQ tests measure only a narrow range of intellectual abilities and are subject to error. Important educational decisions about children should never be based solely on the results of a single IQ score.

Application #2 Advocate for more culturally sensitive methods of assessing intellectual competence. These may include recently developed culture-free tests and nontest observational methods. Qualitative observation of children's performance across a range of developmental areas—music, movement, spatial ability, and social competence, for example—will give a broader picture of intellectual functioning.

Application #3 Plan experiences that enhance multiple intelligences, not solely linguistic or mathematical intelligence. Initiate activities that integrate movement, music, art, and social and interpersonal expression to address those intelligences sometimes neglected in schools.

CRITICAL CONCEPT 2

Piaget has looked at intelligence differently, describing intellectual processes rather than quantifying intelligence with numbers. He has focused as much on how children learn as on what they know. He found that unique thought processes—assimilation and accommodation, decentration, reversibility, and causal thinking—emerge in the primary years. These abilities allow children to acquire new knowledge in math, social studies, science, and other academic areas.

Application #1 Rely on Piaget's descriptions of primary children's thinking to understand and evaluate intellectual development. By asking children to think out loud or explain how they solved problems, you can assess children's acquisition of such mental processes as decentration, reversibility, and causal thinking.

Application #2 Apply Piaget's ideas on the acquisition of map space and time concepts in designing activities and materials in the social studies. Based on Piaget's work, plan map-drawing or map-interpreting experiences that lead to early understanding of geography. Assist children in thinking about the long ago and far away by using literature, old photographs, and classroom visits by grandparents.

Application #3 Apply Piaget's ideas on the acquisition of number, seriation, and transitive reasoning to plan a developmentally appropriate mathematics curriculum. From Piaget's view, providing opportunities for children to make autonomous judgments about amounts, distances, lengths, order, and relationships among objects and events is most important in math learning in the primary grades.

Application #4 Apply Piaget's ideas on classification and understanding natural causes to the planning of a primary-grade science curriculum. Based on Piaget's work, provide opportunities for children to observe and determine the causes of natural phenomena and to categorize objects in a classroom museum.

Application #5 Adhere to Piaget's most basic tenet of learning in the primary years: that children construct knowledge through action on concrete objects. Highly abstract, academic lessons are still inappropriate for children at this age.

CRITICAL CONCEPT 3

There is great variation in children's cognitive development in the primary years. Children of some cultures will be more advanced than Piaget would have predicted, others less so. Such differences may be explained by the diverse life experiences and competencies that are valued by families of different backgrounds.

Application #1 Understand and appreciate cultural differences in such general cognitive abilities as conservation, understanding of space, or mathematical reasoning. Use caution in assessment to ensure that differences in how children think are not misinterpreted as deficits.

Application #2 Plan experiences that represent a range of cognitive abilities so that children of diverse backgrounds are challenged but never overwhelmed.

CRITICAL CONCEPT 4

Vytgotsky has shown that children's learning is enhanced when their teachers or peers guide their problem solving within the zone of proximal development. This zone is a point in a learning experience where a task is just beyond a child's level of understanding. With hints, questions, or modeling, children in this zone can be prompted to accomplish the task on their own.

Application #1 Be cautious not to give children too much help in solving problems. Watch for times when your students are struggling with a challenging problem but show signs they can solve it on their own with just a little help. In these situations, ask guiding questions, give hints, provide demonstrations, provide additional materials, or in other ways enable children to work through the task independently.

Application #2 Play cooperative learning activities to encourage children to assist one another in learning within the zone of proximal development. Assign small groups of children tasks that require much collaboration and discussion. Structure these groups so that they include children who are more or less competent in a particular subject area. Facilitate interactions between "expert" and "novice" learners to promote interactions within the zone of proximal development.

CRITICAL CONCEPT 5

Memory improves during the primary years. One ability that enhances memory at this age is metacognition: the awareness of and ability to regulate one's own thought processes. Children begin to control their own thinking; they can choose to attend to some stimuli and not others, for example, and can rehearse information and skills they wish to retain. Memory and metacognitive strategies will vary among children of different cultures.

Application #1 Initiate memory games in the classroom to help children extend their short- and long-term memories. Examples include the traditional card game "Concentration" and the "Who's Missing?" game, in which children try to guess which classmate has secretly left the room.

Application #2 Suggest strategies that children might use to learn and remember. Hints for remembering, such as "Pay close attention" and "Say these words over to yourself several times," can be understood and used by children of this age.

Application #3 Learn the memory and learning strategies that are most commonly used within a child's family and culture. Students of some cultures may better remember facts if they are incorporated into songs, chants, stories, dances, drawings, and other forms of cultural expression rather than merely being presented in meaningless lists.

CRITICAL CONCEPT 6

Children of some cultural groups perform less well in school. Clashes in cognitive style, poor schools, and negative family attitudes are contributors. Research shows that cultural differences are minimized when the effect of socioeconomic status is controlled. Children of diverse cultural groups who have the same socioeconomic status will be more alike than different in their performance in the classroom.

Application #1   Create multifaceted learning environments that meet a wide range of needs. Plan active, expressive, and artistic learning activities to address the cognitive styles of children of some cultural groups. Collaborative projects that allow much social interaction and language are necessary to support the learning of field-sensitive students.

Application #2   Monitor your own classroom behaviors to be certain that you do not show bias in interactions with children. Ask other professionals to observe your teaching and make note of all comments and questions directed toward individual students in the class. Later, examine this feedback to see whether you are directing more attention or praise to certain groups of students—boys, girls, or children of Euro-American backgrounds, for example.

Application #3   Be cautious not to confuse class and culture. Recognize potential negative effects of poverty on children's development, such as ineffective parenting, risks of violence, and poor health. Also, recognize and appreciate the positive effects of culture on development, such as rich traditions, unique learning styles, and strong family ties.

CRITICAL CONCEPT 7

A number of challenging conditions affect intellectual development and school success. Children with learning disabilities and giftedness often require unique instructional intervention.

Application #1   Recognize the characteristics of children who have intellectual challenges or special needs, including children who are gifted and talented. Identifying and accessing services for children with special needs is a fundamental role of primary teachers in modern American schools.

Application #2   Primary-grade classrooms must contain activities and materials that match the variety of learning abilities and interests represented in the classroom. Each learning center, group activity, and collaborative project must include graded challenges—varied tasks or problems that reflect all levels of cognitive competence. An art center, for example, must contain complex media to inspire a child who is gifted to create an elaborate weeklong project; at the same time, it must include simple materials, such as markers and large paper, that a child with mental retardation can use to scribble. Group time must include both extended group story reading for children who can sit for longer periods and active alternative experiences for those who cannot.

ASSESSING YOUNG CHILDREN: Primary-Age Cognitive Development

Areas of Development	What to Watch For	Indicators of Atypical Development	Applications
General cognitive abilities	Shows an ability to understand the perspectives of others. Reverses operations and thinks about more than one aspect of a problem at a time. Categorizes objects using multiple attributes (e.g., size and shape). Distinguishes between cause and effect in solving problems. Scores near age level on traditional IQ tests.	Poor performance on tasks that require guessing what others are thinking or feeling. Inability to reverse the steps of a task. Continuing to be fooled by the appearance of things and never relying on logic. An inability to identify the causes of simple events. A score below 70 on traditional IQ tests.	Plan a curriculum that addresses the specific cognitive characteristics of concrete operational children. This curriculum should include (a) concrete objects, (b) challenging problems to solve, (c) peer interaction, and (d) thought-provoking teacher questions.

| Specific intellectual skills | Skill in interpreting maps and in distinguishing the long ago from the present. An understanding of how numbers work and an ability to use them to solve real problems. An ability to distinguish natural objects from man-made objects and to place these into simple categories (e.g., plants and animals). A knowledge of what *learning* and *remembering* mean and an ability to regulate these mental processes. | General poor performance on math, science, social studies, and other tasks in school. A lack of ability in just one area of learning (i.e., math) but a high level of competence in other areas. Exceptional intellectual or artistic abilities that are uncharacteristic for one's age level. | Provide problems for children to solve across specific areas of the curriculum: Children can be guided in categorizing objects from nature, guessing about the outcomes of a scientific experiment, or interpreting and making maps. Children can be asked to order historical photographs from oldest to most recent. Prompt children to "remember" and "listen carefully" to enhance memory abilities. |

Interpreting Assessment Data: There are cultural variations in intellectual or school-related abilities. Children in communities that do not use maps, for example, may be less able in map reading, and those in cultures that emphasize math may be advanced in this area. Children who are generally delayed across all areas of intellectual development may have mental retardation. Those who show poor performance in only one area but are competent in others may have a learning disability. These conditions can be addressed through special services delivered in the classroom. Children who show exceptional intellectual or artistic ability may be gifted/talented. The needs of such children are best met by adding new, more challenging and engaging tasks to the curriculum. Simply asking gifted/talented children to do *more* work is not effective.

CHAPTER 16

Language, Literacy, and Schooling

GUIDING QUESTIONS

1. How does phonology advance in the primary years for first- and second-language learners?
2. What are some atypical patterns of phonological development during this developmental period?
3. How does semantics develop during the primary years for first- and second-language learners?
4. What are some atypical patterns of semantic development observed at this age?
5. What are some major advancements in syntax during the primary years for first- and second-language learners?
6. What are the characteristics of atypical syntactic development at this age?
7. What is metalinguistic awareness, and how does it affect first- and second-language acquisition?
8. How does pragmatics develop in the primary years, and what are some social rules of language in school that children this age must acquire?
9. How does culture influence children's acquisition of pragmatics in school?
10. What are some rules for using language in school, and how can these clash with language rules of families from historically underrepresented groups?
11. What are the major approaches to bilingual education, and what are the strategies and stages by which children acquire a second language in school?
12. What are the major stages of writing and reading in the primary years, and how are these influenced by culture and teaching methods?
13. What are the major stages of biliteracy development?
14. What classroom adaptations enhance the language and literacy of children with special needs?

This chapter explores the development of language and literacy in the primary years and the relationship between these areas of development and school life. During the preschool years, children of all linguistic and cultural backgrounds learn the basic syntax, semantics, and phonology of the language spoken within their families and communities. Some refinements occur in these areas in the primary years, but the most significant language advancement during this period is children's ability to use language in a variety of new and different ways.

Children in many cultures must learn a new style of communication: the *language of school*. They must also acquire language that helps them influence peers and make new friends. In most cultures, children learn to read and write conventionally during the primary years. Some children face challenges in learning language and literacy. A child who is delayed in communication abilities may need much adult support in learning the structure and social uses of language. A child who speaks a different language than other students in a classroom must learn not only to speak, read, and write in a new language but also to use it effectively in peer groups and in school.

The following story illustrates this point:

A 6-year-old Korean child who does not speak English is working at the math center near an English-speaking peer. She tries to get the other child's attention to show him a puzzle she has just completed. She calls out to him in her native language. He looks up briefly with a confused expression, then looks down again at the game he is playing.

She tries a new approach. She leans across the table and taps him roughly on the shoulder. He pulls away and calls out across the room to the teacher. "She's bothering me!" he complains. The Korean child, not understanding her peer's words, looks puzzled.

The teacher approaches. "I think Sook wants to show you something," he says to the English-speaking child. "She's asking you in her own language. See? She's showing you her puzzle." Then, to the Korean child, he says, "If you want to get Robert's attention, you could say, 'Look, Robert'!" He points at Robert as he says this. "Look, Robert!" he repeats. The child appears to understand that this is a way of communicating with peers. "Look, Robert," she imitates. Robert smiles, then returns to his work.

The teacher in this vignette has not only assisted the non-English-speaking child in acquiring vocabulary and language structure but also helped her learn a new way of making contact with dominant-culture peers in her classroom. Further, the teacher has assisted a child of the dominant culture in understanding language and communication differences. Facilitating communication in this way is an important role for teachers in modern multicultural classrooms.

FIRST- AND SECOND-LANGUAGE ACQUISITION

Primary-grade children are remarkably competent in their use of language. A brief experiment will help the reader appreciate just how linguistically sophisticated they have become, even at 6 years old. The following statement was uttered by a first-grade child. Read it aloud, paying special attention to the various **articulators** (i.e., tongue, teeth, lips), described in Chapter 12, that are used and to the rules and word meanings that are applied: "The stone was so huge that I couldn't lift it by myself. So Jeremy had to help because he's older and bigger." Notice how your tongue, teeth, and lips move in rapid-fire succession from one position to another as you read the statement. You engaged your vocal cords at just the right times, as when you pronounced the *g* sound in *huge*. You let air pass through your nose to create important nasal tones, such as the *n* sound in *stone* and the *m* sound in *Jeremy*. How is it possible that a child only 6 years old can make such precise movements?

While performing this fantastic feat of articulation, the child is also thinking about word meaning. As you read the passage, did any of the words strike you as particularly complex? Why did the child use *stone* instead of *rock? Huge* instead of *big?* These word pairs have subtle differences in meaning. An advancement in the primary years is an ability to differentiate among words that have similar meanings. This child has come to understand that *huge* implies much greater size (and perhaps carries greater emotional impact) than *big*. These distinctions require complex analysis, yet the child made these word decisions in a split second!

Note that the child is using pronouns. It would seem that one so young might not yet understand that *it* can stand for *stone* and that *he* can stand for *Jeremy*. The child is also applying rules for constructing complex sentences. The agent, action, object, and other critical features of sentences must be expressed in the correct order: *The stone was so huge* rather than *Huge so the stone was*. Each sentence the child speaks contains two distinct ideas that must be connected somehow. The child effectively uses conjunctions (*that* and *because*) to do this. The child has to follow many rules of word order, such as placing the subject *I* before the verb *lift* and inserting the negative *n't* after the verb *could*. Listing all the rules of word order that must be applied to speak this one utterance would be a truly mind-boggling task, yet this 6-year-old can apply every one of them correctly in a matter of seconds.

Now imagine that the child who uttered these sentences speaks a completely different native language. Perhaps in his native tongue, verbs are placed at the ends of sentences. In his own language, he would say, "It I couldn't lift." Suppose that his family's language has no articles. He would be inclined to say, "Stone was so huge." Instead, this child sifts through the two sets of rules in his mind—those from his primary language and those of the new language he is learning—and selects and applies the rules that match the language he is speaking. Many 6-year-olds have learned two languages and can do this with ease!

Primary-age children have become so proficient in language that only minor refinements are needed for them to possess full adult competence.

Phonology

Phonology—the part of language that involves speech sounds, described in Chapter 12—is well developed by the primary years. Children have acquired most of the **phonemes**—that is, individual speech sounds—of their native language by age 5. They may still have difficulty, however, pronouncing some sounds during the first few years of elementary school. In English, the sounds *l, r, s, sh,* and *ch* are still very difficult for many 6- and 7-year-olds. It is common for a first-grader to say "wike" instead of "like" or "wun" in place of "run." These articulation errors usually disappear by age 8. Children whose mispronunciations persist past this age may be in need of special support in school.

Phonology and Second-Language Acquisition. The process of acquiring a second language varies according to family and school circumstances. **Simultaneous second-language learners**—that is, children who are exposed equally to both languages from birth—become quite proficient in both by the end of the preschool years (August & Hakuta, 1998;

articulators: Parts of the body that are responsible for speech production, including the front and back of the tongue, the teeth, the lips, the roof of the mouth, the vocal chords, and the lungs.

phonology: The part of language involving speech sounds, including pronunciation, fluency, and intonation.

phonemes: Individual speech sounds, such as *b, t,* or *ch.*

simultaneous second-language learners: Children who are exposed equally to two languages from birth and become quite proficient in both by the end of the preschool years.

Hernandez et al., 2005). These *bilingual* children have learned to distinguish among and produce the unique sounds of the two languages. Even some *trilingual* preschoolers become so proficient at speech sounds that they sound like native speakers in all three languages (L. W. Hoffman, 1985)!

Successive second-language learners acquire a primary language first and a second language later. A common example is a child who spends the first 5 years of life in Puerto Rico and then moves to the United States during the primary years. Because successive bilingual children learn the sound system of their primary language first, they face greater phonological challenges when learning a second language in school. The new speech system may contain sounds that they cannot pronounce or even hear (Ellis, 2000; Hayes-Harb, 2007).

What do children learning a second language do when confronted with sounds they cannot pronounce? They substitute similar sounds that they do know. Take the example of a Spanish-speaking child learning English. She hears words that contain a hard *s* sound, such as *rose* and *boys*. No such phoneme exists in Spanish, so the child will pronounce these words using a soft *s*, as in *most* and *hoist*. In Spanish, *h* is always silent, so this Spanish-speaking child would pronounce the words *horn* and *hello* as *orn* and *ello*.

Children who speak nonstandard English dialects often engage in the same kinds of substitutions when confronted with standard English word forms in school. In **African American Vernacular English,** defined in Chapter 12, the *th* sound does not exist, so African American children often say *tink* rather than *think* (Klein & Chen, 2001; Labov, 1971; Sligh & Conners, 2003). Children from Boston and other parts of New England often substitute the *ah* sound for *r*, as in *go pahk the cah* (Berger, 2007).

Children who use a different sound system than that of the dominant culture may be teased or corrected, for the first time, in the primary years (Hemmings & Metz, 1990). Their teachers often insist on standard pronunciations in school. Their peers often mimic their unique speech patterns. It is important for professionals who work with children to understand that differences in articulation are not deficits. They must also help other students understand this. Substitutions are, in fact, a creative way for children to solve the problem of pronouncing unfamiliar speech sounds.

Atypical Phonological Development. Three kinds of phonological difficulties that occur in the primary grades require special services: articulation problems, disfluency, and poor voice quality (Ratner, 2008; Rice & Schuele, 1995). These are summarized in Table 16-1.

successive second-language learners: Persons who acquire a primary language first and a second language later.

African American Vernacular English: A form of English spoken by African Americans in many communities in the United States that is as complex and expressive as standard English and includes its own unique phonology, syntax, and semantics.

Challenge	Description
Articulation errors	The child has difficulty pronouncing specific phonemes that are usually acquired by a particular age. A 7-year-old, for example, may not clearly pronounce *b*, *p*, *m*, or *n*—sounds usually learned very early in childhood.
Disfluency	A child stutters in a manner that interferes with communication. Single phoneme misstarts (*b-b-b-b*), facial grimaces, and struggle behaviors may indicate a need for intervention.
Poor voice quality	A child regularly speaks in a highly nasal or hoarse voice.

TABLE 16-1
Phonological Challenges Identified in the Primary Years

Articulation problems relate to an inability to pronounce specific phonemes that are usually acquired by a particular age. For example, a 7-year-old who cannot clearly pronounce the *b, p, m,* or *n* sounds, which are usually learned very early in childhood, may be identified as having articulation difficulties.

One way to determine the severity of speech errors is to test whether children are **stimulable** (described in Chapter 12) for specific sounds. This involves asking children to imitate the sounds they are not articulating clearly. If children can imitate these sounds, their problem is considered less worrisome. If they cannot, intervention may be required. Whether children with phonological impairments are referred for special services will be determined, in part, by whether they are communicating well with peers and teachers in school (Hooper & Edmondson, 2008; Rice & Schuele, 1995). Children whose speech cannot be understood are likely to be referred to a speech and language pathologist, a professional who has received extensive training in identifying and remediating communication problems and disorders. Children who have minor articulation problems but are communicating well with teachers and classmates may not be referred. Their speech may be enhanced informally by the regular teacher in the classroom.

Articulation problems occur for several reasons. They may arise from physiological causes. A child who has a cleft palate—a genetic condition in which the palate did not fully form during prenatal development—may have difficulty making certain speech sounds. A child with cerebral palsy may have trouble coordinating articulators. Another phonological problem identified in the primary years is **disfluency,** or stuttering. All young children stutter. Restarts or whole-word repetitions are very common in childhood discourse (e.g., "The guy...the guy...the guy fell...down"). So common is this sort of disfluency in first or second grade that speech and language pathologists rarely attempt to treat it at this age (Howell, 2007; Rice & Schuele, 1995). When, then, should parents and teachers begin to worry about stuttering? In the early elementary grades, children who have severe problems with disfluency will begin to stutter in different ways and with greater frequency. They will engage in more single-sound or single-syllable repetitions, such as "b-b-b-ball." Their stutters will be prolonged, and there will be longer hesitations in their speech (Howell, 2007). **Struggle behaviors,** such as facial grimaces and contortions of the mouth, may appear (Rice & Schuele, 1995). Children who are disfluent stutter more often—10 or more times as frequently, in fact—than typically developing children. Disfluency is generally considered to be hereditary and is often associated with other conditions, such as neurological impairment (Easterbrooks, 2008; Packman, Code, & Onslow, 2007).

In the primary years, speech and language pathologists work closely with the families of children who stutter. A common approach is to discourage family members from finishing children's sentences or asking them to start over since this adult correction can create stress and exacerbate the problem. Informal work with the children themselves is also customary. Usually, speech and language pathologists do not try to directly reduce stuttering or draw a child's attention to the problem. Instead, they provide a comfortable, relaxed setting in which the child may talk, or they encourage the teacher to do so in the classroom (Rice & Schuele, 1995). Research suggests that a variety of different treatment strategies should be tried, until one is found to be effective with an individual child (Law, 2007).

Poor voice quality is a less common speech disorder identified and treated in the primary years. A teacher may notice that a child is chronically hoarse or has an unusually nasal tone. Such problems may be physiological. Hoarseness can stem from polyps or other growths on the larynx. A cleft palate or cerebral palsy may contribute to nasality. A prompt medical examination is recommended when these characteristics are observed.

The most common source of poor voice quality is **vocal abuse** (Easterbrooks, 2008; Duff, Proctor, & Yairi, 2004). Some children talk so loudly or scream so often they create

articulation problems: An inability to pronounce specific phonemes that are usually acquired by a particular age.

stimulable: A condition in which a child can accurately imitate a particular sound when it is presented to them by an adult even if they do not pronounce it correctly in everyday speech.

disfluency: A speech problem, sometimes called *stuttering,* in which a child engages in prolonged and frequent single-sound repetitions, sometimes accompanied by facial grimaces and contortions of the mouth.

struggle behaviors: Facial grimaces, contortions of the mouth, and other signs of difficulty in producing speech sounds that are indicators of a more serious form of disfluency.

poor voice quality: A speech disorder, sometimes caused by physiological problems such as growths on the larynx or by abuse of the vocal cords, in which a child is chronically hoarse or has an unusually nasal tone.

vocal abuse: A condition caused by loud talking or screaming in which children create callouses, called nodules, on their vocal tissues.

callouses, called nodules, on their vocal tissues. If the causes of the abuse are not treated, children may require surgery to have the nodules removed. A speech and language pathologist may work with families to arrange for quieter home experiences and to discourage the child from yelling. Teachers are encouraged to remind children who habitually scream or talk too loud to lower their voices.

Semantics

Children's **semantics**—the part of language related to word meaning, discussed in Chapter 12—continues to develop throughout childhood. However, the rate at which new words are acquired slows beginning in first or second grade. This is a period not of rapid growth but of refining and coordinating word meanings (Ely, 2001). During this stage, children acquire fuller, more adult definitions for the words they already know. Whereas younger children might think of *big, huge,* and *gigantic* as meaning the same thing, primary-age children come to understand subtle distinctions among these words (Berger, 2007). Children of this age group also acquire fuller meanings of words that describe human character traits—such as *mean* or *shy* (Heyman & Gelman, 1999). Although preschoolers have a general sense of what these words convey, primary-age children can make more sophisticated inferences about how *shy* or *mean* people might behave or what their motives might be. Not only do children learn the fuller meanings of words in the middle years, but they also learn morphemes—parts of words that hold meaning (McBride-Chang, Wagner, Muse, Chow, & Shu, 2005) For example, they can understand a new word, *hopelessness,* by using their knowledge of the morphemes, *-less* and *-ness.*

Primary-age children also begin to construct relationships among the many words they have learned. They create **semantic networks:** internal maps that show connections among words within one's mental dictionary (Cummings, et al., 2006). For example, children begin to understand that some words are opposites, that some hold the same meaning, and that some have similar but subtly different definitions. They understand that some words are labels that represent a whole category of other words. For example, they come to see that *mammals* is a broad term that includes *seals, humans, dogs,* and many other living things.

Semantic networks can be demonstrated most clearly when children are given **free association tasks.** These are tasks in which children are given a word and encouraged to name as many other words as come to mind. When very young children are presented a word—say *throw*—they usually provide a short list of other terms that follow the word in a sentence: *the ball* or *the beanbag.* At about age 7, children respond with longer lists of words that show sophisticated connections in semantics. For example, a child at this age might provide synonyms such as *toss* and *pitch.* They might include words for parallel but different activities, such as *catch, bat, hit,* and *run* (Borghi & Caramelli, 2003; K. Nelson, 1998). The increased complexity of free associations in the primary years is illustrated in Figure 16-1.

Semantics in Bilingual Families. As described in Chapter 12, preschoolers who are bilingual construct one huge vocabulary that consists of words from both languages they are learning. Children of this age who are learning Spanish and English, for example, will at first create a mental dictionary of all words learned. They might become confused about which words to use when speaking a particular language. A sign of this confusion is their frequent use of mixed-language utterances, such as "el kitty blanco."

Primary children who are bilingual begin to differentiate between words from the two languages in their mental dictionary (De Bleser et al., 2003). One factor that influences

semantics: The part of language that has to do with using words and learning word meanings.

semantic networks: A complex organization in one's mental dictionary that shows connections among words and clusters together words with similar meanings.

free association tasks: Tasks to study the connectedness of word meanings in which children are given a word and encouraged to name as many other words as come to mind.

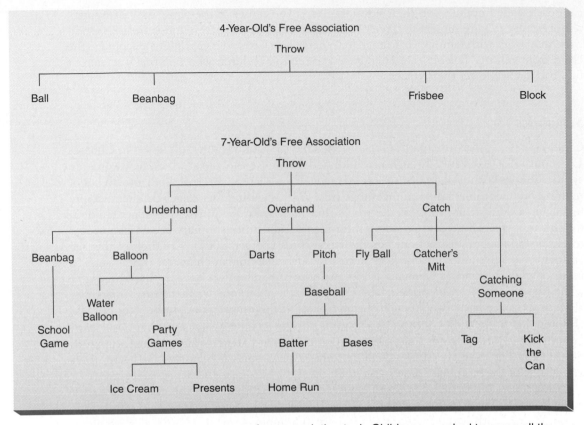

FIGURE 16-1   Two responses to a free association task. Children are asked to name all the words they can think of that go with "throw." The 4-year-old limits responses to things that can be thrown, while the 7-year-old presents a full "semantic network": a complex cluster of many different kinds of related words.

this process is school because, in some cases, the language spoken at school is different from that spoken in the home. In the United States, for example, children who speak both Spanish and English often hear only English spoken in first grade. **Language shock** results when children suddenly discover that their native language is not understood by others. The experience leads some children to more quickly differentiate between the languages they are learning (Arnberg, 1987; August & Hakuta, 1998). "These are the words my peers can understand at school," they learn, "and these are the words they cannot."

Children's experiences with language in the home can also assist them in separating their vocabularies. When one parent speaks one language and the other parent (or perhaps a grandparent) speaks a second language, a child can more readily distinguish the two. In such an environment, the child learns that "these are the words Mom uses, and these are different kinds of words Dad uses."

language shock: Feelings of surprise that result when children who are bilingual suddenly discover that their native language is not understood by others.

Over the course of the primary years, many children successfully separate their languages. Exactly when this occurs varies as a function of the timing and order of language learning. Are two languages learned simultaneously or successively? Do both parents speak the native language, or does one speak one language, one the other? The countless variations in home language environment explain the diversity of second-language learners in school.

Each culture has its own vocabulary. Words describing objects, persons, or events that are of critical importance in one culture may not even exist in another. For example, one of my colleagues who is from Nepal reports that there are numerous words in English that have no meaning in Nepalese. Expressions like *please* and *thank you* have no exact equivalent; in Nepal, such sentiments are communicated with facial expressions and gestures. However, Nepalese words such as *ainsselu*, *chutro*, and *kphal*—names of common berries in Nepal—have no English translation. Some African American children use a street vocabulary that reflects the artistic and playful features of their culture (Klein & Chen, 2001). Common terms such as *jiving* or *dissing* often hold little meaning for peers or teachers from another cultural group. Mismatches in semantics create special challenges for children learning a new language.

Atypical Semantic Development. Some children acquire words more slowly. Often delays in semantic development are associated with more general language problems or other challenging conditions (Easterbrooks, 2008; Weismer & Evans, 2002). Children with mental retardation or learning disabilities, for example, may have limited vocabularies or poor word-retrieval skills.

Children with semantic delays may be unable to identify opposites or synonyms or to generate lists of related terms in a free association task. They may even struggle to correctly name pictures or objects. Sometimes children compensate for difficulty in retrieving words by using *thing* to stand for objects they cannot name. A child with delayed semantics who could not retrieve the word *zipper* compensated by saying, "You know . . . that thing you pull up . . . that goes up on the coat."

Some children may have trouble learning **morphemes**—those small units of language that hold meaning. For some, endings are challenging. A child might say, "Yesterday, my mom play with me" or "There are three ball." Another child might become confused over pronouns and say, "Me going too" or "Him is my friend."

Speech and language pathologists will often work with children on developing a larger vocabulary or understanding word meanings more fully. A growing number of professionals intervene with children within the classroom setting, designing vocabulary enhancement strategies that relate to the school curriculum. The focus of such an intervention may be, for example, learning new words introduced in a science lesson or a story (Rice & Schuele, 1995). Speech and language pathologists also work with families and family service providers to enhance semantics in the home (Stoneman & Manders, 2008; Turnbull & Turnbull, 2001). A labeling strategy might be implemented in which parents energetically strive to name unfamiliar objects or use more descriptive words.

Syntax

Syntax—the part of language related to ordering words to form sentences (see Chapter 12)—continues to advance in the primary years. Children of this age are able to construct very complex sentences by only 6 or 7 years of age. They can speak long declaratives or questions that contain negatives and clauses. However, a few syntactic structures are still challenging to them. Passives (e.g., "The cup was dropped by the girl") are acquired only gradually during childhood. Several studies have shown that English-speaking children misinterpret these when they hear them (Dick, Wulfeck, Krupa-Kwiatkowski, & Bates, 2004; Vasilyeva, Huttenlocher, & Waterfall, 2006). In these studies, primary children were asked to match passive sentences to corresponding pictures. For example, they were presented with the sentence "The farmer was bitten by the cow" and then shown two pictures—one of a cow biting a farmer and another of a farmer biting a cow. When asked to point to the picture that corresponded to

morphemes: Small words or parts of words that hold meaning, such as the past tense *-ed* ending, the plural *-s*, and articles such as *a* and *the*.

syntax: The part of language that involves creating sentences, including word order, sentence length and complexity, and the use of clauses and word endings.

the sentence, subjects invariably pointed to the drawing of the farmer biting the cow. Why? Children in the early elementary years are accustomed to straightforward declarative sentences, such as "I hit the ball." In these sentences, the agent performing the action (*I*) comes first, then the action (*hit*), and finally the object (*ball*). In passive sentences, the object comes first: "The ball was hit by me." Children misinterpret the object to be the agent; that is, in their minds, the sentence becomes "The ball hit me."

Exposure to complex syntax in naturalistic settings may aid children's learning of difficult utterances, like passive sentences. One study found that, when children were read repeated stories that used the passive structure, they were more likely to use passives in their own conversations (Vasilyeva et al., 2006).

Syntax and Bilingual Development. When children learn two different languages, they must learn two sets of syntactic rules. At first they may learn only the syntactic rules of their native language. For a time, they may apply these when speaking in the new language as well. For example, a Spanish-speaking child will learn to form some questions in her native language by placing the verb before the subject. So, when speaking English, she applies the same rule. She may say, "Saw you the boy?" A child who speaks African American Vernacular English (AAVE) may use his home and community syntax when speaking standard English in school (Lipski, 2007). For example, in standard English, the word *do* is inserted to form certain kinds of questions (e.g., "*Do* you swim?"). This rule does not exist in AAVE. So, such a child might initially say, "You swim?"

Some teachers believe that these logical, rule-governed sentences are language errors to be corrected, while others view this early syntax as immature or deficient. These beliefs lead to the misunderstanding and sometimes mistreatment of second-language learners in school. Where do such negative attitudes come from? It has been proposed that a hierarchy of languages exists in any culture (Dale, 1976; J. Edwards, 1981). Some languages are viewed more favorably by dominant society, others less so. In America, standard English is highest on this hierarchy, British–English and French–English dialects are next, and AAVE, Spanish–English, and Appalachian dialect are lowest. These last three languages are often viewed as unsophisticated, primitive, or lower class. Such language preferences are easy to observe in schools. Children who are natives of France or Sweden, for example, are not likely to be harshly corrected by teachers for not speaking standard English. In fact, their dialects might even be considered quaint, charming, or cosmopolitan. However, teachers show great concern about AAVE or Spanish–English syntax (Klein & Chen, 2001).

Children acquire the syntax of a second language in unique stages during the primary years (August & Hakuta, 1998; DeKeyser, 2005; E. L. Wong, 1991). For example, Spanish speakers who are learning English have been found to acquire negatives in the following way:

Stage 1: "The man no like cheese"
Stage 2: "The man not like cheese"
Stage 3: "The man don't like cheese"
Stage 4: "The man doesn't like cheese"

This progression shows why correcting the syntax of children who are learning a second language is ill advised. A child may have just advanced from "no like cheese" to "not like cheese." So, a teacher who responds, "No, it's *doesn't*. Can you say that?" fails to acknowledge the child's significant language achievement. Furthermore, the teacher may be suggesting that this new structure is wrong or bad.

Atypical Syntactic Development. Children with special needs are sometimes delayed in syntactic development. Those with mental retardation, learning disabilities, or general language delay may not be able to understand or speak sentences that are typically learned during the preschool years. For example, typically developing primary-age children can speak and understand embedded clauses (Boloh & Champaud, 1993). They can interpret and even speak sentences such as "The man who talked to the teacher was angry." Children with language delays may interpret this sentence to mean that *both* the man and the teacher are angry (Rice & Schuele, 1995).

Children with such severe syntactic delays are referred to speech and language pathologists. Again, a recent trend is toward providing services within the regular classroom. A speech and language pathologist may guide a child in using or interpreting complex sentences during group time or in naturalistic interactions with peers. Home-based interventions are also implemented. Parents might be encouraged to use more elaborate sentences in their interactions with their children.

Metalinguistic Awareness

One advancement in the primary years that greatly enhances language learning is the emergence of **metalinguistic awareness** (Ferreira & Morrison, 1994; Mertz & Yovel, 2004). This is the ability to think about language itself. Before 6 years of age, children simply speak. Although they may apply the rules of language, structure sentences correctly, and select the right words to convey meaning, they do so subconsciously.

As children enter the primary years, they become more aware of language itself. They can think about and comment on sentence structure, how speech sounds are formed, and the various definitions of words. By age 7, for example, children are able to identify sentences that are grammatically correct or incorrect (Bialystok, 1986). They can critique poorly formed sentences: "No, silly! It should be 'throw the ball,' not 'ball the throw'!"

Primary-age children are able to define words, not simply use them in sentences (Benelli, Belacchi, Gini, & Lucangeli, 2006; Marinellie & Chan, 2006). A 6-year-old illustrates this ability when he explains how hot a summer day is: "It's not just 'hot' because 'hot' doesn't mean hot enough. It's a 'roasting' day. That's better. 'Roasting' means like the stove. It's that hot! A roasting day!"

Primary-age children can define words by relating them to other words they know. For example, an 8-year-old defined the word *huge* as "very, very big, not just 'big.' It's the opposite of 'teeny tiny.'" These abilities show that children can contemplate word meanings. Children's understanding of word meanings can also be observed in their humor. Consider the following classic (if not particularly funny) joke:

> What did the big chimney say to the little chimney?
> What?
> "You're too young to smoke."

Preschoolers might have trouble understanding the joke, but primary-grade children think it is uproariously funny because they now understand that a word can mean two different things. So, they catch the pun.

Phonemic Awareness. Children acquire greater **phonemic awareness**—an awareness of individual speech sounds, syllables, and words—in the elementary years. One problem they begin to overcome is **missegmentation**: an inability to know where the sounds and words of an utterance are divided. As a child, I used to puzzle over what "donzerly" lights were in the National Anthem. Reich (1986) tells the story of a child who misinterpreted a line from a

metalinguistic awareness: An understanding of, and an ability to think and talk about, language itself.

phonemic awareness: The understanding that language is made up of smaller units: words, syllables, and sounds.

missegmentation: An inability to know where the sounds and words of an utterance are divided.

hymn, "Gladly the cross I'd bear," to be "Gladly, the cross-eyed bear." In these examples, children have missegmented utterances. They cannot, as yet, think through the logical sound breaks in sentences. In the primary years, they can contemplate sounds and breaks in language. They can think through better and correct missegmentation errors:

CHILD: (Speaking to her father) Oh! Remember when I was a baby? You said "upyougo." That meant "up" and "you" and "go." Like that. Like "up you go." So, up I'd go (laughs). I get it now.

Awareness of phonology can also be observed in children's humor. Schickedanz, Schickedanz, and Forsyth (1982) provide the following example of a childhood joke. What does it reveal about children's understanding of phonology at this age?

Knock, knock.
Who's there?
Duane.
Duane who?
Duane the tub, I'm dwowning!

This joke shows not only that children are aware of the sounds in their language but also that they have knowledge of typical articulation errors in childhood, such as substituting *w* for *r*.

Phonemic awareness has been found to be very important in learning to read in first and second grade (Castles & Coltheart, 2004; Wagner et al., 1997). Children who can distinguish among individual speech sounds find it easier to learn to read; those who cannot may be at academic risk (Elbro, Borstrom, & Peterson, 1998). In fact, this ability is one of the best predictors of reading proficiency in later childhood. Activities such as reciting nursery rhymes and poetry, singing, and playing with sounds in preschool and kindergarten have been found to enhance this awareness and to promote reading abilities in the elementary years (McIntosh et al., 2007; Neuman et al., 1999; Schickedanz, 1999).

Metalinguistic Awareness and Second-Language Acquistion. Metalinguistic awareness is extremely important in second-language acquisition. When children can reflect on language forms and rules, they are better at differentiating between the two languages they are learning (Jessner, 2008; Roehr, 2008). Several studies have shown that the process of learning a second language can, in turn, enhance metalinguistic awareness (Bialystok, 1997). The struggle to sort out differences between languages may cause bilingual children to think more deeply about language forms and functions.

Pragmatics

Simply speaking correct language forms is not enough to ensure communication. Children must use words, sounds, and sentences effectively to express ideas and get what they need. They must learn to persuade or argue with peers during a game, converse with adults at a family gathering, explain to a parent that a cherished possession was accidentally broken, or entertain siblings with a scary story. Each of these events requires a very different kind of communication. An argument with a peer may include long, flowing, expressive sentences, while an explanation to an angry parent will call for shorter, concise ones. Each situation is guided by different social rules. A discussion with a parent about a misdeed may require rigid adherence to turn-taking and politeness rules since it is usually best not to interrupt or be rude when a parent is angry. A holiday gathering may follow different rules. In many families, the turn-taking rule all but disappears as family members talk and joke all at the same time.

In the primary years, many of the basic social rules of language are acquired. (The social rules of language are called **pragmatics**—see Chapter 12.) Children learn that they must be polite when speaking with adults (Ladegaard, 2004). They say "thank you," make requests instead of demands, and use a pleasant tone when interacting with those in authority. In some languages—Lao and Japanese, for example—children must learn to use special "polite grammatical forms" in addressing adults (Haugh, 2007b; Klein & Chen, 2001).

Primary-age children are able to take turns when speaking to others (Bosch, Oostdijk, & Boves, 2005; Garvey, 1977). The egocentric monologues of the preschool years begin to disappear as children discover the two-way nature of conversations. Children of this age are quite competent at **referential communication**: the ability to adjust language to the view-point of the listener. They are less likely to nod or make gestures during a phone conversation (Hoff-Ginsberg, 1997). They use simpler language when talking to those who are younger (Weppelman, Bostow, Schiffer, Elbert-Perez, & Newman, 2003; Dunn & Kendrick, 1979) and reduce the complexity of their sentences when they realize that listeners cannot understand them (Warren-Leubecker & Bohannon, 2008).

Social rules of language vary, however, from one culture to another. In some communities, collective conversations are the norm. All participants speak spontaneously and simultaneously; turn-taking is not considered an important rule (Cekaite, 2007; Zamborlin, 2007). The rules for politeness vary across cultures. Japanese and Japanese American children are expected to be exceedingly polite in their conversations with anyone—both adults and peers (Haugh, 2007b; Yamamoto & Kubota, 1983). In many Native American and Alaskan Native families, politeness in language is related to the historically defined status of both the speaker and the listener. A very formal, polite style is required when children are speaking to high-status male elders, for example (Blanchard, 1983; Joe & Malach, 1998). In Kenya, polite, respectful interactions toward older siblings are required; older brothers and sisters, in turn, can scold and dominate younger family members. Middle-class American families do not expect children to speak to older siblings in these respectful ways. Bickering and equal-status interchanges are tolerated (B. B. Whiting & Edwards, 1988).

Pragmatics in School. An understanding of the social rules of language is especially important when children enter school. The social rules that govern conversations in the classroom are more numerous and more rigidly enforced than in the home. A number of common school language rules are presented in Table 16-2.

One rule that is common in schools in most cultures is that formal language should be used. Children may not use slang in the classroom, and standard language forms are required in all interactions, especially with teachers. Typical conversation used with peers in the neighborhood will not do, and children who do not speak formally may be corrected by the teacher and even other children.

Formal and informal language styles are referred to as *registers*. In the elementary years, children must learn **register switching**—that is, shifting back and forth between these two very different kinds of language. A child must quickly switch from slang or artful expression with peers on the school bus to correct standard forms in answer to a teacher's question during a math lesson. Switching registers is particularly challenging for children who speak different languages and for children who come from historically underrepresented groups.

Part of the formal language rule is turn-taking and structured conversation. Lessons in school generally are quite orderly: the teacher speaks, the students listen, and a brief time is devoted to questions and answers at the end (Cazden & Beck, 2003; Dickinson, 1985; Klein & Chen, 2001). Children must learn when they may speak and the appropriate ways to seek a turn, such as raising one's hand and waiting to be called on. Learning this rule is particularly challenging for children of cultures in which collective conversations are the norm.

pragmatics: The part of language that involves using words, sentences, and speech sounds to influence people and to accomplish things socially.

referential communication: The ability to adjust language to the viewpoint of the listener. Using simpler language to talk to a younger sibling is an example.

register switching: The ability to shift back and forth between two very different kinds of language (registers), such as between formal language and slang, depending on which is socially acceptable.

TABLE 16-2
Rules of Language Use Common in American Schools

Rule	Description
Formal language	Children are expected to speak standard English without slang or informal, artful expression.
Turn-taking	Children are required to take turns talking. Hand raising and answering questions only when asked are often expected.
Informing/explaining	Children are expected to provide clear, concise information without egocentric "meandering." A succinct, correct answer to questions is often expected.
Requests for information	Children are required to ask clear questions for information. Asking for clarification about assignments or for further explanation of a complex science concept are examples.
Sticking to the main topic	Children are often required to stick to a single topic when talking. Narratives must have a beginning, a middle, and an end.

Besides adopting an overall formal style of language in school, children must learn to use language to accomplish new purposes. A child is often expected to *explain* or *inform* with a great deal more clarity than was previously required. Giving a book report or an answer to a question in a science activity must be delivered in an organized, concise way. Egocentric ramblings, common in the preschool years, are now apt to result in correction: "Sandra, please tell us exactly what the book was about." Such concise dialogue is very difficult for children of some cultural groups. Whereas Americans tend to be very direct in their speech and "tell it like it is" (Klein & Chen, 2001), West Africans value conversation that meanders and digresses and consider succinct speech to be inelegant (Hale-Benson, 1986).

A particularly challenging form of explaining and informing is responding to right-answer questions (Heath, 1996; W. S. Hall, Bartlett, & Hughes, 1988). Parents and child care providers often ask preschoolers open-ended questions such as "What did you do in child care today?" or "What are you playing?" In school, teachers often ask children questions that have only one expected, correct answer (e.g., "What are the three ways that seeds travel from one place to another?"). These questions are not departure points for flowing discussion or open-ended conjecture. To be successful in school, the child must answer these directly, concisely, and accurately. Klein and Chen (2001) argue that this is primarily a Euro-American style of interaction. In some cultures, answering (or asking) single-answer questions is uncomfortable and is viewed as meaningless and inappropriate.

In addition to giving information and answering questions, children must also ask questions. However, question asking has a new purpose in the classroom. No longer do children make inquiries simply to have a curiosity satisfied or a need met. They now ask questions that are vital to school success, such as "Which page do we do for homework?" or "What is the fourth food group again? I forgot." Asking questions is more challenging than it appears since the child must understand the social rules for making inquiries in school: Be concise. Raise your hand. Ask at the right times. Don't interrupt the teacher. Further, the child must learn to phrase the question so that the teacher will know exactly what information is requested.

Children of some cultures use a "topic-chaining" structure in conversation. Euro-American teachers do not always understand or appreciate this artful language style.

Pragmatics, School, and Culture. Rules of language in school are shaped by the values and customs and the status and role assignments of teachers within a particular culture. Not all schools in the world require formal language. B. B. Whiting and Edwards (1988) observed less formal classrooms in Mexico and Okinawa. Their description of a teacher reading a poem in Juxtlahuaca, Mexico, shows that a turn-taking rule is not rigidly enforced:

> Before the teacher finishes, Alberto stands up on his bench, waves his hands, and shouts, "Me, teacher, me." The child who is next to him stands up and cries, "Me, teacher, me." Alberto, the other boy, and several others get up and run toward the teacher, surrounding him . . . so that he might give them a part of the poem. (p. 247)

As described in earlier sections, children from historically underrepresented groups in the United States may have more difficulty acquiring the pragmatics required for success in school. Conversations in typical classrooms in the United States reflect the communication styles of dominant culture (Cazden & Beck, 2003; Dickinson, 1985; Heath, 1996), so children who have learned very different rules of language use may be at a disadvantage. An example of this is the struggle with pragmatics that African American children often face in school. Hale-Benson (1986) contrasts typical school talk with the unique discourse styles of this cultural group. African American children often display an open-ended, artful, expressive style. They joke, tell stories, and even tease and argue in playful ways as they converse. Euro-American teachers sometimes view these modes of communication as inappropriate and even threatening. Playful teasing and arguments, for example, are considered disrespectful and immature.

One characteristic of typical African American discourse is a freedom to verbalize spontaneously. Atang (2004) illustrates this style by describing traditional African American church services. Throughout a typical service, there is much collective verbalization. Testimonials, singing, and welcoming new members are common. Those who "have the spirit" may shout out or move around. Such interactions are in sharp contrast, Lein (1975) notes, to classroom interactions, in which exceedingly long periods of silence are expected and only occasional constrained conversations are allowed. It is easy to see why children from families with such a spontaneous style of interaction would have great difficulty following the turn-taking rule in school.

Hale-Benson cites research suggesting that African American children's communication has a **topic chaining** structure (Michaels, 1980). Conversations flow freely from one subject to another. A single narrative might traverse many different topics that are loosely tied together. Conversations in Euro-American and Chinese communities, in contrast, are more often topic centered. A narrative is likely to have a single theme and a clearly identified beginning, middle, and end. Both conversational styles are expressive; neither is deficient (Jourdain, 2007; Wang & Leichtman, 2000).

Nevertheless, teachers in the United States sometimes view a topic chaining structure as a sign of disorganized thinking or poor communication skills (Hale-Benson, 1986). African American children's free-flowing style clashes with the structured, focused discussions in school. Some teachers vigorously train such children to be more concise and organized in their language and to stick to one topic. Hale-Benson tells of one teacher who tried to correct African American discourse style by implementing a new rule: children were allowed to speak about only one thing at a time during lessons. If they digressed, they were cut off. Needless to say, African American children had great difficulty adhering to this requirement.

Perhaps the most challenging school communication rule for children of some historically underrepresented groups is the formal language requirement. In the classroom, they must switch registers from the more casual, expressive style they use with peers and their family to one that is unfamiliar and unusually concise and conventional. Children who speak a different language or dialect are at a particular disadvantage. To such children, register switching is virtually learning a new language (Heath, 1996; Horton-Ikard & Miller, 2004)!

For example, a Spanish-speaking child who is just learning English may say, "He don't have a pencil." As described earlier, this is a step forward in language learning; at an earlier time, she may have said, "He no have a pencil." However, a teacher might misinterpret this utterance as informal speech or slang and, thus, a violation of the formal language rule. The teacher might respond, "No. We say it correctly in school. We say, 'He *doesn't* have a pencil.'" Likewise, when an African American child uses the rule-governed sentence "He be goin' to the store," the teacher might chastise him for being too casual in his speech.

Most educators have come to believe that helping children learn to switch registers is important for later school success. However, for many children the process takes time, patience, and empathy. Children who come from homes in which only the native language or dialect is spoken will have the greatest difficulty learning the standard English register (Heath, 1996).

Bilingual Education

The term **bilingual education** refers to a variety of strategies used in schools to assist children who speak languages different from that of the dominant culture. Bilingual education is used most often in North America to promote the learning of non-English-speaking children. However, concepts and principles of bilingual education have also been used to teach children who speak nonstandard English dialects, such as African American Vernacular English (Siegel, 2007).

Several models of bilingual education exist. One, called **immersion,** involves placing children who speak one language into a classroom in which a new, second language is spoken primarily. The expectation is that children will be motivated to learn the second language quickly so that they will be able to communicate with peers and teachers and succeed in school. Unfortunately, some immersion classrooms in the United States have been cynically dubbed "submersion" classrooms because children must "sink or swim" in language

topic chaining: A type of conversation, more common in some cultures, that flows freely from one subject to another and does not stick to a single theme or have a clear beginning, middle, and end.

bilingual education: A term used to refer to a variety of strategies used in schools to assist children who speak languages different from that of the dominant culture.

immersion model of bilingual education: A model of bilingual education in which children are taught almost exclusively in the language of the dominant society with the expectation that they will be motivated to learn the second language quickly.

learning without special support (Snow, 1987). Immersion may be professional jargon to mean that no meaningful assistance is given to non-English-speaking children in school. Many non-English-speaking children in America are simply placed in regular classrooms, where they fail to learn a second language well, do poorly in academic subjects, and drop out of school more often than their English-speaking peers (August & Hakuta, 1998; Torres-Guzman, 2007).

Other bilingual models are designed to enhance children's learning in their native language and, at the same time, help them acquire the language of the dominant culture. In the **maintenance/developmental model,** children are taught primarily in their native language so that they acquire the same important school-related skills and concepts as dominant-language children. At the same time, they are introduced to English as a second language (ESL). In one version of the model, children are enrolled in native-language classrooms throughout the primary years and are given special tutoring from ESL teachers.

The **two-way bilingual education model** is preferred by many educators not only because it promotes second-language learning but also because it promotes appreciation for all languages (Barnett et al., 2007). In this approach, both the dominant language and the second language are used equally in the instruction of all children. In one two-way bilingual primary program in New England, Latino children and English-speaking Euro-American children learn both Spanish and English together. Spanish is spoken during mathematics, science, and social studies instruction, and English is spoken during reading and writing. In another program, English is exclusively used on one day and Spanish on the next. Two-way bilingual programs have shown promise in facilitating second-language acquisition among all children, even those who speak the language of the dominant culture (Barnett et al., 2007).

Soto (2007) suggests that what is most important in bilingual education is the overall attitude toward languages that is conveyed in the classroom. She notes that some teachers assume a *subtractive* approach to language teaching, in which the goal is to replace a child's native language or dialect with that of the dominant culture. Research on Southeast Asian immigrant children in America shows the devastating effect of a subtractive model. Although many children were found to learn English quite well, they lost their ability to effectively communicate with their parents and family members (Fillmore, 2005). An *additive* approach is more culturally sensitive, Soto argues. In this approach, children add a new language but maintain and refine their native speaking abilities as well. The goal is to expand the child's linguistic repertoire.

Professionals can advocate for bilingual education programs in their own communities and at a national level. (See the Advocacy and Public Policy box in this chapter for ideas on how to elicit greater public support for such programs.)

Social Strategies in Bilingual Education. Regardless of the type of bilingual education provided, children who do not speak the dominant language of a community will experience a challenging period of transition when they enter school. They often engage in creative social strategies in an attempt to cope with the strangeness of the new classroom environment and to fit in with the dominant-culture peer group (August & Hakuta, 1998; Ellis, 2000; Fillmore, 2005). For example, they may pretend to understand what is being said around them even when they do not. They may smile and nod, join in a group activity, imitate peers, and utter a few simple words in an effort to make others think they can speak the dominant language.

Sometimes children stay close to dominant-culture friends and emulate their speech or behavior. They may assume that what is being said is related to the immediate situation and make guesses about the meanings of words spoken around them. The following story illustrates these coping strategies:

maintenance/developmental model of bilingual education: A model of bilingual education in which children are taught primarily in their native language so that they acquire important school-related skills while at the same time being introduced to English as a second language.

two-way model of bilingual education: A model of bilingual education, preferred by many educators, in which both the dominant language and the second language are used equally in instruction so that all children learn two languages.

ADVOCACY AND PUBLIC POLICY

Supporting Bilingual Education

This chapter discusses the importance of bilingual education for young children in the United States who are English language learners (ELLs)—those whose families' native languages are other than English. The majority of research studies show that bilingual education is effective (National Association for Bilingual Education, 2004). Not only do children in well-designed bilingual programs acquire English as well as or better than children in English-only programs, but they excel in academic subjects such as math and science. In 1974, the U.S. Supreme Court ruled in the landmark *Lau v. Nichols* case that school districts throughout the country must provide adequate services to ELLs. Although the Court did not mandate a particular kind of instructional approach, it identified bilingual education as one approved means of providing these required services to these students.

In spite of this, bilingual education is still under attack in some states. Subtle changes in state and federal laws have undermined the effectiveness of some bilingual programs. For example, the No Child Left Behind Act, discussed in Chapter 15, includes provisions that encourage the rapid teaching of English in order to meet yearly academic progress standards. The act emphasizes the learning of English but not the maintenance of children's native languages. These trends run counter to principles of effective bilingual teaching that include a relaxed pacing that is tailored to the unique language experiences of each child and that focus on competence in two languages, not just English (National Association for Bilingual Education, 2004).

Professionals must work diligently to educate the public and lawmakers about the effectiveness of bilingual programs that are additive (as described in this chapter)—that seek to *add* a new language while maintaining the home language. They can find support for their advocacy efforts from the National Association for Bilingual Education (http://www.nabe.org). This group organizes local, state, and national lobbying efforts to increase federal funding for bilingual programs and to oppose threats to bilingual education as they arise. It posts action alerts about key pieces of pending legislation related to bilingual education on its Website and advises members on advocacy activities. The group publishes a newsletter, two journals, and other articles and books on bilingual education that are helpful in letter-writing and lobbying efforts.

Thi Liên is a 7-year-old Vietnamese student who speaks very little English. She has enrolled in a classroom in which English is the dominant language. She has made a good friend, Jessica. Although the two cannot understand each other's language, they play well together and have become inseparable. As they walk hand in hand along the playground, Cedric approaches them:

THI LIÊN: (Smiles and nods, but says nothing)
JESSICA: (Speaking to Cedric) Know what? My tooth fell out last night.
CEDRIC: (Begins walking around a tire on the playground as she talks) So? Mine fall out all the time.
JESSICA: (Joins Cedric in walking around the tire and laughs) All the time?
THI LIÊN: (Walks on the tire, feigns a laugh) All the time! All the time....
JESSICA: (Picks up Thi Liên's chant) All the time....
CEDRIC: (Joins in the game, walking around the tire and chanting) All the time....

The children continue with the game for many minutes. Thi Liên later reports to her mother that she believes "all the time" is a game you play on the tires.

Thi Liên demonstrates a creative strategy for fitting in. She effectively seeks a common language in play even when she cannot understand the words of her peers. Through smiling, laughter, and playfulness, she has, in all likelihood, convinced her peers that she understands English.

Stages of Production in Bilingual Education. Not all children who are bilingual are as confident as Thi Liên in speaking. Those who have just entered a bilingual setting are often very quiet and reticent to speak. Over time, as children become familiar with teachers and peers, they advance through stages of vocalization or *production* of the second language (Ellis, 2000; H. Hernandez, 2001). In the **preproduction stage,** children in bilingual classrooms are quite silent; they focus on understanding the second language rather than trying to speak it. This is an important period. As they listen, children learn the second language and gradually gain confidence in their ability to speak it. At this early stage, teachers should refrain from asking children to talk since children's efforts to imitate words or phrases may actually inhibit language acquisition.

In the **transition to production stage,** children demonstrate a readiness to make brief verbalizations in the second language. Next, in the **early production stage,** these utterances become longer. Only when they reach the **expansion of production stage** are children able to speak in full sentences or respond in the second language to open-ended questions from teachers or peers. Even at this stage, teachers should not expect perfectly fluent verbal responses. The semantic, syntactical, and phonological features of the child's native language may affect second-language speech even into adulthood (Ellis, 2000). In the final stage, **introduction to written forms,** children show an interest in reading and writing in the second language. Until this point, children are usually encouraged to read and write in their native language. Literacy usually emerges first in the language of a child's own culture (Chamot & O'Malley, 1994; Fillmore, 2005).

LITERACY DEVELOPMENT

Primary-age children's literacy development resembles the process of their oral language learning. They actively construct an understanding of print as they strive for authentic communication. Their motivation for reading and writing—like talking—stems mainly from a desire to acquire meaning from others' writing and to communicate through their own. Most children of every culture will learn to read and write if they are encouraged by families and teachers and provided with a meaningful, print-rich environment.

Writing in the Primary Years

Many children have begun to write by the end of the preschool years. Their writing, which may be composed of scribbles or isolated letters, looks very different from adult text. Vertical lines across paper might represent a whole story, and letters of a child's name might stand for a letter to his or her family. Over time, children's writing looks more and more like adult manuscript or cursive. Chaotic scribbles give way to scribble writing, which runs from the top to the bottom of the page and from left to right, and eventually some letters are incorporated (Clay, 2001; Sulzby, 1995).

Not all children develop through these scribble stages at an early age. Those who have few opportunities to write or have not observed others writing may continue to scribble-write during the early elementary years. Most children of school age, however, have begun to use conventional letters in their writing. They are then likely to progress through three distinct writing stages before they write conventionally (Clay, 2001; Sulzby, 1995). These stages are summarized in Table 16-3.

preproduction stage: A stage of second-language learning in which children are quite silent in the classroom and focus on understanding the second language rather than trying to speak it.

transition to production stage: A stage in second-language learning in which children occasionally make brief verbalizations in the second language during classroom interactions.

early production stage: A stage of second-language learning in which children speak longer utterances in the second language in the classroom.

expansion of production stage: A stage of second-language learning in which children speak in full sentences and respond to open-ended questions in the second language, though with some disfluency.

introduction to written forms stage: A stage of second-language learning in which children speak in full sentences and show an interest in reading and writing in the second language.

TABLE 16-3
Stages of Writing Development in the Primary Years

Stage	Description
Prephonemic stage	Random letters are used to represent whole words or stories. The letters chosen have no relationship to the sounds in the story but are "placeholders for meaning."
Phonemic stage	Letters are used that match some of the sounds in the words or stories being written. A letter matching the beginning sound of a word might be used to represent that whole word (e.g., *p* for *people*).
Transitional stage	The child spells out words using correct letter sounds. However, writing contains much "invented spelling" in which conventions are not followed. For example, the silent *e* is often omitted, as in *mak* for *make*.
Conventional writing	Some children begin writing as adults do during the primary years, using correct spellings and other writing conventions.

Prephonemic Stage. Children who still write using random letters to stand for stories are said to be in the **prephonemic stage of writing.** An example of a prephonemic composition is presented in Figure 16-2.

The child who wrote the story read and reread the text many times over a 4-month period: "Once there were some naughty girls who stole cookies from their friends." The story remained roughly the same on each rereading, suggesting that the letters now represent a permanent idea in the child's mind. However, as can be seen in the figure, the letters have no relationship to the sounds of phonemes in the story. Letters are used merely as "placeholders for meaning" (Temple, Nathan, Burris, & Temple, 1988).

Phonemic Stage. Gradually children enter the **phonemic stage,** in which they begin using consonants that match some of the sounds in the story they are writing; for example, *Bb* might be used to represent *baby*. Often only one or two consonants are used to stand for a complete word. An example of a phonemic composition is presented in Figure 16-3. The text reads, "Dorothy and the Wizard of Oz." For the first time, the child is showing an understanding that letters represent specific phonemes. Children who are encouraged to write independently in the phonemic stage show advancement in a variety of reading abilities—phonological awareness, word identification, and word comprehension (Craig, 2006). This is likely because they focus so intensely on the sounds of letters and letter combinations as they write in this way.

prephonemic stage of writing: A stage of writing in which children use random letters to stand for stories or messages, with no relationship between a letter chosen and the sounds of specific phonemes.

phonemic stage: A stage of writing in which children use consonants that match some of the sounds in the story they are writing.

FIGURE 16-2 Example of a child's prephonemic writing. The child uses conventional letters selected at random to represent ideas.

DOTHE
AD
THEWSR
OVoz

FIGURE 16-3 The child has written "Dorothy and the Wizard of Oz." This young author, who is in the phonemic stage, is now aware of the sounds that letters make and incorporates these into stories and messages.

Transitional Stage. Most children eventually enter a **transitional stage** in which their writing becomes very conventional. During this period, they spell out words using letter sounds and write in full sentences. There are misspellings, though these are often logical errors (K. Young, 2007). For example, the word *make* might be spelled *mak* since the final *e* is silent and seems unnecessary to convey meaning. Because of the creative aspect of constructing words, the phrase "invented spelling" has been used to describe this characteristic of children's writing. Invented spelling has been found to contribute to conventional reading and writing in later childhood (Craig, 2006).

One interesting advancement that occurs during the transitional stage is that children discover that breaks between words must somehow be marked. Children use ingenious methods for doing this. One child began using a heavy dot between words (Sulzby, 1995), while another turned the last letter of each word backward (Pflaum, 1986). A sample of writing in the transitional stage is presented in Figure 16-4.

Many children begin conventional writing during second or third grade. Their writing still contains errors in spelling at this age. Children who have been encouraged to write without anxiety over correct form or spelling often become immensely talented authors in the primary years (Clay, 2001).

Promoting Children's Writing in the Primary Years. Until this point, children's spontaneous creative writing has been discussed—that is, the stages children go through as they create stories, poems, letters, and reports on their own. What role does direct instruction play in learning to write? In what ways do lessons in spelling and handwriting contribute to children's overall writing competence? This is a subject of great debate. Many believe that too great an emphasis on spelling or forming letters in a certain way will impede the writing process. However, research suggests that some teacher guidance in learning to make letters or spell words is helpful as long as this does not inhibit children's true writing (Neuman et al., 1999).

During an editing session, a teacher might show a first-grader how to make a *d* so that others in the class are better able to read her work. Another child might be guided in creating his own personal spelling list of words that he uses often and wishes to remember. Letter and spelling games might be planned. These activities are not useful, however, if they involve simplistic memorization (e.g., the rote spelling out of new words). Children can be encouraged to think and talk about the spellings of words they are wishing to write. In one study, children as young as 6 were found to use at least six different reflective strategies to recall how to spell words, including making analogies to other words and trial-and-error

transitional stage of writing: A stage in writing in which children compose stories or messages in a more conventional way and creative attempts are made to spell out words relying on letter sounds, using "invented spelling."

To mom
i have went away
i wel rome
Bac wen you
go to the mol Let me
Love
Benjamin

FIGURE 16-4 A child has written an angry note to his mother because she would not allow him to go to the mall. His writing is beginning to look conventional. Invented spelling is evident.

experimentation (Rittle-Johnson & Siegler, 1999). Most believe that lessons on isolated writing skills should be made meaningful and active and, whenever possible, connected to children's authentic written work.

A number of specific classroom strategies have been found effective in promoting writing development in the primary classroom (Calkins, 2003; Graves, 2003; Neuman et al., 1999; Dickinson & Neuman, 2006):

1. *Encouraging children to write independently and to use "invented spelling" when unsure of words.* Teachers should provide many opportunities for children to write on their own. When they have difficulty with certain words, teachers should encourage them to "try to write it all by yourself," allowing logical "errors" in spelling. (Contrary to popular wisdom, this strategy has not been found to lead to poor spelling habits later in life. In fact, it has been found to enhance reading and writing ability.)

2. *Creating a writing center.* Teachers can design a special space in the classroom for independent writing. This should include multiple materials for composing—pens, markers, pencils, and a computer, along with lined and unlined paper, blank books, photocopies of children's books with text removed, clipboards, and other innovative materials.

3. *Journaling.* Teachers can provide individual journals for children to write in throughout the school year. They can provide time for children to write in these about events in their daily lives. Sometimes teachers might guide children in writing responses in their journals to a piece of children's literature or a special classroom activity. Periodically, children can be encouraged to read entries from their journals to others in the class.

4. *Establishing a writing workshop.* Teachers can plan a time when all children in a class write together. This might include writing in journals or composing stories or

poems. During this workshop, teachers can conduct *mini-lessons*—brief demonstrations of writing strategies, such as punctuation or grammar. Teachers can also meet with individual children during this time to help them revise, edit, and proofread as well as discuss the content of their compositions. The workshop might culminate in an *author's chair* activity in which several children take a turn reading aloud from their work and receiving suggestions and feedback from peers.

5. **Writing across the curriculum.** Teachers should integrate writing into any curriculum area or any space in the room. Children might write the results of a science experiment in a science journal, compose a play in the drama center, or write reports for a history unit. Children are, thus, encouraged to write in many different forms: stories, informational reports, poems, informal notes, or persuasive letters.

Reading Development

Reading development and writing development are highly interrelated. As children write, they learn to read and vice versa. Among the earliest reading materials are children's own written stories. Children of many cultures also read picture books. As they are read to or as they look at books, children construct understandings of print. Sulzby (1995) has described stages of storybook reading through which most primary-grade children develop. These are summarized in Table 16-4.

Picture-Governed Reading. Children begin reading books by studying the pictures and disregarding print. They point to or name persons or objects that are depicted. They do not, in this early period, tell a coherent story from the book. Their "reading" behaviors are disjointed comments about illustrations. Sulzby (1995) called this the **story not formed stage.**

Somewhat later, children who are read to or have much experience with books will tell a full story as they look at the pictures and turn the pages. Their intonation is that of a storyteller. Their stories approximate events in the actual story. Sulzby named this the **story formed stage.** In the **written language-like stage,** children begin to "read" the story by heart. Their retellings match the actual text, and their intonation is so similar to that of an adult reader that parents or teachers may believe they are actually reading.

During this period, children may begin to notice and comment on print and may map the story over a portion of print. A child studying the title of the book *The Very Hungry Caterpillar* (Carle, 1969) was observed pointing to each word and trying to read the title. She would begin by saying "The" and pointing to the word *The*. (So far, so good.) She would next say the syllable "Ver" and point to *Very* and then say "ry" and point to *Hungry*. When she pronounced the syllable "Hun" and pointed to the word *Caterpillar*, she was out of words and quite confused (Schickedanz, 1982). Such puzzlements stimulate children's interest in how print works and move them toward a major advancement in reading development, *print-governed reading*.

Print-Governed Reading. Once children are aware of and curious about print, their reading responses change significantly. Their reading behaviors now center on the text. In the **print watched/refusal to read and aspectual stage,** children show early conventional reading competence. Refusal to read refers to the child's initial reluctance to use words in reading stories. A child might say, "I don't know the words, but I do know the pictures." This period of doubt gives way to aspectual reading, in which the child selects just one aspect of the reading act—perhaps the memory of certain words or phonics—and uses this strategy exclusively in reading the text.

story not formed stage of reading: A stage of reading in which children point to or name illustrations but do not tell a coherent story as they look at a book.

story formed stage of reading: A stage of reading in which children tell a full story as they look at books, using an intonation of a storyteller and sharing events that approximate events in the actual story.

written language-like stage of reading: A stage of reading in which children "read" a story by heart, with their retellings precisely matching the actual text.

print watched/refusal to read and aspectual stage of reading: A stage of reading in which children initially refuse to read, preferring to listen to adults, but eventually read on their own, relying on only one reading strategy—perhaps the memory of certain words or phonics.

TABLE 16-4
Stages of Storybook Reading

Stage	Description
Picture-Governed Reading	
Story not formed stage	Children point to and make comments about illustrations. No coherent story is told.
Story formed stage	Children tell a story as they point to illustrations and turn pages. The story often resembles the actual story line of the book.
Written language-like stage	Children "read" a storybook by heart. Their retellings match the actual text. Their reading intonations often resemble those of adult readers.
Print-Governed Reading	
Print watched/refusal to read and aspectual stage	Children begin to point to and study the print as adults read. They are often reluctant to read themselves, preferring to observe the reading process. If they do read independently, they rely on just one aspect of reading, such as phonics or sight vocabulary, to construct meaning from print.
Print watched/holistic stage	Children study print and begin to apply multiple reading strategies in order to construct story meaning. They may use phonics, sight vocabulary, and sentence context. Sometimes these strategies are out of balance in that the child relies more heavily on one strategy than another.
Independent reading stage	Children are able to read storybooks independently using a variety of reading strategies, including phonics, sentence context, and sight vocabulary. They are able to coordinate these strategies and select those that are appropriate for a particular text.

This is the period when some primary-grade children laboriously sound out letters without attending to whole words or sentences. Others rely only on whole-word vocabulary and never pay attention to phonics. The following is an example of aspectual reading:

A 6-year-old child with a preference for phonics reading moves along a shelf at a grocery store, sounding out labels of products. He comes to a box of baking soda. He struggles to sound out the letters of the words on the label: "B-A-K-I-N-G." His phonetic reading does not make sense; he has never heard of such a word.

"I give up on that one," he announces to his mother. Then, as an afterthought, he holds the box toward her and asks, "Do you need any baking soda?"

The child in the story is so committed to phonics in reading that he is unable to take advantage of clues from the environment to help decipher a product label. The tendency to center on just one reading strategy is common in early reading development. The particular strategy that a child selects to read may be related to previous experience with print and the method of early reading instruction in school. Children taught phonics, for example, may rely heavily on phonics in reading.

Sulzby (1995) observed that children eventually enter a **print watched/holistic stage** in which they use multiple reading strategies—sight vocabulary, sentence context, and phonics—to acquire meaning from print. Early in this stage, children are somewhat imbalanced in their use of strategies, however. For example, they may still rely mostly on phonics but fall back on context clues or sight vocabulary if this initial strategy does not work. Near the end of the primary years, most children have entered the **independent reading stage,** in which they are able to apply on their own the particular reading strategies that are most helpful for a certain text. A child who cannot sound out a word will quickly reread the whole sentence in order to acquire context clues, for example. Not all children reach this final stage. Intellectual, emotional, family, and school factors will determine adult reading competence.

Promoting Children's Reading in the Primary Years. What is the best way to guide primary-age children through these stages of reading development? A traditional approach was to isolate and teach reading skills directly. Long ago, flash cards were used to enhance sight vocabulary. Context strategies were taught by presenting children with sentences that had missing words. Phonics drill was common. There are very few educators today, however, who believe that reading can be taught in complete isolation of real literature. Most acknowledge that children need to read and be read to for literacy abilities to emerge (Lane & Wright, 2007). Research shows that an ability to comprehend stories and other texts—those that children read and those that are read to them—predicts later reading ability (Booth, MacWhinney, & Harasaki, 2000).

Primary-grade educators do teach specific reading skills, particularly phonics (Stahl, 1992). Studies suggest that instruction in phonics and phonemic awareness enhance reading ability, particularly for those at risk of school failure (Hatcher, Hulme, & Snowling, 2004; Pennington & Lefly, 2001). However, this does not need to include isolated drills. Teaching about sounds, letters, and words can be carried out while reading high-quality literature to children. Games, rhymes, songs, and other activities can teach specific competencies in a playful, active way. Research suggests that a "balanced" approach, which includes both authentic story reading and direct instruction, is most beneficial for children (Pressley, 2005).

Several specific classroom strategies have been found effective in promoting reading development in the primary years (Clay, 2005; McGee & Richgels, 2007; Reutzel & Morrow, 2007; Pressley, 2005):

1. *Reading daily to children, selecting books that provide increasing challenges.* Teachers should read books to children that are both engaging and that continually expand their knowledge of print and story. "Big books" allow children in a group to better see print and illustrations. As children become better readers, teachers should choose books that have increasingly dense text, less repetition, some new and unique words, and more complex plots in order to expand children's literacy understanding.
2. *Encouraging independent reading.* Teachers should provide a wide variety of text types (e.g., high-quality fiction, informational books, poetry) that children may choose from to read independently. Teachers can create a class library for children to visit daily. Books related to various subject areas can be included in all areas of the classroom— the science center, the art area, and even the playground. A silent reading time should be planned when all in the class—including the teacher—read their own books.

print watched/holistic stage of reading: A stage of reading in which children use multiple reading strategies—sight vocabulary, sentence context, and phonics—to acquire meaning from print, though they still rely most on one main strategy, such as phonics.

independent reading stage: A stage of reading in which children are able to apply the particular reading strategies that are most helpful for a certain text and can switch from one strategy to another until they successfully interpret the message.

3. *Implementing guided reading.* Teachers can implement an approach that was originally designed to support children who are experiencing reading difficulties. In this method, the teacher meets with small groups of children to read together a book that is carefully selected for its difficulty level and interest. The teacher *talks through* the book with children first, asking questions about the title, pointing out new words within the text, and discussing the illustrations on each page. Children follow along with their own copy. Eventually, the teacher reads the book to the children, then encourages them to read it independently. They do so quietly but aloud so that the teacher can listen for *points of difficulty*—places where an individual is struggling with the text. When such points occur, the teacher suggests strategies to assist the child in solving reading problems independently.

4. *Demonstrating and modeling strategies for decoding words.* In groups or with in-dividual students, teachers can model specific strategies to use when comprehension breaks down. Teachers might demonstrate the use of phonics strategies, such as recalling a short vowel sound, when this helps a child decode a word. They might teach a sentence context strategy in which they ask the child to read the full sentence or even look at illustrations to guess what an unknown word might be. Many teachers choose to teach these strategies as they come up in real reading situations (e.g., as a child in a guided reading group or during independent reading struggles to decipher a word in a story). Others conduct formal lessons in which they systematically teach all readings skills. Both approaches appear to contribute to reading development.

5. *Introducing new words, building a sight vocabulary.* Teachers can introduce new words in order to promote children's *sight vocabulary*—the collection of words that they can recognize instantly. This can be done informally as teachers read to children. When challenging words come up, the teacher can point them out and define and discuss them. As children read independently, they will come upon common words that they can't recall. The teacher might prompt them to remem-ber these words by defining them and pointing out their letters. More formal methods are used for building sight vocabulary. Teachers may include a *word wall* in the classroom on which are posted the words that both teachers and children select to be remembered. They may engage children in in-depth word studies and *make-a-word* activities, in which similarities in words are studied or words are sorted into families.

6. *Facilitating "grand conversations" about books.* Regardless of the reading skills to be taught in a classroom reading experience, a focus should always be on the content of the reading material. Effort should be made to engage children in "grand conversations" (McGee & Richgels, 2007, p. 264) about what has been read. Such conversations are those that stem from children's comments and questions rather than the teacher's. Almost any reading experience should include the question, "Who has something to say about the story?"

Literacy and Culture

Children of different cultures show distinct aptitudes for and dispositions toward literacy. In a small number of cultures in the world, reading and writing do not exist. Some Aboriginal groups in Australia, for example, have never used a written language (Reynolds, 2001). Literacy is important in most societies, although what is written and read and how literacy is taught vary significantly.

Research on the home literacy environments of African American children illustrates these ideas. Children of low-income African American families have been found to read books less often than children of other groups (Flood, Heath, & Lapp, 1997; Washington, 2002). These families do read but primarily as a source of information. Parents and grandparents read mail, newspapers, magazines, funeral announcements, catalogs, and telephone books. They less often read for recreation.

Storytelling, joking, and music are more highly valued by many African American families. Some parents tell stories to their children more often than they read to them (Hale-Benson, 1986; Mainess, Champion, & McCabe, 2002). Neighbors may gather on front porches to share events in the community, relate family experiences, or discuss disputes with their landlords (Heath, 1988). In this cultural group, artful expression replaces written fiction as an outlet for imagination.

Does this mean that these children are deprived of literacy experiences in the home? One study shows that this is not the case (Pellegrini et al., 1990). In this research, African American parents living in poverty were found to help their children learn to read and write but in different ways than middle-class, Euro-American parents do. In the study, mothers were observed reading to their children in the home. When reading **narrative books**—typical picture books with story lines—they were found to engage in fewer strategies for teaching literacy. Rarely did they ask questions, label illustrations, or summarize plotlines, as middle-class, Euro-American mothers typically do. Taken alone, this finding would suggest that children of these families are not well supported in their literacy development.

However, when these mothers read **expository books**—books containing illustrations and written labels without a plotline—they were as active as middle-class mothers in teaching literacy to their children. The following example, drawn from this research (Pellegrini et al., 1990), illustrates some teaching strategies these mothers used:

MOTHER: (Pointing to text) Chimpanzee.
CHILD: Ooo yeah. Can I see?
MOTHER: What's this? (Points to an illustration of a kitchen sink)
CHILD: Sink. Do that one now.
MOTHER: That's yellow. (Points to boots)
CHILD: My pants are yellow.

Why does reading material make a difference in parent–child literacy interactions? One explanation may be that expository books more closely resemble the kinds of factual reading material—catalogs or church bulletins—that are frequently read within this cultural group. In addition, parents may feel more comfortable with expository text, believing this is the kind of reading that is most important within their own culture. The reading of expository books, which involves naming and discussing illustrations, may be more social and active and more closely match the expressive, interpersonal orientation of many African American families (Hale-Benson, 1986). Similar findings have been reported in studies of Latino mothers and children (Stowe, 2007).

What are the educational implications of research on cultural differences in reading and writing? Literacy programs can be broadened in schools to include all kinds of reading and writing material—magazines, newspapers, catalogs, nonprint books, posters, notes, and fliers as well as books. In addition, storytelling, humor, rhyming, chants, singing, and other modes of self-expression can be incorporated.

Biliteracy

Bilingual children must acquire **biliteracy**—an ability to read and write in two languages. A myth has been that bilingual children take much longer to learn reading and writing.

narrative books: Typical picture books with story lines that may be more familiar to children and families of middle-class, Euro-American backgrounds.

expository books: Books containing illustrations and written labels, without a plotline, that resemble the kind of factual reading that is more common in families of some historically underrepresented groups.

biliteracy: The ability to read and write in two languages.

Once children from bilingual families have learned to speak a second language, they have the additional challenge of learning to read and write in it as well.

Actually, they acquire literacy in their native language at about the same rate as monolingual children and follow roughly the same process (Hough & Nurss, 1992). What takes time is learning written communication in a language that is very different from that spoken in the home. The child's native language and that of the dominant culture may follow very different oral and graphic rules. It is quite remarkable that children acquire second-language literacy as quickly as they do!

Most experts believe that biliteracy begins with the acquisition of verbal skills and early print awareness *within one's native language*. Literacy abilities that children acquire in their own language have been found to help them when they eventually begin to read or write in a second one (Cárdenas-Hagan, Carlson, & Pollard-Durodola, 2007). A next step is the acquisition of *oral* proficiency in the second language. Being able to speak a language to some degree, before trying to read it, makes a great deal of sense. A Spanish-speaking child, for example, would find it very challenging to learn to read or write in English without a solid understanding of this new language. How could she write a coherent English story until she learned to form the article *a*, which does not exist in Spanish? How could she sound out an English word that contained a *v* until she learned the English sound this letter makes (in Spanish, *v* is pronounced "b")? The majority of bilingual education programs stress bilingualism *before* biliteracy.

Only when children acquire a moderate level of bilingualism do most teachers begin to promote reading and writing in the second language. At this point, many challenges still arise. Children may continue to apply the rules of their native language when reading second-language print, as the following example highlights:

> A third-grade child is reading aloud to a teacher. The text he is reading says, "The old man didn't have enough money for dinner." The child reads it this way: "The old man not have enough money for dinner." The teacher says, "Not quite. Try reading it again." The child reads the passage the same way he did before. "Nope," the teacher responds. "Look at this word carefully." He points to the word *didn't* and asks, "What does that say?" The child responds, "Didn't. Oh. I got it now. The old man didn't not have enough money for dinner." He smiles proudly at his teacher.

Why does the child read this way? While he is reading English, he is still applying Spanish language rules. The teacher's efforts to correct him are unsuccessful.

With experience, children begin to note distinctions between rules of their own language and those of a second language. As they do so, they gradually begin to read and write in the new language more conventionally. One advancement that assists in this process is metalinguistic awareness (Bialystok, 2007; Mertz & Yovel, 2004). Although children learning a new language face many challenges in reading and writing, one advantage they have over monolingual children is their ability to think about language itself. This comes from their daily experience of having to listen to and try to separate the rules of two languages. They can think about words and sounds more deeply, and this aids them in acquiring literacy (Bialystok, 2007).

CLASSROOM ADAPTATIONS: LANGUAGE, LITERACY, AND CHILDREN WITH SPECIAL NEEDS

Children with challenging conditions sometimes have language and literacy delays. Throughout this chapter, atypical patterns of language development have been described and strategies proposed for remediation. Teachers are advised to work closely with speech and language pathologists, special educators, and other professionals in addressing the specific language and literacy needs of individual children. A primary teacher's first step is to identify children with language and literacy problems through informal assessment in the classroom (R. B. Lewis & Doorlag, 2005). Listening carefully to the oral language of students is critical. Teachers can audiotape conversations with those for whom they have special concern, later analyzing the tapes in the areas of phonology, semantics, syntax, and pragmatics. Once a referral is made to a speech and language pathologist, a more in-depth evaluation may be conducted. The *Goldman-Fristoe Test of Articulation* (Goldman & Fristoe, 1986) is sometimes used by speech and language pathologists to assess phonology. Syntax, semantics, and phonology may be analyzed using the *Test of Language Development-Primary* (Newcomer & Hammil, 1997).

Literacy growth also can be assessed informally by teachers. As they observe children engaging in reading and writing activities in the classroom, teachers might ask: Do students read and write often? Have they reached the phonemic or transitional stage in their writing (as described in this chapter)? Do they choose to write at all? What is the difficulty level of the books they choose to read? Can they read books that have been written specifically for their age group? Do they show an understanding of what they have read? Do they demonstrate multiple strategies in their reading—phonics, sentence context, and sight vocabulary? Do they display enthusiasm for reading and writing? Teachers may identify some children who have general cognitive delays that impair reading as well as other academic abilities. They may also find that some students have a **specific learning disability in reading.** This is a challenging condition in which children show academic difficulty only in one area—learning to read. The following are key indicators of this exceptionality (Cass & Maddux, 2005; R. B. Lewis & Doorlag, 2005):

1. The child communicates very well orally but reads and writes far below grade level.
2. The child performs well on academic tasks that do not require reading, such as using manipulatives to solve a math problem.
3. The child regularly confuses letters that are similar, such as *d* and *b*.
4. The child regularly confuses similar-looking words, such as *was* and *saw*.
5. The child makes hasty and inaccurate guesses about words when reading without applying any decoding strategies.

When language, reading, or writing difficulties are identified, what strategies can be employed to address them in the classroom? Intensive one-on-one intervention by a

specific learning disability in reading: A challenging condition in which children who show competence in all other academic areas have difficulty learning to read.

professional is sometimes recommended. For example, a tutor may be assigned to instruct a child in a specific language or literacy skill. A more integrated method in which a teacher administers an intervention as part of the natural, day-to-day activities of the classroom has been advocated by some specialists (Guthrie et al., 1998; Hiebert & Raphael, 1996). The following story illustrates this approach:

A 7-year-old, Magda, is delayed in her oral language development. She shows difficulty in pronouncing a number of speech sounds, such as *s,* and has trouble retrieving words. She also is having difficulty learning to read. Working closely with a speech and language pathologist and a special educator, Ms. Schiller, her teacher, plans a special activity for all children in her class during morning group time.

MS. SCHILLER: (Holding up a copy of the classic children's book *Caps for Sale*) Look at this cover. What do you think this book is about?

RAYMOND: (Points) It's about that guy! Look, he's wearing funny clothes.

MS. SCHILLER: Right, he is. Clothes from long ago.

MAGDA: (Points) And he's... he's... got those, uh... those things.

MS. SCHILLER: These? What are these called?

MAGDA: I... don't...

MS. SCHILLER: They're *caps*. Have you heard that word? (Emphasizes the *s* sound in her words) Lots and lots of caps. Look at all the colors! Red caps and blue caps...

TAMIKA: (Points) Black ones!

MS. SCHILLER: Right. They're sort of black, aren't they? They're checkered caps.

MAGDA: Checkered caps.

After further discussion, Ms. Schiller reads to the children, then asks them to use their own copies of the book to dramatize the story. She announces that she will be the narrator and asks Magda to read the part of the peddler and all the other children to be monkeys.

MAGDA: (Playing her role, reading the part of the peddler) Cap, cap for sale...

MS. SCHILLER: Great! Caps-s-s-s for sale! Remember how you make that sound hiss? Caps-s-s-s!

MAGDA: (In a more dramatic intonation) Caps-s-s-s for sale!

The dramatization continues; they come to the part in the story where the monkeys have stolen the peddler's caps.

MAGDA: (Reading) You monkey you!

MS. SCHILLER: Right! You monkeys-s-s-s you!

MAGDA: Monkeys-s-s-s! Give me back my caps!

MS. SCHILLER: And what do the monkeys all say?

ALL CHILDREN: (In unison) Ts-s-s-s-s!

MS. SCHILLER: Isn't that funny? Let's all make that noise, Ts-s-s!

ALL CHILDREN
(INCLUDING MAGDA): Ts-s-s-s-s!

Later that day, the speech and language pathologist, who has been unsuccessful in helping Magda speak the *s* sound, listens in amazement as Magda, on the playground, calls out in clear articulation, to no one in particular, "Caps-s-s-s, caps-s-s-s for sale!"

This vignette illustrates the key elements of a naturalistic intervention technique. The teacher involves all children in the class in an activity; she does not isolate the child with special needs. She addresses several different language and literacy skills within a single, meaningful experience. She selects a story to dramatize that contains sounds Magda and her speech and language pathologist are working on. She takes time in her teaching to emphasize one of these sounds, *s,* and also to quickly teach some new words, *caps* and *checkered.* She supports Magda's reading by selecting a book with simple, repetitive text—a picture book. She prepares Magda for reading by conducting an engaging discussion of the book's cover and creates a motivation for Magda to read by organizing a playful dramatization. Such activities are more authentic and, many believe, more effective than isolated lessons (Hiebert & Raphael, 1996).

suprasegmental aspects of a story: The pacing, pitch, volume, and other modulations of voice that a storyteller uses to make a story exciting.

CHILD GUIDANCE: *Encouraging Children to Tell Stories*

"Once upon a time there was a tiger-man, who was partly a tiger and partly a man. He was like a super human man, and he had special powers. And he lived in the deep, dark forest in a house. It was a ranch house. Not a ranch like with horses, but you know that kind of house? And one day he walked and walked and walked into the jungle and started his adventures."

Thus begins the story of a creative 6-year-old, told to his classmates in a storytelling session in school. Storytelling—the verbal sharing of a tale—contributes uniquely to children's language and literacy development. When children tell or are told stories, they must use their imaginations fully because they have no illustrations, text, or other visual cues to rely on. For example, the tiger-man in the story must be created completely within the child's mind. Storytelling is an important art form in many cultures. In Native American families, for example, storytelling is not only a common form of recreation but also a method of maintaining cultural history and of socializing children (Fiese et al., 1999; Klein & Chen, 2001). Children of some historically underrepresented groups may be more comfortable expressing themselves in a performance-based, storytelling format than in writing (Hale & Franklin, 2001). Sharing tales without books helps children focus on the **suprasegmental aspects of a story**—the pacing, pitch, volume, and other modulations of voice that make a story exciting (Reich, 1986). Storytelling contributes to children's understanding of story structure and genre. In this example, the child shows an understanding of how a traditional fairy tale begins ("Once upon a time . . . ").

Storytelling can be initiated in the classroom in several ways:

1. **Modeling storytelling.** Periodically, during story time, teachers can tell stories rather than read books to children. When doing so, they should use dramatic voices and gestures. Different kinds of tales can be shared—folktales from around the world, fairy tales, and tall tales. Some stories should be told spontaneously to show children the joy of improvising. Teachers might occasionally use storytelling props—a flannel board and cutouts, puppets, or hats.

2. **Collective storytelling sessions.** During group times, teachers can guide children in telling collective stories. Initially, these sessions might be structured. A teacher might begin a story by introducing characters and a plot and then let each child take a turn adding something new to the tale. Eventually, one or a small number of children can share stories spontaneously. They might be encouraged to use storytelling props, such as the flannel board, as they tell their tales.

3. **Storytelling center.** Teachers can create a special center for storytelling that children can visit during free-choice time. This might be located in or near the book center. Here, children can be encouraged to tell stories informally to one another. A variety of materials can be included to promote this:

- A flannel board and cutouts (some related to familiar stories the teacher has shared)
- A simple tape recorder for children to use in recording and playing back their stories
- A full mirror to allow children to watch themselves as they tell stories
- Puppets (some related to familiar stories)
- Hats, coats, or other dress-up items
- A story circle, created on the floor with tape or fashioned from cushions, pillows, or chairs, where storytellers can gather
- Musical instruments to add sound effects or songs to stories (In a classroom I visited in Puerto Rico, a teacher combined the music and storytelling centers. This became the site of many elaborate performances.)

SUMMARY

In the primary years, children have already learned most of the rules of oral language. However, there are many refinements in phonology, semantics, and syntax during this developmental period. These areas of language are affected by culture and the number of languages a child is learning. Those learning two or more languages simultaneously face the special challenge of separating out distinctly different sets of linguistic rules. The emergence of metalinguistic awareness—the ability to think about language itself—supports first- and second-language learning. Children who can think and talk about sounds, word meanings, and sentence structure can acquire complex linguistic rules more readily. A significant advancement in pragmatics in the primary years is learning the social rules of language in school and in other contexts. Children learn register switching—the ability to use different language styles, depending on where they are and to whom they are speaking. Each culture has unique social rules for language, making it difficult for children of some backgrounds to learn the pragmatics of school. Well-designed bilingual programs can help children in the primary grades acquire these various aspects of language.

Children learn to read and write in a conventional way in the primary years, following predictable stages. Specific teaching methods can promote this learning. Literacy development is influenced by culture and the number of languages a child is learning. Children with special needs require extra support in learning to speak, read, and write. Teachers, collaborating with parents, speech and language pathologists, and other professionals, can provide informal interventions within the regular classroom.

RESEARCH INTO PRACTICE

CRITICAL CONCEPT 1

Most of the rules of one's native language are learned by the primary years. Minor refinements occur in the structural aspects of speech—phonology, syntax, and semantics. Metalinguistic awareness—the ability to think about language—is acquired during this period and assists children in language learning.

Application #1   Oral language learning should continue to be a major goal in primary classrooms. Include language-rich activities that allow students to refine their speech sounds, vocabulary, and sentence structure. Storytelling, report giving, open-ended sharing time, and informal social interactions with peers are examples.

Application #2   Promote metalinguistic awareness by guiding children in thinking and talking about their own language. Engage children in discussions about words that rhyme or have dual meanings and the distinct sounds and syllables in poetry, stories, songs, and everyday conversation. Play games in which children identify utterances that are grammatically incorrect or illogical.

CRITICAL CONCEPT 2

A primary area of language growth in the primary years is pragmatics. Children acquire a sophisticated understanding of social uses of language, including the conventions for talking in school. Most children discover that there are certain ways to ask for help, answer questions, or seek information from a teacher that will lead to academic success. They come to understand that, in many classrooms, only formal language is acceptable.

Application #1   A focus of oral language teaching in the primary years should be on pragmatics. Provide children with opportunities to speak in diverse contexts in which varying social rules apply. Encourage them to engage in playful conversations with peers on the playground or in the dramatic play area. Plan experiences for children to talk in whole-group settings. Create cooperative learning projects to help children learn to persuade one another, negotiate, and exchange ideas. Each of these settings will require that children learn a unique set of social language rules.

Application #2   Provide whole-group experiences that give children practice in using different kinds of discourse. Invite children to tell stories or relate events in their lives. Encourage them to present formal reports and give them opportunities to ask and answer questions of you and of their peers. These experiences will assist children in learning the conventions of *school talk*.

CRITICAL CONCEPT 3

Different cultural groups have distinct rules for social language. The styles of discourse of some cultural groups may clash with rules of conversation often required in school. Topic chaining and collective styles of verbal interaction, for example, may not adhere to the rules for orderly conversations emphasized in the classroom. Informal, nonstandard speech styles used in the neighborhood may be viewed as inappropriate by some teachers in American schools. Children of historically underrepresented cultures, then, will find school pragmatics particularly challenging to learn.

Application #1 Provide primary-age children with opportunities to learn the social rules of school while refining their own native discourse patterns. Offer them experiences in giving reports, taking turns talking, and asking questions to seek information in order to promote conventional school talk. At the same time, encourage them to tell stories, provide open-ended accounts of life events, dramatize, and engage in collective conversation using the discourse styles of their own cultures.

Application #2 Introduce children to the concept of register switching—the ability to change one's language based on the pragmatic rules of a particular context. Plan a group discussion to focus on kinds of language that can be used at home or in the neighborhood but not at school. Encourage older primary children to write a story "in the language of your friends" and then to rewrite it using conventional school language. Such experiences help children consciously manipulate their language styles in varying contexts.

CRITICAL CONCEPT 4

For children who are bilingual, the primary years can be a period of rapid linguistic growth within their second language. They may first apply the structures and rules of their native language when speaking in the new language. For example, a child who speaks both Spanish and English says, "The man no like cheese," following rules of Spanish. Eventually, children will be able to separate the two distinct rule systems and speak the second language with accuracy. Special support in school is necessary for this process to occur; a "sink or swim" approach in which no assistance is provided may impede linguistic development. A well-planned bilingual education program can promote the first- and second-language learning of all children.

Application #1 Encourage children who are bilingual to speak in both their native language and the second language they are learning throughout the school day. Thus, language instruction is additive: children are adding a new language without abandoning the language of their families.

Application #2 Understand, accept, and appreciate early linguistic errors among children who are bilingual. Don't correct children who apply rules of their native language when speaking a new, second language. Mistakes are necessary and important in bilingual development.

Application #3 Advocate for bilingual education programs that give special support to children who do not speak the language of dominant society. Create two-way bilingual programs—formally or informally—in which all children in a classroom learn two languages.

CRITICAL CONCEPT 5

Literacy growth is rapid in the primary years as children learn to read and write conventionally. Children's writing progresses in stages from prephonemic writing, in which letters are randomly chosen to represent a message, to phonemic and transitional stages, in which there is a closer association between the letters they use and the sounds of words in the story they are writing. Eventually, they use conventional writing, in which words are spelled accurately. Reading also advances in stages. Children begin by focusing on illustrations rather than print as they "read." Over time, they learn reading strategies—such as phonics or sentence context—and rely on only one of these to read. Finally, they read independently, using a balance of strategies to decode words they don't know.

Application #1 Provide primary age children with print-rich classrooms that offer many opportunities to write in meaningful ways. Stories, journal entries, written observations of scientific experiments, and letters to peers or family members are more significant to children than artificial, isolated-skills instruction.

Application #2 Provide high-quality children's books and other culturally relevant reading materials. Read to children, but also afford much time for independent reading. Signs, posters, sign-up lists, attendance charts, and other types of environmental print also promote reading development.

CRITICAL CONCEPT 6

Children who are bilingual must learn to read and write in two different languages. By acquiring literacy in their native language first, they will more easily learn to read and write in a second language in later years.

Application Encourage children who are bilingual to learn to read in their native language first. If you do not speak the preferred language of a student in class, arrange for a bilingual aid, volunteer, or parent to assist. Read to children and encourage them to write in their native language in various ways. Make available a collection of children's books in the child's native language. Only when children have shown competence in native-language reading and writing is instruction in the second language appropriate.

CRITICAL CONCEPT 7

Some children have language problems in the primary years that require intervention. Articulation errors, disfluency, poor word memory or retrieval, and faulty syntax can all be signs of language disorders.

Application #1   Identify the characteristics of children with speech and language delays and differentiate these from disfluencies and articulation errors that are typical during the primary years. Identifying these delays and seeking special services for children with special language needs are critical responsibilities of elementary teachers.

Application #2   Work closely with speech and language pathologists who are serving children with speech and language delays. Incorporate special speech and language games and activities into the regular classroom that will enhance communication more effectively—and with less social stigma—than pull-out lessons conducted outside the classroom group.

ASSESSING YOUNG CHILDREN: Primary-Age Language and Literacy Development

Areas of Development	What to Watch For	Indicators of Atypical Development	Applications
Oral language abilities	Utters speech sounds that are typically acquired by the child's age. Uses an extensive vocabulary and generates many words on free association tasks. Forms complex sentences that include clauses. Is aware of some language rules and can point out when they have been broken. Uses language effectively in social situations and speaks the "language of school."	Poor articulation that leads peers and teachers to misunderstand the child. Limited vocabulary. Use of short sentences that do not include clauses. Inability to use language to solve social problems. Use of socially inappropriate language in certain contexts, particularly school.	Create a language-rich classroom environment in which children can express themselves in a variety of contexts—large- and small-group conversations, dramatizations, musical performances, and unison readings. Collaborate with the speech and language pathologist to address specific oral language skills of individual children with special needs within the regular classroom. Include activities that focus on specific speech sounds, vocabulary, endings, or sentence structures that are the focus of intervention.

Literacy skills	By age 6, uses letters in writing that match some of the sounds in the story. Uses invented spelling by age 7 and more conventional spelling by age 8. Reads books by heart by age 6. Uses at least one conventional reading strategy—phonics, sentence context, or sight vocabulary—by age 8.	Failure to include some conventional letters in writing by age 6. Absence of any conventional spelling by age 8. Inability to acquire any conventional reading strategies—phonics, sight vocabulary, or sentence context—by age 8.	Provide experiences for children to write across the curriculum—a creative writing center, science journals, or a school post office are examples. Read favorite children's books over and over, then place them in a book center for individual reading. Create a print-rich environment, using signs and labels throughout the classroom. Provide special lap reading or one-on-one writing sessions for children with special needs.

Interpreting Assessment Data: Variations in language and literacy may be due to the specific languages spoken in the home and cultural differences in reading preferences. Children will learn oral language more slowly if they are trying to learn two languages simultaneously. Social language styles may vary depending on cultural tradition. Children whose families converse collectively, for example, may have difficulty learning the turn-taking rule at school. Children of some cultures may prefer different kinds of reading material—magazines or mail-order catalogs. Children learning to read in two languages may acquire conventional reading and writing skills more slowly. Those who display poor language and literacy within their preferred language may be at risk, however. Referral to a speech and language pathologist may be necessary. Classroom interventions, using high-quality children's literature and authentic writing activities (e.g., composing letters, family stories, or journal entries), can remediate some literacy problems.

CHAPTER 17

Social and Emotional Development in the Primary Years

GUIDING QUESTIONS

1. What is a sense of competence, and what common school practices threaten this feeling in the primary years?
2. What are feelings of social acceptance, control, and moral self-worth, and how do these types of self-esteem develop in the primary years?
3. What are inclusive views of self, and how are these influenced by culture?
4. What are cultural competencies, and how are these related to self-esteem?
5. How are feelings of control affected by socialization and prejudice?
6. How are feelings of moral self-worth influenced by culture?
7. What is the myth of self-hatred, and why is prejudice less likely to influence self-esteem in some families?
8. What is identity formation, and what factors lead to strong gender and ethnic identities?
9. How are peer groups, peer rejection and neglect, and friendships different in the primary years than they are during the preschool period?
10. How are peer relations in the primary years influenced by culture and class?
11. What are the basic tenets of Kohlberg's theory of moral development, and what are the major multicultural and feminist criticisms of his viewpoint?
12. What classroom adaptations can be implemented to support the social development of children with serious emotional disturbance, autism, and attention-deficit/hyperactivity disorder?
13. What are invisible handicaps, and how can teachers help their students understand and accept them?

This chapter examines social and emotional development in the primary years. The social worlds of primary-grade children widen considerably as they come into contact with larger and more diverse groups of peers and adults. Children acquire new patterns of social behavior and enter into unique kinds of relationships. Their emerging intellectual abilities allow them to reflect more fully on their peers' behavior and the meaning of friendship, and they form opinions about which characteristics of peers they value and which they dislike. They begin to recognize differences between themselves and others, including racial and class distinctions.

As they advance intellectually, primary-age children are able to study themselves more deeply and form opinions about their own competence and self-worth. They can analyze more accurately what they are good at and not so good at and can discern whether they are smarter, faster, and liked more than their peers—or less so. Because of these advancements, the primary years are a period of great opportunity but also great risk. During this stage, children can come to view themselves as competent and well liked by friends, family

members, and students. They can achieve a sense of pride in themselves and their culture. Or they can suffer self-doubt or feelings of incompetence and powerlessness and come to question the worth of their families or cultural heritage. The following story, adapted from the observations of B. B. Whiting and Edwards (1988), illustrates the potential emotional perils during the primary years:

Andrés, a Juxtlahuacan child in Mexico, has grown up in a supportive extended family. His parents and grandparents have encouraged and appreciated his accomplishments. As one of the oldest children in his village, he has always been the fastest, strongest, and smartest among his peers and siblings. By age 6, he has begun to construct a very positive view of himself; he has had no reason to question his own self-worth or ability.

Andrés attends his first day of school in the center of town, far from his home. He sits quietly as a raucous scene goes on about him. The teacher is asking questions, and the other children in the class are loudly calling out the answers. He is overwhelmed by the experience. He does not speak Spanish, the language used exclusively in the school.

He takes a bold step and tries to speak to the teacher in his native language. "I don't understand, teacher," he calls out. His teacher ignores him and continues responding to the other children's answers. "Teacher!" he says in a loud voice, "I do not understand this." At last the teacher turns to him and hisses loudly: "Sh-sh-sh!"

Later, the teacher asks the child to name letters in Spanish. Andrés cannot understand what she is asking and gives a look of confusion. The teacher says something in Spanish that makes the other students laugh, then moves on to ask another student the same question. Although Andrés cannot understand the teacher's language, he recognizes clearly that he has been ridiculed.

At home that night, Andrés is very quiet. When asked about what has occurred on the first day of school, he does not respond. Finally, with prodding from his grandmother, he tries to describe the experience but breaks down crying: "I can't...[sobs] I can't talk well....I just can't talk like everyone else does...[sobs]."

His grandmother wraps her arms around him and rocks him.

427

As a preschooler, the child in the story had enjoyed a very positive view of himself. He had come to believe that he could accomplish anything and that adults and peers would appreciate him unconditionally. Such beliefs are very common during early childhood. His ordeal on his first day of school, however, has threatened his feelings of competence and pride. Over time, such experiences may lead him to conclude that he is inferior or a bad person.

A SENSE OF COMPETENCE

Erikson's (1963) theory of emotional development has been discussed in previous chapters. Recall that, according to Erikson, one emotional struggle during the preschool years is to achieve a sense of **initiative**. Preschoolers who have acquired initiative will make creative attempts, take risks, and reach out to peers for interaction and friendship. At this age, they feel pride at simply making a good effort or being creative. This all changes in the primary years. Children who are ages 6 to 8 wish to master real skills—the skills possessed by older children and adults. They want to read and write like grown-ups, to excel at sports and other games, and to be strong and smart (Stipek, 1992). It is not enough to try, according to Erikson. Primary children want to succeed!

Children who believe they are successful at mastering real skills are said to have a sense of *industry*, more commonly called **competence**. Erikson has proposed that children who have genuine successes in their early years and whose accomplishments are accepted and appreciated by adults and peers will develop a sense of competence. The opposite state, called *inferiority*, results when children have significant experience with failure. The main psychological work of primary-age children, from Erikson's view, is to come to view themselves as competent persons.

Development of Feelings of Competence

Most preschoolers see themselves as competent (Mantzicopoulos, 2004; Thompson, Goodvin, & Meyer, 2006). For example, in one study, 4-year-olds who had failed several times to complete a difficult task nevertheless reported that they would be successful on their next try (Stipek, 1992). Curry and Johnson (1990) describe preschoolers as "exceedingly optimistic in self-ratings of their abilities and expectations for academic success" (p. 69). Erikson would explain these positive feelings by noting that children of this age are focusing on attempts and initiatives, not on the outcomes of their efforts. Consider the case of the Juxtlahuacan child, Andrés, in the opening vignette. This child may have held positive views of himself in the preschool years because he tried hard, made friends, and was viewed as a good boy by his parents and grandparents. In his early years, it did not matter that he lacked certain skills or knowledge; he made important efforts.

As children approach school age, however, they begin to question their abilities (Cole, Martin, Peeke, Seroczynski, & Fier, 1999; French & Mantzicopoulos, 2007; Verschueren & Marcoen, 1999). What happens during this developmental period to cause this self-doubt? For one thing, primary-age children gain a more accurate understanding of what it means to be smart and good at something. Whereas younger children associate competence with appropriate behavior or hard work, children in the primary grades come to understand that ability at performing school tasks determines "smartness" (Stipek, 1992). In addition, children in the primary years increasingly compare themselves with peers. This leads them to base judgments about their competence on where they stand within their peer group. As early as age 6, children begin to complain that they cannot run as fast, read as well, or learn math as quickly as others.

initiative: Erik Erikson's term for an emotional state, often acquired in the preschool years, in which children assert themselves, make creative attempts, take risks, and reach out to peers. Children whose initiatives are thwarted will experience an opposite emotional state: *guilt*.

competence: Similar to Erikson's term *industry*, an emotional state in which children feel capable because of their successes in and out of school. Repeated failure will result in an opposite emotional state: *inferiority*.

Boys tend to hold more positive views of themselves than girls at this age (French & Mantzicopoulos, 2007; Herbert & Stipek, 2005). In fact, in one study, boys were found to overestimate their abilities, whereas girls tended to underestimate their competence (Cole et al., 1999). A troubling finding of this investigation was that girls' less positive self-assessments were related to anxiety and depression—conditions found to be quite prevalent in the elementary years. Girls who were socially and mentally healthy held much higher views of themselves.

Children who are securely attached to a parent or other caregiver hold more positive views of themselves than those who are not (Ackerman & Dozier, 2005). In one fascinating study, secure attachment to mothers was found to be the strongest predictor of children's positive self-evaluation (Verschueren & Marcoen, 1999). Attachment to fathers was discovered to be less predictive of positive views of self though highly related to other positive childhood traits, such as sociability. Why is there a difference in the influence of mother and father? These authors propose that, in traditional American families, parents play distinct roles, with mothers more often providing comfort and affection. It is this warm caregiving, they contend, that boosts children's views of themselves. An important implication is that children need at least one adult in their lives—whether a mother, father, teacher, or counselor—who provides nurturance.

A Sense of Competence in School

Primary-age children are more likely to consider teacher feedback—both positive and negative—in their assessments of self (Barker & Graham, 1987; Pintrich & Blumenfeld, 1985; Stephan & Maiano, 2007). When a teacher criticizes a primary-grade child's written work, gives a low grade or score on a test, or in other ways provides negative feedback on school performance, the child is likely to feel less competent.

Several common practices in American schools contribute to feelings of inferiority (Stipek & MacIver, 1989). Several of these are summarized in Table 17-1.

Evaluative Symbols. **Evaluative symbols** predominate American public education. These are rewards or indicators of success that are presented publicly by teachers in school. Increasingly, children incorporate this symbolic feedback into their assessments of their own competence (Leondari & Gonida, 2007). In one study (Blumenfeld, Pintrich, & Hamilton, 1986), American elementary children who were asked, "How do you know when someone's smart?" regularly named grades as the primary indicator. Poor grades or failure to earn stars, stickers, or happy faces can have a lasting negative impact on children's feelings of competence.

Public Comparison. In **public comparison**, teachers compare their students with one another, both formally and informally (Stipek, 1992). Charts indicating how many books each child has read or which children have not been behaving appropriately can threaten feelings of competence. More subtle forms of comparison can also lead to negative self-judgments.

The ways in which teachers interact with children can have an effect. For example, a child may never be called on by the teacher because he or she never gets the right answer or takes too long responding. Over time, the message to the child becomes clear: you are a less competent person.

Ability Grouping. In many schools, **ability grouping** is used. Being relegated to a low-ability group can threaten feelings of competence (Trautwein, Lüdtke, Marsh, & Köller, 2006). One second-grader was overheard saying, "I'm in the Tigers group because I can't sit still

evaluative symbols: Rewards or indicators of success—such as grades or stickers—that are presented publicly by teachers in school and that are often incorporated into children's assessments of their own competence.

public comparison: A classroom practice—such as posting a good behavior chart—in which teachers compare their students with one another both formally and informally. This practice can lead to negative self-judgments.

ability grouping: A classroom practice in which children are placed into groups according to ability. Placement in a low-ability group can threaten feelings of competence.

TABLE 17-1

Practices in American Schools That Can Threaten Children's Feelings of Competence

School Practice	Example
Evaluative symbols	First-graders are given stars, stickers, and grades for performing well on academic work. Children who do not perform well do not earn these rewards.
Public comparison	The number of books children have read is indicated with checkmarks on a huge chart at the front of a second-grade classroom. Some children have many checkmarks; others have few.
Ability grouping	Children are placed into high-, middle-, or low-ability reading groups within a third-grade classroom. All students in the class are aware of which group is "slowest" and which is "smartest."
Whole-group instruction	An entire classroom of children is taught a single mathematics lesson. The teacher calls on students to solve problems on the board in front of the other students. Some children can solve the problems; others can't.
Formal relationships	A first-grade teacher welcomes children on the first day of school by presenting a list of rules and expectations. This is in sharp contrast to the smiles and hugs children received on their first day in kindergarten a year ago.

SOURCE: Stipek, D., & MacIver, D. (1989). Developmental change in children's assessment of intellectual competence. *Child Development, 60,* 521–538. Copyright © 1989 Blackwell Publishers. Used with permission.

and listen, and I talk when the teacher says 'stop' and…let's see…oh, I can't read very good either." At a young age, this child can recognize that he has been placed in the slow group. His feelings of competence are threatened.

Whole-Group Instruction. In many elementary schools around the world, children spend the majority of their time being taught in whole groups. In **whole-group instruction**, teachers present the same lesson to all children or ask the same questions regardless of ability level. Children are expected to provide correct responses in front of their classmates. Because all students are engaged in the same tasks at one time, self-comparison with peers is likely. For example, a child might think, "I couldn't solve that math problem, but Hanna and Ezra could!" For some children, being able to perform as well as peers is not possible (Stipek, 1992).

Formal Relationships with the Teacher. Preschool and child care teachers are relatively informal, positive, and accepting of their students. They tend to respond to processes rather than end products and to accept any effort a child makes as satisfactory. In the primary years, however, **formal relationships with the teacher** are more common. Interactions with teachers become more public and more often focus on whether children behave in prescribed ways, accomplish learning tasks successfully, and complete assignments. The transition from the warm, encouraging relationships in child care or preschool to the more formal and evaluative teacher–child relationships can threaten children's feelings of self-worth (Stipek, 1992).

whole-group instruction: The classroom practice of teaching a whole group of students that can lead to self-comparison with peers.

formal relationships with the teacher: The more formal and evaluative teacher–child connections found in elementary schools that can threaten children's feelings of self-worth.

What can teachers do to avoid some of these threats to self-concept? In some classrooms, more small-group or individualized learning projects are provided to reduce academic comparisons with peers. Some teachers emphasize thinking processes rather than right answers; others strive to reduce the amount of public evaluation and ability grouping. Such steps may contribute to children's positive self-assessments in middle childhood.

TYPES OF SELF-ESTEEM

The term **self-esteem** is used to describe a person's overall evaluation of self. A person who has positive feelings of self-worth is said to have high self-esteem, and someone who is unsatisfied with or doubtful about his or her abilities, accomplishments, or interpersonal characteristics is said to have low self-esteem. Erikson (1963) equated a sense of competence with self-esteem in the primary years. His work implies that self-esteem is a single, global psychological trait. Other researchers have challenged this perspective, arguing that two or more types of self-esteem can be differentiated during the primary years (Harter, 2003).

Competence versus Social Acceptance

In several studies, preschool and elementary children were asked to rate themselves on their abilities in many different areas (Davis-Kean & Sandler, 2001; Harter, 2003; Reese, Bird, & Tripp, 2007). Four- to 7-year-old children differentiated between two basic types of self-esteem: *competence*—being good at things, as Erikson described—and **social acceptance**—being liked as a friend or cared for as a family member. The researchers conclude that these two types of self-evaluation are distinct and somewhat unrelated at this age. Children may believe themselves very competent, for example, but not very well liked. Or they may believe that they have many friends or caring relatives but doubt their abilities in school. The following story illustrates these ideas:

A second-grade teacher sits with a group of students in a circle, conducting a self-esteem activity. He asks the children to report things they are very good at and things they would like to learn to do better. The activity is aimed at one child in particular, Twana, who is not doing well in school. The teacher assumes that she suffers low self-esteem, and he hopes the activity will help her see that she has some worthwhile traits and abilities.

The teacher expects that Twana will have trouble coming up with ideas on what she can do well, so he is prepared to assist her in thinking about her strengths. However, she is actually quite vocal when her turn comes:

TWANA: My grandma says, "You're my favorite little granddaughter," and she loves me all the time. And she is always waiting when I get home from school.

TEACHER: (Gently) That's nice. But we're talking about things we can do well. Can you think of something you do very well?

TWANA: Well, my grandma and my sister are always wanting me to tell them stories and jokes. They love it when I tell my jokes. And, know what? I'm going with my sister and some of the older girls to the community center tonight.

TEACHER:. Yes. That's great. Let me ask you a little more about your jokes. Can you tell very funny jokes? Is that something you do well?

self-esteem: A person's overall evaluation of self, including a belief about one's own abilities, accomplishments, or interpersonal characteristics.

social acceptance: A type of self-esteem related to perceptions about how well one is liked by peers and adults.

TWANA: My grandmother says my jokes are just silly, and when I tell her, she
              shakes her head and just puts me right on her lap.
TEACHER: Okay. Well, why don't you think real hard about some things you can do
              very, very well. We'll give Sarah a turn and come back to you in a
              minute.

The teacher in this story has developed an activity that focuses only on one type of self-esteem: competence. His interactions are aimed at helping Twana identify things that she can do well. He has failed to recognize social acceptance as an equally important part of a child's self-assessment. Judging by her comments, Twana clearly holds a very positive view of herself in terms of acceptance. She feels appreciated and loved unconditionally by her family.

Older primary-age children have been found to have even more highly differentiated and diverse types of self-esteem (Davis-Kean & Sandler, 2001; Eccles, Wigfield, Harold, & Blumenfeld, 1993). Seven- and 8-year-olds begin to view themselves as competent or accepted in certain areas but not in others. For example, one child may view herself as very able in math and science but not in reading or athletics. Another may feel very accepted by his family members but not by peers. Some children may have high estimations of their ability to interact with peers in the neighborhood but not with peers at school.

The following vignette shows how feelings of competence can vary depending on context:

A school social worker makes a home visit to the family of an 8-year-old student, Ruben, from her school. The family has moved recently from Puerto Rico, and their child is just learning to speak English. The social worker is concerned because the child is reported to be very quiet and withdrawn. Even on the playground, he stands and watches peers, never joining games or activities. For this reason, he has made no friends and is generally not well liked. She plans to discuss the problem with his mother and grandmother.

When the social worker enters the family apartment, she is shocked by what she sees. Ruben is engaged in active play with his cousin and two neighbor children. He is giving directives to the others in his native language with great confidence. He is not the self-doubting, withdrawn child that his teacher has described; he is bold, self-assured, and gregarious. She quickly rethinks the reasons for her visit and the approach she will take with this family.

This child's self-esteem in the area of peer acceptance appears to be quite high at home, even though he exhibits much self-doubt at school. The social worker has learned that assessments of self-evaluation must include contexts and activities that extend beyond the classroom.

Feelings of Control

Another distinct area of self-evaluation in the primary years is control. **Feelings of control** are related to a person's belief about the ability to control one's own life or make a difference in determining one's destiny (Curry & Johnson, 1990). Children who have acquired an **internal locus of control** are more likely to report that hard work and persistence in solving problems will lead to success. They believe they have the power within themselves to make a difference (Judge, Erez, Bono, & Thoresen, 2002). Children who have an **external locus of control** believe that what happens to them is due to external forces beyond their regulation. They are more likely to report that "It doesn't

feelings of control: A type of self-esteem related to perceptions about the ability to control one's own life or make a difference in determining one's destiny.

internal locus of control: A belief that hard work and persistence will lead to success and that one has the power within oneself to make a difference.

external locus of control: A belief that what happens to a person is due to external forces, that success is beyond one's control, and that failure is inevitable.

matter how hard I try, the teacher will still give me a bad grade" or "No matter what I say, kids in the class won't like me because they're mean."

Children gradually acquire an internal or external locus of control during the primary years. As early as the third grade, some children come to hold such fixed views about their lack of control that their success in all endeavors is hampered. Such children often quit trying to perform well in school because they believe failure is inevitable, that improvement is out of their control (Fincham, Hokoda, & Sanders, 1989).

Feelings of Moral Self-Worth

Another dimension of self-esteem is **moral self-worth** (Curry & Johnson, 1990; Kochanska, 2005). This refers to children's assessments of their goodness or virtue as defined by cultural norms. Primary-age children come to view themselves as *good* or *bad* depending on their social experiences. Children with positive self-esteem in this area come to see themselves as proper, worthwhile, and trustworthy friends and family members.

Three virtues of self-worth—fairness, responsibility, and obedience—are of great importance to children in the primary years (Curry & Johnson, 1990; Damon, 2002). Fairness is of great moral concern in primary-grade classrooms. Frequent arguments erupt about inequitable treatment by the teacher or peers or about the uneven distribution of materials or rewards. Through conflicts over issues of equality, children gradually construct views of themselves as fair or not so fair.

They also develop a sense of responsibility, which is related to being helpful to teachers, parents, friends, and the community. Parents or teachers often nurture this sense with statements such as "You're such a good helper" or "I could never have cleaned up this kitchen without you." Over time, some children come to view themselves as responsible members of the classroom or household; others do not.

Obedience relates to compliance and respect for adults. A certain degree of obedience is expected of children in all cultures. Children who are relatively compliant over time will evaluate themselves as *nice*. Children who are reprimanded regularly in school or at home acquire an opposite view of themselves.

As with other types of self-esteem, children may have positive views of themselves in some areas of moral self-worth and negative views in others. One child may consider himself helpful and nice but not always very obedient. Another may believe she is obedient toward adults but not always fair to peers. Children may hold slightly different self-assessments depending on context. For example, some children enjoy positive feelings of self-worth in school settings but believe themselves to be unkind or unhelpful in the neighborhood.

Integrating the Types of Self-Esteem

Clearly, the development of self-esteem in the primary years is a complex process of self-evaluation. It is quite mind-boggling, in fact, to contemplate the many ways children think about themselves and judge their self-worth at this young age! As discussed previously, the various types of self-esteem are somewhat disconnected in the early years (Harter, 1990). Views of self are splintered into distinct self-appraisals in many different areas of life. Figure 17-1 illustrates the specific areas of self-evaluation that have been discussed in this section.

After age 8, children begin to synthesize their various beliefs about self into a single, global self-esteem. It is not until adolescence, however, that an overall, integrated sense of self-worth emerges (J. D. Brown, 1998; Masden et al., 1995; Thorne & Michaelieu, 1996).

moral self-worth: A type of self-esteem that is related to perceptions about one's goodness or virtue as defined by cultural norms.

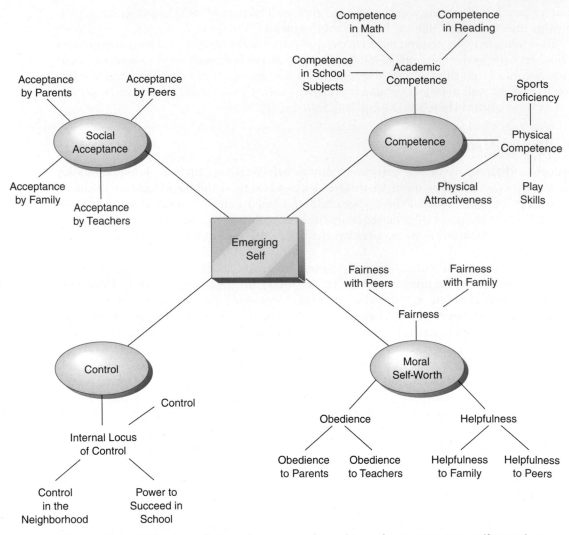

FIGURE 17-1   Self-esteem in the primary years is made up of many separate self-appraisals. During childhood and adolescence, these gradually become integrated into a single, emerging view of self.

SOURCE: Extrapolated from data in Curry & Johnson, 1990; Damon, 1990; Harter, 1990; Stipek, 1992.

SELF-ESTEEM AND CULTURE

Self-esteem in middle childhood is influenced by culture. The worldview, valued competencies, and traditions of a particular cultural group will affect the criteria children use to judge their self-worth.

Inclusive Views of Self

As discussed in previous chapters, some cultures are more collective in thought and action (Klein & Chen, 2001). In such cultural groups, extended families tend to work together toward joint goals, and individual family members often sacrifice personal aspirations for the good of the entire household. Accomplishments of a whole village or neighborhood may be valued more than individual achievements (Yeh & Huang, 2002).

Children of collective cultures hold **inclusive views of self**: evaluations of self that are related to accomplishments or competencies of the entire family or community (Klein & Chen, 2001; Umaña-Taylor, 2004). Their personal self-worth is intricately tied to their views about the groups to which they belong. Inclusive views of self have been found to be prevalent among African American, Mexican American, and Chinese children, for example (Chen, Rubin, & Sun, 1992; Barry & Grilo, 2003). The self-esteem of children of these cultural groups is likely to be related to family and ethnic pride. The children who hold their family, peer group, community, and culture in high esteem are more likely to evaluate themselves in positive ways.

School experiences that emphasize personal achievement may promote positive self-esteem among some children but not in others (Klein & Chen, 2001). Children who have inclusive views of self may not derive feelings of competence from learning to read on their own or by maintaining a high batting average on the playground. Instead, their self-esteem may be based on pride in family literacy or the success of a whole peer group or team. Feelings of social acceptance may depend on being appreciated by one's entire family or ethnic group.

Children who have inclusive views of self may not acquire feelings of control through individual initiative or self-reliance. Instead, a sense of control may come from a belief that one's family or community is powerful and can overcome adversity. A sense of moral self-worth may be based on the view that one's family, community, and cultural group are fair and responsible. When a child's entire ethnic group is subtly portrayed in the media as lazy or dependent on welfare, self-esteem is threatened. When members of one's culture band together and effectively advocate for change in the community, a child's view of self is enhanced.

Culture, then, shapes the very definition of *self*. For children of some groups, proud stories about one's family or the athletic prowess of a neighborhood peer group may be more important indicators of self-esteem than expressions of personal achievement or self-worth.

Cultural Competencies and Criteria for Self-Evaluation

Culture influences the specific criteria children use to evaluate themselves. In the primary years, children make judgments about which abilities are worthwhile or important to learn. Some children may view athletic skill as more important than learning to read, while others believe just the opposite. Some may consider singing or playing a musical instrument to be most critical. In order to acquire positive views of self, children must believe that they are competent at the things they value. A child who believes that reading is very important will derive positive self-esteem from learning to read, while reading achievement will have less effect on a child who does not value this ability.

How do children determine which competencies are important and which are not? Families and culture play a significant role in helping children decide. Parents socialize children to value competencies that are emphasized within a particular cultural group (Ogbu, 1992). Children then assess their own abilities in these areas. One child may weigh storytelling skills more heavily than reading achievement, and another may rely more on social acceptance by peers and family than on grades in school.

The following story shows how diverse cultural groups adopt unique criteria for judging self-worth:

> Karen, a Native American child, has been identified as having learning disabilities. She is enrolled in a second-grade classroom in a regular public school and is struggling academically. A team of professionals interviews the child's teacher and mother about

inclusive views of self: Evaluations of self that are related to accomplishments or competencies of the entire family, community, or other groups to which one belongs.

Children of some cultures have inclusive views of self. Their feelings of competence are tied to the accomplishments of their peer group, family, or community.

Karen's classroom and home experiences and her self-esteem. The two offer quite contrasting perspectives on the child's emotional development:

Teacher's comments: Karen is so quiet and withdrawn that she has made no friends. Her struggles with academic work make her stand out among her peers. Her language is a particular problem: she simply can't learn enough English to communicate effectively. I believe her outward smiles and happy demeanor are just a facade. Inside, I know she's crying. She has a very low opinion of herself.

Mother's assessment: The school calls Karen "learning disabled," but in her family and community we call her "magical." She can draw beautifully. She can draw the old stories better than most adults. Her pictures are on display in our community center. She doesn't speak the language of the school, that's true. But we tell her that English is not as important; Keresan is the language of her people. Words don't matter as much as deeds, anyway. She knows this. She shows us her ideas and her feelings through her actions. Karen is very, very proud of who she is and of her family. She is happy in her real life. Schoolteachers just don't see her in her natural place in the world.

The teacher in this story has assumed that Karen has low self-esteem because she performs poorly in a Western-oriented school. A common misconception among some Euro-American teachers is that children of all cultures base their self-evaluations on criteria defined by the dominant society (Ogbu, 1992; M. B. Spencer, 1988; Trawick-Smith & Lisi, 1994). In fact, Karen holds a very positive view of herself that is unrelated to her competence in school. According to her mother's reports, she is confident about her abilities in areas that matter within her family and culture. She is a gifted visual artist, and her gift is held in high esteem within her community. She can communicate in ways that are important to her cultural group: speaking Keresan and using nonverbal expression. Her positive sense of self is related to her successes and acceptance in her own community.

Culture and Feelings of Control

As previously discussed, feelings of control are part of a child's self-appraisal. A goal of American education has been to instill an internal locus of control—a belief in one's ability to make a difference and to regulate one's own life. Feelings of control vary by culture and gender. In the United States, for example, girls are likely to feel less in control and more helpless than boys (Curry & Johnson, 1990; Dwek & Legget, 1988). Chinese American children also tend to have an external locus of control (Klein & Chen, 2001). Children of this cultural group are more likely to believe that successes or failures are governed by fate, luck, or circumstances beyond their control.

Are these findings cause for concern? The results of some studies suggest that an external locus of control can lead to poor achievement and social adjustment (Fincham et al., 1989). However, this trend may not hold for all children. For girls, an external locus of control has been found to be unrelated to school failure (Dwek & Legget, 1988; Parsons, 1983). Chinese American children who lack feelings of control have, likewise, been found to perform very well in school subjects (Canino & Spurlock, 2000; M. G. Wong, 1988; Knapp & Lo, 2006). Sue and Chin (1983) explain these puzzling research findings by proposing that there are two different reasons that children lack feelings of control in their lives: socialization and prejudice.

Socialization and Control. Some cultures may purposely socialize children to believe in fate and the powerlessness of the individual. In traditional Chinese American families, for example, children are taught to give full regulation of their lives to parents and other family elders (Chao, 2002; Klein & Chen, 2001). According to Yu and Kim (1983), Chinese American children are often trained to abandon urges for "independence and mastery over one's own fate" (p. 160) and to adopt feelings to absolute deference to adults. It is no wonder that Chinese American children exhibit an external locus of control in school. Sue and Chin (1983) propose that the effects of these feelings on school achievement are minimal because children *voluntarily* entrust their lives to external persons or circumstances. These beliefs are in accordance with cultural customs.

Girls may, likewise, be socialized to feel they have less individual control over circumstances (Gilligan, 1993a). Parents often teach their daughters to be reliant on others in solving problems or making decisions. Thus, girls may come to believe that accomplishments are due not to *individual* initiative but to the efforts of all persons in a group. Learning a math concept, for example, may be the result not of a child's own actions but of the efforts of everyone—teachers, peers, and parents—working in concert. Gilligan has suggested that what psychologists call "helplessness" in girls may be simply a reliance on and faith in the help of other people.

Sue and Chin (1983) claim that when an external locus of control is a fundamental part of culture and is taught directly by parents, it causes no harm. Another kind of helplessness, they contend, is more damaging to emotional health—that which stems from prejudice.

Prejudice and Control. Children may have negative experiences that lead them to conclude that they will fail in school or be rejected by peers because of race or gender. They may eventually come to believe that no amount of effort will lead to success. For example, a Puerto Rican child may believe that nothing she does in school will lead to success because of teacher prejudice, or a Chinese American child may be convinced by coaches or peers that because of his ethnic background, he is not aggressive enough to become an athlete. A Euro-American child may be led to believe that because she is a girl, her achievement in mathematics is the result of pure luck.

Even positive stereotypes can lead to reduced feelings of control. The belief that all Chinese American children are bright and hardworking is an example. Students of this cultural group are sometimes given good grades simply because of their ethnicity (Knapp & Lo, 2005; Sue & Chin, 1983). "You must be a good student if you come from a Chinese American family," the thinking goes. Children may eventually see school success as something that is determined by cultural affiliation regardless of one's efforts or accomplishments.

Sue and Chin (1983) express concern about feelings of powerlessness that arise from prejudice. It is one thing to *choose* to trust fate, luck, or the guidance of others, they contend; it is quite another to be truly disempowered because of race or gender bias.

Culture and Feelings of Moral Self-Worth

How children judge their moral self-worth can also be shaped by culture. As discussed earlier, one criterion for determining self-worth is obedience to parents (Damon, 2002). Children believe themselves to be nice or well behaved if they are compliant. How obedient children are expected to be is defined by cultural norms, however, and obedience and respect for adults is required in some cultures more than in others.

In many Japanese American and Chinese American families, absolute submission to parents is required (Chan, 1998; Chao, 2002; Knapp & Lo, 2005). Piety toward parents, other adults, and ancestors is deeply rooted in ancient tradition. Similarly, African American and Mexican American parents often command a high degree of respect and obedience from their children (Nobles, 2007). In fact, some African American parents express disapproval at the more permissive parenting styles of Euro-American families. Within cultural groups that value obedience, this requirement is likely to be weighted heavily in children's self-evaluations. Even a moderate amount of disrespect toward their family members may, over time, lead to negative views of moral self-worth.

In contrast, some middle-class, Euro-American parents are exceedingly permissive (DeCaro & Worthman, 2007; Goodnow & Collins, 1990). Children regularly disobey and argue with adults in these families. Freedom of expression and the individual rights of children are highly valued, so obedience may not be an important criterion when such children judge self-worth.

B. B. Whiting and Edwards (1988) report that, in some societies, children are expected to be obedient in some contexts but not in others. In Ngeca, Kenya, for example, children were observed to be very obedient in school. They regularly complied with their teachers' directives and ran errands for them. Some even tended their teachers' gardens! These same children, however, were found to be relatively disobedient at home. They were observed ignoring parents' demands or requests for help. Parents seemed nonchalant about their children's noncompliance. In this cultural group, obedience at school might be an important standard in assessing self-worth, whereas compliance with parents might not.

Responsibility is another criterion children use in self-evaluation. As mentioned earlier, children who believe themselves to be helpful to their family and community tend to develop positive self-esteem. Expectations for responsibility vary considerably in families, however. The most responsible children tend to be those who live in large non-Western families and whose contributions to the household workload are critical to survival (Hale & Franklin, 2001; B. B. Whiting and Whiting, 1975). Middle-class, Euro-American children are generally less helpful and perform fewer family tasks.

Children who live in families in which obedience and responsibility are valued and respected will base their self-evaluations on these attributes. Moral self-worth depends on being helpful and respectful. In cultures that do not consider such traits crucial, other criteria will be more heavily weighted.

Self-Esteem, Prejudice, and the Myth of Self-Hatred

Several decades ago in the United States, public concern was raised about the self-esteem of children from historically underrepresented groups. It was believed that many children of color, who experienced lives filled with prejudice, hated themselves and wished to be white (Witmer & Kotinsky, 1952). This opinion was based on a series of classic race identification studies in which children were asked to express their preference for dolls or pictures representing various racial groups (Aboud, 1977; J. T. Spencer, 1970). All children—even children of color—were found to prefer and express more positive attitudes toward white dolls than toward black or brown ones. These findings were presented by national committees to the Congress, the U.S. Supreme Court, and the White House Conferences on Children (K. B. Clark, 1952; Joint Commission on the Mental Health of Children, 1970).

Although these concerns were well intentioned, they fostered a new negative racial stereotype, called the **myth of self-hatred**. This is the myth that children of color hate themselves and are to be pitied. I conducted a study that demonstrated this attitude even today among teachers (Trawick-Smith & Lisi, 1994). I presented a photograph of an African American female child to a group of 22 early childhood professionals. Without giving any background about the child's life, family, or abilities, I asked the teachers to write stories about the child. All but three wrote that the child suffered "low self-esteem," and more than half described the child as "feeling helpless" and "alone." These assessments were based solely on a photograph of the child smiling as she played on the playground! Evidently, some teachers automatically assume that children of color suffer low self-esteem and other emotional problems.

The view that children of color hate themselves has been vigorously challenged. Some believe that too much has been made of the doll-and-picture preference studies. Can it be assumed that children suffer negative views of themselves or their race just because they favor white dolls over black ones? More recent research found no connection between doll identification and self-esteem (Nesdale, Durkin, Maass, & Griffith, 2005; M. B. Spencer & Markstrom-Adams, 1990).

Criticisms have also been raised about the methods used in self-esteem studies (Harrison, Wilson, Pine, Chan, & Buriel, 1994). Some argue that the race and attitudes of experimenters may have affected findings. Euro-American researchers may have unconsciously swayed children to express preferences for white dolls or pictures. In doll identification studies, for example, children were found to show greater preference for their own race when researchers were of their own cultural and linguistic background (Annis & Corenblum, 1987; Corenblum & Wilson, 1982). It may be that children respond to doll preference tasks in the way they think researchers expect them to. They may select white dolls if they believe that is the *correct* answer—the one that a white, middle-class researcher is looking for.

Many of the self-esteem studies were conducted prior to the late 1960s. The 1960s and early 1970s were a period of great social and political change in the United States. The civil rights movement was gaining momentum, schools were being desegregated, and African American studies was being incorporated into school curricula. Concepts of "black pride" and "black power" emerged, and "ethnic consciousness" was emphasized. In such a climate, it could be predicted that views about self and culture would become more positive. Indeed, many studies in the late 1960s and early 1970s found that children of color—even those who lived in poverty—were found to have self-esteem as high as *or higher than* their Euro-American, middle-class peers (Hauser, 1972; M. B. Spencer & Markstrom-Adams, 1990). Some researchers during this period have asked children directly about the impact of prejudice (Brigham, 1974; D. T. Campbell, 1976; M. M. Lawrence, 1975; Rosenberg, 1979).

myth of self-hatred:
A well-intentioned misconception that children of color hate themselves and are to be pitied.

Children of color in these studies reported that they were aware of negative attitudes toward their ethnic group in society but stated that they rejected these biases and held positive views of themselves and their cultures.

How can children who experience prejudice maintain positive views of self? A factor that appears to insulate them from bias and hatred is strong ethnic identity and pride (M. B. Spencer & Markstrom-Adams, 1990; Umaña-Taylor & Shin, 2007). Children from historically underrepresented groups who identify proudly with their ethnic heritage and view their communities and families as competent and worthy are more likely to have positive self-esteem (Thompson, Anderson, & Bakeman, 2000; Umaña-Taylor, 2004). This ethnic pride emerges in the primary years as children come to understand and appreciate what it means to be African American, Vietnamese, or Native American.

EARLY IDENTITY FORMATION

During childhood and adolescence, children are engaged in **identity formation**—constructing a clear understanding of themselves. According to Erikson (1963), the formation of identity culminates during adolescence, when young people clarify their roles, personal values, characteristics, and competencies. The process of developing an identity involves answering questions such as "Who am I?" "What am I good at?" "What do I believe in?" and "What groups do I belong to?" Many of these questions take a lifetime to answer.

The roots of identity can be traced to a child's early years. Young children come to view themselves as members of a family—as siblings and sons or daughters. Some may see themselves as kindergartners in Public School Number 14 or as members of Ms. Shultz's T-ball team. Piece by piece, the child's picture of self comes into focus. Gender and ethnic identity are two significant self-discoveries that occur during the early years. Children quickly realize that they are boys or girls and come to understand the behaviors, expectations, and status that accompany each gender. They also come to view themselves as members of an ethnic group. A child in the primary years realizes, for the first time, "I am African American" or "I am Chinese." Some children also discover that they are poor or that their families are better off than others.

Gender Identity

At an early age, children begin to acquire a **gender identity**—that is, they view themselves as boys or girls (Maccoby & Jacklin, 1990; Martin & Ruble, 2004). They describe what it means to be a girl or boy, using physical characteristics to define maleness or femaleness. Primary-age children understand that gender is determined not just by physical appearance. At this age, they begin to view gender as a set of expectations for behavior. A 6-year-old may announce that "boys are rougher and don't cry" or that "girls are quiet and shy."

Initially, children are concerned with the expectations for their *own* gender (Martin & Ruble, 2004). A 6-year-old girl, for example, may hold detailed views of what it means to be a female in her home or school but less complete understandings of what it means to be a male. By age 8, children have more elaborate perspectives about the roles and expectations of both genders. Their beliefs become extremely stereotyped during this age. They adhere to rigid rules about the "rightness" or "wrongness" of gender-stereotypic behavior (Katz & Ksansnak, 1994). For example, a primary-age child responds in the following way to a story about a boy playing with dolls: "He should only play with things that boys play with.... If he doesn't want to play with dolls, then he's right, but if he does want to play with dolls, then he's double wrong" (Maccoby, 1980, p. 236). Double wrong? It is clear from the quotation that a violation of gender rules is more than a minor infringement of

identity formation: The process of constructing a clear understanding of the roles, personal values, characteristics, competencies, and group memberships that define oneself.

gender identity: An understanding and evaluation of one's own gender, including the physical characteristics, behavioral expectations, and social obligations and status that define being a male or female in one's family and culture.

primary-grade protocol. This rigidity is pervasive; even children whose parents have struggled to promote nonstereotyped behavior will show stereotyped views at this age. Such stereotyped beliefs have been found in children in most societies in the world (B. B. Whiting & Edwards, 1988). The good news is that these views become less extreme during later childhood and adolescence.

Children of all societies are socialized to behave and think as boys or girls. Parents particularly fathers—encourage the adoption of gender-appropriate roles (Hastings, McShane, Parker, & Ladha, 2007; Raley & Bianchi, 2006), and both mothers and fathers expect boys to follow more rigid rules of gender behavior than girls (Fagot & Leinbach, 1993).

Ethnic Identity

In the primary years, children also begin to construct an **ethnic identity**: a full understanding and appreciation of behaviors, thinking, values, feelings, and competencies of the ethnic group to which they belong. Research suggests that children who understand that they are part of a particular group and who hold positive opinions of that group are more likely to have high self-esteem (Umaña-Taylor, 2004; Umaña-Taylor & Shin, 2007). Those with this strong ethnic identity are less likely to be psychologically harmed by the experience of prejudice.

Development of Ethnic Identity.   When does an ethnic identity form? As early as 4 years of age, most children can identify their own racial or cultural group. By age 7, many become aware of the distinct cultural groups of peers, teachers, and neighbors (Rutland, Cameron, Bennett, & Ferrell, 2007). In the early primary years, physical characteristics serve as the basis of racial and cultural distinctions. Children at this age use skin color, eyes, hair texture, and other observable traits to define an ethnic group. Not until 8 years of age are children able to identify subtle cultural differences—say, between Chinese American and Japanese American or between Apache and Seminole groups (Nesdale, 2007; Nesdale et al., 2005).

At first, children can identify people of their own culture. For example, by age 5 they can often name persons who belong to their own race or cultural background (Aboud, 1988; Aboud & Doyle, 1993). Statements such as "You're like me 'cause you talk just like I do" are indicators of emerging ethnic affiliation. During the later primary years, children learn to identify those who are from different cultures. For example, an African American 7-year-old might touch the hair of a Euro-American peer and say, "You don't have hair like Nellie and me. It's all straight like everybody else's."

At an earlier age, children may have believed that their ethnic or cultural membership could change, but during the primary years they begin to understand that these are constant. For example, one 4-year-old child reported that a peer's dark skin could "just wash off" (Ramsey, 2004), and 5-year-olds reported that Italian Canadians could become Canadian Indians simply by changing their clothing (Aboud, 1988). By the midprimary years, though, children report, "You're Mexican. You'll be Mexican when you're a mother" or "Once you have brown color, it just stays there."

Evaluations of Ethnicity.   As children come to understand what it means to be a member of a particular cultural group, they also begin to assign a value to that group. Do most children hold positive views of their ethnic heritage? Research findings are mixed. After reviewing a large number of investigations of African American children's attitudes toward ethnicity, Aboud (1987) found that, in 27% of studies, children showed a preference for their own culture, whereas in 57% they showed no preference. Children indicated a preference for Euro-American cultures in only 16% of the studies that he examined.

ethnic identity: An understanding and evaluation of the behaviors, thinking, values, feelings, and competencies of the ethnic group to which people belong.

In other studies, positive ethnic attitudes were found for most but not all children. In one series of investigations, for example, African American children and Native American *boys* were found to value their own cultures very highly (Markstrom, 1987; Markstrom & Mullis, 1986). For Native American girls, however, this was not the case. Across tribal groups, they appear to be at risk of poor ethnic identity (M. B. Spencer & Markstrom-Adams, 1990). Several investigations have shown that preference for one's own race is strongest, and negative attitudes toward other groups is more prevalent, among children of Euro-American cultures (Baron & Banaji, 2006; Ramsey & Myers, 1990). This may reflect biases in the media and other institutions toward this dominant cultural group.

Variation in Ethnic Identity. Some children identify strongly with their cultural group. When asked, "Who are you?" they will name cultural affiliation as a significant defining characteristic. The following story depicts the strong ethnic identity of some 8-year-olds:

A third-grade teacher, Ms. Flores, conducts a sharing time at the beginning of the school day. The topic of basketball comes up. The final game of the National Basketball Association championship series was played the evening before. Many children wish to share their opinions about the game.

MS. FLORES:	So, does anyone else have anything to share? We've talked about basketball quite a bit. Is there anything else you'd like to discuss?
TONY:	They only won 'cause of Shaq.
JOSHUA:	Yeah. Shaquille O'Neal!
ALONZO:	Shaq is a black man. He's black just like me and Raymond. Shaq is like…(laughs)…my father…
TONY:	What?
ALONZO:	…and my brother…and my mother (laughs).
JOSHUA:	(Laughing) Shaq's no mother!
MS. FLORES:	(Trying to change the topic) Well. What else happened over the weekend?
ALONZO:	Shaq's like me, and you, and you (points to peers), but not Sean, and not you….
JOSHUA:	And me.
ALONZO:	No, 'cause he's black. We're black people. You're white. That's different, you know.

The children in this story have a clear and positive view of their ethnicity. They are proud that a sports hero shares their cultural background. Alonzo jokingly makes the case that the basketball star and all others in his ethnic group are related, like family members. His comments are reminiscent of Hale-Benson's (1986) observation that "a strong desire exists among black people to be related to each other" (p. 48). Such self-respecting pronouncements of affiliation are indicators of ethnic identity in the primary years.

Other children do not acquire such well-defined views of their ethnicity. Why? Most psychologists believe that ethnic identity is nurtured within the family (Robbins et al., 2007). Parents or grandparents who are committed to imparting cultural pride will strengthen children's feelings of ethnic affiliation. Parents who believe ethnicity plays a minor role in children's development will not promote a strong cultural identity.

Ethnic Socialization. Socialization is the process of imparting the competencies, values, and expectations of society to children. **Ethnic socialization**, then, involves teaching the beliefs, abilities, roles, and history that are unique to one's own cultural group. When

ethnic socialization: The process of teaching to children the beliefs, abilities, roles, and history that are unique to one's own cultural group.

parents teach children that it is important to be truthful, they are contributing to their child's socialization. Parents of all cultural groups want to impart this message. Examples of ethnic socialization are sharing stories about one's tribal ancestors or teaching the words to a Muslim prayer. These practices provide information that children need to participate in a particular cultural group. A primary goal of ethnic socialization is to inspire a sense of ethnic pride and identity.

Parents from historically underrepresented groups face significant challenges in the ethnic socialization of their children. On one hand, they may wish to teach their sons and daughters the values and competencies that will help them get along in the dominant society. On the other hand, they may also want to teach their children the traditions of their own cultural group. There is often a dual goal, then, in ethnic socialization. Parents want their children to retain their cultural heritage and, at the same time, acquire the knowledge and abilities of mainstream society. Ultimately, many parents wish their children to become **bicultural**: effective members of two distinct cultural groups (Benet-Martínez & Haritatos, 2005; Harrison et al., 1990).

One way parents promote ethnic identity is through **ethnic socialization messages**— statements that guide children in understanding and valuing the uniqueness of their family's cultural heritage. Researchers have identified several kinds of ethnic socialization messages. In a large survey study, African American parents were asked to write down the beliefs or ideas they teach children to help them "to know what it is to be black" (M. C. Thornton, Chatters, Taylor, & Allen, 1990). The most frequent responses are presented in Table 17-2.

As shown in the table, some socialization messages, such as "Be honest and fair," are commonly adopted by families of all cultural groups. Other messages, like "Blacks don't have the same opportunities that whites have," relate to racial restrictions and bias in society. Some messages refer to historical traditions and heritage: "Black people had to cope with great adversity in the past." Others focus on promoting ethnic identity and pride, such as "Realize you're black" and "Take pride in yourself." Over time, such messages can instill accurate and positive views of culture.

Some parents, even those from historically underrepresented groups, do not impart ethnic socialization messages. They may view race or culture as unimportant in child rearing or may worry about the repercussions of instilling positive ethnic views. Some parents are concerned that their children will become arrogant or disrespectful if they acquire ethnic pride, while others fear that children will get into trouble with people of the dominant culture or become prejudiced themselves (M. B. Spencer, 1983). A range of family stressors—poverty

bicultural: A term to describe those who are effective members of two distinct cultural groups.

ethnic socialization messages: Statements that guide children in understanding and valuing the uniqueness of their family's cultural heritage.

Type of Message	Example
Achievement and hard work	"Work hard to get a good education."
Moral virtues	"Respect others. Be honest and fair."
Racial pride	"Never be ashamed of your color."
African American heritage	"Your ancestors had to cope with the cruelty and injustice of slavery."
Acceptance of racial background	"Accept your color; realize you are black."
Positive self-image	"You're as good as anyone else."
Realities of oppression	"Blacks don't have the opportunities that whites have."
Racial equality	"Recognize all races as equal."

**TABLE 17-2
Common Socialization Messages of African American Parents**

SOURCE: Thornton, M. C., Chatters, L. M., Taylor, R. J., & Allen, W. (1990). Sociodemographic and environmental correlates of racial socialization by black parents. *Child Development, 61*, 401–409. Copyright © 1990 Blackwell Publishers. Used with permission.

or drug addiction—can also inhibit ethnic socialization (Phinney & Ong, 2007). Ogbu (1983) warns that children who do not receive an ethnic education from their families are at risk of poor identity development.

Teachers can support children who are at risk of poor ethnic identity. Providing socialization messages in school will complement efforts in the family. It is worthwhile to teach students that all cultural groups have rich, proud histories and traditions and that members of all groups are competent and honorable. An equally important message in school is that prejudice is an evil that persists in society.

PEER RELATIONSHIPS

Peer relationships change significantly in primary years for a variety of reasons. First, children are developing intellectually. As they become less egocentric and more other oriented, they are better able to "put themselves in the shoes" of others and understand their peers' needs and motivations. Children of this age are quite analytical in choosing playmates. They can assess the traits and emotions of peers and make judgments about which characteristics they like and which they don't (Pahl & Pevalin, 2005; Pataki, Shapiro, & Clark, 1994).

As children acquire cognitive and social competence, they can solve social problems independently. They can persuade peers (Trawick-Smith, 1993), enter a playgroup, and strike up a conversation with a stranger (Timler, Vogler-Elias, & McGill, 2007; Putallaz & Wasserman, 1989). When conflicts arise, they can contemplate a range of alternative resolutions (Murphy & Eisenberg, 2002; Stevahn, Johnson, Johnson, Oberle, & Wahl, 2000). In an argument with a friend, for example, they can decide whether to compromise, give a counterargument, give in, or express anger. These growing social understandings cause peer relationships and interactions to become far more complex.

Primary-age children's peer groups are becoming larger and more important in development. At this age, social contacts with family members begin to decline, and peer interactions increase (Feiring & Lewis, 1989; Ladd, 1990). Children rely more and more on peers for companionship, advice, and emotional support (Hartup, 1996).

The Peer Group

Children generally belong to one or more peer groups during the primary years (Gest, Farmer, Cairns, & Xie, 2003). Examples of peer groups are one's classmates in school or the children in one's neighborhood. Primary-age peer groups are more organized than in the preschool years. Each member of a group has a relatively well-defined role, with some children viewed as leaders, others as followers (Trawick-Smith, 1993). Some are well liked, others are not. Larger groups often contain subgroups. Small cliques of children form, and some individuals are ostracized from these. Friendships—pairs of children who are mutually attracted—also exist, as they did in the preschool years. These tend to be longer lasting and more mutually supportive and emotionally satisfying than in earlier years (Cairns et al., 1995; Hartup, 1996). The classroom or neighborhood group, then, contains a complex web of interrelationships. Figure 17-2 illustrates graphically the organization of a primary-age peer group.

Each primary-age peer group to which a child belongs has its own chemistry. Relationships and group status vary from one group to another, depending on composition. A pair of children who are friends in school may not be so close to one another when playing in a neighborhood peer group (Kupersmidt, Griesler, DeRosier, Patterson, & Davis, 1995). A child who is not well liked in the classroom—because of aggression, for example—may be better liked in a neighborhood group composed of more active or aggressive peers (Stormshak et al., 1999).

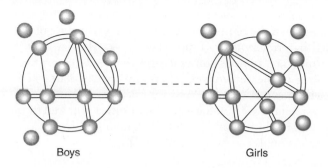

Boys   Girls

FIGURE 17-2   The structure of a primary-age peer group is illustrated graphically. Children are depicted by circles. The strength of relationships is represented by connecting lines: A single line indicates a positive relationship between children who like and respect one another. Double connecting lines indicate friendships. The dotted line represents a casual association; separate male and female peer groups usually emerge in the primary years. Circles without connecting lines represent neglected or rejected children.

Peer relationships within a group transform over time. The leadership of a group may shift. Children who are initially well liked may gradually be rejected, or friendships may dissolve (Jiang & Cillessen, 2005; Dodge, Coie, Pettit, & Price, 1990; Stormshak et al., 1999).

Peer Rejection and Reputation

Some children in peer groups are rejected by others. Those who are rejected can be identified through a sociometric interview, described in Chapter 13, in which all students in a class are asked to name those peers they prefer to play with and those they don't. Primary-grade children who are named often as disliked playmates—that is, those of **rejected sociometric status**—are likely to exhibit a range of academic and social problems that persist into middle and high school (Mayeux, Bellmore, & Cillessen, 2007; Stormshak et al., 1999). In one study, for example, children who were rejected because of aggressive behavior in the primary years were found to commit more delinquent acts, including physical violence, at age 17 (Nagin & Tremblay, 1999).

Reasons for peer rejection in the primary years are more clearly defined than they were in preschool. A 4- or 5-year-old might be shunned because of extreme aggression; "She's mean" might be an explanation a peer gives for avoiding such a child. A 7- or 8-year-old, in contrast, will be avoided for a range of specific behaviors or characteristics. "Spoiled," "bossy," "angry," "fat," "clumsy," and "a tattletale" are terms commonly used to describe a child who is disliked by peers (Rogosch, Cicchetti, & Abner, 1995; Rogosch & Newcomb, 1989). Children in the primary years are said to have a **reputation**, a detailed collection of traits that are assigned to them by peers, fairly or not, that determine their peer status (P. Morrison & Masten, 1991; Zeller, Vannatta, Schafer, & Noll, 2003).

Negative peer reputations take a social and emotional toll. Children sometimes become more and more like what their reputation indicates. A child who has acquired a reputation for being aggressive may become more so, to the point of becoming violent. Another child may become more annoying in school interactions if such behavior is consistent with his reputation among classmates. Sadly, reputations stick with children over time. One study indicates that children's reputations do not become more positive in spite of improvement in their social behaviors (Hetherington, Cox, & Cox, 1979).

Certain clusters of traits are more likely to lead to peer rejection. As in the preschool years, primary-age children who exhibit hostile, aggressive behaviors are more likely to be avoided (Stormshak et al., 1999). Several new causes of rejection also emerge at this age. Some socially withdrawn children, previously overlooked by peers during the preschool

rejected sociometric status: The peer group status of children who are actively avoided by peers and who are named often as undesirable playmates in sociometric interviews.

reputation: A detailed collection of traits that are assigned to children by peers, fairly or not, that determine their peer status and influence later social development.

years, are now actively rejected (Ladd, 2006). This suggests that shyness and timidity may be less tolerated by primary-age children than by preschoolers. Children who are regularly victimized by others are also avoided by primary peer groups (Perren & Alsaker, 2006). These children have been found to exhibit an "anxious vulnerability" that leads to constant assault from bullies. They often acquiesce to the demands of others and cry when attacked. They are often socially anxious and withdrawn.

Anti-bullying programs have been implemented in some schools to protect children from being victimized. (See the Advocacy and Public Policy box in this chapter for descriptions of anti-bullying strategies and ways professionals can become involved.)

Children Who Are Neglected

Some primary-age children are of **neglected sociometric status**. In sociometric interviews, described in Chapter 13, they are never mentioned by peers, in either positive or negative terms. They simply go unnoticed by others at school or in the neighborhood. As in the preschool years, primary children who are neglected tend to be withdrawn (Coplan, Prakash, O'Neil, & Armer, 2004). The following story depicts a neglected first-grade child:

> Early in the school year, a teacher, Ms. Huels, is conducting a cooperative learning experience in science. Children are to gather in teams and solve problems using balances that she has provided. She encourages her students to join with "other children you'd like to work with." In the midst of a flurry of activity to choose teams, one young child stands alone and quiet. Finally, all the other children have gathered around tables in groups. The quiet child remains standing in the center of the classroom.

MS. HUELS:	(Noticing the quiet child) Uh oh. Have you all forgotten someone?
MANY CHILDREN:	What?
MS. HUELS:	Tyrone doesn't have a group!
MANY CHILDREN:	What?
JAMES:	Tyrone? Who's that?
SABRINA:	(Points to quiet child) It's him.
NICOLE:	Oh, *that's* Tyrone. (Laughs) I didn't know who it was!
MS. HUELS:	Tyrone needs to join a group.
ARTIS:	He can come here 'cause he doesn't say anything anyway.
TYRONE:	(Says nothing and moves to Artis's group)

In this story, Tyrone is neglected by his classmates and is not picked as a work partner. In fact, some children do not seem to know his name. A peer announces Tyrone's social reputation with typical primary-grade tact: "he doesn't say anything anyway."

Children may be withdrawn and ignored for different reasons. Some children show a great interest in the activities of peers but are hesitant to join in. Such children sometimes hover around the fringes of peers' play or work in the classroom and passively watch playground activities. They show interest in peer interactions but lack the confidence to act on their desire for friendship. These children may be at risk emotionally; they have been found to be more anxious than other types of withdrawn children (Degnan & Fox, 2007; Coplan, Rubin, Fox, Calkins, & Stewart, 1994; Wentzel & Asher, 1995). Other children may be withdrawn because they choose to be. Rather than hover and watch, they purposely work and play alone (Coplan et al., 2004). These isolated children do not display the same levels of social anxiety as reticent peers. They may be socially competent but simply less interested in extensive interaction.

Research suggests that being shy, playing alone, and even being ignored by peers does not necessarily lead to negative developmental outcomes (Burgess, Wojslawowicz, Rubin,

neglected sociometric status: The peer group status of children who are ignored by their peers and who are rarely mentioned at all in sociometric interviews.

ADVOCACY AND PUBLIC POLICY

Supporting an Anti-Bullying Campaign

This chapter discusses the negative effects of being victimized by peers in school. Professionals and parents must protect children from emotional as well as physical abuse; ridicule from peers can cause the same psychological harm as physical threat (Ladd et al., 1997; Perren & Alsaker, 2006). Professionals are no longer simply looking away when bullying incidents occur and assuming these are just an inevitable part of growing up. School districts around the country are implementing schoolwide anti-bullying programs to address the problem. Professionals can implement such programs in their own schools or classrooms or become involved in the anti-bullying movement on a national level.

More than 100 unique approaches to preventing bullying are available for schools to choose from, online and through published resource and training materials. Two such programs will be presented here as examples. The Anti-Bullying Network (http://www.antibullying.net) is a project funded by the government of Scotland to address problems of bullying in school. The group provides information on anti-bullying strategies to schools through published newsletters and on a Website. It operates a telephone call-in line to those living in Scotland. The network manages a large database of research on anti-bullying programs in operation around the world. It sponsors an annual conference and conducts workshops for teachers and other school personnel working to establish anti-bullying programs. A unique

feature of this program is its focus on professionals, parents, and children themselves. The Website contains a page that gives advice to children who are victimized by their peers.

The Anti-Bullying Network presents a multifaceted approach to reducing bullying behavior: (a) whole-class "circle time" discussions to address interpersonal issues among students; (b) specific strategies for reacting to bullying incidents, including peer mediation and "bully courts"; (c) specific discipline strategies to ensure that bullying does not go unpunished; (d) specific methods for addressing racist and homophobic bullying; and (e) a "peace-building" strategy for resolving conflicts.

Another organization, Operation Respect, promotes anti-bullying programs in the United States. This group has developed and implemented the *Don't Laugh at Me* program (http://www.dontlaugh.org). The program includes a curriculum for grades 2 to 5 and another for grades 6 to 8 that utilizes music, video, and curriculum guides to promote compassionate, safe, and respectful environments in schools. The program includes a well-researched approach to conflict resolution developed by the Educators for Social Responsibility (http://www.esrnational.org). Materials to implement *Don't Laugh at Me* can be ordered free of charge through the group's Website. Professionals can contact the group to organize training workshops in their own schools.

Rose-Krasnor, & Booth-LaForce, 2006). Teachers, parents, and child psychologists can give support to reticent children who desire peer contact but lack skills to achieve it. Interventions to teach social skills, including how to enter a peer group and how to negotiate and resolve conflicts, have been found effective in promoting positive peer relations even in the early elementary years (Garrard & Lipsey, 2007; Stevahn et al., 2000).

Friendships

As described previously, friendships become more important during the primary years. Children express growing concern about having and keeping friends as they advance through the primary grades (Hartup, 1996; Rose, Carlson, & Waller, 2007). Those who have friends are more likely to enjoy school and succeed academically in adolescence (Schneider, Wiener, & Murphy, 1994). Children who do not have friends at this age are more apt to express feelings of loneliness.

An important new role that friendships play is in easing the transition to school (Betts & Rotenberg, 2007; Ladd & Burgess, 1999; Ladd et al., 1997). Children have been found to use friends as a *secure base* for adjusting to and coping with new school experiences. A child who is starting first grade may be less anxious and more eager to attend if a close friend is in the class.

Parents, teachers, and school psychologists often use friendships to help new students adjust to their classrooms. They sometimes arrange for children to sit next to friends from the neighborhood or preschool in the early weeks of school. They facilitate friendships at home, prior to a new school year, by arranging get-togethers during the summer. Teachers give special attention to facilitating at least one friendship for each child in the classroom during early fall. Once children have a friend or two, they can more confidently broaden their interactions to other students.

Although children have a growing number of acquaintances in the primary years, the number of true friendships actually shrinks. By age 8, most children have a small group of true friends. It is not uncommon for girls to have just one best friend during this period (Gilligan, Murphy, & Tappan, 1990).

Friendships are more intimate in the primary years. They provide emotional support and a forum for expressing feelings and disclosing problems (Lloyd & Cohen, 1999; Rose et al., 2007). Some believe that the growing intimacy among friends in the primary years prepares children for opposite-sex love relationships in adolescence and adulthood (T. P. George & Hartmann, 1996). Children are more demanding of their friends at this age. They change friends less often and suffer greater stress when friends move away or a friendship breaks up (Hartup, 1996). Children are often picky about who their friends are; they select peers who have characteristics they admire. In some cases they choose friends who are like them (Güroğlu, van Lieshout, Haselager, & Scholte, 2007; Haselager, Hartup, van Lieshout, & Risen-Walraven, 1998), and best friends are often of the same gender, ethnicity, and socioeconomic status.

Peer Relations, Culture, and Class

Does culture or socioeconomic status influence friendships and peer relations in the primary years? Research findings are somewhat mixed. When asked who their friends are, primary-age

Friendships become more exclusive and longer lasting in the primary years.

children often name peers from their own ethnic background and sometimes from the same socioeconomic group (Beneson, Apostoleris, & Parnass, 1998; Briggs, 2007; Moody, 2001). However, exclusive same-culture friendships and interaction patterns have rarely been observed in elementary classrooms. In fact, most studies of multicultural classrooms reveal that cross-ethnic interaction is common (Howes & Wu, 1990; Lee, Howes, & Chamberlain, 2007). In one study, children as young as 7 reported in interviews that they strongly opposed social exclusion on the basis of ethnicity or racial stereotypes (Killen & Stangor, 2001).

It may be that attitudes vary greatly among individuals in any classroom group. Factors such as previous experience with people of other cultures, family beliefs, and intellectual competence may determine whether ethnicity influences peer relations. Patricia Ramsey (2004) has argued that teachers can facilitate positive attitudes and relationships among children of diverse backgrounds. She proposes that they first assess each student's knowledge and attitudes toward culture and class and then plan classroom activities and informal classroom interactions that will support the needs of individual children.

MORAL DEVELOPMENT

Piaget (1932) believed that, as young children become less egocentric, they acquire an early sense of morality. They begin to understand and adhere to rules and develop a concern for justice. Most preschool children, he proposed, are **premoral**—they do not adhere to clear rules when making moral decisions or playing games. For example, 4-year-olds playing a marble game might change the rules to better their chances of winning. From Piaget's view, such children should not be considered "bad" because they are not intentionally cheating or being dishonest. They are simply limited in their understanding of rules.

Piaget argued that, in the primary years, many children exhibit a sense of **moral realism**. At this stage, moral decisions and games are based on fixed rules. In fact, children of this age are quite rule-bound. In a game of marbles, they might now assert, "I don't care if you can't hit any marbles from there. That's where you shoot from. That's the rule." What is right or wrong at this age is determined by unchangeable rules that come from authority figures: parents, other adults, or God.

The final stage of morality—a sense of **moral relativism**—is achieved in adolescence or adulthood, according to Piaget. In this last stage, situations and intentions are taken into account when making moral judgments. When playing a game, a person might agree to bend the rules to assist another who has physical handicaps or to help a younger player win. According to this view, rules are made by people and can be altered for the higher good.

Elaborating on Piaget's stages, Lawrence Kohlberg (1984) identified three levels of moral development—*preconventional*, *conventional*, and *postconventional*—each containing two stages. These are presented in Table 17-3.

Kohlberg formulated these levels and stages by presenting special stories to elementary and adolescent children and asking for their responses. Each story portrayed a **moral dilemma**, such as the following: "A man's wife is dying. Although a drug is available to save her life, it is too expensive for him to afford. In desperation, he steals the medicine."

After describing the dilemma, Kohlberg would ask his subjects, "Was the man wrong to steal the medicine? Why or why not?" The first question was not as important as the second in assessing a subject's moral development since Kohlberg believed that the *justification* for the moral judgment was more revealing than the judgment itself. One person might say that it is right for the man to steal the medicine because he would not get caught—only a stage 1 answer. Another person might agree that stealing is right because saving a human life is more important than following society's rules—a stage 6 response. The reasoning behind the answer was most critical in evaluating moral development.

premoral: A term to describe children who do not yet understand or adhere to clear rules when making moral decisions or playing games.

moral realism: A stage in moral development in which right and wrong are determined by unchangeable rules that come from authority figures, such as parents.

moral relativism: A stage in moral development in which situations and intentions are taken into account when making moral judgments and rules can be altered for a higher good.

moral dilemmas: Hypothetical stories told to children to evaluate their moral reasoning.

TABLE 17-3

Kohlberg's Stages of Moral Development

Levels and Stages	Definitions of Right and Wrong
Level 1: **Preconventional**	**What's right is what you get rewarded for. What's wrong is what you get punished for.**
Stage 1:	What's right is obeying your parents and not getting punished.
Stage 2:	Actions that lead others to like you or reciprocate your kindness are right. The reason for being nice to people is so they will be nice to you.
Level 2: **Conventional**	**Social rules define what's right. Breaking the rules is wrong.**
Stage 3:	What's right is that which pleases others. Actions that others do not approve of are wrong.
Stage 4:	What's right is obeying laws that have been set down by those in power in society. What's wrong is breaking society's laws.
Level 3: **Postconventional**	**What's right is determined by higher-order moral principles.**
Stage 5:	Rules of society are determined by mutual agreement. Rules that don't work or are destructive may be wrong. Changing the rules can be a morally correct action.
Stage 6:	What's right is governed by universal moral principles. Values such as "life is sacred" and "be kind to others" define what is right, not laws created by humans.

SOURCE: Stages of moral reasoning, pages 176–177, table 2 from *Essays on Moral Development: The Psychology of Moral Development (Vol. II)* by Lawrence Kohlberg. Reprinted by permission of HarperCollins Publishers.

Kohlberg found that most elementary-age children respond to moral dilemmas at the **preconventional level**—stage 1 or 2 (see Table 17-3). They most often resolve these dilemmas by saying that what is right is obeying your parents and the rules and not getting punished. They also justify decisions in terms of being nice so that others will be nice to you. Only in adolescence do some young people reach higher levels of moral reasoning. So, Kohlberg believed that relatively little advancement in moral development occurs during childhood.

Critiques of Kohlberg

Although Kohlberg's theory has been supported by an extensive body of research, a number of criticisms have been raised about his work (Greene & Haidt, 2002).

Moral Behavior versus Moral Reasoning. Some believe that Kohlberg's theory does not adequately emphasize the connections between moral thinking and moral behavior (Eisenberg, 2000). Does one necessarily lead to the other? A child who argues that cheating is wrong in a study of moral reasoning might still cheat in a game with peers, and a young gang member who commits drive-by shootings in a desperate effort to belong may still show very advanced levels of moral thinking. Conversely, a toddler who cannot understand moral dilemma stories, much less answer them in sophisticated ways, may nonetheless share a toy with a peer. Moral

preconventional level: A stage of moral development in which children resolve moral dilemmas by saying that what is right is obeying your parents and the rules and not getting punished. Children at this stage also justify moral decisions in terms of being nice so that others will be nice to you.

reasoning and moral action are not the same, and moral actions often do not advance in clearly defined stages as moral reasoning appears to do. Context, personality, peer relationships, and even biology will affect how children react to real-life moral problems.

Feminist Criticism. Multicultural and feminist scholars have argued that Kohlberg's work reflects the values, social relationships, and interpersonal characteristics of Euro-American males (Genyue, Xu, Cameron, Heyman, & Lee, 2007; Richardson, 2007). Gilligan (1993a) has suggested that a high rating on Kohlberg's moral dilemma scale requires a male-oriented approach to solving problems. She notes, for example, that male children often present cut-and-dried solutions to moral dilemma stories. They take definitive positions on moral issues, based on rules. Females are more hesitant in offering definitive solutions to these stories. They often refuse to judge rightness and wrongness at all, but seek creative, alternative solutions that are beneficial to everyone involved.

For example, one girl's response to Gilligan's dying-wife story was to suggest that the man go to a bank for a loan. She offered this solution because she believed that this would help everyone in the story, including the man who owned the drug. Another girl argued that it would be both right and wrong for the man to steal the drug. It would be right to help his wife, she argued, yet it would also be wrong because, if the man were to go to jail, he would no longer be able to care for his wife. Using traditional research methods, these children might be viewed as lacking moral conviction because of their ambivalence or confusion in solving these problems. Gilligan argues that, to the contrary, a reluctance to take a moral stand may reflect great concern for other people and a need to consider all aspects of a situation fully before making judgments.

Multicultural Criticism. Others have argued that Kohlberg's stages of moral development reflect primarily Western values (Gibbs, Basinger, Grime, & Snarey, 2007). For example, Kohlberg believed that the most moral arguments are those based on concern for all of humankind. In the dying-wife story, a response such as the following would be considered extremely advanced: "The man should steal the medicine because human life is sacred. It is okay to break rules for the benefit of others."

In some cultural groups, however, concerns about one's own family and community may receive highest priority. Consider the example of a Latino child living in a neighborhood in which family and friends have banded together in the face of harsh treatment and racism. The child is taught from a young age to adopt the collective goals of her cultural group. In response to the dying-wife story, this child might say, "It's right for the man to steal to save his wife. She is family. She is Puerto Rican. Puerto Rican people stick together." Although Kohlberg might have construed such a justification as self-oriented or less principled, within the child's culture an argument based on the well-being of one's ethnic group might be considered more ethical than one based on the good of all humans.

Not surprisingly, then, research has shown variations in the acquisition of moral reasoning across cultures (Gibbs et al., 2007). Although Kohlberg's theory provides a useful framework for observing moral development, variations may be expected across groups and individuals.

CLASSROOM ADAPTATIONS: SOCIAL COMPETENCE AND CHILDREN WITH SPECIAL NEEDS

Several challenging conditions in the primary years severely threaten peer relationships and the acquisition of social skills. Among these are serious emotional disturbance, autism, and attention-deficit/hyperactivity disorder. Teachers can adapt classroom activities and interactions to support the social development of children with these disorders.

Serious Emotional Disturbance

Typically developing children may exhibit social conflicts with peers or conduct problems in school. Arguments and even physical fights can erupt in elementary classrooms. Children may misbehave or disobey teachers and parents. The degree to which such behavior is tolerated varies by culture (B. B. Whiting & Edwards, 1988). In some communities inside and outside the United States, a good deal of misbehavior is accepted. In others, rigid rules of conduct are enforced.

A small number of children are more deeply troubled and are said to have **serious emotional disturbance (SED)** (see Chapter 13). They exhibit extreme, negative emotional reactions that go beyond typical misbehavior or peer conflict. They may display disruptive or antisocial behaviors over a long period of time and in many different settings. Some of these children are very aggressive and, as a result, very challenging to live or work with. They sometimes strike out against peers and display oppositional behavior in school. These outward emotional displays have been called *externalizing behavior problems* (Umansky, 2008b; Valiente et al., 2003).

Other children with emotional difficulties are withdrawn, anxious, and sad. They may regularly complain about physical ailments and avoid going to school (Whelen, 1995). These children are said to have *internalizing behavior problems*. Children who outwardly express negative emotions and those who are withdrawn share a common challenge: they have difficulty entering into satisfying relationships with peers and adults (Duhig, Renk, Epstein, & Phares, 2000).

Given the variety of emotional and social problems just described, it is not surprising that professionals do not use a single name for this disorder. Besides *serious emotional disturbance*, some use the term *social and emotional maladjustment*, others *emotional disorder*, to categorize children with these challenges. This emotional impairment, regardless of its name, is almost always accompanied by poor peer relations (Bolger & Patterson, 2001).

What causes SED? Some believe that children are biologically predisposed to social and emotional problems. Having a parent or sibling who has suffered an emotional impairment, for example, increases a child's chances of having SED (O'Connor, Heron, Golding, Beveridge, & Glover, 2003). Fragile X syndrome, a genetic disorder, also has been associated with severe emotional difficulties (Hessl et al., 2002). Others believe that stressful life experiences cause these problems. Chaotic family lives, poor attachment, and violence in the community can all contribute to SED (Margolin & Gordis, 2001). Not surprisingly, child abuse has been linked to SED (Tyler, 2002). Even harsh—though not abusive—discipline practices have been related to this disorder, as have negative parent attitudes toward children (Nix et al., 1999).

A number of strategies have been developed to assist children who have SED. A traditional **behavior modification** approach is often used. In this technique, teachers, parents, or school psychologists articulate specific expectations for behavior and then reward children for meeting those expectations. In spite of advancements in special education, behavior modification continues to be the most widely used strategy for children with SED (Knitzer, Steinberg, & Fleisch, 1990; Whelen, 1995). Caution is urged in using this approach. External rewards may impair **intrinsic motivation**—that is, an internal drive to learn or be accepted (Bénabou & Tirole, 2004). Furthermore, children of some cultural groups may react less positively to praise (Ng et al., 2007).

Other approaches focus on promoting greater self-regulation and intrinsic motivation. In a **modified curricular approach**, the classroom environment, lessons and activities, and student groupings are altered to reduce stress on children who have SED (Bowe, 1999). Rules for sitting absolutely still or being quiet may be relaxed. Teachers may provide material that is easier for children to read, and projects may be planned that incorporate the personal interests of children with SED. Desks or workstations may be arranged so that children with SED interact with peers who have positive affect or who possess superior social skills. Such

serious emotional disturbance (SED): A broad term used to describe children who exhibit negative emotional reactions that go beyond typical misbehavior or upset. Children with SED may exhibit externalizing problems, such as aggression, or internalizing problems, such as withdrawn behavior and anxiety.

behavior modification: A classroom strategy, often used with children with serious emotional disturbance or other special needs, in which adults articulate specific expectations for behavior and then reward children for meeting those expectations.

intrinsic motivation: A desire to learn, behave appropriately, or be accepted that comes from within rather than being imposed externally through rewards or praise.

modified curricular approach: A strategy in which the classroom environment, lessons and activities, and student groupings are altered to reduce stress on children who have serious emotional disturbance or other special needs.

changes in the classroom have been found to increase attention to learning tasks by 30% and reduce disruptive behavior by 67% for children with SED (L. Edwards, 1983).

Whelen (1995) proposes a **trust-building intervention** in which teachers and other professionals interact with children in ways that build positive relationships. The rationale is that, if children who have SED form positive, trusting relationships with adults, they will eventually be able to establish positive peer relations as well. Strategies include *differential acceptance*, in which adults "receive large doses of hate, aggression, and hostility without reacting in kind to the children who transmit them" (p. 312). Whelen asserts that hostile acts by children with SED are expressions of pain and anguish caused by years of abuse or family chaos. Responding with anger to such outbursts will only exacerbate children's negative feelings. He recommends firm but nonhostile and nonpunitive responses to extreme misbehavior.

In the trust-building strategy, teachers or school psychologists go out of their way to be responsive, warm, and empathic (Whelen, 1995). They show great interest in children's comments or accomplishments and attempt to understand and ameliorate children's idiosyncratic fears or dislikes. For example, a teacher who notices that a child is anxious about going outdoors during recess might probe for the source of the child's anxiety rather than expressing intolerance or insisting that the child face the fear. Through conversation, the teacher might learn that the child fears physical assault from peers. Special accommodations could then be made, such as accompanying the child to the playground for a time or inviting the child and a peer to stay behind in the classroom during recess. The result of the trust-building strategy is that children with SED will bond with an adult over time. Once this has occurred, peer interactions and friendships can be facilitated.

Autism and Social Competence

As described in earlier chapters, **autism** inhibits children's social development in numerous ways (S. R. Easterbrooks, 2008). Children with autism have difficulty interpreting the thoughts, motives, and behaviors of others. Often they are unable to pretend, which limits their play interactions. Many children with autism cannot speak; most avoid contact—even eye contact—with peers. It is not surprising that these children are likely to be rejected by classmates and are often unable to make friends.

Autism can vary from mild to severe. Children with milder forms can talk and make contact with others. Can children with mild autism enter into meaningful peer relationships? A recent review of many different studies on the social abilities of children with autism provides a mixed answer to this question (Bellini, Peters, Benner, & Hopf, 2007). These researchers report that school-age subjects with mild autism can make friends and interact positively with peers. However, their relationships are often of poorer quality in terms of companionship, security, and helpfulness. Further, children with autism are more likely than typically developing peers to report that they are lonely. Even those who are befriended by many classmates feel isolated. Interventions to assist children with autism in acquiring social skills are more or less successful, depending on the severity of the condition, the classroom context, and the characteristics of other peers in the classroom group.

Such social skills interventions are not always implemented in schools because of the belief that children with this disorder cannot make friends (Chamberlain, Kasari, & Rotheram-Fuller, 2007; Hurley-Geffner, 1996). Friendship strategies, such as inviting a child with autism and a potential friend to work alone together away from the crowded classroom, might be considered. Parents, guided by recommendations from teachers, might invite potential friends to visit their homes. Adults can guide these friendship pairs by suggesting activities and initiating conversation.

trust-building intervention: A classroom strategy in which professionals interact with children with serious emotional disturbance in ways that build positive relationships with the hope that this will lead to positive peer relations as well.

autism: A condition characterized by a lack of awareness of others, a preference for objects to people, and an intense desire for sameness. Autism can include language delays, self-destructive behavior, repetitive and ritualistic body movements, and difficulty interpreting multiple stimuli.

One promising technique is to guide typically developing peers in making positive contact with children who have autism (Jahr, Eldevik, & Eikeseth, 2000). The first step is to help all children in a classroom understand and be sympathetic to the challenges of this condition. Once students show positive attitudes toward those with this disorder, they can be taught to interact with them in special ways. They might be encouraged to engage peers with autism in turn-taking games—such as playing catch or handing objects back and forth. They might be asked to initiate simple conversations or to play close to peers with this condition. Typically developing peers might be prompted to model social skills, such as asking for help, showing affection, and sharing. This approach has been found to have positive effects on the social development of children with autism that persist well into the elementary years (D. M. Clark & Smith, 1999; I. S. Schwartz & Sandall, 1998).

Because children with autism often lack language skills, teachers might provide alternative communication systems that allow them to make contact with others. Establishing a set of simple, natural gestures to communicate needs (e.g., showing a desire for more juice through pantomime) or teaching sign language has been found to help children with autism to express themselves (Aldred, Green, & Adams, 2004; Cafiero, 1998). Communication boards with photographs or symbols that children can point to may be helpful (Howard et al., 2004).

ADHD and Social Competence

The learning and behavioral difficulties of children with **attention-deficit/hyperactivity disorder (ADHD)** have been described in previous chapters. Because children with ADHD are extremely active, impulsive, and easily distracted, they perform poorly in school and are more likely to break classroom rules (Wicks-Nelson & Israel, 2002). Children with this condition often have trouble forming positive relationships with peers. School-age children with ADHD are more often rejected by classmates (Diamantopoulou, Henricsson, & Rydell, 2005). This rejection emerges quickly within a new group of peers—say, a new classroom of children at the beginning of the school year. Only a month into school, children with ADHD may already be avoided. Once children with ADHD are rejected by a group, they continue to be even when their social behaviors improve (Hinshaw & Melnick, 1995).

Why are some children with ADHD so quickly and irreversibly shunned by peers? One theory holds that they perform behaviors that are disruptive to the activities of other children. Their louder, more active and impulsive interactions might simply drive others away. A study of boys with ADHD supports this view (Hoza, 2007). Compared with typically developing children, those with ADHD were found to be far less persuasive, friendly, conversational, and responsive to their peers and more angry, disruptive, negative, and helpless.

Another explanation for the peer rejection of children with ADHD is that they are less able to understand social situations and the needs of their peers (Milch-Reich, Campbell, & Pelham, 1999). Often they are unable to read accurately the impact of their behaviors on others (Aberson, Shure, & Goldstein, 2007). For example, a child with ADHD might fail to notice that her loud, active interactions are causing peers to move away from her. Children with ADHD often fail to notice and adapt to changes in a social situation. They might continue to perform a behavior that is no longer appropriate because of a shift in situational demands. For example, a child might continue to exhibit loud, playful behavior even when recess is over because he does not understand that a math lesson has begun and it is now time to listen quietly. The following story shows how this inability to read and adapt to new situations can interfere not just with school success but with peer relationships as well:

attention-deficit/hyperactivity disorder (ADHD): A disorder that is characterized by high activity level, impulsiveness, and an inability to pay attention that often leads to poor peer relations and school performance.

A group of 8-year-old children are playing an active, silly game of freeze tag on the playground. The rule is that children run away from one child, Alexander, who is *it*. If they are tagged by him, they must freeze until another child can touch and *free* them. All players scream and joke and run. Colin, a child with ADHD, begins to taunt Alexander: "Ha, ha! You can't get me!" Alexander chases and tags him, laughing and calling, "I did get you! Freeze!" Colin does not freeze, however; he continues with his wild cries. "You aren't going to get me!" He laughs and runs in circles. "Try to get me!"

His peers all stop playing the game. Alexander says, angrily, "No, Colin, you have to freeze now." Other children join in the protest. "He tagged you, so you have to stop." Colin ignores them and calls out in a silly voice, "I'm too fast, I'm too fast! You can't get me!"

One child in the group says, "I'm not going to play because that's not the rule. Colin's not playing it right." The other children mumble agreement, and the game ends.

In this story, Colin initially plays the game very well. His silly, active behaviors are appreciated and encouraged by his peers. It is when the situation changes—when he is tagged by Alexander—that problems arise. He does not seem to understand that he must adapt his behavior at this point in the game. He simply continues with his previous wild interactions. Peers grow angry and leave him.

Teachers, psychologists, and parents may need to adopt a two-pronged strategy for supporting the social interactions of children with ADHD. First, they may need to guide these children in learning specific social behaviors—how to use a quiet voice, to ask rather than demand, or to join a peer activity unobtrusively. In addition, they may need to help children interpret social situations and the impact of their behaviors on others. Asking a child with ADHD, "What happened when you yelled so loud?" or "What do we do differently during this part of the game?" may enhance social understanding.

Invisible Handicaps and Peer Acceptance

The challenging conditions described in this chapter—SED, autism, and ADHD—often lead to greater peer rejection than other types of conditions. Children with hearing impairments or with physically challenging conditions are less likely to be avoided by peers. Why? It is possible that these *visible* handicaps are easier for children to understand (McLean et al., 2003). They can see the apparatus a child uses to hear better or the wheelchair a child uses to move around. Teachers can more easily point out and talk about these conditions with their students. But what does a teacher tell children about a peer with an **invisible handicap**—a disability without easy-to-see physical characteristics, such as autism? What concrete cues can a teacher refer to in explaining ADHD? What is appropriate for a teacher to tell children about a new student who has SED because of child abuse? A first-grade teacher recently shared her thought-provoking and perhaps controversial answers to these questions:

It's simple. You talk openly with all your students about special needs of all kinds. Just as you tell a child, "She needs that thing around her neck to hear better," you also say, "He can get very angry and hit because he's sad sometimes" or "She doesn't answer when children talk to her because she has something called autism." You talk about these things and you let children talk about them. You let them express their concerns and ask any questions they want. If you discuss challenging conditions directly and matter-of-factly, children will be able to understand and appreciate their peers. If you tiptoe around these things, pretend these conditions don't exist, children will not be as accepting. If we want children to appreciate diversity, we can't just pick and choose the handicaps that are easy to talk about!

invisible handicaps: Disabilities without easy-to-see physical characteristics that are more difficult for peers to identify and understand.

CHILD GUIDANCE: *A Conflict Resolution Strategy*

Primary-age children sometimes argue and even fight physically. Often, teachers intervene to resolve such disputes directly. If a child has taken a peer's pencil, a teacher might simply insist that it be returned. If there is loud, angry screaming, a teacher might merely separate the children who are at odds. Aggression might be met with a quick time-out. However, research has shown that even very young children can resolve many of these conflicts on their own with just a little help from adults (Heydenberk & Heydenberk, 2007; Stevahn et al., 2000). When children learn conflict resolution skills, they are better equipped to address problems with peers that arise when no adults are present (e.g., on the school bus or in the neighborhood). As they get older, children who have learned conflict resolution strategies will be less likely to use violence to solve social problems.

A colleague and I created a simple conflict resolution strategy as part of a larger violence prevention program (Andrews & Trawick-Smith, 1996). We trained teachers in using this strategy and interviewed them about its effectiveness. Teachers reported that children learned and could apply the steps of this technique and, within several months of implementation, were more likely to resolve their own disputes without adult assistance. This is how the method works:

Step 1: Introducing the strategy. During a class meeting, teachers introduce the steps of the conflict resolution model, described later. Examples of conflicts and how they are addressed using the strategy are presented. Children are asked to try out the approach through role-playing. A chart is developed that shows graphically how the model works. An example of such a chart is provided in Figure 17-3.

The chart is displayed in a prominent place in the classroom for children to review. The conflict resolution strategy is revisited many times throughout the school year during group time. Children are encouraged to share stories about how they used the method in solving real-life social problems.

Step 2: Keeping children in conflict together. When disputes arise, the next step is for the teacher to move close to the children in conflict and try to keep them together. Quickly separating them, which is a common response to classroom disagreements, is discouraged. (Children should be separated only if they are so angry they cannot talk or if there is a threat of physical harm. In this case, the remaining steps are still followed but after children have cooled down.) An option in this step is to create a *conflict resolution table*, a small table with several chairs that is designated as the place children go to address disputes. The conflict resolution chart can be affixed to the surface of this table.

Step 3: Asking children what happened. The teacher reminds the children who are in conflict about the chart that is posted in the classroom (e.g., "Remember we use the conflict chart when

we have difficulties"). Pointing to the first box on the chart, shown in Figure 17-3, the teacher asks each child to state what has happened to cause the conflict. Each child is given a turn to speak without interruption. The teacher restates each child's view of things so that all others involved will understand that child's perspective (e.g., "So you think you were using the pencil first, but then Jannie took it when you went to your cubby").

Step 3a: Offering insights, if children have none. The teacher gives children time to think about what happened in the dispute, following step 3. However, if none of the children involved have anything to say, the teacher can get the conversation started by offering an insight (e.g., "Well, it looks to me like you're both very angry" or "It seems like she hit you because you knocked over her blocks"). Great care must be taken not to interpret the situation for children when they can do this on their own. In addition, the teacher should only offer interpretations that are accurate and based on direct observation. Nothing undermines the process more than having a teacher state, "I think you hit him," when this did not occur.

Step 4: Asking children for solutions. After all children have stated their interpretations of what occurred, the teacher refers to the next box on the conflict chart (see Figure 17-3) and asks, "What should we do about this?" All children are encouraged to offer resolutions. All suggestions are discussed, even those that may not be appropriate (e.g., "You could give Neddie a whipping!"). Each child involved should be encouraged to offer a solution. If all children talk at once, the teacher can ask that they take turns.

Step 4a: Offering solutions, if children have none. Children should be given time to think of resolutions to their conflict. If children cannot come up with any, however, the teacher can get the conversation started by offering a few suggestions (e.g., "Well, one thing you could do is take turns with the pencil. How could we do that, so you both can use it?" or "I could get another pencil for one of you to use"). Teachers should use this step only if children cannot generate their own solutions. Teachers should offer a number of ideas so that children can still make a choice about which resolution they prefer.

Step 5: Generating multiple solutions to the problem. In step 4, children may come up with only one or two resolutions to their conflict. To promote breadth in social problem solving, the teacher now points to the third box on the conflict chart and says, "That's a good idea! What's something else we could do about the problem?" The point of this step is to help children consider many different solutions to a social dilemma. Children who can generate multiple ideas for resolving a conflict have been found to be less likely to use aggression and more likely to have friends in school (Dodge & Price, 1994; Lemerise & Arsenio, 2000).

Step 6: Agreeing on a solution. After children (and the teacher) have identified several possible solutions to the conflict, the teacher restates each of these for clarity (e.g., "Okay, so Jeremy could help you rebuild your castle, Jeremy could go play somewhere else, or the two of you could start a new building"). The teacher, pointing to box 4 on the conflict chart, now asks which solution all children prefer. When children agree on a solution, the teacher helps them implement it, pointing out that they have reached box 5 on the chart (e.g., "This is great. You're working together and being friends").

How can a teacher do all these things when there are so many other students in the class that need attention? We found that once teachers and children were familiar with this strategy, many conflicts could be resolved in only 2 or 3 minutes (Andrews & Trawick-Smith, 1996)!

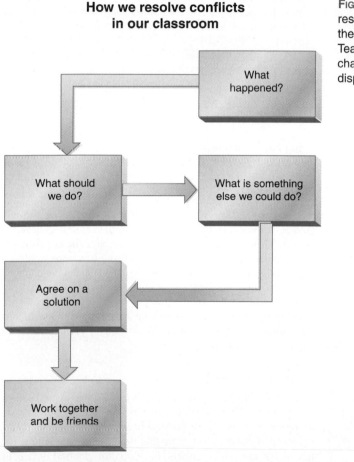

How we resolve conflicts in our classroom

FIGURE 17-3 A sample conflict resolution chart to be posted in the primary-grade classroom. Teachers can refer children to the chart as they help them settle disputes.

SUMMARY

Children's views of themselves and their relationships with others change markedly during the primary years. With emerging cognitive abilities and more frequent evaluation in school, children of this age begin to compare themselves more often with peers. They begin to form judgments about their own competence. They also evaluate themselves on their acceptance by others, the control they have over their own lives, and their moral self-worth. Children may hold positive views of themselves in some of these areas but negative views in others. Those of collective cultures may hold inclusive views of themselves. These are self-evaluations that are based not on individual achievement but rather on the accomplishments, self-sufficiency, and moral worth of their families and communities as a whole. Culture influences the criteria children use to evaluate themselves. Unique cultural competencies, family beliefs about how much control children should have, and experiences with prejudice all affect self-esteem.

In the primary years, children begin to form an identity—an understanding of roles, personal values, characteristics, competencies, and group memberships that define oneself. This includes acquiring an understanding of what it means to be male or female and a member of a particular ethnic group. Children of color whose families instill cultural pride through strong ethnic socialization come to acquire a positive ethnic identity.

Peer groups and friendships in the primary years become more fixed and well defined. Children who are neglected or rejected by their peer group tend to remain in that low status even when they learn more positive social skills. Friendships are relatively permanent and exclusive. Cross-cultural interactions and friendships are common in classrooms where teachers facilitate understanding and cooperation. One factor that influences social interactions is moral reasoning—an ability to think about right and wrong. A traditional view is that primary-age children think about moral dilemmas at a fairly low level. What is right to most children of this age is what will be rewarded or will cause others to be nice to them. Feminist and multicultural scholars have challenged this perspective, citing research showing that children of this age often consider others—particularly members of their family or cultural group—when making decisions about right and wrong.

A number of challenging conditions affect peer relationships. Among these are serious emotional disturbance, autism, and attention-deficit/hyperactivity disorder. Teachers must plan vigorous interventions to help children with these disorders make friends. Teachers must also assist other students in the classroom to understand and accept these invisible handicaps.

RESEARCH INTO PRACTICE

CRITICAL CONCEPT 1

The primary years are a period of social and emotional change. As children's cognitive capacity increases at this age, they are able to engage in a great deal more self-reflection. A more accurate and discerning look at self emerges during this period. Further, children of this age contemplate more fully the meanings of relationships and friendships.

Application #1   Provide children with many opportunities for social experience. They must be able to play, collaborate, and negotiate with peers, even in the primary grades. Only through authentic social interaction are children able to construct an understanding of the social world and their place in it.

Application #2   Provide experiences for children to think and talk about themselves and their peers. Group conversations, for example, about individuals' abilities, interests, and unique characteristics will enhance self-reflection. Children's books about the importance of friendship and feelings associated with peer rejection will stimulate thinking about peer relationships.

CRITICAL CONCEPT 2

According to Erikson, emotionally healthy primary-age children acquire a sense of industry or competence—a belief that they are knowledgeable and skilled. Children will enjoy a sense of competence unless they experience harsh evaluation or frequent failure. Children who receive low grades or negative responses from teachers may come to feel inferior.

Application #1   Provide classroom play and work experiences that lead to true success. Children in the primary years are no longer satisfied with making creative attempts or trying hard; they now seek to master real skills. Activities that challenge their thinking yet are within their level of ability and lead to real learning are necessary for children to feel competent.

Application #2   Avoid evaluative symbols. Although grades, stickers, smiling faces, and improvement charts are intended to motivate children, they may have the opposite effect. Evaluative symbols have been linked to poor achievement and negative beliefs about self.

Application #3   Avoid harsh and public criticism. Classroom interactions should be mainly positive and encouraging. Address misbehaviors of individual children calmly and privately.

CRITICAL CONCEPT 3

Primary children evaluate themselves in other areas besides competence. They acquire a sense of whether they are accepted by peers, family, and teachers. Some develop an internal locus of control—a feeling that one has the power to regulate one's own life. Others develop an external locus of control—a belief that one is mainly powerless and unable to make a difference. Feelings of moral self-worth—that is, of being a good or bad person—are formed. So, children hold many distinct types of self-esteem during the primary years.

Application #1   Show that you unconditionally care for the children in your classrooms. Give the following message, even to the most challenging students: "Sometimes I may not care for your behaviors, but I always deeply care about you as a person." By being responsive, showing interest, and being warm, you can enhance feelings of acceptance.

Application #2   Give over as much control of the classroom to children as is reasonable. Encourage them to solve social or learning problems independently. Implement a group decision-making process in which all children in the class participate in selecting projects or topics to study. Hold group meetings several times a week to air grievances or to raise and solve problems in the classroom. These experiences lead to an internal locus of control in that they help children learn that they have power over their own lives.

Application #3   Be cautious not to threaten children's feelings of moral self-worth when administering reprimands or other discipline strategies. Statements such as "You are so bad!" are global assaults on self-worth and should be replaced by specific comments about inappropriate behavior, such as "You are so loud and silly that other children can't hear the story." Give the message that specific behaviors may be unacceptable but that all children are good and honest.

CRITICAL CONCEPT 4

Children of historically underrepresented groups may hold slightly different views of themselves. Their self-esteem may be more inclusive in that it is based on pride in their family, ethnic group, and community. Some children may base their self-evaluations on very different criteria than children of the dominant culture. In spite of the experience of prejudice that many children of color face, most acquire positive views of self.

Application #1   Understand and appreciate cultural diversity in self-evaluation. Recognize that an inclusive view of self, which is reflected in statements of pride in one's family or community, is an important sign of positive self-appraisal in some children.

Application #2   Redesign typical self-concept activities to accommodate inclusive views of self. Instead of asking children in a group activity to comment on things they do well, ask, "What are some things that you, your family, or your friends do well?" Modify an activity in which children draw themselves to allow children to draw their families or neighborhoods. Ask children to draw, as a group, a mural of all members of the class.

CRITICAL CONCEPT 5

Identity is one factor that influences children's views of themselves. Children who understand and are comfortable with their gender are more likely to have positive self-esteem. Those who strongly identify with and are proud of their ethnic heritage are also more likely to hold more positive views of self. Ethnic identity is often a result of ethnic socialization: the conscious effort of parents or other adults to teach children to understand and have pride in their culture.

Application #1   Create classroom environments in which cultural and gender diversity are celebrated. The first step is to ensure that all children in a class receive the same learning opportunities, encouragements, questions, and contact from the teacher. Monitor your classroom interactions to make certain that your attention is equitably distributed among all students.

Application #2   The curriculum should reflect an appreciation for all cultures and both genders. Photographs of families of diverse backgrounds should be prevalent. Provide children's books that portray competent and likable characters of both genders and all cultures. Study the contributions of both male and female scientists, authors, political leaders, and historical figures from all cultural backgrounds.

Application #3   Integrate the unique histories of historically underrepresented groups—including experiences of oppression—into the curriculum.

CRITICAL CONCEPT 6

Children's peer groups become more complex and organized in the primary years. Children who are more or less popular emerge. Friendships are more intimate and more important. Positive peer relationships in the primary years predict later social adjustment and school success.

Application #1   Provide positive social experiences in the classroom. Offer sociodramatic play, blocks, outdoor activities, and collaborative projects—which are disappearing in many modern primary classrooms—to allow the formation of peer relationships.

Application #2   Intervene in children's play interactions to support positive peer relations. In particular, gently assist rejected or neglected children in entering playgroups, getting peers' attention in positive ways, and resolving conflicts.

Application #3   Facilitate friendships among isolated children. This involves identifying potential friendship pairs and arranging experiences for them to interact in positive ways. Parents can assist by inviting potential friends to visit in their homes.

CRITICAL CONCEPT 7

Children can reflect more competently on moral dilemmas in the primary years. Many base their judgments on whether rules are right or wrong and on a sense of fairness. Cultural and gender variations do exist, however, in how children think about moral problems.

Application #1   Provide group conversations that encourage children to think about and discuss moral dilemmas. For example, tell the classic story of two children who each break a porcelain cup; one of the children does it unintentionally, and the other does it deliberately. Ask your students, "Who is naughtiest?" This activity generates discussions and disagreements and results in advancement in moral reasoning.

Application #2   Provide group games that allow many real-life discussions about moral dilemmas. Disputes about rules, charges of cheating, and disagreements about who won will contribute to moral development.

Application #3 Understand and appreciate diversity in moral reasoning. Children may base moral arguments on what's best for family or community, not rules of society as a whole. Other children may not take a stand on moral issues at all, believing that solutions to these dilemmas cannot be so simply decided. Such arguments, which are more common among females and children of historically underrepresented groups, reflect advanced forms of reasoning that are not appreciated by traditional measures of moral development.

CRITICAL CONCEPT 8

Some children may have serious emotional disturbance (SED), autism, or attention-deficit/hyperactivity disorder (ADHD) in the primary years, conditions that often lead to peer rejection. A variety of causes and remediation strategies have been proposed for these disorders. New techniques for promoting trust and attachment, facilitating friendships, encouraging verbal and nonverbal communication, and helping children interpret social situations have been recommended.

Application #1 Become familiar with and be able to identify the characteristics of children with SED, autism, and ADHD. Negative affect, harsh and often aggressive reactions to others, antisocial or withdrawn behavior, and conduct problems in school are common among children with SED. Children who avoid contact—even eye contact—with others, speak very little, and perform repetitive, ritualistic behaviors may have autism. Those who are highly active, impulsive, and inattentive in ways that interfere with learning and social interactions may have ADHD.

Application #2 In collaboration with special education personnel, adapt the classroom to help children with special needs make friends and interact positively with peers. Arrange desks or workstations so children with SED interact with peers who have positive affect or who possess superior social skills. Ask typically developing peers to make contact with children with autism in order to model social and communication skills. Establish communication boards or a simple system of gestures to help children with this challenging condition express their needs. Coach children with ADHD in how to play and work in less loud, disruptive, or impulsive ways. Guide them in interpreting social situations and noticing the effects of their behaviors on others.

Application #3 Strive to respond in positive and encouraging ways to children with special needs. Patiently accepting a degree of anger and hostility from children with SED, the active and impulsive behaviors of those with ADHD, and a lack of communication and contact from children with autism will promote positive teacher–child relationships. This, in turn, will enhance relationships with peers.

Application #4 Help all students in a class to understand invisible handicaps, such as SED, autism, or ADHD. Although these are difficult conditions to explain to young children, an open dialogue about them will increase empathy and caring. When you are open about disabilities, children will be as well. They will ask questions and more readily enter into relationships with those who have these special needs.

ASSESSING YOUNG CHILDREN: Primary-Age Social and Emotional Development

Areas of Development	What to Watch For	Indicators of Atypical Development	Applications
Emotional health	Displays a positive view of self across four areas: competence ("I can do it!"), moral self-worth ("I'm a good girl/boy!"), social acceptance ("I have lots of friends!"), and control ("I can do it all by myself!"). Holds positive views of one's family and culture ("I'm glad I'm black!").	Expresses feelings of inferiority ("I can't read like everybody else!"). Stops trying to learn, make friends, or complete tasks independently. Expresses a dislike of one's own ethnicity and a preference for others'.	Avoid classroom practices that threaten feelings of competence, such as public comparison, ability grouping, or the overuse of evaluative symbols. Plan activities that help children evaluate their own competence. Help them assess their acceptance by peers and family, their self-reliance, and their moral self-worth. Help children of color acquire positive, inclusive views of themselves by including activities that nurture ethnic pride.

Relationships with others	Is liked by at least some peers. Forms one or more special friendships. Maintains positive relationships with teachers. Has a positive reputation ("a pretty nice person" or "fun to be with").	Is teased, bullied, or in other ways victimized by peers. Is actively avoided or completely ignored. Has no close friends in school or in the neighborhood. Exhibits hostile aggression toward peers. Shows anxiety and withdrawal.	Actively promote positive peer relations by encouraging much social interaction in the classroom. Plan cooperative learning activities in which students of diverse backgrounds are grouped together to complete projects. Pair students with negative reputations with prosocial children and those with like interests or social styles.
Specific social skills	Tries alternative solutions to solve social problems. Effectively persuades peers. Compromises and negotiates. Accurately interprets social situations.	Resolves problems with aggression. Chooses to work and play alone. Engages in behaviors that are considered bizarre by peers.	Guide children in learning specific social skills that lead to peer acceptance, such as persuading others, expressing viewpoints, initiating conversations, and showing kindness. Implement a conflict resolution strategy that allows students to solve their own social problems without adult assistance. Encourage typically developing children to make contact with those with special needs in order to model positive social behaviors and language.

Interpreting Assessment Data: There are cultural differences in social and emotional development. Children of some cultures will evaluate themselves based on their families or cultures. Their self-assessments may be based, for example, on the accomplishments of their parents or community. Some children will base views of self on whether they value their race or ethnic group. Individual achievement may matter less, for example, than having pride in being black or Latino or Asian. Some children will be more or less socially active because of family interactions. Children who have *no* positive relationships with peers may be at risk, however. Those who exhibit extreme aggression or who show great anxiety in social situations may have serious emotional disturbance. Both classroom and family services are required in such cases. Teachers can actively facilitate social skills and peer relationships. Cooperative learning, drama, and outdoor motor play are activities that may promote social development.

CHAPTER 18

Parents, Families, and Children: A Multicultural Perspective

GUIDING QUESTIONS

1. What are the unique strengths and challenges of different types of families in America?
2. What roles do fathers, grandparents, siblings, and "friends who are like family" play in childrearing, and how do these vary across cultures?
3. What are the major parenting styles of families, and how do these differ in their impact on children across cultural groups?
4. How does culture influence parenting beliefs and adult–child interactions, including parent communication, responses to crying, teaching behaviors, and carrying practices?

A theme of this book is that social, physical, and intellectual development vary from one child to the next. A major reason for this variation is diversity in family life and parenting. In this chapter, we will describe the wide variety of families that exist in the country and the world—their structure, composition, challenges, and cultural influences.

Why is it important for professionals who work with young children to know about family diversity? Families adopt unique methods for playing with, carrying, feeding, comforting, educating, and socializing their children. Teachers must understand and appreciate these differences; interactions with children of one family may not be appropriate for those of another, as the following vignette reveals:

> An infant care provider, Ms. Tesdal, has just taken a job in a large urban child care center. She has worked in her own family child care home for years and has raised three children of her own. She believes that she really knows her stuff when it comes to taking care of babies. She is particularly proud of her ability to soothe babies when they are upset. She can spot the onset of distress and knows many tricks for comforting and distracting children. During her first day of work at the new child care center, however, she begins to doubt her abilities in this area.
>
> She quickly discovers that some infants cannot be consoled through snuggling and physical touch, while for others this is the only technique that works. Her old trick of distracting babies who appear on the verge of upset doesn't seem to work its usual magic. With several of the babies in her center, no amount of animated conversation, jiggling of toys, or other stimulation will dissuade them from crying. One baby, in particular, appears to become even more disturbed by these efforts. Some babies don't cry at all, she finds; they seem resistant to affection but like to be bounced and played with.
>
> Ms. Tesdal becomes befuddled and frustrated. Nevertheless, she perseveres. Through observation and interviews with parents, she gradually comes to understand how each baby communicates needs and how those needs are best met.

After years of professional experience, this child care provider has learned a valuable new lesson: not all babies interact with adults in the same way. How is it that this lesson has escaped her until now? Children in her previous family child care home were of very similar cultural and socioeconomic backgrounds. They were primarily sons and daughters of white, middle-class professionals with family lives very much like her own. Her new child care setting includes children of many different cultural and socioeconomic groups. Each baby she now cares for has a different style of communication, a diverse set of needs, and special requirements for having those needs met.

What this caregiver has discovered is that parent–child interactions vary considerably from one family to the next. Parents of some cultural groups are more likely to console their babies by feeding them. Snuggling, distraction, and other techniques—which she had come to believe were universally effective—are not part of some babies' experience. Adult–child interactions are quieter and less active in some cultures. Efforts at stimulation might actually distress these babies further. Infants of some ethnic backgrounds cry very rarely. Their parents may have socialized them to become independent at an earlier age or to express needs less often or less directly.

It is critical for professionals who work with children to understand these diverse patterns of family interaction. Only through a full understanding of parental beliefs, socialization practices, and family relationships can teachers meet the unique needs of individual children.

TYPES OF FAMILIES

What do you picture when you hear the word "family"? Likely you imagine a household with a married mother and father and several children. It may surprise you to know that less than 25% of American families are like this (U.S. Bureau of the Census, 2007). More than 35% of babies are now born to unmarried mothers; 30% of all children under 18 live in single-parent homes (Annie E. Casey Foundation, 2005). There are a growing number of couples who have no children at all. In fact, there are now more American families that don't have children than those that do! In about 10% of families, parents, grandparents, and children all live together, but this percentage is twice as high for families of historically underrepresented groups (Nobles, 2007). Each type of family has different strengths, needs, and challenges.

Nuclear Families

The **nuclear family**—one with just a mother, father, and children living together—has long been viewed as the ideal structure for promoting positive child development (Barton & Coley, 2007). Indeed, nuclear families tend to be better off financially (due largely to the prevalence of two-parent incomes in such families). This socioeconomic advantage may explain, in part, the relatively high level of academic success enjoyed by children living in these families. Nuclear families tend to score higher on a number of measures of health and psychological well-being, including a lower rate of illness and of substance abuse (Barton & Coley, 2007). It is important to note, however, that nuclear families face many of the same challenges that single-parent families do (Amato & Fowler, 2002). Both two- and one-parent families can suffer stressors that lead to parental anxiety and depression, harsh parenting, and poor supervision of children. These, in turn, can result in poor child development. One cause of stress in two-parent families is the need to juggle two careers as well as a busy family life, when two parents are working (Barbour, Barbour, & Scully, 2008). This is a particular problem for mothers, who are often still responsible for most household duties as well as their career responsibilities (Zinn & Eitzen, 2004). One important fact about nuclear families is that they can change in composition over the course of childhood (Tucker & Crouter, 2008). Parents might divorce; a grandparent might become ill and move into the household. Children may begin life with two adults in the home—a mother and father—but live their final years of childhood with just one. It is important for professionals to keep in mind that all families face difficulties and need support, even when both parents are currently living together in the home.

Extended Families

Extended families, in which parents, grandparents, other relatives, and even friends live together, is growing more and more common (U.S. Bureau of the Census, 2007). The following vignette illustrates how this arrangement can be beneficial in child-rearing:

> A director of a child care center has just enrolled a 6-month-old, Hannah, in his infant program. He meets the baby's young mother only briefly and is struck by her youth. Later he learns that she is only 15 years old. Although the infant seems to be healthy, secure, and developing in a positive way, the director believes that special support needs to be provided for this young mother. He invites her to a meeting to discuss ways he might assist her and to recommend a parent education program.
>
> His meeting with the mother is unsatisfying. She is very quiet and does not establish eye contact. She answers his questions by nodding "yes" or "no." He is dismayed by how little she seems to know about babies. After half an hour, they set up a time to meet again. After this interchange, the director can't help but wonder how Hannah has turned out so well.
>
> The young mother brings her own mother—the baby's grandmother—to the second meeting. The director learns that the three of them live together in a small apartment. The conversation that follows is markedly different from the first:

DIRECTOR:	(Talking to both the mother and grandmother) Do you play a lot with Hannah? Do you have toys for her to play with?
MOTHER:	(Looks down and does not answer)
GRANDMOTHER:	(To the young mother, laughing) Tell him what we do with little Hannah. How we play.
MOTHER:	(Looks only at the grandmother) We don't have too many toys.

nuclear family: A family with just a mother, father, and children living together, which has long been viewed as the ideal structure for promoting positive child development.

extended family: A family in which parents, grandparents, other relatives, and even friends live together, which is growing more and more common.

GRANDMOTHER: (Laughing) But we play lots of games. Tell him about "playing faces." That's a game we play. (Looking at the director) My momma played it even with me when I was small. Tell him about that.

MOTHER: (Still doesn't look at the director) We let little Hannah touch our faces or pull our hair. Then we touch her face. It's like a game.

GRANDMOTHER: Oh, that little baby will smile and laugh when we play! We say, "Touch your grandma, touch your mama." And then she touches our eyes and gets her little fingers in our hair. And we touch her right back. I tell my daughter, "You have to talk and touch your baby so she'll get to know you."

As the conversation continues, the director understands why this infant is so secure and healthy. The grandmother is experienced and confident. She has raised her own children and knows how to care for infants. She has clearly been assisting her daughter in learning to become a parent. By the end of the meeting, in fact, the director no longer feels the need to urge this teen mother to take parenting courses. She could get no better instruction, he decides, than from her own mother right at home!

The director in this story at first assumed that the teenage mother was the sole and primary caregiver of her child. It is only when he meets the grandmother that he understands fully the child-rearing dynamic within this home. He now knows that raising Hannah is a collaboration between the mother and grandmother. He has learned that family support services must include all significant adults in a child's life.

Although many different persons may live in the home and care for children in modern, extended families, parenting research still focuses almost exclusively on mothers. Figure 18-1 presents a new, more inclusive definition of the American family.

Children of historically underrepresented groups are more likely to live in extended families (Sarkisian, Gerena, & Gerstel, 2007). This is due partly to financial necessity. African American and Latino families often band together to share resources and housing in the face of poverty and other hardships (Roosa, Morgan-Lopez, Cree, & Specter, 2002). Families of color also tend to be more collective in orientation, as described in earlier chapters. So, they may be more comfortable living with larger groups of relatives.

Because children of so many ethnic groups live in extended families, professionals who care for young children must consider the influence of many different family and non-family adults in children's lives. To gain a multicultural perspective on child rearing, it is necessary to understand the unique roles of such significant persons as grandparents, siblings, friends, and fathers (including those who live outside the home).

FIGURE 18-1   A new conceptualization of the family: children are cared for by a network of relatives and friends, not just parents. In many cultural groups, significant caregiving responsibilities are shared among nonparents.

Single-Parent Families

Nearly 30% of families in the United States are headed by a single parent (Barton & Coley, 2007). There are two reasons this rate has increased in the past few decades: an increase in children born to unmarried mothers and an increase in the rate of divorce. Single-parent households are even more common for African American and Latino families (50% and 44%, respectively). Children living in such families can have difficulties (Lansford, Ceballo, Abbey, & Stewart, 2001). Poor school achievement and classroom conduct problems are more common for students living with a single parent. However, we should be cautious in determining the exact cause of these difficulties. Single parenthood, per se, might not be the culprit but rather the poverty that often accompanies it. As presented in other chapters, poverty is devastating to children's healthy development. Too, family conflict, the loss a child feels when a parent leaves, and other emotional problems related to family break up may contribute. Single parenthood does not appear to have such negative consequences when the influence of these other factors is removed (Lansford et al., 2001).

Garcia Coll (1990) points out that some single-headed households are often not detrimental to child development at all. Although a father or mother may not live with a particular family, other nonparent adults may. These individuals—grandparents, other relatives, older siblings, or friends—perform significant family roles, including child caregiving. Furthermore an absent parent may still remain active in a child's life and provide child rearing and financial support. For these reasons, she cautions professionals not to assume single parenthood necessarily has a negative effect on children.

Gay and Lesbian Families

There are now more than 600,000 households headed by a gay or lesbian couple (U.S. Bureau of the Census, 2007). Approximately 33% of these families have children. For female couples, one or both may have had children from a previous marriage. Adoption of children by gay and lesbian couples is becoming more common. As with all other types of families, gay and lesbian households have both strengths and challenges. Research has found that children in such families develop, in many ways, just as those in other two-parent families do (Lambert, 2005; Tasker, 2000). They tend to be emotionally healthy, perform well in school, and have positive relationships with their peers. They construct an accurate understanding of their own gender as other children do.

Parenting behaviors and overall family climate have been found to be very positive in gay- and lesbian-headed households (Leung, Erich, & Kanenberg, 2005). In fact, gay and lesbian couples with adopted children have been found to demonstrate more positive parenting interactions than heterosexual adoptive parents. The literature is quite conclusive on the effects of growing up in a gay or lesbian household: children are likely to show the same developmental trends as all other children.

What about the stigma associated with living in an atypical family? Are children affected by the bias against their families that is prevalent in our country? Lindsay and colleagues (2006) found that there was great variation in how both parents and children feel about their status within society. Some parents reported that they were very proud of their families and were open about their relationships in the larger community. Not surprisingly, the children of such parents were also likely to show no signs of shame or stigma and were very comfortable discussing their families with peers and teachers. These children were found to be well accepted by both peers and teachers (even those who harbored some negative attitudes toward the concept of gay and lesbian families). In summary, children in these families were reported to feel happy, well supported, and safe.

Sadly, the majority of parents interviewed in this study expressed anxiety about their children being rejected and stigmatized. They were more likely to be secretive about their family relationships and were fearful of rejection by larger society, generally, and by teachers in their children's school, specifically. One factor that differentiated the proud families from the anxious ones was the level of support provided by schools and teachers. The better adjusted parents and children reported having teachers who were open, relaxed, and accepting of gay and lesbian families. These teachers took steps to include discussions of all different kinds of families in their curriculum.

It is not always easy for teachers of some beliefs and family customs to provide this positive support for gay and lesbian families. A deeply devout second-grade teacher from a traditional school in the Deep South expresses her feelings about working with a gay and lesbian family in this way:

> When my principal came in and said, "you have a child of homosexuals joining your class"—that's just how he said it!—I was speechless. Oh, lord, I thought, how will I act around this family? What kinds of things will come up with this child? I was terrified, to be honest. I'd never met a gay person, and I was raised to believe homosexuality is wrong.
>
> But when the family brought their daughter on the first day, they were so friendly and relaxed. They just talked openly about their life, without any worry. Two mothers! Imagine! And all the other children and parents were just nice as could be to them. The child was completely accepted by the group—within days she was as well liked by other students as anyone in the class. Why had I thought she would be troubled or difficult? I believe I learned a real lesson that day about families and about how it's important to accept everyone.
>
> And what about my religious beliefs? Well, I guess you just need to set those aside sometimes in the classroom. For the children. It's all about the children, right? They're the most important thing.

Gay and lesbian families have been found to cope with societal bias and rejection in the same way that families of historically underrepresented groups do (Oswald, 2002). They instill pride in their children by assuring them that their family is as good as any other. They seek social and emotional support from other families. They work closely with their children's teachers to promote academic achievement and social skills. Teachers play an important role in promoting the healthy development of children of gay and lesbian families.

Foster Families

More than 500,000 children in America live in temporary **foster homes** (Children's Defense Fund, 2004; Gibbs, 2007). Most have been removed from their families by protective service agencies because of abuse and neglect by parents. Victims of child abuse are usually placed with foster parents until successful family interventions have been implemented or permanent adoptions arranged. Approximately two-thirds of children placed in foster care are from historically underrepresented groups. African American children remain in foster care longer than do Euro-American children (U.S. Department of Health and Human Services, 2004). One-fifth of children in foster care have developmental disabilities; up to two-thirds have mental health disorders (Kocinski, 1998). Needless to say, foster parenthood is challenging; foster parents need greater training and support to effectively carry out their vital role (Children's Defense Fund, 2004).

Most foster children are placed in the homes of non-relative parents who also have their own children (Child Welfare League of America, 2004). There has been a recent effort to

foster homes: Homes where children are temporarily placed when special circumstances— including abuse and neglect—require that they live away from their families. Children are to live in foster homes until successful family interventions have been implemented or permanent adoptions arranged.

place children in foster care with their own family members—a grandparent or aunt and uncle—so that they remain in the security of their own family and cultural group (Cuddeback, 2004). Although this strategy is well-intentioned—designed to keep families intact—it can jeopardize children's development. Just because an adult is a family member does not always mean she or he will be a good parent. Foster parents who are relatives are often less well trained, less effective in parenting abilities, and have fewer financial resources than non-relative foster parents. Children who grow up in such "kinship care" arrangements are more likely to suffer mental health disorders later in life (Carpenter & Clyman, 2004).

An attempt is also made to keep siblings together when planning foster care arrangements. Children who are able to remain with their siblings show more positive emotional development than those who are separated (Hegar, 2005; Leathers, 2005). However, sibling separation is very common, due to the reluctance of foster parents to take in more than one child. Separated siblings report a greater sense of loss and feelings of not belonging within their new foster family. They are more likely to be disruptive, more likely to be transferred from one foster home to another, and less likely to be permanently adopted.

Some children who are placed in foster homes develop well, particularly if they remain in the same home for the duration of their time away from their birth parents (Barber & Delfabbro, 2006). Certainly, foster care can be preferable to continued exposure to the psychological or physical dangers of an abusive family. However, many children respond poorly to foster care. They have frequent conflicts with foster family members and are more likely to exhibit behavior problems in school (Dance, Rushton, & Quinton, 2002). They tend to lag behind their non-foster-care peers academically (Finkelstein, Wamsley, & Miranda, 2002). One reason may be that many foster parents tend to focus on managing behavior rather than on promoting learning or social skills, as birth parents do. Too, some foster parents are less responsive to the needs of those in their care (Dance et al., 2002). Finally, it is important to remember that many foster children have been victims of abuse and neglect. The long-term consequences of such treatment may be the main reason that children in foster care have so many difficulties.

Foster care is often not a temporary arrangement as it was designed to be. Although the Adoption and Safe Families Act of 1997 has mandated that children be moved from foster care to permanent homes within 18 months, more than half of foster care children remain in temporary placements for longer than this (Children's Defense Fund, 2007). In fact, the average length of stay for children in foster care is almost 3 years (U.S. Department of Health and Human Services, 2008). More troubling is the fact that one-third of children who leave their first placement re-enter foster care in less than 6 months (Children's Defense Fund, 2004). Some children have spent their entire childhoods in the foster care system, moving from one foster home to another and eventually "aging out" when they reach 18. This movement from home to home is especially difficult for infants who are forming attachments to caregivers. Why do foster children move from one placement to another so frequently? Research indicates that the most common reason—representing more than 20% of all changes—is an inability of the foster parents to control a child's behavior (James, 2004).

Adoptive Families

Approximately 3% of American children are adopted (U.S. Bureau of the Census, 2007). The majority of adoptions are into two-parent families, some of which already include biological children. However, the number of adoptions by single parents has increased in recent years. Many adoptions are by non-parent family members, such as grandparents; some are by stepparents who have married into a child's family. Most children who are adopted develop in a healthy way. In fact, they may possess a slightly higher self-esteem than non-adopted children (Juffer & van IJzendoorn, 2007). Although adopted children are no different than their non-adopted peers in intellectual development, some studies have found they lag behind non-adopted children in school achievement (van Ijzendoorn, Juffer, & Poelhuis, 2005).

While the number of adults seeking to adopt young American infants has increased, the number of healthy babies available for adoption in this country has gone down (U.S. Bureau of the Census, 2007). Increasingly, families have adopted babies from other countries—most notably from Russia, Asia, and South America. Do transracial or transcountry adoptions pose special challenges for children or parents? Some children who are adopted by parents of a different race experience confusion about their ethnic or racial identity (Mohanty & Newhill, 2005). "Should I grow up to be a white person, like my parents, or a black person, based on my skin color?" is the question an African American adopted child might struggle with. Such confusion may lead to lower self-esteem, social adjustment problems, and mental health issues, as children approach adolescence. However, many children who are adopted by parents of a different race show typical intellectual, social, and emotional development. The reason some children fare better than others may be due to parenting practices (Baxter, 2006). Children in biracial adoptive families who have parents who accept and promote their racial identity are better adjusted socially and view themselves more positively as persons of color *and* as members of a loving Euro-American family. Interestingly, there may be gender differences in how children in biracial adoptive families adjust to family life and school (Moffatt & Thoburn, 2001). Adopted boys tend to show better adjustment in biracial families than do girls.

FAMILY MEMBERS WHO INFLUENCE CHILDREN'S DEVELOPMENT

Research on parenting and child development has focused extensively on mothers. As American families become more diverse, however, researchers are beginning to study other family members who influence children's lives.

Fathers

Fathers play an important role in children's development. Their involvement in the lives of their children at age 7 has been found to predict their sons' and daughters' mental health and social competence at age 33 (Flouri & Buchanan, 2003)! Fathers and mothers are quite different in the ways they interact with children. Across cultures, fathers are less involved than mothers in the care of children, particularly infants (B. B. Whiting & Edwards, 1988). When they do interact with their sons or daughters, they are more likely to engage in physical play and less likely to assume diapering, feeding, and bathing responsibilities (Tamis-LeMonda, Shannon, Cabrera, & Lamb, 2004). Research suggests that fathers may play this subordinate role because they feel uncomfortable or incompetent in primary caretaking roles (Belsky & Volling, 1987). Fathers have been found to be more active in child rearing when they perceive that their spouse has confidence in their parenting abilities (Bouchard, Lee, Asgary, & Pelletier, 2007). They also tend to become more involved when mothers are not present (M. A. Easterbrooks, 1989). When mothers are available, however, fathers take a backseat. Perhaps this is due to a lack of confidence or in deference to mothers' child-rearing skills. When they do interact with their sons or daughters, fathers tend to be as warm and sensitive as mothers, and children form critical attachments to them. The quality of their interactions is as important in children's long-term development as those of mothers (Brown, McBride, Shin, & Bost, 2007).

Children from some traditionally underrepresented groups are more likely to live in mother-headed families. African American and Puerto Rican children, for example, are much more likely to live without their fathers in the home. Does this circumstance have negative developmental consequences? Research indicates that children whose fathers are absent from the home usually adjust well, if their fathers are positive and accepting and remain active in their lives (Bauserman, 2002). Some developmental problems have been observed among boys living in mother-headed households. Social and behavioral problems can emerge later in life; mother–son relationships can be more strained. Such problems may occur because children adjust less well when the same-sex parent is absent (Camara & Resnik, 1988).

Whether or not fathers live in the home, they must be considered important caregivers, especially for boys, and teachers and child care providers should make every effort to include them (or other significant male role models) in parent programs and conferences. Creativity may be necessary when family disharmony and legal custody issues arise. It should never be assumed, however, that because fathers are not living in the home, they do not matter in children's lives.

Grandparents

In traditionally underrepresented ethnic groups, grandparents are more likely to be directly involved in child-rearing duties (Sudarkasa, 2007). For example, African American

In many families, grandparents serve as primary caregivers for children.

grandmothers have been found to be significantly more active in their relationships with their grandchildren than Euro-American grandparents (Pearson et al., 1990). Having a grandmother living in the home appears to be advantageous for young children of color— particularly those in single-parent families. African American children who live with their single mothers and grandmothers have been found to be emotionally and socially better adjusted than children who lived only with their single mothers (Ruiz & Silverstein, 2007). In fact, children in single-mother/grandmother families show the same positive development as those raised in traditional mother–father homes.

Grandmothers play several key roles in children's lives. They provide an extra pair of hands in caretaking and other family duties. This is particularly important in families with teenage mothers. Grandmothers provide respite so that their daughters can enjoy some semblance of adolescence, finish school, or pursue career goals (Garcia Coll et al., 1998). Grandmothers also teach parenting skills and provide knowledge about child develop-ment to their daughters. In one study, for example, young African American mothers were found to be more knowledgeable about infant care if their own mothers were involved in caretaking (Stevens, 1984). One way that grandmothers teach their daughters parenting skills is through modeling. African American grandmothers have been found to be more responsive and less harsh in their discipline strategies than their teenage daughters (Fuller-Thomson & Minkler, 2002).

An important implication for caregivers is that grandmothers play a role almost equiva-lent in importance to that of parents within some families. It is critical to include all adults with caregiving responsibilities in parent education programs, parent conferences, and all other means of communication with families.

Siblings

Siblings also play an important role in child development (Brody, 2004). Their interactions with younger siblings promote language and cognitive development. They help their broth-ers and sisters understand emotions and acquire theories of the mind. They teach some less positive behaviors as well—such as how to tease and argue. Siblings indirectly shape the be-haviors of younger children by teaching their parents things about parenting. Parents test out and refine their socialization practices on their first-born children. Older siblings "break their parents in," exposing them to all the challenges, difficult decisions, as well as joys, of parenting, prior to a younger sibling's arrival.

Older siblings provide companionship that parents can't. They are often more playful than parents, particularly those parents who may be under stress. Siblings contribute to ethnic socialization—that is, they teach their younger brothers and sisters the roles and competencies that are important in their particular culture (Brody & Murry, 2001; Slonim, 1991). Sometimes they play a direct role in promoting learning. It is not uncommon for an older sister or brother to give the names of objects, provide toys, and stimulate cognitive development. This teaching role becomes even more pronounced as children get older (Brody, 2004).

Families from many traditionally underrepresented groups in the United States include larger numbers of children than Euro-American families (U.S. Bureau of the Census, 2007). Not surprisingly, then, young children of these families are more often played with and cared for by older siblings. In many Puerto Rican, Mexican American, and African American households, for example, older siblings are assigned specific child-rearing responsibilities (Hale & Franklin, 2001). This occurs within cultures outside the United States as well. B. B. Whiting and Edwards (1988) report that children living in India, Okinawa, the Philippines, Mexico, and Kenya are more likely to be cared for by older siblings than are children living in suburban America.

Siblings may play a greater role in some families because of scarce resources. Like grandmothers, a teenage brother or sister can lend an extra pair of hands to allow a parent to pursue a career or attend to other household duties. Siblings are most involved with younger children in large families. The larger and more impoverished the family, the more likely an older brother or sister is to be assigned direct disciplinary or supervisory responsibilities (Dodson & Dickert, 2004). Across cultures, it appears that girls are more likely to be assigned caretaking roles than boys (B. B. Whiting & Edwards, 1988).

Even though in some ethnic groups older siblings assume major child-rearing responsibility, brothers and sisters are rarely included in parenting programs or parent conferences in child care. Professionals might create innovative activities that involve older siblings to a greater extent in early education classrooms.

Friends Who Are Like Family

Children of historically underrepresented groups more often have primary caregivers who are nonfamily members. For example, strong friendship bonds within the African American community often lead to shared child rearing. In African American communities, a system of informal adoption has sometimes evolved in which neighbors or friends care for children outside their own family (Stewart, 2006).

A similar pattern of caregiving has been observed in some Native American cultures (Kawamoto & Cheshire, 1997; Red Horse, 1983). Nonrelated adults of the same culture and community are often invited to join families and to share child care responsibilities. Likewise, in Puerto Rican families, specific persons may be identified as **friends who are like family** (Carrasquillo, 1997; Sanchez-Ayendez, 1988). Although these close friends may have no formal kinship ties, they may be expected to participate in *compadrazgo*, a form of coparenting in which specific duties for meeting social and economic needs of children are assigned (Barnes, 2007). In times of economic hardship, informal adoptions may occur in which friends assume roles identical to those of birth parents. These *padres de crianza* (parents of courtesy) care for children as if they were their own.

These nonfamily caregiving relationships are often misunderstood by mainstream American society. The U.S. legal system does not recognize these ties, and well-intentioned social service and education professionals often underestimate their importance. Child care providers and teachers may wish to consider including friends who are like family in parent programs and activities.

PARENT BELIEFS ABOUT CHILD DEVELOPMENT

Parent–child interactions are influenced by beliefs about what children are like and how they should be treated at each developmental level (Crouch & Behl, 2001; Garcia Coll et al., 1998). These beliefs may come from personal experience; often they reflect the values of one's own family. For example, parents who grew up in families that view infants as fragile and vulnerable might be especially protective and nurturing, whereas parents whose families consider babies to be tough and self-reliant might be less so. Parents who were raised to believe that preschool children are old enough to assume household responsibilities are likely to assign chores or child care duties at a very early age. In contrast, those who grew up in homes where the early years were viewed as a carefree time for unrestricted play are likely to have very different expectations for their young children.

friends who are like family: Close friends within a neighborhood or village who are treated as family members and often share child care responsibilities.

Family beliefs vary from one culture to another. Diversity in beliefs about children can be traced to the unique histories and worldviews of individual cultural groups (Keller, Voelker, & Yovsi, 2005; Garcia Coll et al., 1998). One factor that has shaped the beliefs of some cultural groups is adversity. Families who have faced prejudice and scarce resources hold beliefs about children that are very different from the beliefs of families in the dominant culture.

Poverty and Beliefs About Children

As described throughout this book, poverty poses a significant threat to healthy child development. In the face of scarce resources, families make adaptations in their lives. Often beliefs about children shift as parents struggle to meet basic needs.

Poverty and Beliefs About Infants. Levine (1996) has proposed that parents who have scarce resources or who live in settings where infant mortality is high hold very different beliefs about how babies should be treated. His model of caregiving in high-risk communities is presented in Figure 18-2. As shown in the figure, such parents adopt a **hierarchy of child-rearing concerns**—a prioritizing of child-rearing goals so that basic, physical survival outweighs all other concerns.

In a classic study of parents in impoverished African villages, Levine discovered that parents considered physical survival and health to be the primary goals of infant care, while intellectual stimulation was considered relatively unimportant. These beliefs, Levine notes, lead to distinct caretaking practices. Breastfeeding or quick attention to crying were

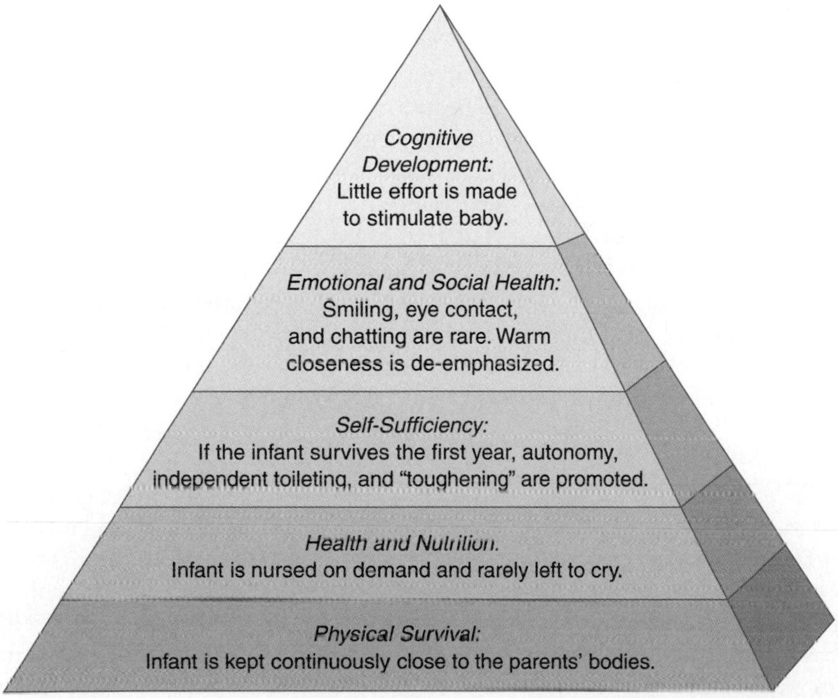

hierarchy of child-rearing concerns: A prioritizing of child-rearing goals by parents living in extreme poverty so that basic, physical survival outweighs all other concerns.

FIGURE 18-2   Parents in communities with an infant mortality rate as high as 60% emphasize different goals in child rearing. They show much greater concern for addressing physical survival and health needs, as indicated by the pyramid's broad base. Concerns about children's cognitive development are minimal, as indicated by the pyramid's narrow tip.
SOURCE: Extrapolated from data in Levine, 1996.

common, but teaching interactions were rare. Levine found that these parents also emphasized self-sufficiency. They would attempt to wean children or teach them to walk at an early age.

Other researchers have described similar parenting patterns in low-income African American families in the United States (Garcia Coll et al., 1998; Hale & Franklin, 2001; Quinlan & Quinlan, 2007). Levine concludes that parents in poor communities wish to protect and nurture their children on the one hand but help them become independent on the other. The message such parents convey to an infant is, "I will do all I can to help get you started in life, but soon you will need to get along on your own."

Other cultural groups in America adopt very different beliefs in the face of poverty. Low-income Mexican American parents have been found to favor dependence and attachment over self-sufficiency in their child rearing (Varela et al., 2004). These families stress learning how to get help from others and relying on family and friends. Poverty influences parental beliefs about infants in a variety of ways, then, depending on cultural values and traditions.

Poverty and Beliefs About Preschoolers. Poverty influences parents' views about preschoolers as well. In some impoverished communities, parents believe that young children should be encouraged to grow up quickly, stand on their own two feet, and contribute immediately to the economic well-being of the family. In some Third World villages, preschoolers as young as age 4 or 5 are assigned child care responsibilities, allowing parents to work outside the home (Harkness & Super, 1996; B. B. Whiting & Edwards, 1988). Children of this age are often expected to tend livestock, weed the garden, and stay on their own for long periods of time.

Poverty may lead to greater expectations for mature behavior. At a very early age, preschoolers may be expected to meet their own personal needs, such as toileting, meal preparation, and personal hygiene. For example, African American mothers and grandmothers of low socioeconomic status have been found to be less tolerant of toileting "accidents" than are middle-class, Euro-American parents (Suizzo, Robinson, & Pahlke, 2007). Parents in Kariobangi, Kenya, have been found to expect mature behavior and absolute obedience from their preschoolers, particularly boys (B. B. Whiting & Edwards, 1988). The rate of compliance among these young children was discovered to be almost twice as high as that for children living in the United States.

Although some of these parenting practices seem harsh and restrictive, they often stem from concern for the child and the family in the face of brutal economic hardship. Such practices are intended to transform immature preschoolers into self-reliant children who can contribute to the survival of the family (Suizzo et al., 2007; Mason, Cauce, Gonzalez, & Hiraga, 1996).

Poverty and Beliefs About Primary Children. Parental beliefs about primary-age children are also influenced by experiences of poverty. Expectations for mature behavior and grown-up contributions to family survival may become even greater during this period. Parents who believe that educational attainment is a means to economic well-being and upward mobility may hold high academic ambitions for their children at this age (Okagaki & Frensch, 1998; Zhan & Sherraden, 2003). Hale-Benson (1986), for example, has described African American families as extremely achievement oriented. Some parents of this cultural group socialize their children to believe that achievement is a way to prosperity not only for oneself but also for the whole family.

Latino parents have also been found to place great emphasis on learning, performing well on tests in school, and completing homework as a means of escaping poverty (C. Chen & Stevenson, 1989). Likewise, Japanese American and Chinese American families show positive dispositions toward schoolwork and urge their children to succeed (Ishii-Kuntz, 1997a, 1997b; Okagaki & Frensch, 1998; W. Yang, 2007). This achievement orientation stems, in part, from the experience of poverty and a drive to better one's family circumstances.

Oppression and Beliefs About Children

The experience of oppression explains some of the cultural diversity in family life and child rearing (Ogbu, 2007). Ethnic groups that have suffered prejudice, community violence, and even slavery over many generations will adopt unique beliefs about children.

Oppression and Beliefs About Infants. Oppression influences beliefs about how babies are cared for. In families who believe that infants should be toughened in preparation for the harsh realities of prejudice, early autonomy and boldness might be major goals. Another family might feel that babies should be taught to seek refuge from racism within the family. In this instance, a caregiving goal might be to create strong family bonds.

Many Puerto Rican parents, for example, believe that family interdependence and banding together with close friends is the way to survive in the face of prejudice (Carrasquillo, 1997; Tamis-LeMonda et al., 2008). A typical socialization goal in Puerto Rican families is **enmeshment**—the ability to become attached to, cooperate with, and rely on others, particularly family members. This goal is evident in parent–infant interactions: Puerto Rican mothers have been found to be particularly indulgent in feeding and nurturing babies (Slonim, 1991). In infant care, these families emphasize attachment rather than separation from the family (Garcia Coll, 1990; R. L. Harwood, 1992; R. L. Harwood, Miller, & Irizarry, 1995).

As mentioned earlier, oppression has caused many African American parents to adopt goals of early self-sufficiency and achievement. They more often seek to achieve weaning and toileting at an early age and are more likely to believe it appropriate to delay responses to infant cries (Klein & Chen, 2001; Liamputtong, 2007; Zeskind, 2008). Their desire is to raise strong individuals who can stand up to the challenges of a biased world.

Oppression and Beliefs About Preschoolers. Families of historically oppressed groups may hold distinct views about how preschoolers should be raised. In some cultures, children of this age are socialized to stand up to those who would oppress them, to fight back when assailed. For example, in some families, young children are taught how to defend themselves physically. In one study, African American mothers and grandmothers were found to be more likely to urge their children to fight back than their Euro-American counterparts (Hale-Benson, 1986). In fact, for these parents and grandparents, the failure to retaliate for an offense could lead to a harsh reprimand or a spanking. These views are in sharp contrast to the dominant society's perspective that childhood aggression is wrong and should be discouraged.

It is easy to see how such family beliefs may clash with typical school regulations against fighting. As a practicing teacher, I have experienced more than one challenging discussion with an angry parent about a *no hitting* rule in the classroom. For some families, fighting back is a way of defending against prejudice; failing to retaliate is seen as a sign of weakness and results in a loss of dignity.

Other cultural groups socialize their preschoolers to be extremely polite and obedient so that they might be assimilated into an inhospitable world. Such families emphasize compliance rather than fighting back or speaking one's mind. Mexican American parents, for example, have been found to emphasize conformity, obedience, and "proper demeanor in public" and to discourage autonomy and self-assertion (Gamble & Modry-Mandell, 2008;

enmeshment: A goal of socialization in some cultures in which children become attached to, cooperate with, and rely on others, particularly their family members.

R. L. Harwood et al., 1995; Knight, Virdin, & Roosa, 1994). Chinese American parents also have been found to value compliance within the dominant culture (Chao, 2002; Greenberger & Chen, 1996; S. A. Miller, 1995). An orientation toward fitting in and "making good" within the dominant society is an effective adaptive strategy that some families use in the face of mistreatment and racial animosity.

Oppression and Beliefs About Primary Children. Parents' beliefs about primary children are influenced by oppression as well. This developmental period is a formative one for acquiring a positive view of self, so young children who are confronted with racism in their schools and communities may be at risk. Parents of some families, then, adopt unique socialization goals aimed at offsetting the negative effects of prejudice. Some African American parents, for example, emphasize racial pride, an understanding of cultural heritage, and the grim realities of racism (Klein & Chen, 2001; Hill, 2001). Socialization messages such as "You are black and as good as anyone else" predominate in adult–child interactions in this culture.

Parenting Beliefs and Professional Practice

Parenting beliefs arise from unique personal and cultural experiences. These beliefs, which represent the thinking of generations of parents within a particular group, are usually logical and contribute to positive development. They are sometimes misunderstood, however, by those of other cultures. In most cases, it should not be the goal of professionals to change what parents believe. The following story illustrates the difficulties that can arise from an attempt to do so:

> Mr. Danforth, a professional in an early intervention program, makes regular home visits to low-income parents with infants and preschoolers. His goal is to support families and teach positive parenting skills in order to offset some of the negative effects of poverty. He is facing a challenge from one particular mother, Ms. Gordon, who seems resistant to his parenting suggestions. She does not follow up on his recommendations for playing with her two young children. She continues to swat her toddler on the hand when he touches things he should not. Mr. Danforth decides to address the problem directly at his next visit.

MR. DANFORTH:	I wanted to talk with you about playing with your children a little more. Remember, we talked about some games you might play? Have you used any of the toys I left?
MS. GORDON:	(Looks down and says nothing)
MR. DANFORTH:	I'm just trying to help you teach your children things. If you play these games, they'll learn and be ready for school.
MS. GORDON:	(Remains silent)
MR. DANFORTH:	I think if you tried using some of these toys, your children wouldn't get into your other things. You wouldn't have to spank hands anymore.
MS. GORDON:	(No response)
MR. DANFORTH:	Okay. I can tell you're upset and don't want to talk about this. I'm sorry I pushed.
MS. GORDON:	(In a very angry tone, tears forming in her eyes) You don't know what's good for my children. I'm their mother, not you!
MR. DANFORTH:	(Looks startled) Well …

MS. GORDON:	(Begins to cry) There's a little boy was killed down the street there. (Points out the window) Got shot. What about that?
MR. DANFORTH:	Tell me what you're feeling about that.
MS. GORDON:	What I'm feeling? I haven't got enough food to eat. There's shooting going on. I just want my children to get by. Want them to live to be grown up. Do you get that?
MR. DANFORTH:	Yes. I understand ...
MS. GORDON:	You're talking about playing and all. I teach my children to survive. Giving them a swat now and then is how I keep them out of trouble. I'm their mother, not you!

Mr. Danforth steps out of his parent education role altogether and just listens and gives support. Ms. Gordon talks on for many more minutes. While driving to his office after this exchange, Mr. Danforth thinks hard about this parent's message. He sees that his approach has been misguided. On a return visit several weeks later, he abandons for now his attempts to teach specific parenting skills. Instead, he focuses on helping Ms. Gordon find additional resources to feed her family.

The home visitor in this story has attempted to impose his own values about child care on a parent of a very different culture and life experience. He misinterprets this mother's disinterest in playing with her children as a lack of concern or knowledge about them. He expects that he can convince her to believe, as he does, that cognitive stimulation and freedom to play are important to children. But these are goals and competencies valued in his world, not hers. It is only when she confronts him with the realities of her life that he comes to see the error of his ways. She behaves as she does for a reason. Learning games seems less important to her than keeping her children out of harm's way in a dangerous neighborhood. Firm discipline may be the only way to ensure the safety of a child who lives in a community filled with violence and racism.

PARENTING STYLES

Beliefs about children and child-rearing goals give rise to differences in overall parenting styles. A **parenting style** is a general approach to socializing children that includes the amount of warmth, communication, and control parents provide, along with their expectations for children's mature behavior. In a classic study, Diana Baumrind (1968) devised a system for categorizing parenting styles, based on these child-rearing elements. Her categories are presented in Table 18-1.

As shown in the table, an **authoritative parenting style** includes a relatively democratic approach to raising children. The authoritative parent is extremely warm and supportive and encourages children to speak their minds and share ideas, even when there are conflicts or misbehaviors. In the end the authoritative parent makes firm decisions about punishments or rules and maintains authority as an adult. Thus, the parent of this style is moderately controlling and has high expectations for mature behavior. This parenting style has been linked to positive outcomes for children and has often been held up as a model for all parents to emulate (Demo & Cox, 2000).

As shown in Table 18-1, Baumrind identified several other parenting styles that she found led to less positive outcomes for children. The **authoritarian parenting style** is one in which the parent is very controlling, allows little discussion (or "talking back") when the parent makes demands, and is less warm. Baumrind and other colleagues found that children of

parenting style: A general approach to socializing children that includes the amount of warmth, communication, and control parents provide, along with their expectations for children's mature behavior.

authoritative parenting style: A parenting style that includes a relatively democratic approach to raising children, in which a parent is warm and supportive and encourages children to speak their minds, even when there are conflicts or misbehavior.

authoritarian parenting style: A parenting style in which the parent is very controlling, allows little discussion about parent demands, and is less warm.

TABLE 18-1
Diana Baumrind's Classification of Parenting Styles

Parenting Style	Description	Expected Child Outcomes
Authoritative	Parent is democratic, warm, and encourages communication when problems arise. Makes final, firm decisions about punishments or rules. Expects a moderate level of maturity in children.	Many children of authoritative parents become highly competent, socially, emotionally, and intellectually. They are more cooperative with teachers and peers and are more independent.
Authoritarian	Parent is very controlling and allows no discussion when making demands. Provides less warmth in interactions.	Many children of authoritarian parents are less independent, have poor relationships with peers, and can be either submissive or aggressive. They tend to be more distrustful of others.
Permissive-Indulgent	Parent provides much warmth and encourages children to "speak their minds." Does not set rules for children and strives to create an environment of complete freedom. Social responsibility and maturity are not emphasized.	Many children of permissive-indulgent parents are less competent socially and intellectually. They are less independent and socially responsible. They have difficulty with self-control and learning rules and routines in school.
Permissive-Neglectful	Parent is generally detached and less warm. Is less responsive to the child's needs or bids for attention. No effort is made to guide or control behavior.	Many children with permissive-neglectful parents are less competent, intellectually and socially. They have difficulty with self-control and exhibit conduct problems in school.

permissive-indulgent parenting style:
A parenting style in which there is much warmth and communication but virtually no control over the child.

permissive-neglectful parenting style:
A parenting style in which parents allow children to behave as they wish, without limits, and in which parents do not offer warmth, communication, or attention.

authoritarian parents are more likely to be submissive, though they might also exhibit aggression and behavior problems in school (Baumrind, 1968; Casas et al., 2006). They are often less independent. A **permissive-indulgent parenting style** is one in which there is much warmth and communication but virtually no control over a child's behavior (Baumrind, 1968). Parents of this style often believe it is best for their children to behave "naturally," in whatever way they choose. They confuse ideas about independence and social responsibility with total permissiveness. In fact, children of permissive-indulgent parents tend to be less independent as they grow older. They often show poor social and intellectual outcomes—less positive outcomes, in fact, than children of authoritarian parents (Milevsky, Schlechter, Netter, & Keehn, 2007).

A final parenting style, presented in Table 18-1, is a **permissive-neglectful parenting style**, in which parents allow children to behave as they wish, without limits, but do not offer warmth or a high degree of communication (Baumrind, 1968). These parents are somewhat detached from their children and unresponsive to their sons' and daughters' needs or bids for attention. Children whose parents are permissive-neglectful are less competent in almost all areas measured—social, emotional, and intellectual. They exhibit behavior problems in school and have difficulty with self-control.

Some multicultural scholars have raised questions about Baumrind's categorization of parents, however (Chao & Tseng, 2002). They note that parents of many cultural groups are more likely to adhere to an authoritarian parenting style. As discussed previously, this more directive approach might stem from experiences with family hardship. Parents of African American, Puerto Rican, Latin American, Turkish, Indian, and Asian families, to name just a few, have been found to exhibit the more controlling pattern of behavior that Baumrind warned against (Rudy & Grusec, 2006). Could children of all of these cultural groups suffer the lower levels of competence presented in Table 18-1, as Baumrind suggests?

New research has shown that the parenting styles Baumrind has proposed may have different effects on children of different cultures. It is well established that authoritarian parenting can lead to poor outcomes for children of Euro-American backgrounds (Steinberg & Silk, 2002). However, a form of this parenting style—one that includes a high degree of control but also a high level of warmth and concern—has a very positive impact on children of many other cultural groups. African American children—particularly girls—have been found to become more competent in later childhood if their parents assume this authoritatian style (Glasgow et al., 1997). Similar findings have been reported for Chinese (Leung, Lau, & Lam, 1998), Puerto Rican (Harwood et al., 1995), and Latino (Lindahl & Malik, 1999) families.

A study by Rudy and Grusec (2006) helps to explain why so-called authoritarian behaviors have a differential impact on various cultural groups. They found that parents of Western European backgrounds were less likely to adhere to an authoritarian parenting style, as predicted by Baumrind. Those in this Western group who did endorse authoritatian approaches were more likely to have strong feelings of anger, hostility, and frustration, and their children scored lower on measures of self-esteem. So, for these Western parents, Baumrind's theory holds up quite well.

Interstingly, findings were nearly the opposite for parents and children of collectivist cultures—those of Egyptian, Iranian, Indian, and Pakistani backgrounds. These parents were more authoritarian in orientation, but this was not related to feelings of anger or hostility. In fact, parents in this group who were authoritarian were happy, emotionally healthy caregivers. These parents appeared to have different reasons for being more directive, unrelated to negative emotions. Further, their use of authoritarian parenting was not related to low levels of self-esteem in their children, as it was for the Western group of parents.

These authors conclude that parenting behaviors have different meanings in different cultures. For Western parents, authoritarian parenting may be a sign of emotional distress. Parents' authoritarian parenting behaviors in this cultural group are likely to be delivered with more anger. This may cause their children to suffer low self-esteem. For parents of collective cultures, authoritarian behaviors may be used to achieve cultural goals, such as maintaining respect for authority and keeping families together. Their children are likely to interpret these behaviors differently than their Western peers. For children in these non-Western cultural groups, authoritarianism is the norm, is viewed more positively, and may confirm for them that their parents truly care about them.

ADULT–CHILD INTERACTIONS

Because of differences in child-rearing beliefs, parents adopt different ways of interacting with their children. Interactions vary across cultural groups in four major ways: communication, responses to crying, teaching, and carrying and holding. These are summarized in Table 18-2.

TABLE 18-2
Cultural Universals and Variations in Parent–Child Interactions

Parenting Interactions	Universals	Variations
Communicating	All parents communicate in some way with their children.	Parents of some cultures use much verbal communication with their children. Others more often communicate through gestures, facial expressions, and physical touch.
Responses to crying	All parents respond in some way to children's crying.	Parents of some cultural groups show distress when their children cry and respond quickly. Others are less concerned by cries and take longer to react. Some use cuddling and feeding as a response; others use a pacifier or physical stimulation.
Teaching	All parents are concerned about the education of their children.	Parents of some cultures believe that teaching is an important part of the parental role. In other cultures, parents believe teachers in school should assume this responsibility.
Carrying and holding	All parents hold and carry their young children.	Some children are bound in slings or cradle boards for much of the day. Others are held in a parent's or grandparent's arms. Some children are held infrequently and move about freely in the home or neighborhood.

Parent Communication

Some characteristics of communication with children are universal. For example, parents in all cultures use exaggerated intonations and unique words and sentences when speaking to their sons and daughters. Such **parentese** includes high-pitched vocalizations and simple sentence structure (Augustyn & Zuckerman, 2007; Bornstein et al., 2002). Parents of all cultures tend to comment on concrete objects, using many nouns, when they talk to their young children (Fonagy, Gergely, & Target, 2007). Why do parents around the world do this? Babies, toddlers, and preschoolers are more attentive and smile more frequently when they are spoken to in these ways (Dominey & Dodane, 2004; Weppelman et al., 2003). Parents of all cultures seem to have an intuitive ability to adapt their speech to children's desires and developmental levels.

There are many cultural differences in adult-to-child language, as well. One example is frequency of verbalization (Klein & Chen, 2001). Some families are very talkative, others quiet. Talkativeness and silence mean very different things in different cultural groups

parentese: A special form of language that parents around the world speak to children that includes exaggerated intonations, unique words, high-pitched vocalizations, and simple sentence structure.

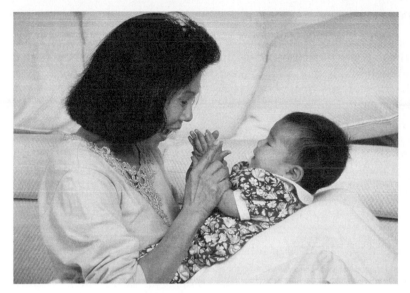

Parents in all cultures speak to their children in "parentese"—a simpler form of communication that promotes language development.

(Irujo, 2004). English-speaking Euro-American parents tend to use lots of language with children. Talkativeness in child–adult interaction has also been observed within Cuban American and Puerto Rican families (Field & Widmayer, 1981).

In contrast, some Mexican American, African American, and Native American parents have been found to be less talkative with children (Haynes & Saunders, 1999; Zepeda, 1986). Navajo and Hopi parents have been described as particularly quiet (Chisholm, 1989; Field, 2002). There are several explanations for why these groups have adopted less verbal interaction patterns. Children of some families may have more passive and less verbal temperaments. Navajo infants and preschoolers, for example, have been found to be timid and quiet. A passive, nonverbal parenting style might be a "good fit" for such children (Garcia Coll et al., 1998). In addition, silence is viewed as a sign of respect in some cultures, and quiet interchanges with children may be an early attempt to impart this concept (Klein & Chen, 2001; Menyuk & Menyuk, 2004).

Quietness within these cultural groups does not mean that there is no communication. Less verbal Hopi mothers communicate quite frequently in nonverbal ways. They may talk less but hold, rub, or bounce young children more (Callaghan, 1981; Cole, 2005). Nsamenang (2004) provides an example of nonverbal communication in his description of the "gifts-giving game" that West African parents play with their toddlers. In this game, an adult offers a child a toy and then entices the toddler to give it back. As the object is passed back and forth, the adult and child are having a kind of conversation that involves turn taking and rules.

Hale-Benson (1986) has observed a high frequency of physical touch and nonverbal communication between African American mothers and their children. She proposes that, because of this parenting style, children of this cultural group are particularly proficient in communicating with body movements, expressions, and gestures.

Because Euro-American parents are very verbal in their interactions with children, some teachers have concluded that frequent speech is desirable. In fact, programs were developed in the 1960s to "bombard" young children with language and to increase parent language use in the home (E. E. Evans, 1975). Such programs did not appreciate diversity of language patterns within families.

Responses to Crying

Crying is the way infants and young children communicate needs, and parents' responses to crying will influence their children's emotional and intellectual development. Parents of different cultures vary in the ways they respond to children's upset. Euro-American mothers vary considerably in how quickly they respond when their babies cry (Palmer, 1991; Zeskind, 2008). Some wait a very long time to respond to infant upset, while others pick up their babies the moment crying begins.

African American mothers and Cuban American mothers, in contrast, have been found to more often adopt a **wait-and-see response to crying** (Ball, 2007; Zeskind, 2008). Their response time is generally slower than that of many Euro-American parents. These parents may delay their responses to ascertain why their children are crying. An overriding concern among these parents is to give just the right amount of attention so that children will be neither "spoiled" nor neglected (Ball, 2007; Garcia Coll et al., 1998).

In some hunter-gatherer societies in Africa, mothers have been found to respond immediately to even the slightest infant whimper (Levine, 1996; B. B. Whiting & Edwards, 1988). In some cases, these mothers carry their babies throughout the day and sleep with them at night (Morelli et al., 2002). In these communities, babies were found to virtually never cry!

The methods that mothers use to soothe crying children also vary across cultures. African American parents prefer using a pacifier or physical stimulation in response to crying, while Euro-American parents more often use physical touch, holding, and breast-feeding (Zeskind, 2008). Cuban American mothers were found to use a combination of a pacifier and cuddling, depending on the circumstances.

Why is there such variation across cultures in responding to cries? It may be that the meaning of crying varies from one cultural group to another. In some populations, crying is viewed as a distress signal and an expression of need. Parents may see their response, then, as an opportunity to nurture attachment and feelings of security. Euro-American mothers, for example, report that infant cries are distressing, arousing, and "sick sounding." Crying induces them to take immediate action (Zeskind et al., 1992).

In other groups, cries are not viewed with such urgency and anxiety. Crying is interpreted as a way of expressing a variety of messages, some of which may require a quick response, others not. For example, when crying is perceived as merely a demand for adult attention, parents might be more cautious about responding too quickly. African American parents report less distress and feelings of urgency when hearing infant cries and express concern about giving cries too much attention (Garcia Coll et al., 1998).

Although parents' responses to crying vary, parents of all cultural groups respond in some way to child upset. That babies of all cultures become attached and secure suggests that there is not one correct way to respond to crying.

Teaching Behaviors

wait-and-see response to crying: A parenting strategy in which parents delay their responses to children's crying in order to ascertain the reasons for crying and to ensure that children will be neither "spoiled" nor neglected.

Parents vary significantly in the ways they attempt to teach their children (Okagaki & Frensch, 1998). Some parents label objects for their children and pose problems and challenges. Others provide educational toys and physical stimulation. Some parents become involved in their children's homework in the primary years. Other parents are less likely to engage in these kinds of activities.

Why is there such variation? In some cultural groups, teaching has been historically valued as a critical component of parenting. Chinese American mothers, for example, more often report that teaching is primarily the responsibility of the family and parents (Chao, 2002; M. S. Steward & Steward, 1974). Not surprisingly, mothers of this culture are very active in instructing children and providing positive feedback on learning tasks (Farver, Natera, & Frosch, 2002). Jewish American families also place great value on learning. From the earliest days of life, many Jewish children are provided cognitive stimulation with the goal of enhancing later academic achievement (Birman & Espino, 2007).

In other cultures, parents are more likely to view teaching as the responsibility of teachers and schools. Euro-American and Mexican American mothers, for example, have been found to view instruction as only one small part of the parental role (M. S. Steward & Steward, 1974; Varela et al., 2004). Teaching activities are not as predominant in interactions with children within these cultures. It is important to note that parents of these cultural groups do value learning. They simply assign the primary teaching role to others, particularly trained educators within schools.

It is also important to understand that parents of different cultures teach children in different ways. Instruction by Mexican American mothers, for example, has been found to be more physical; less verbalization and praising are used (Gibbs & Huang 1997; Varela et al., 2004). In Euro-American families, language is more often a part of teaching interactions. No evidence suggests that a nonverbal style of teaching is any less effective than verbal strategies (Garcia Coll, 1990).

Carrying and Holding Practices

Some children are carried around in a parent's arms all day long for the first 6 months of life. Others are rarely held. Still others spend the day in a sling on a parent's back. It is no wonder that babies and even older children have different preferences in how they are handled by adults. Table 18-3 presents several distinct dimensions of carrying and holding that can differ from one cultural group to another.

Cultural diversity in methods of holding babies has "inspired many misconceptions, stereotypes, and simplistic theories" (Chisholm, 1989, p. 71). For example, carrying

TABLE 18-3 Variations in Carrying and Holding Practices

Carrying and Holding Method	Description
Arm carrying	Babies are held in the parents' arms, either close to the body or balanced on a hip.
Lap holding	Babies are held in a sitting position in an adult's lap.
Carrying device	Babies are strapped to the front or back of an adult's body by a sling, "snugglie," or backpack.
Swaddling	Babies are wrapped tightly in blankets or sheets so that the arms and legs are held fast.
Cradle board	Babies are swaddled, as above, and strapped onto a board in an upright position.
Infrequent carrying	Babies are rarely carried at all but lie freely in a crib or crawl about.

practices in which infants are swaddled or bound have often been viewed as detrimental to children's development, and parents using these methods are sometimes portrayed as misguided or neglectful. Likewise, parents who seldom carry their babies are sometimes viewed as negligent. In fact, carrying and holding methods are a function of cultural norms, the practical demands of work and family life, and the temperament of infants themselves.

In America, babies of many cultures are carried in parents' arms. Backpacks and slings are sometimes used for short periods to travel from one place to another. Commonly, infants are cradled or held in a parent's arms close to the chest, balanced on one hip, or bounced or rocked on a knee or lap. Variation exists among ethnic groups in America in how often children are carried and the age at which children cease to be carried (Greenfield et al., 2003). African American babies are held more often during the day and are carried until later in life than Euro-American infants (Hale-Benson, 1986). Mexican American parents, in contrast, tend to pick up their babies less often than other cultural groups do.

In some cultures, devices are used to carry or hold infants for extended periods. Some Hopi and Navajo infants are held through the day on cradle boards. Infants are swaddled on these boards so that they are unable to easily move any body part but their heads. Although concerns have often been raised about cradle boards, research has shown that this practice has little negative impact on children's physical development (Dennis & Dennis, 1940). Further, although parent–child interchanges are diminished when infants are on the board, rich, full interactions have been found to resume at the end of the day when they are removed (Chisholm, 1989; van Sleuwen et al., 2007). It has been observed that some Navajo infants become so attached to cradle boards that they actually cry to be strapped onto them (Konner, 1993)! It would appear that this practice—so often criticized by Western child specialists—is actually comforting and leads to a sense of security.

In societies that have a high mortality rate, babies are more likely to be strapped against their parents' bodies in slings or packs. In families in urban Zambia, for example, babies are carried in slings on their mothers' backs for much of the day during the first year of life. Most parents gradually reduce the time their children are held in these slings. By age 1, babies are carried far less. Research shows that children who are carried often in slings during the first 6 months of life are actually advanced in development (Goldberg, 1977). These findings challenge the belief that all children must be able to move around freely to grow properly.

How do carrying practices affect teacher–child interactions in school? Some students will seek warm physical contact with peers and teachers. Others, however, will feel less comfortable with physical touch and holding. Professionals can adopt nonphysical methods of showing warmth and caring toward such students.

FAMILY STRESSORS AND RESILIENCE

family stressors: Serious family challenges that threaten healthy family functioning and child development.

Families sometimes face serious challenges that can affect children's development. These are called **family stressors**. This term does not refer to minor day-to-day difficulties that all families face—trying to juggle work and home life or struggling to pay the bills—but to more calamitous circumstances that threaten healthy family functioning. How well a family will cope with such a stressor, when it arises, will depend on what other challenges the family currently faces and what kinds of support and resources they have to resolve the problem.

A way to understand the effects of family stressors is to examine the research on **resilience** in human development (Masten & Obradović, 2006). Resilience is a psychological state in which a child and family possess a range of *protective factors* that help them cope with, and offset, the negative effects of *risk factors* that arise in their lives. (See Chapter 3 for definitions of risk and protective factors.) An example of resilience would be a case where an apartment fire destroyed a family's belongings and residence. The risk factor is obvious—a devastating event has occurred. But the family might have many protective factors that can counterbalance this tragedy and help them to cope. The family may have relatives they can live with temporarily. They may have financial resources that will allow them to rebound. The parents may have a loving relationship and provide warm support to their children. The children may be healthy and emotionally well adjusted. All these things help protect the child and family during this terrible event and allow them to survive, emotionally as well as physically.

In this section we will consider several serious family stressors that affect children's lives. Each will be discussed in terms of risk factors, protective factors, and the potential for families and children to become resilient.

Divorce

More than 1.5 million children will be affected by a family breakup during a given year in the United States. Divorce rates are far higher for families in poverty and those of some historically underrepresented groups—particularly African American and Latino families (Barton & Coley, 2007). The experience of divorce can have a negative effect on the social, emotional, and intellectual development of children. Some children whose parents have divorced will display behavior and academic difficulties in school, lower self-esteem, and less positive relationships with peers (Amato, 2001). But does this research give the full picture? From a risk and resilience perspective, the outcome of a divorce is not so clear cut. Divorce is a risk factor, to be sure, but what protective factors exist for a child that might offset its negative effects?

Studies have shown that divorce can have a negative, neutral, or even positive effect on children's development, depending on the risk and protective factors involved (Hetherington & Kelly, 2002; Kelly, 2007; Kelly & Emery, 2003). Children may have a large number of protective factors that help them cope, including a secure attachment to parents, relative family harmony after the divorce, continued warm contact with the absent parent, and a supportive school and teacher. A number of child characteristics serve as protective factors. Children with "easy going" temperaments tend to be more resilient in such family crises. Even the age of the child may be protective. Young children have an easier adjustment after divorce than do adolescents. The emotional state of parents can be a protective factor. If the parent remaining in the home is free of depression, hostility, drug dependence, or other psychological problems, the family will be more resilient. Sometimes a parent will experience positive feelings of relief and safety after divorce, particularly if the absent parent has been antisocial or abusive. The cumulative effects of these protective elements can reduce or even eliminate the harmful effects of this family stressor.

Addiction and Substance Abuse

As discussed in Chapter 4, parents' addiction to drugs and alcohol can ruin families. Addiction has a particularly devastating effect on children because addicted parents are often highly ineffective parents. One study found that children of alcoholic fathers showed

resilience: A psychological state in which children and families possess enough positive life circumstances or emotional resources to cope with, and offset, risk factors in their lives.

a wide range of behavior problems, from social withdrawal to aggression and conduct problems in school (Fals-Stewart, Kelley, Fincham, Golden, & Logsdon, 2004). These difficulties were most severe and common for those whose addicted fathers were unresponsive, hostile, and unpredictable in their parenting. Similar findings have been obtained in studies on parents' illegal drug use (Fals-Stewart, Kelley, Cooke, & Golden, 2003). Children of drug-addicted parents were found to exhibit serious emotional and social problems at home and school. Children of addicts are more likely to become addicted, themselves, when they become adolescents or adults (Dube, Anda, Felitti, Edwards, & Croft, 2002). Alcoholic and drug-addicted parents are twice as likely to engage in physical child abuse and neglect (Walsh, MacMillan, & Jamieson, 2003).

Such a grim picture this is! Could there be protective factors powerful enough to offset these effects on children's development? Surprisingly, in all of the studies cited here, a number of children were found to be less adversely affected by having an addicted parent. Why? For some children, it was the support of a nurturing, non-addicted mother who helped the child cope with an addicted father. For some children, a supportive school, a special teacher, or the intervention of a community agency helped the family cope. For still others, it was the addicted parent, him- or herself, who was able to provide enough warmth and responsiveness that the child felt secure. Once again, it is the balance between risk and protective factors that makes the difference.

Homelessness

In Chapter 14, homelessness was identified as a growing national family crisis (Proffitt, 2008). Many homeless people live on the streets without any shelter; more than half of them are children. Not surprisingly, families without a place to live suffer a variety of negative outcomes—health problems, hunger, substance abuse, and exposure to violence (Toro, 2007). Only 20% of homeless parents are even able to stay with their children; many children are taken into protective custody (Zlotnick, Robertson, & Tam, 2003). The effects of homelessness on children can be calamitous. Children without homes have been found to become depressed, fearful, aggressive, and disruptive (Buckner, 2008).

Although homelessness always takes a toll on families, in one study, researchers were able to identify two distinct groups of children who are homeless—those who are "higher functioning" and "lower functioning" (Buckner, 2008). The latter group exhibited many of the above-cited behavioral and emotional problems, but the former group did not. Risk and protective factors, once again, may explain this. Children in the higher functioning group were more likely to be securely attached to a parent. They were well cared for, at least emotionally, and had positive interpersonal skills. They had parents who did not have significant mental health problems or addictions. Some of them even attended school (Buckner, Bassuk, & Weinreb, 2002). All of these factors help children and families cope with difficult lives.

Teachers as a Protective Factor

Notice that, in all of these examples, a responsive teacher or school was named as a potential protective factor. In the case of divorce, for example, one of the best predictors of a child's adjustment is a relationship with a warm teacher, who supports the child and family and who maintains predictability, positive expectations for behavior, and clear limits in the classroom (Hetherington & Kelly, 2002). Pedro-Carroll (2005) cites research showing that teachers can play a major role in fostering resilience by addressing the emotional needs of children in crisis and reaching out to their parents before serious psychological difficulties become "rooted." She reports that classroom-based support strategies lead to a reduction in anxiety, behavior, and sleep problems in children and to increases in their healthy adjustment at home and school.

Olsen and Fuller (2008) suggest that teachers consider the following strategies for helping children and families through a crisis:

1. *Listen*. Let both the child and family members know you are available to listen to their concerns and worries related to the child's adjustment. Maintain clear boundaries, however. Any topic regarding the child is appropriate to discuss, but teachers should avoid becoming too enmeshed in personal family issues—such as taking sides or inviting angry comments about other family members or family service professionals.

2. *Provide classroom activities that encourage expression of feelings*. Provide drawing, painting, journal writing, and other self-expressive activities that help children in crisis to communicate fears, confusion, and sadness. Read children's books to the affected child or to the whole class that address the child's family problem. Be cautious to select high-quality books that are reassuring, not frightening. Read such books to the whole class only when the affected child is ready to think about and discuss problems with peers.

3. *Create a safe haven in the classroom, where the child can feel secure*. Often children suffer feelings of insecurity when in family crises. School may be the one place in their lives that is predictable, safe, and non-chaotic. A safe classroom is not only warm and nurturing but includes a predictable schedule, clear limits on behavior, and rules that keep all students safe and happy.

4. *Make referrals*. Assist families in finding the help they need by referring them to professionals within or outside of the school. In many cases, the teacher can communicate directly with families about available services. They can help them to make appointments or arrange for transportation so they can take advantage of these. In some instances—such as a case of suspected child abuse or a parent's drug problem—direct referral to a state or community agency is required.

5. *Provide information and resources to families*. A wealth of resources exist to help families in nearly any crisis. Provide books, pamphlets, or Websites that address a family's particular difficulty. Direct families to support groups, workshops, counseling centers, or other places where they can learn more about coping with their family problem.*

SUMMARY

There are many different types of families in the United States. A family with two married parents and children is no longer the norm. Single-parent, extended, gay and lesbian, and unmarried families are growing more common. Because of this variety in family structure, many different family members play a significant role in childrearing: grandparents, siblings, friends who are like family, and adoptive parents. Actively involved fathers are as important as mothers in promoting positive development. Foster parents—temporary guardians for children who have been abused or neglected—influence children's development.

Families of different backgrounds hold distinct beliefs about children and adopt child-rearing practices that are unique to their community and culture. Beliefs about child development are influenced by cultural tradition and history. Two factors that most affect these beliefs are poverty and oppression. General parenting styles and specific adult–child interactions also are shaped by culture. Although some

---

* Based on Olsen, G. & Fuller, M. L. (2008). *Home–school relations; Working successfully with parents and families*. Boston: Pearson.

parenting behaviors are observed in all families, parents of different cultural groups display distinct forms of communication, responses to crying, teaching behaviors, and carrying and holding practices.

Family stressors—major crises that threaten family functioning and child well being—can have severe or mild consequences, depending on the resilience of the family and child. For those who have many protective factors—warm family relationships, positive mental and physical health, or an easy-going temperament—family stressors may not cause permanent harm. For those children and families whose risk factors outweigh protective ones, negative outcomes can be great.

RESEARCH INTO PRACTICE

CRITICAL CONCEPT 1

There are many different types of families. What constitutes a family in one culture may be quite different in another. Sometimes grandparents, siblings, and even friends live in the home and assume child-rearing responsibilities. Sometimes fathers do not live in the home but still play a critical role. The rich variety of family characteristics reflects the ways that distinct cultural groups have adapted to challenges and life experiences throughout history.

Application #1   In most cases, involve both parents in the programs and activities of the school or center. This is important even when one parent lives outside the child's home. Special effort should be made to communicate with absent fathers and encourage their involvement in the classroom. In the case of an unharmonious relationship between parents, schedule separate parent–teacher conferences.

Application #2   Take care to understand legal issues related to divorce or separation of parents. Some parents may be denied contact with their children by the courts; others may have limited custody. Involving both parents is extremely important; however, in light of the many complex legal issues that arise in modern family life, you should proceed cautiously toward this goal.

Application #3   Be cautious not to assume that living in a single-parent family will impede children's development. In fact, be aware that mother-only homes may not be true single-parent families at all since grandparents and other relatives may play a positive role in child rearing and family life. Appreciate the positive influences on child development of all family members.

Application #4   Involve grandparents who play primary caregiving roles in school or center activities and programs. Invite them to participate in parent–teacher conferences and include them in discussions of classroom problems. Also, ask them to work with children in the classroom. All students will benefit from multigenerational interactions.

Application #5   Involve other family members and friends who have primary caregiving roles in school or center activities and programs as well. Encourage older siblings to work with children in the classroom. Invite aunts, uncles, and even friends who are like family to attend conferences and parent education programs—especially if they are significant caregivers.

Application #6   Plan a curriculum in early childhood education that reflects the diverse family configurations of modern society. Identify children's books, photographs, and curriculum materials that show various types of families. Portray many different kinds of households, such as those headed by mothers and grandmothers, by fathers only, by mothers and partners, and even by mothers and older siblings, throughout the curriculum. Focus discussions of families on caring relationships rather than on blood relations or marital status.

CRITICAL CONCEPT 2

Child development is influenced by family experiences. Families vary greatly across cultures. They hold diverse beliefs about how children should be raised. These beliefs may be shaped by such conditions as poverty and oppression. Families also differ in their styles and methods of adult–child interaction. Some adopt more "authoritarian" approaches to parenting, others "authoritative" methods. Parent communication, responses to crying, teaching behaviors, and holding and carrying practices are also quite diverse from one culture to the next.

Application #1   Learn as much as you can about the beliefs, routines, and traditions of families of the children you serve. Understanding parenting and family life experiences can provide insight into children's development and lead to appreciation of diverse styles of playing and learning.

Application #2   Before children begin school, conduct face-to-face interviews with family members to learn about expectations for behavior, discipline techniques, communication styles, and methods of soothing, feeding, and carrying children. Some family interaction patterns can be replicated in the classroom. For example, you might use more physical and less verbal methods of encouraging a child whose family interacts in these ways. Some family practices, such as physical punishment, may not be compatible with your beliefs or school policies. Openly discuss viewpoints so that consensus about goals and approaches can be achieved.

CRITICAL CONCEPT 3

Families and children face stressors—major crises in their lives—with which they must cope. Those who adjust well to these problems are said to be resilient. They have a range of protective factors—interpersonal traits, family relationships, financial resources, and other positive elements—that outweigh the negative impact of a family stressor. Examples of stressors include divorce, drug and alcohol addiction, and homelessness. With each of these challenges, children do more or less well depending on the balance of protective versus risk factors in their lives.

Application # 1   Help families who are facing crises to get services they need. Make referrals to state and community service agencies when needed. Such services become protective factors that help counterbalance the negative effects of family tragedy.

Application # 2   Provide a "safe haven" for children in school. Create an environment that is nurturing, predictable, and safe. Be responsive and warm, letting children know that you care about them unconditionally and are there to support and listen to them.

Application # 3   Plan curriculum activities that help children to cope with family stressors. High-quality children's literature about divorce, for example, will help children cope with such a problem at home.

Glossary

ability grouping A classroom practice in which children are placed into groups according to ability. Placement in a low-ability group can threaten feelings of competence.

accommodation Piaget's term for a learning process in which humans modify what they already know to make room for new ideas or information.

action research Informal research conducted by teachers and caregivers to answer pressing questions related to teaching, learning, and children's development.

action space An early type of spatial thinking in which young children think about space only in terms of their own movements or actions through it.

affiliative obedience A high level of obedience to elders or respected authorities and a low level of self-assertion that is emphasized more in some cultures than in others.

African American Vernacular English A form of English spoken by African Americans in many communities in the United States that is as complex and expressive as standard English and includes its own unique phonology, syntax, and semantics.

aggression Any action that has the intent of harming another either physically or psychologically, such as hitting, biting, pushing, kicking, or name-calling and other verbal abuse.

alert and waking states States in which newborns are attentive and can explore their world and exercise their senses and motor abilities.

alphabet knowledge The understanding that letters have different shapes and that each is related to a particular sound.

altruistic behaviors Acts of kindness toward other persons, such as sharing a toy, helping with a puzzle, and comforting a crying peer.

amniocentesis A procedure to detect genetic disorders before birth by obtaining a small sampling of amniotic fluid as early as the 12th week of pregnancy.

amnion A protective, fluid-filled sac that forms around the embryo during prenatal development.

anecdotal records A qualitative research method—often used in the classroom—in which children's behavior is observed and recorded in a rich narrative.

articulation problems An inability to pronounce specific phonemes that are usually acquired by a particular age.

articulators Parts of the body that are responsible for speech production, including the front and back of the tongue, the teeth, the lips, the roof of the mouth, the vocal cords, and the lungs.

assertiveness Sticking up for oneself during disputes, such as tugging back a toy that has been snatched away. Assertiveness is not usually considered aggression.

assimilation Piaget's term for a learning process in which humans integrate new ideas or information into what they already know about.

associative play A level of social participation in which children pursue their own individual play themes yet interact often with peers, talking about what they are doing and sharing materials.

attachment The bidirectional process by which infants and other people—particularly parents—form emotional bonds with one another.

attention The ability to focus for an extended period on the important features of a situation or problem.

attention-deficit/hyperactivity disorder (ADHD) A disorder that is characterized by high activity level, impulsiveness, and an inability to pay attention and that often leads to poor peer relations and school performance.

authoritarian parenting style A parenting style in which the parent is very controlling, allows little discussion about parent demands, and is less warm.

authoritative parenting style A parenting style that includes a relatively democratic approach to raising children, in which a parent is warm and supportive and encourages children to speak their minds, even when there are conflicts or misbehavior.

autism A condition characterized by a lack of awareness of others, a preference for objects to people, and an intense desire for sameness. Autism can include language delays, self-destructive behavior, repetitive and ritualistic body movements, and difficulty interpreting multiple stimuli.

autonomy Erikson's term for an emotional state, often acquired in toddlerhood, in which children strive to be independent and separate from parents. Children who are overly restricted will feel *shame and doubt*.

axon A long thread of tissue that extends out from the cell body of a neuron and sends messages to the dendrites of other nerve cells.

babbling A repetitive vocalization by babies that is believed to be play with noise rather than true communication.

behavior modification A classroom strategy, often used with children with serious emotional disturbance or other special needs, in which adults articulate specific expectations for behavior and then reward children for meeting those expectations.

behaviorist theory A theory that holds that most of what humans become is shaped by the environment.

bicultural A term to describe those who are effective members of two distinct cultural groups.

big books Enlarged versions of classic children's books that allow children to see the print and illustrations well.

bilingual education A term used to refer to a variety of strategies used in schools to assist children who speak languages different from that of the dominant culture.

bilingualism The ability to speak two different languages.

biliteracy The ability to read and write in two languages.

body mass index (BMI) A measure of health status, computed by considering weight in relation to height (the formula for calculating BMI is weight/height$^2 \times 703$).

brain lateralization The organization of the brain into right and left hemispheres, with each hemisphere performing unique and specialized functions.

bullying Aggression that is without a clear purpose, often stemming from rage or upset and leading to peer rejection.

by-heart reading A reading behavior in which children recite verbatim the text of a story they have memorized with such accuracy and adult intonation that unknowing teachers or parents will think they are reading conventionally.

case studies A qualitative research method—often used in the classroom—that involves gathering in-depth information on an individual child or family and writing an extensive narrative profiling development.

categorization A mental activity in which children put objects that are alike together. Early categorization is based on one characteristic (e.g., size, color, or shape), later categorization on two or more traits (e.g., placing shapes of the same color together).

causality An understanding of cause and effect, including an ability to see connections between actions—both one's own and others'—and consequences.

causality materials Play materials for infants, such as pull or squeeze toys, that cause things to happen and help children understand cause and effect.

center of gravity The point in the body at which body weight is evenly distributed. Center of gravity is lower in the preschool years, allowing children to perform actions that were impossible in infancy.

cephalocaudal growth gradient The tendency for human development to proceed from the top down so that infants' and children's heads and brains grow more rapidly than their legs and feet.

cerebral palsy A disorder that can be caused by illness, injury, or oxygen deprivation before or during birth that impairs motor coordination, muscle strength, and sometimes hearing and vision.

child care quality The degree to which a child care center includes adequate structural features, such as staff-to-child ratio, available play space and toys, and group size, and dynamic features, such as caregiver warmth and responsiveness.

children of color/children of historically underrepresented groups Children of non-European, non-Caucasian ethnic background. These phrases replace the traditional word *minority*.

chorionic villus biopsy A procedure in which genetic disorders are detected by sampling fetal tissue from the outer membrane of the amniotic sac as early as the ninth week of pregnancy.

chromosomes Chemical structures contained in the nucleus of all human cells that carry all the genetic information necessary for the development of a unique individual.

class meeting A classroom strategy in which children are encouraged to talk openly about cultural and racial differences, share concerns and problems with peers, and resolve conflicts.

classical conditioning A strategy for shaping behavior in which a neutral stimulus is paired with a pleasurable one. Eventually, the subject responds in the same way to the neutral stimulus as to the pleasurable one, even when the pleasurable stimulus is no longer present.

closed-field play Play in which just two children are invited to play together without involvement of other children.

cluster of attachment behaviors The unique set of parenting behaviors of a particular family or culture that lead to the secure attachment of infants.

cognitive development Mental development, including problem solving and the acquisition of knowledge.

cognitive-developmental theory A theory of human development holding that knowledge is actively constructed by the child and that active problem solving, social interaction, and language are necessary for learning.

collective conversations A style of communication, common in many cultures, in which speakers all talk at once, with little turn taking.

collective families Families that are more likely to collaborate in daily life, pooling resources, sharing household tasks and child-rearing responsibilities, making group decisions, and banding together in the face of adversity.

collective monologues Conversations in which children talk *at* one another, not caring whether their messages are getting through to their listeners.

competence Similar to Erikson's term *industry*, an emotional state in which children feel capable because of their successes in and out of school. Repeated failure will result in an opposite emotional state: *inferiority*.

componential intelligence A type of intelligence related to basic processes of thinking, attending, and remembering.

concrete operational stage Piaget's stage of cognitive development that encompasses the elementary years, in which thinking becomes more internal and abstract but in which children still need the support of concrete objects in order to learn.

conflicts and arguments Disagreements among children that can be settled verbally and do not involve aggression.

conservation An understanding that properties and amounts stay the same even when their physical appearances are changed.

conservation of continuous quantity A type of conservation in which children understand that amounts of liquid or other substances stay the same even when they are put in different-size containers.

conservation of number A type of conservation in which children understand that amounts of objects stay the same even if they have been rearranged.

contextual intelligence A type of intelligence—necessary for real-life problem solving—that involves adapting thinking to changes in the environment.

cooperative learning and partnering Classroom strategies in which children work in pairs or groups so that more competent students may be matched with those who have cognitive disabilities.

cooperative play A level of social participation in which children adopt a single, coordinated play theme and plan, negotiate, and differentiate roles in pursuit of a shared goal.

correlational study A type of research in which two traits are measured, and their relationship is examined.

cortisol A hormone that increases in the body with stress and threatens infant brain development by reducing the number of synapses and leaving neurons vulnerable to damage.

cross-sectional study Research in which a trait is studied by examining children of many different ages at one time and developmental trends are determined by comparing one age group to another.

cultural/ethnic diversity Variations in development and behavior that are due to a child's cultural background.

culture The unique collection of beliefs, practices, traditions, valued competencies, world views, and histories that characterize a particular group of people.

cystic fibrosis A genetically derived enzyme disorder, more common in Pueblo Indians and Europeans, that causes mucus to form in the lungs and intestinal tract.

decentration An ability to coordinate two ideas at once and to no longer center on just one phenomenon.

dendrites Elongated tissues on a neuron that receive messages from the axons of other nerve cells.

development The process by which humans change both qualitatively and quantitatively as they grow older.

developmental checklist A classroom observation system in which a teacher or caregiver rates children's attainment of certain developmental milestones, such as revolving conflicts or playing cooperatively with peers.

developmental milestones Specific characteristics that are expected to emerge in children at various age levels.

difficult temperament A disposition that is characterized by harsh and negative reactions to new or frustrating situations, irregular patterns of sleeping or eating, and numerous adjustment problems.

disfluency A speech problem, sometimes called *stuttering*, in which a child engages in prolonged and frequent single-sound repetitions, sometimes accompanied by facial grimaces and contortions of the mouth.

disorganized attachment A category of attachment in which an infant has not securely bonded with a parent or significant other. In the strange situation procedure, babies who have disorganized attachment appear disoriented on their reunion with caregivers and may cling to, push away from, or even ignore them.

DNA (deoxyribonucleic acid) Long, double-stranded molecules that make up chromosomes. Genetic information is carried in DNA within cells.

dominant gene A gene for one trait that overpowers a gene for an alternate trait.

Down syndrome A genetic condition, caused by an extra chromosome that can lead to mental retardation, heart problems, motor delays, and unique physical features such as reduced stature.

Duchenne muscular dystrophy A hereditary disorder affecting motor functioning that is characterized by a steady weakening of skeletal muscles, possibly leading to deterioration of the heart muscle and the need for a wheelchair.

dynamic systems theory A theory that holds that motor action, cognitive development, and behavior are all part of a single, dynamic system in the brain. From this perspective, motor development and brain growth are interrelated.

early childhood development The development of children from conception and birth through age 8.

early production stage A stage of second-language learning in which children speak longer utterances in the second language in the classroom.

easy temperament A disposition in which infants have sunny dispositions, are friendly around strangers, and are easily consoled.

echolalia A language behavior, common in children with autism, in which a child repeats, in a meaningless way, the words, syllables, or sounds spoken by others as if echoing them.

ecological systems theory A theory of development that emphasizes the influence of the many institutions and settings—the community, the school, the political system—within which children live. This theory holds that individual development does not occur in a psychological vacuum but is affected by larger society.

ecology The many different settings or institutions that affect human development.

ego Freud's term for the part of the mind that is rational and regulates and redirects the instinctual impulses of the id.

egocentrism A type of thinking, common in infancy and early childhood, in which children are unable to understand that there are other viewpoints in the world besides their own.

emotional regulation The ability of infants to control and reduce intense feelings by attending intensely to things—a parent's face or a set of keys—that are unrelated to the source of those feelings.

empathy An inborn ability to feel vicariously others' emotions or physical pain.

enmeshment A goal of socialization in some cultures in which children become attached to, cooperate with, and rely on others, particularly their family members.

ethnic identity An understanding and evaluation of the behaviors, thinking, values, feelings, and competencies of the ethnic group to which people belong.

ethnic socialization The process of teaching to children the beliefs, abilities, roles, and history that are unique to one's own cultural group.

ethnic socialization messages Statements that guide children in understanding and valuing the uniqueness of their family's cultural heritage.

ethnography A type of research in which investigators spend significant time working or living with a group—a classroom, a family, or a community—and write qualitative descriptions of their observations.

evaluative symbols Rewards or indicators of success—such as grades or stickers—that are presented publicly by teachers in school and that are often incorporated into children's assessments of their own competence.

event sampling A method of observing children in which a teacher or researcher records the number of times a particular behavior or event occurs.

exosystem The layer of environmental influences on development that is composed of institutions or persons that do not actually touch children's lives but that indirectly affect their experiences. The legal services system or the public assistance office are examples.

expansion A language-teaching technique in which an adult restates a one- or two-word utterance of a child in a more elaborate form.

expansion of production stage A stage of second-language learning in which children speak in full sentences and respond to open-ended questions in the second language, though with some disfluency.

expatiation A language-teaching technique in which an adult restates a one- or two-word utterance of a child but then adds more language, furthering the conversation.

experiential intelligence A type of intelligence that allows humans to use previous experience in learning.

experimental study Research in which a treatment, such as an educational intervention, is administered to subjects. An experimental group receives the treatment, a control group does not, and the researcher compares the outcomes of the two groups.

expository books Books containing illustrations and written labels, without a plotline, that resemble the kind of factual reading that is more common in families of some historically underrepresented groups.

expressive jargon A type of babbling that is so similar to adult speech in complexity and intonation that it sounds as if the baby were speaking in full sentences.

expressive language learning style A style of language learning in which a young child acquires social words, such as *bye-bye* and *no*, earliest in development.

extended family A family in which parents, grandparents, other relatives, and even friends live together and which is growing more common, particularly among historically underrepresented groups.

external locus of control A belief that what happens to a person is due to external forces, that success is beyond one's control, and that failure is inevitable.

extrinsic motivation Motivation to achieve that comes from the outside environment. Learning a skill only to obtain external rewards or praise from others is an example.

feelings of control A type of self-esteem related to perceptions about the ability to control one's own life or make a difference in determining one's destiny.

fetal alcohol syndrome A condition caused by a mother's heavy drinking during pregnancy that can lead to nervous system impairment, mental retardation, hyperactivity, and deficiencies in weight, height, and brain size.

field-independent learners Learners with a cognitive style that allows them to solve problems without much outside assistance and to focus on the specific steps of a task without being distracted by the full external environment, or "the field."

field-sensitive learners Learners with a cognitive style that leads them to rely on the entire environment and everything and everyone in it to solve problems.

fine motor development The ability to coordinate smaller muscles in the arms, hands, and fingers that allows a child to perform such tasks as tying, buckling, zipping, making puzzles, molding clay, cutting with scissors, and drawing.

firm and directive socialization practices Techniques of child guidance, more common in families of traditionally oppressed cultures, in which behavior is closely monitored and regulated in order to keep children safe from danger.

flexible scheduling A classroom strategy in which some children are allowed to take as long as they need on a learning task and others are able to move ahead to more advanced activities if they finish early.

formal operational stage Piaget's most advanced stage of cognitive development that encompasses adolescence and adulthood, in which thinking is purely abstract and not tied to the immediate, physical world.

formal relationships with the teacher The more formal and evaluative teacher–child connections found in elementary schools that can threaten children's feelings of self-worth.

foster homes Homes where children are temporarily placed when special circumstances—including abuse and neglect—require that they live away from their families. Children are to live in foster homes until successful family interventions have been implemented or permanent adoptions arranged.

fragile X syndrome A genetic condition, caused by a brittle or separated X chromosome, that can lead to mental retardation and infantile autism.

free association tasks Tasks to study the connectedness of word meanings in which children are given a word and encouraged to name as many other words as come to mind.

friends who are like family Close friends within a neighborhood or village who are treated as family members and often share child care responsibilities.

frontal cortex A region of the brain that develops rapidly at 8 months of age and is associated with the ability to express and regulate emotions.

functional play A type of play, commonly performed by infants and young children with special needs, that involves repetitive motor action, such as banging objects or repeating body movements again and again.

games with rules A predominant form of play during the primary years that includes rules, strategy, and competition.

gender identity An understanding and evaluation of one's own gender, including the physical characteristics, behavioral expectations, and social obligations and status that define being a male or female in one's family and culture.

general language delay A condition in which a child's language development lags behind that of other children of the same age, with no apparent perceptual or cognitive cause.

genes Segments of DNA molecules, passed along from parents to offspring, that determine the characteristics of a developing human.

gifted and talented A term used to describe children who display a superior intellect and/or talents that are advanced for their chronological age and who are often extremely competent in language and able to grasp complex ideas quickly.

graded challenges The provision of play and learning materials in a classroom that represent varying degrees of difficulty so that children of all abilities can find something meaningful to do.

gross motor abilities Skills, such as running, jumping, throwing, climbing, and kicking, that require the use of large muscles in the legs or arms, as well as general strength and stamina.

guided peer watching A classroom strategy in which caregivers direct children's attention to the play of their peers (e.g., "Let's watch what Charlene is doing").

habituation A psychological process in which infants become so familiar with objects or events that they show disinterest in them. Psychologists have taken advantage of habituation to study what babies know and are able to do.

hands-on/minds-on experience A learning experience that allows children not only to handle objects but also to think deeply about these objects—to order, categorize, describe, compare, or artistically represent them.

hearing impairment A condition caused by a variety of factors that is characterized by deafness or severely limited auditory perception and can lead to language, motor, and other developmental delays.

hemophilia A genetically derived condition that limits blood clotting and can lead to internal bleeding.

heritability ratio A mathematic estimate of the relative role of genetics in determining intelligence.

hierarchy of child-rearing concerns A prioritizing of child-rearing goals by parents living in extreme poverty so that basic, physical survival outweighs all other concerns.

hostile aggression Anger-fueled aggression that is unpredictable, illogical, and unprovoked.

id Freud's term for the part of the mind that contains instinctual urges and strives for immediate gratification but is kept in check by the ego and the superego.

identify formation The process of constructing a clear understanding of the roles, personal values, characteristics, competencies, and group memberships that define oneself.

immersion model of bilingual education A model of bilingual education in which children are taught almost exclusively in the language of the dominant society with the expectation that they will be motivated to learn the second language quickly.

inclusive views of self Evaluations of self that are related to accomplishments or competencies of the entire family, community, or other groups to which one belongs.

independent reading stage A stage of reading in which children are able to apply the particular reading strategies that are most helpful for a certain text and can switch from one strategy to another until they successfully interpret the message.

industry Erikson's term for an emotional state, often acquired in the elementary years, in which children feel competent because of successes in and out of school. Repeated failure will result in an opposite emotional state: *inferiority*.

initiative Erikson's term for an emotional state, often acquired in the preschool years, in which children assert themselves, make creative attempts, take risks, and reach out to peers. Children whose initiatives are thwarted will experience an opposite emotional state: *guilt*.

insecure/ambivalent attachment A category of attachment in which an infant has not securely bonded with a parent or significant other. In the strange situation procedure, babies who have an insecure/ambivalent attachment will alternate between desperate clinging and angry rejection when reunited with a parent.

insecure/avoidant attachment A category of attachment in which an infant has not securely bonded with a parent or significant other. In the strange situation procedure, babies who have an insecure/avoidant attachment may or may not show upset when their mothers leave but will completely ignore them when they return.

instructional pluralism A teaching strategy in which a single unit of instruction includes many different learning options—direct instruction, media presentations, singing, collective brainstorming, guided imagery, creative writing, drawing, drama, or even the recitation of facts.

instrumental aggression Verbal or physical assault that has a logical goal: to get a toy or to chase undesired classmates from a play area, for example.

intelligence quotient (IQ) A formula for expressing an individual's intelligence as a single score, computed by dividing one's mental age—determined by performance on a test—by his or her chronological age—the person's actual age in years. For statistical reasons, the score is then multiplied by 100.

intelligence test A test composed of a series of questions that measure verbal and quantitative reasoning and abstract thinking that is designed to measure innate mental capabilities.

internal locus of control A belief that hard work and persistence will lead to success and that one has the power within oneself to make a difference.

internalized thought A kind of thinking, emerging between 12 and 18 months of age, in which problems are solved by thinking them through, using reflection and mental images.

intersubjectivity The ability to share a common understanding about something with another person.

intrinsic motivation A desire to learn, behave appropriately, or be accepted that comes from within rather than being imposed externally through rewards or praise.

introduction to written forms stage A stage of second-language learning in which children speak in full sentences and show an interest in reading and writing in the second language.

invented spelling An early form of writing in which children use their own, unconventional system of spelling out words, based on their understanding of letters and their associated sounds.

invisible handicaps Disabilities without easy-to-see physical characteristics that are more difficult for peers to identify and understand.

irreversibility A characteristic of preoperational thought in the preschool years in which children are unable to reverse the direction of thinking or action.

isolate behavior A pattern of interaction in which children rarely initiate contact with others, retreat when initiatives are directed toward them, and often prefer to be alone.

kinship Close, supportive relationships with relatives or nonrelatives. Parakinship ties are bonds with people who have no formal blood relations but are like family.

Klinefelter's syndrome A genetically derived condition that can result in sterility, physical malformation, and mental health problems.

labeling and organizing A learning strategy in which learners place objects, events, or ideas they wish to remember into mental categories and then name them.

labor The process of giving birth, which occurs in three stages: dilation, birth of the baby, and expulsion of the placenta.

language differences Variations in language due to cultural or linguistic background, not to be confused with deficits in language caused by challenging conditions.

language shock Feelings of surprise that result when children who are bilingual suddenly discover that their native language is not understood by others.

lap reading A classroom strategy in which adults sit with one or several children in their laps and read favorite books, encouraging them to turn pages, point to illustrations, and ask questions.

learning disabilities (LD) Cognitive disabilities characterized by impairment in some specific aspect of learning, such as writing, speaking, or mathematics, and sometimes including perceptual and attention deficits.

locomotion abilities Skills involving movement from one place to another, such as walking, skipping, and running.

long looking A style of attending in which infants study objects by looking at only one feature for a long period of time. This style causes them to process information more slowly.

long-term memory A type of memory in which certain images, facts, or concepts are drawn from short-term memory and are permanently stored. Some equate long-term memory with knowledge itself.

longitudinal study Research in which a group of children is studied over a long period of time to observe changes in behavior and development at various ages.

macrosystem The layer of environmental influences on development that contains the overarching values, ideologies, laws, worldviews, and customs of a particular culture or society. A society's respect and caring for children is an example.

maintenance/developmental model of bilingual education A model of bilingual education in which children are taught primarily in their native language so that they acquire important school-related skills while at the same time being introduced to English as a second language.

map space A type of spatial thinking in which young children can think about space as a whole and can link directions, locations, and distances together in their minds. This type of thinking allows children to interpret and construct maps.

maturationist theory A theory that holds that most of what humans become is predetermined by genetics and that traits inherited from ancestors simply unfold as children mature.

meiosis A special cell division process that leads to the formation of a father's sperm cell and a mother's ovum.

mental dictionary A child's total vocabulary, including words in all the languages being learned.

mental retardation A condition that may or may not have a clearly identified cause and is characterized by general intellectual impairment and difficulty in adapting well to life events and circumstances.

mesosystem The layer of environmental influences on development that is composed of the interconnections among the persons or organizations within the microsystem. Parent–teacher communication and collaborations between child care centers and public schools are examples.

metacognition The ability to think about and regulate internal cognitive processes, such as learning and remembering.

metalinguistic awareness An understanding of, and an ability to think and talk about, language itself.

microsystem The layer of environmental influences on development that includes all institutions and experiences within the child's immediate environment. The family, the school, and social services agencies are examples.

midwives Childbirth specialists—generally not relatives or doctors—who provide emotional and physical support to mothers during labor and delivery.

missegmentation An inability to know where the sounds and words of an utterance are divided.

mitosis The process of cell division and duplication in which each new cell receives an exact copy of the original cell's chromosomes.

modified curricular approach A strategy in which the classroom environment, lessons and activities, and student groupings are altered to reduce stress on children who have serious emotional disturbance or other special needs.

moral dilemmas Hypothetical stories told to children to evaluate their moral reasoning.

moral realism A stage in moral development in which right and wrong are determined by unchangeable rules that come from authority figures, such as parents.

moral relativism A stage in moral development in which situations and intentions are taken into account when making moral judgments and rules can be altered for a higher good.

moral self-worth A type of self-esteem that is related to perceptions about one's goodness or virtue as defined by cultural norms.

morphemes Small words or parts of words that hold meaning, such as the past tense *-ed* ending, the plural *-s*, and articles such as *a* and *the*.

motor play Spontaneous, repetitive, physical activity, common in infancy, that is nonliteral, intrinsically motivated, self-chosen, and pleasurable.

movement consistency Competence in the performance of basic movement skills, such as running or catching.

movement constancy An ability to adapt basic movement skills to meet varying environmental challenges. Being able to catch balls of different sizes or to run uphill and down as well as on flat surfaces are examples.

multiple classification The ability to categorize objects using more than one attribute.

multiple intelligences A phrase used to indicate that there are many different kinds of intellectual competence in humans, not just a single, general intelligence.

multisensory materials Play materials for infants that encourage the coordination of two or more senses. A brightly colored mobile that also plays music is an example.

myelin A fatty sheath that surrounds the axon and ensures that signals travel efficiently, quickly, and accurately.

myth of self-hatred A well-intentioned misconception that children of color hate themselves and are to be pitied.

narrative books Typical picture books with story lines that may be more familiar to children and families of middle-class, Euro-American backgrounds.

natural childbirth The process of giving birth in a comfortable, family-oriented, and nonmedical way while avoiding the use of drugs.

neglected sociometric status The peer group status of children who are ignored by their peers and who are rarely mentioned at all in sociometric interviews.

Neonatal Behavior Assessment Scale (NBAS) A rating system that assesses newborn functioning by measuring reflexes, states, responses to stimuli, and soothability.

neonatal period A developmental period during the first few weeks after birth when babies have a unique appearance and are more helpless, fragile, and dependent than they will ever be again.

neural cluster A collection of connected brain cells that handle certain movements, such as climbing.

neural map A complex network of neural clusters that connects a whole region of the brain. The formation of neural maps leads to brain organization.

neurons Cells in the brain that transmit and retrieve messages to and from all organs and muscles.

neurotransmitters Chemicals secreted from neurons that are responsible for transmitting messages from one cell to another in the nervous system.

nonconceptual speech An early form of language in which children utter words or phrases without thinking fully about what they mean.

nonverbal thought An early form of mental activity in which children observe objects or events or perform actions without using language.

normative charts Graphic representations of the stages or milestones children pass through as they develop.

nuclear family A family with just a mother, father, and children living together, which has long been viewed as the ideal structure for promoting positive child development.

obesity A serious medical condition in which a child has a body mass index (BMI) that lies above the 95th percentile for his or her particular age group.

object permanence An understanding, usually emerging between 8 and 12 months of age, that objects still exist even if they cannot be seen.

object permanence activities Play activities for infants, such as hiding games, that help children understand that objects exist even if they are out of sight.

onlooker behavior A level of social participation in which a child shows interest in what peers are doing and watches their play but does not interact with them.

open-field play Play in which two children are encouraged to spend time together but with other children present as well.

operant conditioning A form of training in which a desired behavior is immediately rewarded. When this occurs, that behavior is performed more frequently.

otitis media A condition characterized by buildup of fluid behind the eardrum that results in hearing loss and may contribute to articulation problems.

overgeneralization A language characteristic of toddlers and young children in which a word is used to describe more objects, events, or ideas than it should. For example, a child uses the word *car* to stand for cars, trucks, vans, and buses.

overrestriction A language characteristic of toddlers and young children in which a word is used to describe fewer objects, events, or ideas than it should. For example, a child uses the word *shoes* to mean only his or her own shoes.

ovum The egg, contributed by the mother, that will grow into a developing human if fertilized by a sperm cell.

parallel play A level of social participation in which children pursue activities side by side with peers but rarely interact or speak to them.

parentese A special form of language that parents around the world speak to children that includes exaggerated intonations, unique words, high-pitched vocalizations, and simple sentence structure.

parenting style A general approach to socializing children that includes the amount of warmth, communication, and control parents provide, along with their expectations for children's mature behavior.

paying attention A learning strategy in which learners consciously control attention and focus on only one or several relevant phenomena at a time.

perception-based thinking A characteristic of preoperational thought in the preschool years in which children are fooled by what things look or sound like and cannot use logic to overcome mistaken perceptions.

perceptual/motor coordination The ability to integrate movements and perception. Using vision to guide one's hands in drawing or turning the pages of a book are examples.

period of the embryo The second period of prenatal development, from 2 to 8 weeks after conception, when all major organs and structures of the body are formed.

period of the fetus The third period of prenatal development, from 8 weeks after conception to birth, when there is rapid growth and continued development of organs.

period of the ovum The first period of prenatal development, during the first 2 weeks after conception, when the developing human is a rapidly growing shapeless mass of specialized cells.

permissive-indulgent parenting style A parenting style in which there is much warmth and communication but virtually no control over the child.

permissive-neglectful parenting style A parenting style in which parents allow children to behave as they wish, without limits, and who do not offer warmth, communication, or attention.

phonemes Individual speech sounds, such as *b*, *t*, or *ch*.

phonemic awareness The understanding that language is made up of smaller units: words, syllables, and sounds.

phonemic stage of writing A stage of writing in which children use consonants that match some of the sounds in the story they are writing.

phonology The part of language involving speech sounds, including pronunciation, fluency, and intonation.

physical aggression Assaults, including biting, hitting, pushing, or kicking, that are intended to cause physical harm.

pincer grasp An advanced form of grasping, acquired at around age 1, in which the thumb and forefinger are used to hold small objects.

placenta A soft mass that allows the flow of nutrients from the mother to the embryo during prenatal development.

play entry strategies Techniques that young children use to join groups of peers who are already playing.

play-work A type of play in which children integrate play activities with family chores.

poor voice quality A speech disorder, sometimes caused by physiological problems such as growths on the larynx or by abuse of the vocal cords, in which a child is chronically hoarse or has an unusually nasal tone.

popular sociometric status The peer group status of children who are well liked, have many friends, and are named often as desired playmates in sociometric interviews.

postural tone Sufficient muscle strength and control to be able to sit upright or maintain other postures that allow learning and play. Some children with motor challenges lack posture tone and require support.

pragmatics The part of language that involves using words, sentences, and speech sounds to influence people and to accomplish things socially.

preconventional level A stage of moral development in which children resolve moral dilemmas by saying that what is right is obeying your parents and the rules and not getting punished. Children at this stage also justify moral decisions in terms of being nice so that others will be nice to you.

premature births Births in which children are born at least 3 weeks before the end of the 38- to 42-week gestation period or weigh less than 5.5 pounds at the time of delivery. Premature babies have a high mortality rate and may suffer developmental difficulties into childhood.

premoral A term to describe children who do not yet understand or adhere to clear rules when making moral decisions or playing games.

prenatal development The development of the human organism after conception and before birth.

preoperational stage Piaget's stage of cognitive development that encompasses early childhood, in which children use internal thought, including symbols, but still rely on perception and physical cues in the environment for learning.

preoperational thought A kind of thinking used by most young children in which there is still great reliance on perception and physical cues in the environment to learn and solve problems.

prephonemic stage of writing A stage of writing in which children use random letters to stand for stories or messages, with no relationship between a letter chosen and the sounds of specific phonemes.

preproduction stage A stage of second-language learning in which children are quite silent in the classroom and focus on understanding the second language rather than trying to speak it.

preschematic stage A stage of drawing, emerging during the late preschool years, when children begin to create simple representations of the people and things that are important to them. Heads predominate first in this stage; children then progress to adding stick arms, legs, and bodies.

pretend play A form of play in which children transform themselves into make-believe characters, change real objects into imaginary ones, and carry out complex make-believe enactments.

primary circular reactions Actions involving babies' own bodies, usually emerging at 1 month of age, that are performed by accident but then repeated because they produce interesting sensations.

print watched/holistic stage of reading A stage of reading in which children use multiple reading strategies—sight vocabulary, sentence context, and phonics—to acquire meaning from print, though they still rely most on one main strategy, such as phonics.

print watched/refusal to read and aspectual stage of reading A stage of reading in which children initially refuse to read, preferring to listen to adults, but eventually read on their own, relying on only one reading strategy—perhaps the memory of certain words or phonics.

proactive aggression Unprovoked physical or verbal assaults. Children who perform proactive aggression tend to be at risk of being rejected.

productive communication Behavior in which babies convey messages to others, including actual speaking but also gestures, noises, and crying.

propositional logic A kind of reasoning that involves the interpretation of if/then statements, such as "If ——— occurs, then what happens?"

protective factors Conditions that might insulate children from the negative effects of risk factors. Attachment to parents and positive preschool experiences are examples.

proximodistal growth gradient The tendency for human development to proceed from the center of the body out so that infants' and children's trunks develop more rapidly than their appendages and large movements precede the refined use of fingers or toes.

psychoanalytic theory A theory that holds that emotional development is influenced by tensions between internal desires and impulses and the demands of the outside world. The resolution of these tensions is needed to become a healthy adult.

psycholinguists Researchers and other specialists who study children's language abilities.

psychological states Distinct categories of newborn experience or activity, such as sleeping or crying, that vary according to how aroused or alert the infant is.

public comparison A classroom practice—such as posting a good behavior chart—in which teachers compare their students with one another both formally and informally. This practice can lead to negative self-judgments.

qualitative research Research that involves writing a rich description of behaviors and development rather than counting or quantifying observations.

quantitative methods Research methods in which children are observed and their behaviors counted or rated numerically. The numbers that are obtained are then entered into computer programs and analyzed statistically.

questions of different cognitive levels Questions that teachers ask that are of many different difficulty levels so that challenging, open-ended questions are alternated with lower level, simple-answer questions.

rapid eye movement (REM) sleep An important sleep state in which infants spend more time than adults and where the brain is especially active. This state may provide needed exercise for the newborn's nervous system.

reactive aggression Aggression in which children resist or strike out in response to peer mistreatment.

receptive communication The ability to understand language. Receptive communication usually precedes the ability to actually speak language.

recessive gene A gene for one trait that is overpowered by a dominant gene for an alternate trait. A recessive gene expresses itself only when paired with another recessive gene.

referential communication The ability to adjust language to the viewpoint of the listener. Using simpler language to talk to a younger sibling is an example.

referential language learning style A style of language learning in which a young child acquires the names of objects earliest in development.

reflexes Involuntary movements, such as sucking, rooting, and grasping, that are built in to a baby's nervous system. These are present at birth and disappear at about 6 months of age.

Reggio Emilia A region in Italy in which artistic expression is highly valued and where young children are found to create highly representational works of art.

register switching The ability to shift back and forth between two very different kinds of language (registers), such as between formal language and slang, depending on which is socially acceptable.

rehearsal A learning strategy in which learners repeat material verbally or practice actions over and over so they are retained.

rejected sociometric status The peer group status of children who are actively avoided by peers and who are named often as undesirable playmates in sociometric interviews.

reputation A detailed collection of traits that are assigned to children by peers, fairly or not, that determine their peer status and influence later social development.

resilient A descriptor for children who are able to cope and develop in positive directions in spite of terrible circumstances in their lives.

reversibility An ability to mentally or physically reverse the steps of a process to go back to a starting point.

Rh disease A genetic condition, caused by inheriting blood from the father that is incompatible with that of the mother, that can lead to anemia, jaundice, mental retardation, and death.

risk factors Conditions in a child's life that can lead to poor development, including poverty, community violence, and child abuse.

rituals Playful, predictable, often rhythmic routines that children perform and pass on to their siblings and peers in the primary years.

rough-and-tumble play A form of motor play—including wrestling, play fighting, rolling around, and chasing peers—that relieves tension and contributes to social competence but does not lead to aggression.

scaffold To use language and social interaction to guide children's thinking. When scaffolding, adults offer direct solutions to problems, indirectly guide them with hints or questions, or allow them to think completely independently, depending on what they need to learn.

scaffolding A process by which adults give support or guidance for some parts of a task or activity and then gradually give over regulation of the experience to children, allowing them to become more independent in their thinking and actions.

scanning The visual ability to look over all the features of an object and to get a complete picture of what it is like. Babies become competent in scanning an entire object by 3 months of age.

schematic stage A stage of drawing, emerging during the elementary years, in which elaborate, whole scenes of people, houses, trees, and the sun are created. In this stage, figures often are anchored to a ground line, and a patch of blue sky is added above.

scribbling stage The earliest stage of drawing, when children make marks on paper that gradually become more controlled and contain more circular strokes and discrete shapes. Children in this stage eventually tell stories about their scribbles.

secondary circular reactions Repetitive actions in infancy, usually emerging between 4 and 8 months, that are performed on toys or other objects.

secure attachment A category of attachment in which an infant has securely bonded with a parent or significant other. In the strange situation procedure, infants who are securely attached will show some distress on separation from caregivers but quickly re-establish warm interactions when reunited.

self-concept A person's overall view of self, which includes perceptions about traits, abilities, gender, and ethnic affiliation. As children acquire a self-concept, they strive to answer the question, "Who am I?"

self-directed speech A verbal behavior in which children talk to themselves, naming objects or narrating their actions—particularly as they solve problems.

self-esteem A person's overall evaluation of self, including a belief about one's own abilities, accomplishments, or interpersonal characteristics.

semantic networks A complex organization in one's mental dictionary that shows connections among words and clusters together words with similar meanings.

semantics The part of language that has to do with using words and learning word meanings.

sensorimotor stage Piaget's stage of cognitive development that encompasses infancy, in which thinking is limited to using physical action and the senses to know about things.

sensory memory A kind of memory that involves brief recollections of experiences involving the senses. A sensory memory disappears unless it is processed fully in the mind.

separation anxiety A fear of being separated from primary caregivers or left alone that often appears between 6 and 8 months.

seriation The ability to order objects by size or some other dimension. Ordering sticks by length is an example.

serious emotional disturbance (SED) A broad term used to describe children who exhibit negative emotional reactions that go beyond typical misbehavior or upset. Children with SED may exhibit externalizing problems, such as aggression, or internalizing problems, such as withdrawn behavior and anxiety.

sex-typed or gender-stereotyped behaviors Behaviors in which boys and girls exhibit rigid gender expectations of their culture, including toy and playmate preferences and degree of activity, roughness in play, and compliance with adult requests.

short looking A style of attending in which infants take brief looks at many different aspects of an object, looking at one feature, then another. This style allows them to process information more quickly.

short-term memory A type of memory in which experiences are stored in the brain for a short period of time. One can organize, make sense of, reflect on, or in other ways process information in short-term memory.

sibling caretaking A child care arrangement in which an older sibling is assigned direct disciplinary, supervisory, and caregiving responsibilities for a younger brother or sister. Sibling caretaking can promote social development, ethnic socialization, and academic learning.

sickle-cell anemia A genetically derived condition, more common in African Americans, that causes severe pain, heart and kidney problems, and early death.

simple pretense The make-believe use of familiar objects to enact customary routines, such as using a toy cup to pretend to drink.

simultaneous second-language learning Children who are exposed equally to two languages from birth and become quite proficient in both by the end of the preschool years.

single-sound disfluency The most worrisome form of stuttering in which a single sound is repeated (e.g., "b-b-b-b-ball"), often accompanied by tension or facial grimaces, as children struggle to speak.

slow-to-warm-up temperament A disposition in which an infant is wary of strangers, is reluctant to separate from parents, and shows less overt emotions, positive or negative.

small-for-dates Babies who are smaller than expected for their gestational age. Small-for-dates are often full-term babies that are small due to health or nutritional deficiencies.

social acceptance A type of self-esteem that is related to perceptions about how well one is liked by peers and adults.

social cognition The ability to understand social situations, including skill at recognizing the outcomes of one's own behaviors and the actions and motives of others.

social competence The degree to which a person is liked by others and has learned skills to interact effectively in social settings.

social initiative A desire, common in the preschool years, to reach out to others, make social contacts, and try out new social behaviors.

social learning theory A theory that holds that humans learn new behaviors by imitating the people around them. When they are rewarded for this imitation, they will perform these behaviors more frequently.

social participation The degree of children's involvement with peers during play, ranging from unoccupied and onlooking behavior to cooperative play.

social referencing The process by which infants refer to adults' emotional reactions—their voices and facial expressions—to determine how they should feel about persons, objects, or situations.

socialized speech Verbalizations in which children adjust their language to the listener's perspective and level of cognitive ability, including the use of simplified language when talking to younger children and more complex language when talking to older peers or adults.

sociocultural theory A theory that holds that thinking and learning are highly influenced by social interaction, language, and culture.

sociodramatic play A type of pretend play that includes other children and involves complex enactments and intricate themes and story lines.

socioeconomic status (SES) A measure of a family's overall economic and social status, determined by level of education, income, place of residence, and occupation of primary wage earners.

sociometric interview A technique to assess the overall social competence of children in classrooms in which individuals are interviewed about which peers they like to play with and which they do not.

sociometric status A child's relative status in a group of peers—popular, rejected, or neglected—based on a sociometric interview.

sociomoral reasoning An ability to make judgments about right and wrong that may be acquired through the playing of group games.

special needs The needs of children that result from developmental delays or disabilities.

specific learning disability in reading A challenging condition in which children who show competence in all other academic areas have difficulty learning to read.

speech and language pathologist A specially trained professional who works with children with language difficulties. Speech and language pathologists conduct regular speech, language, and hearing screenings and provide home and classroom interventions when serious language difficulties are identified.

speech perception An ability, present at birth, to perceive and process language differently from other sounds.

spina bifida A congenital condition in which the spinal cord and nerve roots are damaged, leading to problems ranging from slight sensory impairments and walking difficulty to paraplegia, severe sensory impairment, incontinence, and retention of fluid in the brain.

standardized tests Tests that are administered to large samples of children, allowing developers to determine how well a typical child performs on test items. In grading these tests, an individual child's scores are compared with those of other children of the same age.

stimulable A condition in which children can accurately imitate a particular sound when it is presented to them by an adult even if they do not pronounce it correctly in everyday speech.

story formed stage of reading A stage of reading in which children tell a full story as they look at books, using an intonation of a storyteller and sharing events that approximate events in the actual story.

story not formed stage of reading A stage of reading in which children point to or name illustrations but do not tell a coherent story as they look at a book.

strange situation procedure A research method used to assess the quality of attachment of babies to their caregivers. The procedure involves observing the responses of a child to a number of conditions, including the departure of a parent and the arrival of a stranger.

stranger anxiety A fear of strangers that often appears between 6 and 8 months of age.

struggle behaviors Facial grimaces, contortions of the mouth, and other signs of difficulty in producing speech sounds that are indicators of a more serious form of disfluency.

successive second-language learners Persons who acquire a primary language first and a second language later.

sudden infant death syndrome (SIDS) A leading cause of death among infants in which a baby stops breathing without a known cause, usually at night.

super-dense infant brain The brain of the infant, which grows more rapidly and has more connections (synapses) among nerve cells than an adult brain.

superego Freud's term for the part of the mind that comprises the conscience, including the values and mores of one's culture.

suprasegmental aspects of a story The pacing, pitch, volume, and other modulations of voice that a storyteller uses to make a story exciting.

symbolic thought A form of thinking in which symbols are used to stand for things that are not present. Language, reading, writing, and pretend play all require symbolic thought.

synapse A juncture between the axon of one neuron and the dendrites of another through which neural messages are transmitted.

syntax The part of language that involves creating sentences, including word order, sentence length and complexity, and the use of clauses and word endings.

tacit knowledge of language A subconscious ability to apply rules of language without thinking about them.

Tay-Sachs disease A genetically derived enzyme, more common in Jews of Eastern European descent, that causes deterioration of the brain and nervous system.

teasing play A form of play, common in some cultures, in which children taunt one another or argue in a nonliteral and nonhostile way. Teasing play is not usually considered aggression.

telegraphic speech Early utterances of young children, such as "Throw ball," that contain only the words necessary to convey the message. Less important words, such as articles, are omitted.

temperament A basic disposition that can be observed throughout a person's development. Babies are born with temperaments that can influence their social relationships and emotional health.

teratogen Environmental agents, such as drugs, radiation, or illness, that threaten the development of the fetus.

thalassemia A genetically derived blood disorder, more common in Asians, that causes damage to vital organs.

theory A system of beliefs about something. A child development theory is a collection of beliefs about why children behave, think, and feel as they do.

theory of the mind A belief about what the mind is, how it works, and how it might be controlled that helps children learn and think at ever-higher levels.

time sampling A research method in which a teacher or researcher observes children at regular time intervals and records interactions that occur during that period.

topic chaining A type of conversation, more common in some cultures, that flows freely from one subject to another and does not stick to a single theme or have a clear beginning, middle, and end.

total communication A system of communication in which manual signals, such as sign language, informal gestures, and facial expressions, are used along with verbalizations to communicate with children with hearing impairment.

tracking The ability to visually follow a moving object with one's eyes. Tracking becomes smoother and more accurate during the first 6 months of life.

transductive reasoning A characteristic of preoperational thought in the preschool years in which children put one immediate event into relationship with another immediate event and assume—sometimes erroneously—that one causes the other.

transition to production stage A stage in second-language learning in which children occasionally make brief verbalizations in the second language during classroom interactions.

transitional stage of writing A stage in writing in which children compose stories or messages in a more conventional way and creative attempts are made to spell out words relying on letter sounds, using "invented spelling."

trust Erikson's term for an emotional state, often acquired in infancy, in which children feel secure and know that basic needs will be met by caregivers. Such experiences as child abuse or neglect will lead infants to an opposite state—*mistrust* of the world and the people in it.

trust-building intervention A classroom strategy in which professionals interact with children with serious emotional distrubance in ways that build positive relationships with the hope that this will lead to positive peer relations as well.

two-way model of bilingual education A model of bilingual education, preferred by many educators, in which both the dominant language and the second language are used equally in instruction so that all children learn two languages.

umbilical cord A cord that transports nutrients from the mother to the fetus during prenatal development.

unidimensional thought A characteristic of preoperational thought in the preschool years in which children focus on only one characteristic of an object or one feature of a problem at a time and have difficulty coordinating more than one idea or activity.

unique/diverse needs The distinct needs of each individual child that are not related to background or disability.

unoccupied behavior A level of social participation in which children show little interest in what is going on around them and do not interact with toys, materials, or peers.

unpredictable substitutions An indicator of possible speech and language delays in which a child uses many different sounds—not just one predictable one—in place of a sound he or she cannot pronounce.

valuing/devaluing Western education Responses of cultural groups to the mainstream educational system. In some cultures, education is viewed as a way to better oneself; in others, children are encouraged to reject mainstream educational institutions.

verbal aggression Nonphysical assaults, such as taunts, teasing, threats, or cruel statements, that are intended to harm others psychologically.

verbal thought A kind of thought in which language and thinking are integrated and mutually supportive. In verbal thought, children use language—such as verbal labels and self-directed speech—to guide learning.

victim status The group status of children who are more likely to be victimized by peers. This status may remain stable over time and can lead to victimization throughout childhood.

visual cliff A research apparatus designed to show that babies have depth perception. Babies are encouraged to crawl out over a clear plastic surface that appears to be a deep drop-off; if they do not, depth perception can be inferred.

visual impairment A condition characterized by blindness or severely limited vision that can impair motor, cognitive, and other areas of development.

visual memory An ability, acquired by 6 or 7 months of age, in which an infant recognizes objects that were seen at an earlier time.

vocal abuse A condition caused by loud talking or screaming in which children create callouses, called nodules, on their vocal tissues.

wait-and-see response to crying A parenting strategy in which parents delay their responses to children's crying in order to ascertain the reasons and to ensure that children will be neither "spoiled" nor neglected.

whole-group instruction The classroom practice of teaching a whole group of students that can lead to self-comparison with peers.

written language-like stage of reading A stage of reading in which children "read" a story by heart, with their retellings precisely matching the actual text.

zone of proximal development A situation in which a problem or task is only slightly above a child's ability level. In this zone, adults can ask questions or give hints that allow the child to solve the problem independently.

zygote A fertilized egg, resulting from the union of sperm and ovum at conception, that contains a full complement of 46 chromosomes.

References

Aaronson, D., & Ferres, S. (1987). The impact of language differences on language processing: An example from Chinese-English bilingualism. In P. Homel, M. Palij, & D. Aaronson (Eds.), *Childhood bilingualism: Aspects of linguistic, cognitive, and social development*. Hillsdale, NJ: Erlbaum.

Abbeduto, L., & Murphy, M. (2004). Language, social cognition, maladaptive behavior and communication in Down Syndrome and Fragile X Syndrome. In M. Rice & S. Warren (Eds.), *Developmental language disorders: From phenotypes to etiologies* (pp. 77–98). London: Routledge.

Abbott, S. (1992). Holding on and pushing away. Comparative perspectives on an Eastern Kentucky child rearing practice. *Ethos, 20*, 33–65.

Aberson, B., Shure, M. B., & Goldstein, S. (2007). Social problem-solving intervention can help children with ADHD. *Journal of Attention Disorders, 11*, 4–7.

Aboud, F. (1977). Interest in ethnic information: A cross-cultural developmental study. *Canadian Journal of Behavioral Science, 9*, 134–146.

Aboud, F. (1985). The development of a social comparison process in children. *Child Development, 56*, 682–688.

Aboud, F. (1987). The development of ethnic self-identification and attitudes. In J. S. Phinney & M. J. Rotheram (Eds.), *Children's ethnic socialization: Pluralism and development* (pp. 32–55). Newbury Park, CA: Sage.

Aboud, F. (1988). *Children and prejudice*. New York: Basil Blackwell.

Aboud, F., & Doyle, A. B. (1993). The early development of ethnic identity and attitudes. In M. E. Bernal & G. P. Knight (Eds.), *Ethnic identity: Formation and transmission among Hispanics and other minorities* (pp. 46–59). Albany: State University of New York Press.

Abrahamsson, N. (2001) *Acquiring l2 syllable margins: Studies on the simplification of onsets and codas in interlanguage phonology*. Ypsilanti, MI: The Liguist List, Eastern Michigan University.

Ackad, T. E. (2007). Television watching, energy intake, and obesity in U.S. children. *The Future of Children, 16*, 19–45.

Ackerman, J., & Dozier, M. (2005). The influence of foster parent investment on children's representations of self and attachment figures. *Journal of Applied Developmental Psychology, 26*(5), 507–520.

Ackermann-Liebrich, U., Voegeli, T., Gunter-Witt, K., Kunz, I., Zullig, M., Schindler, C., et al. (1996). Home versus hospital deliveries: Follow-up study of matched pairs. *British Medical Journal, 313*, 1313–1318.

Acredolo, L. P., & Goodwyn, S. W. (1990). Sign language in babies: The significance of symbolic gesturing for understanding language development. In R. Vasta (Ed.), *Annals of Child Development* (Vol. 7, pp. 1–42). Greenwich, CT: JAI Press.

Adair, J., & Braund, K. (2005). *The history of American Indians* K. Braund (Ed.). Tuscaloosa, AL: University of Alabama Press.

Adams, M. (1990). *Beginning to read: Thinking and learning about print*. Cambridge, MA: MIT Press.

Adams, P. F., & Benson, V. (1991). *Current estimates from the National Health Interview Survey*. Hyattsville, MD: National Center for Health Statistics.

Adelman, H. S. (1992). The classification problem. In W. Stainback & S. Stainback (Eds.), *Controversial issues confronting special education* (pp. 377–469). Boston: Allyn & Bacon.

Adler, S., & King, D. A. (Eds.). (1994). *Oral communication problems in children and adolescents*. Baltimore: Paul H. Brookes.

Adolph. K. E., Vereijken, B., & Shrout, P. E. (2003). What changes in infant walking and why. *Child Development, 74*, 475–497.

Ahnert, L., Pinquart, M., & Lamb, M. (2006). Security of children's relationships with non-parental care providers: A meta-analysis. *Child Development, 77*, 664–679.

Aikens, N., Coleman, C., & Barbarin, O. (2008). Ethnic differences in the effects of parental depression on preschool children's socioemotional functioning. *Social Development, 17*, 137–160.

Ainsworth, M. D. S. (1977). Infant development and mother-infant interaction among Ganda and American families. In P. H. Leiderman, S. R. Tulkin, & A. Rosenfeld (Eds.), *Culture and infancy: Variations in the human experience*. New York: Academic Press.

Ainsworth, M. D. S., Blehar, M. C., Waters, E., & Wall, S. (1978). *Patterns of attachment*. Hillsdale, NJ: Erlbaum.

Aitchison, J. (1987). *Words in the mind: An introduction to the mental lexicon*. London: Basil Blackwell.

Akhtar, N., Carpenter, M., & Tomasello, M. (1996). The role of discourse novelty in early word learning. *Child Development, 67*, 635–645.

Albert, R., & Ha, I. A. (2004). Latino/Anglo-American differences in attributions to situations involving touch and silence *International Journal of Intercultural Relations, 28*, 253–280.

Aldis, O. (1975). *Play fighting*. New York: Academic Press.

Aldred, C., Green, J., Adams, C. (2004). A new social communication intervention for children with autism: Pilot randomised controlled treatment study suggesting effectiveness. *Journal of Child Psychology and Psychiatry, 45*, 1420–1430.

Alexander, G. R., Weiss, J., & Hulsey, T. C. (1991). Preterm birth prevention: An evaluation of programs in the United States. *Birth, 18*, 160–169.

Alexander, G. R., Wingate, M. S., & Boulet S. (2007). Pregnancy outcomes of American Indians: Contrasts among regions and with other ethnic groups. *Maternal and Child Health Journal, 25*, 791–800.

Alexander, M. A., Blank, J. S., & Clark, L. (1991). Obesity in Mexican-American preschool children: A population group at risk. *Public Health Nursing, 8*, 53–58.

Algozzine, R., & Ysseldyke, J. (2006). *Effective instruction for students with special needs: A practical guide for every teacher*. Thousand Oaks, CA: Corwin Press.

Allen, J., Marsh, P., McFarland, C., McElhaney, K., Land, D., Iodl, K., et al. (2007). Attachment and autonomy as predictors of the development of social skills and delinquency during midadolescence. *Journal of Consulting Clinical Psychology, 70*, 56–66.

Almqvist, C., Pershagen, G., & Wickman, M. (2005). Low socioeconomic status as a risk factor for asthma, rhinitis and sensitization at 4 years in a birth cohort. *Clinical & Experimental Allergy, 35*, 612–618.

Alvarez, G., & Cavanagh, P. (2004). The capacity of visual short-term memory is set both by visual information load and by number of objects. *Psychological Science, 15*, 106–111.

Amaro, H., Zuckerman, B., & Cabral, H. (1989). Drug use among adolescent mothers: Profile of risk. *Pediatrics, 84*, 144–151.

Amato, P. (2001). Children of divorce in the 1990s: An update of the Amato and Keith (1991) meta-analysis. *Journal of Family Psychology, 15*, 355–370.

Amato, P., & Fowler, F. (2002). Parenting practices, child adjustment, and family diversity. *Journal of Marriage and Family, 64*, 703–716.

American Association for the Child's Right to Play. (2004). *The case for elementary school recess*. Hempstead, NY: Author.

American Psychiatric Association. (1994). *Diagnostic and statistical manual of mental disorders* (4th ed.). Washington, DC: Author.

American Speech–Language–Hearing Association. (2008). *Facts on newborn hearing loss and screening*. Rockville, MD: Author.

Anderson, C., Gentile, D., & Buckley, K. (2007). *Violent video game effects on children and adolescents*. Oxford: Oxford University Press.

Anderson, D. R., Huston, A. C., Schmitt, K. L., Linebarger, D. L., & Wright, J. C. (2001). Early childhood television viewing and adolescent behavior: The recontact study. *Monographs of the Society for Research in Child Development, 66*, Serial No. 264.

Anderson, M., & Choonara, I. (2006). Drug misuse during pregnancy and fetal toxicity. *Archives of Disease in Childhood - Fetal and Neonatal Edition, 92*, 332–333.

Anderson, N. H., & Cuneo, D. O. (1978). The height + width rule in children's judgements about quantity. *Journal of Experimental Psychology: General, 107*, 335–378.

Anderson, P., & Butcher, K. (2006). Childhood obesity. *The Future of Children, 16*, 19–45.

Anderson, R. M., Giachello, A. L., & Aday, L. A. (1986). Access of Hispanics to health care and cuts in services. *Public Health Reports, 101*, 238–252.

Andrews, L., & Trawick-Smith, J. (1996). An ecological model for early childhood violence prevention. In R. L. Hampton, P. Jenkins, & T. Gullotta (Eds.), *Preventing violence in America* (pp. 233–262). Thousand Oaks, CA: Sage.

Angell, R., & Mason, C. (2008, April) *Object control skill performances by children*. Paper presented at the annual meeting of the American Alliance of Health, Physical Education, Recreation, and Dance, Lubbock, TX.

Anglin, J. M. (1993). Vocabulary development: A morphological analysis. *Monographs for the Society for Research in Child Development, 58*, 10 (Serial No. 238).

Anisfeld, E., Casper, V., Nosyce, M., & Cunningham, N. (1990). Does infant carrying promote attachment? An experimental study of the effects of increased physical contact on the development of attachment. *Child Development, 61*, 1617–1627.

Annie E. Casey Foundation. (2005). *Kids count data book: State profiles of child well-being*. Baltimore: Author.

Annis, R. C., & Corenblum, B. (1986). Effect of test language and experimenter race on Canadian Indian children's racial and self-identity. *Journal of Social Psychology, 126*, 761–773.

Anthony, J., & Petronis, K. R. (1989). Cocaine and heroin dependence compared: Evidence from an epidemiologic field survey. *American Journal of Public Health, 79*, 1409–1410.

Aram, D., & Biron, S. (2004). Joint storybook reading and joint writing interventions among low SES preschoolers: Differential contributions to early literacy. *Early Childhood Research Quarterly, 19*, 588–610.

Ardila, A. & Keating, K. (2007). Cognitive abilities in different cultural context. In B. P. Uzzell, & M. O. Pontón (Eds.), *International Handbook of Cross–Cultural Neuropsychology* (pp. 109–127). London: Routledge.

Arehole, S., Augustine, L. E., & Simhadri, R. (1995). Middle latency response in children with learning disabilities: Preliminary findings. *Journal of Communication Disorders, 28*, 21–38.

Aries, P. (1962). Centuries of childhood. In J. Beck (Ed.), *Toward a sociology of education*, pp. 37–48. Edison, NJ: Transaction Publishers.

Arifeen, S., Black, R. E., Antelman, G., Baqui, A., Caulfield, L., & Becker, S. (2001). Exclusive breastfeeding reduces acute respiratory infection and diarrhea deaths among infants in the Dhaka slums. *Journal of the American Medical Association, 285*, 413–420.

Armor, D. (2006). Can NCLB close the achievement gap? *Teachers College Record*, August 16, 2006.

Armstrong, J., & Reilly, J. (2002). Breastfeeding and lowering the risk of childhood obesity. *Lancet, 359*, 2003–2004.

Armstrong, M. B. (1998). Storybooks to literacy: A collaborative shared reading project. *Infant-Toddler Intervention: The Transdisciplinary Journal, 8*, 365–375.

Arnberg, L. (1987). *Raising children bilingually: The preschool years*. Philadelphia: Multilingual Matters Ltd.

Arsenio, W. F., & Lemerise, E. A. (2004). Aggression and moral development: integrating social information processing and moral domain models, *Child Development, 75*, 987–1007.

Asher, S. R., & Coie, J. D. (1990). *Peer rejection in childhood*. Cambridge: Cambridge University Press.

Asher, S. R., Singleton, L. C., & Taylor, A. R. (1982, April). *Acceptance versus friendships: A longitudinal study of racial integration*. Paper presented at the annual meeting of American Educational Research Association.

Ashkenazy, E., Cohen, A., Ophir-Cohen, M., & Tirosh, E. (2005). *Emotional status and development in children who are visually impaired*. New York: American Foundation for the Blind.

Aslin, R. N. (1987). Motor aspects of visual development in infancy. In P. Salapatek & L. Cohen (Eds.), *Handbook of infant perception* (Vol. 1, pp. 43–113). Orlando: Academic Press.

Aslin, R. N. (1988). Visual perception in early infancy. In A. Yonas (Ed.), *Perceptual development in infancy*. Hillsdale, NJ: Erlbaum.

Atang, C. (2004). The pragmatics of Afrocentric communication patterns: Some implications for African Americans. In J. Gordon (Ed.) *The African presence in Black America*. (pp. 323–334). Trenton, NJ: Africa World Press.

Ataullan, I., & Freeman–Wang, T. (2005). The older obstetric patient. *Current Obstetrics & Gynaecology, 15*, 46–53.

Au, K. (1993). *Literacy instruction in multicultural settings*. Fort Worth, TX: Harcourt Brace Jovanovich.

August, D., Carlo, M., Dressler, C., & Snow, C. (2005). The critical role of vocabulary development for English language learners. *Learning Disabilities Research & Practice, 20*(1), 50–57.

August, D., & Hakuta, K. (Eds.). (1998). *Educating language minority children*. Washington, D. C.: National Academy Press.

Augustyn, M., & Zuckerman, B. (2007). From mother's mouth to infant's brain: Infant-directed speech vs adult-directed speech. *Archives of Disease in Childhood, 92*, 82.

Auslander, M. C., Lewis, D. E., Schulte, L., Stelmachowicz, P. G. (1991). Localization ability in infants with simulated unilateral hearing loss. *Ear and Hearing, 12*, 371–376.

Avis, J., & Harris, P. L. (1991). Belief-desire reasoning among Baka children: Evidence for a universal conception of mind. *Child Development, 62*, 460–467.

Axelson, L., & Dail, P. (1988). The changing character of homeless in the United States. *Family Relations, 10*, 463–469.

Axia, G., & Baroni, M. R. (1985). Linguistic politeness at different age levels. *Child Development, 56*, 918–927.

Axia, V., & Weisner, T. (2002). Infant stress reactivity and home cultural ecology of Italian infants and families. *Infant Behavior and Development, 25*, 255–268.

Axtell, R. E. (1991). *Gestures: The dos and taboos of body language around the world*. New York: John Wiley & Sons.

Azmitia, M., & Hesser, J. (1993). Why siblings are important agents of cognitive development: A comparison of siblings and peers. *Child Development, 64*, 430–444.

Azrin, N., & Foxx, R. (1974). *Toilet training in less than a day*. New York: Simon & Schuster.

Baca Zinn, M., & Eitzen, D. (2004). *Diversity in families*. Boston: Allyn & Bacon.

Baddeley, A. (2001). Is working memory still working? *American Psychologist, 56*, 851–864.

Baer, J., & Schmitz, M. (2007). Ethnic differences in trajectories of family cohesion for Mexican American and non-Hispanic white adolescents. *Journal of Youth and Adolescence, 36*, 583–592.

Bagshaw, D. (2007). Reshaping responses to children when parents are separating: Hearing children's voices in the transition. *Australian Social Work, 60*, 450–465.

Bai, L. (2005). Children at play: A childhood beyond the Confucian shadow. *Childhood, 12*, 9–32.

Bailey, N. (1969). *Bailey scales of infant development*. New York: The Psychological Corporation.

Baillargeon, R., Graber, M., & DeVos, J., & Black, J. (1990). Why do young infants fail to search for hidden objects? *Cognition, 36*, 255–284.

Bakermans-Kranenburg, M., & van IJzendoorn, M., Madigan, S., Moran, G., Pederson, D., & Benoit, D. (2006). Unresolved states of mind, anomalous parental behavior, and disorganized attachment: A review and meta-analysis of a transmission gap. *Attachment & Human Development, 8*, 89–111.

Baldwin, D. A., & Moses, L. J. (1996). The ontogeny of social information gathering. *Child Development, 67*, 1915–1939.

Ball, H. (2007). Nighttime infant care: Cultural practice, evolution, and infant development. In P. Liamputtong (Ed.), *Childrearing and infant care issues* (pp. 47–61). New York: Nova Science Publishers.

Ballard, R. (1976). Ethnicity: Theory and experience. *New Community, 5*, 196–202.

Balogh, R. D., & Porter, R. H. (1986). Olfactory preferences resulting from mere exposure in human neonates. *Infant Behavior and Development, 9*, 395–401.

Bandura, A. (1962). Social learning through imitation. In M. R. Jones (Ed.), *Nebraska Symposium on Motivation*. Lincoln: University of Nebraska.

Bandura, A. (1965). Influence of model's reinforcement contingencies on the acquisition of imitative responses. *Journal of Personality and Social Psychology, 1*, 589–595.

Bandura, A. (1967). The role of modeling processes in personality development. In W. Hartup & N. L. Smothergill (Eds.), *The young child: Reviews of research*. Washington, DC: National Association for the Education of Young Children.

Bandura, A. (1986). *Social foundations of thought and action: A social cognitive theory* Englewood Cliffs, NJ: Prentice Hall.

Bandura, A. (1991). Social cognitive theory of moral thought and action. In W. M. Kurtines & J. L. Gewirtz (Eds.), *Handbook of moral behavior and development* (pp. 45–103). Hillsdale, NJ: Erlbaum.

Banks, J. A. (1995). The historical reconstruction of knowledge about race: Implications for transforming learning. *Educational Researcher, 24*(2), 15–25.

Banks, J. S. (2003). Multicultural education: Historical development, dimensions, and practice. In J. A. Banks & C. Banks (Eds.) *Handbook of research on multicultural education* (pp. 3–29). San Francisco: Jossey-Bass.

Baran, B., & Erdoğan, S. (2007). Children's games in Turkish culture. *Journal of Qafqaz University, 24*, 112–117.

Barbell, K. (1996). *Foster care today: National and South Carolina perspective*. Washington, DC: Child Welfare League of America.

Barber, J., & Delfabbro, P. (2005). Children's adjustment to long-term foster care. *Children and Youth Services Review, 27*, 329–340.

Barbour, C., Barbour, N., & Scully, P. (2008). *Families, schools, and communities: Building partnerships for educating children*. Upper Saddle River, NJ: Prentice Hall.

Barbuto, L. M., Swaminathan, S., Trawick-Smith, J., & Wright, J. L. (2003). The role of the teacher in scaffolding children's interactions in a technological environment: How a technology project is transforming preschool teacher practices in urban schools. In J. Wright, A. McDougal, J. Murnane, & J. Lowe, (Eds.), *Young children and learning technologies* (pp. 13–20). Melbourne: Australian Computer Society, Inc.

Barden, R. C., Ford, M. E., Jensen, A., Rogers-Salyer, M. E., & Salyer, K. (1989). Effects of craniofacial deformity in infancy on the quality of mother-infant interactions. *Child Development, 60*, 819–824.

Barker, G., & Graham, S. (1987). Developmental study of praise and blame as attributional cues. *Journal of Educational Psychology, 79*, 62–66.

Barkley, R. A. (1990). Attention deficit disorders: History, definition, and diagnosis. In M. Lewis & S. M. Miller (Eds.), *Handbook of developmental psychopathology* (pp. 65–76). New York: Plenum.

Barnett, W. S. (1995). Long-term effects of early childhood programs on cognitive and school outcomes. *The Future of Children, 5*(3), 25–50.

Barnes, S. (2007). An intra-ethnic analysis of social affiliations among Latinos in the United States. *Journal of Poverty, 11*, 107–134.

Barnett, W. S., Yarosz, D., Thomas, J., Jung, K., & Blanco, D. (2007). Two-way and monolingual English immersion in preschool education: An experimental comparison. *Early Childhood Research Quarterly, 22*, 277–293.

Baron, A., & Banaji, M. (2006). The development of implicit attitudes: Evidence of race evaluations from ages 6 and 10 and adulthood. *Psychological Science, 17*, 53–58.

Baron-Cohen, S. (1995). *Mindblindness: An essay on autism and theory of mind*. Cambridge, MA: MIT Press.

Baron-Cohen, S. (1997). Autism and symbolic play. *British Journal of Developmental Psychology, 5*, 139–148.

Baron-Cohen, S., & Ring, H. (1994). A model of the mind-reading system: Neuropsychological and neurobiological perspectives. In C. Lewis & P. Mitchell (Eds.), *Children's early understanding of the mind: Origins and development* (pp. 183–207). Hove, England: Erlbaum.

Barratt-Pugh, C., Rohl, M., Oakley, G., & Elderfield, J. (2005). *Better beginnings: An evaluation from two communities*. Perth, Autralia: Edith Cowan University.

Barrett, D. E., Radke-Yarrow, M., & Klein, R. E. (1982). Chronic malnutrition and behavior: Effects of early caloric supplementation on social and emotional functioning at school age. *Developmental Psychology, 18,* 541–556.

Barry, D. T., & Grilo, C. M. (2003). Cultural, self-esteem, and demographic correlates of perception of personal and group discrimination among East Asian immigrants. *American Journal of Orthopsychiatry, 73,* 223–229.

Bartocci, M., Bergqvist, L., Lagercrantz, H., & Anand, K. (2006). Pain activates cortical areas in the preterm newborn brain. *Pain, 122,* 109–117.

Barton, P., & Coley, R. (2007). *The family: America's smallest school.* Princeton, NJ: Educational Testing Service.

Bartz, K. W., & Levine, E. S. (1978). Child rearing by black parents: A description and comparison to Anglo and Chicano parents. *Journal of Marriage and Family,* November, 709–719.

Bassano, D., Eme, P., & Champaud, C. (2005). A naturalistic study of early lexical development. *First Language, 25,* 67–101.

Bassuk, E., & Rubin, L. (1987). Homeless children: A neglected population. *American Journal of Orthopsychiatry, 57,* 279–286.

Batshaw, M. L., & Perret, Y. M. (1992). *Children with disabilities.* Baltimore: Paul H. Brookes.

Bauer, P. J., & Hertsgaard, L. A. (1993). Increasing steps in recall events in 13.5- and 16.5-month-olds. *Child Development, 64,* 1204–1223.

Bauminger, N., & Kasari, C. (2000). Loneliness and friendship in high-functioning children with autism. *Child Development, 72,* 447–456.

Baumrind, D. (1968). Authoritarian versus authoritative parent control. *Adolescence, 3,* 255–272.

Baumrind, D. (1994). The social context of child maltreatment. *Family Relations, 43,* 360–368.

Bauserman R. (2002). Child adjustment in joint-custody versus sole-custody arrangements: A meta-analytic review. *Journal of Family Psychology, 16,* 91–102.

Baxter, C. (2006). Transracial adoption. *Paediatrics & Child Health, 11,* 443–447.

Beal, C. R. (1994). *Boys and girls: The development of gender roles.* New York: McGraw-Hill.

Beasley, A., & Amir, L. (2007). Infant feeding, poverty and human development. *International Breastfeeding Journal, 2,* 14.

Beckman, M., & Edwards, J. (2000). The ontogeny of phonological categories and the primacy of lexical learning in linguistic development. *Child Development, 71,* 240–249.

Beckman, P. (1991). Comparison of mothers' and fathers' perceptions of the effect of young children with and without disabilities. *American Journal on Mental Retardation, 95,* 585–595.

Beckung, E., Hagberg, G., Uldall, P., & Cans, C. (2008). Probability of walking in children with cerebral palsy in Europe. *Pediatrics, 121,* 187–192.

Beckwith, L., & Rodning, C. (1991). Intellectual functioning in children born preterm: Recent research. In L. Okagaki & R. J. Sternberg (Eds.), *Directors of development: Influences on the development of children's thinking.* Hillsdale, NJ: Erlbaum.

Behrman, R. E. (Ed.). (1995). *The future of children: Low birth weight.* Los Angeles: Center for the Future of Children.

Bell, S. M., & Ainsworth, M. D. S. (1972). Infant crying and maternal responsiveness. *Child Development, 43,* 1171–1190.

Bellieni, C., Sisto, R., Cordelli, D., & Buonocore, G. (2004). Cry features reflect pain intensity in term newborns: An alarm threshold. *Pediatric Research, 55,* 142–146.

Bellini, S., Peters, J., Benner, L., Hopf, A. (2007). A meta-analysis of school-based social skills inter-

ventions for children with autism spectrum disorders. *Journal of Remedial and Special Education, 28,* 53–162.

Belsky, J., Friedman, S. L., & Hsieh, K. (2001). Testing a core emotion-regulation prediction: Does attentional persistence moderate the effect of infant negative emotionality on later development? *Child Development, 72,* 123–133.

Belsky, J., & Steinberg, L. D. (1978). The effects of day care: A critical review. *Child Development, 49,* 929–949.

Belsky, J., Vandell, D., Burchinal, M., Clarke-Stewart, K. A., McCartney, K., Owen, M., et al., (2007). Are there long-term effects of early child care? *Child Development, 78,* 681–701.

Belsky, J., & Volling, B. L. (1987). Mothering, fathering, and marital interaction in the family triad during infancy: Exploring family systems processes. In P. Berman & F. Pedersen (Eds.), *Men's transition to parenthood* (pp. 37–63). Hillsdale, NJ: Erlbaum.

Bénabou, R., & Tirole, J. (2003). Intrinsic and extrinsic motivation. *Review of Economic Studies, 70,* 489–520.

Benasich, A. A., & Brooks-Gunn, J. (1996). Maternal attitudes and knowledge of child-rearing: Associations with family and child outcomes. *Child Development, 67,* 1186–1205.

Ben-Avie, M., Comer, J. P., & Joyner, E. T. C., (Eds.). (2004). *Six pathways to healthy child development and academic success.* Thousand Oaks, CA: Corwin Press.

Benelli, B., Belacchi, C., Gini, G., & Lucangeli, D. (2006). 'To define means to say what you know about things': The development of definitional skills as metalinguistic acquisition. *Journal of Child Language, 33,* 71–97.

Benenson, J. F., Apostoleris, N. H., & Parnass, J. (1997). Age and sex differences in dyadic and group interaction. *Developmental Psychology, 33,* 538–543.

Benigno, J. P., & Ellis, S. (2004). Two is greater than three: Effects of older siblings on parental support of preschoolers counting in middle–income families. *Early Childhood Research Quarterly, 19,* 4–20.

Benet-Martínez, V., & Haritatos, J. (2005). Bicultural identity integration (BII): Components and psychosocial antecedents. *Journal of Personality, 73,* 1015–1050.

Bennett, C., Macdonald, G., Dennis, J., Coren, E., Patterson, J., Astin, M., et al. (2008). *Home-based support for disadvantaged adult mothers.* Wiley & Sons.

Bereiter, C., & Engelmann, S. (1966). *Teaching disadvantaged children in the preschool.* Upper Saddle River, NJ: Prentice Hall.

Berenson, G., Frank, G., Hunter, S., Srinivasan, S., Voors, A., & Webber, L. (1982). Cardiovascular risk factors in children: Should they concern the pediatrician? *American Journal of Diseases of Children, 136,* 855–862.

Bergen, D. (2002). The role of pretend play in children's cognitive development. *Early Childhood Research and Practice, 54,* 555–572.

Bergen, D. (2006). The role of pretend play in children's cognitive development. In R. Parker-Rees & J. Willan (Eds.), *Early years: Major themes in education* (pp. 193–204). London: Rouledge.

Berger, K. S. (2008). *The developing person through the life span.* New York: Worth.

Berk, L. E. (2006). *Child development.* (7th ed.). Needham Heights, MA: Allyn & Bacon.

Berk, L. E., & Spuhl, S. T. (1995). Maternal interaction, private speech, and task performance in preschool children. *Early Childhood Research Quarterly, 10,* 145–169.

Berk, L. E., & Winsler, A. (1995). *Scaffolding children's learning: Vygotsky and early childhood education.* Washington, DC: National Association for the Education of Young Children.

Bernardis, P., Bello, A., Pettenati, P., Stefanini, S., & Gentilucci, M. (2008). Manual actions affect vocalizations of infants. *Experimental Brain Research, 184,* 599–603.

Berndt, T. (2007). Children's friendships. In G. Ladd (Ed.), *Appraising the human developmental sciences* (pp. 138–155). Detroit: Wayne State University Press.

Bernard–Opitz, V., Sriram, N., & Naknoda–Sapuan, S. (2001). Enhancing social problem solving in children with autism and normal children through computer–assisted instruction. *Journal of Autism and Developmental Disorders,* 377–394.

Bertenthal, B. I., & Campos, J. (1990). A systems approach to the organizing effect of self-produced locomotion during infancy. In C. Rovee-Collier & L. P. Lipsitt (Eds.), *Advances in infancy research* (Vol. 6). Norwood, NJ: Albex.

Betts, L., & Rotenberg, K. (2007). Trustworthiness, friendships and self-control: Factors that contribute to young children's school adjustment. *Infant and Child Development, 16,* 491–508.

Betz, C. (1994, March). Beyond time out: Tips from a teacher. *Young Children, 49(3),* 10–14.

Bever, T. G. (1970). The cognitive basis for linguistic structures. In J. R. Hayes (Ed.), *Cognition and the development of language.* New York: John Wiley & Sons.

Bhatt, R., Bertin, E., Hayden, A., & Reed, A. (2005). Face processing in infancy: Developmental changes in the use of different kinds of relational information. *Child Development, 76,* 169–181.

Bhushan, V., Paneth, N., & Kiely, J. L. (1993). Impact of improved survival of very low birthweight infants on recent secular trends in the prevalence of cerebral palsy. *Pediatrics, 91,* 1094–1100.

Bhutta, A., Cleves, M. A., Casey, P. H., Cradock, M. M., & Phil, K. (2002). Cognitive and behavioral outcomes of school-aged children who were born preterm. *Journal of the American Medical Association, 288,* 728–737.

Bialystok, E. (1986). Factors in the growth of linguistic awareness. *Child Development, 57,* 498–510.

Bialystok, E. (1997). Effects of bilingualism and biliteracy on children's emerging concepts of print. *Developmental Psychology, 33,* 429–440.

Bialystok, E. (2007). Acquisition of literacy in bilingual children: A framework for research. *Language Learning, 57,* 45–77.

Bialystok, E., McBride-Chang, C., & Luk, G. (2005). Bilingualism, language proficiency, and learning to read in two writing systems. *Journal of Educational Psychology, 97,* 580–590.

Bierman, K. L., Smoot, D. L., & Aumiller, K. (1993). Characteristics of aggressive-rejected, aggressive nonrejected, and rejected nonaggressive boys. *Child Development, 64,* 139–151.

Bigler, R. S., & Liben, L. S. (1992). Cognitive mechanisms in children's gender stereotyping. *Child Development, 63,* 1351–1363.

Birdsong, D. (2004). Second language acquisition and ultimate attainment. In A. Davies & C. Elder (Eds.), *Handbook of applied linguistics* (pp. 82–105). Boston: Blackwell Publishing.

Birman, D., & Ryerson Espino, S. (2007). The relationship of parental practices and knowledge to school adaptation for immigrant and nonimmigrant high school students. *Canadian Journal of School Psychology, 22,* 152–166.

Bishop, M., Hobson, P., & Lee, A. (2005). Symbolic play in congenitally blind children. *Development and Psychopathology, 17,* 447–465.

Bjorklund, D. F. (1997). In search of a metatheory for cognitive development (or, Piaget's dead and I don't feel so good myself). *Child Development, 68,* 142–146.

Bjorklund, D. F. (2005). *Children's thinking: Cognitive developmental function and individual differences.* Pacific Grove, CA: Brooks/Cole.

Bjorklund, D. F., & Bjorklund, B. R. (1992). *Looking at children: An introduction to child development.* Pacific Grove, CA: Brooks/Cole.

Bjorklund, D. F., & Reubens, A. (1997). *Collaborative learning of simple addition strategies between young children and their mothers in the context of a game.* Unpublished manuscript, Florida Atlantic University, Boca Raton, FL.

Bjornstad, G., & Montgomery, P. (2005). *Family therapy for attention deficit-hyperactivity disorder in children and adolescents.* London: Cochrane Collaboration.

Black, R. E., Allen, L., & Bhutta, Z. A. (2008). Maternal and child undernutrition: Global and regional exposures and health consequences. *The Lancet, 371,* 243-260.

Blair, E., & Watson, L. (2006). Epidemiology of cerebral palsy. *Seminars in Fetal and Neonatal Medicine, 11,* 117–125.

Blake, J. (1989). *Family size and achievement.* Berkeley: University of California Press.

Blake, J., & Boysson-Bardies, B. (1992). Patterns in babbling: A cross-linguistic study. *Journal of Child Language, 19,* 51–74.

Blake, R., & Cutler, C. (2003). AAE and variation in teachers' attitudes: A question of school philosophy? *Linguistics and Education, 14,* 163–194.

Blanchard, E. L. (1983). The growth and development of American Indian and Alaskan native children. In G. J. Powell (Ed.), *The psychosocial development of minority children.* New York: Brunner/Mazel.

Blass, E. M., & Ciaramitaro, V. (1994). A new look at some old mechanisms in human newborns: Taste and tactile determinants of state affect and action. *Monographs for the Society of Research in Child Development, 59*(1, Serial No. 239), 1–101.

Blevins-Knabe, B. (1987). Development of the ability to insert into a series. *Journal of Genetic Psychology, 148,* 427–441.

Bloch, M. N., & Adler, S. M. (1994). African children's play and the emergence of the sexual division of labor. In J. L. Roopnarine, J. E. Johnson, & F. H. Hooper (Eds.), *Children's play in diverse cultures* (pp. 148–178). Albany: State University of New York Press.

Bloom, L. (1993). *The transition from infancy to language: Acquiring the power of expression.* Cambridge: Cambridge University Press.

Bugental, D. B., Lyon, J. E., Lin, E. K., McGrath, E. P., & Bimbela, A. (1999). Children "tune out" to the ambiguous communication style of powerless adults. *Child Development, 70,* 214–230.

Blum, N., Taubman, B., & Nemeth, N. (2004). Why is toilet training occurring at older ages?: A study of factors associated with later training. *Journal of Pediatrics, 145,* 107–111.

Blumenfeld, P., Pintrich, P., & Hamilton, V. (1986). Children's conceptions of ability, effort, and conduct. *American Educational Research Journal, 23,* 95–104.

Bodrova, E., & Leong, D. (1996). *Tools of the mind: The Vygotskian approach to early childhood education.* Upper Saddle River, NJ: Merrill/Prentice Hall.

Bodrova, E., & Leong, D. (2003a). Learning and development in preschool children from the Vygotskian perspective. In A. Kozulin, B. Gindis, V. Agevev, and S. Miller (Eds.), *Vygotsky's educational theory in cultural context.* Cambridge: Cambridge University Press.

Bodrova, E., & Leong, D. (2003b). The importance of being playful. *Educational Leadership, 60,* 50–53.

Boets, B., Wouters, J., van Wieringen, A., De Smedt, B., & Ghesquière, P. (2007). Modelling relations between sensory processing, speech perception, orthographic and phonological ability, and literacy achievement. *Brain and Language, 106,* 94–104.

Bogdan, R., & Knoll, J. (1995). The sociology of disability. In E. L. Meyen & T. M. Skrtic (Eds.), *Special education and student disability an introduction: Traditional, emerging, and alternative perspectives* (4th ed., pp. 675–711). Denver, CO: Love Publishing.

Bohannon, J. N., & Bonvillian, J. D. (2001). Theoretical approaches to language acquisition. In J. B. Gleason (Ed.), *The development of language.* Boston: Allyn & Bacon.

Bohlin, G., Hagekull, B., & Andersson, K. (2005). Behavioral inhibition as a precursor of peer social competence in early school age: The interplay with attachment and non–parental care. *Merrill Palmer Quarterly, 51,* 1–19.

Boismier, J. D. (1997). Visual stimulation and wakesleep behavior in human neonates. *Developmental Psychobiology, 10,* 219–227.

Boivin, M., & Hymel, S. (1997). Peer experiences and social self-perceptions: A sequential model. *Developmental Psychology, 33,* 135–145.

Bolger, K. E., & Patterson, C. (2001). Developmental pathways from child maltreatment to peer rejection. *Child Development, 72,* 549–568.

Boloh, Y., & Champaud, C. (1993). The past conditional verb form in French children: The role of semantics in late grammatical development. *Journal of Child Language, 20,* 169–189.

Bonica, C., Arnold, D., Fisher, P., Zeljo, A., & Yershova, K. (2003). Relational aggression, relational victimization, and language development in preschoolers. *Social Development, 12,* 551–562.

Booth, J. R., MacWhinney, B., & Harasaki, Y. (2000). Developmental differences in visual and auditory processing of complex sentences. *Child Development, 71,* 981–1003.

Borghi, A., & Caramelli, N. (2003). Situation bounded conceptual organization in children: From action to spatial relations. *Cognitive Development, 18,* 49–60.

Borke, H. (1975). Piaget's mountain revisited: Changes in the egocentric landscape. *Developmental Psychology, 11,* 240–243.

Bornstein, M. H. (1992). Perception cross the life span. In M. H. Bornstein & M. E. Lamb (Eds.), *Developmental psychology: An advanced textbook* (3rd ed., pp. 155–210). Hillsdale, NJ: Erlbaum.

Bornstein, M. H. (Ed.). (1995). *Handbook of parenting.* Mahwah, NJ: Erlbaum.

Bornstein, M. H. (1998). Stability in mental development from early life: Methods, measures, models, meanings, and myths. In F. Simion & G. E. Butterworth (Eds.), *The development of sensory, motor and cognitive capacities in early infancy: From sensation to cognition* (pp. 299–231). Hove, England: Psychology Press.

Bornstein, M. H. (2002). Measurement variability in infant and maternal behavioral assessment. *Infant Behavior and Development, 25,* 413–432.

Bornstein, M. H., Haynes, O. M., Pascual, L., Painter, K. M., & Galperin, C. (2002). Play in two societies: Pervasiveness of process, specificity of structure. In M. A. Paludi (Ed.), *Human development in cultural context* (pp. 25–31). Upper Saddle River, NJ: Prentice Hall.

Bornstein, M. H., Selmi, A. M., Haynes, O. M., Painter, K. M., & Marx, E. S. (1999). Representational abilities and the hearing status of child/mother dyads. *Child Development, 70,* 833–852.

Borovsky, D., & Rovee-Collier, C. (1990). Contextual constraints on memory retrieval at 6 months. *Child Development, 61,* 1569–1583.

Bosch, L., Oostdijk, N., & Boves, L. (2005). On temporal aspects of turn taking in conversational dialogues. *Speech Communication, 47,* 80–86.

Bosch, L., & Sebastian-Galles, N. (1997). Native-language recognition abilities of four-month-old infants from monolingual and bilingual environments. *Cognition, 65,* 33–69.

Bosco, F., Friedman, O., & Leslie, A. (2006). Recognition of pretend and real actions in play by 1- and 2-year-olds: Early success and why they fail. *Cognitive Development, 21,* 3–10.

Bouchard, G., Lee, C., Asgary, V., & Pelletier, L. (2007). Fathers' motivation for involvement with their children: A self-determination theory perspective. *Fathering: A Journal of Theory, Research, and Practice about Men as Fathers, 5,* 23–40.

Boucher, J. (1996). What could possibly explain autism? In P. Carruthers & P. K. Smith (Eds.), *Theories of theory of mind.* Cambridge: Cambridge University Press.

Bowe, F. G. (2000). *Birth to 5: Early childhood special education.* New York: Delmar.

Bower, T. G. R. (1977). *The perceptual world of the child.* Cambridge, MA: Harvard University Press.

Bowlby, J. (1973). *Attachment and loss: Vol. 2. Separation, anxiety, and anger.* New York: Basic Books.

Boyatzis, C., Matillo, G., & Nesbitt, K. (1995). Effects of "The Mighty Morphin Power Rangers" on children's aggression with peers. *Child Study Journal, 25,* 45–55.

Boyce, G. C., Smith, T. B., Immel, N., Casto, G., & Escobar, C. (1993). Early intervention with medically-fragile infants: Investigating the age-at-start question. *Early Education and Development, 4,* 290–305.

Boyce, W. T., Schaefer, C., Harrison, H. R., Haffner, W. H. J., Lewis, M., & Wright, A. L. (1986). Social and cultural factors in pregnancy complications among Navajo women. *American Journal of Epidemiology, 25,* 217–235.

Boykin, A. W. (1978). Psychological/behavioral verve in academic/task performance. *Journal of Negro Education, 47,* 343–354.

Boykin, A. W. (1994). Harvesting talent and culture: African American children and educational reform. In R. Rossi (Ed.), *Students and schools at risk* (pp. 116–138). New York: Teachers College Press.

Boykin, A. W., & Toms, F. D. (1985). Black child socialization: A conceptual framework. In H. P. McAdoo & J. L. McAdoo (Eds.), *Black children: Social, educational, and parental environments.* Newbury Park, CA: Sage.

Boykin, A. W., Tyler, K., & Miller, O. (2005). In search of cultural themes and their expressions in the dynamics of classroom life. *Urban Education, 40,* 521–549.

Bradley, R. H., & Corwyn, R. F. (2002). Socioeconomic status and child development. *Annual Review of Psychology, 53,* 371–399.

Bradley, R. H., Whiteside, L., Mundfrom, D. J., Casey, P. H., Kelleher, K. J., & Pope, S. K. (1994). Early indications of resilience and their relation to experiences in the home environments of low birth weight, premature children living in poverty. *Child Development, 65,* 346–360.

Bradley, R. M. (1972). Development of taste bud and gustatory papillae in human fetuses. In J. F. Bosma (Ed.), *The third symposium on oral sensation and perception: The mouth of the infant* (pp. 137–162). Springfield, IL: Thomas.

Braga, L. (2007). Developmental perspectives: Culture and neuropsychological development during childhood. In B. P. Uzzell & M. O. Pontón (Eds.), *International Handbook of Cross-Cultural Neuropsychology* (pp. 145–162). London: Routledge.

Brainerd, C. J. (1996). Piaget: A centennial celebration. *Psychological Science, 7,* 191–195.

Brazelton, T. B. (1962). A child-oriented approach to toileting. *Pediatrics, 29,* 121–127.

Brazelton, T. B., Koslowski, B., & Tronick, E. (1971). Study of neonatal behavior in Zambian and American neonates. *Journal of the American Academy of Child Psychiatry, 15,* 97–107.

Brazelton, T. B., & Nugent, J. K. (1995). *Neonatal Behavioral Assessment Scale, 3rd edition.* London: Mackeith Press.

Bredekamp, S., & Copple, C. (1997). *Developmentally appropriate practice in early childhood programs.* Washington, DC: NAEYC.

Breier, B. H., Vickers, M. H., Ikenasio, B. A., Chan, K. Y., & Wong, W. P. (2001). Fetal programming of appetite and obesity. *Molecular and Cellular Endocrinology, 185,* 73–79.

Bremner, J. (2002). The nature of imitation by infants. *Infant Behavior and Development, 25,* 65–67.

Bricker, D., & Cripe, J. J. (1992). *An activity-based approach to intervention.* Baltimore: Paul H. Brookes.

Bridges, A. (1986). Actions and things: What adults talk about to 1-year-olds. In S. A. Kuczaj & M. D. Barrett (Eds.), *The development of word meaning* (pp. 114–136). New York: Springer-Verlag.

Briggs, X. S. (2007). "Some of my best friends are ...": Interracial friendships, class, and segregation in America. *City & Community, 6,* 263–290.

Brigham, J. C. (1974). Views of black and white children concerning the distribution of personality characteristics. *Journal of Personality, 42,* 144–158.

Broberg, A., Lamb, M. E., & Hwang, P. (1990). Inhibition: Its stability and correlates in 16- to 40-month-olds. *Children Development, 61,* 1153–1163.

Brockington, I. (1996). *Motherhood and mental health.* Oxford: Oxford University Press.

Brody, G. H. (2004). Siblings' direct and indirect contributions to child development. *Current Directions in Psychological Science, 13,* 124–126.

Brody, G. H. & Flor, D. (1998). Maternal resources, parenting practices, and child competence in rural, single-parent African American families. *Child Development, 69,* 803–816.

Brody, G. H., & Murry, V. M. (2001). Sibling socialization of competence in rural, single-parent African American families. *Journal of Marriage and Family, 63,* 996–1008.

Brody, G. H., Stoneman, Z., & McKinnon, C. E. (1982). Role asymmetries in interactions among school-aged children, their younger siblings, and friends. *Child Development, 53,* 1364–1370.

Brody, N. (1997). Intelligence, schooling, and society. *American Psychologist, 52,* 1046–1050.

Bronfenbrenner, U. (1995). The bioecological perspective from a life course perspective: Reflections of a participant observer. In P. Moen, G. H. Edler, & K. Luscher (Eds.), *Examining lives in context* (pp. 599–618). Washington, DC: American Psychological Association.

Bronfenbrenner, U. (2006). *The ecology of human development: Experiments by nature and design.* Cambridge: Harvard University Press.

Bronson, G. W. (1990). Changes in infants' visual scanning across the 2- to 14-week age period. *Journal of Experimental Child Psychology, 49,* 101–125.

Bronson, G. W. (1994). Infants' transitions toward adult-like scanning. *Child Development, 65,* 1243–1261.

Brookhart, J., & Hock, E. E. (1976). The effects of experimental context and experiential background on infants behavior toward their mothers and a stranger. *Child Development, 47,* 333–340.

Brooks, P. J., Tomasello, M., Dodson, K. & Lewis, L. (1999). Young children's overgeneralizations with fixed transitivity verbs. *Child Development, 70,* 1325–1337.

Brooks-Gunn, J., Klebanov, P. K., Liaw, F., & Spiker, D. (1993). Enhancing the development of low birth-weight, premature infants. *Child Development, 64,* 736–753.

Brooks-Gunn, J., & Markham, L. (2005). The contributions of parenting to ethnic and racial gaps in school readiness. *The future of children, 15,* 139–168.

Brophy, J., & Everston, C. (1978). Context variables in teaching. *Educational Psychologist, 12,* 310–316.

Brophy-Herb, H., Lee, R., Nievar, M., & Stollak, G. (2006). Preschoolers' social competence: Relations to family characteristics, teacher behaviors and classroom climate. *Journal of Applied Developmental Psychology 28,* 134–148.

Brotman, L., Gouley, K., & Chesir-Teran, D. (2005). Assessing peer entry and play in preschoolers at risk for maladjustment. *Journal of Clinical Child & Adolescent Psychology, 34,* 671–680.

Brown, A. D., & Hernasy, M. A. (1983). The impact of culture on the health of American Indian children. In G. J. Powell (Ed.), *The psychosocial development of minority children* (pp. 39–48). New York: Brunner/Mazel.

Brown, C. (2007). Unpacking standards in early childhood education. *Teachers College Record, 109,* 635–668.

Brown, G., McBride, B., Shin, N., & Bost, K. (2007). Parenting predictors of father-child attachment security: Interactive effects of father involvement and fathering quality. *Fathering, 5,* 197–219.

Brown, J., Hofmeyr, G., Nikodem, V., Smith, H., & Garner, P. (2007). Promoting childbirth companions in South Africa: A randomised pilot study. *BMC Medicine, 5,* 7.

Brown, J. D. (1998). *The self.* New York: McGraw-Hill.

Brown, J. E. (1995). *Nutrition now.* St. Paul, MN: West.

Brown, J. E., & Pollitt, E. (1996, February). Malnutrition, poverty, and intellectual development. *Scientific American, 38*–43.

Brown, J. E., Serdula, M., Cairns, K., Godes, J. R., Jacobs, D. R., Elmer, P., et al. (1986). Ethnic group differences in nutritional status of young children from low-income areas of an urban county. *American Journal of Clinical Nutrition, 44,* 938–944.

Brown, M., & Freeman, N. (2004). Reconceptualizing rough and tumble play: Ban the banning. *Journal of Research in Childhood Education, 12,* 244–263.

Brownell, C. A., & Carriger, M. S. (1990). Changes in cooperation and self-other differentiation during the second year. *Child Development, 61,* 1164–1175.

Bruce, B., & Hansson, K. (2008). Early communication skills: Important in screening for language impairment and neuropsychiatric disorders. *Current Pediatric Reviews, 4,* 53–57.

Brugger, A., Lariviere, L., Mumme, D., & Bushnell, E. (2007). Doing the right thing: Infants' selection of actions to imitate from observed event sequence. *Child Developments 78,* 806–824.

Bruner, J. (1984). Vygotsky's zone of proximal development: The hidden agenda. In B. Rogoff & J. Wertsch (Eds.), *Children's learning in the zone of proximal development* (New Directions in Child Development No. 12). San Francisco: Jossey-Bass.

Bryant, J. B. (2008). Language in social contexts: Communicative competence. In J. B. Gleason (Ed.), *The development of language* (pp. 167–209). Boston: Allyn & Bacon.

Bryen, D. N. (1986). *Inquiries into child language.* Boston: Allyn & Bacon.

Bryne, B., & Fielding-Barnsley, R. (1995). Evaluation of a program to teach phonemic awareness to young children: A 2- and 3-year follow up and a new preschool trial. *Journal of Educational Psychology, 87,* 488–503.

Buckner, J. (2008). Understanding the impact of homelessness on children. *American Behavioral Scientist, 51,* 721–736.

Buckner, J., Bassuk, E., & Weinreb, L. (2002). Predictors of academic achievement among homeless and low income housed children. *Journal of School Psychology, 39,* 45–69.

Buekens, P., Notzon, F., Kotelchuck, M., & Wilcox, A. (2000). Why do Mexican Americans give birth to few low-birth-weight infants? *American Journal of Epidemiology, 152,* 347–351.

Buescher, P., & Horton, S. (2001). Prenatal WIC participation in relation to low birth weight and Medicaid infant costs in North Carolina. *Journal of the American Dietetic Association, 101,* 997–997.

Burchinal, M., & Cryer, D. (2003). Diversity, child care quality, and developmental outcomes. *Early Childhood Research Quarterly, 18,* 401–426.

Burchinal, M. R., Roberts, J. E., Nabors, L. A., & Bryant, D. M. (1996). Quality of center child care and infant cognitive and language development. *Child Development, 67,* 606–620.

Burgess, K., Wojslawowicz, J., Rubin, K., Rose-Krasnor, L., & Booth-LaForce, C. (2006). Social information processing and coping strategies of shy/withdrawn and aggressive children: Does friendship matter? *Child Development, 77,* 371–383.

Burts, D. C., Schmidt, H. M., Durnam, R., Charlesworth, R. & Hart, C. H. (2007). Impact of the developmental appropriateness of teacher guidance strategies on kindergarten children's interpersonal relations. *Journal of Research in Childhood Education, 21,* 290.

Bus, A., van IJzendoorn, M., & Pellegrini, A. (1995). Joint book reading makes for success in learning to read: A meta-analysis on intergenerational transmission of literacy. *Review of Educational Research, 65,* 1–21.

Buschmann, A., Jooss, B., Rupp, A., Dockter, S. Blaschtikowitz, H., Heggen, I., et al. (2008). Children with developmental language delay at 24 months of age: Results of a diagnostic work-up. *Developmental Medicine & Child Neurology, 50,* 223–229.

Bushnell, E., & Boudreau, J. P. (1993). Motor development and the mind: The potential of motor abilities as a determinant of aspects of perceptual development. *Child Development, 64,* 1005–1021.

Bussey, K., & Bandura, A. (1992). Self-regulatory mechanisms governing gender development. *Child Development, 63,* 1236–1250.

Butler, R., Gasson, S. (2005). Self esteem/self concept scales for children and adolescents: A review. *Child and Adolescent Mental Health, 10,* 190–201.

Cafiero, J. (1998). Communication power for individuals with autism. *Focus on Autism and Other Developmental Disabilities, 13,* 113–121.

Cahan, S., Greenbaum, C., Artman, L., Deluya, N., & Gappel-Gilon, Y. (2008). The differential effects of age and first grade schooling on the development of infralogical and logico-mathematical concrete operations. *Cognitive Development, 23,* 258–277.

Cai, J., & Nie, B. (2007). Problem solving in Chinese mathematics education: Research and practice. *ZDM, 39,* 459–473.

Cairns, R. B., Leung, M., Buchanan, L., & Cairns, B. D. (1995). Friendships and social networks in childhood and adolescence: Fluidity, reliability, and interactions. *Child Development, 66,* 1330–1345.

Caldera, Y. M., Huston, A. C., & O'Brien, M. (1989). Social interactions and play patterns of parents and toddlers with feminine, masculine, and neutral toys. *Child Development, 60,* 70–76.

Calkins, L. M. (1986). *The art of teaching writing.* Portsmouth, NH: Heinemann.

Calkins, L. M. (2003). *Units of study for primary writing.* New York: Teachers College Press.

Calkins, S. (2004). Early attachment processes and the development of self-regulation of emotions. In R. F. Baumeister & K. D. Vohs (Eds.), *Handbook of Self-Regulation: Research, Theory, and Applications* (pp. 324–339). New York: Guilford Press.

Call, J., & Tomasello, M. (1999). The nonverbal false belief task: The performance of children and great apes. *Child Development, 70*, 381–395.

Callaghan, J. W. (1981). A comparison of Anglo, Hopi, and Navajo mothers and infants. In T. M. Field, A. M. Sostek, P. Vietze, & P. H. Leiderman (Eds.), *Culture and early interaction* (pp. 115–131). Hillsdale, NJ: Erlbaum.

Callan, D., Tsytsarev, V., Hanakawa, T., Callan, A., Katsuhara, M., Fukuyama, H. et al. (2006). Song and speech: Brain regions involved with perception and covert production. *NeuroImage, 31*, 1327–1342.

Calvert, S. L., Strong, B. L., Jacobs, E., & Conger, E. (2007). Interaction and participation for young Hispanic and Caucasian girls' and boys' learning of media content. *Media Psychology, 9*, 431–445.

Camara, K. A., & Resnick, G. (1988). Interparental conflict and cooperation: Factors moderating children's post-divorce adjustment. In E. M. Hetherington & J. D. Arasteh (Eds.), *Impact of divorce, single parenting, and stepparenting on children* (pp. 169–195). Hillsdale, NJ: Erlbaum.

Cameron, L., Rutland, A. Brown, R., & Douch, R. (2006). Changing children's intergroup attitudes toward refugees: Testing different models of extended contact. *Child Development, 77*, 1208–1219.

Campbell, D. T. (1976). Stereotypes and the perception of group differences. *American Psychologist, 22*, 817–829.

Campbell, F. A., & Ramey, C. T. (1994). Effects of early intervention on intellectual and academic achievement. *Child Development, 65*, 684–698.

Campbell, F. A., & Ramey, C. T. (1995). Cognitive and school outcomes for high-risk African American students at middle adolescence: Positive effects of early intervention. *American Educational Research Journal, 32*, 743–772.

Campbell, S., Spieker, S., Burchinal, M., & Poe, M. (2006). Trajectories of aggression from toddlerhood to age 9 predict academic and social functioning through age 12. *Journal of Child Psychology and Psychiatry and Allied Disciplines, 47*, 791–800.

Campos, B., Keltner, D., Beck, J., Gonzaga, G., & John, O. (2007). Culture and teasing: The relational benefits of reduced desire for positive self-differentiation. *Personality and Social Psychology Bulletin, 33*, 3–16.

Camras, L. A., Oster, M., Compos, J. J., & Bakeman, R. (2003). Emotional facial expressions in Euro-American, Japanese, and Chinese infants. *Annals of the New York Academy of Sciences, 1000*, 1–17.

Canino, I. A., & Spurlock, J. (2000). *Culturally diverse children and adolescents: Assessments, diagnosis, and treatment.* New York: Guilford Press.

Cardenas-Hagan, E., Carlson, C. D. & Pollard-Durodola, S. (2007). The cross-linguistic transfer of early literacy skills: The role of initial l1 and l2 skills and language of instruction. *Language, Speech, and Hearing Services in Schools, 38*, 249–259.

Carle, E. (1969). *The very hungry caterpillar.* Cleveland: Collins-World.

Carlson, S. J., & Ramsey, C. (1995). Assistive technology. In S. K. Campbell (Ed.), *Physical therapy for children.* Philadelphia: W. B. Saunders.

Carlson, S. M., Dorothy, J., Mandell, D. J., & Williams, L. (2004). Executive function and theory of mind: Stability and prediction from ages 2 to 3. *Developmental Psychology, 40*, 1105–1122.

Carmeli, E., Kessel, S., Bar-Chad, S., & Merrick, J. (2004). A comparison between older persons with Down syndrome and a control group: Clinical characteristics, functional status and sensorimotor function. *Downs Syndrome Research and Practice. 9*, 17–24.

Caroli, M., Argentieri, L., Cardone, M., & Masi, A. (2004). Role of television in childhood obesity prevention. *International Journal of Obesity, 28*, 104–108.

Caron, A., Caron, R., & MacLean, D. (1988). Infant discrimination of naturalistic emotional expressions. *Child Development, 59*, 604–616.

Carpenter, B. (2007). The impetus for family-centred early childhood intervention. *Care, Health and Development, 33*, 664–669.

Carpenter, S., & Clyman, R. (2004). The long-term emotional and physical wellbeing of women who have lived in kinship care. *Children and Youth Services Review, 26*, 673–686.

Carrasquillo, H. (1997). Puerto Rican families in America. In M. K. DeGenova (Ed.), *Families in cultural context: Strengths and challenges in diversity* (pp. 109–130). Mountain View, CA: Mayfield.

Carson, D., Perry, C., Diefenderfer, A., & Klee, T. (1999). Differences in family characteristics and parenting behavior in families with language-delayed and language-normal toddlers. *Infant Toddler Intervention, 9*, 259–279.

Carter, A. S., Mayes, L. C., & Pajer, K. A. (1990). The role of dyadic affect in play and infant sex in predicting infant response to the still-face situation. *Child Development, 61*, 764–773.

Carter, J. H. (1983). Vision or sight: Health concerns for Afro-American children. In G. J. Powell (Ed.), *The psychosocial development of minority children.* New York: Brunner/Mazel.

Casas, J., Weigel, S., Crick, N., Ostrov, J., Woods, K., Yeh, E., et al. (2006). Early parenting and children's relational and physical aggression in the preschool and home contexts. *Journal of Applied Developmental Psychology, 27*, 209–227.

Case, T., Repacholi, B., & Stevenson, R. (2006). My baby doesn't smell as bad as yours: The plasticity of disgust. *Evolution and Human Behavior, 27*, 357–365.

Caspi, A., Henry, B., McGee, R. O., Moffitt, T. E., & Silva, P. A. (1995). Temperamental origins of child and adolescent behavior problems: From age 3 to age 15. *Child Development, 66*, 55–68.

Cassidy, J., & Asher, S. R. (1992). Loneliness and peer relations in young children. *Child Development, 63*, 350–365.

Cassidy, J., & Berlin, L. J. (1994). The insecure/ambivalent pattern of attachment: Theory and research. *Child Development, 65*, 971–991.

Cassidy, J., Kirsh, S. J., Scolton, K. L., & Parke, R. D. (1996). Attachment and representations of peer relationships. *Developmental Psychology, 32*, 892–904.

Castles, A., & Coltheart, M. (2004). Is there a causal link from phonological awareness to success in learning to read? *Cognition, 91*, 77–111.

Castrogiovanni, A. (2008). *Incidence and Prevalence of Communication Disorders and Hearing Loss in Children-2008 Edition.* Rockville, MD: American Speech-Language-Hearing Association.

Catherwood, D. (1993). The robustness of infant haptic memory. *Child Development, 64*, 702–710.

Cathey, L. (2006). Stress reactivity and regulation in infancy: Indicators, correlates, and methods of soothing. *Stress, Trauma, and Counseling, 9*, 161–173.

Caudill, W. (1977). Psychology and anthropology: The individual and his nexus. In L. Nader & T. W. Maretzki (Eds.), *Cultural illness and health: Essays in human adaptation* (pp. 67–77). Washington, DC: American Anthropological Association.

Caughy, M. O., O'Campo, P., & Muntaner, C. (2003). When being alone might be better: Neighborhood poverty, social capital, and child mental health. *Social Science & Medicine, 57*, 227–237.

Caughy, M. O., DiPietro, J. A., & Strobino, D. M. (1994). Day-care participation as a protective factor in the cognitive development of low-income children. *Child Development, 65*, 457–471.

Cazden, C., & Beck, S. (2003). In A. Graesser, M. Gernsbacher, & S. Goldman (Eds.), *Handbook of discourse processes* (pp. 165–198). Hillsdale, NJ: Erlbaum.

Cecchini, M., Lai, C., & Langher, V. (2007). Communication and crying in newborns. *Infant Behavior and Development, 30*, 655–665.

Ceci, S. (1991). How much does schooling influence general intelligence and its cognitive components? A reassessment of the evidence. *Developmental Psychology, 27*, 703–722.

Cekaite, A. (2007). A child's development of interactional competence in a Swedish l2 classroom. *The Modern Language Journal, 91* 45–62.

Centers for Disease Control and Prevention. (2004). *Prevalence of overweight among children and adolescents.* Hyattsville, MD: National Center for Health Statistics.

Centers for Disease Control and Prevention. (2008). *Injuries among children and adolescents.* Washington, DC: U.S. Department of Health and Human Services.

Cervantes, C. A., & Callahan, M. A. (1998). Labels and explanations in mother-child emotion talk: Age and gender differentiation. *Developmental Psychology, 34*, 88–98.

Chamberlain, B., Kasari, C., & Rotheram-Fuller, E. (2007). Involvement or isolation? The social networks of children with autism in regular classrooms. *Journal of Autism and Developmental Disorders, 37*, 230–242.

Chamot, A. U., & O'Malley, J. (1994). *The CALLA handbook.* Reading, MA: Addison-Wesley.

Chan, S. (1998). Families with Asian roots. In M. Hanson & E. Lynch (Eds.), *Developing cross-cultural competence: A guide for working with young children and their families* (pp. 22–35). Baltimore: Paul H. Brookes.

Chandra, P., Schiavello, H., Ravi, B., Weinstein, A. & Hook, F. (2002). Pregnancy outcomes in urban teenagers. *International Journal of Gynecology & Obstetrics, 79*, 117.

Chao, R. K. (1994). Beyond parental control and authoritarian parenting style: Understanding Chinese parenting through the cultural notion of training. *Child Development, 65*, 1111–1119.

Chao, R. K. (2002). The parenting of immigrant Chinese and European American mothers: Relations between parenting styles, socialization goals, and parental practices. *Journal of Applied Developmental Psychology, 21*, 233–248.

Chao, R. K., & Tseng, V. (2002). Parenting of Asians. In M. Bornstein (Ed.), *Handbook of parenting* (pp. 59–93). Hillsdale, NJ: Lawrence Erlbaum Associates.

Chavez, A., & Martinez, C. (1979). Consequences of insufficient nutrition on child character and behavior. In D. A. Levitsky (Ed.), *Malnutrition, environment, and behavior* (pp. 238–255). Ithaca, NY: Cornell University Press.

Chavez, L. R., Cornelius, W. A., & Jones, O. W. (1986). Utilization of health services by Mexican immigrant women in San Diego. *Women and Health, 11*, 3–20.

Chavkin, W. (1995). Substance abuse in pregnancy. In B. P. Sachs, R. Beard, E. Papiernik, & C. Russel (Eds.), *Reproductive health care for women and babies* (pp. 305–321). New York: Oxford University Press.

Chen, C., & Stevenson, H. (1989). Homework: A cross-cultural examination. *Child Development, 60*, 551–561.

Chen, C., & Stevenson, H. (1995). Motivation and mathematics achievement: A comparative study of Asian-American, Caucasian-American, and East Asian high school students. *Child Development, 66*, 1215–1234.

Chen, S. (1996). Are Japanese young children among the gods? In D. Schwalb & B. Schwalb (Eds.), *Japanese children rearing: Two generations of scholarship* (pp. 135–146). New York: Guilford Press.

Chen, X., Cen, G., Li, D., & He, Y. (2005). Social functioning and adjustment in Chinese children: The imprint of historical time. *Child Development, 76*, 182–195.

Chen, X., & French, D. (2008). Children's social competence in cultural context. *Annual Review of Psychology, 59*, 591–616.

Chen, X., Rubin, K. H., & Sun, Y. (1992). Social reputation and peer relationships in Chinese and Canadian children: A cross-cultural study. *Child Development, 63*, 1336–1343.

Cherney, I., & London, K. (2006). Gender-linked differences in the toys, television shows, computer games, and outdoor activities of 5- to 13-year-old children. *Sex Roles, 54*, 717–726.

Cherlin, A. J., & Furstenberg, F. F. (1986). *The new American grandparent*. New York: Basic Books.

Chess, S., & Thomas, A. (1987). *Origins and evolution of behavior disorders from infancy to early adult life*. Cambridge, MA: Harvard University Press.

Chess, S., & Thomas, A. (1990). Continuities and discontinuities in development. In L. S. Robins & M. Rutter (Eds.), *Straight and devious pathways from childhood to adulthood* (pp. 98–114). New York: Cambridge University Press.

Childers, J., & Tomasello, M. (2006). Are nouns easier to acquire than verbs? Three experimental studies. In K. Hirsh-Pasek & R. Golinkoff (Eds.), *Action meets word: How children learn verbs*. Oxford: Oxford University Press.

Children's Defense Fund. (2000). *The state of America's children: Yearbook 2000*. Washington, DC: Author.

Children's Defense Fund. (2007). *The state of America's children: Yearbook 2007*. Washington, DC: Author.

Chilmonczyk, B. A., Salmun, L. M., Megathlin, K. N., Neveux, L. M., Palomaki, G. E., Knight, G. J., et al. (1993). Association between exposure to environmental tobacco smoke and exacerbations of asthma in children. *New England Journal of Medicine, 328*, 1665–1669.

Chilton, M., Chyatte, M., & Breaux, J. (2007). The negative effects of poverty & food insecurity on child development. *Indian Journal of Medical Research, 126*, 262–272.

Chisholm, J. S. (1989). Biology, culture, and the development of temperament: A Navajo example. In J. K. Nugent, B. M. Lester, & T. B. Brazelton (Eds.), *The Cultural Context of Infancy* (pp. 341–364). Norwood, NJ: Ablex.

Chomsky, C. (1972). Write now, read later. In C. Cazden (Ed.), *Language in early childhood education*. Washington, DC: National Association for the Education of Young Children.

Christie, J. F. (1983). The effects of play tutoring on young children's cognitive performance. *Journal of Educational Research, 76*, 326–330.

Christie, J. F. (1998). Play: A medium for literacy development. In D. Fromberg & D. Bergen (Eds.), *Play from birth to twelve and beyond* (pp. 50–55). New York: Garland.

Christie, J. F. (2008). The scientifically based reading research approach to early literacy instruction. In L. Justice & C. Vukelich (Eds.), *Achieving excellence in preschool literacy instruction* (pp. 25–40). New York: Guilford Publications.

Christopher, J., & Bickhard, M. H. (2007). Culture, self and identity: Interactivist contributions to a metatheory for cultural psychology. *Culture & Psychology, 13*, 259–295.

Chugani, H. T. (1997). Neuroimaging of developmental nonlinearity and developmental pathologies. In R. W. Thatcher, G. R. J. Lyon, J. Ramsey, & N. Krasnegor (Eds.), *Developmental neuroimaging: Mapping the development of brain and behavior*. San Diego: Academic Press.

Chung, H., & Muntaner, C. (2006). Political and welfare state determinants of infant and child health indicators: An analysis of wealthy countries. *Social Science & Medicine, 63*, 829–842.

Chuoke, M., & Eyman, B. (1997). Play fair—And not just at recess. *Educational Leadership, 54*, 53–55.

Cicchetti, D., & Beeghly, M. (Eds.). (1990). *Children with Down syndrome: A developmental perspective*. Cambridge: Cambridge University Press.

Cicirelli, V. G. (1982). Sibling influence throughout the life span. In M. E. Lamb & B. Sutton-Smith (Eds.), *Sibling relationships* (pp. 73–106). Hillsdale, NJ: Erlbaum.

Cirulli, F., Berry, A., & Alleva, A. (2003). Early disruption of the mother–infant relationship: Effects on brain plasticity and implications for psychopathology. *Neuroscience & Biobehavioral Reviews, 27*, 73–82.

Cizek, G. J. (1995). Crunchy granola and the hegemony of narrative. *Educational Researcher, 24(3)*, 26–28.

Clark, D. M., & Smith, S. W. (1999). Facilitating friendships: Including students with autism in the early elementary classroom. *Intervention in School and Clinic, 34*, 248–251.

Clark, K. B. (1952). The effects of prejudice and discrimination on personality formation. In H. Witmer & R. Kotinsky (Eds.), *Personality in the making*. New York: Harper.

Clark, L., & Redman, R. (2007). Mexican immigrant mothers' expectations for children's health services. *Western Journal of Nursing Research, 29*, 670–690.

Clark, S., & Paechter, C., (2007). Why can't girls play football? Gender dynamics and the playground. *Sport, Education and Society, 12*, 261–276.

Clarke, L. (1988). Invented versus traditional spelling in first graders' writings: Effects on learning to spell and read. *Teaching of English, 22*, 281–309.

Clarke-Stewart, K. A. (1988). "The effects of infant day care reconsidered". *Early Childhood Research Quarterly, 3*, 293–318.

Clarke-Stewart, K. A. (1993). *Daycare*. Cambridge, MA: Harvard University Press.

Clarkson, R. L., Vohr, B. R., Blackwell, P. M., & White, K. R. (1994). Universal infant hearing screening and intervention: The Rhode Island program. *Infants and Young Children: An Interdisciplinary Journal of Special Care Practices, 46*, 65–74.

Clay, M. (2001). *Change over time in children's literacy development*. Portsmouth, NH: Heinemann.

Clay, M. (2005). Literacy lessons: Designed for individuals, part two: Teaching procedures. Portsmouth, NH: Heinemann.

Clements, R. (2007). Is recess a frivolous waste of time with no apparent outcomes? *The Teachers College Record*, February.

Cobco-Lewis, A. B., Oller, D. K., Lynch, M. P., & Levine, S. L. (1996). Relations of motor and vocal milestones in typically developing infants and infants with Down syndrome. *American Journal on Mental Retardation, 100*, 456–467.

Cohen, I. L. (1995). A theoretical analysis of the role of hyperarousal in the learning and behavior of fragile-X males. *Mental Retardation and Developmental Disabilities Research Reviews, 1*, 286–291.

Coie, J. D., Dodge, K. A., Terry, R., & Wright, V. (1991). The role of aggression in peer relations: An analysis of aggression episodes in boys' play groups. *Child Development, 62*, 812–826.

Colburn, N. (1996, September). Fetal alcohol babies face life of problems. *Washington Post*, p. 5.

Cole, D. A., Martin, J. M., Peeke, L. A., Seroczynski, A. D., & Fier, J. (1999). Children's over- and under estimation of academic competence: A longitudinal study of gender differences, depression, and anxiety. *Child Development, 70*, 459–473.

Cole, M. (1990). Cognitive development and formal schooling: The evidence from cross-cultural research. In L.C. Moll (Ed.), *Vygotsky and education* (pp. 89–110). New York: Cambridge University Press.

Cole, M. (2005). Culture in development. In M. Bornstein & M. Lamb (Eds.), *Developmental science: An advanced textbook*. London: Routledge.

Cole, M., & Scribner, S. (1977). Cross-cultural studies of memory and cognition. In R. V. Kail & J. W. Hagen (Eds.), *Perspectives on the development of memory and cognition* (pp. 239–271). Hillsdale, NJ: Erlbaum.

Cole, P., Tamang, B. L., & Shrestha, S. (2006). Cultural variations in the socialization of young children's anger and shame. *Child Development, 77*, 1237–1251.

Coleman, J. M., & Minnett, A. M. (1992). Learning disabilities and social competence: A social ecological perspective. *Exceptional Children, 59*, 234–246.

Colombo, J. (1993). *Infant cognition: Predicting later intellectual functioning*. Newbury Park, CA: Sage.

Colombo, J. (1995). On the neural mechanisms underlying developmental and individual differences in visual fixation in infancy. Two hypotheses. *Developmental Review, 15*, 97–135.

Colombo, J., Frick, J. E., Ryther, J. S., & Gifford, J. J. (1996). Four-month-olds' recognition of complementary-contour forms. *Infant Behavior and Development 19*, 113–119.

Colwell, M., & Lindsey, E. (2005). Preschool children's pretend and physical play and sex of play partner: Connections to peer competence. *Sex Roles, 52*, 497–509.

Comer, J. P. (1985). Empowering black children's educational environments. In H. P. McAdoo & J. L. McAdoo (Eds.), *Black children: Social, educational, and parental environments* (pp. 123–138). Newbury Park, CA: Sage.

Condon, J. C., & Yousef, F. S. (1975). *An introduction to intercultural communication*. Indianapolis: Bobbs-Merrill.

Condon, W. S., & Sander, L. W. (1974). Neonate movement is synchronized with adult speech. *Science, 183*, 99–101.

Cooper, H., Charlton, K., Valentine, J., & Muhlenbruck, L. (2000). Making the most of summer school: A meta-analytic and narrative review. *Monographs for the Society for Research in Child Development, 65*, 1–130.

Cooper, R., & Jordan, W. (2003). Cultural issues in comprehensive school reform. *Urban Education, 38*, 380–397.

Cooper, R. P., & Aslin, R. N. (1990). Preference for infant-directed speech in the first month after birth. *Child Development, 61*, 1584–1595.

Coovadia, H., Rollins, N., Bland, R., Little, K. A., Coutsoudis, Bennish, M., et al. (2007). Mother-to-child transmission of HIV-1 infection during exclusive breastfeeding in the first 6 months of life: An intervention cohort study. *The Lancet, 369*, 1107–1116.

Coplan, R. J., Prakash, K., O'Neil, K., & Armer, M. (2004). Do you "want" to play? Distinguishing between conflicted shyness and social disinterest in early childhood. *Developmental Psychology, 40*, 244–58.

Coplan, R. J., Rubin, K. H., Fox, N. A., Calkins, S. D., & Stewart, S. L. (1994). Being alone, playing alone, and acting alone: Distinguishing among reticence and passive and active solitude in young children. *Child Development, 65*, 129–137.

Copple, C. (2003). Fostering young children's representation, planning, and reflection: A focus in three current early childhood models. *Journal of Applied Developmental Psychology, 24*, 763–771.

Coppola, G., Cassibba, R., & Costantini, A. (2007). What can make the difference? Premature birth and maternal sensitivity at 3 months of age: The role of attachment organization, traumatic reaction and baby's medical risk. *Infant Behavior and Development, 30*, 679–684.

Corapci, F. (2008). The role of child temperament on Head Start preschoolers' social competence in the context of cumulative risk. *Journal of Applied Developmental Psychology, 29,* 1–16.

Corenblum, B., & Wilson, A. E. (1982). Ethnic preference and identification among Canadian Indian and white children: Replication and extension. *Canadian Journal of Behavioral Science, 14,* 50–59.

Corpus, J. H., & Lepper, M. R. (2007). The effects of person versus performance praise on children's motivation: Gender and age as moderating factors. *Educational Psychology, 27,* 487–508.

Correa-Chávez, M., Rogoff, B., & Arauz, R. M. (2005). Cultural patterns in attending to two events at once. *Child Development, 76,* 664–678.

Corsaro, W. (2005). *The Sociology of childhood.* Thousand Oaks, CA: Sage.

Cossrow, N., & Faulkner, B. (2004). Race/Ethnic Issues in Obesity and Obesity–Related Comorbidities. *Journal of Clinical Endocrinology & Metabolism, 89,* 2590–2594.

Cost, Quality, and Child Outcomes Study Team. (1995). *Cost, quality, and child outcomes in child care centers: Public report* (2nd ed.). Denver: University of Colorado, Economics Department.

Costanzo, P. R., & Hoy, M. B. (2007). Intergenerational relations: Themes, prospects, and possibilities. *Journal of Social Issues, 63,* 885–902.

Costabile, A., Smith, P. K., Matheson, L., Aston, J., Hunter, T., & Boulton, M. (1991). Cross-national comparison of how children distinguish serious and playful fighting. *Developmental Psychology, 27,* 881–887.

Cote, L., & Bornstein, M. (2005). Child and mother play in cultures of origin, acculturating cultures, and cultures of destination. *International Journal of Behavioral Development, 29,* 479–488.

Covington, C. Y., Nordstrom-Klee, B., Ager, J., Sokol, R., & Delaney-Black, V. (2002). Birth to age 7 growth of children prenatally exposed to drugs: A prospective cohort study. *Neurotoxicology and Teratology, 24,* 489–496.

Cowan, N. (2007). *Working memory capacity.* London: Taylor and Francis.

Craig, Sharon A. (2006). The effects of an adapted interactive writing intervention on kindergarten children's phonological awareness, spelling, and early reading development: A contextualized approach to instruction. *Journal of Educational Psychology, 98,* 714–731.

Crain, W. (2005). *Theories of development* (5th ed.). Upper Saddle River, NJ: Prentice Hall.

Crais, E. R., & Roberts, J. E. (2003). Assessing communication skills. In M. McLean, D. B. Bailey, & M. Wolery (Eds), *Assessing infants and preschoolers with special needs* (pp. 334–397). Upper Saddle River, NJ: Merrill/Prentice Hall.

Cratty, B. J. (1986). *Perceptual and motor development in infants and children.* Upper Saddle River, NJ: Merrill/Prentice Hall.

Crawford, P., Story, M., Wang, M., Ritchie, L., & Sabry, Z. (2001). Ethnic issues in the epidemiology of childhood obesity. *Pediatric Clinics of North America, 48,* 855–878.

Crespo, C., Smit, E., Troiano, R., Bartlett, S., Macera, C., & Andersen, R. (2001). Television watching, energy intake, and obesity in us children. *Archives of Pediatric and Adolescent Medicine, 155,* 360–365.

Creswell, C., Woolgar, M., Cooper, C., Giannakakis, A., Schofield, E., Young, A., et al. (2008). Processing of faces and emotional expressions in infants at risk of social phobia. *Cognition & Emotion, 23,* 394–417.

Crick, N. R., Casas, J. F., & Mosher, M. (1997). Relational and overt aggression in preschool. *Developmental Psychology, 33,* 579–588.

Crick, N. R., & Dodge, K. A. (1994). A review and reformulation of social information processing mechanisms in children's social adjustment. *Psychological Bulletin, 1154,* 74–101.

Crick, N. R., & Dodge, K. A. (1996). Social information processing mechanisms in reactive and proactive aggression. *Child Development, 67,* 993–1002.

Crick, N. R., & Grotpeter, J. K. (1995). Relational aggression, gender, and social-psychological adjustment. *Child Development, 66,* 710–722.

Crick, N. R., & Ladd, G. W. (1990). Children's perceptions of the outcomes of social strategies. *Developmental Psychology, 26,* 612–620.

Crick, N. R., & Ladd, G. W. (1993). Children's perceptions of their peer experiences: Attributions, loneliness, social anxiety, and social avoidance. *Developmental Psychology, 29,* 244–254.

Crick, N. R., Ostrov, J., & Werner, N. (2006). A longitudinal study of relational aggression, physical aggression, and children's social–psychological adjustment. *Journal of Abnormal Child Psychology, 34,* 127–138.

Cronin, V. (1987, April). *Word association and reading.* Paper presented at the biennial meeting of the Society for Research in Child Development, Baltimore.

Crook, C. K. (1987). Taste and olfaction. In P. Salapatek & L. Cohen (Eds.), *Handbook of infant perception* (Vol. 1, pp. 237–264). Orlando: Academic Press.

Crouch, J., & Behl, L. (2001). Relationships among parental beliefs in corporal punishment, reported stress, and physical child abuse potential. *Child Abuse & Neglect, 25,* 413–419.

Cuddeback, G. (2004). Kinship family foster care: A methodological and substantive synthesis of research. *Children and Youth Services Review, 26,* 623–639.

Cugmas, Z. (2007). Child's attachment to his/her mother, father and kindergarten teacher. *Early Child Development and Care, 177,* 349–368.

Cullinan, D., Epstein, M. H., & Lloyd, J. W. (1983). *Behavior disorders of children and adolescents.* Upper Saddle River, NJ: Merrill/Prentice Hall.

Cummings, A., Čeponienė, R., Koyama, A., Saygin, A., Townsend, J., & Dick, F. (2006). Auditory semantic networks for words and natural sounds. *Brain Research, 115,* 92–107.

Cummins, J. (1987). Bilingualism language proficiency and metalinguistic development. In P. Homel, M. Palij, & D. Aaronson (Eds.), *Childhood bilingualism: Aspects of linguistic, cognitive, and social development* (pp. 57–74). Hillsdale, NJ: Erlbaum.

Cuneo, D. O. (1980). A general strategy for quantity judgements. *Child Development, 50,* 170–179.

Cunningham, A. S., Jelliffe, D. B., & Jelliffe, E. F. P. (1991). Breastfeeding and health in the 1980s. *Journal of Pediatrics, 118,* 659–666.

Curry, N. E., & Johnson, C. N. (1990). *Beyond self-esteem: Developing a genuine sense of human value.* Washington, DC: National Association for the Education of Young Children.

Cutting, A. L., & Dunn, J. (1999). Theory of mind, emotion, understanding, language, and family background: Individual differences and interrelations. *Child Development, 70,* 853–865.

Dale, P. S. (1976). *Language development: Structure and function.* New York: Holt, Rinehart and Winston.

D'Allura (2002). Enhancing the social interaction skills of preschoolers with visual impairments. *Journal of Visual Impairment & Blindness, 96,* 18–37.

Damon, W. (1990). *The moral child.* New York: The Free Press.

Damon, W. (2002). The moral development of the child. *Scientific American* (August) 56–72.

Dance, C., Rushton, A., & Quinton, D. (2002). Emotional abuse in early childhood: Relationships with progress in subsequent family placement. *Journal of Child Psychology and Psychiatry, 43,* 395–407.

Dansky, J. L. (1980). Make-believe: A mediator of the relationship between play and creativity. *Child Development, 51,* 576–579.

Darling–Hammond, L. D. (2004). From "separate but equal" to No Child Left Behind: The collision of new standards and old equalities. In D. Meier & G. Wood (Eds.), *Many children left behind: How the NCLB Act is damaging our children and our schools* (pp. 3–32). Boston: Beacon Press.

Dart, F. E., & Pradhan, P. L. (1967). Cross-cultural teaching of science. *Science, 155,* 649–656.

Davenport, B., Hegland, S., & Melby, J. (2007). Parent behaviors in free-play and problem-solving interactions in relation to problem behaviors in preschool boys. *Early Child Development and Care, 177,* 107–120.

Davidson, J. I. F. (1998). Language and play: Natural partners. In D. Fromberg & D. Bergen (Eds.), *Play from birth to 12: Contexts, perspectives, and meanings* (pp. 175–184). New York: Garland.

Davis, B. L., MacNeilage, P. F., Matyear, C. L., & Powell, J. K. (2000). Prosodic correlates of stress babbling: An acoustical study. *Child Development, 71,* 1258–1270.

Davis, J., Weigensberg, M., Shaibi, G., Crespo, N. Kelly, L., Lane, C., & Goran, M. (2007). Influence of breastfeeding on obesity and type 2 diabetes risk factors in Latino youth with a family history of type 2 diabetes. *Diabetes Care, 30,* 784–789.

Davis, O., Arden, R., & Plomin, R. (2008). g in middle childhood: Moderate genetic and shared environmental influence using diverse measures of general cognitive ability at 7, 9 and 10 years in a large population sample of twins. *Intelligence, 36,* 68–80.

Davis-Kean, P. E., & Sandler, H. M. (2001). A meta-analysis of measures of self-esteem for young children: A framework for future measures. *Child Development, 72,* 887–906.

Dawson, G., Ashman, S. B., Panagiotides, H., Hessel, D., Self, J., Yamada, E., et al. (2003). Preschool outcomes of children of depressed mothers. *Child Development, 74,* 1158–1175.

Dawson, G., & Fischer, K. W. (1994). *Human behavior and the developing brain.* New York: Guilford Press.

Dearing, E., McCartney, K., Marshall, N., & Warner, R. (2001). Parental reports of children's sleep and wakefulness: Longitudinal associations with cognitive and language outcomes. *Infant Behavior and Development, 24,* 151–170.

Deater-Deckard, K. (2005). Parenting stress and children's development. *Infant and Child Development, 14,* 111–115.

De Bleser, R., Dupont, P., Postler, J., Bormans, G., Speelman, D., Mortelmans, L., et al. (2003). The organisation of the bilingual lexicon: A PET study. *Journal of Neurolinguistics, 16,* 439–456.

DeCaro, J., & Worthman, C. (2007). Cultural models, parent behavior, and young child experience in working American families. *Parenting, 7,* 177–203.

DeCasper, A. J., & Spence, M. J. (1991). Auditorially mediated behavior during the perinatal period: A cognitive view. In M. J. S. Weiss & P. R. Zelazo (Eds.), *Newborn attention: Biological constraints and the influence of experience.* Norwood, NJ: Ablex.

Declercq, E., Sakala, C., Corry, M., & Applebaum, S. (2007). Listening to mothers II: Report of the second national U.S. survey of women's childbearing experiences. *Journal of Perinatal Education, 16,* 9–14.

DeGenova, M. K. (1997). *Families in cultural context: Strengths and challenges in diversity.* Mountain View, CA: Mayfield.

Degnan, K., & Fox, N. (2007). Behavioral inhibition and anxiety disorders: Multiple levels of a resilience process. *Development and Psychopathology, 19,* 729–746.

Dei, G. J. S., Mazzuca, J., McIsaac, E., & Zine, J. (1997). *Reconstructing "drop out": A critical ethnography of the dynamics of black students' disengagement from school.* Toronto: University of Toronto Press.

Deitel, M. (2006). The obesity epidemic. *Obesity Surgery, 16,* 377–378.

DeKeyser, R. M. (2005). What makes learning second-language grammar difficult? A review of issues. *Language Learning, 55,* 1–25.

Delcampo, D. S., & Delcampo, R. L. (1998). *Taking sides: Clashing views on controversial issues in childhood and society.* Guilford, CT: Dushkin/McGraw-Hill.

de Castro, B., Slot, N., Bosch, J., Koops, W., & Veerman, J. (2003). Negative feelings exacerbate hostile attributions of intent in highly aggressive boys. *Journal of Clinical and Child and Adolescent Psychology, 32,* 56–65.

de Haan, M., Johnson, M., Maurer, D., & Perrett, D. (2007). Recognition of individual faces and average face prototypes by 1- and 3-month-old infants. *Cognitive Development, 16,* 659–678.

deMarrais, K. B., & LeCompte, M. D. (1998). *The ways schools work.* New York: Addison-Wesley.

deMarrais, K. B., Nelson, P. A., & Baker, J. H. (1994). Meaning in mud: Yup'ik Eskimo girls at play. In J. L. Roopnarine, J. E. Johnson, & F. H. Hooper (Eds.), *Children's play in diverse cultures* (pp. 179–209). Albany: State University of New York Press.

deMause, L. (1974). The evolution of children. In deMause (Ed.), *The history of childhood.* New York: Psychohistory Press.

deMause, L. (1995). *The history of children.* Northvale, NJ: Jason Aronson.

Demmert, W. (2001). *Improving academic performance among Native American students: A review of research.* Charleston, WV: Clearinghouse on Rural Education and Small Schools.

Demo, D., & Cox, M. (2000). Families with young children: A review of research in the 1990s. *Journal of Marriage and Family, 62,* 876–895.

Deng, S., & Roosa, M. W. (2007). Family influences on adolescent delinquent behaviors: Applying the social development model to a Chinese sample. *American Journal of Community Psychology, 40,* 333–44.

Dennis, W., & Dennis, M. G. (1940). The effects of cradling practices upon the onset of walking in Hopi children. *Journal of Genetic Psychology, 56,* 77–86.

Denny, M. (2004). *Gender differences in preschool children's activity level as measured by parent and teacher report.* College Park, MD: Digital Repository at the University of Maryland.

Denzin, N. K., & Lincoln, Y. S. (Eds.). (2001). *Handbook of qualitative research.* Thousand Oaks, CA: Sage.

de Onis, M. (2006). Relationship between physical growth and motor development in the WHO Child Growth Standards. *Acta Paediatrica, 95,* 96–101.

Derman-Sparks, L., Phillips, C. B., & Hilliard, A. G. (1997). *Teaching/learning antiracism: A developmental approach.* New York: Teachers College Press.

DeRosier, M. E., Gillessen, A. H., Coie, J. D., & Dodge, K. A. (1994). Group social context and children's aggressive behavior. *Child Development, 65,* 1068–1079.

Deuchar, M., & Quay, S. (1999). Language choice in the earliest utterances: A case study with methodological implications. *Journal of Child Language, 26,* 461–475.

De Vos, G. (1954). A comparison of the personality differences in two generations of Japanese-Americans by means of the Rorschach Test. *Nagoya Journal of Medical Science, 17,* 153–265.

DeVries, M. W., & DeVries, M. R. (1977). Cultural relativity of toilet training readiness: A perspective from East Africa. *Pediatrics, 60,* 170–177.

DeVries, M. W., & Sameroff, A. J. (1984). Culture and temperament: Influences on infant temperament in three East-African societies. *American Journal of Orthopsychiatry, 54,* 83–96.

DeVries, R. A., & Kohlberg, L. (1990). *Constructivist early education: Overview and comparison with other programs.* Washington, DC: National Association for the Education of Young Children.

DeVries, R. A., Zan, B., Hildebrandt, C., Edmiaston, R., & Sales, C. (2002). *Developing constructivist early childhood curriculum: Practical principles and activities.* New York: Teachers College Press.

Dewey, K. G., Cohen, R. J., & Brown, K. H. (2001). Effects of exclusive breastfeeding for four versus six months on infant motor development. *Journal of Nutrition, 631,* 262–267.

DeWolf, D. M. (2001). Preschool children's negotiation and intersubjectivity in rough-and-tumble play. *Dissertation Abstracts International, 60,* 5833.

De Wolff, M. S., & IJzendoorn, M. H. (1997). Sensitivity and attachment: A meta-analysis on parental antecedents of infant attachment. *Child Development, 68,* 571–591.

Diamantopoulou, S., Henricsson, L., & Rydell, A. (2005). ADHD symptoms and peer relations of children in a community sample: Examining associated problems, self-perceptions, and gender differences. *International Journal of Behavioral Development, 29,* 388–398.

Diaz, J. (1997). *How drugs influence behavior: A neurobehavioral approach.* Upper Saddle River, NJ: Prentice Hall.

Diaz, R. M., & Klinger, C. (1991). Toward an explanatory model of the interaction between bilingualism and cognitive development. In E. Bialystok (Ed.), *Language processing in bilingual children* (pp. 181–197). Cambridge: Cambridge University Press.

Diaz-Guerrero, R. (1987). Historical sociocultural premises and ethnic socialization. In J. S. Phinney & M. J. Rotheram (Eds.), *Children's ethnic socialization.* Newbury Park, CA: Sage.

Dick, F., Wulfeck, B., Krupa-Kwiatkowski, M., & Bates, E. (2004). The development of complex sentence interpretation in typically developing children compared with children with specific language impairments or early unilateral focal lesions. *Developmental Science, 7,* 360–377.

Dickinson, D. K. (1985). Creating and using formal occasions in the classroom. *Anthropology and Education Quarterly, 16,* 47–62.

Dickinson, D. K. (1994). Features of early childhood classroom environments that support development of language and literacy. In J. Duchan, L. Hewitt, & R. Sonnenmeer (Eds.), *Pragmatics: From theory to practice* (pp. 185–201). Upper Saddle River, NJ: Prentice Hall.

Dickinson, D., & Neuman, S. B. (2000). *Handbook of early literacy.* New York: Guilford Press.

Dietz, W. H. (1993). Television, obesity, and eating disorders. *Adolescent Medicine, 75,* 543–549.

Di Leo, J. H. (1982). Graphic activity of young children: Development and creativity. In L. Lasky & R. Mukerji (Eds.), *Art: Basic for young children.* Washington, DC: National Association for the Education of Young Children.

Dilworth, J., Greenberg, M., Kusché, C. (2004). Early neuropsychological correlates of later clock drawing and clock copying abilities among school aged children. *Child Neuropsychology, 10,* 24–35.

Dionne, G., Tremblay, R., Boivin, M., Laplante, D., & Pérusse, D. (2003). Physical aggression and expressive vocabulary in 19-month-old twins. *Developmental Psychology, 39,* 261–273.

DiPietro, J. A., Hodgson, D. M., Costigan, K. A., Hilton, S. C., & Johnston, T. R. B. (1996). Fetal neurobehavioral development. *Child Development, 67,* 2553–2567.

Dixon, S., Graber, J., Brooks-Gunn, J. (2008). The roles of respect for parental authority and parenting practices in parent-child conflict among African American, Latino, and European American families. *Journal of Family Psychology, 22,* 1–10.

Dockrell, J., Campbell, R., & Neilson, I. (1980). Conservation accidents revisited. *International Journal of Behavioral Development, 3,* 423–439.

Dodge, K. A., & Coie, J. D. (1987). Social information processing factors in reactive and proactive aggression in children's peer groups. *Journal of Personality and Social Psychology, 53,* 1146–1158.

Dodge, K. A., Coie, J. D., Pettit, G. S., & Price, J. M. (1990). Peer status and aggression in boys' groups: Developmental and contextual analysis. *Child Development, 61,* 1289–1309.

Dodge, K. A., Lansford, J. E., Burks, V. S., Bates, J. E., Pettit, G. S., Fontaine, R., et al. (2003). Peer rejection and social information processing factors in the development of aggressive behavior problems in children. *Child Development, 74,* 374–393.

Dodge, K. A., & Price, J. M. (1994). On the relation between social information processing and socially competent behavior in early school-aged children. *Child Development, 65,* 1385–1398.

Dodge, K. A., & Rabiner, D. L. (2004). Returning to roots: On social information processing and moral development. *Child Development, 75,* 1003–1008.

Dodson, L., & Dickert, J. (2004). Girls' family labor in low-income households: A decade of qualitative research. *Journal of Marriage and Family, 66,* 318–332.

Dominey, P., & Dodane, C. (2004). Indeterminacy in language acquisition: The role of child directed speech and joint attention. *Journal of Neurolinguistics, 17,* 121–145.

Dondi, M., Simion, F., & Caltran, G. (1999). Can newborns discriminate between their own cry and the cry of another newborn infant? *Developmental Psychology, 35,* 418–426.

Donovan, W., Leavitt, L., Taylor, N., & Broder, J. (2007). Maternal sensory sensitivity, mother-infant 9-month interaction, infant attachment status: Predictors of mother-toddler interaction at 24 months. *Infant Behavior and Development, 30,* 336–352.

Dorosko, S., & Rollins, N. (2003). Infant formula preparation by rural and semi-rural women in South Africa. *Food Policy, 28,* 117–130.

Doucet, S., Soussignan, R., Sagot, P., & Schaal, B. (2007). The "smellscape" of mother's breast: Effects of odor masking and selective unmasking on neonatal arousal, oral, and visual responses. *Developmental Psychobiology, 49,* 129–138.

Dowda, M., Pate, R., Trost, S., Almeida, M., & Sirard, J. (2004). Influences of preschool policies and practices on children's physical activity. *Journal of Community Health, 29,* 183–196.

Dowling, P. T., & Fisher, M. (1987). Maternal factors and low birthweight infants: A comparison of blacks with Mexican-Americans. *Journal of Family Practice, 25,* 153–158.

Dresser, N. (2005). *Multicultural manners: New rules of etiquette for a changing society.* New York: John Wiley & Sons.

Dube, E. F. (1982). Literacy, cultural familiarity, and "intelligence" as determinants of story recall. In U. Neisser (Ed.), *Memory observed: Remembering in natural contexts.* San Francisco: W. H. Freeman.

Dube, S., Anda, R., Felitti, V., Edwards, V., & Croft, J. (2002). Adverse childhood experiences and personal alcohol abuse as an adult. *Addictive Behaviors, 27,* 713–725.

Dubois, L. (2008). Children who consumed sugar-sweetened beverages between meals 1–6 times/week at 2.5–4.5 years of age were more likely to be overweight at 4.5 years of age. *Evidence-Based Nursing, 11,* 1–24.

Dudley-Marling, C. C., & Edmiaston, R. (1985). Social status of learning disabled children and adolescents. *Learning Disability Quarterly*, 8, 189–204.

Duff, M., Proctor, A., & Yairi, E. (2004). Prevalence of voice disorders in African American and European American preschoolers. *Journal of Voice*, 18, 348–353.

Duhig, A. M., Renk, K., Epstein, M., & Phares, V. (2000). Interparental agreement on internalizing, externalizing, and total behavior problems: A meta-analysis. *Clinical Psychology: Science and Practice*, 7, 435–453.

Duncan, G. J., Brooks-Gunn, J., & Klebanov, P. K. (1994). Economic deprivation and early childhood development. *Child Development*, 65, 296–318.

Dunn, J. (1992). Siblings and development. *Current Directions in Psychological Sciences*, 1, 6–9.

Dunn, J. (1993). *Young children's close relationships: Beyond attachment*. Newbury Park, CA: Sage.

Dunn, J. (2005). Commentary: Siblings in their families. *Journal of Family Psychology*, 19, 654–657.

Dunn, J., Cutting, A., & Fisher, N. (2002). Old friends, new friends: Predictors of children's perspectives on their friends at school. *Child Development*, 73, 621–635.

Dunn, J., & Hughes, C. (2001). "I got some swords and you're dead!": Violent fantasy, antisocial behavior, friendship, and moral sensibility in young children. *Child Development*, 72, 491–505.

Dunn, J., & Kendrick, C. (1979). Interactions between young siblings in the context of family relationships. In M. Lewis & L. Rosenblum (Eds.), *The child and its family*. New York: Plenum.

Dunn, J., & McGuire, S. (1992). Sibling and peer relationships in childhood. *Journal of Child Psychology and Psychiatry*, 33, 67–105.

Dunn, J., Slomkowski, C., & Beardsall, L. (1994). Sibling relationships from the preschool period through middle childhood and early adolescence. *Developmental Psychology*, 30, 315–324.

Dunst, C. (2007). Early intervention for infants and toddlers with developmental disabilities. In S. Odom, R. Horner, M. Shell, & J. Blacher (Eds.), *Handbook of developmental disabilities* (pp. 161–180). New York: Guilford Press.

DuPaul, G. J., & Barkley, R. A. (1993). Behavioral contributions to pharmacotherapy: The utility of behavioral methodology in the medical treatment of children with attention deficit hyperactivity disorder. *Behavior Therapy*, 24, 47–65.

Durkin, K. (1995). *Developmental social psychology*. Cambridge, MA: Blackwell.

Dweck, C. S., Goetz, T. E., & Strauss, N. L. (1980). Sex differences in learned helplessness: An experimental and naturalistic study of failure generalization and its mediators. *Journal of Personality and Social Psychology*, 38, 441–452.

Dweck, C. S., & Legget, E. L. (1988). A social-cognitive approach to motivation and personality. *Psychological Review*, 99, 256–273.

Dwivedi, K. N., & Banhatti, R. G. (2005). Attention deficit/hyperactivity disorder and ethnicity. *Archives of Disease in Childhood*, 90, 10–12.

Dyson, L. L. (1993). Response to the presence of a child with disabilities: Parental stress and family functioning over time. *American Journal of Mental Retardation*, 98, 207–218.

Earl, T. R. (2007). Mental health care policy: Recognizing the needs of minority siblings as caregivers. *Journal of Human Behavior in the Social Environment*, 14, 51–72.

Erhardt, D., & Hinshaw, S. P. (1994). Initial sociometric impressions of attention-deficit hyperactivity disorder and comparison boys: Predictions from social behaviors and from nonbehavioral variables. *Journal of Consulting and Clinical Psychology*, 62, 833–842.

Easterbrooks, M. A. (1989). Quality of attachment to mother and to father: Effects of perinatal risk status. *Child Development*, 60, 825–830.

Easterbrooks, S. R. (2008). Communication. In W. Umansky & R. Hooper (Eds.), *Young children with special needs* (pp. 230–276). Columbus, OH: Merrill.

Eaton, W. O., & Yu, A. P. (1989). Are sex differences in child motor activity level a function of sex differences in maturational status? *Child Development*, 60, 1005–1011.

Eaves, L. J., Eysenck, H. J., & Martin, N. G. (1989). *Genes, culture, and personality*. London: Academic Press.

Eccles (Parsons), J. Adler, T. F., Futterman, R., Goff, S. B., Kaczala, C. M., Meece, J. L., et al. (1983). Expectancies, values, and academic behaviors. In J. T. Spence (Ed.), *Achievement and achievement motives* (pp. 75–146). San Francisco: W. H. Freeman.

Eccles, J., Wigfield, A., Harold, R. D., & Blumenfeld, P. (1993). Age and gender differences in children's self- and task-perceptions during elementary school. *Child Development*, 64, 830–847.

Eckman, P. (1972). Universals and cultural differences in facial expressions of emotion. In J. K. Cole (Ed.), *Nebraska Symposium on Motivation* (pp. 46–52). Lincoln: University of Nebraska Press.

Edwards, C. P. (2000). Children's play in cross–cultural perspective: A new look at the six cultures study. *Cross–Cultural Research*, 34, 318–338.

Edwards, C. P., Knoche, L., Aukrust, V., Kumru, A., & Kim, M. (2006). Parental ethnotheories of child development: Looking beyond independence and individualism in American belief systems. In U. Kim, K. Yang, & K. Hwang (Eds.), *Indigenous and cultural psychology: Understanding people in context*. New York: Springer.

Edwards, G., & King, D. (2007). Smoking in pregnancy: A growing health problem. In G. Edwards & S. Byrom (Eds.), *Essential midwifery practice: Public health* (pp. 49–70). Blackwell Publishing.

Edwards, J. (1981). *Ratings of black, white, and Acadian children's speech patterns*. Unpublished manuscript, Mount St. Vincent University, Halifax, Nova Scotia.

Edwards, L. (1983). Curriculum modifications as a strategy for helping regular classroom behavior disordered students. In E. Meyen, G. Vergason, & R. Whelan (Eds.), *Promising practices for exceptional children: Curriculum implications* (pp. 87–104). Denver: Love.

Edwards, S., & Lafreniere, M. (1995). Hand function in the Down syndrome population. In A. Henderson & C. Pehoski (Eds.), *Hand function in the child: Foundations for remediation*. St. Louis, MO: Mosby.

Ehri, L. C., & Roberts, T. (2006). The roots of learning to read and write: The acquisition of letters and phonemic awareness. In D. K. Dickinson & S. B. Neuman (Eds.), *Handbook of early literacy* (pp. 113–134). New York: Guilford Press.

Eilers, R. E., & Oller, D. K. (1994). Infant vocalizations and the early diagnosis of severe hearing impairment. *Journal of Pediatrics*, 124, 199–203.

Eimas, P. D., & Tartter, V. C. (1979). On the development of speech perception. In H. W. Reese & L. P. Lipsitt (Eds.), *Advances in child development and behavior* (Vol. 13, pp. 155–193). New York: Academic Press.

Eisen, A., Schaefer C. E. (2005). *Separation anxiety in children and adolescents: An individualized approach*. New York: Guilford Press.

Eisenberg, N. (1986). *Altruistic emotion, cognition, and behavior*. Hillsdale, NJ: Erlbaum.

Eisenberg, N. (2000). Emotion, regulation, and moral development. *Annual Review of Psychology*, 51, 665–697.

Eisenberg, N., Fabes, R. A., Murphy, B., Karbon, M., Smith, M., & Maszk, P. (1996). The relations of children's dispositional empathy-related responding to their emotionality, regulation, and social functioning. *Developmental Psychology*, 32, 195–209.

Ekman, P. (1994). Strong evidence for universals in facial expressions: A reply to Russell's mistaken critique. *Psychological Bulletin*, 115, 268–287.

Elbro, C. I., Borstrom, I., & Peterson, P. (1998). Predicting dyslexia from kindergarten: The importance of directness of phonological respresentations of lexical items. *Reading Research Quarterly*, 3, 36–60.

Eley, T. C., Lichtenstein, P., & Stevenson, J. (1999). Sex differences in the etiology of aggressive and nonaggressive antisocial behavior: Results from two twin studies. *Child Development*, 70, 155–168.

Elfenbein, H. A., & Ambady, N. (2002). On the universality and cultural specificity of emotion recognition: A meta-analysis. *Psychological Bulletin*, 128, 203–235.

Elkind, D. (1987). *Miseducation: Preschoolers at risk*. New York: Knopf.

Elkind, D. (2007). *The hurried child*. Reading, MA: Addison-Wesley.

Elliott, E., Payne, J., Morris, A., Haan, E., & Bower, C. (2007). Fetal alcohol syndrome: A prospective national surveillance study. *Archives of Diseases in Childhood*, 17, 120–220.

Ellis, R. (1997). *Second language acquisition*. New York: Oxford University Press.

Else-Quest, N., Hyde, J., & Clark, R. (2003). Breastfeeding, bonding, and the mother-infant relationship. *Merrill-Palmer Quarterly*, 49, 495–517.

Ely, R. (2001). Language and literacy in the school years. In J. B. Gleason (Ed.), *The development of language* (pp. 301–349). Boston: Allyn & Bacon.

Endo, Y. (2007). Divisions in subjective construction of teasing incidents: Role and social skill level in the teasing function. *Japanese Psychological Research*, 49, 111–120.

Engle, P., Black, M., Behrman, J., Cabral de Mello, M., Gertler, P., Kapiriri, L., et al. (2007). Strategies to avoid the loss of developmental potential in more than 200 million children in the developing world. *The Lancet*, 369, 229–242.

Entwhistle, D. R. (1966). *Word association of young children*. Baltimore: Johns Hopkins University Press.

Enz, B., & Christie, J. (1997). Teacher play interaction styles: Effects on play behavior and relationships with teacher training and experience. *International Journal of Early Childhood Education*, 2, 55–75.

Erikson, E. H. (1963). *Childhood and society* (2nd ed.). New York: Norton.

Erikson, E. H. (1982). *The life cycle completed: A review*. New York: Norton.

Eron, L. D., & Huesmann, L. R. (1990). The stability of aggressive behavior: Even unto the third generation. In M. Lewis & S. M. Miller (Eds.), *Handbook of developmental psychopathology* (pp. 147–156). New York: Plenum.

Eskes, T. K. (1992). Home deliveries in the Netherlands: Perinatal mortality and morbidity. *International Journal of Gynecology and Obstetrics*, 38, 161–169.

Esposito, B. G., & Koorland, M. A. (1989). Play behavior of hearing impaired children: Integrated and segregated settings. *Exceptional Children*, 55, 412–419.

Evans, E. E. (1975). *Contemporary influences in early childhood education*. New York: Holt, Rinehart and Winston.

Evans, H. J., Fletcher, J., Torrance, M., & Hargreave, T. B. (1981). Sperm abnormalities and cigarette smoking. *Lancet*, 1, 627–629.

Ewen, D., & Matthews, H. (2007). *Families forgotten: Administration's priorities put child care low on the list*. Washington, DC: Center for Law and Social Policy.

Fabes, R. A., Leonard, S. A., Kupanoff, K., & Martin, C. L. (2001). Parental coping with children's negative emotions: Relations with children's emotional and social responding. *Child Development, 72*, 907–920.

Fabricius, W. V., & Cavalier, L. (1989). The role of causal theories about memory in young children's memory strategy choice. *Child Development, 60*, 298–308.

Fagot, B., & Leinbach, M. D. (1993). Gender–role development in young children. *Developmental Review, 13*, 205–224.

Fagot, B., & O'Brien, M. (1994). Activity level in young children. *Merrill-Palmer Quarterly, 40*, 378–398.

Fajardo, B. F., & Freedman, D. G. (1981). Maternal rhythmicity in three American cultures. In T. Field, A. Sostek, P. Vietze, & P. H. Leiderman (Eds.), *Culture and early interaction* (pp. 133–146). Hillsdale, NJ: Erlbaum.

Falbo, T. (1992). Social norms and the one-child family: Clinical and policy implications. In F. Boer & J. Dunn (Eds.), *Children's sibling relationships: Developmental and clinical issues* (pp. 71–82). Hillsdale, NJ: Lawrence Erlbaum Associates.

Falbo, T., & Poston, D. L. (1993). The academic, personality, and physical outcomes of only children in China. *Child Development, 64*, 18–35.

Fals-Stewart, W., Kelley, M., Cooke, C., & Golden, J. (2003). Predictors of the psychosocial adjustment of children living in households of parents in which fathers abuse drugs: The effects of postnatal parental exposure. *Addictive Behaviors, 28*, 1013–1031.

Fals-Stewart, W., Kelley, M., Fincham, F., Golden, J., & Logsdon, T. (2004). Emotional and behavioral problems of children living with drug-abusing fathers: Comparisons with children living with alcohol-abusing and non-substance-abusing fathers. *Journal of Family Psychology, 18*, 319–30.

Fantz, R. L. (1961). The origin of form perception. *Scientific American, 204*, 66–72.

Fantz, R. L. (1963). Pattern vision in newborn infants. *Science, 140*, 296–297.

Fantz, R. L., Fagan, J., & Miranda, S. (1975). Early visual selectivity. In L. Cohen & P. Salapatek (Eds.), *Infant perception: From sensation to cognition* (pp. 249–341). New York: Academic Press.

Farber, B., Mindel, C. H., & Lazerwitz, B. (1988). The Jewish American family. In C. H. Mindel, R. W. Habenstein, & R. Wright (Eds.), *Ethnic families in America: Patterns and variations* (pp. 400–437). New York: Elsevier.

Farrant, A., Boucher, J., & Blades, M. (1999). Metamemory and children with autism. *Child Development, 70*, 107–131.

Farrant, B., Fletcher, J., & Maybery, M. (2006). Specific language impairment, theory of mind, and visual perspective taking: Evidence for simulation theory and the developmental role of language. *Child Development, 77*, 1842–1853.

Farver, J. A., Kim, Y. K., & Lee-Shin, Y. (2000). Within cultural differences: Examining individual differences in Korean American and European American preschoolers' social pretend play. *Journal of Cross-Cultural Psychology, 31*, 583–602.

Farver, J. A. M., Kim, Y. K., & Lee, Y. (1995). Cultural differences in Korean- and Anglo-American preschoolers' social interaction and play behaviors. *Child Development, 66*, 1088–1099.

Farver, J. A. M., Natera, L. X., & Frosch, D. L. (2002). Effects of community violence on inner-city preschoolers and their families. In M. A. Paludi (Ed.), *Human development in multicultural contexts* (pp. 88–91). Upper Saddle River, NJ: Prentice Hall.

Farver, J., Xu, Y., Eppe, S., & Lonigan, C. (2006). Home environments and young Latino children's school readiness. *Early Childhood Research Quarterly, 21*, 196–212.

Fasulo, A., Loyd, H., & Padiglione, V. (2007). Children's socialization into cleaning practices: A cross-cultural perspective. *Discourse & Society, 18*, 11–33.

Fazzi, E., Lanners, J., Ferrari-Ginevra, O., Achille, C., Luparia, A., Signorini, S., et al. (2002). Gross motor development and reach on sound as critical tools for the development of the blind child. *Brain and Development, 24*, 269–275.

Feigenson, L., Dehaene, S., & Spelke, E. (2004). Core systems of number. *Trends in Cognitive Sciences, 8*, 307–314.

Fein, G., & Wiltz, N. (1998). Play as children see it. In D. Fromberg & D. Bergen (Eds.), *Play from birth to twelve and beyond* (pp. 37–49). New York: Garland.

Feingold, A. (1994). Gender differences in personality: A meta-analysis. *Psychological Bulletin, 116*, 429–456.

Feiring, C., & Lewis, M. (1989). The social network of girls and boys from early through middle childhood. In D. Belle (Ed.), *Children's social networks and social supports*. New York: John Wiley & Sons.

Feldman, D. H. (2004). Piaget's stages: The unfinished symphony of cognitive development. *New Ideas in Psychology, 22*, 175–231.

Feldman, R. (1998). *Child development*. Upper Saddle River, NJ: Prentice Hall.

Fenson, L. (1986). The developmental progression of play. In A. Gottfried & C. C. Brown (Eds.), *Play interactions: The contribution of play materials and parental involvement in children's development* (pp. 53–66). Lexington, MA: Heath.

Fenson, L., Dale, P. S., Reznick, J. S., Bates, E., Thal, D. J., & Pethick, S. J. (1994). Variability in early communicative development. *Monographs of the Society for Research in Child Development, 59* (5, Serial No. 242).

Ferber, S., Feldman, R., Kohelet, D., Kuint, J., Dollberg, S., Arbel, E., et al. (2005). Massage therapy facilitates mother–infant interaction in premature infants. *Infant Behavior and Development, 28*, 74–81.

Ferber, S., Feldman, R., & Makhoul, I. (2007). The development of maternal touch across the first year of life. *Early Human Development, 9*, 19–29.

Fergusson, D. M., Horwood, L. J., & Lynskey, M. T. (1993). Maternal smoking before and after pregnancy: Behavioral outcomes in middle childhood. *Pediatrics, 92*, 815–822.

Fernald, A. (1993). Approval and disapproval: Infant responsiveness to vocal affect in familiar and unfamiliar languages. *Child Development, 64*, 657–674.

Fernald, A., & Morikawa, H. (1993). Common themes and cultural variations in Japanese and American mothers' speech to infants. *Child Development, 64*, 637–656.

Fernyhough, C., & Fradley, E. (2005). Private speech on an executive task: Relations with task difficulty and task performance. *Cognitive Development, 20*, 103–120.

Ferreira, F., & Morrison, F. J. (1994). Children's metalinguistic knowledge of syntactical constituents: Effects of age and schooling. *Developmental Psychology, 30*, 663–678.

Ferreiro, E., & Teberosky, A. (1982). *Literacy before schooling*. Exeter, NH: Heinemann.

Fey, M. E., Windsor, J., & Warren, S. F. (Eds.). (1995). *Language intervention: Preschool through the elementary years*. Baltimore: Paul H. Brookes.

Field, M. (2001). Triadic directives in Navajo language socialization. *Language in Society, 30*, 249–263.

Field, T. M., & Widmayer, S. M. (1981). Mother-infant interactions among lower SES black, Cuban, Puerto Rican, and South American immigrants.

In T. M. Field, A. M. Sostek, P. Vietze, & P. H. Leiderman (Eds.), *Culture and early interactions* (pp. 41–60). Hillsdale, NJ: Erlbaum.

Fiese, B. H., Sameroff, A. J., Grotevant, H. D., Wamboldt, F. S., Dickstein, S., & Fravel, D. L. (Eds.). (1999). The stories that families tell: Narrative coherence, narrative interaction, and relationship beliefs. *Monographs of the Society for Research in Child Development, 64*, (Serial No. 257).

Figueroa, R. A. (1980). Field dependence, ethnicity, and cognitive styles. *Hispanic Journal of Behavioral Science, 2*, 10.

Filipek, P., Steinberg-Epstein, R., & Book, T. (2006). Intervention for autistic spectrum disorders. *NeuroRX, 3*, 207–216.

Filippi, V., Ronsmans, C., Campbell, O., Graham, W., Mills, A., Borghi, J. et al. (2006). Maternal health in poor countries: The broader context and a call for action. *The Lancet, 368*, 1535–1541.

Fillmore, M. W. (2005). When learning a second language means losing the first. In M. Suárez-Orozco, C. Suárez-Orozco, & D. Baolin Qin (Eds.), *The new immigration: An interdisciplinary reader* (pp. 289–308). London: Routledge.

Fincham, F. D., Hokoda, A., & Sanders, R. Jr. (1989). Learned helplessness, test anxiety, and academic achievement: A longitudinal analysis. *Child Development, 60*, 138–145.

Finkelhor, D. (2004). The main problem is underreporting child abuse and neglect. In R. Gelles, D. Loseke, R. Gelles, & M. Cavanaugh (Eds.), *Current controversies on family violence* (pp. 299–310). Thousand Oaks, CA: Sage.

Finkelhor, D., & Ormrod, R. (1999, November). *Juvenile Justice Bulletin*. Washington, DC: U.S. Department of Justice, Office of Juvenile Justice and Delinquency Prevention.

Finkelstein, M., Wamsley, M., & Miranda, D. (2002). *What keeps children in foster care from succeeding in school?* New York: Vera Institute of Justice.

Fish, A., Li, X., McCarrick, K., Butler, S., Stanton, B., Brumitt, G., et al. (2008). Early childhood computer experience and cognitive development among urban low-income preschoolers. *Journal of Educational Computing Research, 38*, 97–113.

Fisher, E. (1992). The impact of play on development: A meta-analysis. *Play and Culture, 5*, 159–181.

Fivush, R., Haden, C., & Reese, E. (2006). Elaborating on elaborations: Role of maternal reminiscing style in cognitive and socioemotional development. *Child Development, 77*, 1568–1588.

Fivush, R., & Nelson, K. (2004). Culture and language in the emergence of autobiographical memory. *Psychological Science, 15*, 573–577.

Flavell, J. (1992). Cognitive development: Past, present, and future. *Developmental Psychology, 28*, 998–1005.

Flavell, J. (1996). Piaget's legacy. *Psychological Science, 7*, 200–203.

Flavell, J. (2004). Theory-of-the-mind development: Retrospect and prospect. *Merrill Palmer Quarterly, 50*, 274–290.

Flavell, J., Beach, D., & Chinsky, J. (1966). Spontaneous verbal rehearsal in a memory task as a function of age. *Child Development, 37*, 283–299.

Flavell, J., Green, H. L., & Flavell, E. R. (1995). Young children's knowledge about thinking. *Monographs of the Society for Research in Child Development, 60*(1, Serial No. 243).

Flavell, J., Miller, P. H., & Miller, S. A. (1993). *Cognitive development*. Hillsdale, NJ: Erlbaum.

Flavell, J. H. (1999). Cognitive development: Children's knowledge about the mind. *Annual Review of Psychology, 50*, 21–45.

Flegal, K. M., Ogden, C. L., & Carroll, M. D. (2004). Prevalence and trends in overweight Mexican–American adults and children. *Nutrition Reviews, 62*, 144–148.

Fletcher, K., & Reese, E. (2005). Picture book reading with young children: A conceptual framework. *Developmental Review, 25,* 64–103.

Flood, J., Heath, S. B., & Lapp, D. (1997). *Handbook of research on teaching literacy through the visual and communicative arts.* Cambridge, MA: Harvard University Press.

Flores, G., Tomany-Korman, S., & Olson, L. (2005). Does disadvantage start at home? Racial and ethnic disparities in health-related early childhood home routines and safety practices. *Archives of Pediatric and Adolescent Medicine, 159,* 158–165.

Flouri, E., & Buchanan, A. (2003). The role of father involvement in children's later mental health. *Journal of Adolescence, 26,* 63–78.

Floyd, R. L., Rimer, B. K., Giovino, G. A., Mullen, P. D., & Sullivan, S. E. (1993). A review of smoking in pregnancy. *Annual Review of Public Health, 14,* 379–411.

Fonagy, P., Gergely, G., & Target, M. (2007). The parent-infant dyad and the construction of the subjective self. *Journal of Child Psychology and Psychiatry, 48,* 288–328.

Ford, K., & Labbock, M. (1993). Breastfeeding and child health in the United States. *Journal of Biosocial Science, 25,* 187–194.

Fosnot, C. T. (1996). Constructivism: A psychological theory of learning. In C. T. Fosnot (Ed.), *Constructivism: Theory, perspectives, and practice* (pp. 1–20). New York: Teachers College Press.

Fountas, I., & Pinnell, G. (1996). *Guided reading: Good first teaching for all children.* Portsmouth, NH: Heinemann.

Fox, D. J., & Jordan, V. B. (1973). Racial preference and identification of Black American, Chinese, and White children. *Genetic Psychology Monographs, 88,* 229–286.

Fox, N. A., Kimmerly, N. L., & Schafer, W. D. (1991). Attachment to mother/attachment to father: A meta-analysis. *Child Development, 62,* 210–225.

Fraiberg, S. (1977). *Insights from the blind: Comparative studies of blind and sighted infants.* New York: Basic Books.

Fraley, R. C. (2002). Attachment stability from infancy to adulthood: Meta-analysis and dynamic modeling of developmental mechanisms. *Personality and Social Psychology Review, 6,* 123–151.

Franceschini, M. Thaker, S., Themelis, G., Krishnamoorthy, K., Bortfeld, H., Diamond, S., et al. (2007). Assessment of infant brain development with frequency-domain near-infrared spectroscopy. *Pediatric Research, 61,* 546–551.

Frankland, H., & Turnbull, A. P. (2004). An exploration of the self–determination construct and disability as it relates to the din (Navajo) Culture. *Education and Training in Developmental Disabilities, 39,* 191–205.

Franklin, A., Pilling, M., & Davies, I. (2005). The nature of infant color categorization: Evidence from eye movements on a target detection task. *Journal of Experimental Child Psychology, 91,* 227–248.

Frary, C., Johnson, R., & Wang, M. (2004). Children and adolescents' choices of foods and beverages high in added sugars are associated with intakes of key nutrients and food groups. *Journal of Adolescent Health, 34,* 56–63.

Fraser, A. M., Brockert, J. E., & Ward, R. H. (1995). Association of young maternal age with adverse reproductive outcomes. *New England Journal of Medicine, 332,* 113–117.

Frederickson, N., Simmonds, E., Evans, L., & Soulsby, C. (2007). Assessing the social and affective outcomes of inclusion. *British Journal of Special Education, 34,* 105–115.

Freedman, D. G. (1974). *Human infancy: An evolutionary perspective.* Hillsdale, NJ: Erlbaum.

Freedman, D. G. (1979). Ethnic differences in babies. *Human Nature, 2,* 36–43.

Freeman, N. K. (2007). Preschoolers' perceptions of gender appropriate toys and their parents' beliefs about genderized behaviors: Miscommunication, mixed messages, or hidden truths? *Early Childhood Education Journal, 34,* 357–366.

French, B., & Mantzicopoulos, P. (2007). An examination of the first/second-grade form of the pictorial scale of perceived competence and social acceptance: Factor structure and stability by grade and gender across groups of economically disadvantaged children. *Journal of School Psychology, 45,* 311–331.

French, D. C. (1990). Heterogeneity of peer-rejected girls. *Child Development, 61,* 2028–2031.

Freud, S. (1930). *Civilization and its discontents.* London: Hogarth.

Freud, S. (1938). The history of the psychoanalytic movement. In A. A. Brill (Ed.), *The basic writings of Sigmund Freud.* New York: Modern Library.

Freund, L. S. (1990). Maternal regulation of children's problem solving behavior and its impact on children's performance. *Child Development, 61,* 113–126.

Frick, J. E., Colombo, J., & Saxon, T. F. (1999). Individual and developmental differences in disengagement of fixation in early infancy. *Child Development, 70,* 537–548.

Friedman, J. M., & Polifka, J. E. (1996). *Effects of drugs on the fetus and nursing infant.* Baltimore: Johns Hopkins University Press.

Friedman, W. J., & Laycock, F. (1989). Children's analog and digital clock knowledge. *Child Development, 60,* 357–371.

Frodi, A. M., & Senchak, M. (1990). Verbal and behavioral responsiveness to the cries of a typical infants. *Child Development, 61,* 76–84.

Frost, J. L., Wortham, S., & Reifel, S. (2008). *Play and child development.* Columbus, OH: Merrill.

Frostad, P., & Pijl, S. (2007). Does being friendly help in making friends? The relation between the social position and social skills of pupils with special needs in mainstream education. *European Journal of Special Needs Education, 22,* 15–30.

Fuchs, D., & Fuchs, L. S. (1986). Test procedure bias: A meta-analysis of examiner familiarity effects. *Review of Educational Research, 56,* 243–262.

Fuligni, A. J. (1997). The academic achievement of adolescents from immigrant families: The roles of family background, attitudes, and behavior. *Child Development, 68,* 351–363.

Fuligni, A. J., Witkow M., & Garcia, C. (2005). Ethnic identity and the academic adjustment of adolescents from Mexican, Chinese, and European backgrounds. *Developmental Psychology, 41,* 799–811.

Fuller, B., Holloway, S. D., & Liang, X. (1996). Family selection of child care centers: The influence of household support, ethnicity, and parental practices. *Child Development, 67,* 3320–3337.

Fuller, B., Kagan, S., Caspary, G., & Gauthier, C. (2002). Welfare reform and child care options for low-income families. *The Future of Children, 12,* 97–119.

Fuller-Thomson, E., & Minkler, M. (2002). American grandparents providing extensive child care to their and grandchildren.*The Gerontologist, 41,* 201–209.

Furnham, A., & Davis, S. (2004). Involvement of social factors in stuttering: A review and assessment of current methodology. *Stammering Research, 1,* 112–122.

Furstenberg, F. F., & Cherlin, A. J. (1991). *Divided families: What happens to children when parents part.* Cambridge, MA: 2005 Harvard University Press.

Fusarelli, L. D. (2004). The potential impact of the No Child Left Behind Act on equity and diversity in American education. *Educational Policy, 18,* 71–94.

Fuson, K. C., & Kwon, Y. (1992). Korean children's understanding of multidigit addition and subtraction. *Child Development, 63,* 491–506.

Gable, S., Chang, Y., & Krull, J. (2007). Television watching and frequency of family meals are predictive of overweight onset and persistence in a national sample of school-aged children. *Journal of the American Dietetic Association, 107,* 53–61.

Gadeyne, E., Ghesquière, P., & Onghena, P. (2004). Psychosocial functioning of young children with learning problems. *Journal of Child Psychology and Psychiatry, 45,* 510–521.

Gallahue, D. L., & Ozmun, J. C. (2006). Motor development in young children. In B. Spodek & O. Saracho (Eds.), *Handbook of research on the education of young children* (pp. 105–120). London: Routledge.

Galton Bachrach, V. R., Schwarz, E., & Bachrach, L. (2003). Breastfeeding and the risk of hospitalization for respiratory diseases in infancy: A metaanalysis. *Archives of Pediatric and Adolescent Medicine, 157,* 237–243.

Gamble, W. C., & Modry-Mandell, K. (2008). Family relations and the adjustment of young children of Mexican descent: Do family cultural values moderate these associations? *Social Development, 17,* 358–379.

Gamé, F., Carchon, I., & Vital-Durand, F. (2003). The effect of stimulus attractiveness on visual tracking in 2- to 6-month-old infants. *Infant Behavior and Development, 26,* 135–150.

Gandini, L. (1997a). Foundations of the Reggio Emilia approach. In J. Hendrick (Ed.), *First steps toward teaching the Reggio way* (pp. 14–23). Upper Saddle River, NJ: Merrill/Prentice Hall.

Gandini, L. (1997b). The Reggio Emilia story: History and organization. In J. Hendrick (Ed.), *First steps toward teaching the Reggio way* (pp. 2–13). Upper Saddle River, NJ: Merrill/ Prentice Hall.

Gandour, M. J. (1989). Activity level as a dimension of temperament in toddlers. *Child Development, 60,* 1092–1098.

Gandara, P., Maxwell-Jolly, J., Garcia, E., Asato, J., Gutierrez, K., Stritikus, T., et al. (2000). *The initial impact of Proposition 227 on the instruction of English learners.* Davis: University of California Linguistic Minority Research Institute.

Ganz, J., Simpson, R., & Corbin-Newsome, J. (2008). The impact of the Picture Exchange Communication System on requesting and speech development in preschoolers with autism spectrum disorders and similar characteristics. *Research in Autism Spectrum Disorders, 2,* 157–169.

Garbarino, J., Dubrow, N., Kostelny, K., & Pardo, C. (1992). *Children in danger.* San Francisco: Jossey-Bass.

Garbarino, J., & Kostelny, K. (1993). Neighborhood and community influences on parenting. In T. Luster & L. Okagaki (Eds.), *Parenting: An ecological perspective.* Hillsdale, NJ: Erlbaum.

Garbarino, J., & Kostelny, K. (1996). The effects of political violence on Palestinian children's behavior problems: A risk accumulation model. *Child Development, 67,* 33–45.

Garces, E., Thomas, D., & Curry, J. (2000). *Longer term effects of head start.* Santa Monica, CA: Rand.

Garcia, E. E. (Ed.). (1983). *The Mexican-American child: Language, cognition, and social development.* Tempe: Arizona State University.

Garcia Coll, C. T. (1990). Developmental outcome of minority infants: A process-oriented look into our beginnings. *Child Development, 61,* 270–289.

Garcia Coll, C. T., Hoffman, J., & Oh, W. (1987). The social ecology and early parenting of Caucasian adolescent mothers. *Child Development, 58,* 955–963.

Garcia Coll, C. T., Meyer, E. C., & Brillon, L. (1995). Ethnic and minority parenting. In M. H. Bornstein (Ed.), *Handbook of parenting* (Vol. 2, pp. 189–209). Mahwah, NJ: Erlbaum.

Garcia Coll, C. T., & Pachter, L.M. (2002). Ethnic and minority parenting. In M. Bornstein (Ed.), *Handbook of parenting* (Vol. 4, pp. 1–20). Mahwah, NJ: Erlbaum.

Garcia Coll, C. T., Sepkoski, C., & Lester, B. M. (1981). Cultural and biomedical correlates of neonatal behavior. *Developmental Psychobiology, 14,* 147–154.

Garcia Coll, C. T., Surrey, J. L., & Weingarten, K. (Eds.). (1998). *Mothering against the odds.* New York: Guilford Press.

Gardner, H. (1993). *Frames of Mind: The Theory of Multiple Intelligences.* Jackson, TN: Perseus Books Group.

Gardner, H. (1998). Are there additional intelligences? The case for naturalist, spiritual, and existential intelligences. In J. Kane (Ed.), *Education, information, and transformation.* Englewood Cliffs, NJ: Prentice Hall.

Gardner, H. (2000). *The disciplined mind.* New York: Penguin Books.

Gardner, H. (2006). *Multiple intelligences: New horizons.* New York: Basic Books.

Garner, B. P. (1998). Play development from birth to age four. In D. Fromberg & D. Bergen (Eds.), *Play from birth to twelve and beyond* (pp. 137–145). New York: Garland.

Garner, P. W., Jones, D. C., & Miner, J. L. (1994). Social competence among low-income preschoolers: Emotion socialization practices and social cognitive correlates. *Child Development, 65,* 622–637.

Garner, P. W., & Lemerise, E. A. (2007). The roles of behavioral adjustment and conceptions of peers and emotions in preschool children's peer victimization. *Development and Psychopathology, 19,* 57–71.

Garrard, W., & Lipsey, M. (2007). Conflict resolution education and antisocial behavior in U.S. schools: A meta-analysis. *Conflict Resolution Quarterly, 25,* 9–38.

Garrett, P., Ng'andu, N., & Ferron, J. (1994). Poverty experiences of young children and the quality of their home environments. *Child Development, 65,* 331–345.

Garvey, C. (1977). Play with language and speech. In S. Ervin-Tripp & C. Mitchell-Kernan (Eds.), *Child discourse.* New York: Academic Press.

Garvey, C. (1990). *Play.* Cambridge, MA: Harvard University Press.

Gathercole, S., Pickering, S., Ambridge, B., & Wearing, H. (2004). The structure of working memory from 4 to 15 years of age. *Developmental Psychology, 40,* 177–190.

Geary, D., Bow-Thomas, C., Liu, F., & Siegler, R. (1996). Development of arithmetical competencies in Chinese and American children: Influence of age, language, and schooling. *Child Development, 67,* 2022–2044.

Gelman, S. A., & Gottfried, G. M. (1996). Children's causal explanation of animate and inanimate motion. *Child Development, 67,* 1970–1987.

Gelman, S. A., & Kremer, K. E. (1991). Understanding natural cause: Children's explanations of how objects and their properties originate. *Child Development, 62,* 396–414.

Gelman, S. A., & Williams, E. M. (1997). Enabling constraints for cognitive development and learning: Domain-specificity and epigenesis. In D. Kuhn & R. S. Siegler (Eds.), *Handbook of child psychology: Cognition, perception and language* (Vol. 2). New York: John Wiley & Sons.

Genesee, F., & Nicoladis, E. (2007). Bilingual first language acquisition. In E. Hoff & M. Shatz (Eds.), *Handbook of language development* (pp. 324–342). Cambridge, MA: Blackwell.

Genyue, F., Xu, F., Cameron, C., Heyman, G., & Lee, K. (2007). Cross-cultural differences in children's choices, categorizations, and evaluations of truths and lies. *Developmental Psychology, 43,* 278–293.

George, D. M., & Hoppe, R. A. (1979). Racial identification, preference, and self-concept. *Journal of Cross-Cultural Psychology, 10,* 85–100.

George, T. P., & Hartmann, D. P. (1996). Friendship networks of unpopular, average, and popular children. *Child Development, 67,* 2301–2316.

Gepshtein, Y., Horiuchi, S., & Eto, H. (2007). Independent Japanese midwives: A qualitative study of their practise and beliefs. *Japan Journal of Nursing Science, 4,* 85–93.

Gerken, L. A. (2007). Acquiring linguistic structure. In E. Hoff & M. Shatz (Eds.), *Handbook of language development* (pp. 173–190). Cambridge, MA: Blackwell.

Germo, G. R., Chang, E. S., Keller, M. A., & Goldberg, W. A. (2007). Child sleep arrangement and family life: Perspectives from mothers and fathers. *Infant and Child Development, 16,* 433–456.

Gesell, A. (1933). The Maturation and the patterning of behavior. In C. Murchison (Ed.), *Handbook of child psychology.* Worcester, MA: Clark University Press.

Gesell, A., & Ilg, F. L. (1949). *Child development.* New York: Harper & Row.

Gesell, A., & Thompson, H. (1929). Learning and growth in identical infant twins: An experiment by the method of co-twin control. *Genetic Psychology Monographs, 6,* 1–124.

Gest, S., Farmer, T., Cairns, B., & Xie, H. (2003). Identifying children's peer social networks in school classrooms: Links between peer reports and observed interactions. *Social Development, 12,* 513–529.

Gewirtz, A., Hart-Shegos, E., & Medhanie, A. (2008). Psychosocial status of homeless children and youth in family supportive housing. *American Behavioral Scientist, 51,* 810–823.

Gibbs, D. (2007). *Understanding foster parenting: Using administrative data to explore retention.* Research Triangle Park, NC: RTI International.

Gibbs, J. C., Basinger, K., Grime, R., & Snarey, J. (2007). Moral judgment development across cultures: Revisiting Kohlberg's universality claims. *Developmental Review, 27,* 443–500.

Gibbs, J. C., Potter, G. B., & Goldstein, A. P. (1995). *The EQUIP program: Teaching youth to think and act responsibly through a peer helping approach.* Champaign, IL: Research Press.

Gibbs, J. T., & Huang, L. N. (1997). *Children of color: Psychological interventions with minority youth.* San Francisco: Jossey-Bass.

Gibson, E. J., & Walk, R. D. (1960, April). The visual cliff. *Scientific American,* 64–71.

Gifford-Smith, M., & Brownell, C. (2003). Childhood peer relationships: Social acceptance, friendships, and peer networks. *Journal of School Psychology, 41,* 235–284.

Gilbride, S., Wild, C., Wilson, D., Svenson, L., & Spady, D. (2006). Socio-economic status and types of childhood injury. *Pediatrics, 6,* 1–30.

Gillberg, C., Melander, H., von Knorring, A. L., Janols, L. O., Thernlund, G., Hagglof, B., et al. (1997). Long-term stimulant treatment of children with attention-deficit hyperactivity disorder symptoms: A randomized, double-blind, placebo-controlled trial. *Archives of General Psychiatry, 54,* 857–864.

Gilliam, W. S., & Zigler, E. F. (2001). A critical meta-analysis of all evaluations of state-funded preschool from 1977 to 1998. *Early Childhood Research Quarterly, 15,* 437–440.

Gilligan, C. (1993a). *In a different voice: Psychological theory and women's development.* Cambridge, MA: Harvard University Press.

Gilligan, C. (1993b). Adolescent development reconsidered. In A. Garrod (Ed.), *Approaches to moral development: New research and emerging themes.* New York: Teachers College Press.

Gilligan, C., Brown, L. M., & Rogers, A. G. (1990). Psyche imbedded: A place for body, relationships,

and culture in personality formation. In A. J. Rabin, R. A. Zucker, R. A. Emmons, & S. Frank (Eds.), *Studying persons and lives.* New York: Springer.

Gilligan, C., Murphy, J. M., & Tappan, M. B. (1990). Moral development beyond adolescence. In C. N. Alexander & E. J. Langer (Eds.), *Higher stages of human development* (pp. 41–116). New York: Oxford University Press.

Gillon, G. (2004). *Phonological awareness: From research to practice.* New York: Guilford Publications.

Ginsburg, G. S., & Bronstein, P. (1993). Family factors related to children's intrinsic/extrinsic motivational orientation and academic performance. *Child Development, 64,* 1461–1474.

Girolametto, L., Sussman, F., & Weitzman, E. (2007). Using case study methods to investigate the effects of interactive intervention for children with autism spectrum disorders. *Journal of Communication Disorders, 40,* (6), 470–492.

Girolametto, L., Weitzman, E., & Clements-Baartman, J. (1998). Vocabulary intervention for children with Down syndrome: Parent training using focused stimulation. *Infant-Toddler Intervention: The Transdisciplinary Journal, 8,* 109–125.

Glasgow, K., Dornbusch, S., Troyer, L., Steinberg, L., & Ritter, P. (1997). Parenting styles, adolescents' attributions, and educational outcomes in nine heterogeneous high schools. *Child Development, 68,* 507–529.

Glass, R. M. (2003). Awareness about depression: Important for all physicians. *JAMA, 18,* 3169–3170.

Gleason, J. J. (1990). Meaning of play: Interpreting patterns of behavior of persons with severe developmental disabilities. *Anthropology and Education Quarterly, 21,* 59–77.

Gleitman, L. R., & Gleitman, H. (1992). A picture is worth a thousand words, but that's the problem: The role of syntax in vocabulary acquisition. *Current Directions in Psychological Science, 1,* 31–35.

Glenn, S. M., Cunningham, C. C., & Joyce, P. F. (1981). A study of auditory preferences in non-handicapped infants and infants with Down syndrome. *Child Development, 52,* 1303–1307.

Gmitrova, V., Podhajecká, M., & Gmitrov, J. (2007). Children's play preferences: Implications for the preschool education. *Early Child Development and Care, 177,* 300–333.

Goduka, I. N., Poole, D. A., & Aotaki-Phenice, L. (1992). A comparative study of black South African children from three different contexts. *Child Development, 63,* 500–525.

Gold, R., Kennedy, B., Connell, F., & Kawachi, I. (2002). Teen births, income inequality, and social capital: Developing an understanding of the causal pathway. *Health & Place, 8,* 77–83.

Goldberg, S. (1977). Infant development and mother-infant interaction in urban Zambia. In P. H. Leiderman, S. R. Tulkin, & A. Rosenfeld (Eds.), *Culture and infancy: Variations in the human experience.* New York: Academic Press.

Goldberg, S., Marcovitch, S., MacGregor, D., & Lojkasek, M. (1986). Family responses to developmentally delayed preschoolers: Etiology and the father's role. *American Journal of Mental Deficiency, 90,* 610–617.

Goldenberg, R. L. (1995). Small for gestational age infants. In B. P. Sachs, R. Beard, E. Papiernik, & C. Russell (Eds.), *Reproductive health care for women and babies* (pp. 391–339). New York: Oxford University Press.

Goldfield, B. A., & Snow, C. E. (2001). Individual differences: Implications for the study of language acquisition. In J. B. Gleason (Ed.), *The development of language* (pp. 315–346). Boston: Allyn & Bacon.

Goldin-Meadow, S. (2000). Beyond words: The importance of gesture to researchers and learners. *Child Development, 71,* 231–239.

509

Goldin-Meadow, S., & Morford, M. (1985). Gesture in early language: Studies of deaf and hearing children. *Merrill-Palmer Quarterly, 31,* 145–176.

Goldin-Meadow, S., Mylander, C., & Butcher, C. (1995). The resilience of combinatorial structure at the word level: Morphology in self-styled gesture systems. *Cognition, 56,* 195–262.

Goldman, R. M., & Fristoe, M. (1986). *The Goldman-Fristoe test of articulation.* Circle Pines, MN: American Guidance Service.

Goldsmith, H. H., Buss, K. A., & Lemery, K. S. (1997). Toddler and childhood temperament: Expanded content, stronger genetic evidence, new evidence for the importance of environment. *Developmental Psychology, 33,* 891–905.

Goldsmith, H. H., Lemery-Chalfant, K., Schmidt, N., Arneson, C., & Schmidt, C. (2007). Longitudinal analyses of affect, temperament, and childhood psychopathology. *Twin Research and Human Genetics, 10,* 118–126.

Goldstein, D., Cohn, E., & Coster, W. (2004). Enhancing participation for children with disabilities: Application of the ICF enablement framework to pediatric physical therapist practice. *Pediatric Physical Therapy, 16,* 114–120.

Golomb, C. (2007). Representational conceptions in two- and three-dimensional media: A developmental perspective. *Psychology of Aesthetics, Creativity, and the Arts, 1,* 32–39

Goncu, A. (1993). Development of intersubjectivity in the dyadic play of preschoolers. *Early Childhood Research Quarterly, 8,* 99–116.

Gonzalez, V. (Ed.). (1999). *Language and cognitive development in second language learning.* Boston: Allyn & Bacon.

Gonzalez-Mena, J. (2008). *Diversity in early care and education.* Washington, DC: NAEYC.

Goodman, S. H., Brogan, D., Lynch, M. E., & Fielding, B. (1993). Social and emotional competence in children of depressed mothers. *Child Development, 64,* 516–531.

Goodnow, J., & Collins, W. (1990). *Development according to parents: The nature, sources, and consequences of parent ideas.* Hillsdale, NJ: Erlbaum.

Gopnik, A., & Choi, S. (1990). Do linguistic differences lead to cognitive differences? *First Language, 10,* 199–215.

Gopnik, A., & Choi, S. (1995). *Beyond names for things: Young children's acquisition of verbs.* Hillsdale, NJ: Erlbaum.

Gopnik, A., Choi, S., & Baumberger, T. (1996). Cross-linguistic differences in early semantic and cognitive development. *Cognitive Development, 11,* 197–227.

Gordon, A., El Ahmer, O., Chan, R., Al Madani, O., Braun, J., Weir, D., Busuttil, A., & Blackwell, C., et al. (2002). Why is smoking a risk factor to for Sudden Infant Death Syndrome? *Child Care, Health, and Development, 28,* 23–25.

Gottfried, G., & Gelman, S. (2005). Developing domain-specific causal-explanatory frameworks: The role of insides and immanence. *Cognitive Development, 20/*(1), 137–158.

Graham, L. (2006). From ABCs to ADHD: The role of schooling in the construction of behaviour disorder and production of disorderly objects. *International Journal of Inclusive Education, 12,* 7–33.

Grantham-McGregor, S., Cheung, Y., Cueto, S., Glewwe, P., Richter, L., & Strupp, B. (2007). Developmental potential in the first 5 years for children in developing countries. *The Lancet, 369,* 60–70.

Grantham-McGregor, S., Powell, C., Walker, S., Chang, S., & Fletcher, P. (1994). The long-term follow-up of severely malnourished children who participated in an intervention program. *Child Development, 65,* 428–439.

Grantham-McGregor, S., Walker, S., & Chang, S. (2000). Nutritional deficiencies and later behavioural development. *Proceedings of the Nutrition Society, 59,* 47–54.

Graves, D. H. (2003). *Writing: Teachers and children at work.* Portsmouth, NH: Heinemann.

Gray, D. (2008). *Counting Eskimo words for snow.* Cambridge: Language in Use.

Green, J. A., Jones, L. E., & Gustafson, G. E. (1987). Perception of cries by parents and nonparents: Relation to cry acoustics. *Developmental Psychology, 23,* 370–382.

Greenbaum, C., & Landau, R. (1982). The infant's exposure to talk by familiar people: Mothers, fathers, and siblings in different environments. In M. Lewis & I. Rosenblum (Eds.), *The social network of the developmenting infant,* (pp. 229–247). New York: Plenum.

Greenberger, E., & Chen, C. (1996). Perceived family relationships and depressed mood in early and late adolescence: A comparison of European and Asian Americans. *Developmental Psychology, 32,* 707–716.

Greene, J., & Haidt, J. (2002). How (and where) does moral judgment work? *Trends in Cognitive Sciences, 6,* 517–523.

Greenfield, P. M. (1966). On culture and conservation. In J. S. Bruner, R. R. Oliver, & P. M. Greenfield (Eds.), *Studies in cognitive development* (pp. 225–256). New York: John Wiley & Sons.

Greenfield, P. M. (1995, Winter). Profile: On teaching, culture, ethnicity, race, and development. *Society for Research in Child Development Newsletter,* 3–4, 12.

Greenfield, P. M., Keller, H., Fuligni, A., & Maynard, A. (2003). Cultural pathways through universal development. *Annual Review of Psychology, 54,* 461–490.

Greydanus, J. (2004). Student preferences for teaching styles: Gender, student achievement levels, ethnicity. In L. McCoy (Ed.), *Studies in teaching: 2004 research digest* (pp. 53–64). Winston-Salem, NC: Wake Forrest University.

Gribble, K. D. (2007). A model for caregiving of adopted children after institutionalization. *Journal of Child and Adolescent Psychiatric Nursing, 20,* 14–26.

Griffith, D. R., Azuma, S. D., & Chasnoff, I. J. (1994). Three year outcome of children exposed prenatally to drugs. *Journal of the Academy of Child and Adolescent Psychiatry, 33,* 20–27.

Grogan-Kaylor, A. (2005). Corporal punishment and the growth trajectory of children's antisocial behavior. *Child Maltreatment, 10,* 283–292.

Groome, L. J., Swiber, M. J., Atterbury, J. L., Bentz, L. S., & Holland, S. B. (1997). Similarities and differences in behavioral state organization during sleep periods in the perinatal infant before and after birth. *Child Development, 68,* 1–11.

Gros–Louis, J., West, M., Goldstein, A., & King, A. (2006). Mothers provide differential feed back to infants' prelinguistic sounds. *International Journal of Behavioral Development, 30,* 509–516.

Gross, M. (2003). *Exceptionally gifted children.* London: Routledge.

Grossmann, K., Grossmann, K. E., Fremmer-Bombik, E., Kindler, H., Scheuerer-Englisch, H., & Zimmermann, P. (2002). The uniqueness of the child-father attachment relationship: Fathers' sensitive and challenging play as a pivotal variable in a 16-year longitudinal study. *Social Development, 11,* 301–337.

Grossmann, K., Grossmann, K. E., Spangler, S., Suess, G., & Unzner, L. (1985). Maternal sensitivity and newborn responses as related to quality of attachment in Northern Germany. In I. Bretherton & E. Waters, *Growing points in attachment theory. Monographs of the Society for Research in Child Development, 50,* (Serial No. 209).

Grove, N., Cusick, B., & Bigge, J. (1991). Conditions resulting in physical disabilities. In J. Bigge (Ed.), *Teaching individuals with physical and multiple disabilities* (pp. 1–15). Upper Saddle River, NJ: Merrill/Prentice Hall.

Guisande, M., Tinajero, M., & Almeida, L. (2007). Field dependence–independence (FDI) cognitive style: An analysis of attentional functioning. *Psicothema, 19,* 572–577.

Grund, A., Krause, H., Siewers, M., Rieckert, H., & Müller, M. (2001). Television watching and frequency of family meals is predictive of overweight onset and persistence in a national sample of school-aged children. *Journal of the American Dietetic Association, 107,* 53–61.

Gunderson, L. (1991). *ESL literacy instruction: A guidebook to theory and practice.* Upper Saddle River, NJ: Regents/Prentice Hall.

Gunnar, M. R. (1996). *Quality of care and buffering of stress physiology: Its potential for protecting the developing human brain.* Minneapolis: University of Minnesota Institute of Child Development.

Guntheroth, W. G., Lohmann, R., & Spiers, P. S. (1990). Risk of Sudden Infant Death Syndrome in subsequent siblings. *Journal of Pediatrics, 116,* 520–524.

Guralnick, M. J. (1993). Developmentally appropriate practice in the assessment and intervention of children's peer relations. *Topics in Early Childhood Special Education, 13,* 344–371.

Guralnick, M. J. (2005). Early intervention for children with intellectual disabilities: Current knowledge and future prospects. *Journal of Applied Research in Intellectual Disabilities, 18,* 313–324.

Güroğlu, B., van Lieshout, C., Haselager, G., & Scholte, R. (2007). Similarity and complementarity of behavioral profiles of friendship types and types of friends: Friendships and psychosocial adjustment. *Journal of Research on Adolescence, 17,* 357–386.

Gushurst, C. A. (2003). Child abuse: Behavioral aspects and other associated problems. *Pediatric Clinics of North America, 50,* 919–938.

Gustafson, G. E., & Harris, K. L. (1990). Women's responses to young infants' cries. *Developmental Psychology, 26,* 144–152.

Gustafson, G. E, Wood, R., & Green, J. (2000), Can we hear the causes of infant crying? In R. Barr, B. Hopkins, & J. Green (Eds.), *Crying as a sign, a symptom, and a signal.* Cambridge: Cambridge University Press.

Guthrie, H. (1986). *Introductory nutrition.* St. Louis: Times Mirror/Mosby.

Guthrie, J. T., Cox, K. E., Anderson, E., Harris, K., Mazzoni, S., & Rach, L. (1998). Principles of integrated instruction for engagement in reading. *Educational Psychology Review, 10,* 177–199.

Gutman, L., McLoyd, V., & Tokoyawa, T. (2005). Financial strain, neighborhood stress, parenting behaviors, and adolescent adjustment in urban African American families. *Journal of Research on Adolescence, 15,* 425–449.

Haby, M., Vos, T., Carter, R., Moodie, M., Mar Wick, A., Magnus, A., Tay–Teo, V., & Swinburn, B. (2006). A new approach to assessing the health benefit from obesity interventions in children and adolescents: The assessing cost–effectiveness in obesity project. *International Journal of Obesity, 30,* 1463–1475.

Hack, M., Klein, N. K., & Taylor, H. G. (1995). Long-term developmental outcomes of low birth weight infants. In *The future of children: Low birth weight* (pp. 176–197). Los Altos, CA: The David and Lucille Packard Foundation.

Hagan, L., & Kuebli, J. (2007). Mothers' and fathers' socialization of preschoolers' physical risk taking. *Journal of Applied Developmental Psychology, 28,* 2–14.

Hagerman, R. J. (1996). Biomedical advances in developmental psychology: The case of Fragile X syndrome. *Developmental Psychology, 32,* 416–424.

Haight, W., & Black, J. (2001). A comparative approach to play: Cross-species and cross-cultural perspectives of play in development. *Human Development, 44,* 228–234.

Haight, W. L., Wang, X., Fung, H., Williams, K., & Mintz, J. (1999). Universal, developmental, and variable aspects of young children's play: A cross-cultural comparison of pre-tending at home. *Child Development, 70,* 1477–1488.

Haith, M. M. (1990). Progress in the understanding of sensory and perceptual processes in early infancy. *Merrill-Palmer Quarterly, 36,* 1–26.

Hale, J. (1994). *Unbank the fire: Visions for the education of African-American children.* Baltimore: Johns Hopkins University Press.

Hale, J. (2001). *Learning while black: Creating educational excellence for African American children.* Baltimore: Johns Hopkins University Press.

Hale-Benson, J. E. (1986). *Black children: Their roots, culture, and learning styles.* Baltimore: Johns Hopkins University Press.

Halford, G. S., Maybery, M. T., O'Hare, A. W., & Grant, P. (1994). The development of memory and processing capacity. *Child Development, 65,* 1338–1356.

Halford, J., Gillespie, J., Brown, V., Pontin, E., & Dovey, T. M. (2004). Effect of television advertisements for foods on food consumption in children. *Appetite, 42,* 221–225.

Halgunseth, L. C. (2004). Continuing research on Latino families. In M. Coleman, & L. H. Ganong (Eds.), *Handbook of contemporary families: Considering the past, contemplating the future* (pp. 333–351). Thousand Oaks, CA: Sage.

Hall, C. (2006). Self-reported aggression and the perception of anger in facial expression photos. *The Journal of Psychology: Interdisciplinary and Applied, 140,* 255–267.

Hall, D. G., & Graham, S. A. (1999). Lexical form class information guides word-to-object mapping in preschoolers. *Child Development, 70,* 78–91.

Hall, G. S. (1893). *The content of children's minds.* New York: Kellogg.

Hall, W. S., Bartlett, E., & Hughes, A. T. (1988). Patterns of information requests. In D. Slaughter (Ed.), *Black children and poverty: A developmental perspective* (pp. 11–28). San Francisco: Jossey-Bass.

Hallinan, M., & Sorenson, A. (1983). The formation and stability of instructional groups. *American Sociological Review, 48,* 838–851.

Hallinan, M., & Teixeira, R. A. (1987). Opportunities and constraints: Black-white differences in the formation of interracial friendships. *Child Development, 58,* 1358–1371.

Hamilton, B., Miniño, A., Martin, J., Kochanek, K., Strobino, D. & Guyer, B. (2007). Annual summary of vital statistics: 2005. *Pediatrics, 119,* 345–360.

Hamilton, C. E. (2000). Continuity and discontinuity of attachment from infancy through adolescence. *Child Development, 71,* 690–694.

Hanawalt, B. A. (2002). *Medievalists and the study of childhood.* Cambridge: Oxford University Press.

Hancox, R. J., Milne, B. J., & Poulton, R. (2004). Association between child and adolescent television viewing and adult health: A longitudinal birth cohort study. *Lancet, 364,* 257–262.

Hansen, J., & Bowey, J. A. (1994). Phonological analysis skills, verbal working memory, and reading ability in second-grade children. *Child Development, 65,* 938–950.

Harder, T., Bergmann, R., Kallischnigg, G., & Plagemann, A. (2005). Duration of breastfeeding and risk of overweight: A meta-analysis. *American Journal of Epidemiology 162,* 397–403.

Hardman, M., & Jones, L. (1999). Sharing books with babies: Evaluation of an early literacy intervention. *Educational Review, 51,* 221–229.

Harkin, T. (2007). Preventing childhood obesity: The power of policy and political will. *American Journal of Preventive Medicine, 33,* 165–166.

Harkness, S., & Super, C. (Eds.). (1996). *Parents' cultural belief systems: Their origins, expressions, and consequences.* New York: Guilford Press.

Harlaar, N., Spinath, F. M., Dale, P. S., & Plomin, B. (2005). Genetic influences on early word recognition abilities and disabilities: A study of 7–year–old twins. *Journal of Child Psychology and Psychiatry, 46,* 373–384.

Harpaz-Rotem, I., Murphy, R.A., Berkowitz, S., Marans, S., & Rosensheck, R. A. (2007). Clinical epidemiology of urban violence: Responding to children exposed to violence in ten communities. *Journal of Interpersonal Violence, 22,* 1479–1490.

Harris, J. C. (1995). *Developmental neuropsychiatry.* New York: Oxford University Press.

Harris, S. (1986). Evaluation of a curriculum to support literacy growth in young children. *Early Childhood Research Quarterly, 1,* 333–348.

Harrison, A. O. (1985). The black family's socializing environment: Self-esteem and ethnic attitude among black children. In H. P. McAdoo & J. L. McAdoo (Eds.), *Black children: Social, educational, and parental environments* (pp. 174–193). Newbury Park, CA: Sage.

Harrison, A. O., Wilson, M. N., Pine, C. J., Chan, S. Q., & Buriel, R. (1990). Family ecologies of ethnic minority children. *Child Development, 61,* 347–362.

Harrison, A. O., Wilson, M. N., Pine, C. J., Chan, S. Q., & Buriel, R. (1994). Family ecologies of ethnic minority children. In G. Handel & G. G. Whitchurch (Eds.), *The psychosocial interior of the family* (pp. 187–210). New York: Aldine de Gruyter.

Harrist, A., & Bradley, K. D. (2006). You can't say you can't play: Intervening in the process of social exclusion in the kindergarten classroom. In R. Parker-Rees (Ed.), *Early years education: Major themes in education* (pp. 125–150). London: Routledge.

Harrist, A. W., Zaia, A. F., Bates, J. E., Dodge, K. A., & Pettit, G. S. (1997). Subtypes of social withdrawal in early childhood: Sociometric status and social-cognitive differences across four years. *Child Development, 68,* 278–294.

Hart, C. H., Burts, D. C., & Charlesworth, R. (1997). Integrated developmentally appropriate practice: From theory and research to practice. In C. H. Hart, D. C. Burts, & R. Charlesworth (Eds.), *Integrated curriculum and developmentally appropriate practice: Birth to age eight.* Albany: State University of New York Press.

Hart, C. H., Burts, D. C., Durland, M.A., Charlesworth, R., DeWolf, M., & Fleege, P. O. (1998). Stress behaviors and activity type participation of preschoolers in more and less developmentally-appropriate classrooms: SES and sex differences. *Journal for Research in Childhood Education, 12,* 176–197.

Hart, C. H., DeWolf, D. M., Wozniak, P., & Burts, D. (1992). Maternal and paternal disciplinary styles: Relations with preschoolers' playground behavior orientations and peer status. *Child Development, 63,* 879–892.

Hart, C. H., Ladd, G. W., & Burleson, B. R. (1990). Children's expectations of the outcomes of social strategies: Relations with sociometric status and maternal disciplinary styles. *Child Development, 61,* 127–137.

Hart, C. H., Olsen, S. F., Robinson, C. C., & Mandleco, B. L. (1997). The development of social and communicative competence in childhood: Review and a model of personal, familial, and extrafamilial processes. *Communication Yearbook, 20,* 305–373.

Harter, S. (1990). Causes, correlates, and the functional role of global self-worth: A life span perspective. In R. J. Sternberg & J. Kolligan (Eds.), *Competence considered* (pp. 67–97). New Haven, CT: Yale University Press.

Harter, S. (2003). The development of self-representation during childhood and adolescence. In M. R. Leary & J. Tangney (Eds.), *Handbook of self and identity* (pp. 610–642). New York: Guilford Press.

Hartshorn, K., & Rovee-Collier, C. (2003). Does infant memory expression reflect age at encoding or age at retrieval? *Developmental Psychobiology, 42,* 283–291.

Hartup, W. W. (1996). The company they keep: Friendships and their developmental signficance. *Child Development, 67,* 1–13.

Hartup, W. W., & Laursen, B. (1993). Conflict and context in peer relations. In C. H. Hart (Ed.), *Children on playgrounds: Research perspectives and applications* (pp. 44–84). Albany: State University of New York Press.

Hartup, W. W., Laursen, B., Stewart, M. A., & Eastenson, A. (1988). Conflict and friendship relations of young children. *Child Development, 59,* 1590–1600.

Hartup, W. W., & Moore, S. G. (1990). Early peer relations: Developmental significance and prognostic implications. *Early Childhood Research Quarterly, 5,* 1–17.

Harwood, R. L. (1992). The influence of culturally derived values on Anglo and Puerto Rican mothers' perceptions of attachment behavior. *Child Development, 63,* 822–839.

Harwood, R. L., Miller, J. G., & Irizarry, N. L. (1995). *Culture and attachment: Perceptions of the child in context.* New York: Guilford Press.

Haselager, G. J. T., Hartup, W. W., van Lieshout, C. F. M., & Riksen-Walraven, J. M. A. (1998). Similarities between friends and nonfriends in middle childhood. *Child Development, 69,* 1198–1208.

Haskett, M. E., & Kistner, J. A. (1991). Social interactions and peer perceptions of young physically abused children. *Child Development, 62,* 979–990.

Haskins, R. (1985). Public school aggression among children with varying day-care experience. *Child Development, 56,* 689–703.

Hastings, P., McShane, K., Parker, R., & Ladha, F. (2007). Ready to make nice: Parental socialization of young sons' and daughters' prosocial behaviors with peers. *The Journal of Genetic Psychology, 168,* 177–200.

Hatcher, P. J., Hulme, C., & Ellis, A. W. (1994). Ameliorating early reading failure by integrating the teaching of reading and phonological skills: The phonological linkage hypothesis. *Child Development, 65,* 41–57.

Hatcher, P. J., Hulme, C., & Snowling, M. (2004). Explicit phoneme training combined with phonic reading instruction helps young children at risk of reading failure. *Journal of Child Psychology and Psychiatry, 45*(2), 338–358.

Haugh, M. (2007a). The co-constitution of politeness implicature in conversation. *Journal of Pragmatics 39,* 84–110.

Haugh, M. (2007b). Emic conceptualisations of (im)-politeness and face in Japanese: Implications for the discursive negotiation of second language learner identities. *Journal of Pragmatics, 39,* 657–680.

Hauser, S. T. (1972). Black and white identity development: Aspects and perspectives. *Journal of Youth and Adolescence, 1*(2), 113–130.

Hay, D. F., Caplan, M., Castle, J., & Stimson, C. A. (1991). Does sharing become increasingly "rational" in the second year of life? *Developmental Psychology, 27,* 987–993.

Hay, D. F., Payne, A., & Chadwick, A. (2004). Peer relations in childhood. *Journal of Child Psychology and Psychiatry, 45,* 84–108.

Hayes-Harb, R. (2007). Lexical and statistical evidence in the acquisition of second language phonemes. *Second Language Research, 23*, 65–94.

Haynes, W., & Saunders, D. (1999). Joint book–reading strategies in middle class African American and white mother-child dyads. *Journal of Children's Communication Development, 20*, 9–18.

Haywood, K., & Getchell, N. (2005). *Life span motor development.* Champaign, IL: Human Kinetics.

Hazen, N. (1982). Spatial exploration and spatial knowledge: Individual and developmental differences in very young children. *Child Development, 53*, 826–833.

Heath, S. B. (1988). Language socialization. In D. Slaughter (Ed.), *Black children and poverty: A developmental perspective* (pp. 11–28). San Francisco: Jossey-Bass.

Heath, S. B. (1996). What no bedtime story means: Narrative skills at home and school. In D. Brenneis & R. K. S. Macaulay (Eds.), *The matrix of language: Contemporary linguistic anthropology* (pp. 12–38). Boulder, CO: Westview Press.

Heath, S. B. (2004). Ethnographies in communities: Learning the everyday life of America's subordinated youth. In J. A. Banks & C. Banks (Eds.), *Handbook of research on multicultural education* (pp. 146–162). San Francisco: Jossey-Bass.

Heckman, J. J., Hsee, J., & Rubinstein, Y. (2000). *The GED is a mixed signal: The effect of cognitive and non-cognitive skills on human capital and labor market outcomes.* Chicago: University of Chicago Press.

Hegar, R. (2005). Sibling placement in foster care and adoption: An overview of international research. *Children and Youth Services Review, 27*, 717–739.

Helms, J. E. (1992). Why is there no study of cultural equivalence in standardized cognitive ability testing? *American Psychologist, 47*, 1083–1101.

Hemmings, A., & Metz, M. H. (1990). Real teaching: How high school teachers negotiate societal, local, community, and student pressures when they define their work. In R. Page & L. Valli (Eds.), *Curriculum differentiation: Interpretive studies in the U.S. secondary schools* (pp. 290–356). Albany: State University of New York Press.

Henderson, H., Marshall, P., Fox, N. A., & Rubin, K. H. (2004). Psychophysiological and behavioral evidence for varying forms and functions of nonsocial behavior in preschoolers. *Child Development, 75*, 251–263.

Henry, B., Caspi, A., Moffit, T. E., & Silva, P. A. (1996). Temperamental and familial predictors of violent and nonviolent criminal convictions. *Developmental Psychology, 32*, 614–623.

Heo, K. H., Squires, J., & Yovanoff, P. (2008). Cross-cultural adaptation of a pre-school screening instrument: Comparison of Korean and US populations. *Journal of Intellectual Disability Research, 52*, 195–206.

Herbert, J., & Stipek, D. (2005). The emergence of gender differences in children's perceptions of their academic competence. *Journal of Applied Developmental Psychology, 26*, 276–295.

Herman-Giddens, M. E., Slora, E. J., Wasserman, R. C., Bourdony, C. J., Bhapkar, M. V., Koch, G. G., & Hasermeir, C. M. (1997). Secondary sexual characteristics and menses in young girls seen in office practice: A study from the Pediatric Research in Office Settings Network. *Pediatrics, 99*, 505–512.

Hernandez, A., Li, P., & MacWhinney, B. (2005). The emergence of competing modules in bilingualism. *Trends in Cognitive Sciences, 9*, 220–225.

Hernandez, D. (1993). *America's children.* New York: Russell Sage Foundation.

Hernandez, H. (1997). *Teaching in multilingual classrooms: A teacher's guide to context, process, and content.* Upper Saddle River, NJ: Merrill/Prentice Hall.

Herrera, G., Alcantud, F., Jordan, R., Blanquer, A., Labajo, G., & De Pablo, C. (2008). Development of symbolic play through the use of virtual reality tools in children with autistic spectrum disorders. *Autism, 12*, 143–157.

Herrnstein, R. J., & Murray, C. (1994). *The bell curve: Intelligence and class structure in American life.* New York: Free Press.

Hertsgaard, L., Gunnar, M., Erickson, M. F., & Nachmias, M. (1995). Adrenocortical responses to the strange situation in infants with disorganized, disoriented attachment relationships. *Child Development, 66*, 1100–1106.

Hessl, D., Glaser, B., Dyer-Friedman, J., Blasey, C., Hastie, T., Gunnar, M., & Reiss, A. (2002). Cortisol and behavior in Fragile X syndrome. *Psychoneuroendocrinology, 27*, 855–872.

Hesslinger, B., Thiel, T., van Elst, L., Hennig, J., & Ebert, D. (2001). Attention-deficit disorder in adults with or without hyperactivity: Where is the difference? A study in humans using short echo (1) H-magnetic resonance spectroscopy. *Neuroscience Letters, 304*, 117–119.

Hestenes, L., & Carroll, D. (2000). The play interactions of young children with and without disabilities: Individual and environmental influences. *Early Childhood Research Quarterly, 15*, 229–246.

Hetherington, E. M. (1993). Overview of the Virginia Longitudinal Study of Divorce and Remarriage with a focus on early adolescence. *Journal of Family Psychology, 7*, 39–56.

Hetherington, E. M., Bridges, M., & Insabella, G. M. (1998). What matters? What does not? Five perspectives on the association between marital transitions and children's adjustment. *American Psychologist, 53*, 167–184.

Hetherington, E. M., Cox, M., & Cox, R. (1979). Play and social interaction in children following divorce. *Journal of Social Issues, 35*, 26–49.

Hetherington, E. M., & Kelly, J. (2002). *For better or for worse: Divorce reconsidered.* New York: W. W. Norton & Company.

Hetzroni, O., & Tannous, J. (2004). Effects of a computer-based intervention program on the communicative functions of children with autism. *Journal of Autism and Developmental Disorders, 34*, 95–113.

Hewes, D. W. (1982). Preschool geography: Developing a sense of self in time and space. *Journal of Geography, 81*, 94–97.

Heydenberk, W., & Heydenberk, R. (2007). More than manners: Conflict resolution in primary level classrooms. *Early Childhood Education Journal, 35*, 119–126.

Heyman, G. D., & Gelman, S. A. (1999). The use of trait labels in making psychological influences. *Child Development, 70*, 604–619.

Hicks, L. E., Langham, R. A., & Takenaka, J. (1982). Cognitive and health measures following early nutritional supplementation: A sibling study. *American Journal of Public Health, 72*, 1110–1118.

Hiebert, E. H., & Raphael, T. E. (1996). Psychological perspectives on literacy and extensions to educational practice. In D. C. Berliner & R. C. Calfee (Eds.), *Handbook of educational psychology* (pp. 12–21). New York: Macmillan.

Hill, S., & Flom, R. (2007). 18- and 24-month-olds' discrimination of gender-consistent and inconsistent activities. *Infant Behavior and Development, 30*, 168–173.

Hill, S. A. (2001). Class, race, and gender dimensions of child rearing in African American families. *Journal of Black Studies, 31*, 494–508.

Himmelmann, K., Beckung, E., Hagberg, G., & Uvebrant, P. (2006). Gross and fine motor function and accompanying impairments in cerebral palsy. *Developmental Medicine and Child Neurology 48*, 417–423.

Hine, J., & Wolery, M. (2006). Using point-of-view video modeling to teach play to preschoolers with autism. *Topics in Early Childhood Special Education, 26*, 83–93.

Hinitz, B. F. (1987). Social studies in early childhood education. In C. Seefeldt (Ed.), *The early childhood curriculum: A review of current research* (pp. 237–255). New York: Teachers College Press.

Hinshaw, S. P., & Melnick, S. M. (1995). Peer relationships in boys with attention-deficit hyperactivity disorder with and without comorbid aggression. *Developmental Psychopathology, 7*, 627–647.

Hinshaw, S. P., Zupan, B. A., Simmel, C., Nigg, J. T., & Melnick, S. (1997). Peer status of boys with attention-deficit hyperactivity disorder: Predictions from overt and covert antisocial behavior, social isolation, and authoritative parenting beliefs. *Child Development, 68*, 880–896.

Hirst, W., & Manier, D. (2008). Towards a psychology of collective memory. *Memory, 16*, 183–200.

Hitz, R., & Driscoll, A. (1988). Praise or encouragement. New insights into praise: Implications for early childhood teachers. *Young Children, 43*(5), 6–13.

Ho, D. Y. F. (1994). Cognitive socialization in Confucian heritage cultures. In P. M. Greenfield & R. R. Cocking (Eds.), *Cross-cultural roots of minority child development* (pp. 285–314). Hillsdale, NJ: Erlbaum.

Hock, E., McBride, S., & Gnezda, M. T. (1989). Maternal separation anxiety: Mother-infant separation from the maternal perspective. *Child Development, 60*, 793–802.

Hodnett, E., Downe, S., Edwards, N., & Walsh, D. (2008). *Home-like versus conventional institutional settings for birth.* New York: John Wiley & Sons.

Hoff-Ginsberg, E. (1997). *Language development.* Pacific Grove, CA: Brooks/Cole.

Hoffman, H. J., & Hillman, L. S. (1992). Epidemiology of the Sudden Infant Death Syndrome. *Clinics in Perinatology, 19*(4), 717–737.

Hoffman, L. W. (1975). The value of children to parents and the decrease in family size. *Proceedings of the American Philosophical Society, 119*, 430–438.

Hoffman, L. W. (1985). The changing genetics/socialization balance. *Journal of Social Issues, 41*, 127–148.

Hoffman, L. W. (1991). The influence of family environment on personality: Accounting for sibling differences. *Psychological Bulletin, 110*, 187–203.

Hoffman, M. L. (1988). Interaction of affect and cognition in empathy. In C. E. Izard & J. Kagan (Eds.), *Emotions, cognition, and behavior.* New York: Cambridge University Press.

Hofhuis, W., de Jongste, J. C., Merkus, P. (2003). Adverse health effects of prenatal and postnatal tobacco smoke exposure on children. *Archives of Disease in Childhood, 88*, 1086–1090.

Hogan, D., & Park, J. (2003). Family factors and social support in the developmental outcomes of very low-birth weight children. *Clinics in Perinatology, 27*, 433–459.

Holden, G. W. (1988). Adults thinking about a child rearing problem: Effects of experience, parental status, and gender. *Child Development, 59*, 1623–1632.

Hollich, G. J., Hirsh-Pasek, K., & Golinkoff, R. M. (2000). Breaking the language barrier: An emergentist coalition model for the origins of word learning. *Monographs of the Society for Research in Child Development, 65*(3), 1–138.

Holloway, S. D., & Reichhart-Erikson, M. (1988). The relationship of day care quality and children's free-play behavior and social problem-solving skills. *Early Childhood Research Quarterly, 3*, 39–53.

Holstrum, W., Gaffney, M., Gravel, J., Oyler, R. F. & Ross, D. S. (2008). Early intervention for children with unilateral and mild bilateral degrees of hearing loss. *Trends in Amplification, 12,* 35–41.

Honey, E., Leekam, S., Turner, M., & McConachie, H. (2007). Repetitive behaviour and play in typically developing children and children with autism spectrum disorders. *Journal of Autism and Developmental Disorders, 37,* 1107–1115.

Hooper, S. R., & Edmondson, R. (2008). Developmental stages and factors affecting development. In W. Umansky & S. R. Hooper (Eds.), *Young children with special needs* (pp. 30–71). Upper Saddle River, NJ: Merrill.

Hopkins, B., & Westra, T. (1990). Motor development, maternal expectations, and the role of handling. Prentice Hall. *Infant Behavior and Development, 13,* 117–122.

Hopper, T. E. (1996). *Play is what we desire in physical education: A phenomenological analysis.* EDRS: ED 3918805.

Horton-Ikard, R., & Miller, J. (2004). It is not just the poor kids: The use of AAE forms by African-American school-aged children from middle SES communities. *Journal of Communication Disorders, 37,* 467–487.

Horwood, L. J., Darlow, B. A., & Mogridge, N. (2001). Breastmilk and cognitive ability at 7 and 8 years. *Fetal and Neonatal Journal, 84,* 23–27.

Hough, R. A., & Nurss, J. R. (1992). Language and literacy for the limited English proficient child. In L. O. Ollila & M. J. Mayfield (Eds.), *Emerging literacy* (pp. 42–70). Boston: Allyn & Bacon.

Houwen, S., Visscher, C., Lemmink, K., & Hartman, E. (2008). Motor skill performance of school–age children with visual impairments. *Developmental Medicine & Child Neurology, 50,* 139–145.

Howard, V. F., Williams, B. F., Port, P. D., & Lepper, C. (2004). *Very young children with special needs: A formative approach for the 21st century.* Columbus, OH: Merrill.

Howe, M. L. (1995). Interference effects in young children's long-term retention. *Developmental Psychology, 31,* 579–596.

Howell, P. (2007). Signs of developmental stuttering up to age eight and at 12 plus. *Clinical Psychology Review, 27,* 287–306.

Howes, C. (1983). Patterns of friendship. *Child Development, 54,* 1041–1053.

Howes, C., Droege, K., & Matheson, C. C. (1994). Play and communicative competence processes within long-term and short-term friendship dyads. *Journal of Social and Personal Relationships, 11,* 401–410.

Howes, C., Phillips, D., & Whitebook, M. (1992). Thresholds of quality in child care centers and children's social and emotional development. *Child Development, 63,* 449–460.

Howes, C., & Wu, F. (1990). Peer interactions and friendships in an ethnically diverse school setting. *Child Development, 61,* 537–541.

Hoyert, D. L., Mathews, T. J., Menacker, M. F., Strobino, D. M., & Guyer, B. (2006). Annual Summity of vital statistics: 2004. *Pediatrics, 117,* 168–183.

Hoza, B. (2007). Peer functioning in children with ADHD. *Ambulatory Pediatrics, 7,* 101–106.

Hoza, B., Waschbusch, D. A., Pellham, W. E., Molina, B. S. G., & Milich, R. (2000). Attention-deficit hyperactivity disordered and control boys' responses to social success and failure. *Child Development, 71,* 432–446.

Hsu, H. (2004). Antecedents and consequences of separation anxiety in first-time mothers: Infant, mother, and social-contextual characteristics. *Infant Behavior and Development, 27,* 113–133.

Huffman, L. C., Bryan, Y. E., Pederson, F. A., Lester, B. M., Newman, J. D., & Del Carmen, R. (1994). Infant cry acoustics and maternal ratings of temperament. *Infant Behavior and Development, 17,* 45–53.

Hughes, C., & Dunn, J. (2007). Children's early relationships with other children. In C. Brownell & C. Kopp (Eds.), *Transitions in early socioemotional development: The toddler years.* New York: Guilford.

Hughes, C., Jaffee, C., Happé, F., Taylor, A., Caspi, A., & Moffitt, T. (2005). Origins of individual differences in theory of mind: From nature to nurture? *Child Development, 76,* 356–370.

Hughes, F. P. (1998). Play in special populations. In O. Saracho & B. Spodek (Eds.), *Multiple perspectives on play in early childhood education.* Albany: State University of New York Press.

Hughes, F. P. (1999). *Children, play and development 3rd edition.* Boston: Allyn & Bacon.

Hull, J. N., & Simpson, P. S. (1985). *Breastfeeding across cultures.* New York: Academic Press.

Hummel, I., Roudnitzky, N., Kempter, W., & Laing, D.G. (2007). Intranasal trigeminal function in children. *Developmental Medicine & Child Neurology, 49,* 849–853.

Humphry, R. A., & Hock, E. (1989). Infants with colic: A study of maternal stress and anxiety. *Infant Mental Health Journal, 10,* 263–272.

Hunt, C., & Hauck, F. R. (2006). Sudden Infant Death Syndrome. *Canadian Medical Association Journal, 174,* 1861–1869.

Huntington, L., Hans, S. L., & Zeskind, P. S. (1990). The relationship among cry characteristics, demographic variables, and developing test scores in infants prenatally exposed to methadone. *Infant Behavior and Development, 13,* 533–538.

Hurley, D. S. (2000). *Developing fine and gross motor skills: Birth to three.* New York: Imaginart.

Hurley-Geffner, C. M. (1996). Friendship between children with and without developmental disabilities. In R. L. Koegel & L. K. Koegel (Eds.), *Teaching children with autism: Strategies for promoting positive interactions and improving learning opportunities* (pp. 105–127). Baltimore: Paul H. Brookes.

Hurt, E., Hoza, B., & Pelham, W. (2007). Parenting, family loneliness, and peer functioning in boys with attention-deficit/hyperactivity disorder. *Journal of Abnormal Child Psychology, 35,* 543–555.

Huston, A. C. (Ed.). (1991). *Children in poverty: Child development and public policy.* New York: Cambridge University Press.

Huston, A. C., & Alvarez, M. M. (1990). The socialization context of gender role development in early adolescence. In R. Montemayor, G. R. Adams, & T. P. Gullotta (Eds.), *From childhood to adolescence: A transitional period?* (pp. 156–179). Newbury Park, CA: Sage.

Huston, A. C., McLoyd, V. C., & Garcia Coll, C. T. (1994). Children and poverty: Issues in contemporary research. *Child Development, 65,* 275–282.

Huttenlocher, P. R. (1994). Synaptogenesis synapse elimination and neural plasticity in the human cerebral cortex. In C. A. Nelson (Ed.), *Threats to optimal development: Integrating biological, physiological, and social risk factors: Minnesota Symposium on Child Psychology* (Vol. 27, pp. 35–54). Hillsdale, NJ: Erlbaum.

Hyde, J. S., & Delamater, J. (1999). *Understanding human sexuality.* New York: McGraw-Hill.

Hymel, S., Rubin, K., Rowden, L., & LeMare, L. (1990). Children's peer relationships: Longitudinal prediction of internalizing and externalizing problems from middle to late childhood. *Child Development, 61,* 2004–2021.

Iarocci, G., Virji-Babul, N., & Reebye, P. (2006). Merging family, developmental research, early intervention, and policy goals for children with Down syndrome. *Journal of Policy and Practice in Intellectual Disabilities, 3,* 11–21.

IBFAN. (2004). *Monitoring the baby feeding industry.* Toronto: Author.

Ilg, F. L., & Ames, L. B. (1965). *School readiness: Behavioral tests used at the Gesell Institute.* New York: Harper & Row.

Ingersoll, B., & Schreibman, L. (2006). Teaching reciprocal imitation skills to young children with autism using a naturalistic behavioral approach: Effects on language, pretend play, and joint attention. *Journal of Autism and Developmental Disorders, 36,* 487–505.

Ingersoll, E. W., & Thoman, E. B. (1999). Sleep/wake states of newborn infants: Stability, developmental change, diurnal variation, and relation with caregiving activity. *Child Development, 70,* 1–10.

International Reading Association. (2004). *No Child Left Behind and U.S. education policy.* Newark, DE: Author.

Ipsa, J., & Halgunseth, L. (2004). Talking about corporal punishment: Nine low-income African American mothers' perspectives. *Early Childhood Research Quarterly, 19,* 463–484.

Irizarry, J. (2007). Ethnic and urban intersections in the classroom: Latino students, hybrid identities, and culturally responsive pedagogy. *Multicultural Perspectives, 9,* 21–28.

Irujo, S. (2004). An introduction to intercultural differences and similarities in nonverbal communication. In J. S. Wurzel (Ed.), *Toward multiculturalism: A reader in multicultural education.* Yarmouth, ME: Intercultural Press.

Irvine, J. J., & York, D. E. (1995). Learning styles and culturally diverse students: A literature review. In J. A. Banks (Ed.), *Handbook of research in multicultural education* (pp. 484–497). New York: Macmillan.

Isabella, R. A. (1993). Origins of attachment: Maternal interactive behavior across the first year. *Child Development, 64,* 605–621.

Ishii-Kuntz, M. (1997a). Chinese American families. In M. K. DeGenova (Ed.), *Families in cultural context: Strengths and challenges in diversity* (pp. 109–130). Mountain View, CA: Mayfield.

Ishii-Kuntz, M. (1997b). Japanese American families. In M. K. DeGenova (Ed.), *Families in cultural context: Strengths and challenges in diversity* (pp. 131–154). Mountain View, CA: Mayfield.

Ivanenko, Y. P., Dominici, N., & Lacquaniti, F. (2007). Development of independent walking in toddlers. *Exercise & Sport Sciences Reviews, 35,* 67–73.

Iwata, F., Hara, M., Okada, T., Harada, K., & Li, S. (2003). Body fat ratios in urban Chinese children. *Pediatrics International, 45,* 190–192.

Izard, C. E. (2002). Translating emotion theory and research into preventive interventions. *Psychological Bulletin, 128,* 796–824.

Izard, C. E., & Harris, P. (1995). Emotional development and developmental psyschopathology. In D. Cicchetti & D. J. Cohen (Eds.), *Developmental psychology: Vol. 1. Theory and methods* (pp. 467–503). New York: John Wiley & Sons.

Jacklin, C. N. (1989). Female and male: Issues of gender. *American Psychologist, 44*(2), 127–133.

Jackson, F. M. (2006). *Black infant mortality.* Washington, DC: Joint Center for Political and Economic Studies.

Jackson, G., & Cosca, C. (1974). The inequality of educational opportunity in the Southwest: An observational study of ethnically mixed classrooms. *American Educational Research Journal, 11,* 219–229.

Jackson, M., Barth, J. M., Powell, N., & Lochman, J. (2006). Classroom contextual effects of race on children's peer nominations. *Child Development, 77,* 1325–1337.

Jackson-Maldonado, D., Thal, D., Marchman, V., Bates, E., & Gutierrez-Clellan, V. (1993). Early lexical development in Spanish-speaking infants and toddlers. *Journal of Child Language, 20,* 523–549.

513

Jahr, E., Eldevik, S., & Eikeseth, S. (2000). Teaching children with autism to initiate and sustain cooperative play. *Research in Developmental Disabilities*, 21, 151–169.

James, S. (2004). Why do foster care placements disrupt? An investigation of reasons for placement change in foster care. *Social Service Review*, 78, 601–627.

Janesick, V. J. (1995). Our multicultural society. In E. L. Meyen & T. M. Skrtic (Eds.), *Special education and student disability* (pp. 713–728). Denver: Love.

Jankowski, J. J., Rose, S. A., & Feldman, J. F. (2001). Modifying the distribution of attention in infants. *Child Development*, 72, 339–351.

Janzen, L., & Nanson, J. & Block, G. (1993, March). *Neuropsychological evaluation of preschoolers with fetal alcohol syndrome*. Paper presented at the biennial meeting of the Society for Research in Child Development, New Orleans.

Jarrett, O., & Quay, L. (1983, April). *Cross-racial acceptance and best friend choices in racially balanced kindergarten and first-grade classrooms*. Paper presented at the biennial meeting of the Society for Research in Child Development, Detroit.

Jason, J. M., & Jarvis, W. R. (1987). Infectious disease: Preventable causes of infant mortality. *Pediatrics*, 80, 335–341.

Jenkins, J. M., & Astington, J. W. (1996). Cognitive factors and family structure associated with theory of the mind development in young children. *Developmental Psychology*, 32, 70–78.

Jensen, A. R. (1969). How much can we boost IQ and scholastic achievement? *Harvard Educational Review*, 39(1), 1–123.

Jensen, J. V. (1962). Effects of childhood bilingualism. *Elementary English*, 39, 132–143.

Jessner, U. (2008). Language awareness in multilinguals: Theoretical trends. *Encyclopedia of Language and Education*, 6, 2103–2115.

Jiang, X., & Cillessen, A. (2005). Stability of continuous measures of sociometric status: A meta-analysis. *Developmental Review*, 25, 1–25.

Jiao, S., Ji, G., & Jing, Q. (1996). Cognitive development of Chinese urban only children and children with siblings. *Child Development*, 67, 387–395.

Joe, J. R., & Malach, R. S. (1998). Families with Native American roots. In M. Hanson & E. Lynch (Eds.), *Developing cross-cultural competence* (pp. 127–164). Baltimore: Paul H. Brookes.

Johannemann, T., Conkright, L., Warner, B., Altimier, L., & Swehla, M. (2007). Safe sleep: One organization's approach to enhancing patient safety. *Newborn and Infant Nursing Reviews*, 7, 86–90.

John, R. (1988). The Native American family. In C. H. Mindel, R. W. Habenstein, & R. Wright (Eds.), *Ethnic families in America: Patterns and variations*. New York: Elsevier.

Johnson, D. W., Johnson, R., Dudley, B., Ward, M., & Magnuson, D. (1995). The impact on peer mediation training on the management of school and home conflicts. *American Educational Research Journal*, 32, 829–844.

Johnson, J. E., Christie, J. F., & Wardle, F. (2005). *Play, development and early education*. Boston: Allyn & Bacon.

Johnson, K., DesJardin, J., Barker, D., Quittner, A., & Winter, M. (2008). Assessing joint attention and symbolic play in children with cochlear implants and multiple disabilities: Two case studies. *Otology & Neurotology*, 29, 246–250.

Johnson, L. B., & Staples, R. (2005). *Black families at the crossroads: Challenges and prospects*. San Francisco: Jossey-Bass.

Johnson, M. H. (1997). *Developmental cognitive neuroscience: An introduction*. Oxford: Blackwell.

Johnson, M. H. (2000). Functional brain development in infants: Elements of an interactive specialization framework. *Child Development*, 71, 75–81.

Johnson, M. H., Dziurawiec, S., Ellis, H., & Morton, J. (1991). New borns' preferential tracking of face-like stimuli and its subsequent decline. *Cognition*, 40, 1–19.

Johnson, S. F., McCarter, R. J., & Ferencz, C. (1987). Changes in alcohol, cigarette, and recreational drug use during pregnancy: Implications for intervention. *American Journal of Epidemiology*, 126, 695–702.

Johnson– Powell, G., Yamamoto, J., Wyatt, G., & Arroyo, W. (1997). *Transcultural child development: Psychological assessment and treatment*. New York: John Wiley & Sons.

Joint Commission on the Mental Health of Children. (1970). *Crisis in child mental health: Challenge for the 1970s*. New York: Harper & Row.

Jones, D. C., Swift, D. J., & Johnson, M. A. (1988). Nondeliberate memory for a novel event among preschoolers. *Developmental Psychology*, 24, 641–645.

Jones, L., Rothbart, M., & Posner, M. (2003). Development of executive attention in preschool children. *Developmental Science*, 6, 498–504.

Jourdain, S. (2007). Pragmatics: A multidisciplinary perspective. *The Modern Language Journal*, 91, 125.

Jordan, B. (1993). *Birth in four cultures*. Prospect Heights, IL: Waveland.

Judge, T. A., Erez, A., Bono, J. E., & Thoresen, C. J. (2002). Are measures of self-esteem, neuroticism, locus of control, and generalized self-efficacy indicators of a common core construct? *Journal of Personality and Social Psychology*, 83, 693–710.

Juel, C. (1991). Beginning reading. In R. Barr, M. Kamil, P. Mosenthal, & P. Pearson (Eds.), *Handbook of reading research* (pp. 759–788). New York: Longman.

Juffer, F. & van IJzendoorn, M. (2007). Adoptees do not lack self-esteem: A meta-analysis of studies on self-esteem of transracial, international, and domestic adoptees. *Psychological Bulletin*, 133, 1067–1083.

Jusczyk, P. W. (1995). Language acquisition: Speech sounds and phonological development. In J. L. Miller & P. D. Eimas (Eds.), *Handbook of perception and cognition* (pp. 263–301). Orlando: Academic Press.

Jusczyk, P. W., Cutler, A. I., & Redanz, N. J. (1993). Infants' preference for the predominant stress patterns of English words. *Child Development*, 64, 675–687.

Justice, L., Sofka, A., & McGinty, A. (2007). Targets, techniques, and treatment contexts in emergent literacy intervention. *Seminars in Speech and Language*, 28, 14–24.

Justice, L., & Vukelich, C. (Eds.). (2007). *Achieving excellence in preschool literacy instruction*. New York: Guilford Publications.

Kacerguis, M. A., & Adams, G. R. (1979). Implications of sex-typed childrearing practices, toys, and mass media materials in restricting occupational choices of women. *Family Coordinator*, 28, 368–375.

Kagan, J. (1977). The uses of cross-cultural research in early development. In P. H. Leiderman, S. R. Tulkin, & A. Rosenfeld (Eds.), *Culture and infancy: Variations in the human experience* (pp. 271–286). New York: Academic Press.

Kagan, J. (1994). *Galen's prophecy*. New York: Basic Books.

Kagan, J., Arcus, D., Snidman, N., Feng, W. Y., Hendler, J., & Greene, S. (1994). Reactivity in infants: A cross-national comparison. *Developmental Psychology*, 30, 342–345.

Kagan, J., Kearsley, R. B., & Zelazo, P. R. (1978). *Infancy: Its place in human development*. Cambridge, MA: Harvard University Press.

Kagan, J., Reznick, J., & Snidman, N. (1988). Biological bases of childhood shyness. *Science*, 240, 167–171.

Kagan, J., Snidman, N., & Arcus, D. (1993). On the temperamental categories of inhibited and uninhibited children. In K. H. Rubin & J. Asendorpf (Eds.), *Social withdrawal, inhibition, and shyness in childhood*. (pp. 19–28). Hillsdale, NJ: Erlbaum.

Kalmuss, D., Namerow, P. B., & Cushman, L. F. (1991). Teenage pregnancy resolution: Adoption versus parenting. *Family Planning Perspectives*, 23, 17–23.

Kalyan-Masih, V. (1985). Cognitive performance and cognitive style. *International Journal of Behavioral Development*, 8, 39–54.

Kamii, C. (1982). *Number in preschool and kindergarten: Implications of Piaget's theory*. Washington, DC: National Association for the Education of Young Children.

Kamii, C. (1985). *Young children reinvent arithmetic*. New York: Teachers College Press.

Kamii, C. (1989). *Young children continue to invent arithmetic: 2nd grade*. New York: Teachers College Press.

Kamii, C., & DeVries, R. (1980). *Group games in early education*. Washington, DC: National Association for the Education of Young Children.

Kao, G., & Thompson, J. (2003). Racial and ethnic stratification in educational achievement and attainment. *Annual Review of Sociology*, 29, 417–442.

Kaplan, P. S. (1995). *Pathways for exceptional children*. St. Paul, MN: West.

Kaplan-Sanoff, M., Brewster, A., Stillwell, J., & Bergen, D. (1988). The relationship of play to physical/motor development and to children with special needs. In D. Bergen (Ed.), *Play as a medium for learning and development*. Portsmouth, NH: Heinemann.

Karoly, L. (1998). *Investing in our children: What we know and don't know about the costs and benefits of early childhood interventions*. Santa Monica, CA: Rand.

Karweit, N., & Wasik, B. (1996). The effects of story reading programs on literacy and language development of disadvantaged preschoolers. *Journal of Education for Students Placed at Risk*, 4, 319–348.

Kasari, C., Sigman, M., Yirmiya, N., & Mundy, P. (1993). Affective development and communication in young children with autism. In A. Kaiser & D. Gray (Eds.), *Enhancing children's communication* (pp. 39–48). Baltimore: Paul H. Brookes.

Kass, C., & Maddux, C. (2005). *A human development view of learning disabilities: From theory to practice*. Springfield, IL: Charles C. Thomas.

Kathuria, R., Serpell, R. (1999). Standardization of the Panga Munthu test—a nonverbal cognitive test developed in Zambia. *The Journal of Negro Education*, 67, 228–241.

Katz, G. S., Cohn, J. F., & Moore, C. A. (1996). A combination of vocal, dynamic, and summary features discriminates between three pragmatic categories of infant-directed speech. *Child Development*, 67, 205–217.

Katz, P. S., & Ksansnak, K. R. (1994). Developmental aspects of gender role flexibility and traditionality in middle childhood and adolescence. *Developmental Psychology*, 30, 272–282.

Kaufman, A. S., & Kaufman, N. L. (1983). *Kaufman Assessment Battery for Children: Interpretive manual*. Circle Pines, MN: American Guidance Service.

Kaur, G., & Chhikara, S. (2008). Assessment of multiple intelligence among young adolescents. *Journal of Human Ecology*, 23, 7.

Kavšek, M. (2004). Predicting later IQ from infant visual habituation and dishabituation: A meta-analysis. *Journal of Applied Developmental Psychology*, 25, 369–393.

Kavšek, M. (2007). Infant perception of static two-dimensional transparency information. *European Journal of Developmental Psychology, 10*, 56–74.

Kawamoto, W. T., & Cheshire, T. C. (1997). American Indian families. In M. K. DeGenova (Ed.), *Families in cultural context: Strengths and challenges in diversity* (pp. 15–34). Mountain View, CA: Mayfield.

Kearins, J. M. (1981). Visual-spatial memory in Australian Aboriginal children of desert regions. *Cognitive Psychology, 13*, 434–460.

Keating, D. (1996). A grand theory of development. *Monographs for the Society for Research in Child Development, 61*, 94–116.

Keating, E., & Mirus, G. (2003). Examining interactions across language modalities: Deaf children and hearing peers at school. *Anthropology & Education Quarterly, 34*, 115–135.

Kelishadi, R. (2007). Childhood overweight, obesity, and the metabolic syndrome in developing countries. *Epidemiologic Reviews, 29*, 62–76.

Kellam, S. G., Ensminger, M. E., & Turner, R. J. (1977). Family structure and the mental health of children. *Archives of General Psychiatry, 34*, 1012–1022.

Keller, H., Demuth, C., & Yovsi, R. D. (2008). The multi-voicedness of independence and interdependence: The case of the Cameroonian Nso. *Culture & Psychology, 14*, 115–144.

Keller, H., Voelker, S., & Yovsi, R. D. (2005). Conceptions of parenting in different cultural communities: The case of West African Nso and Northern German women. *Social Development, 14*, 158–180.

Kelly, D., Quinn, P., Slater, A., Lee, K., Gibson, A., Smith, M., Ge, L., & Pascalis, O. Three–month–olds, but not newborns, prefer own–race faces. *Developmental Science, 8*, 34–36.

Kelly, J. (2007). Children's living arrangements following separation and divorce: Insights from empirical and clinical research. *Family Process, 46*, 35–52.

Kelly, J., & Emery, R. (2003). Children's adjustment following divorce: Risk and resilience perspectives. *Family Relations, 52*, 352–362.

Kelly, M. L., & Tseng, H. (1992). Cultural differences in child rearing: A comparison of immigrant Chinese and Caucasian American mothers. *Journal of Cross-Cultural Psychology, 23*, 444–455.

Kelly, Y., Sacker, A., Schoon, I., & Nazroo, J. (2006). Ethnic differences in achievement of developmental milestones by 9 months of age: The Millennium Cohort Study. *Developmental Medicine & Child Neurology, 48*, 825–830.

Kennedy, H., Shannon, M., Chuahorm, U., & Kravetz, M. (2004). The landscape of caring for women: A narrative study of midwifery practice. *Journal of Midwifery & Women's Health, 49*, 14–23.

Keogh, B. K., & Sears, S. (1991). Learning disabilities from a developmental perspective: Early identification and prediction. In B. Y. L. Wong (Ed.), *Learning about learning disabilities* (pp. 80–154). Upper Saddle River, NJ: Merrill/Prentice Hall.

Keogh, J. (1977). The study of movement skill development. *Quest* (Monograph No. 28), 76–80.

Kern, L., & DuPaul, G. (2008). Intervention for young children with, and at–risk for, ADHD. *The ADHD Report, 16*, 6–10.

Kerr, B. A. (1991). *Handbook for counseling the gifted and talented*. Alexandria, VA: American Counseling Association.

Kesner, J. (2000). Teacher Characteristics and the Quality of Child–Teacher Relationships. *Journal of School Psychology, 38*, 133–149.

Kessen, W. (1965). *The child*. New York: John Wiley & Sons.

Khandke, V., Pollitt, E., & Gorman, K. (1999, April). *The role of maternal literacy in child health and cognitive development in rural Guatamala*

Paper presented at the biennial meeting of the Society for Research in Child Development, New Orleans.

Kilbride, J. E., & Kilbride, P. L. (1975). Sitting and smiling behavior of Baganda infants. *Journal of Cross-Cultural Psychology, 6*, 88–107.

Killen, M., & Stangor, C. (2001). Children's social reasoning about inclusion and exclusion in gender and race peer group contexts. *Child Development, 72*, 174–186.

King, A. Y. C., & Bond, M. H. (1985). The Confucian paradigm of man: A sociological view. In W. S. Tseng & D. Y. H. Wu (Eds.), *Chinese culture and mental health* (pp. 29–45). New York: Academic Press.

King, M. L. (2007). Concepts of childhood: What we know and where we might go. *Renaissance Quarterly, 60*, 371–407.

Kinsler, A. (2006). *The perceived impact of No Child Left Behind on third-through fifth-grade elementary science classrooms*. Unpublished doctoral dissertation, East Tennesee State University.

Kirk, S. A. (1972). Ethnic differences in psycholinguistic abilities. *Exceptional Children, 39*, 112–118.

Kirkham, N., Slemmer, J., & Johnson, S. (2002). Visual statistical learning in infancy: Evidence for a domain general learning mechanism. *Cognition, 83*, 35–42.

Kisilevsky, B. S., Fearon, I., & Muir, D. W. (1988). Fetuses differentiate vibroacoustic stimuli. *Infant Behavior and Development, 21*, 25–46.

Kisilevsky, B. S., & Muir, D. W. (1984). Neonatal habituation and dishabituation to tactile stimulation during sleep. *Developmental Psychology, 20*, 367–373.

Kisilevsky, B. S., Muir, D. W., & Low, J. A. (1992). Maturation of human fetal responses to vibroacoustic stimulation. *Child Development, 63*, 1497–1508.

Kistka, Z., Palomar, L., Lee, K., Boslaugh, S., Wangler, M., Cole, F., et al. (2007). Racial disparity in the frequency of recurrence of preterm birth. *American Journal of Obstetrics and Gynecology, 196*, 131.

Kita, S., & Ide, S. (2007). Nodding, *aizuchi*, and final particles in Japanese conversation: How conversation reflects the ideology of communication and social relationships. *Journal of Pragmatics, 39*, 1242–1254.

Kitamura, S., Thanavishuth, C., Burham, D., & Luksaneeyanawin, S. (2001). Universality and specificity in infant–directed speech: Pitch modifications as a function of infant age and sex in a tonal and non–tonal language. *Infant Behavior and Development, 24*, 372–392.

Klahr, D., & MacWhinney, B. (1997). Information processing. In W. Damon (Ed.), *Handbook of child psychology* (pp. 631–678). New York: Wiley.

Klebanov, P., & Brooks-Gunn, J. (2008). Differential exposure to early childhood education services and mother–toddler interaction. *Early Childhood Research Quarterly, 12*, 1–37.

Kleigman, R. M., Behrman, R. E., Jenson, H. B., & Stanton, B. F. (Eds.). (2007). *Nelson textbook of pediatrics* (18th ed.) Philadelphia: Saunders.

Klein, M. D., & Chen, D. (2001). *Working with children from diverse backgrounds*. Albany, NY: Delmar.

Klerman, L., & Parker, M. (1991). *Alive and well? A research and policy review of health programs for poor young children*. New York: National Center for Children in Poverty.

Klerman, L. (1991). The health of poor children: Problems and programs. In A. C. Huston (Ed.), *Children in poverty*. New York: Cambridge University Press.

Klerman, L. (2000). Family planning: Needs and opportunities. In M. C. McCormick & J. E. Siegel

(Eds.), *Prenatal care: Effectiveness and implementation* (pp. 271–284). Cambridge: Cambridge University Press.

Klesges, R. C., Coates, T. J., Brown, G., Sturgeon–Tillisch, J., Moldenhauer, L. M., Holzer, B., Woolfrey, J., & Vollmer, J. (1983). Parental influences on children's eating behavior and relative weight. *Journal of Applied Behavioral Analysis, 16*, 371–378.

Klibanoff, R. S., & Waxman, S. R. (2000). Basic level object categories support the acquisition of novel adjectives: Evidence from preschool children. *Child Development, 71*, 649–659.

Knapp, R. G., & Lo, K. (2006). House, home, family: Living and being Chinese. Honolulu: University of Hawai'i Press.

Knight, G. P., Cota, M. K., & Bernal, M. E. (1993). The socialization of cooperative, competitive, and individualistic preferences among Mexican American children: The mediating role of ethnic identity. *Hispanic Journal of Behavioral Sciences, 15*, 291–309.

Knight, G. P., Virdin, L. M., & Roosa, M. (1994). Socialization and family correlates of mental health outcomes among Hispanic and Anglo American children: Consideration of cross-ethnic scalar equivalence. *Child Development, 65*, 212–224.

Knitzer, J., Steinberg, Z., & Fleisch, B. (1990). *At the schoolhouse door*. New York: Bank Street College of Education.

Knoff, H. (2007). Teasing, taunting, bullying, harassment, & aggression. In J. Zins, M. Elias, & C. Maher (Eds.), *Bullying, victimization, and peer harassment: A Handbook of Prevention*, (pp. 299–312). New York: Haworth Press.

Kochanska, G. (2001). Emotional development in children with different attachment histories: The first three years. *Child Development, 72*, 474–490.

Kochanska, G. (2002). Committed compliance, moral self, and internalization: A mediational model. *Developmental Psychology, 38*, 339–351.

Kochenderfer-Ladd, B., & Wardrop, J. L. (2001). Chronicity and instability of children's peer victimization experiences as predictors of loneliness and social satisfaction trajectories. *Child Development, 72*, 134–151.

Kocinski, J. M. (1998). Foster care. *State Government News, 41*, 16–19.

Kodroff, J. K., & Roberge, J. J. (1975). Developmental analysis of the conditional reasoning abilities of primary-grade children. *Developmental Psychology, 11*, 21–28.

Kohlberg, L. (1984). *Essays on moral development: Vol. 2. The psychology of moral development*. San Francisco: Harper & Row.

Kohlberg, L., & Ullian, D. Z. (1974). Stages in the development of psychosexual concepts and attitudes. In R. C. Friedman, R. M. Richart, & R. L. Vande Wiele (Eds.), *Sex differences in behavior* (pp. 224–249). New York: John Wiley & Sons.

Kohn, A. (2001). Five reasons to stop saying, "Good job." *Young Children, 56*(5), 24–28.

Kollins, S. H., & Greenhill, L. (2006). Evidence base for the use of stimulant medication in preschool children with ADHD. *Infants & Young Children. Attention–Deficit/Hyperactivity Disorder, 19*, 132–141.

Koman, L., Smith, B., & Shilt, J. (2004). Cerebral palsy. *The Lancet, 363*, 1619–1631.

Konner, M. (1993). *Childhood*. Boston: Little, Brown.

Konner, M. (2007). Evolutionary foundations of cultural psychology. In S. Kitayama & D. Cohen (Eds.), *Handbook of Cultural Psychology* (pp. 77–108). New York: Guilford Press.

Kong, E., Beckman, M., & Edwarck, J. (2007). Fine–grained phonetics and acquisition of Greek voiced stops. *ICPHS, 15*, 865–868.

Kovacs, D. M., Parker, J. G., & Hoffman, L. W. (1996). Behavioral, affective, and social correlates

515

of involvement in cross-sex friendships in elementary school. *Child Development, 67,* 2269–2286.

Kramer, L., Perozynksi, L. A., & Chung, T. (1999). Parental responses to sibling conflict: The effects of development and parent gender. *Child Development, 70,* 1401–1414.

Kropp, J. P., & Haynes, O. M. (1987). Abusive and nonabusive mothers' ability to identify general and specific emotion signals of infants. *Child Development, 58,* 187–190.

Kumanyika, S. K., Huffman, S. L., Bradshaw, M. E., Waller, H., Ross, A., Serdula, M., & Paige, D. (1990). Stature and weight status of children in an urban kindergarten population. *Pediatrics, 85,* 783–790.

Kumanyika, S. K. (2007). The obesity epidemic: Looking in the mirror. *American Journal of Epidemiology, 166,* 243–245.

Kupersmidt, J. B., Coie, J. D., & Dodge, K. A. (1990). Predicting disorder from peer social problems. In S. R. Asher & J. D. Coie (Eds.), *Peer rejection in childhood.* New York: Cambridge University Press.

Kupersmidt, J. B., Griesler, P. C., DeRosier, M. E., Patterson, C. J., & Davis, P. W. (1995). Childhood aggression and peer relations in the context of family and neighborhood factors. *Child Development, 66,* 360–375.

Kyratzis, A. (2004). Talk and interaction among children and the co-construction of peer groups and peer culture. *Annual Review of Anthropology, 33,* 625–649.

Labasse, L., Neal, A., Lester, B. M. (2005). Assessment of infant cry: Acoustic cry analysis and parental perception. *Mental Retardation and Developmental Disabilities Research Reviews, 11,* 83–93.

Labov, W. (1971). Stages in the acquisition of standard English. In W. Labov (Ed.), *Readings in American dialectology* (pp. 1–43). New York: Appleton-Century-Crofts.

Ladd, G. W. (1990). Having friends, keeping friends, making friends, and being liked by peers in the classroom: Predictors of children's early school adjustment? *Child Development, 61,* 1081–1101.

Ladd, G. W. (2005). *Children's peer relations and social competence.* New Haven, CT: Yale University Press.

Ladd, G. W. (2006). Peer rejection, aggressive or withdrawn behavior, and psychological maladjustment from ages 5 to 12: An examination of four predictive models. *Child Development, 77,* 822–846.

Ladd, G. W. (2007). Social learning in the peer context. In O. Saracho & B. Spodek (Eds.), *Contemporary perspectives on socialization and social development* (pp. 133–164). Charlotte, NC: Information Age Publishing.

Ladd, G. W., & Burgess, K. B. (2001). Do relational risks and protective factors moderate the linkages between childhood aggression and early psychological and school adjustment? *Child Development, 72,* 1579–1601.

Ladd, G. W., & Coleman, C. C. (1997). Children's classroom peer relationships and early school attitudes: Concurrent and longitudinal associations. *Early Education & Development, 8,* 51–66.

Ladd, G. W., Kochenderfer, B. J., & Coleman, C. C. (1996). Friendship quality as a predictor of young children's early school adjustment. *Child Development, 67,* 1103–1118.

Ladd, G. W., Kochenderfer, B. J., & Coleman, C. C. (1997). Classroom peer acceptance, friendship, and victimization: Distinct relational systems that contribute uniquely to children's school adjustment? *Child Development, 68,* 1181–1197.

Ladegaard, H. (2004). Politeness in young children's speech: Context, peer group influence and

pragmatic competence. *Journal of Pragmatics, 36,* 2003–2022.

Lahr, M. B., Rosenberg, K. D., & Lapidus, J. (2007). Maternal-infant bedsharing: Risk factors for bedsharing in a population-based survey of new mothers and implications for SIDS risk reduction. *Maternal and Child Health Journal, 11,* 277–286.

Laidra, K., Pullmann, H., & Allik, J. (2007). Personality and intelligence as predictors of academic achievement: A cross-sectional study from elementary to secondary school. *Personality and Individual Differences, 42,* 441–451.

Lamaze, F. (1958). *Painless childbirth.* London: Burke.

Lamb, M. E. (1981). The development of father-infant relationships. In M. E. Lamb (Ed.), *Nontraditional families: Parenting and child development* (pp. 1–46). Hillsdale, NJ: Erlbaum.

Lamb, M. E. (1987). *The father's role: Cross-cultural perspectives.* Hillsdale, NJ: Erlbaum.

Lamb, M. E. (2005). Attachments, social networks, and developmental contexts. *Human Development, 48,* 108–112.

Lambert, R., & McCarthy, C. (Eds.). (2006). *Understanding teacher stress in an age of accountability.* Greenwich, CT: Information Age Publishing.

Lambert, S. (2005). Gay and lesbian families: What we know and where to go from here. *The Family Journal, 13,* 43–51.

Lancy, D. F. (1996). *Playing on the mother-ground: Cultural routines for children's development.* New York: Guilford Press.

Landau, R. (1982). Infant crying and fussing. *Journal of Cross-cultural Psychology, 13,* 427–443.

Landau-Stanton, J., & Clements, C. D. (1993). *AIDS. Health and mental health: A primary sourcebook.* New York: Brunner/Mazel.

Landrine, H. (1995). *Bringing cultural diversity to feminist psychology.* Washington, DC: American Psychological Association.

Landry, S. H., & Chapieski, M. L. (1989). Joint attention and infant toy exploration: Effects of Down syndrome and prematurity. *Child Development, 60,* 103–118.

Lane, H., & Wright, T. (2007). Maximizing the effectiveness of reading aloud. *The Reading Teacher, 60,* 668–675.

Langlois, J. H., Ritter, J. M., Casey, R. J., & Sawin, D. B. (1995). Infant attractiveness predicts maternal behaviors and attitudes. *Developmental Psychology, 31,* 464–472.

Langone, J. (1998). Technology. In W. Umansky & S. R. Hooper (Eds.), *Young children with special needs* (pp. 308–339). Columbus, OH: Merrill.

Lansford, J., Ceballo, R., Abbey, A., & Stewart, A. (2001). Does family structure matter? A comparison of adoptive, two-parent biological, single-mother, stepfather, and stepmother households. *Journal of Marriage and the Family, 63,* 840–851.

Lanvers, V. (2001). Language alternation in infant bilinguals: A developmental approach to codeswitching. *International Journal of Bilingual Education and Bilingualism, 52,* 437–464.

Laosa, L. M. (1980). Maternal teaching strategies in Chicano and Anglo-American families: The influence of culture and education on maternal behavior. *Child Development, 51,* 759–765.

Larroque, B., Kaminski, M., Dehaene, P., Subtil, D., Delfosse, M. J., & Querleu, D. (1995). Moderate prenatal alcohol exposure and psychomotor development at preschool age. *American Journal of Public Health, 85,* 1654–1661.

Larson, M. C., White, B. P., Cochran, A., Donzella, B., & Gunnar, M. R. (1998). Dampening the cortisol response to handling at 3 months in human infants and its relations to sleep, circadian cortisol activity, and behavioral distress. *Developmental Psychobiology, 33,* 327–337.

Larson, M. S. (2001). Interactions, activities and gender in children's television commercials: A content analysis. *Journal of Broadcasting & Electronic Media, 45,* 41–56.

Larzelere, R. E. (2006). A review of the outcomes of parental use of nonabusive discipline or customary physical punishment. *Pediatrics, 98,* 824–828.

Larzelere, R. E., & Kuhn, B. R. (2005). Comparing child outcomes of physical punishment and alternative disciplinary tactics: A meta-analysis. *Clinical Child and Family Psychology Review, 8,* 1–37.

Lauteslager, P. E. M. (1995). Motor development in young children with Down syndrome. In A. Vermeer & W. E. Davis (Eds.), *Physical and motor development in mental retardation* (pp. 96–129). New York: Karger.

Law, J. (2007). Behavioral stuttering treatments are effective but no one treatment approach is more effective over other treatment approaches. *Evidence-Based Communication Assessment and Intervention, 1,* 14–15.

Lawrence, M. M. (1975). *Young inner city families: Development of ego strengths under stress.* New York: Behavior.

Lawrence, R. (1991). Breastfeeding trends: A cause for action. *Pediatrics, 88,* 867–868.

Laws, G., & Gunn, D. (2004). Phonological memory as a predictor of language comprehension in Down syndrome: A five-year follow-up study. *Journal of Child Psychology and Psychiatry, 45,* 326–337.

Leaper, C. (1994). *New directions for child development: Vol. 65. Childhood segregation: Causes and consequences.* San Francisco: Jossey-Bass.

Leaper, C., Anderson, K. J., & Sanders, P. (1998). Moderators of gender effects on parents' talk to their children. *Developmental Psychology, 34,* 3–27.

Leaper, C. & Friedman, C. (2007). The socialization of gender. In J. Grusec & P. Hastings (Eds.), *Handbook of Socialization: Theory and research* (pp. 561–587). New York: Guilford Press.

Leathers, S. (2005). Seperation from siblings: Associations with placement adaptation and outcomes among adolescents in long-term foster care. *Children and Youth Services Review, 27,* 793–819.

Leboyer, F. (1975). *Birth without violence.* New York: Random House.

Lederberg, A. R., Chapin, S. L., Rosenblatt, V., & Vandell, D. L. (1986). Ethnic, gender, and age preferences among deaf and hearing preschool peers. *Child Development, 57,* 375–386.

Lederberg, A. R., & Mobley, C. E. (1990). The effect of hearing impairment on the quality of attachment and mother-toddler interaction. *Child Development, 61,* 1596–1604.

Lederer, S. (2002). Collaborative pretend play: From theory to therapy. *Child language teaching and therapy, 18,* 233–255.

Lee, B. J., & Mackey-Bilaver, L. (2007). Effects of WIC and Food Stamp Program participation on child outcomes. *Children and Youth Services Review, 29,* 501–517.

Lee, C., Brown, C., Hains, S., & Kisilevsky, B. (2007). Fetal development: Voice processing in normotensive and hypertensive pregnancies. *Biological Research For Nursing, 8,* 272–282.

Lee, E., & Mock, M. R. (2005). Chinese families. In M. McGoldrick, J. Giordano, & J. Garcia-Preto (Eds.), *Ethnicity and family therapy* (pp. 302–318). New York: Guilford.

Lee, J. S., & Ginsburg, H. (2007). Preschool teachers' beliefs about appropriate early literacy and mathematics education for low- and middle-socioeconomic status children. *Early Education & Development, 18,* 111–143.

Lee, L., Howes, C., & Chamberlain, B. (2007). Ethnic heterogeneity of social networks and cross-ethnic friendships of elementary school boys and girls. *Merrill-Palmer Quarterly, 53*, 325–346.

Lee, V. E., Burkham, D. T., Zimles, H., & Ladewski, B. (1994). Family structure and its effect on behavioral and emotional problems of adolescence. *Journal of Research on Adolescence, 4*, 129–142.

Leerkes, E. M., & Siepak, K. (2006). Attachment linked predictors of women's emotional and cognitive responses to infant distress. *Attachment & Human Development, 8*, 11–32.

Lefly, H. P. (1976). Acculturation, child-rearing, and self-esteem in two North American Indian tribes. *Ethos, 5*, 385–401.

Leibold, L., & Werner, L. (2007). Infant auditory sensitivity to pure tones and frequency-modulated tones. *Infancy, 12*, 225–233.

Lein, L. (1975). Black American migrant children: Their speech at home and school. *Council on Anthropology and Education Quarterly, 6*, 1–11.

Leiser, D., & Halachmi, R. (2006). Children's understanding of market forces. *Journal of Economic Psychology, 27*, 6–19.

Lemerise, E. A., & Arsenio, W. F. (2000). An integrated model of social processes and cognition in social information processing. *Child Development, 71*, 107–118.

Lemerise, E. A., Gregory, D. S., & Fredstrom, B. (2005). The influence of provocateurs' emotion displays on the social information processing of children varying in social adjustment and age. *Journal of Experimental Child Psychology, 90*, 344–366.

Leondari, A., & Gonida, E. (2007). Predicting academic self-handicapping in different age groups: The role of personal achievement goals and social goals. *British Journal of Educational Psychology, 77*, 595–611.

Lerner, J. W. (1997). *Learning disabilities. Theories, diagnosis, and teaching strategies.* Boston: Houghton Mifflin.

Leslie, A., Knobe, J., & Cohen, A. (2006). Acting intentionally and the side-effect effect: Theory of mind and moral judgment. *Psychological Science, 17*, 421–427.

Lester, B. M. (1987). Prediction of developmental outcome from acoustic cry analysis in term and preterm infants. *Pediatrics, 80*, 529–534.

Lester, B. M., & Brazelton, T. B. (1982). Cross-cultural assessment of neonatal behavior. In H. Stevenson & D. Wagner (Eds.), *Cultural perspectives on child development* (pp. 20–53). San Francisco: Freeman.

Leung, K., Lau, S., & Lam, W. (1998). Parenting styles and academic achievement: A cross-cultural study. *Merrill-Palmer Quarterly, 44*, 157–172.

Leung, P., Erich, S., & Kanenberg, H. (2005). A comparison of family functioning in gay/lesbian, heterosexual and special needs adoptions. *Children and Youth Services Review, 27*, 1031–1044.

Leve, L. D., & Fagot, B. J. (1997). Gender-role socialization and discipline processes in one- and two-point families. *Sex Roles, 36*, 1–21.

Leventhal, A., Martin, R., Seals, R., Tapia, E., & Rehm, L. P. (2007). Investigating the dynamics of affect: Psychological mechanisms of affective habituation to pleasurable stimuli. *Motivation and Emotion, 31* 145–157.

Levine, R. A., Levine, S., Dixon, S., & Richman, A. (1996). *Child care and culture: Lessons from Africa.* Cambridge: Cambridge University Press.

Levy, F., Hay, D. A., McStephen, M., Wood, C., & Waldman, I. (1997). Attention deficit-hyperactivity disorder: A category or a continuum? Genetic analysis of a large-scale twin study. *Journal of the American Academy of Child and Adolescent Psychiatry, 36*, 737–744.

Lewin, N. (2005). The No Child Left Behind Act of 2001: The triumph of school choice over racial desegregation. *Georgetown Journal on Poverty Law and Policy, 1*, 95–112.

Lewis, M., Feiring, C. K., & Rosenthal, S. (2000). Attachment over time. *Child Development, 71*, 707–720.

Lewis, M., & Ramsey, D. S. (1999). Effect of maternal soothing on infant stress response. *Child Development, 70*, 11–20.

Lewis, R. B., & Doorlag, D. H. (2003). *Teaching special students in general education classrooms.* Columbus, OH: Merrill Prentice Hall.

Lewis, V., Norgate, S., Collis, G., & Reynolds, R. (2000). The consequences of visual impairment for children's symbolic and functional play. *British Journal of Developmental Psychology, 18*, 449–464.

Lewkowicz, D. J. (1996). Infants' response to the audible and visible properties of the human face. *Developmental Psychology, 32*, 347–366.

Li, P., Zhao, X., & MacWhinney, B. (2007). Dynamic self-organization and early lexical development in children. *Cognitive Science: A Multidisciplinary Journal, 31*, 581–612.

Li, S., & Leader, S. (2007). Economic burden and absenteeism from influenza-like illness in healthy households with children (5–17 years) in the US. *Respiratory Medicine, 101*, 1244–1250.

Liamputtong, P. (2007). On childrearing and infant care: A cross-cultural perspective. In P. Liamputtong (Ed.), *Childrearing and infant care issues,* (pp. 3–29). New York: Nova Science Publishers.

Liben, L., & Downs, R. (2003). Investigating and facilitating children's graphic, geographic, and spatial development. *Journal of Applied Developmental Psychology, 24*, 663–679.

Lieber, J. (1993). A comparison of social pretend play in young children with and without disabilities. *Early Education and Development, 41*, 148–161.

Lieberman, E., & Ryan, K. J. (1989). Birth-day choices. *New England Journal of Medicine, 321*, 1824–1825.

Lieberman, A., Weston, D. R., & Pawl, J. H. (1991). Preventive intervention and outcome with anxiously attached dyads. *Child Development, 62*, 199–209.

Lienhardt, G. (1961). *Divinity and experience: The religion of the Dinka.* Oxford: Clarendon Press.

Lillard, A. S. (1995, March). *Children's understanding of pretense intentions.* Paper presented at the biennial meeting of the Society for Research in Child Development, Indianapolis.

Lillard, A. S. (2007). Pretend play in toddlers. In C. Brownell & C. Kopp (Eds.), *Socioemotional development in the toddler years.* New York: Guilford Press.

Lindahl, K., & Malik, N. (1999). Marital conflict, family processes, and boys' externalizing behavior in Hispanic American and European American families. *Journal of Clinical Child Psychology, 28*, 12–24.

Lindsay, J., Perlesz, A., Brown, R., McNair, R., de Vaus, D., & Pitts, M. (2006). Stigma or respect: Lesbian-parented families negotiating school settings. *Sociology, 40*, 1059–1077.

Lindsey, D. (1991). Factors affecting the foster care placement decision: An analysis of national survey data. *American Journal of Orthopsychiatry, 61*, 272–281.

Lindsey, E. (2002). Preschool children's friendship and peer acceptance: Links to social competence. *Child Study Journal, 32*, 1–17.

Linebarger, D., & Walker, D. (2005). Infants' and toddlers' television viewing and language outcomes. *American Behavioral Scientist, 48*, 624–645.

Lipski, J. (2007). English, Spanish, or Spanglish: Truth and consequences of U.S. Latino bilingualism. In N. Echávez-Solano, & K. Dworkin, V. Méndez (Eds.), *Spanish and Empire* (pp. 197–218). Nashville: Vanderbilt University Press.

Lipworth, L., Bailey, L. R., & Trichopoulos, D. (2000). History of breastfeeding in relation to breast cancer risk. *Journal of the National Cancer Institute, 92*, 302–312.

Little, C. (2005). A closer look at gifted children with disabilities. In S. Johnsen & J. Kendrick (Eds.), *Teaching gifted students with disabilities* (pp. 17–36). Austin, TX: Prufrock Press.

Liu, J., Probst, J., Martin, A., Wang, J., & Salinas, C. (2007). Disparities in dental insurance coverage and dental care among U.S. children: The National Survey of Children's Health. *Pediatrics, 119*, 12–21.

Lloyd, B., & Howe, N. (2003). Solitary play and convergent and divergent thinking skills in preschool children. *Early Childhood Research Quarterly, 18*, 22–41.

Lloyd, P., & Cohen, E. (1999). Peer status in the middle school: A natural treatment for unequal participation. *Social Psychology of Education, 3*, 193–216.

Lockl, K., & Schneider, W. (2006). Precursors of metamemory in young children: The role of theory of the mind and metacognitive vocabulary. *Metacognition and Learning, 1*, 15–31.

Lockman, J. J., & Thelen, E. (1993). Developmental biodynamics: Brain, body, behavior connections. *Child Development, 64*, 953–959.

Loe, I., & Feldman, H. (2007). Academic and educational outcomes of children with ADHD. *Ambulatory Pediatrics, 7*, 82–90.

Loeber, R., & Dishion, T. J. (1983). Early predictors of male delinquency: A review. *Psychological Bulletin, 94*, 68–99.

Logan, O. L. (1991). *Motherwit: An Alabama midwife's story.* New York: Plume.

Lollis, S. P. (1990). Effects of maternal behavior on toddler behavior during separation. *Child Development, 61*, 99–103.

Loo, K., Ohgi, S., Zhu, H., Howard, J. & Chen, L. (2005). Cross-cultural comparison of the neurobehavioral characteristics of Chinese and Japanese neonates. *Pediatrics International, 47*, 446–451.

Loomes, C., Rasmussen, C., Pei, J., Manji, S., & Andrew, G. (2008). The effect of rehearsal training on working memory span of children with fetal alcohol spectrum disorder. *Research in Developmental Disabilities, 29*, 113–124.

Lorenz, K. (1971). *Studies in animal and human behavior* (Vol. 2). Cambridge, MA: Harvard University Press.

Losonsky, G. A., Santosham, M., Sehgal, V. M., Zwahlen, A., & Moxon, E. R. (1984). Haemophilus influenza disease in the White Mountain Apaches. *Pediatric Infectious Disease, 3*, 539–547.

Love, J. M., Harrison, L., Sagi-Schwartz, A., van IJzendoorn, M. H., Ross, C., Ungerer, J. A., et al. (2003). Child care quality matters: How conclusions may vary with context. *Child Development, 74*, 1021–1033.

Lovett, S. B., & Pillow, B. H. (1991, April). *The development of the comprehension-memory distinction.* Paper presented at the biennial meeting of the Society for Research in Child Development, Seattle.

Lowenfeld, V. (1947). *Creative and mental growth.* New York: Macmillan.

Lozoff, D. (1989). Nutrition and behavior. *American Psychologist, 44*, 231–236.

Lozoff, B. (1990). Has iron deficiency been shown to cause altered behavior in infants? In J. Dobbing (Ed.), *Brain, behaviour, and iron in the infant diet* (pp. 107–131). London: Springer-Verlag.

Lozoff, B., Corapci, F., Burden, M., Kaciroti, N., Angulo-Barroso, R., Sazawal, S. et al. (2005). Preschool-aged children with iron deficiency anemia show altered affect and behavior. *Journal Nutrition, 137*, 683–689.

Lu, M. (2000). *Language development in the early years.* Bloomington, IN: ERIC Clearing House on Reading, English, and Communication.

Ludemann, P. M. (1991). Generalized discrimination of positive facial expressions by 7- and

10-month-old infants. *Child Development, 62,* 55–67.

Luecke-Aleska, D., Anderson, D. R., Collins, P. A., & Schmitt, K. L. (1995). Gender constancy and television viewing. *Developmental Psychology, 31,* 773–780.

Lundy, B., Jones, N., Field, T., Nearing, G., Davalos, M., Pietro, P., et al. (1999). Prenatal depression effects on neonates. *Infant Behavior and Development, 22,* 119–129.

Luo, J. (2007). Rethinking Piaget for a developmental robotics of object permanence. *Development and Learning, 11,* 235–240.

Luo, Y., Baillargeon, R., Brueckner, L., & Munakata, M. (2003). Reasoning about a hidden object after a delay: Evidence for robust representations in 5-month-old infants. *Cognition, 88,* 23–32.

Lurie, S., Glezerman, M., Sadan, O. (2005). Maternal and neonatal effects of forceps versus vacuum operative vaginal delivery. *International Journal of Gynecology & Obstetrics, 89,* 293–294.

Luthar, S. S., Cicchetti, D., & Becker, B. (2000). Research on resilience: Response to commentaries. *Child Development, 71,* 573–575.

Luyster, R., Kadlec, M., Carter, A., & Tager-Flusberg, H. (2008). Language assessment and development in toddlers with autism spectrum disorders. *Journal of Autism and Developmental Disorders, 38,* 1426–1438.

Lynch, E. W. (1998). Developing cross-cultural competence. In E. W. Lynch & M. J. Hanson (Eds.), *Developing cross-cultural competence: A guide for working with young children and their families.* Baltimore: Paul H. Brookes.

Lynn, R. (2002). Racial and ethnic differences in psychopathic personality. *Personality and Individual Differences 32,* 273–316.

Lyons-Ruth, K. (2006). Play, precariousness, and the negotiation of shared meaning: A developmental research perspective on child psychotherapy. *Journal of Infant, Child, and Adolescent Psychotherapy, 5,* 142–159.

Lyons-Ruth, K., Connell, D. B., Grunebaum, H. U., & Botein, S. (1990). Infants at social risk: Maternal depression and family support services as mediators in infant development and security of attachment. *Child Development, 61,* 85–98.

Lyons-Ruth, K., Easterbrooks, M. A., & Cibelli, C. D. (1997). Infant attachment strategies, infant mental lag, and maternal depressive symptoms: Predictors of internalizing and externalizing problems at age 7. *Developmental Psychology, 33,* 681–692.

Lyytinen, P. (1995). Cross-situational variation on children's pretend play. *Early Child Development and Care, 105,* 33–41.

Maccoby, E. M. (1980). *Social development: Psychological growth and the parent-child relationship.* New York: Harcourt Brace Jovanovich.

Maccoby, E. M. (1989, August). *Gender and relationships: A developmental account.* Paper presented at the biennial meeting of the Society for Research in Child Development, New Orleans.

Maccoby, E. M. (1999). *Two sexes: Growing apart, growing together.* New York: Belknap Press.

Maccoby, E. M., & Jacklin, C. N. (1990). Gender segregation in childhood. In H. Reese (Ed.), *Advances in child development and behavior* (pp. 161–206). New York: Academic Press.

MacDonald, K., & Parke, R. D. (1986). Parent-child physical play: The effect of sex and age of children and parents. *Sex Roles, 15,* 367–378.

MacGowan, R. J., MacGowan, C. A., Serdula, M. K., Lane, J. M., Joesoef, R. M., & Cook, F. H. (1991). Breastfeeding among women attending women, infants, and children clinics in Georgia, 1987. *Pediatrics, 87,* 361–366.

MacGregor, S. N., & Chasnoff, I. J. (1993). Substance abuse in pregnancy. In C. Lin, M. S. Verp, & R. E. Sabbagha (Eds.), *The high-risk fetus: Pathophysiology, diagnosis, management.* New York: Springer-Verlag.

Magnuson, M. (2000). Infants with congenital deafness: On the importance of early sign language acquisition. *American Annals of the Deaf, 145,* 6–14.

Mainess, K., Champion, T., & McCabe, A. (2002). Telling the unknown story complex and explicit narration by African American preadolescents—preliminary examination of gender and socioeconomic issues. *Linguistics and Education, 13,* 151–173.

Makin, J. W., & Porter, R. H. (1989). Attractiveness of lactating females' breast odors to neonates. *Child Development, 60,* 803–810.

Mallik, S., & Spiker, D. (2004). *Effective early intervention programs for low birth weight premature infants.* Montreal, Quebec: Center of Excellence for Early Childhood Development.

Malina, R. M., & Bouchard, C. (1991). *Growth, maturation, and physical activity.* Champaign, IL: Human Kinetics.

Malinosky-Rummel, R., & Hansen, D. J. (1993). Long-term consequences of childhood physical abuse. *Psychological Bulletin, 114,* 68–79.

Malone, D. M., Stoneman, Z., & Langone, J. (1994). Contextual variation of correspondences among measures of play and developmental level of preschool children. *Journal of Early Intervention, 18,* 199–215.

Mandansky, D., & Edelbrock, C. (1990). Cosleeping in a community sample of 2- and 3-year-old children. *Pediatrics, 86,* 197–280.

Mandell, D., Davis, J., Bevans, K., & Guevara, J. (2008). Ethnic disparities in special education labeling among children with attention-deficit/hyperactivity disorder. *Journal of Emotional and Behavioral Disorders, 16,* 42–51.

Mangelsdorf, S. C. (1992). Developmental changes in infant-stranger interaction. *Infant Behavior and Development, 15,* 191–208.

Mangelsdorf, S. C., Plunkett, J. W., Dedrick, C. F., Berlin, M., Meisels, S. J., McHale, J. L., et al. (1996). Attachment security in very low birth weight infants. *Developmental Psychology, 32,* 914–920.

Mangelsdorf, S. C., Shapiro, J., & Marzolf, D. (1995). Developmental and temperamental differences in emotion regulation in infancy. *Child Development, 66,* 1817–1828.

Mangione, P. (1992). *Infant/toddler caregiving: A guide to culturally sensitive care.* Sacramento: California State Department of Education.

Mantzicopoulos, P. (2004). I am really good at puzzles, but I don't get asked to play with others: Age, gender, and ethnic differences in Head Start children's self-perceptions of competence. *The Journal of Genetic Psychology, 165,* 51–65.

Marchman, V., & Fernald, A. (2008). Speed of word recognition and vocabulary knowledge in infancy predict cognitive and language outcomes in later childhood. *Developmental Science* (Online Early Articles).

Marcon, R. A. (2002). Moving up the grades: Relationships between preschool model and later school success. *Early Childhood Research and Practice, 4,* 1–24.

Maretzki, T. W., & Maretzki, H. (1963). Taira: An Okinawan village. In B. B. Whiting (Ed.), *In six cultures: Studies of child rearing* (pp. 73–157). New York: John Wiley & Sons.

Margai, F., & Henry, N. (2003). A community-based assessment of learning disabilities using environmental and contextual risk factors. *Social Science & Medicine, 56,* 1073–1085.

Margolin, G., & Gordis, E. (2000). The effects of family and community violence on children. *Annual Review of Psychology, 51,* 445–479.

Marinellie, S., & Chan, Y. (2006). The effect of word frequency on noun and verb definitions: A developmental study. *Journal of Speech, Language, and Hearing Research, 49,* 1001–1021.

Marino, D. (2007). Water and food safety in the developing world: Global implications for health and nutrition of infants and young children. *Journal of the American Dietetic Association, 107,* 1930–1934.

Mariscal, M., Palma, S., Llorca, J., Pérez-Iglesias, R., Pardo-Crespo, R., & Delgado-Rodríguez, M. (2006). Pattern of alcohol consumption during pregnancy and risk for low birth weight. *Annals of Epidemiology, 16,* 432–438.

Markides, K. S., & McFarland, C. (1982). A note on recent trends in the infant mortality-socioeconomic status relationship. *Social Forces, 61,* 268–276.

Markman, E. M. (1992). Constraints on word learning: Speculations about their nature, origins, and domain specificity. In M. R. Gunnar & M. P. Maratsos (Eds.), *Minnesota Symposium on Child Psychology* (Vol. 25, pp. 59–101). Hillsdale, NJ: Erlbaum.

Markstrom, C. A., (1987, April). *A comparison of psychosocial maturity between four ethnic groups during middle adolescence.* Paper presented at the biennial meeting of the Society for Research in Child Development, Baltimore.

Markstrom, C. A., & Mullis, R. L. (1986). Ethnic differences in the imaginary audience. *Journal of Adolescent Research, 1,* 289–301.

Marschark, M. (1993). *Psychological development of deaf children.* New York: Oxford University Press.

Marschark, M., Convertino, C., Macias, G., Monikowski, C., Sapere, P., & Seewagen, R. (2007). Understanding communication among deaf students who sign and speak: A trivial pursuit? *American Annals of the Deaf, 152,* 415–424.

Martin, C. L. (1993). New directions in investigating children's gender knowledge. *Developmental Review, 13,* 184–204.

Martin, C. L., & Ruble, D. (2004). Children's search for gender cues. Cognitive perspectives on gender development. *Current Directions in Psychological Science, 13,* 67–70.

Martin, C. L., Wood, C. H., & Little, J. K. (1990). The development of gender stereotype components. *Child Development, 61,* 1891–1904.

Martin, J., & Ross, H. (2005). Sibling aggression: Sex differences and parents' reactions. *International Journal of Behavioral Development, 29,* 129–138.

Martini, M. (1994). Peer interactions in Polynesia: A view from the Marquesas. In J. L. Roopnarine, J. E. Johnson, & F. H. Hooper (Eds.), *Children's play in diverse cultures* (pp. 73–103). Albany: State University of New York Press.

Mason, C., Cauce, A. M., Gonzalez, N., & Hiraga, Y. (1996). Neither too sweet, nor too sour: Problem peers, maternal control, and problem behavior of African American adolescents. *Child Development, 67,* 2115–2130.

Masten, A. S., Coatsworth, J. D., Neemann, J., Gest, S. D., Tellegen, A., & Garmezy, N. (1995). The structure and coherence of competence from childhood through adolescence. *Child Development, 66,* 1635–1659.

Masten, A. S., & Obradovic, J. (2006). Competence and resilience in development. *Annals of the New York Academy of Sciences, 1094,* 13–27.

Mather, N. (1992). Whole language reading instruction for students with learning disabilities: Caught in the cross-fire. *Learning Disabilities Research and Practice, 7,* 87–95.

Mathes, P., Pollard-Durodola, S. D., Cardenas-Hagan, E. Linan–Thompson, S., & Vaughn, S. (2007). Teaching struggling readers who are native Spanish speakers: What do we know? *Language, Speech, and Hearing Services in Schools, 38,* 260–271.

Matheson, C., & Wu, F. (1991, April). *Friendship and social pretend play.* Paper presented at the biennial

518

meeting of the Society for Research in Child Development, Seattle.

Mathews, T. J., & MacDorman, M. F. (2007). Infant mortality statistics from the 2004 period linked birth/infant death data set. *National Vital Statistics Reports*, 55, 1–32.

Mattison, E., & Aber, M. (2007). Closing the achievement gap: The association of racial climate with achievement and behavioral outcomes. *American Journal of Community Psychology*, 40, 1–12.

Maugh, T. H. (1998, November 24). Researchers make key attention deficit disorder finding. *Hartford Courant*, p. 7.

Mauldon, J., & Luker, K. (1996). The effects of contraceptive education on method use at first intercourse. *Family Planning Perspectives*, 28, 19–24, 41.

Maurer, D., Stager, C., & Mondloch, C. (1999). Cross-modal transfer of shape is difficult to demonstrate in one-month-olds. *Child Development*, 70, 1047–1057.

Mayeux, L., Bellmore, A., & Cillessen, A. (2007). Predicting changes in adjustment using repeated measures of sociometric status. *The Journal of Genetic Psychology*, 168, 401–424.

Maynard, A. E. (2002). Cultural teaching: The development of teaching skills in Maya sibling interactions. *Child Development*, 73, 969–982.

Mayson, T., Harris, S., & Bachman, C. (2007). *Gross motor development of Asian and European children on four motor assessments: A literature review*. Pediatric Physical Therapy, 19, 148–153.

McAdoo, H. P. (1985). Racial attitude and self-concept of young black children over time. In H. P. McAdoo & J. L. McAdoo (Eds.), *Black children: Social, educational, and parental environments* (pp. 213–242). Newbury Park, CA: Sage.

McAdoo, H. P. (2007). Religion and African American families. In H. P. McAdoo (Ed.), *Black families* (pp. 97–100). Newbury Park, CA: Sage Publishing.

McBride Chang, C., Wagner, R., Muse, A., Chow, B., & Shu, H. (2005). The role of morphological awareness in children's vocabulary acquisition in English. *Applied Psycholinguistics*, 26, 415–435.

McCall, R. B., & Carringer, M. S. (1993). A meta-analysis of infant habituation and recognition memory performance as predictors of later IQ. *Child Development*, 64, 57–79.

McCarton, C. M., Brooks-Gunn, J., Wallace, I. F., Bauer, C. R., Bennett, F. C., Bernbaum, J. C., et al. (1997). Results at age 8 years of early intervention for low-birth-weight premature infants. *Journal of the American Medical Association*, 277, 126–132.

McClelland, M., Acock, A., & Morrison, F. (2006). The impact of kindergarten learning-related skills on academic trajectories at the end of elementary school. *Early Childhood Research Quarterly*, 21, 471–490.

McCoach, D., & Siegel, D. (2003). *Factors that differentiate under-achieving gifted students from high-achieving gifted students*. Washington, DC: National Association for Gifted Children.

McCormick, K. (2003). Assessing cognitive development. In M. McLean, D. B. Bailey, & M. Wolery (Eds.), *Assessing infants and preschoolers with special needs* (pp. 268–304). Upper Saddle River, NJ: Merrill/Prentice Hall.

McCormick, M., Brooks-Gunn, J., Buka, S., Goldman, J., Yu, J., Salganik, M., et al. (2006). Early intervention in low birth weight premature infants: Results at 18 years of age for the Infant Health and Development Program. *Pediatrics*, 117, 771–780.

McCune, L. (1995). A normative study of representational play at the transition to language stage. *Developmental Psychology*, 31, 198–206.

McCurdy, K., Gannon, R. A., Daro, D. (2003). Participation patterns in home-based family support programs: Ethnic variations. *Family Relations*, 52, 3–11.

McDowell, K. D., Lonigan, C. J., & Goldstein, H. (2007). Relations among socioeconomic status, age, and predictors of phonological awareness. *Journal of Speech, Language, and Hearing Research*, 50, 1079–1092.

McElwain, N., Halberstadt, A., & Volling, B. (2007). Mother- and father-reported reactions to children's negative emotions: Relations to young children's emotional understanding and friendship quality. *Child Development*, 78, 1407–1425.

McEvoy, M. A., & Odom, S. L. (1996). Strategies for promoting social interaction and emotional development of infants and young children with disabilities and their families. In S. L. Odom & M. E. McLean (Eds.), *Early intervention/early childhood special education: Recommended practices*. Austin, TX: PRO-ED.

McGee, L. M., & Richgels, D. J. (2007). *Literacy's beginnings: Supporting young readers and writers*. Boston: Allyn & Bacon.

McGlothlin, H., & Killen, M. (2005). Children's perceptions of intergroup and intragroup similarity and the role of social experience. *Journal of Applied Developmental Psychology*, 26, 680–698.

McGuckian, M., & Henry, A. (2007). The grammatical morpheme deficit in moderate hearing impairment. *International Journal of Language & Communication Disorders*, 42, 17–36.

McIntosh, B., Crosbie, S., Holm, A., Dodd, B., & Thomas, S. (2007). Enhancing the phonological awareness and language skills of socially disadvantaged preschoolers: An interdisciplinary programme. *Child Language Teaching and Therapy*, 23, 267–286.

McKenzie, B. E., Skouteris, H., Day, R. H., Hartman, B., & Yonas, A. (1993). Effective action by infants to contact objects by reaching and learning. *Child Development*, 64, 415–429.

McKeough, A. (1992). A neo-structural analysis of children's narrative and its development. In R. Case (Ed.), *The mind's staircase: Exploring the conceptual underpinning of children's thought and knowledge* (pp. 58–114). Hillsdale, NJ: Erlbaum.

McLean, M., Bailey, D. B., & Wolery, M. (2004). *Assessing infants and preschoolers with special needs*. Upper Saddle River, NJ: Merrill/Prentice Hall.

McLean, M., & Odom, S. (1993). Practices for young children with and without disabilities: Comparison of DEC and NAEYC identified practices. *Topics in Early Childhood Special Education*, 13(3), 274–292.

McLoyd, V. C. (1986). Social class and pretend play. In A. W. Gottfried & C. C. Brown (Eds.), *Play interactions: The contribution of play materials and parental involvement to children's development* (pp. 175–196). Lexington, MA: Heath.

McLoyd, V. C. (1990a). The impact of economic hardship on black families and children: Psychological distress, parenting, and socioemotional development. *Child Development*, 61, 311–346.

McLoyd, V. C. (1990b). Minority children: Introduction to the special issue. *Child Development*, 61, 263–266.

McLoyd, V. C. (1998). Changing demographics in the American population: Implications for research on minority children and adolescents. In V. C. McLoyd & L. Steinberg (Eds.), *Studying minority adolescents: Conceptual, methodological, and theoretical issues* (pp. 3–28). Mahwah, NJ: Erlbaum.

McLoyd, V. C. (2006). The legacy of Child Development's 1990 special issue on minority children: An editorial retrospective. *Child Development*, 77, 1142–1148.

McLoyd, V. C., Aikens, N. L., & Burton, L. M. (2006). Childhood poverty, policy, and practice. In K. Renniger & I. Siegel (Eds.,) *Child psychology and practice*, pp. 700–775. Hoboken, NJ: Wiley.

McLoyd, V. C., & Randolph, S. M. (1984). The conduct and publication of research on Afro-American children: A content analysis. *Human Development*, 27, 65–75.

McLoyd, V. C., & Steinberg, L. (1998). *Studying minority adolescents: Conceptual, methodological, and theoretical issues*. Mahwah, NJ: Erlbaum.

McLoyd, V. C., & Wilson, L. (1992). Telling them like it is: The role of economic and environmental factors in single mothers' discussions with their children. *American Journal of Community Psychology*, 20, 419–444.

McMurray, B. (2007). Moo-cow! Mummy! More! How do children learn so many words? *Significance*, 4, 159–163.

McNeely, M. J., Fujimoto, W. Y., Leonetti, D. L., Tsai, E. C., & Boyko, E. J. (2007). The association between birth weight and visceral fat in middle-age adults. *Obesity*, 15, 816–819.

McNeil, C., Capage, L., & Bennett, G. (2002). Cultural issues in the treatment of young African American children diagnosed with disruptive behavior disorders. *Journal of Pediatric Psychology*, 27, 339–350.

Mcquaid, N., Bigelow, A., McLaughlin, J., & MacLean, K. (2008). Maternal mental state language and preschool children's attachment security: Relation to children's mental state language and expressions of emotional understanding. *Social Development*, 17, 61–83.

Meadan, H., Monda-Amaya, L. (2008). Collaboration to promote social competence for students with mild disabilities in the general classroom. *Intervention in School and Clinic*, 43, 158–167.

Mejia, D. (1983). The development of Mexican-American children. In G. J. Powell (Ed.), *The psychosocial development of minority children*. New York: Brunner/Mazel.

Mejía-Arauz, R., Rogoff, B., Dexter, A., & Najafi, B. (2007). Cultural variation in children's social organization. *Child Development*, 78, 1001–1014.

Mellor, S. (1990). How do only children differ from other children? *Journal of Genetic Psychology*, 151, 221–230.

Mendez, J., Fantuzzo, J., & Cicchetti, D. (2002). Profiles of social competence among low-income African American preschool children. *Child Development*, 73, 1085–1100.

Menn, L., & Stoel-Gammon, C. (2008). Phonological development: Learning sounds and sound patterns. In J. B. Gleason (Ed.), *The development of language* (pp. 59–100). Boston: Allyn & Bacon.

Menyuk, P., & Menyuk, D. (2004). Communicative competence: A historical and cultural perspective. In J. S. Wurzel (Ed.), *Toward multiculturalism: A reader in multicultural education*. Yarmouth, ME: Intercultural Press.

Mercer, J. (1972, September). IQ: The lethal label. *Psychology Today*, 44–47.

Mercuri, E., & Barnett A. L. (2003). Neonatal brain MRI and motor outcome at school age in children with neonatal encephalopathy: A review of personal experience. *Neural Plasticity*, 10, 5–57.

Mertz, E., & Yovel, J. (2000). Metalinguistic awareness. In J. Östman, J. Verschueren, J. Blommaert, & C. Bulcaen (Eds.), *Handbook of pragmatics* (pp. 122–144). New York: Kluwer.

Messier, J., Ferland, F., & Majnemer, A. (2008). Play behavior of school age children with intellectual disability: Their capacities, interests and attitude. *Journal of Developmental and Physical Disabilities*, 20, 193–207.

Meyer, C. A., Klein, E. L., & Genishi, C. (1994). Peer relationships among 4 preschool second language learners in "small-group time." *Early Childhood Research Quarterly*, 9, 61–85.

Michaels, S. (1980, March). *Sharing time: An oral preparation for literacy*. Paper presented at the Ethnography in Education Research Forum, Philadelphia.

Michelsson, K., Rinne, A., & Paajanen, S. (1990). Crying, feeding, and sleeping patterns in 1 to 12 month–old infants. *Child Care, Health, and Development*, 116, 99–111.

Miernyk, K., Parkinson, A., Rudolph, K., Petersen, K., Bulkow, L., Greenberg, D., et al. (2000). Immunogenicity of a heptavalent pneumococcal conjugate vaccine in Apache and Navajo Indian, Alaska Native, and non–Native American children aged <2 years. *Clinical Infectious Diseases*, 31, 34–41.

Milch-Reich, S., Campbell, S. B., & Pelham, W. E. (1999). Developmental and individual differences in children's on-line representations of dynamic social events. *Child Development*, 70, 413–431.

Milevsky, A., Schlechter, M., Netter, S., & Keehn, D. (2007). Maternal and paternal parenting styles in adolescents: Associations with self-esteem, depression and life-satisfaction. *Journal of Child and Family Studies*, 16, 39–47.

Millar, W. S., Weir, C. G., & Supramaniam, G. (1992). The influence of perinatal risk status on contingency learning in 6- to 13-month-old infants. *Child Development*, 63, 304–313.

Miller, A., & Miller, E. (1973). Cognitive developmental training with elevated boards and sign language. *Journal of Autism and Childhood Schizophrenia*, 3, 65–85.

Miller, J. L., & Eimas, P. D. (1996). Internal structure of voicing categories in early infancy. *Perception and Psychophysics*, 58, 1157–1167.

Miller, P. H., & Aloise, P. A. (1989). Young children's understanding of psychological causes of behavior: A review. *Child Development*, 60, 257–285.

Miller, P. H., & Seier, W. L. (1994). Strategy utilization deficiencies in children. In H. W. Reese (Ed.), *Advances in child development and behavior* (Vol. 25, pp. 107–156). New York: Academic Press.

Miller, S. A. (1995). Parents' attributions for their children's behavior. *Child Development*, 66, 1557–1584.

Miller, S. R., & Coll, E. (2007). From social withdrawal to social confidence: Evidence for possible pathways. *Current Psychology*, 26, 86–101.

Miller-Jones, D. (1988). The study of African-American children's development: Contributions to reformulating developmental paradigms. In D. T. Slaughter (Ed.), *Black children and poverty: A developmental perspective* (pp. 75–92). San Francisco: Jossey-Bass.

Mills, D., Plunkett, K., Prat, C., & Schafer, G. (2005). Watching the infant brain learn words: Effects of vocabulary size and experience. *Cognitive Development* 20, 19–31.

Milson, A. (2007). Learning and teaching with maps. *The Professional Geographer*, 59, 282–284.

Milunsky, A. (1989). *Choices, not chances*. Boston: Little, Brown.

Milunsky, A. (1992). *Genetic disorders and the fetus: Diagnosis, prevention, and treatment*. Baltimore: John Hopkins University Press.

Miscione, J. L., Marvin, R. S., O'Brien, R. G., & Greenberg, M. T. (1978). A developmental study of preschool children's understanding of the words "know" and "guess." *Child Development*, 49, 1107–1113.

Mishra, R. C. (2001). Cognition across cultures. In D. Matsumoto (Ed.), *The Handbook of Culture & Psychology*, (pp. 119–136). Oxford: Oxford University Press.

Mitchell, E. A., Ford, R. P. K., Stewart, A., Taylor, B. J., Becroft, D. M. O., Thompson, J. M. D., et al. (1993). Smoking and Sudden Infant Death Syndrome. *Pediatrics*, 91, 893–896.

Mitchell, P. R., & Kent, R. D. (1990). Phonetic variation in multisyllable babbling. *Journal of Child Language*, 17, 247–265.

Mitchell-Copeland, J., Denham, S. A., & DeMulder, E. K. (1997). Q-Sort assessment of child-teacher relationships and social competence in the preschool. *Early Education and Development*, 8, 27–39.

Mize, J., & Ladd, G. W. (1990). A cognitive-social learning approach to social skills training with low-status preschool children. *Developmental Psychology*, 26, 388–397.

Moeller, M. P. (2007). Current state of knowledge: Psychosocial development in children with hearing impairment. *Ear & Hearing*, 28, 729–739.

Moely, B. E., Hart, S. S., Leal, L., Santulli, K. A., Rao, N., Johnson, T., et al. (1992). The teacher's role in facilitating memory and study strategy development in the elementary school classroom. *Child Development*, 63, 653–672.

Moffatt, P., & Thoburn, J. (2001). Outcomes of permanent family placement for children of minority ethnic origin. *Child & Family Social Work*, 6, 13–21.

Moffitt, T., Caspi, A., Harrington, H., Milne, B., Melchior, M., Goldberg, D., et al. (2007). Generalized anxiety disorder and depression: childhood risk factors in a birth cohort followed to age 32. *Psychological Medicine*, 37, 441–452.

Mohanty, J., & Newhill, C. (2005). Adjustment of international adoptees: Implications for practice and a future research agenda. *Children and Youth Services Review*, 28, 384–395.

Molfese, D. L., Freeman, R. B., & Palermo, D. S. (1975). The ontogeny of brain lateralization for speech and nonspeech stimuli. *Brain and Language*, 2, 356–368.

Moll, H., & Tomasello, M. (2006). Level 1 perspective–taking at 24 months of age. *British Journal of Developmental Psychology*, 24, 603–613.

Moody, J. (2001). Race, school integration, and friendship: Segregation in America. *American Journal of Sociology*, 107, 679–716.

Moore, D., Oates, J., Hobson, R., & Goodwing J. (2008). *Cognitive and social factors in the development of infants with Down Syndrome*. Southsea, England: Down Syndrome Education International.

Moore, G. A., Cohn, J., & Campbell, S. (2001). Infant affective responses to mother's still face at 6 months differentially predict externalizing and internalizing behaviors at 18 months. *Developmental Psychology*, 37, 706–714.

Moore, J. L., Ford, D., & Milner, H. R. (2005). Recruitment is not enough: Retaining African American students in gifted education. *Gifted Child Quarterly*, 49, 51–67.

Moore, K. L., & Persaud, T. V. (1993). *The developing human: Clinically oriented embryology*. Philadelphia: Saunders.

Mordkowitz, E. R., & Ginsburg, H. P. (1987). Early academic socialization of successful Asian-American college students. *Quarterly Newsletter of the Laboratory for Comparative Human Cognition*, 9, 85–91.

Mörelius, E., Nelson, N., & Gustafsson, P. (2007). Salivary cortisol response in mother-infant dyads at high psychosocial risk. *Child Care, Health and Development*, 33, 128–136.

Morelli, G. A. (1986). *Social development of 1-, 2-, and 3-year-old Efe and Lese children within the Ituri Forest of Northeastern Zaire*. Unpublished doctoral dissertation, University of Massachusetts, Amherst.

Morelli, G. A., Rogoff, B., Oppenheim, D., & Goldsmith, D. (2002). Cultural variations in infants' sleeping arrangements: Questions of independence. In M. A. Paludi (Ed.), *Human development in multicultural contexts* (pp. 31–37). Upper Saddle River, NJ: Prentice Hall.

Morgan, H. (1976). Neonatal precocity and the black experience. *Negro Educational Review*, 27, 129–134.

Morgan, J. L., & Saffran, J. R. (1995). Emerging integration of sequential and suprasegmental infor-

mation in preverbal speech segmentation. *Child Development*, 66, 911–936.

Morrison, G. M., & Polloway, E. A. (1995). Development and risking conditions. In E. L. Meyen & T. M. Skrtic (Eds.), *Special education and student disability* (pp. 213–270). Denver: Love.

Morrison, P., & Masten, A. S. (1991). Peer reputation in middle childhood as a predictor of adaptation in adolescence: A seven-year follow-up. *Child Development*, 62, 991–1007.

Morrongiello, B., & Sedore, L. (2005). The influence of child attributes and social-situational context on school-age children's risk taking behaviors that can lead to injury. *Journal of Applied Developmental Psychology*, 26, 347–361.

Morrow, L. (1994). *Integrated language arts: Controversy to consensus*. Upper Saddle River, NJ: Prentice Hall.

Morrow, L., & Rand, M. (1991). Preparing the classroom environment to promote literacy during play. In J. Christie (Ed.), *Play and early literacy development* (pp. 141–165). Albany: State University of New York Press.

Morse, A. R., Trieff, E., & Joseph, J. (1987). Vision screening: A study of 297 Head Start children. *Journal of Visual Impairment and Blindness*, 81, 200–203.

Morton, M. (2007). Table manners. *Gastronomica*, 7, 6–8.

Mortensen, E. L., Michaelson, K. F., Sanders, S. A., & Reinisch, J. M. (2002). The association between duration of breastfeeding and adult intelligence. *American Journal of Clinical Nutrition*, 70, 525–535.

Most, T. (2007). Speech intelligibility, loneliness, and sense of coherence among deaf and hard-of-hearing children in individual inclusion and group inclusion. *The Journal of Deaf Studies and Deaf Education*, 12, 495–503.

Mõttus, R., Indus, K., & Allik, J. (2008). Accuracy of only children stereotype. *Journal of Research in Personality*, 42, 1047–1052.

Müeller, U. (1999). Structure and content of concrete operational thought: An interpretation in context. *Archives de Psychologie*, 67, 21–35.

Muir, D. (2002). Adult communications with infants through touch: The forgotten sense. *Human Development*, 45, 95–99.

Mulder, M., Baeyens, D., Davidson, M., Casey, B., van den Ban, E., van Engeland, H., & Durston, S. (2008). Familial vulnerability to ADHD affects activity in the cerebellum in addition to the prefrontal systems. *Journal of the American Academy of Child & Adolescent Psychiatry*. 47, 68–75.

Mull, M., Agran, P., Winn, D., & Anderson, C. (2001). Injury in children of low-income Mexican, Mexican American, and non-Hispanic white mothers in the USA: A focused ethnography. *Social Science & Medicine*, 52, 1081–1091.

Mumme, D. L., & Fernald, A. (2003). The infant as onlooker: Learning from emotional reactions observed in a television scenario. *Child Development*, 74, 221–237.

Mumme, D. L., Fernald, A., & Herrera, C. (1996). Infants' responses to facial and vocal emotional signals in a social referencing paradigm. *Child Development*, 67, 3219–3237.

Munroe, R. L., & Munroe, R. H. (1977). Cooperation and competition among East-African and American children. *Journal of Social Psychology*, 101, 145–146.

Murphy, B. C., & Eisenberg, N. (2002). An integrative examination of peer conflict: Children's reported goals, emotions, and behaviors. *Social Development*, 11, 534–557.

Murray, A. D. (1985). Aversiveness is in the mind of the beholder. In B. M. Lester & C. F. Z. Boukydis (Eds.), *Infant crying* (pp. 217–239). New York: Plenum.

Murray, J. (2008). Media violence: The effects are both real and strong. *American Behavioral Scientist, 51*, 1212–1230.

Murray, L., Cooper, P., Creswell, C., Schofield, E., & Sack, C. (2007). The effects of maternal social phobia on mother-infant interactions and infant social responsiveness. *Journal of Child Psychology and Psychiatry, 48*, 45–52.

Murray, L., Hentges, F., Hill, J., Karpf, J., Mistry, B., Kreutz, M., et al. (2008). The effect of cleft lip and palate and the timing of lip repair on mother-infant interactions and infant development. *Journal of Child Psychology and Psychiatry, 49*, 115–123.

Musselman, C., Lindsay, P., & Wilson, A. (1988). An evaluation of trends in preschool programming for hearing-impaired children. *Journal of Speech and Hearing Disorders, 53*, 71–88.

Myers, S., & Johnson, C. (2007). Management of children with autism spectrum disorders. *Pediatrics, 120*, 1162–1182.

Naber, F., Swinkels, S., Buitelaar, J., Dietz, C., Van Daalen, E., Bakermans-Kranenburg, M., van IJzendoorn, M., et al. (2007). Attachment in toddlers with autism and other developmental disorders. *Journal of Autism and Developmental Disorders, 37*, 1123–1138.

Nachmias, M., Gunnar, M., Mangelsdorf, S., Parritz, R. H., & Buss, K. (1996). Behavioral inhibition and stress reactivity: The moderating role of attachment security. *Child Development, 67*, 508–522.

Nagin, D., & Tremblay, R. E. (1999). Trajectories of boys' physical aggression, opposition, and hyperactivity on the path to physically violent and nonviolent juvenile delinquency. *Child Development, 70*, 1181–1196.

Naglieri, J., & Ford, D. (2003). Addressing underrepresentation of gifted minority children using the Naglieri Nonverbal Ability Test (NNAT). *Gifted Child Quarterly, 47*, 155–160.

Naito, M., & Miura, H. (2001). Japanese children's numerical competencies: Age- and schooling-related influences on the development of number concepts and addition skills. *Developmental Psychology, 37*, 217–230.

Nathani, S., Ertmer, D., & Stark, R. (2006). Assessing vocal development in infants and toddlers. *Clinical Linguistics & Phonetics, 20*, 351–369.

National Association for Bilingual Education. (2004). *What is bilingual education?* Washington, DC: Author.

National Association for the Education of Young Children. (2004a). *Reauthorization of IDEA: Key facts.* Washington, DC: Author.

National Association for the Education of Young Children. (2004b). *Advocacy toolkit.* Washington, DC: Author.

National Center for Health Statistics. (2007a). *Health, United States 2007.* Hyattsville, MD: Public Health Service.

National Center for Health Statistics. (2007b). *National Survey of Children's Health.* Hyattsville, MD: author.

National Council of State Legislatures. (2004). *America's newcomers: Funding prenatal care for unauthorized immigrants.* Washington, DC: Author.

National Education Association. (2004). *No Child Left Behind: Improving the law.* Washington, DC: Author.

National Institute of Child Health and Human Development. (2000). The relation of child care to cognitive and language development. *Child Development, 71*, 960–980.

National Institute of Child Health and Human Development, Early Child Care Research Network. (1997). Child care in the first year of life. *Merrill-Palmer Quarterly, 43*, 340–360.

National Institute of Child Health and Human Development, Early Child Care Research Network. (2000). The relation of child care to cognitive and language development. *Child Development, 71*, 960–980.

National Institute of Child Health and Human Development, Early Child Care Research Network. (2003). Does early amount of time spent in child care predict socioemotional adjustment during the transition to kindergarten? *Child Development, 74*, 976–1005.

National Institute of Child Health and Human Development, Early Child Care Research Network. (2005). *Child care and development.* New York: Guilford.

National Institute of Child Health and Human Development, Early Child Care Research Network (2005). Are there long–term effects of early child care? *Child Development, 78*, 681–701.

National Institute of Child Health and Human Development, Early Child Care Research Network. (2008). Social competence with peers in third grade: Associations with earlier peer experiences in childcare. *Social Development* (online early publication).

National Safety Council. (1997). *Accident facts.* Chicago: Author.

Naus, M. J. (1982). Memory development in the young reader: The combined effects of knowledge base and memory processing. In W. Otto & S. White (Eds.), *Reading expository material* (pp. 273–302). New York: Academic Press.

Neal, L., McCray, A., Webb-Johnson, G., & Bridgest, S. (2003). The effects of African American movement styles on teachers' perceptions and reactions. *Journal of Special Education, 37*, 49–57.

Neihart, M. (2007). The socioaffective impact of acceleration and ability grouping. *Gifted Child Quarterly, 51*, 330–341.

Neisser, U., Boodoo, G., Bouchard, T. J., Boykin, A. W., Brody, N., Ceci, S. J., et al. (1996). Intelligence: Knowns and unknowns. *American Psychologist, 51*, 77–101.

Nell, V. (2007). Environmentalists and nativists: The IQ controversy in cross-cultural perspective. In B. Uzzell, M. Ponton, & A. Ardila (Eds.), *International handbook of cross-cultural neuropsychology* (pp. 63–92). London: Routledge.

Nelson, D., & Crick, N. (1999). Rose-colored glasses: Examining the social information processing of prosocial young adolescents. *Journal of Early Adolescence, 19*, 17–38.

Nelson, K. (1996). *Language in cognitive development.* New York: Cambridge University Press.

Nelson, L. J., Hart, C. H., Robinson, C. C., Olsen, S. F., & Rubin, K. (1997, April). *Relations between sociometric status and three subtypes of withdrawn behavior in preschool children: A multi-method perspective.* Paper presented at the biennial meeting of the Society for Research in Child Development, Washington, DC.

Nelson, L. J., Rubin, K., & Fox, N. (2005). Social withdrawal, observed peer acceptance, and the development of self-perceptions in children ages 4 to 7 years. *Early Childhood Research Quarterly, 20*, 185–200.

Nesdale, D. (2007). Development of ethnic prejudice in early childhood: Theories and research. In O. Saracho & B. Spodek (Eds.), *Contemporary perspectives on socialization and social development in early childhood education,* (pp. 213–240). Charlotte, NC: IAP.

Nesdale, D., Durkin, K., Maass, A., & Griffith, J. (2005). Threat, group identification, and children's ethnic prejudice. *Social Development, 14*, 189–205.

Neuhäuser, M., & Krackow, S. (2007). Adaptive-filtering of trisomy 21: Risk of Down syndrome depends on family size and age of previous child. *Naturwissenschaften, 94*, 117–121.

Neuman, S. B. (2006). The knowledge gap: Implications for early education. In S. Neuman & D. Dickinson (Eds.), *Handbook of early literacy research* (pp. 29–40). New York: Guilford Press.

Neuman, S. B., Copple, C., & Bredekamp, S. (2000). *Learning to read and write: Developmentally appropriate practices for young children.* Washington, DC: National Association for the Education of Young Children.

Neuman, S. B., & Roskos, K. (1997). Literacy knowledge in practice: Contexts of participation for young writers and readers. *Reading Research Quarterly, 32*, 10–32.

Neuman, S. B., & Roskos, K. (2005). The state of state pre-kindergarten standards. *Early Childhood Research Quarterly, 20*, 125–145.

New, R. S. (1994). Child's play—Una cosa naturale: An Italian perspective. In J. L. Roopnarine, J. E. Johnson, & F. H. Hooper (Eds.), *Children's play in diverse cultures* (pp. 123–147). Albany: State University of New York Press.

Newcombe, N., & Huttenlocher, J. (1992). Children's early ability to solve perspective-taking problems. *Developmental Psychology, 28*, 635–643.

Newcomer, P. L., & Hammill, D. D. (1997). *Test of language development-primary.* Austin, TX: PRO-ED.

Newman, D. L., Caspi, A., Mofftt, T. E., & Silva, P. A. (1997). Antecedents of adult interpersonal functioning: Effects of individual differences in age 3 temperament. *Developmental Psychology, 33*, 206–217.

Newman, J., Swaminathan, S., & Trawick–Smith, J. (2008 April). *A comparison of video modeling and video self-modeling for teaching social and play behaviors to young children with autism.* Paper presented at the Annual Meeting of the American Educational Research Association, New York.

Ng, F., Pomerantz, E., & Lam, S. (2007). European American and Chinese parents' responses to children's success and failure: Implications for children's responses. *Developmental Psychology, 43*, 1239–1255.

Nguyen, N., Allen, J., Peat, J., Beal, P., Webster, B., & Gaskin, K. (2004). Iron status of young Vietnamese children. *Journal of Paediatrics and Child Health, 40*, 424–429.

NIMH. (2004). *Depression.* Washington, DC: Author.

Nisan, M. (1987). Moral norms and social conventions: A cross-cultural comparison. *Developmental Psychology, 23*, 719–725.

Nix, R. L., Pinderhughes, E. E., Dodge, K. A., Bates, J. E., Pettit, G. S., & McFadyen-Ketchum, S. A. (1999). The relation between mothers' hostile attribution tendencies and children's externalizing behavior problems: The mediating role of mothers' harsh discipline practices. *Child Development, 70*, 896–909.

Nobles, W. W. (1985). *Africanicity and the black family: The development of a theoretical model.* Oakland, CA: Black Family Institute.

Nobles, W. W. (2007). African American family life: An instrument of culture. In H. McAdoo (Ed.), *Black families* (pp. 69–78). Newbury Park, CA: Sage Publishing.

Noll, D. L. (2007). *Activities for social skills development in deaf children preparing to enter the mainstream.* St. Louis: Washington University School of Medicine.

Nsamenang, A. B. (1995). Theories of developmental psychology for a cultural perspective: A viewpoint from Africa. *Psychology and Developing Societies, 7*, 1–19.

Nsamenang, A. B. (2004). *Cultures of human development and education: Challenges to growing up African.* Newbury Park, CA: Sage.

Nugent, J., Lester, B., & Brazelton, T. B. (1989). *The cultural contex of infancy: Vol. 1. Biology, culture, and infant development*. Norwood, NJ: Ablex.

Nutritional status of minority children. (2004). *Morbidity and Mortality Weekly Report, 48*(37), 829–830.

Nwokah, E. E., & Fogel, A. (1990). *Crosscultural differences in baby-talk to infants: The missing link?* Unpublished manuscript, Purdue University.

Nwokah, E. E., & Ikekeonwu, C. (1998). A sociocultural comparison of Nigerian and American children's games. In M. Duncan, G. Chick, & A. Aycock (Eds.) & S. Reifel (Series Ed.), *Play and cultural studies: Vol. 1. Diversions and divergences in fields of play* (pp. 59–76). Greenwich, CT: Ablex.

Nyiti, R. M. (1982). The validity of cultural differences explanations for cross-cultural variation in the rate of Piagetian cognitive development. In P. Wagner & H. Stevenson (Eds.), *Cultural perspectives in child development* (pp. 167–202). New York: Freeman.

O'Connor, T. G., Heron, J., Golding, J., Beveridge, M., & Glover, V. (2002). Maternal antenatal anxiety and behavioural/emotional problems in children: A test of a programming hypothesis. *Journal of Child Psychology and Psychiatry, 44,* 1025–1036.

Oddy, W. H., Peat, J. K., & deKlerk, N. H. (2002). Maternal asthma, infant feeding, and the risk of asthma in childhood. *Journal of Allergy and Clinical Immunology, 110,* 65–67.

Odom, S. (2002). Narrowing the question: Social integration and characteristics of children with disabilities in inclusion settings. *Early Childhood Research Quarterly, 17,* 167–170.

Ogbu, J. U. (1982). Socialization: A cultural ecological approach. In K. Borman (Ed.), *The social life of children in a changing society* (pp. 253–267). Hillsdale, NJ: Erlbaum.

Ogbu, J. U. (1992). Understanding cultural diversity and learning. *Educational Researcher, 21*(8), 5–14.

Ogbu, J. U. (1994). From cultural differences to differences in cultural frames of reference. In P. M. Greenfield & R. R. Cocking (Eds.), *Cross-cultural roots of minority child development* (pp. 365–391). Hillsdale, NJ: Erlbaum.

Ogbu, J. U. (2007). African American education: A cultural ecological perspective. In H. McAdoo (Ed.), *Black families* (pp. 79–94). Newbury Park, CA: Sage Publishing.

Ogura, T., Yamashita, Y., Murase, T., & Dale, P. S. (1993). *Some preliminary findings from the Japanese early communicative development inventory.* Paper presented at the Sixth International Congress for the Study of Child Language, Triste, Italy.

O'Hara, M. (2008). Young children, learning and ICT: A case study in the UK. *Technology, Pedagogy and Education, 17,* 29–40.

Ohgi, S., Arisawa, K., Takahashi, T., Kusumoto, T., Goto, Y., Akiyama, T., et al. (2003). Neonatal behavioral assessment scale as a predictor of later developmental disabilities of low birth-weight and/or premature infants. *Brain and Development, 25,* 313–321.

Okagaki, L., & Frensch, P. A. (1998). Parenting and children's school achievement: A multiethnic perspective. *American Educational Research Journal, 35*(1), 123–144.

Oken, E., Levitan, E., & Gillman, M. (2008). Maternal smoking during pregnancy and child overweight: Systematic review and meta-analysis. *International Journal of Obesity, 32,* 201–210.

Oliver, B., & Plomin, R. (2007). Twins' early development study (TEDS): A multivariate, longitudinal genetic investigation of language, cognition and behavior problems from childhood through adolescence. *Twin Research and Human Genetics, 10,* 96–105.

Oller, D. K., Eilers, R. E., Neal, A. R., & Schwartz, H. K. (1999). Precursors to speech in infancy: The prediction of speech and language disorders. *Journal of Communication Disorders, 32,* 223–245.

Oller, D. K., Eilers, R. E., Urbano, R. & Cobo-Lewis, A. B., (1997). Development of precursors to speech in infants exposed to two languages. *Journal of Child Language, 24,* 407–425.

Olsen, G., & Fuller, M. L. (2008). *Home–school relations: Working successfully with children and families.* Boston: Pearson.

Olsho, L. W., Koch, E. G., Carter, E. A., Halpin, C. F., & Spetner, N. B. (1988). Pure tone sensitivity of human infants. *Journal of the Acoustical Society of America, 84,* 1316–1324.

Olson, C. M., & Strawderman M. S. (2008). The relationship between food insecurity and obesity in rural childbearing women. *The Journal of Rural Health, 24,* 60–66.

Olson, H. C., Sampson, P. D., Barr, H., Steissguth, A. P., & Bookstein, F. L. (1992). Prenatal exposure to alcohol and school problems in late childhood: A longitudinal prospective study. *Development and Psychopathology, 4,* 341–359.

Olson, L. M., Becker, T. M., Wiggins, C. L., Key, C. R., & Samet, J. M. (1990). Injury mortality in American Indian, Hispanic, and non-Hispanic white children in New Mexico. *Social Sciences Medicine, 30,* 479–486.

Olusanya, B. (2005). Can the world's infants with hearing loss wait? *International Journal of Pediatric Otorhinolaryngology, 69,* 735–738.

Olvera-Ezzell, N., Power, T. G., & Cousins, J. H. (1990). Maternal socialization of children's eating habits: Strategies used by obese Mexican-American mothers. *Child Development, 61,* 395–400.

Olvera-Ezzell, N., Power, T. G., Cousins, J. H., Guerra, A. M., & Trujillo, M. (1994). The development of health knowledge in low-income Mexican-American children. *Child Development, 65,* 416–427.

Olweus, D. (1993). *Bullying at school.* Oxford: Blackwell.

Ormrod, J. E. (2007). *Educational psychology: Developing learners.* Upper Saddle River, NJ: Prentice Hall.

Ostrov, J., & Keating, C. (2004). Gender differences in preschool aggression during free play and structured interactions: An observational study. *Social Development, 13,* 255–277.

Oswald, R. (2002). Resilience within the family networks of lesbians and gay men: Intentionality and redefinition. *Journal of Marriage and Family, 64,* 374–383.

Overton, W., & Ennis, M. (2006). Cognitive-developmental and behavioral-analytic theories: Evolving into complementarity? *Human Development, 49,* 143–172.

Owens, J. A. (2004). Sleep in children: Cross-cultural perspectives. *Sleep and Biological Rhythms, 2,* 165–173.

Owens, R. E. (1994). Development of language, communication, and speech. In G.H. Shames, E. H. Wigg, & W. A. Second (Eds.), *Human communication disorders.* New York: Macmillan.

Owens, R. E. (1996). *Language development.* Boston: Allyn & Bacon.

Oyen, A., & Bebko, J. M. (1996). The effects of computer games and lesson context on children's mnemonic strategies. *Journal of Experimental Child Psychology, 62,* 173–189.

Packman, A., Code, C., & Onslow, M. (2007). On the cause of stuttering: Integrating theory with brain and behavioral research. *Journal of Neurolinguistics, 20,* 353–362.

Padilla, A. M., Lindholm, K. J., Chen, A., Duran, R., Hakuta, K., Lambert, W., et al. (1991). The English-only movement: Myths, reality, and implications for psychology. *American Psychologist, 46,* 120–131.

Pahl, R., & Pevalin, D. (2005). Between family and friends: A longitudinal study of friendship choice. *The British Journal of Sociology, 56,* 433–450.

Paik, H., & Comstock, G. (1994). The effects of television violence on antisocial behavior: A meta-analysis. *Communication Research, 21,* 516–546.

Palfrey, J. S., Hauser-Cram, P., Bronson, M., Warfield, M., Sirin, S., & Chan, E. (2005). The Brookline early education project: A 25-year follow-up study of a family-centered early health and development intervention. *Pediatrics, 116,* 144–152.

Palmer, J. T. (1991, April). *Maternal responses to infant cries: Effects of context and acoustical properties of crying.* Paper presented at the biennial meeting of the Society for Research in Child Development, Seattle.

Paludi, M. A. (2001). Overview: Cultural influences on development in infancy. In M. A. Paludi (Ed.), *Human development in multicultural contexts* (pp. 16–24). Upper Saddle River, NJ: Prentice Hall.

Pamplona, M., Ysunza, A., Gonzalez, F. (2008). Linguistic development in stuttering children. *The Open Otorhinolaryngology Journal, 2,* 1–6.

Pan, B. A., & Gleason, J. B. (2008). Semantic development: Learning the meanings of words. In J. B. Gleason (Ed.), *The development of language* (pp. 100–156). Boston: Allyn & Bacon.

Pan, H. L. W. (1994). Children's play in Taiwan. In J. L. Roopnarine, J. E. Johnson, & F. H. Hooper (Eds.), *Children's play in diverse cultures* (pp. 31–50). Albany: State University of New York Press.

Pan American Health Organization. (2002). *Quantifying the benefits of breastfeeding: A summary of the evidence.* Washington, DC: Author.

Paneth, N. S. (1995). The problem of low birth weight. In R. E. Behrman (Ed.), *The future of children: Low birth weight* (pp. 19–34). Los Angeles: Center for the Future of Children.

Pangrazi, R. (2006). *Dynamic physical education for elementary school children.* Upper Saddle River, NJ: Benjamin Cummings.

Parcel, G. S., Simons-Morton, B. G., O'Hara, N. M., Baranowski, T., Kolbe, L. J., & Bee, D. E. (1987). School promotion of healthful diet and exercise behavior: An integration of organizational change and social learning theory interventions. *Journal of School Health, 57,* 150–156.

Parcel, T. L., & Menaghan, E. G. (1994). *Parents' jobs and children's lives.* New York: Aldine de Gruyter.

Paris, S. G., & Lindauer, B. K. (1977). Constructive aspects of children's comprehension and memory. In R. V. Kail & W. Hagen (Eds.), *Perspectives on the development of memory and cognition* (pp. 35–60). Hillsdale, NJ: Erlbaum.

Park, J., Vincent, D., & Hastings-Tolsma, M. (2007). Disparity in prenatal care among women of colour in the USA. *Midwifery, 23,* 28–37.

Parker, J. G., Rubin, K. H., Price, J. M., & DeRosier, M. E. (1995). Peer relationships, child development, and adjustment. In D. Cicchetti & D.J. Cohen (Eds.), *Developmental psychopathology: Vol. 2. Risk, disorder, and adaptation* (pp. 96–161). New York: John Wiley & Sons.

Parten, M. B. (1932). Social participation among preschool children. *Journal of Abnormal and Social Psychology, 27,* 243–269.

Pataki, S. P., Shapiro, C., & Clark, M. S. (1994). Children's acquisition of appropriate norms for friendships and acquaintances. *Journal of Social and Personal Relationships, 11,* 427–442.

Pate, R., Pfeiffer, K., Trost, S., Ziegler, P., & Dowda, M. (2004). Physical activity among children attending preschools. *Pediatrics, 114,* 1258–1263.

Paterson, S., Heim, S., Friedman, J., Choudhury, N., & Benasich, A. (2006). Development of structure and function in the infant brain: Implications for cognition, language and social behaviour. *Neuroscience & Biobehavioral Reviews, 30*, 1087–1105.

Patz, J. A., & Dennis, C. W. (2008). Sensorimotor development. In W. Umansky & R. Hooper (Eds.), *Young children with special needs* (pp. 94–154). Upper Saddle River, NJ: Prentice Hall.

Paul, R. (1999). Early speech perception and production. *Journal of Communication Disorders, 32*, 247–250.

Pearce, N., Foliaki, S., Sporle, A., & Cunningham, C. (2004). Genetics, race, ethnicity, and health. *British Medical Journal, 328*, 1070–1072.

Pearson, B. Z., Fernandez, S., Lewedeg, V., & Oller, D. K. (1997). The relation of input factors to lexical learning by bilingual infants. *Applied Psycholinguistics, 18*, 41–58.

Pearson, J. L., Hunter, A. G., Ensminger, M. E., & Kellam, S. G. (1990). Black grandmothers in multigenerational households: Diversity in family structure and parenting involvement in the Woodlawn Community. *Child Development, 61*, 434–442.

Peck, C., Odom, S., & Bricker, D. (Eds.). (1993). *Integrating young children with disabilities into community programs.* Baltimore: Paul H. Brookes.

Pederson, D. R., & Moran, G. (1995). A categorical description of infant-mother relationships in the home and its relation to Q-sort measures of mother-infant interaction. *Monographs of the Society for Research in Child Development, 60*, Serial No. 244.

Pedro-Carroll, J. (2005). Fostering resilience in the aftermath of divorce: The role of evidence-based programs for children. *Family Court Review, 43*, 52–64.

Peirano, P., Algarin, C., & Uauy, R. (2003). Sleep-wake states and their regulatory mechanisms throughout early human development. *The Journal of Pediatrics, 143*, 70–79.

Peleg, O., Halaby, E., & Whaby, E. (2006). The relationship of maternal separation anxiety and differentiation of self to children's separation anxiety and adjustment to kindergarten: A study in Druze families. *Journal of Anxiety Disorders, 20*, 973–995.

Pellegrini, A. D. (1995a). Boys' rough-and-tumble play and social competence: Contemporaneous and longitudinal relations. In A. Pellegrini (Ed.), *The future of play theory* (pp. 107–126). Albany: State University of New York Press.

Pellegrini, A. D. (1995b). *School recess and playground behavior.* Albany: State University of New York Press.

Pellegrini, A. D. (2005). *Recess: Its Role in Education and Development.* London: Routledge.

Pellegrini, A. D., & Perlmutter, J. C. (1988). Rough-and-tumble play on the elementary school playground. *Young Children, 43*(2), 14–47.

Pellegrini, A. D., Perlmutter, J. C., Galda, L., & Brody, G. H. (1990). Joint reading between black Head Start children and their mothers. *Child Development, 61*, 443–453.

Pellegrini, A. D., & Smith, P. K. (1999). Physical activity play: The nature and function of a neglected aspect of play. In M. Hertzig & E. Farber (Eds.), *Annual progress in child psychiatry and child development* (pp. 5–36). Hove, England: Psychology Press.

Pellis, S., & Pellis, V. (2007). Rough-and-tumble play and the development of the social brain. *Current Directions in Psychological Science, 16*, 95–98.

Pennington, B. F., & Lefly, D. L. (2001). Early reading development in children at family risk for dyslexia. *Child Development, 72*, 816–833.

Pepler, D. J., & Ross, H. S. (1981). The effects of play on convergent and divergent problem solving. *Child Development, 52*, 1202–1210.

Perlman, M., Claris, O., Hao, Y., Pandit, P., Whyte, H., Chipman, M., et al. (1995). Secular changes in the outcomes to 18 to 24 months of age of ex-

tremely low birth weight infants. *Journal of Pediatrics, 126*, 75–87.

Perlmutter, B. F., Crocker, J., Cornday, D., & Garstecki, D. (1983). Sociometric status and related personality characteristics of mainstreamed and learning disabled adolescents. *Learning Disability Quarterly, 6*, 20–30.

Perner, J., Frith, U., Leslie, A. M., & Leekam, S. R. (1989). Exploration of the autistic child's theory of the mind: Knowledge, belief, and communication. *Child Development, 60*, 689–700.

Perner, J., Ruffman, T., & Leekam, S. R. (1994). Theory of mind is contagious: You catch it from your sibs. *Child Development, 65*, 1228–1238.

Perren, S., & Alsaker, F. (2006). Social behavior and peer relationships of victims, bully-victims, and bullies in kindergarten. *Journal of Child Psychology and Psychiatry, 47*, 45–57.

Perrin, J., Bloom, S., & Gortmaker, S. (2007). The increase of childhood chronic conditions in the United States. *JAMA., 297*, 255–259.

Perris, E. E., Myers, N. A., & Clifton, R. K. (1990). Long-term memory for a single infancy experience. *Child Development, 61*, 1796–1807.

Perry, B. D. (1996). Incubated in terror: Neurodevelopmental factors in the "cycle of violence." In J. D. Osovsky (Ed.), *Children, youth and violence: Searching for solutions* (pp. 44–68). New York: Guilford Press.

Perry, D., Dunne, M., McFadden, L., & Campbell, D. (2007). Reducing the risk for preschool expulsion: Mental health consultation for young children with challenging behaviors. *Journal of Child and Family Studies, 17*, 44–54.

Peskin, J., & Astington, J. (2004). The effects of adding metacognitive language to story texts. *Cognitive Development, 19*, 253–273.

Pesonen, A., Räikkönen, K., Keskivaara, P., & Keltikangas-Järvinen, L. (2003). Difficult temperament in childhood and adulthood: Continuity from maternal perceptions to self-ratings over 17 years. *Personality and Individual Differences, 34*, 19–31.

Peterson, C., Wellman, H., & Liu, D. (2005). Steps in theory-of-mind development for children with deafness or autism. *Child Development, 76*, 502–517.

Peterson, L., Ewigman, B., & Kivlahan, C. (1993). Judgements regarding appropriate child supervision to prevent injury: The role of environmental risk and child age. *Child Development, 64*, 934–950.

Petitto, L. A., Holowka, S., Sergio, L., Levy, B., & Ostry, D. (2004). Baby hands that move to the rhythm of language: Hearing babies acquiring sign languages babble silently on the hands. *Cognition, 93*, 43–73.

Petitto, L. A., & Marentette, P. F. (1991). Babbling in the manual mode: Evidence for the ontogeny of language. *Science, 251*, 1493–1496.

Petterson, S. M., & Albers, B. (2001). Effects of poverty and maternal depression on early child development. *Child Development, 72*, 1794–1813.

Pflaum, S. W. (1986). *The development of language and literacy in young children.* Upper Saddle River, NJ: Merrill/Prentice Hall.

Phillips, D., McCartney, K., Scarr, S., & Howes, C. (1987a). Selective review of infant day care research: A cause for concern. *Zero to Three, 7*, 18–21.

Phillips, D., Mekos, D., Scarr, S., McCartney, K., & Abbott–Shim, M. (2000b). Within and beyond the classroom door: Assessing quality in child care centers. *Early Childhood Research Quarterly, 15*, 475–496.

Phillips, D. A., Voran, M., Kisker, E., Howes, C., & Whitebrook, M. (1994). Child care for children in poverty: Opportunity or inequity? *Child Development, 65*, 472–492.

Philpott, R. H. (1995). Maternal health care in the developing world. In B. Sachs, R. Beard,

E. Papiernik, & C. Russell (Eds.), *Reproductive health care for women and babies* (pp. 226–245). New York: Oxford University Press.

Phinney, J. S., & Ong, A. D. (2007). Ethnic identity development in immigrant families. In J. Lansford, K. Deater–Deckard, & M. Bornstein (Eds.), *Immigrant families in contemporary society* (pp. 51–68). New York: Guilford Press.

Phinney, J. S., & Rotheram, M. J. (1987). Children's ethnic socialization: Themes and implications. In J. S. Phinney & M. J. Rotheram (Eds.), *Children's ethnic socialization: Pluralism and development* (pp. 274–292). Newbury Park, CA: Sage.

Phinney, J. S., & Tarver, S. (1988). Ethnic identity search and commitment in black and white eighth graders. *Journal of Early Adolescence, 8*, 265–277.

Piaget, J. (1930). *The child's conception of physical causality.* London: Routledge & Kegan Paul.

Piaget, J. (1932). *The moral judgement of the child.* New York: Free Press.

Piaget, J. (1952). *The origins of intelligence in children.* New York: International Universities Press.

Piaget, J. (1954). *The construction of reality in the child.* New York: Basic Books.

Piaget, J. (1959). *Language and thought of the child.* London: Routledge & Kegan Paul.

Piaget, J. (1962). *Play, dreams, and imitation in childhood.* New York: Norton.

Piaget, J. (1965). *The child's conception of number.* New York: Norton.

Piaget, J. (1971). *The construction of reality in the child.* New York: Ballantine.

Piaget, J., & Inhelder, B. (1963). *The child's conception of space.* London: Routledge & Kegan Paul.

Piaget, J., Inhelder, B., & Szeminska, A. (1960). *The child's conception of geometry.* New York: Basic Books.

Pickens, J. (1994). Perception of auditory-visual distance relations by 5-month-old infants. *Developmental Psychology, 30*, 537–544.

Pine, J. M., Lieven, E. V. M., & Rowland, C. F. (1997). Stylistic variation at the "single-word" stage: Relations between maternal speech characteristics and children's vocabulary composition and usage. *Child Development, 68*, 807–819.

Pinon, M. F., Huston, A. C., & Wright, J. C. (1989). Family ecology and child characteristics that predict young children's educational television viewing. *Child Development, 60*, 846–856.

Pintrich, P., & Blumenfeld, P. (1985). Classroom experience and children's self-perceptions of ability, effort, and conduct. *Journal of Educational Psychology, 77*, 646–657.

Pizzo, P. A., & Wilfert, M. (Eds.). (1994). *Pediatric AIDS: The challenge of HIV in infants, children, and adolescents.* Baltimore: Williams & Wilkins.

Plomin, R. (1995). Genetics and children's experiences in the family. *Journal of Child Psychology and Psychiatry, 36*, 33–68.

Plomin, R. (2008). *Behavioral genetics.* New York: Worth Publishers.

Plomin, R., DeFries, J. C., McClearn, G. E., & Rutter, M. (1997). Genotype-environment interaction and correlation in the analysis of human behavior. *Psychological Bulletin, 84*, 309–322.

Plumert, J. M. (1994). Flexibility in children's use of spatial and categorical organizational strategies in recall. *Developmental Psychology, 30*, 738–747.

Poag, C. K., Goodnight, J. A., & Cohen, R. (1985). The environments of children: From home to school. In R. Cohen (Ed.), *The development of spatial cognition* (pp. 71–114). Hillsdale, NJ: Erlbaum.

Poest, C. A., Williams, J. R., Witt, D. D., & Atwood, M. E. (1990). Challenge me to move: Large muscle development in young children. *Young Children, 45*(5), 4–10.

Polit, D. (1982). *Effects of family size.* Bethesda, MD: National Institutes of Health.

Pollard, N. L. (1998). Development of social interaction skills in preschool children with autism: A review of the literature. *Child & Family Behavior Therapy*, 20, 1–16.

Pollitt, E. (1994). Poverty and child development: Relevance of research in developing countries to the United States. *Child Development*, 65, 283–296.

Pollitt, E., Golub, M., Gorman, K., Grantham-McGregor, S., Levitsky, D., Schurch, B., et al. (1996). A reconceptualization of the effects of undernutrition on children's biological, psychosocial, and behavioral development. *SRCD policy report*, 10(5). Ann Arbor, MI: Society for Research in Child Development.

Pollitt, E., Gorman, K. S., Engle, P. L., Martorell, R., & Rivera, J. (1993). Early supplementary feeding and cognition: Effects over two decades. *Monographs of the Society for Research in Child Development*, 58, Serial No. 235.

Pollock, L. A. (1987). *A lasting relationship: Parents and children over three centuries*. Hanover, NH: University Press of New England.

Polman, H., Orobio de Castro, B., Koops, W., van Boxtel, H. W., & Merk, W. W. (2007). A meta-analysis of the distinction between reactive and proactive aggression in children and adolescents. *Journal of Abnormal Child Psychology*, 35, 522–535.

Poncin, Y., Sukhodolsky, D., McGuire, J., & Scahill, L. (2007). Drug and non-drug treatments of children with ADHD and tic disorders. *European Child & Adolescent Psychiatry*, 16, 78–88.

Ponza, M. (2004). Looking at WIC. *Journal of the American Dietetic Association*, 104, 1074–1074.

Poolton, J., Masters, R., & Maxwell, J. P. (2007). The development of a culturally appropriate analogy for implicit motor learning in a Chinese population. *The Sport Psychologist*, 21, 375–382.

Pope, A. W., Bierman, K. L., & Mumma, G. H. (1991). Aggression, hyperactivity, and inattention-immaturity: Behavior dimensions associated with peer rejection in elementary school boys. *Developmental Psychology*, 27, 663–671.

Porter, R. H., Makin, J. W., Davis, L. B., & Christensen, K. M. (1992). Breast-fed infants respond to olfactory clues from their own mother and unfamiliar lactating females. *Infant Behavior and Development*, 15, 85–93.

Porter, R. H., & Winberg, J. (1999). Unique salience of maternal breast odors for newborn infants. *Neuroscience & Biobehavioral Reviews*, 23, 439–449.

Posada, G., Jacobs, A., Carbonell, O., Alzate, G., Bustamante, M., & Arenas, A. (1999). Maternal care and attachment security in ordinary and emergency contexts, *Developmental Psychology*, 36, 1379–1388.

Posner, J. K., & Vandell, D. L. (1994). Low-income children's after-school care: Are there beneficial effects of after-school programs? *Child Development*, 65, 440–456.

Potter, E. (1982, March). *Demands upon children regarding quality of achievement: Standard setting in preschool classrooms*. Paper presented at the annual meeting of American Educational Research Association, New York.

Powlishta, K., Serbin, L., & Moller, L. (1993). The stability of individual differences in gender typing: Implications for understanding gender segregation. *Sex Roles*, 29, 723–737.

Prathanee, B., Thinkhamrop, B., & Dechongkit, S. (2007). Factors associated with specific language impairment and later language development during early life: A literature review. *Clinical Pediatrics*, 46, 22–29.

Prendeville, J., Prelock, P., & Unwin, G. (2006). Peer play interventions to support the social competence of children with autism spectrum disorders. *Seminars in Speech and Language*, 27, 32–46.

Pressley, M. (2005). *Reading instruction that works: The case for balanced teaching*. New York: Guilford Press.

Pressley, M., & McCormick, C. B. (1995). *Advanced educational psychology for educators, researchers, and policy makers*. New York: HarperCollins.

Price-Williams, D. R., Gordon, W., & Ramirez, M. (1969). Skill and conservation. *Developmental Psychology*, 1, 769.

Prior, M., Smart, D., Sanson, A., & Oberklaid, F. (2000). Does shy-inhibited temperament in childhood lead to anxiety problems in adolescence? *Journal of the American Academy of Child & Adolescent Psychiatry*, 39, 461–468.

Prizant, B., & Duchan, J. (1981). The functions of immediate echolalia in autistic children. *Journal of Speech and Hearing Disorders*, 46, 241–249.

Proctor, M., Moore, L., Gao, D., Cupples, L., Bradlee, M., Hood, M., et al. (2003). Television viewing and change in body fat from preschool to early adolescence: The Framingham Children's Study. *International Journal of Obesity*, 27, 827–833.

Proffitt, B. (2008). *Homeless children and youth*. Nashville: National Health Care for the Homeless Council.

Punch, S. (2007) "You can do nasty things to your brothers and sisters without a reason": Siblings' backstage behaviour. *Childhood and Society*, 21, 235–236.

Pungello, E. P., Kupersmidt, J. B., Burchinal, M. R., & Patterson, C. J. (1996). Environmental risk factors and children's achievement from middle school to early adolescence. *Developmental Psychology*, 32, 755–767.

Pupillo, J. (2007). Toilet training 101: Potty training in less than a day? Or child-directed bowel and bladder control? A recent report supports the use of either of these training methods. *AAP News*, 28, 16.

Purhonen, M., Kilpeläinen-Lees, R., Valkonen-Korhonen, M., Karhu, J., & Lehtonen, J. (2004). Cerebral processing of mother's voice compared to unfamiliar voice in 4-month-old infants. *International Journal of Psychophysiology*, 52, 257–266.

Putallaz, M., Grimes, C., Foster, K., Kupersmidt, J., Coie, J., & Dearing, K. (2007). Overt and relational aggression and victimization: Multiple perspectives within the school setting. *Journal of School Psychology*, 45, 523–547.

Putallaz, M., & Wasserman, A. (1989). Children's naturalistic entry behavior and sociometric status: A developmental perspective. *Developmental Psychology*, 25, 297–305.

Quay, S. (2003). Cross-linguistic structures in simultaneous bilingualism. *Journal of Child Language*, 30, 925–930.

Quiggle, N. L., Garber, J., Panak, W. F., & Dodge, K. A. (1992). Social information processing in aggressive and depressed children. *Child Development*, 63, 1305–1320.

Quigley, S., & Paul, P. (1987). Deafness and language development. In S. Rosenberg (Ed.), *Advances in applied psycholinguistics* (Vol. 1, pp. 180–219). Cambridge: Cambridge University Press.

Quigley, S., Power, D., & Steinkamp, M. (1977). The language structure of deaf children. *Volta Review*, 79, 73–84.

Quilligan, J. E. (1995). Obstetrics and gynecology. *Journal of the American Medical Association*, 273, 1700–1702.

Quinlan, R. J., & Quinlan, M. B. (2007). Parenting and cultures of risk. *American Anthropologist*, 109, 164–179.

Quiroga, T., Lemos-Britton, Z., Mostafapour, E., Abbott, R., & Berninger, V. (2002). Phonological awareness and beginning reading in Spanish-speaking ESL first graders: Research into practice. *Journal of School Psychology*, 40, 85–111.

Quintana, S. M., Chao, R. K., Cross, W., Hughes, D., Nelson-Le Gall, S., Aboud, F., et al. (2006). Race, ethnicity, and culture in child development: Contemporary research and future directions. *Child Development*, 77, 1129–1141.

Rafferty, Y., & Shinn, M. (1991). The impact of homelessness on children. *American Psychologist*, 46, 1170–1179.

Rah, Y., & Parke, R. (2008). Pathways between parent-child interactions and peer acceptance: The role of children's social information processing. *Social Development*, 17, 341–357.

Raikes, H., & Thompson, R. A. (2005). Links between risk and attachment security: Models of influence. *Journal of Applied Developmental Psychology*, 26, 440–455.

Rakoczy, H. (2006). Pretend play and the development of collective intentionality. *Cognitive Systems Research*, 7, 113–127.

Rakoczy, H. (2007). Play, games, and the development of collective intentionality. *New Directions in Child and Adolescent Development*, 115, 53–67.

Raley, S., & Bianchi, S. (2006). Sons, daughters, and family processes: Does gender of children matter? *Annual Review of Sociology*, 32, 401–421

Ramey, C., Campbell, F., & Blair, C. (1998). Enhancing the life course for high-risk children. In J. Crane (Ed.), *Social programs that work* (pp. 184–199). New York: Russell Sage Foundation.

Ramey, C. T., & Landesman-Ramey, S. (1996). *Prevention of intellectual disabilities: Early intervention to improve cognitive development*. Birmingham: University of Alabama Civitan International Research Center.

Ramey, C. T., & Ramey, S. L. (1998). Early intervention and early experience. *American Psychologist*, 53, 109–120.

Ramsey, P. G. (1989a, April). *Friendships, groups, and entries: Changing social dynamics in early childhood classrooms*. Paper presented at the biennial meeting of the Society for Research in Child Development, Kansas City, MO.

Ramsey, P. G. (1989b, April). *Successful and unsuccessful entry attempts: An analysis of behavioral and contextual factors*. Paper presented at the biennial meeting of the Society for Research in Child Development, Kansas City, MO.

Ramsey, P. G. (1995). Growing up with the contradictions of race and class. *Young Children*, 50(6), 18–22.

Ramsey, P. G. (2004). *Teaching and learning in a diverse world: Multicultural education for young children*. New York: Teachers College Press.

Ramsey, P. G., & Myers, L. C. (1990). Young children's responses to racial differences: Relations among cognitive, affective, and behavioral dimensions. *Journal of Applied Developmental Psychology*, 11, 49–67.

Ratner, N. B. (2008). Atypical language development. In J. Berko–Gleason (Ed.), *The development of language* (pp. 369–406). Boston: Allyn & Bacon.

Raval, V., Goldberg, S., Atkinson, L., Benoit, D., Myhal, N., Poulton, L., et al. (2001). Maternal attachment, maternal responsiveness and infant attachment. *Infant Behavior and Development*, 24, 281–304.

Raver, C., Gershoff, E., & Aber, J. (2007). Testing equivalence of mediating models of income, parenting, and school readiness for white, black, and Hispanic children in a national sample. *Child Development*, 78, 96–115.

Reagon, K., Higbee, T., & Endicott, K. (2006). Teaching pretend play skills to a student with autism using video modeling with a sibling as model and play partner. *Education and Treatment of Children*, 29, 517–526.

Red Horse, J. (1983). Indian family values and experiences. In G. J. Powell (Ed.), *The psychosocial development of minority children* (pp. 258–272). New York: Brunner/Mazel.

Reese, E., Bird, A., & Tripp, G. (2007). Children's self-esteem and moral self: Links to parent-child conversations regarding emotion. *Social Development, 16*, 460–478.

Reich, P. A. (1986). *Language development*. Englewood Cliffs, NJ: Merrill/Prentice Hall.

Reid, B. V. (1984). An anthropological reinterpretation of Kohlberg's stages of moral development. *Human Development, 27*, 56–74.

Reid, S., Salmon, K., & Lovibond, P. (2006). Cognitive biases in childhood anxiety, depression, and aggression: Are they pervasive or specific? *Journal of Cognitive Therapy and Research, 30*, 531–549.

Reilly, J., Methvan, E., McDowell, Z., Hacking, B., Alexander, D., Stewart, Z., & Kelnar, C. (2003). Health consequences of obesity. *Archives of Disease in Childhood, 88*, 748–752.

Reiser, J., Yonas, A., & Wikner, K. (1976). Radial localization of odors by human newborns. *Child Development, 47*, 856–859.

Reiss, A. J., & Roth, J. A. (Eds.). (1993). *Understanding and preventing violence*. Washington, DC: National Academy Press.

Rennie, F., & Mason, R. (2007). The development of distributed learning techniques in Bhutan and Nepal. *The International Review of Research in Open and Distance Learning, 8*.

Rettig, M. (1994). The play of young children with visual impairments: Characteristics and interventions. *Journal of Visual Impairment and Blindness, 88*, 410–420.

Reunamo, S. & Nurmilaakso, M. (2007). Vygotsky and agency in language development. *European Early Childhood Education Research Journal, 15*, 313–327

Reutzel, D., & Morrow, L. (2007). Promoting and assessing effective literacy learning classroom environments. In J. R. Paratore & R. L. McCormack (Eds.), *Classroom literacy assessment: Making sense of what students know.* (pp. 33–49). New York: Guilford Press.

Rey-López, J., Vicente-Rodríguez, G., Biosca, M., & Moreno, L. (2007). Sedentary behaviour and obesity development in children and adolescents. *Nutrition, Metabolism and Cardiovascular Diseases, 18*, 242–251.

Reynolds, A. J. (2004). Research on early childhood interventions in the confirmatory mode. *Children and Youth Services Review, 26*, 15–38.

Reynolds, A. J., & Temple, J. A. (1998). Extended early childhood intervention and school achievement: Age thirteen findings from the Chicago Longitudinal Study. *Child Development, 69*, 231–246.

Reynolds, R. (2001). *Education of Aboriginal groups in Australia*. Unpublished manuscript, Eastern Connecticut State University.

Reznick, J. S., & Goldfield, B. A. (1992). Rapid change in lexical development in comprehension and production. *Developmental Psychology, 28*, 406–413.

Ricci, D., Romeo, D., Serrao, F., Cesarini, L., Gallini, F., Cota, F., Leone, D., Zuppa, A., Romagnoli, C., Cowan, F., & Mercuri, E. (2008). Application of a neonatal assessment of visual function in a population of low risk full-term newborns. *Early Human Development, 84*, 277–280.

Rice, M. L., & Schuele, C. M. (1995). Speech and language impairments. In E. L. Meyen & T. M. Skrtic (Eds.), *Special education and student disability* (pp. 339–376). Denver: Love.

Richardson, J. (2007). Contemporary feminist perspectives on social contract theory. *Ratio Juris, 20*, 402–423.

Richman, A. L., Miller, P. M., & Levine, R. A. (1992). Cultural and educational variations in maternal responsiveness. *Developmental Psychology, 28*, 614–621.

Richmond, M., Stocker, C., & Rienks, S. (2005). Longitudinal associations between sibling relationship quality, parental differential treatment, and children's adjustment. *Journal of Family Psychology, 19*, 550–559.

Rittle-Johnson, B., & Siegler, R. S. (1999). Learning to spell: Variability, choice, and change in children's strategy use. *Child Development, 70*, 332–348.

Rivara, F. P., & Barber, M. (1985). Demographic analysis of childhood pedestrian injuries. *Pediatrics, 76*, 375–381.

Rivara, F. P., & Mueller, B. A. (1987). The epidemiology and causes of childhood injuries. *Journal of Social Issues, 43*, 13–31.

Robbins, M., Szapocznik, S., Feaster, D., Mayorga, C., Dillon, F., & Burns, M., (2007). The impact of family functioning on family racial socialization processes. *Cultural Diversity and Ethnic Minority Psychology, 13*, 313–320.

Roberts, J. E., Burchinal, M. R., & Clark–Klein, S. M. (1995). Otitis media in early childhood and cognitive, academic, and behavioral outcomes at 12 years of age. *Journal of Pediatric Psychology, 20*, 645–660.

Roberts, J. E., Burchinal, M., & Durham, M. (1999). Parents' report of vocabulary and grammatical development of African American preschoolers: Child and environmental associations. *Child Development, 70*, 92–106.

Roberts, J., & Hanson, L. (2007). Best practices in second stage labor care: Maternal bearing down and positioning. *Journal of Midwifery & Women's Health, 52*, 238–245.

Robertson, S., Featherstone, D., Gacic-Dobo, M., & Hersh, B. (2008). Rubella and congenital rubella syndrome: A global update. *PanAmerican Public Health, 14*, 305–315.

Robins, L. N., & Mills, J. L. (1993). *Effects of in utero exposure to street drugs*. Washington, DC: National Institute of Child Health and Human Development.

Robinson, A., & Stark, D. (2002). *Advocates in action: Making a difference for young children*. Washington, DC: National Association for the Education of Young Children.

Robinson, C., Anderson, G., Porter, C., Hart, C., & Wouden-Miller, M. (2003). Sequential transition patterns of preschoolers' social interactions during child-initiated play: Is parallel-aware play a bidirectional bridge to other play states? *Early Childhood Research Quarterly, 18*, 3–21.

Robinson, J. L. (2000). Are there implications for prevention research from studies of resilience? *Child Development, 71*, 570–572.

Robinson, N. M., & Noble, K. D. (1991). Social-emotional development and adjustment of gifted children. In M.C. Wang, M.C. Reynolds, & H. J. Walberg (Eds.), *Handbook of special education: Research and practice* (pp. 29–50). New York: Pergamon Press.

Robinson, S. M., & Deshler, D. D. (1995). Learning disabilities. In E. L. Meyen & T. M. Skrtic (Eds.), *Special education and student disability* (pp. 171–212). Denver: Love.

Rodriguez, C., & Moore, N. B. (1995). Perceptions of pregnant/parenting teens. *Adolescence, 30*, 685–706.

Rodriquez, A. (1983). Educational policy and cultural plurality. In G. J. Powell (Ed.), *The psychosocial development of minority group children* (pp. 499–514). New York: Brunner/Mazel.

Roedell, W. C. (1984). Vulnerabilities of highly gifted children. *Roeper Review, 6*, 127–130.

Roehr, K. (2008). Linguistic and metalinguistic categories in second language learning. *Cognitive Linguistics, 19*, 67–106.

Roemmich, J., Epstein L., Raja S., & Yin L. (2007). The neighborhood and home environments: Disparate relationships with physical activity and sedentary behaviors in youth. *Annals of Behavioral Medicine, 33*, 29–38.

Rogers, S., Hepburn, S., Stackhouse, T., & Wehner, E. (2003). Imitation performance in toddlers with autism and those with other developmental disorders. *Journal of Child Psychology and Psychiatry, 44*, 763–781.

Rogoff, B. (1986). The development of strategic use of context in spatial memory. In M. Perlmutter (Ed.), *Perspectives on intellectual development* (pp. 107–123). Hillsdale, NJ: Erlbaum.

Rogoff, B. (1990). *Apprenticeship in thinking*. New York: Oxford University Press.

Rogoff, B. (1997). Cognition as a collaborative process. In D. Kuhn & R. S. Siegler (Eds.), *Cognition, perception, and language.* (pp. 679–744). New York: John Wiley & Sons.

Rogoff, B. (2001). *Everyday cognition: Its development in social context*. New York: Replica Books.

Rogoff, B. (2003). *The cultural nature of human development*. New York: Oxford University Press.

Rogoff, B., Mistry, J., Goncu, A., & Mosier, C. (1993). Guided participation in cultural activity by toddlers and caregivers. *Monographs of the Society for Research in Child Development, 58*, (Serial No. 236).

Rogosch, F. A., Cicchetti, D., & Abner, J. L. (1995). The role of child maltreatment in early deviations in cognitive and affective processing abilities and later peer relationship problems. *Development and Psychopathology, 7*, 591–609.

Rogosch, F. A., & Newcomb, A. F. (1989). Children's perceptions of peer reputations and their social reputations among peers. *Child Development, 60*, 597–610.

Rommelse, N., Altink, M., Martin, N., Buschgens, C., Faraone, S., Buitelaar, J. et al. (2008). Relationship between endophenotype and phenotype in ADHD. *Behavioral and Brain Functions, 4*, 11–17.

Rommelse, N., Altink, M., Oosterlaan, J., Buschgens, C., Buitelaar, J., De Sonneville, L., et al. (2007). Motor control in children with ADHD and non-affected siblings. *Journal of Child Psychology and Psychiatry, 48*, 1071–1079.

Romney, K., & Romney, R. (1963). The Mixtecans of Juxtlahuaca, Mexico. In B. B. Whiting (Ed.), *In six cultures: Studies of child rearing* (pp. 25–41). New York: John Wiley & Sons.

Roopnarine, J. L., Hossain, Z., Gill, P., & Brophy, H. (1994). Play in the East Indian context. In J. L. Roopnarine, J. E. Johnson, & F. H. Hooper (Eds.), *Children's play in diverse cultures* (pp. 9–30). Albany: State University of New York Press.

Roopnarine, J. L., Johnson, J. E., & Hooper, F. H. (Eds.). (1994). *Children's play in diverse cultures*. Albany: State University of New York Press.

Roosa, M. W. (2000). Some thoughts about resilience versus positive development, main effects versus interactions, and the value of resilience. *Child Development, 71*, 567–569.

Roosa, M. W., Morgan-Lopez, A. A., Cree, W. K., & Specter, M. M. (2002). Ethnic culture, poverty, and context: Sources of influence on Latino families and children. In J. M. Contreras, K. A. Kerns & A. M. Neal-Barnett (Eds.), *Latino children and families in the United States current research and future directions*. Westport, CT: Praeger.

Rose, A., Carlson, W., & Waller, E. (2007). Prospective associations of co-rumination with friendship and emotional adjustment: Considering the socioemotional trade-offs of co-rumination. *Developmental Psychology, 43*, 1019–1031.

Rose, S. A., & Feldman, J. F. (1995). Prediction of IQ and specific cognitive abilities at 11 years from infancy measures. *Developmental Psychology, 31,* 685–696.

Rose, S. A., & Feldman, J. F. (1996). Memory and processing speed in preterm children at eleven years: A comparison with full-terms. *Child Development, 67,* 2005–2021.

Rose, S. A., Feldman, J. F., & Jankowski, J. J. (2001). Attention and recognition memory in the first year of life: A longitudinal study of preterms and full-term. *Developmental Psychology, 37,* 135–151.

Rose, S. A., Feldman, J. F., & Jankowski, J. J. (2004). Infant visual recognition memory. *Developmental Review 24,* 74–100.

Rose, S. A., Futterweit, L. R., & Jankowski, J. J. (1999). The relation of affect to attention and learning in infancy. *Child Development, 70,* 549–559.

Rosen, C. S., Schwebel, D. C., & Singer, J. L. (1997). Preschoolers attributions of mental states in pretense. *Child Development, 68,* 1133–1142.

Rosen, W. D., Adamson, L. B., & Bakeman, R. (1992). An experimental investigation of social referencing: Mothers' messages and gender differences. *Developmental Psychology, 28,* 1172–1178.

Rosenberg, M. (1979). *Conceiving the self.* New York: Basic Books.

Rosenblith, J. F. (1992). *In the beginning.* Thousand Oaks, CA: Sage.

Rosenstein, D., & Oster, H. (1988). Differential facial responses to four basic tastes in newborns. *Child Development, 59,* 1555–1568.

Roskos, K., & Neuman, S. B. (1998). Play as an opportunity for literacy. In O. Saracho & B. Spodek (Eds.), *Multiple perspectives on play in early childhood education* (pp. 100–115). Albany: State University of New York Press.

Ross, B., Gelman, S., & Rosengren, K. (2005). Children's category-based inferences affect classification. *British Journal of Developmental Psychology, 23,* 1–24.

Ross, D. S., Holstrum, W., Gaffney, M., Green, D., Oyler, R. F., & Gravel, J. (2008). Hearing screening and diagnostic evaluation of children with unilateral and mild bilateral hearing loss. *Trends in Amplification, 12,* 27–34.

Ross, J. G., & Pate, R. R. (1987). The national children and youth fitness study: II. A summary of findings. *Journal of Physical Education, Recreation, and Dance, 58,* 51–56.

Rosser, P. L., & Randolph, S. M. (1989). Black American infants: The Howard University Normative Study. In K. Nugent, B. M. Lester, & T. B. Brazelton (Eds.), *The cultural context of infancy: Vol. 1. Biology, culture, and infant development.* Norwood, NJ: Ablex.

Rothbart, M. K. (2007). Temperament, Development, and Personality. *Current Directions in Psychological Science, 16,* 207–212.

Rothbart, M. K., & Bates, J. E. (1998). Temperament. In N. Eisenberg & W. Damon (Eds.), *Handbook of child psychology: Vol. 3. Social, emotional, and personality development* (5th ed., pp. 105–176). New York: John Wiley & Sons.

Rothbaum, F., & Morelli, G. (2005). Attachment and culture: Bridging relativism and universalism. In W. Friedlmeier, P. Chakkarath, & B. Schwarz (Eds.), *Culture and human development: The importance of cross-cultural research for the social sciences* (pp. 99–124). Hove, England: Psychology Press.

Rothbaum, F., Weisz, J., Pott, M., Miyake, K., & Morelli, G. (2000). Attachment and culture: Security in the United States and Japan. *American Psychologist, 55,* 1093–1104.

Rothbaum, F., Weisz, J., Pott, M., Miyake, K., & Morelli, G. (2001). Deeper into attachment and culture. *American Psychologist, 56,* 827–828.

Rothstein–Fisch, C., Trumbull, E., Issac, A., Daley, C., & Pérez, A. (2001, April). *When helping someone else is the right answer.* Paper presented at the annual meeting of the American Educational Research Association, Seattle.

Rotenberg, K. J., & Sliz, D. (1988). Children's restrictive disclosure to friends. *Merrill-Palmer Quarterly, 34,* 203–215.

Rovee-Collier, C. (1997). Disassociations in infant memory: Retention without remembering. In J. D. Osofsky (Ed.), *Handbook of infant development* (2nd ed.). New York: Wiley.

Rovee-Collier, C., Griesler, P. C., & Earley, L. A. (1985). Contextual determinants of retrieval in 3-month-old infants. *Learning and Motivation, 16,* 139–157.

Rovee-Collier, C., Hayne, H., & Colombo, M. (2001). *The development of implicit and explicit memory.* Philadelphia: John Benjamins Publishing Company.

Roy, J. D. (1987). The linguistic and sociolinguistic position of Black English as related to situation and social class. In P. Homel, M. Palij, & D. Aaronson (Eds.), *Childhood bilingualism: Aspects of linguistic, cognitive, and social development* (pp. 231–243). Hillsdale, NJ: Erlbaum.

Rubin, K. H. (1980). Fantasy play: Its role in the development of social skills and social cognition. In K. H. Rubin (Ed.), *Children's play.* San Francisco: Jossey-Bass.

Rubin, K. H. (1982). Nonsocial play in preschoolers: Necessary evil? *Child Development, 53,* 651–657.

Rubin, K. H., & Asendorpf, J. (1993). Social withdrawal, inhibition, and shyness in childhood: Conceptual and definitional issues. In K. H. Rubin & J. Asendorpf (Eds.), *Social withdrawal, inhibition, and shyness in children* (pp. 3–17). Hillsdale, NJ: Erlbaum.

Rubin, K. H., & Coplan, R. (2007). Paying attention to and not withdrawing from social withdrawal and social isolation. In G. Ladd (Ed.), *Appraising the human developmental sciences* (pp. 156–185). Detroit: Wayne State University Press.

Rubin, K. H., Fein, G. G., & Vandenberg, B. (1983). Play. In E. M. Hetherington (Ed.) & P. H. Mussen (Series Ed.), *Handbook of child psychology: Vol. 4. Socialization, personality, and social development.* New York: John Wiley & Sons.

Rubin, K. H., Hymel, S., LeMare, R. S. L., & Rowden, L. (1989). Children experiencing social difficulties: Sociometric neglect reconsidered. *Canadian Journal of Behavioral Science, 21,* 94–111.

Rubin, K. H., Maioni, T. L., & Hornung, M. (1976). Free play behaviors in middle and lower class preschoolers: Parten and Piaget revisited. *Child Development, 47,* 414–419.

Rubin, K. H., & Mills, R. S. L. (1988). The many faces of social isolation in childhood. *Journal of Consulting and Clinical Psychology, 6,* 916–924.

Rubin, K. H., Stewart, S. L., & Coplan, R. J. (1995). Social withdrawal in childhood: Conceptual and empirical perspectives. In T. H. Ollendick & R. J. Prinz (Eds.), *Advances in clinical child psychology* (Vol. 17, pp. 157–196). New York: Plenum.

Rudy, D., & Grusec, J. (2006). Authoritarian parenting in individualist and collectivist groups: Associations with maternal emotion and cognition and children's self-esteem. *Journal of Family Psychology, 20,* 68–78.

Ruiz, S., & Silverstein, M. (2007). Relationships with grandparents and the emotional well-being of late adolescent and young adult grandchildren. *Journal of Social Issues, 63,* 793–808.

Russ, S., & Kaugars, A. (2001). Emotion in children's play and creative problem solving. *Creativity Research Journal, 13,* 211–219.

Rutland, A., Cameron, L., Bennett, L., & Ferrell, J. (2005). Interracial contact and racial constancy: A multi-site study of racial intergroup bias in 3-5 year old Anglo-British children. *Journal of Applied Developmental Psychology, 26,* 699–713.

Rutter, M. (1996). Autism research: Prospects and priorities. *Journal of Autism and Developmental Disorders, 26,* 257–275.

Ryan, A. S., Rush, D., Krieger, F. W., & Lewandowski, G. E. (1991). Recent declines in breastfeeding in the United States. *Pediatrics, 88,* 719–727.

Sabornie, E. J., & deBettencourt, L. U. (1997). *Teaching students with mild disabilities at the secondary level.* Upper Saddle River, NJ: Merrill/Prentice Hall.

Sadeh, A., Raviv, A., & Gruber, R. (2000). Sleep patterns and sleep disruption in school-age children. *Developmental Psychology, 36,* 291–301.

Sadker, M. P., Sadker, D. M., & Klein, S. (1991). The issue of gender in elementary and secondary education. In G. Grant (Ed.), *Review of research in education* (Vol. 17, pp. 269–334). Washington, DC: American Educational Research Association.

Sadler, T. W. (1996). Embryology and experimental teratology. In J. A. Kuller, N. C. Cheschier, & R. C. Cefalo (Eds.), *Prenatal diagnosis and reproductive genetics* (pp. 218–226). St. Louis, MO: Mosby.

Sagi, A., & Hoffman, M. (1976). Emphatic distress in the newborn. *Developmental Psychology, 12,* 175–176.

Sagi, A., van IJzendoorn, M., H & Koren-Karie, N. (1991) Primary appraisal of the strange situation: A cross-cultural analysis of preseparation episodes. *Developmental Psychology, 27,* 587–596.

Sahler, O. J. Z. (1983). Adolescent mothers: How nurturant is their parenting? In E. R. McAnarney (Ed.), *Premature adolescent pregnancy and parenthood* (pp. 37–59). New York: Grune & Stratton.

Sallis, J., Prochaska, J., & Taylor, W. (2000). A review of correlates of physical activity of children and adolescents. *Medicine & Science in Sports & Exercise, 32,* 963–975.

Salmon, A. (2008). Promoting a culture of thinking in the young child. *Early Childhood Education Journal, 35,* 457–461.

Salzinger, S., Feldman, R. S., Hammer, M., & Rosario, M. (1993). The effects of physical abuse on children's social relationships. *Child Development, 64,* 169–187.

Samuelson, L. K., & Smith, L. B. (2000). Grounding development incognitive processes. *Child Development, 71,* 98–106.

Sanchez, Y. M. (1997). Families of Mexican origin. In M. K. DeGenova (Ed.), *Families in cultural context: Strengths and challenges in diversity* (pp. 61–83). Mountain View, CA: Mayfield.

Sánchez-Alonso, S. & Vovides, Y. (2007). Integration of metacognitive skills in the design of learning objects. *Computers in Human Behavior, 23,* 585–595.

Sanchez-Ayendez, M. (1988). The Puerto Rican American family. In C. H. Mindel, R. W. Habenstein, & R. Wright (Eds.), *Ethnic families in America: Patterns and variations.* New York: Elsevier.

Sanchez-Burks, J., & Lee, F. (2007). Culture and workways. In S. Kitayama (Ed.), *Handbook of cultural psychology* (pp. 346–369). New York: Guilford Press.

Sanders, K. M., & Harper, L. V. (1976). Free play fantasy behavior in preschool children: Relations among gender, age, season, and location. *Child Development, 47,* 1182–1185.

Sandstrom, M. (2007). A link between mothers' disciplinary strategies and children's relational aggression. *British Journal of Developmental Psychology, 25,* 399–407.

Sann, C., & Streri, A. (2007). Perception of object shape and texture in human newborns: Evidence from cross-modal transfer tasks. *Developmental Science, 10,* 399–410

Sansavini, A., Bertoncini, J., & Giovanelli, G. (1997). Newborns discriminate the rhythm of multisyllabic stessed words. *Developmental Psychology, 33,* 3–11.

Sanson, A., Hemphill, S., & Smart, D. (2004). Connections between temperament and social development: A review. *Social Development, 13,* 142–170.

Santelli, J. S., Lindberg, L. D., Finer, L. B., & Singh, S. (2007). Explaining recent declines in adolescent pregnancy in the United States: The contribution of abstinence and improved contraceptive use. *American Journal of Public Health, 197,* 150–156.

Santosham, M., Reid, R., Chandran, A., Millar, E., Watt, J., Weatherholtz, R., Donaldson, C. Croll, J., Moulton, L., et al. Thompson, C. Siber, G., & O'Brien, K. (2007). Contributions of Native Americans to the global control of infectious diseases. *Vaccine, 25,* 2366–2374.

Sarkisian, N., Gerena, M., & Gerstel, N. (2007). Extended family integration among Euro and Mexican Americans: Ethnicity, gender, and class. *Journal of Marriage and Family, 69,* 40–54.

Sata, L. S. (1983). Mental health issues of Japanese-American children. In G. J. Powell (Ed.), *The psychosocial development of minority children* (pp. 362–372). New York: Brunner/Mazel.

Saudino, K. J., & Eaton, W. O. (1989, July). *Heredity and infant activity level.* Paper presented to the International Society for the Study of Behavioral Department, Jybaskyla, Finland.

Saunders, G. (1988). *Studies in bilingual development.* Hillsdale, NJ: Erlbaum.

Scafidi, F. A., Field, T. M., Schanberg, S. M., Bauer, C. R., Vega-Lahr, N., Garcia, R., et al. (1986). Effects of tactile/kinesthetic stimulation on the clinical course and sleep/wake behavior of preterm neonates. *Infant Behavior and Development, 9,* 91–105.

Scarlett, W. G. (1983). Social isolation from agemates among nursery school children. In M. Donaldson, R. Grieve, & C. Pratt (Eds.), *Early childhood development and education.* New York: Guilford Press.

Scarr, S. (1993). Biological and cultural diversity: The legacy of Darwin for development. *Child Development, 64,* 1333–1353.

Scarr, S. (1998). American child care today. *American Psychologist, 53,* 95–108.

Scarr, S., Weinberg, R. A., & Waldman, I. D. (1993). IQ correlations in transracial adoptive families. *Intelligence, 17,* 541–555.

Schaal, B. (1986). Presumed olfactory exchanges between mother and neonate in humans. In J. S. Le Camus & J. Cosnier (Eds.), *Ethology and psychology* (pp. 101–110). Toulouse: Privat, I. E. C.

Scheiner, E., Hammerschmidt, K., Jürgens, U., & Zwirner, P. (2004). The influence of hearing impairment on preverbal emotional vocalizations of infants. *Journal of Phoniatrics, 56,* 27–40.

Scher, A., & Mayseless, O. (2000). Mothers of anxious/ambivalent infants: Maternal characteristics and child care context. *Child Development, 71,* 1629–1639.

Schickedanz, J. A. (1982). "Hey! This book's not working right!" In J.F. Brown (Ed.), *Curriculum planning for young children.* Washington, DC: National Association for the Education of Young Children.

Schickedanz, J. A. (1999). *Much more than the ABCs: The early stages of reading and writing* (2nd ed.). Washington, DC: National Association for the Education of Young Children.

Schickedanz, J. A., Schickedanz, D. I., & Forsyth, P. D. (1982). *Toward understanding children.* Boston: Little, Brown.

Schirrmacher, R., & Englebright Fox, J. (2008). *Art and creative development for young children* (6th ed.). Albany, NY: Delmar.

Schlesinger, H. S., & Meadow, K. P. (1972). *Sound and sign: Childhood deafness and mental health.* Berkeley: University of California Press.

Schneider, B. H., Wiener, J., & Murphy, K. (1994). Children's friendships: The giant step beyond peer relations. *Journal of Social and Personal Relationships, 11,* 323–340.

Scholl, T. O., Hediger, M. L., & Belsky, D. H. (1994). Prenatal care and maternal health during adolescent pregnancy: A review and meta-analysis. *Journal of Adolescent Health, 15,* 444–456.

Schwartz, A. J. (1971). The culturally advantaged: A study of Japanese-American pupils. *Sociology and Social Research, 55,* 341–353.

Schwartz, I. S., & Sandall, S. R. (1998). Outcomes for children with autism: Three case studies. *Topics in Early Childhood Special Education, 18,* 132–144.

Schwebel, D. C., & Plumert, J. M. (1999). Longitudinal and cocurrent relations among temperament, ability estimation, and injury proneness. *Child Development, 70,* 700–712.

Schwebel, D. C., & Gaines, J. (2007). Pediatric unintentional injury: Behavioral risk factors and implications for prevention. *Journal of Developmental & Behavioral Pediatrics, 28,* 245–254.

Schweinhart, L. J., & Weikart, D. P. (1996). *Lasting difference: The High/Scope preschool curriculum comparison study through age 23.* Ypsilanti, MI: High/Scope Press.

Schweinhart, L. J., & Weikart, D. P. (2006). The High/Scope preschool curriculum comparison study. In R. Parker-Rees & J. Willan (Eds.), *Early years education* (pp. 116–146). London: Routledge.

Scott-Little, C., Kagan, S. L., & Frelow, V. (2003). Standards for preschool children's learning and development: Who has standards, how were they developed, and how are they used? Greensboro, NC: SERVE Publications.

Sebanc, A. (2003). The friendship features of preschool children: Links with prosocial behavior and aggression. *Social Development, 12,* 249–268.

Sebastián-Gallés, N. (2007). Biased to learn language. *Developmental Science, 10,* 713–718.

Seefeldt, C. (1987). The visual arts. In C. Seefeldt (Ed.), *The early childhood curriculum: A review of current research.* New York: Teachers College Press.

Seefeldt, C. (1998). Social studies in the integrated curriculum. In C. H. Hart, D. C. Burts, & R. Charlesworth (Eds.), *Integrated curriculum and developmentally appropriate practice.* Albany: State University of New York Press.

Segal, N. L., McGuire, S., Havlena, J., Gill, P., & Hershberger, S. (2007). Intellectual similarity of virtual twin pairs: Developmental trends. *Personality and Individual Differences, 42,* 1209–1219.

Seitz, V., & Apfel, N. H. (1994). Effects of a school for pregnant students on the incidence of low birthweight deliveries. *Child Development, 65,* 666–676.

Seligman, M., & Darling, R. (2007). *Ordinary families, special children: A systems approach to childhood disability.* New York: Guilford Press.

Sellwood, M. (2008). Review of NICE guidelines on routine postnatal infant care. *Archives of Disease in Childhood, 93,* 10–13.

Seo, S. (2006). A study of Korean working mothers with infants: Implications for research and social policy. *Early Child Development and Care, 176,* 479–492.

Serbin, L. A., Powlishta, K. K., & Gulko, J. (1993). The development of sex-typing in middle childhood. *Monographs of the Society for Research in Child Development, 58*(2, Serial No. 232).

Serpell, R. (1979). How specific are perceptual skills? A cross-cultural study of pattern reproduction. *British Journal of Psychology, 70,* 365–380.

Settings, M. (2006). Position of the American Dietetic Association: Child and adolescent food and nutrition programs. *Journal of the American Dietetic Association, 106,* 1467–1475.

Shafer, H. H., & Kuller, J. A. (1996). Increased maternal age and prior anenploid conception. In J. A. Kuller, N. C. Cheschier, & R. C. Cefalo (Eds.), *Prenatal diagnosis and reproductive genetics* (pp. 23–28). St. Louis, MO: Mosby.

Shaked, M., Gamliel, I., & Yirmiya, N. (2006). Theory of mind abilities in young siblings of children with autism. *Autism, 10,* 173–187.

Shames, G. H., & Wig, E. H. (1986). *Human communication disorders.* Upper Saddle River, NJ: Merrill/Prentice Hall.

Shatz, M., Grimm, H., Wilcox, S. A., & Niemeier-Wind, K. (1989, April). *The uses of modal expression in conversation between German and American mothers and their two-year-olds.* Paper presented at the biennial meeting of the Society for Research in Child Development, Kansas City, MO.

Shavelson, R. J., & Bolus, R. (1982). Self-concept: The interplay of theory and methods. *Journal of Educational Psychology, 74,* 3–17.

Shayer, M., & Adhami, M. (2003). Realising the cognitive potential of children 5–7 with a mathematics focus. *International Journal of Educational Research, 39,* 743–775.

Shenkin, S., Starr, J. M., Pattie, A., Rush, M. A., Whalley, L. J., & Dreary, I. J. (2001). Birth weight and cognitive function at age 11 years. *Archives of Disease in Childhood, 85,* 189 196.

Shepard, L. (1994). The challenges of assessing young children appropriately. *Phi Delta Kappan, 76,* 206–213.

Shi, L., Macinko, J., Starfield, B., Xu, J., Regan, J., Politzer, R., & Wulu, J. (2004). Primary care, infant mortality, and low birth weight in the states of the USA. *Journal of Epidemiology and Community Health, 58,* 374–380.

Shibusawa, T. (2005). Japanese families. In M. McGoldrick, J. Giordano, & N. Garcia-Preto (Eds.), *Ethnicity and family therapy* (pp. 339–348). New York: Guilford.

Shin, H., Bjorklund, D., & Beck, E. (2007). The adaptive nature of children's overestimation in a strategic memory task. *Cognitive Development, 22,* 197–212.

Shirley, M. M. (1933). *The first two years.* Minneapolis: University of Minnesota Press.

Shonkoff, J. P., Hauser-Cram, P., Krauss, M. W., & Upshur, C. C. (1992). Development of infants with disabilities and their families. *Monographs of the Society for Research in Child Development, 57,* (Serial No. 230).

Shonkoff, J. P., & Phillips, D. (Eds.). (2000). *From neurons to neighborhoods: The science of early childhood.* Washington, D.C.: National Academies Press.

Shore, C. (2006). Play and language: Individual differences as evidence of development and style. In D. Fromberg & D. Bergen (Eds.), *Play from birth to 12: Contexts, perspectives, and meanings* (pp. 165–174). New York: Routledge.

Shore, R. (1997). *Rethinking the brain: New insights into early development.* New York: Families and Work Institute.

Short, K., Harste, J., Burke, C., & Short, C. (1996). *Creating classrooms for authors and inquirers.* Portsmouth, NH: Heinemann.

Shu, X. O., Linet, M. S., Steinbuch, M., Wan, O., Buckley, J., Neglia, J., et al. (1999). Breastfeeding and risk of childhood acute leukemia. *Journal of the National Cancer Institute, 91,* 1765–1772.

Shulman, S., Elicker, J., & Sroufe, L. A. (1994). Stages of friendship growth in preadolescence as related to attachment history. *Journal of Social and Personal Relationships, 11,* 341–361.

Shulruf, B., Hattie, J., & Dixon, R. (2007). Development of a New Measurement Tool for Individualism and Collectivism. *Journal of Psychoeducational Assessment, 25,* 385–401.

Siegel, J. (2007). Creoles and minority dialects in education: An update. *Language and Education, 21*, 66–86.

Siegel, L. S., McCabe, A. E., Brand, J., & Mathews, J. (1978). Evidence for the understanding of class inclusion reasoning in preschool children: Linguistic factors and training effects. *Child Development, 49*, 688–693.

Siegler, R. S. (2000). The rebirth of children's learning. *Child Development, 71*, 26–35.

Siegler, R. S. (2004). Turning memory development inside out. *Developmental Review, 24*, 469–475.

Siegler, R. S. (2007a). Learning about learning. In G. Ladd (Ed.), *Appraising the human development sciences* (pp. 67–82). Detroit: Wayne State University Press.

Siegler, R. S. (2007b). Cognitive variability. *Developmental Science, 10*, 104–109.

Signorielli, N., & Lears, M. (1992). Children, television, and conceptions about chores: Attitudes and behaviors. *Sex Roles, 27*, 157–170.

Silver, E., & Stein, R. (2001). Access to care, unmet health needs, and poverty status among children with and without chronic conditions. *Ambulatory Pediatrics, 1*, 314–320.

Silverman, L. K. (1989). Invisible gifts, invisible handicaps. *Roeper Review, 22*, 37–42.

Silverman, L. K. (1995). Gifted and talented students. In E. L. Meyen & T. M. Skrtic (Eds.), *Special education and student disability* (pp. 377–414). Denver: Love.

Silverman, L. K., Chitwood, D. G., & Waters, J. L. (1986). Young gifted children: Can parents identify giftedness? *Topics in Early Childhood Special Education, 6*(1), 23–38.

Silverman, W.K., La Greca, A. M., & Wasserstein, S. W. (1995). What do children worry about? Worries and their relation to anxiety. *Child Development, 66*, 671–686.

Silverstein, M., & Ruiz, S. (2006). Breaking the chain: How grandparents moderate the transmission of maternal depression to their grandchildren. *Family Relations, 55*, 601–612.

Simmons, I., & Dye, J. (2003). *Grandparents living with grandchildren.* Washington, D. C.: U.S. Bureau of Census.

Simpson, R. L., de Boer-Ott, S. R., & Smith-Myles, B. (2003). Inclusion of learners with autism spectrum disorders in general education settings. *Topics in Language Disorders, 23*, 116–133.

Singer, J., & Singer, D. (1998). "Barney and Friends" as entertainment and education: Evaluating the quality and effectiveness of a television series for preschool children. In J. Asamen & G. Berry (Eds.), *Television, Research Paradigms, and Social Behavior,* (pp. 305–367). Thousand Oaks, CA: Sage.

Singleton, D. (2007). How integrated is the integrated mental lexicon? In Z. Lengyel & J. Navracsics (Eds.), *Second language lexical processes: Applied linguistic and psycholinguistic perspectives.* Clevedon, UK: Multilingual Matters.

Singleton, J. L., & Newport, E. (2004). When learners surpass their models: The acquisition of American Sign Language from inconsistent input. *Cognitive Psychology, 49*, 370–407.

Sirvis, R. P., & Caldwell, T. H. (1995). Physical disabilities and chronic health impairments. In E. L. Meyen & T. M. Skrtic (Eds.), *Special education and student disability* (pp. 533–564). Denver: Love.

Skinner, B. F. (1948). *Walden two.* New York: Macmillan.

Skinner, B. F. (1957). *Verbal behavior.* Upper Saddle River, NJ: Merrill/ Prentice Hall.

Skounti, M., Philalithis, A., & Galanakis, E. (2007). Variations in prevalence of attention deficit hyperactivity disorder worldwide. *European Journal of Pediatrics, 166*, 117–123.

Skrtic, T. M. (1995). The crisis in professional knowledge. In E. L. Meyen & T. M. Skrtic (Eds.), *Special education and student disability* (pp. 567–608). Denver: Love.

Slater, A. (1998). *Perceptual development: Visual, auditory, and speech perception in infancy.* Levittown, PA: Taylor & Francis.

Slaughter, V., Heron, M., & Sim, S. (2002). Development of preferences for the human body shape in infancy. *Cognition, 85*, 71–81.

Slaughter-Defoe, D. T., Nakagawa, K., Takanishi, R., & Johnson, D. J. (1990). Toward cultural/ecological perspectives on schooling and achievement in African- and Asian-American children. *Child Development, 61*, 363–383.

Slavin, R. (1997). *Educational psychology: Theory and practice.* New York: McGraw-Hill.

Sligh, A. C., & Conners, F. A. (2003). Relation of dialect to phonological processing: African American Vernacular English vs. Standard American English. *Contemporary Educational Psychology, 28*, 205–228.

Slonim, M. B. (1991). *Children, culture, and ethnicity: Evaluating and understanding the impact.* New York: Garland.

Small, M. Y. (1990). *Cognitive development.* San Diego: Harcourt Brace Jovanovich.

Smilansky, S. (1968). *The effects of sociodramatic play on disadvantaged preschool children.* New York: John Wiley & Sons.

Smilansky, S. (1990). Sociodramatic play: Its relevance to behavior and achievement in school. In E. Klugman & S. Smilansky (Eds.), *Children's play and learning: Perspectives and policy implications* (pp. 18–42). New York: Teachers College Press.

Smilansky, S., & Shefatya, L. (1990). *Facilitating play: A medium for promoting cognitive, socioemotional, and academic development in young children.* Gaithersburg, MD: Psychosocial & Educational Publications.

Smith, B. A., & Blass, E. M. (1996). Taste-mediated calming in premature, preterm, and full-term human infants. *Developmental Psychology, 32*, 1084–1089.

Smith, F. (1988). *Understanding reading.* Hillsdale, NJ: Erlbaum.

Smith, H. (2007). The social and private worlds of speech: Speech for inter- and intramental activity. *The Modern Language Journal 91*, 341–356.

Smith, L. (1989). A model of perceptual classification in children and adults. *Psychological Review, 96*, 125–144.

Smith, P. K. (1997). *Play fighting and fighting: How do they relate?* Lisbon: ICCP.

Smith, T. M., & Kane, H. D. (1998). Intervention. In W. Umansky & S. R. Hooper (Eds.), *Young children with special needs* (pp. 372–406). Columbus, OH: Merrill.

Snidman, N., Kagan, J., Riordan, L., & Shannon, D. C. (1995). Cardiac function and behavioral reactivity during infancy. *Psychophysiology, 32*, 199–207.

Snow, M. A. (1986). *Common terms in second language education: Center for Language and Research.* Los Angeles: University of California.

Snow, C., Burns, S., & Griffin, P. (1998). *Preventing reading difficulties in young children.* Washington, DC: National Academy Press.

Sorce, J. F., Emde, R. N., Campos, J., & Klinnert, M. D. (1985). Maternal emotional signalling: Its effect on the visual cliff behavior of 1-year-olds. *Developmental Psychology, 21*, 195–200.

Soto, L. D. (1991). Understanding bilingual/bicultural young children. *Young Children, 46*(2), 30–36.

Soto, L. D. (2002). *Making a difference in the lives of bilingual/bicultural children.* New York: Peter Lang.

Soto, L. D., & Negron, L. (1994). Mainland Puerto Rican children. In J.L. Roopnarine, J.E. Johnson, & F.H. Hooper (Eds.), *Children's play in diverse cultures.* Albany: State University of New York Press.

Sousa, D. (2006). *How the special needs brain learns.* Thousand Oaks, CA: Corwin Press.

Southgate, V., van Maanen, C., & Csibra, C. (2007). Infant pointing: Communication to cooperate or communication to learn? *Child Development, 78*, 735–740.

Speltz, M. L., Endriga, M. C., Fisher, P. A., & Mason, C. A. (1997). Early predictors of attachment in infants with cleft lip and/or palate. *Child Development, 68*, 12–25.

Spencer, M. B. (1970). *The effects of systematic social and token reinforcement on the modification of racial and color-concept attitudes in preschool-aged children.* Unpublished master's thesis, University of Kansas.

Spencer, M. B. (1983). Children's cultural values and parental child rearing strategies. *Developmental Review, 3*, 351–370.

Spencer, M. B. (1985). Racial variations in achievement prediction: The school as a conduit for macrostructural cultural tension. In H. P. McAdoo & J. L. McAdoo (Eds.), *Black children: Social, educational, and parental environments* (pp. 85–112). Beverly Hills, CA: Sage.

Spencer, M. B. (1988). Self-concept development. In D. Slaughter (Ed.), *Black children and poverty: A developmental perspective* (pp. 59–74). San Francisco: Jossey-Bass.

Spencer, M. B. (1990). Development of minority children: An introduction. *Child Development, 61*, 267–269.

Spencer, M. B. (1999). Social and cultural influences on school adjustment: The application of an identity-focused ecological perspective. *Educational Psychologist, 34*, 43–57.

Spencer, M. B. (2006). Revisiting the 1990 special issue on minority children: An editorial perspective 15 years later. *Child Development, 77*, 1149–1154.

Spencer, M. B., & Markstrom-Adams, C. (1990). Identity processes among racial and ethnic minority children in America. *Child Development, 61*, 290–310.

Spencer, P. E. (1996). The association between language and symbolic play at two years: Evidence from deaf toddlers. *Child Development, 67*, 867–876.

Spencer, P. E., & Meadow-Orlans, K. P. (1996). Play, language, and maternal responsiveness: A longitudinal study of deaf and hearing infants. *Child Development, 67*, 3176–3191.

Spieker, S. J., Larson, N. C., Lewis, S. M., Keller, T. E., & Gilchrist, L. (1999). Developmental trajectories of disruptive behavior problems in preschool children of adolescent mothers. *Child Development, 70*, 443–458.

Spiers, P. S., & Guntheroth, W. G. (1994). Recommendations to avoid the prone sleeping position and recent statistics for Sudden Infant Death syndrome in the United States. *Archives of Pediatric and Adolescent Medicine, 148*, 141–146.

Spiker, D., Ferguson, J., & Brooks-Gunn, J. (1993). Enhancing maternal interactive behavior and child social competence in low birth weight, premature infants. *Child Development, 64*, 754–768.

Spinks, A., Nagle C., Macpherson A., Bain, C., & McClure, R. (2008). Host factors and childhood injury: The influence of hyperactivity and aggression. *Journal of Developmental and Behavioral Pediatrics, 29*, 117–123.

Spinrad, T., & Stifter, C. (2006). Toddlers' empathy-related responding to distress: Predictions from negative emotionality and maternal behavior in infancy. *Infancy, 10*, 97–121.

Spock, B., & Rothenberg, M. B. (1985). *Dr. Spock's baby and child care.* New York: Dutton.

Sporns, O., & Edelman, G. M. (1993). Solving Bernstein's problem: A proposal for the development of coordinated movement by selection. *Child Development, 64*, 960–981.

Spring, J. H. (1996). *The cultural transformation of a Native American family and its tribe, 1763–1995.* Hillsdale, NJ: Erlbaum.

Sroufe, L. A. (1997). Psychopathology as an outcome of development. *Development and Psychopathology, 9*, 251–268.

Stack, D. M., & Muir, D. W. (1992). Adult tactile stimulation during face-to-face interactions modulates five-month-olds' affect and attention. *Child Development, 63*, 1509–1525.

Stahl, S. A. (1992). Saying the "p" word: Nine guidelines for effective phonic instruction. *The Reading Teacher, 45*, 618–625.

Stangor, C., & Ruble, D. N. (1989). Differential influences of gender schemata and gender constancy on children's information processing and behavior. *Social Cognition, 7*, 353–372.

Staples, R. (1988). The black American family. In C. H. Mindel, R. W. Habenstein, & R. Wright (Eds.), *Ethnic families in America: Patterns and variations.* New York: Elsevier.

State of Connecticut. (2005). *Preschool assessment framework.* Hartford, CT: author.

Steele, C. M. (1997). A threat in the air: How stereotypes shape intellectual identity and performance. *American Psychologist, 52*, 613–629.

Stefanini, S., Caselli, M., & Volterra. V. (2007). Spoken and gestural production in a naming task by young children with Down syndrome. *Brain and Language, 101*, 208–221.

Stein, M., Colarusso, C., McKenna, J., & Powers, N. (2001). Cosleeping (bedsharing) among infants and toddlers. *Journal of Developmental & Behavioral Pediatrics, 22*, 67–71.

Steinberg, L., & Silk, J. (2002). Parenting adolescents. In M. Bornstein (Ed.), *Handbook of Parenting* (pp. 103–134). Hillsdale, NJ: Lawrence Erlbaum Associates.

Steiner, J. E. (1979). Human facial expressions in response to taste and smell stimulation. In H. W. Reese & L. P. Lipsitt (Eds.), *Advances in child development and behavior* (Vol. 13). Orlando: Academic Press.

Steinhausen, H., Blattmann, B., & Pfund, F. (2007). Developmental outcome in children with intrauterine exposure to substances. *European Addiction Research, 13*, 94–100.

Stenberg, G. (2003). Effects of maternal inattentiveness on infant social referencing. *Infant and Child Development, 12*, 399–419.

Stephan, Y., & Maiano, C. (2007). On the social nature of global self-esteem: A replication study. *The Journal of Social Psychology, 147*, 573–575.

Sternberg, R. J. (2000). The concept of intelligence. In R. J. Sternberg (Ed.), *Handbook of intelligence.* New York: Cambridge University Press.

Sternberg, R. J. (2003). A broad view of intelligence: The theory of successful intelligence. *Consulting Psychology Journal: Practice & Research, 55*, 139–154.

Sternberg, R. J. (2004). Culture and intelligence. *American Psychologist, 59*, 325–338.

Sternberg, R. J., & Wagner, R. K. (1993). The egocentric view of intelligence and job performance is wrong. *Directions in Psychological Science, 2*, 1–5.

Stevahn, L., Johnson, D. W., Johnson, R. T., Oberle, K., & Wahl, L. (2000). Effects of conflict resolution training integrated into a kindergarten curriculum. *Child Development, 71*, 772–784.

Stevens, J., Harman, J., & Kelleher, K. (2008). Race/ethnicity and insurance status as factors associated with ADHD treatment patterns. *Journal of Child and Adolescent Psychopharmacology, 15*, 88–96.

Stevens, J. H. (1984). Black grandmothers' and black adolescent mothers' knowledge about parenting. *Developmental Psychology, 20*, 1017–1025.

Stevens, J. H., & Duffield, B. N. (1986). Age and parenting skill among black women in poverty. *Early Childhood Research Quarterly, 1*, 221–235.

Stevenson, H., Chen, C., & Uttal, D. H. (1990). Beliefs and achievement: A study of black, white,

and Hispanic children. *Child Development, 61*, 508–523.

Stevenson, H. W., Chen, C., & Lee, S–Y. (1993). Mathematics achievement of Chinese, Japanese, and American children: Ten years later. *Science, 259*, 53–58.

Stevenson-Hinde, J., & Shouldice, A. (1995). Maternal interactions and self-reports related to attachment classifications at 4.5 years. *Child Development, 66*, 583–596.

Steward, J. F., Popkin, B. M., Guilkey, D. K., Akin, J. S., Adair, L., & Flieger, W. (1991). Influences on the extent of breastfeeding. *Demography, 28*, 181–199.

Steward, M. S., & Steward, D. S. (1974). Effect of social distance on teaching strategies of Anglo-American and Mexican-American mothers. *Developmental Psychology, 10*, 797–807.

Stewart, P. (2006). Who is kin? Family definition and African American families *Journal of Human Behavior in the Social Environment, 15*, 163–181.

Stipek, D. (1992). The child at school. In M. H. Bornstein & M. E. Lamb (Eds.), *Developmental psychology: An advanced textbook* (pp. 579–625). Hillsdale, NJ: Erlbaum.

Stipek, D., & Byler, P. (2001). Academic achievement and social behaviors associated with age of entry into kindergarten. *Journal of Applied Developmental Psychology, 22*, 175–189.

Stipek, D., Freiler, R., Daniels, D., & Milburn, S. (1995). Effects of different instructional approaches on young children's achievement and motivation. *Child Development, 66*, 209–233.

Stipek, D., & Greene, J. (2001). Achievement motivation in early childhood: Cause for concern or celebration? In S. Golbeck (Ed.), *Psychological perspectives on early childhood education* (pp. 64–91). Mahwah, NJ: Erlbaum.

Stipek, D., & MacIver, D. (1989). Developmental change in children's assessment of intellectual competence. *Child Development, 60*, 521–538.

Stipek, D., Recchia, S., & McClintic, S. (1992). Self-evaluation in young children. *Monographs of the Society for Research in Child Development, 57*(no. 1, Serial No. 226).

Stoel-Gammon, C., & Vogel Sosa, A. (2007). Phonological development. In E. Hoff & M. Shatz (Eds.), *Handbook of language development* (pp. 238–256). Cambridge, MA: Blackwell.

Stoltzfus, E. (2002). *Background data on child welfare.* Washington, DC: Congressional Research Service.

Stone, S., & Christie, J. (1996). Collaborative literacy learning during sociodramatic play in a multiage (K–2) primary classroom. *Journal of Research in Childhood Education, 10*, 123–133.

Stoneman, Z., & Manders, J. E. (2008). Partnerships with families. In W. Umansky & S. R. Hooper (Eds.), *Young children with special needs* (pp. 72–93). Upper Saddle River, NJ: Merrill.

Stormshak, E. A., Bellanti, C. J., Bierman, K. L., & the Conduct Problems Prevention Research Group. (1996). The quality of sibling relationships and the development of social competence and behavioral control in aggressive children. *Developmental Psychology, 32*, 79–89.

Stormshak, E. A., Bierman, K. L., Bruschi, C. B., Dodge, K. A., Coie, J. D., & the Conduct Problems Prevention Group. (1999). The relation between behavior problems and peer preference in different classroom contexts. *Child Development, 70*, 169–182.

Story, M., Mays, R., Bishop, D., Perry, C., Taylor, G., Smyth, M., et al. (2000). 5-a-Day Power Plus: Process evaluation of a multicomponent elementary program to increase fruit and vegetable consumption. *Health Education and Behavior, 27*, 187–200.

Stowe, R. (2007). *Home literacy experiences of low-income, urban, Mexican American kindergarten*

students. Manhattan, KS: K-State Research Exchange, Kansas State University.

Strachan, T., & Read, A. P. (1996). *Human molecular genetics.* New York: John Wiley & Sons.

Streri, A., & Féron, J. (2005). The development of haptic abilities in very young infants: From perception to cognition. *Infant Behavior and Development, 28*, 290–304.

Striano, T., & Rochaf, P. (2000). Emergence of selective social referencing in infancy. *Infancy, 1*, 253–264.

Strickland, D., & Schickedanz, J. (2004). *Learning about print in preschool: Working with letters, words, and beginning links with phonemic awareness.* Newark, DE: International Reading Association.

Stuart, S., & Yen, S. (2006). Reforming federal testing policy to support teaching and learning. *Educational Policy, 20*, 495–524.

Sudarkasa, N. (2007). African American female-headed households: Some neglected dimensions. In H. McAdoo (Ed.), *Black families* (pp. 172–183). Newbury Park, CA: Sage Publishing.

Sudhalter, V., & Braine, M. D. S. (1985). How does comprehension of passives develop? *Journal of Child Language, 12*, 455–470.

Sue, S., & Chin, R. (1983). The mental health of Chinese-American children: Stressors and resources. In G. J. Powell (Ed.), *The psychosocial development of minority children* (pp. 385–400). New York: Brunner/Mazel.

Sugden, D., & Keogh, J. (1990). *Problems in movement skill development.* Columbia, SC: University of South Carolina Press.

Suizzo, M., Robinson, C., & Pahlke, E. (2008). African American mothers' socialization beliefs and goals with young children: Themes of history, education, and collective independence. *Journal of Family Issues, 29*, 287–316.

Sulzby, E. (1995). *Emergent writing and reading in 5 and 6 year olds: A longitudinal study.* Norwood, NJ: Ablex.

Sulzby, E., & Teale, W. (1987). *Young children's storybook reading: Longitudinal study of parent-child interaction and children's independent functioning* (Final Report to the Spencer Foundation). Ann Arbor: University of Michigan.

Summerbell, C., Waters, E., Edmunds, L., Kelly, S., Brown, T., & Campbell, K. (2008). *Interventions for preventing obesity in children.* London: Cochrane Collaboration.

Sumsion, J. (2005). Male teachers in early childhood education: Issues and case study. *Early Childhood Research Quarterly, 20*, 109–123.

Sun, M., & Rugolotto, S. (2004). Assisted infant toilet training in a Western family setting. *Journal of Development and Behavioural Pediatrics, 25*, 99–101.

Super, C. (1990). Cross-cultural research on infancy. In J. Oates & S. Sheldon (Eds.), *Cognitive development in infancy* (pp. 23–48). New York: Pscychology Press.

Super, C., Herrera, M. G., & Mora, J. O. (1990). Long-term effects of food supplementation and psychosocial intervention on the physical growth of Colombian infants at risk of malnutrition. *Child Development, 61*, 29–49.

Susser, M., & Stein, Z. (1994). Timing in prenatal nutrition: A reprise of the Dutch Famine Study. *Nutritional Reviews, 52*, 84–94.

Sutton, C. K., & Broken Nose, M. A. (2005). American Indian families. In M. McGoldrick, J. Giordano, & N. Garcia-Preto (Eds.), *Ethnicity and family therapy* (pp. 41–54). New York: Guilford Press.

Sutton-Smith, B. (1983). One hundred years of change in play research. *Association for the Anthropological Study of Play Newsletter, 9*(2), 13–17.

Sutton-Smith, B. (1999). The rhetorics of adult and child play theories. In S. Reifel (Ed.), *Advances in* early childhood education and day care: Vol. 10. Foundations, adult dynamics, teacher education, and play (pp. 149–162). Stamford, CT: JAI.

Sutton-Smith, B., & Roberts, J. M. (1970). The cross-cultural and psychological study of games. In G. Luschen (Ed.), The cross-cultural analysis of sport and games (pp. 64–98). Champaign, IL: Stipes.

Suzuki, L., & Aronson, J. (2005). The cultural malleability of intelligence and its impact on the racial/ethnic hierarchy. Psychology, Public Policy, and Law, 11, 320–327.

Svejda, M., & Campos, J. (1982). The mother's voice as a regulator of the infant's behavior. Paper presented at the International Conference on Infant Studies, Austin, TX.

Swain, J., Lorberbaum, J., Kose, S., & Strathearn, L. (2007). Brain basis of early parent-infant interactions: Psychology, physiology, and in vivo functional neuroimaging studies. Journal of Child Psychology and Psychiatry, 48, 262–287.

Swanton, J. (2006). Chickasaw society and religion. Lincoln, NE: University of Nebraska Press.

Tafoya, N., & Del Vecchio, A. D. (2005). Back to the future: An examination of the Native American holocaust experience. In M. McGoldrick, J. Giordano, & N. Garcia-Preto (Eds.), Ethnicity and family therapy (pp. 55–63). New York: Guilford.

Tager-Flusberg, H. (2008). Putting words together: Morphology and syntax in the preschool years. In J. B. Gleason (Ed.), The development of language (pp. 135–166). Boston: Allyn & Bacon.

Takeuchi, M. (1994). Children's play in Japan. In J. L. Roopnarine, J. E. Johnson, & F. H. Hooper (Eds.), Children's play in diverse cultures (pp. 51–72). Albany: State University of New York Press.

Takahashi, K. (1990). Are the key assumptions of the strange situation procedure universal? A view from Japanese research. Human Development, 33, 23–30.

Tallal, P. (1987). Developmental language disorders. In Learning disabilities: A report to the U.S. Congress. Washington, DC: Interagency Committee on Learning Disabilities.

Tamis-LeMonda, C. S. (2004). Conceptualizing fathers' roles: Playmates and more. Human Development, 47, 220–227.

Tamis-LeMonda, C. S., & Bornstein, M. H. (1991). Individual variation, correspondence, stability, and change in mother and toddler play. Infant Behavior and Development, 14, 143–162.

Tamis-LeMonda, C. S., Shannon, J. D., Cabrera, N., & Lamb, M. (2004). Fathers and mothers at play with their 2- and 3-year-olds: Contributions to language and cognitive development. Child Development, 75, 1806–1820.

Tamis-LeMonda, C., Way, N., Hughes, D., Yoshikawa, H., Kalman, R., & Niwa, E. (2008). Parents' goals for children: The dynamic coexistence of individualism and collectivism in cultures and individuals. Social Development, 17, 183–209.

Tan, A. L. (2004). Chinese American children and families: A guide for educators and service providers. Olney, MD: Association for Childhood Education International.

Tanner, J. M. (1990). Fetus into man: Physical growth from conception to maturity (3rd ed.). Cambridge, MA: Harvard University Press.

Tardiff, T., Gelman, S. A., & Xu, F. (1999). Putting the "noun bias" in context: A comparison of English and Mandarin. Child Development, 70, 620–635.

Tasker, F. (1999). Children in lesbian-led families: A review. Clinical Child Psychology and Psychiatry, 4, 153–166.

Tavecchio, L. W. C., & van IJzendoorn, M. H. (Eds.). (1987). Attachment in social networks: Contributions to the Bowlby-Ainsworth attachment theory. Amsterdam: Elsevier.

Taylor, A. R., & Machida, S. (1994, April). Parental involvement: Perspectives of Head Start parents and teachers. Paper presented at the annual meeting of American Educational Research Association, New Orleans.

Taylor, P. D., & Poston, L. (2007). Developmental programming of obesity in mammals. Experimental Physiology, 92, 287–298.

Teele, D. W., Klein, J. O., Chase, C., Menvuk, P., Rosner, B. A., & the Greater Boston Otitis Media Study Group. (1990). Otitis media in infancy and intellectual ability, school achievement, speech, and language at age 7 years. Journal of Infectious Diseases, 162, 685–694.

Teisl, M., & Cicchetti, D. (2008). Physical abuse, cognitive and emotional processes, and aggressive/-disruptive behavior problems. Social Development, 17, 1–23

Temple, C., Nathan, R., Burris, N., & Temple, F. (1988). The beginnings of writing. Newton, MA: Allyn & Bacon.

Terpstra, J., & Tamura, R. (2008). Effective social interaction strategies for inclusive settings. Early Childhood Education Journal, 35, 405–411.

Terrel, T. D. (1981). The natural approach to bilingual education. In California Department of Education, Schooling and language minority students: A theoretical framework (pp. 117–146). Los Angeles: California State University, School of Education, Evaluation, Dissemination, and Assessment Center.

Teti, D. M., & Ablard, K. E. (1989). Security of attachment and infant-sibling relationships. Child Development, 60, 1519–1528.

Thelen, E. (1995). Motor development: A new synthesis. American Psychologist, 50, 79–95.

Thelen, E., & Smith, L. B. (1994). A dynamic systems approach to the development of cognition and action. Cambridge, MA: Bradford/MIT Press.

Thomas, A., & Chess, S. (1977). Temperament and development. New York: Brunner/Mazel.

Thomas, R. M. (1999). Human development theories: Windows on culture. Belmont, CA: Wadsworth.

Thomas, R. M. (2004). Comparing theories of child development. Belmont, CA: Wadsworth.

Thompson, C. P., Anderson, L. P., & Bakeman, R. A. (2000). Effects of racial socialization and racial identity on acculturative stress in African American students. Cultural, Diversity and Ethnic Minority Psychology, 6, 196–210.

Thompson, D. A., & Christakis, D. A. (2005). The association between television viewing and irregular sleep schedules among children less than 3 years of age. Pediatrics, 116, 851–856.

Thompson, D. R., & Siegler, R. S. (2000). Buy low, sell high: The development of an informal theory of economics. Child Development, 71, 660–677.

Thompson, R. A. (1988). The effects of infant day care through the prism of attachment theory: A critical appraisal. Early Childhood Research Quarterly, 3, 273–282.

Thompson, R. A. (1997). Sensitivity and security: New questions to ponder. Child Development, 68, 595–597.

Thompson, R. A. (1998). Early sociopersonality development. In N. Eisenberg & W. Damon (Eds.), Handbook of child psychology: Vol. 3. Social, emotional, and personality development (5th ed.). New York: John Wiley & Sons.

Thompson, R. A., Goodvin, R., & Meyer, S. (2006). Handbook of preschool mental health: Development, disorders, and treatment. New York: Guilford Press.

Thompson, R. A., & Limber, S. P. (1990). Social anxiety in infancy: Stranger and separation reactions. In H. Leitenberg (Ed.), Handbook of social and evaluation. New York: Plenum.

Thornberg, R. (2006). The situated nature of preschool children's conflict strategies. Educational Psychology, 26, 109–126.

Thorne, A., & Michaelieu, Q. (1996). Situating adolescent gender and self-esteem with personal memories. Child Development, 67, 1374–1390.

Thornton, M. C., Chatters, L. M., Taylor, R. J., & Allen, W. (1990). Sociodemographic and environmental correlates of racial socialization by black parents. Child Development, 61, 401–409.

Thornton, S. (1999). Creating the conditions for cognitive change: The interaction between task structures and specific strategies. Child Development, 70, 588–603.

Tillery, K. L., & Smoski, W. J. (1994, May). Clinical implications of the auditory processing abilities of children with attention deficit-hyperactivity disorder. Paper presented at the Central Auditory Processing: Consensus Development Conference, American Speech-Language Hearing Association, Rockville, MD.

Timberlake, J. M. (2007). Racial and ethnic inequality in the duration of children's exposure to neighborhood poverty and affluence. Social Problems, 54, 319–342.

Timler, G., Vogler-Elias, D., & McGill, K. (2007). Strategies for promoting generalization of social communication skills in preschoolers and school-aged children. Topics in Language Disorders: Social Communication Problems and Peer Interactions, 27, 167–181.

Timm, J., Chiang, B., & Finn, B. D. (1999). Acculturation in the cognitive style of Laotian Hmong students in the United States. In F. Schultz (Ed.), Annual editions: Multicultural education, 1999/2000 (pp. 188–194). Guilford, CT: Dushkin/McGraw-Hill.

Tobin, J. J., Wu, D. Y. H., & Davidson, D. H. (1989). Preschool in three cultures: Japan, China, and the United States. New Haven, CT: Yale University Press.

Todd, P. E. & Wolpin, K. (2007). The production of cognitive achievement in children: Home, school, and racial test score gaps. Chicago: University of Chicago.

Tomasello, M. (2000). The item-based nature of children's early syntactic development. Trends in Cognitive Sciences, 4, 156–163.

Tomasello, M., & Mervis, C. B. (1994). Commentary: The instrument is great, but measuring comprehension is still a problem. Monographs of the Society for Research in Child Development, 59, (Serial No. 242).

Tooby, J., & Cosmides, L. (1992). Psychological foundations of culture. In J. Barkow, J. Tooby, & L. Cosmides (Eds.), The adapted mind: Evolutionary psychology and the generation of culture (pp. 19–136). New York: Oxford University Press.

Toro, P. A. (2007). Toward an international understanding of homelessness. Journal of Social Issues, 63, 461–481.

Torres, V. M. (2005). A cultural model of pregnancy: A comparison between Mexican physicians and working-class women in Tijuana, B. C. The Social Science Journal, 42, 81–96.

Torres-Guzman, M. (2007). Dual language programs: Key features and results. In O. Garcia & C. Baker (Eds.), Bilingual education: An introductory reader (pp. 50–63). Clevedon, UK: Multilingual Matters.

Tracy, J. L., & Robins, R. (2007). Emerging insights into the nature and function of pride. Current Directions in Psychological Science, 16, 147–150.

Trautwein, U., Lüdtke, O., Marsh, H., Köller, O., & Baumert, J. (2006). Tracking, grading, and student motivation: Using group composition and status to predict self-concept and interest in ninth-grade mathematics. Journal of Educational Psychology, 98, 788–806.

Trawick-Smith, J. (1988). Let's say you're the baby, OK?: Play leadership and following behavior in young children. Young Children, 43(5), 51–59.

Trawick-Smith, J. (1990). Effects of realistic vs. nonrealistic play materials on young children's symbolic transformation of objects. *Journal of Research in Childhood Education, 5,* 27–36.

Trawick-Smith, J. (1991). The significance of toddler pretend play in child care. *Early Child Development and Care, 68,* 10–18.

Trawick-Smith, J. (1992). A descriptive study of persuasive preschool children: How they get others to do what they want. *Early Childhood Research Quarterly, 7*(1), 95–115.

Trawick-Smith, J. (1993, April). *A content analysis of the Early Childhood Research Quarterly.* Paper presented at the annual meeting of the American Educational Research Association, Atlanta.

Trawick-Smith, J. (1994). *Interactions in the classroom: Facilitating play in the early years.* Upper Saddle River, NJ: Merrill/Prentice Hall.

Trawick-Smith, J. (1998a). A qualitative analysis of metaplay in the preschool years. *Early Childhood Research Quarterly, 13,* 433–452.

Trawick-Smith, J. (1998b). School-based play and social interactions. In D. Fromberg & D. Bergen (Eds.), *Play from birth to 12: Contexts, perspectives, and meanings.* New York: Garland.

Trawick-Smith, J. (1998c, March). *A sociocultural model of children's play: Observations of Puerto Rican children on the island and the mainland.* Paper presented at the annual meeting of the American Educational Research Association, San Diego.

Trawick-Smith, J. (2000, April). *Drawing back the lens on play: A frame analysis of the play of children from Puerto Rico.* Paper presented at the annual meeting of the American Educational Research Association, Atlanta.

Trawick-Smith, J. (2001, April). The play frame and the fictional dream: The bidirectional relationship between metaplay and story writing. In S. Reifel & M. Brown (Eds.), *Advances in early education and day care: Vol. 1. Early education and care, and reconceptualizing play* (pp. 322–338). New York: JAI Press.

Trawick-Smith, J. (2005). Play and the curriculum. In J. Frost, S. Wortham, & S. Reifel (Eds.), *Play and child development* (pp. 212–245). Columbus, OH: Merrill.

Trawick-Smith (2008, March). *Teacher-child play interactions in preschool: An empirical test of Vygotsky's theory.* Paper presented at the American Educational Research Association, New York.

Trawick-Smith, J., & Lisi, P. (1994). Infusing multicultural perspectives in an early childhood development course: Effects on the knowledge and attitudes of inservice teachers. *Journal of Early Childhood Teacher Education, 15,* 8–12.

Trehub, S. E., Schneider, B. A., Thorpe, L. A., & Judge, P. (1991). Observational measures of auditory sensitivity in early infancy. *Developmental Psychology, 27,* 40–49.

Trehub, S., & Shenfield, T. (2007). Acquisition of early words from single-word and sentential contexts. *Developmental Science, 10,* 190–198.

Trommsdorff, G., Friedlmeier, W., & Mayer, B. (2007). Sympathy, distress, and prosocial behavior of preschool children in four cultures. *International Journal of Behavioral Development, 31,* 284–293.

Tronick, E. Z. (2007). *The Neurobehavioral and Social-Emotional Development of Infants and Children.* New York: W. W. Norton & Company

Tronick, E. Z., Thomas, R. B., & Daltabuit, M. (1994). The Quecha Manta pouch: A caregiving practice for buffering the Peruvian infant against multiple stressors of high altitude. *Child Development, 65,* 1005–1013.

Tucker, K., & Young, F. W. (1989). Household structure and child nutrition. *Social Indicators Research, 21,* 201–221.

Tucker, M., & Crouter, A. (2008). Enduring couples in varying sociocultural contexts. *Family Relations, 57,* 113–116.

Turati, C., & Simion, F. (2002). Newborns' recognition of changing and unchanging aspects of

schematic faces. *Journal of Experimental Child Psychology, 83,* 239–261.

Turbiville, V. P., & Turnbull, A. P. & Turnball, H. R. (1995). Fathers and family-centered early intervention. *Infants and Young Children, 7,* 12–19.

Turchi, M., Duarte, L., & Martelli, C. (2008). Mother-to-child transmission of HIV: Risk factors and missed opportunities for prevention. *Journal of Public Health, 23,* 390–401.

Turiel, E. (2002). *The culture of morality: Social development, context, and conflict.* Cambridge: Cambridge University Press.

Turnbull, A. P., & Turnbull, H. R. (2001). *Families, professionals, and exceptionality: Collaborating for empowerment.* Upper Saddle River, NJ: Merrill/Prentice Hall.

Turner, P. J. (1993). Attachment to mother and behavior with adults in preschool. *British Journal of Developmental Psychology, 11,* 75–89.

Turner, P. J., & Gervai, J. (1995). A multidimensional study of gender typing in preschool children and their parents: Personality, attitudes, preferences, behavior, and cultural differences. *Developmental Psychology, 31,* 759–772.

Tyler, K. (2002). Social and emotional outcomes of childhood sexual abuse: A review of recent research. *Aggression and Violent Behavior, 7,* 567–589.

Uccelli, P., & Páez, M. (2007). Narrative and vocabulary development of bilingual children from kindergarten to first grade: Developmental changes and associations among English and Spanish skills. *Language, Speech, and Hearing Services in Schools, 38,* 225–236.

Umaña-Taylor, A. J. (2004). Ethnic identity and self-esteem: Examining the role of social context. *Journal of Adolescence, 27,* 139–146.

Umaña-Taylor, A. J., & Shin, N. (2007). An examination of ethnic identity and self-esteem with diverse populations: Exploring variation by ethnicity and geography. *Culture, Diversity, and Ethnic Minority Psychology, 13,* 178–186.

Umansky, W. (2008a). Cognitive development. In W. Umansky & S. R. Hooper (Eds.), *Young children with special needs* (pp. 188–225). Upper Saddle River, NJ: Merrill.

Umansky, W. (2008b). Emotional and social development. In W. Umansky & S. R. Hooper (Eds.), *Young children with special needs* (pp. 276–307). Upper Saddle River, NJ: Merrill.

Umansky, W., & Hooper, S. R. (2008). *Young children with special needs.* Upper Saddle River, NJ: Prentice Hall.

UNICEF. (2004a). *Protecting, promoting, and supporting breastfeeding.* New York: Author.

UNICEF. (2004b). *The state of the world's children 2004.* New York: Author.

United Nations. (2004). *Convention on the rights of the child.* New York: Author.

Unnever, J.D. (2005). Bullies, aggressive victims, and victims: Are they distinct groups? *Aggressive Behavior, 31,* 153–171.

Ursin, G., Bernstein, L., Wang, Y., Lord, S., Deapen, D., Liff, J., Norman, S., Weiss, L., Daling, J., Marchbanks, P., Malone, K., Folger, S., McDonald, J., Burkman, R., Simon, M., Strom, B., & Spirtas, R. (2004). Reproductive factors and risk of breast carcinoma in a study of white and African-American women. *Cancer, 101,* 353–362.

U.S. Bureau of the Census. (2001). *Current population survey annual demographic supplement.* Washington, DC: U.S. Government Printing Office.

U.S. Bureau of the Census. (2004). *U.S. interim projections by age, sex, race, and Hispanic origin.* Washington, DC: Author.

U.S. Bureau of the Census. (2007). *Current population reports.* Washington, DC: U.S. Government Printing Office.

U.S. Department of Agriculture. (2004). *Household food security in the United States 2002.* Washington, DC: Author.

U.S. Department of Education. (2004). *Twenty-five years of progress in educating children with disabilities through IDEA.* Washington, DC: Author.

U.S. Department of Education. (2007). *The nation's report card: Overview of NAEP.* Washington: Author.

U.S. Department of Health and Human Services. (2008). *Trends in the well-being of America's children and youth.* Washington, DC: Author.

Utall, D. (2005). Spatial symbol and spatial thought: Cross-cultural, developmental, and historical perspectives, on the relation between map use and spatial cognition. In L. Namy (Ed.), *Symbol Use and Symbolic Representation* (pp. 3–24). London: Routledge.

Vaish, A., & Striano, T. (2004). Is visual reference necessary? Contributions of facial versus vocal cues in 12-month-olds' social referencing behavior. *Developmental Science, 7,* 261–269.

Valatis, R., Hersch, R., & Passarelli, L. (2003). Breastfeeding is protective against dental flourasis. *Canadian Journal of Public Health, 19,* 411–417.

Valenzuela, M. (1990). Attachment in chronically underweight young children. *Child Development, 61,* 1984–1996.

Valero de Bernabé, J., Soriano, T., Albaladejo, R. Juarranz, M., Calle, M., Martinez, D., & Dominguez-Rojas, V. (2004). Risk factors for low birth weight: A review. *European Journal of Obstetrics & Gynecology and Reproductive Biology, 116,* 3–15.

Valiente, C., Eisenberg, N., Smith, C., Reiser, M., Fabes, R., Losoya, S., et al. (2003). The relations of effortful control and reactive control to children's externalizing problems: A longitudinal assessment. *Journal of Personality, 71,* 1171–1196.

Vandell, D. (2007). Early child care: The known and the unknown. In G. Ladd (Ed.), *Appraising the human developmental sciences* (pp. 272–289). Detroit: Wayne State University Press.

van den Boom, D. C. (1995). Do first year intervention efforts endure? Follow-up during toddlerhood of a sample of Dutch irritable infants. *Child Development, 66,* 1798–1816.

Vandewater, E., Shim, M., & Caplovitz, A. (2004). Linking obesity and activity level with children's television and video game use. *Journal of Adolescence, 27,* 71–85.

van Dijk, J. J. M., Mayhew, P., & Killias, M. (1990). *Experiences of crime across the world: Key findings from the 1989 International Crime Survey.* Deventer, The Netherlands: Kluwer Law and Taxation Publishers.

van Haasrert, I., de Vries, L., Helders, P., & Jongmans, M. (2006). Early gross motor development of preterm infants according to the Alberta Infant Motor Scale. *Journal of Pediatrics, 149,* 617–622.

van IJzendoorn, M. H. (1995). Adult attachment representation, parental responsiveness, and infant attachment: A meta-analysis on the predictive validity of the Adult Attachment Interview. *Psychological Bulletin, 117,* 387–403.

van IJzendoorn, M. H., & DeWolf, M. S. (1997). In search of the absent father—Meta-analysis of infant-father attachment: A rejoinder to our discussants. *Child Development, 68,* 604–609.

van IJzendoorn, M. H., Goldberg, S., Kroonenberg, P. M., & Frenkel, O. J. (1992). The relative effects of maternal and child problems on the quality of attachment: A meta-analysis of attachment in clinical samples. *Child Development, 63,* 840–858.

van IJzendoorn, M., & Hubbard, F. (2000). Are infant crying and maternal responsiveness during the first year related to infant-mother attachment at 15 months? *Attachment & Human Development, 2,* 371–391.

van IJzendoorn, M. H., Juffer, F., & Klein Poelhuis, C. (2005). Adoption and cognitive development: A meta-analytic comparison of adopted and non-adopted children's IQ and school performance. *Psychological Bulletin, 131,* 301–316.

van Lier, P., Boivin, M., Dionne, G., Vitaro, F., Brendgen, M., Koot, H., et al. (2007). Kindergarten children's genetic vulnerabilities interact with friends' aggression to promote children's own aggression.. *Journal of the American Acadamy of Child and Adolescent Psychiatry, 46,* 1080–1087.

van Sleuwen, B., Engelberts, A., Boere-Boonekamp, M., Kuis, W., Schulpen, T., & L 'Hoir, M. (2007). Swaddling: A systematic review. *Pediatrics, 120,* 1097–1106.

Varela, R., Vernberg, E., Sanchez-Sosa, J., Riveros, A., Mitchell, M., & Mashunkashey, J. (2004). Parenting style of Mexican, Mexican American, and Caucasian-non-Hispanic families: Social context and cultural influences. *Journal of Family Psychology, 18,* 651–657.

Vasilyeva M., Huttenlocher J., & Waterfall H. (2006). Effects of language intervention on syntactic skill levels in preschoolers. *Developmental Psychology, 42,* 164–174.

Vaughn, B., Colvin, T., Azria, M. R., Caya, L., & Krzysik, L. (2001). Dyadic analyses of friendship in a sample of preschool-age children attending Head Start: Correspondence between measures and implications for social competence. *Child Development, 72,* 862–878.

Vaughn, S. B., Hogan, A., Kouzekanani, K., & Shapiro, S. (1990). Peer acceptance, self-perceptions, and social skills of learning disabled children prior to identification. *Journal of Educational Psychology, 82,* 101–106.

Ventura, S. J. (1987). Births of Hispanic parentage, 1983 and 1984. *Monthly Vital Statistics Report, 36,* 1–19.

Verdeli, H., Ferro, T., Wickramaratne, P., Greenwald, S., Blanco, C., & Weissman, M. M. (2004). Treatment of depressed mothers of depressed children: Pilot study of feasibility. *Depression and Anxiety, 19,* 51–58.

Verschueren, K., & Marcoen, A. (1999). Representation of self and socioemotional competence in kindergartners: Differential and combined effects of attachment to mother and to father. *Child Development, 70,* 183–201.

Vig, S. (2007). Young children's object play: A window on development. *Journal of Developmental and Physical Disabilities, 19,* 201–215.

Vijver, F., & Tanzer, N. (2004). Bias and equivalence in cross-cultural assessment: An overview. *Revue Européenne de Psychologie Appliquée, 54,* 119–135.

Vinden, P. G. (1996). Junín Quechua children's understanding of mind. *Child Development, 67,* 1707–1716.

Volbrecht, M., Lemery-Chalfant, K., Aksan, N., Zahn-Waxler, C., & Goldsmith, H. (2007). Examining the familial link between positive affect and empathy development in the second year. *The Journal of Genetic Psychology, 168,* 105–130.

Vondra, J. I., & Barnett, D. (1999). Atypical attachment in infancy and early childhood among children at developmental risk. *Monographs of the Society for Research in Child Development, 64,* (Series No. 258).

Vouloumanos, A., & Werker, J. (2007). Listening to language at birth: Evidence for a bias for speech in neonates. *Developmental Science, 10,* 159–164.

Vukelich, C. (1991, December). *Learning about the functions of writing: The effects of three play interventions on children's development and knowledge about writing.* Paper presented at the annual meeting of the National Reading Conference, Palm Springs, CA.

Vukelich, C. (1994). Effects of play interventions on young children's reading of environmental print. *Early Childhood Research Quarterly, 9,* 153–170.

Vygotsky, L. S. (1962). *Thought and language.* Cambridge, MA: MIT Press.

Vygotsky, L. S. (1976). Play and its role in the mental development of the child. In J. Bruner, A. Jolly, & K. Sylva (Eds.), *Play: Its role in development and evolution.* New York: Basic Books.

Vygotsky, L. S. (1978). *Mind and society: The development of higher mental processes.* Cambridge, MA: Harvard University Press.

Wade, K., Black, A., Ward-Smith, P. (2005). How mothers respond to their crying infant. *Journal of Pediatric Health Care, 19,* 347–353.

Wagner, R. K., Torgesen, J. K., Rashotte, C. A., Hecht, S. A., Barker, T. A., Burgess, S. R., et al. (1997). Changing relations between phonological processing abilities and word-level reading as children develop from beginning to skilled readers: A 5-year longitudinal study. *Developmental Psychology, 33,* 468–479.

Wahab, Z. (1974, April). *Teacher-pupil transactions in biracial classrooms: Implications for instruction.* Paper presented at the annual meeting of Pacific Sociological Association, San Jose, CA.

Wake, M., Poulakis, Z., Hughes, E. K., Carey-Sargeant, C., & Rickards, F. W. (2005). Hearing impairment: A population study of age at diagnosis, severity, and language outcomes at 7–8 years. *Archives of Disease in Childhood, 90,* 238–244.

Walker, D., Greenwood, C., Hart, B., & Carta J. (1994). Prediction of school outcomes based on early language production and socioeconomic factors. *Child Development, 65,* 606–621.

Walker, H. M. (1995). *The acting out child: Coping with classroom disruption.* Longmont, CO: Sopris West.

Walker, L. J. (1984). Sex differences in the development of moral reasoning: A critical review. *Child Development, 55,* 677–691.

Walker, S., & Berthelsen, D. (2007). The social participation of young children with developmental disabilities in inclusive early childhood programs. *Electronic Journal for Inclusive Education, 2,* 2–28.

Walker, S., Wachs, T., Meeks Gardner, J., Lozoff, B., Wasserman, G., Pollitt, E., & Carter, J. (2007). Child development: Risk factors for adverse outcomes in developing countries. *The Lancet, 369,* 145–157.

Wallander, J. L., & Noojin, A. B. (1995). Mothers' report of stressful experiences related to having a child with a physical disability. *Children's Health Care, 24,* 245–256.

Wallis, C. (1986, January 20). Cocaine babies. *Time, 20.*

Walsh, C., MacMillan, H., & Jamieson, E. (2003). The relationship between parental substance abuse and child maltreatment. *Child Abuse & Neglect, 27,* 1409–1425.

Wan, C., Fan, C., Lin, G., & Jing, Q. (1994). Comparison of personality traits of only and sibling children in Beijing. *Journal of Genetic Psychology, 155,* 377–389.

Wang, D. (2004). Family background factors and mathematics success: A comparison of Chinese and U.S. students. *International Journal of Educational Research, 41,* 40–54.

Wang, D., & Li, H. (2007). Nonverbal language in cross-cultural communication. *English Teaching, 4,* 66–70.

Wang, Q., & Leichtman, M. D. (2000). Same beginnings, different stories: A comparison of American and Chinese children's narratives. *Child Development, 71,* 1329–1346.

Wang, Y. Z., Wiley, A. R., & Zhou, X. (2007). The effect of different cultural lenses on reliability and validity in observational data: The example of Chinese immigrant parent-toddler dinner interactions. *Social Development, 16,* 777–799.

Ward, D., Saunders, R., & Pate, R. (2006). *Physical activity interventions in children and adolescents.* Champaign, IL: Human Kinetics.

Warfield, M. E., Hauser-Cram, P., Krauss, M. W., Shonkoff, J. P., & Upshur, C. C. (2000). The effect of early intervention services on maternal well-being. *Early Education and Development, 11,* 499–517.

Warneken, F., & Tomasello, M. (2006). Altruistic helping in human infants and young chimpanzees. *Science, 311,* 1301–1303.

Warren, A. R., & Tate, C. S. (1992). Egocentrism in children's telephone conversations. In R. M. Diaz & L. E. Berk (Eds.), *Private speech: From social interaction to self-regulation* (pp. 245–264). Hillsdale, NJ: Erlbaum.

Warren, W. H. (2006). The dynamics of perception and action. *Psychological Review, 113,* 358–389.

Warren-Leubecker, A., & Bohannon, J. N. (2008). Pragmatics: Language in social contexts. In J. B. Gleason (Ed.), *The development of language* (pp. 327–368). Upper Saddle River, NJ: Merrill/Prentice Hall.

Warren-Leubecker, A., & Tate, C. (1986, October). *Is preschoolers' speech egocentric?* Paper presented at the Boston University Conference on Language Development, Boston.

Washington, J. (2001). Early literacy skills in African-American children: Research considerations. *Learning Disabilities Research & Practice, 16,* 213–221.

Washington, V. (1980). Teachers in integrated classrooms: Profiles of attitudes, perceptions, and behavior. *The Elementary School Journal, 80,* 192–201.

Washington, V. (1982). Racial differences in teacher perceptions of first and fourth grade pupils on selected characteristics. *Journal of Negro Education, 51,* 60–72.

Watamura, S., Donzella, B., Kertes, D., & Gunnar, M. (2004). Developmental changes in baseline cortisol activity in early childhood: Relations with napping and effortful control. *Developmental Psychobiology, 45,* 125–133.

Waters, E., & Cummings, E. M. (2000). A secure base from which to explore close relationships. *Child Development, 71,* 164–172.

Watson, J. B. (1928). *Psychological care of the infant and child.* New York: Norton.

Waxman, S., & Braun, I. (2005). Consistent (but not variable) names as invitations to form object categories: New evidence from 12-month-old infants. *Cognition 95,* 59–68.

Wegman, M. E. (1994). Annual summary of vital statistics—1993. *Pediatrics, 94,* 792–803.

Wehren, A., DeLisi, R., & Arnold, M. (1981). The development of noun definition. *Journal of Child Language, 8,* 165–175.

Weinfield, N. S., Sroufe, L. A., & Egeland, B. (2000). Attachment from infancy to adulthood in a high-risk sample: Continuity, discontinuity, and their correlates. *Child Development, 71,* 695–702.

Weinfield, N., Whaley, G., & Egeland, B. (2004). Continuity, discontinuity, and coherence in attachment from infancy to late adolescence: Sequelae of organization and disorganization. *Attachment & Human Development, 6,* 73–97.

Weinraub, M., & Lewis, M. (1977). The determinants of children's responses to separation. *Monographs of the Society for Research in Child Development, 42,* (Serial No. 172).

Weismer, S., & Evans, J. (2002). The role of processing limitations in early identification of specific language impairment. *Topics in Language Disorders. Information Processing: Implications for Assessment and Intervention, 22,* 15–29.

Weiss, S., Wilson, P., Hertenstein, P., & Campos, R. (2000). The tactile context of a mother's caregiving: Implications for attachment of low birth weight infants. *Infant Behavior and Development, 23,* 91–111.

Weitzman, M., Gortmaker, S., & Sobol, A. (1990). Racial, social and environmental risks for childhood asthma. *American Journal of Diseases of Children, 144,* 1189–1194.

Welteroth, S. (1999). Play, special children, and special circumstances. In J. E. Johnson, J. F. Christie, & T. D. Yawkey (Eds.), *Play and early childhood development* (pp. 154–188). New York: Longman.

Wender, P. H. (1995). *Attention-deficit hyperactivity disorder in adults*. New York: Oxford University Press.

Wendland-Carro, J., Piccinini, C. A., & Millar, W. (1999). The role of an early intervention on enhancing the quality of mother-infant interaction. *Child Development, 70*, 713–721.

Wenner, J. A., & Bauer, P. J. (2000). Bringing order to the arbitrary: One- to two-year-olds' recall of event sequences. *Infant Behavior and Development, 22*, 585–590.

Wentworth, N., Benson, J. B., & Haith, M. M. (2000). The development of infants' reaches for stationary and moving targets. *Child Development, 71*, 576–601.

Wentzel, K. R., & Asher, S. R. (1995). The academic lives of neglected, rejected, popular, and controversial children. *Child Development, 66*, 754–763.

Weppelman, T., Bostow, A., Schiffer, R., Elbert-Perez, E., & Newman, R. (2003). Children's use of the prosodic characteristics of infant-directed speech. *Language & Communication, 23*, 63–80.

Werker, J. F., & Desjardins, R. N. (1995). Listening to speech in the first year of life: Experimental influences on phoneme perception. *Current Directions in Psychological Science, 4*, 76–81.

Werker, J., Pons, F., Dietrich, C., Kajikawa, S., Fais, L., & Amano, S. (2007). Infant-directed speech supports phonetic category learning in English and Japanese. *Cognition, 103*, 147–162.

Werker, J., & Tees, R. (2002). Cross-language speech perception: Evidence for perceptual reorganization during the first year of life. *Infant Behavior and Development, 25*, 121–133.

Werker, J., & Yeung, H. (2005). Infant speech perception bootstraps word learning. *Trends in Cognitive Sciences, 9*, 519–527.

Werner, E. E. (1995). Resilience in development. *Current Directions in Psychological Science, 3*, 81–85.

Werner, E. E., & Smith, R. S. (1992). *Overcoming the odds: High-risk children from birth to adulthood*. Ithaca, NY: Cornell University Press.

Whalen, C. K., & Henker, B. (1992). The social profile of attention-deficit hyperactivity disorder: Five fundamental facets. *Child and Adolescent Psychiatric Clinics of North America, 1*, 395–410.

Whelen, R. J. (1995). Emotional disturbance. In E. L. Meyen & T. M. Skrtic (Eds.), *Special education and student disability* (pp. 271–338). Denver: Love.

White, S. (1989). Backchannels across cultures: A study of Americans and Japanese. *Language and Society, 18*, 59–76.

Whitebread, D., Anderson, H., Coltman, P., Page, C., Pino Pasternak, D., & Mehta, S. (2005). Developing independent learning in the early years. *Education 3–13, 33*, 40–50.

Whitebrook, M., Phillips, D., & Howes, C. (1993). *National child care staffing study revisited*. Oakland, CA: Child Care Employee Project.

Whitesell, N., Mitchell, C., Kaufman, C., & Spicer, P. (2006). Developmental trajectories of personal and collective self-concept among American Indian adolescents. *Child Development, 77*, 1487–1503.

Whiting, B. B., & Edwards, C. P. (1988). *Children of different worlds*. Cambridge, MA: Harvard University Press.

Whiting, B. B., & Whiting, J. W. M. (1975). *Children of six cultures: A psycho-cultural analysis*. Cambridge, MA: Harvard University Press.

Whitney, M. P., & Thoman, E. B. (1994). Sleep in premature and full-term infants from 24-hour home recordings. *Infant Behavior and Development, 17*, 223–234.

Whyatt, B. (2008). Two languages, two cultures, one mind: A study into developmental changes in the students' view of language as a tool in cross-cultural communication. *Studies in Contemporary Linguistics, 43*, 133–147.

Wicks-Nelson, R., & Israel, A. C. (2002). *Behavior disorders of childhood*. Upper Saddle River, NJ: Merrill/Prentice Hall.

Widmayer, S. M., Peterson, L. M., Larner, M., Carnahan, S., Calderon, A., Wingerd, J., et al. (1990). Predictors of Haitian-American infant development at twelve months. *Child Development, 61*, 410–415.

Wiedmann, M., & Garfield, C. (2007). *Maternal depression and child development: Strategies for primary care providers*. Lisle, IL: Family Practice Education Network.

Wilcock, A., Kobayashi, L., Murray, I. (1997). Twenty-five years of obstetric patient satisfaction in North America: A review of the literature. *Journal of Perinatal and Neonatal Nursing, 101*, 36–47.

Wilcox, J., Baird, D. D., Weinberg, C. R., Hornsby, P. P., & Herbst, A. L. (1995). Fertility in men exposed prenatally to diethylstilbestrol. *New England Journal of Medicine, 332*, 1411–1416.

Wilens, T., Adler, A., Adams, J., Sgambati, S., Rotrosen, J., Sawtelle, R., et al. (2008). Misuse and diversion of stimulants prescribed for ADHD: A systematic review of the literature. *Journal of the American Academy of Child & Adolescent Psychiatry, 47*, 21–31.

Wiley, E., Mathis, W., & Garcia, D. (2005). *The impact of adequate yearly progress requirement of the Federal No Child Left Behind Act on schools in the Great Lakes Region*. East Lansing, MI: Greater Lakes Center for Education Research and Practice.

Williams, D. C., & Kantor, R. (1997). The challenge of Reggio Emilia's research: One teacher's reflections. In J. Hendrick (Ed.), *First steps toward teaching the Reggio Emilia way* (pp. 112–126). Upper Saddle River, NJ: Merrill/Prentice Hall.

Willis, W. (1998). Families with African-American roots. In M. Hanson & E. Lynch (Eds.), *Developing cross-cultural competence: A guide for working with young children and their families* (pp. 121–150). Baltimore: Paul H. Brookes.

Wilson, B. (2008). Media and children's aggression, fear, and altruism. *The Future of Children, 18*, 87–118.

Winsler, A., Diaz, R. M., Espinosa, L., & Rodriguez, J. L. (1999). When learning a second language does not mean losing the first: Bilingual language development in low-income, Spanish-speaking children attending bilingual preschool. *Child Development, 70*, 349–362.

Wise, F., & Miller, N. B. (1983). The mental health of the American Indian child. In G. J. Powell (Ed.), *The psychosocial development of minority children*. New York: Brunner/Mazel.

Wise, P. H. (1995). Infant mortality: Confronting disciplinary fragmentation in research and policy. In B. P. Sachs, R. Beard, E. Papiernik, & C. Russel (Eds.), *Reproductive health care for women and babies* (pp. 375–390). New York: Oxford University Press.

Witherington, D., Campos, J., Anderson, D., Lejeune, L., & Seah, E. (2005). Avoidance of heights on the visual cliff in newly walking infants. *Infancy, 7*, 285–298.

Witmer, H. L., & Kotinsky, R. (1952). *Personality in the making: The report on the Midcentury White House Conference on Children*. New York: Harper & Row.

Wolf, S., & Heath, S. B. (1995). *The braid of literature: Children's worlds of reading*. Cambridge, MA: Harvard University Press.

Wolff, P. H. (1966). The causes, controls, and organization of behavior in the neonate. *Psychological Issues, 5*, 1–105.

Wolff, P. H. (1969). The natural history of crying and other vocalizations in early infancy. In B. M. Foss (Ed.), *Determinants of infant behavior: IV. Proceedings of the Fourth Tavistock Study Group on Mother-Infant Interaction* (pp. 81–109). New York: Wiley.

Wong-Fillmore, L. (1976). *The second time around: Cognitive and social strategies in second language acquisition*. Unpublished doctoral dissertation, Stanford University.

Wong, E. L. (1991, April). *Asian-Americans and bilingualism*. Paper presented at the biennial meeting of the Society for Research in Child Development, Seattle.

Wong, M. G. (1988). The Chinese American family. In C. H. Mindel, R. W. Habenstein, & R. Wright (Eds.), *Ethnic families in America: Patterns and variations* (pp. 230–257). New York: Elsevier.

Wood, A., Saudino, K., Rogers, H., Asherson, P., & Kuntsi, J. (2007). Genetic influences on mechanically-assessed activity level in children. *Journal of Child Psychology and Psychiatry and Allied Disciplines, 48*, 695–702.

Wood, D. L., Valdez, R. B., Hayashi, T., & Shen, A. (1990). Health of homeless children and housed poor children. *Pediatrics, 86*, 858–866.

Wood, R., & Gustafson, G. (2001). Infant crying and adults' anticipated caregiving responses: Acoustic and contextual influences. *Child Development, 72*, 1287–1300.

Woodward, A. L., & Markman, E. M. (1998). Early word learning. In D. Kuhn & R. S. Siegler (Eds.), *Handbook of child psychology: Vol. 2. Cognition, perception, and language*. New York: John Wiley & Sons.

World Health Organization. (2008). *The WHO global data bank on breastfeeding and complementary feeding*. Geneva, Switzerland: WHO.

Wright, B. A., Bowen, R. W., & Zecker, S. (2000). Nonlinguistic perceptual deficits associated with reading and language disorders. *Current Opinion in Neurobiology, 10*, 482–486.

Wright, J. (1991). Poverty, homelessness, health, nutrition, and children. In J. H. Kryder-Coe, L. M. Salamon, & J. M. Molnar (Eds.), *Homeless children and youth: A new American dilemma* (pp. 71–104). New Brunswick, NJ: Transaction.

Wright, J. L., & Samaras, A. S. (1986). Play worlds and microworlds. In P. F. Campbell & G. G. Fein (Eds.), *Young children and microcomputers*. Englewood Cliffs, NJ: Prentice Hall.

Wu, L. (2007). Children's graphical representations and emergent writing: Evidence from children's drawings. *Early Child Development and Care, 177*, 235–253.

Wyver, S., & Spence, S. (1999). Play and divergent problem solving: Evidence of a reciprocal relationship. *Early Education and Development, 10*, 419–444.

Yablo, P., & Field, N. (2007). The role of culture in altruism: Thailand and the United States. *Psychologia, 50*, 236–251.

Yajnik, C. S. (2007). Obesity epidemic in India: Intrauterine origins? *Proceedings of the Nutrition Society, 63*, 387–396.

Yamamoto, J., & Iga, M. (1983). Emotional growth of Japanese-American children. In G. J. Powell (Ed.), *The psychosocial development of minority children* (pp. 167–180). New York: Brunner/Mazel.

Yamamoto, J., & Kubota, M. (1983). Emotional development of Japanese-American children. In G. J. Powell (Ed.), *The psychosocial development of minority children* (pp. 237–247). New York: Brunner/Mazel.

Yamazaki, Y. (2005). Learning styles and typologies of cultural differences: A theoretical and empirical comparison. *International Journal of Intercultural Relations, 29*, 521–548.

Yang, B., Ollendick, T. H., Dong, Q., Xia, Y., & Lin, L. (1995). Only children and children with siblings in the People's Republic of China. *Child Development, 66*, 1301–1311.

Yang, C., & Hahn, H. (2002). Cosleeping in young Korean children. *Journal of Developmental & Behavioral Pediatrics, 23*, 151–157.

Yang, W. (2007). Gifted or not, parental perceptions are the same: A study of Chinese American parental perceptions of their children's academic achievement and home environment. *Diaspora, Indigenous, and Minority Education, 1*, 217–234.

Yeh, C. J., & Huang, K. (2002). The collectivistic nature of ethnic identity development among Asian-American college students. In M. A. Paludi (Ed.), *Human development in cultural context* (pp. 154–158). Upper Saddle River, NJ: Merrill.

Yeh, S. (2006). Reforming federal testing policy to support teaching and learning. *Educational Policy, 20*, 495–524.

Yip, R. (1990). The epidemiology of childhood iron deficiency. In J. Dobbing (Ed.), *Brain, behavior, and iron in the infant diet* (pp. 27–42). London: Springer-Verlag.

Yoon, J., Hughes, J., Cavell, T., & Thompson, B. (2000). Social cognitive differences between aggressive–rejected and aggressive–nonrejected children. *Journal of School Psychology 38*, 551–570.

Yoshinaga-Itano, C., & Apuzzo, M. L. (1998). Identification of hearing loss after age 18 months is not early enough. *American Annals of the Deaf, 143*, 380–387.

Young, D. (2007). Management of opioid dependence in pregnancy: A review of the evidence. *International Journal of Mental Health and Addiction, 5*, 187–194.

Young, K. (2007). Developmental stage theory of spelling: Analysis of consistency across four spelling-related activities. *Australian Journal of Language and Literacy, 30*, 203–220.

Youngblade, L. M., & Dunn, L. (1995). Individual differences in young children's pretend play with mother and sibling: Links to relationships and understanding of other peoples' feelings and beliefs. *Child Development, 66*, 1472–1492.

Younger, A. J., & Daniels, T. M. (1992). Children's reasons for nominating their peers as withdrawn: Passive withdrawal versus active isolation? *Developmental Psychology, 28*, 955–960.

Yu, C., Ballard, D., & Aslin, R. (2005). The role of embodied intention in early lexical acquisition. *Cognitive Science: A Multidisciplinary Journal, 29*, 961–1005.

Yu, K. H., & Kim, L. I. C. (1983). The growth and development of Korean-American children. In G. J. Powell, J. Yamamoto, A. Romero, & A. Morales. (Eds.), *The psychosocial development of minority children* (pp. 147–158). New York: Brunner/Mazel.

Yuko, T., Masaharu, T., & Masako, K. (2007). The influence of toddler temperament on the childcare anxiety. *Kawasaki Medical Welfare Journal, 16*, 221–227.

Yuzawa, M., Bart, W., & Yuzawa, M. (2000). Development of the ability to judge relative areas: Role of the procedure of placing one object on another. *Cognitive Development, 15*, 135–152.

Zahn-Waxler, C., Radke-Yarrow, M., Wagner, E., & Chapman, M. (1992). Development of concern for others. *Developmental Psychology, 28*, 126–136.

Zamborlin, C. (2007). Going beyond pragmatic failures: Dissonance in intercultural communication. *Intercultural Pragmatics, 4*, 21–50.

Zametkin, A. J., Nordahl, T. E., Gross, M., King, A. C., Semple, W. E., Rumsey, J., et al. (1990). Cerebral glucose metabolism in adults with hyperactivity of childhood onset. *New England Journal of Medicine, 323*, 1361–1366.

Zarbatany, L., Van Brunschot, M., Meadows, K., & Pepper, S. (1996). Effects of friendship and gender on peer group entry. *Child Development, 67*, 2287–2300.

Zareai, M., O'Brien, M., & Fallon, A. (2007). Creating a breastfeeding culture: A comparison of breastfeeding practices in Australia and Iran. *Breastfeeding Review, 15*, 15–20.

Zeece, P. (2007). The style of reading and reading in style. *Early Childhood Education Journal, 35*, 41–45.

Zeifman, D. (2004). Acoustic features of infant crying related to intended caregiving intervention. *Infant and Child Development, 13*, 111–122.

Zeller, M., Vannatta, K., Schafer, J., & Noll, R. (2003). Behavioral reputation: A cross-age perspective. *Developmental Psychology, 39*, 129–139.

Zepeda, M. (1986, April). *Early caregiving in a Mexican origin population.* Paper presented at the International Conference on Infant Studies, Los Angeles.

Zero to Three. (2004). *Improving early intervention services for infants and toddlers with disabilities and their families.* Washington, DC: Author.

Zeskind, P. S. (1983). Cross-cultural differences in maternal perceptions of cries of low- and high-risk infants. *Child Development, 54*, 1119–1128.

Zeskind, P. S. (2008). Impact of the cry of the infant at risk on psychosocial development. In R. Tremblay, R. Barr, R. Peters, & M. Boivin (Eds.), *Encyclopedia on early childhood development* [online]. Montreal, Quebec: Center of Excellence for Early Childhood Development.

Zeskind, P. S., Klein, L., & Marshall, T. R. (1992). Adult's perceptions of experimental modifications of durations of pauses and expiratory sounds in infant crying. *Developmental Psychology, 28*, 1153–1162.

Zhan, M., & Sherraden, M. (2003). Assets, expectations, and children's educational achievement in female-headed households. *Social Service Review, 77*, 191–211.

Zhang, Q., & Wang, Y. (2004). Socioeconomic inequality of obesity in the United States: Do gender, age, and ethnicity matter? *Social Science & Medicine, 58*, 1171–1180.

Zhang, W., & Fuligni, A. (2006). Authority, autonomy, and family relationships in urban and rural China. *Journal of Research on Adolescence, 16*, 527–537.

Zhou, Z., Peverly, S., Boehm, A., & Chongde L. (2000). American and Chinese children's understanding of distance, time, and speed interrelations. *Cognitive Development, 15*, 215–240.

Zigler, E. F. (1998). By what goals should Head Start be assessed? *Children's Services: Social Policy, Research, and Practice, 1*, 5–18.

Zigler, E. F., & Finn-Stevenson, M. (2007). From research to policy and practice: The school for the 21st century. *Journal of Orthopsychiatry, 77*, 175–181.

Zimmerman, F., Christakis, D., Meltzoff, A. (2007). Television and DVD/video viewing in children younger than two years. *Archives of Pediatric and Adolescent Medicine, 161*, 473–479.

Zive, G., Frank–Sophrer, J. F., Sallis, T., & McKenzie, J. (2003). Determinants of dietary intake in a sample of White and Mexican–American Children. *Journal of the American Dietetic Association, 98*, 1282–1289.

Zlotnick, C., Robertson, M., & Tam, T. (2003). Substance use and separation of homeless mothers from their children. *Addictive Behaviors, 28*, 1373–1383.

Zuniga, M. E. (1998). Families with Latino roots. In E. Lynch & M. Hanson (Eds.), *Developing cross-cultural competence: A guide for working with young children and their families* (pp. 209–250). Baltimore: Paul H. Brookes.

Author Index

Subject Index